The Routledge Handbook of Language and Professional Communication

The Routledge Handbook of Language and Professional Communication provides a broad coverage of the key areas where language and professional communication intersect and gives a comprehensive account of the field.

The four main sections of the *Handbook* cover:

- Approaches to professional communication
- Practice
- Acquisition of professional competence
- Views from the professions.

This invaluable reference book incorporates not only an historical view of the field, but also looks to possible future developments. Contributions from international scholars and practitioners, focusing on specific issues, explore the major approaches to professional communication and bring into focus recent research.

This is the first handbook of language and professional communication to account for both pedagogic and practitioner perspectives and as such is an essential reference for postgraduate students and those researching and working in the areas of applied linguistics and professional communication.

Contributors: Natasha Artemeva, Vijay Bhatia, Stephen Bremner, Patrice M. Buzzanell, Saul Carliner, Winnie Cheng, Marta Chromá, Isabel Corona, Stephani Currie, George Anthony David Dass, Bertha Du-Babcock, Matt Falconer, Gail Forey, Janna Fox, Finn Frandsen, Jeremy P. Fyke, Michael B. Goodman, David Grant, Elizabeth de Groot, Christoph A. Hafner, Michael Handford, Peter B. Hirsch, Janet Holmes, Winni Johansen, Alan Jones, Sujata S. Kathpalia, Koo Swit Ling, Becky S. C. Kwan, William Littlewood, Jane Lockwood, Jane Lung, Carmen Daniela Maier, Meredith Marra, Lindsay Miller, Catherine Nickerson, Daniel Nyberg, Anne Peirson-Smith, Robyn V. Remke, Priscilla S. Rogers, Graham Smart, Alina Wan, Yunxia Zhu.

Vijay Bhatia is an Adjunct Professor at Macquarie University and University of Malaya. He is the author of *Analysing Genre: Language Use in Professional Settings* (1993) and *Worlds of Written Discourse: A Genre-based View* (2004).

Stephen Bremner is an Associate Professor in the Department of English at City University of Hong Kong. His main research interests are workplace writing and the ways in which students make the transition from the academy to the workplace.

The Routledge Handbook of Language and Professional Communication

Edited by
Vijay Bhatia and Stephen Bremner

LONDON AND NEW YORK

First published in paperback 2017

First published 2014
by Routledge
2 Park Square, Milton Park, Abingdon, Oxon OX14 4RN

and by Routledge
711 Third Avenue, New York, NY 10017

Routledge is an imprint of the Taylor & Francis Group, an informa business

© 2014, 2017 selection and editorial matter, Vijay Bhatia and Stephen Bremner; individual chapters, the contributors

The right of the editors to be identified as the authors of the editorial matter, and of the authors for their individual chapters, has been asserted in accordance with sections 77 and 78 of the Copyright, Designs and Patents Act 1988.

All rights reserved. No part of this book may be reprinted or reproduced or utilised in any form or by any electronic, mechanical, or other means, now known or hereafter invented, including photocopying and recording, or in any information storage or retrieval system, without permission in writing from the publishers.

Trademark notice: Product or corporate names may be trademarks or registered trademarks, and are used only for identification and explanation without intent to infringe.

British Library Cataloguing in Publication Data
A catalogue record for this book is available from the British Library

Library of Congress Cataloging in Publication Data
The Routledge handbook of language and professional communication / edited by Vijay Bhatia and Stephen Bremner.
pages cm. – (Routledge handbooks in applied linguistics)
1. Communication–Study and teaching. 2. Language and language–Study and teaching.
I. Bhatia, V. K. (Vijay Kumar), 1942–
P91.3.R685 2014
302.2'071–dc23
2013025674

ISBN: 978-0-415-67619-9 (hbk)
ISBN: 978-1-138-28178-3 (pbk)
ISBN: 978-1-315-85168-6 (ebk)

Typeset in Bembo
by Taylor & Francis Books

Contents

List of figures ... ix
List of tables ... x
Notes on contributors ... xi

Introduction ... xvi

Section 1: Approaches to professional communication ... 1
   A. *General theoretical frameworks*

1 Analysing discourse variation in professional contexts ... 3
   Vijay Bhatia

2 Corpus analyses of professional discourse ... 13
   Winnie Cheng

3 A situated genre approach for business communication education in cross-cultural contexts ... 26
   Yunxia Zhu

4 Stretching the multimodal boundaries of professional communication in multi-resources kits ... 40
   Carmen Daniela Maier

   B. *Broad disciplinary frameworks*

5 Business communication ... 50
   Catherine Nickerson

6 Business communication: A revisiting of theory, research and teaching ... 68
   Bertha Du-Babcock

Contents

7   Research on knowledge-making in professional discourses: The use of theoretical resources   85
    Graham Smart, Stephani Currie and Matt Falconer

8   Technical communication   99
    Saul Carliner

9   The complexities of communication in professional workplaces   112
    Janet Holmes and Meredith Marra

10 Electronic media in professional communication   129
    Michael B. Goodman and Peter B. Hirsch

11 The role of translation in professional communication   147
    Marta Chromá

    C. Specific disciplinary frameworks

12 Management communication: Getting work done through people   165
    Priscilla S. Rogers

13 Business and the communication of climate change: An organisational discourse perspective   193
    David Grant and Daniel Nyberg

14 Professionalising organisational communication discourses, materialities and trends   207
    Patrice M. Buzzanell, Jeremy P. Fyke and Robyn V. Remke

15 Corporate communication   220
    Finn Frandsen and Winni Johansen

16 Corporate communication and the role of annual reporting: Identifying areas for further research   237
    Elizabeth de Groot

Section 2: Practice   255
A. Pedagogic perspectives

17 A blended needs analysis: Critical genre analysis and needs analysis of language and communication for professional purposes   257
    Jane Lung

18	The changing landscape of business communication *Sujata S. Kathpalia and Koo Swit Ling*	274
19	Methodology for teaching ESP *William Littlewood*	287

B. *Disciplinary perspectives*

20	English for Science and Technology *Lindsay Miller*	304
21	Communicative dimensions of professional accounting work *Alan Jones*	321
22	Professional communication in the legal domain *Christoph A. Hafner*	349
23	Communication in the construction industry *Michael Handford*	363
24	Offshore outsourcing: The need for appliable linguistics *Gail Forey*	382
25	Media communication: Current trends and future challenges *Isabel Corona*	400
26	The public relations industry and its place in professional communication theory and practice: Past, present and future perspectives *Anne Peirson-Smith*	419

Section 3: Acquisition of professional competence 441

27	Communities in studies of discursive practices and discursive practices in communities *Becky S. C. Kwan*	443
28	The formation of a professional communicator: A socio-rhetorical approach *Natasha Artemeva and Janna Fox*	461
29	Collaborative writing: Challenges for research and teaching *Stephen Bremner*	486

30 Training the call centre communications trainers in the Asian BPO industry   501
    Jane Lockwood

31 Credentialing of communication professionals   521
    Saul Carliner

Section 4: View from the professions   533

32 Banking   535

33 Law   547

34 Accounting   555

35 PR   562

Appendix: View from the professions – questions   570
Index   571

List of figures

0.1	ESP and professional communication	xviii
1.1	Discourse and genre analysis in professional communication	4
1.2	Interdiscursivity in genre-based analysis of professional communication	8
2.1	A sample concordance for 'thank you' in HKCSE	14
4.1	The multi-resources kits	47
10.1	Tweets with Kony or #StopKony	131
11.1	Verbal communication chart	152
11.2	The process of bilingual translation	153
12.1	Competing values communication framework illustrates the relationships between four basic types of communication and valued characteristics	179
12.2	Profile of a relatively newly hired employee with a liberal arts background whose communication is 'now' too transformational whereas it 'should be' more informational for his responsibilities as an analyst	180
12.3	Profile of a memo that needs to be a bit more persuasive	181
15.1	Degree of strategic coordination	227
17.1	The micro and macro aspects of social reality in workplace communication	267
17.2	BNA (Blended Needs Analysis) framework of language and professional communication at the workplace	268
17.3	Key aspects of needs analysis	270
19.1	Two dimensions of learning	295
20.1	A classification of English courses	305
20.2	Architecture of the technological learning environment	317
21.1	Professional capability framework	328
21.2	Professional practice as the recruitment of disciplinary knowledge and communicative competence for the realisation and promotion of interests, values and agendas	332
23.1	Relationships among speakers	369
23.2	Organisational chart	370
23.3	Language and practice relationship	371
23.4	Engineer drawing	374
27.1	A hierarchical relationship of texts at JRC	451
27.2	Discourse flow of land surveying project management	452
30.1	Workplace ESP syllabus development	512
30.2	Call centre ESP syllabus development	513

List of tables

3.1	Breakdown of the learning activities	31
3.2	A breakdown of the communicative purposes students identified	33
3.3	The NZ and Chinese managers' views on the English invitation	35
12.1	*Financial Times* top 51 global MBA programs shows growth in programs outside the United States	167
12.2	English language perspective compared to Business English Lingua Franca perspective	174
12.3	Association of Business Communication Outstanding Researcher Award recipients who are known for their management communication research recommend readings from their work	185
19.1	Analytic and experiential approaches to language learning and teaching	295
19.2	The 'communicative continuum' as a framework for teaching methodology	298
20.1	EST teaching contexts	306
21.1	Two sets of four skills, as identified by researchers (A) and auditors (B)	334
24.1	Summary of discourse marker functions	388
27.1	Discourse processes and products among parties in external communication	450
27.2	Discourse processes and products among parties in internal communication	450
31.1	Certificates available from professional associations	525
31.2	Certifications available to professional communicators	526

Notes on contributors

Natasha Artemeva is Associate Professor at Carleton University, Canada. Her research focuses on applications of activity-based rhetorical genre theory to the study of school-to-work transitions in engineering, mathematics, and other fields. Her work has received awards from the National Council of Teachers of English, USA.

Vijay Bhatia is an Adjunct Professor at Macquarie University and University of Malaya. His research interests include genre analysis, ESP and professional communication. Two of his books, *Analysing Genre: Language Use in Professional Settings* and *Worlds of Written Discourse: A Genre-based View*, are widely used by researchers in genre theory.

Stephen Bremner is an Associate Professor in the Department of English at City University of Hong Kong. His main research interests are workplace writing and the ways in which students make the transition from the academy to the workplace.

Patrice M. Buzzanell is Professor of Communication in the Brian Lamb School of Communication (and Professor of Engineering Education by Courtesy) at Purdue University, USA. Her research centres on the intersections of communication, career and gender.

Saul Carliner is an Associate Professor, eLearning Fellow, and Director of the Education Doctoral Program at Concordia University, Canada. He is editor-in-chief of the *IEEE Transactions on Professional Communication*, a Fellow and past international president of the Society for Technical Communication, and a past board member of the STC Certification Commission.

Winnie Cheng is an Associate Dean, Faculty of Humanities, and Professor of English and Director of the Research Centre for Professional Communication in English (RCPCE), Department of English, The Hong Kong Polytechnic University.

Marta Chromá is a teacher and researcher in legal English, legal linguistics and translation at Charles University in Prague, Czech Republic. She focuses on the issues of linguistic and legal interpretation of legal concepts and texts for the purposes of translation and translational lexicography.

Isabel Corona (PhD) is a Senior Lecturer in English Studies at the Universidad de Zaragoza (Spain). Her main research interests are genre analysis and multimodality in academic and legal texts and in professional media discourse. She is a member of the research group InterLAE (www.interlae.com).

Notes on contributors

Stephani Currie recently completed an MA degree in Applied Linguistics and Discourse Studies at Carleton University, Canada. Her research focused on the role of ideology in discursive constructions of climate change established by various environmental organisations.

George Anthony David Dass was a partner at Shahrizat, Rashid and Lee for over 25 years. He continues as a consultant and a board member of Perbadanan Insurans Deposit Malaysia, and also of United Bintang Berhad in Malaysia.

Bertha Du-Babcock is an Associate Professor teaching (intercultural) business communication and Communication Strategies in Business Projects at City University of Hong Kong. She also is the Vice-President for the Asia and Pacific Region of the Association for Business Communication.

Matt Falconer recently completed an MA degree in Applied Linguistics and Discourse Studies at Carleton University, Canada, and is currently an intern with the Council of Canadian Academies, a non-profit organisation providing independent, expert assessments of science relevant to public concerns. While this is his first publication, Matthew's research has also focused on tutor training in a Canadian university's academic writing centre.

Gail Forey is an Associate Professor at the Hong Kong Polytechnic University. She has carried out research and published in the areas of discourse analysis, systemic functional linguistics, written and spoken workplace discourse, language education and teaching development. Gail edited a book in 2010 with Jane Lockwood, *Communication and the Workplace*, which is directly relevant to the present chapter and discusses the BPO industry from different perspectives.

Janna Fox is an Associate Professor at Carleton University, Canada. Her research focuses on assessment, teaching, and the development of academic literacies in culturally and linguistically diverse settings. She holds a 3M National Teaching Fellowship in recognition of contributions to scholarship and leadership in Canadian higher education.

Finn Frandsen is Professor of Corporate Communication and Director of the Centre for Corporate Communication (CCC) at the Department of Business Communication, School of Business and Social Sciences, Aarhus University, Denmark.

Jeremy P. Fyke is an Assistant Professor, Communication Studies and Strategic Communication, in the J. William and Mary Diederich College of Communication at Marquette University, USA. His research focuses on consulting, leadership development, ethics and discourses of social change.

Michael B. Goodman is Professor and Director of the MA in Corporate Communication at Baruch College, The City University of New York, and Director of CCI Corporate Communication International. He is Visiting Professor at Aarhus University (Denmark), Hong Kong Polytechnic University, and Universita IULM (Italy). He has published widely, including *Corporate Communication: Strategic Adaptation for Global Practice*, with Peter B. Hirsch.

David Grant is Co-Dean and Professor of Organisational Studies at the University of Sydney Business School, Australia. His current research interests focus on the application of discourse theory and analysis to organisational change and leadership.

Notes on contributors

Elizabeth de Groot is Assistant Professor in Communication and Information Studies at the Radboud University Nijmegen, the Netherlands. Her research interests involve the use and effectiveness of English and multimodality in international business texts.

Christoph A. Hafner trained as a lawyer and is now Assistant Professor in the Department of English at City University of Hong Kong. His research interests include legal discourse, academic and professional literacies, and language learning and technology. In addition to his other publications, he has co-authored a book (with Rodney H. Jones) entitled *Understanding Digital Literacies: A Practical Introduction*, published by Routledge in 2012.

Michael Handford is Professor of the Institute for Innovation in International Engineering Education at the University of Tokyo, and works on professional and intercultural discourse analysis. He is the co-editor, with JP Gee, of *The Routledge Handbook of Discourse Analysis*.

Peter B. Hirsch is Executive Vice President, Director of Reputation Risk for Ogilvy Public Relations. With more than 30 years experience in public relations, he counsels global corporations on issues of corporate reputation and risk management.

Janet Holmes holds a Chair in Linguistics and is Director of the Wellington Language in the Workplace Project at Victoria University of Wellington, New Zealand. She teaches and researches in the area of sociolinguistics, specialising in workplace discourse and language and gender.

Winni Johansen is Professor of Corporate Communication and Director of Study of the Executive Master's in Corporate Communication (EMCC) at the Department of Business Communication, School of Business and Social Sciences, Aarhus University, Denmark.

Alan Jones is a Senior Research Fellow in the Department of Linguistics, Macquarie University, Sydney, and a Visiting Fellow in Anthropology at the Australian National University in Canberra. Research interests include discourse analysis, English for Specific Purposes, and professional communication.

Sujata S. Kathpalia is Senior Lecturer at the Language and Communication Centre, Nanyang Technological University, Singapore, where she teaches academic writing courses. Her research interests include genre analysis, academic writing and English language teaching.

Becky S.C. Kwan is Associate Professor of English at City University of Hong Kong where she teaches on a variety of theory and ESP courses. Her areas of research include thesis writing, academic discourse, genre analysis and doctoral publishing.

Koo Swit Ling, Deputy Director, Language and Communication Centre, Nanyang Technological University, Singapore, is currently teaching Professional Communication to engineering students. Her research interests include business communication, classroom teaching, and language learning.

William Littlewood taught in secondary schools and teacher education before moving to Hong Kong in 1991. He has published widely in the field of language teaching and is now Honorary Professor at the Language Centre at the Hong Kong Baptist University.

Notes on contributors

Jane Lockwood is an Associate Professor in the Department of English at City University of Hong Kong and her research interests involve English for Specific Purposes curriculum and assessment design. She has also developed 'train the trainer' education programmes for Asian workplace settings.

Jane Lung has been working closely with language specialists, subject specialists, ESP practitioners and language teachers in a number of research projects. She has interests in discourse analysis, genre analysis, corpus linguistics and professional communication including legal, business and promotional genres, as well as language teaching and learning. She is an Associate Professor at Macao Polytechnic Institute.

Carmen Daniela Maier is an Associate Professor and member of the Centre for Business Communication and of the Knowledge Communication Research Group at Business and Social Sciences, Aarhus University, Denmark. Her main research interest is the theoretical and methodological development of multimodal analysis of knowledge communication.

Meredith Marra investigates workplace discourse (including meeting talk and workplace identities) as a core member of the Wellington Language in the Workplace Project team. She currently teaches sociolinguistics from first year to PhD level at Victoria University of Wellington.

Lindsay Miller is Associate Professor in the Department of English at City University of Hong Kong. He has been responsible for designing, developing and teaching a wide variety of ESP courses in the department, mostly English for Science and English for Engineering.

Catherine Nickerson is a Professor in the College of Business at Zayed University in the United Arab Emirates. She is currently working on research on the impact of language and languages in the Islamic business world.

Daniel Nyberg is Professor in Sustainability at Nottingham University, UK. His main research interest is investigating how organisations take part in negotiating and shaping how we, as individuals, organisations and societies, respond to global or societal phenomena.

Anne Peirson-Smith is an Assistant Professor in the Department of English at City University of Hong Kong teaching courses on advertising copywriting, fashion communication, public relations and popular culture. Her research focuses on the discourses of fashion branding, advertising and public relations. She is co-author of *Public Relations in Asia Pacific: Communicating Across Cultures* (2009).

Robyn V. Remke is Associate Professor of Intercultural Communication and Management at the Copenhagen Business School in Denmark. Her interests focus on organisational irrationality and resistance in public welfare organisations, organisational diversity and women's leadership. She is the immediate past-president of the Organisation for the Study of Communication, Language, and Gender.

Priscilla S. Rogers, Associate Professor at the University of Michigan Ross School of Business, teaches in Global MBA and Executive Education programs, trains for diverse companies and is an Association for Business Communication Outstanding Researcher Award recipient.

Graham Smart is an Associate Professor of Applied Linguistics and Discourse Studies at Carleton University, Canada. He has published research on writing in professional and academic settings, including *Writing the Economy: Activity, Genre and Technology in the World of Banking*, an ethnographic study of the discourse practices and collaborative knowledge-making activity of economists at Canada's central bank. His current research focuses on the discourses and argumentation of various social actors in the debate over global climate change.

Alina Wan is a PhD student at City University of Hong Kong. Her research relates to communicative practices in the accountancy profession. She has published in this area in the journal *English for Specific Purposes*.

Yunxia Zhu is Senior Lecturer at UQ Business School, University of Queensland, Australia. Her research interests include cross-cultural communications and management and written communication. She has published extensively in these areas and her works have appeared in books, book chapters and prestigious international journals such as *Management International Review, Journal of Business Ethics, Academy of Management Learning and Education, Discourse & Communication, Discourse Studies, Discourse & Society, Text,* and *Journal of Business and Technical Communication*. She also has extensive consulting experience with companies and government agencies in Australia and China.

Introduction

Vijay Bhatia and Stephen Bremner

The *Handbook of Language and Professional Communication* is an attempt to introduce current research and practice in the field of language teaching and learning in professional contexts to a wide audience, which includes not only newly initiated professional communicators, teachers and trainers, but also researchers in the field of professional communication. In addition to bringing readers up to date on the current understanding of professional communication, the *Handbook* also takes them a step further in making them aware of the most recent thinking on the issues confronting the field. The *Handbook* is multidimensional and multiperspective in its design and implementation, and brings together not only researchers from a wide range of disciplines, such as English for Specific Purposes, business communication, management communication, corporate communication, organisational communication, and translation, but also practising professional communicators from the field.

Professional communication

Professional communication, like many other terms in applied linguistics, has been variously understood, interpreted and used in published literature. Broadly interpreted, it refers to the use of all forms of semiotic resources (linguistic as well as multimodal) in and for academic as well as professional contexts, both spoken and written. This interpretation is common in English for Specific Purposes (ESP) and business communication literature.

A narrower interpretation is common in Business and Technical Communication (BTC) literature, which incorporates sub-disciplinary contexts, and often includes management communication, corporate communication, organisational, and institutional communication. Professional communication is also sometimes viewed as incorporating what is generally referred to as workplace communication.

In addition to these interpretations, professional communication also has some overlap with 'Writing In the Disciplines' (WID), or even 'Writing Across the Curriculum' (WAC), although these two are mostly concerned with communication in academic and disciplinary contexts, whereas professional communication most often refers to communication in the world of work. Although these two types of writing programmes (WID and WAC) address different audiences and may claim different motivations, they do seem to have some synergy and overlap with professional communication. A fourth possibility, historically strong but not very common today, is the use of professional communication to refer to what is popularly known as mass communication, media communication, and sometimes new media communication.

Although all the somewhat different forms of communication outlined above have common and overlapping interests, in that most of them are concerned with communication issues in specific academic, professional, institutional or other workplace contexts, they essentially draw their inspirations from different theoretical orientations, some paying more attention to texts (use of language) while others regard context of use as more central. However, none of these approaches ignore either the text or the context completely. In theory, they all tend to work within their specific frameworks; in pedagogical practice, however, they often have overlapping use of resources. ESP approaches, for instance, have traditionally been driven by discourse and genre analyses of academic and professional discourses (which draw on a strong British tradition in the analysis of specialised genres, as in Swales 1990, and Bhatia 1993), or rhetorical theory (which likewise heavily relies on the American tradition in rhetoric and genre, as in Devitt 1991, 2004), whereas others have drawn their strengths from either general communication theories, or from more specific management or organisational theories (as in Reinsch 1996; Rogers 1998, 2000, and 2001; Jameson 2000, 2001). However, in spite of these different theoretical and disciplinary orientations, most of these approaches have the same ultimate objective, that is to be able to understand and appreciate how professional communication is used in their specific contexts, and how best they can teach and train professionals to communicate appropriately in their specific contexts to achieve their disciplinary and/or professional objectives. And since their concerns are somewhat similar or shared, they are more likely to benefit from an integration of one another's approaches and available work. There have been a number of studies published in the last few years, particularly in business communication, which have been using discourse and genre frameworks to enrich their understanding of issues in various areas of business, management, and organisational communication (as evidenced in Bargiela-Chiappini and Nickerson 1999; Nickerson 1998; Chia 2000; Rogers 2000 and 2001; Grant, Keenoy and Oswick 2001; Louhiala-Salminen 2002; Boje, Oswick and Ford 2004; Rogerson-Revell 2007; Charles 2007; and a number of others). These recent developments (see Bhatia 2007) encourage a synergetic integration of various approaches and frameworks.

Integrated view of professional communication

This view favouring integration of various approaches is further strengthened by the fact that in more recent pedagogic practice there appears to be a considerable interest in incorporating methodologies and insights from seemingly different approaches to professional communication, certainly more than was the case a few years ago. Considering the situation today and what it is likely to be in years to come, this *Handbook of Language and Professional Communication* takes a broader perspective on professional communication than has been taken traditionally.

Professional communication thus integrates three main areas of study: English for Specific Purposes (ESP), which draws its inspiration in turn from analysis of disciplinary variation within the framework of register or genre analysis, the second area. The third main tradition that seems to have influenced current thinking in professional communication consists of business communication, management communication and corporate communication. Unlike ESP, none of these sub-areas of communication studies have been seriously influenced by register or genre analysis until recently (see Bhatia 2007 for a detailed review). Instead, they have drawn their strength from various communication theories. The focus in these sub-dimensions of professional communication has been primarily on text-external factors, including context. However, as Bhatia and Bhatia (2011) point out, although at least two of these approaches to professional communication, i.e. ESP and business communication studies, developed almost independently of each other, and remained separate for a long time, they seem to have been brought together by their common interest in the analysis of discourse variation in professional communities, which makes discourse and genre analysis a key contributor to the current integration of ESP and business communication we have called professional communication.

In this volume, we give more substance to this integrated view of professional communication by referring to some of the main developments in recent research in all three areas: analysis of discourse variation in professional communities, ESP, and various other contributors to professional communication, such as business communication, management communication, corporate communication, and organisational communication. This integrated view of *English for professional communication* can be visually represented as follows:

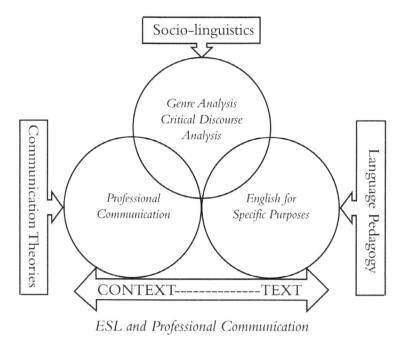

Figure 0.1 ESP and professional communication

Taking this broad integrated perspective on professional communication, the proposed *Handbook* will essentially incorporate not only an historical view of the field, but will also lead readers in the direction in which we think it is likely to develop in the coming years. This has been achieved by specially solicited papers from some of the best-known and most well-established scholars and practitioners in their respective fields to give their understanding of specific issues relating to professional communication and also to project their views about its future development. The main objectives of this *Handbook* thus are:

- To provide an overview of the key contributors to professional communication,
- To make readers aware of the major approaches to professional communication,
- To bring into focus the recent research in professional communication, and
- To argue for the integration of various dimensions of professional communication.

Organisation of the Handbook

The *Handbook* has four major sections:

1 Approaches to professional communication

The first section of the *Handbook* consists of three separate and yet conceptually interrelated sub-sections, which share an overlapping concern with theoretical inputs to various areas of professional communication. They provide, though in varying degrees, some indications of the various kinds of inspiration that have provided strength to individual strands of professional communication.

A General theoretical perspectives

This section reflects the underlying philosophy and some of the key components of theoretical frameworks that have inspired and contributed to the present-day understanding of what we have referred to here as professional communication, while at the same time illustrating its development through a range of ideas and approaches.

In the first chapter, 'Analysing discourse variation in professional contexts', Vijay Bhatia introduces one of the most established and most popular frameworks for the analysis of discourse variation in language use in academic and professional contexts. Although his starting point is the development of discourse and genre analysis of academic and professional discourses, his focus is on both text and context: text as the object of analysis, and context as text-external phenomenon that makes such textual genres possible in real academic and professional contexts. He concludes by suggesting the integration of genre as discursive practice and context as professional practice.

Winnie Cheng, in her chapter 'Corpus analyses of professional discourse' explains a popular research approach used to empirically analyse variation in language use in professional contexts. This corpus-driven approach, based on large quantities of textual data, has brought an increasing amount of credibility to analyses of discourse variation, and hence is being widely used in ESP and business communication studies. Based on reviews of some of the key contributions to the field, Cheng offers a very comprehensive introduction to this immensely useful approach, illustrating her chapter with insights from instances of professional discourses.

Yunxia Zhu, in the next chapter, proposes a situated genre approach for cross-cultural business communication and education, which she explains as a genre learning process in professional contexts. Drawing on the experiences of Chinese students learning English business writing in New Zealand as an example, she claims that the situated model can help learners guide their learning processes to achieve an in-depth understanding of communication genres through active participation in class. This research finding with its focus on student knowledge construction has implications for professional communication learning and education in general.

In the final chapter of this sub-section, Carmen Daniela Maier introduces multimodality as a methodological tool, exploring specific aspects of professional communication. Looking beyond language and across several media, she focuses on the present and future communicative potential and challenges provided by the simultaneous appearance of more complex communicative tools of multiliterate generations, who create, disseminate and use these tools in broad multidisciplinary contexts. She also investigates several types of multi-resources kits that are meant to facilitate new forms of inter-institutional and inter-professional communication and interaction related to the context of the film business.

B Broad disciplinary frameworks

The first part of this section contains five chapters concerned with the ways in which researchers have traditionally approached professional communication, looking at the diverse theories that have informed research and analysis. The intention is, on the one hand, to help readers understand the various perspectives from which professional communication has been viewed, and on the other, to help readers recognise commonalities among the theories and frameworks employed in the field in order to consider ways in which they might be combined and integrated in subsequent research.

Catherine Nickerson, in her chapter 'Business communication' traces the historical development of business communication as an academic discipline from the beginning of the 1990s to its present-day evolution. She provides an insightful overview of published work based on some of the key international journals and other related publications in the field of business communication research and pedagogy. She identifies some of the most important theoretical and methodological frameworks that have influenced business communication researchers and practitioners in the field, discussing how business communication has made a substantial contribution to our understanding of professional communication. She also identifies a number of common trends in business communication in recent research and pedagogical approaches, and speculates on how these may shape the future of the discipline in the course of the next ten years.

Bertha Du-Babcock, in her chapter, revisits theory, research, and teaching in business communication to claim that since theories in this field are proliferating as researchers strive to explain a more complex and diversified global communication environment, they may either be leading to a theory jungle that explains business communication from different positions or to an orchard representing different yet complementary aspects of business communication. She argues that to prevent a jungle from emerging, it is important to distinguish the goals and methods of each research study and to integrate concepts from all of the various approaches whereby they contribute to a better understanding of the field of business communication.

Drawing on a corpus of research studies of the discursive dimension of knowledge-making in the natural sciences, Graham Smart, Stephani Currie and Matt Falconer explore how theory is employed in qualitative empirical research for the purposes of framing, data analysis, and further theory-building in scientific communication. Their analysis of a corpus of ten research studies is intended to help graduate students and early-career scholars in reading and producing qualitative empirical research in the natural sciences, and more generally in professional communication.

In the next chapter Saul Carliner offers a useful and comprehensive account of the field of technical communication, which he defines as a broad field that includes any form of communication about technical or specialised topics, or that communicates by using technology, or provides instructions about how to do something, or a combination of these. For him, the discipline of technical communication has many roots, including in writing, cognitive psychology, and linguistics, and their underlying philosophies, though most technical communicators take a broad view that focuses on designing content for users. The profession of technical communication, he claims, has a growing body of literature rooted in peer-reviewed and professional publications and conferences, and has established quality standards as part of its awards programmes.

Janet Holmes and Meredith Marra, in 'The complexities of communication in professional workplaces', review research on the analysis of workplace communication, focusing on interaction in workplace contexts. They identify a rich and diverse number of theoretical frameworks that have been developed for the analysis of workplace communication, along with a

Introduction

range of contrasting and complementary methods of data collection. Within a broad sociolinguistic framework, their review describes some of the significant theoretical orientations, key issues and methodologies relating to workplace communication. They also consider likely directions for future research in this area.

In our view, there are two additional areas of concern that have potential relevance to and synergy with professional communication. These are the use of electronic media, and translation, which are becoming increasingly relevant because of their shared interest in theories of discourse and communication. The first chapter in this sub-section concerns the importance of new media in present-day professional communication, while the second addresses the challenges of dealing with professional communication issues in the context of translation settings.

This sub-section opens with a chapter by Michael B. Goodman and Peter B. Hirsch, who highlight how electronic media – Web 2.0 – has created internal and external communication challenges for corporations, what they are, and some of the ways in which companies deal with them. They also point out the key challenges: these include globalisation, employee use of social media in a networked enterprise, news aggregation and timely corporate responses in an instantaneous media environment, and the use of electronic media in the regulated environment of investor relations.

Marta Chromá, in the next chapter, considers translation in and as professional communication. She introduces basic translational theories relevant in professional settings, outlining the process of translation and comparing specific aspects within three different domains of professional communication – engineering, commerce and law – as diverse backgrounds for translation, and finally indicates basic assumptions regarding the future position of translation in professional communication.

C Specific disciplinary frameworks

This sub-section brings together five chapters introducing four very specific and different sub-disciplinary frameworks that have become established in their own right. Each of the chapters deals with one discipline, drawing strength from somewhat different disciplinary concepts, which include management, organisational, institutional and corporate communication.

Priscilla S. Rogers in her chapter describes the historical development of management communication, identifying its unique focus relative to other professional communication fields, and its core content related to managers' communication activities. Management communication, she explains, examines managers' effective use of writing and speaking to get work done with and through people. Her sources for this important overview of management communication include a range of key journals in the field, in addition to descriptions and syllabi of related courses from some top business schools.

In the next chapter, David Grant and Daniel Nyberg provide a framework to analyse prevalent organisational discourses communicated and employed within contemporary organisations. The use of the framework is illustrated with examples based on studies of how business engages with climate change and the emerging discourse of sustainability to highlight how discourses are operating at different levels – societal, organisational and individual – that form organisational realities. The framework serves as a useful means by which to understand inter- and intra-organisational dynamics, which also allows us to theorise and give examples of the possibility for corporations to shape and reshape discursive formations.

In the next chapter, Patrice M. Buzzanell, Jeremy P. Fyke and Robyn V. Remke discuss organisational communication for scholars in professional communication, noting how recent inquiry in their field can contribute to professional communication. Their chapter provides overviews of organisational communication from the earliest reviews to current reframings, at the same time encouraging emerging research trends that underlie organisational-professional communication intersections. They point out that although organisational and professional communication have quite distinctive orientations, both of them attend to intersections between discourse and materialities, as well as theory and practice, and power, authority, and agency.

The next chapter, by Finn Frandsen and Winni Johansen, is a state-of-the-art account of the field of corporate communication, defined both as a specific organisational practice and also as a young and emerging academic discipline. They discuss the historical conditions and drivers that have triggered the rise of corporate communication as a new strategic management tool in private and public organisations, distinct from other related disciplines such as public relations, organisational communication, marketing communication and business communication, by identifying key concepts such as corporate *identity, image* and *reputation, integration,* and *stakeholder relations*.

Elizabeth de Groot in the following chapter develops the theme of corporate communication further by identifying it as a management instrument that focuses on the orchestration of all internal and external communication activities, in order to generate and convey a consistent corporate story based on which favourable relationships are established with stakeholders. Drawing on her extensive work on corporate disclosure practices, she identifies several of the theoretical and analytical issues that scholars in the fields of corporate communication and corporate reporting currently face.

2 Practice

This section addresses the varied ways in which professional communication practitioners, both in ESP and business communication contexts, have been handling various issues confronting the teaching and learning of language in professional contexts in order to prepare students to make the transition from the academy to the workplace. This section addresses two major kinds of perspectives: pedagogical, such as needs analysis, curriculum design, materials development, and appropriation of relevant pedagogies, especially focusing on innovative aspects of methodology, both from ESP and business communication; and secondly, disciplinary perspectives such as English for science and technology, engineering, accountancy, law, business processing outsourcing, public relations, and media communication.

A Pedagogic practices

In the first chapter, on needs analysis for professional communication, Jane Lung examines different approaches to determining language and communication needs in the workplace. She introduces a blended approach to needs analysis by combining Critical Genre Theory with traditional needs analysis approaches as a tool to determine the actual needs of learners in specific professional communication contexts. She illustrates the approach by looking into the future English language communicative needs of students in the hotel industry and identifies the typical skills and activities required and desired by the respondents to improve their effective professional communication in English.

Based on a survey of practitioners and a review of current research, the next chapter, by Sujata Kathpalia and Koo Swit Ling, attempts to reach a deeper understanding of the emergence and development of professional practices in business contexts, specifically to determine how workplace communication has changed due to technological advances in the context of globalisation with its focus on flexibility, mobility and diversity. With a focus on programme design in professional communication, they examine these changing trends in the use of communication modes such as websites, instant messaging, emailing, audio and video conferencing that have given rise to new communicative processes and multimodal genres that integrate text, speech, graphics, recorded sound and movies, affecting discourse in ways that were not possible in the past. They investigate these shifts in communication practice in order to capture snapshots of the changing landscape to better equip old and new employees with the dynamically changing world of business discourse.

In the next chapter William Littlewood reviews how teaching methodology has been dealt with, focussing on published books and chapters for ESP teachers rather than research articles. He considers whether there is in fact an identifiable 'ESP methodology' which is separate from that for general EFL, and claims that at the level of principles for language teaching, a single framework embraces both domains. He then considers attempts to formulate context-free principles that inform a context-sensitive methodology relevant to ESP and professional communication teaching strategies and instructional materials.

B Disciplinary perspectives

This sub-section looks at the different disciplinary fields for which professional communication programmes are designed and implemented, always keeping in mind the ways in which practising specialists achieve their academic and professional objectives. This section has several chapters on principles and insights from specific sites of practical and pedagogical engagement.

This section on ESP practice opens with an historical review of the research into English for Science and Technology by Lindsay Miller. He points out how English for Science and Technology (EST) has moved along with trends in linguistic theory. Based on research impacts on pedagogy and a review of textbooks in EST, he shows how materials development in EST has moved from a focus on accuracy, to fluency, to socio-cultural agency. This he illustrates by examining case studies of materials and courses in EST, suggesting ways to prepare EST students for the ever more complicated world of dealing with multi-genres in EST that are emerging due to the multiliteracies students are expected to have in the twenty-first century.

Alan Jones, in the next chapter of this section, highlights the cross-functional roles of accounting professionals, in particular their involvement in strategic management and responsibility for adding value to commercial operations. He rightly claims that all this entails a very high level of interpersonal skills along with the ability to articulate policies and decisions both lucidly and persuasively. In order to give more substance to this view, he identifies and problematises key aspects of what counts as professional communicative expertise in the context of specific professions, especially accounting. Taking a top-down functionalist orientation, he describes the types of work accountants do, what they need to know to do this, and the kinds of social-institutional problems they engage with on a daily basis, in order to conceptualise professional expertise in terms of skills and attributes.

In the next chapter, Christoph A. Hafner provides an overview of the existing research into professional communication in the legal domain. He argues that, in order to reach a satisfactory understanding of specialised legal genres and interactions, it is necessary to go beyond a focus on texts and take into account the full socio-cultural context, in particular the discursive practices of the legal professional community, which are shaped by the social goals of those practices, as well as the jointly held tacit system of values and beliefs of community members. He reviews three main areas of scholarly activity in professional legal communication research: 1 descriptive studies of written professional genres, 2 interpretive studies of talk and interaction, and 3 studies of multilingual and multicultural legal contexts, before speculating as to how the study of professional legal communication might usefully develop in the future.

Drawing on a discourse-based project in the construction industry, Michael Handford outlines how what he calls the 'construction communication' process is structured, with particular reference to the different parties involved. He looks at how communication within the industry is portrayed in academic and professional studies, and the types of research that have been conducted. He then considers how studies in professional discourse might be operationalised to have practical relevance in construction contexts, and goes on to outline an appropriate methodology, demonstrating how it has been applied to audio, video and ethnographic data collected on a Hong Kong construction project.

In the next chapter, Gail Forey, based on her work in the Business Process Outsourcing (BPO) industry, focuses on the differences between written and spoken discourse in order to build a bridge between what we know within applied linguistics and how language is understood in the workplace. Using the framework of Systemic Functional Linguistics (SFL), she claims that if the industry wants to hire and train Customer Service Representatives (CSRs) to deal effectively with customer service enquiries, it may be futile to test and train potential employees through models of written language. Drawing on her data from actual BPO industry interactions, she argues for an evidenced-based understanding of significant features of spoken language in the BPO industry to help change how language is perceived within the industry.

Isabel Corona, in her chapter, attempts to clarify the current state of media communication, by taking a threefold perspective: media as a discipline, media as professional practice, and media as object of research by discourse analysts. For her, media as a discipline is concerned with media studies in tertiary education as part of communication studies; media as professional practice involves encompassing a multiplicity of professions and practices, with an increasing demand for both specialised knowledge and adaptability to respond to evolving new media texts and genres and globalising contexts for production and dissemination processes; and media as object of research responds to an increasing demand for interdisciplinarity as shown by the current trends and methodological approaches in the study of media discourse. The chapter thus tries to find some common ground for an integrated view of the problems and challenges posed by technological, social and globalisation factors that have a strong impact on the current developments in media studies, practice and research.

In the final chapter of this section, Anne Peirson-Smith outlines some of the main theories and debates surrounding the current role of public relations as professional practice and as a subject for academic study. After defining public relations, its history and origins, and its role within the integrated marketing communications framework, she focuses on the rationale behind public relations, stakeholder relationships, the development of public relations, and the application of professional communication theories to analyse and direct public relations activities. She also speculates where public relations education and practice are heading in the future, given the rapidly changing nature of communication brought on with the application and dominance of new technology.

3 Acquisition of professional competence

This section addresses the varied ways in which people become competent performers in professional settings, looking at how professional competence is acquired, whether as a participating member of a particular discourse community or community of practice, or as a student being prepared to make the transition from the academy to the workplace.

In the first chapter in this section, Becky S. C. Kwan discusses the notion of community in professional communication, which has been variously used and interpreted in Applied

Introduction

Linguistics, particularly in the context of discursive practices, in a wide range of academic and professional settings. The notion of *community* has been linguistically modified in a variety of ways, as we see in examples such as *discourse community, community of practice*, and *scientific community*, which have now become widely invoked in the literature on acquisition of professional competence. She provides a brief overview of the epistemic origins of the three community notions, how they have been characterised, how they have been taken up in early and current studies of professional communication, and what the plethora of language studies have revealed about discursive practices in specific communities. She also proposes directions that future studies of discursive practices in specific communities may consider.

In contrast to Becky S. C. Kwan's focus on discursive practices in the acquisition of professional competence, Natasha Artemeva and Janna Fox adopt a socio-rhetorical approach as they consider the formation of a professional communicator, highlighting the notion of portability as it pertains to the transition from academia to the workplace. They point out that whereas the ESP tradition has continued to focus to a large extent on the *textual* realisations of oral and written professional communication by non-native speakers of English, the Writing Studies tradition in North America has investigated academic and workplace writing as situated within socio-cultural, historical, or *rhetorical* contexts of predominantly English-speaking students and professionals.

In his chapter 'Collaborative writing: Challenges for research and teaching', Stephen Bremner looks at the role of collaborative writing in professional communication, considering the definitions and taxonomies that have emerged from research. A central issue is the extent to which collaborative writing activity is entwined in the contexts in which it takes place; he considers the implications this has for research aimed at defining and delineating collaborative writing, and the challenges that this constitutive relationship between writing and context poses for teaching. He concludes the chapter with a look at research areas related to collaborative writing that might be worthy of further investigation.

In the next chapter Jane Lockwood addresses two key issues: the training of professionals in call centres, the nature of knowledge and skills required of English language communications trainers, and the nature of Customer Service Representative (CSR) communication breakdown that they are expected to prevent and remediate. In order to address these issues, she outlines the context of the call centre worksite and then describes how CSRs are currently being supported through English language communications training and coaching in the workplace. Situating this discussion within research in the English for Specific Purposes (ESP) discipline, on the one hand, and business management research as it relates to training in the workplace, on the other, she offers an analysis of communication breakdown in call centres, finally suggesting what might go into ESP call centre communication 'train the trainer programmes' and briefly discussing how these could be implemented.

The final chapter in this sub-section is by Saul Carliner, who discusses credentialing of practising professionals as a significant development in the practice of professional communication. Credentialing for him refers to the process of formal recognition of the accomplishments of communication professionals. Credentialing is intended to recognise professional expertise and provide a 'seal of approval' to hiring managers. He outlines the types of existing credentials, which include certification (voluntary validation of demonstrated competence in a particular field by a third party assessor), licensure (required validation of demonstrated competence in a particular field by a third party assessor, required to practise a profession), certificates (successful completion of a particular programme of study), degrees (completion of an approved curriculum of study at an accredited institution), and accreditation (validation that an academic programme meets the essential requirements).

4 View from the professions

Since the *Handbook of Language and Professional Communication* concerns professionals in the field as much as it does academic scholars, including research students and faculty in universities, it is necessary to balance what academics think and claim about the nature, function, teaching and learning of professional communication with reactions, views, and perspectives of practitioners from the professions. In order to achieve this balance, this section considers the views of practitioners from four relevant fields. The editors of the *Handbook* interviewed well-established and very experienced professionals from banking, law, accounting, and public relations in an attempt to explore the extent to which their perspectives converge with or diverge from the views of researchers in those fields, particularly in areas such as the acquisition of professional expertise in their respective professions. The interviews were generally about an hour long, based on a set of pre-designed questions. Section 4 presents the authentically approved transcripts of these interviews. The section also includes the set of questions we had for our guidance. The four specialists are:

- Banking: A very senior and experienced banker, who would like to remain anonymous.
- Law: George Anthony David Dass, Partner, Shahrizat, Rashad and Lee, Kuala Lumpur, Malaysia.
- Accounting: A Hong Kong accountant, who would like to remain anonymous, interviewed by Alina Wan.
- PR: The managing director of a PR company, who would like to remain anonymous.

Concluding remarks

We have been fortunate to have some of the most established and experienced scholars in the field of professional communication write for this volume, and we have been able to cover a diverse range of areas to offer a truly stimulating collection of informative and scholarly contributions. We are sure that whatever your interests and motivations, you will find some of these chapters in this *Handbook* useful and inspiring, as we have in putting it together. To help newly initiated researchers to explore a particular area more rigorously we have encouraged authors to include suggestions for further reading, in addition to extensive lists of references in specific areas. As professional communication as a field of study and professional practice is still relatively new, we believe this *Handbook* will prove to be a thought-provoking experience for researchers old and new.

Bibliography

Bargiela-Chiappini, F., and Nickerson, C. (eds) (2001). *Writing Business: Genres, Media and Discourse*, London: Longman.
Bhatia, Vijay K. (1993). *Analysing Genre: Language Use in Professional Settings*, Harlow: Longman.
——(2004). *Worlds of Written Discourse: A Genre-Based View*, London and New York: Continuum.
——(2007). 'Discursive practices in disciplinary and professional contexts', *Linguistic and Human Sciences*, 2(1), 5–28.
Bhatia, Vijay K., and Bhatia, Aditi (2011). 'Business communication', in James Simpson (ed.) *Routledge Handbook of Applied Linguistics*, London: Routledge Publications.
Boje, D., Oswick, C., and Ford, J. (eds) (2004). 'Language and organization: The doing of discourse', *Academy of Management Review*, 29(4), 571–77.
Charles, M. (1996). 'Business communications: Interdependence between discourse and the business relationship', *English for Specific Purposes*, 15(1), 19–36.

Chia, Robert, (2000). 'Discourse analysis as organizational analysis', *Organization*, 7(3), 513–18.
Devitt, A. (1991). 'Intertextuality in tax accounting: Generic, referential and functional', in C. Bazerman and J. Paradis (eds), *Textual Dynamics of the Professions,* Madison: University of Wisconsin Press, 337–57.
——(2004). *Writing Genres*, Carbondale: Southern Illinois University Press.
Grant, D., Hardy, C., Oswick, C., Phillips, N., and Putnam, L. (eds) (2004). *Handbook of Organizational Discourse*, London: Sage Publications.
Grant, D., Keenoy, T., and Oswick, C. (eds) (2001). 'Organizational discourse: Key contributions and challenges', *International Studies of Management and Organization*, *31*(3), 5–24.
Jameson, D. A. (2000). 'Telling the investment story: A narrative analysis of shareholder reports', *Journal of Business Communication*, *37*(1), 7–38.
——(2001). 'Narrative discourse and management action', *Journal of Business Communication*, *38*(4), 476–511.
Louhiala-Salminen, L. (2002). 'The fly's perspective: Discourse in the daily routine of a business manager', *English for Specific Purposes*, *21*(3), 211–31.
Nickerson, C. (1998). 'Corporate culture and the use of written English within British subsidiaries in the Netherlands', *English for Specific Purposes*, *17*(3), 281–94.
Reinsch, N. L. (1996). 'Business communication: Present, past, and future', *Management Communication Quarterly*, *10*(1), 27–49.
Rogers, P. S. (1998). 'National agendas and the English divide', *Business Communication Quarterly*, *61*(3), 80.
——(2000). 'CEO presentations in conjunction with earning announcements: Extending the construct of organizational genre through competing values profiling and user-needs analysis', *Management Communication Quarterly*, *13*(3), 426–85.
——(2001) 'Convergence and commonality challenge business communication research', *Journal of Business Communication*, *38*(1), 14–23.
Rogerson-Revell, P. (2007). 'Using English for international business: A European case study', *English for Specific Purposes*, *26*, 130–120.
Swales, J. M. (1990) *Genre Analysis: English in Academic and Research Settings*, Cambridge: Cambridge University Press.

Section 1
Approaches to professional communication

A. General theoretical frameworks

1
Analysing discourse variation in professional contexts

Vijay Bhatia

Much of research in English for Specific Purposes (ESP), and to some extent in professional communication, has been inspired by descriptions of discourse variation in academic and professional contexts. Although professional communication represents the development that integrates ESP and Business Communication as two main areas of study (see Bhatia and Bhatia 2011), with ESP drawing its inspiration from applied linguistics, and Business Communication from communication theory, both of them have come to benefit from the outcomes of analysis of various forms of academic and disciplinary discourses within the various frameworks of discourse analysis, in particular from genre analysis. In more recent years critical discourse and genre analytical frameworks have also started influencing the current thinking in organisational communication, management communication, and corporate communication, all of which are often grouped under professional communication (see Chia 2000; Boje, Oswick and Ford 2004; Grant *et al.* 2004; Bhatia 2007). In the early sixties, only ESP relied heavily on descriptions of discourse variation, and none of the other areas of professional communication took studies in discourse and genre analysis seriously, relying on various communication theories instead. The focus in these individually somewhat diverse areas of professional communication was primarily on text-external factors, including context, whereas in ESP the focus was on text-internal aspects, such as lexico-grammar and rhetorical organisation. However, in more recent years, the focus in all areas of professional communication has been shifting towards disciplinary variations in professional and academic discourses and practices in addition to various theories of communication, thus integrating text-internal as well as text-external factors in professional communication. In this chapter I would like to introduce some of the key developments in the field of discourse and genre analysis and their applications to various forms of professional communication, which can be represented as shown in Figure 1.1.

Analysing functional variation as register

As mentioned earlier, ESP has always drawn its inspiration from applied linguistics, particularly from sociolinguistics, through the analyses of functional variation in language use in academic as well as professional contexts. The earliest forms of analysis of language variation can be traced back to the work of Halliday, McIntosh and Strevens (1964), who defined functional variation

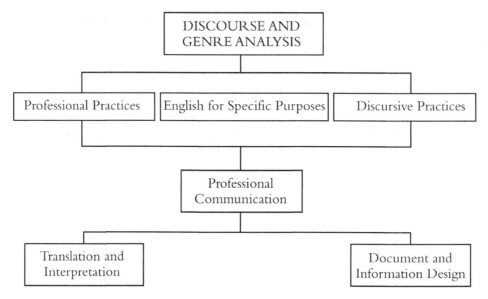

Figure 1.1 Discourse and genre analysis in professional communication (adapted from Bhatia 2012)

in language use as *register*, drawing evidence from statistical significance of lexico-grammatical features. As Swales (2000) pointed out, register analysis gave early ESP practitioners a mechanism to relate findings of linguistic analysis to pedagogic materials through what he called 'thin' descriptions of ESP discourses. However, he cautioned that this resource lacked 'a perception of discourse itself' and 'the means for analyzing and exploiting it' (2000: 60), which was rectified in later work on genre analysis.

In subsequent years numerous studies appeared identifying and describing typically characteristic features of various academic and professional registers, such as scientific English, business English, and legal English. However, it is a common perception that outsiders to a discourse or professional community are not able to follow what specialists write and talk about even if they are in a position to understand every word of what is written or said (Swales 1990), and even being a native speaker in such contexts is not necessarily helpful if one does not have sufficient awareness or understanding of the conventions of such specialised discourses and genres situated in specific professional practices. Thus in subsequent years, ESP inspired a new tradition for the analysis of academic and disciplinary discourses within the framework of *genre analysis*, which, as Widdowson (1998) points out, was a significant advance on register analysis. Referring to the work done by Swales (1990) and Bhatia (1993), he claims that it 'seeks to identify the particular conventions for language use in certain domains of professional and occupational activity'. He further points out that it is 'a development from, and an improvement on, register analysis because it deals with discourse and not just text: that is to say, it seeks not simply to reveal what linguistic forms are manifested but how they realise, make real, the conceptual and rhetorical structures, modes of thought and action, which are established as conventional for certain discourse communities' (1998: 9).

The rationale for such developments has been that communication is not simply a matter of putting words together in a grammatically correct and rhetorically coherent textual form, but more importantly, it is also a matter of having a desired impact on how a specifically relevant discourse or professional community views it, and how the members of that community negotiate meaning in professional contexts. It is a matter of understanding 'why members of a specific disciplinary or professional community communicate the way they do' (Bhatia 1993), which requires the discipline-specific knowledge of how professionals conceptualise issues and talk about them in order to achieve their disciplinary and professional objectives.

Analysing functional variation as genre

In its early conceptualisations, genre analysis sought thicker functional descriptions of discourse variation, often going beyond the immediate context of situation, attempting to offer a grounded description of language use in educational, academic, or professional settings. Genre analysis thus reflected more than mere linguistic descriptions of texts, invariably offering explanation for language use in conventionalised and institutionalised settings. Genre analysis, as pointed out in Bhatia (2004), is viewed as the study of situated linguistic behaviour in institutionalised academic or professional settings, whether defined in terms of *typification of rhetorical action*, as in Miller (1984), Bazerman (1994), and Berkenkotter and Huckin (1995); *regularities of staged, goal oriented social processes*, as in Martin, Christie and Rothery (1987), and Martin (1993); or *consistency of communicative purposes*, as in Swales (1990) and Bhatia (1993). Genre theory, in spite of these seemingly different orientations, covers a lot of common ground. The most important feature of this view of language use is the emphasis on conventions that all three manifestations of genre theory consider very central to any form of generic description. Genre essentially refers to language use in a conventionalised communicative setting in order to give expression to a specific set of communicative goals of a disciplinary or social institution, which gives rise to stable structural forms by imposing constraints on the use of lexico-grammatical as well as discoursal resources (Bhatia 2004).

The second important aspect of genre theory is that although genres are typically associated with recurring rhetorical contexts, and are identified on the basis of a shared set of communicative purposes with constraints on allowable contributions in the use of lexico-grammatical and discoursal forms, they are not static. Berkenkotter and Huckin (1995: 6) aptly point it out when they say 'genres are inherently dynamic rhetorical structures that can be manipulated according to conditions of use'.

These two features of genre theory – emphasis on conventions and propensity for innovation – may appear to be contradictory in character; one tends to view genre as a rhetorically situated and highly institutionalised textual activity, having its own generic integrity, whereas the other assigns genre a natural propensity for innovation and change, which is often exploited by the expert members of the specialist community to create new forms in order to respond to novel rhetorical contexts or to convey 'private intentions within the socially recognised communicative purposes' (Bhatia 1995: 1). How do we explain this seeming contradiction between 'generic integrity' on the one hand, and 'propensity for innovation' on the other?

Going back to Berkenkotter and Huckin, we find that although genres are associated with typical socio-rhetorical situations and in turn, they shape future responses to similar situations, they have always been 'sites of contention between stability and change' (1995: 6). Situations, and more importantly rhetorical contexts, may not always recur exactly in the same way, though they may still have a considerable overlap. It may be that a person is required to respond to a somewhat changing socio-pragmatic need, encouraging her or him to negotiate her or his response in the light of recognisable or established conventions. It may also be that she or he may decide to communicate 'private intentions' within the rhetorical context of a 'socially recognized communicative purpose' (Bhatia 1995). Bhatia (2004) discusses the example of a letter from a company chairman to the shareholders, in which he finds expert manipulation of generic resources to convey a positive image about a company's somewhat negative performance. In contexts such as these it is often possible for established members of a professional community to manipulate institutionalised generic resources, thus exploiting the 'tactical freedom' available to expert professionals to negotiate individual responses to recurring and novel rhetorical situations. It is true that there are regularities of various kinds, in the use of lexico-grammatical, discoursal, and generic resources; there are rhetorical situations, which often recur, though not exactly in the same form, or manner, but at the same time, there are expert and well-established users of language in specific disciplinary cultures who try to exploit, appropriate, and even bend generic conventions and thus expectations in order to be innovative and effective in their use of language. All these factors make the real world of discourse complex and yet interesting.

In the last two decades genre theory has become one of the most favoured tools for the analysis of professional discourse. The frameworks and methods of language description have also become increasingly sophisticated, focusing more on context, rather than just the text. It has also become increasingly multidimensional and multi-perspective (Bhatia 2004), in that it has integrated a number of different methodologies, such as textography (Swales 1998), interpretive ethnography (Smart 2006), corpus analysis (Hyland 2000; Cheng, this volume), participant-perspectives on specialist discourses (Louhiala-Salminen 1996; Rogers 2000), cross-cultural and intercultural perspectives (Gimenez 2001; Vergaro 2004; Planken 2005; Vuorela 2005; Zhu, this volume), multimodal analysis (Brett 2000; O'Halloran 2006; Maier, this volume), and observation analysis (Louhiala-Salminen 2002), to name only a few. However, the implication for professional communication is that text-based analyses within register or genre analysis have been found to be increasingly inadequate in explaining and accounting for the typical relationship between 'discursive' and 'professional' practices (Bhatia 2004, 2008a, 2008b, and 2010) of various professional communities. In the light of this need to analyse 'professional' practices, Bhatia (2008a, 2008b, and 2010) argues for a much deeper understanding of context in all its varied forms, including studies of how participants undertake these discursive tasks, perform professional actions, and what they achieve through these discursive and professional activities and practices.

In its recent developments, genre analysis started exploring more comprehensively what Bhatia (2010) calls 'socio-pragmatic space' to raise a number of other interesting issues, in particular those that question some of the basic assumptions about the integrity of generic descriptions. This has prompted investigations into variations in 'discursive practices' leading to critical examination of 'professional practices', with focus on the achievement of successful outcomes in professional actions, rather than just on the writing of grammatically correct and acceptable texts. In this context, Livesey (2002: 7–9) points out that 'formal and surface features of texts' must be studied in 'the narratives of context' leading to what he calls 'a creative-critical moment of understanding' thus revealing 'the ideological meaning of particular texts' and the interests they serve.

Bremner (2008: 308) also argues in favour of a more comprehensive understanding of interdiscursive voices in any system of activity. He points out that,

> If we take the social constructionist view of genres and contexts as inherently dynamic, as mutually constitutive (Berkenkotter and Huckin 1993; Goodwin and Duranti 1992; Smart 2006), and also recognize that genres are interconnected in wider systems of activity, then we need to look at the ways in which genres influence other genres in the system. A key feature of intertextuality to consider, then, is that it is not simply a link between texts, but a phenomenon that helps shape other texts: as genres combine to achieve different goals, they contribute to the development of new genres as they are recontextualised (Linell 1998). Thus the generic, linguistic and rhetorical choices that a writer makes will be

influenced by the texts that precede or surround the text under construction, and will in turn have an effect on the final textual product.

Bhatia (2004, 2008a, and 2010) argues that the study of conventional analyses of genres or even 'genre sets' (Devitt 1996) or 'systems of genres' (Bazerman 1994) that are used to fulfil the professional goals of specific disciplinary or professional communities may not be sufficient to understand the complexities of professional communication. He claims that a comprehensive understanding of the motives and intentions of professional practices is possible only if one looks beyond the textual constraints to analyse the multiple discourses, actions and voices that play a significant role in the formation of specific discursive acts within the contexts of specific institutional and organisational practices and cultures. He develops the notion of 'interdiscursivity' as a function of appropriation of contextual and text-external generic resources within and across professional genres and professional practices, to which we shall return in the next section.

Interdiscursivity in professional communication

Interdiscursivity in professional communication has become one of the most important concepts that seem to be crucial to the study of professional genres and practices (Bhatia 2010). Within the concept of genre and professional practice, one can see expert professional writers constantly operating within and across generic boundaries creating new but essentially related and/or hybrid (both mixed and embedded) forms to give expression to their 'private intentions' within the socially accepted communicative practices and shared generic norms (Bhatia 1995; Fairclough 1995). Interdiscursivity is invariably across discursive events that may be genres, professional activities, or even more generally professional cultures. It is often based on shared generic or contextual characteristics across two or more discursive constructs, and some understanding of these shared features is a necessary condition to an adequate understanding of the new construct. Interdiscursivity thus can be viewed as a function of *appropriation of generic resources* across three kinds of contextual and other text-external resources: genres, professional practices, and professional cultures.

From the point of view of genre theory, especially in the context of professional communication, it is necessary to distinguish appropriations across text-internal and text-external resources, the former often viewed as intertextuality, and the latter as interdiscursivity. Intertextuality operates within what we refer to as 'textual space' (Bhatia 2004) and has been widely studied (Kristeva 1980; Foucault 1981; Bakhtin 1986; Fairclough 1995); however, a vast majority of appropriations often take place across text-external semiotic resources at other levels of professional, institutional and disciplinary discourses, such as genres, professional, institutional, and disciplinary practices, and professional, institutional and disciplinary cultures to meet socially shared professional, institutional, and disciplinary expectations and objectives, and sometimes to achieve 'private intentions'. These latter forms of appropriations that operate in what could be viewed as 'socio-pragmatic space' (Bhatia 2004) are essentially interdiscursive in nature. It may be pointed out that often all these appropriations, whether text-internal or text-external, discursively operate simultaneously at all levels of discourse to realise the intended meaning, and have been widely used in the recontextualisation, reframing, resemiotisation or reformulations of existing discourses and genres into novel or hybrid forms. In addition to this, appropriation of generic resources is also very common in various forms of hybrids, such as mixing, embedding and bending of genres (see for details Bhatia 2004, 2008a, 2008b, and 2010). The general picture representing interdiscursivity in genre theory can be summarised as in Figure 1.2.

I would like to claim that interdiscursivity operates at all levels of text-external use of resources, e.g. generic, professional practice, and professional culture; it also allows a more

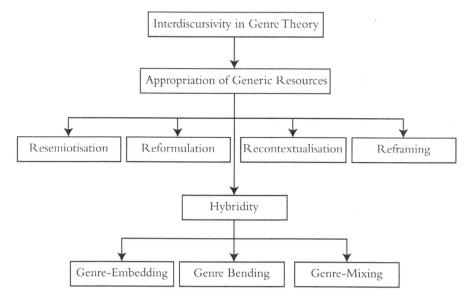

Figure 1.2 Interdiscursivity in genre-based analysis of professional communication (Bhatia 2012: 25)

rigorous and comprehensive analysis of genres in and as professional practice. At the same time, it also encourages evidenced-based studies of professional and institutional practices and cultures through the genres that are typically used in such contexts.

This idea of studying professional practice through interdiscursive use of linguistic and other semiotic resources within socio-pragmatic space is very much the central focus of what I have referred to elsewhere as 'critical genre analysis' of professional communication as part of professional practices (see Bhatia 2008a, 2010). Critical genre analysis contributes significantly to our understanding of organisational and institutional practices, in addition to its current applications to discursive and professional practices, in both academic as well as professional contexts. Critical genre analysis is meant to explain and clarify how professional communication is actually constrained and eventually realised, and in what ways this meaning is intended to be part of professional practices, as well as providing insights into what goes into its production, reception and the consumption of knowledge. This emphasis on academic and professional practice, in addition to discursive actions, encourages a further perspective on genre analysis, with a focus on what I would like to call 'discursive performance', which extends the scope of analysis from genres as discursive products to the professional practice that all discursive acts tend to accomplish. In the final section of the chapter I would like to give more substance to what I have referred to as 'Critical Genre Analysis' (CGA).

Critical Genre Analysis of professional discourse

Critical Genre Analysis (CGA) is an attempt to extend genre theory beyond the analyses of textual resources used in professional genres to understand and demystify professional practices or actions in academic as well as professional contexts. In spite of apparent similarities with Critical Discourse Analysis (CDA), CGA is very different.

CDA draws on critical theory as cultural critique, and focuses on social relations of domination, typically grounded in class relations, including race and gender, specifically focussing on their oppressive sides. It thus tends to analyse social structures in such a way that they are viewed as invulnerable. It encourages recognition of domination without offering resources for action against such practices. CDA thus examines social structures and relations and analyses them in such a way that the analysis highlights the use of power and domination to represent oppressive actions in somewhat unequal social settings.

Critical Genre Analysis, on the other hand, is a way of 'demystifying' professional practice through the medium of genres. An interesting aspect of this analysis is that it focuses as much on generic artifacts, as on professional practices; as much on what is explicitly or implicitly said in genres, as on what is not said; as much on socially recognised communicative purposes, as on 'private intentions' (Bhatia 1995) that professional writers tend to express in order to understand professional practices or actions of the members of corporations, institutions and professional organisations. In CGA, therefore, no professional, institutional, or organisational practices are assumed, but are systematically analysed and negotiated. They seem to be in a constant struggle between competing interests. CGA with its focus on practice considers individual members of professional organisations, though bound by their common goals and objectives, as still having enough flexibility to incorporate 'private intentions' within the scope of professionally shared values, genre conventions, and professional cultures (Bhatia 1995). A notion of practice thus describes the relation between shared values and flexibility as dynamically complex, in that institutional and organisational ideologies and constraints are often conventionalised and standardised, but not always static or inflexible. In professional communication, a theory of practice is a function of organisational and institutional structures as evident in the everyday activities of professionals, and conditions of production and reception are crucial. Not only this, in professional communication in the age of computer-mediated communication, CGA also considers the overwhelming power and influence of technology in professional life. Thus professional practices give shape to actions in specific professional contexts, and they get established so long as the members of the professional community continue to follow the conventions which are shared by the members of a specific professional discourse community. CGA makes a commitment, not only to describe, but also to explain, clarify, and 'de-mystify' professional practice. In this sense, CGA is not an initiative to change the professional practices of individual disciplinary, institutional, and corporate communities, but to understand how professional writers use the language to achieve the objectives of their professions.

Concluding remarks

I have made an attempt in this chapter to present a broad overview of register and genre-based frameworks for the analysis of discourse variation in professional contexts. In doing so, I have also highlighted the recent developments in the field of genre analysis, particularly the effort to go beyond the textual artifacts to investigate context of various kinds, including interdiscursivity as crucial to a comprehensive understanding of professional communication.

It may be pointed out that research in areas such as the relationship between discursive activities and professional practices in most disciplinary, professional and institutional contexts (Bhatia 2008a, 2008b) is still in its early stages, and a lot more work is needed before we can find convincing answers to the question that Bhatia (1993) raised, that is, 'why do most professionals use the language they way they do?' For instance, we still have no comprehensive understanding of what makes a novice accounting student into a good accountant, or how we identify, train, and appraise a good manager, marketing executive, or a public relations expert. What is the role of language in the development of specialist expertise in a particular professional field? What are the core competencies that are needed to make a person a competent professional? Are these competencies teachable? Is it possible to assess the acquisition of such expertise? Although we seem to be a long way from any kind of definite and convincing answers to some of these questions, and a lot more work is needed, we seem to be heading in the right direction.

To conclude, I would like to suggest a few directions in which research in future is likely to go. In my view, there is a need to integrate ESP with current research in other areas of professional communication. This will also encourage a more comprehensive view of professional communication. In addition to this, the field of professional communication can be enriched by integrating insights from and about professional practices, which can be and have, in recent genre analytical studies, been successfully undertaken with insightful conclusions. If we can continue to explore some of these perspectives, I feel that we will be very close to demystifying some of the hitherto hidden complexities associated with acquisition of specialist professional and disciplinary competence.

Related topics

corpus analysis of professional discourse; business communication; needs analysis; professional communication in legal domain; communities in discursive practices.

Key readings

Bargiela-Chiappini, F. and Nickerson, C., (eds) (2002). *Writing Business: Genres, Media and Discourse*, London: Longman. (This offers a good collection of papers on various aspects of professional communication studies, often combining ESP and Business Communication studies.)

Bhatia, V. K. (2004). *Worlds of Written Discourse: A Genre-Based View*, London and New York: Continuum. (It offers a comprehensive genre analytical framework for the study of discursive and professional practices in a number of different business and disciplinary contexts.)

Bhatia, V.K. (2010). 'Interdiscursivity in professional communication', *Discourse and Communication*, 21/1, 32–50. (This offers a comprehensive understanding of interdiscursivity in genre theory.)

Bhatia, V. K., John Flowerdew and Rodney Jones, (eds) (2008). *Advances in Discourse Studies*, London and New York: Routledge. (It offers a broad view of some of the key approaches to discourse analysis, covering a range of approaches, discourses and frameworks.)

Swales, J. M. (1990). *Genre Analysis: English in Academic and Research Settings*, Cambridge: Cambridge University Press. (This is a very comprehensive account of the genre theory, in particular focusing on academic communication.)

Bibliography

Bakhtin, M. M. (1986). *Speech Genres and Other Late Essays*, Austin: University of Texas Press.

Bazerman, C. (1994). 'Systems of genres and the enhancement of social intentions', in Aviva Freedman and Peter Medway (eds), *Genre and New Rhetoric* (pp. 79–101), London: Taylor & Francis.

Berkenkotter, C. and Huckin T. N. (1995). *Genre Knowledge in Disciplinary Communication-Cognition/Culture/Power*, NJ: Lawrence Erlbaum Associates, Publishers.

Bhatia, V. K. (1993). *Analysing Genre: Language Use in Professional Settings*, Harlow: Longman.

——(1995). 'Genre-mixing and in professional communication: The case of "private intentions" v. "socially recognised purposes"', in P. Bruthiaux, T. Boswood and B. Bertha (eds), *Explorations in English for Professional Communication* (pp. 1–19), Hong Kong: City University of Hong Kong.

——(2004). *Worlds of Written Discourse: A Genre-Based View*, London: Continuum International.

——(2007). 'Discursive practices in disciplinary and professional contexts', *Linguistic and Human Sciences*, 2(1), 5–28.

——(2008a). 'Genre Analysis, ESP and Professional Practice', *English for Specific Purposes*, 27, 161–74.

——(2008b). *Towards Critical Genre Analysis*, in V. K. Bhatia, John Flowerdew and Rodney Jones (eds), *Advances in Discourse Studies* (pp. 166–77), London: Routledge Publications.

——(2010). 'Interdiscursivity in professional communication', *Discourse and Communication*, 21/1, 32–50.

Bhatia, V. K. and Bhatia, Aditi (2011). 'Business communication', in James Simpson (ed.), *Routledge Handbook of Applied Linguistics*, London: Routledge Publications.
Boje, D., Oswick, C. and Ford, J. (eds) (2004). 'Language and organization: The doing of discourse', *Academy of Management Review, 29*(4), 571–77.
Bremner, Stephen (2008). 'Intertextuality and business communication textbooks: Why students need more textual support', *English for Specific Purposes*, 27, 306–21.
Brett, P. (2000). 'Integrating multimedia into the Business English curriculum: A case study', *English for Specific Purposes*, 19, 269–90.
Cheng, W. (2014). 'Corpus analyses of professional discourse', in V. K. Bhatia and Stephen Bremner (eds), *Handbook of Professional Communication*, London: Routledge Publications.
Chia, Robert (2000). 'Discourse analysis as organizational analysis', *Organization*, 7(3), 513–18.
Devitt, A., (1996): 'Genre, genres, and the teaching of genre', *College Composition and Communication*, 47, 605–16.
Duranti, Alessandro and Goodwin, Charles (eds) (1992). *Rethinking Context: Language as Interactive Phenomenon*, Cambridge: Cambridge University Press.
Fairclough, N. (1995). *Critical Discourse Analysis: The Critical Study of Language*, London: Longman.
Foucault, M. (1981). *The Archaeology of Knowledge*, New York: Pantheon Books.
Gimenez, J. C. (2001). 'Ethnographic observations in cross-cultural business negotiations between non-native speakers of English: An exploratory study', *English for Specific Purposes*, 20, 169–93.
Grant, D., Hardy, C., Oswick, C., Phillips, N. and Putnam, L. (eds) (2004) *Handbook of Organizational Discourse*, London: Sage Publications.
Halliday, M. A. K., McIntosh, A. and Strevens, P. (1964). *The Linguistic Sciences and Language Teaching*, London: The English Language Book Society and Longman Group Ltd.
Hyland, K. (2000). *Disciplinary Discourses: Social Interactions in Academic Writing*, Harlow: Pearson Education Ltd.
Kristeva, J. (1980). 'Word, dialogue and novel', in J. Kristeva (ed.), *Desire in Language* (pp. 64–91), Oxford: Blackwell.
Linell, P. (1998). 'Discourse across boundaries: On recontextualizations and the blending of voices in professional discourse', *Text, 18*(2), 143–57.
Livesey, S. M. (2002). 'Interpretive acts: New vistas in qualitative research in business communication', *Journal of Business Communication, 39*(1), 6–12.
Louhiala-Salminen, L. (1996). 'The business communication classroom vs. reality: What should we teach today?' *English for Specific Purposes*, 15(1), 37–51.
——(2002). 'The fly's perspective: Discourse in the daily routine of a business manager', *English for Specific Purposes*, 21, 211–31.
Maier, C. D. (2014). 'Stretching the multimodal boundaries of professional communication in multi-resources kits', in V. K. Bhatia and Stephen Bremner (eds), *Handbook of Professional Communication*, London: Routledge Publications.
Martin, J. R., Christie, F. and Rothery, J. (1987). 'Social processes in education: A reply to Sawyer and Watson (and others)', in I. Reid (ed.), *The Place of Genre in Learning: Current Debates* (pp. 46–57), Geelong: Deakin University Press, Australia.
Martin, J. R. (1993). 'A contextual theory of language', in Bill Cope and Mary Kalantzis (eds), *The Powers of Literacy – A Genre Approach to Teaching Writing* (pp. 116–36), Pittsburgh: University of Pittsburgh Press.
Miller, C. R. (1984). 'Genre as social action', *Quarterly Journal of Speech*, 70, 157–78, also published in A. Freedman and P. Medway (eds) (1994) *Genre and the New Rhetoric* (pp. 23–42), London: Taylor and Francis.
O'Halloran, K. (2006). *Multimodal Discourse Analysis: Systemic Functional Perspectives*, London: Continuum.
Planken, Brigitte (2005). 'Managing rapport in lingua franca sales negotiations: A comparison of professional and aspiring negotiators', *English for Specific Purposes*, 24, 381–400.
Rogers, P. S. (2000). 'CEO presentations in conjunction with earning announcements: Extending the construct of organizational genre through competing values profiling and user-needs analysis', *Management Communication Quarterly* 13(3), 426–85.
Smart, G. (2006). *Writing the Economy: Activity, Genre and Technology in the World of Banking*, London: Equinox.
Swales, J. M. (1990). *Genre Analysis: English in Academic and Research Settings*, Cambridge: Cambridge University Press.

——(1998). *Other Floors Other Voices: A Textography of a Small University Building*, London: Lawrence Erlbaum Associates, Publishers.
——(2000). 'Language for specific purposes', *Annual Review of Applied Linguistics, 20*, 59–76.
Vergaro, C. (2004). 'Discourse strategies of Italian and English sales promotion letters', *English for Specific Purposes Journal, 23*, 181–207.
Vuorela, T. (2005). 'How does a sales team reach goals in intercultural business negotiations? A case study', *English for Specific Purposes, 24*, 65–92.
Widdowson, H. G. (1998). 'Communication and community: The pragmatics of ESP', *English for Specific Purposes, 17*(1), 3–14.
Zhu, Y. (2014). 'A situated genre approach for business communication education in cross-cultural contexts', in V. K. Bhatia and Stephen Bremner (eds) *Handbook of Professional Communication*, London: Routledge Publications.

2
Corpus analyses of professional discourse

Winnie Cheng

Introduction

In Biber and Reppen's (2012) four-volume collection of corpus linguistic research papers, corpus linguistics (CL) is described as 'a research approach to investigate the patterns of language use empirically, based on analysis of large collections of natural texts' which has 'revolutionized the study of language variation and use: what speakers and writers actually do with the lexical and grammatical resources of a language' (Book Description, 2012). Indeed a similar view is expressed by many others; for example, Halliday (1993: 24) regards CL as re-uniting the activities of data gathering and theorising, which leads to a qualitative change in our understanding of language, and Tognini-Bonelli (2001: 1) considers CL to be 'a new philosophical approach to linguistic enquiry'. Generally speaking, CL researchers analyse corpora – phonemic, textual, multimodal and so on – with the aim of finding 'probabilities, trends, patterns, co-occurrences of elements, features or groupings of features' (Teubert and Krishnamurthy 2007: 6) to arrive at generalisations.

CL is primarily quantitative; nevertheless, in most recent CL studies, a combination of quantitative and qualitative techniques is employed, by obtaining statistical findings using text analysis software and tools in order to identify trends and other ideas for follow-up qualitative analysis. The value of frequency data, as noted by Handford and Matous (2011: 91) on spoken corpora, illustrates the combination of methods: 'as a first step, quantitative analyses of fully transcribed complete encounters allow for the texts to be prized open with an attractive degree of interpretive objectivity'. Qualitative analysis can take the form of concordance or discourse analysis. A concordance, 'a collection of the occurrences of a word-form, each in its own textual environment' (Sinclair 1991: 32), serves as a useful source of data for making a number of inquiries in language use and meaning. Figure 2.1 shows a sample of 20 lines of the concordance for 'thank you' in the Hong Kong Corpus of Spoken English (HKCSE).

CL studies can be corpus-driven, corpus-based, corpus-assisted, or corpus-informed, depending on why and how a corpus is used for carrying out research. In recent years, CL methods have been applied to a number of linguistic inquiries in sounds and intonation, words, phraseology, grammar and lexical semantics, and CL research conducted in conversation analysis, discourse and genre analysis, and pragmatics. Conrad (2002), for instance, notes that CL methods have

```
1    well  a: yeah  A: you speak English very well  a: * oh thank you    A: ** (inaudible)  a: so would you mind    (pause)   a:
2        (pause)  a: your receipt thank you   (pause)   B: okay thank you  a: yes (.) enjoy your flight bye bye  B056     B1: oh t
3    conclude this presentation  a1:        ** mm         ** thank you   a1: thank you er for your comments   b2: so shall we
4        a7: ((Cantonese))  a1: ((Cantonese: okay thanks)) * thank you   a7:            ** thank you   a1:  now but er who had he
5    ave no reason to say no  B: great b: * alright  B: ** thank you   also um I don't need a room made up but can I get a new
6    h thank you   B: (inaudible)  b: (inaudible) tired b: thank you  (.) and Mister V__ do you have any check in baggage  B:
7    the floor no okay and then er thank you very much  a:  thank you  ((applause))              1       1       A028
8    ny evening work (.) * yeah a:          ** mhm (.) * thank you   B:        ** and the salary is I think in the region o
9    nd then er filling that in have you got a pen  a3: oh thank you   B: the pen is there  a1: yeah a pen here thank you
10   hich case just knock on the door and come in  a: okay thank you   B: okay * thanks  a:       ** thank you  A1:       **
11   thanks * very much  a2:                  ** thank you  a3: thank you   B: thanks  B084    a1: so this is (.) this is erm (.)
12   n the fifth floor  x: okay * thank you  b1:       ** thank you  B010    b: good afternoon  B: er reservation   b: yes
13   share and even increase our market share (.) okay  B4: thank you  b1: quite a bit it's actually very hard to er to tr
14   you also guide us as to where the increases come from thank you   b1: sales of funds partly because of seasonal because
15   )  b2: exactly  b1: okay thank you both very much  b3: thank you   b1: that's all we have for you this week join us again
16   r designs magazine  B1: okay (.) good  a1: that's it thank you   B2: erm just saying so yesterday we we passed on to W
17       (inaudible) that that's why I am saying a slim chance thank you  b2: that's all  a1: thank you (do you have any more qu
18   ate sixteen  B: six- close to sixteen  b: yep  B: okay thank you   bye  b: bye  B046    a: so er (.) for- any baggage chec
19   vy pleasure (pressure) er on the provision of services thank you  chairman  b2: er thank you the Professor Lee may be wh
20   t I will hand it to the to Nicole Leung   (pause)   a11: thank you  Daisy and now I would like to talk about the reservatio
```

Figure 2.1 A sample concordance for 'thank you' in HKCSE

been used to address such discourse-level phenomena as 'characteristics associated with the use of a language feature', 'realizations of a particular function', 'characterizing a variety of language', and 'mapping the occurrences of a feature through entire texts' (p. 75). Sinclair (1996, 2004) postulates an abstract model of lexical description that accounts for the internal structure of a lexical item (Sinclair 2004: 141–48). The model comprises 'five categories of co-selection', two obligatory and three optional, which are put forward as components of a lexical item. The lexical item 'reconciles the paradigmatic and syntagmatic dimensions of choice at each choice point' (p. 141). The first obligatory category is the 'core', which is 'invariable, and constitutes the evidence of the occurrence of the item as a whole' (p. 41). The other obligatory category is the semantic prosody, the determiner of the meaning of the whole lexical item that expresses the 'function' of the lexical item and shows 'how the rest of the item is to be interpreted functionally' (p. 41). The three optional components are collocation, colligation and semantic preference. Collocation is 'co-occurrence of words'; colligation is 'co-occurrence of grammatical choices'; and semantic preference refers to 'the restriction of regular co-occurrence to items which share a semantic feature' (p. 141).

A review of the recent literature shows that in CL research, the nature and communicative purpose of corpus data examined in different studies varies widely. A broad way of classifying the corpora is general language and specialised corpora. An example of a recently compiled specialised corpus is the Corpus of American Soap Operas (SOAP) consisting of '100 million words in more than 22,000 transcripts of ten American soap operas from 2001 and 2012' (http://corpus2.byu.edu/soap/overview.asp). Many specialised corpora are small, such as the group of online profession-specific corpora created by the Research Centre of Professional Communication in English of The Hong Kong Polytechnic University, in collaboration with professional associations. The corpora include the Hong Kong Financial Service Corpus, 7.3 million words; Hong Kong Engineering Corpus, 9.2 million words; and Corpus of Research Articles, 5.7 million words. Others have investigated a specific type of specialised corpora, namely academic and educational corpora, such as academic research articles (e.g., Mur-Dueñas 2011; Peacock 2011; Murillo 2012) and learner corpora (Rankin and Schiftner 2011; Ädel 2011).

Many CL studies have examined general language corpora; for instance, Moon's (2011) study of English denominal adjectives in – *like* in the British National Corpus (BNC), Grant's (2012) study of lexis in the spoken Wellington (NZ) corpus, and Parviainen's (2012) investigation into the Asian varieties of English 'use of clausal-final focus particles *also* and *any* in sentences' (p. 226) in the International Corpus of English (ICE). A major general American English corpus is the Corpus of Contemporary American English (COCA), which consists of five genres, namely spoken, popular magazines, fiction, newspapers, and academic journals of rather balanced representation (Davies 2009).

A recent study of COCA was conducted by Hardy and Colombini (2011) who examined the nominal uses of the 'heavily metaphorized and often contested concept' (p. 462) of risk in COCA in order to investigate 'further the seemingly self-contradictory negative and positive semantics of risk' (p. 464). The study employed corpus analysis methods including 'frequency analysis, concordance contextual analysis, collocational analysis, and a variation on distinctive-collexeme analysis' (p. 462). It was found that across the five genres of COCA, the occurrence of the noun lemma RISK in descending order of frequency is academic discourse, magazines, spoken discourse, newspapers and fiction. Collocational analysis shows that 'infection' is the most frequent collocate of RISK and the most frequent phrasing is 'risk of infection' (p. 480). Another finding is 'concentration of both RISK and negatively medical RISK in magazine and academic genres', indicating that these two genres use the negatively medical discourse of RISK more frequently (p. 472). Hardy and Colombini (2011) found that when RISK collocates with 'worth taking', 'RISK is still inherently negative' (p. 482).

A review of CL research studies in professional communication

This chapter delimits the scope of review by focusing on specialised, professional 'genre- and topic-specific corpora' (Fuertes-Olivera 2007: 219), written and spoken, in a wide range of professional contexts, including business, political, heath care, public, media, and legal contexts. The review includes methods of study and the main findings of these CL studies, as well as their applications in various situations and implications for research and teaching and learning. A number of these studies reviewed combine corpus linguistic methods with conversation analysis, (critical) discourse analysis and pragmatics. The chapter ends with projection about the future development of the use of corpus approaches and methods in the study of professional communication.

A variety of professional genres, written and spoken, have been examined with the use of CL methods, including corporate annual report narratives (Rutherford 2005), press releases, research and analysis reports, trade policy reviews of different countries, ministerial conferences (Fuertes-Olivera 2007), legal cases (Hafner and Candlin 2007), financial disclosure genres of earnings presentations and earnings releases (Camiciottoli 2010), Enron emails (Kessler 2010), the meeting subcorpus of Cambridge and Nottingham Business Corpus (CANBEC) (Handford 2010), interactions between engineers and foremen on a construction site (Handford and Matous 2011), and media reports (Cheng and Lam 2012), to name a few recent ones.

The Business English Corpus (BEC), one million words with 56 per cent from written and 44 per cent spoken business genres, was used in Nelson (2006). Nelson's (2006) study is concerned with the statement that 'collocates themselves can have a semantic patterning that is not random' (p. 218). He compared the key words of the BEC with the BNC Sample (2 million words), and found that 'the business world revolves around recurring semantic sets: people, institutions, places and money' (p. 231). His analysis of the semantic associations of 10 selected key words by manually examining the concordances of these words shows that some words have unique semantic prosodies while others have shared ones; for example, 'company-customer relations' is specific to the word 'customer' and 'company hierarchy and status' is shared by 'manager', 'staff', and 'status' (p. 223). However, some words were found to have the same semantic associations in the BEC and the BNC; for example, '*send* – documents; *big* – people; *global* – people and *package* – computers' (p. 230). In addition, Nelson found 'unique business-related' semantic associations (p. 230), with 'global' and 'package' occurring in the BEC much more frequently than in the BNC.

The 10-million-word Wolverhampton Corpus of Business English (WBE Corpus) contains web-based English texts collected during a period of six months in 1999–2000 from different countries (Fuertes-Olivera 2007). The corpus mostly (99.3 per cent) contains written official documents, including 'press releases, research and analysis reports, trade policy reviews of different countries, ministerial conferences' and the rest (0.7 per cent) account for transcripts of speeches. The WBE Corpus has been examined to find out the feature of lexical gender, namely forms of address, professional titles, and generic man. Findings confirmed the '"Male-As-Norm" underlying principle of lexical gender' (Fuertes-Olivera 2007: 230) due to male dominance in particularly management positions in business settings. The study also found in professional settings greater use of *Ms* than *Mrs* and *Miss* combined, showing some impact of the non-sexist language campaign, and greater use of 'generic *person*' than 'generic *man*', indicating the use of lexical means to indicate 'dual gender reference' (p. 231).

Ooi (2000, 2008) examined a unique corpus that contains web-based electronic gaming texts, such as 'the manufacturer's product descriptions, gaming reviews, gaming weblogs and discussion forums for gaming participants' (p. 3). With the use of the integrated corpus linguistic tool *Wmatrix* (Rayson 2001), Ooi (2008) compared the corpus of electronic gaming genre (G-Corpus) with the one-million-word BNC Written Sample and one-million-word BNC Spoken Sampler respectively to conduct content category analysis, followed by lexeme analysis, namely 'shmup' or 'shoot-'em-up', 'vertically', 'frag', 'NPC', and 'cheap'. Findings were then discussed by using Sinclair's (1996) abstract model of the lexical item and Hoey's (2005) lexical priming model, as well as some popular online dictionaries in order to study the semantic and attitudinal meanings of these lexemes in the G-Corpus.

A well-known business corpus that has been investigated in a number of ways is the Enron email dataset, which, after duplicate entries have been removed, consists of over 12.6 million words of over 500,000 emails (Kessler 2010). The dataset has been examined by several researchers to address different research questions, including 'email classification and threading behaviour among email users (Klimt and Yang 2004), social networking analysis (Corrada-Emmanuel *et al.* 2005), document classification (Bekkerman 2007), and linking trends (Shetty and Adibi 2005)' (Kessler 2010: 264). Similarly, Kessler (2010) used the Enron email corpus to investigate the polysemic nature of the word 'virtual'. The choice of Enron was because the company is 'tech savvy' with 'high proclivity for use of neologism' and the company itself is 'a virtual company' (p. 262). Kessler (2010) found that the word 'virtual' occurring in the co-text of the email message makes 'broad reference to nearly anything computer related, including computer business, computer based simulation and varied forms of computer mediated communication' and illustrates 'inauthenticity, hyperbole and potential deception' (p. 262). The study concluded that the word 'virtual' is increasingly polysemic, and potentially increasingly ambiguous in meaning and use.

The professional genre of accounting narratives in the UK Operating and Financial Review (OFR) was examined by Rutherford (2005). He divided the corpus into seven groups of companies, classified into loss-making, least profitable, most profitable, largest, smallest, highest geared (leveraged) and lowest geared. The study conducted word frequency analysis, which is 'straightforward, objective, and economical to use' (p. 374). Findings showed that the genre of accounting narratives, in a similar way to unregulated accounting narratives, uses 'language biased toward the positive (the "Pollyanna effect")', despite authoritative guidance that the PFR should be expressed in neutral terms' (p. 349). The Pollyanna effect, which is used as 'a form of impression management' (p. 373), was found to be more profound in poorly performing companies.

Also in financial services, Camiciottoli (2010) examined two corpora of financial disclosure genres, earnings presentations and earnings releases, from the same 25 companies and in the same financial periods, specifically studying the use of contrastive, additive and resultative discourse connectives. Comparative word profile analysis showed greater use, and a wider range, of discourse connectives in the oral financial genre, showing that presentations are 'carefully structured and planned' due to the top executives' persuasive intention to emphasise success and downplay failure, while 'exhibiting their oratory competence at the same time', compared to the less 'rhetorically motivated' (p. 661) staff press officers. Then concordance analysis of the most frequent discourse connectives in both spoken and written financial corpora, *however, in addition/additionally,* and *as a result,* in each corpus was conducted so as to determine their communicative functions. Camiciottoli's (2010) corpus study concluded that discourse connectives are the defining feature of financial earnings presentations.

Related to the legal profession, Hafner and Candlin (2007) compiled a corpus with 114 legal cases, suggesting that judgements in the corpus resemble such legal genres as letters of advice, legal opinions, and pleading submissions in lexico-grammatical patterns and language functions, and that examination of a specific legal genre helps students to learn 'the complex intertextuality and interdiscursivity that is characteristic of legal discourse' (p. 307). The corpus was utilised to demonstrate the value of an online concordancer and collocation tool as a means for law students, as novices, to develop competence in writing for legal purposes, and hence to acquire professional expertise. Hafner and Candlin's (2007) findings showed an increase in the use of the tool and resources among students from the second to the fourth year of study, and more appropriate use as 'an aid to composition' (p. 312) in terms of finding 'quick and convenient solutions to their language problems' (p. 314).

Political texts and discourses, specifically English EU documents, are useful data for corpus linguistic research (e.g., Trebits 2008, 2009; Jablonkai 2010). Trebits (2008) examined the Corpus of EU English (CEUE) and found prevalent technical and non-technical lexical elements and collocation patterns. Trebits (2009) compared the use of conjunctions in the CEUE with the BNC, and found, in descending order of frequencies, additives, temporals, causals, adversatives, clarifying conjunctions, hypothetical conjunctions, and continuitives. In Jablonkai (2010), the English EU Discourse Corpus was examined in terms of lexical bundles. The corpus comprised EU legal texts, legislative preparatory documents, documents related to EU funds, and other documents issued by EU institutions, totalling 241 texts and 1.1 million words. For each of the four text categories, there were many genres; for example, the EU legal texts consist of treaties, international agreements, regulations, directives, decisions, recommendations, opinions, common positions CFSP, and judgements of the Court of Justice (p. 256). When compared to the structural types of lexical bundles in textbooks and academic prose (Biber *et al.* 2004), Jablonkai (2010) found a higher number of lexical bundles with verb phrases and fairly high frequencies of occurrences in EU texts, as well as similarities in both the structural and functional classification of lexical bundles in EU texts and Biber *et al.*'s (1999) textbooks and academic prose.

The findings, or evidence, from specialised corpora have been discussed in terms of heightening the learners' awareness of various features of the language, including lexical, grammatical and textual aspects (Gavioli 2005; Walker 2011). Walker (2011) demonstrates how corpus evidence can be successfully used in addressing 'searching and demanding questions' (p. 111) about words and phrases from non-native English speakers who are senior managers in global companies. Using the general language corpus Bank of English (BoE) (450 million words) and the British National Commercial Corpus (6.3 million words) (BNC), Walker (2011) identified a collocational profile for selected items first in the BoE and then in the BNC. This was followed by studying the respective concordances to identify the semantic sets. Based on corpus evidence, the advice given to a senior manager is to say '*I am responsible for human resources* or *I manage the*

Human Resources Division', but not '*I am in charge of human resources* or *I run the Human Resources Division*' (p. 110). The reason is that *I run* or *I am in charge of* seem to be associated with power, and hence reflect 'a top-down management style' (p. 110).

Some CL research studies compared business English textbooks and specialised corpora of written business English, suggesting that corpus evidence be considered when selecting or designing materials for business English instruction. Sznajder (2010), for instance, first identified words and phrases that express the conceptual metaphors of war, health and sports taught in a textbook of business English. The researcher then searched a sample of a million-word corpus of business periodical and journal articles (BPJA) manually. The corpus sample searches also included metaphor collocational patterns and metaphor synonyms. The study concluded that the selection of metaphors for explicit language instruction is only partly supported by corpus evidence, including frequency data. Based on the conclusions, Sznajder (2010) suggested the use of business corpus data to 'allow students and teachers to inquire into the meaning and form of frequent metaphorical expressions and their context of use' (p. 40).

CL studies have also been conducted in metaphor and word play in Chinese. Han (2011) conducted research into the use of 'playful, humorous, and creative metaphors' (p. 3476) in 1016 items of Chinese online entertainment news obtained from the Entertainment Channel of the online news portal people.com.cn. A word list was first generated, from which potential metaphorical expressions were noted. Then the concordances of the words were manually examined to determine the metaphorical sense of the words. The last step was to group the different metaphorical senses into such lexical domains as 'WAR, MARTIAL ARTS and FOOD'. The study identified two patterns of playful metaphors, namely 'a blend of war metaphors with popular cultural formats such as computer games and martial arts fiction' and 'the playful exploitation of food metaphors that are originally invented by Chinese Internet users' (p. 3476). Examples of war metaphors are 'SPORTS IS A CHAPTER NOVEL OF WAR' and 'NEWS EVENTS ARE ROLE-PLAYING MARTIAL ARTS GAMES' (p. 3478). Han (2011) concluded that these play metaphors 'creatively and amusingly exaggerate the superficial triviality of the personal actions of entertainers' and thus have 'the potential to promote or even hype the news content' (p. 3487).

The use and meaning of media language and discourse has been another subject of CL study. Bednarek (2012), for instance, investigated key words and trigrams, and their concordances, in contemporary American English television dialogue from seven fictional series, comprising the genres of crime, mystery, medical, comedy, and drama, with the spoken American National Corpus ('ANCS') as the reference corpus. The study focused on the characteristic 'over-represented key words/trigrams and their potential to indicate informality and emotionality' (p. 35) in television series. Bednarek (2012) found that informality, the expression of emotion, involvement and specific communicative situations are key defining features of the language of television across about 80 per cent of the television series and different television genres (p. 35), as illustrated in the 'core' features of 'key word forms involving first- and second-person pronouns (*me, I'm, your, you're*)' and 'the specific key words *hey, sorry, gonna, gotta, man, thanks, please* and *hell*' (p. 42). Findings also demonstrate the more informal nature of the television corpus, compared to the ANCS, as in the greater frequency of semi modals (*gonna, gotta*), the expletive *hell*, the informal *hey*, and the informal words *mom, dad, guy*, and *boss* in the television series. In addition to informality, Bednarek (2012) identified higher frequency of expressions of emotion in the television dialogue, compared to unscripted conversation in the ANCS. Features of emotional language include evaluative language, emotional lexis, modal verbs, lexical repetition, intensification, exclamations/interjections, expletives and taboo words, emphasis, and expressive speech acts (p. 48). The study further found that the key words/trigrams '*hey, man, need to talk, out of here, I told you, I want you, you want me, want me to, why, what are you, why don't you, who are you, why are you, are you doing*' (p. 49) are used in the expression of emotion and stance, specifically 'in the context of negative emotions associated with conflict, confrontation or other problematic issues that characters face' (p. 56). The study also examined under-represented, unusually infrequent negative key words and trigrams and found the functional categories of vague language, narrative-like language, discourse markers, non-fluency features, as well as identifiers and quantifiers (p. 58). Based on the results of both positive and negative key words and trigrams, Bednarek (2012) concluded that there exists 'a fictional television register' that is 'characterised by its high degree of emotionality' (p. 60).

Many CL studies have analysed spoken professional texts and discourses. In their applied corpus study in clinical linguistics, Adolphs *et al.* (2004) examined the NHS Direct corpus, which contained 17 phone calls made by the researchers to NHS Direct in Nottingham in 2002, without awareness of the health advisers and nurses. With the use of the CANCODE as a reference corpus, key word analysis was conducted to reveal qualitative features. Examples include the use of pronouns for hearer involvement, backchannel responses to invite the patient to 'explain their symptoms and invite further elaboration' (p. 17), the use of 'able' and direct quoting of instructions from another source by the health professional to 'make the advice appear authoritative' (p. 20), and the use of convergence codas to summarise the event of the preceding interaction before the phone call ends.

Two spoken corpora of simulated 'new-relationship sales negotiations' (Planken 2005: 384) were compared in terms of interactional (safe) talk and personal pronouns. Participants, who speak English as a lingua franca, in each corpus are dyads of professionals and students of international business communication respectively. Pronoun use was considered to be 'indicators of the negotiator relationship' (p. 384), and pronouns examined were 'you' (as indicator of other-orientedness) and inclusive 'we' (cooperativeness) versus inclusive 'we' (professional distance), and 'I' (self-orientedness). Corpus searches on pronoun use are complemented by qualitative conversation analysis, showing that student negotiators underuse institutional 'we' and so are 'unsuccessful at maintaining professional distance, and thus, at creating a professional identity within the negotiation event' (p. 382).

Office hour academic consultations were studied by Reinhardt (2010), where two professional groups, international teaching assistants (ITAs) in training in simulation situations and practising academic professionals in MICASE, were compared in their use of directive language in their consultations with students in order to 'inform instruction in advanced spoken English for academic purposes' (Reinhardt 2010: 94). Comparative findings showed that the ITAs in training, as a group, underuse modal and periphrastic modal constructions that 'promote inclusion' and overuse directive vocabulary constructions that 'may restrict choice and promote dependence', which can be attributed to '(lack of) instruction or exposure, or to the influence of individual L1s and backgrounds' (Reinhardt 2010: 100).

The genre of business meetings has been examined in a number of corpus linguistic studies based on the DIRECT project in Brazil, including the use of modals in Portuguese in Brazilian meetings (Barbara and Berber Sardinha 2005), and the predominate use of pronouns in a corpus of ten Brazilian meetings that indicates 'the important role of the interpersonal metafunction' in these meetings (Barbara and Berber Sardinha 2005). Handford (2010) examined the keywords of the meeting subcorpus (900,000 words) of the Cambridge and Nottingham Business Corpus (CANBEC), when compared to the Socialising and Intimate subcorpora (SOCINT) from Cambridge and Nottingham Corpus of Discourse in English (CANCODE). He found some statistically significant features that are characteristic of business meetings. They are five interpersonal features which invoke different 'social dimensions and discursive practices in business meetings' (p. 92):

1 *Pronouns*: signalling the social relationship.
2 *Backchannels*: signalling listener solidarity.
3 *Vague language*: signalling solidarity over knowledge.
4 *Hedges*: negotiating power over knowledge.
5 *Deontic modality*: negotiating power over actions.

(Handford 2010: 92)

In a later study, Handford and Matous (2011) compared the statistically significant lexico-grammatical items in a corpus of spoken communication recorded on a construction site in Hong Kong that involved Japanese engineers and Hong Kong foremen, with SOCINT and CANBEC as reference corpora. The items identified were interpersonal items, such as deontic modality, hedges and fillers, certain back channels (*hmm*, *yah* and *hai*), the discourse marker *so*, and the pronoun *we* as well as place deixis. Construction words that were statistically significant were *boulder*, *shift* and *slope*. When key word analysis was performed by comparing the Hong Kong construction site corpus with the SOCINT and then the CANBEC respectively, differences were found; for example, evaluative nouns and action verbs were found to be statistically significant in the HK-SOCINT key words.

Pauses in conversational narrative in the Narrative Corpus (NC), extracted from the BNC, were examined by Rühlemann, Bagoutdinov and O'Donnell (2011) in order to find out how pauses in conversational narrative were used and why pauses in conversational stories were more frequent. A software tool was used to examine 'collocation patterns around pause words and elements' (p. 202). Major observations of the study were that '*er*, *erm* and short silent pauses are more frequent in story-telling' (p. 225) whereas long silent pauses were more frequent in the non-narrative general conversation. The researchers suggested three reasons for the observations:

(i) the need for narrators, in the opening utterance of the story, to provide specific information to orient listeners to the situation in which the events unfolded, (ii) the need to coordinate narrative clauses to match the story events, and (iii) the preference of narrators to present speech, thought, emotion and gesture using direct-mode discourse presentation.

(Rühlemann, Bagoutdinov, and O'Donnell 2011: 198)

In recent years, researchers have increasingly adopted a 'methodological synergy' (Baker *et al.* 2008) between CL and critical discourse analysis (CDA). Cheng and Lam (2010, 2012), for example, investigated journalistic and media corpora, combining the theories and methods of corpus linguistics and critical discourse analysis. The tools used for corpus analysis are *ConcGram 1.0* (Greaves 2009) and *Wmatrix 3.0* (Rayson 2008). *ConcGram 1.0* (Greaves 2009) is a corpus linguistic program designed to uncover the co-occurrence of words fully and in an automated way. *Wmatrix* is a web-based software tool for corpus analysis and comparison. The corpus examined in their 2008 study consisted of 5,000 articles collected from a leading English newspaper in Hong Kong in two periods before and after the change of sovereignty in 1997, with a focus on changes in the representation of human rights issues. Sinclair's (1996, 2004) model of five categories of co-selection to study the extended units of meaning of the lexical item was applied to analyse instances of 'human rights' in the corpus as a lexical item. Cheng and Lam's (2010) findings show that the newspaper has changed its representation of human rights issues, particularly in China and Hong Kong, over the decade, reflecting an ideological shift in the newspaper's stance in response to the current situations in both local and world politics. The authors concluded that human rights concerns are not merely a nationalistic, but also a culturally dynamic, phenomenon. In their 2012 study, Cheng and Lam examined four self-compiled corpora that contained a range of written texts concerned with the handover of Hong Kong from Britain to the People's Republic of China (PRC): two Western media corpora with texts published in 1996–98 and 2006–8, and two Chinese media corpora with texts published in 1996–98 and 2006–8. Western media's perceptions of, and relations with, Hong Kong ten years on were discussed, substantiated with findings obtained from key word, concgram (Cheng, Greaves and Warren 2006; Cheng, Greaves, Sinclair and Warren 2009), semantic field, and concordance analyses. The products of *ConcGram 1.0* (Greaves 2009) are termed 'concgrams', defined as comprising all of the permutations of the association of two or more words, irrespective of whether the words occur in different sequence relative to one another (i.e. positional variation, AB and BA) or when one or more words drop between the co-occurring words (i.e. constituency variation AB and ACB) (Cheng, Greaves and Warren 2006). Findings show that Western media discourses in 1996–98 expressed negative views about political issues, and placed a stronger focus on the general business environment of Hong Kong; however, such views and perceptions had been replaced by 'an increasing emphasis on political-related issues and individual political views in the new politicalised Hong Kong in 2006–8' (p. 14). Findings also show that the Chinese media have changed, as revealed 'in the increase in quoting Hong Kong political parties or individuals' unfavourable views about the political situation in Hong Kong' (p. 14). Cheng and Lam's (2012) corpus and CDA study gives insights into the new image of Hong Kong through the eyes of the West and helps to re-evaluate the relations and power balance between the West and China.

The term 'human rights' was studied by Mooney (2012) who built a discursive profile of 'human rights' through comparing British and American print media corpora. Discursive profiling was performed by manually cataloguing key usages of the term, followed by studying 'frequent and salient collocations of the keywords in question' (p. 171). Mooney identified a number of fields that are common to both corpora, including activists and advocacy, law, institutions, legal processes and actors, less than abuse, breach/violation, abstract values, abuses in other countries, disparaging, protection, and association with criminals, all of which are associated with legal human rights (LHR). Further comparison of two 'human right' British and American print media corpora revealed that the singular and individual human right is associated with bare human rights (BHR), defined as 'those which are necessary for bodily human Life' (p. 169). Human rights, found to be associated with basic right and specific rights, such as marriage, medical care, right to life and water, were regarded as universal and outside the law, but not subject to social and cultural norms. Mooney (2012) hence argued that BHR can 'form a defensible basis' (p.79) for the meaning of LHR, and constitute a 'reasonable and viable way to ensure the future of legal human rights' (p. 169).

Another corpus-assisted CDA study (Koteyko 2012) found 'discursive (re)construction of market-based solutions to climate change' (p. 24) by examining lexical compounds of 'carbon' retrieved from UK national newspapers each year between 1990 and 2009. Based on frequency of tokens of carbon-compounds and lexical productivity, i.e., 'the capacity of producing different forms from a specific lexeme or root' (p. 27), Koteyko identified two major groups of compounds that denote 'a reduction or even elimination of carbon dioxide emissions' (p. 27) and are related to finance. Koteyko (2012) also examined the chronological appearance of the carbon-compounds and found 'both continuities and changes in the discursive presentation of climate change mitigation' (p. 33). The study concludes that the discursive framing by means of lexical productivity functions to 'restrict the debate on climate change mitigation scenarios by relying on calculation and monetization emissions as the starting point' (p. 24).

Forchtner and Kølvraa (2012) combined CL, the discourse-historical approach (DHA) in CDA (Reisigl and Wodak 2001), and theories of narrativity (Somers 1994; Labov 2006) and conceptual history (Koselleck 2004) arguing that 'the specific narratives of a common European past ultimately serve to legitimate the contemporary identity constructions and political priorities of the EU' (p. 382). The researchers examined a corpus of 62 'speculative speeches' (p. 377) delivered by leading politicians in the European Union between 2001 and 2007 at commemorative events, celebrations, anniversaries, and milestone events, with a focus on the politicians' 'emerging memory frames' that 'narrate their symbolic boundaries in a more inclusive way by admitting past wrongdoings' (p. 377). The first step of data analysis involved corpus downsizing. The corpus was examined to generate a word list, followed by collocates of 'Europe', and then the concordances of collocates. After that, clusters around 'Europe' were examined, resulting in retaining 32 relevant clusters, classified into Koselleck's (2004) three dimensions in the conceptual construction of collective identities: temporal (e.g., *building Europe, division of Europe, Europe is now*), spatial (e.g., *Central and Eastern Europe, citizens of Europe, Eastern Europe*), and hierarchical (e.g., *democratic Europe, Europe of peace, Europe stands*) clusters. Specific texts were then analysed in detail through CDA. Findings show that the EU politicians' self-critical narratives about a bitter past differentiates between Europe that has learned and the external 'other' that has not, and hence 'can become the foundation of European superiority expressed in ambitions to "teach the world"' (p. 398).

In another corpus and CDA study of political discourse, Edwards (2012) was interested in studying the development of British National Party (BNP) discourse by comparing the 2005 and 2010 BNP manifestos, and specifically examined the discursive techniques adopted by the British National Party and the way in which 'their language is changing to appeal to a wider electoral base' (p. 245). Hence, the study was designed to examine 'the formulation of the "in-group"' (p. 247) by identifying node words such as self-reference words, i.e., first-person pronouns and 'BNP', and node words that vary significantly in frequencies between the two manifesto corpora, e.g., 'British' and 'the British', 'natives' and 'indigenous peoples', 'white' and 'humans'. The concordances of these node words were then analysed 'to identify their referents, contexts and relevance' (p. 248). The study concluded that 'in-group' categories such as nationhood seems to be invoked to imply inclusivity; however, the closer study of 'our' and 'British' revealed that BNP racism is disguised in the 'seemingly moderate discourse' (p. 245); the use of 'indigenous' and 'white' showed an increase in 'the appropriation of the discourse of victimhood and the racialisation of crime' (p. 256); and the use of 'human' only for derision and attack pointed to the opposite of inclusivity.

Future directions for CL research

The foregoing review of previous studies shows that previous CL studies conducted in professional contexts have examined a range of textual data in different types of discourse and genres. Departing from mainstream textual corpus linguistic analysis, Gu (2006) adopted a CL approach to multimodal and multimedia discourse analysis with the analytic unit being a social situation, comprising activity type, task/episode, and the participants' behaviour of talking and doing, acts, prosodic units of illocutionary force, and so on. His corpus consists of 'video streams with synchronized sounds' (p. 127). In the context of his study, Gu defines a corpus linguistic approach as first, digitalising a multimodal text so that it becomes processable by the computer; second, segmenting the nondiscrete streams of flowing images into 'discrete units that correspond to the analytic units of the content'; and third, coining a metalanguage to annotate the segmented units (p. 146). Gu illustrates his approach with some professional or social situations, including 'a group of archaeologists excavating a recently discovered ancient tomb', which was televised live by China Central TV (p. 140), the Beijing Foreign Studies University (BFSU) sixtieth anniversary ceremony, and 'a group of tourists taking a rafting tour down the valley of Wuyi Mountain, Fujian Province, South China' (pp. 143–44).

This chapter concludes that the future directions for corpus linguistic research, whether or not combined with other approaches and methodologies in language and communication such as those for (critical) discourse and genre analysis, lexical semantics, pragmatics, and intercultural communication, should aim to extend beyond single modality corpora and to build and examine multimodal and multimedia corpora (e.g., Gu 2006) so as to more fully understand and describe the 'probabilities, trends, patterns' (Teubert and Krishnamurthy 2007: 6) and co-occurrences of elements and features in the interactions and inter-relationships revealed in various modes of communication in professional settings. As Edlund, Heylen and Paggio (2012) point out, 'multimodal corpora are becoming a core research asset and they provide an opportunity for interdisciplinary exchange of ideas, concepts and data' (p. 5). Future CL research should consider language, spoken or written, to be 'situated action, where linguistic and non-linguistic actions are intertwined with the dynamic conditions given by the situation and the place in which the actions occur' (Edlund, Heylen and Paggio 2012: 5).

Related topics

general and specialised language corpora; discipline and profession-specific corpora; corpus linguistic methods; multimodal corpora

Key readings

Biber, D. and Reppen, R. (eds) (2012). *Corpus Linguistics 4 Volumes*, London: Sage. (A collection of 60 previously published articles and chapters classified into four volumes: lexical studies, grammar, varieties and methods and applications.)

Cheng, W. (2012). *Exploring Corpus Linguistics: Language in Action*, London: Routledge. (Combining the author's long experience and involvement in many research projects over the years to illustrate how different corpus linguistic theories and methods can be effectively used to study different practical linguistic phenomena and features.)

Sinclair, J. McH. and Mauranen, A. (2006). *Linear Unit Grammar: Integrating Speech and Writing*, Amsterdam/ Philadelphia: John Benjamins. (Proposes the linear approach that describes the role of natural chunking in discourse, especially spoken discourse.)

Bibliography

Ädel, A. (2011). 'Rapport building in student group work', *Journal of Pragmatics*, *43*, 2932–47.

Adolphs, S., Brown, B., Carter, R., Crawford, P. and Sahota, O. (2004). 'Applying corpus linguistics in a health care context', *Journal of Applied Linguistics*, *1*(1), 9–28.

Baker, P., Gabrielatos, C., Khosravinik, M., Krzyżanowski, M., McEnery, T. and Wodak, R. (2008). 'A useful methodological synergy? Combining critical discourse analysis and corpus linguistics to examine discourses of refugees and asylum seekers in the UK press', *Discourse & Society*, *19*(3), 273–306.

Barbara, L. and Berber Sardinha, T. (2005). 'Cultural stereotype and modality: A study into modal use in Brazilian and Portuguese meetings', in G. Forey and G. Thompson (eds), *Text Type and Texture: In Honour of Flo Davis* (pp. 246–62), Liverpool: School of English, University of Liverpool.

Bednarek, M. (2012). "Get us the hell out of here': Key words and trigrams in fictional television series', *International Journal of Corpus Linguistics*, *17*(1), 35–63.

Bekkerman, R. (2007). 'Document classification on Enron email dataset'. Available from http://people.cs.umass.edu/~ronb/enron_dataset.html (accessed 22 November 2012).

Biber, D., Johansson, S., Leech, G., Conrad, S. and Finegan, E. (1999). *Longman Grammar of Spoken and Written English*, London: Longman.

Biber, D., Conrad, S., and Cortes, V. (2004). 'If you look at ... : Lexical bundles in university teaching and textbooks', *Applied Linguistics*, *25*, 371–405.

Biber, D. and Reppen, R. (eds) (2012). *SAGE Benchmarks in Language and Linguistics: Corpus Linguistics* (Vols. 1–4), London: Sage Publications Ltd.

Book description, Biber, D. and Reppen, R. (eds) (2012). *SAGE Benchmarks in Language and Linguistics: Corpus Linguistics* (Vols. 1–4), London: Sage Publications Ltd. Available from www.amazon.com/Corpus-Linguistics-SAGE-Benchmarks-Language/dp/0857029649 (accessed 22 October 2012).

Camiciottoli, B. C. (2010). 'Discourse connectives in genres of financial disclosure: Earnings presentations vs. earnings releases', *Journal of Pragmatics*, 42, 650–63.

Cheng, W., Greaves, C. and Warren, M. (2006). 'From n-gram to skipgram to concgram', *International Journal of Corpus Linguistics*, 11(4), 411–33.

Cheng, W., Greaves, C., Sinclair, J. McH, and Warren, M. (2009). 'Uncovering the extent of the phraseological tendency: Towards a systematic analysis of concgrams', *Applied Linguistics*, 30(2), 236–52.

Cheng, W. and Lam, P. (2010). 'Media discourses in Hong Kong: Change in representation of human rights', *Text & Talk*, 30(5), 507–27.

Cheng, W. and Lam, P. W. Y. (2012). 'Western perceptions of Hong Kong ten years on: A corpus-driven critical discourse study of public discourse', *Applied Linguistics*, 2012, 1–19, DOI:10.1093/applin/ams038.

Conrad, S. (2002). 'Corpus linguistic approaches for discourse analysis', *Annual Review of Applied Linguistics*, 22(1), 75–95.

Corrada-Emmanuel, A., McCallum, A., Smyth, P., Steyvers, M. and Chaitanya, C. (2005). 'Enron email dataset. Workshop on Link Analysis, Counterterrorism and Security', SIAM Intrenational Conference in Data Mining, 23 April 2005, Newport Beach, California, USA.

Davies, M. (2009). 'The 385+ million word Corpus of Contemporary American English (1990–2008+): Design, architecture, and linguistic insights', *International Journal of Corpus Linguistics*, 14(2), 159–90.

Edlund, J., Heylen, D. and Paggio, O. (2012). 'Proceedings of LREC workshop on multimodal corpora for machine learning: How should multimodal corpora deal with the situation?' 22 May 2012, Istanbul, Turkey.

Edwards, G. O. (2012). 'A comparative discourse analysis of the construction of "in-groups" in the 2005 and 2010 manifestos of the British National Party', *Discourse & Society*, 23(3), 245–58.

Forchtner, B. and Kølvraa, C. (2012). 'Narrating a "new Europe": From "bitter past" to self-righteousness?' *Discourse & Society*, 23(4), 377–400.

Fuertes-Olivera, P. A. (2007). 'A corpus-based view of lexical gender in written Business English', *English for Specific Purposes*, 26, 219–34.

Gavioli, L. (2005). *Exploring Corpora for ESP Learning*, Amsterdam: John Benjamins.

Grant, L. E. (2012). 'Culturally motivated lexis in New Zealand English', *World Englishes*, 31(2), 162–76.

Greaves, C. (2009). *ConcGram 1.0: A Phraseological Search Engine*, Amsterdam: John Benjamins.

Gu, Y. G. (2006). 'Multimodal text analysis: A corpus linguistic approach to situated discourse', *Text & Talk*, 26(2), 127–67.

Hafner, C. A. and Candlin, C. N. (2007). 'Corpus tools as an affordance to learning in professional legal education', *Journal of English for Academic Purposes*, 6, 303–18.

Halliday, M. (1993). 'Quantitative studies and probabilities in grammar', in M. Hoey (ed.), *Data, Description, Discourse* (pp. 1–25), London: HarperCollins.

Han, C. (2011). 'Reading Chinese online entertainment news: Metaphor and language play', *Journal of Pragmatics*, 43, 3473–88.

Handford, M. (2010). *The Language of Business Meetings*, Cambridge: Cambridge University Press.

Handford, M. and Matous, P. (2011). 'Lexicogrammar in the international construction industry: A corpus-based case study of Japanese-Hong Kongese on-site interactions in English', *English for Specific Purposes*, 30, 87–100.

Hardy, D. E. and Colombini, C. B. (2011). 'A genre, collocational, and constructional analysis of RISK', *International Journal of Corpus Linguistics*, 16(4), 462–85.

Hoey, M. (2005) *Lexical Priming: A New Theory of Words and Language*, London: Routledge.

Jablonkai, R. (2010). 'English in the context of European integration: A corpus-driven analysis of lexical bundles in English EU documents', *English for Specific Purposes*, 29, 253–67.

Kessler, G. (2010). 'Virtual business: An Enron email corpus study', *Journal of Pragmatics*, 42, 262–70.

Klimt, B. and Yang, Y. (2004). 'Introducing the Enron corpus', First Conference on Email and Anti-Spam (CEAS), Mountain View, CA. Available from ftp://ftp.research.microsoft.com/users/joshuago/conference/papers-.pdf (accessed 11 December 2012).

Koselleck, R. (2004). *Futures Past: On the Semantics of Historical Time*, New York: Columbia University Press.

Koteyko, N. (2012). 'Managing carbon emissions: A discursive presentation of "market-driven sustainability" in the British media', *Language & Communication*, 32, 24–35.

Labov, W. (2006). 'Narrative pre-construction', *Narrative Inquiry*, *16*(1), 37–45.
Moon, R. (2011). 'English adjectives in-*like*, and the interplay of collocation and morphology', *International Journal of Corpus Linguistics*, *16*(4), 486–513.
Mooney, A. (2012). 'Human rights: Law, language and the bare human being', *Language & Communication*, *32*, 169–81.
Mur-Dueñas, P. (2011). 'An intercultural analysis of metadiscourse features in research articles written in English and in Spanish', *Journal of Pragmatics*, *43*, 3068–79.
Murillo, S. (2012). 'The use of reformulation markers in Business Management research articles: An intercultural analysis', *International Journal of Corpus Linguistics*, *17*(1), 64–90.
Nelson, M. (2006). 'Semantic associations in Business English: A corpus-based analysis', *English for Specific Purposes*, *25*, 217–34.
Ooi, B. Y. V. (2000). '"Language Games" on the World Wide Web: Analysing the language of electronic gaming', in H. Heffer and H. Sauntson (eds), *Words in Context: A Tribute to John Sinclair on his Retirement* (pp. 110–19), Birmingham: ELR Discourse Analysis Monograph 18.
——(2008). 'The lexis of electronic gaming on the web: A Sinclarian approach', *International Journal of Lexicography*, *21*(3), 311–23.
Parviainen, H. (2012). 'Focus particles in Indian English and other varieties', *World Englishes*, *31*(2), 226–47.
Peacock, M. (2011). 'A comparative study of *introductory it* in research articles across eight disciplines', *International Journal of Corpus Linguistics*, *16*(1), 72–100.
Planken, B. (2005). 'Managing rapport in lingua franca sales negotiations: A comparison of professional and aspiring negotiators', *English for Specific Purposes*, *24*, 381–400.
Rankin, T. and Schiftner, B. (2011). 'Marginal prepositions in learner English: Applying local corpus data', *International Journal of Corpus Linguistics*, *16*(3), 412–34.
Rayson, P. (2008). *Wmatrix Corpus Analysis and Comparison Tool*, Lancaster: Lexical Analysis Software.
——(2001). *Wmatrix: A Web-based Corpus Processing Environment*, Computing Department, Lancaster University, UK. Available at http://ucrel.lancs.ac.uk/wmatrix/.
Reinhardt, J. (2010). 'Directives in office hour consultation: A corpus-informed investigation of learner and expert usage', *English for Specific Purposes*, *29*, 94–107.
Reisigl, M. and Wodak, R. (2001). *Discourse and Discrimination: Rhetorics of Racism and Anti-semitism*, London: Routledge.
Rühlemann, C., Bagoutdinov, A. and O'Donnell, M. B. (2011). 'Windows on the mind: Pauses in conversational narrative', *International Journal of Corpus Linguistics*, *16*(2), 198–230.
Rutherford, B. A. (2005). 'Genre analysis of corporate annual report narratives: A corpus linguistics-based approach', *Journal of Business Communication*, *42*(4), 349–78.
Shetty, J. and Adibi, J. (2005). 'Discovering important nodes through graph entropy: The case of Enron email database', Workshop on Link Discovery: Issues, Approaches and Applications, ACM SIGKDD Conference, 21–24 August 2005, Chicago, IL.
Sinclair, J. McH. (1991). *Corpus, Concordance, Collocation: Describing English Language*, Oxford: Oxford University Press.
——(1996). 'The search for units of meaning', *Textus*, *9*(1), 75–106.
——(2004). *Trust the Text*, London and New York: Routledge.
Somers, M. (1994). 'The narrative constitution of identity: A relational and network approach', *Theory and Society*, *23*, 605–49.
Sznajder, H. S. (2010). 'A corpus-based evaluation of metaphors in a business English textbook', *English for Specific Purposes*, *29*, 30–42.
Teubert, W. and Krishnamurthy, R. (2007). 'General introduction', in W. Teubert and R. Krishnamurthy (eds), *Corpus Linguistics: Critical Concepts in Linguistics* (pp. 1–37), London and New York: Routledge.
Tognini-Bonelli, E. (2001). *Corpus Linguistics at Work*, Amsterdam; Philadelphia: John Benjamins.
Trebits, A. (2008). 'English lexis in the documents of the EU – A corpus-based exploratory study', Eötvös Loránd University: *Working Papers in Language Pedagogy*, *2*, 38–54.
——(2009). 'Conjunctive cohesion in English language EU documents – A corpus-based analysis and its implications', *English for Specific Purposes*, *28*, 199–210.
Walker, C. (2011). 'How a corpus-based study of the factors which influence collocation can help in the teaching of business English', *English for Specific Purposes*, *30*, 101–12.

3
A situated genre approach for business communication education in cross-cultural contexts

Yunxia Zhu

Introduction

Cross-cultural communication is becoming increasingly important with the rapid development of internationalisation and globalisation. This international trend is also evident in the tertiary education sector. With an increasing number of students from foreign countries,[1] especially from Asia, coming to study in the USA, UK, Canada, Australia and New Zealand (NZ) in the past two decades, the student composition in the tertiary institutions of these countries is changing. Instructors on professional communication programmes are often challenged with issues of finding appropriate models to teach students from different cultural and linguistic backgrounds. What were assumed to be good models for teaching professional communication may not be appropriate for a class of mixed cultural backgrounds.

As expected cross-cultural education has attracted extensive research attention in cross-cultural management and communication (e.g. Chen and Starosta 1996; Egan and Bendick 2008; Earley and Ang 2003; Earley and Mosakowski 2004; Kim 1991). Yet, cross-cultural issues so far have not drawn sufficient research attention from professional communication (e.g. business writing), education and learning. Relevant cross-cultural theories such as Hofstede's individualism vs. collectivism, and Confucian long-term orientation have been used extensively in exploring how cultural values shape the way international students learn in a foreign context. These cross-cultural dimensions, although useful and comprehensive to a certain extent for understanding cultures (e.g. Al-Olayan and Karande 2000; Albers-Miller 1996), are also known as sophisticated stereotypes and generalisations of cultures (Osland *et al.* 2000). Hence it is imperative to incorporate alternative perspectives into cross-cultural research. A salient perspective derives from cross-cultural discursive competence, which may offer nuanced views about cultures through the use of language.

Although extensive research (e.g. Swales 1990; Bhatia 2004) has been done on discursive competence using a genre-based approach in English professional communication, little research has been conducted on achieving discursive competence (Bhatia 2004) in cross-cultural contexts. There is also a practical imperative for conducting such a study. For example, Andrews and Henze (2009) found that it is important to incorporate local knowledge in teaching business writing for a study abroad programme. Likewise, other researchers (Carter *et al.* 2007;

Nickerson 2001; Schneider and Andre 2005; Yu 2011) also expressed a similar practical concern about the importance of local situated knowledge in industry. It is therefore imperative to develop new models to promote situated learning for professional communication. It is also timely for such a study as an increasing number of researchers have drawn our attention to the discourse in organisational settings (e.g. Cornelissen 2008; Hardy *et al.* 2000; Levina and Orlikowski 2009; Phillips *et al.* 2004; Zhu 2008; Zhu and Hildebrandt, 2012) and their research suggests that organisational discourse is vital for institutional practice and activities.

In order to fill the above particular research gap, this paper proposes a situated genre approach based on genre theory (e.g. Bhatia 2004; Martin 2009; Swales 1990), situated cognition (Brown *et al.* 1989), and cross-cultural persuasion to enhance international students' cross-cultural generic competence in business communication education. A situated genre approach is defined as genre learning process in a professional context, aiming to incorporate real-world practices (Lave and Wenger 1991). Cross-cultural generic competence is defined as the competence of using written communication fluently in a cross-cultural context (Zhu 2008). The major contribution of this paper mainly lies in extending the genre approach to the learning of business communication in a cross-cultural context.

Specifically, this paper examines issues in the teaching of written business communication, looking in particular at teaching sales Expo letters used in organisational settings. The various types of written communication found in workplace settings constitute an important topic for business communication courses. This topic is chosen for two reasons. First, as indicated in Eunson (2004), the lack of written communication skills can create barriers to accomplishing specific tasks of management, not to mention the blunders of business communication that often occur due to lack of communication skills in cross-cultural contexts. Second, and also more importantly, we should explore how to use international students' knowledge as a resource (Connor 2004; Zhu 2008) and bring this into play in their learning processes.

This paper has four sections. First, it examines a range of current issues relating to business communication education. Second, it develops a situated genre model for cross-cultural contexts, which also aims to solicit international students' contributions to learning and education. In particular, it discusses in what way this approach can help to enhance student generic competence through situated learning and peripheral participation (Lave and Wenger 1991). Third, the proposed model is applied to Chinese students' learning experience of one particular written genre – English sales Expo invitations. Finally, implications for cross-cultural professional communication learning and education in general are highlighted and discussed.

Genre approach

According to Hyland (2007), genre approaches see ways of writing as purposeful, socially situated responses to particular contexts and communities. This view echoes other genre-based views such as the notion of genre as social action (Miller 1984). Likewise, genre is seen as characterised by communicative purposes and shared by a particular discourse community (Swales 1990).

In the context of this study, genre is further conceptualised 'as a form of situated cognition embedded in disciplinary activities' (Berkenkotter and Huckin 1995: 3). In a similar light, genre is seen as related to social constructivism within the sociology of knowledge (Berger and Luckmann 1966; Bergmann and Luckmann 1995; Schutz and Luckmann 1974). According to this view, genres are 'socially constructed models' that respond to recurrent communicative problems. Furthermore, the social stocks of knowledge are not statically transmitted, rather they are 'being built up, maintained, transmitted and also modified in communicative processes' via 'prepatterned' conventions (Gunthner and Knoblauch 1995: 5).

Genre researchers also point to the importance of understanding genre from the expert members' perspective. For example, Berkenkotter and Huckin (1995) stress the intimate link between genre and disciplinary knowledge and point out that genre should be studied in relation to the discipline's norms, values, and ideology. Their view coincides with Paltridge's (1995) explanation of institutional understanding on the part of the members of the discourse community, who understand 'the function of genre from the perspective of the actor or the insider'. The insiders are the managers who are also the users of genres, and thus understand the 'typical regularities and organisation' of genre (Bhatia 1993) as well as being familiar with the genre strategies of their discourse community. Their views about 'regularities' and 'strategies' (Bhatia 1993; Rutherford 2005) can offer us some interesting clues for identifying significant patterns within genre conventions, and will therefore be incorporated in this study.

Although the regularities and patterns of genre conventions are relatively stable, they are rather dynamic and can be constructed and re-constructed by intertextuality. The concept of intertextuality originates from Bakhtin's (1986) 'dialogic interaction' in writing processes, by which he means that an utterance is linked to other utterances like a dialogue in a complex organising system. Kristeva (1986) employs intertextuality as a property of text, which makes reference to previous texts. In this way, a text is no longer regarded as static and constrained by existing structure, and it actually interacts with the writer's or the reader's pre-acquired knowledge of other types of text or genres. Fairclough (1992) applies intertextuality as an important construct to investigate the relationship between genres as social action and the concurrent social structures. Here Fairclough points to intertextuality as part of an essential genre system and as a response to social structures and social change.

We can infer from the above discussion that intertextuality focuses on genre creation, genre construction, and genre interaction through a system of interactive texts within a community and across communities (Orlikowski and Yates 1994).

The above discussion also indicates that a genre approach offers insights for training students to become professional members of the discourse community. Yet, questions about how to use this approach in cross-cultural learning still remain:

1. How can we help international students to learn a genre of written business communication situated in a foreign culture they are not familiar with?
2. In what way can they contribute to learning using their existing knowledge as resources of learning?

To answer these questions, we need to understand the concept of situated cognition and culture, hence the following review of both areas.

Situated cognition

Situated cognition is composed of two important aspects, namely soliciting legitimate peripheral participation (LPP) (Lave and Wenger 1991) and providing alternative world views in classroom contexts (Brown et al. 1989).

Firstly, in terms of LPP, Lave and Wenger (1991: 29) note that 'learners inevitably participate in communities of practitioners and that the mastery of knowledge and skill requires newcomers to move toward full participation in the sociocultural practices of a community'. Lave and Wenger also point out that LPP is a process that differs from intentional instruction. For example, tailors learn how to make clothes in a reversed order of learning from specific skills such as sewing straight lines, which will prepare them to become a professional tailor later. This principle of peripheral participation can also apply to learning written business communication in order to achieve high-level competence. Lave and Wenger's view ties in well with process-oriented learning, and LPP involves a process that goes beyond the classroom to include mastery of real-world social skills and practical generic competence. This kind of participation can be extremely crucial for enhancing international students' generic competence. According to Rowley-Jolivet and Carter-Thomas (2004), non-native speakers tend to have a lower level of genre awareness and rhetorical appropriacy.

Secondly, Brown *et al.* (1989) proposed the imperative of practising situated cognition in classrooms by bringing changes to the school culture of teaching textbook content. They offered an example of solving mathematics problems from the mathematician's perspective. In this way, students can think beyond the limitations of the textbook and reflect on real world experiences. So teachers need to proactively provide students with opportunities that may convey these experiences and provide alternative views to students.

Based on the above literature review, a situated genre approach in cross-cultural contexts can be defined as applying a genre approach with cross-cultural competence and locally situated knowledge. Specifically, high-level competence involves interactions between novices and experts (e.g. for novices to learn from the experts' views); students thus need to get involved in the processes to understand genres beyond the text, and involve themselves in the processes in which genres are produced as much as possible in order to achieve a high-level generic competence. However, since the context in question is a cross-cultural context, cross-cultural knowledge in areas such as persuasion should be seen as an important resource for learning and education.

Cross-cultural persuasion

Cultural dimensions are useful concepts for understanding persuasion across cultures. According to Hofstede (1991), cultures can be divided into individualist and collectivist, based on how 'self' is related to 'the other'. The former refers to cultures such as the USA, Australia and NZ, which have a focus on individual achievement and business objectives. The latter alludes to cultures such as Japan, China and Hong Kong where group interest and long-term relationships are seen as important. For example, one particular way of establishing long-term relationships in the Chinese culture is through *guanxi*, or personal relationships and connections (Zhu *et al.* 2006).

Culture serves as a basis for reasoning and persuasion, and different cultures may resort to different types of rhetoric and persuasion (Hall 1976). Here Aristotle's and Confucius' views on rhetoric are discussed as a point of comparison. These two sets of rhetorical theories are essential for understanding modern Western and Chinese persuasion (Campbell 1998; Lü 1998). Aristotle, as a major representative of Greek rhetoric, developed a wide range of concepts in rhetoric, and the most relevant to this study are the persuasive appeals or orientations including *ethos* (character and standards), *pathos* (emotion) and *logos* (reason and evidence). Aristotle (1991) places major importance on *logos*, treating *pathos* only as secondary to the logical presentation of an argument. This stress on *logos* has a fundamental influence on today's business communication textbooks (e.g. Eunson 2004; Murphy *et al.* 1997).

Similar persuasive orientations are also in existence in the Confucian rhetorical tradition (Garret 1993; Lü 1998). Confucian rhetoric is based mainly on his philosophy of *ren tao* or the way of humans and the moral codes he prescribes in his teachings. To him, *ren* (benevolence) is seen as the highest standard of moral perfection. In order to achieve these virtues, Confucius sets the highest standards for adequate conduct in these five key role relationships between ruler and subject, neighbour and neighbour, father and son, husband and wife, and older brother and younger brother, among which four are hierarchical relationships. These relations are related to *pathos* and are often advocated as important forms of effective persuasion in specific genres of Chinese business communication (Zhu 2000a, 2000b, 2011).

Confucian persuasive orientations have a strong influence on today's Chinese writing in general, including business letter writing. Li (1990), for example, advocates that *qing* (feelings) has great persuasive power and complements *li* (reason). *Qing* and *li* can thus be seen as essential elements in Chinese persuasion. This principle also permeates business writing in China. As Li (1990) puts it, feelings and intuitive thinking are still an important element in business writing with which the writer can create a specific effect of persuasion on the reader. This effect is particularly relevant for Chinese invitations, which are often described as a type of *liyi xin* or 'letters of social etiquettes', or *shejiao xin* or 'letters of social networking'. The meaning of *shejiao* or 'social networking' is readily apparent; however, *liyi xin* or 'letters of social etiquettes' needs some explanation. According to Zhuge and Chen (1994: 361), *liyi* means etiquettes and ceremonies. Accordingly, Chinese sales Expo invitations are treated as a form of etiquette for building relationships in which *qing* or 'feelings' plays an important role.

It can be inferred from the above discussion that Chinese students may have already learned the Chinese rhetorical traditions. Their knowledge should not be seen as conflicting knowledge in relation to English written communication, but rather these differences in persuasion represent a continuum of different expectations for written business communication. Their knowledge of persuasion can be used as a resource for further re-construction of written communication that fits into different genre regularities of different cultures.

Cross-cultural learning model

In light of the conceptualisation of the situated genre approach, this paper proposes a cross-cultural learning model taking into account peripheral participation and intertextuality, and also paying attention to the previous knowledge of the international student. The model consists of the following processes:

1. Living sociocultural contexts across cultures through internship
2. Learning persuasive orientations and communicative purposes
3. Learning to write texts and incorporating peripheral participation and intertextuality
4. Incorporating authentic data and managers' views.

The first process provides contextualised knowledge about business texts in specific cultures. Similar background knowledge is also stressed in the field of cross-cultural management (Earley and Mosakowski 2004), and genre learning (e.g. Nickerson 2001; Zhu 2000b). This process offers cultural knowledge for understanding persuasive orientations of cultures that will be further reinforced by student internship experiences (Liebman 1988).

In the second process, students compare persuasive orientations and communicative purposes. More importantly, they can also apply theories to written business communication practice. For example, English rhetorical theory can be used to identify persuasive orientations in English business genres, while Chinese persuasion theories can be introduced as a guideline for identifying persuasive orientations in Chinese business genres.

The third process provides an opportunity for students to learn written business communication through real-life experience, and they can apply the knowledge they learned in the classroom, for example practising various strategies relating to rhetorical structure and intertextuality. This is also the most important process for incorporating student peripheral participation (Lave and Wenger 1991), which can be carried out through internship or other relevant industry learning experience. It should also be learned in relation to previous processes as a situated textual realisation of persuasive orientations and communicative purposes.

The fourth process involves learning generic praxis about how a particular genre is used. During this process, students will have the opportunity to have access to authentic texts relating to appropriate written communication skills in class. This process also incorporates business managers' or insiders' views on effective communication. Business managers are the experts and their views will reflect the relevant stock of knowledge of the discourse community. In this way, this process targets a high level of learning and competence close to mastery of real-world skills. Students can also test their learning by comparing their views with those of the managers, thereby identifying gaps in learning, which, in turn, are likely to inspire them to learn from these professional members.

In sum, these processes complement each other and the totality of them forms part of a systematic nexus of learning and community practice, in which students learn theories, apprentice themselves in industry, test their understanding in light of the professional members' views, and eventually achieve generic fluencies and competence across cultures (Leki 1991).

Applying the situated genre model

This section illustrates teaching and learning briefly, using Chinese students' experience of learning to write English sales Expo invitations in tutorials as an example. The tutorial activity involves a specific project requiring students to re-write a Chinese sales Expo invitation in English. This invitation was an effective invitation since it had succeeded in bringing a great number of participants to a Chinese trade fair. The particular tutorial group were in the final year of an undergraduate programme on a business communication course at a tertiary institute in NZ. All students had some internship experience in business organisations in NZ.

The following specific steps were taken for this project. The students were asked to re-write the Chinese sales Expo invitation in English supposing their company is to promote their Expo in NZ. The activity was arranged across three tutorial sessions and activities (see Table 3.1).

As shown in Table 3.1, each of the three tutorial sessions involves completing specific tasks, has clear learning objectives and targets different stages of competence. For example, the first tutorial focuses on assigning the first re-writing task and deals initially with the first three learning processes relating to understanding communicative purposes and persuasive orientations. These activities mainly target a high-level discursive competence relating to world experience

Table 3.1 Breakdown of the learning activities

	Task 1	Task 2	Task 3
Tut 1 (Day 1)	Overview of activities	Brainstorming session on communicative purposes	Assigning re-writing task with summary notes
Tut 2 (Day 7)	Submitting Version 1	Incorporating Chinese and NZ managers' views	Re-writing task (Version 2) with summary notes
Tut 3 (Day 10) Reflective journal	Submitting Version 2	Brainstorming session	Debriefing session

(Brown *et al.* 1989). The final tutorial is reflective of the whole writing process and students are expected to reflect on their learning experience in relation to achieving cross-cultural competence in this particular context.

At the first tutorial session, a brief overview of Chinese and English sales invitations was also given to students. Here is the background information and specific requirements I distributed to the students during the session:

1. Re-write the Chinese invitation (due at the 2nd tutorial) in English: Suppose you are a sales manager in a Chinese exhibition company. Now your company is arranging promotional tours in NZ. You need to re-write this letter based on your internship experience. Secondly, you are asked to write a summary note in bullet-point form about what criteria you followed for re-writing the invitation.
2. Revise the English sales invitation (Version 2; due at the 3rd tutorial) with a summary note for this new version. You will have a chance to discuss your work in comparison with the Chinese and NZ managers' views[2] about Expo invitation writing, which will be distributed during this tutorial.
3. Submit your final version at the 3rd tutorial and debrief on the implications of this writing exercise at the tutorial.

The above class activities were conducted with two tutorial groups, each composed of five Chinese students, who participated according to the above requirements and completed the project. Findings from these tutorial sessions will be referred to in the following detailed discussion of each of the learning processes.

Learning and comparing the sociocultural contexts through internship

The major objective of this first learning process is to help to build students' world schemata. First, students need to be acquainted with the social and economic environments in relevant cultures. English sales invitations are a written genre used to promote trade fairs. Major teaching points should include an introduction to the market economy prevalent in the West, such as Australia and NZ, and to the marketing strategies relevant to this type of economy.

These two learning points can be helpful. The first point is to discuss the economic reform and changes that have occurred in the Chinese economy since 1978. These changes have led to the increasing popularity of sales invitations. The second point is to draw students' attention to the use of marketing strategies alongside the economic reforms. For example, the use of the AIDA (attention, interest, desire and action) model and stress on sales promotions were discussed as an illustration here as an additional teaching point. In individualistic countries such as NZ, people tend to stress individual autonomy, and reducing imposition upon the invitee is likely to be the major persuasive strategy. In contrast, people from high context cultures such as China prefer to adopt a collaborative and host-like attitude. Therefore it is essential for Chinese invitations to employ a respectful tone to indicate adequate *qing* or 'feelings' towards the reader. In this regard, reference can be made to relevant Chinese scholars' views (such as Zhuge and Chen 1994) to indicate the importance of *li yi* or 'social etiquettes' and politeness rituals for invitation writing.

This background information was discussed in the first session as guidance to solicit students' input and reflections, and was also meant to help them understand different expectations regarding the persuasive orientations of invitations.

Table 3.2 A breakdown of the communicative purposes students identified

English sales invitation	Chinese sales invitation
To invite the reader to Expo	To invite the reader to Expo
To attract reader's attention	To attract reader's attention
To give positive appraisal	To give positive appraisal
To persuade the reader to attend	To persuade the reader to attend
To achieve a positive image	To achieve a positive and respectful image
	To build a host–guest relationship

Learning persuasive orientations and communicative purposes

This process focused on different persuasive orientations found in English and Chinese business genres. As noted earlier, English sales Expo invitations have an emphasis on *logos* while Chinese tend to stress both *qing* and *li*. Theories from target cultures, in this case both English and Chinese, can be referred to where relevant to help students understand persuasive orientations in business writing.

As part of the participation in classroom teaching and learning, students were encouraged to identify communicative purposes themselves first in a brainstorming session. They came up with various purposes. They also tried to justify their findings with relevant persuasive orientations and link them to the sociocultural environments they had learned about so far. After sufficient discussion and clarification amongst students, they were able to identify the two sets of communicative purposes (see Table 3.2).

As shown in Table 3.2, the similarity exhibited in these purposes in both English and Chinese sales Expo invitations lies in the fact that they can be divided into two kinds: inviting the reader to the Expo and advertising the Expo and the exhibits. These two types of purpose are related to the application of *logos* and *pathos*. Students were able to identify the differences and similarities without any difficulty by referring to the previous teaching points as well as their work experience. On the face of it English and Chinese genres displayed similarities in terms of promoting trade fairs. However, students also realised they exhibited significant differences in the use of politeness rituals, as shown in the emphasis on respectful image and host–guest relationships in the Chinese genre.

This difference served as a further discussion point to highlight the importance of establishing a host–guest relationship with the reader, which exhibited stronger '*pathos*' in the Chinese sales invitations compared to the English invitations. Students agreed that in Chinese culture, a host was supposed not only to show hospitality and kindness, but also to extend this to a long-term relationship, which would help the promotion of the product. Intercultural theories relating to face and cultural values (such as Hofstede 1991; Hall 1976; Gao and Ting-Toomey 1998) were also referred to at this point, which helped students interpret cultural differences in sales Expo invitation writing.

Learning to write texts and incorporating LPP and intertextuality

The third process, learning to write the text, involves peripheral participation and situated learning. This is also the process linking theories with practice. The Chinese students were beginning a process of making reference to the authentic English texts actually used in the NZ business contexts on their internship websites. In other words, they were establishing a new set of schemata for writing English sales Expo invitations while making reference to their prior knowledge.

According to their summary notes, their writing criteria appeared to be based on three sets of knowledge during this process:

1 Situated knowledge about English sales invitations
2 Intertextual knowledge about Chinese sales invitations
3 Intercultural knowledge about differences and similarities across genres.

First and foremost, their situated and contextualised knowledge gained through peripheral participation turned out to be very helpful. The students had some access to invitations in the workplace. In addition, they were also exposed to internet websites containing similar information about sales exhibitions besides invitations letters, which is also an instance of intertextuality in application. They thus had first-hand experience about what English sales Expo invitations should be like. For example, they commented that they preferred a personal salutation such as 'Mr Smith' in their first draft of the re-written invitations to the more impersonal but more respectful *jing qizhe* or 'Respected Reader' used in the original Chinese invitation, since they learned that sales invitations were often sent to individuals in NZ. Another student commented on the informal use of polite closing in the English sales invitation, which also differs from that of the Chinese. This process reminds us of Lave and Wenger's (1991) analogy about the apprentice learning sewing with straight lines, which may eventually constitute part of the garment-sewing process. The basic first-hand experience of using appropriate personal salutations thus helps to prepare the students towards an expert mastery of writing English sales Expo invitations.

Intertextualised knowledge about Chinese sales Expo invitations was also helpful in this process. For example, they realised that some linguistic features to do with the AIDA promotional strategies were very much similar across cultures and their knowledge about Chinese invitations was used as reference in this process. This was reflected in keeping most of the content moves from the original invitation. Students noted that they were overjoyed about this finding since they could use and transfer their knowledge to the new learning environment.

Finally, they commented that they had benefited from their enhanced intercultural knowledge through comparing the English and Chinese texts. For example, they could work out the similarities and differences in terms of invitation rituals and writing conventions. In doing so, they have acquired two sets of schemata for writing both English and Chinese sales invitations, hence gaining competence in fluency in both cultures, and especially in the new NZ culture.

Using authentic data and incorporating managers' views

The fourth process incorporates authentic data and managers' views in the second tutorial. Some research has been done on the importance of using authentic data and native speakers' views for teaching (Bhatia 1993; Zhu 2000b). Specifically, the objective of the tutorial was to expose the students to the managers' views of both cultural groups towards the English sales Expo invitations.

The NZ and Chinese managers' views on this English invitation were incorporated into the learning and teaching process. For example, students compared their understanding of the English sales invitations with managers' views. The managers' views, provided by ten NZ and ten Chinese managers via focus group interviews, are summed up in Table 3.3 for ease of discussion.

Table 3.3 The NZ and Chinese managers' views on the English invitation

The NZ managers' comments	The Chinese managers' comments
This is an excellent letter which starts straight to the point.	The letter does not have the *ketaohua* 客套 ' or 'polite rituals' as would be expected of Chinese invitations.
This letter is quite clear in structure, and the writer gives necessary details.	The purpose of the letter is clear. It is short and easy to understand and there is no exaggeration.
The style of the letter is quite professional and yet calm. No flowery expressions and exaggerations are included.	It is polite using a friendly and informal approach.

The students commented that the NZ managers' views and, in particular, the first two views further confirmed the persuasive orientations learned in the previous processes. The NZ managers explicitly emphasised the importance of clarity in style and idea development. Chinese managers' comments pointed to a different kind of expectation relating to politeness rituals. Students also commented on the informal tone (you approach) used by the English invitation. However, they indicated that they shared a similar view with the NZ managers about the stress on clarity of style for writing English letters. At this point, one student referred to the brevity of invitations he received during his internship as further confirmation of his findings. Managers' views have thus triggered further learning. This is also an instance to show that the knowledge this student gained through peripheral participation earlier has been built into part of his knowledge structure and can be retrieved under appropriate learning circumstances such as this. The incorporation of managers' views not only helped trigger this process but also offered an insider's perspective into the understanding of effective persuasion.

Furthermore, students also identified gaps in their knowledge in this process. For example, managers' views on the informal and friendly tone of the English invitation offered new insight. This 'gap', they agreed, should be the focus for the revision. As such, the managers' views on this helped them reach a higher level of generic competence.

Implications for cross-cultural generic competence

The final tutorial was a debriefing process that started with similar brainstorming sessions to those used in the earlier processes. It was student-led, focusing on what they had learned. Here is a summary of what they discussed at the tutorial.

First of all, they discussed theoretical implications in relation to real-world learning experience as in this case. Students can have a thorough understanding of the sociocognitive approach in a situated context, and learn to apply this approach as an important tool to build relevant knowledge structures in similar situations.

The second implication was that peripheral participation and situated learning were an effective way of learning, in which students were exposed to an abundance of knowledge and communication skills. In this way, student internship and work experience were seen as an essential part of peripheral participation, which equipped them with situated knowledge and fluency of cultures gradually. As shown in this case, both types of situated cognition (Brown *et al.* 1989) of real work experience (internship) and managers' views were applied to class. The Chinese students' learning and unlearning processes illustrated well the importance and absolute necessity of having this kind of participatory experience. In a less direct manner, the use of authentic data and managers' views can also help students enhance their generic competence. The incorporation of these data has actually further initiated student reflections on their own previous industry participatory experience.

Third, students can enhance their generic competence through effective use of intertextuality. For example, understanding universal features of promotional strategies helped students greatly. They also made reference to previous knowledge of writing Chinese Expo invitations. Re-writing the Chinese invitation in English actually helped them to reflect on their previous knowledge.

Conclusion

This paper proposed and applied the situated genre approach to cross-cultural education, using teaching and learning business writing in the NZ context as an example. As shown in the case described here, learning took place through two kinds of situated cognition incorporating peripheral participation and managers' views. The education and learning processes represented a combination of classroom teaching, peripheral participation, unlearning existing knowledge, and reconstructing texts. These activities complemented each other with the aim of bringing student initiatives into play.

This study has contributed to cross-cultural learning by going beyond using culturally stereotypical dimensions and applying discursive competence to specific cultural contexts. Specifically, it views soliciting international students' knowledge structure as a resource of learning. The case study indicates that there is potential for instructors to explore new ways of learning, which will encourage international students' participation and contribution. Business communication education should be seen as a dialogue between students, the professional members of the discourse community and the authentic texts or other real-life practices, in which the instructor serves only as a facilitator to ensure that the dialogues take place applying process-oriented learning in the new cultural context.

Related topics

business communication; discourse variation in professional communities; a situated genre approach for business communication; workplace communication; management communication

Key readings

Miike, Y. (2008). 'Toward an alternative metatheory of human communication: An Asiacentric vision', in M. K. Asante, Y. Miike and J. Yin (eds), *The Global Intercultural Communication Reader* (pp. 57–72), New York: Routledge. (This paper focuses on the culture-specific perspective of human interactions and communication.)

Tanaka, H. and Bargiela-Chiappini, F. (2011). 'Asian business discourse(s)', in J. P. Gee and M. Handford (eds), *The Routledge Handbook of Discourse Analysis* (pp. 455–69), London: Routledge. (This paper offers insight about different types of discourse in the business contexts in Asia.)

Zhu, Y. and Bargiela-Chiappini, F. (in press). 'Balancing emic and etic: Situated learning and ethnography of communication in cross-cultural management education', *Academy of Management Learning and Education*, 12(3), 380–95. (This paper proposes a new approach based on ethnography of communication and language for learning cultures as situated knowledge.)

Notes

1 In this paper, all terms such as 'international students', and 'students from foreign countries' refer to those who speak English as a second or foreign language.
2 These managers' views were collected from two focus group interviews (one Chinese and one NZ group) before the experiment. Each group was composed of ten managers from three international trade companies in Auckland and Zhengzhou, where the Chinese invitation was collected. The managers were chosen based on their experience of writing business letters. Therefore their attitudes can be taken to represent professional attitudes, and reflect the shared conventions of the business community. One of the interview tasks was to let them reflect on general criteria for good writing for sales Expo invitations in their own culture. I gave them this scenario for them to reflect on: Supposing you were to write a trade fair invitation to your potential customers, what criteria do you think are appropriate? We recorded and decoded all their discussions and finally came up with a summary of their views.

Bibliography

Albers-Miller, N. (1996) 'Designing cross-cultural advertising research: A closer look at paired comparisons', *International Marketing Review*, 13(5), 59–75.
Al-Olayan, F. S. and Karande, K. (2000). 'A content analysis of magazine advertisements from the United States and the Arab world', *Journal of Advertising*, 29(3), 69–82.
Andrews, D. C. and Henze, B. (2009). 'Teaching professional writing to American students in a study abroad program', *Business Communication Quarterly*, 72(1), 5–20.
Aristotle (1991). *Aristotle on Rhetoric: A Theory of Civic Discourse*, George A. Kennedy (trans.), New York: Oxford.
Bakhtin, M. M. (1986). 'The problem of speech genres', in C. Emerson and M. Holquist (eds), V. W. McGee (trans.), *Speech Genres and Other Late Essays* (pp. 60–102), Austin: University of Texas Press.
Berger, P. and Luckmann, T. (1966). *The Social Construction of Reality*, Garden City, NY: Doubleday.
Bergmann, J. R. and Luckmann, T. 1995. 'Reconstructive genres of everyday communication', in U. Quasthoff (ed.), *Aspects of Oral Communication* (pp. 289–304), Berlin: de Gruyter.
Berkenkotter, C. and Huckin, T. N. (1995). 'Rethinking genre from a sociocognitive perspective', in C. Berkenkotter and T. N. Huckin (eds), *Genre Knowledge in Disciplinary Communication: Cognition/Culture/Power* (pp. 1–25), Hillsdale: Lawrence Erlbaum.
Bhatia, V. K. (1993). *Analysing Genre: Language Use in Professional Settings*, New York: Longman Group, UK Limited.
——(2004). *Worlds of Written Discourse: A Genre-based View*, London: Continuum.
Brown, J. S., Collins, A. and Duguid, S. (1989). 'Situated cognition and the culture of learning', *Educational Researcher*, 18(1), 32–42.
Campbell, C. P. (1998). 'Rhetorical ethos: A bridge between high-context and low-context cultures?' in S. Niemeier, C. P. Campbell and R. Dirven (eds), *The Cultural Context in Business Communication* (pp. 31–47), Philadelphia: John Benjamins.
Carter, M., Ferzli, M. and Wiebe, E. (2007). 'Writing to learn by learning to write in the disciplines', *Journal of Business & Technical Communication*, 21(3), 278–302.
Chen, G. M. and Starosta, W. J. (1996). 'Intercultural communication competence: A synthesis', *Communication Yearbook*, 19, 353–83.
Connor, U. (2004). 'Intercultural rhetoric research: Beyond texts', *Journal of English for Academic Purposes*, 3(4), 291–304.
Cornelissen, J. P. 2008. 'Metonymy in language about organizations: A corpus-based study of company names', *Journal of Management Studies*, 45(1), 79–99.
Earley, P. C. and Ang, S. (eds) (2003). *Cultural Intelligence: Individual Interactions across Cultures*, Stanford, CA: Stanford University Press.
Earley, P. C. and Mosakowski, E. (2004). 'Cultural intelligence', *Harvard Business Review*, 82(10), 1–9.
Egan, M. L. and Bendick, Jr, M. (2008). 'Combining multicultural management and diversity into one course on cultural competence', *Academy of Management Learning and Education*, 7(3), 387–93.
Eunson, B. (2004). *Communicating in the 21st Century*, Singapore: Wiley.
Fairclough, N. L. (1992). *Discourse and Social Change*, Cambridge: Polity Press.
Gao, G. and Ting-Toomey, S. (1998). *Communicating Effectively with Chinese*, London: Sage.

Garrett, M. (1993). 'Classical Chinese conceptions of argumentation and persuasion', *Argumentation and Advocacy*, 29, 105–115.
Gunthner, S. and Knoblauch, H. (1995). 'Culturally patterned speaking practices: The analysis of communicative genres', *Pragmatics*, 5(1), 1–32.
Hall, E. T. (1976). *Beyond Culture*, Garden City, New York: Anchor.
Hardy, C., Palmer, I. and Phillips, N. (2000). 'Discourse as a strategic resource', *Human Relations*, 53(9), 1227–48.
Hofstede, G. (1991). *Cultures and Organizations: Software of the Mind*, New York: McGraw-Hill.
Hyland, K. (2007). 'Genre pedagogy: Language, literacy and L2 writing instruction', *Journal of Second Language Writing*, 16(3), 148–64.
Kim, Y. Y. (1991). 'Intercultural communication competence: A systems-theoretic view', in S. Ting-Toomey and F. Korzenny (eds), *International and Intercultural Communication Annual: Vol 12. Theories in Intercultural Communication* (pp. 259–75), Newbury Park, CA: Sage.
Kristeva, J. (1986). 'Word, dialogue and novel', in T. Moi (ed.), *The Kristeva Reader*, Oxford: Blackwell.
Lave, J., and Wenger, E. (1991). *Situated Learning: Legitimate Peripheral Participation*, Cambridge: Cambridge University Press.
Leki, I. (1991). 'Twenty-five years of contrastive rhetoric: Text analysis and writing pedagogies', *TESOL Quarterly*, 25(1), 123–42.
Levina, N. and Orlikowski, W. J. (2009). 'Understanding shifting power relations within and across organizations: A critical genre analysis', *Academy of Management Learning and Education*, 52(4), 672–703.
Li, D. (ed.) (1990). *Caijng yingyong xiezuo* (On the writing of practical documents in finance and economics), Beijing: Zhongguo Caizheng Jingji Chubanshe.
Liebman, J. (1988). 'Contrastive rhetoric: Students as ethnographers', *Journal of Basic Writing*, 7(2), 6–27.
Li, Xiaoming. (1996). *'Good Writing' in Cross-cultural Context*, Albany: SUNY.
Lü, X. (1998). *Rhetoric in Ancient China, Fifth to Third Century B.C.E.*, Columbia: University of South Carolina Press.
Martin, J. R. (2009). 'Genre and language learning: A social semiotic perspective', *Linguistics and Education*, 20(1), 10–21.
Miller, C. R. (1984). 'Genre as social action', *Quarterly Journal of Speech*, 70(2), 151–67.
Murphy, H. A., Hildebrandt, H. W. and Thomas, J. P. (1997). *Effective Business Communication*, New York: The McGraw-Hill Companies, Inc. (The first edition: 1972).
Nickerson, C. (2001). 'The relevance of the corporate context for the teaching of business English: Taking real life business practices into account',' *Teaching English for International Business*, 1(1), 4–12.
Orlikowski, W. and Yates, J. (1994). 'Genre repertoire: The structuring of communicative practices in organizations', *Administrative Science Quarterly*, 39, 541–74.
Osland, J. S., Bird, A., Delano, J. and Matthew, J. (2000). 'Beyond sophisticated stereotyping: Cultural sensemaking in context', *Academy of Management Executive*, 14(1), 65–77.
Paltridge, B. (1995). 'Working with genre: A pragmatic perspective', *Journal of Pragmatics*, 24, 393–406.
Phillips, N., Lawrence, T. B. and Hardy, C. (2004). 'Discourse and institutions', *Academy of Management Review*, 29, 635–652.
Rowley-Jolivet, E., and Carter-Thomas, S. (2004). 'Genre awareness and rhetorical appropriacy: Manipulation of information structure by NS and NNS scientists in the international conference setting', *English for Specific Purposes*, 24(1), 41–64.
Rutherford, B. A. (2005). 'Genre analysis of corporate annual report narratives: A corpus linguistics-based approach', *Journal of Business Communication*, 42(4), 349–78.
Schneider, B. and Andre, J. (2005). 'University preparation for workplace writing', *Journal of Business Communication*, 42(2), 195–218.
Schutz, A. and Luckmann, T. (1974). *The Structures of the Life-World*, R. M. Zaner and T. H. Engelhardt Jr (trans.), London: Heinemann.
Swales, J. (1990). *Genre Analysis: English in Academic and Research Settings*, Cambridge: Cambridge University Press.
Yu, H. (2011). 'Integrating intercultural communication into an engineering communication service class tutorial', *IEEE Transactions on Professional Communication*, 54(1), 83–96.
Zhu, Y. (2000a). 'Structural moves reflected in English and Chinese sales letters', *Discourse Studies*, 2(4), 525–48.
——2000b. 'Building knowledge structures in teaching cross-cultural sales genres', *Business Communication Quarterly*, 63(4), 49–68.

——(2005). *Written Communication across Cultures: A Sociocognitive Perspective on Business Genres*, Amsterdam: John Benjamins.
——(2008). 'From cultural adaptation to cross-cultural discursive competence', *Discourse and Communication*, 2(2), 185–205.
——(2011). 'Building intercultural alliances: A study of moves and strategies in initial business negotiation meetings', *TEXT & TALK*, 31(1), 101–26.
Zhu, Y. and Hildebrandt, H. W. (2012). 'Effective persuasion of international business sales letters: An emic-etic perspective', *Management International Review*, DOI 10.1007/s11575-012-0154-z.
Zhu, Y., Nel, P. and Bhat, R. (2006). 'A cross cultural study of communication strategies for building business relationships', *International Journal of Cross Cultural Management*, 6(3), 319–41.
Zhuge, R. and Chen, X. (eds). (1994). *Duewai maoyi wenshu xiezuo* (Practical writings in foreign trade), Beijing: Renmin Daxue Chubanshe.

4
Stretching the multimodal boundaries of professional communication in multi-resources kits

Carmen Daniela Maier

Introduction

In order to detect and explain some of the contemporary shifts in professional communication, it is necessary to address the manifestation of processes of variation, recontextualisation and emergence both at the level of discourse and genre, and at the level of specific practices. This involves the exploration of new communicative tools that are created, disseminated and used by multiliterate individuals. It also involves the examination of how these individuals' professional identities and roles are dynamically shaped in interactions across various professional and academic settings. Such investigations are made possible through a multimodal approach to the communication and representation of these dynamic processes at the above-mentioned levels.

In this chapter, I attempt to exemplify how to approach multimodally a couple of issues related to the contemporary representation and communication of professional identities. The multimodal exploration is meant to provide an understanding of the communicative nuances that can be added when language is accompanied by other semiotic modes. The illustrative examples used in this chapter are taken from multi-resources kits designed to facilitate new forms of inter-institutional and inter-professional communication and interaction related to the context of the film business (see also Maier 2008 and forthcoming). Between 2004 and 2008, two series of novel multi-resources kits were launched by Kodak Company and by the oldest German film and television university, Konrad Wolf. These communicative tools are designed by and for professionals specialised in visuals who are able to use and exploit the latest technological developments. Both sets of kits appear in challenging moments for the respective communities: the community of film stock users is struggling to maintain its position in the film business, while the emerging 3D community is struggling to consolidate a position in the same business. In both situations, the multi-resources kits facilitate fast and nuanced communication of professional knowledge that can be routinely accessed by professional filmmakers and professionals-to-be in various contexts. The latest technological developments have influenced the kits' 'sites of appearance and the media of dissemination' (Kress 2010: 133), as they have appeared and have been disseminated across professional and academic settings. The two series of kits have been chosen for a detailed scrutiny because of the multimodal ways in which they represent and communicate the filmmakers' professional identity and their roles related to academic settings. In approaching these issues, I focus on how the dynamic character of filmmakers' professional identity allows them to take roles as *expert practitioner*, *aspirant* or *educator* in concordance with the requirements of specific communication and/or interaction settings. I have also multimodally identified educator roles related to the formal academic settings (*lecturer*, *instructor* and *trainer*), and roles related to the informal ones (*advisor* and *counsellor*).

After introducing multimodality as a methodological approach, this chapter attempts to show how by using this approach in the exploration of multi-resources kits, aspects of the representation and communication of the above-mentioned role changes can be revealed.

Multimodality

A multimodal approach offers the research means necessary for engaging with various semiotic entities be they texts or interactions that are designed with the help of several other semiotic modes apart from language. It permits the researcher to address both how each semiotic mode contributes to making meaning, and how the multimodal interplay can reinforce, complement or subvert the mono-modal meanings. Among the main issues of multimodal research, there should be mentioned: the identification of semiotic modes and their individual contribution to meaning making in complex texts and interactions, the explanation of the interplay of semiotic modes and its contribution to meaning making, and the capture of the simultaneous orchestration of several semiotic modes for revealing the multiplication of meanings.

Researchers in multimodality highlight the fact that communication has been multimodal in all historical, social and cultural contexts, and that the present technological developments have made it possible to 'transform what can be seen and by whom it can be seen' (Jewitt 2009: 3). Without confining multimodal communication to the present, Jewitt links the increasing interest in multimodality in a variety of fields with the fact that 'the need to understand the complex ways in which speech and writing interact with "non-verbal" modes can no longer be avoided' (Jewitt 2009: 3).

Both the definition of modes and the modes' interplay are recurrent themes in multimodal research. Certainly, the concept of 'mode' can and has been defined in various ways. Taking a social semiotic perspective, Kress defines a mode as 'a socially shaped and culturally given resource for making meaning (Kress 2009: 55), and he emphasises that, '*socially*, what counts as a mode is a matter for the community and its social-representational needs' (Kress 2010: 87). Jewitt defines the concept by contrasting it with the concept of 'medium':

> Medium refers to how texts are disseminated, such as printed book, CD-ROM, or computer application. Mode refers to any organized, regular means of representation and communication, such as still image, gesture, posture, speech, music, writing, or new configurations of the elements of these.
>
> *(Jewitt 2004: 184)*

Stöckl classifies the semiotic modes into modes, sub-modes, peripheral modes and medial variants that 'shift or blend (mode overlapping) and mix (mode mixing)' (Stöckl 2004: 9). In her multimodal (inter)action analysis, Norris also addresses the ways in which modes take different positions, gaining or losing primacy at different points in the process of communication, as they are used in 'modal aggregates' (Norris 2012: 17) in order to convey specific meanings. Processes of intersemiotic shift, namely the transpositions of meanings from one semiotic mode to another, are discussed by Iedema by employing the concept of resemiotisation, which 'is meant to provide the analytical means for (1) tracing how semiotics are translated from one into the other as social processes unfold, as well as for (2) asking why these semiotics (rather than others) are mobilized to do certain things at certain times' (Iedema 2003: 29).

The interplay of semiotic modes is a central theme in the specific agenda of multimodality because researchers in multimodality consider that this interplay is 'significant for meaning making, practices and shape of knowledge' (Jewitt 2012: 99). From this perspective, the meaning making processes take place both at the level of one semiotic mode and at the level of its interaction with other modes. In order to account for the complex systems of relations that can appear between semiotic modes, researchers as Lim (2004), Macken-Horarik (2004), Martinec and Salway (2005), Unsworth (2006) and Van Leeuwen (2005) have provided conceptual tools relevant for various contexts from textbooks to videos and homepages.

A multimodal approach to the analysis of complex texts and interactions also implies a detailed transcription that has to precede any analytical endeavour relating to the multimodal dimension of the respective texts or interactions. The multimodal transcription is a fundamental means of providing transparency by revealing layers of patterns at both micro level and macro level of the data. Therefore, in order to gain accurate and relevant information about the data, multimodal researchers have also been preoccupied with finding transcription procedures and concordancing tools that could capture multimodal data. Researchers such as Baldry and Thibault (2006) have contributed to the creation of online computer-assisted tools for storage, retrieval, and comparative analyses of multimodal corporate texts in order to account for recurrent patterns of meaning and generic structures. Bateman (2008) has also provided tools for processing multimodal page-based corpora, proposing the GeM model as a corpus of annotation scheme.

Before concluding this short presentation of multimodal issues, it might be relevant to mention that, according to multimodal researchers, 'multimodality can be understood as a theory, a perspective or a field of enquiry or a methodological application' (Carrey 2009: 12). However, O'Halloran argues that the development of theories and methodologies meant 'to account for multimodal phenomena across multiple domains of application' should be considered 'evidence that such a field is emerging to take its place alongside other established fields such as linguistics' (O'Halloran and Smith 2011: 2).

In what follows, I intend to show how a multimodal perspective can be used in order to explore the consequences of employing several semiotic modes for the communication and representation of professional identities and roles in the multi-resources kits. As only certain issues relating to the multimodal approach have been included in this chapter, the multimodal transcription has not been incorporated. The multimodal transcription that has been necessary in order to structure the explorative work that will be presented in this chapter, has been made at the level of shot and sequence in the case of genres as filmed interviews, symposium trailers and panel discussions.

Multi-resources kits

Kodak Company's multi-resources kits were created and disseminated in professional and academic settings during the launching of the most technologically advanced line of film stock products ever made, *Kodak Vision 2*. The CDs of *Embracing the Power of Light* (2005), *Light and Shadow in Perfect Harmony* (2005) and *When Words Aren't Enough* (2006) are dedicated to sharing professional knowledge that encompasses information, facts and benefits relating to the expanded *Kodak Vision 2* film family. Knowledge about the practical professional collaboration between cinematographers and laboratories and post-production houses is also included. In *The Difference*, 'industry veterans discuss the unique attributes of film and digital capture' (*The Difference* 2004). Apart from a digital video disc, *The Difference* also provides a booklet in which commentaries of 19 professional filmmakers are included together with stills from their work and brief enumerations of their professional achievements. In the digital video disc, their commentaries, both as voice-over and as filmed interviews, accompany excerpts from feature films, commercials, documentaries, location coverage, stills from features and from location coverage, and footage from preservation facilities.

Inside Out, the series of multi-resources kits created during 2006–8 in connection with annual international symposiums on digital production of film and TV held by Konrad Wolf University, target film and TV executives, practitioners, and teachers and students who are interested in how film and TV production will develop in the digital era. The participants are also offered an opportunity to familiarise themselves with digital high-end systems. The communication of professional knowledge from the domain of digital film and TV is accompanied in these kits by the communication of knowledge about the actual events and participants.

Some of these multi-resources kits incorporate several media embedded in each other. Apart from digital video discs and booklets, the series include several other media that are embedded. For example, photography, film and video are both visually and verbally present in both booklets and digital video discs. Furthermore, the medium of film is also aurally represented in *The Difference* as the specific sound of film running through the camera can be continuously heard while the titles of the digital video disc's chapters are displayed on the screen. The internet is represented through links that facilitate access to more professional knowledge outlets existing on the homepages related to the two institutional entities. The medium of radio is also present in *Insight Out* series. The modal aggregates used by these media include several semiotic modes and submodes: first the visual mode manifested through the submodes of still and moving images, and animated and static writing; secondly, the auditory mode manifested through the submodes of speech, sound and music.

The multimedia kits are supported across these semiotic modes and media by a complex system of genres belonging to academic, advertising and professional practices. In the Kodak kits, apart from interviews, feature films, commercials and documentaries, there are also featurettes, namely shorter feature films, represented either in excerpt form or in their entirety. The CDs dedicated to the *Kodak Vision 2* film family are organised in chapters, each chapter being dedicated to a new type of film. Each chapter includes featurettes and documentaries about the shooting of those featurettes. The documentaries are accompanied by the voice-over of the expert practitioners who contributed to the making of the respective featurettes. The chapters also communicate professional knowledge about features, benefits and technical curves of the new types of film, which is displayed in PDF files. In the *Insight Out* series, the fluid boundaries between academic, advertising and professional practices are also reflected in the various genres that appear in booklets and/or digital video discs: lectures, panel discussions, radio interviews, television broadcasts, product brochures, commercials, trailers and journal articles. Some of the genres lose their generic integrity when reframed in the multi-resources kits. For example, in *The Difference*, due to the advertising and professional discourses that are mixed in the filmed interviews with expert professionals, they cannot be classified either as testimonials or lectures. Both on and off screen, the experts share their professional experience and knowledge, but they do so by highlighting how the usage of film stock has contributed to the building of professional identity. The fact that the interviews are also interspersed with many excerpts from other genres (features, sitcoms, documentaries or commercials) contributes also to this blurring of boundaries. Other genres do preserve their generic integrity – although sometimes only excerpts are provided – but, by being embedded in the multi-resources kits, their expected communicative purposes are overshadowed by new meta-communicative purposes that permeate the overall discourse of the kits.

Professional identities and roles

Addressing professionals and professionals-to-be, these two series of multi-resources kits are dynamic arenas for sharing highly specialised professional knowledge that not only 'create conditions of homogeneity between insiders' (Bhatia 2004: 192), but also facilitate the inclusion of outsiders. Although the professionals interacting in and with these multi-resources kits belong to different communities, possess various types and levels of expertise, and are driven by specific professional goals and objectives, they do share broad communicative purposes in these kits. These meta-communicative purposes are related to the maintenance and/or consolidation of the above-mentioned challenged positions. In order to back up his statements and to highlight their relevance, John Walker, a producer, cinematographer and director, claims at the beginning of his interview that 'right now, is the best time to be a film maker, ever, in the history of film making' (*The Difference* 2004).

The shared meta-communicative purposes, the basic common professional knowledge and the wish for strong collaborative ties surface implicitly and explicitly in all multi-resources kits in complex multimodal structures building a shared platform for interaction and communication. Simultaneously, the kits also contribute to the reinforcement or building of the professional identities of those who are represented in them and of those who use them. For example, in his filmed lecture about ARRI HD cameras, Dr Hans Kiening reminds the symposiums' participants that 'internationally and scientifically we have agreed upon a system of standardized test images' (*Insight Out* 2007). As a technical director, Dennis Rettowski, in a journal article embedded as a PDF file in one of the kits, also claims that 'shooting straight onto a disk recording system without being able to retain an original negative is an idea most cinematographers feel uncomfortable with' (*Insight Out* 2006). In the Kodak series, the emphasis on professional collaborations in particular is recurrent: 'Now it's easier than ever for cinematographers to collaborate with labs and post houses. Insert this CD to find out how' (*When Words Aren't Enough* 2006).

What mainly separates the professionals communicating in and through these kits and their users is merely the level of specialised knowledge and the degree of professional expertise. To help in eliminating these gaps, the kits use the interplay of semiotic modes to communicate not only domain-specific knowledge but also knowledge about outstanding members of the professional communities affected by the above-mentioned challenging situations in the film business. Their context-related roles that they take in various situations can be discerned in a nuanced way by focusing on how each semiotic mode and the multimodal interplay of several semiotic modes contribute to their representation.

In the Kodak kits, the professional identities of experts are visualised through still and moving images in interviews with superimposed captions disclosing their professional field and achievements. Examples from previous film productions (shots from feature films, commercials or documentaries) and shots with the film crew on location are sometimes accompanied by the voice-over commentaries of the respective expert. The professional identity of the filmmakers is multimodally communicated as the shots visualise their generic competence and professional expertise, while the commentaries reinforce verbally these visualised proofs. However, the verbal mode contributes to this reinforcement as well by disclosing the discursive competence of the expert as a person who can share professional knowledge. From being a renowned practitioner, the expert is able to become an educator using discursive strategies meant to diminish the usual distance existing between experts and aspirants: confessions related to their past experiences, doubts or mistakes, and advice related to future decisions. For example, John Bowring, a director of photography and managing director, confesses both in the booklet and in the filmed interview: 'When I first started in television, I said, Bowring, you're a bloody idiot … ' (*The Difference* 2004). John Walker discloses that 'as a producer who invests in making my own films … if I'd chosen to go the digital capture route 15 years ago, I would have invested about 100,000 in equipment every year' (*The Difference* 2004). The relevance of this excerpt from his filmed interview is highlighted as the excerpt is also resemiotised in the booklet with white letters underlined with green lines. In his interview, he gives also his personal advice about acquiring professional expertise: 'To a young film maker, I wouldn't discount film, but it requires a discipline. I personally like that discipline, because the tension of film focuses you' (*The Difference* 2004). Ferne Pearlstein, another director of photography, relates the development of her professional identity to past choices in a personal way: 'I feel very lucky that I actually learnt how to be a filmmaker with film. I feel like it made me a better filmmaker. It made me think things through in a different way' (*The Difference* 2004).

The distance between experts and aspirants is also diminished visually because the experts are no longer 'behind the scenes' as their professions require, and the kits' users can have eye contact with them, see their facial expressions, and hear their voices. As in any professional domain, for professionals-to-be, seeing and hearing experts who are the 'stars' of their profession strengthen the inspiring effect of the experts' words. By maintaining eye contact with the viewer, the experts' facial expressions and gaze (in close up shots), and body language (in medium and long shots) reinforce convincingly the meaning of their words. Sound-wise, the rhythm and tone of their words have the same persuasive effect. Furthermore, apart from visual appearance, hesitations, pauses, rhetorical questions or the repetition of certain words also reveal the individual identity of the experts. Many of the experts address the viewer directly by using the 'you' personal pronoun. This can be seen, for example, in the interview with Matthew Libatique, director of photography, when he confesses: 'You know, film making is the best classroom there is … Every time I make a film, I'm learning something new because I have to research something, a world perhaps that I'm not involved in' (*The Difference* 2004). In this way, even if they don't maintain eye contact with their viewers, the small distance between professionals and professionals-to-be is still maintained. Certainly, both the choice of words, and the confessional and informal tone of their explanations enrich the representation of their identity when they are sharing their professional experience and expertise on or off screen.

The filmed interviews are also interspersed with excerpts from their well-known works accompanied by the voice-over commentaries of the experts. Still and moving images from locations with the experts 'in action' are also used while the experts explain off screen what kind of challenges they faced and what solutions they have found. When excerpts from the filmed interviews are also resemiotised in the booklet, these are also personalised by using different fonts in different colours for each expert. Nevertheless, the inclusion of photos of hardware, flow graphs and general workflow diagrams in the digital video discs or CDs reinforce the experts' high professional status, and the level and types of expertise needed in their professional practices. The complex modal aggregates that represent professional identities are organised at several levels in different ways, first, at the level of the specific genres of the multimodal kits, and secondly at the level of the whole kit. At the level of the whole multi-resources kit *The Difference* (2004), the visual aggregate of the booklet cover's still image (a surfer balancing on a huge wave) and the static written text on the first image of the DVD ('artistic discipline, artistic freedom') represent the essence of a filmmaker's professional identity that the multi-resources kit intends to communicate, namely the dichotomy between technology and art. The idea of a balancing act is recurrent in these multi-resources kits and it is used to represent multimodally not only the professional identity of a filmmaker, but the profession as such too. In *Light and Shadow in Perfect Harmony* (2005), the user is addressed imperatively on the left side of the CD's cover, 'behold the beauty of balance', while on the right side, the medium shot of a woman's legs running barefoot with her high heeled shoes in her hand reinforces the verbal advice.

Implicitly, Nick Powell talks also about a sort of balancing act when, in his filmed interview about the *Insight Out* symposiums, he characterises them as being a way for 'people in the industry and in education to compare notes especially about the meeting of technology and creative content' (*Insight Out*, 2008). So, in the multi-resources kits of *Insight Out*, not only is the representation of how the gap between experts and aspirants is bridged relevant, but also the bridging of the gap between the professional and academic practices has a high representational value. These kits are supposed to represent and communicate both domain specific knowledge and knowledge about the interactions occasioned by the symposiums, while the professionals belonging to various professional communities are represented as changing their roles several times in the context of the symposiums. These changes are related to the knowledge they have about film and TV digitalisation:

> as participants in these symposiums, renowned directors of photography can become learners due to their lack of expertise in digital film, or they can maintain and even enhance their expert status given by their professional identity due to a high level of expertise in digital film.
>
> *(Maier forthcoming)*

The experts meeting in these symposiums are both expert practitioners and academics, and their level of expertise is validated multimodally in the kits through the credentials displayed on both still and moving images in filmed lectures or interviews. The blurring of boundaries between the roles of these professional filmmakers is also highlighted in their own words: 'I'm a Director of Photography and a Film Director as well. I do documentaries and at the film academy in Vienna, I teach the camera class' (Interview with Christian Berger, *Insight Out*, 2006). CVs, interview transcripts, and the introduction of experts by the symposiums' organisers in the booklets are also meant to verbally assist in strengthening the representation of their professional identity and roles in the kits.

The different roles they take during the symposiums can also be detected by viewing the moving and still images that show them involved in the formal and informal activities of the symposiums. Obviously, the prevalence of certain types of shots in the kits is meant to visualise the changing distance between the expert and the other participants when involved in these different symposiums' activities. As lecturers, the experts are usually shown in long shots while sharing their knowledge in concordance with the common rules of academic practice: speaking in front of a group of people, using a PowerPoint presentation and answering questions at the end of the lecture. Close-up shots or medium shots are also used especially when the question and answer session is filmed in order to show the closer relation between the expert and the person asking a question. As instructors or trainers, they are generally shown in medium shots surrounded by a group of people while explaining the working of various appliances used in recording, editing or storing digital images. When playing the roles of advisers or counsellors during informal events at the symposiums, for example, coffee breaks, the experts are shown in close-up or medium shots while talking with a single person or a smaller

MULTI-RESOURCES KITS

MULTIMODAL REPRESENTATION OF:				MULTIMODAL REPRESENTATION ACROSS:	
Shared meta-communicative purposes				Academic genres	Research studies (pdf files)
^				^	Lectures (pdf, PP, filmed)
Basic common professional knowledge				^	Panel discussions (filmed)
Collaborative ties				Professional film genres	Features & featurettes
^				^	Sitcoms
Professional identities				^	Documentaries
Context-related roles	expert	Practitioner		Advertising genres	TV broadcasts
^	^	^		^	Event trailers
^	^	^		^	Press articles
^	^	educator	lecturer and instructor	^	Product presentation (brochures and pdf)
^	^	^	advisor and counsellor	^	Photos
^	^	^	^	^	Advertisements
^	aspirant	^	^	^	Interviews (filmed, transcripts)

Figure 4.1 The multi-resources kits

group. Verbally, the behind-the-scenes accounts illustrate the amount of experience they have in dealing with difficult professional issues. For example, Benjamin Bayer, a director of photography, explains the technical challenges in his filmed interview: 'During preproduction, the challenge for the camera and art department was to handle depth of field in a way it would not limit the actors in performing fast movements' (*Insight Out*, 2006). The participants in the symposiums disclose their professional identity in more general or personal ways too. For example, David Serge confesses: 'I have a soft spot for visual effects' (*Insight Out*, 2008). Solo Avital states in a close-up shot of the film trailer dedicated to the symposium: 'I am a great admirer of the digital because it generates greater freedom to the creative people' (*Insight Out*, 2007).

As in the case of the filmed interviews embedded in *The Difference*, these filmed interviews also bridge the gap between participants in the symposiums and the users of the multi-resources kits multimodally, because both the choice of words, speech characteristics, and the close-up images of the participants' faces brings them closer to the users. And, in the same way, the kits' PDF files loaded multimodally with technical descriptions and explanations reinforce the experts' high professional status, and the level and types of expertise needed in their professional practices. Figure 4.1 summarises how and what is multimodally represented in the multi-resources kits.

Conclusions

I have chosen to explain in this chapter a few multimodal aspects of professional identity representations in multi-resources kits that have appeared in film-related professional and academic settings in challenging moments for the film business.

The shared meta-communicative purposes, the basic common professional knowledge and the wish for strong collaborative ties that make possible inter-institutional and inter-professional forms of communication and interaction are represented in the kits together with the changing roles that professionals can take in these contexts. Whether they belong or attempt to belong to the challenged professional community of film stock users or to the emerging 3D professional community, the professionals and the professionals-to-be are faced with the chance to (re)think, (re)assess and (re)state their professional identity, and the multi-resources kits reflect these processes in a complex mixture of genres and discourses. The multi-resources kits reflect how these professionals belonging (or striving to belong) to film-related professional and academic settings can change their roles in accordance with the specific requirements of multi-disciplinary interactions.

I have tried to show how these professional identities and changing roles represented in the multi-resources kits can be understood in greater detail when semiotic modes other than language are taken into consideration. The modal aggregates designed to represent and communicate the above-mentioned dynamic changes shift their composition (and the dominance of certain semiotic modes inside them) in concordance with the specific communicative purposes of the experts and aspirants engaged in the multi-disciplinary interactions.

Far from being a full-fledged multimodal analysis, this chapter is meant to indicate some of the directions in which a researcher could look if a multimodal approach is to be adopted. It is my conviction that, regardless of (sub-)disciplinary contexts and frameworks, future research in professional communication might not be able to ignore the multimodal aspect because communication is and will become more and more multimodal due to the continuous development of technologies and the complex requirements faced by multiliterate generations of professionals.

Related topics

media communication; electronic media; knowledge-making; professional discourse; genre analysis

Key readings

Kress, G. and Van Leeuwen, T. (2001). *Multimodal Discourse: The Modes and Media of Contemporary Communication*, London, England: Routledge. (In this book, an introduction to the main concepts and assumptions of the multimodal approach is provided.)

Kress, G. and Van Leeuwen, T. (2006). *Reading Images. The Language of Visual Design*, London: Routledge. (Drawing on a wide range of examples, this book presents a series of methodological tools for analysing how images produce meaning.)

Norris, S. and Maier, C.D. (eds) (forthcoming). *Texts, Images and Interactions: A Reader in Multimodality*, New York: De Gruyter. (This textbook introduces the topic of multimodality in a systematic way so that it can be used in teaching situations and/or for self-study.)

Royce, T. D. and Bowcher, W. L. (eds) (2007). *New Directions in the Analysis of the Multimodal Discourse*, London: Lawrence Erlbaum Associates. (Taking a social semiotic view of multimodal communication, this book accounts for the various facets of multimodality in a range of texts and contexts.)

References

Baldry, A. and Thibault, P.J. (2006). *Multimodal Transcription and Text Analysis. A Multimedia Toolkit and Coursebook with Associated On-line Course*, London: Equinox.

Bateman, J. (2008). *Multimodality and Genre. A Foundation for the Systematic Analysis of Multimodal Documents*, NY: Palgrave Macmillan.

Bhatia, V. K. (2004). *Worlds of Written Discourse. A Genre-based View*, London: Continuum.

——(2008). 'Towards critical discourse analysis', in V. K. Bhatia, J. Flowerdew and R. H. Jones (eds) *Advances in Discourse Studies* (pp. 166–78), London: Routledge.

——(2010). 'Interdiscursivity in professional communication', *Discourse and Communication*, 4(1), 32–50.

Carrey, J. (2009). 'Introduction', in J. Carrey, *The Routledge Handbook of Multimodal Analysis* (pp. 11–14), London: Routledge.

Iedema, R. (2003). 'Multimodality, resemiotization: extending the analysis of discourse as multi-semiotic practice', in *Visual Communication*, 2(1), 29–57.

Jewitt, C. (2004). 'Multimodality and new communication technologies', in P. Levine and R. Scollon (eds), *Discourse and Technology: Multimodal Discourse Analysis* (pp. 184–96), Washington DC: Georgetown University Press.

——(2009). 'Introduction', in C. Jewitt (ed.), *The Routledge Handbook of Multimodal Analysis* (pp. 1–13), London: Routledge.

——(2012). 'Technology and reception as multimodal remaking', in S. Norris (ed.), *Multimodality in Practice: Investigating Theory-in-practice-through-methodology* (pp. 97–115), London: Routledge.

Kress, G. (2009). 'What is mode?' in C. Jewitt (ed.), *The Routledge Handbook of Multimodal Analysis* (pp. 1–13), London: Routledge.

——(2010). *Multimodality: A Social Semiotic Approach to Contemporary Communication*, London: Routledge.

Lim, V. F. (2004). 'Developing an integrative multi-semiotic model', in K. L. O'Halloran (ed.) *Multimodal Discourse Analysis. Systemic-functional Perspectives* (pp. 220–47), London: Continuum.

Macken-Horarik, M. (2004). 'Interacting with the multimodal text: Reflections on image and verbiage in ArtExpress', *Visual Communication*, 4(3), 5–26.

Maier, D. C. (2008). 'Multimodal communication of specialized knowledge in interactive corporate materials', *The International Journal of Learning*, 14, 7–15.

——(forthcoming). 'Transgeneric multimodal designs across business and academic communication: The case of multimedia kits', in P. Evangelisti-Allori, V. K. Bhatia and J. A. Bateman (eds), *Evolution in Genres: Emergence, Variation, Multimodality*, Bern: Peter Lang.

Martinec, M. and Salway, A. (2005). 'A system for image-text relations in new (and old) media', *Visual Communication*, 4(3), 337–71.

Norris, S. (2012). 'Teaching touch/response – feel', in S. Norris (ed.), *Multimodality in Practice: Investigating Theory-in-practice-through-methodology* (pp. 7–19), London: Routledge.

O'Halloran, K.L. and Smith, B.A. (2011). *Multimodal Studies*, in K. L. O'Halloran and B.A. Smith, *Multimodal Studies. Exploring Issues and Domains* (pp. 1–13), London: Routledge.

Stöckl, H. (2004). 'In between modes: Language and image in printed media', in E. Ventola, C. Charled and M. Kaltenbacher (eds), *Perspectives on Multimodality* (pp. 9–30), Amsterdam: John Benjamins.

Unsworth, L. (2006). 'Towards a metalanguage for multiliteracies education: Describing the meaning making resources of language-image interaction', *English Teaching: Language and Critique*, 5(1), 55–76.

Van Leeuwen, T. (2005). *Introducing Social Semiotics*, New York: Routledge.

B. Broad disciplinary frameworks

5
Business communication

Catherine Nickerson

Introduction

In the course of the past two decades, business communication (BC) has become perhaps one of the best-established discipline-based approaches to communication. As the name suggests, it has two primary concerns, i) to understand more about how people communicate within their own business organisations, and ii) to understand more about how business people communicate with other people outside of their own organisations, who may or may not be engaged in business. More specifically, as the Finnish scholar Louhiala-Salminen (2009) observes, the goal of BC research is to develop and disseminate 'knowledge that increases the effectiveness and efficiency of business operations' (2009: 307). As a result, BC can best be viewed as 'an integrated "umbrella" concept covering all formal and informal communication within a business context, using all possible media, involving all stakeholder groups, operating both at the level of the individual employee and that of the corporation' (2009: 312). Eight years earlier, writing from the perspective of a US scholar, Rogers (2001) had already observed 'we do appear to share an interest in providing practical knowledge that can enhance the communication effectiveness of all kinds or organizational stakeholders, particularly related to business' (Rogers 2001: 21). As a broad disciplinary framework then, embedded in the exigencies of business operations, BC draws on and has overlaps with many other disciplines such as management communication, corporate communication and intercultural communication, while at the same time, it also refers to theoretical frameworks, including genre and discourse analysis, and rhetoric and conversational analysis, all of which are also discussed in this volume.

As an academic discipline, BC is taught and researched at various institutions around the world, often (but not always) within a business school affiliated to a university. In some of these contexts BC scholars also hold senior positions at the level of professor, an indication that the discipline has reached maturity. At the same time, however, Lawrence and Galle (2011) discuss a survey of the ABC's membership, which reveals that at least for the North American context, many BC professionals now hold non-tenure track positions as BC instructors, and that furthermore, this trend is likely to continue in the future as part of a national trend in the US to hire non-tenure-track faculty. At least half of the business communication faculty they surveyed in 2007, for instance, held non-tenure track positions. They comment, the community of academic business communication professionals is difficult to define. We are full-time, part-time, tenured, and nontenured. We hold appointments in business schools and other social sciences as well as in the liberal arts. We are primarily a teaching faculty, but many of us are required or expected to conduct research, publish, engage in service activities, and advise students.

(Lawrence and Galle 2011: 334)

The community is clearly diverse, and there are differences in focus both within the US and in different parts of the world, with more opportunity for BC research in some contexts than in others. Louhiala-Salminen (2009) identifies two prominent European examples where this is the case: the master's programme at the School of Business at the University of Aarhus in Denmark (corporate communication) and the master's and doctoral programmes at what is now the Aalto University School of Economics (international BC). And in recent years, the European ABC in particular has also hosted an additional symposium for doctoral candidates, which has started to make an impact on the published work representing the discipline; for instance, the Special Issue of the *JBC* which appeared in October 2011 on 'Displaying Competence', contains a number of examples of the work of young European BC scholars, located in universities such as Aarhus in Denmark, Vienna in Austria, Ghent in Belgium, Helsinki in Finland, and Verona in Italy. Other examples from around the world where there is an active interest in research, include Baruch College in New York (corporate communication), Anderson UCLA (management communication), Marshall USC (management communication), Copenhagen Business School (intercultural communication, management and international culture, and communication studies), Radboud University Nijmegen (business communication), Singapore Management University (management and organisation), City University Hong Kong (English for the business and corporate world), and Hong Kong Polytechnic University (research centre for professional communication in English). As these suggest, it is not always easy to identify BC programmes, or to locate BC scholars and practitioners, and as I will go on to discuss below, there may indeed be considerable overlap in the disciplinary frameworks that BC scholars refer to, as well as in the topics and skills that are included in a BC teaching programme. At my own university, Zayed University in the United Arab Emirates, for instance, we teach several modules in business communication, all of which aim to help our students to understand how to optimise the efficiency and effectiveness of business operations; within those modules we refer to BC, alongside discourse and genre analysis, intercultural and cross-cultural communication, management communication, organisation communication and corporate communication, depending on what we are focusing on. BC maintains its own professional organisation – the Association for Business Communication (ABC) – supported by both international and regional groups, and it supports two journals, *The Journal of Business Communication* (*JBC*), which has a focus on research, and *The Business Communication Quarterly* (*BCQ*), which has a focus on praxis, pedagogy and research related to teaching. As I have suggested above, BC scholars encompass a broad spectrum of interests and backgrounds, from the management communication scholars and rhetoricians in the North American context, through the applied linguists and document design specialists who dominate the European scene, on to the scholars in Asia, many of whom are also applied linguists, whose work has most recently been characterised by the maintenance of close ties with business people and the discussion of what it means to communicate in a professionally competent way.

In this chapter, I will first trace the historical development of BC as an academic discipline from the beginning of the 1990s to the present day. I will consider the initial discussions on BC in terms of its formation as a discipline and its subsequent evolution, and I will provide an overview of the published work within the *JBC* and *BCQ* in the last five and a half years, together with other related publications, that illustrate how BC research and pedagogy has indeed contributed to an increase in the 'effectiveness and efficiency of business operations'. I will identify the most important theoretical frameworks that have influenced BC researchers and practitioners located in different parts of the world, together with the related analytical and methodological approaches that they have used, and I will also discuss how BC as a discipline has made a substantial contribution to our understanding of professional communication, competence and practice as it relates to business. In doing so, I will also showcase the work of a number of key individuals whose work has made a lasting contribution to the formation of the discipline. Finally, in the last part of the chapter I will pinpoint a number of common trends in BC in the most recent research and pedagogical approaches, and I will speculate on how these may shape the future of the discipline in the course of the next ten years.

Historical development

As Louhiala-Salminen (2009) observes, the discussion of the formation of the discipline began in earnest in the mid to late 1990s, with a series of publications in the *Journal of Business & Technical Communication* (e.g. Reinsch 1996), the *Business Communication Quarterly* (e.g. Charles 1998) and perhaps most notably the *Journal of Business Communication*, where a special issue that appeared in 1998 was focused on discipline formation (Graham and Thralls 1998). The ABC in particular, and the publications it supports, has encouraged the discussion on discipline formation that continues to the present day. Lawrence and Galle (2011) comment as follows,

> As an organization and group of scholars, the Association for Business Communication (ABC) and its members have been a highly self-reflective group. Looking back over decades of Association journal issues, we can easily find articles that attempt to help define our field and our identity as researchers, instructors, and professionals (e.g., Daniel 1983; Forman 1993, 1998; Gieselman 1982; Kostelnick 1998; Krapels and Arnold 1996; Rogers 2001; Rogers, Campbell, Louhiala-Salminen, Rentz and Suchan 2007; Shaw 1993).
>
> *(2011: 319–20)*

Although the scholars involved in the initial discussions, and indeed those that came later, represented different scholarly traditions roughly divided by the Atlantic, there was, and remains, 'a shared goal for research' and 'a general understanding of the utilitarian goal of developing and disseminating knowledge that increases the effectiveness and efficiency of business operations' (Louhiala-Salminen 2009: 307). As I have suggested above, it is this shared goal that best defines BC as a discipline and that unites those scholars that are interested in contributing to it, rather than the adherence to any one theory or methodological approach. In order to understand how communication contributes to the effectiveness and efficiency of business operations, BC is therefore characterised by a need to understand how things work in practice, in other words, to unpack how people 'get their work done' through communication (Bargiela-Chiappini, Nickerson and Planken 2007; 2013: 3). In a recent discussion on BC as a discipline, Cyphert (2009) traces a shift in emphasis in the 40-year period since the formation of the ABC, in that on the basis of a survey of the membership in 2007 and 2008, she can conclude that 'Members continue to highly value pedagogical relevance, but the Association for Business Communication clearly attracts research-active academics' (2009: 262). The indication is that the original emphasis on praxis that was inherent in the North American membership in particular at the foundation of the Association has gradually accommodated the need to also refer to empirical research, with this shift becoming most especially apparent during the past decade. Until very recently, the *JBC* and *BCQ* have published the plenary addresses of the winners of the Outstanding Researcher Award and Outstanding Teaching Award respectively, and these publications have also contributed to discipline formation through dissemination amongst the ABC's membership. Notable contributions of this type in the *JBC* for instance have included Charles (2007) who introduces the concept of Business English as a lingua franca (BELF), Fann Thomas (2007) who discusses the relationship between the workplace and academia, Dulek (2008) who reflects on the impact of academic citations systems on the BC community in particular, and Jameson (2009a) who discusses the contribution that BC scholars could make to help make a difference in the current economic crisis. These, and their pedagogical counterparts in the *BCQ*, have raised a number of issues of relevance for the Association either in terms of research direction, e.g. BELF, or in terms of approach, e.g. academia versus the workplace.

BC researchers are concerned with investigating how communication works in business organisations and then with making recommendations as to how to make things better. This also explains why the collection of empirical data has also been so influential, while at the same time accounting for why the BC community has encompassed a variety of different approaches and has not relied on any one particular theoretical approach; although BC scholars may belong to a particular research tradition, often as a consequence of their geographical location, they have generally selected an appropriate theoretical model and methodological approach that can most effectively lead to a better understanding of a particular set of data. As discussed elsewhere in this volume, genre analysis (in the English for Specific Purposes tradition), for instance, has evolved as a way to understand a set of data, rather than working with a set of data to define and refine an established model – and there are obvious parallels with the evolution of BC as it exists today as a broad academic discipline. As a result, many BC scholars, particularly those based in Europe and Asia, have chosen to use a genre approach. In addition, as a scholarly community, BC has increasingly drawn on the views and experience of scholars from all over the globe, most especially in the development of a research tradition. Since 1999, for instance, when the first European ABC Convention was held in Helsinki in Finland, there have been regular opportunities for BC scholars to meet and exchange ideas, not only in North America, but also in Europe and in the Asia-Pacific Region. As a result, the *JBC* in particular has increasingly showcased the work of scholars from around the world, as I will discuss in the next section, and both the *JBC* and the *BCQ*, and other publications of relevance to the discipline, now exhibit a concern with issues such as the impact of multicultural workforces on the communication that takes place within business (e.g. Jameson 2007a; Goby 2009) and the undeniable influence of English on global business as a dominant lingua franca (Nickerson 2005; Louhiala-Salminen, Charles and Kankaanranta 2005; Charles 2007).

Key publications

The Association for Business Communication supports two journal publications; the *Journal of Business Communication* (*JBC*), which publishes scholarly research relevant for the development of BC as an academic discipline, and the *Business Communication Quarterly* (*BCQ*), which has a focus on both BC praxis and pedagogy. Rentz (2009) has suggested that the *JBC* is a 'niche' journal, which means that it is 'essential to the scholarly conversation in specialty areas that are not well served by bigger, mainstream journals' (2009: 404). She goes on to observe that journals of this nature are of importance for career advancement, particularly for new members of the community. Many BC scholars have published in both journals, a reflection of the dual nature of the discipline as maintaining a focus on both research and pedagogy.

A review of work published in the *JBC* over the past five years, from January 2007 until April 2012, reveals the increasing presence of European scholars, alongside their US counterparts, together with a small number of contributions from scholars located in the Asia-Pacific region. Of the 22 issues of the journal that appeared within that timeframe, 15 include at least one contribution from outside of the US, compared to only seven issues that were US-only. In addition, six issues either included an equal number of US and non-US contributors, or the non-US contributors were in the majority. As I will go on to discuss below, those issues where non-US contributors dominated, were also in three of the four Special Issues of the journal that were published during that time. In keeping with the overarching goal of BC research to contribute to an increase in the efficiency and effectiveness of business operations, the journal in this period has included a wide variety of different types of communication or relevance to the business context, alongside an equally diverse set of theories, approaches to the analysis, and research methods. The written forms of communication include press releases, email, internal corporate writing, corporate homepages, mission statements, annual reports, investors prospectuses, audit reports, CSR reporting, performance appraisals, direct mail, CEO's speeches, advertising slogans, recruitment advertisements, earning forecasts, CEO profiles and PowerPoint presentations. The spoken forms of communication are dominated by meetings in various different contexts, but in addition, the journal also includes studies of call centre communication transactions, negotiations, mentoring interactions, small talk, listening, face-to-face versus online interactions, supervisory communication, coaching and conference calls. In addition, a number of general topics of relevance to the contemporary business enterprise are also discussed, including the role played by emerging economies and cyberspace, intercultural BC, the interface between the workplace and academia, BELF, crisis communication, women's issues in the workplace, leadership communication, socialisation in business organisations, employee involvement, sustainability and CSR communication in general, language policies, diversity and identity, client communication, visual communication, and closely related to this, multimodality. As I discussed in the introduction to this chapter, the theories referred to and the analytical approaches taken are generally a reflection of the geographical location of the author or authors of the individual publication, with the general observation that the work is data-driven rather than being theory-driven. Therefore, for instance, the three US scholars represented in the January 2007 issue refer to Sproull and Kiesler's (1991) work on computer-mediated communication, to Weick's (1995) work on sensemaking, and to Daft and Lengel's (1984) media richness theory respectively, whereas the European scholar who completes the issue, refers to Bhatia's (1993) theory on genre. Other theories and analytical approaches that characterise the contributions to the journal include social constructionism (US scholars), narrative theory (US scholars), action research (Australian scholars), content analysis (US scholars), rhetorical genre analysis (US scholars), Conversation Analysis-Ethnography (US and European scholars), Discourse Analysis and Rhetoric (US and European scholars), Accommodation Theory (US and European scholars), Macro-theories on intercultural communication (European scholars), framing (US scholars), and Lemke's theory of hypermodality (European scholars). The data-driven nature of the majority of the contributions, also means that the journal encompasses a range of different methodologies to collect and analyse the data, including survey research and structured interviews, experimental investigations, close text analyses, extended literature reviews, case studies, and both descriptive and prescriptive accounts of a particular set of data. The methodology selected was unrelated to the geographical location of the author or authors, but was driven by the nature of the data and the theory or analytical approach selected in its investigation. Finally, in the last five years, the *JBC* has published four Special Issues on corporate reporting (April 2008; July 2008), on discourse analysis (January 2009), on language matters (April 2010; October 2010), and on displaying competence (October 2011). With the exception of the two issues dedicated to work on corporate reporting, where the majority of the contributors are based in the US, all three remaining Special Issues are dominated by scholars located in different parts of Europe, a clear indication of the shift within the ABC and the *JBC* towards a more global membership and audience.

The *BCQ* over the same time period, from March 2007 until June 2012, has not shown the same increase in material published by scholars from around the world, an indication perhaps that the pedagogical tradition most closely associated with BC has largely remained within the borders of North America. Until the September of 2011, the *BCQ* published a combination of research articles related to BC pedagogy and praxis, together with shorter commentaries often in the form of a column on topics such as Focus on Teaching, and Focus on Business Practices. Since September 2011, editorial policy has been to include fewer, longer, pieces as research articles, such that the June 2012 issue consists of seven research articles, four on general topics related to BC pedagogy, e.g. Kindles and e-books, Plain Language, instructor credibility and information literacy, and three additional articles all on the topic of communicating negative messages. Over the five and half year period from 2007 to 2012, 136 authors appeared in the journal as either authors or co-authors of the research articles, and of these 136, 111 were located in the United States, and only 25 in the rest of the world (Canada, Hong Kong, Australia, New Zealand, Finland, Mexico, Italy, Belgium, Singapore and the United Arab Emirates). Of these 25, with the exception of six authors located in Canada, and four in Australia, the rest were more or less equally distributed over the eight remaining locations. What this clearly indicates is that as far as scholarly contributions to the discipline are concerned related to pedagogy, the field is dominated by North America. The June 2009 issue provides a useful example of the topics that are covered in the journal. The research articles cover learning styles and technology mediated learning (Dufrene, Lehman, Kellermanns and Pearson 2009), an employer survey of resumes and cover letters (Schullery, Ickes and Schullery 2009), and curriculum design (Sharifi, McCombs, Fraser and McCabe 2009). These are followed by an Innovative Assignment Column that deals with writing for business (Seifert 2009), and four contributions to a Focus on Teaching Column, where the discussion is about how to manage student teams (Jameson 2009b; Wills and Clerkin 2009; Barker and Stowers 2009; Cox and Friedman 2009). In this issue, although unusual since most of the issues do have one or more non-US contributors, all the authors are located in the US. In other issues of the *BCQ*, the topics that are covered include literacy (Jameson 2007b), memos and critical thinking (Carrithers and Bean 2008), curriculum design for leadership and communication (Tuleja and Greenhalgh 2008), cross-disciplinary approaches to teaching BC (Laster and Russ 2010), improving student proofreading and editing skills (Enos 2010), accounting communication (Jones, 2011), ethics in financial reporting (Crawford Camiciottoli 2011), and the use of e-portfolios in business communication courses as tools for employment (Okoro, Washington and Cardon 2011). The research articles carried in the journal therefore provide BC practitioners with a range of different ideas on a variety of different topics of relevance to the day to day business of teaching and training. Outside of the research articles, in the issues of the journal up to September 2011, numerous other BC practitioners have also made lasting contributions to the development of the pedagogy associated with the discipline. In the March 2007 issue, for instance, the Focus on Teaching Column looks at BC and English as a second language, and in doing so, it brings together perspectives from researchers located in places such as the US (Jameson 2007c; Worley and Dyrud 2007; Penrose 2007), New Zealand (Campbell 2007; Zhu 2007), Spain (Ruiz-Garrido 2007) and Finland (Kankanranta and Louhiala-Salminen 2007). Similarly, in the same issue, the Focus on Business Practices Column, with an emphasis on Communicating Diversity at Work, brings together contributions from scholars in the US (Scott 2007), New Zealand (Cruickshank 2007), South Africa (Grant 2007) and Turkey (Usluata and Bal 2007). As is the case with *BCQ*'s research article contributions, the discussions in columns such as these, and the innovative assignments that are showcased in the journal, all provide BC practitioners with a useful resource of ideas related to teaching and to curriculum design. For the time being, it may be true to say that the *BCQ* maintains a largely US perspective, of particular relevance for practitioners working within the US system, often in a business school. However, as BC programs begin to be established in other parts of the world, and issues such as accreditation become of increasing relevance outside of North America, it seems plausible that the *BCQ* will follow the same path as the *JBC* and become more rather than less global in perspective in the future.

In addition to the ABC's own journals, BC scholars have also regularly published in journals such as the *English for Specific Purposes Journal* (e.g. Planken et al. 2010; Louhiala-Salminen 2002; Nickerson 2005; Planken 2005; Charles 1996), the *Journal of Business and Technical Communication* (e.g. Goby 1999; Tebeaux 1999; Rogers 2006), the *Management Communication Quarterly* (e.g. Livesey 2002; Rogers 2000) and the *IEEE Transactions on Communication* (e.g. de Groot et al. 2011; Louhiala-Salminen and Kankaanranta 2011). These publications have focused on a variety of different business genres, such as advertisements (Planken et al. 2010), CEO presentations (Rogers 2000), and annual general reports (de Groot et al. 2011), as well as discussing general trends in global business, such as the dominance of BELF (Nickerson 2005; Louhiala-Salminen and Kankaanranta 2011), the communication challenges posed by new technologies (Rogers 2006) and the impact of the discussion around sustainability on multinational corporations (Livesey 2002). The range of journals in which BC scholars have successfully published is also a reflection of the 'integrated umbrella' under which work in BC falls (Louhiala-Salminen 2009), together with the diversity of research approaches taken by those who are active in the discipline, from the work in language and applied linguistics that characterises the *English for Specific Purposes Journal*, through to the discourse and rhetoric influenced accounts that characterise the *Management Communication Quarterly* and the *Journal of Business and Technical Communication*. It's also interesting to note that several of these scholars have also appeared in journals that represent very different research traditions, the unifying factor in each case being the empirical investigation of the communication that takes place in business organisations. It is clear that there has been a considerable amount of overlap between the cognate disciplinary frameworks as discussed in the present volume, particularly between BC, technical communication, intercultural communication and management communication. St Clair Martin, Davis and Krapels (2012) provide a useful comparative report on the top six journals selected by the ABC's membership as significant for professional advancement. The six journals reviewed are as follows: *Academy of Management Journal*, *Academy of Management Review*, *Administrative Science Quarterly*, *Journal of Business and Technical Communication*, *Journal of Business Communication* and *Management Communication Quarterly*.

Evidence for this overlap can also be found in a number of the journal Special Issues and edited collections relevant for BC, that have proliferated since the 1990s. These collections have contributed to the development of the discipline, particularly in showcasing work by BC scholars from different parts of the world within one academic space. The UK-based Italian researcher Francesca Bargiela-Chiappini has been the driving force behind many of these publications, and although her own research interests as a sociolinguist fall closer to the business discourse end of the spectrum than to the BC end, her work as an editor has nonetheless had a lasting impact on the formation of the BC discipline. The earlier projects that she was associated with primarily included work by scholars located both in Europe and the Asia-Pacific region, and most recently, she has also showcased the work of scholars in North America. The 1997 edited collection on spoken communication, for instance, co-edited with Sandra Harris (Bargiela-Chiappini and Harris 1997), primarily focuses on the language and languages used in business meetings in business contexts such as Hong Kong (Bilbow 1997), the UK (Collins and Scott 1997) and the US and Japan (Yamada 1997). It provides an early account of how language works in business organisations, which has had a lasting influence on those BC researchers with a background in applied linguistics. Likewise the edited collection that appeared two years later, Bargiela-Chippini and Nickerson (1999), which provided a similar account of written business communication, as exemplified by the contributions made by Akar and Louhiala-Salminen (1999) for business faxes, Mulholland (1999) and Nickerson (1999) for email, Van Nus (1999) for sales letters, and Vandermeeren (1999) for an early discussion on the use of languages in the European business context, including English as a lingua franca. Following on from this, Bargiela-Chiappini went on to co-edit a Special Issue of the *International Review of Applied Linguistics in Language Teaching* on business discourse (Bargiela-Chiappini and Nickerson 2002), a Special Issue of the *Journal of Intercultural Studies* on intercultural business communication (Bargiela-Chiappini and Nickerson 2003), a co-edited volume on Asian business discourse (Bargiela-Chiappini and Gotti 2005), alongside a two-part Special Issue of the *Journal of Asian Pacific Communication* (2005; 2006), and most recently an edited *Handbook of Business Discourse* (Bargiela-Chiappini 2009a) with contributions from a broad range of BD and BC scholars from around the world. Publications such as these have run parallel to and been influential on the development of BC as a discipline, particularly in initially bringing the work of non-US scholars to a wider audience, and then in helping to identify the unifying characteristics of global BC research and praxis.

Finally in this section, two book length volumes have also been of influence on the discipline. The first of these is the 2007 volume on BD by Bargiela-Chiappini, Nickerson and Planken (2007), republished in 2013, and the second the 2010 volume by Koester (2010) on workplace discourse which builds on her earlier volumes (Koester, 2004; 2006). As in the case of the edited collections and Special Issues that I have profiled above, these volumes have both shaped and been shaped by developments in BC alongside several other disciplines. Bargiela-Chiappini *et al.* (2007; 2013) provide an overview of the development of BD, the application of BD research in teaching, consultancy and the development of teaching materials, and the different methods of analysis that can be used in researching BD. The work of numerous BC scholars and practitioners is included throughout and the volume reflects the sometimes overlapping and sometimes complementary nature of the two disciplines. Louhiala-Salminen (2009) includes an interesting discussion on the distinction between the two, and concludes that it is largely a question of degree rather than of actual difference, in that whereas BD may be more textual in approach, BC may be more con-textual. As a result, as Louhiala-Salminen observes, where a project falls on the BD/BC cline 'is often a matter for the researchers to decide' (2009: 305). In a similar way, Koester's 2010 volume also demonstrates the overlap between BC and workplace communication (as discussed elsewhere in the present volume). Koester takes an (ESP) genre approach in discussing her data, and many of the same concerns are dealt with in the volume that are also inherent in BC research and praxis, including the identification of the genres used in the workplace, the impact of English as a lingua franca on workplace communication, and the teaching of English for business purposes.

Geographical trends

As Louhiala-Salminen (2009) suggests, the BC research tradition in North America originally grew out of rhetoric. It has also been influenced by scholars with a background in speech communication. Notable BC scholars working within this tradition include Sharon Livesey, Mark Zachry and the late Margaret Baker Graham (e.g. Livesey 1999, 2001, 2002; Livesey, Hartman, Stafford and Shearer, 2009; Graham 2006; Graham and Thralls 1998; Zachry 2009). Livesey's work, in particular, provides a series of examples of BC in the North American rhetoric and discourse tradition. Over the past decade, she has completed a number of critical analyses, using a qualitative approach and rhetorical discourse analysis, to unpack the corporate discourse realised by corporations such as Shell, McDonald's and Exxon Mobil. Outside of this tradition, although not unrelated to it, scholars such as Janis Forman, Priscilla Rogers and Daphne Jameson have contributed greatly to the development of BC as a discipline since the nineties, working with collaborative writing processes, rhetorical genre analysis, and narrative theory respectively (e.g. Forman 2004; Rogers 2001; Rogers, Gunesekera and Ling Yang 2011; Jameson 2001). In addition to this empirical work, the North American BC community has also had a major influence on the teaching of BC, in that many active BC scholars have also written the best-selling BC textbooks in use around the globe (e.g. Andrews 2002; Beamer and Varner 2005; Guffey and Loewy, 2010; Locker and Kaczmarek 2010; Shwom and Gueldenzoph Snyder 2011). In many ways, the North American BC tradition has therefore determined the praxis of BC, at least in contexts where BC is taught as a skill set for people either working in business already or for those who aspire to do so in the future. Although several scholars have observed that there is a pressing need for BC textbooks originating in other parts of the world (e.g. Nair-Venugopal 2009), it seems likely that North American teaching materials will continue to dominate the market for the time being.

In Europe the development of the BC tradition has been somewhat different than that in North America. Many European BC scholars are also applied linguists, often with a background in English for Specific Business Purposes (ESBP), and many would also consider themselves primarily as business discourse (BD) analysts, while at the same time observing the shared BC research goal to contribute to the effectiveness and efficiency of business operations. There is an obvious overlap between BC and BD within the European tradition, and as a result, much of what Nickerson and Planken (2009) discuss in terms of business discourse research in Europe is also the case for much of the work that falls within European BC. They identify five characteristics that have influenced BD research in Europe as follows: the influence of applied linguistics and ESBP; the reference to authentic data, both spoken and written; the investigation of business English alongside other European languages; the contextualisation of the analysis through reference to the business context; and a neutral, i.e. non-critical, approach to the analysis (adapted from Nickerson and Planken 2009; 18). Many of the prominent BC scholars located in Europe have been influenced by these five characteristics, including Mirjaliisa Charles, Leena Louhiala-Salminen, Gina Poncini, Pamela Rogerson-Revell, Brigitte Planken and Julio Gimenez (e.g. Louhiala-Salminen, Charles and Kankaanranta 2005; Charles 2007; Poncini 2004; Planken 2005; Gimenez, 2006; Rogerson-Revell, 2010). Over the course of the past decade, they, and others, have looked at many of the different forms of communication that are used in business organisations, including fax (Louhiala-Salminen 1997), email (Louhiala-Salminen 1999; Gimenez 2006), meetings (Poncini 2004; Rogerson-Revell 2010), and negotiations (Charles 1996; Planken 2005). In addition, working with Anne Kankaanranta, Charles, Louhiala-Salminen and Planken, have also established Business English as a lingua franca (BELF) as being of major interest to European BC (e.g. Louhiala-Salminen, Charles and Kankaanranta 2005; Kankaanranta and Planken 2010; see also Bhatia and Bremner 2012 for further discussion on this point). As I will discuss below, this is likely to continue to be of interest to BC scholars in the future.

Outside of the ESBP-applied linguistics tradition, European BC research has also been influenced by the field of document design, particularly in Belgium and the Netherlands.

Bargiela-Chiappini, Nickerson and Planken (2007; 2013) provide the following definition of document design:

> Simply put, Document Design, as a field of research can be explained as the study of what makes a document work, whether it is a brochure circulated by a local council, a tax form, an instructional manual or a mission statement. Document design studies the instruments and tools that can be used to convey the correct and appropriate message to the readers that the message is aimed at.
>
> *(2007: 202; 2013: 236)*

It is not difficult to see how work aimed at improving the quality of documents used in business organisations would also contribute directly to an improvement in the efficiency and effectiveness of business operations. Notable studies using this approach include Gerritsen, Korzilius, Van Meurs and Gijsbers (2000) on TV commercials, Van Meurs, Korzilius and Hermans (2004) on job advertisements, and de Groot (2008) on annual general reports. Several of the most recent studies using the approach have also looked at the use of BELF in advertising alongside other European languages, e.g. Planken, Van Meurs and Radlinska (2010), Gerritsen, Nickerson, Van Hooft, Van Meurs and Korzilius (2010), as characteristic of the way in which business organisations communicate with consumers in the European market. BC studies such as these have therefore drawn on document design, alongside both BD approaches and a discussion on the impact of BELF.

In the Asia-Pacific and Middle East region, the development of BC research and praxis has been similar to that in Europe. As is the case in Europe, many scholars with an interest in BC who are located in the Asia-Pacific region are applied linguists, also often teaching and conducting research in the ESP tradition as ESBP. Because English has become increasingly prominent as the language of Asian business, including in the emerging economies in the Gulf Region, the teaching of Business English has also increased in relevance throughout the region and with it the importance of BC. As Nickerson (2012) observes,

> in Hong Kong, for instance, the emphasis has been on the attainment of professional competence through good communication skills. Business communication scholars located in Hong Kong have consequently focused their efforts not on linguistic competence (or language proficiency), but on understanding what it means to communicate effectively in order to achieve professional goals.

The large number of scholars located in Hong Kong who have published research that falls within the remit of BC, means that the discipline has been heavily influenced by work completed in business organisations where English is used in business alongside Cantonese, and increasingly, Mandarin Chinese (Putonghua). In addition, the region, both in Hong Kong and beyond, has been characterised by empirical research within business organisations, and the development of relationships with professional business people in order to understand more about what it means to achieve professional competence. Perhaps it is here, more than any other region in the world, that the overlap between professional communication and business communication is at its most obvious, since the work done on professional communication has also included the communication that takes place in business organisations. BC scholars located in the Asia-Pacific region and the Middle East have looked at a wide range of communication genres used in business organisations, including meetings (e.g. Chew 2005; Yeung 1998; 2000; 2003; Handford 2010; Yamada 2002; Briguglio 2005; Du-Babcock and Babcock 2007), sales information (e.g. Zhu 2000; 2005), electronic forms of communication (e.g. Akar and Louhiala-Salminen 1999; Habil and Rafik-Galea 2005), internal written documents (e.g. Li So-mui and Mead 2000; Baxter, Boswood and Peirson-Smith 2002), application letters (e.g. Bhatia 1993; Al-Ali 2004), and the conversations that take place in the call centre industry (e.g. Forey and Lockwood 2007). The 2009 edited collection, co-edited by Cheng and Kong (Cheng and Kong 2009) showcases the work of several researchers in the Asia-Pacific region, with an interest in the communication that takes place within business organisations (e.g. Bargiela-Chiappini 2009b; Jung 2009; Cheng 2009; Kong 2009). The individual contribution made by Cheng in particular, exemplifies the type of work carried out in Hong Kong, in identifying what constitutes communicative competence in four key industries in the Hong Kong economy: financial services, tourism, trade and logistics, and professional services. Her conclusions underline the importance of BC skills for the Hong Kong economy and the way in which empirical research of this nature can also be useful in identifying fruitful areas of enquiry for the future for BC scholars and practitioners. Cheng writes,

> The most popular language courses are English writing, business or industrial English, and Putonghua. Communications courses are also popular, and the content includes customer service skills, negotiation skills, social skills and presentation skills. These courses aim to enhance the spoken and written presentation and reporting skills of their members.
>
> *(2009: 46)*

Work such as this clearly shows the investigation of empirical data in order to contribute to the main goal associated with BC, increasing the efficiency and effectiveness of business operations.

One final project located in the Asia-Pacific region, also contributes empirical research to the overarching goal of BC in furthering our understanding of how communication works within business organisations. The Language in the Workplace Project (LWP) at the University of Wellington in New Zealand (www.victoria.ac.nz/lals/lwp/) is a major project that has looked at how people use language in different organisations, including business organisations. It has included topics such as women's language, humour and leadership (e.g. Holmes 2005; Holmes and Marra 2004; Holmes and Stubbe 2003). Although the scholars involved with the LWP would consider themselves as BD researchers rather than BC researchers, their work has nonetheless been influential on BC in the region, and the work that has been done on the communication that takes place in business organisations as part of the LWP would certainly contribute to an increase in the efficiency and effectiveness of business organisations. The LWP has also generated a set of resource materials based on the empirical data collected during the project, including the 2002 publication on successful communication in factory teams by two of the LWP scholars, Maria Stubbe and Pascal Brown (Stubbe and Brown 2002). It provides an invaluable set of resources both for research and praxis of relevance for BC.

The applied linguist Vijay Bhatia, working in the ESP tradition, has been a major influence on the work of BC researchers in both Europe and the Asia-Pacific region. Bhatia's approach (e.g. Bhatia 1993; 2004) has lent itself to the work of numerous BC researchers, particularly those interested in written genre, because of its focus on the description of empirical data, rather than on the application of any one theory. Bhatia's understanding of genre also facilitates a prescriptive approach on the basis of the data analysis. Both the description of empirical data, and the subsequent discussion on the implications of the analysis, can be seen as contributing to the overarching goal associated with both BC research and teaching. BC scholars who have used a genre approach include Leena Louhiala-Salminen in her analysis of fax communication (Louhiala-Salminen 1997), Catherine Nickerson in her discussion on corporate email (Nickerson 2000), Elizabeth de Groot in her exploration of annual general reports (de Groot 2008) and Michael Handford in his full-length re-application of Bhatia's work to business meetings (Handford 2010). Bhatia's influence has been extensive on the development of BC as a discipline over the past two decades. Handford's work in particular demonstrates its usefulness, not only in understanding written business genres, but also in unpacking what happens in the communication that takes place in spoken business events such as business meetings. Most recently, working with Stephen Bremner, Bhatia has turned his attention to the increasing overlap between English for Business Purposes and Business Communication, which the authors believe should be integrated in the design of English for Business Communication programmes (Bhatia and Bremner 2012; Bremner 2010). It seems likely that this approach, and Bhatia's approach in general, will continue to be of influence into the next decade.

The future of BC

In this overview of what constitutes business communication as a broad disciplinary framework, I have identified a number of areas that will continue to shape the future of the discipline. Firstly, BC research will become increasingly multinational in both the work that is published and in the topics discussed in the classroom. This will continue the trend that is apparent in the work that has appeared in the *JBC* and *BCQ*, and also in other journals, books and edited collections of relevance for the discipline. Although US-based textbooks will continue to dominate the teaching materials market for the time being, it is likely that BC scholars based in other parts of the world will also develop materials appropriate for their local student populations, and that these will eventually lead to the publication of local textbooks. Secondly, there will be continuing interest in research and teaching related to global business, including the use of BELF and the use of multimodality, together with the focus on the corporate discourse surrounding sustainability. It is possible that BC researchers and practitioners will therefore turn more attention to corporate communication than has already been the case, and as a result, that the integrated BC umbrella will broaden rather than narrow its frame of reference. Thirdly, BC scholars will continue to refer to the cognate disciplinary frameworks, both broad and narrow, and similarly, they will continue to select an appropriate method of analysis or approach depending on the data they are investigating. Despite this, however, it is likely that the BC community will become more rather than less cohesive as scholars become more familiar with each others' work in different parts of the world. The availability of journal publications and other publications online will facilitate this process, and it is likely that BC will be represented in further landmark publications that bring a number of scholars together in the formation and eventual maturation of the discipline. Finally, it seems likely that the pressures of globalisation will lead to a renewed interest in the teaching of BC, particularly the interaction between English BC and BC in other languages, and that this will in turn lead to more formal BC programmes in different parts of the world.

Related topics

discourse variation in professional contexts; communication in professional workplaces; management communication; corporate communication; business communication pedagogy

Key readings

Bargiela-Chiappini, F. (ed.) (2009a) *Handbook of Business Discourse*, Edinburgh: Edinburgh University Press. (A landmark publication that includes contributions from numerous BC scholars from around the world.)

Bargiela-Chiappini, F., Nickerson, C. and Planken, B. (2007; 2013). *Business Discourse*. Basingstoke: Palgrave Macmillan. (A detailed account of BD and BC research.)

Bhatia, V.K. and Bremer, S. (2012). 'English for business communication', *Language Teaching*, 45(4), 410–45. (A recent review of research and pedagogical scholarship on English for business.)

Fann Thomas, G. (2007). 'How can we make our research more relevant? Bridging the gap between workplace changes and business communication research', *Journal of Business Communication*, 44(3), 283–96. (A discussion on the relevance of research for the workplace exemplifying the North American BC approach.)

Lawrence, H. and Galle, W.P. (2011). 'Tenure, status and workload: Fundamental issues among business communication faculty', *Journal of Business Communication*, 48(3), 319–43.

Bibliography

Akar, D. and Louhiala-Salminen, L. (1999). 'Towards a new genre: A comparative study of business faxes', in F. Bargiela-Chiappini and C. Nickerson (eds), *Writing Business: Genres, Media and Discourses* (pp. 227–54), Harlow: Longman.

Al-Ali, M. N. (2004). 'How to get yourself on the door of a job: A cross-cultural contrastive study of Arabic and English job application letters', *Journal of Multilingual and Multicultural Development*, 25(1), 1–23.

Andrews, D. (2002). *Technical Communication in the Global Community*, Upper Saddle River, NJ: Prentice Hall.

Bargiela-Chiappini, F. (2005). 'Asian business discourse(s)', Special issue of the *Journal of Asian Pacific Communication*, Part 1, 15(2).

——(2006). 'Asian business discourse(s)', Special issue of the *Journal of Asian Pacific Communication*, Part 2, 16(1).

——(ed.) (2009a) *Handbook of Business Discourse*, Edinburgh: Edinburgh University Press.

——(2009b). 'Business communication across cultures: A theoretical perspective', in W. Cheng, and K. C. C. Kong (eds), *Professional Communication. Collaboration Between Academics and Practitioners* (pp. 19–30), Hong Kong: Hong Kong University Press.

Bargiela-Chiappini, F. and Gotti, M. (eds) (2005). *Asian Business Discourse(s)*, Bern: Peter Lang.

Bargiela-Chiappini, F. and Harris, S. (eds) (1997). *The Languages of Business: An International Perspective*, Edinburgh: Edinburgh University Press.

Bargiela-Chiappini, F. and Nickerson, C. (eds) (1999). *Writing Business: Genres, Media and Discourses*. Harlow: Longman.

——(2002). 'Business discourse: Old debates, new horizons', *International Review of Applied Linguistics in Language Teaching, (IRAL)*, 40(4), 273–381.

——(eds) (2003). 'Special issue on intercultural business communication', *Journal of Intercultural Studies*, 24(1), 1–79.

Bargiela-Chiappini, F., Nickerson, C. and Planken, B. (2007; 2013). *Business Discourse*, Basingstoke: Palgrave Macmillan.

Barker, R. T. and Stowers, R. H. (2009). 'Team virtual discussion board: Toward multipurpose written assignments', *Business Communication Quarterly*, 72(2), 227–30.

Baxter, R., Boswood, T. and Peirson-Smith, A. (2002). 'An ESP program for management in the horse-racing business', in T. Orr (ed.), *English for Specific Purposes* (pp. 117–46), Alexandria, VA: TESOL, Inc.

Beamer, L. and Varner, I. (1994; 2005). *Intercultural Communication in the Global Workplace*, Boston: Irwin.

Bhatia, V. K. (1993). *Analysing Genre: Language in Professional Settings*, London: Longman.

——(2004). *Worlds of Written Discourse: A Genre-based View*, London: Continuum.

Bhatia, V. K. and Bremner, S. (2012). 'English for business communication', *Language Teaching*, 45(4), 410–45.

Bilbow, G. (1997). 'Spoken discourse in the multicultural workplace in Hong Kong: Applying a model of discourse as "impression management"', in F. Bargiela-Chiappini and S. Harris (eds), *The Languages of Business: An International Perspective* (pp. 21–48), Edinburgh: Edinburgh University Press.

Bremner, S. (2010). 'Collaborative writing: Bridging the gap between the textbook and the workplace', *English for Specific Purposes*, 29, 121–32.

Briguglio, C. (2005). 'Developing an understanding of English as a global language for business settings', in F. Bargiela-Chiappini and M. Gotti (eds) *Asian Business Discourse* (pp. 313–44), Bern: Peter Lang.
Campbell, N. (2007). 'Bringing ESL students out of their shells: Enhancing participation through on-line discussion', *Business Communication Quarterly*, 70(1), 37–43.
Carrithers, D. and Bean, J.C. (2008). 'Using a client memo to assess critical thinking of science majors', *Business Communication Quarterly*, 71(1), 10–26.
Charles, M. (1996). 'Business negotiations: Interdependence between discourse and the business relationship', *English for Specific Purposes*, 15(1), 19–36.
——(1998). 'Europe: Oral business communication', *Business Communication Quarterly*, 61(3), 85–93.
——(2007). 'Language matters in global communication', *Journal of Business Communication*, 44(3), 260–82.
Cheng, W. (2009). 'Professional communicative competences; four key industries in Hong Kong', in W. Cheng and K. C. C. Kong (eds), *Professional Communication: Collaboration Between Academics and Practitioners* (pp. 31–50), Hong Kong: Hong Kong University Press.
Cheng, W. and Kong, K. C. C. (2009). *Professional Communication: Collaboration Between Academics and Practitioners*, Hong Kong: Hong Kong University Press.
Chew, S. K. (2005). 'An investigation of the English language skills used by new entrants in banks in Hong Kong', *English for Specific Purposes*, 24(4), 423–35.
Collins, H. and Scott, M. (1997). 'Lexical landscaping in business meetings', in F. Bargiela-Chiappini and S. Harris (eds), *The Languages of Business: An International Perspective* (pp. 183–210), Edinburgh: Edinburgh University Press.
Cox, P. L. and Friedman, B. A. (2009). 'The team boat exercise: Enhancing team communication midsemester', *Business Communication Quarterly*, 72(2), 230–36.
Crawford Camiciottoli, B. (2011). 'Ethics and ethos in financial reporting: Analysing persuasive language in earnings calls', *Business Communication Quarterly*, 74(3), 298–312.
Cruickshank, P. (2007). 'Immigrant diversity and communication practices in the New Zealand business sector', *Business Communication Quarterly*, 70(1), 87–92.
Cyphert, D. (2009). 'Who we are and what we do, 2008', *Journal of Business Communication*, 46(2), 262–74.
Daft, R. and Lengel, R. (1984). 'Information richness: A new approach to managerial information processing and organizational design', in B. M. Staw and L. L. Cummings (eds), *Research in Organizational Behavior* (pp. 191–233), Greenwich, CT: JAI.
Daniel, C. (1983). 'Remembering our charter: Business communication at the crossroads', *Journal of Business Communication*, 20, 3–11.
Du-Babcock, B. and Babcock, R. D. (2007). 'Genre patterns in language-based communication zones', *Journal of Business Communication*, 43(3), 253–64.
DuFrene, D., Lehman, C. M., Kellermanns, F. W. and Pearson, R.A. (2009). 'Do business communication technology tools meet learner needs?' *Business Communication Quarterly*, 72(2), 146–62.
Dulek, R. (2008). 'Academic research: two things that get my goat – and three that offer meaning', *Journal of Business Communication*, 45(3), 333–48.
Enos, M. F. (2010). 'Instructional interventions for improving proofreading and editing skills of college students', *Business Communication Quarterly*, 73(3), 265–81.
Fann Thomas, G. (2007). 'How can we make our research more relevant? Bridging the gap between workplace changes and business communication research', *Journal of Business Communication*, 44(3), 283–96.
Forey, G. and Lockwood, J. (2007). '"I'd love to put someone in jail for this": An initial investigation of English in the business processing outsourcing (BPO) industry', *English for Specific Purposes*, 26(3), 308–26.
Forman, J. (1993). 'Business communication and composition: The writing connection and beyond', *Journal of Business Communication*, 30, 333–52.
——(1998). 'More than survival: The discipline of business communication and the uses of translation', *Journal of Business Communication*, 35, 50–68.
——(2004). 'Opening the aperture: Research and theory and collaborative writing', *Journal of Business Communication*, 41(1), 27–36.
Gerritsen, M., Korzilius, H., van Meurs, F. and Gijsbers, I. (2000). 'English in Dutch commercials: Not understood and not appreciated', *Journal of Advertising Research*, 40(3), 17–31.
Gerritsen, M., Nickerson, C., van Hooft, A., van Meurs, F. and Korzilius, H. (2010). 'English in product advertisements in non-English-speaking countries in Western Europe: Product image and comprehension of the text', *Journal of Global Marketing*, 23(4), 349–65.
Gieselman, R. (1982). 'Reading, writing, and research: Pedagogical implications', *Journal of Business Communication*, 19(4), 23–38.

Gimenez, J. (2006). 'Embedded business emails: Meeting new demands in international business communication', *English for Specific Purposes*, 25, 154–72.
Goby, V. P. (1999). 'Teaching business communication in Singapore: An issue of language', *Journal of Business and Technical Communication*, 13, 449–456.
——(2009). 'Primacy of cultural over personal attributes demonstrating receptiveness as a key to effective cross-national interactions', *Canadian Social Science*, 5(3), 91–104.
Graham, M. B. (2006). 'Disciplinary practice(s) in business communication, 1985–2004', *Journal of Business Communication*, 43(3), 268–77.
Graham, M. and Thralls, C. (1998). 'Connections and fissures: Discipline formation in business communication', *Journal of Business Communication*, 35(1), 7–13.
Grant, T. (2007). 'Transformation challenges in the South African workplace: A conversation with Melissa Steyn of iNCUDISA', *Business Communication Quarterly*, 70(1), 93–98.
de Groot, E. B. (2008). *English Annual Reports in Europe: A Study on the Identification and Reception of Genre Characteristics in Multimodal Annual Reports Originating in the Netherlands and in the United Kingdom*, Published PhD thesis, Nijmegen/Utrecht: Radboud University Nijmegen/LOT.
de Groot, E., Gerritsen, M., Korzilius, H. and Nickerson, C. (2011). 'There's no place like home. UK-based financial analysts' response to Dutch-English and British-English annual report texts', *IEEE Transactions on Professional Communication, 54(1)*, 1–17.
Guffey, M. E. and Loewy, D. (2010). *Business Communication: Process and Product*, Nashville: South-Western College Publishing.
Habil, H. and Rafik-Galea, S. (2005). 'Communicating at the workplace: Insights into Malaysian electronic business discourse', in F. Bargiela-Chiappini and M. Gotti (eds), *Asian Business Discourse(s)* (pp. 121–43), Bern: Peter Lang.
Handford, M. (2010). *The Language of Business Meetings*, Cambridge: Cambridge University Press.
Holmes, J. (2005). 'Leadership talk: How do leaders "do mentoring", and is gender relevant?' *Journal of Pragmatics*, 37, 1779–1800.
Holmes, J. and Marra, M. (2004). 'Relational practice in the workplace: Women's talk or gendered discourse?' *Language in Society*, 33, 377–98.
Holmes, J. and Stubbe, M. (2003). *Power and Politeness in the Workplace*, Upper Saddle River, NJ: Pearson Education.
Jameson, D.A. (2001). 'Narrative discourse and management action', *Journal of Business Communication*, 38(4), 476–511.
——(2007a). 'Reconceptualizing cultural identity and its role in intercultural business communication', *Journal of Business Communication*, 44(3), 199–235.
——(2007b). 'Literacy in decline: Untangling the evidence', *Business Communication Quarterly*, 70(1), 16–33.
——(2007c). 'Self-directed teams as an enrichment strategy for non-native speakers', *Business Communication Quarterly*, 70(1), 51–55.
——(2009a). 'Economic crises and financial disasters: The role of business communication', *Journal of Business Communication*, 46(4), 499–509.
——(2009b). 'What's the right answer?: Team problem-solving in environments of uncertainty', *Business Communication Quarterly*, 72(2), 215–21.
Jones, C.G. (2011). 'Written and computer-mediated accounting communication skills: An employer perspective', *Business Communication Quarterly*, 74(3), 247–71.
Jung, Y. (2009). 'Indirect requests in Korean business correspondence', in W. Cheng and K.C.C. Kong (eds), *Professional Communication: Collaboration Between Academics and Practitioners* (pp. 93–112), Hong Kong: Hong Kong University Press.
Kankaanranta, A. and Louhiala-Salminen, L. (2007). 'Business communication in BELF', *Business Communication Quarterly*, 70(1), 55–59.
Kankaanranta, A. and Planken, B. (2010). 'BELF competence as business knowledge of internationally operating business professionals', *Journal of Business Communication*, 47(4), 380–407.
Koester, A. (2004). *The Language of Work*, London and New York: Routledge.
——(2006). *Investigating Workplace Discourse*, London: Routledge.
——(2010). *Workplace Discourse*, London: Continuum.
Kong, K. C. C. (2009). 'Interactions of professional, institutional and business discourses in academic settings', in W. Cheng and K. C. C. Kong (eds), *Professional Communication: Collaboration Between Academics and Practitioners* (pp. 113–30), Hong Kong: Hong Kong University Press.

Kostelnick, C. (1998). 'A research consortium that's all over the map – That's our strength, if we use translation to teach each other: A response to Janis Forman's outstanding researcher lecture', *Journal of Business Communication*, 35, 69–73.

Krapels, R. and Arnold, V. (1996). 'The legitimacy of business communication', *Journal of Business Communication*, 33, 331–52.

The Language in the Workplace Project (2012). Available at www.victoria.ac.nz/lals/lwp/ (accessed 27 September 2012).

Laster, N. M. and Russ, T. L. (2010). 'Looking across the divide: Analyzing cross-disciplinary approaches for teaching business communication', *Business Communication Quarterly*, 73(3), 248–64.

Lawrence, H. and Galle, W. P. (2011). 'Tenure, status and workload: Fundamental issues among business communication faculty', *Journal of Business Communication*, 48(3), 319–43.

Li So-mui, F. and Mead, K. (2000). 'An analysis of English in the workplace: The communication needs of textile and clothing merchandisers', *English for Specific Purposes*, 19, 351–68.

Livesey, S. (1999). 'McDonald's and the environmental defense fund: A case of a green alliance', *Journal of Business Communication*, 36, 5–39.

——(2001). 'Eco-identity as discursive struggle: Royal Dutch Shell, Brent Spar, and Nigeria', *Journal of Business Communication*, 38, 58–91.

——(2002). 'The discourse of the middle ground: Citizen Shell commits to sustainable development', *Management Communication Quarterly*, 15, 313–49.

Livesey, S. M., Hartman, C. L., Stafford, E. R. and Shearer, M. (2009). 'Performing sustainable development through eco-collaboration', *Journal of Business Communication*, 46, 4, 423–54.

Locker, K. and Kaczmarek, S. (2010). *Business Communication: Building Critical Skills*, Upper Saddle River, NJ: McGraw-Hill.

Loewy, D. (2010). *Business Communication: Process and Product*, Nashville: South-Western College Publishing.

Louhiala-Salminen, L. (1997). 'Investigating the genre of a business fax: A Finnish case study', *The Journal of Business Communication*, 34(3), 316–33.

——(1999). '"Was there life before them?" Fax and email in business communication', *The Journal of Language for International Business*, 10(1), 24–42.

——(2002). 'The fly's perspective: Discourse in the daily routine of a business manager', *English for Specific Purposes*, 21, 211–31.

——(2009). 'Business communication', in F. Bargiela-Chiappini (ed.), *The Handbook of Business Discourse* (pp. 305–16), Edinburgh: Edinburgh University Press.

Louhiala-Salminen, L., Charles, M. and Kankaanranta, A. (2005). 'English as a lingua franca in Nordic corporate mergers: Two case companies', *English for Specific Purposes*, 24(4), 401–21.

Louhiala-Salminen, L. and Kankaanranta, A. (2011). 'Professional communication in a global business context: The notion of global communicative competence', *IEEE Transactions on Professional Communication*, 54(3), 244–62.

Mulholland, J. (1999). 'E-mail: Uses, issues and problems in an institutional setting', in F. Bargiela-Chiappini and C. Nickerson (eds), *Writing Business: Genres, Media and Discourses* (pp. 57–84), Harlow: Longman.

Nair-Venugopal, S. (2009). 'Malaysia', in F. Bargiela-Chiappini (ed.), *The Handbook of Business Discourse* (pp. 387–99), Edinburgh: Edinburgh University Press.

Nickerson, C. (1999). 'The use of English in electronic mail in a multinational corporation', in F. Bargiela-Chiappini and C. Nickerson (eds), *Writing Business: Genres, Media and Discourses* (pp. 35–56), Harlow: Longman.

——(2000). *Playing the Corporate Language Game: An Investigation of the Genres and Discourse Strategies in English used by Dutch Writers Working in Multinational Corporations*, Amsterdam and Atlanta: Rodopi.

——(2005). 'English as a lingua franca in international business contexts', *English for Specific Purposes*, 24(4), 367–80.

——(2012). 'Unity in diversity: the view from the (UAE) classroom', *Language Teaching, Firstview Articles*, DOI: http://dx.doi.org/10.1017/S0261444812000237.

Nickerson, C. and Planken, B. (2009). 'Europe: The state of the field', in F. Bargiela-Chiappini (ed.), *The Handbook of Business Discourse* (pp. 18–29), Edinburgh: Edinburgh University Press.

Okoro, E. A., Washington, M. C. and Cardon, P. W. (2011). 'Eportfolios in business communication courses as tools for employment', *Business Communication Quarterly*, 74(3), 347–51.

Penrose, J. M. (2007). 'Responding to the unique expectations and needs of graduate students who are nonnative speakers of English', *Business Communication Quarterly*, 70(1), 47–50.

Planken, B. (2005). 'Managing rapport in lingua franca sales negotiations: A comparison of professional and aspiring negotiators', *English for Specific Purposes*, 24(4), 381–400.
Planken, B., van Meurs, F. and Radlinska, A. (2010). 'The effects of the use of English in Polish product advertisements: Implications for English for business purposes', *English for Specific Purposes*, 29, 225–42.
Poncini, G. (2004). *Discursive Strategies in Multicultural Business Meetings*, Bern: Peter Lang.
Reinsch, L. (1996). 'Business communication: Past, present and future', *Management Communication Quarterly*, 10(1), 27–49.
Rentz, K. (2009). 'The importance of "niche" journals to new business communication academics – and to all of us', *Journal of Business Communication*, 46(3), 404–11.
Rogers, P. (2000). 'CEO presentations in conjunction with earnings announcements. Extending the construct of organizational genre through competing values profiling and user-needs analysis', *Management Communication Quarterly*, 13(3), 426–85.
——(2001). 'Convergence and commonality challenge business communication research (Outstanding Researcher Lecture)', *Journal of Business Communication*, 38(1), 79–129.
——(ed.) (2006). 'Special issue on communication challenges from new technology', *Journal of Business and Technical Communication*, 20(3), 246–379.
Rogers, P., Campbell, N., Louhiala-Salminen, L., Rentz, K. and Suchan, J. (2007). 'The impact of perceptions of journal quality on business and management communication academics', *Journal of Business Communication*, 44, 403–26.
Rogers, P. S., Gunesekera, M. and Yang, M. L. (2011). 'Language options for managing: Dana Corporation's Philosophy and Policy Document', *Journal of Business Communication*, 48(3), 256–99.
Rogerson-Revell, P. (2010) 'Can you spell that for us non-native speakers? Accommodation strategies in international business meetings', *Journal of Business Communication*, 47(2), 432–54.
Ruiz-Garrido, M. F. (2007). 'Teaching and learning English for business communication: A case in Spain', *Business Communication Quarterly*, 70(1), 74–79.
Schullery, N. M., Ickes, L. and Schullery, S.E. (2009). 'Employer preferences for résumés and cover letters', *Business Communication Quarterly*, 72(2), 163–76.
Scott, O. L. (2007). 'Diversity issues and practices at work in San Antonio', *Business Communication Quarterly*, 70(1), 82–87.
Seifert, S. (2009). 'Writing for business: A graduate-level course in problem-solving', *Business Communication Quarterly*, 72(2), 200–213.
Sharifi, M., McCombs, G. B., Fraser, L. L. and McCabe, R. K. (2009). 'Structuring a competency-based accounting communication course at the graduate level', *Business Communication Quarterly*, 72(2), 177–99.
Shaw, G. (1998). 'The shape of our field: Business communication as a hybrid discipline', *Journal of Business Communication*, 30, 297–313.
Shwom, B. G. and Gueldenzoph Snyder, L. (2011). *Business Communication: Polishing your Professional Presence*, Upper Saddle River, NJ: Prentice Hall.
Special Issue: The business communication of corporate reporting (2008). *Journal of Business Communication*, 45(2).
Special Issue: The business communication of corporate reporting part 2 (2008). *Journal of Business Communication*, 45(3).
Special Issue: Discourse analysis (2009). *Journal of Business Communication*, 46(1).
Special Issue: Language matters (2010). *Journal of Business Communication*, 47(2).
Special Issue: Language matters part 2 (2010). *Journal of Business Communication*, 47(4).
Special Issue: Displaying competence (2011). *Journal of Business Communication*, 48(4).
Sproull, L. and Kiesler, S. (1991). *Connections: New Ways of Working in the Networked Organization*, Cambridge: MIT Press.
St Clair Martin, J., Davis, B. D. and Krapels, R. H. (2012). 'A comparison of the top six journals selected as top journals for publication by business communication educators', *Journal of Business Communication*, 49(1), 3–20.
Stubbe, M. and Brown, P. (2002). *Talk that Works: Communication in Successful Factory Teams: A Training Resource Kit*, Wellington: School of Linguistics and Applied Language Studies, Victoria University of Wellington.
Tebeaux, E. (1999). 'Designing written business communication along the shifting cultural continuum. The new face of Mexico', *Journal of Business and Technical Communication*, 13, 49–85.

Tuleja, E. A. and Greenhalgh, A. M. (2008). 'Communicating across the curriculum in an undergraduate business program: Management 100 – leadership and communication in groups', *Business Communication Quarterly*, 71(1), 27–43.
Usluata, A. and Bal, E. A. (2007). 'The meaning of diversity in a Turkish company: An interview with Mehmet Oner', *Business Communication Quarterly*, 70(1), 98–102.
Vandermeeren, S. (1999). 'English as a lingua franca in written corporate communication: Findings from a European survey', in F. Bargiela-Chiappini and C. Nickerson (eds), *Writing Business: Genres, Media and Discourses* (pp. 273–92), Harlow: Longman.
van Meurs, F., Korzilius, H. and Hermans, J. (2004). 'The influence of the use of English in Dutch job advertisements: An experimental study into the effects on text evaluation, on attitudes towards the organisation and the job, and on comprehension', *ESP Across Cultures*, 1, 93–110.
van Nus, M. (1999). '"Can we count on your bookings of potatoes to Madeira?" Corporate context and discourse practices in direct sales letters', in F. Bargiela-Chiappini and C. Nickerson (eds), *Writing Business: Genres, Media and Discourses* (pp. 181–206), Harlow: Longman.
Weick, K. E. (1995). *Sensemaking in Organizations*, Thousand Oaks, CA: Sage.
Wills, K. V. and Clerkin, T. A. (2009). 'Incorporating reflective practice in team simulation projects for improved learning outcomes', *Business Communication Quarterly*, 72(2), 221–27.
Worley, R. B. and Dyrud, M. (2007). 'Focus on teaching: Business communication and ESL', *Business Communication Quarterly*, 70(1), 34–36.
Yamada, H. (1997). 'Organisation in American and Japanese meetings: Task versus relationship', in F. Bargiela-Chiappini and S. Harris (eds), *The Languages of Business. An International Perspective* (pp. 117–35), Edinburgh: Edinburgh University Press.
——(2002). *Different Games, Different Rules: Why Americans and Japanese Misunderstand Each Other*, Oxford: OUP.
Yeung, L. (1998). 'Linguistic forms of consultative management discourse', *Discourse and Society*, 9(1), 81–101.
——(2000). 'The question of Chinese indirectness: A comparison of Chinese and English participative decision-making discourse', *Multilingua*, 19(3), 221–64.
——(2003). 'Management discourse in Australian banking contexts: In search of an Australian model of participation as compared with that of Hong Kong Chinese', *Journal of Intercultural Studies*, 24(1), 47–63.
Zachry, M. (2009). 'Rhetorical analysis', in F. Bargiela-Chiappini (ed.), *The Handbook of Business Discourse* (pp. 68–79), Edinburgh: Edinburgh University Press.
Zhu, Y. (2000). 'Rhetorical moves in Chinese sales genres, 1949 to the present', *Journal of Business Communication*, 37, 156–72.
——(2005). *Written Communication across Cultures: A Sociocognitive Perspective on Business Genres*, Amsterdam: John Benjamins.
——(2007). 'Using authentic cross-cultural dialogues to encourage international students' participation in tutorial activities', *Business Communication Quarterly*, 70(1), 43–47.

6
Business communication
A revisiting of theory, research and teaching

Bertha Du-Babcock

Business communication is a global phenomenon where business communicators from around the world are interacting in a diverse, differentiated and expanding global communication environment. Facilitated by the development of telecommunication technologies and due to the expanding volume of international trade as well as globalised business operations, changes in business communication patterns and practices have outpaced the development of an integrated theory to explain fully the evolving patterns of business communication. Differing communication networks have emerged where culture and language differences have impacted the communication among businesspeople from different world areas.

Business communication has grown into a global multi-language system where businesspeople with differing levels of communication competence interact in international and intercultural contexts. In so doing, English has notably become the preferred business language or lingua franca (referred to as Business English as Lingua Franca or BELF by Louhiala-Salminen, Charles and Kankaanranta (2005)) in international business contexts where no shared language is available among interlocutors. As such, English takes on differing roles in different industries and world areas. In today's global business environment interactants are likely to engage in any of three kinds of business communication situations: native speaker to native speaker (NS-NS) with variations, native speaker to nonnative speaker (NS-NNS), and nonnative speaker to nonnative speaker (NNS-NNS).

The study of business communication has gone from a communication environment in which businesspeople come from the same cultural background (most notably the United States) and speak the same language (English) to focus on the present complex, globalised communication environment where English is no longer solely spoken by native English speakers and where many different Englishes are used. To align with the evolution of the business communication environment, research in the field of business communication has also gradually shifted to examining the communication in global communication contexts.

The recognition of business communication as an area of practical application, and the teaching of it, originated in the United States almost a century ago. But a gap has opened between current business communication theorising and the early applied teaching of business communication. While the study of business communication has always been interdisciplinary, the result has been an eclectic but also a disconnected and sometimes contradictory body of research findings, models, and theories. Studies of business communication are based on disciplines such as rhetoric, management, psychology, sociology, anthropology, linguistics, language acquisition, intercultural and interpersonal communication, to name a few, that follow the terminology and conventions of those disciplines, and are not always understood by each other. As a result, the field of business communication is beginning to resemble a theory jungle (Du-Babcock 2009a, Outstanding Researcher Award Plenary Address at the 74th Annual Conference of the Association for Business Communication).

With regard to the teaching of business communication, integration of the expanding volume of theory into practical and operational teaching materials is needed. This need for the teaching of business communication to reflect current practice and theory is made more difficult by a resistance to change due to the effect of functional silos (cited in Suchan and Mirjaliisa 2006). This paper describes and analyses the state of affairs of a changing business communication discipline that is in the midst of a period of transition (see Du-Babcock 2006), and specifically the interrelationships among the practice, research, theory, and teaching of business communication. To analyse these questions and issues, I will first trace the historical development of the business communication discipline in order to present the current and projected states of affairs in perspective, and thereby set the stage for the analysis. Second, I will discuss the diversity of business communication practice in the differing patterns developed in various organisational structures. Third, I will outline the theory, research and teaching of business communication by delineating the different schools and the factors in disintegration (jungle) and integration (orchard). To conclude, I will present my recommendations for the possible movement toward integration and away from the theory jungle, and project future directions for the business communication discipline.

Historical development of business communication practice

The development of business communication in an international context has a long history, stemming from the time when traders from different parts of the world began exchanging their products and merchandise. In the early part of the pre-globalisation period (before 1945), international business communication comprised a very small, insignificant proportion of business communication as commerce largely took place within local regions and consisted of communication about the basic necessities of life. Indeed, throughout history, business communication has been largely local and regional in scope. People communicated in their native languages and with people from the same or similar cultural backgrounds.

International trade and global business entered the period of globalisation (from 1945 to approximately 1970) in the second half of the twentieth century. After the end of World War II, the United States emerged as the sole global economic power. Upon rebuilding, Europe and Japan joined the United States to form a tripartite economic structure that dominated international business. Multinational corporations headquartered in home countries first established sales branches in overseas markets and then moved manufacturing to overseas sites. The movement of manufacturing facilities was spurred by low labour costs in the developing countries (see Babcock and Du-Babcock 2009a) where plants were established. A prominent development, as evidenced in the clothing and shoe industries, was the use of contract manufacturers. The spread of globalisation has increased intercultural communication exchange such that businesspeople are increasingly engaged in global communication environments.

From 1970 to the present period is characterised as larger scale globalisation that has brought more world areas into global business. The concentration of economic activity that was centred around three economic regions (USA, Europe and Japan) throughout the second half of the twentieth century has been moving toward a more globalised system in the twenty-first century. China emerged as a contract manufacturing centre and is now developing its own brands and a large international market. Equal or even more drastic changes can be expected in the future. For example, India is currently entering world markets as China did previously. Africa with its vast natural resources to be developed as well as Central and South America (especially Brazil) can be projected to emerge as significant new areas of international business activity. The development of the world economy has created an international business communication environment characterised by increasing diversity and complexity. That is, a growing trend has resulted in which both native-to-nonnative and nonnative-to-nonnative English speakers interact in differing business communication networks.

Business communication practices also differ among corporations. Corporations (e.g. international, multi-domestic, global, and transnational companies) following different management and structural strategies take on different communication networks in communicating with employees around the world. For instance, the **international company** is based on core operations centred in the home country but with provision of some international operations too, such as marketing and manufacturing. Initially, an international manufacturing company makes and distributes the products mostly in the home market, but with some exports to foreign countries. With only a small volume of exports, an export specialist with language ability located in the marketing department handles sales to foreign customers. This specialist, as volume grows, may well work through sales representatives or agents who are located in the foreign countries. As foreign sales develop, companies may establish international divisions to carry out the marketing function for their foreign markets. In these manufacturing companies, only the employees responsible for exports take a direct role in international business communication.

Global and transnational companies serve as another example to illustrate how business communication operates, creating different global communication networks when compared to international companies. Companies following a global strategy attempt to develop an integrated communication network, and the personnel across organisational units and at all organisational levels are concerned with and communicate about external environmental conditions from all parts of the world. Likewise, companies following transnational strategies concurrently attempt to respond to the demands of globalisation (integration) and the need to develop products tailored to different markets (local responsiveness). In this connection, all personnel in a worldwide division of global and transnational firms are directly and indirectly engaged in the business communication network, thereby increasing the complexity of the global business communication environment.

In the global business communication environment, English plays a major and necessary role as either the major working or the linking language where the businesspeople do not speak each other's language. In these communication networks businesspeople use English to communicate about their work with each other directly (working language) or speak in their own languages and then exchange messages through though link-pin channels (linking language) if their competency levels do not allow them to communicate directly. Consequently, English takes on different roles in the different industry categories. In international organisations, native languages are used and English is the working language only in English-speaking countries. English only comes into play in exporting activities of international organisations. In global organisations, English is the working language regardless of the language spoken in given countries; whereas, in transnational companies English becomes the linking language between headquarters and divisions while local languages are used as the working languages in the various regional and country organisations.

The development of business communication research, theory, and teaching

The development of business communication research, theory, and teaching has followed the changes in business communication practice but has lagged behind these changes. Research, theory, and teaching originated and grew with the parameters of the discipline of business administration and the business school. Other disciplines and academic areas outside of the business school joined the study of business communication. Within the academic field of business administration, business communication has developed in separate streams that have focused on different aspects of the business communication process. In one stream, business communication fits into management and organisational behaviour in terms of research, theory and teaching practices.

The classical management, neoclassical management, and organisational behaviour theories established the foundation for the stream of business communication seen as a part of the management process. In classical management theory, communication was identified either by name or by description as a primary managerial function or as a component of a management function. Henri Fayol (1916; 1949 translated into English), who is seen as the father of the managerial process school of management, listed commanding (communication by superiors) as one of six managerial functions. He set forth [communication] principles to guide managerial practice that were based on his managerial experience. In neo-classical management theory, Chester Barnard (1938) identified the ability to communicate as one of the three necessary elements for creating a formal organisation. The Hawthorne studies (Roethlisberger and Dickson 1939) provided empirical evidence of human differences in the work force and how the first level supervisor stood as the person in the middle (the link-pin) who connected workers and management in the vertical communication process. The emphasis of business communication in classical management and the neo-classical period was on practice and practical application from the management and organisational perspective.

Business communication as a separate discipline originated in the United States about 80 years ago and moved to other parts of the world about two decades ago. The initiation of the discipline was a response to the need to teach managers and their secretaries the essentials of business correspondence. This stream of business communication evolved from the earlier field of business English (where rhetoric and form were emphasised) to a focus on effective and efficient communication (where communicative competence is the emphasis). The principle for this stream was initially based on the assumption that proper and correct English established the basis for effective and efficient communication. As noted by Hagge (1989), business communication in the early stages was rooted in the study of rhetoric as applied to the writing of letters and memos, with emphasis placed on the proper form and correct use of English. The overall pedagogical objective in the early years was to teach American students how to communicate effectively in American business environments. As such, in its early decades, business communication was taught as a practical skill set, and early textbooks outlined *how to* advice for correspondence, report-writing and oral communication. During those years, business communication teachers made little reference to theory, did data collection and called it research, and wrote publications that made almost no reference to any theory.

During the current period of large-scale globalisation, the teaching of practical application in business communication has extended to environments where English is used both as a second language (see Kachru's 1985 outer circle) and as a foreign language (see Kachru's 1985 expanding circle). This stream of business communication has established itself as a formal discipline (Krapels and Arnold 1998; Locker 1998; Rogers 1996) and has become an important subject area and an integral component of business school curricula. Business communication courses also have been developed in other university departments, usually being designated as English for Specific Purposes (ESP) or writing for the professions. The subject matter has expanded to include many genres (correspondence, report writing, oral reporting, oral presentations, stakeholder communication, direct mail, and marketing communication, to name a few) and to include many channels, such as email and video telecommunication. With the information technology revolution first in computerised messages and later in internet connectivity, business communication expanded. Social media such as Facebook and Twitter, and channels such as video telecommunication (Skype), and mobile phone connectivity further expanded the range and nature of business communication. Obviously, global communication means an increased emphasis on exchanges between people of different cultures.

Business communication theory and teaching: Jungle or orchard?

Since the development of communication theory, there have been some 50 theories represented by scholars from different fields of communication. Craig (1999) proposes a vision for communication theory to move towards a 'unifying' rather than a 'disparate' field. The unifying vision, according to Craig (1999: 120), shows how 'various traditions of communication theory' can be engaged in a dialogue on 'the practice of communication'.

Coinciding with Craig's aim of unifying the communication field and Koontz's (1980) views of a management theory jungle, I would argue that business communication as a part of communication theory is in transition (see Du-Babcock 2006), and has taken on the shape of what Koontz describes as a 'theory jungle'. To illustrate, I next discuss the present state of affairs in the theory and teaching of business communication. In doing so, I first provide a brief overview of the five identified approaches to the study and development of business communication theory (Du-Babcock 2009a, Kitty O. Locker Outstanding Researcher Award Plenary Address presented at the 74th Annual Convention of the Association for Business Communication). I then discuss the divergent factors and forces pushing toward the development of a business communication jungle and the convergent factors and forces pushing toward the development of a business communication orchard.

Approaches to the research and teaching of business communication

1 The language approach

The language approach focuses on the study of language and communication in business contexts. There are branches within the language approach: genre/discourse studies, conversational analysis (CA), business English as a lingua franca (BELF), and the plain English approach. With the exception of the plain English approach many of the scholars in this school have backgrounds in applied linguistics.

Genre studies describe and analyse the communication patterns and behaviour of particular groups of people (labelled as 'discourse communities' by Bhatia 2004). This approach has developed from three different traditions: rhetorical genre studies, systemic functional linguistics, and English for Specific Purposes (ESP). Berkenkotter and Huckin (1995) developed five principles that constitute a theoretical framework for genre study. Bhatia can be regarded as one of the major contributors of this approach in relation to business communication in that he directed attention to the study of patterns of business and professional communication, which he labelled professional genres (2004). He also broadened the scope of the approach when he considered genres in all their complexities: both vertically as super-genres with sub-genres within each super-genre and horizontally with interrelations and relatedness to external context and influence (see Bhatia 2004). Yates and Orlikowski (2002) captured the essence of the genre studies approach when they formulated the concept of genre systems, in that they described how genre communities develop distinctive communication patterns that can be organised into genre systems distinguished by their purpose, content, participants, form, time and place. These distinct and related characteristics interactively determine the patterns of communication that develop in different genre communities. Nickerson (2000) and Du-Babcock and Babcock (2007) developed categories for different genres relating to business communication and thereby facilitated the more systematic study and classification of business communication genre patterns.

Discourse analysis (DA) has been taken up in a variety of social sciences disciplines, including linguistics and communication studies in terms of coherent sequences of sentences, propositions, speech acts or turns-at-talk. Unlike traditional linguistics, discourse analysts not only study language use 'beyond the sentence boundary', but also prefer to analyse 'naturally occurring' language use (extracted from Wiki). Consequently, DA is similar to genre studies but more micro in nature. Scholars from language and applied linguistics fields have developed an extensive literature that analyses the textual patterns of different kinds of business communication. These studies are directed toward discovering and contrasting communication patterns by examining texts, including oral texts produced by speakers.

The discourse approach concerns the kinds of tools and strategies people use when engaged in communication. Some scholars have examined business texts (Charles 1996; Kennoy, Oswick and Grant 1997), while others have examined academic texts (Flowerdew 1999; Hyland 2000). For example, Jameson (2000) made an important contribution when she used narrative to analyse the discourse in corporate annual reports. Du-Babcock (1999, 2006), meanwhile, compared the turn-taking and topic management strategies of Hong Kong bilinguals in first- and second-language communication in making strategic management decisions. In her intercultural studies, Du-Babcock (2003, 2005) examined the similarities and differences of communication behaviours between individuals from individualist and collectivist countries when taking part in both intercultural and intra-cultural business meetings.

Other researchers from the European continent (e.g. Charles 1996; Louhiala-Salminen 1996; Louhiala-Salminen, Charles and Kankaanranta 2005; Poncini 2002, 2003) also have investigated language choice and communication in different European languages. Bargiela-Chiappini and Harris (1997), for example, examined the discourse in British and Italian business meetings. The study analysed both structural and pragmatic properties of intra-cultural business meetings (British and Italian) as well as the structural and pragmatic properties in intercultural business meetings that took place in an Anglo-Italian joint venture. Other studies by Poncini (2002, 2003, 2004) examined an Italian company's meetings with its international distributors. Poncini's study shows how the meeting participants constructed their business relationships through their choice of linguistic strategies.

Business English as a lingua franca (BELF) has become a major component of the language approach. Studies conducted from this perspective recognise that English has emerged as the world's largest and most dominant business language. Empirical in nature, and originating in Europe, this approach studies communication networks in and between organisations where interlocutors are non-native English speakers but choose English as shared language in their business interaction. Louhiala-Salminen, Charles and Kankaanranta (2005), Poncini (2004), and Nickerson (2000, 2005; Gerritsen et al. 2007) have studied English language communication among European speakers in various industries. Kameda (2005), concentrating firstly on Japan and also extending to other parts of Asia, has proposed the concept of regional BELFs where vocabularies are developed for specific industries (see also Kameda 2013).

The plain language approach has emerged as a reaction to the overcomplicated and bureaucratic writing that has become the norm in many areas, such as in business contracts and government documents and contracts (Dorney 1988; Center for Plain Language n.d.). Spearheaded by public service organisations such as the Center for Plain Language, documents are analysed and rewritten into more straightforward and understandable language. Working relationships are established with governmental agencies and business organisations whose documents are analysed.

2 The culture approach

The culture approach focuses on how culture affects the communication process. There are different streams that investigate the influence of national, organisational and professional cultures on communication behaviour.

The **National Culture** approach studies the effect of national culture on business communication. In this approach scholars and researchers take cultural theories and apply them to communication processes. One group of scholars draws on underlying disciplines such as psychology, sociology, and cultural anthropology scholars. For instance, scholars draw upon and apply large-scale empirical (e.g. House *et al.* 2012; Hall 1976; Hofstede 2002; Trompenaars 1993) or conceptual studies (Hall 1976) that identify and compare national cultural differences. Individualism-collectivism and high-low context have been the most researched cultural dimensions.

Another group (Cushner and Brislin 1996; Martin and Chaney 2012) searches out and identifies specific cultural habits and behaviours in national cultures that can lead to intercultural miscommunication. The focus is to enable individuals to better communicate with the identified cultures. Centred in the United States, the major thrust has been the interaction of Americans with other cultures. There is an implicit assumption that successful intercultural exchange is accomplished by accommodating the identified culture. This is achieved by following specific cultural practices that are deemed essential or important and avoiding specific practices that are alien or taboo. Lists of dos and don'ts are developed to guide communicators as they interact with new and different cultures.

The **Cultural Intelligence** (CQ) approach is a part of a larger effort to study and compare how people interact with new national cultures. Cultural Intelligence is seen as a construct that determines a person's ability to adjust to new cultural settings. Earley, Ang and Tan (2006) extended the study to business communication in the workplace by explaining to those living and working in another country how to identify and develop their Cultural Intelligence, or CQ.

The **organisational culture** approach, which is embedded in management and organisational behaviour literature, examines the influence of organisational culture on business communication. Influenced by the work of Schein (1992, 1999), this stream contrasts organisational cultures among different levels of organisations and at different states of growth. Scholars include the influence of organisational culture on communication in their theory building and research on leadership, organisational development, or other business related topics. Rather than constituting a distinct group of scholars and researchers, the scholars and researchers from this approach may be primarily associated with their respective academic disciplines. For example, Mintzberg (1980), writing in the business strategy field, differentiated between machine bureaucracy, professional bureaucracy, entrepreneurial organisations, innovative organisations, and multidivisional organisations in the business strategy literature. Although his primary focus was on strategy, he showed how distinctly different organisational cultures have associated communication patterns that develop in these organisational configurations.

Professional culture has not received the same amount of attention as national and organisational culture. Professional culture often appears under the heading of a 'subculture', not even recognised at the same level as national and organisational cultures (Scott *et al.* 2003; Hofstede 1980; Degeling *et al.* 1998). Pierre Bourdieu (2004 as cited in Herkenhoff and Heydenfeldt 2011: 61) points out that people are not born into professions but acquire the 'socially learned predispositions' of their professions. Professional culture can be defined as 'the behaviors that are appropriate and acceptable by each profession' (Boyatzis 1982: 20). The influence of professional culture on business communication has been usually indirectly addressed by the professional genre studies in the language approach. In all, although the literature in the area of professional genre is extensive, there is an absence of studies comparing and integrating the comparative effects and impacts of the differing cultures' influences.

3 The empirical approach

The empirical approach focuses on communication patterns that take place in identified areas or topics of business communication. Scholars in this approach conduct empirical research on identified areas or topics and may make generalisations or construct theories based on the empirical data in their studies. Concepts and models from other approaches are drawn on to guide data collection and to analyse the communication processes. The study of communication can focus on different industries (banking, advertising), contexts (research in negotiation, call centres), and professions (health care delivery), as well as broad conceptual and applied issues such as ethics, conflict management, and crisis management.

4 The interpretation of meaning in the organisations approach

This approach attempts to discover the underlying meaning of the language used in organisational communication. The basic premise of the interpretation of meaning approach is that language is not only content but also context and a way to recontextualise content. The environment in which communication takes place and the relationship of elements in terms of intertextuality are considered in the analysis. Bakhtin (1981) is the spiritual father figure of this stream. Boje, Oswick and Ford (2004) capture the essence of this approach:

> [we] believe the primary focus should be on developing insights into the nature and complexity of organizations (through language), rather than insights into language (through organizations). ... For this reason, we view discourse as the intermingled play of differences in meaning mediated through socially constructed language practices ... We also see this as encompassing the ways in which texts are inter-textual, collectively produced and re-produced, and distributed and re-distributed for consumption and re-consumption across discursive divides. Within this point of view, organizations are in heteroglossia (Bakhtin, 1981): diverse and constantly emerging and changing fragments of contending multi-voiced discourses and speech forms with local (as in micro) and more macro situated contexts.
>
> *(pp. 571–72)*

5 The process or operational approach

The process or operational approach has its roots in the two streams of business communication that focus either on the managerial process or interpersonal communication (individual communicator). This approach has established a framework of operational principles, concepts, and models to guide business communication practice.

The teaching component of this approach originally focused on communicating in an American native-English speaking communication environment, but has broadened its scope to recognise second- and foreign-language speakers of English. It has been exported to other countries as American English textbooks have developed international or foreign editions. In the past two to three decades, most of these foreign editions contain the same content as the US editions, and the only difference is that the foreign editions are put into paperback format to reduce cost. However, publishers are beginning to recognise the need for a less American-specific approach in other countries. For example, the textbooks written by Guffey and Du-Babcock (2010, 2008) have been adapted to better fit an Asian audience and the needs of second-language non-native English speakers.

State of affairs in research, theory, and teaching of business communication

Business communication is in a transitional stage where interacting forces (some divergent and some convergent) are contributing to the possible development of either a business communication theory jungle (leading to fragmentation and confusion) or an orchard (leading to integration and order).

Divergent force leading to a possible theory jungle. The first interacting force is divergent in that the theory relating to business communication has divided and is scattered in different schools or approaches. Craig (1999: 119) noted that 'while the study of communication and communication theory has become a 'rich' and 'flourishing' field, communication theory does not yet exist, and the field of communication has fragmented into 'separate domains' that simply ignore each other'. Researchers and scholars from the different schools are reflecting their different orientations and different academic backgrounds in researching and building models and theories from their differing perspectives. As such, a silo phenomenon (cited in Suchan and Mirjaliisa 2006) is created as these researchers and scholars draw upon differing bodies of literature and use differing concepts and terminologies to describe the business communication process. Each school has concentrated on different aspects of the communication process and has built its own independent body of theory. Specialised genres from each school facilitate communication within their respective disciplines but may not be understandable to scholars outside their own fields. There is little interchange among schools. New research findings and theoretical frameworks are scattered in the specialised literature of underlying disciplines. These new research findings and theories represent a growing but also a dispersed and non-integrated body of business communication theory.

Convergent force leading to possible theory integration. There are some hopeful signs that the research, theory, and teaching of business communication can move toward integration (orchard) and away from disintegration (jungle). These convergent forces have been spurred by changes in the communication environment and technology advancement. These hopeful signs are rooted in several developments. Although not widespread in scope, some scholars are breaking out of their silos and engaging in broader-based research and theory development and in developing frameworks identifying the background factors impacting business communication. Examples of theory integration will be discussed in the next section.

Suggestions for moving toward integration and bringing order to business communication theory

To prevent the communication theory jungle from continuing to grow uncontrollably, this chapter serves as an initial attempt to take on a similar approach to business communication to that suggested by Craig (1999), namely that when developing communication theories, researchers and theorists recognise the existence of similar theories from other fields or disciplines and seek to integrate them. Through the unifying of different approaches, the development of the field of communication can move towards integration into an orchard and away from disintegrating into a denser business communication theory jungle.

To parallel with Craig's proposal, as a general statement and guiding principle, integration should include a multiplicity of research and theoretical approaches, perhaps organising theories by clusters that have similar concerns, but not eliminating any theory or well-designed research approach in the process. In this way researchers from various schools of business communication theory could continue to focus on the particular areas of interest that reflect their academic backgrounds. Subsequently, findings and theories could then be integrated into the process or operational approach. This means that an approach directed toward developing an overall explanation of the business communication process (process or operational approach) becomes the organising framework. Consequently, theories from the language, cultural, interpretation of meaning and empirical approaches can be integrated into the operational approach.

To illustrate, I will use the development of the language-based communication Zones model as an example to elaborate how one theoretical framework has been expanded by integrating it with other established frameworks to attain a more complete international business communication model that includes the essence of language, culture, and knowledge systems. The initial experimental research design of the language-based communication Zones model (Du-Babcock and Babcock 1996) drew on the basic communication model as described in the process approach, which is still included in business communication textbooks. The essence of stage 1 of the Zones model focuses on the division of expatriate communication into direct and mediated link-pin communication. In doing this, Du-Babcock and Babcock (1996) adapted the term and concept of link-pin previously developed by Likert (1967) in his analysis relating to managing organisations with a humanistic orientation.

The 2001 Zones model specified the interactive nature of the communication process, and the model delineated the possible communication channels available to prospective interactants, given their level of language competence. This redefinition makes the model bi-directional and dynamic by explicitly acknowledging that all interactants in the communication transaction have the potential to send and receive messages in a continuing process (Sherblom 1998). In this redefinition the 2001 Zones model drew on theorists who had updated the basic communication model of the process approach. Beamer (1992: 285–86) explained the rationale for this update by stating, 'transmission by itself is not communication, but the conscious perception of signals at the receiver's end is essential for communication to have taken place'. So, when both sides of the dyad, in their roles as receivers, find a linking language where they can recognise the signals sent within their perceptual fields or schema (Widdowson 1983), the conditions for establishing communication zones are satisfied. In this way, the concept of a language competency match or fit was introduced into the theory of business communication.

The 2007 Zones model expanded the conceptual framework by drawing on genre theory and creating three genre categories to classify the patterns of direct communication found in organisations. Consequently, this reconfigured model categorises genre-specific language patterns in relation to professional tasks, commercial tasks, and relational tasks. The genre types include professional genres (specialised languages spoken by professionals within a discipline (see Bhatia 2004: 129)), commercial genres (organisational- and company-specific language used to describe information exchange and commercial transactions, etc.) and relational genres (verbal and nonverbal communications used to create the social fabric of a group by promoting relationships between and among group members/language communicators (Keyton 1999).

To recognise the effect of culture and to complete the initial thinking about the influence of culture on communication, an attempt was made to integrate Victor's (1992) LESCANT model with Du-Babcock and Babcock's link-pin and zones framework. Victor (1992) offered the LESCANT model as an organising framework specifying variables impacting the business communication process. The LESCANT framework identifies seven variables that business communicators can take into consideration as they interact in a global business communication environment. These seven variables consist of language, environment, social system, culture, authority, non-verbal communication, and time concept. Although his list is not exhaustive, it provides a starting point for the identification of factors that impact the global business communication process. The LES variables of Victor's model focus attention on the need to understand the language, environmental, and social systems in which people communicate, while the CANT variables draw attention to four socio-cultural characteristics of particular communicators. The Zones model already had a structure to show how people of varying cultural competencies and differing cultural characteristics could fit their messages into intercultural communication corridors. However, the model did not have a structure to show how individuals with differing knowledge of international systems could exchange messages. So, the integration of these two frameworks added the concept of knowledge corridors to show how people having differing knowledge competency matches communicate in different knowledge corridors.

An ongoing project is to explore the integration of the BELF model with the Zones model. The BELF research by Louhiala-Salminen, Charles and Kankaanranta (2005) demonstrates the effect of language choice on intercultural business communication, while the significance of theoretical advances in BELF is that they show how English as a lingua franca impacts the communication processes among nonnative speakers. The merger employees in their study were of two nationalities (Finns and Swedes); as a result of the merger, at the meetings, employees of the two merged companies who were formerly independent companies represented both cultures in the merged company, the new entity, and two different languages, 'one of which was a foreign language' (Nickerson 2005: 373). The choice of English put both the Finns and Swedes in neutral-language proficiency positions as the use of BELF is nobody's native or first language, and therefore, the 'language superiority' positions are greatly reduced (Du-Babcock and Babcock 2007: 363).

Future directions for research and practice

The framework described above for studying business communication in international business contexts has resulted from research studies by researchers and theorists from different schools, and it can be seen they have significantly contributed to the development of a framework for guiding future research in the field of business communication. Indeed, work of this integrative nature suggests three possible directions for the future development of research and practices in business communication: (1) the development of a shared framework for research that integrates and adapts existing approaches or frameworks; (2) the need for collaborations across the disciplines and across the globe; and (3) bridging the gap between workplace communication practice and business communication research.

Development of a shared framework. As the study of business communication involves many different approaches, it is important to determine whether scholars are looking at the same aspect of communication from different perspectives or examining different aspects of the communication process. As Craig (1999) noted, 'rather than attempting to promote theory construction based on an artificially limited field of communication, an effort should be made to unify the field by assimilating its diversity'. In developing a shared framework, the issue is how to integrate the findings into the growing body of business communication theory, and thus help create the basis for the development of a business communication theory orchard. Scholars would have to look at possible causal variables from other approaches as well as those from their own approaches. The result would be a convergent process of integration as factors from different approaches are brought together, and divergence as factors from different approaches are further investigated and refined. It would also result in movement toward clarity in recognising the multiple theoretical approaches that bring greater understanding of business communication (bringing order to the jungle) and encourage the further development of approaches explaining aspects of business communication (planting an orchard).

The two examples outlined above, which involve integrating the theoretical framework of the Zones model with the LESCANT and the BELF frameworks, provide a competency-based framework that recognises the need for linguistic and intercultural competence and that diagnoses the development of the requisite competence for communicating in different situations and tasks in international business communication. In addition, through the integration of the Zones model and the BELF framework, a mechanism can be introduced to identify communicators' competence match at the beginning of or throughout interactions among communicators, and to apply the framework to different languages that communicators may choose to use. This integrated approach allows a more systematic detection of whether intercultural miscommunication emanates from linguistic competence or deep meanings of exchanged messages in which there are cultural differences.

The example also illustrates that the theoretical framework or concepts from any one school may not be adequate to explain the communication process but rather inter-school models and frameworks are necessary to capture the complexity and diversity of present day and future business communication practice This could mean using a categorising approach where theories would be clustered together according to their research parameters. New findings would first be integrated into the body of theory and then into teaching and training. The gradual integration of models and theories from within and across different approaches would result in a progressively more unified theory. Prior models and frameworks can serve as the foundation for further development and refinement.

The need for collaborations across the disciplines and across the globe. In addition to the development of a shared framework, there is the need for collaborations across the disciplines and across the globe. Forman (2006) suggested that:

> the research issues we address are driven by our own curiosity, heightened by our gaps in knowledge. Those gaps are created to some extent by the functional silos (e.g., English, management, speech communication, information technology) in which we work. That combination of personal curiosity and gaps in knowledge created by our own particular educational backgrounds and the functional areas in which we work makes our research autobiographical: a narrative of what each of us believes we need to know.
>
> *(cited in Suchan and Charles 2006: 395)*

Forman's remarks imply that many researchers have only a partial picture of the larger field, and suggest a pressing need for greater collaboration. Due to advances in technology, there are increasing research efforts at collaboration between institutions and between disciplines. However, these research collaborations are still largely limited by region. Research by Louhiala-Salminen, Charles and Kankaanranta (2005) and Poncini (2002, 2003, 2004) in Europe, and the research by Du-Babcock and Varner (2008) in Hong Kong and the US have addressed some of the research issues within the boundaries of the geography they are investigating. While I agree with Poncini's (2004) call for the need for research in multicultural and multilingual settings, I propose that the future research agenda should involve a 'global focus' in that we cannot examine the research issues only from specific geographical regions, but we also need to compare the findings across the globe.

Let me provide an example to illustrate the possibility and opportunities of internationally collaborative research by describing a project led by Vijay Bhatia. In his research team, Professor Bhatia successfully involved scholars from 25 countries in working on the same research issues related to legal discourse. This research project drew on discourse-based data (e.g. narrative, documentary, and interactional) to examine the extent to which the 'integrity of arbitration principles is maintained in international commercial arbitration practice' (Bhatia 2009: 1). As stated by Bhatia,

> Building on the wide degree of interest created by the focus of the overall project theme, the international research collaboration it enabled, and the excellent research opportunities for interdisciplinary and international teamwork it provided, the research team has undertaken a further research project focusing on the actuality of arbitration practice across linguistic, socio-cultural, political, and legal boundaries.
>
> (cited in Du-Babcock 2009, www.english.cityu.edu.hk/arbitration/)

This longitudinal large-scale discourse analysis study is an example of research collaboration across disciplines and across the globe.

This example illustrates that international research collaborations can facilitate the development of the discipline and improve our effectiveness as researchers. Business communication researchers and theorists should work not only within our discipline with researchers from other cultures and countries (providing firsthand experience in intercultural and multidisciplinary communication) but also outside our discipline with scholars and business professionals (legal specialists in this case) in other disciplines and fields (providing exposure to the knowledge bases and professional genres in different professional fields). These collaborations will allow us to undertake research projects that we could not do individually but also place us in a collaborative and supportive environment to guide our development as researchers and teachers.

Conclusions

Business communicators need understandable frameworks, theories, and models that can help to communicate effectively and efficiently in the increasingly diverse and complex business communication environment. Multiple interacting factors are impacting the communication process. A proliferation of research and theory-building efforts from the different approaches/schools of business communication is trying to explain this complexity and diversity, while instruction and training efforts are moving from an emphasis on a one best way approach to an emphasis on communicative competence. However, the concepts from any one approach may not be adequate to explain the communication process. Instead, inter-school models and frameworks are necessary to capture the complexity and diversity of present day and future business communication practice.

The major challenge in the discipline of business communication is integration that takes on two dimensions. The first dimension is to develop closer connections between practice, theory, and teaching and to reduce the time gap or lag in making these connections. The second dimension is to organise theory drawn from the different approaches/schools to gradually move toward developing a more unified and comprehensive theory.

Research and theory are at a transitional stage with the possibility of moving either toward a business communication jungle with a proliferation of theories and research findings or toward an orchard with a movement toward integration and a more unified theory. Business communication has been an eclectic discipline that has drawn theories from underlying disciplines but is now starting to develop its own set of theories and models. Business communication teaching also faces the challenge of keeping its content relevant to current and future business practice and of integrating research findings and theories into the teaching. Overcoming resistance to change is a major part of the challenge facing teaching.

Related topics

discourse variation in professional contexts; business communication education in cross-cultural contexts; complexities of communication in professional workplaces; organisational communication

Key readings

Du-Babcock, B. and Tanaka, H. (2013). 'A comparison of the communication behaviors of Hong Kong Chinese and Japanese business professionals in intracultural and intercultural decision-making meetings', *Journal of Business and Technical Communication*, 27(3), DOI: 10.1177/1050651913479918. (The study compares the communication behaviours of business professionals from two prominent Asian cultures (Japanese and Hong Kong Chinese) in intercultural and intracultural decision-making meetings.)

Fujio, M. and Tanaka, H. (2010). '"Harmonious disagreement" in Japanese business discourse', in J. Aritz and R. Walker (eds), *Discourse Perspectives on Organizational Communication*, Madison, MI: Fairleigh Dickinson University. (This study presents a Japanese perspective on business discourse, and seeks to bridge the gap between business discourse analysis and the study of organisations in Japan.)

Kankaanranta, A. and Planken, B. (2010). 'Belf competence as business knowledge of internationally operating business professionals', *Journal of Business Communication*, 47, 380–405, DOI: 10.1177/0021943610377301. (The article explores internationally operating business professionals' perceptions of BELF communication and its 'success' at work.)

Sweeney, E. and Zhu, H. (2010). 'Accommodating toward your audience: Do native speakers of English know how to accommodate their communication strategies toward nonnative speakers of English?' *Journal of Business Communication*, 47, 477–504, DOI: 10.1177/0021943610377308. (The study seeks to add to the current debate on English as a lingua franca by analysing the role of native speakers of English in intercultural business negotiations and to what extent they effectively accommodate lingua franca speakers.)

Xu, X. and Du-Babcock, B. (2012). 'Impact of English-language proficiency on Chinese expatriates' adjustment to overseas assignments', *Global Advances in Business Communication*, 1(1), Article 4. Available at: http://commons.emich.edu/gabc/vol1/iss1/4. (The study examines the impact of English-language proficiency on Chinese expatriates' adjustment to overseas assignments.)

Bibliography

Babcock, R. and Du-Babcock, B. (2001). 'Language-based communication zones in international business communication', *Journal of Business Communication*, 38, 372–412.

Babcock, R. and Du-Babcock. (2009). 'Strategic versus non-strategic organization development in overseas Chinese family firms: A comparison of traditional and progressive firms', in Therese F. Yaeger and Peter F. Sorensen (eds), *Strategic Organization Development: Managing Change for Success* (pp. 279–304), Charlotte, NC: Information Age Publishing.

Bakhtin, M. M. (1981). *The Dialogical Imagination*, in M. Holquist (ed.), and C. Emerson and M. Holquist (Trans.), Austin, TX: University of Texas Press.

Bargiela-Chiappini, F. and Harris, S. (1997). *Managing Language: The Discourse of Corporate Meetings*, Amsterdam: Benjamins Publishing.
Barnard, C. I. (1938). *The Functions of the Executive*, Cambridge, MA: The Harvard University Press.
Beamer, L. (1992). 'Learning intercultural communication competence', *The Journal of Business Communication*, 27, 285–303.
Berkenkotter, C. and Huckin, T. (1995). *Genre Knowledge in Disciplinary Communication: Cognition/Culture/Power*, Hillsdale, NJ: Lawrence Erlbaum.
Bhatia, V. J. (2004) *Worlds of Written Discourse*, London: Continuum.
——(18 August 2009). *Exploring the Discourses and Practices of International Commercial Arbitration*, Colloquium presented at the XVII European Symposium on Languages for Specific Purposes, Aarhus School of Business, University of Aarhus, Denmark, 17–21 August 2009.
Boje, D. M., Oswick, C. and Ford, D. J. (2004). 'Language and organization: The doing of discourse', *Academy of Management Review*, 29(4), 571–77.
Bourdieu, P. (2004). *A Sociology of the Professions*, http://journalism.uts.edu.au (accessed 27 August 2013).
Boyatzis, R. (1982). *The Competent Manager: A Model for Effective Performance*, New York, NY: John Wiley & Sons.
Charles, M. (1996). 'Business negotiations: Interdependence between discourse and the business relationship', *English for Specific Purposes*, 15(1), 19–36.
Craig, R. T. (1999). 'Communication theory as a field', *Communication Theory*, 9(2), 119–161.
——(2009). *Reflection on 'Communication Theory as a Field'*, retrieved from www.revuecsp.uqam.ca/numero/n1/pdf/RICSP_Craig_2009.pdf (accessed 27 August 2013).
Cushner, K. and Brislin, R. (1996). *Intercultural Interactions: A Practical Guide* (2nd edn), Thousand Oaks, CA: Sage.
Degeling, P., Kennedy, J. and Hill, M. (2001). 'Mediating the cultural boundaries between medicine, nursing and management – the central challenge in hospital reform', *Health Services Management Research*, 14, 36–48.
Degeling, P., Kennedy, J., Hill, M., Carnegie, M. and Holt, J. (1998). *Professional Subcultures and Hospital Reform – A Study of the Attitudes and Beliefs of Staff of Australian and English Hospitals*, Sydney: The Centre for Hospital Management and Information Systems Research, University of New South Wales.
Dorney, J. M. (1988). 'The plain English movement', *English Journal*, 77(3), 49–51.
Du-Babcock, B. (1999). 'Topic management and turn taking in professional communication: First- versus second-language strategies', *Management Communication Quarterly*, 12(4), 544–74.
——(2003). 'A comparative analysis of individual communication processes in small group behavior between homogeneous and heterogeneous groups'. Proceedings of the 68th Association of Business Communication Convention, Albuquerque, New Mexico, USA, 1–16.
——(2005). 'An analysis of communication behaviors between intra- and inter-cultural decision-making meetings', in F. Bargiela-Chiappini and M. Gotti (eds), *Asian Business Discourse(s)* (pp. 147–168), Bern, Berlin: Peter Lang.
——(2006). 'Teaching business communication: Past, present, and future', *Journal of Business Communication*, 43, 253–64.
——(2009a). 'Is a business communication theory jungle emerging?: Analysis and recommendations' Kitty O. Locker Outstanding Researcher Award Plenary Address at the 74th Annual Convention of the Association for Business Communication. Available at: http://businesscommunication.org/wp-content/uploads/2011/11/2009ORAaddress.pdf (accessed 27 August 2013).
Du-Babcock, B. (2009b). 'English as a business lingua franca: A framework of integrative approach to future research in international business communication', in L. Louhiala-Salminen and A. Kankaanranta (eds), *The Ascent of International Business Communication* (pp. 45–66), Helsinki: Helsinki School of Economics.
Du-Babcock, B. and Babcock, R. (1996). 'Patterns of expatriate-local personnel communication in multinational corporations', *Journal of Business Communication*, 33(2), 141–64.
——(2006). 'Developing linguistic and cultural competency in international business communication', in Juan Carlos Palmer (ed.), *International/Intercultural Business Communication* (pp. 55–82), New York: Peter Lang.
——(2007). 'Genre patterns in language-based communication zones', *Journal of Business Communication*, 44, 340–73.
Du-Babcock, B., and Varner, I. (2008). 'Intercultural business communication in action: Analysis of an international videoconference', in D. Starke-Meyerring and Melanie Wilson (eds), *Designing Globally Networked Learning Environment* (pp. 156–69), AW Rotterdam, The Netherlands: Sense Publishers.

Earley, P. C., Ang, S. and Tan, J. S. (2006). *Developing Cultural Intelligence at Work*, Palo Alto, CA: Stanford University Press.

Fayol, H. (1916). *Administration industrielle et générale*, Paris: H. Dunod et E. Pinat.

——(1949). *General and Industrial Management*, London: Sir Isaac Pitman & Sons. (Translated by C. Storrs.)

Flowerdew, J. (1999). 'Writing for scholarly publication in English: The case of Hong Kong', *Journal of Second Language Writing*, 8(2), 123–145.

Gerritsen, M., Nickerson, C., Van Hooft, A., Van Meurs, F., Nederstigt, U., Starren, M. and Crijns, R. (2007). 'English in product advertisements in Belgium, France, Germany, the Netherlands and Spain', *World Englishes*, 26(3), 291–315.

Griffin, E. (2012). *A First Look at Communication Theory* (7th edition), Boston, MA: McGraw-Hill.

Gudykunst, W. B. (1985). 'The influence of cultural similarity, type of relationship, and self-monitoring on uncertainty reduction processes', *Communication Monographs*, 52, 203–17.

——(2005). *Theorizing About Intercultural Communication*, Los Angeles, CA: Sage.

Guffey, M. E. and Du-Babcock, B. (2008). *Essentials of Business Communication* (First Asian Edition), Singapore: Thomson.

——(2010). *Essentials of Business Communication* (Second Asian Edition), Singapore: Cengage Learning Asia Pte Ltd.

Hagge, J. (1989). 'The spurious paternity of business communication principles', *Journal of Business Communication*, 26, 33–55.

Hall, E. T. (1976). *Beyond Culture*, Garden City, NY: Anchor/Doubleday.

Herkenhoff, L. M. and Heydenfeldt, J. A. (2011). 'A correlational study of professional culture and intraorganizational conflict', *The International Journal of Management and Business*, 2(1), 61–76.

Hofstede, G. (1980). *Culture's Consequences: International Differences in Work-Related Values*, Beverly Hills, CA: Sage.

——(2002). 'The pitfalls of cross-national survey research: a reply to the article by Spector et al. on the psychometric properties of the Hofstede Values Survey Module 1994', *Applied Psychology: An International Review*, 51(1), 170–178.

House, R., Javidan, M., Hanges, P. and Dorfman, P. (2002). 'Understanding cultures and implicit leadership theories across the globe: An introduction to project GLOBE', *Journal of World Business*, 37(3), 3–10.

Hyland, K. (2000). *Disciplinary Discourses: Social Interactions in Academic Writing*, London: Longman.

Jameson, D. A. (2000). 'Telling the investment story: A narrative analysis of shareholder reports', *Journal of Business Communication January*, 37, 7–38,

Kachru, B. B. (1985). 'Standards, codification and sociolinguistic realism: The English language in the outer circle', in R. Quirk and H. Widdowson (eds), *English in the World: Teaching and Learning the Language and Literatures* (pp. 11–36), Cambridge: Cambridge University Press.

Kameda, N. (2005). 'A research paradigm for international business communication', *Corporate Communications: An International Journal*, 10(2), 168–82.

——(2013). 'Future prospects of BELF: Diversion or conversion', *The Doshisha Business Review*, 64(6), 343–57.

Kennoy, T., Oswick, C. and Grant, D. (1997). 'Organizational discourses: Text and context', *Organization*, 4, 147–57.

Keyton, J. (1999). 'Relational communication in groups', in L. R. Frey, D. S. Gouran, and M. S. Poole (eds), *The Handbook of Group Communication Theory and Research* (pp. 192–222), Thousand Oaks, CA: Sage.

Koontz, H. (1980, April). 'The management theory jungle revisited', *Academy of Management Review*, 5(2), 175–88. Retrieved 24 March 2009, from Business Source Premier database.

Krapels, R. H. and Arnold, V. D. (1998). 'Response to Murphy's "Re-viewing business communication"', *Journal of Business Communication*, 35, 149–53.

Likert, Rensis (1967). *The Human Organization: Its Management and Value*, New York: McGraw-Hill. Available from http://en.wikipedia.org/w/index.php?title=Linking_pin_model& oldid = 470875300 (accessed 27 August 2013).

Locker, K. O. (1998). 'The role of the Association for Business Communication in shaping business communication as an academic discipline', *Journal of Business Communication*, 35(1), 14–49.

Louhiala-Salminen, L. (1996). 'The business communication classroom vs reality: What should we teach today?' *Journal of English for Specific Purposes*, 15(1), 37–51.

Louhiala-Salminen, L., Charles, M. and Kankaanranta, A. (2005). 'English as a lingua franca in Nordic corporate mergers: Two case companies', *English for Specific Purposes*, 24, this issue DOI:10.1016/j.esp.2005.02.003.

Martin, J. S. and Chaney, L. H. (2012). *Global Business Etiquette: A Guide to International Communication and Customs* (2nd edn), Santa Barbara, CA: Praeger.

Mintzberg, H. (1980). *The Nature of Managerial Work*, Englewood Cliffs, NJ: Prentice-Hall.

Nickerson, C. (2000). *Playing the Corporate Language Game*, Amsterdam: Rodopi.

——(2002). 'Endnote: Business discourse and language teaching', *IRAL*, *40*(4), 375–81.

——(2005). 'English as a lingua franca in international business contexts', *Journal of English for Specific Purposes*, *24*(4), 367–80.

——(2009). 'The challenge of the multilingual workplace', in L. Louhiala-Salminen, and A. Kankaanranta (eds), *The Ascent of International Business Communication* (pp.193–204), Helsinki: Helsinki School of Economics.

Plain Language (n.d.). In *Center for Plain Language*, Available from http://centerforplainlanguage.org/.

Poncini, G. (2002). 'Investigating discourse at business meetings with multicultural participation', *International Review of Applied Linguistics in Language Teaching*, *40*(4), 345–73.

——(2003). 'Multicultural business meetings and the role of languages other than English', *Journal of Intercultural Studies*, *24*(1), 17–32.

——(2004). *Discursive Strategies in Multicultural Business Meetings*, Frankfurt: Peter Lang.

Roethlisberger, F. and Dickson, W. (1939). *Management and Worker: An Account of a Research Program Conducted by the Western Electric Company*, Hawthorne works. Cambridge, MA: Harvard University Press.

Rogers, P. S. (1996). 'Disciplinary distinction or responsibility', *Management Communication Quarterly*, *10*(1), 112–23.

Schein, E. H. (1992). *Organizational Culture and Leadership* (2nd edn), San Francisco: Jossey-Bass.

——(1996). 'Culture: The missing link in organization studies', *Administrative Science Quarterly*, 1996, *41*, 229–40.

——(1999). *The Corporate Culture Survival Guide: Sense and Nonsense about Culture Change*, San Francisco: Jossey-Bass.

——(2004). *Organizational Culture and Leadership*, San Francisco, CA: Jossey Bass.

Scott, T., Russell, M., Davies, H. and Marshall, M. (2003). 'The quantitative measurement of organizational culture in health care: A review of the available instruments', *Health Serv Res.* 2003 June; *38*(3): 923–45, DOI: 10.1111/1475–6773.00154.

Sherblom, J. (1998). 'Transforming business communication by building on Forman's translation metaphor', *The Journal of Business Communication*, *35*, 7486.

Suchan, J. and Charles, M. (2006). 'Business communication research: Past, present, and future', *Journal of Business Communication*, *43*, 389–97.

Suchan, J. and Mirjaliisa, C. (2006). *Journal of Business Communication*, *43*, 389–97.

Trompenaars, F. (1993). *Riding the Waves of Culture: Understanding Cultural Diversity in Business*, London: The Economist Books.

Victor, D. A. (1992). *International Business Communication*, New York: Harper Collins.

Widdowson, H. G. (1983). *Learning Purpose and Language Use*, Oxford: Oxford University Press.

Yates, J. and Orlikowski, W. J. (2002). 'Genre systems: Structuring interaction through communicative norms', *Journal of Business Communication*, *39*(1), 13–35.

7
Research on knowledge-making in professional discourses
The use of theoretical resources

Graham Smart, Stephani Currie and Matt Falconer

Drawing on a corpus of ten research studies investigating the discursive dimension of knowledge construction in professional discourses, with a focus on knowledge-making in the natural sciences as a test case, this chapter explores how theory is employed in qualitative empirical research for the purposes of framing, data analysis and further theory-building. The aim of the chapter is to look closely at the corpus of ten research studies in order to see how the authors employ theory for these three purposes. We hope that by casting light on how theory is used in such studies, we might help graduate students and early-career scholars in reading and producing qualitative empirical research on professional discourses more generally.

For over 35 years now researchers in a range of scholarly disciplines have been using qualitative empirical methods of inquiry to study the relationship between discourse and knowledge-making in the natural sciences, thereby contributing significantly to the literature of professional communication (e.g., Journet 2010; Latour 2008; Gross 2006; Harris 2005; Shapin 1984; Myers 1991; Bazerman 1988; Fahnestock 1986; Latour and Woolgar 1979; Gusfield 1976). This chapter presents a representative corpus of this work, examining a number of well-cited studies and their uses of theory. The chapter begins with some preliminary background remarks; next, we look briefly at a range of topics frequently addressed in research studies investigating the discursive dimension of knowledge-making in the natural sciences; and then we consider how the authors of the studies in the corpus have used theory for the productive purposes of framing, data analysis and further theory-building. This latter part of the chapter is organised into sections looking at text-based analyses, case studies and ethnographic research. The chapter concludes with a recap of the chapter, a brief discussion of the implications for pedagogy and suggestions for further research.

Some preliminaries

Before continuing with the main concerns of the chapter, we will discuss three issues relevant to what follows: first, the epistemology of the theories employed in and generated through scholarly research, i.e., the nature, genesis, and uses of these theories; second, a distinction between case-study research and ethnography; and third, the contemporary view of rhetoric that is implicit in the chapter.

To begin, then – what is a theory and how is it used in scholarly work? The nature and uses of theory in disciplinary contexts have recently been the subject of lively debate among scientists and philosophers of science (e.g., Gorelick 2011, 2012; Scheiner 2012; Colyvan 2011). The questions of what theories entail and what ends they serve have also been addressed in the fields of medicine and nursing (e.g., Rees and Monrouxe 2010; Reeves, Albert, Kuper and Hodges 2008). And as well, one can find methodologists reflecting on the meaning and functions of theory as it pertains to qualitative empirical research in the social sciences and humanities (e.g., Ely, Vinz, Downing and Anzul 1997; Flinders and Mills 1993; Eisner and Flinders 1994). However, none of these discussions is based on actual investigations of the nature and uses of theory as it figures within a sizeable corpus of published qualitative empirical studies. This chapter enters this under-explored research space by examining a corpus of ten studies that investigate the role of discourse and rhetoric in knowledge-making within the natural sciences, with a view to coming to a better understanding of how theory is applied for different productive ends in these studies (Bazerman 1988; Fahnestock 1986; Journet 2010, 2005; Knorr-Cetina 1981, 1999; Latour and Woolgar 1979; Myers 1985a, 1985b; Shapin 1984).

For our purposes in this chapter, we will define a theory as a generalising, evidence-supported assertion, or 'knowledge claim', regarding the nature of, and sometimes causalities within, a particular realm of material and/or social reality. Viewed this way, theories can be seen as tools for coming to understand and explain physical and/or social phenomena and for predicting probable outcomes or future events related to these phenomena. The next issue to consider is the question of where the theories used in qualitative research come from. A theory may originate as a knowledge claim produced through research within the author's own discipline or it may come from work outside their field; in both cases, the theory either stems from previous qualitative empirical inquiry or is derived from scholarly work of a more philosophical or conjectural nature. Whatever its origins, a knowledge claim's 'career progression' towards the status of an accepted theory depends on academic publication and the preceding gate-keeping activity of editors and peer-reviewers, with further validation of the knowledge claim, or new theory, occurring when other researchers take it up in their own work *as if* it were true.

Finally, a related concern: how might we distinguish between a theory and a concept? In the context of this chapter, we will define a concept as a particular facet of a larger theory. So for example, we might talk about Lev Vygotsky's (1962) theory of cognitive growth and language-learning as a social process involving problem-solving interactions between a child and an adult, while referring to the Zone of Proximal Development as a concept associated with this theory. Two other examples are the theory of genre-as-social-action (Miller 1984, 1994) and the concepts of 'genre system' (Bazerman and Prior 2004), 'addressivity' (Bakhtin 1986), and 'uptake' (Freadman 1994); and the social constructionist theory on the origins and status of scientific knowledge (Knorr-Cetina 1981) and the concept of 'literary transcription' (Latour and Woolgar 1979).

For our purposes here, we also want to make a distinction between case studies and ethnographies, as two distinctly different types of qualitative empirical research. A case study typically focuses on a situation involving one or several individuals, on a pattern of recurrent social interactions, or on a single event, with the researcher spending the time needed to collect data such as documents, interviews and observational field-notes. An ethnography, on the other hand, is a long-term study of a particular community in which the researcher, in the role of participant-observer, remains on-site permanently, or at least visits the site regularly, over an extended period of time. The ethnographer gathers and interprets data comprising documents and in some cases other artifacts; interviews with a representative range of individuals within the community, including outlying nonconformists if these are to be found; and field-notes recording ongoing observations – all with the aim of gradually building an account of the shared lived experience of the community, typically with a focus on some particular aspect of the community's day-to-day activities and shared social reality.

While researchers conducting case studies and ethnographies may use similar methods to gather comparable types of data, the aim of the inquiry is quite different: the goal of case-study research is to produce a description and/or explanation of a particular instance or type of human experience; while an ethnographer strives to produce an account of a community's culture, as expressed through its regular round of daily activities and social interactions, its repertoire of symbolic resources, and its web of shared meanings – all of which combine to constitute a distinctive collective world-view and a particular version of social reality.

The review of qualitative empirical studies of scientific knowledge-making presented in the chapter also assumes a broad view of 'rhetoric' derived from the work of contemporary theorists such as Deidre (formerly Donald) McCloskey (1998), Kenneth Burke (1966), Charles Bazerman (1988), and Chaïm Perelman and Lucie Olbrechts-Tyteca (1969), whose views of rhetoric extend beyond the Aristotelian definition of it as the 'art of discovering the best available means of persuasion' in any given communicative situation (Aristotle, trans. Cooper, 1960). McCloskey describes this theoretical expansion: '[In more recent times] the word [rhetoric] has also been used in a broader ... sense, to mean the study of all the ways of accomplishing things with language' (p. xix). Bazerman goes a step further, expanding the notion of rhetoric to include not only spoken and written language, but also any other semiotic elements used to 'realize human goals and carry out human activities' (p. 6).

This contemporary understanding of rhetoric also implies a broad view of the nature of rhetorical strategies, which goes beyond the Aristotelian notion of *topoi* and appeals of *logos*, *ethos*, and *pathos* and the traditional figures of speech, such as metaphor, analogy, metonymy and synecdoche, to include all instances of the purposeful use of alpha-numeric language, graphic representations, mathematical equations or other symbol-systems to communicate acceptance-seeking meanings to an audience. At the same time, every local sphere of human social activity is seen to have its own particular repertoire of rhetorical conventions for constructing and interpreting knowledge and engaging in argumentation (Barton 1993). As we will see, this view of rhetoric as a domain-specific discursive practice with effects achieved through a wide variety of symbol-based rhetorical strategies accords very well with our intention in this chapter.

Disciplines and frequent topics

Researchers in a number of academic disciplines have explored the role of discourse and rhetoric in the creation of scientific knowledge, including the fields of Writing Studies, Discourse Studies, Applied Linguistics and Science Studies – the latter a cross-disciplinary field of scholarship comprising work in the History of Science, Philosophy of Science, Rhetoric of Science, Sociology of Scientific Knowledge, Anthropology of Science, Science and Technology Studies, Scientific Communication, Medicine Studies, and Public Understanding of Science.

Researchers in these different fields have addressed a range of topics, with the following topics frequently appearing: (a) the collaborative production of scientific 'facts' and established knowledge (Knorr-Cetina 1999; Latour and Woolgar 1979); (b) scientists' reliance, within this epistemic activity, on rhetorical strategies such as Aristotle's appeals and *topoi* (Fahnestock 1999), narrative (Journet 2011), and metaphor (Keller 1995); (c) the re-contextualisation of scientific discourse for public and other audiences (Myers 2003; Paul 2004); (d) the diverse forms of representation found in scientific texts (Lynch and Woolgar 1990); (e) discourse-analytic investigations of argumentation in different sciences (Martin and Veel 1998; Smart 2011, 2012); (f) the discourse of interdisciplinary scientific work and the role of 'boundary rhetoric' (Schryer, Gladkova, Spafford and Lingard 2007; Wilson and Herndl 2007); (g) the rhetorical dynamics of scientific controversies (Thacker and Stratman 1995); (h) the technical and discursive apprenticeship of junior scientists and their concurrent formation of identity (Blakeslee 2001; Tardy 2003); (i) the role of scientific discourse and knowledge in maintaining and transforming social order (Jasanoff 2004); (j) the discursive interface of science and public policy (Graham and Lindeman 2005); and (k) the composing processes of scientists (Florence and Yore 2004; Rymer 1988).

Three methodological approaches and their uses of theory

Collectively, the ten studies of discourse and knowledge-making in the natural sciences that are discussed in this part of the chapter address the first three topics mentioned above: the collaborative production of scientific 'facts' and established knowledge; scientists' reliance, within this epistemic activity, on rhetorical strategies such as Aristotle's appeals and *topoi*, narrative and metaphor; and the re-contextualisation of specialised scientific discourse for lay audiences. These ten studies are divided into three methodological categories: text-based inquiry, case studies and ethnographies. In each case, the discussion of a study includes a description of the research, including the data collected; a discussion of the theoretical resources used by the researcher for purposes of framing, data analysis and/or further theory-building; and an overview of the findings of the study. We will see that the theoretical resources – i.e., theories and individual concepts – employed in the qualitative empirical research studies discussed here are used in three ways: (1) as a conceptual frame for the study as a whole; (2) as an analytical 'lens' for identifying themes, categories, or other patterns in one's data that speak to the research question(s) motivating the study; and (3) for further theory-building. The first use of theory, to serve as a conceptual frame for the study as a whole is somewhat analogous to, or at least perhaps a variation on, Kenneth Burke's (1966) notion of the 'terministic screen': a symbol-constituted interpretive filter that influences how we view the world, a filter that has the effect of directing us towards certain understandings of reality and away from others. An author's use of theory to establish a broad conceptual frame at the outset of a qualitative empirical research study is similar in a way, in that this rhetorical move provides the reader with an interpretive key for construing what follows.

Text-based analyses[1]

One strand of qualitative empirical research exploring the discursive dimension of knowledge-making in the natural sciences focuses entirely on the published texts produced by scientists, including research by Jeanne Fahnestock and Debra Journet in the discipline of Writing Studies and by Stephen Shapin in the Sociology of Scientific Knowledge. Looking at one study of Fahnestock's and two of Journet's, we will see theory being employed as an analytical 'lens' through which the researcher examines a body of data, looking for themes, categories, or other patterns that are meaningful vis-à-vis the research question(s) motivating the study (with these research question(s) stated explicitly or conveyed implicitly), and develops a set of findings that address the research question(s). Then turning to work by Shapin, we will see how he uses theory at the outset of a study to frame his research, signalling that his treatment of the topic will be informed by a particular conceptual perspective.

A recurrent theme in Fahnestock's work (1986, 1988 [co-authored with Mary Secor], 2004) is the shaping influence exerted by audience and other aspects of rhetorical context on scientific discourse and knowledge construction. In investigating this topic, Fahnestock frequently draws on concepts from classical rhetorical theory, such as Cicero's *stasis* – the *stasis* of an argument being its orientation towards one of five categories of subject matter: fact, definition, cause, value (rightness/wrongness), and action (Crowley and Hawhee 1999) – and Aristotle's classification of discourse into three types: 'forensic' (legal or otherwise argumentative), 'deliberative' (policy-related), and 'epideictic' (ceremonial). In some of her work, Fahnestock combines classical rhetoric with contemporary theory such as Bruno Latour and Steve Woolgar's (1979: 75–88) five-level scale of scientific certainty, developed in an ethnographic study discussed later in this chapter, in which the assertions contained in scientists' published work are seen to range from highly certain to openly speculative, depending on their degree of perceived 'facticity': (1) definitively certain statements, self-evident to insiders; (2) statements that are uncontroversial, although accompanied by explanation; (3) slightly qualified statements; (4) statements that are more heavily qualified and carefully hedged; and (5) openly speculative statements.

Fahnestock's (1998) study of the changes in information, language, and argumentative style that occur when scientific reports intended for a specialist audience are adapted for lay readers in popular science magazines offers an especially explicit instance of theory being used for analytical ends. In this study, Fahnestock combines all three theoretical ideas mentioned in the paragraph above in an analytic framework that she uses for interpreting her textual data – four articles from a professional scientific journal and four matching articles from a popular scientific magazine – and developing findings.

First, Fahnestock uses *stasis* theory to distinguish arguments advanced in specialised scientific reports from arguments contained in popular scientific magazines: she points to a shift in *stasis* from arguments of fact and cause in professional scientific reports to arguments of value (rightness/wrongness) and action in the matching articles intended for a lay audience. Second, Fahnestock employs Aristotle's classification scheme of 'forensic', 'deliberative' and 'epideictic' discourse in describing how scientific accounts begin in the scientific literature as forensic, or argumentative, but often become epideictic, or celebratory, when adapted for a lay audience. And finally, Fahnestock draws on Latour and Woolgar's five-level scale of scientific certainty to further distinguish popularised versions of scientific reports from the original professional scientific discourse, finding the former much more inclined towards certainty in its assertions than the latter, which typically contains numerous statements that are cautiously qualified or hedged.

Journet has researched knowledge-making in the field of Evolutionary Biology. In one study (2005), she presents a rhetorical analysis of two influential papers by W. D. Hamilton: 'The Genetical Evolution of Social Behaviour' (1964a) and 'The Genetical Evolution of Social Behaviour II' (1964b). In a second study (2010), Journet examines Richard Dawkins' (1976) use of rhetorical devices in his monograph, *The Selfish Gene*.

In both studies, Journet draws on Kenneth Burke's (1945/1969) theory of dramatism, with its concept of the 'dramatistic pentad', a five-part heuristic (act, scene, agent, agency and purpose) for identifying the motives of social actors in discursive situations, along with Burke's related concept of the ambiguity inherent in metaphors. As Journet herself puts it, she 'use[s] these theoretical frameworks to build a rhetorical reading of Hamilton's articles' (2005: 380) as well as, she might have added, a rhetorical reading of Dawkin's monograph. In the findings from her examination of Hamilton's papers, Journet points to the author's knowledge-building tactic of according agency to organisms and genes. Hamilton uses agent-agency metaphors to depict the evolution of social behaviours as consequent to the 'acts' of organisms and their genes. Here Journet views the ambiguity of metaphor as playing a significant role in Hamilton's work.

Similarly, a key finding from Journet's study of *The Selfish Gene* is that Dawkins also intentionally uses the ambiguity of metaphor as a knowledge-building resource in arguing his highly controversial claim that 'genes are the sole agents of evolution' (p. 31). Journet shows, for example, how the ambiguity associated with the metaphor of 'altruism' in nature enables Dawkins to create a narrative in which the gene appears to have a certain kind of agency.

Shapin's (1984) well-known study of the seventeenth-century English natural philosopher Robert Boyle's pioneering use of written accounts to communicate the results of his air-pump experiments and to achieve authentication of these results, provides an excellent example of theory being used in the early part of a qualitative empirical study to frame the research, indicating to readers that a certain conceptual viewpoint is in play. Indeed, we see this happening immediately, in the abstract of Shapin's journal article:

> Robert Boyle's experimental programme had as its end-product *the generation of indisputable matters of fact*. In this paper I analyze the *resources used to produce these matters of fact*, paying particular attention to linguistic practices. Experimental reports rich in circumstantial detail were designed to enable readers of the text to create a mental image of an experimental scene they did not directly witness. I call this 'virtual witnessing', and its importance was as a means of enlarging the witnessing public. The notion of a 'public' for experimental science is, I argue, essential to *our understanding of how facts are generated and validated*
>
> *(481, italics added)*

Here we see Shapin providing readers with an early unmistakable signal that the study to follow will be conceptually framed by the social constructionist theory of scientific knowledge (Knorr-Cetina 1981). In keeping with this theme of knowledge production in science, Shapin proceeds to construct his own conceptual schema – comprising three 'technologies': material, social, and literary – that informs and organises the discussion of Boyle's *New Experiments Physico-Mechanical* (1660) and other written accounts of his experiments. Focusing on Boyle's use of a 'literary technology', Shapin shows how Boyle's publications, containing both alpha-numerical and visual depictions of experiments, not only embodied new knowledge about the behaviour of air, but were also an implicit claim that while both an experiment *and* multiple trustworthy witnesses to it are necessary for achieving and legitimating new scientific knowledge, this could be accomplished through text-enabled 'virtual public witnessing' of the experiment.

Case studies

In this section, we discuss the research of two scholars who employ a case-study methodology in their work: Charles Bazerman and Greg Myers. Bazerman's research in the field of Writing Studies on the discursive construction of scientific knowledge (and there is a great deal of it!) is primarily historical and text-based (1988, 1991, 1994, 2002). However, his journal article, 'Physicists reading physics: Schema-laden purposes and purpose-laden schema' (1985), presents a case study of the specialised expert reading practices of seven physicists.

In his case study, Bazerman draws on theories from two fields: from Literary Studies he adopts a social constructionist view on reading to explain how readers may interpret texts and produce meanings that differ significantly from the authors' intended meanings (Eco 1979; Iser 1978); and from Cognitive Psychology he takes up the idea of the 'schema', or mental structure of background knowledge, which shapes an individual's perception and understanding of their experiences and, more specifically, also influences their interpretation of the texts they read (Rumelhart and Orotony 1977; Spiro, Bruce and Brewer 1980). Bazerman combines these concepts in an analytical framework that he employs for interpreting interviews, observational field-notes, and texts collected from the seven physicists.

In his findings, Bazerman demonstrates that reading is a constructive activity for the physicists, with their approach to reading in the professional literature of their fields shaped by the common need to locate, read and retain information specifically relevant to their own current research projects. While the physicists share this imperative of efficiently managing their engagement with the scientific literature, at the same time each individual physicist's reading practices are unique, infused with distinctive purposes and schema, or 'personal maps of the field' (1985: 3), that guide the reading.

Myers, publishing in the Sociology of Scientific Knowledge and in Writing Studies, investigates how scientific knowledge is socially constructed through discursive interactions between authors, their colleagues, and the gate-keeping peer-reviewers of scientific research. Two of his studies, published in the same year and best viewed as a complementary pair, are presented in journal articles that examine the writing activities of the same two biologists, with one study looking at the biologists' respective negotiations with journal editors and peer-reviewers (1985a) and the second study looking at the biologists' use of comments from fellow scientists during their production of grant proposals to fund their work (1985b). At the outset of both studies, Myers frames his research, indicating a particular conceptual approach to the topic, with a reference to the theory of the social construction of scientific knowledge (Knorr-Cetina 1981). To give our readers a sense of what this rhetorical move looks like, we will provide excerpts from the introductory paragraphs of Myers' two journal articles:

> Two anthropologists who studied the researchers at the Salk Institute describe the scientists and technicians there as 'a strange tribe who spend the greatest part of their day coding, marking, altering, correcting, reading, and writing' (Latour and Woolgar 1979). ... I would like to read two scientific [grant proposals] as products of a community of researchers, to see what they can tell us about composing as a process of social construction (Knorr-Cetina 1981; Gilbert and Mulkay, 1984).
>
> *(1985b: 219)*

> I would like to look at the processes of review and revision [of two scientific journal articles-in-progress] ... as part of the functioning of a scientific community. I will suggest that the procedures of review and revision of the text can be seen as the negotiation of the status that the scientific community will assign to the text's knowledge claim ... Thus, a close study of these texts may help us see one part of what Bruno Latour and Steve Woolgar call 'The Social Construction of a Scientific Fact'. I present two articles as cases of such negotiation, showing the range of possible claims, interpreting the formal changes in the manuscripts as they affect the status of the claim, and accounting for these changes in terms of the social context.
>
> *(1985a: 593)*

Both these excerpts show us Myers framing what is to follow in the study through an opening reference to Latour and Woolgar's (1979) anthropological research approach and to the social constructionist theory of the textually mediated production of scientific knowledge. In both studies, this social constructionist theory serves as a conceptual frame for the study as a whole, in much the same way that Burke's (1966) 'terministic screen' orients one's interpretation of experience.

Ethnographic research

This part of the chapter looks at three well-cited ethnographies. In our discussion of this work, we will see two rhetorical strategies employed for further theory-building: in the first case, the researchers introduce concepts from the literature approvingly and then use them as a platform for the researchers' own further theory-building; and in the second case, two theories taken from the published literature are used as foils for the researcher's own theory construction, with the researcher challenging the theories, pointing to their deficiencies, and thereby clearing the way for alternative theorising.

In their widely cited volume, *Laboratory Life: The Construction of Scientific Facts* (1979), the sociologists of science Bruno Latour and Steve Woolgar present an extended ethnographic account derived from Latour's field-work in the laboratory of the Salk Institute for Biological Studies in La Jolla, California. During his 21 months of active participant-observation (Adler and Adler, 1987) – in addition to working as a researcher, Latour was also employed part-time as a laboratory technician in the Institute – he had the opportunity to study, closely and over a sustained period of time, the culture and daily round of activities that constitute the work-world of the Institute's scientists.

With the duration of his time in the field, Latour was able to collect for analysis a very large body of data, including the following: a voluminous set of field-notes recording his observations in the laboratory; all the papers published by the Institute's scientists during his stay there; drafts of the scientists' papers-in-progress; various textual and visual representations of data; memoranda and letters exchanged among collaborating colleagues; interviews with each of the scientists working in the Institute as well as interviews with a number of scientists at other professional sites working in the same field; copious notes on discussions in group meetings and in numerous informal conversations with the members of the Institute; and Latour's recorded day-to-day journal reflections arising from his experience as an observer in the laboratory and as a part-time technician. The project's data analysis and write-up began very soon after Latour arrived in the Institute and continued throughout and beyond his time there. Latour regularly shared drafts of his ethnography-in-progress with the participants in the study, factoring in their perspectives, and he also organised several seminars in which the laboratory's scientists discussed their own work as well as Latour's emerging ethnographic account with visiting sociologists and philosophers of science.

Latour and Woolgar state that the primary concern of their research was to address the question, 'how [are] facts constructed in a laboratory?' and that, accordingly, the primary outcome of their ethnography is its detailed description of 'the way in which the daily activities of working scientists lead to the construction of scientific facts' (p. 40). According to Latour and Woolgar's study of the day-to-day routines of the scientists working in the Institute's laboratory, socially constructed 'facts' – assertions about the material world professed to be accurate – and the published papers that argue for the validity of these facts emerge from ongoing micro-processes of negotiations of both technical and political matters among collaborating scientists. Latour and Woolgar describe a scene featuring chains of material substances; various types of 'inscription devices', i.e., equipment able to translate material substances into numbers, graphs, diagrams or similar signs; constant spoken interaction among collaborating scientists, particularly arguments and acts of rhetorical persuasion; and a profusion of texts of diverse kinds.

In the final chapter of their book, Latour and Woolgar – in a rhetorical move found nowhere else in our corpus of ten qualitative empirical studies – explicitly discuss how, in constructing from their data an ethnographic account of 'laboratory life' in the Institute, they have used six concepts drawn from the theoretical work of other scholars for their usefulness as a platform for further theory-building (p. 236). These concepts include the following: 'construction', Karin Knorr-Cetina and Dietrich Knorr's (1978) term for what Latour and Woolgar call the 'slow, practical craftwork' through which scientific knowledge claims are produced; Jean-François Lyotard's (1975) notion of the 'agonistic' or disputatious language and social interaction that characterise political discourse, taken up by Latour and Woolgar in their depiction of the Institute's laboratory as an agonistic field of contending claims and arguments; Gaston Bachelard's (1953) 'materialization', a process through which knowledge resulting from prior intellectual work is built into pieces of new scientific apparatus; the concept of 'credibility', taken from Pierre Bourdieu and Luc Boltanski's (1976) theory of a societal political economy comprising symbolic, cultural, social and economic capital and seen in *Laboratory Life*'s description of the different types of capital – economic, epistemological and psychological – that scientists invest in their daily laboratory work and in their careers more generally; Michel Serres (1977) 'circumstances', a concept that Latour and Woolgar adopt in representing scientific knowledge as the product of 'specific localized practices' and 'idiosyncratic circumstances', rather than the product of some abstract universal circumstance-free realm strictly ruled by the scientific method; and finally, 'noise', a concept taken from Léon Brillouin's (1962) information theory, which is used metaphorically in *Laboratory Life* to refer to the relationship, within the scientific activity of the laboratory, between a given observation or claim and the 'noise' of other equally probable alternatives.

In the excerpt below, Latour and Woolgar illustrate how they have drawn on the first five of these six concepts in building their ethnographic account of the construction of scientific facts in the Institute's laboratory:

> The result of the *construction* of a fact is that it appears unconstructed by anyone; the result of rhetorical persuasion in the *agonistic* field is that the participants are convinced that they have not been convinced; the result of *materialization* is that people can swear that material considerations are only minor components of the 'thought process'; the result of investments in *credibility* is that the participants can claim that economics or beliefs are in no way related to the solidity of science; as to the *circumstances*, they simply disappear from accounts, being better left to political analysis than to an appreciation of the hard and solid world of facts!
>
> (p. 240)

Karin Knorr-Cetina, working in the field of the Sociology of Scientific Knowledge, offers another example of a researcher using theory for different productive purposes in a qualitative empirical study. In her two book-length ethnographies, *The Manufacture of Knowledge: An Essay on the Constructivist and Contextual Nature of Science* (1981) and *Epistemic Cultures: How the Sciences Make Knowledge* (1999), also frequently cited, Knorr-Cetina reports on the physical surrounds, social relations, technical procedures, and discursive practices of 'tribes' of collaborating scientists as observed in their laboratory habitats – spheres of knowledge-making activity that Knorr-Cetina calls 'epistemic cultures' (1999). In order to produce the two ethnographies, she spent extended periods of time watching scientists at work in a range of different laboratories – first, thirteen months in a large multiple-disciplinary scientific research centre in Berkeley, California; and then the better part of a decade in a comparative study of scientists in High-Energy Physics and Molecular Biology laboratories in Germany and Switzerland. The data she collected in these sites included documents of many different types and at various stages of production; a profuse set of field-notes from ongoing observations; interviews with key informants and with scientists in other locations; discussions in team meetings; and conversations involving collaborating scientists in the laboratory.

A key finding from Knorr-Cetina's ethnographic work concerns the relationship between the activity of constructing knowledge through the laboratory's localised and contingent cognition and decision-making, technical procedures, and social interactions, on the one hand, and the scientific paper that subsequently results from this work on the other. Knorr-Cetina shows us that the intended-for-publication scientific paper, with its stylised depiction of laboratory activity and a sustained cogent argument, is very different in nature from the circumstances of its production and is designed not as a faithful account of events in the laboratory, but rather as a rhetorical artifact aimed at a niche in the scientific literature perceived to be available for researchers.

Of particular interest for us here are the different ways in which Knorr-Cetina employs theories and concepts in her published ethnographies; indeed, she uses them for the full range of productive purposes mentioned earlier in the chapter: framing, data analysis and further theory-building. We will describe an example to illustrate the third of these purposes: in constructing a knowledge claim to account for the way that science – with its experimental methods, instruments, and resulting knowledge – evolves over time, Knorr-Cetina (1981: 9–16) employs both Stephen Toulmin and Niklas Luhmann as foils. She first considers the merits of Toulmin's (1972) model of scientific evolution – a model based on the Darwinian theory of biological evolution through innovation, competition, and natural selection – as a plausible explanation for the historical development of science. She also reflects on what Luhmann's (1981) theory of social systems might look like if applied to the development of scientific practice and knowledge. In each case, Knorr-Cetina finds the theory usefully suggestive, but at the same time deficient in significant ways. Her discussion and critique of Toulmin and Luhmann sets the stage for her own alternative theory-building. Knorr-Cetina proposes that scientific development is an historical process characterised by indeterminacy and contingency, a process that occurs through continuously reconstructed practices and knowledge based on the selective 'integration and elimination' of earlier experiences and outcomes, with a consistent move over time towards greater complexity.

Conclusion

In this chapter we have looked at a corpus of ten studies, each of which investigates the discursive dimension of knowledge-making in the realm of the natural sciences, with a view to illustrating three different productive uses of theory in qualitative empirical research investigating professional communication: theory employed for purposes of framing, data analysis, and further theory-building. The impetus for the chapter was our observation that graduate students, as readers and authors of qualitative empirical studies, typically have difficulty recognising the different purposes that theory serves in qualitative empirical research. An additional concern was for early-career professional scholars facing a similar challenge when submitting manuscripts to journals.

Accordingly, our aim in this chapter has been to cast light on the different ways in which theory is used in qualitative empirical research on professional discourses, employing studies of knowledge-making in the natural sciences as a test case, with the hope that this will be of value for graduate students as well as for early-career scholars. And we are reasonably confident in the assertion that developing a greater awareness of the uses of theory, in combination with practice in applied genre analysis focusing on rhetorical moves (Swales 1990, 2004; Bhatia 1993, 2004, and this volume) and discourse structure (Paltridge 1994), will help individuals perform more effectively as readers of qualitative empirical research studies. However, to go further in this direction and suggest with any degree of certainty that this approach will also help individuals as *writers* of such studies, would be a step too far, if we are to conclude this chapter with some confidence in its pedagogical efficacy. Instead, in this regard we will turn to the wisdom of applied linguist John Swales, who has been known to say, when feeling that a discussion is straying too far from research-based claims, 'I think it's time to stop on this topic now, because, after all, that's an empirical question needing further research, isn't it.'

We will end the chapter by considering the question of whether our findings on the uses of theory in qualitative empirical studies of discourse and knowledge-making in the natural sciences can be applied to research on professional communication more broadly. Our experience as readers in the social sciences and humanities would lead us to affirm, anecdotally, that these findings on the uses of theory can indeed be extended to research on other professional discourses; however, again deferring to John Swales' point above, we recognise that any such claim would require examination of research studies investigating different areas of professional communication.

Related topics

English for science and technology; communication in professional workplaces; corpus analyses of professional discourse

Key readings

Bargiela-Chiappini, F. and Nickerson, C. (eds) (1999). *Writing Business: Genres, Media and Discourses*, Harlow, UK and New York: Longman. (A collection of papers using different methodological approaches to examine the functions of a range of written genres in various business contexts.)

Bazerman, C. and Paradis, J. (eds) (1991). *Textual Dynamics: Historical and Contemporary Studies of Writing in Professional Communities*, Madison: University of Wisconsin Press. (A collection of papers investigating the interaction between texts and professional practices in a variety of academic, scientific and business settings.)

Gunnarsson, B.-L. (2009). *Professional Discourse,* London and New York: Continuum. (An extended study of the role of discourse in the business activities of a variety of European professional organisations.)

Sarangi, S. and Candlin, C. (eds) (2011). *Handbook of Communication in Organisations and Professions*, Berlin and Boston: Mouton De Gruyter. (A survey of contributions from Applied Linguistics to the study of communication in professional organisations, employing a range of theoretical and methodological innovations to investigate the discourses embedded in and enabling professional practices.)

Scollon, R. (2008). *Analyzing Public Discourse: Discourse Analysis in the Making of Public Policy*, London and New York: Routledge. (A discourse-analytical study of a range of documents from public-policy consultations, focusing on the possibilities for democratic public discourse in debates on environmental issues.)

Note

1 The larger number of text-based analyses discussed here reflects the fact that there are many more text-based studies of discourse and knowledge construction in the natural sciences than any other type of research. To speculate, the reasons for this could be that case studies and ethnography usually require significantly more time and funding, not to mention ethics approval, and, perhaps, also, that many of the text-based studies published in this area have been produced by scholars with professional training in Literary Studies.

Bibliography

Adler, P. and Adler, P. (1987). *Membership Roles in Field Research*, Newbury Park, CA: Sage.
Aristotle. (1960). *The Rhetoric of Aristotle*, L. Cooper (trans.), New York: Appleton-Century-Crofts.
Bachelard, G. (1953). *Le matérialisme rationnel*, Paris: Presses Universitaires de France.

Bakhtin, M. M. (1986). *Speech Genres and Other Late Essays*, V. W. McGee (trans.), Austin, TX: University of Texas Press.
Barton, E. (1993). 'Evidentials, argumentation, and epistemological stance', *College English*, 55, 745–69.
Bazerman, C. (1988). *Shaping Written Language: The Genre and Activity of the Experimental Article in Science*, Madison: University of Wisconsin Press.
——(1991). *Textual Dynamics: Historical and Contemporary Studies of Writing in Professional Communities*, Madison: University of Wisconsin Press.
——(1994). *Constructing Experience*, Carbondale: Southern Illinois University Press.
——(2002). *The Languages of Edison's Light*, Boston: MIT Press.
Bazerman, C. and Prior, P. (2004). *What Writing Does and How it Does it: An Introduction to Analyzing Texts and Textual Practices*, Mahwaw, NJ: Earlbaum.
Bhatia, V. K. (1993). *Analysing Genre: Language Use in Professional Settings*, London: Longman.
——(2004). *Worlds of Written Discourse: A Genre-based View*, London and New York, Continuum.
Blakeslee, A. (2001). *Interacting with Audiences: Social Influences on the Production of Scientific Writing*. Mahwah, NJ: Lawrence Erlbaum.
Bleich, D. (1978). *Subjective Criticism*, Baltimore: Johns Hopkins University Press.
Bourdieu, P. and Boltanski, L. (1976). 'La production de l'idéologie dominante', *Actes de la recherche en sciences socials*, 2–3, 4–73.
Boyle, R. (1660). *New Experiments Physico-mechanical: Touching the Spring of the Air and their Effects*, London: Miles Flesher.
Brillouin, L. (1962). *Science and Information Theory* (second edition), London: Academic Press.
Burke, K. (1945/1969). *A Grammar of Motives*, Berkeley: University of California Press.
——(1966). *Language as Symbolic Action*, Cambridge, UK: Cambridge University Press.
Colyvan, M. (2011). 'A philosopher's view of theory: A response to Gorelick', *Ideas in Ecology and Evolution*, 4, 11–13.
Crowley, S. and Hawhee, D. (1999). *Ancient Rhetorics for Contemporary Students*, New York: Longman.
Dawkins, R. (1976). *The Selfish Gene*, Oxford: Oxford University Press.
Eco, U. (1979). *The Role of the Reader*, Bloomington: Indiana University Press.
Eisner, E. and Flinders, D. (1994). 'Educational criticism as a form of qualitative inquiry', *Research in the Teaching of English*, 28, 341–57.
Ely, M., Vinz, R., Downing, M. and Anzul, M. (1997). *On Writing Qualitative Research: Living by Words*, Bristol, PA: The Falmer Press.
Fahnestock, J. (1986). 'Accommodating science: The rhetorical life of scientific facts', *Written Communication*, 3, 275–93.
——(1999). *Rhetorical Figures in Science*, New York: Oxford University Press.
——(2004). 'Preserving the figure: Consistency in the presentation of scientific arguments', *Written Communication*, 21, 6–21.
Fahnestock, J. and Secor, M. (1988). 'The stases in scientific and literary argument', *Written Communication*, 5, 427–43.
Flinders, D. J. and Mills, G. E. (eds) (1993). *Theory and Concepts in Qualitative Research: Perspectives from the Field*, New York: Teachers College Press.
Florence, M. K. and Yore, L. D. (2004). 'Learning to write like a scientist: Coauthoring as an enculturation task', *Journal of Research in Science Teaching*, 41, 637–68.
Freadman, A. (1994). 'Anyone for tennis?' in A. Freedman and P. Medway (eds), *Genre and the New Rhetoric* (pp. 43–66), London, UK; Bristol, PA: Taylor & Francis.
Gilbert, G. N. and Mulkay, M. J. (1984). *Opening Pandora's Box: A Sociological Analysis of Scientists' Discourse*, Cambridge: Cambridge University Press.
Gorelick, R. (2011). 'What is theory?' *Ideas in Ecology and Evolution*, 4, 1–10.
——(2012). 'Theory may not be definable and its development is not efficient', *Ideas in Ecology and Evolution*, 5, 25–26.
Graham, M. B. and Lindeman, N. (2005). 'The rhetoric and politics of science in the case of the Missouri River system', *Journal of Business and Technical Communication*, 19, 422–48.
Gross, Alan (2006). *Starring the Text: The Place of Rhetoric in Science Studies*, Carbondale: Southern Illinois University.
Gusfield, J. (1976). 'The literary rhetoric of science: Comedy and pathos in drinking driver research', *American Sociological Review*, 41, 16–34.
Hamilton, W. D. (1964a). 'The genetical evolution of social behaviour I', *Journal of Theoretical Biology*, 7(1), 1–16.

——(1964b). 'The genetical evolution of social behaviour II', *Journal of Theoretical Biology*, 7(1), 17–52.
Harris, R. A. (ed.) (2005). *Rhetoric and Incommensurability*, West Lafayette: Parlor Press.
Iser, W. (1978). *The Act of Reading*, Baltimore: Johns Hopkins University Press.
Jasanoff, S. (2004). 'Science and citizenship: A new synergy', *Science and Public Policy*, 31, 90–94.
Journet, D. (2005). 'Metaphor, ambiguity, and motive in Evolutionary Biology: W. D. Hamilton and the "Gene's Point of View"', *Written Communication*, 22, 379–420.
——(2010). 'The resources of ambiguity: Context, narrative, and metaphor in Richard Dawkins' *The selfish gene*', *Journal of Business and Technical Communication*, 24, 29–59.
——(2011). 'George C. Williams, Kenneth Burke, and "The goal of the fox": Or, genes, organisms, and the agents of natural selection', *Narrative*, 19, 216–28.
Keller, E. F. (1995). *Refiguring Life: Metaphors of Twentieth-century Biology*, New York: Columbia University Press.
Knorr-Cetina, K. (1981). *The Manufacture of Knowledge: An Essay on the Constructivist and Contextual Nature of Science*, Oxford and New York: Pergamon.
——(1999). *Epistemic Cultures: How the Sciences make Knowledge*, Cambridge: Harvard University Press.
Knorr-Cetina, K. and Knorr, D. (1978). 'From scenes to scripts: On the relationship between laboratory research and published papers in science', *Research Memorandum* No. 132. Institute for Advanced Studies, Vienna, Austria, and Cornell University, Ithaca, NY.
Latour, B. (2008). 'A textbook case revisited: Knowledge as mode of existence', in E. Hackett, O. Amsterdamska, M. Lynch and J. Wacjman (eds), *The Handbook of Science and Technology* (third edition) (pp. 83–112), Cambridge: MIT Press.
Latour, B. and Woolgar, S. (1979). *Laboratory Life: The Construction of Scientific Facts*, Princeton, NJ: Princeton University Press.
Latour, B. and Woolgar, S. (1986). *Laboratory Life: The Construction of Scientific Facts*, Princeton, NJ: Princeton University Press.
Luhmann, N. (1981). *Politische Theorie im Wohlfahrtsstaat*, München: Gunter Olzo Verlag.
Lynch, M. and Woolgar, S. (eds) (1990). *Representation in Scientific Practice*, Cambridge: MIT Press.
Lyotard, J. F. (1975). 'For a pseudo-theory', M. Ron (trans.), *Yale French Studies*, 52, 115–27.
Martin, J. R. and Veel, R. (eds) (1998). *Reading Science: Critical and Functional Perspectives on Discourses of Science*, London and New York: Routledge.
McCloskey, D. (1998). *The Rhetoric of Economics*, Madison: University of Wisconsin Press.
Miller, C. (1984). 'Genre as social action', *Quarterly Journal of Speech*, 70, 151–67.
——(1994). 'Genre as social action', in A. Freedman and P. Medway (eds), *Genre in the New Rhetoric* (pp. 23–42), London: Taylor & Francis.
Myers, G. (1985a). 'The social construction of two biologists' articles', *Social Studies of Science*, 15, 593–630.
——(1985b). 'The social construction of two biologists' proposals', *Written Communication*, 2, 219–45.
——(1991) *Writing Biology: Texts in the Social Construction of Scientific Knowledge*. Madison: University of Wisconsin Press.
——(2003). 'Discourse studies of scientific popularization: Questioning the boundaries', *Discourse Studies*, 5, 265–79.
Paltridge, B. (1994). 'Genre analysis and the identification of textual boundaries', *Applied Linguistics*, 15, 288–99.
Paul, D. (2004). 'Spreading chaos: The role of popularizations in the diffusion of scientific ideas', *Written Communication*, 21, 32–68.
Perelman, C. and Olbrechts-Tyteca, L. (1969). *The New Rhetoric: A Treatise on Argumentation*, Notre Dame, IN: University of Notre Dame Press.
Rees, C. E. and Monrouxe, L. V. (2010). 'Theory in medical education research: How do we get there?' *Medical Education*, 44, 334–39.
Reeves, S., Albert, M., Kuper, A. and Hodges, B. D. (2008). 'Qualitative research: Why use theories in qualitative research?' *British Medical Journal*, 337, 631–34.
Reynolds, R. E., Taylor, M. A., Steffensen, M. S., Shirey, L. L. and Anderson, R. C. (1981). *Cultural Schemata and Reading Comprehension*, Reading report 201, Urbana, IL: Center for the Study of Reading.
Rumelhart, D. E. and Orotony, A. (1977). 'The representation of knowledge in memory', in R. Anderson, R. Spiro, and W. Montague (eds), *Schooling and the Acquisition of Knowledge*. Hillside, NJ: Erlbaum.
Rymer, J. (1988). 'Scientific composing process: How eminent scientists write journal articles', in D. Jolliffe (ed.), *Advances in Writing Research* (Vol. 2, pp. 211–250), Norwood, NJ: Ablex.
Scheiner, S. M. (2012). 'The multiple roles of theory: A reply to Gorelick', *Ideas in Ecology and Evolution*, 5, 22–24.

Schryer, C. F., Gladkova, O., Spafford, M. M. and Lingard, L. (2007). 'Co-management in healthcare: Negotiating professional boundaries', *Discourse & Communication*, *1*(4), 452–79.

Serres, M. (1977). *La naissance de la physique dan le texte de Lucrece. Fleuves et turbulences*, Paris: Editions de Minuit.

Shapin, S. (1984). 'Pump and circumstance: Robert Boyle's literary technology', *Social Studies of Science*, *14*, 481–520.

Smart, G. (2011). 'Argumentation across web-based organizational discourses: The case of climate-change debate', in C. Candlin and S. Sarangi (eds), *Handbook of Communication in Organizations and Professions* (pp. 363–86), Berlin and Boston: Walter de Gruyter.

——(2012). 'The discursive production and impairment of public trust through rhetorical representations of science: The case of global climate change', in C. Candlin and J. Crichton (eds), *Discourses of Trust: The Discursive Construction of "Trust" within Applied Linguistic Research*, London and New York: Palgrave Macmillan.

Spiro, R., Bruce, B. and Brewer, W. (eds) (1980). *Theoretical Issues in Reading Comprehension: Perspectives from Cognitive Psychology, Linguistics, Artificial Intelligence, and Education*, Hillsdale, NJ: Erlbaum.

Swales, J. (1990). *Genre Analysis: English in Academic and Research Settings*, Cambridge and New York: Cambridge University Press.

——(2004). *Research Genres: Explorations and Applications*, Cambridge: Cambridge University Press.

Tardy, C. (2003). 'A genre system view of the funding of academic research', *Written Communication*, *20*, 7–36.

Thacker, B. and Stratman, J. (1995). 'Transmuting common substances: The cold fusion controversy and the rhetoric of science', *Journal of Business and Technical Communication*, *9*, 389–424.

Toulmin, S. (1972). *Human Understanding*, Princeton: Princeton University Press.

Vygotsky, L. S. (1962). *Thought and Language*, Cambridge, MA: MIT Press.

Wilson, G. and Herndl, C. (2007). 'Boundary objects as rhetorical exigence: Knowledge mapping and interdisciplinary cooperation at the Los Alamos National Laboratory', *Journal of Business and Technical Communication*, *21*, 129–54.

8
Technical communication

Saul Carliner

The professional practice of technical communication

The professional practice of technical communication is:

> a broad field and includes any form of communication that exhibits one or more of the following characteristics:
>
> - Communicating *about technical or specialized topics*, such as computer applications, medical procedures, or environmental regulations.
> - Communicating *by using technology*, such as web pages, help files, or social media sites.
> - Providing *instructions about how to do something*, regardless of how technical the task is or even if technology is used to create or distribute that communication.
>
> (Society for Technical Communication 2012)

This chapter describes the frameworks for considering the specialty of technical communication within the broader field of professional communication. To provide a context for the discussion, I begin this chapter with a description of the work of technical communicators, drawing first on historical studies of technical communication before the formal rise of the field and continuing with descriptions of modern practice derived from empirical studies. Next, I shift attention to the theories and intellectual foundations that guide professionals in communicating technical content, and then explore their practical applications in the technologies used to prepare and publish technical content and the methods used to evaluate this content. I close the chapter by exploring technical communication as a profession.

The work of technical communicators

Admittedly, technical communication has existed for millennia and, in theory, covers a wide range of topics, from recipes to operating public institutions. For example, the Neues Museum in Berlin exhibits technical documentation from the ancient Near East.

Yu (2009) explores the development of cookbooks in China from 500 BCE. Explaining that cookbooks convey technical information from experts to those who need to know (cooks), she shows how cookbooks became increasingly sophisticated over the years. Others have also found examples of technical communication in previous eras. For example, Tebeaux (1997) presents examples of procedural and public works discourse in Elizabethan times. Loges (1998) reports on testimony before the US Congress in 1859, which credits the publication of a guide for lighthouse operators as the reason that no preventable maritime disaster occurred in the previous year.

> While it is not fair to give the written instructions the entire credit for the improvement [technical advancements were introduced] ... [These] comments regarding how the lights were kept is positive testimony to the value of the documentation.
>
> *(Loges 1998: 452)*

Durack (1998) describes instruction manuals for sewing machines in the early 1900s and their role in reinforcing gender roles.

Although these researchers document the long history of efforts to communicate technical information, the difference between these historical efforts and more recent ones is that the historical documents were written by technical experts who needed to communicate technical information, or writers who did not have access to specialised training in technical communication. What distinguishes technical communication today is that such documents are prepared by people specially trained in the field of technical communication and whose primary job responsibility involves preparing this content. This section of the chapter explores that work. It first describes the types of content that technical communicators produce then describes the role of technical communicators in producing that content.

What technical communicators produce

The identified practice of technical communication did not emerge until the 1940s, with growth in documentation required for sophisticated military products. The field became formalised in the 1950s with the establishment of the first academic programs in technical communication at Carnegie Mellon University (then the Carnegie Institute of Technology) and two professional associations in the United States: the predecessor of the Society for Technical Communication and a Professional Communication Society within the Institute for Electrical and Electronic Engineers (IEEE).

Professional literature in the field suggests that technical communication covers a broad range of materials (Society for Technical Communication 2012), including user guides, online help, and service guides for high technology, telecommunications, and pharmaceutical products. Technical communicators also prepare scientific and technical reports; complex proposals for large sales efforts (such as the sale of military equipment to a government); white papers and other marketing materials for high technology products; e-learning and similar training programs; and government policies.

Empirical studies (such as Carliner forthcoming; Carliner 2004; Spinuzzi 2003) suggest, however, that the primary work of technical communicators has a narrower scope. For example, in his studies of the work of technical communication groups, Carliner (2006, 2004) found that the most common assignments include:

- Developing user assistance for hardware, software, and other technical products and services. User assistance refers to the conceptual material, instructions, and advice that help people make the most effective use of these products. (Because the material they publish focuses on the *use* of a product or service, technical communicators refer to their audiences as *users* rather than readers.) User assistance takes many forms. These include:

- User's guides, which are a type of manual that explains how to use a product (Price and Korman 1993; Weiss 1991).
- Quick references (Johnson and Minson 2010), which summarise this material in compact publications that more easily fit in cramped workspaces.
- Online help (Welinske 2011; Boggan, Farkas and Welinske 1999; Duffy, Palmer and Mehlenbacher 1992), which provides similar information, but online and is primarily used to guide people in using software. Help appears when users press a Help key or choose a Help option in a software application.
- Support websites (Gentle 2012), which provide similar content, but through a website, and also provide helpful tips for more advanced users, as well as solutions to problems that other users have reported. More recently, organisations added *social capabilities* to user assistance. Social capabilities let people other than technical communicators contribute material to user assistance, such as technical experts and customers who already use the product (Gentle 2012).

Technical communicators try to put the 'user' in user assistance by designing the content for easy use. They do so by emphasising the user's perspective, such as writing about tasks users perform rather than characteristics of the product (Waite 1997) that are meaningless outside of the context of use; writing in plain language (Redish 2012); and designing content so users can easily find the information they seek (Redish 2012), called *retrievability*.

- Developing technical support materials, used by trained professionals who offer service to customers as well as by technical experts within customer organisations. This type of content provides users with the information they need to adapt products and services and troubleshoot and solve problems. Often called *service* or *troubleshooting documentation* (Lew 1994), this type of content is primarily intended for people who have special training on the product or service, and often work for the company that produces it.

Like user assistance, service documentation takes many forms. In some instances, it focuses on solving problems. Such documentation often has a procedural element, first walking readers through a series of questions to precisely document the problem, then offering procedures to fix the problem (Lew 1994). In other instances, even experts might have difficulty diagnosing the problem because it is rare – or they may have encountered the problem so many times that they do not need assistance with diagnosing it. Instead, they need factual information about the product or service, from which they can reach knowledgeable conclusions on their own. Technical communicators document such information in *references*, which provide complete technical information. References can be published in print or online or, more recently, as mobile applications used on smart phones and tablets (Welinske 2011) and e-books (Cooper and Rockley 2013).

In contrast to the simplicity emphasised in user assistance, technical communicators emphasise completeness when writing references. Many have particular ways of presenting content that, while not self-evident to readers, let them communicate extensive information to readers in as little space as possible. In such instances, users receive special training in using these references. Furthermore, because technical communicators assume that users of service documentation have formal training, they often use a more technical vocabulary when writing content and might not define terms.

- Developing scientific and engineering content, which is primarily used to promote basic and applied research by scientists and engineers (Society for Technical Communication 2012).

Technical communicators (some of whom refer to themselves as scientific communicators) work on several types of research documents, such as editing research reports by scientists that these scientists will eventually submit to peer-reviewed journals in their fields. Other technical communicators work in engineering firms, editing reports produced by the engineers for their client organisations. In some instances, technical communicators edit reports originally drafted by scientists and engineers. In other instances, technical communicators draft materials for review by scientists and engineers.

Some technical communicators prepare grants and proposals (Society for Technical Communication 2012). Grants are usually prepared for major funding agencies such as the US National Science Foundation and the National Institutes for Health and usually describe proposed research projects worth several hundred thousand or million US dollars. Technical communicators who work in engineering and consulting firms work on proposals for large contracts, usually of a similar financial scope to those for grants. The nature of the contracts can vary, from contracts for a feasibility study for an airport to overseeing the outsourcing of an internal Information Systems group. Some of these proposals can comprise several hundred or more pages. To facilitate the process, many technical communicators use 'proposal generators', repositories of material from earlier proposals that communicators can use as-is or with minor modifications. For example, the repository of content might include information about the organisation, profiles of people likely to work on a project, and work plans from similar projects in the past.

Like other types of technical content, research and engineering reports and proposal writing emphasise clarity, consistency, and conciseness. But most of this writing also adheres to strong genre conventions. For example, many peer-reviewed journals have specific expectations regarding the structure of research articles and the nature of content reported in each part. Similarly, many proposals must report information in the particular order required by the funding agency or prospective client. Despite the technical nature of these proposals, they must also persuade clients to purchase the proposed service or project (Melancon 2010).

- Project documentation, which includes documenting product plans (especially the detailed technical specifications for a product that guide product developers in designing and testing the components to which they are assigned) and status reports used for communication across an entire project team. Although preparing such documentation is often a secondary responsibility for technical communicators, it builds on their competencies of documenting material and provides technical communicators with opportunities to influence the design of products because they can spot issues as they prepare the project documentation.

Although technical communicators emphasise their roles as advocates for the user and in promoting the usability of the products and services they document (Barnum 2010), empirical research suggests that this is only a secondary job responsibility for technical communicators (Carliner 2006, 2004). That is, in most organisations, technical communicators do not have responsibility for the usability of products and services, although some technical communicators in some organisations will.

The role of technical communicators in producing this content

In terms of work processes, empirical evidence suggests that technical communicators often play a central role in the design and development of content (Carliner 2006; Spinuzzi 2003). Such processes involve analysis, design, development, and production (Hackos 2007, 1994) with an emphasis on the process of developing and reviewing drafts (Carliner 2006, 2004).

As part of its project to certify technical communicators, the STC has identified competencies that play a central role in developing technical content (STC Certification Commission 2012b). In turn, these competencies are based on competencies identified by a community college in Seattle, Washington. These competencies include:

1. User, Task, and Experience Analysis – Define the users of the information and analyze the tasks that the information must support.
2. Information Design – Plan information deliverables to support task requirements. Specify and design the organization, presentation, distribution and archival for each deliverable.
3. Process Management – Plan the deliverables schedule and monitor the process of fulfilment.
4. Information Development – Author content in conformance with the design plan, through an iterative process of creation, review, and revision.
5. Information Production – Assemble developed content into required deliverables that conform to all design, compliance, and production guidelines. Publish, deliver, and archive.

(STC Certification Commission 2012a)

Technical communicators play three key roles when developing content:

- Technical writer, who writes the content and usually oversees the project through to publication (Barnum and Carliner 1993). The technical writer usually has ongoing responsibility for the project after publication, such as responding to comments received.
- Technical editor, who reviews draft materials for clarity and flow (called *substantive editing*) and conformance to style guidelines (called *copyediting*), and often prepares materials for production (Rude and Eaton 2010; Tarutz 1992).
- Technical illustrator or graphic designer, who prepares illustrations for a project or adapts them from other sources (such as CAD drawings).

If they remain with an organisation, technical communicators often work with the same content through a series of revisions. For example, technical communicators might write the topics for a help system for the beta version of an app, then revise that content as the organisation prepares new versions of the app and as readers suggest clarifications to it.

Before the advent of desktop publishing, different people typically handled each of these roles. With automated formatting and spell- and grammar-checking capabilities arising, smaller organisations abolished or curtailed technical editing activities. When possible, these organisations have one technical writer check the work of another, called *peer editing*. Similarly, with the advent of computer-aided drawing tools and clip art, many technical communicators assumed the roles of technical illustrators. As a result, many technical communicators perform all three roles.

Project managers typically oversee the work of technical communication projects. These project managers prepare budgets and schedules for projects, identify quality standards and hire staff for them, and oversee ongoing projects to make sure they meet requirements (Hackos 1994). Sometimes, project managers exclusively oversee technical communication efforts. In other organisations, project managers coordinate all work on a project, including development, testing and marketing.

One trend in technical communication is *outsourcing* and *offshoring* of work (Padmanabhan 2007). Outsourcing refers to hiring other organisations to prepare technical content, such as contractors (individuals who work for a company for a defined period of time, as defined in a contract) and agencies (companies that specialise in preparing content for other companies). Offshoring refers to assigning projects to people who work in another country, typically on the other side of an ocean (hence the term, *offshoring*). Offshored workers might also be outsourced, but can work for the same company. For example, several large high tech companies like Oracle and IBM have staffs in India that prepare technical content for products and services developed in North America.

When organisations prepare content for markets other than their own, they typically need to localise and translate it. Localisation refers to efforts to use terminology and examples appropriate to a given market, which often differ from those used where technical communicators develop products and services. For example, people in North America use the term *elevator* to refer to the machine that carries people between floors; in Asia, Australia and Europe, people use the term *lift*. Translation refers to converting the content from a source language (such as English) to a target language (such as Japanese). Translators typically handle both of these tasks. Before the advent of computer-assisted translation, the process of translation and localisation began when technical communicators submitted final drafts of work for production so translated versions of products and services in other markets would not appear until several months after their introduction in their 'home' markets. Although it does not replace translators, computer-aided translation improves their productivity by suggesting initial translations of passages (Folaron 2012). With the advent of the internet, consumers learn about availability of products and services online when companies first introduce them and organisations now feel compelled to release products globally on the same day, rather than one country at a time (Poire 2005). Typically, organisations outsource translation to translation and localisation firms. These firms play a central role in technical communication projects to help their clients control the cost of translation. For example, by more closely managing revisions, organisations can reduce translation costs by limiting the changed content to just that which is most necessary, rather than anything the technical communicator chooses to revise.

When designing and developing technical content, technical communicators also rely on technical experts – that is, the engineers, programmers, scientists, and other technical professionals who develop the products and services or conduct the research communicated by the technical communicator (Price and Korman 1993). These experts provide source material, review drafts of content for technical accuracy, and approve content for publication. This reliance on third parties for content creates tension in the relationships between technical communicators and technical professionals. Common issues include a failure to provide complete technical information about a project, late changes to products and services, resulting in extensive and avoidable revision to the technical content, and a lack of timeliness in reviews or a failure to provide them (Brown 2011).

The discipline of technical communication also encompasses the communication practices of scientific and technical professionals who communicate as part of their jobs, but are not professional communicators. In some instances, these professionals are filling in for a technical communicator (such as a programmer who writes the online help for an application). In other instances, these professionals are supporting their everyday work (such as documenting the plans for a product an engineer is developing). Work processes in these situations are abridged versions of those used by professional technical communicators because communication is an additional job responsibility and these technical professionals have less time to devote to it (Markel 2012). In such instances, professional technical communicators might support the technical professionals.

The discipline of technical communication

Having provided a background on the work of technical communicators, this chapter next turns its attention to the intellectual roots of the discipline. Technical communication has its intellectual roots in three disciplines. Many technical communication scholars were first trained in the humanities, including English literature, composition, and communication studies. For them, the primary roots of the discipline are rhetoric (Rutter 1991). Other technical communication scholars were first trained in education or psychology. For them, the primary roots of the discipline lie in cognitive psychology – especially composition studies, reading and ergonomics (Flower 2003; Schriver 1997; Redish 1993). A third group of technical communication scholars were trained in Applied Linguistics. For some of them, the roots of the discipline lie in discourse analysis (such as Gee 2011) while, for others, the roots of the discipline lie in empiricism associated with cognitive psychology (Charney 1996).

Regardless of the routes that bring professionals and scholars to technical communication, they eventually take a broad view towards the design, development, and assessment of technical content that encompasses pieces of each of these traditions. The primary theories guiding the design of content include a focus on readers (Redish 1993) and the principles of user-centred design (Norman 1998). Other theories certainly provide guidance, including performance-centred design (Marion 2002; Gery 1995) and reading theory (Redish 1993). Dragga (1997) adds ethical concerns to these guiding approaches.

In addition, several theories and approaches guide specific aspects of technical communication. Theories guiding the design development of content include theories of:

- Writing, which focuses on the composition of text and is guided by theories such as task-oriented writing (Waite 1997; Price and Price 2002), problem-based writing (Flower 1981), genre theory (such as Bhatia 1993; Berkenkotter and Huckin 1995; Kress and Van Leuwen 2001) and reader-focused prose (Redish 1993).
- Visual communication, which focuses on the use of visuals to communicate ideas as well as the use of visual devices to aid and influence readers, and is guided by theories such as visual rhetoric (Kostelnick and Hassett 2003; Kress and Van Leuwen 1996; and Bernhardt 1992), and principles of page (Felker, Pickering, Charrow, Holland and Redish 1981) and screen design (Van der Geest and Spyridakis 2000).
- Editing, which focuses on the role of editors as the first readers of documents (Rude and Eaton 2010) and as a means of quality control (Hargis *et al.* 2004) and is guided by an approach called the levels of edit (Van Buren and Buehler 1980).
- Translating and localising documents, which focus on providing content in languages other than the ones in which the content was written and addressing the unique local context, and is guided by theories of intercultural communication (Hoft 1995) and translation.

Until recently, production of documents – that is, the preparation of finished content for publication – has primarily been a practical concern. But increasingly complex systems guide the production process and allow technical communicators to publish content from a single file in print and in various online formats (called *single-sourcing*), only print documents when needed (called *printing on-demand*), create documents as needed from paragraphs and sections of completed documents (called *dynamic publishing*), and partially translate and localise documents with the assistance of computer software (called *computer-assisted translation*) (Carliner 2010). On the one hand, such technological developments let technical communicators produce documents much more quickly than in the past and with little or no assistance from editors, illustrators, publishing professionals, and translators. On the other hand, realising the benefits of these systems adds significant complexity to the process of designing and developing content. For example, to dynamically produce content from several, separate topics, a technical communicator must first tell the system which parts are available and that, in turn, affects design. This, in turn, affects work processes in technical communication groups, because they need to invest more effort in design and development, and use different processes to review documents (O'Keefe and Pringle 2012). In addition, to facilitate some degree of machine translation, technical communicators must restrict the terminology and expressions used in their documents.

These technologies have created new roles for technical communicators, most notably those of the *content strategist*, who helps organisations with the complex design underlying dynamic publishing (O'Keefe and Pringle 2012), and the *content curator*, who selects and edits content from others rather than developing the content on their own (Gentle 2012).

These technologies have also generated new theories and approaches, including single-source documentation, content management (Rockley 2002) and the use of corpus-based approaches to translation (Orr 2006). Theory-driven approaches also guide the process for developing content, including linear, goal-driven processes (Hackos 1994) and flexible, emergent processes like Agile development (Dayton and Barnum 2009).

Several approaches guide the evaluation of technical content, each rooted in a different philosophy about the purposes of content and how to evaluate it. These include usability testing (Barnum 2010), which assesses the ability of users to perform the intended tasks; editing (Rude and Eaton 2010; Eaton, Brewer, Portewig and Davidson 2008), which emphasises readability and adherence to publishing norms; and value added (Redish 1995), which emphasises the financial return to the organisation publishing the content. No consensus exists, however, on the characteristics of quality technical content (Carliner 2003).

The profession of technical communication

A recurring theme in the literature on technical communication is its status as a unique profession (for example, Coppola 2011; Kynell and Savage 2004). The characteristics of a bona-fide profession include control over education about, and entry into, the field, establishing a body of literature, identifying competence in the field and standards of excellence, developing and enforcing a code of ethical professional behaviour, and establishing organisations to oversee all of this (James 2012; Trice and Beyer 1993).

At this time, technical communication does not fully fulfil the criteria for a profession, but does partially fulfil them through efforts that started at least six decades ago.

The first of those efforts was the establishment of professional organisations. The first were the Society of Technical Writers (STW) and the Association of Technical Writers and Editors (ATWE), both founded in the US in 1953 and merged to become the Society for Technical Writers and Editors (STWE) in 1957. STWE renamed itself as the Society for Technical Communication in the 1970s (Wikipedia 2012). Other organisations serving the field emerged. Some are geographically focused, including the Australian Society for Technical Communication, European-based Conseil des Redacteurs Techniques, Technical Communicators Association of New Zealand, German-based tekom, and UK-based Institute for Scientific and Technical Communicators. Some are primarily intended for people who teach technical communication, such as the Association for the Teachers of Techincal Writing (ATTW), Canadian Association for the Study of Discourse and Writing (CASDW), and the Council of Programs in Scientific and Technical Communication (CPTSC). Some are special interest groups of organisations serving technical professionals, such as the Professional Communication Society of the Institute for Electrical and Electronic Engineers (IEEE) and the Special Interest Group on Documentation of the Association of Computing Machinery (ACM). Others focus on narrow specialties within technical communication, including the American Medical Writers Association (AMWA) and the Board of Editors in the Life Sciences (BELS).

Soon after their founding, the professional societies began promoting conversations in their field and building bodies of literature. To promote conversations in the field, the professional organisations launched conferences and similar events. Among the larger conferences in the field are the STC Summit – the Society for Technical Communication Annual Conference – the International Professional Communication Conference of the IEEE Professional Communication Society, and tcworld sponsored by tekom. Commercial conferences are also produced, such as the WritersUA conference focused on professionals who create user assistance (renamed ConveyUX in 2013), LavaCon, a conference originally focused on technical communication managers, Intelligent Content, a conference for people focused on content strategy, and Best Practice, a conference focused on technical communication managers.

Building the body of literature started with the founding of the peer-reviewed journals: *Technical Communication* in 1953 and *IEEE Transactions on Professional Communication* in 1957. These were joined by the *Journal of Technical Writing and Communication* (established in 1971), *Journal of Business and Technical Communication* (established in 1986) and *Technical Communication Quarterly* (established in 1991), replacing an earlier journal, the *Technical Writing Teacher*. Scholars in technical communication also publish in journals whose focus extends beyond technical communication, such as *Business Communication Quarterly, Computers and Composition,* and *Information Design Journal.* To help generate content for its journal, the Society for Technical Communication offered research grants in technical communication, until the program was abolished in the mid-2000s for financial reasons.

The peer-reviewed literature is supplemented by hundreds of academic and trade books (Murphy 2011), professional magazines *Intercom*, published by the Society for Technical Communication, and *TC World,* published by tekom, and various websites and blogs, including the webzine, KeyContent.org, and the blog, I'd Rather Be Writing.

As technical communicators laid the foundation for a profession in the 1950s, universities began formally training technical communicators. As noted earlier, the US-based Carnegie Mellon University established the first academic program in technical communication, followed by ones at the Rensselaer Polytechnic Institute and University of Minnesota. By the 1990s, university-level programs were established throughout the United States and Finland and in community colleges in Canada, China and Germany. In addition, tekom has established its own certificate program in technical communication with a rigorous examination process to provide formal recognition to people who work in the field but do not have a formal education in it.

One of the ongoing challenges for these academic programs is that the faculty in them had dual responsibilities for teaching majors in their field (Barnum 2006) as well as providing service courses – that is, teaching writing to students who specialise in engineering, science, and other technical fields and who do not intend to become professional technical communicators. Because service assignments comprise the majority of the teaching responsibilities for faculty in some academic technical communication programs, teaching and supporting the service course also encompasses much of their research, leading to a divide between the interests of researchers and those of practising professionals (Carliner 1994).

Professional organisations also launched efforts to recognise outstanding work in the field, such as the International Technical Communication Competition sponsored by the Society for Technical Communication that recognises excellence in print and online communication, and the documentation award from tekom. As part of devising the competitions, organisers also develop criteria for award-winning publications, which serves as an initial guide to defining quality in technical communication. In addition, some professional organisations recognise sustained contributions to the profession. For example, the Association of Teachers of Technical Writing and Society for Technical Communication both have honorary ranks of Fellows, which recognise lifelong achievement in the profession.

Perhaps the most controversial initiative in professionalising technical communication is the launch of certification. Certification is the recognition of competence in a profession by a third party (Hale 2012), as evidenced by a demonstration of work. At least as early as the 1970s, the Society for Technical Communication has explored the possibility of launching a certification program but, until 2009, always rejected the possibility (Turner and Rainey 2004). In 2010, STC approved a certification program and launched its first certification in 2012 and a second one in 2013. The first certification, the Certified Professional Technical Communicator^{TM} (CPTC^{TM}), requires that participants have at least five years of experience in the field (or as many as two fewer years, if the applicant has a related degree) and provide an annotated portfolio of work that demonstrates competence in the five areas named earlier in this chapter. The second certification, the Certified Professional Technical Writer^{TM} (CPTW^{TM}), requires that participants have at least three years of experience and provide an annotated portfolio of work that demonstrates competence in the information development and information production competencies. Specialty branches of technical communication, including medical writing and editing in the life sciences also have or will have certification, as do general business communication (through the International Association of Business Communicators), public relations (through the Public Relations Society of America), and training (through the American and Canadian Societies for Training and Development). Proponents of certification say that, in the absence of a formal barrier to entry in the field, certification helps professionals distinguish themselves and employers determine who is most qualified to perform work. Opponents of certification fear that, by tightly defining what technical communication is, it excludes other types of communication that could be thought of as technical. Opponents worry, too, that certification will limit entry into the field.

Conclusion

As suggested in this chapter, technical communication is a relatively young discipline that continues to evolve. But its evolution mirrors, in many ways, those of other branches of communication like marketing communications, business communication, and public relations, although it is somewhat behind those branches in its development. For example, universities and colleges established academic programs in some of those other disciplines before technical communication, professional associations in those other areas formed before those in technical communication, and certification launched as many as 20 years earlier (for example, the International Association of Business Communicators launched its certification at least 20 years before the Society for Technical Communication launched its program). Some technical communicators emphasise the overlap between technical communication and other branches of communication. But when considering this discipline, perhaps the other branches of communication offer a preview of developments to come in this branch.

Trademarks

Certified Professional Technical Communicator, Certified Professional Technical Writer, CPTC, and CPTW are trademarks of the Society for Technical Communication Certification Commission.

Related topics

Electronic media in professional communication; workplace communication; business and the communication of climate change

Key readings

Coppola, N. W. (2011). 'Professionalization of technical communication: Zeitgeist for our age', *Technical Communication*, 58(4), 277–84. (Provides an overview of the challenges of professionalizing technical communication.)
Johnson-Eilola, J. and Selber, S. A. (eds) (2013). *Solving Problems in Technical Communication*, Chicago, IL: University of Chicago Press. (A contemporary look at the profession.)
Schriver, Karen. (1997). *Dynamics of Document Design*, New York: John Wiley & Sons. (A classic that provides an overview of the principles that guide the design of documents.)

References

Barnum, C. M. (2006). 'If I had a crystal ball … ', *Technical Communication*, 53(3), 283–85.
——(2010). *Usability Testing Essentials: Ready, Set … Test!* Burlington, MA: Morgan Kaufmann.
Barnum, C. M. and Carliner, S. (1993). *Techniques for Technical Communicators*, New York: Macmillian.
Berkenkotter, C. and Huckin, T. N. (1995). *Genre Knowledge in Disciplinary Communication: Cognition/Culture/Power*, Hillsdale, NJ: Lawrence Erlbaum Associates.
Bernhardt, S. (1992). 'Seeing the text … ', *Journal of Computer Documentation*, 16(3).
Bhatia, V. (1993). *Analysing Genre: Language Use in Professional Settings*, London: Longman.
Boggan, S., Farkas, D. and Welinske, J. (1999). *Developing Online Help for Windows 95 (TM)* (2nd edn), Reading, MA: Solutions.
Brown, K. (2011). 'Conducting effective team technical reviews', Published at Techwr-l, 8 June 2011. Available at http://techwhirl.com/skills/soft/conducting-effective-team-technical-reviews/ (accessed 18 November 2012).
Carliner, S. (1994) 'Guest editorial: A practitioner's call for the STC to establish a research agenda', *Technical Communication*, 41(4).
——(2003). 'Characteristic-based, task-based, and results-based: The three value systems for assessing professionally produced technical communication products', *Technical Communication Quarterly*, 12(1), 83–100.
——(2004). 'What do we manage? A survey of the management portfolios of large technical communication groups', *Technical Communication*, 51(1), 45–67.
——(2006). 'Productivity and effectiveness: An exploratory study of what managers actually track and report', European Conference on Human Resource Development, Academy for Human Resource Development, Tilburg, the Netherlands, 23 May 2006.
——(2010). 'A taxonomy of technology: A tool for preparing students for internal communications context of organizations', Canadian Association for the Study of Discourse and Writing Annual Conference, Montreal, QC, 29 May 2010.
——(forthcoming). 'Comparing the work portfolios of corporate communication, training, and technical communication managers', To be submitted to the *Journal of Business and Technical Communication*.
Charney, D. (1996). 'Empiricism is not a four-letter word', *College Composition and Communication*, 47(4), 567–93.
Cooper, C. and Rockley, A. (2013). 'Content strategy for mobile devices', 60th Technical Communication Summit, Society for Technical Communication, Atlanta, GA, 7 May 2013.
Coppola, N. W. (2011). 'Professionalization of Technical Communication: Zeitgeist for our age', *Technical Communication*, 58(4), 277–84.

Dayton, D. and Barnum, C. M. (2009). 'The impact of Agile on user-centered design', *Technical Communication*, 56(3), 219–34.
Dragga, S. (1997). 'A question of ethics: Lessons from technical communicators on the job', *Technical Communication Quarterly*, 6(2), 161–78.
Duffy, T. M., Palmer, J.E. and Mehlenbacher, B. (1992). *Online Help: Design and Evaluation*, Norwood, NJ: Ablex Publishing Corporation.
Durack, K. T. (1998). 'Authority and audience-centered writing strategies: Sexism in 19th-century sewing machine manuals', *Technical Communication*, 45(2), 180–96.
Eaton, A., Brewer, P. E., Portewig, T. C. and Davidson, C. R. (2008). 'Examining editing in the workplace from the author's point of view', *Technical Communication*, 55(2), 111–39.
Felker, D. B., Pickering, F., Charrow, V. R., Holland, V. M. and Redish, J. C. (1981). *Guidelines for Document Designers*, Washington, DC: American Institutes for Research.
Flower, L. (1981). *Problem-Solving Strategies for Writing*, Chicago, IL: Harcourt Brace Jovanovich.
——(2003). *Problem Solving Strategies for Writing*, San Diego, CA: Harcourt College Publishing.
Folaron, D. (2012). 'Conversation with Saul Carliner', 29 August 2012, Montreal, QC.
Gee, J. P. (2011). *How to Do Discourse Analysis*, Abingdon: Routledge.
Gentle, A. (2012). *Conversation and Community: The Social Web for Documentation* (2nd edn), Ft. Collins, CO: XML Press.
Gery, G. (1995). 'Attributes and behaviors of performance-centered systems', *Performance Improvement Quarterly*, 8(1), 47–93.
Hackos, J. T. (1994). *Managing Your Documentation Projects*, New York: John Wiley & Sons.
——(2007). *Information Development: Managing Your Documentation Projects, Portfolio, and People*, New York: John Wiley & Sons.
Hale, J. (2012). *Performance-Based Certification: How to Design a Valid, Defensible, Cost-Effective Program* (2nd edn), San Francisco: Pfeiffer.
Hargis, G., Carey, M., Hernandex, A. K., Hughes, P., Longo, D., Rouiller, S. and Wilde, E. (2004). *Developing Quality Technical Information: A Handbook for Writer and Editors* (2nd edn), Boston, MA: IBM Press.
Hoft, N. L. (1995). *International Technical Communication: How to Export Information about High Technology*, New York, NY: John Wiley & Sons.
James, N. (2012). *The Future of Technical Writing in a Converging Communications Profession*, Keynote presentation at 2012 Technical Communicators Association of New Zealand (TCANZ) Conference. Auckland, NZ: 26 October 2012.
Johnson, T. H. and Minson, B. (2010). 'Quick reference guides: Short and sweet documentation', Writers UA website. Available at www.writersua.com/articles/quickref/index.html (accessed 18 November 2012).
Kostelnick, C. and Hassett, M. (2003). *Shaping Information: The Rhetoric of Visual Conventions*, Carbondale, IL: Southern Illinois University Press.
Kress, G. and van Leeuwen, T. (1996). *Reading Images: The Grammar of Visual Design*, London: Routledge.
——(2001). *Multimodal Discourse*, London: Arnold.
Kynell, T. and Savage, J. (2004). *Power and Legitimacy in Technical Communication: Strategies for Professional Status*, Amityville, NY: Baywood Publishing.
Lew, H. K. (1994). 'Developing troubleshooting publications for complex systems: A case study: Troubleshooting router-based internetworks', Proceedings of the 41st Society for Technical Communication Annual Conference, Arlington, VA: Society for Technical Communication.
Loges, M. (1998). 'The value of technical documentation as an aid in training: The case of the U.S. Lighthouse board', *Journal of Business and Technical Communication*, 12(4), 437–53.
Marion, C. (2002). 'Attributes of performance-centered systems: What can we learn from five years of EPSS/PCD competition award winners?', *Technical Communication*, 49(4), 428–43.
Markel, M. (2012). *Technical Communication* (10th edn), Boston, MA: Bedford/St Martin's.
Melancon, L. (2010). 'Answering the call: Toward a history of proposals', *Journal of Technical Writing and Communication*, 40(1), 29–50.
Murphy, A. (2011). 'The top 100 technical communication books of 1991–2010', *Intercom*, 58(7), 6–9.
Norman, D. (1998). *The Design of Everyday Things*, New York, NY: Basic Books.
O'Keefe, S. S. and Pringle, A. S. (2012). *Content Strategy 101: Transform Technical Content into a Business Asset*, Research Triangle Park, NC: Scriptorium.
Orr, T. (2006). 'Introduction to the special issue: Insights from corpus linguistics for professional communication', *IEEE Transactions on Professional Communication*, 49(3), 213–16.

Padmanabhan, P. (2007). 'Technical communication outsourcing: The twelve driver framework tutorial', *IEEE Transactions on Professional Communication*, *50*(2), 109–20.

Poire, E. (2005). 'Managing translations: Achieving quality by coordinating all available resources', Proceedings of the 42nd Society for Technical Communication Annual Conference, Arlington, VA: Society for Technical Communication.

Price, J. and Korman, H. (1993). *How to Communicate Technical Information: A Handbook of Software and Hardware Documentation*, Redwood City, CA: Benjamin/Cummings.

Price, J. and Price, L. (2002). *Hot Text: Web Writing That Works*, Indianapolis, IN: New Riders.

Redish, J.C. (1993). 'Understanding readers', in C. M. Barnum and S. Carliner (eds), *Techniques for Technical Communicators*, New York: Macmillian, 15–41.

——(1995). 'Adding value as a technical communicator', *Technical Communication*, *42*(1), 26–39.

——(2012). *Letting Go of the Words: Writing Web Content That Works* (2nd edn), Waltham, MA: Morgan Kaufmann.

Rockley, A. (2002). *Managing Enterprise Content: A Unified Content Strategy*, Indianapolis, IN: New Riders.

Rude, C. and Eaton, A. (2010). *Technical Editing* (4th edn), Pearson Education. New York, NY: Longman.

Rutter, R. (1991). 'History, rhetoric, and humanism: Toward a more comprehensive definition of technical communication', *Journal of Technical Writing and Communication*, *21*(2), 133–53.

Schriver, K. (1997). *Dynamics of Document Design*, New York: John Wiley & Sons.

Society for Technical Communication (2012). *Defining Technical Communication*. Available at www.stc.org/about-stc/the-profession-all-about-technical-communication/defining-tc (accessed 18 November 2012).

Spinuzzi, D. (2003). *Tracing Genres through Organizations: A Sociocultural Approach to Information Design*, Cambridge, MA: MIT Press.

STC Certification Commission (2012a). *About Certification*. Available at http://stctc.org/showDocument-id-143.php (accessed 26 August 2013).

STC Certification Commission. (2012b). *CPTC Certification*. Available at www.stccert.org/?q=node/180 (accessed 17 November 2012).

Tarutz, J. (1992). *Technical Editing: The Practical Guide for Editors and Writers*, New York, NY: Perseus Books.

Tebeaux, E. (1997). *The Emergence of a Tradition: Technical Writing in the English Renaissance, 1475–1640*, Amityville, NY: Baywood Publishing Company.

Trice, H. M. and Beyer, J. M. (1993). *The Cultures of Work Organizations*, Englewood Cliffs, NJ: Prentice-Hall.

Turner, R. K. and Rainey, K. T. (2004). 'Certification in technical communication', *Technical Communication Quarterly*, *13*(2), 211–34.

van Buren, R. and Buehler, M. F. (1980). *The Levels of Edit*, Pasadena, CA: Jet Propulsion Laboratory.

Van der Geest, T. and Spyridakis, J. (2000). 'Developing heuristics for web communication: An introduction to this special issue', *Technical Communication*, *47*(3), 301–10.

Waite, R. (1997). 'Documenting complex processes: Educating the user and simplifying the task', *Journal of Computer Documentation*, *21*(1).

Weiss, E. (1991). *How to Write a Usable User Manual*, Phoenix, AZ: Oryx Press.

Welinske, J. (2011). *Developing User Assistance for Mobile Apps*, Seattle, WA: WritersUA.

Wikipedia. (2012). 'Society for Technical Communication'. Available at http://en.wikipedia.org/wiki/Society_for_Technical_Communication (accessed 17 November 2012).

Yu, H. (2009). 'Putting China's technical communication into historical context', *Technical Communication*, *56*(2), 99–110.

9
The complexities of communication in professional workplaces

Janet Holmes and Meredith Marra

Introduction

This chapter reviews research on the analysis of workplace communication. Alongside the home and education, the workplace is an important social domain in most people's lives and over the last 20 years sociolinguists have paid increasing attention to interaction in workplace contexts. As a result, a rich and diverse number of theoretical frameworks have developed for approaching the analysis of workplace communication, along with a range of contrasting and complementary methods of data collection. Within a broad sociolinguistic framework, this review describes some significant theoretical orientations, key issues and methodologies, and considers likely directions for future research in this area.

Workplace communication is a broad church covering a wide range of types of written and spoken interaction from large and small business meetings, through professional-client consultations and call-centre interactions, to water-cooler chat, letters, memos and email messages. Different researchers have made distinctions within this broad area, using more specific terms such as business discourse, institutional discourse and professional discourse, but there is little agreement on what exactly is included and excluded from each of these terms. Indeed some researchers use all three interchangeably.

The editors of this volume take a broad and inclusive perspective on what qualifies as professional communication, as does Gunnarsson (2009) who uses 'professional' as a synonym for 'paid-work-related', including skilled and unskilled employees. For Gunnarsson, professional communication contrasts with 'private discourse' (2009: 6); the term covers text and talk 'in professional contexts and for professional purposes' (2009: 5), including talk between professionals and with lay people. She identifies a number of distinguishing features, including the fact that workplace discourse entails domain-specific knowledge and skills, is goal-oriented, and contributes to the construction of the social order within a workplace unit (2009: 6–9). This broad definition is adopted in our discussion below, but it is worth noting the distinctions made by other researchers, since they offer useful alternative perspectives.

Where distinctions are made within the concept of workplace communication, the term *business discourse* tends to be defined in relation to the commercial sector (Koester 2010: 6). Bargiela-Chiappini *et al.* (2007: 3), for example, describe business discourse as 'how people communicate using talk or writing in commercial organizations'. Koester (2010: 5–6) further distinguishes between a narrow perspective that focuses 'only on company-to-company communication' examining how customers and suppliers do business, and a broader view that encompasses company-internal communication, including office talk and meetings. Drew and Heritage (1992: 3) in their seminal *Talk at Work*, define institutional interaction as 'task-related' interaction that involves 'at least one participant who represents a formal organization of some kind'; hence, for these researchers *institutional* interaction entails 'talk between professionals and lay persons' (1992: 3, see also Heritage and Clayman 2010). Sarangi and Roberts (1999: 15–19), by contrast, make a distinction between professional and institutional discourse. They use the term *professional discourse* for the language used by those with specific vocational skills and knowledge, such as lawyers, teachers and scientists. *Institutional discourse* refers to the linguistic features of regulatory practices such as record-keeping (e.g. student records, medical case notes, criminal records). The two types of discourse interact and influence each other in interesting ways, as Sarangi and Roberts discuss in some detail.

Although we have not always maintained such precise distinctions in our own research, they do offer the advantage of encouraging reflection on the similarities and differences between different kinds of workplace discourse, as well as the ways in which they interact. For example, as Sarangi and Roberts (1999: 16) indicate, examining how bottom-up professional interactions engage with top-down institutional rules and categories can illuminate how decision-making is constrained on the one hand, and how institutional change gradually comes about on the other. So, for instance, when an IT professional makes available an easy-to-understand 'translation' of IT technical jargon to the non-IT members of her company, she is challenging the institutional gate-keeping rules by de-mystifying an aspect of her professional discourse. This example also makes it clear that the distinction between professional and client or lay person is remarkably slippery. Moreover, given that many of the roles within commercial organisations are held by professionals of various kinds, business discourse can be regarded as overlapping with both professional discourse and institutional discourse. There seems no point in introducing yet another set of difficult-to-maintain distinctions. It is useful, however to be aware of the overlaps and ambiguities of these terms.

Our own research has focussed predominantly on spoken interaction in the workplace with the analysis of power and politeness, and the construction of professional and social identities, including gender and ethnic identities, as major areas of consideration. We draw on this for exemplification at a number of points in what follows.

Theorising workplace discourse

Workplace communication has been the focus of many different kinds of analysis, reflecting a range of theoretical approaches. Those of most interest here are unified by the researchers' commitment to taking account of contextual information in interpreting the data, and in some cases by their endeavours to relate macro-level socio-cultural constraints to the detail of micro-level face-to-face interaction.[1] We review them in an order that approximately reflects their historical emergence, though all are still very evident in current research on workplace communication. Each approach addresses slightly different goals and makes different assumptions about the role of context and the inherent differences between groups.

The earliest research adopted an **Interactional Sociolinguistics** (IS) framework, and focussed, perhaps not entirely coincidentally, on intercultural workplace interaction and the potential for workplace miscommunication. Gumperz's (1982: 173) 'gravy' analysis is a well-known example. In a British cafeteria, the influence of an Indian woman's native language resulted in strong stress and falling intonation on the word *gravy* when offering it to customers, prosodic contextualisation cues which led the customers to misinterpret her utterance as a peremptory, challenging assertion rather than an offer. More recently Celia Roberts and her colleagues (e.g. Roberts, Davies and Jupp 1992; see also Campbell and Roberts 2007) have further developed this approach, analysing in detail the linguistic and non-linguistic clues which account for how people *interpret* conversational interaction within its ethnographic context, and specifically in job and promotion interviews between immigrants and employers. Campbell and Roberts (2007: 243) argue that interviewers are looking for an effective synthesis of institutional and personal discourses in the production of an 'authentic self', an interesting example of the intersection of institutional and professional constraints alluded to above.

Politeness theory, in a modified form labelled '**neo-politeness theory**' by Holmes (2012; see also Mullany 2006) has also proved a useful framework for a good deal of research on workplace communication. Neo-politeness theory builds on the valuable analytical categories provided by Brown and Levinson's (1987) classic model, but extends the analysis beyond the utterance to encompass extended discourse and negotiated interaction, locating the analysis in specific social (workplace) contexts, and bringing contextual knowledge to bear in interpreting social meaning.

Adopting this framework, the Wellington Language in the Workplace Project (LWP) examined the dimensions of power and politeness in analysing the complex ways in which effective managers integrate transactional and relational objectives in white-collar professional organisations (Holmes and Stubbe 2003). The analysis illustrates how managers explicitly enact authority, giving directives and managing meetings, while also drawing attention to the importance of relationally oriented discourse, such as small talk, social talk, and humour in the workplace, as well as more explicitly face-oriented devices such as hedges and epistemic modals to soften directives.

Focussing on another aspect of relationally oriented workplace discourse, the LWP researchers also explored the value of the concept of the community of practice (Wenger 1998) in analysing workplace communication. The analyses indicate that recordings of workplace discourse are firmly embedded in their social and organisational context. Co-workers typically take a great deal for granted; they share assumptions and often extensive background knowledge and experiences as well, and they use the same jargon. They hold similar values and attitudes towards work and the objectives of their organisation. In other words, colleagues and team members in many workplaces constitute 'communities of practice' – groups who regularly engage with each other in the service of a joint enterprise, and who share a repertoire of resources that enables them to communicate in a kind of verbal shorthand that is often difficult for outsiders to penetrate.

The LWP research sparked a good deal more work in the area, including research that further explored the value of the concept of community of practice in analysing workplace communication (Angouri 2007; Mullany 2007; Chan 2008; Schnurr 2009; Murata 2010; Ladegaard 2011). These researchers have analysed discourse in a wide range of different professional and cultural contexts, from IT companies, through multinational companies and more blue-collar environments. The research in this category typically demonstrates the context-bound nature of workplace interactions, and the influence of a particular community's norms on the interaction amongst that group.

Orienting to another of the weaknesses of canonical Politeness theory, Spencer-Oatey (2000, 2008) developed **Rapport Theory**, a framework that focuses on 'the use of language to promote, maintain or threaten harmonious social relations' (2008: 4), and which aims to encompass a broader cultural framework than Politeness theory. The term 'rapport' provides an interactionally-oriented alternative to the term 'face', which 'seems to focus on concerns for self' (2008: 4), taking little account of the addressee. Rapport Theory includes considerations of face, which (like Brown and Levinson 1987; Leech 1983, and others) Spencer-Oatey considers a universal phenomenon. However, importantly, the theory also includes the concepts of sociality rights and obligations, which take account of the societal expectations of many Asian cultures. Using this approach, Spencer-Oatey and Xing (2003) identified and analysed misunderstandings in meetings between British and Chinese business people, demonstrating the extent to which assumptions about what was considered appropriate attention to sociality rights and obligations differed between members of the two groups. In particular, the British hosts did not accurately understand the relationship between the job titles and roles of different members of the Chinese delegation, and thus did not pay sufficient respect to some from the Chinese perspective. Moreover, they did not pay enough attention to ceremonial meeting conventions, such as a formal welcome and formal allocation of speaking turns, which were considered very important by the Chinese. The analysis emphasises the importance of sociality rights as well as the notion of 'group face', concepts that have proved fruitful in subsequent research within the Rapport Theory framework.

With its 'overtly political agenda' (Kress 1990: 84–85), **Critical Discourse Analysis** (CDA) challenges the hierarchies that exist in workplace contexts, aiming to identify the ways in which power and dominance are produced and reproduced in social practice through the discourse structures of everyday interactions. This theoretical approach is thus well positioned to explore the relationship between institutional constraints and the enactment of professional identity in interaction alluded to above. As outlined by Fairclough (1995, 2003), CDA examines how dominant 'discourses' gradually become culturally entrenched as norms within given social or professional contexts through mundane linguistic interactions. Power is treated as 'a systemic characteristic' (Fletcher 1999: 16), a transformative and non-static feature of interaction (Wodak 1996, 1999; Blommaert 2005). CDA provides a framework to explore ways in which systemic power is constructed and reinforced in interaction, to identify how the dominant group determines meaning, and, more specifically, to describe the processes by which the more powerful person in an interaction typically gets to define the purpose or significance of the interaction and to influence the direction in which it develops. The analyst aims to examine discursive evidence of the covert exercise of power, identifying the unobtrusive, 'naturalised' conversational strategies through which power relations are constructed and reinforced in everyday, unremarkable, workplace interactions (cf. Fairclough 1992).

A good example of how such an approach has been applied to workplace data is provided by Koller (2004), who made use of the CDA lens in her analysis of metaphors in the business world. Her particular interest was the way in which women managers were described in texts (e.g. as corporate killers and warriors) and her analysis highlights a hegemonic masculinity which she claims undergirds business discourse. Her data comprises business magazine articles, and she made use of corpora that allowed her to add quantitative components to her analysis alongside the qualitative interpretations that are more typical of workplace discourse research.

Post-structural theory has also been productively used to examine workplace communication, and especially the relevance of gender identities in professional contexts (Baxter 2006, 2008, 2010; Baxter and Wallace 2009; Cameron 2009). Key principles of this approach are a view of language as social practice, a performative approach to the analysis of aspects of social

115

identity and a concern with power relations in interaction. Using the term 'communicative identities', and focussing in particular on women leaders, Baxter (2006) emphasises the role of the subject as agent of her own performances: social identities are negotiated and constructed through social interactions and practices which shape power relations and meaning. The subject positions of speakers are open to redefinition and being continuously reconstructed through discourse. They are 'fluid, multiple and multi-layered, shifting and often contradictory' (Baxter 2006: xvii).

Using this framework, Baxter has examined communication in a number of different workplace contexts, including business meetings in a multi-national corporation, secondary school classroom discourse, and talk between blue collar workers on a building site (Baxter and Wallace 2009). Like Holmes (2006), Mullany (2007) and Schnurr (2009), she demonstrates that, because they are constantly contending with negative stereotypes and expectations, powerful women not only have to manage the demands that all business leaders face in juggling transactional and relational goals, but they also have to undertake a kind of 'interactional shitwork' (Fishman 1983), i.e. additional conversational work 'to sustain a credible identity as a leader' (Baxter 2010: 113). On a building site, by contrast, talk functioned not only to construct a very masculine identity, but also a very tight-knit, in-group professional identity, which served as a flexible means of 'doing power' over others, and as a form of resistance against more powerful social groups (Baxter and Wallace 2009).

All these frameworks are compatible with a **social constructionist approach**, a theoretical perspective adopted by many researchers particularly in the analysis of workplace identities. Our LWP research illustrates how people draw on a range of linguistic and pragmatic resources to construct particular kinds of leadership identity (Holmes, Marra and Vine 2011; Holmes and Marra 2011), including how they integrate potentially conflicting components of different aspects of their social identity, such as femininity and authority, or mateship and control. Some leaders, for instance, tell hero stories (Olsson 2000; Jackson and Parry 2001), explicitly constructing themselves as decisive leaders who transformed a situation, or even the organisation they work in. Some use amusing anecdotes to address relational needs after a display of overt power. Discourse analysis of workplace narratives provides interesting insights into how exactly their complex professional identities are accomplished (Holmes 2005a; Holmes and Marra 2005). Analysing ways of speaking in ethnically different workplaces, Holmes, Marra and Vine (2011) demonstrate similarities and differences in the ways in which Māori and Pākehā leaders make use of pragmatic, discourse and linguistic resources to construct ethnically and professionally appropriate leadership identities. Humour as a rich pragmatic resource has been analysed by Schnurr (2009) who demonstrates the range of contrasting ways in which female and male leaders construct power in different communities of practice. Similarly, using a social constructionist approach, Mullany (2006, 2007) has analysed gendered talk in British corporations, health care, and media settings. And in a rugby team environment, Wilson (2011) illustrates the different ways in which swearing contributes to the negotiation of different facets of the leadership role of the coach, boss, mentor, motivator and mate at different points in the lead up to a match. These varied examples indicate some of the diverse ways in which research within a social constructionist framework has deepened our understanding of the complexities of professional communication.

This range of theoretical approaches reflects the different questions and assumptions that workplace communication researchers bring to their analysis. An equally important concern is a match between theoretical approach and methodological design, as discussed in the next section.

Data and methodologies

Researchers in the field of workplace communication have used a variety of methodologies for collecting data, including multi-method approaches combining two or more different data-gathering strategies. This data includes both written and spoken workplace communication from a wide range of countries and contexts.

Written data has included questionnaires and surveys (e.g. Lønsmann 2011; Kingsley 2010; Gunnarsson 2009), providing self-reported information from workplace participants about their workplace interactions. **Questionnaires** have been used to gather data about reported usage and attitudes to different types of workplace communication. For example, examining the functions for which people used email at work, Waldvogel's questionnaire (2005) collected information about people's preference for different types of communication (face-to-face, phone, email) in relation to such factors as the sensitivity of the topic and their relationship to the addressee. **Survey research** focussed on business writing is discussed in Bargiela-Chiappini, Nickerson and Planken (2007: 181). They outline surveys of business writing practices by a number of researchers, including multiple language use in multilingual contexts (e.g. Vandermeeren 1999) and the use of English by non-native speakers (e.g. Nickerson 2000). Their useful summary also highlights the relevance of debates surrounding English as a Lingua Franca within the context of business discourse, a concept explored by Louhiala-Salminen and colleagues (2005) using the concept of Business English as a Lingua Franca (BELF).

In addition to these written forms of data collection, some researchers also include **interviews** in their design to further explore information provided by their participants. This has proved a particularly valuable means of eliciting data when considering explicit and implicit language policies, especially in multilingual workplaces (Kingsley 2010; de Bres 2008; Gunnarsson 2010). For these researchers, the goal is often to establish the norms for language practices using survey techniques and questionnaires, with follow-up interviews used to probe particular communication strategies and potential communication issues in more depth.

In fact, interviews are frequently used in a wide range of research on workplace communication, with or without supporting written material. Gunnarsson's (2010) research team interviewed a range of employees in different roles in a Swedish hospital (doctors, nurses, cleaners), and in a large company (office workers, factory workers) as one component in their research on the organisational structure of talk at work. This data provided additional insights into how people construct their workplace identity, a theme also explored by Mullany (2007), Schnurr (2009) and Baxter (2010), for example, all of whom used interviews to elicit self-report accounts of how people 'do leadership' in different organisations.

Similarly, interviews have been used to complement, triangulate, and help interpret data collected using other methods, notably recordings of naturalistic workplace talk (e.g. Schnurr 2009, Holmes et al. 2011; Angouri 2007). In general, these researchers have used semi-structured interview schedules with a list of open questions, which allow them to be responsive to the specific work communication context of the interviewee. As an example, in our own research, we have asked questions such as the following:

- How important are communication skills in this job/industry?
- Are there any really effective communicators in this company/team? Why do you consider them to be effective?
- Is there a formal policy on language use at work?
- Is there an informal policy on language use at work?

- Is it okay to use a language other than English at work?
- Can you remember any instances where the use of English/another language has been (a) beneficial (b) problematic?

The responses to these questions provide useful information on how participants perceive the communicative norms of their workplaces. Our follow-up recordings of workplace interaction indicate the extent to which perceptions match practice. The questions are aimed at contributing to the ethnographic information we collect to supplement our recordings.

Ethnographic approaches to the study of workplace communication are also generally used to complement other methods, and to validate or 'warrant' (Swann 2002; Cameron 2009) particular interpretations of the data. Participant observation, for example, often conducted over a substantial time period, can provide useful access to insider meanings and interpretations (Swann and Maybin 2008: 24; Johnstone 2001). Typically the researchers will be familiar at a general level with the kind of workplace context in which they are collecting data, and so the challenge is firstly to make the familiar more strange (Rampton 2007). This can involve identifying their taken-for-granted assumptions about normal ways of communicating in professional business settings so that they can provide a rich, informative 'thick' (Geertz 1973; Sarangi 2009) ethnographic description, usually recorded in the form of field-notes. Then, most importantly, the ethnographer must identify the specific features of the particular community in which they are working, noting the distinctive communicative norms, jargon, workplace social practices, and appropriate ways of interacting in different workplace contexts within the larger organisation. In many organisations, for example, researchers have found that important business communication often takes place around the edges of formal events, before the meetings start, for example, at morning tea or Friday evening drinks (Holmes *et al.* 2011; Fletcher 2011).

The participant observer in our LWP research was generally selected to match as far as possible the social characteristics of the participants themselves. While observing and making notes on the workplace routines, spaces, artifacts, and comings and goings, s/he would also undertake everyday tasks such as copying material, making coffee and doing errands. The goal was to fade into the background and minimise the impact of the research on the organisation's business. This generally proved a very successful approach to collecting ethnographic material.

But by far the most common method currently used for collecting workplace discourse follows the inspirational lead of the late Michael Clyne (1994) who pioneered recordings of naturally occurring talk in a multicultural Melbourne factory. Our own LWP methodology developed this approach, originally seeking ways of reducing the effect of the 'observer's paradox' (Labov 1972), in particular. The goals of the research are first negotiated with workplace participants who become collaborators, research partners and consultants. Then, typically, volunteers use small individual recorders to collect a range of their everyday work interactions over a period of two to three weeks. In other words, the participants themselves control the data collection in order to obtain material that is as little affected by the recording process as possible. Where possible we also video-record workplace meetings: the video cameras are set up in the corners of the meeting room before anyone arrives, and we disappear till the meetings are over. These procedures help reduce the effects of the observer's paradox, by removing intrusive observers from the workplace context. Participants are obviously conscious of the cameras initially, as illustrated in this excerpt from a managers' meeting.

Example 1[2]

Context: A meeting of the senior managers group at Company S. Joel is on a phone link.

1	Shaun:	I get you two
2		no nah I get you and Dean mixed up quite often mm
3	Chester:	fuck off Shaun
4		[laughter] //[laughter]\
5	Chester:	/[laughs]: for the record:\\
6		[laughter]
7	Neil:	... Joel we're taping the session
8		so we were trying to keep all four letter words out
9		but that //hasn't really worked\
10	Victor:	/[laughs]\\
11		[laughter throughout next turns]
12	Shaun:	Chester was toning down his normal er
13	Victor:	no they insist on us having //+ the normal meetings\
14	Neil:	/yeah yeah\\ (yeah) yeah
15	Chester:	oh right
16	Neil:	it's two minutes thirty seconds into the
17		discussion + they'll be thinking oh that's a record

Here Neil remonstrates, albeit tongue-in-cheek, about the swearing *we were trying to keep all four letter words out* (line 8), Shaun comments that Chester's remark was actually toned down from his normal style (line 12), while Victor humorously challenges his suggestion that they should behave in a way that is not normal *they insist on us having the normal meetings* (line 13). Victor is here referring to our practice of reassuring people that they don't have to change their interactional style because they are being recorded. Neil reinforces this interpretation when he jokes that they had managed to get *two minutes thirty seconds into the discussion* (line 16) before a swear word had occurred. In fact, there is abundant evidence in our recordings that participants soon forgot about the cameras, especially after the first meeting.

Using this methodological approach, we have recorded workplace interaction in a wide range of New Zealand workplaces, including government departments, commercial organisations, small businesses, factories, eldercare facilities and hospital wards. Many other researchers have adopted this methodology, and used it to study workplace communication in banks in Scandinavia (Gunnarsson 2010), engineering companies in the EU (Angouri 2007), and family businesses in Hong Kong (Chan 2008), among other workplace sites. In our research it has proved especially useful in recording meetings for detailed analysis of communicative strategies, including those used in intercultural communication contexts (Holmes *et al.* 2011; see Bargiela-Chiappini and Harris 1997, Spencer-Oatey and Xing 2003 for further examples).

Analytic approaches

Whether the data is written or spoken, self-reported or naturalistic, there is a considerable range of analytic approaches from which to choose. Some researchers are interested in the micro-level detail of the sequencing and joint negotiation of interactions (e.g. Conversation Analysis[3]), some are interested in themes that emerge from the data (e.g. making use of coding software such as NVivo or EXMAraLDA), and some are committed to providing quantitative measures of certain features (e.g. corpus approaches). Because of the range used by workplace communication researchers, we cannot possibly do justice to them all. Instead we choose just two methods of analysis as illustration, describing the way in which researchers consider their theoretical perspective, data collection methods and analytic approaches when addressing their research questions.

Focussing on how social meaning is conveyed and inferred in particular social contexts, an **Interactional Sociolinguistics** framework has proved particularly valuable in studies of cross-cultural workplace communication (Roberts *et al.* 1992), and the ways in which workplace identities are constructed (Vine *et al.* 2008; Mullany 2007; Schnurr 2009). This approach is often valuably enriched with ethnographic observations and interviews that contribute to the interpretation of the data. IS has been described as having an 'eclectic toolbox' for analysis (Bailey 2008: 2317) and identifying discourse features, lexical items, and grammatical strategies which instantiate power, tools which could be found in other approaches. What distinguishes IS is the identification of contextualisation cues – linguistic and discourse features that index contextual information, creating a local practice through which they signal a speaker's stance in interaction and construct an interpretive frame (Gumperz 1982, 1999; Schiffrin 2003).

Example 2 demonstrates ethnic humour in a New Zealand organisation with a conscious orientation to Māori cultural norms and goals. Encouraged by Daniel, the Māori CEO, the meeting members poke fun at Pākehā (New Zealanders with European ancestry) who in the current political climate see strategic advantage in getting on-side with Māori, and specifically with their new Māori neighbours in well-to-do suburbs.

Example 2

Context: Management meeting at Company K.

```
1    Caleb:     multimillion dollar properties up //( )\
2    Daniel:    /[laughs]\\ oh they'll have a happy weekend
3               then won't they
4    Hari:      yeah
5    Daniel:    [laughs]: the neighbours hey:
6    Caleb:     //[laughs]\
7    Hari:      /that's good\\ they love it eh
8    Daniel:    [laughs]: yeah: I bet they love it
9    Hari:      they love they love that stuff
10              //that Māori dynamic\
11   Daniel:    /that cultural colour\\
12   Hari:      yeah
13   Hinerau:   [name] was //saying that they've been\
14   Hari:      /the property values go up\\
15   Hinerau:   coming round to offer offer what they can do
16              whether they can bake or
17   Daniel:    //[laughs] [laughs]: yeah yeah choice:\
18   Hari:      /yeah oh yeah yeah straight up eh\\
19              Māori is the new black eh Caleb?
20   Caleb:     yeah it is
21              [laughter]
```

| 22 | it is it is the new black bro [laughs] |
| 23 | [laughter] |

It will be apparent that interpreting the social meaning of this short excerpt requires extensive local contextual knowledge. Drawing on shared knowledge of covert racism, Daniel makes explicit fun of rich Pākehā who find they have new Māori neighbours: *they'll have a happy weekend then ... I bet they love it ... that cultural colour* (lines 2–3, 8, 11). Hari's comment that *the property values go up* (line 14) is especially telling since the traditional cultural stereotype entails depressed house prices in Māori neighbourhoods. Hari follows this up with another witty comment, using a rich metaphor, *Māori is the new black eh Caleb* (line 19). The metaphor conveys many levels of meaning: using a well-known phrase referring to the current fashionability of the colour black in the clothing industry, it also subtly references black power movements, and ironically satirises the fact that Māori people, with skin colour ranging from light to dark brown, are nonetheless perceived and labelled as 'black' by many Pākehā. The contributors in this example are all Māori, with Daniel leading the humour and encouraging his team in mocking Pākehā hypocrisy.

The example is marked discursively as in-group Māori interaction through features such as the pragmatic tag *eh* (lines 7, 18, 19), a rapidly spreading feature of New Zealand English which has its origins in Māori interaction, and which is strongly associated with Māori ethnicity (Stubbe and Holmes 2000; Meyerhoff 1994; Vine and Marra 2008), as well as the address term *bro*, which is also associated with Polynesian identity (Bell 2000). The use of subversive humour, metaphor, as well as repetition (evident in lines 7, 8, 9 and lines 19, 22) are further features that have been identified as characterising Māori discourse (Benton 1996; Metge 1995). And the syntactic apposition evident in Daniel's comment, *they'll have a happy weekend then won't they ... the neighbours*, also tends to characterise Māori English discourse (Thornton 1985).

The group thus uses a range of discursive strategies and linguistic features to index ethnicity and to construct and maintain solidarity between members of the organisation. This analysis of the social meanings conveyed clearly draws on the researchers' familiarity with the wider social and cultural context in which it was produced, and it will also be apparent that the interpretation is immeasurably enriched by extensive ethnographic observation and interaction with the workplace participants over a protracted period.

The power and status differences that are evident in the analysis above are among a number of features that can take centre stage in an analysis using IS. **CDA**[4] by contrast takes power asymmetries as its explicit focus, aiming to encourage positive social change by unearthing accepted power misuse and abuse. As an analytic lens it thus provides an interesting and stimulating framework for analysing workplace interaction. Many workplaces are structured hierarchically with power relationships constantly constructed and reconstructed in the everyday interactions that constitute the 'business' of organisations. A CDA approach encourages the analyst to look for systemic reasons for participants' use of particular discourse strategies in particular contexts. Power is enacted discursively both through overt strategies such as directives (whether hedged or not), and meeting management stratagems, such as agenda management, turn-allocation and summarising, as well as in more covert ways through subtle appeals to taken-for-granted assumptions about 'the way we do things round here'. It is also worth paying attention, however, to what is achieved by less powerful participants in an interaction in responding to the subtle and not-so-subtle exercise of power by superiors. In any particular interaction, different participants may have different kinds of power, which they make use of in different and often subtle ways in particular contexts (cf. Tannen 1993), through subversive comments or ironic humour, for example (Holmes and Marra 2002). In what follows, we demonstrate some of the more subtle, systemic ways in which power is constructed in workplace interaction.

In most of the workplaces in our data, the most senior person chaired regular meetings of their section or team. In some, however, the chair rotated at each meeting. In such cases, conflicts of authority sometimes arose between the apparent authority of the chair of the meeting, and the institutional status of the manager. The resolution of such an impasse indicated in every case the pervasive and ultimate authority of the most senior person in the organisational hierarchy. Typically, in such cases, the most senior manager needed to merely indicate, sometimes very subtly, that they were unhappy with a decision, or with the direction the discussion was taking. In example 3, Dudley, a senior manager, signals that he is not happy with the suggestion made by Barry who is chairing the meeting.

Example 3

Context: Regular meeting of project team in a commercial organisation. Barry is the Chair. Dudley is the most senior person present.

```
1  Barry:    so soon after that if not sort of at the tail end of that Callum should
2            start to kick in to that those discussions in terms of //+\ =
3  Dudley:   /[inhales]\\
4  Barry:    = scoping it is that how you I mean //(   )\ =
5  Dudley:   /yeah I [exhales]\\ =
6  Barry:    = how to plug Callum in Call-Callum hasn't been really involved
7            in this at all //um\
8  Dudley:   /no and\\ I guess my concern is how does this thing get started
9            because I think it's all very well to to talk about saying. ...
```

The project team is planning the steps in the next phase of their project. Barry proposes that when they reach a particular stage Callum, another member of the project team, should be allocated the task of scoping the project. At this point, Dudley, who rarely contributes explicitly to the team's discussions, simply draws in his breath (line 3). Barry responds by first re-orienting his comment specifically to Dudley *is that how you I mean* (line 4), and then providing a rationale for his suggestion, namely it is time for Callum to get involved in the project (lines 6–7). Using a hedge *I guess my concern is* and a passive construction which avoids specifying an agent *how does this thing get started* (line 8), Dudley expresses his disagreement with Barry's proposal to involve Callum. In what follows, Dudley's view prevails. This demonstrates the institutional authority that Dudley is claiming, despite the fact that Barry is charged with the responsibility of managing this project and team meeting, including making decisions about which staff should undertake any particular task.

In another organisation, the manager regularly brought digressions from the agenda to a close with her humorous stock phrase 'moving right along', even when the project manager was running the meeting. Her regular use of this phrase when chairing meetings meant that when she was not in the chair it was immediately recognised as a signal that she considered a digression had gone on long enough. Such strategies for exercising control in the workplace often develop gradually over time, and consequently managers can assert power and influence with a minimum of effort and overt display. This systemic exercise of power is constructed and reinforced in everyday workplace interactions. A CDA approach allows the analyst to make explicit the taken-for-granted assumptions that are at play about who controls interaction and decisions.

These are just two analytic approaches that are used within workplace discourse. In the brief analysis provided it will also be clear that there is some overlap in the features that are described, despite a different orientation to the data (the first orienting to more socio-cultural description and explanation, and the second adopting a more critical stance, drawing on power as a fundamental analytical dimension). An exercise that carried out multiple analyses of the same piece of workplace data is described in Stubbe *et al.* (2003). The conclusion that was reached there indicates the important decision that analysts make when choosing their approach (2003: 380):

> Each approach therefore provides a slightly different lens with which to examine the same interaction, highlighting different aspects or dimensions of its key features. These are not necessarily in conflict with one another (though in some cases the analyses and/or the theoretical assumptions underlying them are difficult to reconcile); rather, they are complementary in many ways, with each approach capable of generating its own useful insights into what is going on in the interaction, with the proviso that the framework adopted needs to be a good match for the research questions being asked.

Future directions

There is already a wealth of material on professional communication, and the field of workplace discourse continues to grow, almost exponentially. In this final section, we reflect on potential future directions for research, identifying those areas that we anticipate will be influential in this respect.

To date, workplace research has been dominated by a focus on organisations in which English is spoken. Increasingly, however, interest is developing in multilingual business settings and in workplace talk expressed in languages other than English. This emerging focus is led by a number of key research groups, notably those at the University of Geneva (e.g. Filliettaz *et al.* 2008), University of Hamburg (Meyer and Apfelbaum 2010), the Scandinavian academics at Roskilde University (e.g. Lønsmann 2011; Fabricius 2012), Helsinki University (Louhiala-Salminen *et al.* 2005), Uppsala University (e.g. Gunnarsson 2009), and the DYLAN group, which investigates diversity in language use across Europe (e.g. Lüdi *et al.* 2010). The benefit that these researchers bring (alongside the obvious advantage of broadening the scope of the field) is to join together research traditions that have contributed to different literatures on workplace talk based on the language of publication. As those working in English-dominant contexts increasingly recognise the relevance of globalisation and internationalisation (see Blommaert 2010), the broadening of the field is inevitable and offers great potential for dialogue across countries and languages.

Similarly there have been calls for greater dialogue between workplace discourse researchers and those who teach business talk (e.g. Bremner 2010; Bowles 2006). This is a result of the ongoing identification of mismatches between what is being taught and the findings of workplace discourse researchers (e.g. Williams 1988; Chan 2009). Analyses of workplace talk, such as the examples provided in this chapter, offer rich material demonstrating the importance of contextual sensitivity in understanding and interpreting workplace discourse. Clearly, the gap between interactional analysis and teaching materials can be bridged where desirable. It is encouraging to note that researchers and practitioners alike see the benefit of increased interaction and engagement across these disciplines.

One area in which researchers have a particular contribution to make is in the analysis of more than just the linguistic features of workplace interaction. Multimodal discourse analysis offers new insights to enrich our interpretations of workplace talk (see Norris and Jones 2005;

Norris 2011), whether it is in the relevance of the mimicry of gesture for creating shared understanding and rapport in job interviews (e.g. Kusmierczyk 2012) or the way in which vocational educators make use of movement in their teaching practice during apprenticeships (Filliettaz and Losa 2012). This new and exciting area of discourse analysis offers an obvious and welcome extension to workplace discourse analysis.

Clearly communication in professional contexts is anything but straightforward; it is without doubt a complex research area. As the discussion in the introduction to this chapter indicated, even the definition and scope of what counts as professional communication is subject to debate. In this review we have indicated many other factors that contribute to the complexity of workplace discourse research, from the language(s) spoken, to differences based on the industry in which people work, to the different kinds of 'culture' that influence interactions (team, workplace, national, etc). Given the range of factors contributing to workplace talk, it is hardly surprising that the questions researchers are asking are many and varied. In exploring these questions, researchers make use of theoretical stances, data collection techniques, and analytic frameworks that all contribute to the way in which we understand professional communication in its various forms. The subtle and yet important complexities identified in the analysis of professional communication allow us not only to identify areas of potential conflict, but also to appreciate the remarkable success and effectiveness of most workplace communication.

Related topics

business communication; management communication; corporate communication; communities of practice

Key readings

Candlin, C. N. and Sarangi, S. (eds) (2011). *Handbook of Communication in Organisations and Professions* [HAL 3], Berlin: Mouton de Gruyter. (This recent edited collection highlights the current range of applied linguistic research on professional communication.)
Drew, P. and Heritage, J. (eds) (1992). *Talk at Work: Interaction in Institutional Settings*, Cambridge University Press, Cambridge. (This is a seminal collection of studies investigating interaction at work using a Conversation Analysis approach.)
Gunnarsson, B.-L. (2009). *Professional Discourse*, London: Continuum. (Gunnarsson's book exemplifies the approach of Scandinavian researchers and usefully includes a focus on written material.)
Holmes, J. and Stubbe, M. (2003). *Power and Politeness in the Workplace*, London: Pearson. (This book explores various aspects of spoken workplace discourse as investigated by the Wellington Language in the Workplace team using naturalistic data.)
Sarangi, S. and Roberts, C. (eds) (1999). *Talk, Work and Institutional Order: Discourse in Medical, Mediation and Management Settings*, Berlin: Mouton de Gruyter. (This important collection for the field provides a good overview of the scope of the field of workplace discourse.)

Notes

1 There is an extremely fruitful body of research that adopts either a stronger or weaker view of Conversation Analysis (CA) for approaching workplace talk, normally under the heading of institutional interactions as described earlier (see, for example, Heritage and Clayman 2010, Svennevig 2008, Richards 2011 and the range of articles in Drew and Heritage 1992). In terms of approach, CA is normally treated as belonging to a category distinct from other discourse approaches because of theoretical assumptions, traditions and data sources (Wooffitt 2005). For these reasons, we have not discussed CA research in detail in this chapter.

2 Transcription conventions:

[ ] : :	Paralinguistic and editorial information in square brackets; colons indicate start and end.
...	Section of transcript missing
+	untimed pause of approximately one second
//here\	Overlapping talk. Double slashes indicate beginning and end.
/here\\	
( )	Untranscribable talk
(yeah)	Transcriber's best guess at an unclear utterance
=	Turn continues
=	

All names are pseudonyms, and any identifying material has been removed.
3 See note 1 above.
4 This section draws on Holmes (2005b).

Bibliography

Angouri, Jo (2007). 'Language in the workplace: A multi-method study of communicative activity in seven multinational companies situated in Europe', PhD thesis, Colchester: University of Essex.

Bailey, Benjamin (2008). 'Interactional sociolinguistics', *International Encyclopedia of Communication*, 59.

Bargiela-Chiappini, Francesca and Harris, Sandra (1997). *Managing Language: The Discourse of Corporate Meetings*, Amsterdam: John Benjamins.

Bargiela-Chiappini, Francesca, Nickerson, Catherine and Planken, Brigitte (2007). *Business Discourse*, New York: Palgrave Macmillan.

Baxter, J. (2006) *Speaking Out in Public Contexts*, Basingstoke: Palgrave.

——(2008). 'Is it all tough talking at the top? A post-structuralist analysis of the construction of gendered speaker identities of British business leaders within interview narratives', *Gender and Language*, 2(2), 197–222.

——(2010). *The Language of Female Leadership*, London: Palgrave Macmillan.

Baxter, Judith and Wallace, Kieran (2009). 'Outside in-group and out-group identities? Constructing male solidarity and female exclusion in UK builders' talk', *Discourse and Society*, 20(4), 411–29.

Bell, Allan (2000). 'Maori and Pakeha English: A case study', in Allan Bell and Koenraad Kuiper (eds) *New Zealand English*, (pp. 221–48), Wellington: Victoria University Press.

Benton, Richard A. (1996). 'Tokens and tokenism, models and metaphors: Facilitating the reacquisition of Te Reo Māori in the 1990s', Presentation to Applied Linguistics Association of New Zealand Research Seminar, 2 August 1996.

Blommaert, Jan (2005). *Discourse: A Critical Introduction*, Cambridge: Cambridge University Press.

——(2010). *The Sociolinguistics of Globalisation*, Cambridge: Cambridge University Press.

Bowles, H. (2006). 'Bridging the gap between conversation analysis and ESP – an applied study of the opening sequences of NS and NNS service telephone calls', *English for Specific Purposes*, 25, 332–57.

Bremner, S. (2010). 'Collaborative writing: Bridging the gap between the textbook and the workplace', *English for Specific Purposes*, 29, 121–32.

Brown, Penelope and Levinson, Stephen C. (1987). *Politeness: Some Universals in Language Usage*, Cambridge: Cambridge University Press. [Originally published in 1978.]

Cameron, D. (2009). 'Theoretical issues for the study of gender and spoken interaction', in P. Pichler and E. M. Eppler (eds), *Gender and Spoken Interaction* (pp. 1–17), London: Palgrave Macmillan.

Campbell, Sarah and Roberts, Celia (2007). 'Migration, ethnicity and competing discourses in the job interview: Synthesizing the institutional and personal', *Discourse and Society*, 18(3), 243–71.

Chan, Angela (2008). 'Meeting openings and closings in a Hong Kong company', in Hao Sun and Dániel Z. Kádár (eds), *It's the Dragon's Turn: Chinese Institutional Discourse(s)* (pp. 181–229), Bern: Peter Lang.

Chan, Clarice (2009). 'Forging a link between research and pedagogy: A holisitic framework for evaluating business English materials', *English for Specific Purposes*, 28(2), 126–36.

Clyne, Michael (1994). *Inter-cultural Communication at Work*, Cambridge: Cambridge University Press.

de Bres, Julia (2008). 'Planning for tolerability: Promoting positive attitudes and behaviours towards the Māori language among non-Māori New Zealanders', Unpublished PhD thesis: Victoria University of Wellington.

Drew, Paul and Heritage, John (eds) (1992). *Talk at Work: Interaction in Institutional Settings*, Cambridge: Cambridge University Press.

Fabricius, Anne H. (2012). 'The international academic at the crossroads: Between the local and the international at the university', Paper presented at Sociolinguistics Symposium 9, Berlin, 21–24 August 2012.

Fairclough, Norman (1992). *Discourse and Social Change*, Cambridge: Polity Press.

——(1995). *Critical Discourse Analysis*, London: Longman.

——(2003). *Analyzing Discourse: Textual Analysis for Social Research*, London: Routledge.

Filliettaz, L., de Saint-Georges, I. and Duc, B. (2008). *'Vos mains sont intelligentes!': Interactions en formation professionnelle initiale*, Geneva, Université de Genève: Cahiers de la section des sciences de l'éducation, 117.

Filliettaz, L. and Losa, S. (2012). 'Gaining social legitimacy in and across contexts: Apprenticeship in a "dual" training system', Paper presented at Sociolinguistics Symposium 9, Berlin, 21–24 August 2012.

Fishman, Pamela M. (1983). 'Interaction: The work women do', in Barrie Thorne, Cheris Kramarae and Nancy Henley (eds), *Language, Gender and Society* (pp. 89–101), Cambridge, MA: Newbury House.

Fletcher, Jeanette Rae (2011). 'The role of discourse in establishing an enabling context for organizational knowledge creation: An ethnographic study', Unpublished PhD thesis, Victoria University of Wellington, New Zealand.

Fletcher, Joyce K. (1999). *Disappearing Acts: Gender, Power, and Relational Practice at Work*, Cambridge, MA: MIT Press.

Geertz, Clifford (1973). 'Thick description: Towards an interpretive theory of culture', in Clifford Geertz (ed.) *The Interpretation of Cultures* (pp. 3–30), New York: Basic Books.

Gumperz, John (1982). *Discourse Strategies*, Cambridge: Cambridge University Press.

——(1999). 'On interactional sociolinguistic method', in S. Sarangi and C. Roberts (eds), *Talk, Work and Institutional Order: Discourse in Medical, Mediation and Management Settings* (pp. 453–71), Berlin: Mouton deGruyter.

Gunnarsson, Britt-Louise (2009). *Professional Discourse*, London: Continuum.

——2010. 'Multilingualism within transnational companies: An analysis of company policy and practice in a diversity perspective', in H. Kelly-Holmes and G. Mautner (eds), *Language and the Market* (pp. 171–84), Basingstoke and New York: Palgrave Macmillan (Language and Globalization series).

Heritage, John and Clayman, Steven (2010). *Talk in Action: Interactions, Identities and Institutions*, Oxford: Blackwell.

Holmes, Janet (2005a). 'Story-telling at work: A complex discursive resource for integrating personal, professional and social identities', *Discourse Studies*, 7(6), 671–700.

——(2005b). 'Power and discourse at work: Is gender relevant?' in Michelle Lazar (ed.), *Feminist Critical Discourse Analysis* (pp. 31–60), London: Palgrave.

——(2006). *Gendered Talk at Work: Constructing Social Identity Through Workplace Interaction*, Malden, MA: Blackwell.

——(2012). 'Politeness in intercultural discourse and communication', in Christina Bratt Paulston, Scott F. Kiesling and Elizabeth S. Rangel (eds), *The Handbook of Intercultural Discourse and Communication* (pp. 205–28), Oxford: Wiley-Blackwell.

Holmes, Janet and Marra, Meredith (2002). 'Over the edge? Subversive humour between colleagues and friends', *Humor*, 15(1), 65–87.

——2005. 'Narrative and the construction of professional identity in the workplace', in Joanna Thornborrow and Jennifer Coates (eds), *The Sociolinguistics of Narrative* (pp. 193–213), Amsterdam: John Benjamins.

——2011. 'Leadership discourse in a Māori workplace: Negotiating gender, ethnicity, and leadership at work', *Gender & Language*, 5(2), 317–42.

Holmes, Janet, Marra, Meredith and Vine, Bernadette (2011). *Leadership, Discourse, and Ethnicity*, Oxford: Oxford University Press.

Holmes, Janet and Stubbe, Maria (2003). *Power and Politeness in the Workplace*, London: Pearson.

Jackson, Brad and Parry, Ken (2001). *The Hero Manager: Learning from New Zealand's Top Chief Executives*, Auckland: Penguin.

Johnstone, Barbara (2001). *Discourse Analysis*, Oxford: Blackwell.

Kingsley, Leilarna (2010). 'Language policy in multilingual workplaces: Management, practices and beliefs in banks in Luxembourg', Unpublished PhD thesis, Victoria University of Wellington, New Zealand.

Koester, Almut (2010). *Workplace Discourse*, London: Continuum.

Koller, Veronika (2004). 'Businesswomen and war metaphors: Possessive, jealous and pugnacious?' *Journal of Sociolinguistics*, 8(1): 3–22.

Kress, Gunther (1990). 'Critical Discourse Analysis', *Annual Review of Applied Linguistics*, 11, 84–99.

Kusmierczyk, Ewa (2012). '"I consider myself a specialist" – a multimodal perspective on believable professional identity construction in a job interview', Paper presented at Sociolinguistics Symposium 9, Berlin, 21–24 August 2012.
Labov, William (1972). *Sociolinguistic Patterns*, Philadelphia: University of Pennsylvania Press.
Ladegaard, Hans J. (2011). '"Doing power" at work: Responding to male and female management styles in a global business corporation', *Journal of Pragmatics*, 43, 4–19.
Leech, Geoffrey (1983). *Principles of Pragmatics*, London: Longman.
Lønsmann, Dorte (2011). 'English as a corporate language: Language choice and language ideologies in an international company in Denmark', PhD Thesis, Roskilde University, Denmark.
Louihiala-Salminen, L., Charles, M. and Kankaanranta, A. (2005). 'English as a lingua franca in Nordic corporate mergers: Two case companies', *English for Specific Purposes*, 24(4), 401–21.
Lüdi, Georges, Höchle, Katharina and Yanaprasart, Patchareerat (2010). 'Plurilingual practices at multilingual workplaces', in Bernd Meyer and Birgit Apfelbaum (eds), *Multilingualism at Work* (pp. 211–34), Amsterdam and Philadelphia: John Benjamins.
Metge, Joan (1995). *New Growth from Old: The Whanau in the Modern World*, Wellington: Victoria University Press.
Meyer, Bernd and Apfelbaum, Birgit (2010). *Multilingualism at Work: From Policies to Practices in Public, Medical and Business Settings*, Amsterdam: John Benjamins.
Meyerhoff, Miriam (1994). 'Sounds pretty ethnic eh? A pragmatic particle in New Zealand English', *Language in Society*, 23(3), 367–88.
Mullany, Louise (2006). 'Girls on tour: Politeness, small talk, and gender in managerial business meetings', *Journal of Politeness Research*, 2(1), 55–77.
——2007. *Gendered Discourse in the Professional Workplace*, Basingstoke, Palgrave Macmillan.
Murata, Kazuyo (2010). 'A contrastive study of the discourse of business meetings in New Zealand and in Japan', PhD thesis, Victoria University of Wellington.
Nickerson, Catherine (2000). *Playing the Corporate Language Game: An Investigation of the Genres and Discourse Strategies in English used by Dutch Writers Working in Multinational Corporations*, Amsterdam and Atlanta: Rodopi.
Norris, Sigrid (2011). *Identity in (Inter)action: Introducing Multimodal (inter)action Analysis*, Berlin: Mouton de Gruyter.
Norris, Sigrid and Jones, Rodney (eds) (2005). *Discourse in Action: Introducing Mediated Discourse Analysis*, Abingdon: Routledge.
Olsson, Su (2000). 'The "Xena" paradigm: Women's narratives of gender in the workplace', in Janet Holmes (ed.), *Gendered Speech in Social Context* (pp. 178–91), Wellington, New Zealand: Victoria University Press.
Rampton, Ben (2007). 'Neo-Hymesian linguistic ethnography in the UK', *Journal of Sociolinguistics*, 11(5), 584–607.
Richards, Keith (2011). 'Engaging identities: Personal disclosure and professional responsibility', in Jo Angouri and Meredith Marra (eds), *Construction Identities at Work* (pp. 200–22), Basingstoke: Palgrave Macmillan.
Roberts, Celia, Davies, Evelyn and Jupp, Tom (1992). *Language and Discrimination: A Study of Communication in Multi-ethnic Workplaces*, London: Longman.
Sarangi, Srikant (2009). 'Culture', in Gunter Senft, Jan-Ola Ostman and Jeff Verschueren (eds), *Culture and Language Use* (pp. 81–104), Amsterdam: John Benjamins.
Sarangi, Srikant and Roberts, Celia (eds) (1999). *Talk, Work and Institutional Order: Discourse in Medical, Mediation and Management Settings*, Berlin: Mouton de Gruyter.
Schiffrin, Deborah (2003). *Approaches to Discourse*, New York: Wiley.
Schnurr, Stephanie (2009). *Leadership Discourse at Work: Interactions of Humour, Gender and Workplace Culture*, Basingstoke: Palgrave Macmillan.
Spencer-Oatey, Helen (2000). 'Rapport management: A framework for analysis', in Helen Spencer-Oatey (ed.), *Culturally Speaking: Managing Rapport Through Talk Across Cultures* (pp. 11–46), London: Continuum.
——(ed.) (2008). *Culturally Speaking: Managing Rapport Through Talk Across Cultures*, 2nd edn, London: Continuum.
Spencer-Oatey, Helen and Xing, Jianyu (2003). 'Managing rapport in intercultural business interactions: A comparison of two Chinese–British welcome meetings', *Journal of Intercultural Studies*, 24(1), 33–46.
Stubbe, Maria and Holmes, Janet (2000). 'Talking Māori or Pākehā in English: Signalling identity in discourse', in Allan Bell and Koenraad Kuiper (eds), *New Zealand English* (pp. 249–78), Wellington: Victoria University Press.

Stubbe, Maria, Lane, Chris, Hilder, Jo, Vine, Elaine, Vine, Bernadette, Marra, Meredith, Holmes, Janet and Weatherall, Ann (2003). 'Multiple discourse analyses of a workplace interaction', *Discourse Studies*, *5*(3), 351–88.

Svennevig, Jan (2008). 'Exploring leadership conversations', *Management Communication Quarterly*, *21*, 529–36.

Swann, Joan (2002). 'Yes, but is it gender?' in Lia Litosseliti and Jane Sunderland (eds), *Gender Identity and Discourse Analysis* (pp. 43–67), Amsterdam: Benjamins.

Swann, Joan, and Maybin, Janet (2008). 'Sociolinguistic and ethnographic approaches to language and gender', in Kate Harrington, Lia Litosseliti, Helen Sauntson and Jane Sunderland (eds), *Gender and Language Research Methodologies* (pp. 21–28), New York: Palgrave Macmillan.

Tannen, Deborah (1993). *Gender and Conversational Interaction*, Oxford: Oxford University Press.

Thornton, Agatha (1985). 'Two features of oral style in Māori narrative', *Journal of the Polynesian Society*, *94*, 149–77.

Vandermeeren, S. (1999). 'English as a lingua franca in written corporate communication: Findings from a European survey', in Francesca Bargiela-Chiappini and Catherine Nickerson (eds), *Writing Business: Genres, Media and Discourses* (pp. 273–92), Harlow: Longman.

Vine, Bernadette, Holmes, Janet, Marra, Meredith, Pfeifer, Dale and Jackso, Brad (2008). 'Exploring co-leadership talk through interactional sociolinguistics', *Leadership*, *4*(3), 339–60.

Vine, Bernadette and Marra, Meredith (2008). 'EH and Māori men: A vernacular feature at work', Paper presented at 5th Biennial International Gender and Language Association Conference (IGALA5), Victoria University of Wellington, 3–5 July 2008.

Waldvogel, Joan (2005). 'The role, status and style of workplace email: A study of two New Zealand workplaces', Unpublished PhD thesis, Victoria University of Wellington, New Zealand.

Wenger, Etienne (1998). *Communities of Practice: Learning, Meaning and Identity*, Cambridge: Cambridge University Press.

Williams, Marion (1988). 'Language taught for meetings and language used in meetings: Is there anything in common?' *Applied Linguistics*, *9*, 45–58.

Wilson, Nick (2011). *Playing with Language: Examining Leadership Discourse in New Zealand Rugby Teams*, Unpublished PhD thesis, Wellington: Victoria University of Wellington.

Wodak, Ruth (1996). *Disorders of Discourse*, London: Longman.

——(1999). 'Critical discourse analysis at the end of the 20th century', *Research on Language and Social Interaction*, *32*(1–2), 185–93.

Wooffitt, R. (2005). *Conversation Analysis and Discourse Analysis: A Critical Introduction*, London: Sage.

10
Electronic media in professional communication

Michael B. Goodman and Peter B. Hirsch

The use of digital and computer-mediated communications in the era of The Web has created a profound paradox for corporations and organisations. The evolution of the internet and the rapid increase in broadband availability around the world, on the one hand, have placed powerful and efficient tools for communication in the hands of corporate enterprises. On the other, the rich connectivity and transparency of internet-based communications media have created unforeseen challenges for these same corporations.

Web technologies have empowered professional communicators to develop relationships, engage, and communicate with internal and external audiences locally and globally. Electronic or digital media have enabled the rise of the networked enterprise or organisation. There are three types: 1) internally networked organisations (their focus of electronic media use is almost exclusively within their own walls); 2) externally networked organisations (the focus of their use is with customers and business partners); and 3) fully networked enterprises (these organisations integrate electronic media collaboratively in revolutionary ways to break down organisational barriers that slow the flow of information).

Web technologies, however, have also unleashed new global threats to professional organisations. This chapter describes and analyses some of the mistakes that corporations have made in handling these threats, as well as some leading practices being applied by major multinational organisations and corporations in taking advantage of the new technologies to communicate and to manage the attendant risks.

Electronic media on the web include:

Blogs (short for web logs; online journal or databases hosted on a website);
Mash-ups (aggregations of content from different online sources to create a news service);
Microblogging (a form of multimedia blogging such as Twitter that allows users to send brief updates or micromedia such as photos or audio clips and publish them);
Podcasts (a multimedia form of a blog distributed through an aggregator such as iTunes);
Prediction markets (websites that forecast events by aggregating opinions across a wide base of users; also known as – information markets, decision markets, idea futures, event derivatives and virtual markets);

Rating tools (web features that let users provide a numerical quality rating for pieces of content such as product rating features on Amazon.com);
RSS (Really Simple Syndication is an application that allows people to subscribe to online distribution of news, blogs, podcasts or other online information);
Social networking (systems such as Facebook and LinkedIn that allow members of a specific site to learn about other members' skills, talents, knowledge or preferences);
Tagging (software tools such as HTML or XBRL that enable individual users to attach descriptive words and identifiers to pieces of web content);
Wikis (systems for collaborative publication such as Wikipedia that allow many authors to contribute to an online discussion or document)

The contemporary internet has been the subject of much breathless contemplation and the details of its awe-inspiring traffic density are too well known to need describing in detail here. The key statistics for our purposes are those that show the extent to which people all over the world have access to the internet, how much time they spend online, and what they are doing while they are there.

Out of a world population of 6.9 billion, there are 2.4 billion individuals with internet access, according to *Internet World Stats: Usage and Population Statistics* gathered by the Miniwatt Marketing Group, as of June 2012. China alone has 538 million internet users. In September 2009, a global total of 27 billion hours were spent online and in the United States, the average amount of time spent online per week almost doubled to 13 hours between 1999 and 2009, according to Harris Interactive. Among US Baby Boomers, this time exceeded the weekly amount of television viewing. Even Africa, with the lowest internet penetration as a percentage of population (15.6 per cent), can still boast 167 million internet users.

Global challenges

What this means for corporate communicators is that essentially all of its key stakeholders, even in some very remote parts of the world, have access to corporate websites and social media pages, and are not afraid of often posting hostile comments about the company. A recent example is the campaign being orchestrated by Greenpeace to stop Nestle from using allegedly unsustainably harvested palm oil in its chocolate products. Notwithstanding the company's explanation of its strategy and sourcing policies, its Facebook page has become home to hundreds of negative comments, including distortions of a product logo from 'KitKat' to 'Killer'. Nor is this kind of activity just happening on official pages.

One group of individuals has created a site called 'ChangeChevron' dedicated to persuading Chevron to adopt what adherents believe are more sustainable behaviours. The site, which has more than 2,000 fans, has been used very effectively by opponents of the company as a vehicle for articles and films describing what is believed to be the company's criminal behaviour. One such film posted by the Ecuadorian pressure group 'Justicia Now!' is deliberately designed to exert influence on lawsuits that the company faces in the United States about an environmental issue in Ecuador.

And in early 2012, *Kony 2012* a 27-minute online video focused on the atrocities of Ugandan terrorist Joseph Kony posted by Invisible Children went viral and almost 10 million people downloaded and watched the video in less than two days.

As digital communication becomes almost ubiquitous in global business interactions, and more complex, etiquette in communicating online is becoming an issue. Virginia Shea in her book *Netiquette* addresses the need for civil interaction in discourse online (see box).

Electronic media

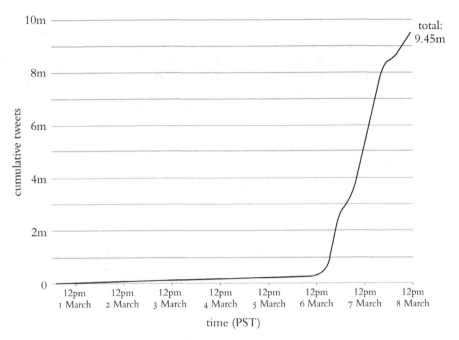

Figure 10.1 Tweets with Kony or #StopKony, 1–8 March 2012

Etiquette online

Shea's core rules of 'Netiquette' are:

Rule 1: Remember the Human
Rule 2: Adhere to the same standards of behaviour online that you follow in real life
Rule 3: Know where you are in cyberspace
Rule 4: Respect other people's time and bandwidth
Rule 5: Make yourself look good online
Rule 6: Share expert knowledge
Rule 7: Help keep flame wars under control
Rule 8: Respect other people's privacy
Rule 9: Don't abuse your power
Rule 10: Be forgiving of other people's mistakes

Internal communication

In addition to the external communications challenges represented by the web, multinational companies are also dealing with the internal or employee communication challenges presented by these new technologies. We can look at these challenges from two perspectives. The first involves the difficulty of managing the corporate brand in an environment in which any employee, whether a full time employee, an intern or even a part-time contractor can associate his or her social media presence with your company name.

Sometimes this 'squatting' is relatively benign, but in other circumstances it can pose a real reputational threat. The Facebook pages of many major corporations, for example, are held hostage by local country business divisions or individual business units. The first John Deere fan page, with 157,000 alleged fans, is listed as being in the name of John Deere in Switzerland and has no recent wall posts of any kind. Intel's official fan page is jostled by fan pages for Gardner's works on emotional intelligence and on some days the number one search result returned to a search for 'Intel' is a page of French students talking about how excited they are about their holidays.

Social media and company policies

These examples demonstrate that corporations have little choice, if they wish to protect their reputations, but to participate in digital and especially social media. Some commentators have suggested that in response to the allegations of using unsustainably harvested palm oil in its chocolate Nestle should simply have shut down its Facebook fan page and started fresh. However, we believe this solution only gives the company's opponents another issue to stir up, and 'sulking' is rarely an effective corporate communication posture. Nestle, as the world's largest food company, has endured boycotts and attacks since the 1970s. It is unlikely to see these attacks diminish by closing a communications platform. In fact, it could be argued that the company should increase the number of platforms through which it can communicate its viewpoint.

In order to organise defensively against online reputational threats, companies need to establish internal and external policies about their expectations for employee social media communications. A company needs to make clear what it will publish, or allow to be published, on the platforms that it controls. IBM and Xerox are two companies that have created effective employee social media policies. These policies are fundamentally a reflection of the communications' policies that have been in place at major corporations for many years. These policies simply ask the following of employees:

- Identify yourself as an employee of the company if writing about industry issues, but make it clear that the opinions expressed are your own
- Do not reveal confidential company information
- Do not disparage the company, its employees or officers
- Do not comment on competitors' business practices

These requirements do not go much further than standard code of business conduct guidelines, but Xerox also offers some more web-specific suggestions. The company's social media directive to employees warns against the temptation to use sarcasm when responding to negative postings. It also offers sound advice on how to respond to such negative responses and whether one should publish negative comments at all. In the spirit of transparency, Xerox suggests, it is advisable to allow any comments that are not obscene, derogatory or defamatory.

Guidelines on responding to external communities offer other challenges. The Japanese car maker Toyota in 2010 faced some of these when its Facebook fan page filled up with customer outrage about the product recall it had announced. The company responded briefly and sincerely to reasonable customer questions and complaints, while publishing more inflammatory postings without response. The net effect of this policy was that other customers in significant numbers posted comments in favour of the company, its products and the steps it was taking to manage the recall. Facebook pages make for a messy environment as a result, but it appears to be preferable to let a certain amount of negative commentary into the public space in order to stimulate the loyalists.

Related to these challenges of handling negative commentary in the digital space is the problem presented by the ubiquity and endurance of web-based information. Companies are faced with reputational challenges every day, many of which involve the allegation that they are engaged in a cover up or are sweeping negative information under the rug. In a web environment, in which content lives forever, what is the appropriate posture with respect to retention and positioning of the information?

Social media strategies

In the 'gotcha' world of web reputation, companies need to practise a high degree of information transparency, for a number of reasons. First among these is that, in spite of earnest attempts by companies to make content – audio and video, as well as written content – disappear, the amoebic nature of the medium means that almost all information that is suppressed grows back somewhere else on the internet. Companies that try to eradicate negative content not only fail but often look foolish in the attempt. It is much more preferable to have past negative events and the company's response available within a few clicks on the company website than to drive searchers to other places on the web where the company's response doesn't appear.

The second principal reason is that in an era of diminished trust in global corporations, the ability for a company to face up to its poor judgment or bad behaviour is seen as a positive act. By allowing negative content to remain available, companies are implicitly acknowledging their flaws and demonstrating to stakeholders of all kinds that they adhere to ordinary human standards of ethics and not the artificial stoic defensiveness that has, in the past, characterised corporate brands.

Emerging, then, from this still evolving engagement of corporations with the web, one can glimpse the outline of leading practices with respect to their online presence:

- Develop a long-term vision for the use of web tools for interaction with different stakeholders commensurate with your corporate brand and business objectives.
- Do not simply replicate the same content across multiple platforms but design content (including navigation and applications) that take advantage of the unique characteristics of each platform.
- Assess your resource allocation to the web to ensure that you can sustain a high refreshment frequency on any platform you use.
- Develop a tolerance for a high level of negativity, especially of the prankish type.

IBM social computing guidelines

Know and follow IBM's business conduct guidelines:

1. IBMers are personally responsible for the content they publish on-line, whether in a blog, social computing site or any other form of user-generated media. Be mindful that what you publish will be public for a long time – protect your privacy and take care to understand a site's terms of service.
2. Identify yourself – name and, when relevant, role at IBM – when you discuss IBM or IBM-related matters, such as IBM products or services. You must make it clear that you are speaking for yourself and not on behalf of IBM.

3 If you publish content online relevant to IBM in your personal capacity use a disclaimer such as this: 'The postings on this site are my own and don't necessarily represent IBM's positions, strategies or opinions.'
4 Respect copyright, fair use and financial disclosure laws.
5 Don't provide IBM's or another's confidential or other proprietary information and never discuss IBM business performance or other sensitive matters publicly.
6 Don't cite or reference clients, partners or suppliers without their approval. When you do make a reference, link back to the source. Don't publish anything that might allow inferences to be drawn that could embarrass or damage a client.
7 Respect your audience. Don't use ethnic slurs, personal insults, obscenity or engage in any conduct that would not be acceptable in IBM's workplace. You should also show proper consideration for others' privacy and for topics that may be considered objectionable or inflammatory – such as politics and religion.
8 Be aware of your association with IBM in online social networks. If you identify yourself as an IBMer, ensure your profile and related content is consistent with how you wish to present yourself with colleagues and clients.
9 Don't pick fights, be the first to correct your own mistakes.
10 Try to add value. Provide worthwhile information and perspective. IBM's brand is best represented by its people and what you publish may reflect on IBM's brand.
11 Don't use IBM logos or trademarks unless approved to do so.

The web and negativity

The web is highly susceptible to prankish humour, invective, and a general mean-spirited tone, much of that directed at institutions such as large multinational corporations. We can trace this meme back to the more relaxed, less nihilistic side of the 1960s protest movements. Even as far back as the early 1960s, Ken Kesey's 'Merry Pranksters' were practising a theatre of irreverence.

More recently, the career of film maker Michael Moore represents the tradition of using humour, albeit heavy-handed, as a type of agitprop against corporations. In films such as *Roger & Me*, *Sicko* and *Capitalism: A Love Story*, Moore uses broad humour to attack corporate interests. And at the other end of the political spectrum, Andrew Breitbart, who worked on the Drudge Report and *The Huffington Post*, created conservative opinion and infotainment at Breitbart.com.

> [H]e understood in a fundamental way how discourse could be profoundly shaped by the pixels generated far outside the mainstream media he held in such low regard. Mr. Breitbart, as much as anyone, turned the web into an assault rifle, helping to bring down Acorn, a community organizing group, with the strategic release of undercover videos made by James O'Keefe, a conservative activist; forcing Shirley Sherrod, an Agriculture Department official, out of her job with a misleadingly edited clip of a speech; and flushing out Representative Anthony D. Weiner, Democrat of New York, when he tried to lie about lewd pictures he had sent via Twitter.

Less watchdog than pit bull (and one who, without the technology of the twenty-first century, might have been just one more angry man shouting from a street corner), Mr Breitbart altered the rules of civil discourse.

Mark Feldstein, a journalism professor at the University of Maryland, said that Mr Breitbart 'used the tools of invective and polemic to change the conversation, to try to turn it to his advantage' (Carr 2012).

In the twenty-first century, sophomoric humour, polemic arguments, vitriol and 'trash-talk' found a rich new breeding ground on the internet. People of every age, demographic and culture flocked to enjoy mockery and abuse of the powerful. The viral nature and visibility of the web has proved to be irresistible to pranksters and provocateurs of every type.

These include the hapless employees of Domino's Pizza, who videotaped and posted to YouTube footage of themselves befouling the company's product. It also included more serious activists such as the environmentalists opposed to Chevron.

On April Fool's Day, 2010, environmental activists organised under the banner 'Fossil Fools' (sic) Day' staged actions in more than 30 cities around the world. Prior to the event, UK pressure group, Rising Tide, published suggestions on its website for 'pulling a prank that packs a punch'. According to dozens of commentators on Twitter, a 'clown army ... tried to drill for custard in front of Chevron CEO John Watson's home' (Change Chevron Facebook Fanpage).

The appetite for making fun of corporations, most enjoyed by 20–30-year-olds most likely to be anti-corporate activists appears to be remarkably free of cultural differences. In practically every country with broadband access to the internet it is possible to find 'prank shows' or 'prank call shows' that bear witness to the homogenisation of global youth culture. When this is fuelled and organised by global NGOs, the pranking or 'punking' of corporates can occur simultaneously all over the world.

This is the ethos that underlines Nestle's current travails concerning palm oil and has for many years inspired activist pranksters, such as the Yes Men, anti-corporate ideologues who have successfully spoofed corporate websites and hosted press conferences pretending to be representatives of actual business organisations.

In 2009, for example, they successfully hosted a press conference at the National Press Club in Washington, DC, pretending to be representatives of the US Chamber of Commerce, which at the time was vigorously opposing climate change legislation. The Yes Men's fake policy U-turn on behalf of the chamber was interrupted by a real representative of the organisation. The resulting confrontation, which was being videotaped, was subsequently viewed more than 66,000 times on YouTube. Their fake press conference announcing that Dow Chemical was planning to admit responsibility for the chemical explosion at Bhopal was viewed 160,000 times and the real news reports of the stunt reached millions of other viewers.

The web and the networked enterprise

We have previously discussed the pitfalls of employees communicating via social media platforms and personal blogs and the need to develop strong social media policies to manage expectations and outputs. In another part of the web, however, new digital technologies are helping companies handle communications with an increasingly diverse set of workers some of whom are not employees. Over the past 20 years, global companies have transformed the way they do business, carving out whole fields of corporate activities that they no longer believed they needed to perform 'in-house', in other words with their own employees, but could outsource to other providers.

The spark for this far-reaching transformation was Michael Porter's groundbreaking work of 1985 called *Competitive Advantage*. Porter argued that what really mattered to the success of a company was its unique ability to create value for its stakeholders and the activities that did so along what he called the 'value chain' were core competencies. All other activities, in this theory, could be outsourced and this is eventually what happened. Starting with support functions such as payroll, security, customer call centres and transportation, companies today have outsourced and created partnerships to do fundamental manufacturing, even some research activities that would once have been closely guarded internal activities. The outcome of a generation of this trend is the 'networked enterprise' in which companies create value with an extensive network of workers and other resources whom they don't employ or control.

Online collaboration

There are two things of relevance to our discussion to note about the networked enterprise. The first is perhaps a truism, namely that when products are researched, manufactured and brought to market by a chain of independent entities, the need for close and effective communication could not be more paramount. The second is that legacy computer and email systems inside large organisations are poorly adapted to facilitating communications between independent parties.

However, new applications such as wikis and internet-based systems known as 'cloud computing' are becoming huge facilitators for networked enterprises. Wikis, accessible to anyone with network access privileges and a web browser, are being used all over the world to facilitate work flow between participants in the networked enterprise. Researchers in a company's Silicon Valley research facility, for example, can participate in wikis with process engineers in the outsourced Mexican manufacturing facilities. These, in turn, can collaborate with independent raw materials suppliers in Asia. Internet-based collaborations such as these have been critical in the growth of innovative products and services that have involved suppliers and partners at a much earlier stage in the development process.

In the past, a company would traditionally not involve components suppliers and outsourced manufacturing partners until relatively late in development, delivering a closed specification for the supplier to bid on.

Today, with sophisticated online collaboration tools, the suppliers and business partners are deeply involved in developing the specifications themselves. The result is faster time to market or, in some cases, early identification of obstacles to success, permitting companies to shut down a research project much earlier in the process saving resources for more promising innovations.

Social media policy

A social media policy can help a company to limit potential disadvantages from the use of social media, and can help the company gain competitive advantages. Ignoring the need for published social media guidelines can impede a company's ability to protect itself and hamper its efforts to compete effectively in the marketplace.

To be effective, a company's social media policy should reflect the company's culture. Here are some items to consider in developing a social media policy:

- Make sure that the policy is readily available on the company's website and intranet.
- Incorporate the company's existing disclosure policy into the social media guidelines.
- Describe the ways in which the company and its employees are authorised to use Twitter and other social media. Companies may find it beneficial to use social media to announce earnings calls. Investor relations tweets should include a hyperlink to full disclaimers and risk factors whenever the tweet involves forward-looking information – this needs to be considered within the 140-character limit.

- Tell employees what should not be discussed in tweets or other social media. This can be done by a clear reference to the company's disclosure policy, or the company may prefer to describe prohibited content more directly.
- Tell employees not to participate in social media when the topic being discussed may be considered a crisis situation or an area in which they are not authorised spokespersons and that disciplinary action may be initiated by the company if they do not follow the guidelines.
- Anyone who is going to be authorised to speak on behalf of the company in social media should have training in applicable securities laws and other applicable laws with examples of how to remain compliant with those rules while using social media.

(NIRI Standards 2012: 47)

News aggregation and automation

The rapidity of the spread of news stories and stunts such as these in the web era is unthinkable without two core technologies of the medium: sharing applications and automated alerts, such as RSS feeds or Google Alerts. These technologies have fundamentally changed the way in which companies need to defend their reputations globally in the culture of the internet. The evolution of sharing applications has been rapid and straightforward, starting with the initial success of bookmarking applications such as Digg, Stumbleupon, Reddit and delicious.com, many of which have morphed from sites on which individuals could store favourite websites and online material to social applications in which friends and online groups can share content on topics of mutual interest.

Really Simple Syndication (RSS) has its roots in the early days of the web, but came into common use around 2003. This extended xml code became one of a series of methods by which individuals could automate the process of finding and receiving information about topics that interested them. The use of this and similar technologies has burgeoned in the intervening years and versions of the concept can be found in use at Google and Yahoo's 'Alert' systems and across social pages such as Facebook.

The impact of these applications for corporate communication and reputation management has been profound. Where it was once necessary to comb countless news sources manually for news about a company or a product or to pay a service to do so, it is now possible for opponents of corporations to receive instant automatic updates on any topic under the sun. This has, in turn, increased the speed with which activist organisations can energise their networks and exhort members to take action.

Clearly, the spread of these automated news services places a new burden on corporations to be ready to respond to a wide range of news stories, especially those that ordinarily would only have found a tiny readership. With RSS feeds, the content of obscure technical journals, publications from other countries, and even the public postings of rulings and directives from foreign governments are pouring into online mail boxes all over the world. The individual with an interest in commercial fishing regulations, the links between cancer and bisphosphenates, or changes in package dimension for breakfast cereal now has the same access to information as the most ardent researcher or journalist.

The borderless nature of the internet also ensures that this flow of information rarely stays within individual countries. A leading US pharmaceutical company, for example, dealt in a conventional manner with a relatively low level concern about the quality and integrity of one of its products that in itself was no threat to human health. In the United States, the story received the kind of news coverage commensurate with these facts. In China, however, product integrity was much more than a passing issue. In the wake of the milk melamine scandal and the pet food and drywall contaminations of 2008–9, the news of quality issues with the product of a leading US company became a huge story that ran for many days.

Risk alert systems

Global companies are adopting a range of new methods and processes to deal with the issues created by the ubiquity of automated 'news' delivery. One leading global professional services firm has responded to the threat by creating a continuously refreshed online database of response statements available for use by country-based spokespeople at any time. Tracking dozens of issues, the global communications team creates position statements as these issues emerge and posts them to the online database. When a company representative faces a question about the issue in a time zone during which global communications headquarters in New York are closed, he or she is able to use a keyword search of the database to find the current position statement of the firm on this issue. Whenever new facts or changing circumstances create a need for the firm's position to be revised or updated, the global team posts the new version to the database. This triggers an automatic alert to anyone around the world who has previously accessed the firm's position on this issue, informing them that new language on the subject has become available.

Notwithstanding the borderless quality of the internet, there are still many issues of importance in one country that do not automatically leap across national or regional borders immediately. However, many issues of reputation have the potential to do so, either spontaneously through mainstream media foreign correspondents or through the propaganda activities of global NGOs. The difficulty for the multinational corporation lies in identifying as best they can those issues that will jump across borders and preparing themselves for the consequences. Without some kind of approach to managing this problem, the communications function of the typical large multinational would soon be overwhelmed by hundreds of issues.

The most common approach is to rely on the professional judgment and experience of communications staff at the local country level as to when an issue needs to be brought to the attention of global leadership. However, expertise in reputation risk management varies widely around the world and many critical issues jump borders before internal alerts have taken place. In addition to the question of expertise, organisational power structures can sometimes militate against timely disclosure and local communicators may be constrained from disclosure to 'corporate' even when they believe they should. One company has addressed this question by creating a 'traffic light' system with three levels of action and triggers for communication:

- Green: a one-country issue with no broader reputational ramifications for which a local spokesperson suffices. No alert to global leadership required.
- Yellow: a one-country issue that potentially poses broader reputational ramifications. Local spokesperson suffices, but alert must be sent to global describing the issue and the position taken.
- Red: a one-country issue with significant reputational ramifications or an issue with potential global impact. Alert global headquarters immediately and confer to select most appropriate spokesperson and agree statement.

While no system of this kind can be foolproof, it does provide a framework for communicators under pressure to think outside their own immediate surroundings to consider the broader global ramifications of the issue they are handling. A recent case illustrates the difficulty of controlling reputational challenges within an individual country.

In 2009, Maclaren USA announced a 'recall' of some of its baby strollers because some American consumers had complained that their children were getting their fingers caught in the collapsible hinges, sometimes with dangerous results. The recall, which Maclaren intended only for the United States, involved customers applying to the company to receive two pieces of cloth to cover the offending hinges and prevent children from inserting their fingers into them. What the company failed to predict was that, as a leading British brand sold throughout the world, their customers outside the US would feel more than somewhat ignored. When the recall was covered in the global media, Maclaren's Facebook page was inundated with comments from outraged upscale parents from India to Australia asking why their children's safety was held to be less important than that of American children. When the company responded by saying that the reason the recall was restricted to the US was because no complaints had been received elsewhere, they were vilified and had to execute an abrupt about face. To its credit, Maclaren made excellent use of social media after it regained its footing and responded quickly to any customer inquiry about the recall and expressed gratitude when thanked or praised. Here is a characteristic exchange on the company's 'wall':

> Hi Maclaren, We live in Italy and need to ask for the hinge kits for our ryder lacoste and also our volo ... is there a phone or email of someone in Italy or should I have them sent to my parents in the US.
> March 12 at 11:03pm · Comment · Like Unlike · View Feedback (1)Hide Feedback (1) · Report
> MACLAREN BABY
> Erin – Please call 0033 (0)1.48.63.11.85 or email info-it@maclaren.fr for those covers. No need to have them sent from the US. Hope this helps!
> March 13 at 3:25pm · Report

The Maclaren recall perfectly illustrates the difficulty of isolating issues geographically in a global digital environment.

In another communications discipline that has become global, new digital tools offer a more positive experience. The field of investor relations is being transformed by electronic media and such digital technology requirements such as XBRL.

Investor relations and digital communication

Use of digital communication – corporate websites, blogs and social media – for publically traded companies offers positive opportunities to reach investors, analysts, media, regulators and the general public. Digital communication also adds additional challenges, because of the investment, legal and financial concepts of materiality, disclosure, and transparency. *Materiality* is 'an event or information that is sufficiently important (or *material*) to have a large impact on a company's stock price ... Material information is information the reasonable investor needs to make an informed decision about investment'. *Disclosure* is the 'release by companies of all information, positive or negative, that might bear on an investment decision, as required by the Securities and Exchange Commission and the stock exchanges'. And *transparency* in financial reporting is the 'ease of understanding, made possible by the full, clear, and timely disclosure of relevant information' (Downes and Goodman 2012).

With the dramatic growth in the use of digital communication, maintaining a corporate website has generally become a leading practice for public companies. Investors, analysts, and others seeking information about public companies review corporate websites as part of their

139

due diligence process. The company website can become the comprehensive repository for relevant information. Leading companies include investor relations contact information on their websites, including phone numbers and email addresses (*NIRI Standards 2012*: 47).

Because much of the information on a company is subject to federal securities laws, companies should post accurate information as they would in an SEC filing. And since SEC regulations forbid it, the National Investor Relations Institute (NIRI) counsels that

> companies should not distribute, post or provide links to analyst reports in order to avoid any implication of the adoption or approval of these reports. Companies may list the covering analysts and/or firms. Companies should also create special archive sections on their websites and regularly move out-of-date content into these areas to indicate that it is historical and not current.
>
> *(NIRI Standards 2012: 48)*

The dissemination process for the earnings information is evolving because of digital technology, the SEC's *Interpretive Guidance for Websites*, as well as changes in the requirements for public companies by stock exchanges such as NYSE and NASDAQ. The 'public disclosure' of company information under securities regulations, including Regulation Fair Disclosure (Reg. FD), calls for broad and non-exclusionary distribution to the public. The company website can qualify as 'public disclosure'. In contrast to past practice of using a wire service to post information, many companies now use their websites as their primary means to disclose and distribute information.

Investment conferences and road shows are an important way to reach out to current and potential investors. Usually the CEO and CFO participate in these events. The IR officer plans the presentations, prepares the slides, and knows what information will be presented. If material, nonpublic information is discussed during these events, the IR officer should disseminate a news release in advance of the presentation, and post the news release and presentation on the IR portion of the company's website. If an unintentional disclosure of material, nonpublic information is made during the presentation, Q&A period, or in one-on-one meetings, in order to avoid violating Regulation FD, the company should issue a news release or file a Form 8-K containing that information as soon as reasonably practicable (but in no event after 24 hours or the commencement of the next day's trading on the New York Stock Exchange), or both. The leading 'practice at investment conferences is to webcast corporate presentations' (NIRI Standards 2012: 44).

Leaders in investor communications have also worked hard to reduce the click stream required to get to different parts of investor pages, as well as to provide access to thought leadership presentations in a variety of audiovisual formats. These are important enhancements of the stakeholder relationship enabled by the web.

XBRL and investor relations

However, there is one transformation made possible by digital innovation that can truly be described as revolutionary, and that is XBRL – eXtensible Business Reporting Language – whose use by the largest 500 US companies was mandated by the Securities and Exchange Commission (SEC) beginning in April 2009.

XBRL is based on a system of meta-tagging data, organised through a series of so-called taxonomies that define which tags mean what in terms of a company's financial statement and balance sheet. XBRL is designed to make a company's financial data more searchable, more comparable, and to be interactive.

Prior to the introduction of XBRL, financial analysts who typically develop their own models were required to update these models manually whenever they received new data from one of their investment companies. Even when this information was received via a digital channel, the data itself was not automatically mergeable with the spreadsheet being used by the analyst.

XBRL makes any financial data using its tags instantly integratable. It makes voluminous data deeply searchable and queryable. As the investor or analyst works with XBRL data, he or she is able to test different financial scenarios by varying any field in the data table without having to manually recreate any data at all. The alignment of the XBRL taxonomies makes it significantly easier for investors to compare one company or industry sector with another, identify inconsistencies or warning signals in the data, and customise their own early-warning signals by type of data. XBRL also reduces the effort that companies make in producing financial information for different purposes – regulatory filings, their websites or printed financial statements.

Companies are exploring social media methods such as Facebook and Twitter to communicate with investors while still complying with the SEC's guidelines for insider trading and Regulation Fair Disclosure (Reg FD). This will be especially true for companies not currently tracked by financial analysts. Since the marginal cost of providing investment analysis for additional companies will drop radically when the manual inputting or transformation of information is eliminated, it will be possible for research houses to offer research on many more companies.

Finally, XBRL helps accomplish a key aim of the SEC: to level the playing field for individual and institutional investors. By making high-quality data available faster for everyone and at less cost, the reliability and value of detailed analysis is significantly enhanced. For the investor relations professional, the reduction in time required for the mere production of financial information for stakeholders facilitates a more intimate and strategic relationship, reducing the stress of sudden surprises, and enabling longer and more trusting engagements.

The ability to generate these more intimate and strategic relationships becomes particularly important in the context of the changing global investment infrastructure in which new players with different cultural assumptions and contexts are having to develop relationships. Chinese investors and sovereign wealth funds from the Middle East and Southeast Asia are investing in Western markets at an unprecedented level. At the same time, Western investors are venturing deeper and deeper into China, Vietnam, Brazil and some African countries. By reducing the time spent on 'mechanical' financial analysis, time becomes available to decipher more complex cultural signals.

Blogs and electronic forums

Statements made by a company's representatives on blogs, whether company-sponsored or third-party blogs, must comply with securities laws. The company is responsible for statements made by or on behalf of the company, and cannot avoid liability by having employees speak in their 'individual' capacities if employees are authorised company spokespersons. The *NIRI Standards 2012* offer these suggested practices for corporate blogs:

> A company is not responsible for third-party statements on blogs or on a company-sponsored blog and has no duty to correct misstatements made by a third party – but not responding to such information may not be practical or prudent from a business perspective. Also, if a company selectively edits or deletes blog entries other than on a pre-established, non-discriminatory basis (for example, the posting is offensive), it might be considered to have approved of, or agreed with, the information that has been posted.

A company should establish a policy that clearly designates which employees are authorized to represent the company in a blog or e-forum (whether sponsored by the company or a third party) and the content that the authorized employees are permitted to post.

If a company decides to sponsor or host a blog, it should establish and publish terms of use designed to limit the company's liability. As part of entering into the blog, users should be required to affirmatively accept these terms. If the company (or someone on behalf of the company) collects personally identifiable information from those who post comments, the company should post and adhere to a privacy policy.

Though some companies use blogs to discuss their products and services, most do not provide forums in which to discuss their results and prospects.

Some companies have incorporated Twitter, Facebook and other social media into their investor relations programs. If your company decides to participate, for example, by having an officer or other designated spokesperson blog or tweet, remember that all communications must be Regulation FD compliant. There also may be other laws and rules that apply. For example, if your company is contemplating or has begun a capital raise, Rules 134 and 135 under the Securities Act of 1933 are likely to apply. These rules permit companies to make limited announcements about public offerings (*NIRI Standards 2012*: 46).

Even if your company is not ready to tweet or blog, it should monitor what is being said about the company, its management, its products and services, and competitors who are doing so. Not monitoring what is being said about the company or its management could result in damage to your company's or its management's reputations. Companies should give serious thought to acquiring Twitter account names that their customers, clients, investors and service representatives would likely consider to be company accounts.

Micro-blogging

When Twitter began in 2006, this short form messaging system in which users 'tweet' 140 character messages seemed destined to be little more than a quaint game. Critics mocked what they believed was the inanity of people with time on their hands tweeting about where they were having their second cup of coffee of the day. The application's lift off is usually traced to the SXSW (South by Southwest) festival in Austin, Texas in 2007, which first brought the service to wide attention.

In the first quarter of 2010, there were more than 4 billion tweets globally and 75 million unique visitors in the month of January. While usage is highest in the United States, there are millions of Twitter profiles in countries all over the world. Twitter currently offers services in English, French, German, Japanese, Italian and Spanish. Nor is it just individuals who are using this service. According to a March 2010 survey by Burson-Marsteller 65 per cent of the Fortune Global 100 have one or more Twitter profiles.

In defiance of its critics, Twitter has already proven itself as a significant tool for information dissemination. Some of these uses are political. In 2009, the US government formally requested that Twitter postpone a scheduled maintenance outage because Iranian protesters were tweeting about their experience in demonstrations following the Iranian election. The service has also proved to be a powerful public service tool during and after public emergencies such as the terrorist attack in Mumbai in 2008 and during the aftermath of the earthquake in Haiti in January 2010. Twitter messages helped emergency services locate survivors and enabled citizens to report looting and violence to the authorities in real time.

What has proved most surprising is the robustness of Twitter as a tool for businesses. The transparent nature of the Twitter universe and its searchability has meant that businesses are being given a real-time insight into the opinions and behaviours of customers and other stakeholders. An early adopter of the technology for business use was Dell the computer company. By proactive scanning of customer tweets using keyword search terms, the company has been able to address customer concerns quickly, identify emerging needs and build customer relationships.

Airlines, such as Jet Blue, have availed themselves of the technology to advise customers about flight delays, how to find lost luggage and send them discounts and other benefits to compensate for difficult travel experiences. The sheer volume of searchable messages has also provided businesses with a unique new research tool that provides time-based information about the needs and concerns of potential customers. Twitter has also begun enabling GPS technologies available on some smart phones so that individuals and businesses can permit their followers to see where they are at all times. While it is yet to be determined how many people will enable this feature, it is reasonable to speculate that a sufficient number of individuals will do so to provide additional insights that will give business new information about their potential customers.

While the various uses of Twitter by businesses are still developing, we believe that companies with a large community footprint and small businesses will benefit most. Power utilities, phone and cable companies, transportation systems are already using Twitter both to learn about service problems directly from customers ('tree on power line at Fourth and Elm'), as well as communicate to customers about rapidly changing conditions ('4:14PM train to Clark's Ridge running 10 minutes late'). Small businesses, as well as retail food chains are using Twitter successfully to promote daily deals and specials. Businesses as small as individual food trucks that move from location to location are able to advertise their daily location to regular customers in real time.

The use of Twitter by small businesses is largely a North American phenomenon at the time of writing, but we believe that the legions of small businesses around the world, which have already adopted mobile phone technologies with alacrity, will find in Twitter and other micro-blogging platforms an essential tool to communicate with customers. These uses will undoubtedly be adapted to local cultures around the world. It is not hard to imagine Twitter as a tool for the 5,000 dabbawalla who deliver 200,000 lunch boxes around Mumbai every day. Vietnamese farmers, often several hours' drive from the markets for their goods could use Twitter to get information about real-time pricing in order to determine whether the journey to market is justified on any given day. Growth in this type of micro-blogging will, in turn, provide new data for companies that serve these small businesses as well as government policy makers to identify new needs and opportunities.

Other platforms

The period 2011–12 witnessed an explosion of new social media platforms that are in the process of proving themselves, as well as a maturation process for the more established media. At the same time, social media communities that came to prominence with a relatively narrow focus have been changing and adding features to attract more time online from web users. Facebook, for example, which was launched as a 'friend' site for individuals, has been at great pains to create page types that are suitable for corporations both large and small. The Facebook timeline feature, which debuted in 2012, has the clear intent to generate lifetime loyalty as its users age and its usership plateaus at close to 1 billion users. YouTube, the web's premier video site, added a 'channel' feature, making it enormously valuable as a business communications tool and enabling companies to own their own real estate on the site. With the arrival of Foursquare (20 million registered users by April 2012), the location-based website for mobile devices, all of the other social platforms have rushed to enable geo-location features to take advantage of the explosion in smart phone use. SIRI, the speech interpretation and recognition interface, available on the latest iPhone will undoubtedly spawn related innovations in speech recognition that will create new challenges and opportunities, especially when it becomes available in non-English languages beyond 2012. While the features of social media platforms will converge, we believe that organisations will continue to create stakeholder management strategies that make use of the specific strengths of each.

Conclusion

It has been a little more than a decade since web technologies emerged to transform the world of corporate communications. What we have learned over the course of this period is that every new communications technology or application creates new tools as well as new threats. Furthermore, the low cost and accessibility of these technologies creates a scale of usage with previously unthinkable speed. The scale, speed and democratisation of usage created by the low cost of entry have produced a very high degree of innovation in usage. This innovation has been encouraged by companies such as Google, Facebook and Twitter who have made the creativity of third-party developers an essential element in their success. As a result, many new technologies have stumbled into uses and markets never envisaged. This has been a healthy process, by and large, but it brings with it a large challenge for corporate communications users. This challenge is that web technologies, more so than other recent innovations, require active participation.

Every industry, indeed individual companies, can only establish the benefits and risks of social media by experimenting with them. That is what customers and other stakeholders are doing. Communications professionals at global corporations must do the same, learning from mistakes, trying out different uses in what Ray Jordan, former chief communications officer at Johnson & Johnson, has called a perpetual beta test. Over time, we will see more clearly which uses of these media will create long-term value and what the resource allocation for these new platforms needs to be.

Related topics

business communication; technical communication; management communication: getting work done through people; business and the communication of climate change: an organisational discourse perspective; corporate communication; corporate communication and the role of annual reporting

Key readings

Bhargava, Rohit (2012) *Likeanomics*. Hoboken, NJ: John Wiley & Sons. (This book traces the pathways used by organisations to build, maintain and regain trust in the age of the internet.)
'IBM Social Computing Guidelines: Blogs, wikis, social networks, virtual worlds and social media'. Available at www.ibm.com/blogs/zz/en/guidelines.html (accessed February 2012). (IBM has set the standard for organisations and their commercial and professional use of social media.)

Logan, Robert (2010). *Understanding New Media: Extending Marshall McLuhan*, New York: Peter Lang. (This book investigates the impact of 'new media' using the concepts and methods of Marshall McLuhan, and how it is changing our world.)

Schmidt, E. and Cohen, J. (2013) *The New Digital Age: Reshaping the Future of People, Nations and Business*, NY Knopf. (This work by Google founder, Eric Schmidt, thoughtfully shifts the debate from the future of apps to how technology truly interacts with power in today's world.)

Shirky, Clay (2010). *Cognitive Surplus: How Technology Makes Consumers into Collaborators*, New York: Penguin Books. (The author of *Here Comes Everybody: The Power of Organizing Without Organizations*, examines the transformative power that is the result of the use of new digital technology to leverage shared resources and talent.)

Bibliography

Appleyard, Bryan (2011). 'The digital generation', *RSA Journal*, Winter, 18–23.

Bennett, Drake (2012). 'Ten years of inaccuracy and remarkable detail: Wikipedia', *Bloomberg Businessweek*, 10–16 January 2012, 57–61.

Bhargava, Rohit (2012). *Likeanomics*, Hoboken, NJ: John Wiley & Sons, Inc.

Bugeja, Michael (2005). *Interpersonal Divide: The Search for Community in A Technological Age*, New York: Oxford.

Bughin, Jacques, Byers, Hung, Angela and Chui, Michael (2011). 'How social technologies are extending the organization', *McKinsey Quarterly The Online Journal of McKinsey and Company*. Available at www.mckinseyquarterly.com (accessed November 2011).

Bughin, Jacques, and Chui, Michael (2010). 'The rise of the networked enterprise: Web2.0 finds its payday', *McKinsey Quarterly The Online Journal of McKinsey and Company*. Available at www.mckinseyquarterly.com (accessed December 2010).

Carr, David (2011) 'The great mashup of 2011', *The New York Times*, 3 January 2011, B 1 and B6.

——(2012). 'The provocateur', *The New York Times*, 15 April 2012, Sunday Styles, 1 & 10.

Change Chevron (2010). *Facebook Fan Page*. Available at www.facebook.com/search/?ref=search&q=Intel&init=quick#!/pages/Lyss-Switzerland/John-Deere/14754086861?ref=ts (accessed 9 April 2010).

Downes, J. and Goodman, J. E. (2010). *Dictionary of Finance and Investment Terms*, Eighth Edition, Barron's Educational Series, New York: Hauppauge.

Eviltwinbooking (2010). *Yes Men Fix the Chamber of Commerce*. Available at www.youtube.com/watch?v=D67LYEacBoE (accessed 9 April 2010).

Falkenrath, Richard (2012). 'Google must remember our right to be forgotten', *Financial Times*, 16 February 2012, 9.

Financial Times (2011). 'Cybersecurity', *Financial Times Special Report*, 1 November 2011.

——(2012). 'Connected business: Special report', *Financial Times*, 25 January 2012.

Ghonim, Wael (2012). *Revolution 2.0: The Power of the People Is Greater Than the People in Power: A Memoir*, Boston: Houghton Mifflin Harcourt.

Goodman, J. David (2012a). 'Twitter's new policy on blocking posts is attacked and defended'. Available at 28 January 2012 from http://thelede.blogs.nytimes.com (accessed 27 January 2012).

——(2012b). 'Backlash aside, charities see lessons in a web video'. Available at www.nytimes.com/2012/03/16/us/backlash-aside-charities-see-lessons-in-a-web-video.html?_r=1&scp=9&sq=kony%202012&st=cse (accessed 16 March 2012).

Goodman, M. and Hirsch P. (2010). *Corporate Communication: Strategic Adaptation for Global Practice*, New York, NY: Peter Lang Group.

IBM (2012). 'IBM social computing guidelines: Blogs, wikis, social networks, virtual worlds and social media'. Available at www.ibm.com/blogs/zz/en/guidelines.html (accessed February 2012).

Intel Corp. (2010). *Facebook Fan Page*. Available at Facebook website www.facebook.com/search/?ref=search&q=Intel&init=quick#!/Intel?ref=search&sid=507624095.2257522700.1 (accessed 9 April 2010).

Harris Interactive (2009). *Internet Users Now Spending 13 Hours a Week Online*. Available at http://news.harrisinteractive.com/profiles/investor/ResLibraryView.asp?BzID=1963&ResLibraryID=35164&Category=1777 (accessed 22 December 2009).

John Deere (2010). *Facebook Fan Page*. Available at www.facebook.com/search/?ref=search&q=Intel&init=quick#!/pages/Lyss-Switzerland/John-Deere/14754086861?ref = ts (accessed 9 April 2010).

Lessig, Lawrence (2008). *Remix: Making Art and Commerce Thrive in the Hybrid Economy*, New York: Penguin.
Levinson, Paul (2009). *New New Media*, Boston: Allyn & Bacon.
Livingston, Geoff with Solis, Brian (2007). *Now is Gone: A Primer on New Media for Executives and Entrepreneurs*, Baltimore: Bartleby Press.
Logan, Robert (2010). *Understanding New Media: Extending Marshall McLuhan*, New York: Peter Lang.
Maclaren USA (2010). *Facebook Fan Page*. Available at www.facebook.com/#!/MACLAREN?ref=ts (accessed 9 April 2010).
Miniwatt Marketing Group (2011). *Internet World Stats: Usage and Population Statistics*, 31 December 2011. Available at www.internetworldstats.com/stats.htm (accessed 26 March 2012).
National Investor Relations Institute (NIRI) (2012). Available at www.NIRI.org (accessed 2012).
Palmer, Maija (2012). 'The netiquette of working life', *Financial Times*, 7 February 2012, 10.
Perry, Tekla S. (2008). 'Gordon Moore's next act', *IEEE Spectrum*, May 2008, 40–43.
Pew Research Center (2012). 'Pew internet and American life project 2012'. Available at http://pewinternet.org (accessed 2012).
Porter, Michael E. (1985). *Competitive Advantage*, New York, NY: Free Press.
Razorfoundation (2010). *Bhopal Disaster – BBC – The Yes Men*. Available at www.youtube.com/watch?v=LiWlvBro9eI (accessed 9 April 2010).
RSS (2010). In *Wikipedia*. Available at http://en.wikipedia.org/wiki/RSS (accessed 2 April 2010).
Schmidt, E. and Cohen, J. (2013). *The New Digital Age: Reshaping the Future of People, Nations and Business*, New York: Knopf.
SEC *Interpretive Guidance for Websites*. Release Nos. 34–58288, IC-28351; File No. S7-23-08. August 2008.
Seel, Peter B. (2012). *Digital Universe: The Global Telecommunication Revolution*, Malden, MA: Wiley.
Shea, Virginia (2012). *Netiquette*, Albion Books, Online version at www.albion.com/netiquette/ (accessed 27 April 2012.
Shirky, Clay (2010). *Cognitive Surplus: How Technology Makes Consumers into Collaborators*, New York: Penguin Books.
Taylor, Paul (2012). 'Customer must be king in the web world', *Financial Times: Special Report the Connected Business*, 25 January 2012.
Toyota (2010). *Facebook Fan Page*. Available at www.facebook.com/search/?ref=search&q=Intel&init=quick#!/toyota?ref=ts (accessed 9 April 2010).
Wyld, David C. (2007). *The Blogging Revolution: Government in the Age of Web 2.0*, Washington, DC: IBM Center for The Business of Government.
Xerox (2010). *Xerox Social Media Guidelines*. Available at www.xerox.com/downloada/en/s/Social_Media_Guidelines.pdf (accessed 9 April 2010).
Zittrain, Jonathan (2008). *The Future of the Internet – And How to Stop It*, New Haven: Yale University Press.

11
The role of translation in professional communication

Marta Chromá[1]

Professional discourse, as suggested in earlier chapters, can be viewed from many perspectives, and the methodologies used to analyse the process would differ depending on the purpose of the research.

Communication at a workplace is a multifarious process fully determined by the environment in which it is pursued. Interlingual translation becomes an issue where speakers of different languages are to join the discourse, whether one working language serves as a means of communication in a non-native environment or more languages are used to smooth the interaction among individual actors.

The first traces of translation and translators in professional communication date back to Ancient Rome: every public official had translators in his staff (*interpretes* in Latin) whose function was to mediate oral and written communication of his superior with Greeks, i.e. Latin and ancient Greek being the source and target languages (Skřejpek 2007: 29). In addition, during the Roman Empire there was a special office entitled *ab epistulis Latinis*, which was charged with translating all relevant correspondence with the Greek-speaking part of the Empire and as such served as a foreign department of its own (Skřejpek 1991: 89).

Since Ancient Rome, the practice of translation in professional settings has expanded, diversified and included dozens of languages all over the world. Today translation between languages may be relevant in all chains of both vertical and horizontal communication in various organisations; however, its extent and scope may vary substantially.

The purpose of this chapter is (1) to introduce basic translational theories relevant in professional settings; (2) to outline the process of translation and to compare selected aspects within three different domains of professional communication – engineering, commerce and law, as diverse backgrounds for translation; and (3) to indicate basic assumptions regarding the future position of translation in professional communication.

Approaches to translation

Translation in its simplest definition as a transfer of information from one code to another has existed 'since time immemorial', i.e. when human beings started to interact, mostly as a subconscious process aimed at preserving their lives. With the development of their verbal contact, the transfer became a more conscious, intentional and planned activity. It was the practice of translation, not theory, that was the subject of debates over the centuries and comments found, for example, in the texts of Cicero or Horace in Ancient Rome, Étienne Dolet in the Renaissance, or Martin Luther in the Protestant Reformation, to name just a few (cf. Nord 1997: 4; Munday 2001: 18–29). One of the most famous translators in the early Christian history, St Jerome, has been recognised as the patron of the guild of translators at least in Europe.

Although the practice of translation and its occasional theoretical contemplations date back hundreds of years, the creation of consistent theories of translation did not become a topic of academic and research papers and publications until as late as the twentieth century. With an accelerating and diversifying world and life, many more people and fields were affected by, and dependent upon, translation of various texts. With practical translation playing a more and more significant role in virtually all spheres of life, translational theories have attempted to critically analyse, or even anatomise, existing translational practices, and have intended to set principles, methods and rules in order to help improve the practice of translation and the competence of translators. Needless to say, an unequivocal response to the general question of what a 'good' translation is has not been found despite various attempts in history to prescribe certain rules and concrete steps to be followed (cf. Malmkjær 2005: 5–8); very often, one would resort to an answer incorporating the purpose of translation which would significantly determine the evaluation of its quality.

There have been various approaches to the study of translation spanning the ranges from source text (ST) orientation theories to a target text (TT) focus, from purely linguistic theories to pragmatic and semiotic views upon translation, including the attention paid to the role of an ultimate recipient of the translated text in the very process of translation. The process of translating by itself is an excellent way of discovering relations between languages (i.e. in a comparative analysis), looking for linguistic differences (through a contrastive analysis), and identifying cultural differences (cross-cultural pragmatics), which all may have a significant impact upon the creation of the target text.

The work of a few theoreticians in translation will be sketched in order to introduce basic approaches to translation, which are pertinent to a translator's work even today. In 1958, Jean-Paul Vinay and Jean Darbelnet published their *Stylistique comparée du français et de l'anglais* in which they outlined strategies and procedures applicable to translation. They saw just two methods, or strategies, available to a translator: *direct (literal) translation* and *'oblique' translation*, the latter meant as departing from straight procedures of transposing the text from one language into another (Venuti 2000: 84) and close to what is usually termed *free* translation. The choice between the strategies would remain with the translator, having considered the potential of a source text and using any, or a combination, of seven procedures, used for smaller units of a text, such as sentences, phrases or words. Of the seven procedures, the three that determine direct translation are: (a) borrowing (e.g. source language (SL) words preserved in the target text, such as Czech *robot* in English and other languages), (b) calque (as a special kind of borrowing, also termed 'loan' translation, e.g. English *loan-word* and German *lehnwort*), and (c) word-for-word exchange (or literal translation); the other four are choices typical of oblique translation: (d) transposition (replacing one word class with another without changing the meaning of the message), (e) modulation (changing the point of view of the message), (f) equivalence (at the level of words, phrases, or larger units), and (g) adaptation (when a cultural issue contained in the ST is missing in the target language (TL) culture (Venuti 2000: 85–92)). All seven strategies still remain part of a translator's decision-making: they represent elementary operations aimed at transmitting and preserving the specificity of the SL in the TT.

Unlike his predecessors, Eugene Nida (1964) turns his attention to the reader and measures equivalence in translation by a reader's reaction. He distinguishes two types of equivalence – *formal* and *dynamic*, the former also termed as *gloss* translation with the aim of 'permitting the reader to identify himself as fully as possible with a person in the source language context, and to understand as much as he can ... ' (Venuti 2000: 129). The latter type is very close to Newmark's free translation (see below). As the title of his major work suggests (*Toward a Science of Translating*), Nida tried to consolidate his extensive practical experience in Bible translating and recent achievements particularly in semantics and pragmatics into the scientific study of translation processes. More than 40 years later, Nida retreats from *science* back to *theory* admitting that 'Translating is not a separate science, but it often does represent specialized skills [...]'; at the same time, however, he preserves his initial affinity with semantics and pragmatics adding cultural anthropology and theories of communication as disciplines which, on the one hand, assist a translator in applying his or her skills, and may help understand objective translational processes on the other (2006: 11).

Peter Newmark, although criticised for his prescriptivism (Munday 2001: 46, or Malmkjær 2005: 5), elaborates on the dichotomy of translation being either *literal* or *free*, the former based upon the SL as the main determinant of the translated text, whilst the latter emphasises the TL as the main factor in producing the translated text. Methods focusing on the SL are word-for-word translation, literal translation, faithful translation and semantic translation; the TL is focused upon in adaptation, free translation, idiomatic translation and communicative translation (1988: 45–47). What is primarily relevant in his classification is the distinction between semantic and communicative translation, the former strongly dependent upon the language of the source text (ST), i.e. 'translation at the author's level' (1988: 285). Communicative translation, i.e. 'translation at the readership's level' (1988: 282) concentrates on an accurate transfer of the ST message to the TT and attempts to bring various elements suggesting foreign culture, in the widest sense of the word, closer to the reader; in this sense, 'communicative translation explains' (1988: 48). This pragmatic aspect may cause the TT to be perceived by its readers better than the ST can be by its original audience. The communicative translation strategy in this sense may be useful for example in tourism (brochures, leaflets or advertisements) where, in order to attract potential visitors, the translator should (at least generally) reflect on their expectations.

The interpretive theory of translation was introduced by the French École Supérieure d'Interprètes et de Traducteurs almost 40 years ago (Lederer 2003) and during those years spread over to other training centres for translators and interpreters; its basic premise is that understanding the source text (ST), i.e. interpreting the ST using one's linguistic, extra-linguistic and encyclopaedic knowledge, thus identifying its sense, requires that context be considered at all levels of the meaning construction (word/phrase, sentence, text, discourse). This theory may be considered a pre-stage of a semiotic approach to translation to a certain extent, emphasising interpretive aspects of a translator's work interlinked with his or her cognitive background employed in a particular context of communication.

Functional theories of translation are fully oriented at the target text and its addressees. A functional approach to translation is primarily represented in the work of Katharina Reiss (1971 in Venuti 2000), Hans Josef Vermeer (1978) and Christiane Nord (1997). Reiss speaks of a 'TL text that is functionally equivalent to a SL text' (2000: 160) and elaborates on the premise that a particular text type has a particular function and that function should be preserved in the TT. Three basic types of text are distinguished, namely *informative* (simple communication of content), *expressive* (communication of artistically organised content) and *operative* (communication content with a persuasive character) (2000: 163). Informative and operative texts are pertinent to professional communication: the former would prevail in technical fields (e.g. servicing manuals), the latter, encompassing letters, reports, proposals, contracts, etc., would be found in almost all domains of professional discourse.

Hans Vermeer is the 'father' of the *skopos* theory. The Greek word *skopos* means *purpose* and the main premise is that 'any (form of translational) action has an aim, a purpose' (in Venuti 2000: 221). The functions and purposes of the ST and the TT may (significantly) differ as the ST is produced for an audience within the 'source' culture and its translation into the TT would serve a different audience with a different cultural background. This is true particularly of literary texts considering their emotive (expressive) and poetic functions (in Jakobson's terms, 1960: 353), which are deeply culture-bound, but also of legal texts, as law is a field of knowledge deeply culturally rooted. On the other hand, the purpose of the ST and the TT may be identical in the most precise meaning of this attribute, such as in the majority of *informative* text types mentioned above (e.g. an operating manual for a mobile phone). As Vermeer argues, 'every translation can and must be assigned a skopos' and 'the skopos of a translation is the goal or purpose, defined by the commission and if necessary adjusted by the translator' (in Venuti 2000: 230).The term *commission* is meant as an initiative to translate, either on one's own or someone else's initiative (in Venuti 2000 : 229). Christiane Nord expands, and elaborates on, various aspects of the skopos theory, extending it to the training of translators and interpreters. Nord claims (1991: 8) that a translation must fulfil certain requirements, which are defined by translation 'instructions' (assignments) in order to be suitable for a certain purpose. Her dichotomy of *documentary* and *instrumental* translation is of major importance to the analysis of translation process; the former 'serves as a document of a source culture communication between the author and the ST recipient' whilst the latter 'is a communicative instrument in its own right, conveying message directly from the ST author to the TT recipient' having the same or analogous function as the ST (1991: 72). Instrumental translation in this sense applies widely to various manuals and instructions for how to handle or operate particular machines or other devices, and also covers (maybe quite surprisingly) legislative texts issued by the institutions of the European Union and translated into all 23 national or official languages of the EU Member States (but not to legislation passed in individual countries).

Recently, pragmatic and semiotic aspects of translation have been paid more attention. For example, Mona Baker in her seminal book (1992) not only analyses equivalence at linguistic levels (words, collocations, phrases, grammar), but also focuses on the word order and its role in translation and on the pragmatic aspects of translation. She reintroduces the concept of functional sentence perspective (FSP), originally presented by Vilém Mathesius within the Prague Linguistic Circle as early as 1929, followed by other Czech linguists Jan Firbas (e.g. 1956, 1986) and František Daneš (e.g. 1974), and built upon, but modified, by Michael Alexander Kirkwood Halliday into his systemic functional grammar (1985). The gist of the traditional understanding of the FSP lies in the theme-rheme dichotomy: the former suggests what is known, the latter expresses what is new (a speaker-oriented distinction). Should discourse be considered, the theme is what the clause is about and links the clause back with preceding parts of the discourse, the rheme 'is what the speaker says about the theme. It is the goal of discourse.' (Baker 1992: 121–22). Elaborating on the model of the speaker-oriented thematic structure and the hearer-oriented information structure of the text (what is known and what is new to the text addressee), Baker analyses text equivalence comparing the communicative potential of texts in various languages (such as Chinese, Arabic, Japanese or Brazilian Portuguese) from a translator's perspective and suggesting some strategies for resolving the tension between syntactic and communicative functions in translation (1992: 167). Considering pragmatic equivalence, i.e. how the translated text is perceived by its audience in a given communicative context, Baker explores the question of *making sense* in cross-cultural communication focusing on coherence (as the network of conceptual relations underlying the surface text) (1992: 218) and the Gricean implicature (what is meant rather than what is explicitly said by the speaker), and offers strategies for a translator to deal with those issues.

Roman Jakobson (1959) laid down the fundaments of the theory of translation based on his semiotic and functional approach to languages. Understanding translation as interpretation, Jakobson (1959: 232) distinguishes the following: intralingual translation or *rewording* in the same language; interlingual translation or *translation proper* between two or more languages; and intersemiotic translation or *transmutation* is an interpretation of verbal signs by means of signs of nonverbal sign systems. Paraphrasing Jakobson I would call the intralingual translation 'interpretation proper' as this is the stage when the translator tries to identify the message (in its widest sense including the form, content and functions) to be conveyed, to understand it and possibly to reword it should such rephrasing help transfer it into the target language. Jakobson's *translation proper* is transmission across temporal, geographic, and linguistic boundaries. Jakobsonian intralingual translation creates the initial, but crucial or even critical, stage of interlingual translation as the translator may transmit to another language only such information (message) that he or she finds in the source text, i.e. what sense he or she identifies in the source text at its individual levels and how it can be interpreted in its complexity as a type of (social) discourse. Since Jakobson's era, the concept of intersemiotic translation has acquired wider dimensions for translating law: law may be regarded as a dual semiotic system composed of the language in which it is expressed and the discursive system expressed by that language (Jackson 1997: 3). Interlingual translation of a legal text is intersemiotic translation (Tomášek 1991: 147) as it represents a process where one dual semiotic system should be replaced by the other, preserving the purpose and characteristics of the source text to the extent expected and required by the recipient of the translation (the extent may differ depending on the purpose of the translation). The core factor of the interlingual legal translation is the translator's ability to reasonably interpret the source text, identifying, for example, the genre of the legal discourse, the genre of the source text (text-type), its narrative repertoire, legal concepts and their reflection in terminology, etc.

The semiotic approach to translation as an inclusion of (social or cultural) context and discourse interpretation into a translator's work in order to avoid shifts in various functions of a text (e.g. ideational or interpersonal) and discourse is crucial particularly in texts dealing with areas of knowledge, fields or subjects that are deeply culturally rooted, such as law or literary works. Context in our understanding is both the external (objective) environment of the communication (such as situational circumstances, cultural factors, etc.) and the internal (subjective) environment of a participant in the communication referred to as *cognitive environment* (Gutt 2000: 27). The latter includes information that can be perceived in the external environment, derived from preceding utterances, retrieved from memory (knowledge stored there), etc. As Gutt points out successful communication depends on the meeting of the sender's and receiver's assumptions. In other words, contextual information about the communicator and the world allows the interpreter to deduce the communicator's purposes, and the communicator's beliefs about the world and the way it normally works (Kramer 2003: 179). In addition, making sense of language involves understanding what the speaker/writer is doing, not merely what is being said/written (Jackson 1995: 10). Since translation is mediated communication, the potential of misinterpreting and misunderstanding is much higher as the translator's cognitive background (assumptions) plays a crucial role (in addition to other factors such as a possibly different external environment including a varying time span). Cultural differences occur in everyday professional communication where, for example, business representatives of different cultural backgrounds exchange official letters to formally commence their talks on a deal: translators (on both sides of the deal) should, and are expected to, establish felicitous conditions for the representatives' interaction, being aware of those (social or cultural) contextual differences that may hinder communication.

The process of translation

Interpretation as a pre-stage of translation

Interpretation in the sense of Jakobson's *intralingual* translation has acquired more attention with pragmatic and semiotic aspects being included in translational theories. Bilingual translation is social interaction; it is a type of discourse fully dependent on a go-between or intermediary – the translator. Describing unilingual verbal communication, Jakobson (1960: 353) emphasises the context known to both the addresser and the addressee, their common code and physical and mental connection enabling them to interact. Lecercle notes that with interpretation involving a pragmatic setting 'we must discover not merely the meaning of the text but its addressee' (1999: 17). Jakobson's description may be visualised as in Figure 11.1, with the double-ended arrow suggesting that the contact between the addresser and addressee may be reciprocal or interactive in order to facilitate their efficient communication, i.e. their exchanging of understanding.

Traditionally, the translator intervenes in communication between the addresser and the original addressee where the code, and often the context, used by the former is unknown to the latter but their communication should be facilitated for various reasons. An emphasis placed on the presumed function of the target text (not its actual perception by the recipient), which predetermines the translation strategy (i.e. approaches, methods and procedures), has been mentioned. Simplistically described, the translator as a communication intermediary first becomes a substitute addressee and after his 'processing' the original message he acts as a substitute addresser to convey the 'processed' message to the presumed original addressee. *Message* is understood here in a wider sense as a substance (content) of communication expressed in a certain format (e.g. the text). The 'processing' phase is composed of several steps to take: first the translator tries to understand and interpret (decode) the source language message in its immediate linguistic and wider social and cultural context; then he transmits the interpreted message to the target language (the code of the final addressee); finally, the translator should adapt, if necessary, the transmitted information in a way corresponding to the purpose of translation, to the function of the target text and possibly to the expectations of the ultimate addressee (see Figure 11.2).

It should be noted, however, that the 'contact' between the addresser and the addressee in Jakobson's sense, i.e. the communication channel, is far from being straightforward, particularly where the communication is mediated by a translator. Transmission of the original message to the ultimate recipient may span centuries, with substantially different cultures and potentially remote linguistic codes built upon nonconforming means of interpreting social realities (cf. Nida 1964). Lecercle terms this disconnect between the original text and its interpreters as *temporality*

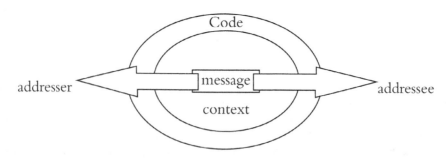

Figure 11.1 Verbal communication chart

Figure 11.2 The process of bilingual translation

of interpretation; he sees an interpreter of the original text as an 'interventionist' as interpretation shifts the decision on what the meaning is to the interpreter 'intervening' in the original intentions of the author. Translation, he points out, 'implies a fading of intention of meaning as source of the text, the coming to the forefront of language and of the text' (1999: 22). This might leave us slightly incredulous of the potential of interlingual translation as 'we cannot simply construct versions of other people's central terms as if we could understand them perfectly. ... we have to recognize that the most we can attain is an imperfect understanding and approximation' (White 1994: 44).

However doubtful one can be, it is more than obvious that translation between languages is feasible and attainable and even powerful; for example, the European Union is built upon the idea of multilingualism, which in practice also means that all laws, whatever particular form they may have, and many other documents, are translated into the 23 official languages of the EU.

A translator's approach to, and results of, interpretation depend on many factors, which, to simplify the issue, may be divided into 'objective' (external) and 'subjective' (internal) factors. The objective factors encompass all issues beyond the translator's control, such as the quality of drafting and clarity of the source text, or its topic and text-type/genre (for example an informational leaflet for a new chocolate to be placed on the market can generally be considered 'easier' to interpret and translate than homologation documents to prove that the new version of a car meets local regulatory standards). The translator's knowledge, skills, and experience on the one hand, and their ability to organise their work (for example, to avoid time constraints) on the other hand, create the subjective factors of translation; interpretive skills of a particular translator logically belong to the subjective factors.

Cognitive factors

As our main concern is translation in professional communication, which covers non-literary genres and spans various branches of knowledge and profession from business, law, medicine or science to technology and engineering, one important aspect of translation, and interpretation as its pre-stage, should not be omitted. Texts required to be translated are very often narrowly specialised in their topic, rich in terminology, using specific syntactic or textual means in individual type-texts and discursive strategies applicable to the profession at issue. In order to interpret the ST meaningfully the translator should possess some knowledge of the subject matter (factual knowledge), or should have at least general understanding of the discipline. For example, the annual financial statement of a company, a lease contract, medical report or a patent application for a new invention to be registered are specialised technical documents not only because of the subject-area terminology used, but also because they deal with specific issues requiring expert knowledge to compile such texts; naturally, the requirement of the same or nearly the same cognitive background to interpret such texts properly and to transmit the interpreted information to the TL may be justified. Although Venuti comments on his translation of a philosophic text (2003: 237), and philosophy is an academic discipline rather than part of professional communication, his experience that

> translating the work of this contemporary French philosopher requires that one be a specialist in a certain sense, possessing a knowledge not only of the French language, but of Continental philosophical traditions, and not only of translation practices between French and English, but of the discursive strategies that have been used to translate Derrida's writing over the past thirty years

is fully applicable to many fields of professional communication. Gunnarsson treats the same issues from the perspective of professional discourse pragmatics (2009: 18):

> Every profession has a certain way of viewing reality, a certain way of highlighting different aspects of the surrounding world. Socialization into a profession means learning how to discern the relevant fact, how to view the relations between factors. ... If we consider a professional group as a whole, we see that its professional language has developed as a means of expressing this professional view of reality. ... Attitudes and norms are also built into the cognitive structures.

It is not just the SL code and the code of a particular profession in the SL environment that are relevant for the initial interpretation of the sense of the ST; the translator should, in addition to his proficient linguistic skills, be also aware of the code of the profession in the target language environment so that he can efficiently place his translated text in that context allowing for an adequate interpretation of the TT by its ultimate TL recipient. This is typical of disciplines whose conceptual repertoire is primarily abstract and the discourse strongly culturally determined, such as law. For example, contracts are part of everyday business practice and if translated in a way that certain provisions are unclear to one or both parties relying on the TT, and the parties act upon a misinterpreted clause, it may lead to a breach of contract ending up even in court. However, a general practice in many businesses has been that translators are hired primarily for their linguistic competences and general translational skills, irrespective of their specialist knowledge. This is the practice invoked by the system of university education and degrees for translators who are trained as linguists possessing translational skills; just a few subject specialists, sufficiently proficient in languages, get professionally engaged in translating in the domain of their expertise.

Equivalence in translation

Whatever theory of, and approach to, translation is discussed, sooner or later the concept of equivalence becomes an issue. Emery claims that 'a definition of equivalence will have a direct bearing on a definition of translation' (2004: 143). House admits that the notion of equivalence creates the conceptual basis of translation and is essential for translation criticism; following Albrecht (1990) House argues that 'equivalence is always and necessarily relative', evaluating the phrase *absolute equivalence* as a contradiction in terms (1997: 25). It appears obvious that the concept of equivalence is not confined just to the theory of translation, but also, and even more, to its practice, since a traditional core objective of a translator's work has been to identify the meaning of the ST at all its levels and to reach an equivalent effect (cf. Newmark 1988: 49) in the TL upon a potential target recipient. As suggested by Pym (2010: 6), the concept of equivalence is based upon assumption that 'on some level, a source text and a translation can share the same value ... and that this assumed sameness is what distinguishes translations from all other kinds of texts'. As the focus of translational theories has shifted from the strong orientation on the source text to emphasising the purpose of translation, which may determine the mode and process of a translator's work, the understanding of equivalence has also slightly modified. In skopos theory, equivalence means adequacy to a purpose that requires that the TT serve the same communicative function as the ST (Nord 1997: 36).

The issue of equivalence is applicable to all levels of a text — lexical units, phrases, sentences, paragraphs and the text as a whole, but a question arises as to whether the translator may seek, and can reach equivalence and equivalent effect at a higher level, such as discourse. For example, a British *letter of claim* (formerly called *statement of claim*), no matter how excellent the translator's translation into Czech may be, can never be used for the commencement of a civil action before a Czech court as neither the formal nor substantive elements required by Czech law would be preserved; as a result, the communicative function of the ST would not be preserved in the TT, but the TT may serve other communicatively relevant functions in the TL environment. Another example of a shift in the communicative function would be (in some countries) a translation of a university diploma awarding the degree in law: the degree in the country of issuance allows the holder to practise law (with all necessary training stages, if applicable). Its translation by an authorised translator (sworn, certified, court-appointed) would serve merely as evidence of the acquired degree to be submitted in a complex administrative procedure in the TL country aimed at receiving the official approval to practise law. On the other hand, the translation of a birth certificate by a specially authorised translator would be of the same discursive value in the TL environment.

Since terminology plays a significant role in the language of any profession, whether 'genuine' terminology used in specialist texts or adapted in professional jargon or slang, lexical equivalence is usually a focus particularly for novice translators. Equivalence at the level of lexis and smaller syntactic units is the core of translational specialist dictionaries, which serve as the first aid to those not experienced in a respective subject-area.

Attaining equivalence in the translation of terms in culture-specific branches of knowledge, such as law, and culture-specific nomenclatures in other fields (e.g. names of institutions), should go with conceptual analysis of a particular term. The core of the analysis is to compare concepts expressed by particular terms in both the source and target languages in order to measure the degree of equivalence between potential equivalent terms. It is based upon a premise that every term, whether one-word or multiverbal, possesses certain essential elements and certain accidental characteristics. As suggested by Šarčević (2000: 238) for the language of law (but her conclusions are generally applicable), where concepts in the source language and target language expressed by the respective terms share all of their essential elements and most of their accidental characteristics, *near* equivalence would be reached. This would apply to most terminology in technology and engineering. *Partial* equivalence is attained where concepts in the source language and target language share most of their essential elements and only some of their accidental characteristics; this may be the case of translating *equity* in the sentence 'Home equity loan interest rates may cost less than borrowing from other sources', since no substantive equivalent for 'home equity' can be found in the TL (e.g. Czech in this particular case) and the translational solution would be an explicative 'equivalent' based upon the original English definition of this term (e.g. the market value of residential premises minus outstanding mortgage payments). *Non-equivalence* is identified where concepts in the source language and target language share few or none of their essential elements and no accidental characteristics. Whilst the first two types of equivalence could be satisfied with a functional or substantive equivalent in the target law, non-equivalence would be compensated for by an explanatory or descriptive equivalent (cf. Zgusta 1971: 319) or it is solved through semantic calques (such as many English terms within stock-exchange terminology if translated into other languages). The term *functional* equivalence is used in general translation theory (e.g. Newmark 1988: 83); a functional equivalent is understood to result from a cultural componential analysis and serves as the most accurate way of translating (deculturalising) a cultural word. The selection of a functional equivalent is based upon the comparative semantic and genre analysis of the source text and corresponding texts in the target language and it is to fulfil the same role as the original term in the ST. The English *Old Bailey* would be 'deculturalised' in a way that its TL equivalent would correspond to 'the Central Criminal Court in London' to transmit the descriptive information.

Translation may require not only a comparative conceptual analysis of the source term and its potential equivalent in the target language but also a comparative research into a wider (extra-linguistic) context. For example, *debriefing* was traditionally used within military forces as questioning to obtain secret information from the hostile side; later, it was an instruction to employees not to reveal classified or secret information; most recently (in experimental social sciences), it denotes a discussion at the end of an experiment when the researcher reveals the background to the subject and explains the reasons for any concealed steps taken that were necessary for the success of the research. The translator should not only identify the context and the meaning of 'debriefing' in the ST, which is an easier part, but also search into a similar context in the TL environment and find out whether a similar concept is applicable and, if so, what TL term is used.

Having considered various definitions of translating and equivalence, Emery (2004: 149) offers his definition of translation covering the polysemous nature of the term *translation* (process and product). He defines translation in terms of pragmatic meaning as a two-fold concept composed of the process of translating (the rendering of an SL text's pragmatic meaning into a TL text in line with TL expectancy norms) and equivalence as a product (i.e. the notion of a TL text purporting to be a rendering of a particular SL text's pragmatic meaning). Translating as a process involves both interpretation of a text/author's meaning (as expressed in an SL code) and analysis of the factors that govern the translator's choice in rendering this meaning into a TL code in line with TL expectancy norms (2004: 146).

Translation within an organisation

Professional communication is confined here to communication within business entities in the widest sense of the term, excluding communication within academia and scientific research. The need for translation at a workplace, or generally in professional communication, will be determined by many factors that can be simplistically subdivided into objective and subjective, the former at both macro- and micro-levels of communication, the latter applicable just at the micro-level.

Objective factors at a macro-level are those that cannot be influenced by communication parties and encompass what Gunnarsson (2009: 24) in her analysis of professional discourse calls societal framework systems encompassing technical and economic framework, socio-cultural framework (such as cultural specifics and primary social values), legal and political framework, identified through legislation and the system of government, and linguistic framework, all four being horizontally interwoven. There are significant differences in the translational load between a multilingual society (e.g. Switzerland) and a unilingual country partly detached from the rest of the world by the decision of its political establishment; those differences would apply to all professional domains (e.g. wide vs. limited possibilities to publish academic texts abroad, multiple vs. no international companies doing business locally, global companies vs. purely local industry, extensive vs. limited incoming tourism, etc.). Objective factors at a micro-level would determine the very environment of a communicative event, such as an order by the management to translate dozens of pages of a servicing manual overnight as the client is to arrive unexpectedly.

Subjective factors are those within the control (real or assumed) of the parties to the communication. Proficiency in foreign languages required as a means of interaction in a particular professional environment, or its absence, the decision as to who is to translate the respective text, what the function of translation would be, how experienced and/or well-organised a translator may be, etc., fall within the category of subjective factors at a micro-level.

Every organisation is defined by its own 'culture' usually reflected in, and governed by, its code of conduct or mission statement. Salvi (2011: 27) points out that 'this culture is reinforced through all manners of language, evidenced in all types of corporate communication, both external and internal, such as press releases [...] the semantics of job title and descriptions, [...]'. She acknowledges the reciprocal function of language which 'reflects corporate culture and massively creates it'. For example, slogans as short memorable phrases identifying a company or its products particularly in advertisements are an essence of a respective corporate culture. Needless to say, slogans as such are very difficult to translate into other languages as their main goal is to attract the attention of potential customers/clients in a particular geographical area determined by a particular language and culture (in the widest sense of the term inclusive of social values, patterns and standards). Many global corporations opt for their slogans to be confined to English without their 'localisation' through translation into the language of a respective community: translation in its standard meaning discussed above would not efficiently work, as the issue of equivalence would be reduced to an equivalent effect upon the TT recipient not necessarily attainable by pure linguistic means. In addition, potential clientele is lured not only through a written phrase but also by its audio version often recorded in a smooth, tender and appealing voice, which is to stimulate affectionate feelings in listeners, and English often appears to 'sound better' than a local language in this respect. The use of English in a non-English market environment is to bring a flair of something special, enticing people to 'be in' if they buy the respective product. Thus a traditionally Czech producer of cars, Škoda, uses its English slogan 'Simply Clever' even in Czech media for the Czech native community to imply that Škoda 'goes global', or the Finnish electronic giant Nokia is 'Connecting People' worldwide in English. On the other hand, Volkswagen preserving its German 'Das Auto' in most markets implies prototypical German accuracy, perfection, excellence and reliability in their cars, and this background message, if translated, would be lost. Tesco Stores in the Czech market opted for the Czech slogan 'Na všem záleží' (literal translation would be 'everything matters') as a free equivalent of their original English phrase 'Every Little Helps'. Linguistic equivalence is partial, but the pragmatic effect of this phrase, i.e. how the phrase is by implicature perceived by the respective language community, is very near.

Contextual background for translation

Translation is used in multilingual settings to assist interaction of potential communication partners if they cannot use the same language code. This may be caused by an inability to speak, or write in, the language of the other partner, or because the local law or internal protocol require so. Translation can serve within an organisation in all chains of both vertical and horizontal communication (in-house purposes); in addition, translation is relevant in communication between the organisation and the outer world (external purposes). It should be noted that English is very often either the source or target language since (a) it has become a sort of lingua franca even in professional (trade, banking, technology, etc.) communication among partners with different linguistic backgrounds, and (b) the practice of professional communication at the middle and top management level suggests that where just one communication partner is unable to speak the working language (other than English) of the respective communicative event he or she participates in (such as a meeting), all other actors in the event switch to English; this seems to be standard in most global enterprises (including banks), but the trend has expanded to smaller businesses having just one branch in a country different from its headquarters (e.g. cross-border ventures). Texts arising from such interaction are often written in both the working language and English. It may happen that identification of which is the source and which the target language could be quite impossible as parts of the text, such as a transcript of a meeting, can be compiled from notes taken during the meeting in English, some parts may be reconstructed in the working language; the decision as to which language version would be drafted first quite often depends on the language of the more extensive initial written notes, comments, etc., and also on the subjective preference of the drafter.

Three different professional contexts were chosen to exemplify differences and/or sameness in the role of translation in those domains, namely an international special technology manufacturer, a foreign car producer and an international law firm. A special technology manufacturer (STM) either opens its branch in another country or joins an existing local business; the former option means that the company brings over not only its know-how, technologies, etc. but also its corporate culture including the modes of internal communication. Translation plays a crucial role at the outset of business of any kind as all administrative procedures aimed at establishing the company are performed, and legal documents written, in the local language. As a result, almost all texts relevant in the establishing of a new foreign company are in both languages (the local language and the corporate language of the foreign manufacturer). The latter option opens space for mingling or amalgamation of the culture of the established domestic business and new approaches brought in by the newcomer; moreover, the initial administrative and legal procedure is usually easier and less extensive and the volume of translated texts is smaller.

A foreign car producer (FCP) either intentionally introduces its original corporate culture (habits, patterns, rules, etc.) into the local environment, which is usually the approach of Japanese car companies, or relies on a locally attained good reputation of their cars (imported earlier) and on local agents, dealers and servicing companies, which results in the voice of corporate culture not being as strong in internal communication. The role of translation in the first case is substantial: all documents are in the local language and in English, and selected (by the management) texts may be required to be translated into the native language of the owner (Japanese). Another interesting aspect can be seen within Japanese car producers having their branches in Central Europe, namely the varying English proficiency level of their management: those on the top of a company hierarchy possess quite limited English language skills, therefore substantial documents are subject to relay translation from the local language into English and then to Japanese. The strongest English proficiency appears to be possessed by the middle management hired from the local and international professional community. Limited or even no English skills are possessed by local workers (e.g. servicemen); recently even specialised professionals, such as accountants, have been hired primarily for their expertise in book-keeping under the local law, with basic English proficiency being an advantage in obtaining the job but not disqualifying *conditio sine qua non*.

An international law firm (ILF), when establishing in a new country, is in the same position as any other business, i.e. certain documents are statutorily required to be in the local language, but should also be in the official language of the firm's headquarters usually for the archives.

In-house purpose translation

The scope and extent of in-house translations depend on many factors; one of them is the organisational structure of the entity along with its size, which determines levels of management, decision-making systems, the scope of the staff's involvement in the decision-making, or market or production orientation, etc. Another factor having an impact on the extent of translation for in-house purposes is the composition of the workforce in terms of their foreign language proficiency. A small manufacturer moving his business to another country and hiring employees primarily in the country of the company's origin would preserve its original (office) language and locally hired people would be required to be proficient in that language, thus the need for translation in everyday communication within that business would be marginal; however, there may be a local administrative and legal rule that certain 'organisational' text-types, such as the code of conduct, house rules, safety instructions, various labels, door tags, etc., must exist in the local language. On the other hand, a large supranational enterprise subdivided functionally and geographically into many different divisions and departments, dependent on the expertise of, and hiring, local professionals, would require a significant volume of internal documents to be translated; very often, a quasi-bilingual environment is created and parallel texts are produced – one in the original language of the enterprise, which is primarily English in most supranational and global businesses, and one in the local language. This applies mainly to 'organisational' text-types, but also certain genres reflecting the purpose and course of business may be included: various kinds of internal *memoranda* can be directed to subordinate personnel not proficient in the corporate language, which introduce modifications to the assignments of those personnel or inform them of the latest developments (*'top-down'* address); memos written by lower staff in the local language, informing the superior (management) of the progress in a particular deal (*'bottom-up'* address) can also be translated. A range of internal *reports* are translated in order to, for example, display outcomes of practical research so that persons at all levels of the organisation may become acquainted with the results. Internal *proposals* can also be found among documents subject to translation, particularly where they are addressed to senior staff and suggest any improvement (in organisation, production, technological processes, etc.).

It should be noted that genre rules for these simple documents may vary among languages. Translators should consider both the format and the content, the latter being a decisive factor in this type of interlingual communication; this is why translation sometimes glides into merely conveying the main message while losing the essential features of the source text. Moreover, there are differences in the load of translation of internal documents among a special technology manufacturer, foreign car producer and an international law firm. The first two (STM and FCP) rely primarily on local specialists and other workers and the environment is far from being bilingual, as the expertise and special technical and manual skills of employees are relevant, not their linguistic competence. As a result, internal memoranda, reports, proposals or other simple communications should often be translated and the target language would depend on the top-down or bottom-up direction in the interaction. Internal documents to be translated are often drafted in jargon characterised by technical vocabulary, can be elliptical in structure, and contain a lot of metaphors, acronyms and abbreviations typical of a respective professional context or even of a particular job. Texts are usually translated by linguistically competent staff, not by professional translators; this is why translations of internal documents from English into the local language are often rather 'casual', informal and linguistically neglectful, containing many English loan-words and phrases (with the local language inflection, if applicable) not yet established in the standard local language, but familiar to the corporate employees within the given context.

On the other hand, internal texts of an ILF would almost exclusively be in the corporate language (English) as virtually all employees in such firms have English proficiency as part of their qualifications; the role of translation within in-house communication would be marginal. However, some genres, such as a legal memorandum, need not exist in the local legal system and local lawyers, however fluent they may be in English, should learn what proper formats and different purposes of this text-type are relevant in the English-speaking legal environment (which may be part of their university education).

External purpose translation

Translations done in order to facilitate communication of an organisation with external actors play a much more important role as they form a strong component in establishing positive and effective relations with the outer environment, which, in turn, may be beneficial for the organisation.

Recipients of texts which an organisation is expected to translate in order to establish, or promote, the relationship with actors outside, can be generally subdivided into two types according to their legal nature, namely (a) private individuals or entities in the local market, such as customers, clients, contractors, business partners, cooperating enterprises, other manufacturers, competing businesses, etc., and (b) public institutions, such as administrative agencies, judicial bodies or other institutions (e.g. tax offices), which are statutory addressees of a diverse range of documents to be submitted in the local language. The pragmatic aspect of translated texts for these two groups would differ: whilst translations for the local market (in the widest sense of the phrase) MIGHT achieve their purpose, translations to be submitted to local administration or courts MUST correspond in the form, content and purpose to the local rules and conventions.

Texts subject to translation can also be subdivided into two large categories according to their culture-sensitivity: (a) technical documentation, such as handling instructions, user instructions, servicing and operation manuals, installation manuals, etc., are usually less culturally susceptible than (b) informational texts (e.g. business or official letters, memoranda, proposals, reports), policy documents (e.g. white papers, position papers or missions) or legal documents (e.g. contracts, complaints, petitions).

The main reason why technical documentation should be translated into the local language is the localisation of the respective item or product. Although the quality of translation may have an impact on the success or failure of that item or product on the local market, a considerable number of producers resort to the assistance of electronic translators, sometimes of a dubious quality, without any subsequent review of the 'translated' text by a human translator or a TL proof-reader or a local expert trying to follow the instructions and decide whether the target text makes technical sense in relation to the respective product or item.

Both STM and FCP have a large portion of their translational load assigned to technical documentation. The main difference between these two organisations subsists in the volume of translated texts for the purpose of marketing and advertising, as STM would address highly focused potential users and FCP aims at attracting the attention of the largest possible number of potential local buyers irrespective of their technical background. Texts dealing with narrowly specialised technology are aimed at a quite limited number of readers, such as specialised manufacturers of products built upon or including that technology, i.e. the ultimate recipient of the translation will primarily be a professional with some specialist knowledge in the field. There will be a minimum communication asymmetry between the ST author and the TT recipient in their expertise, which would require the translator to be sufficiently knowledgeable of the subject-matter of the ST, relevant terminology and (marginally) corresponding text-patterns in the TL. In addition to highly specialised technical texts for their servicing companies, FCP produces marketing texts directed to potential buyers, which include technical information, but manipulated to a certain extent in order to highlight presumed advantages and positives for the potential buyers. Linguistic means and psychological methods of persuasiveness used in the ST should be adapted in the TT to the local environment, particularly where the source culture and the target culture are remote. Due to a certain degree of asymmetry in communication partners (buyers of cars are primarily lay people, whilst producers are specialists in the field), this adaptation is quite often done by local marketing specialists knowing well (or presumed to know well) the needs, habits and values of the respective market; in such cases, the translator's task would be 'just' to convey the principal information into the TL, i.e. precise (direct) translation would be applicable with respect to the technical issues in the ST, and free (dynamic) translation would be permissible for the rest of the ST. Most businesses of a STM or FCP type use the services of translation agencies, which are more or less specialised in particular subject-areas, or offer specialised translators. The quality of their translation is usually hard to evaluate as not many available SL or TL subject specialists are sufficiently proficient in the other language to be able to assess the precision of, and correspondence between, the ST and the TT.

As a matter of principle, ILF hires and educates legally competent translators, or even establishes its own translational department. The main reason is that law is a deeply culturally rooted discipline as its primary purpose is to regulate the life of a specifically identified community. Where members of different communities enter into legal relations, a certain clash of cultures may occur, as law, more than any other field of humanities, is built upon, and reflects, local social patterns, habits, values and conventions. It means that translating law in a way that makes sense to the TT recipient, is based and dependent upon a translator's legal literacy in both the SL and TL legal systems. This requirement applies to all text-types within private law, such as contracts, wills, deeds, etc., and to all text-types within public law, such as judicial documents or legislation. An increasing number of potential clients in all spheres of business have become aware of the specificity of legal translation; their demands for competent legal translators have resulted in the formation of translation agencies specialised only in legal translation and focused on producing competent and quality legal translations.

Conclusions

Over the last sixty years, the focal point of translation theories has shifted; in many respects, it has followed the main trends in linguistics and human sciences generally. An emphasis upon the source text, its linguistic means and their exact transmission into the target language was replaced by a focus on the target text, its recipients and their expectations. The following individual stages of the process of translation have been studied and analysed: the identification of linguistic means in the ST, as well as their interpretation, the construction of the meaning of the ST as a whole, the modes of transfer of all layers of interpreted information into the TL and their 're-creation' into the TT reflecting the purpose of translation as well as the expectations of potential final recipients, and making sense of the TT in the TL environment. The study of translation processes has also expanded: purely linguistic means and processes were enhanced by sociolinguistic views, pragmatic applications and semiotic approaches, following the line *WORD-phrase-sentence-TEXT-register-context-DISCOURSE-environment-CULTURE*.

Although new translational theories have been incorporated in the training and education of translators and interpreters, the general practice of translation has not been susceptible to radical shifts and changes as the theories are. The reason may partly be that not all people who earn their living by translating texts in various fields are translators by education; they follow their own translational patterns empirically proved to be 'correct', i.e. a person initiating their translation (e.g. their client) has not provided any negative feedback or refused to pay for the finished translation due to its poor quality. Moreover, many translators (professionally trained or not) often resort to sources available through the internet considering them reliable; however, a significant number of translators are not fully capable of discerning the applicability or inapplicability to their translation of 'solutions' found due to, for example, the improper context or origin of such solutions.

Professional communication more than any other segment of communication is getting more and more globalised, tending to resort to the use of just one language in order to ease, and to make cheaper, interaction between and among individual actors. Although this has become reality in some professional contexts (e.g. business in the widest sense of the word), other contexts are, and will be in the future, dependent on local languages, which will nurture the practice of translation in professional settings. Unless there is one global language spoken by all people in the world, bilingual or even multilingual professional communication mediated by translators and supported by translations will survive: there will always be local groups of potential clients, customers or employees speaking just their own mother tongue, which differs from the language of respective providers of services, manufacturers and other entrepreneurs intending to establish themselves on the local market.

Despite many attempts to replace human translation with translation made by computers, and despite strong hopes, and large funds invested, in those attempts, PC translators have been of varying quality particularly those covering 'minor' languages and languages of different typology. Even though an efficient PC translator might be effective for rather simple informational texts, it should be noted that any product of a PC translator should always be 'checked' by a human translator, or at least by a TL speaker to determine whether the translated text makes sense in the respective context.

Related topics

business communication; technical communication; corporate communication; professional communication in the legal domain

Key readings

Baker, Mona (2011). *In Other Words: A Coursebook on Translation*, London and New York: Routledge. (The essential textbook on the theory and practice of translation and their applications in the training of translators.)

Cronin, Michael (2003). *Translation and Globalization*, London: Routledge. (A critical study and analysis of the impact of new technologies and globalised economy upon translation.)

Malmkjær, Kirsten (2005). *Linguistics and the Language of Translation*. Edinburgh: Edinburgh University Press. (An analysis of the relationship between the knowledge of language and the translation skills framed by contemporary approaches to translation.)

Nord, Christiane (1997). *Translating as Purposeful Activity: Functionalist Approach Explained*, Manchester: St. Jerome Publishing. (The essential textbook on the functionalist approach to translation, extremely relevant in translating professional discourse.)

Venuti, Lawrence (2000). *The Translation Studies Reader*, London: Routledge. (A selection of the relevant segments of texts written by the leading theoreticians in the field of translation.)

Note

1 This chapter was drafted as part of PRVOUK 06 (Public Law in the Context of Europeanization and Globalization) within Charles University Research Development Schemes.

Bibliography

Albrecht, Jörn (1990). 'Invarianz, Äquivalenz, Adäquatheit', in R. Arntz, G. Thome (Hrsg.) *Übersetzungswissenschaft: Ergebnisse und Perspektiven.* Festschrift für Wolfram Wilss zum 65. Geburtstag. Tübingen: Narr. 71–81.
Baker, Mona (1992). *In Other Words: A Coursebook on Translation*, London and New York: Routledge.
Daneš, František (1974). *Papers on Functional Sentence Perspective*, Praha: Academia.
Emery, Peter G. (2004). 'Translation, equivalence and fidelity: A pragmatic approach', *Babel*, *50*(2), 143–67.
Firbas, Jan (1956). 'Poznámky k problematice anglického slovního pořádku z hlediska aktuálního členění větného' [Some notes on the problem of English word order from the point of view of functional sentence perspective], *Sborník prací filozofické fakulty brněnské univerzity*, A *4*, 93–107.
——(1957). 'K otázce nezákladových podmětů v současné angličtině: Příspěvek k teorii aktuálního členění větného' [On the problem of non-thematic subjects in contemporary English: A contribution to the theory of functional sentence perspective], *Časopis pro moderní filologii*, *39*, 165–73.
——(1972). 'On the interplay of prosodic and non-prosodic means of functional sentence perspective', in V. Fried (ed.), *The Prague School of Linguistics and Language Teaching*, London: Oxford University Press.
——(1986). 'On the dynamics of written communication in the light of the theory of functional sentence perspective', in C. R. Cooper and S. Greenbaum (eds), *Studying Writing: Linguistic Approaches*, New York: Sage.
Gunnarsson, Britt-Louise (2009). *Professional Discourse* (Continuum Discourse Series), London and New York: Continuum International Publishing Group.
Gutt, Ernst-August (2000). *Translation and Relevance: Cognition and Context*, Manchester: St Jerome Publishing.
Halliday, M. A. K. (1976). *Systems and Function in Language*, London: Oxford University Press.
——(1985). *An Introduction to Functional Grammar*, London: Edward Arnold.
House, Julianne (1997). *Translation Quality Assessment: A Model Revisited*, Tübingen: Gunther Narr Verlag.
Jackson, Bernard S. (1995). *Making Sense in Law*, Liverpool: Deborah Charles Publications.
——(1997). *Semiotics and Legal Theory*, Liverpool: Deborah Charles Publications.
Jakobson, Roman (1959). 'On linguistic aspects of translation', in R. A. Brower (ed.), *On Translation* (pp. 232–39), Cambridge, MA: Harvard University Press [Reprinted in Venuti 2000].
——(1960). 'Closing statement: Linguistics and poetics', in T. Sebeok, *Style in Language* (pp. 350–77), Cambridge MA: MIT Press.
Kramer, Adam (2003). 'Common sense principles of contract interpretation (and how we've been using them all along)', *Oxford Journal of Legal Studies*, (Summer), *23*(2), 173–96.
Lecercle, Jean-Jacques (1999). *Interpretation as Pragmatics*, London: Macmillan Press Ltd.
Lederer, Marianne (2003). *Translation: The Interpretive Model*, Manchester: St Jerome.
Malmkjær, Kirsten (2005). *Linguistics and the Language of Translation*, Edinburgh: Edinburgh University Press.
Munday, Jeremy (2001). *Introducing Translation Studies. Theories and Applications*, London and New York: Routledge.
Newmark, Peter (1988). *A Textbook of Translation*, 1st edn, London: Prentice Hall Europe, 7th impression Harlow: Pearson Education, 2003.
Nida, Eugene A. (1964). *Toward a Science of Translating with Special Reference to Principles and Procedures involved in Bible Translating*, Leiden: E. J. Brill [parts reprinted in Venuti 2000].
——(2006). 'Theories of translation', *Pliegos de Yuste*, No. 4, I, 2006, 11–14, retrieved from www.pliegosdeyuste.eu/n4pliegos/eugeneanida.pdf
Nord, Christiane (1991). *Text Analysis in Translation*, Amsterdam / Atlanta: Rodopi.
——(1997). *Translating as Purposeful Activity. Functionalist Approach Explained*, Manchester: St Jerome Publishing.
Pym, Anthony (2010). *Exploring Translation Theories*, London and New York: Routledge.
Reiss, Katharina (1971). 'Type, kind and individuality of text: Decision making in translation', in L. Venuti (ed.) (2000), *The Translation Studies Reader* (pp. 160–71), London Routledge.
Salvi, Rita (2011). 'Changes, chances and challenges in describing intercultural professional interactions', in R. Salvi and H. Tanaka (eds), *Intercultural Interaction in Business and Management* (pp. 22–44), Linguistic Insights 146, Bern: Peter Lang.

Salvi, Rita and Tanaka, Hiromasa (eds) (2011). *Intercultural Interaction in Business and Management*, Linguistic Insights 146, Bern: Peter Lang.

Šarčević, Susan (2000). *New Approach to Legal Translation*, The Hague, London, Boston: Kluwer Law International.

Skřejpek, Michal (1991). 'Studie z dějin římské ústřední správy za principátu: Císařské kanceláře, jejich činnost a byrokratizace', *AUC-IURIDICA*, No. 2–3, 19–139.

——(2007) 'Státní úřady a úředníci v antickém Římě', in *Právnický stav a právnické profese v minulosti* (pp. 15–34), Praha: Havlíček Brain Team.

Tomášek, Michal (1991). 'Právo – interpretace a překlad', *Translatologica Pragensia V*, Acta Universitatis Carolinae Philologica, 4–5/1991. Praha: Karolinum, 147–54.

Venuti, Lawrence (2000). *The Translation Studies Reader*, London: Routledge.

——(2003). 'Translating Derrida on translation: Relevance and disciplinary resistance', *The Yale Journal of Criticism*, 16(2), 237–62.

Vermeer, Hans J. (1978). 'Ein Rahmen für eine allgemeine Translationstheorie', *Lebende Sprachen*, 23(1): 99–102. Reprinted in Vermeer (1983), 48–88.

——(1989). 'Skopos and commission in translational action', trans. Andrew Chesterman, in L. Venuti (ed.) (2000) *The Translation Studies Reader* (pp. 221–32), London: Routledge.

Vinay, J. P. and Darbelnet J. (1958) (1977). *Stylistique comparée du français et de l'anglais*. Paris: Didier.

——(1995). *Comparative Stylistics of French and English: A Methodology for Translation*, trans. J. C. Sager and M.-J. Hamel, Amsterdam and Philadelphia, PA: John Benjamins [parts reprinted in Venuti 2000].

White, James Boyd (1994). *Justice as Translation: An Essay in Cultural and Legal Criticism*, Chicago, London: The University of Chicago Press.

Zgusta, Ladislav (1971). *Manual of Lexicography*, Praha: Academia, The Hague: Mouton.

C. Specific disciplinary frameworks

12
Management communication
Getting work done through people

Priscilla S. Rogers

Management communication examines managers' effective use of writing and speaking to get work done with and through people (Hill 2003; Suchan and Dulek 1998; Dulek and Fielden 1990; Kotter 1982). A major objective of the field is 'to develop and disseminate knowledge that increases the effectiveness and efficiency of managers' (Smeltzer 1996: 22). As Smeltzer, Glab and Golen (1983) noted: 'Management views communication as a means to an end, something to be exploited in the service of organizational objectives after weighing the cost-benefit considerations' (p. 74). Academics in management communication have sought to facilitate this goal from a social constructionist perspective that does not ignore the fundamental responsibility to treat each other and the planet respectfully.

Managers are individuals with decision-making responsibilities for an organisation or its sub-units (Hill 2003; Reinsch 1991). They spend most of their time interacting with others, diagnosing unstructured problems, developing and implementing plans, managing information, and relaying decisions about strategic goals, financial support and assigned tasks (Kotter 1982). Success involves developing, motivating and retaining outstanding employees (O'Rourke 2010; Mintzberg 1973). Managers also need to access the impact of oral and written messages in recurring situations and to implement modifications to achieve organisational goals (e.g., Suchan 2006). Academics in management communication have originated and appropriated frameworks and tools to assist managers with these activities, although much more developmental work remains to be done.

This chapter describes: (1) the historical development of management communication, (2) its unique focus relative to other professional communication fields, and (3) its core content related to managers' communication activities. Sources used for this overview included: journals focusing on communication enactment that are most read by academics in professional communication fields; the publications of Association for Business Communication Outstanding Researcher Award (ORA) recipients who are known for their work on management communication; and the descriptions and syllabi on the websites of the *Financial Times*' top business schools. Also contributing were publications on the nature of managerial work and discussions with ORA researchers over many years including recent emails and phone calls.[1] A descriptive rather than an empirical piece, this chapter was also influenced by a personal commitment over three decades to develop frameworks and tools that help managers see, shape, and evaluate workplace communications.

Priscilla S. Rogers

Management communication is a widely dispersed, interdisciplinary field. Academics invested in its development must persevere to crystallise the field's theoretical propositions and paradigms, like the devotees of organisational communication have done since the formative work of Charles Redding and Karl Weick. This chapter offers a step toward formalising this specialised field.

Historical development

Management communication emerged with the development of graduate business education, particularly the Masters of Business Administration (MBA). Although 'universities formed business schools and departments to train managers, beginning with the University of Pennsylvania's Wharton School in 1881', and although the study of business communication has been around for over a century (Russell 1991: 126), the academic area of management communication is relatively new (Knight 1999).[2]

Impetus to develop management communication in academe came with the American Assembly of Collegiate Schools of Business (AACSB) accreditation standard stipulating that business programs provide graduate training in written and oral communication.

> C.I.3.C *Standard*: Basic skills in written and oral communication, quantitative analysis, and computer usage should be achieved either by prior experience and education, or as part of the MBA curriculum.
>
> (AACSB 1991: 20, quoted in Smeltzer 1996)[3]

Shortly thereafter, in 1979, instructors from top-ranked US business schools who were charged with teaching management communication convened at Yale University to share syllabi, discuss teaching methods, and target areas for research. The group adopted the name Managerial Communication Association or 'MCA' (Munter 1989b).

In 1984, MCA members voted by a small margin to retain their 'by-invitation only' membership, which some viewed as an impediment to the growth of the field. But individual MCA members have not been isolationists. Members Paul Feingold, Christine Kelly, and JoAnne Yates played a critical role by founding and editing the *Management Communication Quarterly* (*MCQ*). Others published two of the few textbooks in the field: Mary Munter's (2012) popular *Guide to Managerial Communication* and James O'Rourke's (2010) *Management Communication: A Case-Analysis Approach*, which in its fourth edition won the Association for Business Communication Distinguished Publication Award. MCA members have shared their research and pedagogical materials by lecturing in a wide variety of business schools around the world and by participating in the Association for Business Communication.

An international organisation in existence for some time, the Association for Business Communication (ABC) has been another forum for developing management communication. Within ABC, the MBA Consortium has spearheaded regular conference sessions on management communication pedagogy. The ABC's research journal, the *Journal of Business Communication* along with the *Journal of Business and Technical Communication* (originated at Iowa State University in 1987) are primary publication sites for management communication research and are two of the most read journals by academics in professional communication fields (Rogers, Campbell, Louhiala-Salminen, Rentz and Suchan 2007; Lowry, Humphreys, Malwitz and Nix 2006). Also, since the ABC began giving the Outstanding Researcher Award in 1990, over half of its recipients have been known for their management communication research.

While most of the business schools offering MBA or MBA-type degrees remain in the United States (see Table 12.1) graduate business degrees have mushroomed globally and, with

Table 12.1 Financial Times top 51 global MBA programs shows growth in programs outside the United States

25 US	Stanford; Harvard; Wharton; Columbia; MIT; Chicago; Berkeley; Duke; Northwestern; NYU; Dartmouth; Yale; Cornell; Michigan; UCLA; Carnegie; Darden; Emory; Georgetown; Rice; Indiana; Penn State; Rochester; Texas A&M; University of Texas at Austin
16 Europe	London; Insead; IE; Iese; IMD; HEC; Oxford; Rotterdam, SDA; Cambridge; Warwick; Manchester; Esade; Cranfield; Cass; Imperial
04 China	Hong Kong UST; Ceibs; CuHK; Uni of Hong Kong
03 Singapore	Insead; NUS; NTU
02 India	Ahmedabad; Indian School
02 Australia	AGSM; Melbourne
01 Brazil	Coppead
01 Canada	Toronto

Source: *Global MBA rankings 2012* (2012). Retrieved 28/10/12, from http://rankings.ft.com/businessschoolrankings/global-mba-rankings-2012

them, a wide variety of management communication and related courses (Knight 2005). Consider the following examples reported on the websites of the *Financial Times*' top ten programs in October 2012:

- Stanford Graduate School of Business offered a varied collection of communication courses, including *Strategic Communication, Interpersonal Dynamics at Work, Negotiations* and *How to Make Ideas Stick.*
- University of Pennsylvania Wharton School of Business had diverse offerings – *Management Communication, Negotiations, Advanced Persuasive Speaking, Advanced Persuasion and Data Display* and *Communication Challenges for Entrepreneurs: Pitching Your Business.* Wharton also provided a Writing Center for MBAs.
- MIT Sloan Business School covered writing and speaking skills for management in a course titled *Communication for Leaders* and offered an *Advanced Managerial Communication* course emphasising interpersonal skills and how to run meetings.
- INSEAD's communication course called *The Art of Communication*, focused on individual and group presentation, including the production of effective visual aids.
- IE (Instituto de Empresa) Business School had a *Communication Skills* course covering techniques such as structuring a message for high impact and developing an authentic communicative style.
- IESE (Instituto de Estudios Superiores de la Empresa) Business School had two courses covering many topics associated with organizational communication: *Managing People in Organizations* (which covered management styles, sources of authority, hierarchical communication and organizational cultures) and *Communication and Interpersonal Relations* (which looked at relations with superiors, group dynamics and group decision-making).
- Hong Kong University of Science and Technology (UST) Business School offered a management communication core course and relevant electives, such as the course titled *Maximizing Your Leadership Potential.*

Some MBA programs, like the University of Michigan's Ross Business School, also require MBAs to complete consulting projects for organisations (domestic, international, corporate, entrepreneurial or nonprofit). These real-world projects give MBAs the opportunity to apply critical thinking and analytical tools they have learned in core courses, to develop teamwork skills and to improve their communication skills by preparing project proposals, status reports, final written reports and final oral presentations (Pawlik, Rogers and Shwom 2010).

Although graduate business schools around the world have not yet settled on a standard way to deliver management communication training, external interest in graduates who are skilled communicators has not waned. The Graduate Management Admission Council's survey of 2,825 representatives from over 2,000 companies in 63 countries worldwide found that employers seek good oral and written communication skills as their *highest criterion* (89 per cent) when hiring MBA graduates, even to a greater degree than proven ability to perform (73 per cent), strategic skills (69 per cent), and core business knowledge (69 per cent) (Murray 2009).

Focus of management communication

In 1996 Smeltzer wrote that management communication had no solid focus, definition, or distinctive content. He concluded that:

> communication scholars who would like to identify themselves as specialists in management communication have an ambiguous professional self-construct. They do not know what is central, distinctive, and enduring about their profession.
>
> (p. 7)

Management communication is interdisciplinary, drawing from rhetoric, composition, linguistics, and social science generally. This complicates the task of identifying its core theoretical constructs. In 1988, Shelby described management communication as a patchwork discipline that picks content on the basis of what is intuitive, convenient or practical rather than on the basis of a well-articulated rationale (see also Feingold 1987). Not long thereafter, Suchan (1991: 1) characterised management communication as 'still a fledgling area'.

One can argue that management communication remains fledgling. No PhD programs have emerged to train faculty who continue to be sourced from diverse fields. *Management Communication Quarterly*, the research journal named for the field and initiated by its devotees, has through a succession of editors become the 'flagship' and 'defining' journal for *organisational* communication (Putnam 2012: 510, 511). Management communication courses are delivered under diverse names with less standardisation of content than one finds in business and corporate communication. For example, only four of the 25 top non-US programs that Knight (2005) investigated used 'management communication' as the course title. Globally, course content incorporates a wide range of topics, such as corporate communication, cross-cultural management, interpersonal skills and leadership. Methods of delivery 'do not seem to follow any particular model' (Knight 2005: 139). The ABC Outstanding Researchers known for their work in management communication draw from a wide variety of theoretical frameworks, none of which emerged as dominant in surveying these researchers for this chapter. And although Knight concluded in 1999 that management communication training of some sort appeared to have 'a permanent home in professional graduate management education' (p. 22), it is not clear that this will remain the case, particularly as some MBA programs are now downsizing from two-year to one-year programs.

Although management communication is less developed than other professional communication fields, a review of research and teaching content suggests a definitional perspective: *Management communication focuses on the manager and the enactment of communication related to management activities in organisational contexts.* Of particular interest are oral and written texts that managers originate, receive, and encounter from co-workers, suppliers, customers and other stakeholders (Shelby 1988). As O'Rourke (2010) wrote in his textbook for managers: 'An understanding of language and its inherent powers, combined with the skill to speak, write, listen, and form interpersonal relationships, will determine whether you will succeed as a manager' (p. 1).

Management communication has been distinguished from other professional communication fields for some time (Shelby 1993). For example, we know that business communication shares a keen interest in oral and written texts, including language issues, content development, structure and format. But business communication looks at these textual concerns for business more broadly. Business communication is tied to undergraduate education in business schools; management communication to the MBA.

By contrast, corporate communication concerns 'the corporation's voice and the images it projects of itself on a world stage populated by various ... constituencies' (Argenti and Forman 2002: 4). It is an arm of upper-management involving public investor relations, crisis communication, corporate image and corporate social responsibility. It has an underlying marketing function. Specialists, like the PhDs trained in corporate communication at the Aalto University School of Business, learn how to produce external communications, like annual reports, CEO blogs and scripts for CEO presentations to the investment community. By contrast, management communication is interested in the day-to-day communications of middle managers.

Organisational communication is closely aligned with organisational behaviour and communication studies generally, giving far less attention to the enactment of oral and written communications. Sometimes 'organisational' and 'management' communication are used interchangeably and there have been efforts to 'create a shared space' for organisational communication and communication fields that focus on enactment (Aritz and Walker 2012: 5). However, at present, there is not much cross-fertilisation. For example, Hartelius and Browning (2008) published a literature review on the application of rhetorical theory in 'managerial research' but cited neither of the most-read journals noted earlier that focus on language, writing, speaking, and organisational genre. What Munter (1989a) wrote years ago remains representative of how organisational communication differs from professional communication fields concerned with enactment:

> [I]f you see the word *organizational* in the title, the course – taught at either the graduate or undergraduate levels – will emphasize the effects of the organization on communication: communication networks, information flow and direction, hierarchies, motivation, and so on. The communication skills, if any, tend to be interpersonal and small group communication, rather than writing and speaking.
>
> *(p. 270)*

Management communication's interest in writing and speaking distinguishes it from organisational communication. Its focus on *the textual life of the manager* differentiates it from the broader field of business communication and the more specialised corporate communication.

Managers' core communicative activities

If management communication is the study of the written and oral textual life of the manager who must get work done with and through people, then what is its content? What communication activities do managers engage in? What does research and pedagogical literature tell us about these activities?

The following five core communication activities were derived from literature on the nature of managerial work, a review of most-read journals by academics in the field, the publications of award-winning researchers, course descriptions and the author's own experience in the field.

- Predicting audience response
- Selecting workplace language
- Seeing and shaping organisational genres
- Diagnosing communication effectiveness
- Using discourse interaction

These activities are offered as a *preliminary rather than comprehensive* list. They could comprise the topics in a primer on management communication, much like those taught in core courses in accounting, finance, marketing, and operations. These activities appear in some form or fashion in research and pedagogical materials, although they have not been pulled together like this. All require more research attention.

Predicting audience response

Predicting how audiences will respond to messages is a critical aspect of managing communication to get work done with and through people. 'Management skills are *responsive*,' observed McKnight (1991: 205). Clampitt (1991) compared a manager's communicative task to dancing. The better you know your partner, the more effective your communication will be. As Munter (2012) wrote:

> You not only need to know where *you* want the audience to be as a result of your communication, you also need to figure out where *they* are right now ... The more you can learn about your audience – who they are, what they know, what they feel, and how they can be persuaded – the more likely you will be to achieve your desired outcome.
>
> (p. 10)

The audiences that managers communicate with to 'achieve desired outcomes' are many and diverse, however. Managers oversee various employee groups, report to upper management and board members, negotiate with different suppliers and labour union leaders, serve customers and investors, interact with local communities and government officials, respond to reporters interested in their successes or failures, and more. These audiences have unique needs, views, and interests that may converge or conflict and that change over time. Their work responsibilities, language skills, and communication habits also differ.

But workplace audiences also intermingle. They form informal and formal networks independent of management. They are known to gossip, become Facebook friends, meet for social events, become upset with each other, and rail against management. Meanwhile, effective managers build networks of their own, including hundreds of individuals both inside and outside their organisations (Ibarra and Hunter 2007; Cross and Parker 2004; Watts 2004; Cross, Borgatti and Parker 2002). These networks intersect forming complex relationships that shift over time as circumstances change. For example, during employee contract negotiations, labour union leaders and employees coalesce; management and their backers retrench, while reporters and their constituent readers clamour for information from both sides.

In this complicated communicative environment *it is not possible for managers to determine fully who is talking to whom and what their audiences know, do not know, or need to know*. Nor can managers dictate how their messages will be received. Whether a message gets read, heard, interpreted, or acted upon as intended, depends on many situational and personal factors beyond a manager's control. At best, managers guess how audiences will respond. Communicating to achieve desired work outcomes with multiple audiences is a *predictive* activity not a prescriptive one.

Bases for predictive analysis

Predicting how audiences will respond to messages in management contexts is not as simple as seeking answers to demographic questions about age, sex, education, social position, cultural background and the like. Managers need to focus their analyses around the needs of workplace participants. Considered individually, these needs are many, varied and difficult to coral. Looking at *shared* needs is less unruly and potentially fruitful for predictive analysis.

Two needs relevant to most workplace participants are: (1) the need for work productivity and (2) the need for cooperative relationships. Absent productivity and cooperative relationships, organisations have difficulty remaining viable. Pay, promotions and jobs may be jeopardised. These potentialities are no secret and bring workplace participants together when times are tough, such as when management and unions need to reach agreement so that an automotive company can survive an economic downturn. Using these basic shared needs as a framework for predicative analysis seems like a sensible point of departure.

Seeing that *work gets done productively* is a critical aspect of a manager's job. Predictive analysis to increase productivity examines message relevance:

- Will this message waste receivers' time?
- Will receivers fail to understand how this message is relevant to them?
- Is there some probability that receivers will trash or ignore this message?

A 'yes' answer to any one of these questions suggests that a message is faulty in its structure and content, unnecessary, or directed to the wrong audience. Related to this, Mathas and Stevenson (1976) provided a helpful way to select receivers. They divided receivers into three groups:

- *Primary* receivers must reach a decision or act upon the message.
- *Secondary* receivers are likely to be affected by the action or decision.
- *Intermediate* receivers are gatekeepers who determine if and when others receive the message.

Shaping messages for primary receivers is key but sometimes it is also necessary to engender goodwill or demonstrate message urgency with intermediate receivers (like secretaries or deputy assistants) as they may prevent successful delivery. Reaching primary receivers also involves analysing their media preferences and timing. These considerations suggest questions like these:

- What communication media is likely to reach primary receivers expediently? What are receivers' media preferences?
- When are primary receivers most available to receive this message?
- Will any intermediate receivers stop this message from being delivered? If so, how might these intermediate receivers be persuaded to deliver the message or how might they be sidestepped?
- Should this message be directed to any secondary receivers?

To do their job, *managers must also build cooperative relationships* with a large number of people – subordinates, peers, superiors and a variety of organisational outsiders (Hill 2003; Stewart 1988; Kotter 1982; Mintzberg 1973). Workplace relationships are tied to organisational roles, responsibilities, and situations that carry with them various expectations for communication. Managers are often expected to mentor employees, to assign work tasks that are reasonable, and to appraise their performance with thoughtfulness and objectivity. Managers need employees to be receptive, to learn, to complete assigned tasks, and to perform those tasks well. Managers must devise plans, persuade superiors to support those plans, and get employees to enact them. Managerial success depends upon cooperation. When a manager has good communication skills, these relationships may evolve into highly functional partnerships (Clampitt 1991).

Key to relationship building is communicative civility and polite concern for the feelings or face needs of others (Holmes and Stubbe 2003; Brown and Levinson 1987). This expectation persists, even in contentious situations, including when individuals and groups disagree or become belligerent. A manager is a 'professional' after all and, as such, must subjugate personal feelings to bigger organisational goals.

There are also issues related to the political environment and the organisation's reporting relationships and reward systems. In a hierarchical environment, it is fair to predict that relationships may be hurt if messages skip the queue, for example. Observing the chain of command may also have negative consequences for a reporting manager, however. That manager may go unrecognised for an original idea by those who have reward power, for example. This makes the question of who should and should not receive messages enormously complex – 'Should I "cc" or "bcc" upper management or would they find this a waste of their time?' 'If I "cc" upper management, will my direct boss be upset?' 'What are the trade-offs?'

All in all, the need to build cooperative relationships can guide predication, raising targeted questions, such as these:

- Who should and should not receive this message?
- How are receivers likely to react to this message? Will it surprise them? Are they likely to ignore it, dismiss it, consider it or accept it?
- What face issues may come into play? Could this message embarrass or hurt receivers? How might these face issues be mitigated?
- Am I the best person to deliver this message? Will receivers expect this message to come from me? Will they see it as important, affirming or threatening?
- Is this the best time to deliver this message? Are work pressures or relational tensions too great to relay this message now? Is this a religious holiday for them? Should the message be delayed?
- Should this message be delivered face-to-face or in some other oral or written format?
- If this message were leaked, would it damage our relationship? Should this message be oral, private and undocumented at present?
- Should this message invite receivers to express their views or is it wise to wait and see how they respond first?

Finally, a comprehensive resource on predictive audience analysis in organisational contexts is Young's (2011) book titled *How Audiences Decide*. Young identifies the types of decisions that audiences are asked to make in professional contexts, for example whether to comply, staff, employ, invest, or provide financial support. He then describes the criteria that audiences use to make such decisions and provides examples to illustrate how these criteria can help managers formulate messages that get read, understood and acted upon. Young's analysis is relevant to the productivity and relational concerns of managers. For example, consider the decision criteria employees may use when responding to a manager's request for cost-cutting measures or longer working hours:

- Are the circumstances significant enough to merit my manager's request?
- Will my sacrifice be appreciated?
- Will my manager do his/her part?
- Does my manager share my values?

By identifying decision criteria that audiences use and examples of textual options that may address these criteria, Young (2011) provides a wonderful resource for management communication research and teaching.

Selecting workplace language

Eccles and Nohria (1992) noted that to 'see management in its proper light, managers need first to take language seriously' (p. 205). 'Without the right words, used in the right way,' they continued, 'it is unlikely that the right actions will occur. Words do matter – they matter very much' (p. 209). This conclusion raises a basic question: What are the right words used in the right way? Across management contexts, the answer is 'it depends'. Managers' workplace environments are both idiosyncratic and interactively complex. Formulaic approaches may be irrelevant. Communicating effectively is not a repetitive process that can be applied straight-away in different situations (Kent 1993). Thus managers need to develop a repertoire of options from which to choose and to follow the protocols of Business English Lingua Franca (BELF) when interacting with non-native speakers of English in some contexts.

Developing a repertoire of options

What does it mean for managers to 'take language seriously' as Eccles and Nohria (1992) suggest? It means developing a repertoire of linguistic and rhetorical options from which to choose and observing the relative effectiveness of those options in the workplace. Research has elaborated options that are highly useful for managers to know. Three examples are: (1) direct and indirect structuring, (2) use of narrative, and (3) sentence-level tools.

Direct (high-impact) or indirect (low-impact) structuring are both useful depending upon the nature of the workplace situation and the manager's goals (Suchan and Colucci 1989; Fielden and Dulek 1983). For example, research on advance organisers (subject lines, introductions, headings and meeting agendas) that introduce the specific topic at the onset of the message are shown to help users more efficiently comprehend a message (Rogers 1990). Advance organisers work well for informational messages, particularly when receivers are suffering from information overload (Hemp 2009; Fann-Thomas and King 2006). But an indirect structure may have a better chance of success if receivers are in the habit of using it for a particular task, or if they are likely to dismiss the message outright without explanation or proof first, or if the news is bad or face threatening (Suchan and Dulek 1990).

Narratives (or stories) are an option that should not be dismissed in preference for probative statistics. Jameson (2001) described narratives as having 'an internal logic strong enough to link the component events into a unified whole with a point that is more than the sum of the parts' (p. 478). She found that narratives were a means for managing conflicts involving incompatible demands, that they could soften receiver resistance to arguments based on statistical evidence or theory, and that they impacted a manager's power to inform and influence (see also Forman 2013; Jameson 2000; Bal 1997; Suchan 1995). 'Storybuilding', the collective group activity of organising disparate facts and experiences into a sequence that implies cause and effect, helped managers 'challenge corporate policies, advocate change, and influence important constituencies' (Jameson 2001: 477).

Sentence-level choices that managers need to know include constructions that have been dismissed as ineffective in some business communication textbooks, such as passives, nominalisations, expletive constructions, and hedging particles. But research shows that such constructions are expedient choices for some management situations. For example, Hagge and Kostelnick (1989) found that 'suggestion letters' written by auditors in a Big Eight accounting firm consistently employed 'both the mandative subjunctive and the modals could, should, might, may, and would ... to convey the sense of uncertainty inherent in the auditing process and to mitigate the impositive force of directive [r]ecommendations' (p. 321). They also found that extensive use of agentless passives (such as 'are not documented' and 'have been returned') in sections of letters that defined a problem in a client's organisation effectively removed references to the individual or organisation that caused the problem. As Brown and Levinson (1987) observed in 'Politeness: Some Universals in Language Usage', the passive coupled with a rule of agent deletion is perhaps the means par excellence in English of avoiding reference to persons involved in FTAs [Face Threatening Acts] (p. 194; see also Rogers et al. 2004; Rogers and Lee-Wong 2003).

In summary, managers need to develop a repertoire of linguistic and rhetorical alternatives from which to choose.

Using Business English Lingua Franca (BELF)

For managers who work across cultures with non-native speakers of English, using the right words in the right way involves learning the protocols of Business English Lingua Franca (BELF). BELF is a 'simplified English' without complex sentences, idiomatic expressions, jargon, or unusual words (Kankaanranta and Planken 2010: 392; Rogerson-Revell 2010; Kankaanranta and Louhiala-Salminen 2010 and 2007; Louhiala-Salminen and Charles 2006; Louhiala-Salminen and Kankaanranta 2005; Nickerson 1998). Two recurring protocols characterise BELF: (1) focus on content comprehension and (2) 'let it pass' strategies.

As an instrument for getting work done with non-native speakers of English, BELF focuses on user comprehension of content rather than on grammatical or syntactical correctness (Table 12.2).

Table 12.2 English language perspective compared to Business English Lingua Franca perspective

	English language perspective	Business English Lingua Franca perspective
Speaker/writer aims to...	Emulate native speaker	Get job done
Non-native speaker seen as...	Learner who slows down work and requires patience	Communicator in his/her own right
Main communication concerns	Language errors	Increasing English vocabulary and responding more quickly
Important culture...	Host country culture	Global business culture
Goal of non-native speaker is to:	Increase of understanding of 'perfect' English	Increase understanding of 'Englishes' for global business

Errors that disrupt understanding matter, such as unclear pronoun references and lack of subject-verb agreement. Accent errors, like missing articles or incorrect plurals that do not impede understanding, are ignored (Rogers and Rymer, 2001). A Japanese manager may never master the use of 'a', 'an', and 'the', although he interacts regularly with employees at a manufacturing plant where English is the native language. He can relax knowing that communication effectiveness is not dependent on English language mastery in every respect, nor will his business associates expect mastery.

BELF's focus on content comprehension invites users to engage in a number of distinctive practices (Kankaanranta and Planken 2010). BELF interactions are known to include a good deal of checking and re-checking – 'Do you understand my meaning?' Delivery tends to be slower and more formal procedurally and linguistically. Procedural formality involves topic control and turn taking. For example, in meetings individuals may be invited to speak with their turns directed through a chairperson. Formal procedures of this kind act 'as a barrier to spontaneous, self-selected turns, with some NNSE [Non-native speakers of English] participants feeling they lack the ability to use the appropriate formal register to claim turns or interrupt' (Rogerson-Revell 2010: 447; see also Du-Babcock 1999). Linguistic formality may involve frequent nominalisations, passive rather than active voice, and Latinate words learned in English language courses. Words and phrases from users' native languages may be interspersed with English.

Effective BELF users are also shown to ignore linguistic anomalies. Firth (1996) called this the 'let it pass' strategy, which disregards the surface features of talk in the interest of making meaning together. A characteristic of 'let it pass' is lack of other repair. One participant's non-traditional usage will go uncorrected and may be even replicated by participants who know better in an attempt to identify (Rogerson-Revell 2010; Sweeney and Hua 2010). Participants may also admit their own linguistic limitations – 'I don't know if I say this the best way.' Small talk about safe topics, like music or food, may be interjected to build rapport and solidarity (Pullin 2010).

The consequences of not knowing BELF's idiosyncrasies for international management communication is just beginning to become known. One dramatic example from the discipline of finance is Brochet, Naranjo and Yu's (2012) discovery that linguistic complexity in conference calls held in English by non-US firms contributed to reductions in trading volume and in price movement. Negative market responses were even more pronounced when there was a greater presence of foreign investors. The 'form in which financial information is presented', they concluded, 'can impose additional processing costs by limiting investors' ability to interpret the reported financials' (see abstract).

Managers who communicate in global environments need to know how BELF works. This is particularly true for native English speakers (Kankaanranta and Planken 2010). Sweeney (2010) characterised this as 'the native speaker problem', that is, the native speaker continuing 'to speak idiomatically, using complicated or obscure vocabulary, and bringing with them their cultural communication norms' (p. 480).

In summary, managers must take language seriously. This involves choosing strategies that are best suited for different contexts. A large repertoire of linguistic and rhetorical options from which to choose and knowledge of BELF will enable this.

Seeing and shaping genre

Organisational genres are another communication tool for managing. Organisational genres are typified messages recognised by their form, content and the actions they engender (Bakhtin

1986; Miller 1984; Yates 1989b; Swales 1990 and 2004; Yates and Orlikowski 1992; Orlikowski and Yates 1994; Spinuzzi 2003). They are often associated with work roles (e.g. Nickerson 2000). The status report a project team delivers to their supervising manager, the flowsheet on which a nurse records patient information in a hospital's emergency room, and the post-audit letter a tax accountant completes to examine the accuracy of the Internal Revenue Service's calculations for penalty assessment are organisational genres (Pawlik, Rogers and Shwom 2010; Østerlund 2007; Devitt 1991).

Research shows that organisational genres comprise an infrastructure for managing communicative activities. They channel, sequence, and expedite recurring work. They facilitate organised interaction among individuals with vastly different responsibilities (Yates and Orlikowski 2002; Nickerson 1998, 2000; Zachery 2000). They serve as collaborative tools and documentation (Winsor 1999; Freedman, Adam and Smart 1994).

Organisational genres originated to meet the need for structured and efficient work processes as businesses grew and record keeping and reporting became more complex (Yates 1989a). For example, the memorandum with its innovative subject line replaced the letter. The subject line directs a writer to surface the topic of the memo and it facilitates efficient filing and retrieval.

But more than this, genres draw attention to the kind of work activities that are important. For example, the standard quarterly financial report with its expectation that figures be displayed in tables rather than solely elaborated in prose, not only makes quarterly results easier for users to see, but also exerts pressure on reporting employees to focus on profit-making activities – e.g., we should streamline the XYZ manufacturing process so that we have more profits to report next year.

Genres may also be modified to redirect work activities as organisational goals change (Bremner 2012). The dean who added 'media citations' to the categories in the faculty annual report is an apt example. Intent on elevating his business school's MBA in the *Business Week* rankings, the dean wanted faculty to produce research that would impact managerial practices and, thereby, get reported in trade magazines and the popular press. Whether the higher MBA ranking that followed can be attributed to the addition of 'media citations' to the faculty reporting genre is unclear. But the author of this chapter did modify her publication activities as a consequence of this change.

Genre sets and systems

Sometimes genres are clustered into sets and systems that sequence the flow of work and compile information for discussion and retrieval (Østerlund 2007; Spinuzzi 2004). Genre sets comprise a full range of genres for one side of a multiparty interaction, such as the set of deliverables that consulting teams produce at the beginning, middle and end of project work – contracting documents, status reports, and final presentations (Pawlik, Rogers and Shwom 2010). Contracting documents become instruments for benchmarking team progress when status reports are delivered, for example.

Genre systems comprise an intermingling of two or more genre sets, such as the genre sets that nurses, doctors, and clericals use as they move a patient through the emergency room. Nurses regularly update patient flowsheets; doctors consult these flowsheets to complete their reports; clerks compile all these genres for future reference when patients are released (Østerlund 2007). Functioning as they should, genre systems provide an iterative, systematic means for individuals with different work responsibilities and interdependencies to interact effectively. But effective function requires genre oversight.

Need for genre management

Managers are not always attentive to the potential of genres or the need to manage them. Genres can become so ingrained in work routines that they go unmanaged. Sometimes genres can fail to produce desired results or become abused. They can be diluted in their use if they do not serve the best interest of their users (Bremner 2012). An automotive company's Dealer Contact Report (DCR) is a case in point. Field managers were expected to complete DCRs to describe decisions for handling customer problems at car dealerships. But some field managers ignored the required DCR format. Instead of elaborating on the Problem, Recommendation, Action and Timetable categories specified on the DCR, they ignored these categories and simply wrote narrative chronological accounts of their discussions with dealers. Field managers said narratives were easier to write and were appreciated by their district managers who were eager to hear stories about dealerships. But their narratives did not provide the kind of documentation that upper management needed to follow-up on cases or to defend company decisions if a case were taken to court. Therefore, training was implemented to show field managers why they needed to follow the dictates of the DCR genre and to help them do so expeditiously (Rogers 1989).

Organisational genres offer 'perceived fixity' that can stabilise, direct and expedite work activities (Østerlund 2007: 83). But genres can also lose their power if their form and content requirements are abused or ignored. Shaping genres that meet workplace needs, reinforcing their diligent use, revising and replacing them when work needs change, comprise a managerial endeavour of some complexity and consequence.

Diagnosing communication effectiveness

Managers also need diagnostic skills to monitor and improve communications. This is not easy. Managers must evaluate the effectiveness of messages and of the individuals who deliver them in light of contextual and discursive realities (Bhatia 2008). Approaches that work for one context may not work in another context. Jobs and situational demands change and with them the communicative competencies needed to do them well. Messages must be crafted for receivers with different and changing expectations and obligations.

Managers are confronted with multiple questions related to communication effectiveness: What types of communications are required for this job at this juncture in the life of the organisation? Who possesses the skills to communicate well in this job? Is the employee assigned to this job meeting its communication requirements? If not, where is improvement needed? Am I communicating job requirements clearly? Will this message achieve what we want it to achieve with its receivers? Managers use a variety of diagnostic tools to address such questions.

Hiring and placement

There are a slew of tools to measure personality traits, communication style, and communication competence generally. Sometimes managers employ these to facilitate hiring or placement decisions. Two examples are Richmond, McCroskey and Johnson's (2003) and Richmond and McCroskey's (1990) Nonverbal Immediacy Scale and the 'SocioCommunicative' Style Scale. Although first published in 1962, the Myers-Briggs Type Indicator assessment, which measures how individuals are inclined to view the world and make decisions, remains popular for matching employees with jobs. Also used are assessment centres, which place candidates in simulated situations like those they would encounter in a particular job. For example, candidates for a managerial position might be given a simulated in-basket exercise. How candidates process in-basket messages suggests their ability to discern the relative importance of messages, to select appropriate media for responding, and to delegate.

Performance appraisal and message monitoring

Providing employees with 'feedback about performance is one of the most important communication tasks of the manager' (Clampitt 1991: 147). Organisations develop appraisal genres for this purpose, which typically incorporate some assessment of communication skills. But regular informal feedback is also important. Clampitt (1991) provides a useful overview on performance feedback in Communicating for Managerial Effectiveness.

Templates for evaluating various components of individual messages have also been developed, such as the Analysis of Argument Measure – which scores the use of claims, data, and warrant in persuasive messages based on Toulmin's (1958) definitive work on the components of an argument – and the Persuasive Adaptiveness Measure for Managerial Writing, which scores the extent to which a message adapts the readers' perspective (Rogers 1994). Challenged to provide new MBA students with a baseline assessment of their managerial writing skills using the Graduate Management Admissions Test Analytical Writing Assessment, Rogers and Rymer (2001) developed four basic tools: the Task Tool evaluates how well a piece of writing fulfils the assigned task and meets reader expectations; the Coherence Tool assesses if a message forms a meaningful whole for readers; the Reasoning Units Tool examines how logically convincing readers find claims and support in the writing, and the Error Interference Tool identifies errors that impede reader understanding and/or hurt the writer's credibility. Managers can use such tools to help employees improve their skills.

Competing Values Framework

Used for management evaluation and training in Asia, Europe, and the United States, the Competing Values Framework (CVF) is a multifaceted tool for diagnosing the effectiveness of individual messages and communicative performance on the job. Rather than evaluating effectiveness against some absolute standard, this tool asks managers to compare a message or an employee's performance as it is 'now' against what it 'should be' for the situation or the job (Quinn, Hildebrandt, Rogers and Thompson 1991; Rogers and Hildebrandt 1993). The 'now' and 'should be' scheme is dynamic; it accommodates contextual variability.

In brief, the CVF was empirically built by asking communication experts to associate a comprehensive list of valued communication characteristics with four types of communication: relational, informational, promotional and transformational. Experts' responses were subjected to multidimensional scaling, which revealed relationships between the valued characteristics and the types of communication. The resulting CVF identifies sets of characteristics most strongly associated with each type of communication, as shown in Figure 12.1. For example, the characteristics 'open, candid and personal' are highly valued for relational communications, whereas promotional communications are expected to be more conclusive, decisive and action-oriented.

The CVF further illustrates the relationships between relational, informational, promotional, and transformational types of communication. Each type of communication is visualised as a quadrant. Quadrants that are side-by-side share characteristics. For example, being 'dependable, accurate, and factual' is valued for highly relational and informational communications; being 'innovative, creative, and original' is valued for highly transformational and promotional communications. Types of communication in quadrants located across from each other have

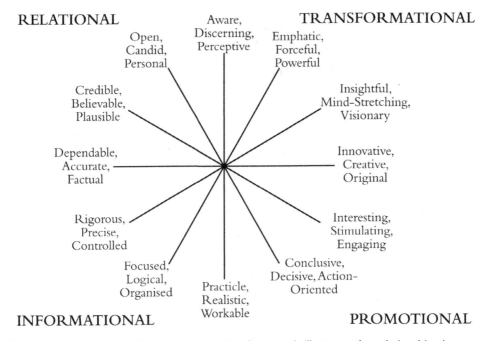

Figure 12.1 Competing values communication framework illustrates the relationships between four basic types of communication and valued characteristics

'competing values'. For example, there is a tension between the characteristics 'open, candid and personal' expected when relating and the characteristics 'conclusive, decisive and action-oriented' needed to promote. The fact that some characteristics are competing suggests that while all the characteristics are valued, the extent to which they are targeted depends upon the goal of the communication – a highly promotional communication will tend to be more conclusive and action-oriented; a highly relational communication more personal and open. In brief, the CVF provides a conceptual map for understanding the qualities most expected for different types of communication (Quinn *et al*. 1991).

By attaching a seven-point scale to each set of valued characteristics, the CVF becomes an instrument for evaluating individual messages or the extent to which an individual is communicating to meet the demands of his or her job (Rogers and Hildebrandt 1993). For job evaluation, data is collected from workplace associates (such as subordinates, peers, superiors, suppliers and customers). These associates use a 1–7 point scale to score the importance of each set of characteristics for an individual's job – where that individual's communication is 'now' (N) and where it 'should be' (SB). These scores are then averaged and used to create profiles. N scores are connected with a solid line; SB scores with a dotted line, as shown in Figure 12.2. Characteristics on which N and SB match suggest strengths. Where N and SB differ by two points or more, improvement is needed. Associate profiling has been used to train medical staff at Detroit's Henry Ford Hospital and to help new entrants into the Ross School of Business's Global MBA Program assess their skills, for example. Individuals can also score their own communication for their job to create 'self profiles' and set personal goals, as is done by participants in a Singapore government officer training program.

Individual messages can also be scored on N and SB, as shown in Figure 12.3. For example, the CVF was used to evaluate the effectiveness of CEO presentations of poor earnings at the

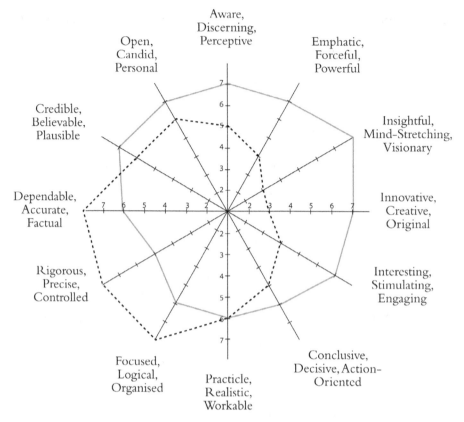

Figure 12.2 Profile of a relatively newly hired employee with a liberal arts background whose communication is 'now' too transformational whereas it 'should be' more informational for his responsibilities as an analyst

New York Society of Security Analysts (Rogers 2000) and the effectiveness of email messages to customers at TVS Logistics in Chennai, India.

More evaluative instruments that account for unique contextual communicative demands need to be developed for management communication.

Using discourse interaction

Another core activity for managers is using 'discourse interaction'. Couture and Rymer (1991) originated the term 'discourse interaction' to describe oral and written discussions about documents as they are planned, drafted and revised. These interactions may be dyadic, within groups, or across groups. When writers discuss their drafts with supervising managers and when groups collaborate on writing or use document cycling (passing a document back and forth between writers and various parties), they are engaged in discourse interaction.

Discussions about oral texts have also been characterised as discourse interaction (Pawlik, Rogers and Shwom 2010). Examples include a project team planning their oral status report, a CEO and his deputy debating how to frame an upcoming presentation of poor earnings, and a manager giving feedback on a consulting team's presentation rehearsal. Such interactions about oral and written discourse are pervasive in the communicative life of a manager.

Management communication

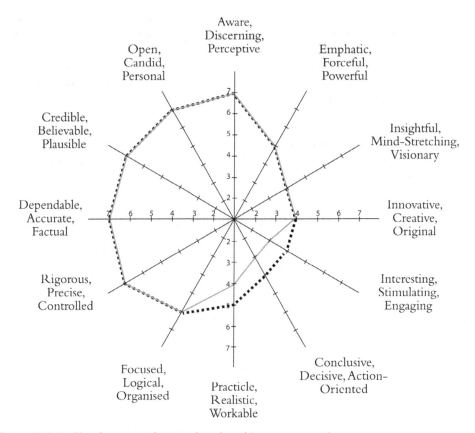

Figure 12.3 Profile of a memo that needs to be a bit more persuasive

Research suggests that discourse interaction can enhance the text under discussion and also benefit discussants and their organisation in a variety of ways. Discourse interaction in management contexts is instrumental in getting work done. As Ede and Lunsford (1986) noted about collaborative writing:

> Working with someone else gives you another point of view. There is an extra voice inside your head; that can make a lot of difference. Others can see things about what I am doing or what I am saying that I can't see.
>
> *(p. 29)*

When talking about discourse under construction, discussants discover new ideas, learn about procedures, practices and others' views, explore possible political implications, discover weaknesses, unearth disagreements, surface ethical concerns and reach consensus. For example, Rogers and Horton (1992) observed 19 groups composing documents together in two different environments – one with computers and projection capabilities, the other with flipcharts and notepads. In both environments group discussion of the documents spawned a deep analysis of rhetorical complexities including the ethical dimensions of language choices. Groups developed a shared voice for talking about the issues. Cross (2001) discovered that a large-scale collaboration involving participants from multiple departments in the composing processes, helped participants form a 'collective mind' despite episodes of 'apathy, cacophony, and anticonsensual revolt' (p. 57). These and other studies suggest the value of discourse interaction for managing (e.g., Forman 1992).

Discourse interaction also presents the manager with an opportunity to guide what is not said, what is said, and how it is said. It can function as a powerful teaching tool. Consider what the writer would learn if a supervisor provided feedback like this:

> You can wait to email this. Ulrich won't even look at it until after quarterly earnings are reported. By the way, send it as an email attachment and use a memo format. Include more details about the customer and get yourself out of it. Keep it objective. Don't use 'I'. It's his turf, not yours.

This supervisor provides information on timing and distribution, genre use, the level of detail required, and the appropriateness of self-reference. This could have been reinforced with a summary:

> So the next time you prepare this report for Ulrich, consider his schedule, use a memo format, provide more supporting detail, and keep the tone neutral, not personal.

Research shows that the potential benefits of discourse interaction are not fully recognised by managers, however. Consider the contrasting views of the writers and supervising mangers that Couture and Rymer (1991) studied. Writers reported that supervisor input brought clarity to important aspects of the writing assignment and surfaced considerations that were not apparent before the interaction, such as content that should and should not be included to keep a supervisor out of trouble, make the department look good, or to help sell something (Couture and Rymer 1991: 96, 99). Discourse interaction was also reported to move the project along. For example, one writer observed that discussing a document with his supervisor was the point at which they worked out the technical details of the project, such as work commitments, scheduling and overall cost (Couture and Rymer 1991, 1993).

By contrast, supervisors were largely oblivious to these benefits. They viewed these interactions as an unfortunate necessity to correct grammatical errors, clarify misunderstandings, point out where more elaboration was needed, and explain reporting requirements. Supervisors expressed resentment over the need for discourse interaction. 'Professionals,' like the writers reporting to them, 'should not have to be told what to do' (Couture and Rymer 1991: 99). While supervisors acknowledged that the writers were inexperienced, they failed to observe that interactions were contributing significantly to the mentoring process and to the work itself. As Couture and Rymer (1991) concluded:

> Writers and managers may have radically different perspectives on the function of discourse interaction, inhibiting them from collaborating effectively ... The disparity in their perceptions, we believe, causes much of this interaction to be minimally effective.
>
> *(pp. 97–98, 99)*

Research on collaborative writing suggests that discourse interaction can fail if it is not managed well. Forty-two per cent of the respondents to Lunsford and Ede's (1990) well-known survey on writing collaboration reported that their group writing was 'not too productive' or 'not at all productive' (p. 50; see also Ede and Lunsford 1986). Locker (1992) watched a team produce 13 inadequate document drafts before the writing task was assigned to a new team. A writing group that Cross observed (1990) took 77 days to compose the cover letter for an annual report and their final version failed to address audience needs and contained poor explanations and redundancies.

To date, managing discourse interaction to get work done has received little research attention. Compiling directives for collaborative writing (e.g., Cross 2011, 1994, 1990; Locker 1992; Paradis, Dobrin and Miller 1985) and document drafting (e.g., Shwom and Hirsch 1994), and considering how they might be used to achieve management goals, is a place to begin.

Other management communication activities

The proposed five activities for managing the oral and written texts to get work done with and through people should be viewed as starter kit. Other foundational constructs that merit elaboration include:

- Systems theory (Suchan 2006; Suchan and Dulek 1998)
- Network theory (Ibarra and Hunter 2007; Cross and Parker 2004)
- Media selection (Lengel and Daft 1968; Yates and Orlikowski 1992, 2002)
- Cultural identity and cultural intelligence theory (Jameson 2007; Earley and Ang 2003; Nickerson 1998; Thomas 1998; Hildebrandt and Liu 1991).
- Interpersonal communication (Iacoboni 2008; Stone, Patton and Heen 2000; Tannen 1995), including building credibility and trust (Thomas, Zolin and Hartman 2008), doing 'empathy work' (Clark et al. 2013), and conflict management (Thomas, Thomas and Schaubhut 2008).

Day-to-day communicative activities that managers need to master include information management and persuasion. Managing information requires decisions about what information to share and retrieve, as well as ways to get information heard and understood despite overload (Hemp 2009; Reinsch, Turner and Tinsley 2008). Managers need to employ textual strategies that help readers and listeners comprehend and process information quickly (e.g., Kostelnick and Hassett 2003). Young (2011) provides a thorough list of textual aids to perception, attention, sentence-level comprehension, and information integration. Heath and Heath (2007) describe techniques for making information 'sticky' so that its impact is long lasting.

Persuading is also essential for managing (Hill 1997). 'Communication is almost always an attempt to control change – either by causing it or by preventing it,' Hanna and Wilson observed in *Communicating in Business and Professional Settings* (1998: 21). Reinsch and Shelby (1997) found that managers' most challenging situations involved 'conflict or the necessity of persuading someone' (p. 18). Theories of persuasion and compliance gaining have been applied to management activities (e.g., Shelby 1986, 1988, 1991). Commonly used for management communication teaching are Toulmin's (1958) components of an argument (claim, data, warrant, qualification and rebuttal) and the six principles of persuasion (reciprocity, commitment and consistency, social proof, authority, liking and scarcity) that Cialdini (2009) laid out in his book *Influence: Science and Practice*. Tests of evidence and logical fallacies are also explored, including in Huff's (1954) classic book *How to Lie With Statistics*, which is complemented by Seife's (2010) recent publication titled *Proofiness: The Dark Arts of Mathematical Deception*.

Conclusion

In summary, the field of management communication is newer than other professional communication fields. It shares with business and corporate communication a keen interest in effective speaking and writing on behalf of organisations. But it differs from these fields and from organisational communication in its focus on the oral and written texts that the manager creates, receives, and is responsible to manage to get work done with and through people. The manager's role requires ability to predict how various audiences will respond to textual choices, to develop a repertoire of language options from which to choose, to use BELF strategies when working with non-native speakers of English in some contexts, to see and shape genres to manage recurring events, to diagnose the communication effectiveness of messages and employees, to use discourse interaction as a learning and consensus-building vehicle, to manage information so that it gets understood and remembered, to persuade to cause or prevent change, and much more. Research provides some frameworks and tools that can be rallied to assist managers with this work, but much more remains to be done.

Related concepts

needs analysis of language; genre analysis; collaborative writing

Key readings

Couture, B., and Rymer, J. (1991). 'Discourse interaction between writer and supervisor: A primary collaboration in workplace writing', in M. M. Lay and W. M. Karis (eds), *Collaborative Writing in Industry: Investigations in Theory and Practice* (pp. 87–108), Farmingdale, NY: Baywood. (Illustrates the prevalence and value of 'talk about discourse' that managers need to see and use to get work done through people.)

Jameson, D. A. (2001). 'Narrative discourse and management action', *Journal of Business Communication*, 38(4), 476–511. (Shows the power of narratives as a management tool for conveying contextual complexities, resolving conflict, influencing corporate decisions, building a cohesive group.)

Nickerson, C. (2000). *Playing the Corporate Language Game. An Investigation of the Genres and Discourse Strategies in English Used by Dutch Writers Working Within Multinational Corporations*, Amsterdam-Atlanta: Rodopi. (Illustrates the complexity of Business English Lingua Franca and genre use in management contexts.)

Rogers, P. S. and Hildebrandt, H. W. (1993). 'Competing values instruments for analyzing written and spoken messages', *Human Resources Management*, 32(1), 121–42. (Provides a conceptual framework for planning and diagnosing communication effectiveness in diverse management contexts.)

Suchan, J. (2006). 'Changing organizational communication practices and norms: A framework', *Journal of Business and Technical Communication*, 20(1), 5–47. (Argues that managers who want to change communication practices must not only introduce new skills but must alter the way employees habitually think and talk about communication.)

Notes

1 Special thanks to Randolph Barker, Geoff Cross, Ron Dulek, Gail Thomas, Janis Forman, Herb Hildebrandt, Daphne Jameson, Catherine Nickerson, Lamar Reinsch, Jone Rymer, Jim Suchan and JoAnne Yates for directing me to studies they have conducted and theories that influence their teaching of management communication. I asked these recipients of the Association for Business Communication Outstanding Research Award (who are known for their work on management communication) the following question: Which two or three of *your* publications most influence your management communication research and teaching? Their answers helped with this chapter and are provided in Table 12.3.

2 In the early 1980s scholars were comparing organisational and business communication with no reference to managerial communication. Although management communication is a young field, it has ancient roots. Rhetoric began to be developed as a formal area of knowledge with ties to business in the fifth century BCE (Reinsch 1996; Kennedy 1963).

Table 12.3 Association of Business Communication Outstanding Researcher Award recipients who are known for their management communication research recommend readings from their work

Researcher	Which three of your publications most influence your management communication research and/or teaching?
Randolph Barker	Stutts, N. and Barker, R. T. (1999). 'The use of narrative paradigm theory in audience value conflict identification', *Management Communication Quarterly, 13*(2), 209–44.
	Barker, R. T. and Camarata, M. (1998). 'The role of communication in creating and maintaining a learning organization: Preconditions, indicators and disciplines', *The Journal of Business Communication, 35*(4), 443–67.
	Barker, R. T., Pearce, C.G. and Johnson, I. W. (1992). 'An investigation of perceived managerial listening ability', *Journal of Business and Technical Communication, 6*(4), 438–57.
Geoffrey Cross	Cross, G. A. (2011). 'Envisioning collaboration: Group verbal-visual composing in a system of creativity book review', *IEEE Transactions on Professional Communication, 54*(2), 215.
	Cross, G. A. (2001). *Forming the Collective Mind: A Contextual Exploration of Large-Scale Collaborative Writing in Industry.* Cresskill, NJ: Hampton Press.
	Cross, G. A. (1994). *Collaboration and Conflict: A Contextual Exploration of Group Writing and Positive Emphasis.* Cresskill, NJ: Hampton Press.
Ronald E. Dulek	Suchan, J. and Dulek, R. E. (1998). 'From text to context: An open systems approach to research', *The Journal of Business Communication, 35*, 87–110.
	Fielden, J.S. and Dulek, R. E. (1984). 'How to use bottom-line writing in corporate communications', *Business Horizons, 27*(4), 24–30.
	Dulek, R. E. and Annette Shelby, A. (1981). 'Writing principles stressed by business communication instructors', *Journal of Business Communication, 18*(2), 41–50.
Janis Forman	Forman (2013). *Storytelling in Business: The Authentic and Fluent Organization*, CA: Stanford University Press.
	Forman, J. & Rymer, J. (1999). 'Defining the genre of the "case write-up"', *Journal of Business Communication, 36*(2), 103–33.
	Forman, J. (ed.) (1992). *New Visions of Collaborative Writing.* Portsmouth, New Hampshire: Boynton/Cook Publishers.
Herbert W. Hildebrandt	Hildebrandt, H. W. (1998). 'International/intercultural communication: A comparative study of Asian and US managers', *World Communication Journal, 17*(1), 49–68.
	Hildebrandt, H. W. and Liu, J. (1991). 'Communication through foreign languages: An economic force in Chinese enterprises'. *Journal of Asian Pacific Communication: The Economics of the Language in the Asian Pacific, 2*(1).
	Quinn, B., Hildebrandt, H. W., Rogers, P. S. and Thompson, M. (1991). 'A competing values framework for analyzing presentational communication in management contexts', *Journal of Business Communication, 28*(3), 213–31.
Daphne A. Jameson	Jameson, D. A. (2007). 'Reconceptualising cultural identity and its role in intercultural business communication', *Journal of Business Communication, 44*(3), 199–235.
	Jameson, D. A. (2001). 'Narrative discourse and management action', *Journal of Business Communication, 38*(4), 476–511.
	Jameson, D. A. (2000). Telling the investment story: A narrative analysis of shareholder reports. *Journal of Business Communication, 37*(1), 7–38.

Table 12.3 (continued)

Researcher	Which three of your publications most influence your management communication research and/or teaching?
Catherine Nickerson	Nickerson, C. (2000). *Playing the Corporate Language Game: An Investigation of the Genres and Discourse Strategies in English used by Dutch Writers Working within Multinational Corporations*. Amsterdam-Atlanta: Rodopi.
	Nickerson, C. (1999). 'Genre theory and intercultural communication. The usefulness of genre theory in the investigation of organisational communication across cultures', *Document Design 1*(3), 202–15.
	Nickerson, C. (1998). 'Corporate culture and the use of written English within British subsidiaries in the Netherlands', *English for Specific Purposes, 17*(3), 281–94.
N. Lamar Reinsch, Jr.	Reinsch, N. L., Jr., Turner, J. W. and Tinsley, C. H. (2008). 'MultiCommunicating: A practice whose time has come?' *Academy of Management Review, 33*(2), 391–403.
	Patel, A., and Reinsch, N. L. (2003). 'Companies can apologize: Corporate apologies and legal liabilities', *Business Communication Quarterly, 66*(1), 9–25.
	Reinsch, N. L., Jr., and Shelby, A. N. (1997). 'What communication abilities do practitioners need? Evidence from MBA students', *Business Communication Quarterly, 60*(4), 7–29.
Priscilla S. Rogers	Clark, C. M., Murfett, U. M., Rogers, P.S. and Ang, S. (2013). 'Is empathy effective for customer service? Evidence from call center interactions', *Journal of Business and Technical Communication, 27*(2), 123–53.
	Rogers, P. S., Ho, M., Thomas, J., Wong, I. and Cheng, C. (2005). 'Preparing new entrants for subordinate reporting: A decision-making framework', *Journal of Business Communication, 41*(2), 1–32.
	Rogers, P. S. and Hildebrandt, H. W. (1993). 'Competing values instruments for analyzing written and spoken messages', *Human Resources Management, 32* (1), 121–42.
Jone Rymer	Rogers, P. S. and Rymer, J. (2001). 'Analytical tools to facilitate transitions into new writing contexts: A communicative perspective', *Journal of Business Communication, 38*(2), 112–52.
	Rogers, P. S. and Rymer, J. (1995). 'What is the relevance of the GMAT analytical writing assessment for management education? A critical analysis, Part 1', *Management Communication Quarterly, 8*(3), 347–67.
	Couture, B. and Rymer, J. (1991). 'Discourse interaction between writer and supervisor: A primary collaboration in workplace writing', in M. M. Lay and W. M. Karis (eds), *Collaborative Writing in Industry: Investigations in Theory and Practice* (pp. 87–108). Farmingdale, NY: Baywood.
Jim Suchan	Suchan, J. (2006). 'Changing organizational communication practices and norms: A framework', *Journal of Business and Technical Communication, 20*(1), 1–43.
	Suchan, J. (1995). 'The influence of organizational metaphors on writers' communication roles and stylistic choices', *The Journal of Business Communication, 32*(1), 7–29.
	Suchan, J. and Dulek, R. (1990). 'A reassessment of clarity in written managerial communications', *Management Communication Quarterly, 4*(1), 87–99.

Table 12.3 (continued)

Researcher	Which three of your publications most influence your management communication research and/or teaching?
Gail Fann Thomas	Thomas, G. F. and Stephens, K. (2011). 'Problematizing political space through discursive analysis: The case of the United States Coast Guard and the live fire zones on the Great Lakes,' *Discourse Perspectives on Organizational Communication*. Madison, NJ: Fairleigh Dickinson University Press Communication Series.
	Thomas, G. F., Zolin, R. and Hartman, J. L. (2009). 'The central role of communication in developing trust and its effects on employee involvement', *Journal of Business Communication, 46*(3), 287–310.
	Thomas, K. W., Thomas, G. F., and Schaubhut, N. (2008). 'Conflict styles of men and women at six organizational levels', *International Journal of Conflict Management, 2*(14), 148–66.
JoAnne Yates	Yates, J. and Orlikowski, W. J. (2002). 'Genre systems: Structuring interaction through communicative norms', *Journal of Business Communication, 39*(1), 13–35.
	Yates, J. and Orlikowski, W. J. (1992). 'Genres of organizational communication: A structurational approach to studying communication and media', *Academy of Management Review, 17*(2), 299–326.
	Yates, J. (1989). *Control through Communication: The Rise of System in American Management*. Baltimore, NY: The Johns Hopkins University Press.

3 Founded in 1916, the Association to Advance Collegiate Schools of Business, now known as AACSB International, 'advances quality management education worldwide through accreditation, thought leadership, and value-added services' (AACSB International, www.aacsb.edu/about/default.asp, accessed October 2012). In 2005, Knight found that at the MBA level, communication was no longer mentioned specifically in the AACSB International standards, but communication appears throughout the interpretative guidelines (www.aacsb.edu).

References

American Assembly of Collegiate School of Business. (n.d.) *Standards for Business and Accounting Accreditation*. Available at www.aacsb.edu/ (accessed October 2012).
Argenti, P. A. and Forman, J. (2002). *The Power of Corporate Communication: Crafting the Voice and Image of Your Business*, New York, NY: McGraw-Hill.
Aritz, J. and Walker, R. C. (2012). *Discourse Perspectives on Organizational Communication*, Madison: Fairleigh Dickinson University Press.
Bakhtin, M. M. (1986). *Speech Genres and Other Late Essays*, W. McGee (trans.), Austin, TX: University of Texas Press.
Bal, M. (1997). *Narratology: Introduction to the Theory of Narrative* (2nd edn), Toronto: University of Toronto Press.
Bhatia, V. K. (2008). 'Genre analysis, ESP and professional practice', *English for Specific Purposes, 27,* 161–74.
Bremner, S. (2012). 'Working with genre systems: Accommodating multiple interests in the construction of organizational tests', in P. Gillaerts, E. de Groot, S. Dieltjens, P. Heynderickx and G. Jacobs (eds), *Researching Discourse in Business Genres*, Berlin: Peter Lang.
Brochet, F., Naranjo, P. and Yu, G. (2012). 'Causes and consequences of linguistic complexity in non-U.S. firm conference calls', *Harvard Business School Working Paper No. 2154948,* http://papers.ssrn.com/sol3/papers.cfm?abstract_id=2154948.
Brown, P. and Levinson, S. C. (1987). *Politeness: Some Universals in Language Usage*, Cambridge, United Kingdom: Cambridge University Press.
Cialdini, R. B. (2009). *Influence: Science and Practice*, Boston, MA: Pearson/Allyn and Bacon.

Clampitt, P. G. (1991). *Communicating for Managerial Effectiveness*, Newbury Park, CA: Sage Publications.
Clark, C., Murfett, U., Rogers, P. S. and Ang, S. (2013). 'Is empathy effective for customer service? Evidence from call center interactions', *Journal of Business and Technical Communication*, 27(2), 123–53.
Couture, B. and Rymer, J. (1991). 'Discourse interaction between writer and supervisor: A primary collaboration in workplace writing', in M. M. Lay and W. M. Karis (eds), *Collaborative Writing in Industry: Investigations in Theory and Practice* (pp. 87–108), Farmingdale, NY: Baywood.
——(1993). 'Situational exigence: Composing processes on the job by writer's role and task value', in R. Spilka (ed.), *Writing in the Workplace: New Research Perspectives* (pp. 4–20), Carbondale, IL: Southern Illinois University.
Cross, G. A. (1990). 'A Bakhtinian exploration of factors affecting the collaborative writing of an executive letter of an annual report', *Research in the Teaching of English*, 24, 173–202.
——(1994). *Collaboration and Conflict: A Contextual Exploration of Group Writing and Positive Emphasis*, Cresskill, NJ: Hampton Press.
——(2001). *Forming the Collective Mind: A Contextual Exploration of Large-scale Collaborative Writing in Industry*, Cresskill, NJ: Hampton Press, Inc.
——(2011) 'Envisioning collaboration: Group verbal-visual composing in a system of creativity book review', *IEEE Transactions on Professional Communication*, 54(2), 215.
Cross, R., Borgatti, S. and Parker, A. (2002). 'Making invisible work visible: using social network analysis to support strategic collaboration', *California Management Review*, Winter 44(2), 25–46.
Cross, R. and Parker, A. (2004). *The Hidden Power of Social Networks: Understanding How Work Really Gets Done in Organizations*, Harvard Business School Press.
Devitt, A. (1991). 'Intertextuality in tax accounting: Generic, referential, and functional', in C. Bazerman and D. R. Russell (eds), *Textual Dynamics of the Professions: Historical and Contemporary Studies of Writing in Professional Communities* (pp. 336–57), Madison, WI: University of Wisconsin Press.
Du-Babcock, B. (1999). 'Topic management and turn taking in professional communication: First- versus second-language strategies', *Management Communication Quarterly*, 12, 544–74.
Dulek, R. E. and Fielden, J. S. (1990). *Principles of Business Communication*, New York: Macmillan Publishing Co.
Earley, P.C. and Ang, S. (2003). *Cultural Intelligence: Individual Interactions Across Culture*, Palo Alto, CA: Stanford Business Books.
Eccles, R. G. and Nohria, N. with Berkley, J. D. (1992). *Beyond the Hype: Rediscovering the Essence of Management*, Washington, DC: Beard Books.
Ede, L. S. and Lunsford, A. A. (1986). 'Collaborative learning: Lessons from the world of work.' *Writing Program Administration*, 9(3), 17–26.
Fann-Thomas, G. and King, C. (2006). 'Reconceptualizing e-mail overload', *Journal of Business and Technical Communication*, 20(3), 252–87.
Feingold, P. (1987). 'The emergence of management communication', *Management Communication Quarterly*, 1, 121–23.
Fielden, J. S. and Dulek, R. E. (1983). *Bottom Line Business Writing*, Upper Saddle River, NJ: Prentice Hall Trade.
Firth, A. (1996). 'The discursive accomplishment of normality: On "lingua franca" English and conversation analysis', *Journal of Pragmatics*, 26, 237–59.
Forman, J. (1992). *New Visions of Collaborative Writing*, Portsmouth, New Hampshire: Boynton/Cook Publishers.
——(2013). *Storytelling in Business: The Authentic and Fluent Organization*, Stanford, CA: Stanford University Press.
Freedman, A., Adam, C. and Smart, G. (1994). 'Wearing suits to class: Simulating genres and simulations as genres', *Written Communication*, 11(2), 193–226.
GMAC (Graduate Management Admission Council) (n.d., distributed 1994, May). *The GMAT Analytical Writing Assessment: An Introduction*, Santa Monica, CA: GMAC.
Hagge, J. and Kostelnick, C. (1989). 'Linguistic politeness in professional prose: A discourse analysis of auditors' suggestion letters, with implications for business communication pedagogy', *Written Communication*, 6, 312–39.
Hanna, M. S. and Wilson, G. L. (1998). *Communicating in Business and Professional Settings* (4th edn), New York: McGraw-Hill Co. Inc.
Hartelius, E. J. and Browning, L. S. (2008). 'The application of rhetorical theory in managerial research: A literature review', *Management Communication Quarterly*, 22(1), 13–39.
Heath, C. and Heath, D. (2007). *Made to Stick: Why Some Ideas Survive and Others Die*, New York: Random House.

Hemp, P. (2009). 'Death by information overload', *Harvard Business Review*, 83–123.
Hildebrandt, H. W. and Liu, J. (1991). 'Communication through foreign languages: An economic force in Chinese enterprises', *Journal of Asian Pacific Communication – the Economics of Language in Asian Pacific*, 2(1), 45–67.
Hill, L. A. (1997). *Becoming a Manager: How New Managers Master the Challenges of Leadership* (2nd edn), Boston, MA: Harvard Business Press.
——(2003). *Becoming a Manager: How New Managers Master the Challenges of Leadership*, Boston, MA: Harvard Business School Press.
Holmes, J. and Stubbe, M. (2003). *Power and Politeness in the Workplace: A Sociolinguistic Analysis of Talk at Work*, London: Pearson Education.
Huff, D. (1954). *How to Lie With Statistics*, New York, NY: W.W. Norton & Company, Inc.
Iacoboni, M. (2008). *Mirroring People: The New Science of How we Connect With Others*, New York: Farrar, Straus, and Giroux.
Ibarra, H. and Hunter, H. (January 2007). 'How leaders create and use networks', *Harvard Business Review*.
Jameson, D. A. (2000). 'Telling the investment story: A narrative analysis of shareholder reports', *Journal of Business Communication*, 37(1), 7–38.
——(2001). 'Narrative discourse and management action', *Journal of Business Communication*, 38(4), 476–511.
Jameson, D. A. (2007). 'Reconceptualizing cultural identity and its role in intercultural business communication', *Journal of Business Communication*, 44(3), 199–235.
Kankaanranta, A. and Louhiala-Salminen, L. (2007). 'Business communication in BELF.' *Business Communication Quarterly*, 70(1), 55–59.
——(2010). '"English? – Oh, it's just work!": A study of BELF users' perceptions', *English for Specific Purposes*, 29, 204–9.
Kennedy, G. (1963). *The Art of Persuasion in Greece*, Princeton, NJ: Princeton University Press.
Kent, T. (1993). *Paralogic Rhetoric: A Theory of Communicative Interaction*, London: Lewisburg Bucknell University Press.
Knight, M. (1999). 'Management communication in US MBA programs: The state of the art', *Business Communication Quarterly*, 62(8), 9–32.
——(2005). 'Management communication in non-U.S. MBA programs: Current trends and practices', *Business Communication Quarterly*, 68, 139–79.
Kostelnick, C. and Hassett, M. (2003). *Shaping Information: The Rhetoric of Visual Conventions*, Carbondale, IL: Southern Illinois University.
Kotter, J. P. (1982). *The General Managers*, NY: The Free Press, Macmillan, Inc.
Lengel, R. H. and Daft, R. L. (1968). 'The selection of communication media as an executive skill', *The Academy of Management EXECUTIVE*, 2(3), 225–32.
Livingston, J. S. (1971). 'Myth of the well-educated manager', *Harvard Business Review*, 49, 79–89.
Locker, K. O. (1989). *Business and Administrative Communication*, Boston, MA: Richard D. Irwin, Inc.
——(1992). 'What makes a collaborative writing team successful? A case study of lawyers and social workers in a state agency', in J. Forman (ed.), *New Visions of Collaborative Writing* (pp. 37–62), Portsmouth, New Hampshire: Boynton/Cook Publishers.
Louhiala-Salminen, L., Charles, M. and Kankaanranta, A. (2005). 'English as the lingua franca of international business communication: Whose English? What English?' in J. Palmer-Silveira, M. Ruiz-Garrido and I. Fortanet-Gomez (eds), *Intercultural and International Business Communication* (pp. 27–54), Bern, Switzerland: Peter Lang.
Lowry, P. B., Humphreys, S., Malwitz, J. and Nix, J. C. (2006). 'A scientometric study of business and technical communication journal quality ratings', *IEEE Transactions on Professional Communication* (IEEETPC), 50(4), 352–78.
Lunsford, A. and Ede, L. (1990). *Singular Texts/Plural Authors: Perspectives on Collaborative Writing*, Carbondale: Southern Illinois UP.
Mathas, J. C., and Stevenson, D. (1976). *Designing Technical Reports: Writing for Audiences in Organizations*, Indianapolis: Bobbs-Merrill.
McKnight, M. R. (1991). 'Management skill development: What it is. What it is not', in J. D. Bigelow (ed.), *Managerial Skills: Explorations in Practical Knowledge*, Newbury Park, CA: Sage Publications.
Michigan Ross School of Business (November, 2012). *What is MAP?* Available at www.bus.umich.edu/MAP/Dev/WhatisMAP.htm (accessed 2012).
Miller, C. (1984). 'Genre as social action', *Quarterly Journal of Speech*, 70, 151–67.
Mintzberg, H. (1973). *The Nature of Managerial Work*, New York: Harper & Row.

Munter, M. (1989a). 'What's going on in business and management communication courses', in M. Kogen (ed.), *Writing in the Business Professions* (pp. 267–78), Urbana, IL: National Council of Teachers of English & The Association for Business Communication.

——(Winter 1989b). 'Nostalgia corner: MCA history', *MCA Newsletter*.

——(2012). *Guide to Managerial Communication: Effective Business Writing and Speaking*, 9th edition, Boston: Prentice Hall.

Munter, M., Rogers, P. S. and Rymer, J. (2003). 'Business e-mail: Guidelines for users', *Business Communication Quarterly*, 66(1), 26–40.

Murray, M. (2009). *Corporate Recruiters Survey*. Available at www.gmac.com/market-intelligence-and research/research-library/employment-outlook/2009-corporate-recruiters-survey-report.aspx (accessed November 2012).

Nickerson, C. (1998). 'Corporate culture and the use of written English within British subsidiaries in the Netherlands', *English for Specific Purposes*, 17(3), 281–94.

——(2000). *Playing the Corporate Language Game: An Investigation of the Genres and Discourse Strategies in English Used by Dutch Writers Working Within Multinational Corporations*, Amsterdam-Atlanta: Rodopi.

Orlikowski, W. J. and Yates, J. (1994). 'Genre repertoire: The structuring of communicative practices in organizations', *Administrative Science Quarterly*, 39, 541–74.

O'Rourke, J. S. (2010). *Management Communication: A Case-analysis Approach*. (4th edn), Upper Saddle River, NJ: Prentice Hall.

Østerlund, C. (2007). 'Genre combinations: A window into dynamic communication practices', *Journal of Management Information Systems*, 23(4), 81–108.

Paradis, J. G. (1991). 'Text and action: The operator's manual in context and in court' in C. Bazermann and J. G. Paradis (eds), *Textual Dynamics of the Professions* (pp. 256–78), Madison, WI: University of Wisconsin Press.

Paradis, J., Dobrin, D. and Miller, R. (1985). 'Writing at Exxon ITD: Notes on the writing environment of an R & D organization', in L. Odell and D. Goswami (eds), *Writing in Nonacademic Settings* (pp. 281–307), New York: The Guilford Press.

Park, D. B. (2011). 'Analyzing audiences', *College Composition and Communication*, 37(4), 478–88.

Pawlik, L., Rogers, P. S. and Shwom, B. (2010). 'Static products or working texts? The function of communication deliverables in project work', Association for Business Communication International Conference Proceedings, Chicago, IL.

Pullin, P. (2010). 'Small talk, rapport, and international communicative competence: Lessons to learn from BELF', *Journal of Business and Technical Communication*, 47(4), 455–76.

Putnam, L. L. (2012). 'Looking back, looking forward: A tribute to MCQ and my colleagues', *Management Communication Quarterly*, 26(3), 510–20.

Quinn, R. E., Hildebrandt, H. W., Rogers, P. S. and Thompson, M. P. (1991). 'A competing values framework for analyzing presentational communication in management contexts', *Journal of Business Communication*, 28(3), 213–31.

Reinsch, N. L. (1991). 'Editorial: What is business communication?', *Journal of Business Communication*, 28(4), 305–10.

——(1996). 'Business communication: Present, past, and future', *Management Communication Quarterly*, 10(1), 27–49.

Reinsch, N. L. Jr. and Shelby, A. N. (1997). 'What communication abilities do practitioners need? Evidence from MBA students', *Business Communication Quarterly*, 60(4), 7–29.

Reinsch, N. L., Turner, J. W. and Tinsley, C. H. (2008). 'MultiCommunicating: A practice whose time has come?' *Academy of Management Review*, 33(2), 391–403.

Richmond, V. P. and McCroskey, J. C. (1990). 'Reliability and separation of factors on the assertiveness-responsiveness scale', *Psychological Reports*, (67), 449–50.

Richmond, V. P., McCroskey, J. C. and Johnson, A. D. (2003). 'Development of the nonverbal immediacy scale (NIS): Measure of self- and other-perceived nonverbal immediacy', *Communication Quarterly*, 51(4), 504–17.

Rogers, D. P. (1978). 'The content of organizational communication texts', *Journal of Business Communication*, 16(1), 57–64.

Rogers, P. S. (1989). 'Choice-based writing in managerial contexts: The case of the dealer contact report', *Journal of Business Communication*, 23(3), 197–216.

——(1990). 'A taxonomy for the composition of memorandum subject lines: Facilitating writer choice in managerial contexts', *Journal of Business and Technical Communication*, 4(2), 21–43.
——(1994). 'Analytic measures for evaluating managerial writing', *Journal of Business and Technical Communication*, 8(4), 380–407.
——(2000). 'CEO presentations in conjunction with earnings announcements: Extending the construct of organizational genre through competing values profiling and user needs analysis', *Management Communication Quarterly*, 13(3), 484–545.
Rogers, P. S., Campbell, N., Louhiala-Salminen, L., Rentz, K. and Suchan, J. (2007). 'The impact of perceptions of journal quality on business and management communication academics', *Journal of Business Communication*, 44(4), 403–26.
Rogers, P.S. and Hildebrandt, H. W. (1993). 'Competing values instruments for analyzing written and spoken messages', *Human Resources Management*, 32(1), 121–42.
Rogers, P., Ho, M., Thomas, J., Wong, I. and Cheng, C. (2004). 'Preparing new entrants for subordinate reporting: A decision-making framework', *Journal of Business Communication*, 41(2), 1–32.
Rogers, P. S. and Horton, M. S. (1992). 'Exploring the value of face-to-face collaborative writing', in J. Forman (ed.), *New Visions of Collaborative Writing*, Portsmouth, NH: Boynton/Cook Publishers.
Rogers, P. S. and Lee-Wong, L. (2003). 'Re-conceptualizing politeness to accommodate dynamic tensions in subordinate-to-superior reporting', *Journal of Business and Technical Communication*, 17(4), 379–412.
Rogers, P. S. and Rymer, J. (1995a) 'What is the relevance of the GMAT analytical writing assessment for management education? A critical analysis, Part 1', *Management Communication Quarterly*, 8(3), 347–67.
——(1995b). 'What is the functional value of the GMAT analytical writing assessment for management education? Part 2', *Management Communication Quarterly*, 8(4), 477–94.
——(2001). 'Analytical tools to facilitate transitions into new writing contexts: A communicative perspective', *The Journal of Business Communication*, 38(2), 112–52.
Rogerson-Revell, P. (2007). 'Using English for international business: A European case study', *English for Specific Purposes*, 26, 130–120.
——(2010). 'Can you spell that for us nonnative speakers? Accommodation strategies in international business meetings', *Journal of Business Communication*, 47(4), 432–454.
Russell, D. R. (1991). *Writing in the Academic Disciplines, 1870–1990: A Curricular History*, Carbondale, IL: Southern Illinois University Press.
Seife, C. (2010). *Proofiness: The Dark Arts of Mathematical Deception*, New York, NY: Penguin Group.
Shelby, A. N. (1986). 'The theoretical bases of persuasion: A critical introduction', *Journal of Business Communication*, 23(1), 5–29.
——(1988). 'A macro theory of management communication', *Journal of Business Communication*, 30(3), 13–28.
——(1991). 'Applying the strategic choice model to motivational appeals: A theoretical approach', *Journal of Business Communication*, 28, 187–212.
——(1993). 'Organizational, business, management, and corporate communication: An analysis of boundaries and relationships', *Journal of Business Communication*, 30, 241–67.
Shwom, B. L. and Hirsch, P. L. (1994). 'Managing the drafting process: Creating a new model for the workplace', *Bulletin of the Association for Business Communication*, 57(2), 1–8.
Smeltzer, L. R. (1996). 'Communication within the manager's context', *Management Communication Quarterly*, 10(1), 5–26.
Smeltzer, L. R. Glab, J. and Golen, S. (1983). 'Managerial communication: The merging of business communication, organizational communication, and management', *The Journal of Business Communication*, 20(4), 71–78.
Spinuzzi, C. (2003). *Tracing Genres Through Organizations: A Sociocultural Approach to Information Design*, Cambridge, MA: MIT Press.
——(2004). 'Describing assemblages: Genre sets, systems, repertoires, and ecologies', *Computer Writing and Research Lab White Paper Series*: #040505–2.
Stewart, R. (1988). *Managers and Their Jobs*, 2nd Edition, Hampshire: Macmillan Press.
Stone, D., Patton, B. and Heen, S. (2000). *Difficult Conversations: How to Discuss What Matters Most*, New York, NY: Penguin Books.
Suchan, J. (1991). 'Toward an understanding of managerial communication', Paper presented at the meeting of the Association for Business Communication, Honolulu, HI.
——(1995). 'The influence of organizational metaphors on writers' communication roles and stylistic choices', *The Journal of Business Communication*, 32(1), 7–29.

——(2006). 'Changing organizational communication practices and norms: A framework', *Journal of Business and Technical Communication*, 20(1), 5–47.
Suchan, J. and Colucci, R., (1989). 'Communication efficiency between high-impact and bureaucratic written communication', *Management Communication Quarterly*, 2(4), 452–84.
Suchan, J. and Dulek, R. (1998). 'From text to context: An open systems approach to research in written business communication', *The Journal of Business Communication*, 35, 87–110.
——(1990). 'A reassessment of clarity in written managerial communications', *Management Communication Quarterly*, 4(1), 90–97.
Swales, J. M. (1990). *Genre Analysis: English in Academic and Research Settings*. Cambridge, United Kingdom: Cambridge University Press.
——(2004). *Research Genres: Exploration and Applications*, Cambridge: Cambridge University Press.
Sweeney, E. and Hua, Z. (2010). 'Accommodating toward your audience: Do native speakers of English know how to accommodate their communication strategies toward nonnative speakers of English?' *Journal of Business and Technical Communication*, 47(4), 477–504.
Tannen, D. (1995). *Talking From 9 to 5: Women and Men at Work*, New York, NY: HarperCollins Books.
Thomas, G. F., Zolin, R. and Hartman, J. (2008). 'The central role of communication in developing trust and its effect on employee involvement', *Journal of Business Communication*, 46(3), 287–310.
Thomas, J. (1998). 'Contexting Koreans: Does the high/low model work?' *Business Communication Quarterly*, 61(4), 9–22.
Thomas, K. W., Thomas, G. F. and Schaubhut, N. (2008). 'Conflict styles of men and women at six organizational levels', *International Journal of Conflict Management*, 2(14), 148–66.
Toulmin, S. (1958). *The Uses of Argument*, Cambridge, UK: Cambridge University Press.
Watts, D. (2004). *Six Degrees, The New Science of Networks*, New York: W. W. Norton & Co.
Wikipedia (2013). *Myers-Briggs Type Indicator*. Available at http://en.wikipedia.org/wiki/Myers-Briggs_Type_Indicator (accessed 3 April 2013).
Winsor, D. A. (1999). 'Genre and activity systems: The role of documentation in maintaining and changing engineering activity systems', *Written Communication*, 16(2), 200–24.
Yates, J. (1989a). *Control through Communication: The Rise of System in American Management*, Baltimore: The Johns Hopkins University Press.
——(1989b). 'The emergence of the memo as a managerial tool', *Management Communication Quarterly*, 2(4): 485–510.
Yates, J. and Orlikowski, W. J. (1992). 'Genres of organizational communication: A structurational approach to studying communication and media', *Academy of Management Review*, 17(2), 299–326.
——(2002). 'Genre systems: Structuring interaction through communicative norms', *Journal of Business Communication*, 39(1), 13–35.
Young, R. O. (2011). *How Audiences Decide: A Cognitive Approach to Business Communication*, New York: Routledge.
Zachery, M. (2000). 'Communicative practices in the workplace: A historical examination of genre development', *Technical Writing and Communication*, 30(1), 57–79.

13
Business and the communication of climate change

An organisational discourse perspective

David Grant and Daniel Nyberg

It has been suggested that it is perhaps now more appropriate to talk about an emerging discursive rather than linguistic 'turn' in the social sciences (Torfing 2005). This observation seems especially pertinent in relation to organisation and management theory, where we have seen an increasing interest in an approach to the study of organisations that has been termed organisational discourse studies (ODS) (Grant *et al.* 2004; Alvesson and Karreman 2000, 2011; Hardy and Grant 2012). The value of this approach is highlighted by Mumby and Clair (1997: 181) where they discuss the nature of the relationship between organisations and discourse:

> When we speak of organizational discourse, we do not simply mean discourse that occurs *in* organizations. Rather, we suggest that organizations exist only in so far as their members create them through discourse. This is not to claim that organizations are nothing but discourse, but rather that discourse is the principal means by which organization members create a coherent social reality that frames their sense of who they are.

The reach of organisations is such that they impact in some way, on almost every aspect of our daily lives and remind us of the importance of understanding organisational discourse more broadly. Specifically, it reminds us that, through their communicative practices and activities, organisations and their members have the capacity to shape identities and democratic processes. The study of organisational discourse thus extends to how organisations are engaged in framing the social reality of actors locally and globally.

Among ODS scholars, the creation of social reality is understood in terms of how discourses are produced, distributed and consumed through 'texts', which comprise both linguistic (e.g. spoken and written language) and non-linguistic (e.g. non-verbal communication and symbolic actions, pictures, symbols and images) media (Hardy and Phillips 2004). Discourse is not then a solely linguistic phenomenon and, as an intrinsic part of practice, a discourse is not limited to a linguistic arena. Rather discourses shape and reshape organisational realities and confer meaning on social and political events (Chouliaraki and Fairclough 1999). Broadly following the work of Foucault (see e.g. 1979, 1980, 1998), we are interested in how discursive practices take part in shaping the discursive formations that regulate 'what can be said, how it can be said, who can speak and in which name, and what kind of strategies that can be realized at the level of discourse' (Torfing 2005: 7). This approach emphasises the productive aspects of power in shaping identities, capacities and relations. By studying organisational discourses and the texts therein, it is possible to understand the 'conduct of conduct' that influences the conditioning of possibilities for social actors as well as the modifications of discourses through what is said and done (Foucault 2007: 192–93). More specifically, the study of how these everyday texts are produced, distributed and consumed in organisations enables us to understand the relationship of these to both local identities and societal social structures (Mumby and Clair 1997).

In this chapter, we provide a framework to analyse prevalent organisational discourses communicated and employed within contemporary organisations. The framework draws on the insights provided by a number of organisational and linguistic scholars inspired by Foucault (e.g. Fairclough 1992; Phillips and Hardy 1997; Oswick *et al.* 2000; Grant and Shields 2002; Parker 1992). It distinguishes between concepts (categories, ideas and theories), objects (material arrangements) and subjects (actors or positions having voice) in investigating how organisational discourses are (re)produced and changed. All three of these aspects of discourse, though distinct, are also inter-related, and it is this feature of the framework that makes it a useful means by which to understand inter- and intra-organisational dynamics. In adopting this framework we apply it somewhat differently to those previous studies that have used it. This allows us to theorise and give examples of the possibility for corporations to shape and reshape discursive formations. In particular, it allows us to understand and study how through these organisations' communicative practices the construction of the concept of 'climate change' occurs and how this in turn influences our capacity to make sense of, and act in response to what has been described as *the* major social, political and economic challenge of this century (Stern *et al.* 2006).

As we present our framework, we provide examples based on studies of how business engages with climate change and the emerging discourse of sustainability to highlight how discourses are operating at different levels – societal, organisational and individual – that form organisational realities. For instance, at the societal level, different macro discourses shape how we interpret and experience events such as climate change, and affect how organisations respond to these events. At an organisational level, specific discourses, such as environmental management or sustainability, are brought into being as sustainability practices and policies that influence behaviour and organisational outcomes. Finally, at an individual level, constructs such as identity provide organisational members with reflective tools to interrogate and manage themselves and others. How organisations respond to climate change and the adaptation of sustainability is then dependent on available societal discourses, how local organisational discourses are connected to these, and to what extent organisational actors identify with these discourses (Nyberg and Wright 2012; Wright *et al.* 2012).

Our application of the framework to these illustrative examples leads us to observe that it has several important properties that make it particularly useful for analysing organisations and their communicative practices. First, in demonstrating the significance of concepts, the framework allows us to understand the powerful discursive constructs that provide both objects and subjects with positions – concepts influence what objects and subjects are. Second, through demonstrating their significance, the framework makes it possible to understand the limits of concepts to frame and interpret a situation and the relevant subjects. We argue that often the material situation influences the concepts used and the subjects that are given voice. Finally, the framework provides a more detailed understanding of how subjects' positions allow them to draw upon powerful concepts in framing objects. In short, actors use concepts to produce material effects. The application of the framework in this way allows us to bring forward the role of discourse in shaping social and political interpretations.

Discursive constructions of knowledge and ignorance

In their everyday communication, organisations produce texts that establish relations between concepts, objects and subjects. *Discursive concepts* represent the constructions that arise out of ideas and are the 'theories through which we understand the world and relate to one another' (Phillips and Hardy 1997: 167). Participation in the formulation of concepts via discourse is in itself a political act since the concept may well redefine and transform the world to which it is applied. Proponents of a concept will believe that it is correct and valid and will seek to use it to change social structures and relationships. At the same time, they may encounter resistance to its accomplishment from those whose evaluation of the concept is unfavourable and propose their own alternative concepts. The contestability of concepts is well illustrated in the case of climate change. Despite increasing consensus within the scientific community that climate change is a reality, there has been an intense level of debate concerning whether or not the phenomenon exists, with a range of underlying theories and ideas being widely contested in the political arena and wider society (Dunlap and McCright 2011; Nyberg et al. 2013).

Though related to discursive concepts, *discursive objects* differ in an important way: ' ... concepts exist only in the expressive order; they exist in the realm of ideas. Objects on the other hand, are part of the practical order; they are real in the sense of existing in the material world' (Phillips and Hardy 1997: 168). One cannot therefore think of objects as being inanimate; unlike concepts, they can exist in a physical sense and have an ontological reality. However, the social accomplishment of a concept requires that it be applied to, or become, an object. Changing the concept stands to change the way in which the object itself is socially accomplished, acknowledged and related to (Phillips and Hardy 1997: 168). Continuing with the example of climate change, recent catastrophes such as Hurricane Sandy in 2012 and the Australian bushfires of 2013 were clear material events. They were objects that with their devastating and unquestionable effects made the concept of climate change a reality. However, again, it was mainly the scientific community that saw these events as objectification of climate change and as evidence of a looming catastrophe. For wider society the material events were mainly connected to the weather, instead of climate.

Whether a discursively constructed concept 'works' once it becomes an ontological reality – an object – can only be assessed by paying particular attention to the relevant *discursive subjects*. Individuals who are the focus of a particular discourse are not simply passive receptacles of that discourse, but are active social agents with their own interests and subjectivities who are seeking to establish their own social and power relations (Phillips and Hardy 1997: 170). Thus, it becomes important to know how discursive subjects react to a particular discourse. In the case of climate change, how society and organisational actors make sense of the concept of climate change is dependent on which actors and positions have a voice in the co-construction of reality. For example, whether an organisation acts upon climate change as a threat, opportunity or not at all is dependent on the actors influencing decision-making processes within the organisation. This point is brought home in a recent study by Wright, Nyberg and Grant (2012). The study shows how environmental and sustainability managers sought to negotiate and enhance their positions within organisations so as to be able to influence the nature and extent of their employers' response to climate change.

Everyday talk both constitutes local discourses and reproduces their effects; everyday talk illuminates the relationship between discourse and the construction of social reality. Dominant local discourses constrain actors' possibilities and reproduce 'knowledge' and 'truths' concerning how concepts, objects and subjects are understood and made sense of. Such discourses influence how we make sense of concepts such as climate change, whether material effects, such as changing weather patterns, gain object status in relation to climate change, and the identity of subjects who are in a position to influence the discursive production of knowledge and truths about climate change. The relation between these constructs can, at times, be conflicting or even paradoxical. Further, several competing discourses can be present simultaneously. The internal discursive conflicts and the plurality of discourses creates 'space of action'; that is the opportunity to challenge dominant discourses and change how we make sense of ourselves and surrounding social realities (Holmer-Nadesan 1996). Organisations and other groups thus take part in a contest where they seek to shape social reality. How actors make sense of societal discourses, such as climate change is influenced by dominant discourses. This alignment of dominant discourses with their interests goes on both consciously and unconsciously.

With the growing power of multinational corporations, a clear distinction between what is termed the 'market' and what is termed 'education', 'health care' and the 'environment', is increasingly difficult to sustain. Instead, the latter terms are often conflated or are used interchangeably with the former. We have thus witnessed an increased involvement by corporations in environmental and social challenges such as human rights, global warming or deforestation (Scherer and Palazzo 2008: 426). With this increased influence comes the ability of corporations, through their discursive production of texts, to shape social reality, and how we make sense of and act in the world. Acting in a complex and ambiguous world, organisational communications often take part in simplifying the operational environment in order for members to make sense of it. Drawing upon available discourses, organisations produce versions of their operational environment that necessarily exclude concepts, theories and versions of the world which are in tension or contradiction with their own (Rayner 2012). Organisations engage not only in producing particular 'truths' or 'knowledge', but also in producing ignorance (McGoey 2007). These productions of knowledge/ignorance can be both conscious and unconscious articulations that form the discourses that locally produced texts engage with. While most of these articulations are not strategically aimed towards changing surrounding discourses, however, in prioritising certain concepts others are marginalised. By including particular versions or interpretations, others are excluded and even forgotten. As Derrida (1988) convincingly argued, this leads to the privilege in binary hierarchies of certain concepts, subjects and objects over others. For example, discrimination in terms of age, gender and sexuality that occur in organisations can be caused by the unconscious consumption and distribution of the privileged positions that are supported by the prevailing discourses.

However, organisations also engage more strategically in challenging or undermining concepts or theories that threaten their ability to pursue market competitiveness and profit (Rayner 2012). For example, Oreskes and Conway (2010) illustrate how the tobacco industry funded scientists and research to undermine the evidence between second-hand smoking and cancer. In doing this, they successfully delayed regulations that would impact the sale and consumption of cigarettes. Their research illustrates how the operational context is a political arena. How organisations respond to their environment is then not determined by the situation, but rather how the situation is framed or situated (Barley 2010; Grint 2005). Large organisations and industries, such as those in tobacco or oil, have the capacity to persuade stakeholders and influence what is seen as a legitimate response to a situation or problem.

With the capacity to frame the situation or problem, how organisations respond to a problem can even be dependent on available solutions. The complex relationship between understanding problems and understanding their relationship to solutions was discussed by Rittel and Webber

(1973) who, in the context of urban planning, differentiated between *Tame* and *Wicked problems*. Grint (2005) adapted Rittel and Webber's analysis to further suggest how organisations are active in constituting the context of the situations. Grint suggests that tame problems, can be complex but there is a known solution and correct procedure for solving them. They are problems that can be (and have previously been) solved, such that leaders leave it to others to apply the known solution and apply the correct procedures in order to solve them. Wicked problems are not easily solvable because they are novel and may be difficult to resolve such that we have to learn to live with them. The solution to a wicked problem often generates another problem and they often appear to have no right or wrong solutions. Different stakeholders will likely have different approaches and understandings of them and understanding them is developed through construction of the solution. The construction of the solution is achieved through dialogue, collaboration and the securing of collective consent. Grint further added *Critical problems* to the typology. These are often depicted as a self-evident crisis and generate widespread uncertainty. Critical problems are argued as providing no time for discussion or dissent or worrying about 'procedures' if these delay resolution. In solving them coercion, given the circumstances, is often deemed to be in the public interest and necessary. These problems are often characterised as a 'crisis'; self-evident in nature and demanding swift actions with limited consultations (Grint 2005). Using the empirical cases of Shell's problem with Brent Spar, Kennedy's response to the Cuban missile crisis, and the invasion of Iraq, Grint (2005) illustrates how the responses to these situations were dependent on whether the problems were seen as tame, wicked or critical. The actors had the capacity to influence and persuade groups of the 'reading' of the situations; how the problem was understood was dependent on the ideas for solving it (see also Rittel and Webber 1973).

Grint (2005) illustrates through these empirical cases how leaders frame particular problems as tame, wicked or critical in order to suit their purposes. We believe that this framework lends itself well to our discourse-based analysis of corporate communication strategies and how these are used by organisations to shape their operational environments and legitimise particular activities (or lack thereof). Through producing and distributing texts that influence surrounding discourses, organisations shape the context which justifies solutions in response to the environment. Fairclough (2003) in discussing policy documents makes a similar point. Political policy documents are written to portray inevitable actions by the problem at hand. Fairclough (2003: 99) refers to a famous expression of the former British Prime Minister Margaret Thatcher: 'there is no alternative', which was referred to as the 'TINA' principle. Similar to the TINA principle, in constituting the contextual discourses, corporate strategies limit available alternatives for other actors; the framing of the situation ensures that only certain responses make sense. Particular actions, supported by dominant discourses, become normalised. The demands of the situation are thus constructed to fit the organisation's favoured engagements.

However, different organisations may have different agendas in addressing a shared environment or common problem. Contested situations suggest the possibility for different sub-sections of society, industry and organisations to have different definitions of the problem as well as diverse potential solutions without challenging each others' motivations too deeply. This further allows for a range of strategies to manage the contested and ambiguous situations (Rayner 2012). For example, dependent on favoured responses and strategies to deal with climate change, organisations can articulate the problems with climate change differently. This may further differ so as to influence internal and external audiences. Any analysis of business responses to climate change thus requires knowledge of the organisational context and the various actors and their interests that are at play in order to understand corporate strategies and communication in relation to this issue.

The remaining sections of this chapter employ a discourse analytical tool that distinguishes between concepts (categories, ideas and theories), objects (material arrangements) and subjects (actors or positions having voice) in investigating how organisations are responding to climate change and their subsequent engagement with sustainability. The ideas and theories (concepts) underlying the debate on climate change are contested, dismissed and supported by various corporations and industries; organisations engage in a wide range of contextual policies and practices (objects) in response to the 'issue' of climate change; and, scientists, environmentalists and corporate managers (subjects) produce numerous texts in shaping the debate about climate change. Previous studies that have employed this analytical framework, have used it in a way that sequences concept first, followed by object, followed by subject. This has enabled them to demonstrate how concepts and objects ultimately impact on the subject. In a departure from this convention, we are concerned with the idea that through a combination of the concept and subject, it is the object that is impacted. We suggest that though this process corporations have actively constructed climate change as either a tame or wicked problem rather than a crisis and, in doing this, have avoided the challenge to capitalism's raison-d'être: economic growth. Using the framework in this way illustrates its dynamism; dependent on your analytical focus – discourse as concept, subject or object – it is an explanatory prism that can be altered to illuminate various social phenomena.

Concepts

The concept of climate change has rapidly emerged as *the* major social, political and economic issue of this century (Hansen 2009; Stern *et al.* 2006). Indeed, the escalation of texts produced in relation to climate change has made it almost impossible for corporations to not engage with climate change at some level. There is consequently awareness among corporations that the implications of climate change as an issue and the proposed political situations in responding to climate change are profound. Since the economic system that corporations are part of is largely based upon the continuing use of fossil fuels and the increasingly escalating production of greenhouse gases, organisations are 'forced' to manage the, often uncomfortable, knowledge of climate change by giving the concept meaning in relation to their particular situation and industry.

However, what counts as 'true', 'objective' and as a 'fact' in relation to climate change is not a scientific discovery, but rather the negotiation between contending accounts of 'reality'. In many countries during the early stages of the twenty-first century, the belief that climate change is happening and that it is caused by humans is supported by a minority of the population. For example, a World Bank (2009) study reported that only a minority of people thought that there is a scientific consensus on the urgent need to address climate change – Russia (23 per cent), the US (38 per cent), Japan (43 per cent) and Indonesia (33 per cent). Whether climate change is a problem is then dependent on particular groups' ability to persuade people that it is an urgent issue. Indeed, in responding to the challenge of climate change, corporations have employed a range of strategies to avoid it becoming a critical problem and a crisis. A crisis would, arguably, demand forms of state authoritarianism and legitimate disrupting of corporate technologies and processes; force discontinuing of services and products; and enforce new regulations and taxes. Rather, the corporate strategies have communicated climate change as a wicked or tame problem. These corporate strategies are, of course, dependent on the industry and interest of the organisation.

Some corporations have engaged with climate change only to reject the concept as a wicked problem without any clear solution and in favour of the status quo. The argument has varied between claiming that the scientific evidence is unreliable, wrong, or produced with a hidden agenda (Levy and Egan 2003). The problem of climate change thus lacks a clear definition and it would be dangerous to act upon vague or unreliable empirical evidence. In line with this, corporations have even actively lobbied and campaigned against the regulation of greenhouse gas emissions, promoting counter-discourses of climate change denial (Dunlap and McCright 2011; Nyberg et al. 2013). For example, Livesey's (2002: 128) analysis of four ExxonMobil advertorials published on the Op-Ed page of *The New York Times* as paid for opinion pieces during 2000 suggested that the oil company's argument was 'that the problem is not global warming, but the wrong-headed, if not arrogant, views of climate scientists (and the misguided government representatives and the public who trust them), who "believe they can predict changes in climate decades from now"'. As Livesey's (2002: 136) analysis shows 'from the corporate perspective, then, climate science, as a young and contentious field (with a "range of views" and given to "debate"), does not present an adequate basis for decision and action'.

This dismissal of the scientific community's conceptualisation of climate change and its ability to predict its consequences has further been highlighted by a range of studies illustrating how corporations have invested heavily in producing texts used for political lobbying and public relations as well as distributed through the funding of activist groups promoting climate change denial (Dunlap and McCright 2011; Oreskes and Conway 2010). A similar process of producing and distributing dismissal and denial has occurred in Australia, where mining and manufacturing companies in association with conservative think-tanks have produced a range of texts to question the science of climate change through funding of climate sceptic groups, authored opinion pieces for media outlets, networking with sympathetic journalists, as well as paid advertisements and marketing within political campaigns (Hamilton 2007; Pearse 2009). Corporations in both the US and Australia have successfully taken part in discursive activities that have created enough doubt about the problem of climate change that responses to it have been stymied.

By contrast, other organisations have constructed climate change as a *tame* problem. Rather than creating doubt about the wickedness of the concept, these corporations have sought to accommodate their strategies within a difficult and challenging new environment. Similar to other business opportunities and threats in their ever changing regulatory and economic context, this tame problem 'only' requires reassessing their strategies and investing in new technologies (Hoffman 2007; Orsato 2009). The tameness of climate change as a problem is well illustrated by a report by the Economist Intelligence Unit (2011) based on a survey of more than 700 global executives from a range of industry sectors from the Asia-Pacific, Middle East and Africa, Western Europe, North America and Latin America, which found that two-thirds of businesses see climate change as an opportunity. Common arguments among these types of corporations are that the problem can be addressed by restructuring markets to tackle environmental concerns (Mol and Sonnenfeld 2000). Indeed, as the survey shows, environmental sustainability is presented as a business opportunity for new products, markets and forms of technological innovation. Following this, we have seen corporations increasingly embrace discourses of 'corporate sustainability' and 'green' products and services. These discourses have also led to new roles and departments in organisations, such as sustainability managers and consultants, who are charged with making their corporations 'sustainable' and 'good corporate citizens'.

The texts produced, distributed and consumed to represent climate change as a tame or wicked problem are all to counter-weight the narrative of crisis expressed by environmental organisations such as Greenpeace and the emergency expressed by international bodies of scientists producing the IPCC (2007) reports. As Rayner (2012: 117) argues:

It seems odd that climate science has been held to a 'platinum standard' of precision and reliability that goes well beyond anything that is normally required to make significant decisions in either the public or private sectors. Governments have recently gone to war based on much lower-quality intelligence than that which science offers us about climate change. Similarly, firms embark on product launches and merges on the bases of much lower-quality information.

Through their communication strategies, corporations have worked hard to avoid the uncertainty that arguably would come with the construction of climate change as a crisis and the acuteness of responses then required.

Subjects

In order for a concept, or a particular interpretation of a concept, to gain meaning for other actors and be legitimised as a valid position, the particular understanding needs to be embedded in a context. Corporations cannot simply produce texts to suit their needs and interests. To shape other texts and subsequently broader discourses, the interests of corporations are required to be connected to interests or identities of other actors or subject positions. The texts and interpretations of concepts need to be 'made relevant by and for participants' (Van Dijk 1997: 16). As such, corporations are engaged in hegemonic struggles with different groups and other corporations to shape social reality in ways that serve their particular interests (Mumby and Clair 1997). In this 'war of positions' (Gramsci 1971), corporations engage simultaneously in two manoeuvres to mobilise coalitions and gain legitimacy. These are: 1) to make their particular claim or interest generally or universally accepted principles; and 2) to demonstrate that certain actors' interests and identities overlap with their own while others do not (Laclau 1996; Laclau and Mouffe 2001).

By engaging in these types of discursive activities corporations can generate new meanings of concepts that help the enactment of material practices in their particular situation (Hardy et al. 2000). 'Discourse shapes the subjective experience and the actions of those participating in it and, in doing so, helps to produce their subjectivities' (Hardy and Phillips 1999: 4). Corporate communications in particular, can be seen as a means by which to shape relations among actors through the ways they represent their interests and connect them to each other (Fairclough and Wodak 1997). In this way the production of texts transforms the discursive structures, that is, what can be said, when it can be said, who has the legitimacy or has the right to say something, and how this is understood. Corporate communication can stabilise the discursive structure so that certain actors are privileged, legitimate and a warranted voice, while others are marginalised, illegitimate, and even silenced. The reproduction of the discursive structure strengthens certain actors where it modifies the discourse so that it is useful for their interests (Hardy and Phillips 2004).

For most corporations the overlap of their interests and identities with those of other actors is communicated to immediate stakeholders, such as employees, customers and investors, through 'normal' business activities. In response to climate change, such connection of interests has been undertaken through initiatives related to organisational sustainability or corporate social responsibility. In their research on how businesses respond to climate change, Nyberg and Wright (2012) show how corporations established a chain of equivalence between the corporation and a range of relevant actors. For example, in including their customer base, the corporations commonly developed new products and services, such as 'low-carbon' beer, recyclable office equipment, and 'hybrid' and 'electric cars'. The corporations communicated this through marketing strategies and created a corporate identity as a green company. This was expressed by one sustainability manager of a large energy company, who was envious of a competitor:

> [T]hey are often held up as they're the 'green energy company' because all their marketing material is around 'green'. So you go to them if you want your green power because their ads are saying 'green'.
>
> *(Nyberg and Wright 2012: 1827)*

These 'green' products and marketing their sustainability together with increased energy efficiency, also addressed investors' concerns. Similarly, Nyberg and Wright show how the identities of the employees are included in the frontier of the climate change positioning. In addressing climate change, corporations communicated this to employees and allowed them to engage in a range of sustainability projects enabling employees to incorporate organisational claims as part of their identity. The environment generally, and addressing climate change more particularly, was seen as a topic that engendered passion and emotion in working for the organisation and it provided sources of meaning beyond the conventional monetary rewards. This is particular pertinent for sustainability and environmental managers, who are charged with making their corporations 'sustainable' and 'good corporate citizens' (see also Wright, Nyberg and Grant 2012).

The study by Nyberg and Wright (2012) also found that in mobilising a coalition of interests and legitimating their positions, corporations engaged NGOs as well as other corporations to legitimate and strengthen their position. It showed that environmental sponsorships and engagement with green NGOs, such as WWF, were presented as promoting a favourable image of how the corporations engaged with climate change and legitimised their position. Several of the companies examined by Nyberg and Wright were prominent in advocating for greater government action on climate change and had established coalitions of business leaders to promote this issue. How the corporations could capitalise on the urgent concept of climate change was explained by a sustainability manager for a global construction and mining company:

> [T]he opportunity here is for us to build new businesses out of a new carbon economy essentially and we've done a lot of work on that. We've formed an industrial energy division to take advantage of those opportunities. We've got partnerships with a number of renewable energy technology providers.
>
> *(Nyberg and Wright 2012: 1826)*

Nyberg and Wright's (2012) findings suggest that with broad coalitions of actors supporting corporate claims, the best way to address climate change is 'business as usual'. The 'tame' problem of climate change is a business opportunity validated by the new internal positions of environmental or sustainability managers as well as a range of external stakeholders.

While many corporations have engaged in politics of inclusion by connecting their interests to a range of subject positions, others have engaged in exclusion by emphasising difference rather than equivalence. In drawing the boundaries of the political struggle over climate change, the focus is here on those who should be kept out, rather than those who are invited in. Instead of trying to claim that our knowledge of climate change is uncertain and that it is a wicked problem, the emphasis has here instead been on portraying certain actors, or subject positions, as wicked.

Fossil fuels industry led by corporations with their associations, such as ExxonMobil, Peabody Coal and the American Petroleum Institute, have built coalitions with other associations, such as the US Chamber of Commerce, National Associations of Manufacturers and conservative think-tanks to mount attacks on IPCC and individual scientists (Dunlap and McCright 2011). Parallels can be drawn here with the attack mounted on Rachel Carson by the major chemical corporations in the US who manufactured the pesticides that she criticised in her book *Silent Spring* (1962). At the book's publication, Carson was portrayed as hysterical and as an extremist in an attempt to undermine the credibility of her message. Such charges are levelled today at those who seek to challenge or question whether the activities of corporations are contributing to environmental degradation (Mann 2012). In Australia, the demonisation of climate scientists culminated with a conservative newspaper corporation publishing a map showing where a famous Australian climate scientist lived.

In sum, climate scientists and others seeking to project climate change as a real and evident crisis can be seen to have been demonised and excluded from relevant debate by suggesting that their positions lack credibility and are against the general good or welfare of society. Silencing and marginalising actors who voice climate change as a critical problem ensures that, in many countries, the debate that does occur about this issue generally frames it as a tame or wicked problem and therefore in ways that suit other more powerful actors' interests.

Objects

Above we have made it clear that climate change is not an objective phenomenon or scientific truth. This means that, while the material effects of climate change exist 'out there', the truth of climate change does not. How climate change is interpreted is dependent on the temporally dominant truth regimes available for actors to make sense of the events. Climate change can thus 'bite back' and challenge the dominant regimes, by confronting them with weather events or climate alterations that cannot be explained or represented by the available or hegemonic discourses and constructions of climate change.

The identity of objects is determined by their situation in discursive articulations and practices. This is not to suggest that discourse analysis ignore the material, but rather that the emphasis is on how the material a) acquires meaning through the discursive articulations and b) is entangled with the possible articulations (Hardy and Grant 2012). They are mutually implicated (Barad 2007). Object materiality and identity in the discursive realm can then, in turn, provide limits for discursive articulations and practices. Organisational policies and practices regarding climate change and sustainability are then dependent on local context with the particular qualified objects, such as CSR or sustainability reports legitimating broader discourses as well as how the effects of climate change are interpreted and their entanglement with the discourses of sustainability.

As suggested above, the climate change debate has led to a range of policies and practices (objects) implemented in organisations to address climate change: products such as fuel efficient cars, carbon neutral beers, reports establishing corporate GHG emissions; services by environmental consultants and accounting firms to help corporations to adapt to and mitigate the effects of climate change; and, despite the polarised debate in countries like Australia, Canada and the US, we have seen new policies including a Carbon Reduction Scheme in Australia directed towards the major corporate GHG pollutants. Even so, the polarised debate in these countries about the concept of climate change has resulted in its limited 'weight' as an object (Iedema, 2007). With the exception of the academic community, where climate change has obtained more noticeable traction, climate change is either put into practice as a 'tame' problem with common business practices suitable to address it, or as a 'wicked' problem, with no right or wrong solution to what is seen as an uncertain and debatable concept.

Thus, while the physical existence of climate change is objectified in the academic community through record temperatures and increases in other extreme weather events, these are still not linked to the concept of climate change by most of the population in countries like Australia and the US where many of these events are taking place. Moreover, this is despite predictions that climate change will further 'bite back' through, for example, dramatic temperature changes that will lead to sectors of the Earth no longer being suitable for human habitation, rising sea levels swallowing island nations, catastrophic weather events, and the acidification of oceans with major effect on the fish stocks. We assert that corporate communication will increasingly struggle to incorporate these physical events into their conceptualisation of climate change as 'tame' or 'wicked'. There is a disconnect between how corporations have made sense of the concept of climate change through their 'lame' practices of CSR reporting and greening initiatives and the scientific prevailing discourse of climate change as a 'crisis'. In short, the current objectification of climate change by corporations is unsustainable.

Conclusion

In this chapter we have sought to demonstrate how ODS can open up analytical space for more informative accounts of how discourses are communicated and employed within and among contemporary organisations. We have also sought to show how these processes frame the social reality of actors locally and globally. The specific ODS framework of analysis that we have adopted in order to achieve this distinguishes between concepts (categories, ideas and theories), objects (material arrangements) and subjects (actors or positions having voice) (Fairclough 1992; Phillips and Hardy 1997; Oswick et al. 2000; Grant and Shields, 2002; Parker 1992). Drawing on this framework enabled us to vividly demonstrate the capacity of social constructionist process and outcome focused research to challenge, innovate and progress more conventional approaches to the study of organisations and organising. More specifically, we believe that we have shown how the framework can be used to offer organisation and communication scholars valuable insight into how businesses engage with the issue of climate change while at the same time allowing space for more progressive and bolder ways of interacting with the topic. This has been achieved where, in contrast to previous studies, we have employed the framework in a way that sequences concept first, followed by object, followed by subject. Doing so has enabled us to show how, through a combination of the concept and subject of climate change, it is climate change the object that is impacted.

Our discourse-based analysis of corporate communication strategies draws attention to how organisations frame particular problems as tame, wicked or critical in order to suit their purposes. In this instance, we show how this plays out where corporate communication attempts to position physical events (objects) indicative of climate change as being commensurate with their current conceptualisation of the issue as a 'tame' or 'wicked' problem. Our analysis leads us to conclude that the challenge for corporations is to conceptualise and make sense of the increased physical presence of climate change in more meaningful ways than has so far been the case and without it turning into a critical problem. Could they achieve this? We suggest that with the increasingly obvious effects of climate change, its physical point of reference needs to change. Continued corporate communication of climate change as a tame problem could, for example, see arguments for increased adaption and mitigation strategies, which would have limited impact on the global rise in temperature and frequency of extreme weather events. Alternatively, the conceptualisation of climate change as 'wicked' will perhaps lead to more extreme measures of geo-engineering. The current power of large corporations to influence how we make sense of phenomena and to shape what we take to be our social reality suggests that their communicative practices will be influential in how societies make sense of, and act on, climate change.

Related topics

management communications; corporate communications; public relations and professional communications

Key readings

Grant, D., Hardy, C., Oswick, C. and Putnam L. (eds) (2004). *The Sage Handbook of Organizational Discourse*, London: Sage. (This Handbook provides an introduction to organisational discourse theory generally and includes several chapters relevant to understanding and analysing professional communication.)

Nyberg, D. and Wright, C. (2012). 'Justifying business responses to climate change: Discursive strategies of similarity and difference', *Environment and Planning A*, 44, 1819–35. (This article employs discourse analysis in order to examine a range of corporate responses to climate change.)

Oreskes, N. and Conway, E. M. (2010). *Merchants of Doubt: How a Handful of Scientists Obscured the Truth on Issues from Tobacco Smoke to Global Warming*, New York: Bloomsbury Press. (*Merchants of Doubt* convincingly and entertainingly examines the strategies employed by key actors in order to delay efforts designed to minimise smoking and stop climate change.)

Phillips, N. and Hardy, C. (1997). 'Managing multiple identities: Discourse, legitimacy and resources in the UK refugee system', *Organization*, 4(2), 159–85. (This article provides a detailed explanation of the concept, object, subject discursive analytical framework and provides a useful illustration of its applicability in analysing communications.)

Bibliography

Alvesson, M. and Karreman, D. (2000). 'Varieties of discourse: On the study of organizations through discourse analysis', *Human Relations*, 53(9): 1125–49.

——(2011). 'Decolonializing discourse: Critical reflections on organizational discourse analysis', *Human Relations*, 64, 1121–46.

Barad, K. (2007). *Meeting the Universe Halfway: Quantum Physics and the Entanglement of Matter and Meaning*, Durham, NC: Duke University Press.

Barley, S. R. (2010). 'Building an institutional field to corral a government: A case to set an agenda for organization studies', *Organization Studies*, 31(6), 777–805.

Carson, R. (1962). *Silent Spring*, Boston: Houghton Mifflin.

Chouliaraki, L. and Fairclough, N. (1999). *Discourse in Late Modernity*, Edinburgh: Edinburgh University Press.

Derrida, J. (1988). *Limited Inc.*, Evanston: Northwestern University Press.

Dunlap, R. E. and McCright, A. M. (2011). 'Organized climate change denial', in J. S. Dryzek, R. B. Norgaard and D. Schlosberg (eds), *The Oxford Handbook of Climate Change and Society* (pp. 144–60), Oxford: Oxford University Press.

Economist Intelligence Unit (2011). *Adapting to an Uncertain Climate: A World of Commercial Opportunities*, London: UK Trade and Investment.

Fairclough, N. (1992). *Discourse and Social Change*, Cambridge, MA: Polity Press.

——(2003). *Analysing Discourse: Textual Analysis for Social Research*, London: Routledge.

Fairclough, N. and Wodak, R. (1997). 'Critical discourse analysis', in T. A. van Dijk (ed.), *Discourse as Structure and Process*, Vol. 2. (pp. 258–84), London: Sage.

Foucault, M. (1979). *Discipline and Punish: The Birth of the Prison*, London: Penguin.

——(1980). *Power/Knowledge: Selected Interviews and other Writings 1972–1977*, Brighton: Harvester Press.

——(1998). *The Will to Knowledge: The History of Sexuality*, Vol. 1, London: Penguin.

——(2007). *Security, Territory, Population*, London: Palgrave.

Gramsci, A. (1971). *Selections from Prison Notebooks*, London: Lawrence and Wishart.

Grant, D., Hardy, C., Oswick, C. and Putnam, L. (2004). 'Introduction – Organizational discourse: Exploring the field', in D. Grant, C. Hardy, C. Oswick and L. Putnam (eds), *The Handbook of Organizational Discourse* (pp. 1–36), London: Sage.

Grant, D. and Shields, J. (2002). 'In search of the subject: Researching employee reactions to HRM', *Journal of Industrial Relations*, 44(3), 313–34.

Grint, K. (2005). 'Problems, problems, problems: The social construction of "leadership"', *Human Relations*, 58(11), 1467–94.

Hamilton, C. (2007). *Scorcher: The Dirty Politics of Climate Change*, Melbourne: Black Inc.

Hansen, J. (2009). *Storms of my Grandchildren: The Truth about the Coming Climate Catastrophe and our Last Chance to Save Humanity*, New York: Bloomsbury.

Hardy, C. and Grant, D. (2012). 'Readers beware: Provocation, problematization and ... problems', *Human Relations*, 65(5), 547–66.

Hardy, C., Palmer, I. and Phillips, N. (2000). 'Discourse as a strategic resource', *Human Relations*, 53(9), 1227–48.

Hardy, C. and Phillips, N. (1999). 'No joking matter: Discursive struggle in the Canadian refugee system', *Organization Studies*, 20(1), 1–24.

———(2004). 'Discourse and power', in D. Grant, C. Hardy, C. Oswick and L. L. Putnam (eds), *The SAGE Handbook of Organizational Discourse* (pp. 299–316), London: Sage.

Hoffman, A. J. (2007). *Carbon Strategies: How Leading Companies are Reducing their Climate Change Footprint*, Ann Arbor, MI: University of Michigan Press.

Holmer-Nadesan, M. (1996). 'Organizational identity and the space of action', *Organization Studies*, 17, 49–81.

Iedema, R. (2007). 'On the multi-modality, materiality and contingency of organization discourse', *Organization Studies*, 28(6), 931–46.

IPCC (2007). *Climate Change 2007: Synthesis Report*, Geneva: IPCC.

Laclau, E. (1996). *Emancipations*, London: Verso Press.

Laclau, E. and Mouffe, C. (2001). *Hegemony and Socialist Strategy*, London: Verso Press.

Levy, D. and Egan, D. (2003). 'A neo-Gramscian approach to corporate political strategy: Conflict and accommodation in the climate change negotiations', *Journal of Management Studies*, 40(4), 803–29.

Livesey, S. M. (2002). 'Global warming wars: Rhetorical and discourse analytic approaches to ExxonMobil's corporate public discourse', *Journal of Business Communication*, 61(4), 343–75.

Mann, M. E. (2012). *The Hockeystick and the Climate Wars: Dispatches from the Front Lines*, New York: Columbia University Press.

McGoey, L. (2007). 'On the will to ignorance in bureaucracy', *Economy & Society*, 36(2), 212–35.

Mol, A. P. and Sonnenfeld, D. A. (2000). 'Ecological modernisation around the world: An introduction', in A. P. Mol and D. A. Sonnenfeld (eds), *Ecological Modernisation Around the World: Perestives and Critical Debates* (pp. 3–14), London: Frank Cass.

Mumby, D. and Clair, R. D. (1997). 'Organizational discourse', in T. A. van Dijk (ed.), *Discourse as Social Interaction: Discourse Studies, Vol. 2 – A Multidisciplinary Introduction* (pp. 181–205), Newbury Park, CA: Sage.

Nyberg, D., Spicer, A. and Wright, C. (2013). 'Incorporating Citizens: Corporate Political Engagement with Climate Change in Australia', *Organization*, 20(3), 433–53.

Nyberg, D. and Wright, C. (2012). 'Justifying business responses to climate change: Discursive strategies of similarity and difference', *Environment and Planning A*, 44, 1819–35.

Oreskes, N. and Conway, E. M. (2010). *Merchants of Doubt: How a Handful of Scientists Obscured the Truth on Issues from Tobacco Smoke to Global Warming*, New York: Bloomsbury Press.

Orsato, R. J. (2009). *Sustainability Strategies: When Does it Pay to be Green*, London: Palgrave Macmillan.

Oswick, C., Keenoy, T. and Grant, D. (2000). 'Discourse, organizations and organizing: concepts, objects and subjects', *Human Relations*, 52(9), 1115–24.

Parker, I. (1992). *Discourse Dynamics*, London: Routledge.

Pearse, G. (2009). 'Quarry vision: Coal, climate change and the end of the resources boom', *Quarterly Essay*, 33, 1–122.

Phillips, N. and Hardy, C. (1997). 'Managing multiple identities: discourse legitimacy and resources in the UK refugee system', *Organization*, 4(2), 159–85.

Rayner, S. (2012). 'Uncomfortable knowledge: The social construction of ignorance in science and environmental policy discourses', *Economy and Society*, 41(1), 107–25.

Rittel, H. W. J. and Webber, M. M. (1973). 'Dilemmas in a general theory of planning', *Policy Sciences*, 4, 155–69.

Scherer, A. G., and Palazzo, G. (2008). 'Globalization and corporate social responsibility', in A. Crane, A. McWilliams, D. Matten, J. Moon and D. Siegel (eds), *The Oxford Handbook of Corporate Social Responsibility* (pp. 413–31), Oxford: Oxford University Press.

Stern, N., Peters, S., Bakhshi, V., Bowen, A., Cameron, C., Catovsky, S., Crane, D., Cruickshank, S., Dietz, S., Edmonson, N., Garbett, S.-L., Hamid, L., Hoffman, G., Ingram, D., Jones, B., Patmore, N., Radcliffe, H., Sathiyarajah, R., Stock, M., Taylor, C., Vernon, T., Wanjie, H. and Zenghelis, D. (2006). *Stern Review: The Economics of Climate Change*, London: HM Treasury.

Torfing, J. (2005). 'Discourse theory: Achievements, arguments, and challenges', in D. Howarth and J. Torfing (eds), *Discourse Theory in European Politics* (pp. 1–32), Hampshire: Palgrave.

Van Dijk, T. A. (1997). 'Discourse as interaction in society', in T. A. van Dijk (ed.), *Discourse as Structure and Process*, Vol. 2. (pp. 1–37), London: Sage.

World Bank (2009). *Public Attitudes toward Climate Change: Findings from a Multi-country Poll*, Washington DC: The World Bank.

Wright, C., Nyberg, D. and Grant, D. (2012). '"Hippies on the Third Floor": Climate Change, Narrative Identity and the Micro-Politics of Corporate Environmentalism', *Organization Studies*, *33*(11), 1451–75.

14
Professionalising organisational communication discourses, materialities and trends

Patrice M. Buzzanell, Jeremy P. Fyke and Robyn V. Remke

As a field, organisational communication began because of a confluence of national and global events. These events included military training needs and changing labour force requirements and interests, as well as growing appreciation for how communication enables particular processes and outcomes and how communication constitutes realities locally and globally (see Ashcraft, Kuhn and Cooren 2009; Axley 1984; Redding 1972, 1985; Jablin and Putnam 2001; Jablin et al. 1987; Putnam and Nicotera 2009; Tompkins and Redding 1988). Scholars conceptualised organisational communication in various ways. Organisational communication has been positioned as both antecedent and effect, clusters of metaphorical schema and problematics, and as the process through which organisation itself is constituted and performed (see Corman and Poole 2000; Mumby and Stohl 1996; Putnam and Nicotera 2009; Putnam and Boys 2006; Robichaud and Cooren 2012). Shared by but different in organisational and professional communication, this constitutive approach centred on discourse and text offers value in current and emerging trends in research and practice.

In taking the constitutive approach to communication, Kuhn (2012) describes what this lens means in scholarship and practice. To Kuhn, taking communication seriously means 'portraying communication as constitutive of social realities' with a focus on the production of meanings in social action; 'seeing organizations not as containers for communication, not merely settings inside of which communication occurs, but intrinsically *as* communication'; 'staying in the realm of communicational events both conceptually and methodologically' with mindfulness that communication is always contextually, politically and materially situated; and 'eradicating simplistic assumptions about meaning convergence as the *telos* of communication' while embracing the ambiguities, contradictions, and logics of difference in which order and disorder co-influence each other and operate as significant analytical frames (pp. 548–50). This constitutive nature of communication underlies both organisational and professional communication with the former examining a broader range of phenomena about diverse collectivities on micro through macro levels and in private-public realms, and the latter studying specific professional exigencies and findings that correspond with understandings about, or more effective, practices in professions. Organisational communication scholars increasingly have expressed interest in the nature, expectations surrounding, and meanings/meaningfulness of particular types of work (e.g. Barley, Leonardi and Bailey 2012; Buzzanell and Lucas 2013; Cheney et al. 2008; Gabor 2011; Kisselburgh, Berkelaar and Buzzanell 2009) and of being professional in local and global contexts (Cheney and Ashcraft 2007; Ellingson 2011; Lammers and Garcia 2009; Meisenbach 2008). They have not delved as deeply into the discursive and material practices that create and sustain professions and professionals through documents, logics and arguments, and identity formations through text development, reports, websites and other discourses and materialities. Similarly, professional communication researchers have delved into how professionals understand their communities of practice, how materials are generated for organisational goals, and where there can be greater academician-practitioner collaborations (Cheng and Kong 2009). For professional communication scholars, texts are contested sites for training and for informing practitioners about daily practices. Power and agency are significant considerations insofar as accreditations, certifications, policies, reports and other texts have profound consequences. Inattention to political dynamics, cultural underpinnings, and document specifications can affect professions' (de)legitimisation and (de)institutionalisation. In sum, organisational and professional communication have distinctive orientations. Yet both attend to intersections between discourse and materialities, as well as theory and practice; both examine power, authority and agency.

Because our chapter discusses organisational communication for scholars in professional communication, we organise our chapter (a) by providing overviews of organisational communication from the earliest reviews to current reframings (Part I); (b) by noting recent inquiry can contribute to professional communication (Part II); and (c) by encouraging emerging research trends that underlie organisational-professional communication intersections (Part III). In Part I, we incorporate different levels – individual and interactional (micro) through organisational or institutional (meso), and societal, cultural, and global (macro discourses) – and varied organisational contexts in which professional might have different meanings. Furthermore, we highlight diverse metatheoretical traditions, communication theories, and methodologies (for overviews, see Carbaugh and Buzzanell 2010; Craig 1999; May and Mumby 2005; Putnam and Mumby 2014). We integrate some classic materials as springboards for later discussion. We note key scholars' research programs, acknowledging that our limited depth and breadth does not do justice to their work and to the many others who have contributed greatly to organisational communication.

In Part II, we utilise several decision criteria to focus on current organisational communication research that can inform and be informed by professional communication. Here we use particular conceptualisations. For organisational communication, Mumby (2007) notes that 'in simple terms' such scholars investigate:

> the dynamic relationships between communication processes and human organizing. Communication is conceived as foundational to, and constitutive of, organizations, while organizations are viewed as relatively enduring structures that are both medium and outcome of communication processes. While research has focused traditionally on corporate organizational forms, recently the field has broadened its scope to study nonprofit and alternative organizations.
>
> *(2007: 3290)*

In contrast, the IEEE (2013) delimits professional communication as 'include[ing] the study, preparation, production, delivery, use, improvement, and promotion of human communication in all media in engineering and other technical and professional environments'. Bhatia (2010) enlarges the scope of professional communication by focusing on text and context:

The interesting thing about professional communication is that what you see as the ultimate product is the text, which is made possible by a combination of very complex and dynamic range of resources, including those that in linguistic and earlier discourse analytical literature are viewed as lexico-grammatical, rhetorical and organizational. Other contributors to the construction of professional artefacts are conventions of the genre in question, the understanding of the professional practice in which the genre is embedded, and the culture of the profession, discipline or institution, which constrains the use of textual resources for a particular discursive practice. In other words, any instance of professional communication simultaneously operates and can be analysed at these four levels, as text, as representation of genre, as realization of professional practice, and as expectation of professional culture.

(2010: 33)

In keeping these definitions in mind, we focus primarily on empirical research that has been conducted within the last decade, noting trends and pragmatic implications. We use this overview to generate areas of interest for both organisational and professional communication scholars and practitioners in Part III, Emerging research directions.

Part I: Overview of organisational communication

In this section, we overview the conceptual, empirical and methodological landscape of organisational communication. From its very beginnings and continuing today, organisational communication has been interdisciplinary – drawing from organisational sociology, administrative science, management, industrial/organisational psychology, organisational behaviour and human resources, and training and development, amongst others – grounded in practice as well as theory, and diverse in terms of methodologies (see Barnett and Thayer 1988; Buzzanell and Stohl 1999; Farace, Monge and Russell 1977; Goldhaber and Barnett 1988; Jablin *et al.* 1987; Redding 1985; Tompkins and Redding 1988). This diversity is evident in the various ways in which scholars have reviewed the field and have noted trends at different points in time.

For instance, in early reviews, organisational communication was organised by traditions, such as Putnam and Cheney's (1985) communication channels and climate, organisational networks and superior-subordinate communication, that were grounded in social science and oriented more toward communication as essential in more effective, efficient and satisfying workplaces consistent with managerialist concerns. With Putnam and Paconowky's (1983) *Communication and Organizations: An Interpretive Approach*, emphases shifted toward linguistic and performative turns, questioning how organisation members make sense of, express, and work through the politics and practices of their everyday lives. With the interpretive turn also came attention to critical, feminist, postmodern, and postcolonialist means of understanding organisational life and organising processes (e.g. Ashcraft and Mumby 2004; Broadfoot and Munshi 2007; Buzzanell 1994, 2000; Deetz 1992; Mumby 1988; Pal and Buzzanell 2013) as well as greater attention to difference (e.g. Ashcraft and Allen 2003; Mumby 2011). Although much early structuration work had been qualitative, organisational communication scholars also used quantitative and mixed methodological approaches to ask how organisational members were enabled and constrained in their abilities to act and how structures were (re)constructed through human interaction in contexts ranging from seemingly intractable human conflicts to technologies and work-family policies (e.g. Contractor, Monge and Leonardi 2011; DeSanctis and Poole 1994; Haslett 2011; Kirby and Krone 2002; Poole and DeSanctis 1992; Nicotera and Mahon 2013).

In some cases, these materials provided insight into the ways individuals learn about professions and 'doing' professional, mostly through a sideways glance at socialisation experiences, politics and ethical dilemmas, and stories about everyday work life (e.g. Allen 2000; Ashcraft 2000), rather than a direct examination of professionals and professions and of text as the primary site of investigation. More recently, scholars in different fields, including organisational communication, have used computational social science with its emphases on big data and integration of internet and social media to better understand and predict everyday human behaviour and fields (Lazer et al. 2009).

Although the sites, methodologies, and research questions have expanded, core issues are ever present in organisational communication. Scholars have sought broader ways to characterise organisational communication. Mumby and Stohl (1996) centred organisational communication's distinctiveness around problematics or underlying concerns of voice, rationality, organisation and organisation-society, problematics that have continued to be critiqued and extended in terms of whose voice, what rationalities, and how organisation are prioritised and afforded or denied legitimacy (Broadfoot and Munshi 2007). Furthermore, Putnam (2012) argued that organisation and organisation-society would continue to be central problematics in organisational communication scholars' pursuit of greater internationalisation, engagement and understanding of the contradictions and complexities in organising.

Within the last decade, these problematics along with increased engagement with social and global issues have been recurring trends in and challenges for organisational communication scholarship. Echoing organisational communication's past and looking toward the future, Jones et al. (2004) encourage pursuit of research responding to several challenges: theoretical and methodological innovation, ethics and macrolevel issues, new organisational structures and technologies, organisational change as well as diversity and intergroup aspects, and importance of voice and multilevel analyses. Seibold et al. (2009) pose new questions about areas that have long traditions in organisational communication – organisational socialisation and assimilation, organisational culture, innovation diffusion and organisational change – and future possibilities for applied communication scholarship and engagement. Most recently, Rooney, McKenna and Barker (2011) traced patterns throughout the history of *Management Communication Quarterly* through an intellectual structure approach that maps concepts graphically. Their findings not only dovetailed with *MCQ* editors' assessments of journal content but also with others' trends in organisational communication. Of interest to professional communication researchers and practitioners, Rooney et al. (2011) concluded their computer-assisted text analyses by saying: 'Clearly, the communication "fields" of professional and technical writing, as well as spoken and interpersonal communication, have been jettisoned, allowing the journal to shape its identity more toward an organizational studies centre focused on communication and discourse' (p. 605). Perhaps these fields have been 'jettisoned' but there remain points of convergence for, as Bhatia (2010) notes, professional communication analyses integrate 'textual and intertextual resources, generic conventions, professional practices, and professional cultures in the context of which the other three are invariably embedded' (p. 34).

Part II: Current research directions

Professional cultures and the broader environments in which they are embedded are characterised by risk, economic instabilities, growth of entrepreneurships and fast-paced technological change (Neff 2012). In these environments, workers attempt to fashion flexible but branded selves in face-to-face and mediated contexts, as their identities constantly change to be reflexive and employable (Hearn 2008; Kuhn 2006; Lair, Sullivan and Cheney 2005). Identities are (re)formed by a complex 'assemblage' of discursive resources that stand at the intersection of the person–organisation–society relationship (Kuhn 2006). Regarding identities, what it means to 'do' professional can be ascertained by current organisational communication research on (a) cybervetting and employer-applicant expectations, (b) requirements to work constantly yet also have career and personal life sustainability; (c) meaning/meaningfulness of work that affords dignity; and (d) discursive approaches to traditional research areas, such as leadership and organisational change management.

First, emerging research on cybervetting and employer-applicant expectations indicates that use of internet and social media has become normative. Cybervetting is the 'process by which organizational representatives [and applicants] use publicly accessible nongovernmental, non-institutional online tools or sites such as search engines or SNS to gather information about current or prospective employees [and organisations for which they might become members]' (Berkelaar 2010: 18). Through an extractive process available via information and communication technologies (ICTs), individuals gather and use information about others' perceived professionalism, interests, social networks and other details relying on visual, textual and technological cues – noting that it is not simply about deleting 'red flags' because most individuals and organisations need to have an online presence (Berkelaar 2010). For employers, cybervetting is risk work – taking and mitigating risk – as well as reputation management. Berkelaar and Buzzanell (2012) argue that cybervetting entails a 'paradigm shift in how employers communicatively constitute 'the right fit' in contemporary personnel selection … with practical implications for personnel selection, work, and careers' (2012: 3) as well as professions and what it means to do professional work. Yet, there still are not adequate organisational documents and policies that operate simultaneously to afford adequate transparency, privacy, and network building for career and personal relationships within local and global contexts – research areas fitting within purviews of organisational and professional communication scholars.

Second, organisational communication scholars are delving into work-life balance or, as we refer to the phenomenon, the paradoxical requirements to work constantly yet also have career and personal life sustainability. Researchers have studied how individuals and groups engage in work at offices, through telework and other nonstandard arrangements, and use technology (presumably) to manage tensions between and feel satisfaction with career and home, family, community, and/or leisure (e.g. Edley 2004; Fonner and Roloff 2010; Golden, Kirby and Jorgensen 2006; Golden and Geisler 2007; Hylmö and Buzzanell 2002; Kirby and Buzzanell 2014; Leonardi, Treem and Jackson 2010). According to Gregg (2011) knowledge workers are caught in ever expanding work that they see as necessary given their often precarious positions in today's market economy. They also view work expansion as inevitable given workplace technologies and expectations to keep ahead of fast breaking changes and reputational or brand challenges. Professionals' long work hours actually may result more from their enjoyment of the work itself and the many satisfactions that are derived from work accomplishment. They also may fail to define some activities, such as email, as work itself. What aspects of certain genres, such as email and work-life policies promote such contradictions could be answered in part through organisational and professional communication research.

Third, organisational communication researchers are investigating the meaning and meaningfulness of work and how people construct dignity and career choice (Buzzanell and Lucas 2013). In 2008, Cheney *et al.* recommended use of communicative approaches and empirical, interpretive, and critical perspectives in this area. They explicated work meaning/meaningfulness by examining an array of concepts (e.g. central life interest, job satisfaction, work-life balance, life satisfaction, perspectives on career, spirituality and the meaning of leisure). Using an intersubjective approach that acknowledges historical, economic and cultural contexts, Cheney *et al.* considered basic work perceptions (e.g. unpleasant labour, personal expressions of intrinsic and extrinsic worth, and means to transcendent goals). Scholars have enlarged the boundaries used to define work (e.g. unpaid work; Medved 2007), have argued for inclusion of race and other forms of difference (Parker 2003), and have reframed stigmatised work (Meisenbach 2010) and choice (Buzzanell and Lucas 2013). Moreover, scholars have noted that individuals' search for deeper meanings in their (work) lives are subjugated by dominant discourses – 'secular hegemony' – that regard spirituality as a private experience (Buzzanell and Harter 2006; Harter and Buzzanell 2007). Overall, public and private experiences of spirituality can be studied and blended in ways that enhance the meaning(fulness) of work experiences (Feldner 2006).

Fourth, fresh insights into traditional research areas, such as leadership and organisational change management, have been gained through discursive approaches. From the dominant psychology perspective, leadership ontologically tends to be predispositional, cognitive, and trait-based (Fairhurst 2007, 2008). Thus, leadership has been largely fixed with research exploring individual leaders, situations and/or styles. By contrast, discursive approaches are rooted in social constructionist ontological stances (Barge and Fairhurst 2008) whereby leadership is performed or "brought off" in discourse' (Fairhurst 2007: 5). Leadership is thus a performance, one that happens through the interaction of texts, where communication is primary. Stated differently, 'leadership [is] a lived and experienced *social* activity in which persons-in-conversation, action, meaning, and context are dynamically interrelated' (Barge and Fairhurst 2008: 228) with pragmatic applications (Fairhurst 2011).

Besides leadership, organisational communication has witnessed a resurgence of interest in change management, consulting, and organisation development (OD) through discursive approaches (Hearn and Ninan 2003; Jian 2007a, 2007b; Mumby 2005; Seo, Putnam and Bartunek 2004; Tracy 2004). The interest in discursive perspectives can be seen in calls for a 'new OD' that emphasises dialogic processes (Bushe and Marshak 2009). Dialogic OD recognises that change happens *not* when consultants diagnose problems and then prescribe courses of action. Rather, change happens when 'people become aware of the variety of stories people have about themselves and each other and understand their own part in creating unproductive patterns of interaction' (2009: 353). Dialogic OD differs from diagnostic perspectives mainly because of the marked shift from positivist and diagnostic traditions, which focus on objective, empirical measurement of 'what's wrong' followed by ways to 'fix' problems. Dialogic OD includes: appreciative inquiry, which discovers what is good and best within an organisation (Cooperrider, Barrett and Srivastva 1995; Preskill and Catsambas 2006); social constructionism, which focuses on how assumptions about organising are created, maintained and transformed through language (Barrett *et al.* 1995); and narrative, linguistic and discursive turns, which explore how organisational actors make sense of their daily lives and the role that language and contradiction play in the processes (Bisel and Barge 2010; Fyke and Buzzanell, in press; Heracleous and Barrett 2001; Marshak and Grant 2008; Oswick *et al.* 2005). Overall, organisational communication scholarship and practice can still be regarded as secondary in scholarship and practice in OD, change management and consulting (see Barge 2009). However, the discursive approach combined with examination of online and offline texts through professional communication promises creative insights into change.

Part III: Emerging research directions

In this section, we extend points from the previous section to focus on research directions that are emerging in organisational communication but also have application to professional communication. Although many trends span micro through macro levels and utilise diverse theoretical and analytic lenses, we discuss two that underlie many topics and that examine discourse and text as well as materialities: communication as constitutive of organising (CCO) and a discursive approach to difference.

First, organisational communication scholars are developing CCO and its implications not only for making communication central in organisation theorising but also for offering unique ways of approaching societal and global challenges. To understand CCO, scholars have reconsidered the role of communication whereby 'meaning is negotiated and productive of thought and action' (Jian, Schmisseur and Fairhurst 2008: 302; see also Putnam 2008). Jian *et al.* (2008) argue that communication is the 'doing' while discourse is the 'done'.

From a CCO perspective, organisations are recognised as discursive constructions (Fairhurst and Putnam 2004) where different messages and interaction processes constitute the organisation (McPhee and Zaug 2009). For McPhee and Zaug, organisations must develop and maintain relations to at least four 'audiences': members through membership negotiation; themselves through control and self-structuring; internal groups and subgroups through coordinated activity; and external stakeholders through institutional positioning. Communication is a necessary but insufficient condition for organising to actually occur (Bisel 2010). However, an overemphasis on communication as the constitutive element can fail to account for other elements such as the material, spatial and temporal aspects of organising (Reed 2010). Cooren and Fairhurst (2009; see also Haslett 2012) have extended McPhee and Zaug's model by suggesting how researchers can 'scale up' from the micro (i.e. local interactions) to the macro (i.e. structures, rules) and consider both as constitutive of organising. They attend to the interplay of human and non-human actors as agents of organising, as evidenced by burgeoning work on materialities.

Central to the materialities literature is the belief that since the linguistic turn in organisation studies (in the early 1980s), matter has taken a backseat to the role of language in scholars' understanding of organisational processes. Interested in overcoming the duality of language and matter, scholars have explored multimodality, materiality and linguistic resources in organisational life. The myriad non-human elements involved in organising can be categorised in several ways, but we focus here on Ashcraft *et al.*'s (2009) objects, sites and bodies. This three-part typology provides an entrée for future research to bridge material and discursive realities and professional and organisational communication. Research under the heading of objects investigates the material and ideational qualities of organisational documents and texts such as memos, titles, work orders and signs (Ashcraft *et al.* 2009; Cooren 2004). Cooren (2004) shows that non-human actors (e.g. memos, reports, signs) have the ability to inform (e.g. memos inform office personnel about important events), deny (e.g. reports deny an organisation's participation in an act), and indicate (e.g. a sign that warns of a security system and cameras on the premises). Using actor network theory, Brummans, Cooren and Chaput (2009) show how anyone or anything that makes a difference in a configuration or network is considered an agent. How agents become present and have agency in particular ways are issues explicated through examination of talk during meetings.

Besides objects, sites bridge material-discursive realities. Sites supply the infrastructure requisite for communication and organising; communication likewise affects the infrastructure, in a constitutive fashion (e.g. office layout). Barley *et al.* (2012) and Leonardi (2011) discuss how disciplinary sites and material objects in collaborations affect the logic of arguments and resolution of engineering design and innovation considerations (for discussion of communication in engineering design presentations, see Buzzanell and Zoltowski, in press). Finally, recent work considering bodies recognises that communication is an embodied process and that the physical body can be altered as a result of communication (e.g. for embodiment and institutionalisation of occupation and profession, including stigmatised work; see Ellingson 2011; Gabor 2011; Lammers and Garcia 2009). In short, new and productive intersections between, and unique contributions of, organisational and professional communication can be made visible through the CCO lens (e.g. Robichaud and Cooren 2012).

Second, a discursive approach to difference underscores the complex, nuanced, and contradictory ways in which individuals and collectivities make sense of and create documents, including policies, that privilege and marginalise, include and exclude. Difference does not mean simply representational diversity in workplaces but also the occupational and institutional ways in which membership, logics, priorities and pathways to innovation are determined (e.g. multidisciplinary collaborations; see Leonardi 2011). Furthermore, issues of diversity and inclusion result from both the realities of an ever-shrinking world and intentional attempts to create more representative and equal workplaces. For many industrialised countries, immigration and workplace migration have led to a more international workforce. With increased diversity come challenges in terms of aging workforce, glass ceilings, wage disparities, disciplinary knowledge, and differences in cultures, amongst other issues (e.g., Shen *et al.* 2009). Organisational communication scholars urge critical and in-depth treatment of these issues, 'in a sustained and coherent manner' with attention to political consequences (Mumby 2011: ix; Allen 2011; Zanoni *et al.* 2010). Their focus on the ways difference is constituted communicatively offers insight into the everyday construction of difference through dialectics of privilege and marginalisation and through identity construction.

Difference is a consequence of organisational practices and interpersonal interactions rather than a precondition for these social processes (Mumby 2011). Identity, in this perspective, relates to difference as the flipside of a piece of paper; whereas identity usually denotes stability and regularity it cannot, in practice, arise independently of dynamics of differentiation and variation. The identity of one individual or group appears in and through the relational differences from other individuals and groups, and difference, similarly, cannot be considered without having recourse to the identities which it relates. Put otherwise, difference becomes constitutive of identity; it is 'both the mechanism through which meanings and identities are organized and the product – intended or unintended – of everyday organizing and collective sensemaking' (Mumby 2011: ix).

Using a discursive lens means, first, that difference is constructed at micro through macro-levels in varied ways, including but not limited to gender, age, nationality, race and occupations, and with a look inward as well as toward others. Second, the indeterminacy of difference is premised upon a move to seeing differences as the outcomes of dynamic processes that are, in turn, constitutive of identities. This understanding of difference provides a more fruitful starting point for researchers as well as practitioners who are interested in promoting the management and practice of diversity.

Specifically, organisations have created diversity strategies and management policies, but they remain controversial (Zanoni and Janssens 2003). This is in part because they transcend traditional organisational (public) boundaries into private realms. Diversity management practices – such as diversity sensitivity training, work/family balance policies, and recruitment and hiring strategies – are the places where private matters (e.g. gender) meet public performance in paradoxical ways (Remke and Nøholm Just 2013). Similarly creativity thrives on difference in expertise, background, class and other identity aspects but collaborating and innovating remain difficult (Leonardi 2011). In examining discursive-material processes of difference, organisational and professional communication specialists may understand and document more fully the inclusionary practices and complexities of human organising.

Conclusion

In this chapter, we begin by providing an overview of organisational communication then note several trends in its research and practice: cybervetting, career and personal life sustainability; meaning/meaningfulness and dignity of work, and discursive approaches to leadership and organisational change management. We conclude with emerging research directions. Specifically the communication as constitutive of organising (CCO) and difference frameworks hold promise for fully realising the importance of organisational communication approaches and of productive linkages with professional communication.

Related topics

organisational communication; management communication, corporate communication, professional communication; discourse variation in professional communities

Key readings

Cheney, G. and Ashcraft, K. (2007). 'Considering "the professional" in communication studies: Implications for theory and research within and beyond the boundaries of organizational communication', *Communication Theory, 17*, 146–75. (This article discusses 'professional' as a contested term whose meanings and materialities lay at the intersections of organisational, health, rhetorical, critical-cultural, interpersonal and legal communication.)

Ellingson, L. (2010). 'The poetics of professionalism among dialysis technicians', *Health Communication*, 1–12. (This essay integrates several different ways of knowing. The author describes discursive, embodied and material constructions of professional identity and professional communication in health care contexts.)

Kong, K. (2013). *Handbook of Professional Communication*, Cambridge, UK: Cambridge University Press. (This Handbook defines and provides an agenda for future research in professional communication. It can function as a source for ways to conduct different kinds of professional discourse research.)

Lammers, J. and Garcia, M. (2009). 'Exploring the concept of "profession" for organizational communication research: Institutional influences in a veterinary organization', *Management Communication Quarterly, 22*, 357–84. (This article maintains that 'profession' often is used uncritically by researchers but the disparate aspects – knowledge, self-management, internal motivation, service orientation and participation in knowledge communities beyond the workplace – are unified by work.)

Bibliography

Allen, B. J. (2000). '"Learning the ropes": A black feminist standpoint analysis', in P.M. Buzzanell (ed.), *Rethinking Organizational and Managerial Communication from Feminist Perspectives* (pp. 177–208), Thousand Oaks, CA: Sage.

——(2011). *Difference Matters* (2nd edn), Prospect Heights, IL: Waveland.

Ashcraft, K. (2000). 'Empowering "professional" relationships: Organizational communication meets feminist practice', *Management Communication Quarterly, 13*, 347–92.

Ashcraft, K. and Allen, B. J. (2003). 'The racial foundation of organizational communication', *Communication Theory, 13*, 5–38.

Ashcraft, K., Kuhn, T. and Cooren, F. (2009). 'Constitutional amendments: "Materializing" organizational communication', *Academy of Management Annals, 3*, 1–64.

Ashcraft, K. and Mumby, D. K. (2004). *Reworking Gender: A Feminist Communicology of Organization*, Thousand Oaks, CA: Sage.

Axley, S. R. (1984). 'Managerial and organizational communication in terms of the conduit metaphor', *Academy of Management Review, 9*, 428–37.

Barge, J. K. (2009, November). *Positive Organizational Communication Scholarship: Prospects and Challenges*, Paper presented to the National Communication Association conference, held in Chicago, IL.

Barge, J. K. and Fairhurst, G. T. (2008). 'Living leadership: A systemic constructionist approach', *Leadership*, 4, 227–51.
Barley, W., Leonardi, P. and Bailey, D. (2012). 'Engineering objects for collaboration: Strategies of ambiguity and clarity at knowledge boundaries', *Human Communication Research*, 38, 280–308.
Barnett, G. and Thayer, L. (eds) (1997). *Organization Communication: Emerging Perspectives V: The Renaissance in Systems Theory*, Greenwich, CT: Ablex.
Barrett, F. J., Thomas, G. F. and Hocevar, S. P. (1995). 'The central role of discourse in large-scale change: A social construction perspective', *Journal of Applied Behavioral Science*, 31, 352–72.
Berkelaar, B. (2010). 'Cybervetting: Exploring the implications of online career capital for career capital and human capital decisions', Unpublished dissertation, Purdue University, W. Lafayette, IN.
Berkelaar, B. and Buzzanell, P. M. (2012). 'Reconceptualizing fit in personnel selection: Employers' sensemaking about cybervetting', Unpublished manuscript.
Bhatia, V. K. (2010). 'Interdiscursivity in professional communication', *Discourse & Communication*, 21, 32–50.
Bisel, R. S. (2010). 'A communicative ontology of organization? A description, history, and critique of CCO theories for organization science', *Management Communication Quarterly*, 24, 124–31.
Bisel, R. S. and Barge, J. K. (2011). 'Discursive positioning and planned change in organizations', *Human Relations*, 64, 257–83.
Broadfoot, K. and Munshi, D. (2007). 'Diverse voices and alternative rationalities: Imagining forms of postcolonial organizational communication', *Management Communication Quarterly*, 21, 249–67.
Brummans, B., Cooren, F. and Chaput, M. (2009). 'Discourse, communication and organizational ontology', in F. Bargiela-Chiappini (ed.), *The Handbook of Business Discourse* (pp. 53–67), Edinburgh, Scotland, UK: Edinburgh University Press.
Bushe, G. R. and Marshak, R. J. (2009). 'Revisioning organization development: Diagnostic and dialogic premises and patterns of practice', *Journal of Applied Behavioral Science*, 45, 348–68.
Buzzanell, P. M. (1994). 'Gaining a voice: Feminist organizational communication theorizing', *Management Communication Quarterly*, 7, 339–83.
——(ed.) (2000). *Rethinking Organizational and Managerial Communication from Feminist Perspectives*, Thousand Oaks, CA: Sage.
Buzzanell, P. M. and Harter, L. (2006). '(De)centering and (re)envisioning the secular hegemony of organizational communication theory and research', *Communication Studies*, 57, 1–3.
Buzzanell, P. M. and Lucas, K. (2013). 'Constrained and constructed choice in career: An examination of communication pathways to dignity', *Communication Yearbook*, 37, 3–31.
Buzzanell, P. M. and Stohl, C. (1999). 'The Redding tradition of organizational communication scholarship: W. Charles Redding and his legacy', *Communication Studies*, 50, 324–36.
Buzzanell, P. M. and Zoltowski, C. (2014). 'Get your message across: The art of gathering and sharing information', in D. F. Radcliffe and M. Fosmire (eds), *Integrating Information into Engineering Design* (pp. 159–70), West Lafayette, IN: Purdue University Press.
Carbaugh, D. and Buzzanell, P. M. (eds) (2010). *Distinctive Qualities in Communication Research*, New York: Routledge.
Cheney, G. and Ashcraft, K. (2007). 'Considering "the professional" in communication studies: Implications for theory and research within and beyond the boundaries of organizational communication', *Communication Theory*, 17, 146–75.
Cheney, G., Zorn, T. E., Planalp, S. and Lair, D. J. (2008). 'Meaningful work and personal/social well-being: Organizational communication engages the meanings of work', *Communication Yearbook*, 33, 137–86.
Cheng, W. and Kong, K. (eds) (2009). *Professional Communication: Collaboration between Academics and Practitioners*, Hong Kong: Hong Kong University Press.
Contractor, N. S., Monge, P. R. and Leonardi, P. M. (2011). 'Multidimensional networks and the dynamics of sociomateriality: Bringing technology inside the network', *International Journal of Communication*, 5, 682–720.
Cooperrider, D. L., Barrett, F. and Srivastva, S. (1995). 'Social construction and appreciative inquiry: A journey in organizational theory', in D. Hosking, P. Dachler and K. Gergen (eds), *Management and Organization: Relational Alternatives to Individualism* (pp. 157–200), Aldershot: Avebury.
Cooren, F. (2004). 'Textual agency: How texts do things in organizational settings', *Organization*, 11, 373–93.
Cooren, F. and Fairhurst, G. T. (2009). 'Dislocation and stabilization: How to scale up from interactions to organization', in L. L. Putnam and A. M. Nicotera (eds), *Building Theories of Organization: The Constitutive Role of Communication* (pp. 117–52), New York, NY: Routledge.
Corman, S. R. and Poole, M. S. (eds) (2000). *Perspectives on Organizational Communication: Finding Common Ground*, New York, NY: Guilford.

Craig, R. (1999). 'Communication theory as a field', *Communication Theory*, 9, 119–61.
Deetz, S. (1992). *Democracy in an Age of Corporate Colonization: Developments in Communication and the Politics of Everyday Life*, Albany: SUNY Press.
DeSanctis, G. and Poole, M. S. (1994). 'Capturing the complexity in advanced technology use: Adaptive Structuration Theory', *Organization Science*, 5, 121–47.
Edley, P. (2004). 'Entrepreneurial mothers' balance of work and family: Discursive constructions of time, mothering, and identity', in P. M. Buzzanell, H. Sterk and L. H. Turner (eds), *Gender in Applied Communication Contexts* (pp. 255–73), Thousand Oaks, CA: Sage.
Ellingson, L. (2011). 'The poetics of professionalism among dialysis technicians', *Health Communication*, 26, 1–12.
Fairhurst, G. T. (2007). *Discursive Leadership: In Conversation with Leadership Psychology*, Los Angeles, CA: Sage.
——(2008). 'Discursive leadership: A communication alternative to leadership psychology', *Management Communication Quarterly*, 21, 510–21.
——(2011). *The Power of Framing: Creating the Language of Leadership*, San Francisco, CA: Jossey-Bass.
Fairhurst, G. T. and Putnam, L. (2004). 'Organizations as discursive constructions', *Communication Theory*, 14, 5–26.
Farace, R. V., Monge, P. R. and Russell, H. M. (1977). *Communicating and Organizing*, Reading, MA: Addison-Wesley.
Feldner, S. (2006). 'Living our mission: A study of university mission building', *Communication Studies*, 57, 67–86.
Fonner, K. L. and Roloff, M. E. (2010). 'Why teleworkers are more satisfied with their jobs than office-based workers: When less contact is beneficial', *Journal of Applied Communication Research*, 38, 336–61.
Fyke, J. and Buzzanell, P. M. (in press). 'The ethics of conscious capitalism: Wicked problems in leading change and changing leaders', *Human Relations*.
Gabor, E. (2011). 'Turning points in the development of classical musicians', *Journal of Ethnographic & Qualitative Research*, 5, 138–56.
Golden, A. G. and Geisler, C. (2007). 'Work-life boundary management and the personal digital assistant', *Human Relations*, 60, 519–51.
Golden, A., Kirby, E. and Jorgensen, J. (2006). 'Work-life research from both sides now: An integrative perspective for organizational and family communication', *Communication Yearbook*, 32, 143–96.
Goldhaber, G. M. and Barnett, G. A. (eds) (1988). *Handbook of Organizational Communication*, Norwood, NJ: Ablex.
Gregg, M. (2011). *Work's Intimacy*, Cambridge, UK: Polity.
Harter, L. M. and Buzzanell, P. M. (2007). '(Re)storying organizational communication theory and practice: Continuing the conversation about spirituality and work', *Communication Studies*, 58, 223–26.
Haslett, B. (2012). *Communicating and Organizing in Context: The Theory of Structurational Interaction*, New York, NY: Routledge.
Hearn, A. (2008). '"Meat, Mask, Burden": Probing the contours of the branded "self"', *Journal of Consumer Culture*, 8, 197–217.
Hearn, G. and Ninan, A. (2003). 'Managing change is managing meaning', *Management Communication Quarterly*, 16, 440–45.
Heracleous, L. and Barrett, M. (2001). 'Organizational change as discourse: Communicative actions and deep structures in the context of informational technology implementation', *Academy of Management Journal*, 44, 755–78.
Hylmö, A. and Buzzanell, P. M. (2002). 'Telecommuting as viewed through cultural lenses: An empirical investigation of the discourses of utopia, identity, and mystery', *Communication Monographs*, 69, 329–56.
Institute of Electrical and Electronics Engineers (IEEE). (2013). Available at www.ieee.org/membership-catalog/productdetail/showProductDetailPage.html?product=MEMPC026 (accessed 2013).
Jablin, F. M. and Putnam, L. L. (eds) (2001). *The New Handbook of Organizational Communication: Advances in Theory, Research, and Methods*, Thousand Oaks, CA: Sage.
Jablin, F. M., Putnam, L. L., Roberts, K. H. and Porter, L. W. (eds) (1987). *Handbook of Organizational Communication: An Interdisciplinary Perspective*, Newbury Park, CA: Sage.
Jian, G. (2007a). 'Unpacking unintended consequences in planned organizational change: A process model', *Management Communication Quarterly*, 21, 5–25.
——(2007b). '"Omega is a four-letter word": Toward a tension-centered model of resistance to information and communication technologies', *Communication Monographs*, 74, 517–40.
Jian, G., Schmisseur, A. M. and Fairhurst, G. T. (2008). 'Organizational discourse and communication: The progeny of Proteus', *Discourse and Communication*, 2, 299–320.

Jones, E., Watson, B., Gardner, J. and Gallois, C. (2004). 'Organizational communication: Challenges for the new century', *Communication Theory*, 722–50.
Kirby, E. and Buzzanell, P. M. (2014). 'Communicating work-life', in L. L. Putnam and D. K. Mumby (eds), *The SAGE Handbook of Organizational Communication* (3rd edn, pp. 351–73), Thousand Oaks, CA: Sage.
Kirby, E. and Krone, K. (2002). '"The policy exists but you can't really use it"': Communication and the structuration of work-family policies', *Journal of Applied Communication Research*, 30, 50–77.
Kisselburgh, L., Berkelaar, B. and Buzzanell, P. M. (2009). 'Discourse, gender, and the meanings of work: Rearticulating science, technology, and engineering careers through communicative lenses', *Communication Yearbook*, 33, 258–99.
Kuhn, T. (2006). 'A "demented work ethic" and a "lifestyle firm": Discourse, identity, and workplace time commitments', *Organization Studies*, 27, 1339–58.
——(2012). 'Negotiating the micro-macro divide: Thought leadership from organizational communication for theorizing organization', *Management Communication Quarterly*, 26, 543–84.
Lair, D., Sullivan, K. and Cheney, G. (2005). 'Marketization and the recasting of the professional self: The rhetoric and ethics of personal branding', *Management Communication Quarterly*, 18, 307–343, DOI: 0.1177/0893318904270744.
Lammers, J. and Garcia, M. (2009). 'Exploring the concept of "profession" for organizational communication research: Institutional influences in a veterinary organization', *Management Communication Quarterly*, 22, 357–84.
Lazer, D., Pentland, A., Adamic, L., Aral, S., Barabási, A.-L., Brewer, D., Christakis, N., Contractor, N., Fowler, J., Gutmann, M., Jebara, T., King, G., Macy, M., Roy, D. and Van Alstyne, M. (2009, February 6). 'Computational social science', *Science*, 323, 721–23.
Leonardi, P. (2011). 'Innovation blindness: Culture, frames, and cross-boundary problem construction in the development of new technology concepts', *Organization Science*, 22, 347–69.
Leonardi, P., Treem, J. and Jackson, M. (2010). 'The connectivity paradox: Using technology to both decrease and increase perceptions of distance in distributed work arrangements', *Journal of Applied Communication Research*, 38, 85–105.
Long, Z., Kuang, K. and Buzzanell, P. M. (2013). 'Legitimizing and elevating telework: Chinese constructions of a nonstandard work arrangement', *Journal of Business and Technical Communication*, 27, 243–62.
Marshak, R. J. and Grant, D. (2008). 'Organizational discourse and new organization development practices', *British Journal of Management*, 19, S7-S19.
May, S. and Mumby, D. K. (eds) (2005). *Engaging Organizational Communication Theory and Research: Multiple Perspectives*, Thousand Oaks, CA: Sage.
McPhee, R. D. and Zaug, P. (2009). 'The communicative constitution of organizations: A framework for explanation', in L. L. Putnam and A. M. Nicotera (eds), *Building Theories of Organization: The Constitutive Role of Communication* (pp. 21–48), New York: Routledge.
Medved, C. (2007). 'Investigating family labor in communication studies: Threading across historical and contemporary discourses', *Journal of Family Communication*, 7, 1–19.
Meisenbach, R. (2008). 'Working with tensions: Materiality, discourse, and (dis)empowerment in occupational identity negotiation among higher education fund-raisers', *Management Communication Quarterly*, 22, 258–87.
——(2010). 'Stigma management communication: A theory and agenda for applied research on how individuals manage moments of stigmatized identity', *Journal of Applied Communication Research*, 38, 268–92.
Mumby, D. K. (1988). *Communication and Power in Organizations: Discourse, Ideology, and Domination*, Norwood, NJ: Ablex.
——(2005). 'Theorizing resistance in organization studies: A dialectical approach', *Management Communication Quarterly*, 19, 19–44.
——(2007). 'Organizational communication', in G. Ritzer (ed.), *The Encyclopedia of Sociology* (pp. 3290–99), London: Blackwell.
——(ed.) (2011). *Reframing Difference in Organizational Communication Studies: Research, Pedagogy, Practice*, Thousand Oaks, CA: Sage.
Mumby, D. K. and Stohl, C. (1996). 'Disciplining organizational communication studies', *Management Communication Quarterly*, 10, 50–72.
Neff, G. (2012). *Venture Labor: Work and the Burden of Risk in Innovative Industries*, New York: Routledge.
Nicotera, A. and Mahon, M. (2013). 'Between rocks and hard places: Exploring the impact of structurational divergence in the nursing workplace', *Management Communication Quarterly*, 27, 90–120.
Oswick, C., Grant, D., Michelson, G. and Wailes, N. (2005). 'Looking forwards: Discursive directions in organizational change', *Journal of Organizational Change*, 18, 383–90.

Pal, M. and Buzzanell, P. M. (2013). 'Breaking the myth of Indian call centers: A postcolonial analysis of resistance', *Communication Monographs*, 80, 199–219.

Parker, P. S. (2003). 'Control, resistance, and empowerment in raced, gendered, and classed work contexts: The case of African American women', *Communication Yearbook*, 27, 257–91.

Poole, M. S. and DeSanctis, G. (1992). 'Microlevel structuration in computer-supported group decision making', *Human Communication Research*, 19, 5–49.

Preskill, H. and Catsambas, T. T. (2006). *Reframing Evaluation Through Appreciative Inquiry*, Thousand Oaks, CA: Sage.

Putnam, L. L. (2008). 'Images of the communication-discourse relationship', *Discourse and Communication*, 2, 339–45.

——(2012). 'Looking back, looking forward: A tribute to MCQ and my colleagues', *Management Communication Quarterly*, 26, 510–20.

Putnam, L. L. and Boys, S. (2006). 'Revisiting metaphors of organizational communication', in S. R. Clegg, C. Hardy, W. Lawrence and W. Nord (eds), *Handbook of Organization Studies* (pp. 541–76), Thousand Oaks, CA: Sage.

Putnam, L. L. and Cheney, G. (1985). 'Organizational communication: Historical development and future directions', in T. W. Benson (ed.), *Speech Communication in the Twentieth Century* (pp. 130–56), Carbondale, IL: Southern Illinois University Press.

Putnam, L. L. and Mumby, D. K. (eds) (in press). *Handbook of Organizational Communication* (3rd edn), Thousand Oaks, CA: Sage.

Putnam, L. L. and Nicotera, A. M. (eds) (2009). *Building Theories of Organization: The Constitutive Role of Communication*, New York, NY: Routledge.

Putnam, L. L. and Paconowsky, M. (eds) (1983). *Communication and Organizations: An Interpretive Approach*, Beverly Hills, CA: Sage.

Redding, W. C. (1972). *Communication in the Organization: An Interpretive Review of Theory and Research*, New York: Industrial Communication Council, Inc.

——(1985). 'Stumbling toward identity: The emergence of organizational communication as a field of study', in R. McPhee and P. K. Tompkins (eds), *Organizational Communication: Traditional Themes and New Directions* (pp. 15–54), Beverly Hills, CA: Sage.

Reed, M. (2010). 'Is communication constitutive of organization?' *Management Communication Quarterly*, 24, 151–57.

Remke, R. and Nøholm Just, S. (2013, February). *Irrational Practices – Toward a Relational Theory of Diversity*, Paper presented to the Diversity and Difference in the Contemporary Workplace conference, held at Copenhagen Business School, Copenhagen, Denmark.

Robichaud, D. and Cooren, F. (eds) (2012). *Organization and Organizing: Materiality, Agency, Discourse*, New York: Routledge.

Rooney, D., McKenna, B. and Barker, J. (2011). 'A history of ideas in *Management Communication Quarterly*', *Management Communication Quarterly*, 25, 583–611.

Seibold, D., Lemus, D., Ballard, D. and Myers, K. K. (2009). 'Organizational communication and applied communication research: Intersections and integration', in L. R. Frey and K. N. Cissna (eds), *Routledge Handbook of Applied Communication* (pp. 331–54), New York: Routledge.

Seo, M., Putnam, L. L. and Bartunek, J. M. (2004). 'Dualities and tensions of planned organizational change', in M. S. Poole and A. H. Van de Ven (eds), *Handbook of Organizational Change and Innovation* (pp. 73–107), New York, NY: Oxford University Press.

Shen, J., Chanda, A., D'Netto, B. and Monga, M. (2009). 'Managing diversity through human resource management: An international perspective and conceptual framework', *International Journal of Human Resource Management*, 20, 235–51.

Tompkins, P. K. and Redding, W. C. (1988). 'Organizational communication – Past and present tenses', in G. M. Goldhaber and G. A. Barnett (eds), *Handbook of Organizational Communication* (pp. 5–33), Norwood, NJ: Ablex.

Tracy, S. J. (2004). 'Dialectic, contradiction, or double bind? Analyzing and theorizing employee reactions to organizational tension', *Journal of Applied Communication Research*, 32, 119–46.

Zanoni, P. and Janssens, M. (2003). 'Deconstructing difference: The rhetoric of human resource managers' diversity discourses', *Organization Studies*, 25, 55–74.

Zanoni, P., Janssens, M., Benschop, Y. and Nkomo, S. (2010). 'Unpacking diversity, grasping inequality: Rethinking difference through critical perspectives', *Organization*, 17, 1–21.

15
Corporate communication

Finn Frandsen and Winni Johansen

Introduction

From the early 1990s and until now, corporate communication has been institutionalised both as an organisational practice, as an academic discipline, and as a widespread designation for how private companies handle, or should handle, their external and internal communication, from corporate branding and corporate social responsibility to crisis and change communication. However, it is not only private companies that have adopted this new strategic approach to communication; many other types of organisations, including private non-for-profit organisations as well as public authorities and institutions, are also navigating in challenging complex and dynamic contexts similar to those of the business world and need a more strategic, integrated and stakeholder-oriented approach to their external and internal communication activities. Although the name of the discipline obviously expresses something different, corporate communication has become relevant to many types of organisations other than private companies.

The aim of this chapter is to present a state of the art of the field of corporate communication defined both as a specific organisational practice and as a young and emerging academic discipline. The focus throughout the chapter will be on *research* in corporate communication. The chapter is divided into four sections: (1) a section on the historical conditions and drivers that have triggered the rise of corporate communication as a new strategic management function in private and public organisations; (2) a section on the definitions of corporate communication and how corporate communication differs from related disciplines such as public relations, organisational communication, marketing communication and business communication; (3) a section on the core themes in research on corporate communication (including key concepts such as corporate *identity, image* and *reputation, integration* and *stakeholder relations*); and, finally, (4) a section on the critique of corporate communication including a 'critique of the critique'. The chapter ends with a short section on academic resources (e.g. information on research centres, international conferences and journals such as *Corporate Communications: An International Journal*) that may prove useful in the study of corporate communication.

A short history of corporate communication: from organisational practice to academic discipline

The European Communication Monitor (ECM) is a large survey, which has been conducted every year since 2007 by the European Public Relations Research and Education Association (EUPRERA) in collaboration with the European Association of Communication Directors and the *Communication Director* magazine. In 2011, the survey included a series of questions headlined 'Credibility of public relations and alternative concepts' (Zerfass *et al.* 2011: 18–29). More than 2,000 respondents from 43 European countries were asked about the concepts they would prefer to use concerning their profession or occupation. 67.9 per cent answered *corporate communication* (in particular private companies), 61.3 per cent answered *strategic communication* (in particular governmental organisations), 55.7 per cent preferred *communication management* (many of them nonprofit organisations), 46.7 per cent *public relations* (especially consulting agencies) and 34 per cent *business communication* (in particular private companies).

Why have so many alternative concepts – and in particular the concept of corporate communication (but not for example public relations) – become so popular in Europe recently? The researchers behind the European Communication Monitor explain that this is due to the fact that the concept of public relations evokes too many 'negative connotations'. It seems reasonable to assume that such associations may have an impact on the choice of a *name* for a profession or occupation. However, if we take a closer look at the *content* of the organisational practice, that is, the various disciplines practised by corporate communication professionals (for a list of disciplines, see Goodman 2006 and Goodman and Hirsch 2010), it will soon become clear that we need to find a more sophisticated explanation.

According to North American management and corporate communication scholar Paul Argenti, who is the author of *Corporate Communication* (1994), one of the first and still most popular textbooks within the field, the first large corporate communication department was established by Mobil Oil at the beginning of the 1970s. The director of the department, Herb Schmertz, was at the same time one of the first communications executives who was also a member of the board of directors. Argenti identifies a series of changes, first and foremost the growing negative attitude towards the business world, as the reason why the development of a new 'totally integrated corporate communication function' started. The role played by the Chicago-based accounting firm Arthur Andersen in the spectacular Enron scandal in 2001 is used as an illustrative example. Unfortunately, Argenti's historiography remains within a North American context (see also Goodman and Hirsch 2010).

Dutch communication and organisation scholar Joep Cornelissen, author of another influential textbook, also entitled *Corporate Communication* (2011), has established a more general historical framework consisting of three different sets of drivers, which according to Cornelissen might explain why private companies have started implementing a corporate communication function:

1 Market- and environment-based drivers, which first of all comprise the many new stakeholder groups having different expectations and demands, and the increased possibility for individuals to enact different stakeholder roles. For example, the employee is not just an employee, but may also serve as an investor or as a client regarding one and the same company. A high degree of coordination is needed if the companies wish to communicate with stakeholders who have strong and conflicting interests (cf. the idea of a claims culture);
2 Communication-based drivers, which first of all comprise the growing number of messages and media to which the members of society are exposed with or against their will, or which

they can use for specific communicative purposes (cf. the new social media). Cornelissen talks about 'message clutter', while other scholars prefer over-communication, or they talk about a new attention economy. Also here, a high degree of coordination is needed if the companies want to get their messages through and want them to appear as clear and consistent across various types of media; and

3   Organisational drivers, comprising, among other things, the increased demand from the top management or the communication department for effectiveness and positioning of the company. In order to meet this demand the communication department must replace the traditional tactical approach to communication (a business communication approach) with a new strategic approach where the communication strategy is in alignment with and anchored in an overall business and corporate strategy.

At the same time as corporate communication has been institutionalised as a new organisational practice in private and public organisations (as briefly described and explained above), it has also developed into a new academic discipline supported by its own research environments, international conferences and publication outlets (for more details, see the short section on academic resources at the end of this chapter). In the following two sections, we will take a closer look at some key definitions of corporate communication, and at some core themes in research on corporate communication.

Definitions and delimitations: What is corporate communication?

What is corporate communication? And how does corporate communication differentiate itself from related disciplines such as public relations, organisational communication, marketing communication and business communication?

Shelby (1993) is one of the few scholars who have attempted to identify boundaries and relations between the various disciplines within the field of strategic communication. Unfortunately, her attempt to do this took place at the very beginning of the history of corporate communication, in the early 1990s, that is, before this still rather young discipline had gained any kind of maturity. Shelby defines corporate communication very briefly and with a slight touch of negativity: first as 'an umbrella for a variety of communication forms and formats' and then as '[a] cafeteria from which choices are made' (Shelby 1993: 255). The 'communication forms and formats' included in the organisational practice vary from organisation to organisation. As we will see later, Shelby (1993) thus neglects what first of all characterises corporate communication as a discipline: the perspective that makes the forms and formats selected by a specific company *cohere*.

Since the beginning of the 1990s, a series of more or less well-developed academic definitions of corporate communication has been formulated. Below we have listed some of the most widespread and typical definitions (presented in chronological order):

> Corporate communication is an instrument of management by means of which all consciously used forms of internal and external communication are harmonized as effectively and efficiently as possible, so to create a favourable basis for relationships with groups upon which the company is dependent.
>
> *(van Riel 1995: 26; see also van Riel 1997)*

> Corporate communication is the term used to describe a variety of strategic management functions. Depending on the organization, corporate communication includes: public

relations; crisis and emergency communication; corporate citizenship; reputation management; community relations; media relations; investor relations; employee relations; government relations; marketing communication; management communication; corporate branding and image building; advertising.

(Goodman and Hirsch 2010: 15; see also Goodman 2006)

Corporate communication is a management function that offers a framework for the effective coordination of all internal and external communication with the overall purpose of establishing and maintaining favourable reputations with stakeholder groups upon which the organization is dependent.

(Cornelissen 2011: 5)

To these explicit definitions one may add a series of more implicit or fragmented definitions, that is, definitions that are spread over one or more sections or chapters in a book or an article. This is the case, for example, with Argenti (1994), whose attention is directed towards concepts such as the strategy of the organisation (objectives, resources), its constituencies and the messages to be communicated (channels, structure) (see also Argenti 1996). Another example is Belasen (2008) who inserts corporate communication in the so-called Competing Values Framework based on the idea that corporate communication professionals try to meet stakeholder expectations, which are inconsistent or in conflict with each other (for a more detailed overview of corporate communication definitions, see Hübner 2007: 11–19).

If we try to emphasise what is common to the definitions listed above, we reach the following synthesis:

- Corporate communication is a *strategic management function*, that is, a function that not only takes a strategic approach to communication activities as such (based on a specific communication strategy, for example), but which also ties this approach to the overall strategy of the company (mission, vision, corporate strategy);
- Corporate communication *integrates* external and internal communication activities with each other based on the idea that this will lead to the most effective and efficient form of communication. These communication activities are distributed among a series of *disciplines*, which are selected and combined from company to company (cf. Shelby's (1993) umbrella term);
- The purpose of integrating external and internal communication activities is to build, maintain, change and/or repair one or more positive images and/or reputations. However, corporate communication also includes other types of communication disciplines and cannot be reduced to corporate branding;
- The building, maintenance, change and/or repair of positive images and/or reputations take place inside relationships with the external and internal stakeholders of the company (clients, investors, suppliers, competitors, media, local community, employees, etc.).

Based on the definitions mentioned above, and the attempt to synthesise the common elements, it is possible to delimit corporate communication regarding related disciplines within communication research. Corporate communication differs from public relations, organisational communication, marketing communication and business communication by involving and communicating with *all* types of external and internal stakeholders, by integrating the corresponding external and internal communication activities, and by applying a strategic perspective on communication. Marketing communication is also a strategic discipline, but the focus is on only one type of stakeholder, that is, the clients. Traditionally, public relations and organisational communication have concentrated on either external communication (for example, the media) or internal communication (for example, the employees). And business communication often only applies an operational or tactical perspective. However, today, there seems to be a new and promising tendency to 'build bridges' between one or more of these disciplines (cf. Christensen and Cornelissen 2011).

Core themes in research on corporate communication

In this section, we will take a closer look at some of the core themes in research on corporate communication, mostly themes that cut across the various disciplines included in the concept of corporate communication helping us with characterising corporate communication vis-à-vis related disciplines (cf. the previous section). The three (sets of) core themes that we have selected for a more detailed inspection are: (1) *corporate identity, image or reputation* representing a cluster of key concepts, which many see as the most important within corporate communication (cf. the definitions mentioned above); (2) *integration* of verbal and behavioural activities at various communicative and organisational levels; and (3) *relations* between the organisation and its stakeholders. For each of these (sets of) core themes we will briefly show how research has developed, and where it stands today. In general, one may say that whereas corporate identity, image and reputation form an area where a lot of research has been done, research on integration and stakeholder relations is still lagging behind.

Corporate identity, image and reputation

The concepts of *corporate identity, image and reputation* concern the overall goal of corporate communication: to build, maintain, change and/or repair positive images and/or reputations among the external and internal stakeholders of the company (cf. the previous section). In this section, we will take a detailed look at the comprehensive research that has been conducted on each of the three key concepts including their interrelationship, development and application. Thus, the focus is on the 'symbolic capital' of the company.

Corporate identity

The field of identity studies is huge, but is mainly dominated by the following disciplines: corporate communication, marketing, organisation studies, and graphic design studies (visual symbolism). So far, identity has been studied through three different lenses: (1) a functionalist approach viewing identity as a fact, (2) an interpretative approach defining identity as a socially constructed phenomenon, and (3) a postmodern or critical approach focusing on power relationships within the organisational context (cf. Balmer and Greyser 2003).

The concept of identity originates from the Latin word *idem*, 'same'. It is a rich and complex concept covering a whole range of different understandings. In an organisational context the concept refers to *what a company is and stands for*. Inside this context, identity comes in two important versions: corporate identity and organisational identity. The corporate identity tradition stems primarily from brand management and the marketing management tradition, whereas organisational identity is mostly situated within organisation studies.

Corporate identity initially focused on how an organisation appears and differentiates itself in relation to its external stakeholders. Among many early scholars, especially within corporate branding, there was a strong focus on visual symbolism (logo/design) and brand architecture

(Olins 1989), a tradition sometimes referred to as *the visual school of identity* (Balmer 1995). However, among most corporate communication scholars of today, a broader view – the so-called *strategic school of identity* – has emerged highlighting the planned processes linking strategy, philosophy and values of an organisation with its image and reputation.

Cees van Riel, one of the first European corporate communication scholars and author of *Principles of Corporate Communication* (1995), defines corporate identity in the following way: 'Corporate identity is the self-presentation of an organization: it consists in the cues which an organization offers about itself via the behaviour, communication, and symbolism which are its forms of expression' (van Riel 1995: 36). From this organisation-centric perspective, corporate identity is seen as a strategic and deliberate choice of the expressive identity of the company, vis-à-vis its external stakeholders and controlled by management, as opposed to organisational identity, which focuses on what is going on, inside the company, among the employees.

Organisational identity refers to how the members of an organisation understand, perceive and live the questions of 'who we are' and 'what we stand for'. The concept originates from organisation behaviour studies and has undergone an important transformation over time (cf. Hatch and Schultz 2004).

In early organisational identity theory, scholars were interested in research topics such as the characteristics of organisational identity (Albert and Whetten (1985), who see identity as the 'core, distinctive, and enduring features' of an organisation); the concept of organisational identification (Ashforth and Mael 1989); and the interaction between image and identity in organisations (Dutton and Dukerich 1991). More recently, the field has become puzzled with the complexity and dynamics of multiple identities (Pratt and Rafaeli 1997; Balmer and Greyser 2002); identity as narratives (Czarniawska-Joerges 1994; Johansen 2012), the interdependence of culture, identity and image (Hatch and Schultz 2001); and the linkage between internal and external communication forming organisational identity (Cheney and Christensen 2001).

Today, however, scholars have started comparing and combining the two concepts of identity to such an extent that they are merging. Hatch and Schultz (2000) suggest that '[i]nstead of choosing between corporate or organizational identity, we advocate combining the understandings offered by all the contributing disciplines into a single concept of identity defined at the organizational level of analysis' (p. 19). Similarly, Balmer and Greyser (2003) suggest that we conceive the concepts of 'corporate identity and organizational identity as alter egos' (Balmer and Greyser 2003: 33).

Image and reputation

The concept of corporate image dates back to the 1950s and has since then been used and defined in many different ways. However, there seems to be a certain consensus among scholars that although image is a broad term, it comprises a number of attributes, functional (tangible elements) as well as emotional (attitudes, feelings). Image is about the perception of an organisation by its different stakeholders (Dowling 2001; Cornelissen 2011).

One of the most widespread definitions of image stems from Australian marketing professor Graham Dowling, who defines image in the following way: 'An image is the set of meanings by which an object is known and through which people describe, remember and relate to it. That is the result of the interaction of a person's beliefs, ideas, feelings and impressions about an object' (Dowling 1986: 110). The object in question can be a person as well as a product and an organisation. Over time, the idea of a corporate image as a unitary monolithic phenomenon has been abandoned in favour of (a) complex multiple corporate image(s), where different images are shaped depending on the perceptions and stakes of each group of stakeholders. This means that the images of companies can be diverse and conflicting, making it difficult for them to communicate in a clear and consistent way. Some scholars have suggested that companies solve this problem by using ambiguity or hypocrisy as a strategy in their communication (cf. Eisenberg 1984 and Brunsson 1991).

When it comes to the relationship between corporate image and reputation, the two concepts have often been considered synonyms and applied randomly. Today, however, most scholars within the field of corporate communication consider them to be two distinct but interrelated concepts, based on two different dimensions: *time* and *values*.

The first dimension is related to reputation as a time-based construct. Whereas image can be considered a snapshot that develops here and now in the minds of stakeholders as their immediate response to one or more cues from or about a particular organisation at a single point in time, reputation can be considered the result of an accumulation of past images of an organisation established *over time* (Cornelissen 2011: 255). Schultz (2005: 43) also applies a time dimension when she defines reputation as 'the longitudinal judgement of who the company is and what it stands for among multiple stakeholders'. This means that a negative event such as a crisis may have an instant but ephemeral effect on the image of a company, whereas reputational damage is built up over time.

The second dimension is related to reputation as a value-based construct. Values are about ideals and beliefs, personal or social preferences for what is considered to be an appropriate way of acting for an organisation. Values form the basis for an overall evaluation of the company. North American scholar and director of the Reputation Institute Charles J. Fombrun defines corporate reputation as 'the overall estimation in which a company is held by its constituents' based on a series of values such as 'reliability, credibility, social responsibility and trustworthiness' (Fombrun 1996: 37; see also Dowling 2001 who also makes a value-based distinction between image and reputation).

Today, reputation research seems to be mainly concerned with three questions. The first question is about reputation management. How can a company create and maintain a favourable reputation? This explains part of the growing interest in areas such as CSR and crisis management. The second question is about the measurement of reputations. What are the components of a reputation, and how can they be measured? The Reputation Institute in New York, founded by Charles Fombrun and Cees Van Riel, has established a Reputation Quotient model, replaced in 2006 by the Global RepTrak™ Pulse, which is based on a reputation model. The model combines seven 'rational' dimensions, that is, product/services, innovation, workplace, governance, citizenship, leadership, and performance. Within each of these seven dimensions, the degree of admiration, trust, good feeling and overall esteem is measured. The third and last question is about the alignment, interrelationship and balance between strategy (management), identity (organisational culture), image and reputation (stakeholders), and the importance for a company of not having too large gaps between these different views of an organisation.

Over the years, *Corporate Communication: An International Journal* has published a series of articles and special issues (cf. vol. 4 no. 4, 1999, on 'Corporate identity' and vol. 14 no. 1, 2009, on 'Explicating corporate identity') presenting new research on the concepts of corporate and organisational identities. Unfortunately, the interest for theory-building and empirical studies within the area of image and reputation has not been quite as burning.

Integration

Integration is another hallmark of corporate communication. Besides that, it is also an area where the discipline cherishes certain ambitions. 'Corporate communications conceives itself as the integrated communication discipline *par excellence*, supplying an all-encompassing framework that includes all possible communication disciplines' (Christensen, Firat and Torp 2008: 424).

We can define integration as the *strategic coordination* of various communicative and organisational activities, entities and disciplines that a majority of practitioners and researchers as per tradition have practised and studied in isolation from each other, for example external communication versus internal communication, or public relations versus marketing communication. However, now and then there has been an attempt to build bridges between the disciplines. At the end of the 1970s, scholars started discussing the advantages of integrating public relations and marketing communication within the framework of a new paradigm defining the two disciplines as 'partners' rather than 'rivals' (Kotler and Mindak 1978; for a detailed account of this discussion, see Cornelissen 2011).

Formulated in an abstract way, the formal and explicit coordination of activities, entities and disciplines takes place within a more-or-less *continuum* where the two extremes are represented by *no coordination* and *complete coordination* respectively. Between these two extremes, lies a series of more or less tight or loose coordinations (see Figure 15.1).

Thus, integration is not just one thing, but several things. There exist *degrees of coordination*. This is the reason why we cannot just, as has been done by some researchers, equate integration with complete coordination, an approach to corporate communication characterised by the somehow unrealistic ideal and idea of many managers that their company will be able to communicate 'as with one voice'.

The choice of degree of coordination for a specific set of communication activities depends more precisely on: (1) the purpose of the coordination, (2) the situation, and (3) the understanding of strategy, management and organisation. If the purpose is to communicate in a clear and consistent way over time in order to create a favourable image or reputation among the external and internal stakeholders of the organisation, the company can try working with a more tight form of coordination (= corporate branding). The same is the case if the company wants to avoid contradicting itself when it has to account for its involvement in a crisis situation (= crisis communication). This line of thought has much in common with the understanding of strategy as a rational, linear and sequential planning process and the idea of management as top-down control and the organisation as a formal and tightly coupled structure.

However, there are also purposes, situations and understandings of strategy, management and organisation where a more loose type of coordination will be the best solution, e.g. if the company finds it necessary to communicate in a more ambiguous way in order to meet the expectations of many different groups of stakeholders, or if the company wants to encourage the 'many voices' of the organisation, formal as well as informal, to communicate freely with each other to strengthen the power of innovation.

Integration also takes place at various *levels of coordination*. This is an idea fostered not only in corporate communication, but also within the field of integrated marketing communication (IMC), an approach to marketing communication, equally interested, if not more, in integrated communication, that has developed almost at the same time as corporate communication. Based on this idea of levels, it is for example possible to distinguish between the following levels of coordination:

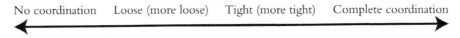

Figure 15.1 Degree of strategic coordination

- Integration of messages and inside a message (content integration)
- Integration of external and internal communication
- Integration of disciplines within internal communication (e.g. management communication and employee communication) and within external communication (e.g. public relations and marketing communication)
- Integration of departments in organisation (e.g. different types of organisational design)
- Integration of communication strategy, business strategy and corporate strategy.

Thus, while there are these different levels of coordination, outlined above, within which it seems possible to integrate different types of activities, it is also possible for integration to take place across two or more of these levels. This applies for example to the integration of a brand promise delivered by a company in its product branding or corporate branding, and the fulfilment of this promise in words, pictures or actions at the levels mentioned above, that is, the classic alignment of words and deeds. It also applies to the integration of a company and its stakeholders, or what Zerfaß (2008), inspired by Anthony Giddens (1984), terms *social integration*. Here we have an 'outside-in' perspective (and not an 'inside-out' perspective as at the other levels of coordination) focusing on the interdependence between the organisation and its stakeholders and the adaptation of the former's interpretations, interests (ends) and actions (means). In this case, we transcend not only the traditional levels of coordination (message, external and internal communication, etc.), but the very understanding of integration.

Finally, besides degrees and levels of strategic coordination, corporate communication also investigates *models of coordination*, that is, the set of procedures that the companies decide to implement to create and secure integration.

An early, but still rather popular model of coordination is van Riel's (1995) theoretical integration framework called *common starting points* (CSPs). Van Riel, who has a background in marketing, defines common starting points as 'central values that function as the basis for undertaking any kind of communication envisioned by an organization' (van Riel 1997: 302; see also van Riel 1995). This approach, which brings together strategy, identity and image, is presented more precisely as a method 'to manage ambiguities' in communication. The outcome of the application of the CSP model is the so-called corporate marketing mix involving and combining all types of communication, especially the following three different categories: (1) management communication, (2) marketing communication, and (3) organisational communication, which surprisingly enough also includes public relations. More recently, van Riel has added the concept of the *sustainable corporate story* (SCS) to the common starting points. The idea behind this model of coordination is to create consistency and distinctiveness in the messages produced by the company by building on and offering a realistic (based on the identity), relevant (offers added value for stakeholders), responsive (allows for two-way communication) and sustainable story about the company's origin, mission and vision (van Riel 2000).

Another and even more recent example of a model of coordination is Belasen's (2008) application of the Competing Values Framework (CFV) to corporate communication. This framework was initially based on research to identify indicators of organisational effectiveness (Quinn and Rohrbaugh 1983). The answer to this question was that companies must learn to navigate between *conflicting values* (represented by four models, each one containing a different set of effectiveness criteria: the human relations model, the open system model, the rational goal model and the internal process model). Belasen claims that 'the value of the Competing Values Framework for Corporate Communication (CVFCC) is in providing a broader and integrative interpretation of corporate communication environments by addressing diverse stakeholders' (Belasen 2008: 27).

As claimed at the beginning of this section, research on integration is not very extensive compared to the research undertaken from a corporate communication perspective within the area of corporate identity, image and reputation. Most of the research on integration has been conducted within the field of integrated marketing communication. Nevertheless, there are a few important publications. Some scholars have tried to rethink the concept of integration in communication as co-creation in a study of how a company is challenged by consumer resistance (Johansen and Andersen 2012). Other scholars have studied how the concept of integration can be applied to internal communication (Kalla 2005). Yet other scholars are asking: Is the ideal achievable? (Massie and Anderson 2003). However, the most important contribution to the study of integration lies first and foremost in the critique of the concept (see Christensen, Torp and Firat 2005; Torp 2009; Christensen, Firat and Cornelissen 2009). We will return to this critique in the next section.

Stakeholder relations

The last core theme in research on corporate communication to be examined is *relationship*, more precisely the relationship between a company and its external and internal stakeholders. This is another area where corporate communication differs from related disciplines. Public relations scholars, for example, prefer to talk about *publics*, whereas marketing communication scholars talk about *target groups*.

Although the stakeholder concept was coined and introduced already in the early 1960s, it was not until the publication of R. E. Freeman's seminal book *Strategic Management: A Stakeholder Approach* in 1984 that the concept got access to management and organisation studies, and later on to corporate communication (Friedman and Miles 2006). Freeman defines stakeholders as 'groups and individuals who can affect or are affected by the achievement of an organization's mission' (Freeman 1984: 52). He then places the concept within a strategic framework containing three levels: (1) a 'rational' level focusing on stakeholder mapping (key question: who are the stakeholders of the organisation?), (2) a 'process' level (key question: how do the organisational processes fit with the stakeholder map?), and (3) a 'transactional' level (key question: how can the organisation interact with its stakeholders?). The more these three levels are coordinated, the higher the Stakeholder Management Capability of the organisation is.

In its early version, Freeman's stakeholder approach to strategic management was based on a philosophy of voluntarism. According to this philosophy, organisations with high Stakeholder Management Capability must design and integrate communication processes with multiple stakeholders; negotiate explicitly with stakeholders on critical issues and seek voluntary agreements; overspend on understanding stakeholder needs; integrate boundary spanners into the strategy formulation processes in the organisation; be proactive anticipating stakeholder concerns and trying to influence the stakeholder environment; allocate resources in a manner consistent with stakeholders' concerns; and think in 'stakeholder-serving' terms (Freeman 1984: 78–80). Today, Freeman has moved in an even more philosophical direction, presenting stakeholder theory as a new philosophy of capitalism (Freeman *et al.* 2010).

Since the mid-1980s, stakeholder theory in general, and the stakeholder concept in particular, have been developed further and redefined several times, either in a more strategic or in a more normative direction (cf. the overview in Friedman and Miles 2006). But to what extent has it been developed within the field of corporate communication?

Parmar *et al.* (2010) have listed the *disciplines* or research areas where the stakeholder theory has been applied: (1) strategic management, (2) finance, (3) accounting, marketing and management (organisational behaviour, human resource management, etc.) (see also Freeman *et al.* 2008).

Laplume *et al.* (2008) have established a similar list, this time, however, of *research themes* in stakeholder theory. A total of five broad themes are identified in the period from 1985 to 2007: (1) stakeholder definition and salience (Which stakeholders should managers pay attention to? Which stakeholders do they really care about?), (2) stakeholder actions and responses (How do stakeholders influence companies? When will stakeholder groups mobilise? When will they support companies?), (3) company actions and responses (How do companies gain stakeholder support? How do/should companies manage stakeholders? How do/should they balance stakeholder interests?), 4) company performance (What is the relationship between stakeholder management and company performance? What is the relationship between stakeholder management and CSR? What other organisational outcomes are affected by stakeholder management?), and (5) theory debates (What are the normative foundations of stakeholder theory? What are the problems of stakeholder theory? Which theories does stakeholder theory compete with?).

As we can see, corporate communication is neither to be found on the list of disciplines, nor on the list of research themes. This is rather surprising, especially if we take into consideration how crucial, yes, even defining a role the stakeholder concept is ascribed in corporate communication (cf. section two of this chapter; Cornelissen 2011, chapter 3). Perhaps the explanation of the absence is very simple: so far, the stakeholder has not really been defined in *communicative* terms, but has remained an under-theorised concept imported from management and organisation studies.

This would also explain why not all corporate communication scholars are talking about stakeholders, why they sometimes do it in a problematic way, and why some of them take the concept of stakeholder for granted. Argenti (1994) uses the concept of constituency, without ever mentioning stakeholders. Van Riel and Fombrun (2007) use the stakeholder concept in their stakeholder linkage model, but mix it up with the concept of target groups (a marketing concept based on a transmission model). And Goodman (1994) uses the concept of stakeholder as if we all know what it means.

Recently, there has been a growing interest in studying and redefining stakeholder theory and the stakeholder concept within the field of corporate communication. The Finnish communication scholar Vilma Luoma-aho has played a key role in this new understanding of stakeholders. Replacing the traditional stakeholder maps with a more *dynamic* type of stakeholder, Luoma-aho and Vos (2010) claim that the interaction between companies and stakeholders has changed due, among other things, to the new media landscape: a change from the old situation characterised by organisation centrism and stakeholder control to a new situation characterised by the existence of multiple issues arenas to which stakeholders can contribute in a more active way. According to the two authors, these arenas will be the new focus for corporate communicators in the future. Luoma-aho (2010) has renewed our understanding of stakeholders by adding *emotions* to the traditional stakes and by making a distinction between *faith-holders* (positive emotions) and *hate-holders* (negative emotions). Finally, Luoma-aho and Paloviita (2010) have also contributed to a new understanding of stakeholders by demonstrating that we need to include *non-human* influences (e.g. infrastructure, technology and market trends) to better describe the complex corporate environment in which the companies are navigating. They see Bruno Latour's actor-network theory (ANT) as an approach that can help us in explaining how and why stakeholders represent both human and non-human entities.

The growing interest in the study of stakeholders from a corporate communication perspective also includes a stakeholder approach to internal communication (Welch and Jackson 2007) and internal crisis communication (Frandsen and Johansen 2011); studies of how the organisation-stakeholder relationship transforms into dialogue or co-creation (Johansen and Nielsen 2011;

Kantanen 2012); studies of how organisations communicate with multiple stakeholders or integrate them in their communication (Hutt 2012); and studies of how different groups of stakeholders interpret the company's communication differently (Helm 2007).

A critique of corporate communication: towards flexibility

Over the last two decades, corporate communication has been criticised, directly or indirectly, by scholars coming from related disciplines within the field of communication research.

This applies to the academic discipline of public relations, where James E. Grunig has accused the concept of *image* of focusing too strongly on the symbolic, and not behavioural, dimension of the relationship between an organisation and its stakeholders (Grunig 1993). This criticism is still influential today, forming part of the theoretical background of Grunig's distinction between a symbolic, interpretive paradigm and a strategic management, behavioural paradigm (Grunig 2006; see also Kim and Ni 2010). Corporate communication has also been criticised by scholars from organisational communication, although the criticism this time is directed towards another aspect, that is, the concept of *integration* and the idea that strategic coordination will make the communication of a company more effective and efficient.

In the middle of the 1990s, Cees van Riel used a body metaphor that is well-known in Western philosophy (Plato, Hobbes, Bentham), in his account of the overall purpose of corporate communication:

> This overview clusters around three focal responsibilities in corporate communication: identity, reputation, and orchestration of communication. The term corporate should be interpreted in the context of the Latin word *corpus*, meaning *body*, or, in a more figurative sense, *relating to the totality*. In other words, specialists working in areas of identity, reputation, and communication orchestration relate their work to, and are guided by, the needs of the organisation.
>
> *(van Riel 1997: 305)*

It is exactly this body metaphor that two Danish researchers Lars Thøger Christensen and Mette Morsing (joined by North American communication scholar George Cheney in 2008) have turned into the thread of their critique of the concept of integration (Christensen, Morsing and Cheney 2008: 6–9). It is not so much a critique of corporate communication as such; it is more the discipline of integrated marketing communication, or the generalised term of integrated communication, which is under accusation. The critique is first and foremost a critique of the *management ideal* or managerial 'mindset' often associated with corporate communication. 'Corporate communication is a managerial vision of managing *all* communications that involve the organization as a whole' (Christensen, Morsing and Cheney 2008: 9). This management ideal is based on the following basic assumptions:

- Integration will make a company's communication more clear, consistent and continuous over time, and thereby also more effective;
- The more communicative and organisational levels that are integrated (cf. above), the more effective the communication will be;
- The more tightly coupled the organisation of the company, the more effective the communication will be;

- Integration can and must be surveilled and controlled by a centralised unit (communication department);
- Integration will always be the best solution for the company independent of purpose and situation.

This ideal may seem very promising, especially if you share the same idea concerning the 'nature' of communication, organisation and management. However, Christensen, Morsing and Cheney (2008) claim that eventually this type of strategic coordination will make the companies more vulnerable. Today, the business world is again and again confronted with different, or even conflicting, expectations and demands from its stakeholders. At the same time, businesses are operating in markets and societies that have become more complex and dynamic due to globalisation, new information and communication technology, and a growing sense of uncertainty. Taking this development into consideration, the solution according to Christensen, Morsing and Cheney (2008) is not to follow the road leading to absolute integration, but to apply a *flexible* integrated approach: 'To acknowledge and adapt to environmental complexity, the project of corporate communications needs to balance central control with flexibility and decentralization' (Christensen, Morsing and Cheney 2008: 182; see also Christensen, Firat and Torp 2008).

In his ground breaking book *Images of Organization*, Gareth Morgan emphasises the paradoxical nature of metaphors: 'Metaphor is inherently paradoxical. It can create powerful insights that also become distortions, as the way of seeing created through a metaphor becomes a way of *not* seeing' (Morgan 2006: 5). If we apply this perspective to the body metaphor introduced by Christensen, Morsing and Cheney (2008) in their critique of corporate communication, the following 'way of not seeing' appears: the trunk or torso (the central part of the body, or 'the organization as a whole') is highlighted, and the arms and legs are neglected.

In a similar way, corporate communication seems to be reduced to corporate branding forgetting about the stakeholder approach and the other autonomous, yet mutually related disciplines within corporate communication, such as investor relations, community relations, issues management, change communication and crisis communication, are neglected. This reduction is closely related to another reduction: the reduction of integration to complete *co-ordination* (the ideal of communication 'with one voice'), a degree of integration that fits well with corporate branding, but perhaps not so well with more stakeholder differentiated disciplines.

The reduction of corporate communication to corporate branding also appears in the definition of the discipline proposed by the three critics: 'The ambition of corporate communications is to project a consistent image of the organization across multiple audiences' (Christensen, Morsing and Cheney 2008: vi). Here the terms 'image' and 'stakeholder' ('*across* multiple audiences') are in the singular form, distinguishing this definition from Cornelissen's (2011) definition where the terms 'reputation' and 'stakeholder' are in plural form.

Lars Thøger Christensen and his colleagues will claim that corporate communication risks becoming a simple 'umbrella term' where corporate communication is defined in terms of *other* communication disciplines (Christensen, Morsing and Cheney 2008: 3; see also Christensen and Cornelissen 2011: 385–86). There is such a risk, no doubt about that, but only if you forget about the stakeholder approach where differentiation is a possibility, and only if you forget that the communication department of a company serves many other purposes than just corporate branding, and that many of the other communication disciplines are often collaborating independently of the corporate branding activities of the company (e.g. issues management and stakeholder management).

Academic resources: research centres, international conferences and CCIJ

A group of academic centres conducting research, teaching, and/or disseminating knowledge about corporate communication, have been created around the world. The oldest of these centres is the Corporate Communication Centre, established at Rotterdam School of Management, Erasmus University (the Netherlands) in 1997 under the guidance of Professor Cees van Riel. Almost as old is Corporate Communication International (formerly known as the Corporate Communication Institute) at Baruch College, City University of New York, founded and led by Professor Michael Goodman since 1999. CCI has conducted a series of surveys examining how corporate communication has developed as an organisational practice in the United States, Europe, South Africa and China (*Corporate Communication Trends and Practices*).

Among the other academic centres are the Centre for Corporate Communication, created at Aarhus University (Denmark) in 2001, which is one of the largest communication research centres in Europe with its more than 30 senior and junior researchers; and the Centre for Corporate Communication, created at BI Norwegian Business School in 2007, which works in close collaboration with partners from the business world in Norway.

The two largest international conferences on corporate communication are the Conference on Corporate Communication, organised every year by CCI, and the International Conference on Corporate and Marketing Communications, held every year. So far, only one journal has been dedicated to the field of corporate communication, namely *Corporate Communications: An International Journal* (*CCIJ*), established in 1995 and published four times a year.

Related topics

business communication; management communication; organizational communication and discourse; and public relations

Key readings

Barnett, M. L., Jermier, H. M. and Lafferty, B. A. (2006). 'Corporate reputation: The definitional landscape', *Corporate Reputation Review*, 9(1), 26–38. (Provides an overview of the many different definitions of corporate reputation.)
Carroll, C. (ed.) (2013). *Handbook of Communication and Corporate Reputation*, Boston: Wiley-Blackwell. (A handbook partly devoted to corporate communication.)
Elving, W. J. L. (2012). 'Corporate communication positioned within communication studies – *Corporate Communications, an International Journal*: The journal and its history, scope and future developments', *The Review of Communication*, 12(1), 66–77. (A comparison of corporate communication and other disciplines within communication studies.)
Illia, L. and Balmer, J. M. T. (2012). 'Corporate communication and corporate marketing: Their nature, histories, differences and similarities', *Corporate Communications: An International Journal*, 17(4), 415–33. (A comparison of corporate communication with corporate marketing.)
Kornberger, M. (2010). *Brand Society: How Brands Transform Management and Lifestyle*, Cambridge: Cambridge University Press. (A study of the consequences of working and living in a brand society.)

Bibliography

Albert, S. and Whetten, D. A. (1985). 'Organizational identity', in L. L. Cummings and M. M. Staw, (eds), *Research in Organizational Behavior*, 7, 263–95, Greenwich, CT: JAI Press.
Argenti, P. A. (1994). *Corporate Communication*, Boston, MA: Irwin McGraw-Hill. Second edition (2008).
——(1996). 'Corporate communication as a discipline: Toward a definition', *Management Communication Quarterly*, 10(1), 73–97.

Ashforth, B. E. and Mael, F. (1989). 'Social identity theory and the organization', *Academy of Management Review*, 14(1), 20–39.
Balmer, J. M. T. (1995). 'Corporate branding and connoisseurship', *Journal of Grand Management*, 21(1), 22–46.
Balmer, J. M. T. and Greyser, S. A. (2002). 'Managing the multiple identities of the corporation', *California Management Review*, 44(3), 72–86.
——(eds) (2003). *Revealing the Corporation: Perspectives on Identity, Image, Reputation, Corporate Branding, and Corporate-Level Marketing*, London: Routledge.
Belasen, A. T. (2008). *The Theory and Practice of Corporate Communication: A Competing Values Perspective*, Los Angeles: Sage.
Brunsson, N. (1991). *The Organization of Hypocrisy: Talk, Decisions, and Action in Organizations*, Copenhagen: Copenhagen Business School Press.
Cheney, G., and Christensen, L. T. (2001). 'Organizational identity: Linkages between "internal" and "external" organizational communication', in F. M. Jablin and L. L. Putnam (eds), *The New Handbook of Organizational Communication* (pp. 231–69), Thousands Oaks, CA: Sage.
Christensen, L. T. and Cornelissen, J. (2011). 'Bridging corporate and organizational communication: Review, development and a look to the future', *Management Communication Quarterly*, 25(3), 383–414.
Christensen, L. T., Firat, A. F. and Cornelissen, J. (2009). 'New tensions and challenges in integrated communications', *Corporate Communications: An International Journal*, 14(2), 207–19.
Christensen, L. T., Firat, A. F. and Torp, S. (2008). 'The organization of integrated communications: Toward flexible integration', *European Journal of Marketing*, 42(3/4), 423–52.
Christensen, L. T., Morsing, M. and Cheney, G. (2008). *Corporate Communications: Convention, Complexity, and Critique*, Los Angeles: Sage.
Christensen, L. T., Torp, S. and Firat, A. F. (2005). 'Integrated marketing communication and postmodernity: An odd couple?' *Corporate Communications: An International Journal*, 10(2), 156–67.
Cornelissen, J. (2011). *Corporate Communications: A Guide to Theory and Practice*, London: Sage. Third edition.
Corporate Communication: An International Journal (1999). Special issue on 'Corporate identity', 4(4).
Corporate Communication: An International Journal (2009). Special issue on 'Explicating corporate identity', 14(1).
Czarniawska-Joerges, B. (1994). 'Narratives of individual and organizational identities', in Deetz, S. (ed.), *Communication Yearbook*, vol. 17, Newbury Park: Sage.
Dowling, G. (1986). 'Managing your corporate image', *Industrial Marketing Management*, 15, 109–15.
——(2001). *Creating Corporate Reputations: Identity, Image and Performance*, Oxford: Oxford University Press.
Dutton, J. E. and Dukerich, J. M. (1991). 'Keeping an eye on the mirror: Image and identity in organizational adaptation', *Academy of Management Journal*, 34, 517–54.
Eisenberg, E. M. (1984). 'Ambiguity as strategy in organizational communication', *Communication Monographs*, 5(3), 227–42.
Fombrun, C. J. (1996). *Reputation: Realizing Value from the Corporate Image*, Boston, MA: Harvard Business School Press.
Frandsen, F. and Johansen, W. (2011). 'The study of internal crisis communication: Towards an integrative approach', *Corporate Communications: An International Journal*, 16(4), 347–61.
Freeman, R. E. (1984). *Strategic Management: A Stakeholder Approach*, Boston: Pitman.
Freeman, R. E., Harrison, J. S. and Wicks, A. C. (2008). *Managing for Stakeholders: Survival, Reputation and Success*, Boston: Yale University Press.
Freeman, R. E., Harrison, J. S., Wicks, A. C., Parmar, B. L. and De Colle, S. (2010). *Stakeholder Theory: The State of the Art*, Cambridge, UK: Cambridge University Press.
Friedman, A. L. and Miles, S. (2006). *Stakeholders: Theory and Practice*, Oxford: Oxford University Press.
Giddens, A. (1984). *The Constitution of Society: Outline of the Theory of Structuration*, Cambridge: Polity Press.
Goodman, M. B. (1994). *Corporate Communications: Theory and Practice*, Albany: State University of New York Press.
——(2006). 'Communication practice and pedagogy at the dawn of the new millennium', *Corporate Communications: An International Journal*, 11(3), 196–213.
Goodman, M. B. and Hirsch, P. B. (2010). *Corporate Communication: Strategic Adaptation for Global Practice*, New York: Peter Lang.
Grunig, J. E. (1993). 'Image and substance: From symbolic to behavioral relationships', *Public Relations Review*, 19(2), 121–39.
——(2006). *After 50 Years: The Value and Values of Public Relations*, The Institute for Public Relations: 45th Annual Distinguished Lecture, The Yale Club, New York. November 9, 2006.

Hatch, M. J. and Schultz, M. (2000). 'Scaling the tower of Babel: Relational differences between identity, image, and culture in organizations', in M. Schultz, M. J. Hatch and M. Holten Larsen (eds), *The Expressive Organization: Linking Identity, Reputation, and the Corporate Brand* (pp. 11–35), Oxford: Oxford University Press.

——(2001). 'Are the strategic stars aligned for your corporate brand?' *Harvard Business Review*, 79(2), 3–4, 128–34.

——(2004). *Organizational Identity: A Reader*, Oxford: Oxford University Press.

Helm, S. (2007). 'One reputation or many? Comparing stakeholder's perceptions of corporate reputation', *Corporate Communications: An International Journal*, 12(7), 238–54.

Hübner, H. (2007). *The Communicating Company: Towards an Alternative Theory of Corporate Communication*, Heidelberg: Physica Verlag.

Hutt, R. W. (2012). 'The extent and patterns of multi-stakeholder communications in annual reports', *Corporate Communications: An International Journal*, 17(3), 323–35.

Johansen, T. S. (2012). 'The narrated organization: Implications of a narrative corporate identity vocabulary for strategic self-storying', *International Journal of Strategic Communication*, 6(3), 232–45.

Johansen, T. S. and Andersen, S. E. (2012). 'Co-creating ONE: Rethinking integration within communication', *Corporate Communications: An International Journal*, 17(3), 272–88.

Johansen, T. S. and Nielsen, A. E. (2011). 'Strategic stakeholder dialogues: A discursive perspective on relationship building', *Corporate Communications: An International Journal*, 16(3), 184–91.

Kalla, H. K. (2005). 'Integrated internal communications: A multidisciplinary perspective', *Corporate Communications: An International Journal*, 10(4), 302–14.

Kantanen, H. (2012). 'Identity, image and stakeholder dialogue', *Corporate Communications: An International Journal*, 17(1), 56–72.

Kim, J.-N. and Ni, L. (2010). 'Seeing the forest through the trees: The behavioral, strategic management paradigm in public relations and its future', in R. L. Heath (ed.), *The SAGE Handbook of Public Relations* (pp. 35–57), Thousand Oaks, CA: Sage.

Kotler, P. and Mindak, W. (1978). 'Marketing and public relations: Should they be partners or rivals?' *Journal of Marketing*, 43(19), 13–20.

Laplume, A. O., Sonpar, K. and Litz, E. A. (2008). 'Stakeholder theory: Reviewing a theory that moves us', *Journal of Management*, 34(6), 1152–89.

Luoma-aho, V. (2010). *Emotional Stakeholders: A Threat to Organizational Legitimacy?* Paper presented at the 60th Annual Conference of the International Communication Association, Singapore, 22–26 June.

Luoma-aho, V. and Paloviita, A. (2010). 'Actor-networking theory for today's corporate communications', *Corporate Communications: An International Journal*, 15(1), 49–67.

Luoma-aho, V. and Vos, M. (2010). 'Towards a more dynamic stakeholder model: Acknowledging multiple issues arenas', *Corporate Communications: An International Journal*, 15(3), 315–31.

Massie, L. and Anderson, C. L. (2003). 'Integrating communications: Is the ideal achievable?' *Corporate Communications: An International Journal*, 8(4), 223–28.

Morgan, G. (2006). *Images of Organization*, Thousand Oaks, CA: Sage. Second edition.

Olins, W. (1989). *Corporate Identity: Making Business Strategy Visible Through Design*, London: Thames and Hudson.

Parmar, B. L., Freeman, R. E., Harrison, J. S., Wicks, A. C., Purnell, L. and De Colle, S. (2010). 'Stakeholder theory: The state of the art', *The Academy of Management Annals*, 4(1), 403–45.

Pratt, M. G. and Rafaeli, A. (1997). 'Organizational dress as a symbol of multilayered social identities', *Academy of Management Journal*, 40, 862–98.

Quinn, R. E. and Rohrbaugh, J. (1983). 'A spatial model of effectiveness criteria: Towards a competing values approach to organizational analysis', *Management Science*, 29(3), 363–377.

Riel, C. van (1995). *Principles of Corporate Communication*. London: Prentice Hall.

——(1997). 'Research in corporate communication: An overview of an emerging field', *Management Communication Quarterly*, 10(2), 288–309.

——(2000). 'Corporate communication orchestrated by a sustainable corporate story', in M. Schultz, M. J. Hatch and M. Holten Larsen (eds), *The Expressive Organization: Linking Identity, Reputation, and the Corporate Brand* (pp. 157–81), Oxford: Oxford University Press.

——(2005). 'Defining corporate communication', in P. S. Brønn and R. W. Berg (eds), *Corporate Communication: A Strategic Approach to Building Reputation*, Oslo: Gyldendal Akademisk.

Riel, C. van and Fombrun, C. J. (2007). *Essentials of Corporate Communication: Implementing Practices for Effective Reputation Management*, London: Routledge.

Schultz, M. (2005). 'A cross-disciplinary perspective on corporate branding', in M. Schultz, Y. M. Antorini and F. F. Csaba (eds), *Corporate Branding: Purpose, People, Process*, Copenhagen: Copenhagen Business School Press.

Shelby, A. N. (1993). 'Organizational, business, management, and corporate communication: An analysis of boundaries and relationships', *Journal of Business Communication*, *30*(3), 241–67.

Torp, S. (2009). 'Integrated communications: From one look to normative consistency', *Corporate Communication: An International Journal*, *14*(1), 190–206.

Welch, M. and Jackson, P. R. (2007). 'Rethinking internal communication: A stakeholder approach', *Corporate Communications: An International Journal*, *12*(2), 177–98.

Zerfaß, A. (2008). 'Corporate communication revisited: Integrating business strategy and strategic communication', in A. Zerfaß, B. van Ruler and S. Krishnamurthy (eds), *Public Relations Research: European and International Perspectives and Innovations: Festschrift for Günter Bentele* (pp. 65–96), Wiesbaden: GWV Fachverlage.

Zerfass, A., Verhoeven, P., Tench, R., Moreno, A. and Vercic, D. (2011). *European Communication Monitor 2011. Empirical Insights into Strategic Communication in Europe. Results of an Empirical Survey in 43 Countries*, Brussels: EACD, EUPRERA.

16
Corporate communication and the role of annual reporting

Identifying areas for further research

Elizabeth de Groot

Introduction: Corporate communication

Stronger stakeholder demands, an increase in planned and unplanned media presence, homogeneity in products, internationalisation, a growing need for more cost efficiency ... These are several of the major developments that led to the introduction of the concept of corporate communication in the final decades of the twentieth century. Corporate communication has been defined as a management function that focuses on the orchestration of all internal and external communication activities. Its purpose is to generate and convey a consistent corporate story based on which favourable relationships are established with stakeholders who determine the company's bottom line (Cornelissen 2011; Van Riel and Fombrun 2007). This means that corporate communication entails the coordination of a complex set of communication activities that need to reflect a 'coherent and unambiguous' picture of 'what the organization is and what it stands for' (Christensen, Morsing and Cheney 2008: 3). It needs to do this, moreover, for stakeholder groups that have specific interests in the company. Based in a philosophy that regards the company as a whole, corporate communication combines activities in marketing communications, employee communications, investor relations or PR in an attempt to build strategic affiliations with customers, employees, investors or other publics who may fulfil multiple stakeholder roles and who may reside in domestic or foreign markets that require specific stakeholder approaches (e.g. Cornelissen 2011; Torp 2009). In recent years, the corporate communication function has been further complicated by new trends in ethics and technology (Goodman 2012). Accounting incidents and environmental disasters have raised stakeholder concerns about companies' transparency and social responsibility, leaving companies with the task of presenting themselves as 'reliable and trustworthy institutions with nothing to hide' (Cornelissen 2011: 23). At the same time, the flight of Web 2.0 has not only caused a growth in verbal and visual communication media such as social networks, blogs or video sharing services but has also caused an increase in uncontrollable stakeholder-generated content that can be shared rapidly and broadly (Aula 2010).

While companies are currently wrestling with the realisation and professionalisation of integrated corporate communication under technological and stakeholder pressures, from a scholarly perspective there seems to be an ambiguous understanding of the theoretical starting points and analytical challenges of such communication (cf. Torp 2009). With regard to current research in corporate communication, moreover, Christensen and Cornelissen (2011: 384) argue that it is primarily concerned with 'the controlled handling and organization of communication' but without much direct attention for actual communication actions and processes. This chapter seeks to contribute to a more concrete understanding of some of the theoretical and analytical issues in today's corporate communication field, in particular in relation to the genre of the annual report (Bhatia 2008). It aims to point at several areas for future annual report research that have emerged *because of* the fact that the annual report – as an Investor Relations tool – is an integral part of a corporate communication strategy (Stanton and Stanton 2002). These research areas will be discussed after describing the role of investor relations and the annual report in corporate communication.

Corporate communication and investor relations

Corporate communication has a distinctive position within communication. Management communication, for example, focuses on communication in terms of managerial roles and strategic activities, organisational communication often looks at how communication shapes internal organisational systems and behaviour, and business communication articulates pragmatic communication skills within internal or external professional contexts (Elving *et al.* 2012). Additionally, corporate communication considers communication as a management *function* that helps fulfil corporate objectives by aligning management's envisioned corporate identity – i.e. its desired personality in terms of values and culture – with the perceptions internal and external stakeholders have of the company (Cornelissen 2011; Van Riel and Fombrun, 2007). According to Gray and Balmer, it is responsible for 'the aggregate of messages from both official and informal sources, through a variety of media, by which the company conveys its identity to its multiple audiences or stakeholders' (1998: 696).

The stakeholder perceptions that are formed based on corporate communication messages comprise (a) incidental mental pictures activated by everyday encounters with the company – e.g. through a newspaper article on its CSR activities – and (b) an overall company assessment that evolves and is imprinted over time as a result of multiple encounters – e.g. through newspaper articles on the company's CSR activities, product advertisements reflecting its brand values, or annual reports presenting its financial results. While the former are generally referred to as corporate images, the latter concerns corporate reputation (Chun 2005). Van Riel and Fombrun (2007) explain that the corporate images established through corporate communication activities – e.g. social image, product image, financial image – collectively form the input for corporate reputation. Research has shown that a favourable reputation may positively influence a company's performance, for example with regard to market value (e.g. Smith, Smith and Wang 2010), but also in terms of customer loyalty (e.g. Walsh *et al.* 2009) or employer attractiveness (e.g. Cable and Turban 2003).

In line with the key concepts of corporate communication, many studies in this field have revolved around corporate identity, images, reputation, branding, coordination of communication activities, stakeholder theory and corporate citizenship (Christensen and Cornelissen 2011; Scott 2012). Corporate communication research has focused primarily on the corporate sender as well as on the management and effect of communications in general; it has paid relatively little attention to the polyphonic messages inherent in corporate communication and how the verbal and non-verbal languages used in them signal meaning to stakeholders in diverse social backgrounds (Christensen and Cornelissen 2011). This is an interesting gap in research, given that the essence of corporate communication is translating intended company meanings into corresponding stakeholder beliefs about the company.

There is one communication discipline within corporate communication for which this research gap seems to apply in particular: investor relations (e.g. Dolphin 2004). Whereas investor relations (IR) was initially used simply for the distribution of financial results to analysts and investors, today it serves as a strategic management function by means of which companies 'identify, establish, maintain and enhance ... relationships' with capital providers (investors) as well as opinion formers (e.g. analysts, journalists) (Dolphin 2004: 26). Its purpose is twofold. On the one hand, it is intended to inform stakeholders by providing transparent insight into performance details and shareholder structure. On the other hand, IR is also meant to attract and commit (financial) stakeholders to the company by stimulating positive images and – in the long term – a favourable reputation (Hoffmann and Fieseler 2012). Companies employ various IR genres to address the multi-faced audience in domestic and foreign investor communities; for example, they use CEO webcasts or CFO presentations for investors and analysts, annual general meetings for investors, journalists and authorities, and press releases, corporate websites or annual reports for any stakeholder with a performance-related interest in the company (e.g. Dolphin 2004).

As with other corporate communication activities, the ability of IR genres to help construe positive images and build favourable relationships depends on their congruity with stakeholders' needs and self-concepts. Following signalling theory, this requires that managers try to reduce the information asymmetry between the company and its stakeholders by communicating *signals* that enable these stakeholders to form impressions of the company (Hussainey and Salama 2010). With regard to IR, investors need these signals to determine whether they think a company is investment worthy. For investors, for example, messages about environmental responsibility can serve as a signal of the company's sustainable character and thus future market position (Hussainey and Salama 2010). In order for these signals to be effective, moreover, they need to *appeal* to the individual stakeholders. In terms of social identity theory, this means that IR genres need to communicate a corporate character that is conceived of as relevant and desirable by the individual stakeholders (e.g. being ethical). In other words, IR genres are to make stakeholders identify with the company; based on the message in IR genres, stakeholders should 'perceive an overlap between the company's organizational attributes and their own individual attributes' (Aspara and Tikkanen 2011: 1450). More overlap between company and stakeholder attributes will cause stronger company identification, which in turn will result in a stronger disposition toward appreciating the company for its qualities and supporting its welfare, e.g. by buying shares. Throughout the past decade, the IR discipline has had a difficult task in establishing stakeholder identification and good reputations. IR genres have been heavily criticised and scrutinised as a result of fraudulent financial reporting practices by large multinationals such as Enron or Ahold. This has raised worldwide bids for increased trustworthiness and transparency in IR.

The annual report genre

The annual report is generally regarded as one of the most important IR tools (Courtright and Smudde 2009). It is a statutory document, which at the same time needs to fulfil the expressive, informative and relational functions of the IR discipline (Ditlevsen 2012). Consistent with developments in IR, the annual report has been observed to have metamorphosed from a financial factsheet into 'a marketing and public relations document' that reflects the company's awareness of its diverse audiences (Campbell, McPhail and Slack 2009: 909). Ditlevsen explains that the annual report is intended to provide an equity story that appeals to potential and current stakeholders by presenting 'the company as an investment case' (2012: 379). The story it tells needs to convince stakeholders that the company will be able to meet its strategic objectives and that, therefore, present and future investments in the company are potentially successful and legitimate. Within annual reports, the story is conveyed through two kinds of information: narrative and numerical. Numerical information is presented in the financial accounts – e.g. the balance sheet, cash flow statement – in the back of the report and is subject to (inter)national reporting regulations. Narrative information precedes the financial statements and discloses 'who the company is and what its values are, what its businesses are and how successful they have been, and how the company manages its environments and interacts with its stakeholders' (Courtright and Smudde 2009: 258). Narrative information is provided, for example, in the CEO's foreword, the Strategy Overview, the Operating and Financial reviews, the Governance review and the CSR review.

Similar to other corporate communication tools such as CEO's personnel letters (internal communication, e.g. Hendriks and van Mulken 2012), press releases (PR, e.g. Catenaccio 2008) or earnings calls (IR, e.g. Crawford Camiciottoli 2010), the annual report can be classified as a professional *genre*. This means that it is a conventionalised text type that has been recognised over time to repeatedly fulfil particular communicative purposes within a given community of senders and receivers (Bhatia 1993). As is evident from its history, the annual report genre is shaped by and shapes the specific communicative context in which it is used (Rutherford 2005). Developments in business and accounting have adapted the 'rules of engagement' for the annual report: the focus of its purposes has shifted, its reader audience has extended and, consequently, its content and form have changed. Senders' recurrent implementation of these changes and receivers' subsequent acceptance of these changes have caused the annual report genre to be redefined throughout the years.

While the annual report was initially a tool for the corporate sender to satisfy the fact-based information needs of national investors and analysts, today's annual report is also used to inform and persuade media, customers, authorities, employees, suppliers and NGOs around the globe (Rowbottom and Lymer 2010). Thus, annual reports no longer have only an informative purpose; they also have a promotional purpose. Information about the corporate mission, strategy and performance needs to be accurate and transparent, but is generally presented in a way that encourages favourable perceptions of the company. This is particularly the case in the narrative sections, where the absence of disclosure regulations leaves room for creative authorship and impression management (Ditlevsen 2012; de Groot 2008). In the narrative sections, impression management is executed primarily through colourful photographs, voluntary themes such as corporate profile or CSR, and stylistic devices such as markers of emphasis ('definitely'), interaction ('as you can see'), justification (attributing losses to external causes) or even obfuscation through confusing sentence structures (Courtis 2004; Hooghiemstra 2008; Hyland 1998; Stanton and Stanton 2002).

Several studies have explained the importance of the annual report genre within corporate communication by referring to its link with corporate identity, image and reputation. Since the verbal and visual messages in annual reports have been observed to reflect company-specific ideologies, strategies and operations, they are seen as one of management's strong vehicles 'for constructing corporate identity … as part of their equity stories' (Ditlevsen, 2012: 387, 390): by the very expression of the company's personality and performance, these reports reinforce a particular mental picture among stakeholders about for example its ethical, social, innovative, financial and commercial character. Courtright and Smudde (2009: 258) add that the annual report 'is an organization's opportunity to truly influence how its constituencies view it, bolstering its identity and public image through what is said and how it is said'. This means that apart from constructing the corporate identity, annual reports are also used to evoke favourable corporate images upon reading the text and viewing the pictures. Given the many aspects of corporate personality and performance that an annual report can convey, such images are likely to be multidimensional (e.g. social or financial). In the long term, the corporate images established through the annual report will inform the corporate reputation (Courtright and Smudde 2009). Geppert and Lawrence (2008) explain how annual report texts can influence the market value and non-financial assessment aspects of a company's reputation. They argue that by highlighting past achievements and stakeholder-friendly (future) initiatives, annual report texts can positively affect perceptions about the company's financial status. Additionally, annual report texts have the potential to influence the perceived reliability, credibility and transparency of the company based on the choice of words, voluntary themes, language style and images used in these texts.

According to Tregidga, Milne and Lehman, there is a particular lack of research into the 'meaning', 'effects' and 'process and context' of annual reports (2012: 224, 225). They argue that most studies have focused on the content, linguistic structures and readability of this genre as well as on its production and position within corporate communication. To be able to obtain a better theoretical understanding of the communication actions that constitute the genre, Tregidga et al. (2012) suggest scholars should further investigate how annual reports relate to other corporate communication genres (e.g. in PR), how they contribute to the company's accountability and its interaction with stakeholders and how they are used in particular social contexts. In line with these suggestions for future research, the following sections will further elaborate on four specific research areas: the interdependence between annual reports and other corporate communication genres, multimodality in annual reports, response to annual reports, and the cultural background of annual report users.

The annual report as part of the corporate story

At the basis of corporate communication is a corporate story, which is designed to capture 'the "essence" of the company' and 'to frame corporate communication' in the long term (Van Riel and Fombrun 2007: 148). Corporate stories generally involve descriptions of the company's heritage, philosophy, ethics, activities, abilities, strengths and future course. They are intended to present and familiarise both internal and external stakeholders with a unique and appealing picture of the corporate identity (Gill 2011). As such, corporate stories provide companies with a tangible reputation platform, i.e. a proclamation of the core positioning that is adopted company-wide in all communication practices and that helps establish a desired reputation over time (Van Riel and Fombrun 2007). They can make a crucial contribution to the integration of all internal and external corporate communication genres, since they include key messages that potentially allow the company to speak as 'a single entity' (Johansen and Andersen 2012: 276). However, a major challenge inherent in communicating a predetermined corporate story is maintaining its recognisability across different media and genres. While some digital genres – such as IKEA's corporate website – may enable companies to convey the full corporate story, some print or audio-visual genres require fragmentation of the story and can only convey parts of it. Accommodation of the corporate story is often needed not only as a result of limitations of the medium – e.g. IKEA's total story can hardly be told in a TV or print ad – but also as a consequence of the purpose of the genre – e.g. IKEA's product ads primarily aim at promoting to consumers the specific product qualities rather than the qualities of the whole company. It has been argued that, apart from (partial) overlap in story content, consistency in composition and style across corporate communication activities are needed 'to provide the opportunity for shared meaning and mutual understanding across a diverse audience' (Gill 2011: 21). Thus, coherence in message construct across genres is essential to the recognisability of the fragmented corporate story.

Given that today's annual report genre aims 'to proactively construct a particular visibility and meaning' for the company and its achievements (Stanton and Stanton 2002: 478), it plays an important role in corporate story-telling. Moreover, it often includes texts that are produced by senders in different departments (e.g. management, finance, marketing, communications) and which are focused on a variety of company-related topics (e.g. corporate history and identity, management structure, product or divisional performance, research and development, HRM and CSR activities, financial results). Hence, it is likely that the content, style and structure of the annual report are tied to multiple genres in other corporate communication disciplines, such as the corporate website, press releases about product innovation or employee newsletters. Little is known, however, about how exactly the annual report contributes to the integral construction of the corporate story. Stanton and Stanton argue that studies of the company annual report (CAR) have fallen short 'of establishing that the CAR is used as a part of an integrated … communication system' (2002: 488). It thus seems that further research is needed into the 'very complex and dynamic range of resources' of which the annual report is a product (Bhatia 2010: 33).

To date, *discourse* scholars in particular have looked at the annual report genre as an integrated instrument of the corporate communication strategy. Most have done so in terms of the annual report's intertextual and interdiscursive relations to other corporate communication discourses and genres. Intertextuality involves in-text, language-based references to other texts. It can encompass explicit references to other text types, literal references to the language use in other texts or sequential references to information in prior texts (Devitt 1991). While intertextuality rests on text-internal resources, interdiscursivity results from text-external resources. Interdiscursivity refers to the creation of a hybrid text based on 'appropriating or exploiting established conventions' that are typically associated with the discourse in other professional genres, practices and cultures (Bhatia 2010: 35). Texts that are interdiscursively related to other texts may embed (part of) the context-based features contained in these other texts, e.g. communicative purpose, communication modes, sender-reader orientations, or cultural norms.

With regard to the annual report, Bhatia (2008) suggests that this is likely to include explicit *intertextual* references to other IR genres such as earnings announcements or notes from annual general meetings. Conversely, Crawford Camiciottoli (2010) finds that executives may explicitly refer to the annual report to direct listeners of earnings calls to further information on corporate performance. Hendriks and Van Mulken (2012) indicate, moreover, that, compared to external CEO forewords in annual reports, internal CEO letters contain overlapping verbal information about corporate achievements (e.g. strategy, performance and markets themes). Henry (2008) also proposes that there is likely to be an *interdiscursive* overlap in purpose (informational-promotional) and verbal style (biased attributions) between the annual report and other IR genres such as the earnings press release. Solbjørg Skulstad (1996) furthermore shows that the rhetorical style of chairman's statements in environmental reports corresponds with the rhetorical style of chairman's statements in annual reports, i.e. for the use of interactional speech acts ('we explain', or 'I report'). Alternatively, in their analysis of male and female portrayals in annual reports, Anderson and Imperia (1992) suggest there is a strong resemblance between the company's visualisation of gender ideologies in the annual report and in product advertisements. Other scholars have elaborated on the interdiscursive nature of the annual report by referring to the multiple discourses that are represented in this genre. In their study of chairman's statements, for example, Merkl-Davies and Koller observe the use of 'discourses of finance (emphasizing financial performance based on numbers), accounting (emphasizing accuracy and factuality), and public relations (emphasizing promotion and corporate image)' (2012: 182). They confirm the results of Bhatia's (2010) analysis of full annual reports, which in addition showed the use of legal discourse (e.g. disclaimers for forward-looking statements).

Research on the intertextual and interdiscursive features of annual reports has clearly marked a first step towards identifying the genre's integration in corporate communication and its contribution to corporate story-telling. Applying such research specifically within the frame of particular corporate stories and in relation to multiple IR and other corporate communication genres is likely to further enhance our understanding of the annual report as a corporate communication tool (Stanton and Stanton 2002). More specifically, this would further 'reveal the intricacies of the construction ... and especially exploitation of these corporate genres in achieving their corporate objectives within the requirements of disclosure practices imposed by corporate governance bodies and rating agencies' (Bhatia 2010: 45).

The annual report and its multimodal story

Stories about companies' history, ideologies or achievements can be expressed through both verbal and non-verbal modes of communication. In order to bring the corporate story alive and strengthen stakeholders' sensory experiences with the story, these communication modes are often combined (cf. Van Riel and Fombrun 2007). Kress and Van Leeuwen (2001) refer to this as multimodal communication. Despite the omnipresence of pictorial images in particular, however, most studies on corporate communication genres seem to uphold a 'primacy of language in the constitution of socially constructed reality' (Bell and Davison 2012: 3). It appears that within relevant fields such as management and organisation, marketing and accounting, the focus has been on the role of verbal modes in realising the purpose of the genre, while the visual modes have remained relatively unexplored (Bell and Davison 2012). Scholars in the field of corporate communication seem to have discussed the visualisation of the corporate story primarily in relation to corporate visual identity (CVI) and corporate branding, which provide somewhat restricted insights with regard to the visual corporate story. Studies on CVI, for example, specialise in analysing visual elements such as logos, typography or colour (e.g. van den Bosch, de Jong and Elving 2005). And studies on corporate branding often briefly illustrate the contribution of photos in the overall development of common corporate meanings (e.g. Hatch and Schultz 2003).

Considering that pictures contribute to identifying and promoting the company just as much as logos or symbols do, there still is a pressing need for 'critiques of the visual image and conceptual frameworks of visual rhetoric, to be developed to underpin systematic analyses of the modus operandi of the visual' in multimodal corporate communication genres (Davison 2009: 887). Images in corporate communication genres reinforce or complement words by leaving impressions of tangible as well as intangible company achievements or attributes, e.g. delivered end products or social responsibility. Different from words, which tend to encourage a logical and structured understanding of the message, images appeal to the senses and more easily trigger feelings towards, immersion with and perceptual understanding of information presented in the images or in the coinciding words (Kress and Van Leeuwen 2001; Salzer-Mörling and Strannegård 2004).

The imbalance between verbal and visual analysis is also evident in annual report research, although the number of studies of pictures in annual reports seems to have increased throughout the past decade. *Verbal* research has taken various angles to look at the what and how of corporate story-telling in annual reports. The content of the annual report has been investigated in terms of genre-induced themes (e.g. de Groot et al. 2006), or legally required and voluntary informational items (e.g. Meek, Roberts and Gray 1995). Studies of verbal themes have shown, for example, that annual report texts include information on finance, management, CSR or marketing and expectations of future results (e.g. Merkl-Davies, Brennan and McLeay 2011; Osborne, Stubbart and Ramaprasad 2001). Several studies have also pointed out how the structuring of annual report texts helps to build writer-reader relationships (e.g. Garzone 2005; Solbjørg Skulstad 1996) and influences their readability level (e.g. Clatworthy and Jones 2001). From a stylistic perspective, moreover, lexico-grammatical research has exposed the use of informative as well as persuasive language (Hyland 1998; Rutherford 2005) and the formulation of biased cause-effect relationships in annual report texts (e.g. Tsang 2002).

Studies of pictures in annual reports have largely been conducted separately from verbal studies. They have often been based on distinctive theoretical approaches from aesthetics, semiotics, rhetoric, ethical philosophy and sociology (Bell and Davison 2012). *Visual* studies have indicated that although pictures may offer visual evidence of the company's factual reality, they are predominantly used for the purpose of impression management (David 2001; Duff 2011). As Ditlevsen concludes, pictures 'are used strategically in annual reports to construct a corporate identity that is aligned with company strategy in order to position companies as attractive to investors and other stakeholders' (2012: 391). Research on the content of photographs has indicated that they reflect corporate ideologies e.g. concerning gender relations or minority representation (in Benschop and Meihuizen 2002; Bernardi, Bean and Weippert 2005; Duff 2011). Visual themes have also been observed to refer to corporate globalisation, corporate change, corporate power, product features or consumer lifestyle (e.g. McKinstry 1996; de Groot et al. 2006; Preston, Wright and Young 1996; Preston and Young 2000). Only a few visual analyses have focused on the structural and stylistic role of photographs in annual reports. Visual style in annual reports, for example, has been characterised as professional yet often emphasising corporate 'myths' such as high status of products and management, entrepreneurial creativity, or trustworthiness (David 2001; Davison 2010).

Apart from the need for more research on images in annual reports, the visual studies conducted so far leave room for further investigations in specific areas. Since nearly all examine pictures separately from words and do not align visual with verbal analyses (Bell and Davison 2012), there is still limited insight into how messages are established through the multimodal relationships omnipresent in reporting genres such as the printed annual report, the company's reporting web pages or financial webcasts (e.g. de Groot 2008). Also, the interdisciplinary set of theories these studies often apply present substantial challenges for the conceptualisation of visual meaning, since it requires 'the skill and imagination to make leaps and connections, the need for adequate expertise in more than one discipline, with the accompanying risk of amateurism' (Pink, Kurti and Afonso 2004, in Bell and Davison 2012: 5). Despite the cross-pollination strength of interdisciplinarity, more demarcated theoretical frames would contribute to a more solid definition of visual analysis, of what it entails and why it is a research field in its own right like linguistic analysis is. Bell and Davison (2012) suggest, for example, that a first step in demarcating frameworks could involve categorisation of visual research by type of visual data used (e.g. still versus moving) or professional discipline (e.g. marketing, accounting). Except for some quantitative studies by Benschop and Meihuizen (2002), Bernardi et al. (2005) and Duff (2011), moreover, most analyses of annual report pictures rely on qualitative descriptions that can hardly be used for generalisations about pictorial meaning. The large number of qualitative studies is likely to be a logical result of 'the inherently ambiguous and polysemic nature of the visual' (Bell and Davison 2012: 4), which makes objective quantification of visual elements difficult. Quantitative studies of annual report pictures have often focused on rather straightforward content elements such as gender, colour of skin, formality of dress or formality of location. It appears that more detailed and rhetorical analyses of annual report pictures, e.g. of their structural and stylistic functionality, remain laborious and hard to validate (de Groot 2008). Future research on annual reports thus faces the challenge of developing theoretical and analytical frameworks that facilitate systematic and consistent analyses of pictures in relation to words.

Stakeholder response to annual reporting

The basic premise of corporate communication is that stakeholders provide material (e.g. finance, labour) as well as immaterial (e.g. positive word of mouth, reputation) resources which can be made accessible to a company through communication (Van Riel and Fombrun 2007). Accordingly, building stakeholder relationships is a fundamental motivation of corporate communication genres. While companies have long focused on profit maximisation and shareholder relationships in particular, since the 1980s there has been a growing awareness of companies' broader position in society and the multiple stakeholder groups they depend on and need to manage (Johansen and Nielsen 2011). This is also reflected in the composition of the stakeholder audience of specific IR genres such as the annual report, which presently addresses employees or suppliers besides private and institutional shareholders (e.g. Rowbottom and Lymer 2010). Bhattacharya, Korshun and Sen explain that the quality of company-stakeholder relationships 'is commensurate with the benefits stakeholders receive from their interactions with the company' (2009: 260). For corporate communication genres, it is therefore important that they express the mutual advantage of the association between company and stakeholder; they need to indicate that by contributing to the company's resources stakeholders are enabled and acquire personal benefits. This suggests that stakeholders should 'be addressed in relation to the stake(s) they hold and that communication must be adjusted to these stake(s)' (Johansen and Nielsen 2011: 206). The returns to stakeholder can be specified as functional (instrumental benefit), psycho-social (psycho-social well-being) and value-based (desirable end-state). Investors, for example, may consider stock returns a functional benefit, financial success a psycho-social benefit and personal accomplishment a value-based benefit. For employees, these benefits may include job retention, a secure professional life and safety, respectively (Bhattacharya et al. 2009; Johansen and Nielsen 2011).

Monitoring and tuning into stakeholder interests seems to be crucial to current corporate communication practices, given the rise of new media and the subsequent growth in stakeholder-generated messages. Online media cause 'less corporate control over stakeholder relations and easy communications between stakeholder groups', e.g. through online social networks or blogs (Aula 2010: 44). Here, dissatisfied stakeholders especially may form a reputation risk, as they can quickly and widely distribute their own unfavourable picture of the company. This implies that the messages companies *can* control, and which often are the basis for uncontrolled messages, had better be appealing to stakeholders (Argenti 2011). Hence the importance of stakeholder response research that provides insight into how a message can enhance stakeholder affiliation with the company.

Numerous studies have tested the effect of corporate communication messages in terms of corporate, brand or product attitudes, identification and behavioural intentions. Such studies have been carried out in particular by scholars in marketing communications (e.g. McQuarrie and Phillips 2005), but have also been regularly conducted within the disciplines of internal communications (e.g. Burmann, Zeplin and Riley 2009), and CSR communications (e.g. Sen, Bhattacharya and Korschun 2006). However, studies on stakeholders' message reception are still relatively uncommon in the IR discipline, which means that with regard to IR genres such as the annual report there is still a limited understanding of its effectiveness within corporate communication. Tregidga *et al.* argue that 'it would be interesting to know whether reporting information met or even exceeded readers' expectations' (2012: 227). Existent research on the response to annual reports has covered a limited set of verbal content and style features, and has involved only a few of the target groups of the genre. Several studies have identified positive investment effects of specific CSR information in annual reports (Alniacik, Alniacik and Genc 2011; Holm and Rikhardsson 2008; Milne and Patten 2002). Others have examined investors' investment intentions as well as their perceptions of management and corporate reputation in relation to annual report texts with distinctive cause-effect descriptions or (im)plausible performance explanations (Barton and Mercer 2005; Cianci and Kaplan 2010). Also, some studies have found that the accuracy of analyst disclosures is related to the readability of the company's annual reports (Lehavy, Li and Merkley 2011).

In the light of recent developments in corporate communication and IR, it appears that there are ample opportunities to extend the scope of research on the response to annual reports. Firstly, such research could focus for instance on the concepts of accountability and ethics. Drawing on Legitimacy Theory, these concepts refer to the social contract companies maintain with all their stakeholders. Presently, all corporate reporting – be it verbal or visual – is expected to include transparent reflections on the societal and environmental impacts of the company's activities and its responsibility for past and future performance. Previous studies have observed, however, that companies may manage these concepts rather creatively in annual reports, i.e. obfuscating negative information and avoiding responsibility (e.g. Hrasky 2012; Merkl-Davies and Koller 2012). To date, little is known about stakeholders' legitimacy perceptions of the verbal and visual messages in annual reporting. In order to fill this gap, future research could look into the effect of content and style in multimodal annual reports in terms of social concern, credibility, responsibility and/or openness in particular. Or, it could analyse what factors determine the legitimacy and accountability of annual report texts in the eyes of the stakeholders (Healy and Palepu 2001).

A related, under-explored research area involves stakeholder response to the tone of voice in annual report texts. Several studies have indicated that performance disclosures in annual reports may be characterised by a high degree of positive language and a good news bias, regardless of the corporate results. Whether stakeholders expect companies to express 'a robust attitude' towards reporting or prefer a factual representation, is still unclear; hence, there is room 'to begin the work of establishing how effective preparers' attempts to manage the language of such communication really are' (Rutherford 2005: 373, 374).

Thirdly, follow-up studies may consider stakeholder response to different corporate reporting media. Interactive and social media in particular seem to become increasingly important for reporting practices (Bonsón and Flores 2011). Research on the effect of financial reporting – in times of crisis – may be inspired for example by Schultz, Utz and Göritz (2011: 25), who found that crisis communication via Twitter elicited less negative stakeholder responses than blogs and newspaper articles. Existent annual report studies so far have examined the production and reception of one-way, print and website reporting only, which suggests that there is still considerable opportunity for the analysis of the effect of company engagement in 'firm-investor interactions and communications ... that are prevalent on ... social media platforms' (Saxton 2012: 289).

A fourth proposal for further research relates to the stakeholder audience of annual reports. Although there is evidence of the use of annual reports by non-financial audiences such as employees, customers or special interest groups (Rowbottom and Lymer 2010), response analyses have focused primarily on financial stakeholders. A full understanding of the actual usefulness of the annual report would thus require additional effect studies among internal, non-financial stakeholder audiences, who may have their own expectations with regard to the report's multimodal content and style.

A final suggestion for further analysis concerns the stakeholder-as-viewer. As has been discussed, the corporate story in annual reports is often told in part through pictures. These pictures generally aim to imprint qualitative impressions of the company in the minds of stakeholders (Davison 2010). Yet, 'the role of the viewer in creating interpretations' – for instance in relation to photographic content or style – has hardly received attention in the IR discipline (Bell and Davison 2012: 13).

Telling the corporate story in international annual reports

As markets and stakeholder audiences internationalise, research on the design and effect of multimodal corporate communication genres cannot ignore the potential intervention of culture-specific communication values and norms. Cultural studies have shown that particular social groups internalise such values and norms and can be distinguished from other social groups based on these values and norms (e.g. Hofstede 2001 in Hornikx and O'Keefe 2009). Within the *business* context, national culture can be defined as the set of social values, beliefs and conventions that underlie business objectives, structures, policies and relationships (Varner 2000). Drawing on corporate communication and genre theories, it can be argued that national culture is likely to have a fundamental impact on multinationals' communication activities: it can shape both the production and reception of these activities (e.g. Balmer and Wilson 1998; Bhatia 1993). From a *sender* viewpoint, national culture is an environmental feature that co-determines the company's identity – i.e. its soul or personality and management processes – and subsequently affects management's internal and external stories about the corporate identity (Cornelissen and Elving 2003). A vivid case in which culture functions as a frame of reference for corporate identity and corporate story involves British Airways: its personality is interwoven with Britishness – e.g. calmness, efficiency, politeness, sophistication – and its corporate visual identity, advertising and service encounters repeatedly emphasise its British heritage (Balmer, Stuart and Greyser 2009).

At the same time, cultural frames of reference also tend to play a role in the *receiver*'s interpretation of the corporate story. Successful transmission of the corporate story would mean that the receiver shares cultural reference frames with the corporate sender of the story and conceives of the story as recognisable, meaningful and (legally) protectable (e.g. Fox 2011). Miscommunication may occur, however, when receivers and senders rely on distinctive reference frames and have different expectations as to the intentions and design of the story. This can be explained based on Byrne's (1971) Similarity-Attraction paradigm, which assumes that individuals who feel similar to members in a group (e.g. the company) in terms of values, norms, attitudes and behaviours automatically experience attraction and desire towards that group (in Francis 1991). Whereas dissimilarity generally results in conflicts of understanding and in an individual's rejection of the other, 'perceived similarity between the self and the other may positively influence perceptions of liking, appropriateness, reliability, capability or cooperativeness' (de Groot *et al.* 2011: 5). Hence, more overlap between cultural reference frames is likely to facilitate the interpretation of intended meanings and to encourage positive reactions to corporate messages.

Research in marketing communications in particular has looked at the influence of cultural values and norms in the design and response to corporate communication genres (see for an overview Hornikx and O'Keefe 2009). The main question this research puts forward is whether international corporate messages are or should be (1) locally adapted as a result of pronounced cultural differences or (2) globalised as a result of a convergence of markets (e.g. Papavassiliou and Stathakopoulos 1997). Since the research results have been equivocal, the current status quo with regard to the adaptation-globalisation debate is that standardised messages are relevant whenever possible and adapted messages are relevant whenever required (cf. Taylor and Johnson 2002). Ambiguity with respect to the circumstances that determine or necessitate the adaptation and globalisation of corporate communication messages particularly remains within the areas of IR communications and corporate reporting. Here, limited knowledge is available on the role of culture in the across-the-border establishment of 'quality and meaning and ... accountability' (Tregidga *et al.* 2012: 226).

Existing research on the annual report genre has often omitted culture-related factors that may come into play when annual reports are produced and consumed in different nations. This is remarkable, given the importance multinationals ascribe to the (English) annual report for 'communicating corporate image and performances over a large international audience and the opening of markets' (Maitra and Goswami 1995: 198). Effectively interfacing with stakeholders from different cultural backgrounds is thus crucial to the success of the annual report. So far, cross-cultural comparisons of *design* have focused on the overall disclosure of financial and non-financial information in US and European annual reports (e.g. Meek *et al.* 1995) or have specifically documented the verbal and visual themes in annual report texts from Europe and the Americas (e.g. Conaway and Wardrope 2010; de Groot *et al.* 2006). Others have identified culture-dependent disclosures on CSR activities and corporate strategy in European or emerging markets (e.g. Alon *et al.* 2010; Santema *et al.* 2005). Contrastive *reader response* analyses where stakeholders evaluate annual report messages including local versus foreign communication conventions are particularly rare. Only a few studies have compared the effects of these conventions, for instance with regard to preferences for distinctive verbal information or pictorial style among European, American and Asian readers (de Groot *et al.* 2011; Van der Laan-Smith *et al.* 2010; Maitra and Goswami 1995).

Both the design and response studies have observed shared as well as culture-specific preferences for annual reporting practices. But the basis for concluding that companies should therefore consider cultural subtleties 'when relating "universal" financial information to stakeholders with different perspectives' (Conaway and Wardrope 2010: 144) is still rather thin. Accordingly, further multicultural research is needed to substantiate insight into the convergence or divergence of corporate story constructions and interpretations among annual report users. For example, successive analyses could specifically compare the design of annual reports originating in emerging and emerged markets, or investigate the effect of Western-based annual reports among stakeholders in emerging markets. In addition to measuring the response to annual report texts and images across cultures, future research could also look at the cross-cultural effectiveness of corporate reporting media. Recent studies have shown, for instance, that stakeholders from different cultures engage more or less actively in new media such as social networking sites (Shu-Chuan and Sejung 2011). This suggests that the success of social media platforms aimed at encouraging the sharing of financial information is likely to be culture-dependent.

Conclusion

The present chapter set out to identify several of the theoretical and analytical issues scholars in the fields of corporate communication and corporate reporting currently face or may wish to deal with in the future. As was shown, many of these issues stem from recent developments in international stakeholder demands, new media, corporate accountability and integrated communications. Management-based sources were used to explain the role of corporate reporting within the broader corporate communication frame. These academic sources indicated that corporate reporting – the annual report in particular – helps to make manifest the corporate identity and to establish images and reputations. As such, the chapter has illustrated that the annual report genre is an integral part of a multinational's total set of international communication activities for internal as well as external stakeholders.

The literature review has pointed out that the analysis of the rhetorical potential of the annual report – like the analysis of other corporate communication genres – rests on several fundamental theoretical assumptions, related to signalling theory, social identity theory, and genre theory. While considering these fundamental assumptions, moreover, it has shown that specific areas for further research may require specific theoretical approaches. The annual report's relationships with other corporate communication genres that constitute the corporate story, for instance, can be mapped with the help of theoretical insights into intertextuality and interdiscursivity. Additionally, an analytical frame combining semiotics, rhetorical theory and sociology would seem to enable the systematic identification of visual communication in annual reports. And response analyses that focus on the perceptions stakeholders hold toward the company based on the annual report, may draw on stakeholder theory or legitimacy theory. Finally, the chapter proposed that cultural studies and the similarity-attraction paradigm form relevant starting points for the analyses of the design and effect of international annual reports. Thus, the literature review suggests that future annual reporting research – seen within a corporate communication frame – requires a highly interdisciplinary approach.

The discussion of the role of annual reports within corporate communication also points to suggestions for future research that may be applicable to other genres in IR or additional corporate communication disciplines. This is because these genres are subject to similar developments and pressures in today's corporate communication. For example, genres in CSR communication such as the company's sustainability report are also conditioned by multimedia trends, increased stakeholder activism, and internationalisation of a broad stakeholder audience (e.g. authorities, special interest groups). Therefore, the chapter has indirectly opened up opportunities for further investigations beyond the scope of the annual report genre.

Related topics

corporate communication genres; interdiscursivity; multimodality; stakeholder response; cultural context

Key readings

Cho, C. H., Phillips, J. R., Hageman, A. M. and Patten, D. M. (2009). 'Media richness, user trust, and perceptions of corporate social responsibility: An experimental investigation of visual web site disclosures', *Accounting, Auditing & Accountability Journal*, 22(6), 933–52. (Financial stakeholders participate in an experiment that measures their response to different levels of visual and interactive online reporting.)

Haigh, M. M., Brubaker, P. and Whiteside, E. (2013). 'Facebook: Examining the information presented and its impact on stakeholders', *Corporate Communications, An International Journal*, 18(1), 52–69. (Investor relations research can be inspired by this study, which investigates the information companies present on Facebook and its impact on stakeholders.)

Helm, S. (2007). 'The role of corporate reputation in determining investor satisfaction and loyalty', *Corporate Reputation Review*, 10(1), 22–37. (A marketing scholar analyses the interplay between corporate reputation, satisfaction of investors, and investor loyalty.)

Hooghiemstra, R. (2003). *The Construction of Reality*. Rotterdam, ERIM. (This study is based on the notion that accounting narratives are intended to impression-manage; it includes a cross-cultural comparison of reporting style in the US, the Netherlands and Japan.)

Van der Laan Smith, J., Adhikari, A. and Tondkar, R. H. (2005). 'Exploring differences in social disclosures internationally: A stakeholder perspective.' *Journal of Accounting and Public Policy*, 24(2), 123–51. (The authors provide a contextual rationale for the comparative analysis of reporting content across the US and Scandinavia.)

Bibliography

Alniacik, U., Alniacik, E. and Genc, N. (2011). 'How corporate social responsibility information influences stakeholders' intentions', *Corporate Social Responsibility and Environmental Management*, 18, 234–45.

Alon, I., Lattemann, C., Fetscherin, M., Li, S. and Schneider, M.-A. (2010). 'Usage of public corporate communications of social responsibility in Brazil, Russia, India and China (BRIC)', *International Journal of Emerging Markets*, 5(1), 6–22.

Anderson, C. J. and Imperia, G. (1992). 'The corporate annual report: A photo analysis of male and female portrayals', *Journal of Business Communication*, 29(2), 113–28.

Argenti, P. A. (2011). 'Digital strategies for powerful corporate communications', *The European Financial Review*, February–March, 61–64.

Aspara, J. and Tikkanen, H. (2011). 'Corporate marketing in the stock market: The impact of company identification on individuals' investment behaviour', *European Journal of Marketing*, 45(9/10), 1446–69.

Aula, P. (2010). 'Social media, reputation risk and ambient publicity management', *Strategy & Leadership*, 38(6), 43–49.

Balmer, J. M. T. and Wilson, A. (1998). 'Corporate identity: There is more to it than meets the eye', *International Studies of Management and Organisations*, 28(3), 12–31.

Balmer, J. M. T., Stuart, H. and Greyser, S. A. (2009). 'Aligning identity and strategy: Corporate branding at British Airways in the late twentieth century', *California Management Review*, 51(3), 6–23.

Barton, J. and Mercer, M. (2005). 'To blame or not to blame: Analysts' reactions to explanations of poor management performance', *Journal of Accounting and Economics*, 39, 509–33.

Bell, E. and Davison, J. (2012). 'Visual management studies: Empirical and theoretical approaches', *International Journal of Management Reviews*, doi: 10.1111/j.1468–2370.2012.00342.x

Benschop, Y. and Meihuizen, H. E. (2002). 'Keeping up gendered appearances: Representations of gender in financial annual reports', *Accounting, Organizations and Society*, 27(7), 611–36.

Bernardi, R. A., Bean, D. F. and Weippert, K. M. (2005). 'Minority membership on boards of directors: The case for requiring pictures of boards in annual reports', *Critical Perspectives on Accounting*, 16(8), 1019–33.

Bhatia, V. (1993). *Analysing Genre: Language Use in Professional Settings*, London: Longman.

——(2008). 'Genre analysis, ESP and professional practice', *English for Specific Purposes*, 2, 161–74.

——(2010). 'Interdiscursivity in professional communication', *Discourse and Communication*, 21(1), 32–50.

Bhattacharya, C., Korschun, D. and Sen, S. (2009). 'Strengthening stakeholder–company relationships through mutually beneficial corporate social responsibility initiatives', *Journal of Business Ethics*, 85, 257–72.

Bonsón, E. and Flores, F. (2011). 'Social media and corporate dialogue: The response of global financial institutions', *Online Information Review*, 35(1), 34–49.

Bosch, A. L. M. van den, de Jong, M. D. T. and Elving, W. J. L. (2005). 'How corporate visual identity supports reputation', *Corporate Communications: An International Journal*, 10(2), 108–16.

Burmann, C., Zeplin, S. and Riley, N. (2009). 'Key determinants of internal brand management success: An exploratory empirical analysis', *Journal of Brand Management*, 16(4), 264–84.

Cable, D. M. and Turban, D. B. (2003). 'The value of organizational reputation in the recruitment context: A brand equity perspective', *Journal of Applied Social Psychology*, 33, 2244–66.

Campbell, D., McPhail, K. and Slack, R. (2009). 'Face work in annual reports: A study of the management of encounter through annual reports, informed by Levinas and Bauman', *Accounting, Auditing & Accountability Journal*, 22(6), 907–32.

Catenaccio, P. (2008) 'Press releases as a hybrid genre: Addressing the informative/promotional conundrum', *Pragmatics*, 18(1), 9–31.

Christensen, L. T. and Cornelissen, C. (2011). 'Bridging corporate and organizational communication: Review, development and a look to the future', *Management Communication Quarterly*, 25(3), 383–414.

Christensen, L. T., Morsing, M. and Cheney, G. (2008). *Corporate Communications: Convention, Complexity, and Critique*, Los Angeles, London etc.: Sage.

Chun, R. (2005). 'Corporate reputation: Meaning and measurement', *International Journal of Management Reviews*, 7(2), 91–109.

Cianci, A. A. and Kaplan, S. E. (2010). 'The effect of CEO reputation and explanations for poor performance on investors' judgments about the company's future performance and management', *Accounting, Organizations and Society*, 35, 478–95.

Clatworthy, M. and Jones, M. J. (2001). 'The effect of thematic structure on the variability of annual report readability', *Accounting, Auditing & Accountability Journal*, 14(3), 311–26.

Conaway, R. N. and Wardrope, W. J. (2010) 'Do their words really matter? Thematic analysis of U.S. and Latin American CEO letters', *Journal of Business Communication*, 47(2), 141–68.

Cornelissen, J. P. (2011). *Corporate Communications: A Guide to Theory and Practice* (3rd edn), London: Sage Publications, Ltd.

Cornelissen, J. P. and Elving, W. J. L. (2003). 'Managing corporate identity: An integrative framework of dimensions and determinants', *Corporate Communications: An International Journal*, 8(2), 114–120.

Courtis, J. K. (2004). 'Corporate report obfuscation: Artefact or phenomenon?' *British Accounting Review*, 36(3), 291–312.

Courtright, J. L. and Smudde, P. M. (2009). 'Leveraging organizational innovation for strategic reputation management', *Corporate Reputation Review*, 12(3), 245–69.

Crawford Camiciottoli, B. (2010). 'Earnings calls: Exploring an emerging financial reporting genre', *Discourse and Communication*, 4(4), 343–59.

David, C. (2001). 'Mythmaking in annual reports', *Journal of Business and Technical Communication*, 15(2), 195–222.

Davison, J. (2009). 'Icon, iconography, iconology: Visual branding, banking and the case of the bowler hat', *Accounting, Auditing & Accountability Journal*, 22(6), 883–906.

——(2010). '[In]visible [in]tangibles: Visual portraits of the business élite', *Accounting, Organizations and Society*, 35(2), 165–83.

Devitt, A. J. (1991). 'Intertextuality in tax accounting: Generic, referential, and functional', in C. Bazerman and J. Paradis (eds), *Textual Dynamics of the Professions*, Madison: University of Wisconsin Press.

Ditlevsen, M. G. (2012). 'Revealing corporate identities in annual reports', *Corporate Communications: An International Journal*, 17(3), 379–403.

Dolphin, R. R. (2004). 'The strategic role of investor relations', *Corporate Communications: An International Journal*, 9(1), 25–42.

Duff, A. (2011). 'Big four accounting firms' annual reviews: A photo analysis of gender and race portrayals', *Critical Perspectives on Accounting*, 22(1), 20–38.

Elving, W., van Ruler, B., Goodman, M. and Genest, C. (2012). 'Communication management in the Netherlands: Trends, developments, and benchmark with US study', *Journal of Communication Management*, 16(2), 112–32.

Fox, R. (2011). 'Naming an organisation: A (socio)linguistic perspective', *Corporate Communications: An International Journal*, 16(1), 65–80.

Francis, J. N. P. (1991). 'When in Rome? The effects of cultural adaptation on intercultural business negotiations', *Journal of International Business Studies*, 22(3), 403–28.

Garzone, G. (2005). 'Letters to the shareholders and chairman's statements: textual variability and generic integrity', in P. Gillaerts and M. Gotti (eds), *Genre Variation in Business Letters* (pp. 179–204), Bern, etc.: Peter Lang.

Geppert, J. and Lawrence, J. E. (2008). 'Predicting firm reputation through content analysis of shareholders' letter', *Corporate Reputation Review*, 11(4), 285–307.

Gill, D. R. (2011). 'Using storytelling to maintain employee loyalty during change', *International Journal of Business and Social Science*, 2(15), 23–32.

Goodman, M. B. (2012). 'Transformation and the corporate communication profession', *Corporate Communications: An International Journal*, 17(3), 233–40.

Gray, E. R. and Balmer, J. M. T. (1998). 'Managing corporate image and corporate reputation', *Long Range Planning*, 31(5), 695–702.

Groot, E. B. de (2008). *English Annual Reports in Europe: A Study on the Identification and Reception of Genre Characteristics in Multimodal Annual Reports Originating in the Netherlands and in the United Kingdom*, Published PhD thesis, Nijmegen/Utrecht: Radboud University Nijmegen/LOT.

Groot, E. B. de, Korzilius, H., Nickerson, C. and Gerritsen, M. (2006). 'A corpus analysis of text themes and photographic themes in managerial forewords of Dutch-English and British annual general reports', *IEEE Transactions on Professional Communication*, 49(3), 217–35.

Groot, E. B. de, Korzilius, H., Gerritsen, M. and Nickerson, C. (2011) 'There's no place like home: UK-based financial analysts' response to Dutch-English and British-English annual report texts', *IEEE Transactions on Professional Communication*, 54(1), 1–17.

Hatch, M. J. and Schultz, M. (2003). 'Bringing the corporation into corporate branding', *European Journal of Marketing*, 37(7/8), 1041–64.

Healy, P. and Palepu, K. (2001). 'Information asymmetry, corporate disclosure, and the capital markets: A review of the empirical disclosure literature', *Journal of Accounting and Economics*, 31, 405–40.

Hendriks, B. and Mulken, M. van (2012). 'Dear worker: A corpus analysis of internal CEO's letters', in P. Gillaerts and E. B. de Groot (eds), *Researching Discourse in Business Genres. Cases and Corpora* (pp. 73–95), Bern, etc.: Peter Lang.

Henry, E. (2008). 'Are investors influenced by how earnings press releases are written?' *Journal of Business Communication*, 45(4), 363–407.

Hoffmann, C. and Fieseler, C. (2012). 'Investor relations beyond financials: Non-financial factors and capital market image building', *Corporate Communications: An International Journal*, 17(2), 138–55.

Hofstede, G. (2001). *Culture's Consequences: Comparing Values, Behaviors, Institutions, and Organizations Across Nations* (2nd edn), Thousand Oaks, CA: Sage.

Holm, C. and Rikhardsson, P. (2008). 'Experienced and novice investors: Does environmental information influence investment allocation decisions?' *European Accounting Review*, 17(3), 537–57.

Hooghiemstra, R. (2008). 'East–West differences in attributions for company performance', *Journal of Cross-Cultural Psychology*, 39(5), 618–29.

Hornikx, J. and O'Keefe, D. J. (2009). 'Adapting consumer advertising appeals to cultural values: A meta-analytic review of effects on persuasiveness and ad liking', *Communication Yearbook*, 33, 39–71.

Hrasky, S. (2012). 'Visual disclosure strategies adopted by more and less sustainability-driven companies', *Accounting Forum*, 36(3), 154–65.

Hussainey, K. and Salama, A. (2010). 'The importance of corporate environmental reputation to investors', *Journal of Applied Accounting Research*, 11(3), 229–41.

Hyland, K. (1998). 'Exploring corporate rhetoric: Metadiscourse in the CEO's letter', *Journal of Business Communication*, 35(2), 224–44.

Johansen, T. S. and Nielsen, A. E. (2011). 'Strategic stakeholder dialogues: A discursive perspective on relationship building', *Corporate Communications: An International Journal*, 16(3), 204–17.

Johansen, T. S. and Andersen, S. E. (2012). 'Co-creating ONE: Rethinking integration within communication', *Corporate Communications: An International Journal*, 17(3), 272–88.

Kress, G. and van Leeuwen, T. (2001). *Multimodal Discourse: The Modes and Media of Contemporary Communication*, London: Arnold.

Lehavy, R., Li, F. and Merkley, K. (2011). 'The effect of annual report readability on analyst following and the properties of their earnings forecasts', *The Accounting Review*, 86(3), 1087–115.

Maitra, K. and Goswami, D. (1995). 'Responses of American readers to visual aspects of a mid-sized Japanese company's annual report: A case study', *IEEE Transactions on Professional Communication*, 38(4), 197–203.

McKinstry, S. (1996). 'Designing the annual reports of Burton PLC from 1930 to 1994', *Accounting, Organizations and Society*, 21(1), 89–111.

McQuarrie, E. F. and Phillips, B. J. (2005). 'Indirect persuasion in advertising: How consumers process metaphors presented in pictures and words', *Journal of Advertising*, 34(2), 7–20.

Meek, G. K., Roberts, C. B. and Gray, S. J. (1995). 'Factors influencing voluntary annual report disclosures by U.S., U.K. and continental European multinational corporations', *Journal of International Business Studies*, 26(3), 555–72.

Merkl-Davies, D. M. and Koller, V. (2012). '"Metaphoring" people out of this world: A Critical Discourse Analysis of a chairman's statement of a UK defence firm', *Accounting Forum*, 36(3), 178–93.

Merkl-Davies, D. M., Brennan, N. M. and McLeay, S. J. (2011). 'Impression management and retrospective sense-making in corporate narratives: A social psychology perspective', *Accounting, Auditing & Accountability Journal*, 24(3), 315–44.

Milne, M. J. and Patten, D. M. (2002). 'Securing organizational legitimacy: An experimental decision case examining the impact of environmental disclosures', *Accounting, Auditing & Accountability Journal*, 15(3), 372–405.

Osborne, J. D., Stubbart, C. I. and Ramaprasad, A. (2001). 'Strategic groups and competitive enactment: A study of dynamic relationships between mental models and performance', *Strategic Management Journal*, 22(5), 435–54.

Papavassiliou, N. and Stathakopoulos, V. (1997). 'Standardization versus adaptation of international advertising strategies: Towards a framework', *European Journal of Marketing*, 37(7), 504–27.

Pink, S., Kurti, L. and Afonso, A. I. (eds) (2004). *Working Images: Visual Research and Representation in Ethnography*, London: Routledge.

Preston, A. M., Wright, C. and Young, J. J. (1996). 'Imag[in]ing annual reports', *Accounting, Organizations and Society*, 21(1), 113–37.

Preston, A. M. and Young, J. J. (2000). 'Constructing the global corporation and corporate constructions of the global: A picture essay', *Accounting, Organizations and Society*, 25(4–5), 427–49.

Riel, C. B. M. van and Fombrun, C. J. (2007). *Essentials of Corporate Communication: Implementing Practices for Effective Reputation Management*, New York: Routledge.

Rowbottom, N. and Lymer, A. (2010). 'Exploring the use and users of narrative reporting in the online annual report', *Journal of Applied Accounting Research*, 11(2), 90–108.

Rutherford, B. A. (2005). 'Genre analysis of corporate annual report narratives: A corpus linguistics-based approach', *Journal of Business Communication*, 42(4), 349–78.

Salzer-Mörling, M. and Strannegård, L. (2004). 'Silence of the brands', *European Journal of Marketing*, 38(1/2), 224–38.

Santema, S., Hoekert, M., Van de Rijt, J. and Van Oijen, A. (2005). 'Strategy disclosure in annual reports across Europe: A study on differences between five countries', *European Business Review*, 17(4), 352–66.

Saxton, G. D. (2012). 'New media and external accounting information: A critical review', *Australian Accounting Review*, 22, 286–302.

Schultz, F., Utz, S. and Göritz, A. (2011). 'Is the medium the message? Perceptions of and reactions to crisis communication via Twitter, blogs and traditional media', *Public Relations Review*, 37(1), 20–27.

Scott, P. B. (2012). 'How is the study of communication changing?' *Corporate Communications: An International Journal*, 17(3), 350–57.

Sen, S., Bhattacharya, C. B. and Korschun, D. (2006). 'The role of corporate social responsibility in strengthening multiple stakeholder relationships: A field experiment', *Journal of the Academy of Marketing Science*, 34(2), 158–66.

Shu-Chuan, C. and Sejung, M. C. (2011). 'Electronic word-of-mouth in social networking sites: A cross-cultural study of the United States and China', *Journal of Global Marketing*, 24(3), 263–81.

Smith, K. T., Smith, M. and Wang, K. (2010). 'Does brand management of corporate reputation translate into higher market value?' *Journal of Strategic Marketing*, 18(3), 201–21.

Solbjørg Skulstad, A. (1996). 'Rhetorical organization in chairmen's statements', *International Journal of Applied Linguistics*, 6(1), 43–62.

Stanton, P. and Stanton, J. (2002). 'Corporate annual reports: Research perspectives used', *Accounting, Auditing & Accountability Journal*, 15(4), 478–500.

Taylor, C.R. and Johnson, C. (2002). 'Standardized vs. specialized international advertising campaigns: What we have learned from academic research in the 1990s', *New Directions in International Advertising Research*, 12, 45–66.

Torp, S. (2009). 'Integrated communications, from one look to normative consistency', *Corporate Communications: An International Journal*, 14(2), 190–206.

Tregidga, H., Milne, M. and Lehman, G. (2012). 'Analyzing the quality, meaning and accountability of organizational reporting and communication: Directions for future research', *Accounting Forum*, 36(3), 223–30.

Tsang, E. W. K. (2002). 'Self-serving attributions in corporate annual reports: A replicated study', *Journal of Management Studies*, 39(1), 51–65.

Van der Laan Smith, J., Adhikari, A., Tondkar, R. H. and Andrews, R. L. (2010). 'The impact of corporate social disclosure on investment behavior: A cross-national study', *Journal of Accounting and Public Policy*, 29(2), 177–92.

Varner, I. I. (2000). 'The theoretical foundation for intercultural business communication: A conceptual model', *Journal of Business Communication*, 37(1), 39–57.

Walsh, G., Mitchell, V., Jackson, P. and Beatty, S. (2009). 'Examining the antecedents and consequences of corporate reputation: A customer perspective', *British Journal of Management*, 20(2), 187–203.

Section 2

Practice

A. Pedagogic perspectives

17
A blended needs analysis
Critical genre analysis and needs analysis of language and communication for professional purposes

Jane Lung

> If a group of learners' needs for a language can be accurately specified, then this specification can be used to determine the content of a language program that will meet these needs.
>
> *(Widdowson 1981: 1)*

Introduction

The rapidly changing world of work has caused profound and fundamental changes to work practices, employment and recruitment patterns, and the need to develop new vocational skills, such as language, literacy, communication and learning to learn. It is thus putting greater demands and challenges on the competencies of employees in the workplace as well as on their trainers.

Globalisation has also created an increasing demand for effective communication and proficiency in English (Candlin 2006; Huhta 2010; Sajavaara 2006; Takala 2008). In recent years a trend has emerged whereby the communicative needs of students and what they need to do with the language have very much come to the fore. Thus, instead of just examining linguistic structures and lexicons when designing ESP (English for Specific Purposes) or English for Professional Communication Purposes (EPCP) or Language for Specific Purposes (LSP) courses, detailed empirical analysis of language situations in actual language use is now being brought into play. In this way the specific learner-needs for communication in a particular situation are analysed and instructional materials gathered accordingly. Such factors as the reasons for learning, anticipated place and time of usage, those whom the speaker will likely interact with, activities involved, skills needed (e.g. listening, speaking, reading, writing, translation) are all taken into consideration in what could be called a 'needs analysis'. However, this chapter aims at going one step further by showing how critical genre analysis (CGA) also needs to be applied in order to assist in determining what the actual 'needs' are.

The theory of needs analysis

Needs analysis emerged in the 1960s and became important with the increasing demand for specialised language programmes in the 1970s, especially in the field of business and industry. It is considered as 'a necessary step' to be taken before developing an ESP course, the idea being that it is important to 'design a foreign language course which is relevant and as efficient as possible for the target group' (Koster 2004: 5). However, it is also used for very general purposes to obtain 'information both on the individual and groups of individuals who are to learn a new language and on the use which they are expected to make of it when they have learnt it' (Richterich 1983: 2) or simply as 'a procedure for establishing the specific needs for learners' (Ellis 2003: 345–46).

Mountford (1981) identifies three sets of methodological problems in relation to needs analysis: (i) the problem of perception (whose needs), (ii) the problem of principle (the content in the needs analysis) and (iii) the problem of practice (how the needs analysis is undertaken). As the concept of needs appears elusive, Van Hest and Oud-de Glas (1990) state that such a concept must be defined before any foreign language needs are identified, and they relate needs analysis to the subject of needs (requirers/users), the character of needs (use, lack, key asset) and the object of needs (language, skills situations and linguistic content). Brown looks at needs analysis from an educational perspective and maintains that it is

> the systematic collection and analysis of all subjective and objective information necessary to define and validate defensible curriculum purposes that satisfy the language learning requirements of students within the context of the particular institutions that influence the learning and teaching situation.
>
> *(2006: 102)*

However, Hyland (2003) sees needs analysis from the utilisation perspective and suggests that different methodologies be utilised to evaluate the findings of needs analysis before, during and after a language course.

In view of this, needs analysis is also called needs assessment, which is used to collect information for curriculum development that will meet the needs of a particular group of learners. Its main purpose is filling in the 'gap' of what a language programme 'lacks' (Brown 1995; Songhori 2008). Richards (2001: 51) considers needs analysis 'as procedures used to collect information about learners' needs'. While needs analysis is used to collect and analyse data in order to determine what learners 'want' and 'need' to learn, Soriano (1995) points out that it is also an evaluation to measure the effectiveness of a programme and whether the programme meets the needs of the learners. To identify what learners have to know and what learners feel they need to know, Hutchinson and Waters (1992) define needs analysis on the basis of 'necessities' and 'wants'. The main purpose is to fill in the 'gap' of the learners' required proficiency in the target situation and their existing proficiency. In view of this, Witkin and Altschuld (1995) define needs analysis as a 'gap' between 'what is' and 'what should be', focusing on the current state of affairs and the desired state of affairs. All these definitions provide the concept of needs analysis around the terms 'necessities', 'lacks', 'wants' and 'gaps'. While needs refers to a target situation or goal situation, the learning refers to a process or a product.

Brindley (1984) describes needs as subjective or objective, and Vandermeeren (2005) further subdivides language needs into subjective need, unconscious need, subjective unmet need and objective unmet need. When defining a subjective need, it emerges that such is the case when an employee feels the need for a foreign language but has not (yet) been faced with a real work situation where it is needed. An unconscious need might arise when a manager claims, for example, that the department does not need a foreign language yet some people in the department deal with customers speaking that language. Further, reports of difficulties, when using a foreign language, as for example from secretaries, may be symptoms of subjective unmet needs. On the other hand, an objective unmet need could be identified if a company enters a new market and does not have any speakers of that language.

Dudley-Evans and St John (1998) summarise the content of needs analysis:

A Professional information about the learners in relation to the target situation and the objective needs
B Personal information about the learners in relation to their wants, means and subjective needs as well as factors affecting their learning such as learning experience and cultural information
C Target language information about the learners to analyse their present situation
D The gap between (A) and (C) to understand what the learner lacks
E Language learning information to identify the learners' learning needs and how they can learn effectively
F Professional communication information about the target situation by conducting linguistic analysis, discourse analysis, genre analysis
G Learner preferences such as what participants want from the course
H Information about the environment in which the course will be run by conducting means analysis

In addition to the above components, objective needs also include the needs of the company, the professional field and the societal situation.

From the foregoing it can thus be seen that needs analysis involves gathering material that can form the basis of a curriculum that will fit the needs of a particular group of students, the needs involving tests, materials, teaching activities and evaluation strategies, the analysis, and measures of effectiveness i.e. establishing the extent to which the resulting programme meets those learners' needs. In the matter of needs, however, teachers, learners, administrators, employees and other stakeholders may all have different ideas as to what these are. Other common factors, such as staffing, time and cultural attitudes can also be taken into consideration when conducting a 'needs analysis'. Research studies in needs analysis in ESL and EFL settings include both academic ESP programmes (Al-Busaidi 2003; Bosher and Smalkowski 2002; Eggly et al. 1999; Rattanapinyowong et al. 1988; Shi et al. 2001) and professional ESP programmes (Al-Bazzaz 1994; Al-Gorashi 1988; Almulhim 2001).

In relation to the sources of needs analysis information, Chambers (1980: 27) states, 'Whoever determines needs largely determines which needs are determined'. While learners are usually considered as the primary source of information (Auerbach and Burgess 1985), Long (2005) questions the sufficiency of the information given because 'pre-experience' or 'pre-service' learners may not understand what will be expected in the workplace. He suggests that other sources may be considered, including 'in-service' informants and professionals working in expert positions; experienced teachers; subject specialists; applied linguists; written sources in the field; and employers such as managers, foremen and human resources departments (Long 2005).

Needs analysis methods

As to the methods used to determine the needs of the individuals involved, Long (2005) provides a comprehensive classification of language needs analysis methods. Surveys may be conducted, interviews engaged in and non-expert intuitions as well as expert intuitions brought into play. At the same time, language audits, participant and non-participant observations, diaries, journals and logs may also be formulated. Finally, content analysis, register analysis, computer-aided corpus analysis and triangulation analysis all share in arriving at a needs analysis.

Approaches to needs analysis

In regard to the foregoing, different models involving different methods have approached the field of 'needs analysis'. In the mid-1970s, linguistic and register analyses were used as needs were seen as discrete language items of vocabulary and grammar. However, Munby's Communicative Syllabus in 1978 put the focus of needs analysis on the learner's needs and consequently the notions of target needs and situation have become prominent. The main three approaches are defined as target-situation analysis (TSA), present situation analysis (PSA) and pedagogic needs analysis (PNA).

Target situation analysis (TSA) started with Munby's (1978) model of the Communication Needs Process, which detailed a set of procedures for discovering target situation needs, such as (1) *Why is the language needed?* (2) *How will the language be used?* (3) *What will the content areas be?* (4) *Where will the language be used?* (5) *When will the language be used?* These questions provide a communicative needs profile for a specified group of learners, thus specifying the skills and linguistic forms needed in the target situation. It consists of nine components: participant, purposive domain, setting, interaction, instrumentality, dialect, target level, communicative event, and communicative key. Questions in relation to each of these components are asked about the use of the target language in order to identify the learner's real world communicative requirements. In this way preparation is made for the learner's future use of the language by converting the needs profile into a communicative competence specification presented in the form of a syllabus (Jordan 1997).

In respects to 'needs analysis' and in order to provide a general profile of the language situation to be used as input for the actual course design, the four skills (i.e. listening, speaking, reading and writing) are analysed along with the various job-related activities in terms of receptive and productive skills (Jordan 1997). In language teaching such information guides the classroom teaching process and enables priorities to be set. For example, the interpersonal mode is used to link the receptive and productive skills with the interpretive mode relying on receptive skills and the presentational mode (Brecht and Walton 1995).

Present situation analysis (PSA), proposed by Richterich and Chancerel (1980), provides a second major model of needs analysis and functions as a complement to TSA (Robinson 1991; Jordan 1997) because it attempts to identify what learners are like at the beginning of a language course and 'estimates strengths and weaknesses in language, skills, learning experiences' (Dudley-Evans and St John 1998: 125). The learners themselves, the teaching establishment, and the user-institution such as place of work are considered as the sources of information (Jordan 1997). Data from these can provide information about the learners' present abilities.

Thus, needs analysis may be seen as a combination of TSA and PSA. However, to enhance learning and to achieve the desired goals, other approaches such as pedagogic needs analysis have been proposed.

West's (1998) pedagogic needs analysis (PNA) contains three elements of needs analysis: deficiency analysis, strategy analysis or learning needs analysis, and means analysis. He argues that PNA can compensate for the shortcomings of TSA by collecting data about the learner and the learning environment. Deficiency analysis can be matched with what Hutchinson and Waters (1987) define as lacks and it considers learners' present needs or wants as the route to cover from the point in the present situation to a point in the target situation. Strategy analysis or learning needs analysis is concerned with the learner's view of learning and gives information about what the learner needs to do in order to learn. Allwright (1982 cited in West 1994), a pioneer in the field of strategy analysis, maintains that the examination of learners' preferred learning styles and strategies offers a picture of the learners' conception of learning. Means analysis gives information about the environment in which the course will be run (Dudley-Evans and St John 1998), and the practicalities and constraints in implementing needs-based language courses (West 1998). Swales (1989 cited in West 1994) lists five factors relating to the learning environment that should be considered by curriculum specialists: (1) classroom culture; (2) EAP staff; (3) pilot target situation analysis; (4) status of service operations; (5) study of change agents.

In subsequent years, discourse analysis shifted attention to finding out how sentences were combined into discourse, resulting in a textual focus on the level above the sentence. On the basis of his observations, West (1998) maintains that although the discourse analysis approach concentrates more on how sentences are used when communicating, it only offers limited guidance on how these units fit together to form texts. Thus, the shortcoming of the discourse analysis approach is that it does not take sufficient account of the academic or professional context in which communication takes place (Dudley-Evans and St John 1998; Songhori 2008). Nevertheless, the discourse analysis approach has a bearing on needs analysis when the context or setting is stipulated.

Interestingly, Bhatia (1993) states that the main benefit of a genre approach to teaching and learning specialist English is to see the relevant connection between the use of language on one hand and the purpose of communication on the other. He also encourages the need to be aware of why the members of a specialist discourse community use language the way they do. Flowerdew (2011) comments that most ESP practitioners view genres as action, in other words as staged, purposeful, communicative events. Thus Bhatia (1993) views genre analysis as the study of linguistic behaviour in an academic or professional setting, or, put another way, as language in action; because genre analysis takes communicative purposes into account, it is useful in analysing what constitutes needs analysis.

Bhatia, in more recent works (2008, 2010, 2012 and this volume) advocates critical genre analysis (CGA), a specific approach to the study of genre, as a further stage in the development of written discourse studies. 'Critical genre theory offers a complementary methodological alternative in the form of a discourse-based investigation of a range of professional, organizational and institutional practices' (2010: 466). In his 2004 work he describes the historical development of written discourse analysis, showing how it is accomplished at three stages: textualisation, organisation, and contextualisation. He explains that contextualisation includes both the immediate text and the context in which the text is placed, and that it incorporates both the communicative purpose and the communicative context (Bhatia 2004). He also proposes a multi-dimensional and multi-perspective view of genre analysis, which includes three overlapping spaces of analysis: (1) Textual Space, where discourse can be analysed as text and as textual knowledge; (2) Socio-Cognitive Space, where discourse can be analysed as genre and as genre knowledge on the one hand, and as professional expertise and as professional practice on the other; (3) Social Space, where discourse can be analysed as social practice and as social pragmatic knowledge. The multi-perspective view presents two opposite poles: the pedagogical perspective on the one end of the continuum (going from the text towards the social practice) and socio-critical perspective on the other end (going from the social practice towards the text) (see Bhatia 2004: 19, for details). Moving from text to context and from discursive to professional practice, Bhatia (2007 and 2008) moves a step further towards critical genre analysis, which, as he points out, focuses on professional practice, suggesting interdiscursive links between discursive and professional practices in the context of specific professional, corporate and institutional cultures. (See Bhatia 2010 for a detailed account of interdiscursivity in professional genres.)

Critical genre analysis (CGA) is thus an approach

> to the analysis of professional genres, while at the same, extending the scope of the construction, interpretation and use of professional genres by focusing on the academic and professional 'practices' that most academics and professional experts are engaged in as part of their daily routine within what Bhatia (2010) calls 'socio-pragmatic space' in which such professional genres invariably function.
>
> *(Bhatia 2012: 17)*

Thus, CGA is used not only to describe, but also to 'demystify' professional practices or action in typical academic and professional contexts through the medium of genres. Bhatia (2012) further states that this approach focuses on both generic artifacts and professional practices; on what is explicitly said and implicitly communicated or even not said in and through genres; as well as on socially recognised communicative purposes and individuals' 'private intentions'. As critical genre analysis is a new approach to the investigation of a range of professional, organisational and institutional practices, this chapter aims to undertake this approach to the subject of needs analysis and to show how critical genre analysis as a tool also needs to be applied in order to assist in determining what the actual 'needs' are in the workplace.

To illustrate, the following sections take up the case of applying critical genre analysis to examine the needs of hoteliers at the workplace by using Bhatia's multi-perspective and multi-dimensional genre analytical framework. Such an approach is an integrated analysis of mixed methodologies – both quantitative and qualitative in nature – that include surveys, language audit, text analysis and interviews with specialist informants involving introspection about needs of hoteliers.

Discursive professional practices in hospitality and hotel industry

Hospitality is defined as 'friendly, welcoming behavior towards guests or towards strangers in the part of the country where you live' (Collins 2000). Such a theme of friendliness and generosity is a rather narrow and one-way process without clear parameters in contrast to the contemporary view that hospitality is connected to human interactions. King (1995) suggests hospitality embraces four distinct characteristics:

1. It is conferred by a host on a guest who is away from home.
2. It is interactive, involving the coming together of a provider and receiver.
3. It is comprised of a blend of tangible and intangible factors.
4. The host provides for the guest's security as well as psychological and physiological comfort.

Tideman (1983), Pfeifer (1983) and Jones (1996) see hospitality as the provision and consumption of certain types of products (food, beverage and lodging). Burgess (1982), Cassee and Reuland (1983) and King (1995) consider hospitality as an exchange process that generates mutual benefits for the parties involved. Meanwhile Cassee and Reuland (1983) maintain that hospitality is a 'harmonious' combination of these concepts of hospitality and motive. Thus, the concept of hospitality involves 'a harmonious mixture of food, beverage, and/or shelter, a physical environment, and the behavior and attitude of people' (1983: 144). Hence, the product component lays the foundation for the concept of hospitality and the notion of exchange is undisputable. However, hospitality is more than the provision of food, beverage and/or lodging, and is something greater than hospitable behaviour. Nonetheless, it is possible to take advantage of such a concept to revisit the core value of hospitality and the communicative needs involved by examining the communicative characteristics of discursive practices in hotels and the hoteliers' experience of the actualities of interaction in 'critical sites of engagement' (Scollon 2001).

The duties of hoteliers may vary from one hotel to another depending on the hotel's size, location and the type of business it attracts. For instance, dealing mainly with holidaymakers, the small resort hotel requires a different work schedule from a large hotel located in the centre of a big city. In a large, busy town or city hotel, a hotelier deals mainly with receiving and welcoming visitors, the registration of all arrivals and general queries concerning the accommodation of visitors. Advanced reservations in this type of hotel may also be their duty, but in principle, the hotel employs separate staff to deal with this. Thus, there is a certain amount of clerical work involved in keeping the records of visitors.

A hotel is required to offer a 24 hour service to its visitors, and the employees are divided into teams or 'brigades', which will have a duty roster comprising shift-work covering morning and early afternoon and the late afternoon and evening. With flights arriving and leaving at all hours of the night, the hotel requires as large a night brigade as during the day. Life in a reception office is not only made up of 'meeting people', nor does it entail the normal working hours usually related to businesses outside the hotel and catering industry. There are many records to be kept either manually, electronically or by computer, and these make up the bulk of the work of a hotel receptionist. Regardless of whether the employee is a male or a female, whether s/he is working during the day or at night, the basic work is the same. It entails receiving and welcoming visitors to the hotel, the maintaining of all records relating to the visitors' stay, and in most cases, the very important task of selling the hotel's accommodation. Other tasks include writing letters, memos, emails and faxes, reports, phone conversations, meetings and presentations. Each of these functions is very closely linked with the others and cannot easily be separated into different categories.

Blended needs analysis in the hotel industry

In view of the preceding and to illustrate how a 'needs analysis' might proceed, this section will continue by looking into the English language communicative needs in the hotel industry to identify the typical skills and activities required and wanted by the respondents to improve their effective professional communication in English. After that, it will go on to discuss why traditional needs analysis approaches are not sufficient and how critical genre analysis as a tool also needs to be applied in order to assist in determining what the actual 'needs' of hotels are.

As a typical example of a location where the demand for English is becoming more and more important, especially in the hospitality industry, Macao has been chosen, with the needs of its foremost industry demonstrating how a 'needs analysis' can be used to good effect. It can be readily discerned that English language courses for hospitality purposes should be based on a communicative use of language rather than formal linguistic categories representing the grammatical rules of language. By conducting a needs analysis, this research identifies the typical skills and activities required and wanted by the respondents to improve their effective professional communication in English. The sample is composed of 140 hoteliers from 20 hotels in Macao.

The questionnaire design for this study is based on the previous literature, involving needs analysis (Alharby 2005; Almulhim 2001) and the principles of designing questionnaires in second language research (Brown 1995; Jordan 1997). It seeks to answer the following questions:

1 To what extent is the English language used by hotel professionals in hotels in Macao?
2 What level of reading, writing, listening and speaking skills in the English language are required for conducting different tasks in the hotel industry?
3 When graduating from college, do hotel professionals feel that they are prepared, in terms of their English language competence, to meet the communication needs of their workplace?

The questionnaire was divided into four parts. Part One was used to obtain the biographical data of the respondents such as their job titles and their year of graduation. Part Two was used to answer the first research question by seeking information about the usage of English in hotel training and how respondents perceived the importance of using English as a tool of communication at their workplace. Part Three was used to answer the second research question by seeking information about which of the four language skills were more emphasised in the hotel industry and about the importance of each of the four skills in various job-related activities. Part Four was used to answer the third research question by seeking information about perceived English language ability before and after college and the relevance of English courses at college to the tasks performed in the workplace.

The results of the survey indicate that English is not only extensively used by hotel professionals in hotels in Macao, it also plays an important role in helping them to perform daily tasks effectively. The majority of the respondents perceived English as playing an important role in their workplace, acknowledging that more than 50 per cent of their work would be conducted in English. The importance of using English language was also reflected in the respondents' hospitality training as English was the medium of instruction. In relation to the extent of English use in the workplace, just below 80 per cent of respondents reported that they had had to communicate with co-workers who only spoke English.

The results also indicate that the majority of respondents felt that an excellent level or a good level of the four skills enabled them to perform their job effectively. Dealing with hotel guests and engaging in phone conversations placed greater demands on listening and speaking skills when compared to dealing with colleagues. This suggests that when designing English programmes for hotel professionals, dialogues representing interactions between hotel guests as well as during phone conversations should be included. Letters, memos, emails and faxes, research, forms/applications, reports and the use of computers would require a high level of reading and writing skills. Among these tasks, emails, faxes and reports were perceived to place the greatest demands on reading and writing skills. These results suggest that when designing English programmes for hotel professionals, more emphasis should be put on reading and writing those particular text-types. A high level of proficiency in reading, writing, listening and speaking skills in English is required for conducting different tasks in hotels, such as meetings, instructions/explanations, and presentations. The results also indicate that there are the differences between the perceptions of the importance of the receptive and productive skills. For example, while presentations were perceived to place the greatest demands on both listening and speaking in equal measure, listening skills were perceived as being more important than the other three skills when having meetings. Thus, it would also be difficult to prioritise any skill sets over the others. The most crucial point is when designing an English programme for hotel professionals, the activities involved should reflect the real situations that the learners encounter in their real life workplace situations. For example, while authentic hotel-related materials should be used for reading and writing practice, real-life dialogues should also be used, representing hotel encounters for listening and speaking practice.

To compare the respondents' perceptions of their English language proficiency before and after college, the results indicated most of the respondents said that they had improved their English language proficiency, especially those who felt their English before college was poor and who now reported that their English was satisfactory. However, the overall improvement did not seem to measure up to the standard required in the workplace when considering the importance of having a high level of English proficiency to perform daily tasks effectively, and 58 per cent viewed their English language college courses as being only 'somewhat' or 'slightly' relevant to their workplace needs.

To identify the crucial sites of engagement in respect to the competency needs of hoteliers, it is necessary to analyse the talk at work. Drew and Heritage (1992: 37) rightly point out that 'all analyses of institutional interaction – from ethnographic to sociolinguistic – connect talk to its institutional context by citing extracts of interaction in order to exhibit features of action and social relations that are characteristics of particular settings'. Since the reception desk is the focal point of the hotel, there is a need to examine spoken genres employed there, for example, while dealing with complaints – a task that the respondents in the current study considered as one of most important tasks that they had in their daily practices.

The communicative purpose of dealing with complaints is to achieve a mutually agreed solution, and the moves consist of (1) describing a problem situation; (2) comprehending and interpreting the problem; (3) generating a solution. To achieve the communicative purpose, the employee has to deal with the guest's feelings as well as with the problem. When dealing with the guest's feelings, the employee needs to remain polite and listen to the guest with empathy, patience and attention. S/He also needs to apologise with an assertive rather than a passive strategy by using appropriate body language and facial expressions; trying to explain the situation, but not seeking blame or being defensive by arguing with the guests. When dealing with the problem, the employee needs to let the guest tell him/her what exactly the guest wants by using open- and closed-ended questions. He/she also needs to build on the guest's idea whenever possible and tries to get a mutually agreed solution by looking for a win-win solution so as to make both the guest and the hotel benefit. Language skills such as listening, speaking and paraphrasing certainly play an important role. The language required in the speech acts includes apologising, giving feedback and showing understanding in dealing with the guest's feelings, seeking and confirming information about what exactly the guest wants, while giving explanations and making suggestions to solve the problem. The turn-takings are well ordered – one party speaks and then the next one speaks, and the basic register is distinctly cooperative, efficient and slightly formal but friendly.

From the foregoing, it can be seen that it is useful to interview specialist informants as they are in a position to explain clearly 'what expert members of the disciplinary culture do when they exploit language in order to accomplish generic goals' (Bhatia 1993: 35–36). One of the senior managers interviewed confirmed that the core value of handling disappointed and disruptive guests is being positive and enthusiastic. The hoteliers have the responsibility to handle disappointed guests. However, they need to be tactful because the guests are the customers. When the guests find that they have been somehow treated unfairly or have become the victims, they could perceive this as an insult or that they are being ignored. Together with disrespect, the embarrassment could finally push the guests over the edge and make the situation even worse. Thus, dealing with the guests' feelings and showing an understanding that the guests have suffered is crucial. It is also vital to work with reality and seek a mutually agreed solution. Arguing with the guests will not help the situation. By demonstrating a helpful attitude in solving the guests' difficulties and providing a mutually beneficial solution, the hoteliers are showing their eagerness and sincere service. In this way, not only do hoteliers serve the guests physically, but they also look after their affective domain. For instance, when attempting to understand and meet the unspoken needs of their guests, hoteliers try their best to demonstrate their care and interest for them in order to build up rapport. Thus, the issues relating to the participant relationships and the social components of communication in workplace contexts also need to be considered.

The analysis of the related texts has also shown that hoteliers' interpretation is an event that is both linguistically and analytically complex. Not only do they need to have recourse to a range of linguistic and discoursal strategies, they also need to understand the social components in the communicative contexts at their workplace in order to achieve the communicative purposes and maintain the participant relationships. This, in turn, can increase the guests' perception of service quality.

Thus, applied linguistic theory and existing needs analysis practice seem to be insufficient to analyse the actual needs of a dynamic and exciting industry as the world becomes a global village. Managers and workers alike need to cope with a vast array of challenges due to the changing nature of the industry. For instance, the hospitality industry is not just a relationship based on hosts and guests by providing food, drinks and sometimes accommodation. It is an exchange process within which the exchange transaction contains three components: products (food, beverage and accommodation), employee behaviour, and the physical environment (Reuland et al. 1985). Tideman (1983) and Pfeifer (1983) suggest that when the needs of guests away from home, such as food, beverage and lodging, are offered at a price that is acceptable to them, then this could be reasonably be defined as hospitality. Thus the relationship between hotels and guests is no longer hosts and guests, but becomes more critical – sellers and buyers. Buyers are customers, but not guests. It is a business, but not a home and thus the relationship is economic, but not philanthropic (Slattery 2002).

Slattery (2002) identifies three levels of context in hospitality: the industry context, the corporate context, and the venue context. When considered in terms of the industry context, the hospitality industry is becoming diverse and complex, encompassing a wide range of venues whose primary function may be something other than hospitality. An outstanding example of this is that seen in Las Vegas where there are 29 venues of which each contain more than 1000 rooms. Each venue might include a major casino, a restaurant campus, at least one theatre, a conference and exhibition centre, a shopping mall and a health club, with some going as far as an aquarium or a circus, while the Bellagio and the Venetian each incorporate an art gallery. True, Macao may not yet have aspired to all of these, but the fact that such fabulously complex venues exist may be a harbinger of what is soon to come, with hospitality extending far beyond the minimals of renting rooms and selling drinks. Critical genre analysis and needs analysis must obviously be at the ready for such expansion.

In terms of the corporate context, as the hospitality industry consolidates, with its chains replacing unaffiliated venues as the key operators in the industry, opportunities to offer careers to graduates rather than mere operational jobs, become obviously greater as does the need for good communication skills. The variety of interactions can widen considerably, and might involve a range of partners, including suppliers, lenders, investors, investment banks, property developers, management consultants and demand processors such as travel agents, tour operators, etc. Here again the need for good communication skills is evident.

In terms of the venue context, the more complex a hotel venue becomes, the greater the need for unambiguous interaction between staff and hospitality customers. Not only are products bought within the venue but also facilities and services. Thus hospitality management academics focus on how problems can be solved within these contexts. For this reason graduates in this field need to gain effective conceptual understandings of the industry at the same time

A blended needs analysis

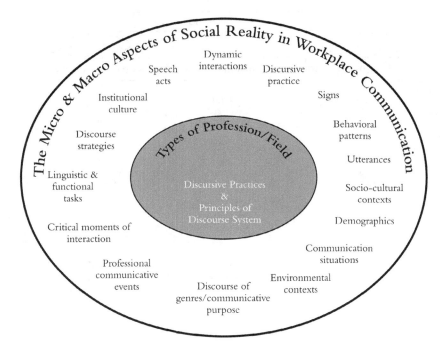

Figure 17.1 The micro and macro aspects of social reality in workplace communication

focusing on research activities that will contribute to its development, all of this relying heavily on a working knowledge of what has become the accepted means of communication within the industry – English.

Thus, to examine the needs of language and communication in the workplace, traditional needs analysis approaches are not sufficient. It is essential to incorporate critical genre analysis as a tool to extend the understanding of discourse or genres to a wider spectrum, in order to assist in determining what the actual 'needs' are. Bhatia (2004) identifies disciplines in terms of their content and in part by the field of discourse. He further asserts that disciplines, even when overlapping between register, still retain their typical characteristics and can be discerned in terms of the specific knowledge, methodologies and shared practices of community members. As shown in Figure 17.1, professional communication at the workplace involves the micro and macro aspects of social reality. While language skills, discourse of genres, communicative events and speech acts can be identified as the micro aspects, the global environment, society and culture as well as communication situations can be identified as the macro aspects. These aspects must be considered when analysing the actual needs in workplace communication.

It is further asserted that the language of the workplace constitutes a professional environment consisting of discourse communities, professions and their discourses as well as interdiscursive practice within the community, involving various communicative events such as meetings (Brown and Yule 1987; Schiffrin 1994; Schiffrin *et al.* 2006). In order to understand the workplace communication, a blended needs analysis (BNA) framework of language and professional communications at the workplace is required (Figure 17.2), blending the traditional needs analysis approaches with critical genre analysis (CGA). While language and discourse form the base of the framework, language and communication is the springboard to achieve the social and institutional goals. Two pillars connect the base and the springboard. They are the

Jane Lung

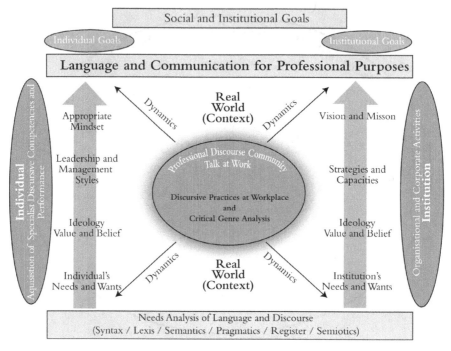

Figure 17.2 BNA (Blended Needs Analysis) framework of language and professional communication at the workplace

individual pillar and the institution pillar, representing the individual perspective and the institutional perspective, respectively. The individual pillar contains four essential elements: (1) an individual's needs and wants; (2) his/her ideology, values and beliefs; (3) his/her management and leadership styles; and (4) his/her appropriate mindset. These four elements must mirror the corresponding institutional pillar's (1) needs and wants; (2) value and ideology; (3) strategies and capacities; as well as (4) vision and mission. While the elements in the individual pillar are reflected in the individual's specialist discursive competencies (Bhatia 2004) and performance, those of the institutional pillar are reflected in the corporate activities. The core of the framework is discursive practices at the workplace and Bhatia (2004: 124) states that such practices 'include factors such as the choice of genre and mode of communication to suit a particular professional action'. The blurred area surrounding the core represents the evolving interdiscursivity created by the force and motion of the real world.

Hence, Figure 17.2 illustrates that traditional needs analysis approaches form the base to help identify the specific language and discourse required in the profession in general terms; mastering English is essential in hospitality students in their current studies and future career. However, there is also a need to have knowledge about the communication environment, issues involved, the pursued processes and goals as well as the vision and mission of a corporation. Thus, in order to determine what the actual 'needs' of hotels are, critical genre analysis has been used not only to describe, but also to 'demystify' professional practices or action in typical academic and professional contexts through the medium of genres. Thus, when conducting a needs analysis, a blended needs analysis (BNA) considers three perspectives: (1) the individual perspective; (2) the institution perspective; and (3) most importantly, the social and societal perspective, thus going beyond a mere (though essential) needs analysis and addressing the aforementioned perspectives.

Conclusion

To sum up, it can be seen that the hotel workers in the study reported here perceived the need for all four of the language skills (speaking, listening, writing, reading) in slightly varying degrees and in some cases the differences were so small that it was difficult to judge which sets of skills were more important. Thus it would be very difficult to prioritise one set of skills above another, the most important criterion being that the activities reflect the real-life situations that the students encounter in their real-life hotel situations. However, although after leaving college most of the respondents viewed their English as satisfactory, the overall improvement did not seem to measure up to the standard required in the workplace, with their college English courses not sufficient to help them with the tasks performed in the workplace. In this connection, many of them viewed their English language college courses as being only 'somewhat' or 'slightly' relevant to their work-place needs. Thus on examining the curricula of the respondents' English college courses, it was seen that these were not sufficient to prepare them to meet the communication needs of their work-place.

In view of this and as deduced from the earlier sections of this chapter these needs are now being addressed and a blended needs analysis (BNA) framework of professional communications at the workplace is provided. There is a need to blend the traditional needs analysis approaches with critical genre analysis (CGA) in order to analyse the actual communication needs at workplace. This framework looks into the communication environment, professional practices, issues involved as well as the vision and mission of a corporation and individuals from different perspectives (individual, institutional, social and societal) and aspects (micro and macro). This has application to a particular group of students in a particular location that has its own particular needs which, having been identified, can now serve as a basis for developing tests, materials, teaching activities and evaluation strategies leading to activities that meet their specific needs, which in turn are assessed or evaluated. These 'lacks' as it were, having now been identified can then be addressed to fill the gap between the 'current state of affairs' and the 'desired state of affairs'. Thus priorities are set for the specific situation and language teaching proceeds in a way that will best serve the needs of the learner.

At the same time, for those who feel that their college preparation was not adequate, complementary courses in English for hospitality professions could be designed specifically and this on an ongoing basis. Of course, in this respect it is not sufficient to design only one generic curriculum for English for hospitality purposes. Instead, these could be designed to incorporate each field of the hospitality profession. Not only that, but an evaluation could be carried out to test how the new courses meet the intended communicative needs. No doubt work such as this could open up opportunities to discern the communicative differences that occur from day to day between the various hotel professionals such as front office managers, guest relations managers and service centre agents, etc. Figure 17.3 sums up the key aspects of needs analysis: (1) the types of needs; (2) components in needs analysis; (3) approaches to needs analysis and their informants; (4) methods of needs analysis.

To conclude, the study reports how, by taking a blended approach to needs analysis that incorporates the principles of Bhatia's critical genre analysis (CGA), we can gain a more comprehensive and realistic picture of the needs of current students in the hospitality industry and thereby provide curriculum and course designers with the kinds of information required to determine more explicitly what these actual needs are. Bhatia's (2008) key point is brought to the fore, that of seeing the relevant connection between the use of language on the one hand and the purpose of communication and the context of communication on the other, focusing on language in action and in context. It is thus seen that because critical genre analysis takes

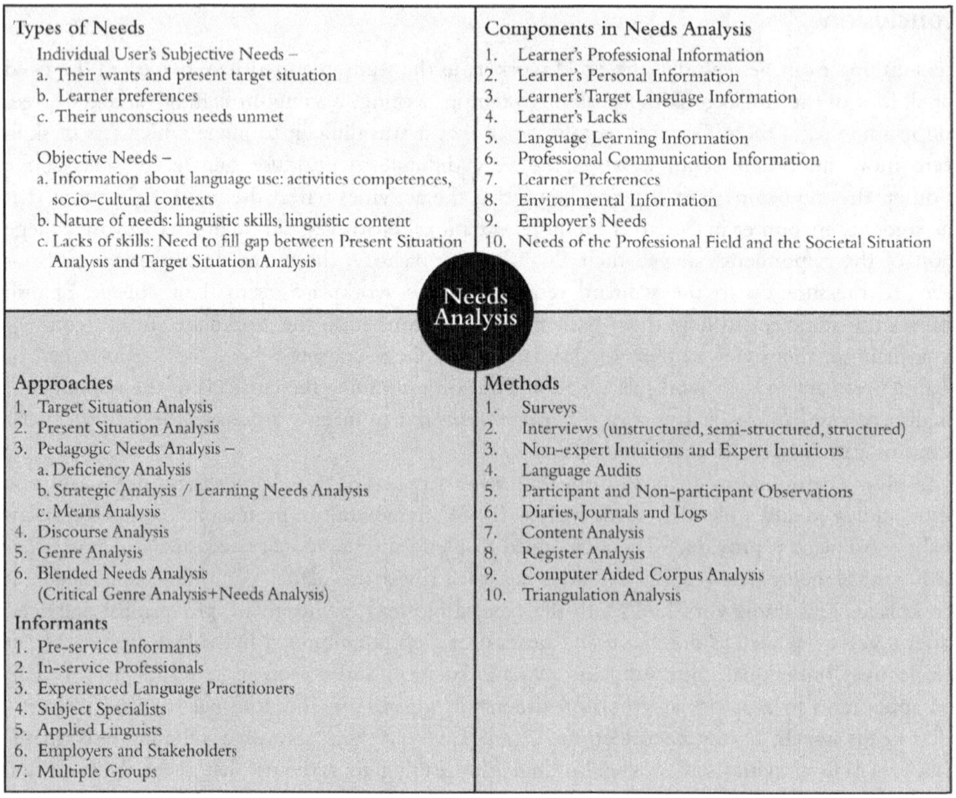

Figure 17.3 Key aspects of needs analysis

Types of Needs
- Individual User's Subjective Needs –
  - a. Their wants and present target situation
  - b. Learner preferences
  - c. Their unconscious needs unmet
- Objective Needs –
  - a. Information about language use: activities competences, socio-cultural contexts
  - b. Nature of needs: linguistic skills, linguistic content
  - c. Lacks of skills: Need to fill gap between Present Situation Analysis and Target Situation Analysis

Components in Needs Analysis
1. Learner's Professional Information
2. Learner's Personal Information
3. Learner's Target Language Information
4. Learner's Lacks
5. Language Learning Information
6. Professional Communication Information
7. Learner Preferences
8. Environmental Information
9. Employer's Needs
10. Needs of the Professional Field and the Societal Situation

Approaches
1. Target Situation Analysis
2. Present Situation Analysis
3. Pedagogic Needs Analysis –
   - a. Deficiency Analysis
   - b. Strategic Analysis / Learning Needs Analysis
   - c. Means Analysis
4. Discourse Analysis
5. Genre Analysis
6. Blended Needs Analysis (Critical Genre Analysis+Needs Analysis)

Informants
1. Pre-service Informants
2. In-service Professionals
3. Experienced Language Practitioners
4. Subject Specialists
5. Applied Linguists
6. Employers and Stakeholders
7. Multiple Groups

Methods
1. Surveys
2. Interviews (unstructured, semi-structured, structured)
3. Non-expert Intuitions and Expert Intuitions
4. Language Audits
5. Participant and Non-participant Observations
6. Diaries, Journals and Logs
7. Content Analysis
8. Register Analysis
9. Computer Aided Corpus Analysis
10. Triangulation Analysis

academic and professional practices into account, it is useful in analysing what might supplement needs analysis in order to determine what the actual needs of a specific workplace are.

While increasing work is being done in this field today it can be seen that both needs analysis and critical genre analysis can be combined and interwoven proving complementary in the roles they play. It is hoped that continuing work in this field will provide a significant role for programme designers to develop an applicable and practical ESP/EPCP/LSP programme, addressing the very real needs of their students particularly when meeting the challenges of the hospitality industry.

Acknowledgements

Part of the research reported here is drawn from an MPI funded project under the contract number: RP/ESCE-02/2009.

Related topics

discourse variation in professional contexts; critical genre analysis; professional discourse and discursive practices; communication in professional workplaces; methodology for teaching ESP; acquisition of professional competence

Key readings

Bhatia, V. K. (2004). *Worlds of Written Discourse: A Genre Based View*, London: Continuum. (Bhatia proposes a multiperspective model of discourse analysis, which moves genre theory away from simplified and idealised contexts into the real world of discourse and the tension that exists between the world of written discourse and its representation in applied genre-based literature.)

Bhatia, V. K. (2012). 'Critical reflections on genre analysis', *Iberica*, 24, 17–28. (Bhatia attempts to critically reflect on a general overview of genre analysis as it applies to the analysis of professional genres, at the same time focussing on the academic and professional practices that most academics and professional experts are engaged in.)

Bhatia, V. K., Cheng, W., Du-Babcock, B. and Lung, J. (2008). *Language for Professional Communication: Research, Practice and Training*, Hong Kong: City University of Hong Kong, Asia-Pacific LSP and Professional Communication Association, and The Hong Kong Polytechnic University. (This book presents a widely diverse set of papers from an equally diverse geographically and institutionally based authorship, and represents a force for exchange and innovation in three aspects: research, practice, and training.)

Brown, J.D. (2009). 'Foreign and second language needs analysis', in M. H. Long and C. J. Doughty (eds), *The Handbook of Language Teaching*, Oxford: Blackwell. (Brown addresses three basic questions that arise relating to needs analysis [needs assessment], along with details emerging from such a consideration.)

Hall, D. R. (ed.) (2013). *Needs Analysis for Language Course Design: A Holistic Approach to ESP*, Cambridge: Cambridge University Press. (This book provides further assistance for language teachers with the need to design language courses, drawing on past models of needs analysis along with the latest research into language usage in professional and vocational contexts.)

Bibliography

Al Bazzaz, A. A. (1994). *The Students' Low Achievement in Business English at the College of Business Studies in Kuwait: An Analysis of the Students' Educational and Occupational Language Requirements*, United Kingdom: University of Sussex.

Al-Busaidi, S. S. (2003). *Academic Needs of EFL Learners in the Intensive English Language Program at Sultan Qaboos University in the Sultanate of Oman*, Illinois: University of Illinois at Urbana-Champaign.

Al-Gorashi, A. K. (1988). 'The English Communication Needs of Military Cadets in Saudi Arabia as Perceived by Junior Officers in the Saudi Army and Air Defense', Unpublished PhD dissertation, Indiana: Indiana University.

Al-Kamookh, A. A. (1981). *A Survey of the English Language Teachers' Perceptions of the English Language Teaching Methods in the Intermediate and Secondary Schools of the Eastern Province in Saudi Arabia*, Kansas: University of Kansas.

Alharby, M. (2005). *ESP Target Situation Needs Analysis: The English Language Communicative Needs as Perceived by Health Professionals in the Riyadh Area*. Available from: http//ebookbrowse.com/alharby-majid-200505-phd-pdf-d372628168.

Almulhim, A.M. (2001). *An English Language Needs Assessment of Saudi College-of-technology Students with Respect to a Number of Business Sectors in Saudi Arabia*, United States – Mississippi: The University of Mississippi.

Auerbach, E. R. and Burgess, D. (1985). 'The hidden curriculum of survival ESL', *TESOL quarterly*, 19(3), 475–95.

Bhatia, V. K. (1993). *Analysing Genre: Language use in Professional Settings*, London: Longman.

——2004. *Worlds of Written Discourse: A Genre Based View*, London: Continuum.

——2007. 'Interdiscursivity in critical genre analysis', in A. Bonini, D. C. Figueiredo and F. Rauen (Orgs.), *Proceedings from the 4th International Symposium on Genre Studies (SIGET)*. Tubarão: Unisul, v. 1. 391–400.

——(2008). 'Towards critical genre analysis', in V. K. Bhatia, J. Flowerdew and R. Jones (eds), *Advances in Discourse Studies* (pp. 166–77), Routledge.

——2010. 'Accessibility of discoursal data in critical genre analysis: International commercial arbitration practice', *Linguagem em (Dis)curso, Palhoça, SC*, 10(3), 465–83.

——2012. 'Critical reflections on genre analysis', *Iberica*, 24, 17–28.

——(this volume). 'Analysing discourse variation in professional contexts.'

Bosher, S. and Smalkowski, K. (2002). 'From needs analysis to curriculum development: Designing a course in health-care communication for immigrant students in the USA', *English for Specific Purposes*, *13*(1), 3–21.
Brecht, D. R. and Walton, A. R. (1995). 'The future shape of language learning in the new world of global communication: Consequences for higher education and beyond', in R. Donato and R. M. Terry (eds), *Foreign Language Learning: The Journey of a Lifetime* (pp. 110–52), Lincolnwood, IL: National Textbook Company.
Brindley, G. (1984). *Needs Analysis and Objective Setting in the Adult Migrant Education Service*, Sydney: Adult Migrant Education Service.
Brown, G. and Yule, G. (1987). *Discourse Analysis*, Cambridge: Cambridge University Press.
Brown, J. D. (1995). *The Elements of Language Curriculum: A Systematic Approach to Program Development*, New York: Heinle and Heinle.
——(2006). 'Research methods for applied linguistics: Scope, characteristics and standards', in A. Davies and C. Elder (eds), *The Handbook of Applied Linguistics* (pp. 476–500), Oxford: Blackwell.
Burgess, J. (1982). 'Perspectives on gift exchange and hospitable behavior', *International Journal of Hospitality Management*, *1*(1), 49–57.
Candlin, C.N. (2006). 'Accounting for interdiscursivity: Challenges for professional expertise', in M. Gotti and D. Giannone (eds), *New Trends in Specialized Discourse Analysis* (pp. 1–25), Bern: Peter Lang Verlag.
Cassee, E. H. and Reuland, R. (1983). 'Hospitality in hospitals', in E. H. Cassee and R. Reuland (eds), *The Management of Hospitality* (pp. 143–63), Oxford: Pergamon.
Chambers, F. (1980). 'A re-evaluation of needs analysis', *English for Specific Purposes Journal*, *1*(1), 25–33.
Collins (2000). *Collins English Dictionary*, 5th edn, Glasgow: HarperCollins.
Drew, P. and Heritage, J. (1992). *Talk at Work: Interaction in Institutional Settings*, Cambridge: Cambridge University Press.
Dudley-Evans, T. and St John, M. (1998). *Developments in ESP: A Multidisciplinary Approach*, Cambridge: Cambridge University Press.
——(2002). *Developments in ESP: A Multidisciplinary Approach*, Cambridge: Cambridge University Press.
Eggly, S., Musial, J. and Smulowitz, J. (1999). 'The relationship between English language proficiency and success as a medical resident', *English for Specific Purposes*, *18*(2), 201–8.
Ellis, R. (2003). *Task-based Language Learning and Teaching*, Oxford: Oxford University Press.
Flowerdew, J. (2011). 'Action, content and identity in applied genre analysis for ESP', *Lang. Tech*, *44*(4), 516–28, DOI: 10.1017/s026144481000042x.
Huhta, M. (2010). 'Language and communication for professional purposes – Needs analysis methods in industry and business and their yield to stakeholders'. Available at https://aaltodoc.aalto.fi/bitstream/handle/123456789/4731/isbn9789522482273.pdf?sequence=1
Hutchinson, T. and Waters, A. (1987). *English for Specific Purposes: A Learning-Centered Approach*, Cambridge: Cambridge University Press.
——(1992). *English for Specific Purposes: A Learning Centered Approach*, Cambridge: Cambridge University Press.
Hyland, K. (2003). 'Genre-based pedagogies: a social response to process', *Journal of Second Language Writing*, *12*(1), 17–29.
Jones, P. (1996). 'The hospitality industry', in P. Jones (ed.), *Introduction to Hospitality Operations* (pp. 1–20), London: Cassell.
Jordan, R. R. (1997). *English for Academic Purposes: A Guide and Resource Book for Teachers*, Cambridge: Cambridge University Press.
King, C. A. (1995). 'What is hospitality?', *International Journal of Hospitality Management*, *14*(3), 219–34.
Koster, C. (2004). *A Handbook on Language Auditing*, Amsterdam: Editions 'de Werelt'.
Long, M. H. (2005). *Second Language Needs Analysis*, Cambridge: Cambridge Applied Linguistics.
Mountford, A. (1981). 'The what and the why and the way', in Aupelf/Goethe Institut/British Council, *Triangle. English For Specific Purposes* (pp. 19–34), Quebec: Aupelf.
Munby, J. (1978). *Communicative Syllabus Design*, Cambridge: Cambridge University Press.
Pfeifer, Y. (1983). 'Small business management', in E. H. Cassee and R. Reuland (eds), *The Management of Hospitality* (pp. 189–202), Oxford: Pergamon.
Rattanapinyowong, W., Vajanabukka, R. and Rungruangsri, P. (1988). 'A study of the academic English needs of medical students', *pasaa*, *18*(1), 32–39.
Reuland, R., Choudry, J. and Fagel, A. (1985). 'Research in the field of hospitality', *International Journal of Hospitality Management*, *4*(4), 141–46.

Richards, J. C. (2001). *Curriculum Development in Language Teaching*, Cambridge, UK; New York: Cambridge University Press.

Richards, J. C., Platt, J. T. and Weber, H. (1985). *Longman Dictionary of Applied Linguistics*, Harlow, Essex, England: Longman.

Richterich, J.C. (1983). *Case Studies in Identifying Needs of Adult Learners*, Oxford: Council of Europe.

Richterich, R. and Chancerel, J. L. (1980). *Identifying the Needs of Adults Learning a Foreign Language*, 1977, Strasbourg: Council of Europe, Pergamon Press.

Robinson, P. (1991). *ESP Today: A Practitioner's Guide*, UK: Prentice Hall International (UK) Ltd.

Sajavaara, K. (2006). 'Kielipolitiikka ja kielikoulutuspolitiikka' (Language policy and language education policy), Presentation 10 March 2006, KIEPO. Available at www.jyu.fi/hum/laitokset/solki/tutkimus/projektit/kiepo/tavoitteet/Kielipolitiikka_FSFT.pdf.

Schiffrin, D. (1994). *Approaches to Discourse*, Cambridge, US: Blackwell.

Schiffrin, D., Tannen, D. and Hamilton, H. (2006). *The Handbook of Discourse Analysis*, Malden, MA: Blackwell.

Scollon, R. (2001). *Mediated Discourse: The Nexus of Practice*, London: Routledge.

Shi, L., Corcos, R. and Storey, A. (2001). 'Using student performance data to develop an English course for clinical training'. *English for Specific Purposes*, *20*(3), 267–91.

Slattery, P. (2002). 'Finding the hospitality industry', *Journal of Hospitality, Leisure, Sport and Tourism Education*, *1*(1), 19–28.

Songhori, M.H. (2008). 'Introduction to needs analysis', *English for Specific Purposes*, World issue 4, 2008. www.esp-world.info.

Soriano, F. I. and University Of Michigan, School Of Social Work (1995). *Conducting Needs Assessments: A Multidisciplinary Approach*, Thousand Oaks: Sage Publications.

Takala, S. (2008). 'Plurilingualism – can it help solve the current crisis in our language education?' Presentation at Turku School of Economics 26 September 2008. Unpublished slide series.

Tideman, M. C. (1983). 'External influences on the hospitality industry', in E. H. Cassee and R. Reuland (eds), *The Management of Hospitality* (pp. 1–24), Oxford: Pergamon.

Van Hest, E. and Oud-de-Glas, M. (1990). *A Survey of Techniques used in the Diagnosis and Analysis of Foreign Language Needs in Industry*, Brussels: Lingua.

Vandermeeren, S. (2005). 'Foreign language need of business firms', in M. H. Long (ed.), *Second Language Needs Analysis* (pp. 159–81), Cambridge: Cambridge University Press.

West, R. (1994). 'Needs analysis in language teaching', *Language Teaching*, *27*(1), 1–19.

——(1998). *ESP-State of the Art*, paper presented at Networking for ESP – An Anti-Conference. Switzerland.

Widdowson, H. G. (1981). 'English for specific purposes: Criteria for course design', in L. Selinker, E. Tarone and V. Hanzeli (eds), *English for Academic and Technical Purposes: Studies in Honor of Louis Trimble* (pp. 1–11), Cambridge, MA: Newbury House.

Witkin, B. R. and Altschuld, J. W. (1995). *Planning and Conducting Needs Assessments: A Practical Guide*, Thousand Oaks: Sage Publications.

18
The changing landscape of business communication

Sujata S. Kathpalia and Koo Swit Ling

Introduction

Communication, whether written or spoken, plays an important role in the business world and is at the core of all work-related activities within and across organisations. Communication is essential for the survival of any organisation whether it is for developing and maintaining internal relationships between employees or external relationships with clients, partners, mass media, government officials or politicians. Business practices have not only emerged over time through the use of written and spoken discourse among practitioners but have also been reshaped to meet the changing needs of modern society. In particular, the internet and recent technological advances have created new forms of communication in the workplace, resulting in the globalisation of business communication and a transformation of traditional means of spoken communication (e.g. meetings, negotiations, conferences, etc.) and written communication (e.g. letters, memos, reports, contracts, etc.) in the work context (Gunnarsson 2009). This has implications not only for practitioners but also instructors at tertiary institutions who train students to cope with the demands of their working lives in order to interact and communicate in a professionally appropriate way.

Traditionally, courses in business communication at universities have focused on letter writing, memos, proposals, and business presentations. Although these genres are still relevant in today's business world, the internet has had a tremendous impact on these by introducing a variety of new channels of communication that require special skills. As such, videoconferencing is not the same as face-to-face meetings, email is not an electronic version of memos and instant messaging is not merely a written version of telephone calls. Videoconferencing, email, instant messaging and other innovations support different kinds of communication and have different characteristics when compared to the traditional channels of communication. For instance, one key aspect that differentiates these channels is the concept of media richness, with some of these channels being 'low bandwidth' and others being 'high-bandwidth', depending upon the breadth and depth of communication cues that can be transmitted (Wallace 2004). Based on this concept, lower bandwidth channels would be letters and email on one end of the scale, face-to-face interaction on the high end and videoconferencing in the middle. Communication channels, however, do not just vary along a continuum of media richness; they have other differences based on the inherent qualities of the medium. An email, for instance, has certain advantages over face-to-face conversations due to the convenience of multiple addressing, permanent digital records, and computer processing that make it more useful in certain business contexts. Given the choice of business genres and the multiplicity of channels available, the decision of selecting a suitable one and using it effectively becomes challenging for students who have just entered the workforce. Therefore, in the interim phase when electronic communication media are multiplying, students may need direct and what seem like superficial netiquette tips for using different channels of communication effectively in the workplace.

Based on a survey implemented on practitioners and review of current research, this chapter attempts to reach a deeper understanding of the emergence and development of, and change in professional practices and discourse in the Singapore business context. Specifically, the goal is to determine how workplace communication has changed due to technological advances that have coincided with globalisation and its focus on flexibility, mobility and diversity. As company websites also play an important role in the 'modern technologised business world', these will be examined to discover the changing trends of business discourse to meet the needs of internal and external communication, particularly in relation to organisational image-building. In fact every aspect of workplace communication has been affected by technology, whether it is written or spoken discourse. For instance, communication modes such as websites, instant messaging, emailing, audio and video conferencing have given rise to new communicative processes and multimodal genres that integrate text, speech, graphics, recorded sound and movies, affecting discourse in ways that was not possible in the past. Given this change in the world of business communication, it is timely to investigate these shifts in communication practice in order to capture snapshots of the changing landscape to better equip old and new employees with the dynamically changing world of business discourse.

Methodology

Singapore's population is slightly over 5 million and it has the highest level of internet penetration at 77.2 per cent in South East Asia. According to the Singapore SEO Consultant (n.d.), the total number of internet users in Singapore is 3,658,400, with internet subscriptions ranging from 7,806,700 for 3G mobile subscriptions, 1,237,000 for residential broadband subscription and 87,700 for corporate broadband subscriptions. Given the high rate of internet usage as Singapore progresses steadily into the twenty-first century, changes in the way people communicate in businesses have occurred but these changes have not been sufficiently captured and documented. Therefore a survey questionnaire was designed to study how people communicate in the workplace and how effective the communication channels have been in serving their communication needs.

The five-page questionnaire comprised demographic questions along with six main questions on workplace communication. There were five specific demographic questions on company name, type of industry, size of company (including information on whether it was local or global), appointment in company and age of respondent. In the main section of the questionnaire, there were six main questions with several sub-divisions based on the various channels of communication. The questions focused on obtaining information on the use of company websites (Question 1), online applications for routine matters (Question 2), time spent on various channels (Question 3), channels of communication for inter and intra office communication (Question 4), preference for and effectiveness of these channels (Question 5), and targeted audience of the channels (Question 6). In terms of form, the questions ranged from yes-no questions to multiple choice, ranking and short answer questions.

A pilot run was conducted with four participants from the target population to ensure that the questionnaire was comprehensive in terms of addressing the research questions and reader friendly from the respondents' perspective. Based on the feedback received, the questions as well as the layout were revised before the actual survey. The questionnaires were distributed electronically over a one-month period to people in different sectors, including service, manufacturing and technology sectors.

Altogether, 32 completed questionnaires were received, covering a range of sectors, ages and corporate levels. Face-to-face interviews were conducted with 10 per cent of the respondents for clarifications and further information on workplace communication in their companies/sectors. The responses were computed to obtain relevant information on inter and intra office communication and websites of companies from each of these sectors were also analysed for further insights into corporate communication, particularly in relation to public engagement. The findings and discussion of these are presented in the next section.

Results and discussion

The overall findings of the survey show that although there is an increase in computer mediated channels of communication in the workforce, they have not completely substituted traditional channels and modes of communication. While company websites are popular with large, medium and small size organisations for image-building purposes, the level of deployment varies depending upon the expenditure and expertise available to the companies for creating and maintaining these sites. As for the intranet, although most organisations have some form of intranet communication, the extent of use varies from routine administrative applications to sophisticated knowledge-building and collaborative software designed for promoting organisational knowledge and interaction. As for everyday communication, a combination of traditional (e.g. face-to-face and telephone communication) as well as new modes of communication (e.g. teleconferencing, videoconferencing, text messages and intranet chat) continue to be used in the workplace, with a slight increase in the use of computer mediated communication in the last five years. The detailed findings in relation to the frequency of use and preferences of respondents are provided below.

(i) Company websites

The evolution of the World Wide Web has enabled companies to enhance their corporate image and promote their products/services using a range of different media and multimodal resources in the form of images, sounds, animation and videos. Through the integrated deployment of these resources, companies have been able to reach millions of users, including customers, investors and stakeholders. Therefore it is not surprising that companies, whether large multinational corporations or small family-run businesses, have taken advantage of the internet and created company websites in order to gain visibility, obtain new customers and build their brands (Bargiela-Chiappini 2009). This is reflected in the current survey that revealed that most of the respondents (97 per cent) belong to companies that have websites irrespective of their sector and/or size. The only difference is that they come in different sizes, ranging 'from the simple one- or two-page presentation of a small company to the vastly stratified websites of global companies representing self-contained virtual worlds, populated with music, animation, videos, games etc' (Bargiela-Chiappini 2009). In terms of genres, these websites have a proliferation of genres from company mission/vision statements, press-releases, advertisements, announcements of sponsored events to company reports, targeted at different groups of users.

These genres seem to span the corporate functions of transactional e-commerce, the interpersonal and socialising function of public relations and the promotional function of corporate image-building. The sophistication with which these functions are achieved depends upon the level of investment as well as commitment towards building and maintaining the websites, with the smaller organisations providing simple hyperlinks to relevant company information in comparison to innovative Web designs of bigger companies that are constantly pushing the boundaries of current technology.

(ii) Intranet communication

The intranet is an internal company online Web that provides an organisation-wide electronic link and 24-hour access to employees from work or any other location round the clock. It uses the same technology as the internet but has the advantage of restricting access to qualified users for routine HR processes as well as other company related information. In our survey, 70 per cent of our respondents confirmed that they used the intranet for routine application for leave, expense claims and medical claims. In fact, intranets of companies are becoming increasingly more complex as they are being used not only for routine HR processes but also for communication (through chat, email and/or blogs), Web publishing of corporate knowledge (employee manuals, benefits documents, company policies, business standards, news feeds, employee training, etc.), and business operations and management. The benefits of intranet communication are many. First of all, it is cost effective, saving the company money on printing as well as conserving the environment. In addition, it is a platform that enhances collaboration among employees, promotes corporate culture and provides live updates on changes in relation to company policies, employee benefits and new schemes. According to Guenther and Braun (2001: 18), 'the underlying reason to put an intranet in place is to provide a fabric for sharing and collaboration based on a central repository that acts as an authoritative source of organisational knowledge'. To sum up, the intranet clearly provides productivity benefits by empowering employees in several ways, whether it is for collaboration on projects with colleagues, to access company information or for administrative purposes.

(iii) Channels of communication: Preference and frequency of use

The channels of communication at a broad level include both written and spoken modes of business communication. The written modes usually include the traditional genres such as letters, reports, and proposals whereas the newer modes of communication include email, text messages and intranet chat. As for oral modes of communication, oral presentations, telephone and face-to-face communication would be the traditional means while teleconferencing and videoconferencing belong to the more recent methods of communication. To determine whether there have been changes in the business world in relation to these traditional and modern ways of communication, questions in the survey requested information on the perceived time spent on these channels of communication at present and in the past (i.e. five years ago) as well as questions in relation to the respondents' preferences in relation to some of these channels.

In terms of time spent, only 50 per cent of the respondents provided a comparison between the past and present modes of communication. This could be due to the employment history of our respondents, many of whom are young and have joined the workforce in recent years. Out of those who provided comparative figures, only 50 per cent indicated that dependence on traditional modes of communication (e.g. face-to-face and telephone communication) is decreasing while that on newer modes (e.g. emails, teleconferencing, videoconferencing, text messages and intranet) is increasing. As for written genres of reports, proposals and even oral communication, there was no consistent pattern as the type of written and oral communication depends on one's role in an organisation as well as the nature of service provided by the company depending upon its sector.

The findings reveal that the internet has not only added many new choices for communication in the workplace but also altered the use of many of the old choices of communication. This does not mean that the old channels are obsolete or that the new channels are better or more productive than the traditional channels of communication. According to Wallace (2004: 82–83), 'the range of new communication channels make the selection and use of an appropriate channel more complicated' as the sender now has to choose between a growing list of channels which include a 'face-to-face meeting, a cell phone call, a call to the individual's office number, a voice mail message, a formal business letter, an interoffice memo, a fax, email, instant message, videoconference, a notice on the Intranet, or a handwritten note'. The key to successful communication in the workplace is not only to choose an appropriate channel in a particular situation but also to take into consideration the bandwidth of a channel when making a decision. The advice based on findings of a study (Trevino, Webster and Stein 2000) is to use low bandwidth channels such as email, letters and memos for straightforward, factual and unambiguous messages as they are leaner in terms of communication cues (such as nonverbal cues) that they can transmit. However, high bandwidth channels which include face-to-face communication, telephone or interactive videoconferencing (stated in descending order of media richness) are recommended for more complex and sensitive issues that have the potential for misinterpretation and misunderstanding.

The other factors that determine choice of a particular medium also depend on the cost of the channel and the size of the audience, with face-to-face communication being more expensive when employees are separated geographically and email being the most convenient for reaching a large number of people instantaneously. The choice of channel could also be influenced by media symbolism in that an individual's selection could be determined by the impression s/he believes a particular medium will make on the recipient, whether it signals a desire for teamwork, a sense of urgency or a need for formality (ibid.). On the other hand, a medium's symbolism could be linked to an organisation and its corporate culture, with some companies preferring face-to-face meetings while others rely heavily on email communication. According to the social influence theory, the choice of a channel is determined by organisational norms and the symbolism placed on particular channels within the organisation but in reality there is considerable variety in choice of channels as employees end up choosing channels for diverse reasons (ibid.). To complicate matters further, choice of a medium could also be due to cultural factors, with some cultures placing a higher value on face-to-face communication over the new electronic communication media.

As for preferred modes of communication, the majority of respondents preferred face-to-face communication over email, telephone and intranet chat for both internal (78 per cent within the company) and external (59 per cent with clients) communication. While intranet chat is the least preferred at 6 per cent, there is a close tie between email (12.5 per cent) and telephone (9.4 per cent) communication for internal communication but a larger gap between the two (email – 28 per cent and telephone – 6 per cent) for external communication. That face-to-face communication is ranked as the most preferred mode of communication is no surprise as it 'is the richest medium because it has the *highest* availability of communication cues and is preferable in times of organisational uncertainty and equivocality' (Kupritz and Cowell 2011). No matter how sophisticated the virtual environment is, it does not provide the objective conditions in the physical environment that enable 'perception, memory and emotional management' for optimal engagement in work processes (Wise and Augustin 2000: 130). According to Kupritz and Cowell's study (2011), face-to-face communication is particularly favoured among employees for human resource information that is private, personal or sensitive, including information about annual reviews, promotions, discipline and legal concerns. However in the same study, employees indicated that it was productive and even critical to receive non-confidential information such as meeting times, training times, policy changes, system problems and information with numerous details through email. This goes to show that both mediums play an important role in organisations as each serves a different role and is effective for disseminating different kinds of information.

As for telephone communication, it seems to follow closely behind email communication as the preferred channel of communication in the present study. This is not surprising as it is a high-bandwidth channel in comparison to email communication in that it has the advantage of communicating nuances of tone, using natural language and getting immediate feedback from the sender. It not only offers additional bandwidth in terms of media richness but is also a familiar channel of communication in comparison to the newer interactive modes such as videoconferencing. According to media richness theory, videoconferencing falls somewhere between telephone and face-to-face communication while email falls between the telephone and letter in terms of the availability of multiple channels of communication (Wallace 2004). However, the reason why email is still preferred over telephones could be because communication channels do not only vary along a continuum of media richness but have other advantages. For instance, email communication has several advantages over face-to-face or telephone conversations that make it an attractive choice in business contexts, being particularly convenient for multiple addressing through distribution lists, storage of permanent digital records of email exchanges as well as message sorting and searching features.

Apart from email communication, other technologies such as instant messaging are emerging in the business context. In comparison to email, instant messaging has fewer norms, leans more towards speech and provides immediate feedback from recipients. Although the use of instant messaging as a business communication tool was nonexistent until the late 1990s, according to Wallace (2004: 109) 'it appears to be filling a role on the fringes of email and telephone conversations, in which short and quick text exchanges with immediate response work well'. Based on the present study, instant messaging appears to be the least preferred means of communication; however it is too early to make any predictions regarding its use in the business context in the future. As expected, the response to it as an effective communication tool is mixed, with some believing that it will be the next killer app in business settings while others being sceptical of its usefulness. Whether it will hinder or improve productivity remains to be seen but it may be useful in certain specialised contexts such as technical support and sales jobs which rely on quick exchange of information to accomplish tasks. In these specialised contexts, instant messaging may prove to be a valuable time-saving tool due to its unique characteristics of brevity and informality, which liberates people from adhering to the usual social norms of polite greetings, closings and other civilities.

The preference of one medium of communication over another may also be related to diversity in experience with new media. Research has shown that people's attitude plays an important role in choice and use of media but that this can change with exposure and familiarity with the medium as well as with the message topics, organisational context and styles of their communication partners (Wallace 2004). Based on a study on email communication, Carlson and Zmud (1999) proposed the Channel Expansion Theory, emphasising the important role that experience with new media played on changing people's attitudes towards that media. The perceptions of their study participants towards email were enhanced by positive experiences with the media, knowledge about the topic of the message and familiarity with the communication partner. Similarly, it is expected that knowledge-building experiences with other new and emerging media will change our perceptions and improve our use of the media with time.

(iv) Efficiency of channels

Apart from the frequency of use of channels, the efficiency of channels from the users' perspective is relevant for any study on workplace communication. Therefore, our questionnaire sought the respondents' views on whether they found the use of certain traditional and newer channels of communication effective. Contrary to expectations, in spite of the availability of alternative modes of communication in our internet age, the channels that our respondents considered to be the most effective with a 97 per cent response rate were the traditional modes of communication such as face-to-face communication and telephone calls. The only other mode of communication that they considered equally effective was email communication, which is understandable as it was the first mode of internet communication introduced in workplaces and has been in existence since the early 1980s. As for teleconferencing and videoconferencing, 70 per cent and 60 per cent of our respondents considered these channels to be effective whereas text messaging and intranet chatting, the most recent channels to gain entry into the workplace, were at the lower end of the spectrum in terms of efficiency at 56 per cent and 46 per cent respectively.

It must be acknowledged that face-to-face meetings are the most effective way to communicate in the workplace as they enable business associates to not only transmit information (especially equivocal information) speedily and receive immediate feedback but also build a personal and trustworthy atmosphere among them. According to researchers, teleconferencing (Fowler and Wackerbarth 1980) and videoconferencing (Denstadli, Julsrud and Hjorthol 2012) are unsatisfactory for tasks that are complex and involve interpersonal features. In spite of their shortcomings, the use of teleconferencing and videoconferencing has grown tremendously since the 1970s and 1990s respectively. Perhaps one reason for the increased use of these alternative audio-only and audio-visual modes of communication in business settings is that they fulfil different but complementary functions when compared to face-to-face meetings. For instance, Lu and Peeta's study (2009) has shown that the context of a meeting is the key factor influencing the choice between mediums, with face-to-face meetings being preferred for negotiations and problem-solving while videoconferencing is chosen for more straightforward information exchange.

Face-to-face meetings and videoconferencing seem to be motivated by nonhomogeneous needs in organisations. According to Denstadli *et al.*'s survey-based study (2012), the key advantages of videoconferencing are that it improves efficiency in exchanging information and making decisions, saves time in the planning and duration of meetings, and reduces strain resulting from travelling from one place to another. As for the disadvantages, it seems like it is not suitable for meetings with unknown people and for developing new business contacts. Therefore, the choice between face-to-face meeting and videoconferencing seem to be motivated by relational and task-related dimensions as well as time and travel constraints. This applies to the present study in which face-to-face meetings are considered to be more effective than virtual meetings, whether teleconferencing or videoconferencing. However, they are still rated quite high in terms of efficiency in second and third place, indicating that these modes are not meant to substitute face-to-face meetings but serve alternate functions in the business organisations. What makes one virtual mode more popular than another among the respondents could be due to several reasons – the context of the meeting (information-giving or problem solving), the relationship between the participants (known or unknown), the size of their organisations (multi unit or single unit), the position of the respondents (managerial or non-managerial), and their access to facilities for teleconferencing and videoconferencing within the organisation.

The use of text-based chat was nonexistent in business settings and only emerged as a tool for communication in the late 1990s. However, it was called instant messaging rather than chat to give it a more serious flavour as an information exchange tool meant for gathering business intelligence rather than for social interactions among employees (Wallace 2004). That it is not considered by the survey respondents in the current study to be as effective a mode of communication as some of the other virtual channels of communication could be attributed to the newness of the channel. In fact, business communication texts have only recently started including instant messaging as a legitimate tool in business contexts. Other reasons could be its perception as a tool for social interaction and its limitations as a medium in that it is constrained by short text messages, which tend to be informal as they are composed synchronously, with little scope for editing. Yet, some respondents believe that it is the next killer app in certain specialised contexts in the technical and service sectors where information is required immediately and in companies where employees are distributed around the globe. In fact, instant messaging can be a productive communication tool in companies where business is dependent upon speedy communication. Many companies are therefore installing privately operated networks that are restricted to authenticated employees and that have special features for monitoring their employees' online chats. It is only through regular use of this channel that businesses will be able to ascertain its value and correct use in the particular business setting.

(v) Relationship between channels and audience

The choice of a channel of communication is often determined by the targeted audience/reader in many communication situations, including the business context. We anticipated that there would be differences in the selection of channels among employees depending upon whether the communication was internal or external as well as the direction of the communication (i.e. vertical or horizontal). The last question in the survey questionnaire was therefore aimed to determine the respondents' choice of channel in these two scenarios.

As expected, the findings revealed that over 90 per cent of respondents were likely to use traditional channels (e.g. face-to-face and telephone) and familiar internet channels (e.g. email) for communication internally and externally with colleagues at all levels, including superiors, peers and juniors. Survey findings for the more popular virtual channels of teleconferencing and videoconferencing were divided, with 25–30 per cent of respondents indicating that they would use these channels for both external and internal communication but the remaining respondents preferring to use them exclusively, either for external or internal communication. This finding is contradictory to that of Denstadli *et al*'s survey-based study (2012) in which respondents preferred to use videoconferencing for intraorganisation communication as they felt that it is not an effective mode for communicating with unknown people and for building client relationships. As for texting and instant messaging, the findings were more skewed towards the use of these channels for internal communication, with more respondents preferring to use these channels with peers or juniors rather than superiors.

Preferences for particular channels could be due to several reasons ranging from inherent characteristics and availability of the channels to the level of formality and familiarity with the channels. The new media innovations that have emerged from the internet 'support different kinds of communication with characteristics that are not the same as the phone call or a face-to-face meeting' (Wallace 2004: 112), making them more suitable for use in special circumstances rather than in all business situations.

Business communication curriculum: pedagogical implications

(i) Current business communication courses

It is a well-known fact that the professional competence of graduating students is dependent on their communication competence and familiarity with workplace genres. To ensure that students leave university well equipped for the workplace, business communication courses are offered at most overseas and local universities. Topics covered in these courses usually include *communication theories* (basic communication models, persuasive communication theories, group communication theories, etc.), *written communication* (letters, memos, and reports), *public speaking* (presentations, visual aids, delivery, etc.), *mediated communication* (mainly email), and *employment communication* (resumes, cover letters and interviews). Other topics include *interpersonal communication* (nonverbal communication, conflict resolution, negotiations, etc.), *group communication* (meetings, role of participants and leaders), *organisational communication* (company's communication practices) and *intercultural communication*. Although this is a comprehensive list of possible topics included in business courses, there are institutional variations depending upon the number of business communication and related courses offered at a particular university. In addition, there are other variables such as students' academic level, teacher's experience, course duration and class time that affect the coverage of topics.

In the past, business communication courses at tertiary level traditionally focused on letter writing, memos, reports, proposals and business presentations but the internet has triggered a transformation in the syllabi. The question to consider is whether computer mediated communication in the business world has rendered the syllabi at most universities obsolete or has supplemented traditional means of workplace communication with net-centric methods of communication. A bird's eye view of the business communication syllabi of the three main universities (available on their websites) in Singapore shows that the focus is on traditional topics such as the communication process, writing skills in relation to business documents (letters, memos and email), report writing skills, employment communication, intercultural communication skills, interpersonal skills and oral presentation skills. In two of the universities, these topics are either covered in a single course of four academic units or span two courses of two academic units each. As for the third university, only the core topics of written and spoken communication are handled in the introductory business communication course, with separate courses being offered on interpersonal, intercultural, organisational, creative and mediated communication.

In the context of mediated communication, it was noted that all the universities cover email communication extensively but there is no mention of teleconferencing, videoconferencing or instant/text messaging in the syllabus except in one of the universities, which offers a dedicated course on digital media. This is reflective of business communication courses in US universities where instructors spend more time on email instruction rather than on other technological advancements (Russ 2009). The lack of emphasis on some of these digital modes of communication could be because they are fairly new in the workplace. However, this reason cannot justify the omission of these topics in the business curriculum given the importance of digital media in the twenty-first-century workplace.

(ii) Enhanced business communication curriculum for the future

Given the complex communication environment of the twenty-first century, the current business communication curriculum and pedagogy needs to be enhanced by incorporating some aspects of digital media communication into the current courses. Du-Babcock (2006: 261) aptly describes the future challenges of business professionals as learning 'how to communicate in an information-overload environment, how to encode and decode messages within interactants at varying competency levels, and how to use and choose among communication media and technologies'. To ensure that undergrad students are well prepared for the transforming workplace, business communication academics need to extend their discipline and teaching to encompass a combination of traditional and digital means of communication which tend to coexist and are deployed for different communication situations and needs. In order to bridge the gap between the old and new modes of workplace communication, it becomes necessary to examine the similarities and differences between them and to suggest specific practice activities for university students.

To begin with, students may not be aware that different channels of communication serve different purposes and are suited for different kinds of business communication. Research on employees' perception in relation to communication channels has shown that they prefer face-to-face communication over digital modes of communication for information that is private, personal or sensitive. With particular reference to email, participants felt that it is productive for conveying information related to meeting times, training times, policy changes, system problems and complex information (Kupritz and Cowell 2011). As for videoconferencing, while it is considered to be a good tool for meetings on well defined areas of concern and to communicate the progress of ongoing projects with known people, it is not recommended for use in situations where more creative interaction is required, especially with unfamiliar people (Panteli and Dawson 2001; Denstadli, Julsrud and Hjorthol 2012). Given the fact that different communication channels play specific roles in business organisations, the first step in business communication courses would be to raise student awareness regarding the effectiveness of the many channels of communication in different settings. The next step would be to examine closely the characteristics and functions of the channels that make them particularly suited to these settings.

Although there are some similarities between audio/video conferencing and face-to-face meetings, the digital nature of the former has given rise to some key differences. For instance research on teleconferencing has shown that in comparison to face-to-face meetings, there are fewer interruptions, overlaps and pauses but more attempts at identification of self and others; small talk is restricted to the beginning and end with no side comments among participants; and there is frequency of back channels to signal feedback or desire to take the floor (Halbe 2012). Due to lack of body language signals, these features along with paralanguage signals such as intonation and silence play an important role in communication, especially when attempting to read between the lines. As for videoconferencing, research has shown that it is not a substitute for face-to-face meetings as it is effective mainly for intra-organisational communication among known participants involved in virtual projects (Denstadli, Julsrud and Hjorthol 2012). It lacks the advantages of face-to-face meetings, which include transmitting equivocal information, enabling immediate feedback and building a personal, authentic and trustworthy atmosphere among participants. Given that these modes of communication have unique characteristics and serve complementary functions in different business settings, it becomes imperative to prepare students for the proper use of these channels in the workplace.

Rather than expecting students to cope with teleconferencing and videoconferencing on their own, it would be beneficial to incorporate activities in relation to these digital media in the business communication curriculum. An introductory activity could be an analysis of a recorded telephone or video conference. Students could work on small-scale projects to compare the similarities and differences between face-to-face meetings and these new modes of communication using the criteria of pauses, speaker selection, turn taking, overlaps, back channels and interruptions. As mentioned earlier, there are fewer interruptions, overlaps and pauses in teleconferencing, small talk is restricted to the beginning or end of calls, side comments are non-existent and back channels occur frequently as they are the only means of communicating attention (Halbe 2012). Similarly, videoconferencing has its own unique characteristics such that it tends to be more structured than physical meetings, disallowing spontaneous interjections and blurring non-verbal signals (Panteli and Dawson 2001). Once students are aware of the subtle differences in these digital modes, they could be given a meeting topic and agenda to simulate real-life telephone and video conferences in small groups using Skype or other similar platforms that are freely available on the internet. As a post-activity task, they could be asked to use their institutions' instant messaging platform to discuss their experience of having participated in the activities.

Another aspect that should be taken into consideration in designing a business communication curriculum is the changing landscape of business communication in today's corporate world. The emergence of mediated discourses has made it possible for business organisations to connect with people located in different parts of the world, with different cultural backgrounds and different levels of proficiency and competency in English. In such a complex and diverse business communication environment, business students need to be trained to communicate effectively with multilingual and multicultural people with varying linguistic competencies, using different professional genres and communication technologies. We cannot expect our students to cope with this rapidly changing business communication environment on their own. We should, therefore, include in our syllabuses practice tasks as well as straightforward and useful netiquette tips that they will need to cope with the challenges presented by the new media. For instance, to make students realise that virtual presence in a videoconference is not the same as physical presence in a face-to-face meeting, it would be useful to train them to call a participant by name before posing a question to him/her as eye contact and gestures are not easily picked up on a screen (Panteli and Dawson 2001). As students gain more experience with the different modes of electronic communication, they will be able to improve and refine their usage of these channels. However, in the interim period, it is our responsibility as educators not only to provide them with specific training in the use of different electronic business communication tools but also advice on their suitability in different settings.

One way of integrating the use of digital media in our current business communication courses could be through projects which involve communication between students from universities in different countries. Du-Babcock (2006) describes one such effort based on a short project between US and Hong Kong students to solve a business case via videoconferencing and a more extensive research project involving the analysis of different business practices using a variety of digital media. In addition to these project topics, students could compare Corporate Social Research initiatives or corporate websites in their respective countries, particularly from the perspective of high-context or low-context communication styles in different cultures (Usunier 2012). Such projects are particularly useful for students as language competency and communication patterns of participants differ depending upon whether they are first or second language speakers of English and whether their cultural orientations are personality-centred (i.e. proactive style) or situational (i.e. reactive style). Through collaborations with universities abroad, business communication teachers can provide real time practice to students to communicate in a multinational and global environment using new communication technologies.

It seems like the business scenario of the future requires students to be able to communicate in a variety of professional genres, with people of diverse linguistic and cultural competencies using a range of communication technologies. To meet these challenges, Du-Babcock (2006: 257) rightly points out that teachers of business communication need to 'learn how to teach in this changing communication environment, in which the basic communication process and underlying communication process remain constant but individuals are communicating via cell phones, videoconferences, and so on, rather than – and in addition to – via letters, memos, and face-to-face meetings'. Therefore to prepare students for their future workplaces, the goal of business communication teachers should be to expand their courses to include new strategies and technologies within the existing framework of business communication.

Conclusion

In this chapter, based on a survey conducted on practitioners and review of current research, an attempt is made to reach a deeper understanding of the emergence, development and change in professional practices and discourse in the Singapore business context. The study has shown that new electronic media has had an impact on organisational communication, changing the way people communicate in the workplace. Even though the transformation is gradual, with most organisations continuing to use the traditional means of communication along with the new technologies, our students need to be ready for the future workplace. To achieve this, educators need to embrace new technologies by incorporating them into their introductory business courses at university. As students gain more experience with new digital channels, they will be able to use them more effectively to fulfil varying communication needs in the dynamically changing landscape of the twenty-first century workplace.

Related topics

transformation in business communication; impact of technological advances; new digital channels and workplace communication; implications for business communication curriculum

Key readings

Berg, R. W. (2012). 'The anonymity factor in making multicultural teams work: Virtual and real teams', *Business Communication Quarterly*, 75(4), 404–24. (According to this paper, members of a dysfunctional multicultural team contributed in a more balanced manner in anonymous virtual teams than in a real-team setting though team members believed that their input was also heard and appreciated in the real-team setting.)

Lam, C. (2013). 'The efficacy of text messaging to improve social connectedness and team attitude in student technical communication projects: An experimental study', *Journal of Business and Technical Communication*, 27(2), 180–208. (This study provides empirical evidence for using short-messaging service (SMS) in team contexts as students in the SMS-only group had better communication and connectivity compared to students in the non-SMS group.)

Pazos, P., Chung J. M., and Micari, M. (2013). 'Instant messaging as a task-support tool in information technology organizations', *Journal of Business Communication*, 50(1), 68–86. (This paper investigates the use of instant messaging (IM) in information technology organisations and reports that there is a greater use of IM in collaboration tasks than cognitive conflict tasks.)

Bibliography

Bargiela-Chiappini, F. (2009). *The Handbook of Discourse*, Edinburgh: Edinburgh University Press.
Carlson, J. R. and Zmud, R. W. (1999). 'Channel expansion theory and the experiential nature of media richness perceptions', *Academy of Management Journal*, 42(2), 157–71.

Denstadli, J. M., Julsrud, T. E., and Hjorthol, R. J. (2012). 'Videoconferencing as a mode of communication: A comparative study of the use of videoconferencing and face-to-face meetings', *Journal of Business and Technical Communication*, 26(1), 65–91.

Du-Babcock, B. (2006). 'Teaching business communication: Past, present, and future', *Journal of Business Communication*, 43(3), 253–64.

Fowler, G. and Wackerbarth, M. (1980). 'Audio teleconferencing versus face-to-face conferencing: A synthesis of the literature', *Western Journal of Speech Communication*, 44, 236–52.

Guenther, K. and Braun, E. (2001). 'Knowledge management benefits of intranet'. Available at www.onlineinc.com/onlinemag (accessed 9 May 2012).

Gunnarsson, B-L. (2009). *Professional Discourse*, London, New York: Continuum.

Halbe, D. (2012). '"Who's there?" Differences in the features of telephone and face-to-face conferences', *Journal of Business Communication*, 49(1), 48–73.

Kupritz, V. W. and Cowell, E. (2011). 'Productive management communication: Online and face-to-face', *Journal of Business Communication*, 28(1), 54–82.

Lu, J. L. and Peeta, S. (2009). 'Analysis of the factors that influence the relationship between business air travel and videoconferencing', *Transportation Research Part A*, 43, 709–21.

Panteli, N. and Dawson, P. (2001). 'Video conferencing meetings: Changing patterns of business communication', *New Technology, Work and Employment*, 12(2), 88–98.

Russ, T. L. (2009). 'The status of the business communication course at U.S. colleges and universities', *Business Communication Quarterly*, 72(4), 395–413.

Singapore SEO Consultant (n.d.) *Singapore Internet Statistics 2013*. Available at www.larrylim.net/singapore-Internet-usage-statistics.htm (accessed 2 May 2013).

Trevino, L. K., Webster, J. and Stein, E. W. (2000). 'Making connections: Complementary influences on communication media choices, attitudes, and use', *Organization Science: A Journal of Institute Management Sciences*, 11(2), 163–83.

Usunier, J.-C. (2012). 'The influence of high- and low-context communication styles on the design, content, and language of business-to-business web sites', *Journal of Business Communication*, 47(2), 189–227.

Wallace, P. (2004). *The Internet in the Workplace: How New Technology is Transforming Work*, Cambridge: Cambridge University Press.

Wise, J. and Augustin, S. (2000). *Enhancing Employees' Experiences of Workplace Environments: A Workshop Illustrating what Evolutionary Psychology is Teaching us About Workplace Designs* [Abstract], Proceedings of the 31st Environmental Design Research Associaton (p. 130), Oklahoma: Environmental Design Research Association.

19
Methodology for teaching ESP

William Littlewood

Introduction

First I will clarify the direction from which this article has been written. My main interest and experience are not in the 'ESP' part of the title but in the 'methodology'. For several years I did indeed teach ESP at undergraduate level – mainly to science students but also to students of the arts and social sciences (including business) – but was never really aware of doing a different job from what I had done before. Of course I made efforts to adapt my teaching to the purposes, needs and interests of the specific students I was teaching, but this was no different from what I had always been doing. So in the domain of methodology, my experience has reflected the view of Hutchinson and Waters (1987: 18): 'ESP is *not* different from any other form of language teaching, in that it should be based in the first instance on principles of effective and efficient learning'.

My first step in preparing this article was to search for what I had been missing in the ESP journals that would illuminate for me any special ESP methodology that I had not been applying in my own teaching. Mostly it turned out to be the proverbial search for the needle in the haystack. A title about seminars would look promising – but it would say little about alternative ways to conduct them effectively and everything about the discourse that they display. As if this discourse did not depend in large part on how the seminars were conducted! An article about plagiarism would say a lot about students' strategies for plagiarising but offer few practical ideas on how to motivate and help them to avoid it by finding their own voice. ESP researchers seemed to be very interested in investigating an almost endless number of aspects of specialist language and discourse (especially in written texts) but less interested in exploring ways to help students gain access to them.

There are notable exceptions. There are, for example, the investigations of problem-based learning by Barron (2002) and Wood and Head (2004); Esteban and Canado's (2004) exploration of ways of 'making the case-method work'; Flowerdew's (2010) account of how she devised and implemented a business proposal module; Lee and Swales' (2006) discussion of a corpus-based course; Zappa-Hollman (2007) on academic presentations; and a number of studies that investigate genre-based pedagogy and how instruction can move 'from the assistance of more knowledgeable others to gradually more independent text generation' (Belcher 2006:

141; see also Johns 2009). On the whole, however, an examination of the articles published over recent years in the specialist journal *English for Specific Purposes* confirms Paltridge and Starfield's (2011: 116) statement that 'research in ESP has remained close to its earlier textual or transcriptual roots' and been dominated by the same 'text/discourse analytic perspective' (106) that Master (2005) had identified several years earlier. (Master cites data from a 2002 survey by Hewings which reveals that in the years 1997–2001, 49 articles in *English for Specific Purposes* had focused on text and discourse analysis, 10 on programme description, 9 on needs analysis and syllabus design, and a meagre 6 on materials and methods.)

In the present article, the first main section will survey how teaching methodology has been dealt with not in research articles but in published books and chapters for ESP teachers. Here we find a respectable number of individual chapters that discuss ESP methodology, as well as handbooks that offer a wide variety of individual techniques. Most of these publications present methods and techniques in a 'state-of-the-art' manner without problematising them or considering alternatives. The second main section will address the question of whether there is in fact an identifiable 'ESP methodology' that is separate from that for general EFL. Since my own answer to that question (as I indicated above) is that at the level of principles for language teaching, a single framework embraces both domains, the third and final major section will shift to that higher level. It will consider attempts to formulate context-free principles that can inform what Kumaravadivelu (2006: 20) calls 'a context-sensitive postmethod pedagogy that encompasses location-specific teaching strategies and instructional materials'. This description includes, of course, the various contexts of ESP. By extension, too, the same methodological principles may be applied to teaching other languages for special purposes (LSP).

ESP methodology: a neglected field?

In response to Hyland and Hamp-Lyons' (2002) 'state-of-the-art' introduction to the first issue of the *Journal of English for Academic Purposes*, Watson Todd (2003) elaborates on a similar view to the one presented above: that the field of English for academic purposes (EAP) had made impressive efforts in analysing *what* needs to be taught (e.g. the nature of the specialist communication and texts that constitute the students' learning goals) but devoted comparatively little attention to *how* it needs to be taught (i.e. the learning experiences that are needed if students are to achieve these goals). A similar concern had earlier led Hutchinson and Waters (1987) to propose their 'learning-centred approach' to ESP. Hutchinson and Waters made the more radical claim that earlier stages of ESP had been 'fundamentally flawed, in that they are all based on descriptions of language *use*' (1987: 14) rather than language *learning*. ESP should start by analysing not students' special 'target needs' (e.g. the registers, discourse types and situations that they will encounter) but rather their 'learning needs' and the experiences that will enable them to acquire competencies that can be used in *any* situation. Hutchinson and Waters' proposal provoked reactions mainly because it queried the principle of 'specificity' (of language and context) that is encoded in the very label of English for *specific* purposes (see e.g. the commentary of Cheng 2011: 46–47) but it also contained the clear message that the field should pay more attention to principles and processes of learning and teaching. Indeed the text provides what is still one of the most useful discussions of learning and teaching principles in the ESP literature.

In the more than two decades that have followed the publication of Hutchinson and Waters (1987), it would not be true to say that teaching methodology has not received attention in the field of ESP. With few exceptions, however, the treatment of methodology has focused on describing or recommending techniques and there has been little discussion of a higher-level framework that would guide teachers in the choice of these techniques or illuminate their function in relation to each other and the goal of specialist communicative competence. Strategic advice of this kind has mainly taken the form of vague suggestions to use a range of methods and adapt one's approach to specific learners. Here I will mention just a few milestones in the published literature, restricting myself to material that has appeared in book or book-chapter form.

- Robinson's (1991) book has a chapter in which she discusses 'what methodological options are available in ESP' and advocates mainly 'tasks, used here as an overall term and including role plays and simulations, case studies, projects and oral presentations' (p. 47). There is some discussion of how the teacher may deal with task-based learning in the classroom (e.g. whether explicit attention to language should come before or after the task and the danger of disrupting an activity through ongoing error correction). However, tasks are not placed in a higher-level methodological framework which might seek to explain their role in the teaching-and-learning process and guide teachers in whether to select one of these options rather than others at particular stages of instruction.
- Ellis and Johnson (1994) include more detailed practical classroom recommendations. They suggest ways of using 'framework materials' – 'diagrammatic representations' which represent concepts such as cause and effect, interactions such as business meetings, or ways of expressing ideas such as describing situations – which can serve as a useful basis for students to generate language. They also recommend ways of exploiting authentic materials in class and give advice on how to manage activities (notably role plays and simulations). Their concluding advice on 'methodologies' is that 'there is no one "best" methodology' and the choice depends on the specific situation, but that 'methodologies that put the learners at the centre of the learning process are likely to be the most effective when working with professional people' (1994: 219). The principles that might guide this choice of methodology and the strategies for implementing a learner centred approach are not further elaborated.
- Dudley-Evans and St John (1998) include a chapter on 'classroom practice and beyond'. These authors are amongst the few who believe that there is 'a distinguishable ESP methodology' (which is different from EFL teaching) because (a) the learners have specialist knowledge and (b) they bring different cognitive and learning processes (including learning styles) from their specialist field. The implication they draw is similar to that described by Robinson (1991): 'in addition to language-learning activities, the ESP classroom uses tasks and activities that reflect the learners' specialist world' (p. 187) and often a 'deep-end strategy [which] takes performance as its starting point' (p. 190) is appropriate. The authors include useful practical considerations but again we lack a broader framework that might help teachers to decide on a balance between the (analytical? form-focused?) 'language learning activities' and the tasks that are 'often' (when not?) a more appropriate starting point.
- Jordan (1997) provides more extensive and in-depth discussion of teaching methodology (here: for EAP). In seven separate chapters on the 'study skills' he gives advice on matters such as increasing students' reading speed (p. 146), using mnemonics to help students to memorise vocabulary (p. 161) and developing oral presentation skills (pp. 201–4). Significantly for the present discussion, before embarking on this detailed treatment of specific skills and techniques, he addresses the need for a higher-level framework of guiding principles. In what sometimes becomes a labyrinth of partially overlapping accounts from the ESP and general EFL literature, he lists, for example, four 'methodological principles' (p. 109), to which are added nine fundamental 'principles of learning' (p. 110), five 'principles of communicative methodology' (p. 111), four 'purposes of communicative activities' (p. 112) and

five 'principles for a communicative exercise typology' (p. 112). In conclusion, he presents (pp. 124–25) a diagram giving a 'synthesis of the methodological aspects' of EAP. The diagram distinguishes an 'activity' (e.g. problem-solving, discussion, role-play) from a 'task/exercise/technique' (e.g. information transfer, reformulation, cloze) and also incorporates factors related to educational aids, language/material, organisation and teacher's role.

- Johns (1999) is one of the few publications (albeit only a chapter in an encyclopaedia) which is dedicated specifically to pedagogical principles in LSP. Building on the notion of specificity referred to above, Johns points out that each pedagogical situation and each group of learners has unique characteristics, including teachers' and learners' theories of how language is learned, perceptions of the teacher/learner relationship, present needs and interests, anxieties and learning styles. So 'no single approach ... is appropriate for all pedagogical situations' (1999: 633). She discerns three main trends: learner-centred approaches, genre-based approaches and task-based approaches.

- In a comprehensive coverage of practical issues in teaching business English, Donna (2000) includes two substantial chapters (about 200 pages in all) that deal with 'day-to-day concerns' such as presenting language and error correction and 'developing students' skills' in domains such as talking to clients and telephoning. Her advice on selecting methods is to use 'a range of methods ... selected to suit individual students' (p. 69) and follow certain principles such as giving students models of language, contextualising language practice realistically and encouraging the use of language for communication. She gives a large number of activities for practising relevant skills such as leaving messages on answering machines and apologising for arriving late.

- There are several other useful handbooks that consist almost entirely of descriptions of specific classroom activities, procedures and techniques. For example, Harding (2007) describes some 70 small-scale activities, each lasting between 15 and 60 minutes, in which students practise components of specialist discourse such as explaining the function of equipment, using the language of charts and graphs, and even smiling on the phone. The activities in Emmerson and Hamilton (2005) are even shorter and more numerous: no fewer than 129 'five-minute activities' that focus on individual skills and aspects of language used in Business English. Guse (2011) describes activities (mostly of about 40 minutes) that focus on each of the four major skills, as well as on vocabulary and grammar. One special feature is the import into EAP of collaborative learning structures such as 'rotating trios' and 'jigsaw'.

- A rare initiative to develop a coherent and explicitly justified framework for developing an ESP methodology is found in Basturkmen (2006). One of Basturkmen's explicit aims in the book is to compensate for the lack of discussion in the ESP literature of theory and ideas about learning and teaching (she mentions Hutchinson and Waters 1987, as a notable exception). ESP has been preoccupied with 'practical aspects of course and materials design and with language descriptions' (2006: 5) and paid little attention to 'the views of learning implicit in [for example] project work and task-based learning' (ibid.). To help fill this gap, she includes two substantial sections that explore learning and teaching. Section B on 'learning' contains two chapters that discuss respectively the conditions that support learning (acculturation, input and interaction). Section C on 'teaching' draws the implications of these views of learning for 'methodologies' (where she draws a broad distinction between 'input-based strategies' and 'output-based strategies') and 'objectives' (to reveal subject-specific language use; to develop target language competencies; to teach underlying knowledge; to develop strategic competence; to foster critical awareness). Unfortunately she does not develop these topics further in her 2010 book, though one key aspect of developing a course in ESP is surely to explore an appropriate methodology for actually teaching it.

We will mention Basturkmen's suggested methodological framework later in the context of discussing other principles proposed in the TESOL and EFL literature.

ESP methodology – How 'specific' is it?

The controversy aroused by Hutchinson and Waters' (1987) book concerned mainly the way it seemed to question the specificity of the language and contexts of ESP. However it also has clear implications for the methodology of ESP. If learning ESP is fundamentally the same as learning any other kind of language, then teaching also is guided by the same principles. Hutchinson and Waters themselves draw this implication when they state: 'There is, in other words, no such thing as an ESP methodology, merely methodologies that have been applied in ESP classrooms, but could just as well have been used in the learning of any kind of English' (1987: 18).

The same view emerges from most of the publications reviewed in the previous section. For example, Robinson (1991: 47) states that the same 'methodological options' are available in ESP as in general ELT and 'there is very little difference from general ELT'. Ellis and Johnson (1994: 12), referring to Business English, express a similar view: 'Many learning tasks and activities will be the same as on a General English course, especially for teaching structures, vocabulary and social English'. Those writers who advise teachers to use 'a range of methods ... selected to suit individual students' (Donna 2000: 69) and design 'a unique curriculum and collection of classroom activities ... for each group of students and teachers in every new context' (Johns 1999: 633) are obviously assuming that teachers can select from a general 'pool' of activities available to all language teachers. Of the authors cited above, only Dudley-Evans and St John (1998: 187) perceive 'a distinguishable ESP methodology' in which, because of the learners' specialist knowledge and experience, the 'deep-end strategy' will often be more appropriate than the familiar PPP sequence (present, practise, perform). But this is really an instance of their own general language teaching principle that 'there is no best way' and teachers should 'select and adapt their methodology to match the learners' needs' (ibid.).

We can infer from the two previous sentences that whether or not we identify a 'distinguishable methodology' depends largely on our level of analysis. As Rodgers (2011) argues, the concept of 'methodology' is itself problematic:

- At the more concrete level of classroom implementation, methodology can be defined as 'the variety of ways teachers use to activate the learning process – the techniques, activities, etc. locally appropriate to particular learning/teaching situations' (Rodgers 2011: 341). At this level we are indeed likely to distinguish techniques and activities that comprise an ESP methodology in the sense that they are more appropriate in, say, an adult ESP situation than in an adolescent EFL situation. These might include activities that implement the 'deep-end strategy' mentioned by Dudley-Evans and St John (1998) (e.g. case studies, role-play, simulation, project work, problem-based learning, genre-based learning) in addition to more controlled activities focused on specific language, functions or skills. A rich variety of activities at this practical level can be found in the ESP literature, including the practical handbooks reviewed above (e.g. Harding 2007) and textbooks such as those reviewed by McDonough (2010).
- At a more abstract level, methodology can also be defined as '*a set of general principles* that in one way or another inform the variety of local practices' (Rodgers 2011: 342; emphasis added). They not only inform present practices but are also capable of generating new practices in the individual teacher's pedagogy, guiding the teacher's choice of practices, and showing how these practices relate to each other and to the students' goals. At this level,

'methodology' is a cognitive framework that can give direction and coherence to our choice of activities and guide us in implementing them. It is part of the 'theory and ideas' about learning and teaching that Basturkmen (2006: 4) finds lacking in ESP discussions. Methodology in this sense transcends the specific world of ESP. It embraces ESP in the same way as it embraces, say, English for young learners, and asks: What are the specific features of these contexts, these learners and these teachers, so that we can take these features into account in developing an appropriate pedagogy based on sound principles?

It is to methodology in this sense that the next section will turn.

Methodological principles for teaching ESP

The goal of teaching is learning. The fundamental premise of Hutchinson and Waters' (1987) book is that ESP teaching 'must be based on an understanding of the processes of language *learning*' (p. 14). Similarly, one of the aims of Basturkmen's (2006) book is to examine the 'different ideas about language learning' that are incorporated in the methodologies for ESP such as genre-based and deep-end approaches (pp. 3–4). Indeed in the wider ELT literature it is axiomatic that the practice of teaching must be underpinned by 'a core set of theories and beliefs about the nature of language, of language learning, and a derived set of principles for teaching a language' (Richards and Rodgers 2001: 244).

Accordingly in this section we will look at how 'beliefs about the nature of language' and 'beliefs about the nature of learning' have evolved during the period of ESP's development. The section that follows will then address the 'principles for teaching a language' that constitute the third component of Richards and Rodgers' framework.

Beliefs about the nature of language

The history of ESP is usually said to have begun in the 1960s and it continues, of course, into the present day. This means that most of its development has been contemporaneous with the development of the 'communicative approach' in the wider field of language teaching. ESP and the communicative approach have influenced each other mutually and many of the key works of the 1970s (e.g. Wilkins 1976; Widdowson 1978) had an equally seminal effect in both ESP and general ELT. Indeed one could say that ESP implements the principles of the communicative approach in the domain of learning English for specific rather than general purposes. That is one reason why the ESP literature has needed to make comparatively few detailed statements about the principles that inform its teaching methodology: it has drawn on the same principles as general ELT.

A major impetus in the development of both general ELT and ESP was the realisation (in the early 1970s) that structural accounts of language do not provide an adequate basis for language teaching. Language teaching began to work with communication-oriented frameworks such as Michael Halliday's 'functional' view of language and Dell Hymes' concept of 'communicative competence' (excerpts from both of these writers can be found in Brumfit and Johnson 1979). Analyses of communication and communicative competence reveal the complex relationships that exist between structures and meanings, especially when we consider not only the conceptual meanings of sentences but also the communicative functions they perform in situations. For example, an apparently straightforward declarative sentence such as *The door's open* could function as an explanation ('that's why it's so cold'), a reassurance ('don't worry, you'll be able to get out'), a request ('close it, please'), and in many other ways, depending on the situation. Conversely, a request could be expressed not only through the above sentence but also more directly through, for example, *Would you mind closing the door?* or simply *Close the door, please.* The selection of one form rather than another is governed by linguistic factors, situational factors, and conventions of social appropriacy. In order to communicate both effectively and appropriately, learners must therefore be aware of the links between language forms and all aspects of meaning (conceptual, functional and social) and be able to express and interpret specific links in specific situations. Moreover, it is not enough to learn to do this for individual utterances. Communication is a process of interaction, in which meanings are developed and negotiated over longer stretches of discourse. It is therefore necessary to learn ways of structuring information and creating cohesive links over longer stretches of writing, ways of opening and closing conversations, disagreeing without producing confrontation, and so on. These ideas are embodied in the influential and still widely cited framework for analysing communicative competence proposed by Canale and Swain (1980) and Canale (1983). (For further discussion, see for example Harley *et al.* 1990 and Benati 2009). Here I have adapted the terminology slightly and also added a fifth dimension to the four proposed in Canale:

- *Linguistic competence* includes the knowledge of vocabulary, grammar, semantics and phonology that have been the traditional focus of second language learning.
- *Sociolinguistic competence* consists primarily of knowledge of how to use language appropriately in social situations, e.g. conveying suitable degrees of formality, directness and so on.
- *Discourse competence* enables speakers to engage in continuous discourse, e.g. by linking ideas in longer written texts, maintaining longer spoken turns, participating in interaction, opening conversations and closing them.
- *Pragmatic competence* enables second language speakers to use their linguistic resources to convey and interpret meanings in real situations, including those where they encounter problems due to gaps in their knowledge.
- *Sociocultural competence* includes awareness of the cultural knowledge and assumptions that affect the exchange of meanings and may lead to misunderstandings in intercultural communication, e.g. the use of gestures or attitudes to punctuality.

The development of ESP (as outlined, for example, in Hutchinson and Waters 1987: 9–15, Ellis and Johnson 1994: 3–5, and more recently Belcher 2009, Paltridge 2009 and Gnutzmann 2011) shows the influence of this expanding concept of communicative competence. In the early stages of ESP, the emphasis was on teaching the structural and lexical characteristics of specialist subject 'registers'. In the 1970s the focus shifted to how this language is used to express important communicative functions and to compose coherent discourse within a specialist domain. At the same time there has been increasing emphasis on developing pragmatic skills for using language in relevant situations and on gaining access to the specialist 'discourse community'. This involves also acquiring an extended sense of identity (see, for example, Belcher and Lukkarila 2011; Hamp-Lyons 2011; Paltridge and Starfield 2011). This expansion of scope obviously has important implications for methodology: the structure-based drills that may be effective for increasing students' command of the passive voice in scientific reports will not be adequate in helping them to find their own voice within a community of scientists, for which the notion of the classroom as a 'participatory learning community' (Belcher 2006) offers more hope.

Beliefs about the nature of language learning

As well as extending our notions of what communicative competence involves in ESP and general ELT (i.e. the goals of language teaching), the period of ESP's development has also been accompanied by broader conceptions of the learning processes that can help students towards these goals.

Before the 1970s, language learning was seen predominantly (and often exclusively) from an 'analytic' perspective and as a form of skill learning. Items of language (e.g. structures, functions, lexical items) are isolated by the teacher and taught as 'part-skills'; the learners practise them separately in order to make them as automatic as possible; subsequently they engage in 'whole-task' practice in which they have to integrate the separate items in order to communicate. These stages underlie the familiar 'PPP' (Presentation – Practice – Performance) sequence described in many teachers' handbooks. One of the main contributions of work in the early 1970s was to expand this analytic dimension by adding a functional-communicative element, so that learners are more aware of the functional and social aspects of the language they are practising. For example, they may carry out a controlled pair-work activity in which they 'make suggestions' in various situations and later engage in a less controlled role play based on a similar situation.

The skill-learning model retains its influence and validity (it is explored by, for example, Johnson 1996; McLaughlin 1987; Mitchell and Myles 2004) but it is now joined by a view of learning as a process of holistic development, which occurs when students use language for communication. The experience of natural, untutored second language acquisition has been particularly important in showing that through participating in interaction and other forms of communicative language use, learners not only consolidate their capacity to use their existing knowledge of the language but actually extend this knowledge. Studies of learners' 'inter-language' (surveyed in, e.g. Lightbown and Spada 2006; Littlewood 2004a; Ortega 2009) highlight some of the internal processes by which this takes place as well as how output and interaction push learners to refine their language knowledge. This 'experiential' perspective on learning has gained in prominence over the years and is especially relevant in ESP, where learners have often already acquired an extensive analytic knowledge of the language but need to integrate this knowledge into an effective performance system.

The analytic and experiential approaches to learning are analysed in, e.g. Allen 1983, Stern 1990 and 1992. Table 19.1 below (adapted from Stern 1992) compares some of the features of the two approaches.

The left-hand and right-hand columns represent two extremes of a continuum. Actual learning activities will usually be somewhere in-between or the focus may change in the course of an activity e.g. from focus on communication to focus on language.

The complementary roles of the two dimensions in contributing to communicative competence may be represented as in Figure 19.1.

It should again be noted that the two dimensions are at two ends of a continuum and that most specific learning activities will have features of each, to varying degrees. For example, in many of the information-transfer tasks included in textbooks and practical handbooks, learners use pre-taught forms but engage in communicating new information with them. On the other hand, in role-plays and problem-solving, the main focus is on communication but learners may sometimes focus analytically on specific forms that cause difficulties.

Principles of language teaching methodology

There have been many decades of debate and experimentation in the field of language teaching methodology (surveyed for example in Littlewood 1999; Larsen-Freeman 2000; Richards and Rodgers 2001; Rodgers 2011). This has left teachers with an immense range of learning activities to choose from. In the field of ESP, a wide selection of these is offered in textbooks and handbooks such as those mentioned earlier (e.g. Emmerson and Hamilton 2005; Harding 2007;

Table 19.1 Analytic and experiential approaches to language learning and teaching

Analytic approach	←↔→	Experiential approach
Focus is on learning language as discrete items.	←↔→	Focus is on using language for communication.
Learning and teaching are organised around discrete language patterns and vocabulary.	←↔→	Learning and teaching are organised around communication e.g. tasks.
Language is often experienced without a context (i.e. is 'decontextualised').	←↔→	Language is experienced in the context of meaning and communication.
Controlled practice of language patterns is important.	←↔→	Communicative use of language is important.
Students aim to produce formally correct sentences.	←↔→	Students aim to achieve communicative outcomes.
Accuracy is very important.	←↔→	Fluency is very important.
Feedback focuses on form (e.g. through error correction).	←↔→	Feedback focuses on meaning (formal errors are less important).
Reading and writing are emphasised.	←↔→	Speaking is given at least as much time as reading and writing.
Activity tends to be teacher-centred.	←↔→	Activity tends to be student-centred.
There is a lot of whole-class teaching.	←↔→	There is a lot of pair or group work.

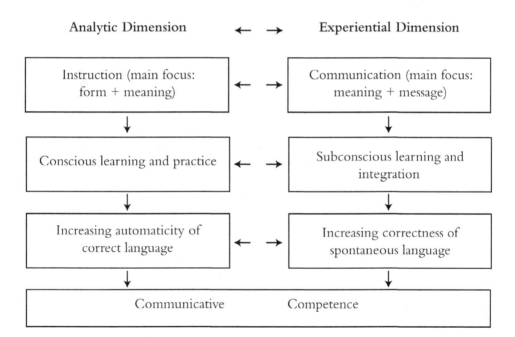

Figure 19.1 Two dimensions of learning

and Guse 2011). Self-contained 'methods' such as the audio-lingual approach and situational language teaching embody explicit principles for selecting from this range and sequencing activities. But few people now believe that there is a single 'best method' (Prabhu 1990), since every teacher, teaching context and group of learners is different. We have entered a so-called 'postmethod' era (e.g. Kumaravadivelu 2003 and 2006; Allwright and Hanks 2009; Littlewood 2011 and 2012) in which the object of our enquiry is not to find or prove the best method but to clarify principles according to which each teacher can develop an approach that is sensitive to his or her specific context. There have been several main ways of approaching this search.

Teachers' 'sense of plausibility'

One way of addressing the question is to start from the 'sense of plausibility' (Prabhu 1990) of experienced teachers and develop a 'teacher-generated theory of classroom practice' (Senior 2006: 270). Breen *et al.* (2001) followed this approach when they worked from 18 teachers' accounts of their own practices and their reasons for adopting them. They found reasonable consensus on about a dozen principles, such as taking account of individual differences and making it easier for students to remember what is taught. In the field of ESP, a similar approach is adopted (at a more global level) by Watson Todd (2003), who studies 'reports of teaching and learning practices' and identifies six approaches that are especially widespread. These are:

1   focusing on inductive learning
2   using process syllabuses
3   promoting learner autonomy
4   using authentic materials and tasks
5   integrating technology in teaching
6   using team teaching.

(Watson Todd 2003: 151–52)

These are all approaches that may be implemented through a variety of specific techniques appropriate to the context where learning and teaching take place.

Principles of instructed language learning

A second approach is to start from principles of second language learning and use these as a basis for proposing optimal ways of facilitating this learning. Ellis (2005a, 2005b) and Erlam (2008) worked in this way. Based on research into second language acquisition, they propose 10 'principles of effective instructed language learning':

1   Instruction needs to ensure that learners develop both a rich repertoire of formulaic expressions and a rule-based competence
2   Instruction needs to ensure that learners focus predominantly on meaning
3   Instruction needs to ensure that learners also focus on form
4   Instruction needs to be predominantly directed at developing impexlicit knowledge of the L2 while not neglecting expexlicit knowledge
5   Instruction needs to take into account the learner's 'built-in syllabus'
6   Successful instructed language learning requires extensive L2 input
7   Successful instructed language learning also requires opportunities for output
8   The opportunity to interact in the L2 is central to developing L2 proficiency
9   Instruction needs to take account of individual differences in learners
10 In assessing learners' L2 proficiency it is important to examine free as well as controlled production.

(Formulation by Erlam 2008: 257)

We find two examples of a similar approach within the field of ESP. Hutchinson and Waters (1987: 128–30) list eight 'basic principles of language learning' (it is a developmental process; an active process; a decision-making process; not just a matter of linguistic knowledge; not the learners' first experience with language; an emotional experience; to a large extent incidental; not systematic). They go on to describe model lessons in which the principles are realised. Basturkmen (2006) draws on second language acquisition research to suggest two essential conditions for second language learning (that it depends on acculturation and requires input and interaction) and elaborates on two basic explanations for learning (that it involves the individual's cognitive processes and results from social activity). She goes on to outline a methodological framework based on the concepts of input and output which she had introduced earlier:

- Input-based strategies:
    - Predominantly input
    - Input to output
- Output-based strategies:
    - Predominantly output
    - Output to input

She gives examples of specific methods and materials that implement these strategies.

Accumulated professional experience illuminated by language teaching theory

A third approach is that taken by Kumaravadivelu (2003) and Littlewood (2004b, 2011). These writers have proposed frameworks to guide classroom practice based on accumulated classroom experience as well as current language teaching theory. Kumaravadivelu's (2003) framework consists of 10 'macro-strategies' for language teaching. Here they are paraphrased:

1. Provide the maximum possible number of learning opportunities
2. Facilitate classroom interaction with a communicative purpose
3. Minimise perceptual misunderstandings
4. Activate students' intuitive capacity for independent discovery
5. Foster conscious awareness of aspects of language
6. Contextualise the linguistic input
7. Integrate the language skills
8. Promote learner autonomy
9. Raise students' cultural consciousness
10. Ensure social relevance.

Other teachers may have a different set of priorities. Many would want to include, for example, more explicit attention to motivation, learning strategies and practice opportunities leading to memorisation.

Littlewood's (e.g. 2004b, 2011) framework is an attempt to combine the broader view of communication mentioned earlier with the continuum from analytic learning (where the focus is mainly on form) to experiential learning (where the focus is mainly on the communication of meanings). Along this continuum, five categories (which overlap conceptually and in practice) locate activities in relation to each other and the goal of communicative competence (see Table 19.2).

With ESP students who have mastered the key structures of the language, much of the learning is likely to take place at the right-hand end of the continuum. This is where 'tasks' are

Table 19.2 The 'communicative continuum' as a framework for teaching methodology

Analytic learning			→		Experiential learning
Non-communicative learning	Pre-communicative language practice	Communicative language practice		Structured communication	Authentic communication
Focusing on the structures, vocabulary and sounds of language, how they are formed and what they mean, e.g. through substitution exercises, inductive 'discovery' and awareness-raising activities	Practising language with some attention to meaning but not communicating new messages to others, e.g. describing visuals or tables, answering questions about texts available to all	Practising pre-taught language but in a context where it communicates new information, e.g. information gap activities, carrying out simple surveys		Using language to communicate in situations which elicit pre-learnt language but with some degree of unpredictability, e.g. structured role-play, simple problem-solving	Using language to communicate in situations where the meanings are unpredictable, e.g. more creative role-play, more complex problem-solving, discussion, simulations, case-based learning
Focus on forms and meanings		↑			Focus on meanings and messages

Methodology for teaching ESP

located, as these are usually defined in the literature, i.e. as communication-oriented activities with a context, purpose and non-linguistic outcome (see for example Ellis 2003; Norris 2009; Nunan 2004). However, even with proficient learners, teachers may often organise non-communicative or pre-communicative work in order to remedy gaps in the students' linguistic repertoire or to teach features of specialist language use.

Within the field of ESP, an early initiative to create a methodological framework based on both theory and professional experience was that of Widdowson (1978), whose seminal book was referred to earlier. Widdowson's distinction between 'linguistic skills' and 'communicative abilities' can be related to the model of communicative competence described earlier. It emphasises the need to move from 'usage' (which depends on knowledge of grammatical rules) to 'use' (in which we 'use our knowledge of the language system in order to achieve some kind of communicative purpose', 1978: 3). Widdowson proposes a range of learning activities to achieve this aim, such as 'rhetorical transformation' and 'information transfer'. As I suggested in a '30 years later' review of the book (Littlewood 2008), if we add to this framework more opportunities for learners to use language to express their own meanings, this early proposal can form the starting point for a more inclusive framework with three major stages. The stages combine to form an integrated strategy for helping students to develop communicative competence in relevant professional fields:

1 *Activities for language awareness and appropriation.* These focus on the language itself and seek to extend students' competence in aspects of its grammar, vocabulary and pronunciation.
2 *Activities for communicative awareness.* These focus on facilitating students' awareness of the features of language use in relation to their target field, for example, the key genres and how language conveys meanings in communicative events. But the student is an 'observer of ESP communication' rather than an ESP communicator.
3 *Activities for communicative experience.* Here the focus is on language use in contexts such as discussions, role-plays, simulations, and producing relevant genres. These activities serve also as the bridge between the classroom and real discourse communities outside the classroom.

A similar framework underlies much current genre-based teaching (e.g. Belcher 2009), which starts from current language skills (stage 1 in the above framework), moves through genre awareness and analysis (stage 2), and progresses towards collaborative and finally independent generation of texts (stage 3). The framework may prove fruitful not only for analysing other aspects of the methodological principles for ESP and taking the field further, but also for forging a link with earlier stages in the development of ESP.

Conclusion: Some issues and challenges

As indicated in the previous section, if we analyse methodology at the level of universal principles, ESP provides just one set of specific contexts for the 'context-specific pedagogy' that *all* teachers are urged to design. If, however, we look at the specific techniques contained in handbooks such as those reviewed in the second main section, it is clear that many of these techniques (such as 'smiling over the phone') have a distinctive ESP flavour. In between, there are many methods that are used in general EFL but have become special features of ESP approaches (e.g. case-based learning, genre-based learning and project work). At what level and in what ways, then, can ESP methodology be described as 'special'? The pedagogy of ESP would benefit from more discussion of possible overall frameworks in which general principles and specific techniques are seen in systematic relation with each other and with students' communicative goals. This will also help clarify the relationship between general EFL methods research (of which there is a lot) and specific ESP methods research (of which there is little).

Many specific learning activities are more urgently in need of investigation in ESP simply because they are so common and so much learning depends on them. Problem-based learning, case-based learning, corpus-based learning, oral presentations and genre-based learning were mentioned earlier. It is not enough to study the discourse in activities such as these because the nature of the discourse depends crucially on the kinds of organisation and interventions that the teacher chooses to make. An apparently minor change in how, say, a tutorial is organised or presented, or how a tutor intervenes, can have a major effect on the kinds of student participation and interaction that ensue. In this area, research outside ESP (such as the six-category intervention analysis of Heron 1999) may serve as a fruitful impetus for investigation. The field of collaborative learning also provides a rich source of ideas for experimenting with different interactional structures (e.g. Littlewood 2009).

ESP is oriented towards specific areas of discourse activity outside the classroom. Bremner (2010) shows how the tasks suggested in a range of textbooks are inadequate to bridge the gap between the classroom and the workplace. He argues the need for more authentic collaborative activities. Basturkmen (2006: 85–90) sees it as a basic condition for learning that learners 'become socially and psychologically integrated into their target discourse community' either through 'induction' in the classroom or through direct links with that community on an adjunct or apprenticeship basis. An essential task for future pedagogical research is to seek ever more effective ways of helping teachers 'bridge the gap between the ideal world of the classroom and the real world of professional practice' (Bhatia 2008: 171) either by creating imagined discourse communities within the classroom itself or by forging real links between the classroom and the discourse community outside it.

Related topics

business communication: a revisiting of theory, research, teaching; a blended needs analysis: critical genre analysis and needs analysis of language and communication for professional purposes; the formation of a professional communicator: a socio-rhetorical approach; collaborative writing: challenges for research and teaching

Key readings

Basturkmen, H. (2006). *Ideas and Options in English for Specific Purposes*, Mahwah, NJ: Lawrence Erlbaum. (Amongst other issues, Basturkmen addresses the lack of discussion so far, in the field of ESP, about theories of learning and teaching, and proposes a framework for developing an ESP methodology.)
Belcher, D. (ed.) (2009). *English for Specific Purposes in Theory and Practice*, Ann Arbor: University of Michigan Press. (The chapters provide comprehensive discussion of issues in various areas of ESP. The book refers to matters related to methodology and recognises the importance of addressing them.)
Donna, S. (2000). *Teach Business English*, Cambridge: Cambridge University Press. (Donna gives advice on principles to follow in developing methods for ESP, suggests a wide range of activities for practising relevant skills, and deals with many day-to-day concerns such as approaches to error correction.)
Hutchinson, T. and Waters, A. (1987). *English for Specific Purposes: A Learning-centred Approach*, Cambridge: Cambridge University Press. (This text has had an important influence on attitudes to ESP in relation to general ELT and includes insightful discussion of the nature of learners' needs and implications for methodology.)
Jordan, J. J. (1997). *English for Academic Purposes: A Guide and Resource Book for Teachers*, Cambridge: Cambridge University Press. (Focusing mainly on EAP, Jordan provides extensive discussion of teaching methodology and gives advice on a range of practical matters related to teaching strategies and techniques.)

Bibliography

Allen, J. P. B. (1983). 'A three-level curriculum model for second language education', *Canadian Modern Language Review*, *40*(1), 23–43.

Allwright, D. and Hanks, J. (2009). *The Developing Learner: An Introduction to Exploratory Practice*, Basingstoke: Palgrave Macmillan.

Barron, C. (2002). 'Problem-solving and EAP: Themes and issues in a collaborative teaching venture', *English for Specific Purposes*, *22*(3), 297–314.

Basturkmen, H. (2006). *Ideas and Options in English for Specific Purposes*, Mahwah, NJ: Lawrence Erlbaum.

——(2010). *Developing Courses in English for Specific Purposes*, Houndmills, Basingstoke: Palgrave Macmillan.

Belcher, D. (2004). 'Trends in teaching English for specific purposes', *Annual Review of Applied Linguistics*, *24*, 165–86.

——(2006). 'English for specific purposes: Teaching to perceived needs and imagined futures in worlds of work, study and everyday life', *TESOL Quarterly*, *40*(1), 133–56.

——(2009). 'What ESP is and can be: An introduction', in D. Belcher (ed.), *English for Specific Purposes in Theory and Practice* (pp. 1–20), Ann Arbor: University of Michigan Press.

Belcher, D. and Lukkarila, L. (2011). 'Identity in ESP context: Putting the learner front and centre in needs analysis', in D. Belcher, A. Johns and B. Paltridge (eds), *New Directions in English for Specific Purposes Research* (pp. 73–93), Ann Arbor: University of Michigan Press.

Benati, A. G. (ed.) (2009). *Issues in Second Language Proficiency*, London: Continuum.

Bhatia, V. K. (2008). 'Genre analysis, ESP and professional practice', *English for Specific Purposes*, *27*(2), 161–74.

Breen, M. P., Hird, B., Hilton, M., Oliver, R. and Thwaite, A. (2001). 'Making sense of language teaching: Teachers' principles and classroom practices', *Applied Linguistics*, *22*(4), 470–501.

Bremner, S. (2010). 'Collaborative writing: Bridging the gap between the textbook and the workplace', *English for Specific Purposes*, *29*(2), 121–32.

Brumfit, C. J. and Johnson, K. (eds) (1979). *The Communicative Approach to Language Teaching*, Oxford: Oxford University Press.

Canale, M. (1983). 'From communicative competence to communicative language pedagogy', in J.C. Richards and R.W. Schmidt (eds), *Language and Communication* (pp. 2–27), London: Longman.

Canale, M. and Swain, M. (1980). 'Theoretical bases of communicative approaches to second language teaching and testing', *Applied Linguistics*, *1*(1), 1–47.

Cheng, A. (2011). 'ESP classroom research: Basic considerations and future research questions', in D. Belcher, A. M. Johns and B. Paltridge (eds), *New Directions in English for Specific Purposes Research* (pp. 44–72), Ann Arbor: University of Michigan Press.

Donna, S. (2000). *Teach Business English*, Cambridge: Cambridge University Press.

Dudley-Evans, T. and St John, M. J. (1998). *Developments in English for Specific Purposes*, Cambridge: Cambridge University Press.

Ellis, M. and Johnson, C. (1994). *Teaching Business English*, Oxford: Oxford University Press.

Ellis, R. (2003). *Task-based Learning and Teaching*, Oxford: Oxford University Press.

——(2005a). 'Principles of instructed language learning', *Asian EFL Journal*, *7*(3), 1–16.

——(2005b). 'Principles of instructed language learning', *System*, *33*(2), 209–24.

Emmerson, P. and Hamilton, N. (2005). *Five-minute Activities for Business English*, Cambridge: Cambridge University Press.

Erlam, R. (2008). 'What do you researchers know about language teaching? Bridging the gap between SLA research and language pedagogy', *Innovation in Language Teaching and Learning*, *2*(3), 253–67.

Esteban, A. A. and Canado, M. L. P. (2004). 'Making the case method work in teaching business English: A case study', *English for Specific Purposes*, *23*(2), 137–61

Flowerdew, L. (2010). 'Devising and implementing a business proposal module: Constraints and compromises', *English for Specific Purposes*, *29*(2), 108–20.

Gnutzmann, C. (2011). 'Language for specific purposes vs. general language', in K. Knapp, B. Seidlhofer and H. Widdowson (eds), *Handbook of Foreign Language Communication and Learning* (pp. 517–44), Berlin/New York: Walter de Gruyter.

Guse, J. (2011). *Communicative Activities for EAP*, Cambridge: Cambridge University Press.

Hamp-Lyons, L. (2011). 'English for academic purposes', in E. Hinkel (ed.), *Handbook of Research in Second Language Teaching and Learning, Volume II* (pp. 89–105), New York: Routledge.

Harding, K. (2007). *English for Specific Purposes*, Oxford: Oxford University Press.

Harley, B., Allen, J. P. B. and Swain, M. (eds) (1990). *The Development of Second Language Proficiency*, Cambridge: Cambridge University Press.
Heron, J. (1999). *The Complete Facilitator's Handbook*, London: Kogan Page.
Hutchinson, T. and Waters, A. (1987). *English for Specific Purposes: A Learning-centred Approach*, Cambridge: Cambridge University Press.
Hyland, K. and Hamp-Lyons, L. (2002). 'EAP: Issues and directions', *Journal of English for Academic Purposes*, 1(1), 1–12.
Johns, A. M. (1999). 'Language for special purposes: Pedagogy', in B. Spolsky (ed.), *Concise Encyclopedia of Educational Linguistics* (pp. 633–39), Oxford: Pergamon.
——(2009). 'Tertiary undergraduate EAP: Problems and possibilities', in D. Belcher (ed.), *ESP in Theory and Practice* (pp. 41–59), Ann Arbor: University of Michigan Press.
Johnson, K. (1996). *Language Teaching and Skill Learning*, Oxford: Blackwell.
Jordan, J. J. (1997). *English for Academic Purposes: A Guide and Resource Book for Teachers*, Cambridge: Cambridge University Press.
Kumaravadivelu, B. (2003). *Beyond Methods: Macrostrategies for Language Teaching*, New Haven, CT: Yale University Press.
——(2006). 'Dangerous liaison: Globalization, empire and TESOL', in J. Edge (ed.), *(Re-)Locating TESOL in an Age of Empire* (pp. 1–26), Basingstoke: Palgrave Macmillan.
Larsen-Freeman, D. (2000). *Techniques and Principles in Language Teaching* (2nd edn), New York: Oxford University Press.
Lee, D. and Swales, J. (2006). 'A corpus-based EAP course for NNS doctoral students: Moving from available specialized corpora to self-compiled corpora', *English for Specific Purposes*, 25(1), 56–75.
Lightbown, P. M. and Spada, N. (2006). *How Languages are Learned* (3rd edn), Oxford: Oxford University Press.
Littlewood, W. T. (1999). 'Second language teaching methods', in Bernard Spolsky (ed.), *The Concise Encyclopedia of Educational Linguistics* (pp. 658–68), Oxford: Pergamon.
——(2004a). 'Second language learning', in A. Davies and C. Elder (eds), *The Handbook of Applied Linguistics* (pp. 500–24), Oxford: Blackwell.
——(2004b). 'The task-based approach: Some questions and suggestions', *ELT Journal*, 58(4), 319–26.
——(2008). 'Thirty years later: Henry Widdowson's *Teaching Language as Communication*', *International Journal of Applied Linguistics*, 18(2), 212–17.
——(2009). 'Chinese learners and interactive learning', in T. Coverdale-Jones and P. Rastall (eds), *Internationalising the University: The Chinese Context* (pp. 206–22), Basingstoke: Palgrave Macmillan.
——(2011). 'Communicative language teaching: An expanding concept for a changing world', in E. Hinkel (ed.), *Handbook of Research in Second Language Teaching and Learning, Volume II* (pp. 541–57), New York: Routledge.
——(2012). 'Communication-oriented language teaching: Where are we now? Where do we go from here?' *Language Teaching* (access through Cambridge Journals *first view*).
McDonough, J. (2010). 'English for special purposes: A survey review of current materials', *ELT Journal*, 64(4), 462–77.
McLaughlin, B. (1987). *Theories of Second-language Learning*, London: Edward Arnold.
Master, P. (2005). 'Research in English for specific purposes', in E. Hinkel (ed.), *Handbook of Research in Second Language Teaching and Learning* (pp. 99–115), Mahwah, NJ: Lawrence Erlbaum.
Mitchell, R. and Myles, F. (2004). *Second Language Learning Theories*, London: Arnold.
Norris, J. M. (2009). 'Task-based teaching and testing', in M. J. Long and C. J. Doughty (eds), *The Handbook of Language Teaching* (pp. 578–594), Chichester: Wiley Blackwell.
Nunan, D. (2004). *Task-based Language Teaching*, Cambridge: Cambridge University Press.
Ortega, L. (2009). *Understanding Second Language Acquisition*, London: Hodder Education.
Paltridge, B. (2009). 'Afterword: Where have we come from and where are we now?' in D. Belcher (ed.), *ESP in Theory and Practice* (pp. 289–96), Ann Arbor: University of Michigan Press.
Paltridge, B. and Starfield, S. (2011). 'Research in English for specific purposes', in E. Hinkel (ed.), *Handbook of Research in Second Language Teaching and Learning, Volume II* (pp. 106–21), New York: Routledge.
Prabhu, N. S. (1990). 'There is no best method – Why?' *TESOL Quarterly*, 24(2), 161–76.
Richards, J. C. and Rodgers, T. S. (2001). *Approaches and Methods in Language Teaching* (2nd edn), Cambridge: Cambridge University Press.
Robinson, P. (1991). *ESP Today: A Practitioner's Guide*, Hemel Hempstead: Prentice Hall.

Rodgers, T. (2011). 'The methodology of foreign language teaching', in K. Knapp, B. Seidlhofer and H. Widdowson (eds), *Handbook of Foreign Language Communication and Learning* (pp. 341–72), Berlin/New York: Walter de Gruyter.
Senior, R. (2006). *The Experience of Language Teaching*, Cambridge: Cambridge University Press.
Stern, H. H. (David) (1990). 'Analysis and experience as variables in second language pedagogy', in B. Harley, J. P. B. Allen and M. Swain (eds), *The Development of Second Language Proficiency* (pp. 93–109), Cambridge: Cambridge University Press.
——(1992). *Issues and Options in Language Teaching*, Oxford: Oxford University Press.
Watson Todd, R. (2003). 'EAP or TEAP?' *Journal of English for Academic Purposes*, *2*(2), 147–56.
Widdowson, H. G. (1978) *Teaching Language as Communication*, Oxford: Oxford University Press.
Wilkins, D. (1976). *Notional Syllabuses*, Oxford: Oxford University Press.
Wood, A. and Head, M. (2004). '"Just what the doctor ordered": The application of problem-based learning to EAP', *English for Specific Purposes*, *23*(1), 3–17.
Zappa-Hollman, S. (2007). 'Academic presentations across post-secondary contexts: The discourse socialization of non-native English speakers', *Canadian Modern Language Review*, *63*(4), 455–85.

B. Disciplinary perspectives

20
English for Science and Technology

Lindsay Miller

Introduction

This chapter reviews English for Science and Technology (EST): past, present and future trends. The development of EST courses started in the early 1960s and we see, by examining EST textbooks and courses, how different approaches have moved from a focus on accuracy, to fluency to socio-cultural agency. The chapter provides several case studies illustrating course development and argues that the future for EST course development lies in our ability to deal with a number of approaches to teaching and learning in the twenty-first century, where students have to deal with emerging multiple-genres and have multi-literacies.

English for Science and Technology sits within the overall context of English for Specific Purposes (ESP). We generally separate the teaching of ESP from teaching General English (GE) language for a number of reasons. Firstly, we believe that ESP has its own distinct methodology, which is different from that used with GE students. Secondly, the research agenda that ESP draws upon relates to the disciplines that inform it. Thirdly, a central feature of ESP courses is the application on practical outcomes (Dudley-Evans and St John 1998). This means that we tend to focus on the specific needs of learners taking ESP courses; the texts that they use, and the communicative tasks they are required to perform.

ESP is not a new phenomenon. As long as men have been travelling the world and trying to speak with people of other languages there has been a need to communicate for specific purposes, usually for trading purposes (see Howatt 1984). However, since the 1960s ESP has taken on a major role in the teaching of English as a Foreign or Second Language. There are three main reasons why ESP developed so significantly and uniquely in the past half century (Hutchinson and Waters 1987):

1 After the Second World War (1945) there was an expansion of scientific, technical and economic activity around the world. The main economic power was the US and therefore the language that was used in all this activity was English. For example, the Middle East became an important provider of oil to Western countries and so the exploration and development done by the West was manned by English-speaking engineers working alongside locals.

English for Science and Technology

2 There has been a significant development in the way languages are taught post-1960. Previously, language was analysed and rules memorised (the grammar-translation approach, for instance). With the advent of communicative teaching methods, we began to explore the real use of languages and what people used them for socially and professionally.
3 The way in which learners acquired languages became a hot topic in the early 70s and we began to understand that different learners used different skills and strategies in the way they learned languages. Therefore, the focus on the learner became more important than it previously had been.

Post-1960, a greater understanding of the different types of communicative contexts learners needed English for meant that we had to distinguish more clearly the types of English courses we developed – for instance, English for scientists might be for biology, physics, or engineering, each of which had different course requirements. It would have been of little use to an Egyptian structural engineer to study only social English if what he required was to be able to read specification documents about bridge construction, for instance. Figure 20.1 shows how English courses can be generally divided (based on Jordan 1997). What may be of interest in this figure is that EST is not marked. That is because EST is subsumed into the whole of ESP – it falls into all of the sub-categories in the ESP dimension. An EST course can be developed for a nurse working in a hospital (English for Occupational Purposes: EOP), for a technical student studying to be an electrician in a vocational institute (English for Vocational Purposes: EVP), for a doctor learning to work in an English speaking country (English for Professional Purposes: EPP), for undergraduate physics students requiring English for a variety of communication purposes at university (English for General Academic Purposes); or for a post-graduate biology student preparing to write a thesis (English for Specific Academic Purposes: ESAP). Of course, EST can be classified more specifically by grouping science courses such as life sciences and physical sciences together, and Engineering and Technology courses together (see Swales 1988).

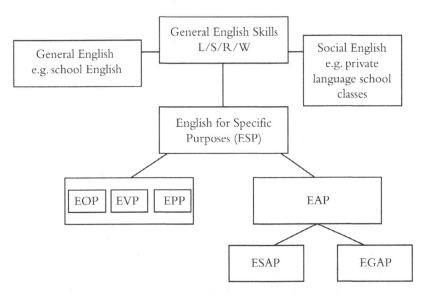

Figure 20.1 A classification of English courses (adapted from Jordan 1997)

Lindsay Miller

Table 20.1 EST teaching contexts

Where	Who	Context
Zagazig University, Egypt	Engineering Students	ESAP. These were undergraduate students who studied mostly in Arabic but needed revision of general English grammar and some knowledge of technical terminology to be able to read some of their engineering books which were written in English.
Petroleum Development Oman, Sultanate of Oman	Technicians	EGAP. These were young Omani technicians working in an oil company who had been selected for further study on a variety of diploma courses in the UK. Their language training in Oman was to help them cope with both everyday life in the UK, and to help them follow their technical courses.
Jeddah Oil Refinery, Saudi Arabia	General Grade Staff	EOP (basic literacy). These general grade older male staff were Saudi nationals who were illiterate in Arabic and English. They were identified as 'helpers' around the oil refinery. As this is a dangerous environment to work in these workers had to be able to read and understand basic English signage around the refinery – most of the signs related to the working environment, e.g. 'danger' 'electricity' 'toxic'.
The British Council, London, UK	PhD students (Nuclear Physics)	ESPA (thesis writing). These were Korean students on British Council scholarships who were having difficulty in presenting their work, both written and orally, in English to their supervisors, and get the necessary feedback. They mostly needed to improve their written language skills in order to write their theses. The sessions were one-on-one with the tutor.
City University of Hong Kong, Hong Kong	Undergraduate Engineering, and Science Students	ESAP. These were second language engineering students in an English medium university. Therefore, they needed all four language skills, in an academic context, in order to pass their degree programmes.

To illustrate this point about the variety of EST contexts, I will refer to my own career as an ESP teacher. Table 20.1 shows the different contexts I have worked in over the past 25 years. As can be seen from the table, I have worked in a variety of EST contexts, and with complete beginners and advanced level students. Each of the contexts required a different approach to material development and teaching – the most obvious being the contrast between situation 3 and 4 in the table. Each situation in Table 20.1 constitutes a unique context in which the learners' needs were paramount to the development of the course material and delivery of the course. Furthermore, as the EST courses I have been involved with range over a 25-year period of time, different pedagogical approaches have evolved so that the course of engineering students I taught in situation 1, in Egypt, bears no resemblance to the English for Engineering courses I currently teach in Hong Kong. EST course design is sensitive to the contemporary needs of the learners and has to keep up-to-date with developments in the specific fields it is helping learners deal with, something that I will illustrate in this chapter.

ESP is often seen as an *approach* to teaching and learning rather than a *product* in itself. 'The foundation of ESP is the simple question: Why does this learner need to learn a foreign language?' (Hutchinson and Waters 1987: 19). Therefore, the starting point for each ESP course is to attempt to discover what the specific needs of the learners are – this relates to the primacy of needs analysis, a central focus of all ESP courses. There have been several attempts to define exactly what ESP is. Based on Streven's (1988) definition of ESP, Dudley-Evans and St John (1998: 4–5) defined ESP courses as having three absolute characteristics and five variable characteristics:

Absolute characteristics:

1 ESP is designed to meet specific needs of the learner;
2 ESP makes use of the underlying methodology and activities of the disciplines it serves;
3 ESP is centred on the language (grammar, lexis, register), skills, discourse and genres appropriate to these activities.

Variable characteristics:

1 ESP may be related to or designed for specific disciplines;
2 ESP may use, in specific teaching situations, a different methodology from that of general English;
3 ESP is likely to be designed for adult learners, either at a tertiary level institution, or in a professional work situation. It could, however, be used for learners at secondary school level;
4 ESP is generally designed for intermediate or advanced students;
5 Most ESP courses assume basic knowledge of the language system, but it can be used with beginners.

The task for the ESP developer is to ensure that all the absolute characteristics and as many as possible of the variable characteristics in the above definition are accommodated within an ESP course. This may require some collaboration between language teaching experts and discipline experts, or at least some knowledge by the curriculum developer of the most important technical and semi-technical vocabulary, specific notions and functions and other general communicative events required by the learners.

Historical perspective of EST

English for Science and Technology has a well-plotted history. However, because of their practical nature, EST courses have not always been made available for everyone to see – the courses tend to be designed and delivered on-site and materials kept in-house. This is partly due to the very specialised nature of some courses, e.g. an English course for sanitation engineering in Indonesia may not be very useful for engineers working in Africa who may have very different problems to deal with. Also the teachers who developed the first EST courses had fewer publishing opportunities to make the course materials available to a wider audience, compared with nowadays when anything can be uploaded onto the internet. Notwithstanding these problems, we can still identify some pioneering work in EST course design by looking at publications of articles in journals (most notably *The ESP Journal*), and also some well-known published textbooks.

Swales (1988) provides us with an excellent selection of articles and textbooks that illustrate the development of ESP from the early 1960s until the early 1980s. Swales starts his review of the field with C. L. Barber's 1962 article 'Some Measurable Characteristics of Modern Scientific Prose'. This seminal article demonstrated how the descriptive techniques of Halliday, McIntosh and Strevens (1964) could be transposed into teachable contexts for science and technology students. Barber's article also provided us with an argument to distinguish between general English courses and EST courses. The distinctions presented in 1962 were in line with the lexico-grammatical approach in use in language classes at that time and so focused mostly on the description of which parts of grammar, and which words, were 'more useful' for EST students to learn. Swales maintains that Barber's work set the scene for more investigations into how to teach science students English and pointed to the direction of using frequency analysis to examine syntax and vocabulary within specific texts.

Over the next 20 years or so teachers, researchers and writers in ESP have contributed greatly to the debate about approaches to language teaching and learning. This has included presenting such issues as *the communicative use of language* (Allen and Widdowson 1974a); *notions* and *functions* (Bates and Dudley-Evans 1976); *use of authentic materials* (Philips and Shettlesworth 1978); *task-based learning* (Herbolich 1979); *team teaching* (Jones and Dudley-Evans 1980) and *discipline-specific teaching methods* (Widdowson 1983). Many of these issues, brought to our attention via the EST contexts, are now part of general English courses.

Textbook development

'ESP is essentially a materials and teaching-led movement' (Dudley-Evans and St John 1998: 19). As such, it is worthwhile to look at how EST textbooks have been written over the past 50 years to see the approaches used and methods advocated. In a recent survey of ESP textbooks, McDonough (2010) received over 60 books to review. The ESP textbook market is alive and well and covers many specific areas in English language learning. When examining EST textbooks we see clearly delineated periods of development. I group these into five generations of textbook development:

First-generation EST textbooks (1960–1968)

An example of a first-generation textbook is Herbert (1965) *The Structure of Technical English*. This 28 short unit textbook uses a register analysis lexico-grammatical approach to introduce students to science and technology topics: e.g. reactor cooling systems; liquid pumps; suspension bridges. Each unit has a reading passage often accompanied with simple line drawings. Then, students are introduced to a word study section that highlights special features in the text, and some grammatical examples. There are structural practice exercises after each feature of the text has been introduced. For instance:
  Section 8

1   Reading – Condensation and condensers
2   Word study
    i   Produce, product, production
    ii Consume, consumption
    iii Withdraw, extract, abstract
3   Pattern
    i   Means (by + noun or–ing)
    ii Purpose (clause)
    iii Noun + Noun

Second-generation EST textbooks (1969–78)

In this period a rhetorical and discourse analysis approach was used with many EST textbooks, for instance Ewer and Latorre (1969) *A Course in Basic Scientific English*. During this period we also saw the publications of textbooks with a wider-angle approach using general science as the background for the input texts. The *Focus* series adopted a 'rhetorical-communicative' approach (Allen and Widdowson 1974b) while the *Nucleus* series of textbooks used the concept of notions and functions as a way to organise content (Bates and Dudley-Evans 1976, *Nucleus: General Science*). The Nucleus series of textbooks put the emphasis on oral forms of scientific English. Although these textbooks appeared to be moving away from the lexico-grammatical approach they still rely heavily on written exercises and students learning 'useful' grammar and vocabulary – as determined by the often non-specialist textbook writer. Visuals were integral to the texts in these books although there was little or no recorded material. The Nucleus series did provide a Teacher's Book, which helped non-specialised teachers work with the material.

Third-generation EST textbooks (1980–89)

As we moved into the 1980s the communicative approach and a study skills approach to language teaching became the most popular teaching methodology used in both general and specific contexts. Although EST course design had always been focused on the learners' needs, the communicative approach took the focus off form and placed it onto function. Hutchinson and Waters' (1984) *Interface: English for Technical Communication* is an example of a third-generation EST textbook.

Interface is a ten unit textbook for intermediate learners of EOP or EAP. It was intended for use with a group of general EST students and there is a wide range of topics and themes: using tools, electricity, computers. The technical content was a way into the lexical/grammatical teaching points. *Interface* used a communicative approach and there is a variety of exercises to stimulate students' interest and cater to different learning styles: cloze sentences, note-taking, labelling diagrams, completing charts and listening to taped texts, which lead towards completing a final task at the end of each unit. The Teacher's Book clearly advocates the communicative approach and offers the teachers advice on how to present the exercises and an answer key for their reference.

Fourth-generation EST textbooks (1990–99)

The main focus in what I refer to as the fourth-generation of EST textbooks is the clear link between the learning of English and professional development. In contrast to early EST textbooks with titles like *General Science,* the titles of many EST textbooks are now written for specific groups of learners: *English for Information Systems* (Hick 1991); *English for Electrical and Mechanical Engineering* (Glendinning and Glendinning 1995). During this period there was also an increase in the variety of supplementary materials accompanying the textbooks. Video and audio recordings not only allowed students more opportunities to see or hear authentic language in use but also helped sell these textbooks in an ever increasing competitive market. Textbooks in this era tend to be task-based, include a variety of authentic written and audio texts, and the activities and tasks are situated within professional contexts.

Another focus of fourth-generation textbooks, especially for specific EAP purposes, was the use of genre-analysis as a way of heightening students' awareness of how texts are constructed. One example of this is Swales and Feak's (1994) *Academic Writing for Graduate Students*. This task-based textbook allows students practice in how to construct texts specifically for their discipline and also shows students how specific texts such as emails and conference abstracts can be constructed.

Fifth-generation EST textbooks (2000–)

As we move into the twenty-first century there has been a greater interest in multi-media and multi-modality. Warschauer (2000) states that information technologies have transformed the ways in which we communicate and work with each other in English: the international language. This has to be considered when we look at EST courses in the future. Recent EST textbooks place a stronger focus on interpersonal communication, and the use of technology (e.g. McCullagh and Write 2008: *Communication Skills in English for the Medical Practitioner*, and Grice and Greenan 2008: *English for Nursing*), and recently produced in-house materials by Hafner (2012) show how elements of multi-modality can be incorporated into an EST course. The review by McDonough (2010) gives us a good idea of the scale of EST textbooks currently on the market, which nearly all have multi-modality elements included in them.

In contrast to the first-generation textbooks that were printed in black and white with a few line drawings, fifth-generation textbooks all have a variety of text and task types; have clear rubrics for students to follow; combine text with highly illustrative graphics; are colourful in design and presentation; and there is often a clear link between the language introduced and practised in the workplace. There is nearly always supporting material for each textbook: CDs, DVDs, online web links. In addition, all EST textbooks now have accompanying Teacher's Books with guidelines on how to present the material and answer keys.

Case studies in EST

In this section I present three case studies of EST courses to show how such courses can be designed and used in different contexts. Each case study is based on published work and constitutes a real situation where a course has been specifically developed for a particular group of learners. Textbooks were not used in any of these case studies, but, rather, the course designer developed materials to match the specific needs of the learners. As reported on in section 2, given the large number of EST textbooks on the market now it may seem strange not to use one of them. However, each course developer had his or her own reasons for customising the course materials, as will be seen. The case studies are from the academy, the workplace, and for career development, and show different types of learners in Hong Kong, Australia and Argentina.

Case Study 1: The academy

In an English for Engineering course, Miller (2002a) reports on an EST course designed for a homogeneous group of Chinese first-year undergraduate students at a university in Hong Kong. The main focus of this course was to ensure that these students, starting on their university life, were given help in reading scientific texts and listening to engineering lectures – the main skills identified from the needs analysis. The course designer adopted a task-based and strategy-based approach to developing the materials, and there was also a strong focus on fostering learner independence. The materials for this course came from a variety of popular engineering journals and newspaper reports about science, and a series of talks about the process of manufacturing engineering designed for high school students in the USA. The rationale for using these materials was that the materials were authentic but not too difficult for either the students or teachers to understand, and were similar to what the students would be required to deal with in the first year of study. The focus of the teaching materials was not to teach engineering, but the skills the students needed to develop their confidence in reading scientific texts. The listening material was chosen for a similar reason – it had face validity in that it was about engineering, but it was not so specific that it would confuse the teacher or students. Therefore, the main course objectives for this EST course were: 1) to be able to read and learn from semi-technical articles from popular manufacturing journals and newspapers; 2) to be able to listen and to learn from transactional types of academic lectures on engineering topics. In addition to these course objectives there was also an emphasis on heightening the students' awareness of their learning strategies when reading science articles or listening to lectures, and focusing on learner autonomy so that the students could further develop their language skills after the course ended. A typical activity on this course was:

Listening activity

Stage 1 Pre-listening: Students were given the topic of the talk they would listen to, e.g. quality control, and they had to brainstorm the type of vocabulary they expected to hear.
Stage 2 While-listening: Students were given skeleton notes, which had the main heading and subheading of the talk. They had to try and write notes onto the handout.
Stage 3 Post-listening: Students compared their notes with each other and discussed which parts were easy or difficult for them. This discussion was then extended into a general discussion about what type of information would be important to listen for in such a talk, and why.

Follow-up:
Students were asked to practise one of the note-taking skills in their next engineering lecture (e.g. focus on how the lecturer moves from one part of the talk to another) and write a comment about this in their learner diaries.

A special feature of this EST course, as stated by Miller, was the need to design materials that would be accessible to the teacher as well as the learner. EST courses often suffer from teachers who do not have a directly relevant scientific or technical background and who may be unsure of the specific genres they are working in. Therefore, an EST course at university needs to cater to such teaching staff. Another interesting feature of this course is the changing roles expected of both teacher and learner. Miller describes the learners who have come directly from high school as needing 'control' in order for the course to proceed in some sort of orderly fashion. Even although these were young adults, course management was an issue and the teacher was recommended to treat the students in a strict fashion until the classroom rules were established, after which a more relaxed atmosphere was attempted. As EST courses are often aimed at adult learners this additional role, of disciplinarian, is often overlooked. The outcome of the English for Engineering course was a heightened awareness of the students about how to approach their academic reading and listening.

Case Study 2: The workplace

Hussin (2002) reports on an English for Nurses course where non-native English speaking nurses learn how to work in a hospital environment in Australia. This course was designed for heterogeneous linguistic groups of SE Asian nurses. Some of the main concerns when designing this course were i) all the participants were professionals and had to be treated as such; ii) as nurses in their own countries they may have held high positions and may not be used to some of the cultural aspects of working in an Australian hospital; and iii) all were immigrants and may have emotional needs as well as linguistic-related needs.

The course objectives here were to prepare the nurses to have a working knowledge of English so as to be able to perform routine tasks in the hospital; to be able to communicate with other nurses and doctors on professional issues related to patient care; and to write case reports on the patients under their care. Therefore, as the course had a strong workplace element the classes were divided between in-class language work, and on-the-ward practice. The course was also delivered by both a language specialist and a nursing professional. A typical activity on this course would be as follows:

Writing activity

Stage 1: In class discussing of what a nursing care plan is.
Stage 2: Look at an authentic nursing care plan and focus attention on aspects of the text at the discourse level.
Stage 3: Provide the nurses with a series of manipulation texts tasks (language exercises).
Stage 4: As a homework task, construct a nursing care plan and receive feedback on it.
Stage 5: Write a real nursing care plan for their practicum.

Some important features of this English for Nurses course were: 1) the English teacher had to collaborate with other professionals in order to create a course that would meet the demands of a practising nurse in an Australian hospital; 2) the English teacher's role was focused on being the provider of not only linguistic knowledge but also cultural information; 3) there was an element of negotiation in the syllabus as not all the students had similar backgrounds and so some may have required more help, others less; 4) the language teacher also had to supervise the placements to ensure that the course met the workplace needs of the students; and 5) the language teacher also had to act as a counsellor at times to help the students adjust to their new living and working environments.

As can be seen from this English for Nursing course, there was a need for the course materials to have a strong correlation to the actual working environment, and the language teacher's roles go far beyond what might be expected of a teacher – something a textbook might not be able to offer. The outcome for this course was the students' ability to pass their practicum, a demonstration of their ability to work in English in their professional environment.

Case Study 3: Career development

In English for Brewing, Orsi and Orsi (2002) describe an unusual EST course for workers in the brewing industry. This course was developed in Argentina and taught in-house at one of the main breweries. As far as I am aware, no EST textbook for the brewing industry has been published, possibly due to the small market. The students on this course were all adults learners between the ages of 30 and 55 and were all colleagues in the company. The learners had full-time jobs and attended the intensive English course during lunchtime or after work. The main aim of the course was that these employees often had to travel overseas to represent the company and so had a need to be able to talk about the brewing industry in English to either native English speakers, or other non-native English speakers. The course objectives were mainly on listening and speaking, with a secondary focus on reading and writing. All four skills were practices within a brewery context – with the terminology that contained, e.g. acetaldehyde; balling degrees; diacetyl; fermentation. Apart from helping the employees transfer their knowledge about brewing from Spanish into English, the course also had to help the learners develop their confidence in using English to talk about their work when they travelled overseas – from both social and technical perspectives. For instance, it was discovered that apart from being able to talk about the chemistry of brewing, being able to listen to and tell jokes in English were valuable skills for their learners as this helped maintain social and professional contact with people they met at seminars and on promotional tours.

The syllabus for this course was skills-based using authentic materials provided by the company. Manuals about the brewing industry were used, as was a video on the brewing process. Material was specially prepared based on the authentic sources, and the syllabus reflected the learners' profile and individual needs. A typical activity for this course was:

Reading activity

Stage 1: Read authentic texts related to brewing (e.g. advertisements).
Stage 2: Engage in a variety of reading skills (right/wrong statements; matching words; answering open-ended questions).
Stage 3: Critically discuss the text used in the class.

Some special features of this English for Brewing course are 1) the teacher had to negotiate most of the syllabus with the students as they had to tell her what was important in their work; 2) the learners had to cooperate with the teacher in providing the non-specialist teacher with specialist information about their industry; 3) the learners had to suspend their roles as workers and become students in the workplace; 4) the teacher had to deal with cultural issues related to telling jokes (e.g. obscenities). The outcome of this course was more difficult to observe than for Case Studies 1 and 2, as the employees would only know if the course had been successful once they travelled overseas to represent their company – and possibly if their jokes worked.

Future directions in EST

In this final section I discuss some approaches, old and new, which I think have to be considered in the development of EST courses in the future. The approaches I consider are: learner autonomy, project-based learning, multi-literacies, genre, and ethnography. After a brief discussion on each area I will illustrate what I think the future directions for EST course development might be with a final example, Case Study 4.

Learner autonomy approach

'Learner autonomy' is a concept that was introduced into language learning via EST course design in the 1960s. This was mostly due to the practical nature of such courses and the need for learners to find out for themselves what they needed to learn. The term became more widely used in general language learning after Holec (1981) defined it as the ability to take control over one's learning. Therefore, the concept behind encouraging a learner autonomy approach in EST course design is not new. What is new is the myriad of opportunities learners now have to access English, mostly electronically, and the ways in which the language is used in professional contexts (e.g. the surge in email communications in the workplace and the sharing of files). A learner autonomy approach to EST course design encourages learners to participate in their learning more fully (Miller 2009), and has to be an aspect of all EST course design in the future.

Project-based learning approach

Once more, project-based learning is not a new idea. It is a way of encouraging cooperation among learners in achieving an outcome, or task. Project-based learning relies heavily on cooperative learning, the characteristics of which are: positive interdependence; individual accountability; promotive interaction; equal participation; equal opportunities for success; and group processing (Johnson et al. 2006). When asking students to engage in project-based learning we encourage them to focus not only on their individual understanding and learning, but also on helping other students learn – that is, the group becomes the learning agent (Suthers 2006) and communities of learners (Lave 1993) are established. The concept of a community of learners fits well with communities of practice (Lave and Wenger 1991) in the science and technology workplace where groups of colleagues collaborate to solve problems and work to achieve a project outcome.

Genre-based approach

Attention has been paid to how texts (often written texts) are constructed in EST contexts (see Hyland 2010). Since the early 1960s material developers have tried to reproduce sample texts in their EST course materials to reflect the actual types of documents learners have to deal with. In early efforts attention was mostly on linguist forms and vocabulary (see Section 2 above); by paying attention to specific features of texts tutors could speed up the learning process in specific English courses (Hutchinson and Waters 1987). More recently EST course developers have gone beyond the purely descriptive nature of written texts and focused more on the 'language description as explanation' (Bhatia, 1993: 10–12), and paid attention to the *how* as much as the *what*. Based on the work of Swales (1993) and Bhatia (1993) we have gone from a 'thin' description of texts (a surface linguistic analysis) to a more 'thick' description of texts (a deep functional analysis), and a better understanding of how texts are constructed within social contexts for their intended audiences.

Examining genres in professional contexts allows us to address a number of fundamental principles of EST course design: by varying the types of genres we allow our students access to we raise their consciousness of how language is used (Swales 1990); the focus on genres also sensitises learners to the need to understand the rhetorical demands of communicative situations in a range of specific domains (Bhatia 1993); and this sensitivity may result in students developing transferrable skills (Flowerdew 1993), which has become a feature in the modern day (technology-driven) workplace. For these reasons it is therefore advisable to re-examine the types of EST courses and ensure that we cater to the changing text-types and situational contexts our learners will have to deal with.

Multi-literacies approach

As we move into the twenty-first century we have to consider the enormous impact technology is having on literacy development, and the role EST course development can play in this. Information and Communications Technologies (ICTs) play an ever increasing role in the daily lives of our students (see Conole et al. 2008). It has ' … changed *how* people learn languages' (Warschauer 2005: xiv), and so, not only do course designers have to consider the use of ICTs in learning, but also consider how the multi-literacies that are now becoming familiar within their social contexts can be utilised in the classroom. 'Multi-literacies' is a term coined by the New London Group (1996) as a way of showing how multiple modes of communication (e.g. linguistic, graphical, audio) often operate concurrently in helping to communicate ideas and thoughts nowadays. Belcher (2004: 177), for instance, notes that the proliferation of computer-mediated communication has led to the development of emerging genres that draw on new forms of representation, and states:

One of the resulting challenges for ESP researchers will be to find ways to facilitate practitioners' conceptualisation and operationalisation of a more broadly inclusive multiliteracies approach to fostering and assessing genre competence ...

Ethnographic approach

Based on the extensive ethnographic work of Flowerdew and Miller (1992, 1995, 1996a, 1996b, 1997, 2000 and 2008), and Miller (2002b, 2007 and 2009) the use of multiple research tools for uncovering issues relevant to teaching university students in general and engineering students in particular have been investigated. In addition to a more traditional approach to conducting needs analysis for EST course design an ethnographic approach allows us to uncover the 'untold' stories of students' lives and gain a better perspective on what they bring to the learning context. For instance, Flowerdew and Miller (1995, 1996a) outline four main cultural dimensions to six socio-cultural features lectures that may often be overlooked by tutors preparing students on EST courses. Meanwhile, Miller (2002a) alerts us to the multiple dimensions students cope with when listening to talks in engineering. Such features of students' learning may not be obvious when conducting a basic needs analysis. In addition to this 'thick' description of the learning context, Flowerdew and Miller (2008) also bring in aspects of social structure and individual agency that have to be considered when teaching in an EST context. We need to gain as complete an understanding as possible of our students' needs and wants in order to offer them courses that suit their purposes, and build on their previous experiences.

Case Study 4: The new EST course design

In the past few years I have been working with my colleagues at The City University of Hong Kong in developing a new approach to teaching science students on one of our EST courses for biology, chemistry and mathematics students (see Hafner and Miller 2011; Miller, Hafner and Ng 2012; and Hafner, Miller and Ng 2012). Prior to the new course design, these students took an EGAP course and had to complete the following tasks:

- Read scientific articles and write summaries of the main points in the articles.
- Present, in class, in groups of 3, an oral report on a scientific experiment.
- Write a lab report (with the data from the oral report) using the Introduction, Methods, Results, Discussion (IMRD) protocol.

This type of course is similar in format to Case Study 1 reported on earlier and is a standard approach to an EST course design. However, with the 'new' dimensions of EST course design in mind (see above), we set about re-designing the course.

Prior to re-designing the course, an extensive needs analysis was undertaken by the tutors. This included the following:

1 A review of the existing course materials constrained by the fact that we had to retain the main course intended learning outcomes, the overall structure of the teaching pattern and type of materials used.
2 Discussions with programme leaders of the students' host departments to find out what the lecturers thought their students lacked in terms of English language skills. One of the main areas of concern reported was the students' ability to present scientific ideas clearly and accurately in English (in both written and spoken modes).

3 A review of students' work to identify the typical genres that students were engaged with in their discipline, and to evaluate apparent English language strengths and weaknesses.
4 Interviews with students from the existing course to see what types of language skills they thought should be the main focus in a revamped course. Students frequently referred to their desire for better oral proficiency skills.
5 An extensive review of the literature on areas such as learner autonomy, new literacies, project-based learning and course design.

We had several considerations in mind when we started to re-design the EST course:

1 The existing course aimed to cover too many skills in a one-semester period (39 hours over a 13-week period).
2 We wanted to engage the students in their learning. For instance, students were already familiar with writing lab reports, so we wanted to do something different that might motivate them to consider how science can be communicated through diverse forms of representation, especially orally.
3 Our students were *au fait* with technology – all students had their own laptop computers and many made use of a variety of technological communication tools (email, chat rooms, blogs, Whatsapp etc.). Therefore, we wanted to capitalise on the students' interest in using technology in the new course design.

The main change to the course was the introduction of a scientific video documentary to replace the existing oral presentation. When giving a traditional oral presentation, students usually stand in front of the class and frequently read from notes, sometimes with reference to PowerPoints. In our revamped course design, we asked students to prepare a 10-minute scientific documentary, in the form of a digital video, which would be uploaded to YouTube and shared through a course weblog. Students were encouraged to make the presentation of their documentaries as creative and entertaining as possible. We offered a choice of two different topics: a study of the blind spot in the human eye; a study of the sense of smell and taste in humans. The two topics were generic enough for the English tutors to support (see comments in Case Study 1), but also had strong scientific underpinnings, requiring students to do background research, formulate hypotheses, collect and interpret data. When they were complete, all videos were viewed in a class sharing session and oral feedback was given by both, classmates and tutors. Examples of our students' work can be seen at www1.english.cityu.edu.hk/acadlit/index.php?q = node/21. The new course met all the criteria for an ESP course as suggested by Dudley-Evans and St John's absolute and variable characteristics.

Architecture of the technological learning environment

In order to support student learning, we created a 'technological learning environment', with a full range of technological tools and resources to help students plan, construct and share their digital scientific documentaries. The design of this technological learning environment was based on a modular system that included an online learning management system supported by our university for course administration, a course weblog that served as a venue for students to engage in reflective discussions on coursework and learning, digital video cameras and editing software for video production, online resource website with support for video editing software in the form of screencasts, and the YouTube platform to share videos (which were also embedded in the course blog). Figure 20.2 shows the architecture of the technological

English for Science and Technology

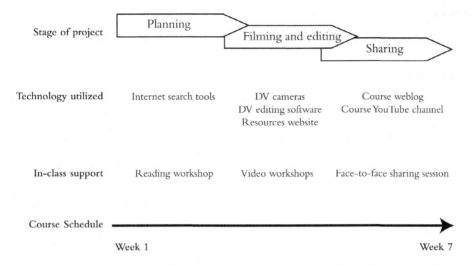

Figure 20.2 Architecture of the technological learning environment (from Hafner and Miller 2011)

learning environment and how the technology supported different stages of the English for Science project.

This newly designed EST course integrates new media and technology in order to engage students in new forms of multimodal representation and share the students' finished works through a world-wide internet platform (YouTube and the course weblog). Students on our EST course created a multimodal scientific documentary that they seemed proud of and invested heavily in. They were prepared to share their work not only with their tutor, or other classmates, but with a wider online audience. The documentary, which was constructed for a 'real' audience that students could relate to, acted as a useful bridge to the more academic scientific genres treated on the course. When they re-presented their study in the form of a written lab report students had to consider how to recontextualise their findings for a specialist audience. As a result, a number of 'teachable moments' arose as students reflected on the different audience and purpose of the written genre, and how this affected the language and even visual representation of their work.

Conclusion

English for Science and Technology is a well-established enterprise within the framework of English for Specific Purposes. In the past 50 years, or so, course design in ESP has moved from a structural approach to a cognitive approach to a socio-cognitive approach, and from accuracy to fluency to agency. We are able to trace this development with the help of research articles published in journals, and from examining the approaches taken to textbook development from the early 1960s to nowadays.

The future of EST course development lies in our ability to cater to the increasingly sophisticated professional communication needs of our learners. The internet and multimedia support new moves in EST course design and I believe that integrating aspects of new literacies into our EST courses and making use of a technology-driven pedagogy will help to cater to our twenty-first century EST learners' needs – which is, after all, the driving force for all ESP course design.

Related topics

ESP course development; learner autonomy; project-based learning; new technologies

Key readings

Dudley-Evans, T. and St John, M. J. (1998). *Developments in English for Specific Purposes: A Multi-disciplinary Approach*, Cambridge: Cambridge University Press. (This book reviews the main developments in the field of ESP from its early beginnings till the later 1990s. The book is essential reading for all ESP course developers and offers many useful and practical examples of what to consider when developing an ESP course.)

Hafner, C. A. and Miller, L. (2011). 'Fostering learner autonomy in English for Science: A collaborative digital video project in a technological learning environment', *Language Learning & Technology, 15*(3), 201–23. (This paper illustrates the main features of a new approach to designing an English for Science course outlined in this chapter. The integration of an autonomy-based pedagogical approach in a technology learning environment is highlighted. The paper also makes reference to other important developmental work in the area of EST course design.)

Orr, T (ed.) (2002). *English for Specific Purposes*, Alexandria: TESOL Inc. (This book presents 12 innovative case studies written by practitioners of ESP course design and development. The case studies represent different countries and contexts and are presented in a way that the reader can adapt the ideas to the local situation.)

Swales, J. (1988). *Episodes in ESP: A Source and Reference Book on the Development of English for Science and Technology*, New York: Prentice Hall. (This is an excellent historical review of the most important works published in ESP from the early 1960s until the late 1980s. Swales selects the most influential papers/ books and comments on the impact each has had on the way we think about ESP course design, and how we go about developing specific courses.)

Bibliography

Allen, J. P. B. and Widdowson, H. G. (1974a). 'Teaching the communicative use of English', *International Review of Applied Linguistics, 12*(1), 1–20.

——(eds.) (1974b). *English in Focus Series*, Oxford: Oxford University Press.

Barber, C. L. (1962). 'Some measurable characteristics of modern scientific prose', in *Contributions to English Syntax and Phonology*, Stockholm: Almquist & Wiksell.

Bates, M. and Dudley-Evans, T. (1976). *Nucleus: English for Science and Technology. General Science*. London and Harlow: Longman.

Bhatia, V. K. (1993). *Analysing Genre: Language Use in Professional Settings*, London: Longman.

Belcher, D. D. (2004). 'Trends in teaching English for specific purposes', *Annual Review of Applied Linguistics, 24*, 165–86.

Conole, G., de Laat, M., Dillion, T. and Darby, J. (2008). '"Disruptive technologies", "pedagogical innovation": What's new? Findings from an in-depth study of students' use and perception of technology', *Computers & Education, 50*, 511–24.

Dudley-Evans, T. and St John, M. J. (1998). *Developments in English for Specific Purposes: A Multi-disciplinary Approach*, Cambridge: Cambridge University Press.

Ewer, J. R. and Latorre, G. (1969). *A Course in Basic Scientific English*, London: Longman.

Flowerdew, J. (1993). 'An educational or process approach to the teaching of professional genres', *ELT Journal, 47*(4), 305–16.

Flowerdew, J. and Miller, L. (1992). 'Student perceptions, problems and strategies in L_2 lectures', *RELC Journal, 23*(2), 60–80.

——(1995). 'On the notion of culture in second language lectures', *TESOL Quarterly, 29*(2), 345–74.

——(1996a). 'Lectures in a second language: Notes towards a cultural grammar', *English for Specific Purposes Journal, 15*(2), 121–40.

——(1996b). 'Lecture perceptions, problems and strategies in second language lectures', *RELC Journal, 27*(1), 23–46.

——(1997). 'The teaching of academic listening comprehension and the question of authenticity', *English for Specific Purposes Journal, 16*(1), 27–46.

—— (2000). 'Chinese lecturers' perceptions, problems and strategies in lecturing in English to Chinese speaking students', *RELC Journal, 33*(2), 116–38.

—— (2008). 'Social structure and individual agency in second language learning: Evidence from three life histories', *Critical Inquiry in Language Studies, 5*(4), 201–24.

Glendinning, E. H. and Glendinning, N. (1995). *English for Electrical and Mechanical Engineering*, Cambridge: Cambridge University Press.

Grice, T. and Greenan, J. (2008). *English for Nursing*, Cambridge: Cambridge University Press.

Hafner, C. A. (2012). *GE2401: English for Science*, Hong Kong: Department of English, City University of Hong Kong.

Hafner, C. A. and Miller, L. (2011). 'Fostering learner autonomy in English for science: A collaborative digital video project in a technological learning environment', *Language Learning & Technology, 15*(3), 201–23.

Hafner, C.A., Miller, L. and Ng, C. (2012). 'Digital video projects in English for academic purposes: Students' and lecturers' perceptions and issues raised', in C. Berkenkotter, V. K. Bhatia and M. Gotti (eds), *Insights into Academic Genres*, Bern: Peter Lang.

Halliday, M. A. K., McIntosh, A. and Strevens, P. (1964). *The Linguistic Sciences and Language Teaching* (Longmans' Linguistic Library), London: Longmans.

Herbert, A. J. (1965). *The Structure of Technical English*, London: Longman.

Herbolich, J. B. (1979). 'Box Kites', *English for Specific Purposes, 29*, English Language Institute, Oregon State University, Corvallis, Oregon, USA.

Hick, S. (1991). *English for Information Systems*, Hemel Hempstead: Prentice Hall.

Holec, H. (1981). *Autonomy and Foreign Language Learning*, Oxford: Pergamon.

Howatt, A. P. R. (1984). *A History of English Language Teaching*, Oxford: Oxford University Press.

Hussin, V. (2002). 'An ESP program for students of nursing', in T. Orr (ed.), *English for Specific Purposes*, Alexandria: TESOL Inc.

Hutchinson, T. and Waters, A. (1984). *Interface: English for Technical Communication*, London: Longman.

—— (1987). *English for Specific Purposes*, Cambridge: Cambridge University Press.

Hyland, K. (2010). 'Constructing proximity: Relating to readers in popular and professional science', *Journal of English for Academic Purposes, 9*, 116–27.

Johnson, D. W., Johnson, R. and Johnson Smith, K. A. (2006). *Active Learning: Cooperation in the Classroom*, Edina, MN: Interaction Book Company.

Jones, T. F. and Dudley-Evans, A. (1980). 'An experiment in team-teaching of overseas postgraduate students of transportation and plan biology', *ELT Documents 106: Team Teaching in ESP*, The British Council, London: ETIC.

Jordan, R. R. (1997). *English for Academic Purposes: A Guide Book and Resource for Teachers*, Cambridge: Cambridge University Press.

Lave, J. (1993). 'The practice of learning', in S. Chaiklin and J. Lave (eds), *Understanding Practice: Perspectives on Activity and Context*, Cambridge: Cambridge University Press.

Lave, J. and Wenger, E. (1991). *Situated Learning: Legitimate Peripheral Participation*, Cambridge: Cambridge University Press.

McCullagh, M. and Wright, R. (2008). *Communication Skills in English for the Medical Practitioner*, Cambridge: Cambridge University Press.

McDonough, J. (2010). 'English for specific purposes: A survey review of current materials', *ELT Journal, 64*(4), 462–77.

Miller, L. (2002a). 'English for engineers in Hong Kong', in J. Murphy and P. Byrd (eds), *Understanding the Courses we Teach: Local Perspectives on English Language Teaching*, Ann Abor: The University of Michigan Press.

—— (2002a). 'Towards a model for lectures in a second language', *Journal of English for Academic Purposes, 1*(2), 145–62.

—— (2007). 'Issues in lecturing in a second language: Lecturer's behaviour and students' interpretations', *Studies in Higher Education, 32*(6), 747–60.

—— (2009). 'Engineering lectures in a second language: What factors facilitate students' listening comprehension?', *Asian EFL Journal, 11*(2), 8–30.

Miller, L., Hafner, C. A. and Ng, C. (2012). 'Project-based learning in a technologically enhanced learning environment for second language learners: Students' perceptions', *E–Learning and Digital Media, 9*(2), 183–95.

New London Group. (1996). 'A pedagogy of multiliteracies: Designing social futures', *Harvard Educational Review, 66*(1), 60–92.

Orsi, L. and Orsi, P. (2002). 'An ESP program for brewers', in T. Orr (ed.) *English for Specific Purposes*, Alexandria: TESOL Inc.

Philips, M. K. and Shettlesworth, C. C. (1978). 'How to arm your students: A consideration of two approaches to providing materials for ESP', in *ELT Documents: ESP*, The British Council, London.

Strevens, P. (1988). 'ESP after twenty years: A re-appraisal', in M. Tickoo (ed.), *ESP: State of the Art*, Singapore: SEAMEO Regional Language Centre.

Suthers, D. D. (2006). 'Technology affordances for intersubjective meaning making: A research agenda for CSL', *International Journal of Computer-Supported Collaborative Learning*, *1*(3), 315–37.

Swales, J. (1988). *Episodes in ESP: A Source and Reference Book on the Development of English for Science and Technology*, New York: Prentice Hall.

——(1990). *Genre Analysis: English in Academic and Research Setting*, Cambridge: Cambridge University Press.

——(1993). 'Discourse communities and the evaluation of written text', in J. E. Alatis (ed.), *Georgetown University Round Table on Languages and Linguistics 1992*, Washington, DC: Georgetown University Press.

Swales, J. and Feak, C. B. (1994). *Academic Writing for Graduate Students: A Course for Non-native Speakers of English*, Ann Arbor: The University of Michigan Press.

Warschauer, M. (2000). 'The changing global economy and the future of English teaching', *TESOL Quarterly*, *34*(3), 511–35.

——(2005). 'Sociocultural perspectives on CALL', in J. Egbert and G. M. Petrie (eds), *CALL Research Perspectives*, Mahawah, NJ: Lawrence Erlbaum.

Widdowson, H. G. (1983). *Learning Purpose and Language Use*, Oxford: Oxford University Press.

21
Communicative dimensions of professional accounting work

Alan Jones

Introduction

Despite the establishment of professional bodies and the promulgation of professional standards and a rigorously worked out conceptual framework, professional accounting work was long conceptualised as a purely technical and routine field of activity. As such it was viewed as a technical adjunct to the core activities of business and management. However, beginning in the last quarter of the twentieth century, there has been increasingly widespread recognition that accountancy constitutes a thoroughly pervasive set of social and epistemological practices that affects fundamentally how business is conducted and how business organisations and institutions operate. Nowadays it is widely acknowledged that accounting is a pivotal social institution and that professional accounting work[1] is a crucial 'device for intervening in the functioning of organizations and society' (Potter 2005: 267; see also Ahrens 1997; Hopwood and Miller 1994) while remaining in essence an objectivating and calculative one. The underlying epistemology of accounting and auditing nowadays influences countless aspects of our everyday lives (Power 1999; Dean 1999). Meanwhile, as a set of professional practices, accounting has experienced unprecedented shifts of focus and functional expansions. The types of services offered by accounting firms have expanded from traditional audit work; such firms now offer a broad range of commercially oriented services (Sin, Reid and Dahlgren 2011). These changes have not been confined to professional services firms, and both the trend and pace of change are continuing and affect all the sub-fields of accounting practice and every practising accountant is being affected in one way or another.

The new and largely cross-functional roles being assumed by accountants, their involvement in strategic management and their responsibility for adding value to commercial operations all entail a very high level of interpersonal skills along with the ability to articulate policies and decisions both lucidly and persuasively. Like professionals more generally, accountants are nowadays expected be capable of building and sustaining trust-based relationships, and doing this entails that they espouse new levels of openness, informality and cooperativeness in their interactions with clients and their employees, as well as with colleagues and clients (Misztal 2000, 2001). These developments clearly put a priority on an individual's communicative and interactional abilities.

However, professional communicative expertise was until relatively recently conceptualised as an optional extra in accounting. And it is still often considered, by employers of new graduates, to be something that will improve to the required standard after a certain length of time in the workplace (Gray and Murray 2011: 289). At the same time, employers want to employ graduates who are 'work-ready' and hiring practices will certainly reflect a preference for candidates who already possess high-level communication abilities. As such abilities become ever more central to the roles enacted by accountants in the contemporary workplace, their development should no longer be left to chance. Moreover as applied linguists we have a special interest in identifying and problematising key aspects of what counts as professional communicative expertise in the context of specific professions. The following discussion focuses on developments in Australia and New Zealand, but many of the points I make will have broader relevance, e.g. for other countries and other professions. I will summarise an understanding of communication in professional contexts that is becoming increasingly widespread, and in which communication is viewed as a necessary dimension of professional practice and the negotiation of meaning that such practice essentially consists of. However, adopting a top-down, functionalist orientation, I begin by describing the types of work accountants do, what they need to know to do this, and the kinds of social-institutional problems they engage with on more-or-less a daily basis.

Domains and levels of practice

Professional accountants work in or across a number of specialised domains, or sub-fields, as well as across levels of expertise (or *competence* as it is commonly called in accounting circles). They can work for government departments, or within business organisations, or in firms run by accountants (where they offer services to private individuals or organisations). Some take up teaching positions. Practising accountants specialise in topics such as commercial and corporation law, tax law and compliance, auditing, assurance, insolvency and reconstructions, and information or accounting systems. Many accounting professionals nowadays are involved in business consulting, business valuations, litigation support, forensic accounting, fraud examination, and other such services that entail the embedding of their specialised knowledge and skills in complex social, economic, legal and/or commercial contexts.

Traditionally the two main recognised domains of accounting work have been financial accounting and management accounting. Financial accounting covers the preparation and interpretation of financial statements and their communication to the users of the accounts, primarily users external to the organisation producing the accounts (e.g. banks and government departments). Management accounting involves reporting internally, to the owners and management of an organisation who need access to reliable financial information to be able to discharge their own functions of stewardship, planning, control and decision making. An important component of management accounting is cost accounting, which deals with cost ascertainment and cost control. More specialised subfields of accounting work, of more recent origin, are social responsibility accounting and human resource accounting. Social responsibility accounting measures social costs incurred by the enterprise and social benefits created. Human resource accounting is an attempt to *identify quantity* and report investments made in human resources of an organisation that are not presently accounted for under conventional accounting practice.

An influential study by Birkett (1993) identified the competencies required by practitioners in five subfields at three different levels of expertise or experience: competent, proficient and expert. The discrete abilities needed to function at each level are regarded as cumulative, that is as building upon one another and developing over time. Birkett conceived of competency as a highly integrated and dynamic capacity, explaining that it 'relates to the way in which individual attributes (knowledge, skills and attitudes) are drawn on in performing tasks in particular work contexts (job performance). Neither contextual task performance nor individual attributes constitute competence; *it is the relation between the two that does*' (1993: 4; emphasis added). Birkett later (2002, 2003), in writing about management accountants, distinguished five levels of experience and implicitly expertise:[2]

1   the novice practitioner level
2   assistant practitioner level
3   competent practitioner level
4   proficient practitioner level
5   expert practitioner level.

For the profession generally, each level of expertise is characterised by a distinct appropriate position in the business hierarchy, by specific activities, and by specific expectations regarding performance. Birkett's early research was commissioned by the Institutes of Chartered Accountants in Australia and New Zealand and has influenced training and development in the field ever since. It is often incorporated into research instruments (questionnaires, etc.) or forms the starting point of further investigations. His work on management accountants is much cited (see Birkett 2002, 2003).

Traditional conceptions of accounting work

Accounting in general (and financial accounting in particular) is still often described in terms of recording and reporting financial facts or situations, and justified in terms of its 'usefulness' with regard to business decision-making. Very recently, in connection with the development of new minimum standards for accounting education in Australia, we read that the chief goal of accounting work is 'to assist resource allocation decisions and compliance' (Hancock, Freeman and Associates 2010: 7). Hancock *et al.*'s summary of accounting practices (ibid.) is reproduced below.

> Accounting practices undertaken to assist resource allocation decisions and compliance include, but are not restricted to:
>
> - recording and summarising transactions and other economic events
> - application and interpretation of accounting standards in the preparation of financial statements
> - analysis of the operations of business (for example, performance measurement; management control; decision analysis)
> - financial analysis and projection (for example, analysis of historical trends for budgeting; analysis of financial ratios for budgeting or raising funds; analysis of cash flow from operations; analysis of financial risks in light of operating in an uncertain future economic climate).

This description is by most standards very superficial yet it is typical of most 'official' definitions of accounting work and is still found in introductory textbooks. Some preliminary observations can be made here. Clearly recording and summarising economic events ('recognising' them as such, to use the technical terminology of accounting) depends on the application of complex, detailed definitions, which in Australia are provided in the official Statement of Accounting Concepts (SAC 4: 'Definition and Recognition of the Elements of Financial Statements').[3] Accounting standards are published in the same way by the Australian Accounting Standards Board and are known as AASB standards. AASB 1018, to give an example, takes up approximately 27 pages of small print, contains worked examples, and is framed in the kind of format and language generally found in legal documents. These are all conceptually dense texts, reflecting what is known as the conceptual framework of accounting, and accounting practice consists largely in the interpretation and application of the categories and principles contained in these texts to the flux of business transactions that are on the whole motivated by very different axioms and principles. Yet analysis of business operations and projections based on such analyses, are also part of the work of the accountant.

Accounting practice 'is not conducted in isolation but is informed by various perspectives including social, ethical, economic, regulatory and global' (Hancock, Freeman and Associates 2010: 7). Thus the interpretation and *use* of the formally defined categories and principles described above – which constitute accountancy as a codified discourse (Llewellyn and Milne 2007) – are processes that must themselves be richly *contextualised*, at a number of different levels, possibly simultaneously. These matters are taken up in more detail in a later section that summarises research conducted in discourse or practice oriented frameworks. What is relevant here, however, is the fact that recent research into student learning has established a firm link between students' conceptions of professional work in their intended field and their current approaches to learning and learning outcomes (Abrandt Dahlgren *et al.* 2008; Abrandt Dahlgren *et al.* 2006; Jones and Sin 2005; Reid and Petocz 2004). This research is grounded in more general findings about student learning (Van Rossum and Schenk 1984; Entwistle and Ramsden 1983). So it is clearly of considerable importance that we define the field (along with its sub-fields) as accurately – i.e. as realistically – as possible, for the benefit of students and other relative novices.

Conceptualising professional expertise in terms of skills and attributes

One response of employers, the professional accounting organisations and accounting academics to the changes to professional practice mentioned above and the new demands they make on accounting graduates was an emphasis on developing generic skills (or generic attributes, or graduate attributes) in education and training (see American Institute of Certified Public Accountants 1999; Canadian Institute of Chartered Accountants 2005; Australian Society of CPAs and the Institute of Chartered Accountants in Australia 1997). This is succinctly acknowledged in a recent version of the Professional Accreditation Guidelines for Higher Education Programs put out by the Australian Society of Certified Practising Accountants and the Institute of Chartered Accountants in Australia (2009: 12):

> The professional bodies expect that accounting students will acquire a set of generic skills, therefore they require the teaching of generic skills in the core curriculum. The teaching of generic skills and their development in students should be planned and systematically implemented in curriculum design. It is recommended that generic skills be developed in an integrated fashion throughout the various course areas taught rather than be treated separately.

The Australian Society of Certified Practising Accountants (ASCPA)[4] and the Institute of Chartered Accountants in Australia (or ICAA) issued a joint statement in 1996 urging all accredited accounting programs at tertiary level to explicitly teach a range of generic skills (Australian Society of CPAs and Institute of Chartered Accountants in Australia 1996). In 2000 this had become a condition of accreditation. The emphasis on generic skills had grown out of extensive research carried out by William Birkett using surveys and focus groups.[5] His findings were summarised as a taxonomy of generic skills that was subsequently promulgated by the bodies. This taxonomy of skills (based on Birkett's attempt to define 'competency-based standards' for the profession in Australia) owed much to Bloom's well-known taxonomy of educational objectives (Bloom 1956; see Birkett 1993: 13–14; Birkett 2003).[6] This set of generic skills is still in common use, either in its original form (Institute of Chartered Accountants in Australia and CPA Australia 2009; Jones and Sin 2003) or as the basis for more developed lists or taxonomies (Whitefield and Kloot 2006). It is reproduced in the Appendix below. However, it is crucial to point out that the skills listed by the professional bodies in the above-mentioned document are not so much generic as discipline-specific (based as they are on Birkett's detailed surveying of accounting practitioners).

More recent research has established the skills that employers consider most important for accounting graduates in the first decade of the twenty-first century. Findings of Kavanagh and Drennan (2008: 293; Table 5) generally agree with those in earlier surveys, in Australia and elsewhere, in identifying the top four skills required by employers (in order) as,

1 analytical thinking/problem solving, i.e. cognitive, generic skills or abilities
2 business awareness/real life experience, i.e. practical, individual skills, attributes
3 basic accounting skills, i.e. technical, discipline-specific skills
4 ethics/fraud awareness/professionalism, i.e. attributes of character, identity

Employers indicated more informally that they expected every accounting graduate would possess basic accounting and analytical skills (Kavanagh and Drennan 2008). In addition, they wanted graduates to possess a range of other capabilities of the kind sometimes referred to as 'soft skills'. These are widely thought to be properly 'generic', i.e. transferable from one discipline or one field of practice to another. Employers identified certain types of communicative ability as *explicitly* communicative (oral communication, written communication), but other capabilities named clearly also entail communication skills (e.g. teamwork, interpersonal skills):

> There was also demand for oral communication skills, ethical awareness/professional skills, teamwork, written communication and a 'whole of business', contextual or interdisciplinary approach to the information that accounting outputs provide. Employers emphasised the need for graduates to develop interpersonal skills and be aware of the need for continuous learning in order to be up to date with a changing, increasingly global environment.
> *(Kavanagh and Drennan 2008: 294)*

The same employers ranked two explicit categories of communication skills/attributes immediately after the four categories given above, i.e.,

5 Communication: oral/face to face
6 Communication: written

These were followed by three categories that implicitly entail face-to-face communication and varying levels and types of linguistic and discursive expertise:

7 Interdisciplinarity: able to work across/knowledge of other disciplines
8 Teamwork/cooperation/participation
9 Interpersonal/facilitation/skills.

Oral communication and *written communication* are represented as being analytically (and I would add artificially) distinct from the abilities needed to carry out the tasks in which these activities are normally embedded or of which they form an intrinsic part (Bhatia 2006, 2008b). *Interdisciplinarity* suggests interdiscursivity, a sophisticated communicative capability that involves a command of functionally distinct discourses. While *teamwork/cooperation/participation* skills and *interpersonal/facilitation* skills clearly entail face-to-face communication and, in a work context, the inherently communicative capacity to negotiate tasks, roles and outcomes while simultaneously building and sustaining relationships.

Use of the term 'skills' or 'attributes' is often a matter of personal preference, and sometimes the two terms are used interchangeably, without any clear or explicit distinction being made (e.g., Jones 2010; Kavanagh and Drennan 2008). On the whole, the term 'attribute' connotes a more complex and a more integrated capability than the term 'skill' (Barrie 2004). The following definition from Bowden *et al.* (2000) probably represents a fairly widely accepted Australian understanding of the meaning of the term:[7]

> Graduate attributes are the qualities, skills and understandings a university community agrees its students should develop during their time with the institution. These attributes include, but go beyond, the disciplinary expertise or technical knowledge that has traditionally formed the core of most university courses. They are qualities that also prepare graduates as agents for social good in an unknown future.

It is worth noting in passing that the current discourse of generic skills and/or generic attributes reflects a fairly recent emphasis by the Australian and New Zealand governments on work-readiness and workplace productivity, now seen as the central goals of education, including professional education. As noted above, this agenda has been taken up and is indeed enforced by many professional bodies, including those in accounting.

The generic skills agenda has long been criticised, and for a variety of reasons. Clanchy and Ballard (1995) were among the first to highlight the definitional problems that beset skills constructs, and hence the research and recommendations centring on them. Barnett (1994) and Hyland and Johnson (1998) were among those pointing to the questionable pedagogic value of teaching from skills lists. Sarangi (2005) and Dall'Alba and Barnacle (2007) are more recent critics, questioning whether students can become fully competent and versatile professionals through a focus on discrete skills and warning that such an emphasis may undermine the kind of skilfulness that emerges from an inner transformation. But much criticism of the skills agenda has in fact been quite constructive, suggesting how the contextualisation of such skills could provide them with concrete meaning and make it possible to develop them in context-specific instructional programs. Thus Anna Jones (who generally writes in terms of 'attributes') notes that '[r]ecent research finds that generic attributes are intrinsically complex and there is a range of ways of defining and conceptualising these attributes' (2010: 7). She summarises her position as follows:

> This paper does not assume that generic attributes are utterly context-dependent nor that they exist only relative to their context. Rather, it assumes that, although there is the possibility for abstraction and generalisability, the way in which the attributes are conceptualised cannot be understood in isolation from the social and cultural context within which they exist.
>
> (Jones 2010: 7)

Jones cites numerous studies to support the argument that generic attributes in accounting are in fact 'shaped' by disciplinary and professional knowledge and skills (2010: 10) – a point I will take up again below. She emphasises that:

> What is clear from this is that the skills which accounting graduates need are an integration of so called 'generic' skills and accounting knowledge.
>
> *(2010: 10)*

> The disciplinary context is of the utmost importance because it forms the knowledge-base out of which these skills arise and from which these skills are defined. Employers may have yet another knowledge base (or series of bases) which they assume to be universal.
>
> *(2010: 12)*

It is easy to list some the most intransigent problems faced by the so-called generic skills agenda: the inherent complexity of professional practice and the capabilities entailed in it; the fact that generic skills or attributes are intrinsically related to content knowledge and its application; and finally the now notorious problem of the transferability of skills or attributes acquired in one context to another. Jones and Sin (2003), responding to the practical needs of the accounting profession in Australia with its obligatory skills list, developed a method for fostering the listed skills indirectly, by engaging students in richly contextualised tasks and task-based discussions (the intervention is evaluated in Sin, Jones and Petocz 2007). More recently there have been several attempts to 'embed' generic skills and/or attributes in the core curriculum, related in some ways to the initiative by Jones and Sin (2003), but the degree to which the skills/attributes are actually embedded – rather than in practice added on – varies considerably. Hocking and Fieldhouse (2011) provide a useful critique of approaches to 'embedding' that ignore basic insights of research into academic literacy, reminding us that developing expertise in a discipline or profession takes place at the level of epistemology and identity, while describing an initiative they themselves undertook in an unrelated field.

I next examine models of professional expertise that attempt to integrate all the various capabilities identified so far as necessary to or helpful in effective practice.

Towards an integrated or 'organic' model of professional expertise

Some of the most insightful models of professional expertise have aimed to integrate a diverse set of capabilities in an organic fashion, that is, as functionally interdependent. Below I reproduce what is to my mind one of the most comprehensive models of integrated knowledge and skills to have been developed so far, the Professional Capability Framework.[8]

Wells et al. (2009) note that while this framework recognises the importance of generic *and* job or profession specific skills (D and E), it also recognises that such skills are not sufficient for effective professional performance. It is at least equally important to possess:

- a high level of social and personal emotional intelligence (A);
- a contingent way of thinking, i.e. an ability to 'read' what is going on in new situations (B);
- a capacity to discern and assess the potential outcomes of alternative courses of action (B);
- a set of 'diagnostic maps' developed from handling previous practice problems in the unique work context (C).

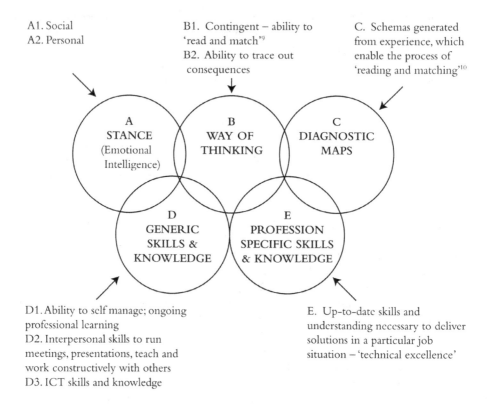

Figure 21.1 Professional capability framework (reproduced from Scott 2003)

While we will not attempt a rigorous definition of emotional intelligence here (see Goleman 1995), it is worth pointing out that certain characteristics of emotional intelligence according to Goleman (self awareness and impulse control, persistence, zeal and self-motivation, empathy and social deftness) are assets for the type of critical-dialectical discourse that Mezirow (2003) claims underlies meta-cognitive reasoning and transformative learning. Kemmis, an authority on learning and development, puts these claims in terms of practical reason (2005: 391):

> As a way of thinking, practical reasoning may indeed involve drawing on resources of what those authors call 'professional practice knowledge', but it involves drawing on more than that 'store' of knowledge. It also involves drawing on understandings about one's own and others' intentions, understandings, meanings, values and interests, and on one's own and others' reflexive, unfolding understandings of the situation in which one is practising at any given moment.

The work of Scott and his colleagues on the Professional Capability Framework has repeatedly confirmed the importance of intellectual capabilities, specifically Way of Thinking (which combines cognitive intelligence with creativity) and Diagnostic Maps (which are developed through reflection on experience). Scott's Diagnostic Maps resonate with research on expertise that has recognised that expert practitioners develop an intuitive or 'tacit' ability to recognise significant patterns (Dreyfus and Dreyfus 1986; Benner and Tanner 1987; Sally Candlin 2002; but cf. Whitehead 2005). However, in this regard it is important to recall that for many practical purposes (e.g. mentoring and pedagogical ones) knowledge needs to be articulated, or discursively 'elaborated' (Bordage 1994), i.e. made explicit. It is only in this way that the expert practitioner's premises and reasoning processes are made contestable and negotiable, and only in this way that their expertise can be shared.

In the next section I summarise some recent discourse and practice oriented research into professional accounting work and examine its implications.

Professional accounting work as discourse, interpretation and practice

Recent empirical work using qualitative methods as well as, and sometimes instead of, quantitative methods, has introduced the notion of practice *as discourse* and helped re-define some of the communicative challenges faced by accountants in general and auditors in particular. The challenging organisational role of auditors has been the focus of considerable attention, along with the communicative strategies practitioners employ to cope with the challenges (e.g. Goodwin 2002; van Peursem 2005; Hollindale, Kent and McNamara 2008). More generally, the interpersonal resource and communicative capacity required of all accounting practitioners are now seen to be just as complex and task-critical as in fields such as health care, the law, or social service delivery.[11] It has long been recognised that accountants frequently experience role conflict and role ambiguity (Bame-Aldred and Kida 2007; Senatra 1980). Van Peursem (2005) has shown how internal auditors, for example, must manage ambiguity across workplace functions and discourses, on the level of interpersonal, face-to-face communication. Van Peursem notes that internal auditor effectiveness depends crucially on the ability to communicate informally 'on many levels to many parties' and thus 'gently influence' an organisation's processes and decision-making (2005: 508). As she puts it (509):

> Perhaps most revealing from these data, however, is that these internal auditors who seem to be most effectively addressing the tension of their role are also those who resolve those tensions through somewhat ambiguous means. That is, these internal auditors seem to serve best where they can skilfully walk the line between providing advice to management and, at the same time, provide assurance to others. It is thus a revelation of the study to understand that role ambiguities, and occasionally conflicts, may themselves be a key to achieving that balance.

Beginning in the 1990s, there has been an explicit 'turn to discourse' in investigations of professional accounting work, especially as regards its role in organisations. Ahrens (1997) highlights the role of face-to-face communication in negotiating action plans and outcomes in business organisations. As he puts it: 'Accounting talk ... emerges as a medium for the creative mobilisation of accounting in everyday work' (1997: 618). Through talk management accountants influence decision making, but this is not an unproblematic process. Accounting talk comes up against other kinds of talk (sales talk, production talk, human resources talk, etc.) with which it becomes creatively intertwined. Outcomes – in the shape of decisions, explicitly or tacitly arrived at – typically reflect the domination of accounting talk (Ahrens 1997: 624). However, this domination does not occur all at once, but rather through an incremental blurring – in talk – of the boundaries between the *interests* of the accounting practitioner and those of other organisational stakeholders, and 'a blending of their particular ways of understanding the organisation' (1997: 618). In Ahrens' words (ibid.),

> talking accounting becomes a way of tailoring financial information to a particular operational decision-making scenario. The thought of organisational members who talk about

accounting implies a distinction between an accounting to which that talk can refer and the processes in which it is drawn upon and 'used' for decision-making.

It is clear that accounting talk can, however, in certain situations, function as a mode of generating financial management information for specific purposes by combining estimates of the financial effects of action with operational, more tacit knowledge. Through such a combination, talk becomes creative. The distinction between the 'practice' of accounting and its 'use' is blurred. Together, 'practitioner' and 'user' order, rearrange and combine accounting with sales expertise. At the micro-level of organisational action, local perceptions of relevant information are reproduced, but also shaped, through the creative oral intertwining of accounting and other organisational knowledge.

Meanwhile interviews of accounting professionals carried out by Sin (2011) have allowed us to identify the crucial role played by communicative expertise in the establishment and maintenance of trust in the often fragile and frequently tested interpersonal relationships that are so central to much accounting work, especially in the audit function (see also Jones and Sin 2013).

A more recent theoretical focus on 'practice' (drawing on Bourdieu 1977; also Giddens 1984) has encouraged scholars to conceptualise accounting work as a 'skilful practical activity' in social contexts that are themselves, in part at least, constituted through intentional actions and sense-making processes (Ahrens and Chapman 2007a: 24). In other words (quoting from Ahrens and Chapman 2007a: 1–2),

> the orderly properties of the social arrangements around accounting have been conceived as a direct outcome of practical activity, avoiding analytical distinctions between high-level structures and low-level action. Accounting cannot be understood simply with reference to its supposed functional properties because it is implicated in the shaping of its own context.

The discourse-focused approach to professional communication in-and-around accounting has been elaborated in important ways by Llewellyn and her colleagues (see especially Llewellyn and Milne 2007), who argue that accounting discourses are 'codified' discourses. By this they mean that the various discourses of accounting (corresponding to different areas of practice) incorporate 'codes' that range from such formal and explicit codes as regulations, standards and policies to the informal and generally unverbalised codes that are enshrined in professional norms, ceremonies and rituals (Llewellyn and Milne 2007). Llewellyn and Milne enlarge on the relevant term as follows (p. 806):

> By 'codified' [3] we mean that accounting is cast into systematic forms that prescribe codes for practices. Like a recipe, rule, guideline, template, protocol or law, accounting tells people how to do things. For example, 'discounted cash flow' tells managers how to make investment decisions through a particular way of valuing their likely returns. So accounting prescribes practice in the financial world, but accounting itself is also the result of pre-scriptions. For example, a balance sheet is the outcome of a particular way of accountants following codes to represent assets and liabilities. Codification fixes financial realities. Once particular codified rules are adopted the history of the underlying economic realities becomes ' … legally and socially irreversible … ' (Suzuki, 2003) as the ability is 'un-pick' the codes, to recover what was represented, is lost.

The textual entities here referred to as regulations, standards and policies naturally incorporate, entextualise and legitimise the concepts, conceptual relations, assumptions and principles that make up the knowledge base of accounting practice (Park and Bucholtz, 2009). And we cannot adequately conceptualise the interpretive and meaning-making activities of individual practitioners that are contingently and ongoingly achieved in the midst of workplace negotiations, problem-solving and decision-making without recognising that these activities have as their central semiotic resource that whole systematic network of concepts, relations, assumptions and principles.

Interpretive approaches to accounting that paved the way for its conceptualisation in terms of discourse and practice can be traced back to Child (1972) who argued that organisational actors must exercise choice in balancing general strategic objectives with possible specific actions. Hopwood (1989) developed this approach further, seeking to promote the study of accounting practices 'as finely graded, highly specific contingencies in the minds of organisational members who seek to put them to use for their specific priorities' (as summarised in Ahrens and Chapman 2007b: 106; cf. Scott et al., above). In his attempt to redefine the work of accountants Hopwood wrote of 'a deep interpenetration between the technical practices of accounting, the meanings and significances that are attributed to them and the other organisational practices and processes in which they are embedded' (Hopwood 1989: 37). As well as being used to inform decisions regarding future actions (a function that has traditionally been foregrounded), accounting was now seen as 'a vital resource for making sense of past decisions and the present to which they have lead [sic]' (Ahrens and Chapman 2007a: 2). Thus researchers have started to focus upon the uses of accounting qua discourse and interpretive practice in processes of organisational learning, negotiation, persuasion and rationalisation. The ultimate, cumulative effect of interpretive studies has been to establish the flexibility and variability of accounting practices (Dent 1986) and the way in which accounting, as an ideology and indeed a Discourse (in Gee's expanded sense of the word),[12] pervades and constrains all of the major functions of an organisation.

It seems that, for many purposes, accounting can be envisaged as a system of meanings and attitudes i.e. values, and as one with hegemonic tendencies. These meanings and values are realised as a discourse (or Discourse), i.e. as a system of interpretations and practices. Its realisation implicates a number of levels or strata that range from institutionalised practical genres (*activity types*) to speech genres (and *discourse types*) and discursive/communicative *strategies* (see Figure 21.2 and discussion). The concrete rearrangements that are the outcomes of accounting as discourse, interpretation and practice can be conceptualised as *materialised meanings* – i.e. as the resemiotisation of more abstract sets of meanings (Iedema 2001, 2003) – and of the values that are attached to these meanings.

Communication as a dimension of professional expertise – the role of knowledge

The upshot of these recent insights and findings for professional accounting practice is that both language and communication, instead of being seen as add-ons, must be understood as preconditions for, and inherent dimensions of, such work. Following Llewellyn and Milne (2007), all of the problems and indeed the dilemmas that accountants struggle to resolve in their everyday work, and all of the socially and institutionally situated decisions they make in doing so, intimately involve linguistically realised categories. These categories constitute the knowledge base that characterises and legitimates the profession, a unique semiotic resource. Accounting work, by and large, involves negotiating the nature and import of these categories for different parties in different contexts of use. Use of these categories in social contexts – which presupposes mastering a body of knowledge – involves the control and skilled manipulation of

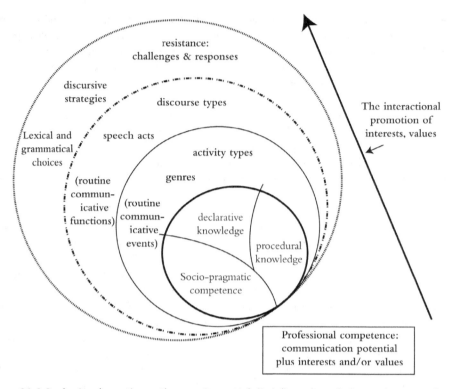

Figure 21.2 Professional practice as the recruitment of disciplinary knowledge and communicative competence for the realisation and promotion of interests, values and agendas

practice genres, discourse genres and interpersonal/rhetorical strategies and is an intrinsically moral practice. As Bowker and Star (1999: 156) put it:

> Few have looked at the creation and maintenance of complex classifications as a kind of *work practice*, with its attendant financial, skillful, and moral dimensions.

Anna Jones (2010: 15) has recently expanded upon the problems inherent in the dualistic understanding that separates knowledge and practice that is implicit in much of the generic skills literature.

Many current debates about generic skills or attributes often still suggest that there is disciplinary knowledge ('content') and there are skills or attributes that can be bolted onto this knowledge or, at best, be embedded in it. The position here is that generic skills and attributes are part of the epistemology and practice of disciplines and professions. In so far as they can be analytically distinguished, they enact discursively constructed content, or knowledge. Skills and attributes are thus shaped by the disciplinary epistemologies and professional practices that they embody and realise. This means that they will not exist in identical form in each discipline.

With reference to accounting, Jones notes (2010: 15–16, emphasis added):

> [Accounting] has a unique disciplinary and professional culture and with this comes particular knowledge creation and verification practices as well as professional ethics and practices. It is evident from the literature on generic skills in accounting that *skills, conceptual knowledge*

and the professional context are integrated. For example, solving a problem may require the ability to identify information, analyse and interpret it using particular accounting concepts, make recommendations or evaluations and communicate the findings either orally or in writing in an appropriate format, all within an ethical framework.

As Jones also notes (ibid.), dualistic understandings are inherently reductionist and stand in the way of a unified approach to teaching and learning.

Expert *knowledge* (knowledge of categories and conceptual taxonomies) is used in two main ways in accounting talk. It can appear overtly – on the surface of discourse – in problem-solving talk, when there is a question of recognising or refusing to recognise items proposed to be credited to or debited from financial statements. However, classification and numerical analysis also play a powerful covert role when in multifunctional meetings (as described by Ahrens 1997) management accountants ensure that profit margins remain at the forefront of everyone's thinking and are the deciding factor in decision-making. But to do so they need to be able to deploy a wide range of interactional and discursive strategies to manipulate meaning on a number of different levels simultaneously and implicitly.

Communication as a dimension of professional expertise – discursive strategies

The focus on discourse and discursive practices (see above) has provided valuable insights into exactly how communicative expertise becomes manifest in interactions. Practitioners themselves are becoming aware of the strategies they use. Jones and Sin (2013) found that experienced accountants across a range of workplace contexts recognise the need to aspire to skilful practice (what Schön, 1983, called 'artful doing'), particularly in performing certain types of communicative function: probing for sensitive financial information without endangering or irrevocably damaging interpersonal relationships; explaining complex concepts or unsatisfactory outcomes, both to lay persons and to specialists; giving advice on sensitive financial matters tactfully, persuasively and confidentially; and participating effectively in difficult negotiations that typically involve advising, persuading, compromising, and resolving disagreements and conflicts.

Janet Holmes, with colleagues at the Language in the Workplace Project (LWP) in New Zealand,[13] emphasise the crucial importance of 'meshing both transactional and relational dimensions of workplace interaction' (Holmes and Riddiford 2010). That is, effective communication in the workplace is instrumental in getting things done, but must also function to develop and sustain good interpersonal relationships with everyone involved in that process. Transactional objectives must also be achieved without flouting the norms of the workplace culture – norms that are set by the culture at large but that vary in important ways from site to actual site. Discourse analyses based on transcripts of authentic workplace communication have established that effective interactants deploy situation-specific strategies in order to achieve their ends.[14] The strategies identified include the ability to skilfully integrate social talk into daily work routines (Holmes 2000, 2005), to tell stories (Holmes 2005, 2006; Holmes and Marra, 2011) and to make use of humour (Holmes 2005; Holmes and Marra 2006; Holmes and Riddiford 2010). Effective managers usually control a subtly calibrated repertoire of linguistic templates for giving directives or for making requests that are intimately affected by the relationships of the actors and the communicative purpose of the interaction (Vine 2004). More generally, expecting differences (Marra 2008) and indeed expecting things to go wrong, communicatively and interactionally (Scollon and Scollon 2001: 22–23), while having the resources to cope with eventualities such as these are hallmarks of expert communicators.

Research carried out by accounting academics should not be ignored as a frequent source of authentic practitioner insights into communicative strategies. Much has been published, in particular, on the difficult and inherently conflictual nature of auditor-client negotiations where there are often disagreements over what should be recognised in financial statements and how. This kind of research is typically survey-based and the survey instruments used may incorporate categories established by social psychologists. For example, Hollindale, Kent and McNamara (2011), using a broad list of negotiating tactics drawn from McLaughlin, Carnevale and Lim (1991), had respondents group the tactics in terms of i) relative importance and ii) similarity. The authors, using factor analysis, were able to identify four main sets of skills (see A below); the auditors themselves manually identified four somewhat different sets (B below). I list the two sets of general negotiation skills in Table 21.1.

Sample tactics from A. 1) are: 'Have them prioritize the issues'; 'Tell them that their position is against the spirit of the relevant accounting standard'; 'Remind the other party of the responsibility of directors to ensure the accounts present a true and fair view'. Clearly these are what an applied linguist would call discursive strategies and as applied linguists we should be setting about finding out how they are realised interactionally.

Table 21.1 Two sets of four skills, as identified by researchers (A) and auditors (B)

A. Ranked in terms of importance	B. Grouped in terms of similarity
1 contending: forcing/asserting	1 appealing to authority
2 compromising	2 contending: forcing/asserting
3 problem solving	3 context setting
4 accommodating	4 facilitating

Towards a unified theory of professional practice

As we saw above, communication in the context of professional accounting has frequently been represented in terms of discrete skills or attributes. Whatever value such models may have, they directly or indirectly represent communication as a separate domain, essential perhaps but ancillary to practice. Skills/attributes based models have in fact proved useful in developing more innovative curricula in tertiary institutions and more explicit approaches to teaching and assessment. However, I take issue with this approach on theoretical grounds, and devise what I hope is a richer and more authentic model of professional practice – *as* discourse and *as* communication. In doing so I also try to go beyond the kinds of organic/integrative models illustrated above – valid and practically useful as these too may be – by representing professional practice dynamically and agentively as the intentional, goal focused furtherance (i.e. the 'realisation') of interests, orientations and agendas. The professional's resources (procedural and declarative types of knowledge as well as sociopragmatic competencies) are envisaged as a potential for (communicative) action – a potential that, in practice, is realised in successively more situated, more specific, and (correspondingly) less routinised instantiations of that potential (Figure 21.2).

Candlin (2006) summarises and builds upon conceptual advances by Levinson (1979) and Sarangi (2000) to devise a sophisticated tri-stratal model in which *activity types*, *discourse types*, and situated *communicative strategies* constitute a 'neat and nested arrangement' where units at each successive level redound with and particularise those at prior levels (2006: 21). As Candlin puts it (2006: 23; italics in the original):

[W]e can imagine a *nested arrangement* in which activity types with their focus on *setting* are realized through particular practices with their associated discourse types, themselves focused on *forms of talk*, which in turn draw strategically on a range of communicative resources, i.e. what people actually perform. These strategies are then realized by actual usages of language or in other semiotic modes: what they actually say, write, display, do. Of course, there is no one-to-one relationship here, although it may turn out to be the case, as Sarangi (2000) indicates, that particular activity types typically are linked to sets of discourse types and that they, in turn, in the context of this or that event, draw on preferred selections of communication strategies.

Candlin gives the example of a medical consultation, which can be seen as an activity type; this potentially contains – and is realised by – a range of characteristic discourse types such as *history-taking, troubles talk, counselling, advising,* and *instructing*; and each of these is in turn realised through a range of 'often overlapping and hybridized strategies': *talking plainly, talking obliquely, giving face and deference, justifying actions, hypothesising, envisaging outcomes* etc. All of these 'goal-focused, purposive strategies' are ultimately realised by particular choices of language and other ancillary semiotic modes, selected from the participants' professional-communicative resources and shaped by their control of relevant discourses. An accountant typically takes part in a range of formal and informal meetings and interactions that, as more or less conventionalised activity types, shape communication in terms of discourse types and strategies. Although these have not been exhaustively described we can identify the following critical meeting-types: initial face-to-face meetings with new clients, annual reviews, regular budget meetings and regular team meetings. Accountants employed in organisations also participate in various types of cross-functional meetings where their contribution is often vital. Accountants also engage in more or less structured one-on-one interactions, such as when they interview staff members as part of an internal audit process. Some of the discourse types that appear in medical consultations would certainly be used in the aforementioned meetings and interactions, as would some of the strategies mentioned.

Discourse types like *advising* and *instructing* can be subject to further analysis; for example, instances of *advising* and the way these respond pragmatically and strategically to unforeseen challenges can be further specified in terms of their location within a 'pragmatic space' (Candlin and Lucas 1986; see also Willing 1992; Holmes, Stubbe and Vine 1999). Sometimes also the precise function of a stretch of talk remains unclear, while sometimes this can only be identified in retrospect (Slembrouck and Hall 2011: 492–93). And certain discursive strategies like *expressing uncertainty* (Lingard *et al.* 2003) can be mapped across a wide range of possible linguistic realisations. However, allowing for this kind of fuzziness and overlap, the tri-stratal system suggested by Candlin allows us to conceptualise the multi-layeredness of the meaning making that takes place in professional accounting work and, to a very large degree, constitutes it.

Clearly, in practice, activity types, discourse types and discursive strategies are inextricably linked, interdependent, and *simultaneously enacted*. While meaning on the more abstract and time-stable levels (activity types) tends to be highly conventional and constraining, meaning on the more contingent and dynamic levels of realisation (discourse types and strategies) is reactively, responsively and innovatively constructed.[15] Figure 21.2 represents these levels or strata and their interrelationships, which all together constitute professional practice, as progressively realised dimensions of professional expertise – conceptualised here as a set of resources for meaningful action in a given field, and hence as *potential*. The arrow on the right signifies the driving force of interested intentionality, without which meaning making is essentially meaningless – *where meaning stands for interest and value*. In this schema it is the meaning-maker who is the source of semiotic energy.

The one concept that underpins and unifies the schema represented above is the concept of *genre,* very broadly understood. As used here, genre includes the kinds of typified actions that respond to the 'exigences' of typified situations (Halliday 1978; Miller 1994: 157, 158; Bhatia 1993, 1999, 2004, 2006; and see Kamberelis 1995). Thus all of the more conventionalised situations and practices that make up professional competence and expertise in accounting can be classed as genres, just as are (more commonly) conventionalised modes of oral and written communication. The latter mediate the former; or, as Bhatia (2010: 48) has it, professional goals and interests are advanced, mediated and (I now add) *realised by* discursive practices that in turn creatively and strategically exploit familiar textual genres and the audience's expectations of these. Although exigence is a social not a personal given, it presents the individual with a set of affordances, in the sense of determinate possibilities for communicative action. Miller remarks (1994: 158):

> Exigence must be seen neither as a cause of rhetorical action nor as intention, but as social motive. [...] It is an understanding of social need in which I know how to take an interest, in which one can intend to participate.

To expand briefly on this, *exigence* delimits and determines a range of appropriate discursive-communicative responses (i.e. speech acts and discourse types) to a typified situation (what we have referred to as an activity type). That said, it does not determine the semiotic (here, especially linguistic) realisation of these responses, which range from the particular communicative strategies employed to the grammatical and lexical choices made at the level of an individual sentence or utterance. The latter reflect each individual's own creative exploitation of the meaning-potential germane to a particular field or professional domain.

Professional development – future directions for research and facilitation

Srikant Sarangi and Christopher Candlin have mapped out a future agenda for the linguistic study of professional practice (2010, 2011).[16] They view professional communication as an essential aspect of professional practice and call for:

> an applied linguistics which addresses not only the realized forms of language and discourse but the structure and texture of the practices themselves – how these are framed and organized, and how such framings are diversified across the participants in distinctive sites of engagement.
>
> *(Sarangi and Candlin 2011: 6)*

This resonates with amplification of the notion of genre and genre knowledge discussed above (Bhatia 1993, 1999). Sarangi and Candlin call here (as they have called before) for a new type of collaborative interdisciplinary and interprofessional research enterprise that will cross the traditional boundaries between practitioners and researchers while drawing on the diverse perspectives and insights of a range of contributory disciplines or 'knowledges' (2011). Collaborative research that combines the 'insider' knowledge and insights of the practitioner with the analytic language awareness of the applied linguist is envisaged as opening up important new vistas and new possibilities in the field of education and training (Sarangi 2002).

The question that remains is this: How can these newer, deeper and more holistic understandings of professional practice, in accounting as elsewhere, be used to scaffold and enrich the trajectory that most if not all practitioners follow, from novice to competent, proficient and ultimately expert practitioner? There seem to be three possible approaches that we might label informally as 'from the top down', 'from the inside out', and 'from the bottom up'. The first places the chief emphasis on identity and values, the second on the role of expert knowledge and understandings, while the third foregrounds the types of communicative and interactional expertise that in a sense operationalise the previous two approaches.

We can, for instance, aim to transform novices from the top down – starting, that is, with their conceptions of professional practice and their personal values, in short, their self-identity as professional practitioners (Mezirow 1991; Reid and Petocz 2004; Lucas and Tan 2007; Sin, Reid and Jones 2012). Professional identity can in some respects be regarded as a *habitus* (Bourdieu 1977; Wacquant 2005), comprising largely unconscious dispositions to see, think and act in certain ways and to value certain goals and outcomes over others (Goodwin 1994). The subtle but often quite directive processes whereby individuals develop such a habitus have been described in considerable detail for medicine (e.g. Sinclair 1997) and for law (e.g. Mertz 2007). So far nothing similar exists for relatively newer professions, such as accountancy. But it is clear that accredited teaching institutions and the accrediting professional bodies bear much of the responsibility for this, as well as all employing organisations.

Secondly – working from the inside out, as we may say – we can foreground the role that specialised knowledge plays, not just in legitimating but in lending substance to professional practice. It is possible to represent the trajectories followed by practitioners, as they progress from novice to expert, in terms of the specialised knowledge (perhaps knowledges) that they need to acquire along their way. The role of language in the acquisition of specialised knowledge is often seen as predominantly communicative and interactional (Wells 1999; Mercer and Howe 2012). However, it can also be viewed as predominantly cognitive and representational (see Vosniadou 1994; diSessa and Sherin 1998; but also the seminal work by Halliday and Martin on taxonomies of scientific knowledge, as in Halliday and Martin 1993). Mohan (1986) developed an influential content-based teaching-and-learning schema known as the Knowledge Framework (KF). However, while the KF functions as a heuristic tool for the analysis of content, it has nothing to say about teaching methods (Early, Potts and Mohan 2005: 66); in practice it is frequently combined with a social constructivist pedagogy drawing on Vygotskian (socio-cultural) understandings of language use. More recently, European researchers working within the framework of Content and Language Integrated Learning (CLIL) (e.g. Maljers, Marsh, Wolff, Genesee, Frigols-Martín and Mehisto 2010) have moved beyond content-focused language teaching, aiming for an equipollent mutually reinforcing focus on subject-matter learning and language development. A closely related initiative called Language in Content Instruction (LICI) (Järvinen 2009) resonates with my own moves towards a 'linguistically scaffolded curriculum' (Jones and McCracken 2007). The most innovative theoretical work in this area is currently being carried out in Sweden where researchers are developing a framework for conceptual learning that may supersede the approaches mentioned above as it accounts for individual learning trajectories and individual-idiosyncratic modes of meaning-making. The Swedish researchers emphasise the active epistemological role of language in incremental conceptual learning. They focus initially on the learner's perspective, but go on to examine ways in which conceptual learning can be 'scaffolded' in and through dialogue with expert knowers who are attuned to the often idiosyncratically encoded meanings and understandings of the learner (see Anderberg 2000; Anderberg, Svennson, Alvegård and Johansson 2008; Alvegård, Anderberg, Svensson and Johansson 2010).[17]

Finally, and starting in a sense from the bottom up, professional development can focus on the overtly communicative, interactional and indeed linguistic dimension of professional expertise. As noted above (see Figure 21.2) this can be seen to consist of three realisational layers. Most fundamentally, there is the ability of a practitioner to exploit 'genre knowledge' (see Berkenkotter and Huckin 1995; Bhatia 1999; Candlin 1999) in order to perform appropriately and strategically across a wide variety of more or less routinised professional 'activity types'.[18] Genre knowledge is complemented and to a large extent implemented by the ability to deploy skilled interactional routines or discourse types (Sarangi 2000; Candlin 2006), which are again largely conventionalised. However, the foregoing two abilities add up to very limited type of professional expertise unless practitioners are also able to come up with a broad range of contingent and dynamic discursive-communicative strategies to cope with unexpected scenarios or problems (Sarangi 2000; Candlin 2006; Holmes, Stubbe and Vine 1999).

Our understanding of the ways in which expert professional knowledge – with all its inherent uncertainties – is interactionally deployed and how professional identities are enacted and transformed in practice has benefitted greatly from applied linguistic work focusing on the microgenesis of selves and relationships in and through face-to-face interaction – that is to say, talk. Some of most focused and rigorous work on this has been done by Janet Holmes and her colleagues (Holmes 2005, 2006; Holmes and Riddiford 2010). The type of person who can effectively deal with the kinds of complex social and cultural situations that are characteristic of the modern workplace needs a broad repertoire of interactional abilities and a special type of interactional skilfulness. Thus the 'habitus' reflects and projects the persona, intimately linking two crucial levels of our model (see Figure 21.2).

Holmes and Riddiford (2010), much like Senatra (1980) and van Peursem (2005) before them, acknowledge the ambiguities inherent in professional work in organisations, where one must balance professionalism with collegiality. They describe the kind of abilities and skilfulness required as socio-pragmatic proficiency. The same authors elsewhere define socio-pragmatic competence succinctly as 'the ability to accurately interpret and appropriately express social meaning in interaction' (2011: 377). They argue (2010) that this capability is best developed through reflection. In line with Schön's seminal work on reflection on and in professional practice, they state that

> The most essential ability needed by anyone attempting to operate in any kind of workplace, and the one that trainers and developers must attempt to foster, is the ability to reflect on one's interactions and to analyse and eventually 'understand and relate to' the social lifeworld that their interlocutors inhabit.
>
> *(quoting Byram 1997: 20)*

This definition of reflection resonates with what Baartman and de Bruijn (2011) call critical (self-)reflection which, when combined with an openness to change, can lead to the transformative integration of separately acquired knowledge, skills and capabilities.

There is increasing emphasis nowadays on the essential role of first-hand experience in learning, and accounting students are strongly urged to obtain work experience through internships (e.g. Lucas and Tan 2007). However, the benefits of workplace experience are limited without reflection on the experience gained, and shared or guided reflection seems to work best. The education and training of professionals is currently benefitting from a wide range of new technologies that aid such reflection on practice. But Candlin, Maley, Crichton and Koster (1995) show that effective programs can be designed using few specialised technical resources. In an innovative program devised for lawyers and focusing on lawyer-client conferencing, they used joint reflection on transcripts of interactions to stimulate participants' awareness of critical moments in these interactions and to trigger a joint critical appraisal of the strategies employed. The procedure was experiential and participatory and was organised as a pedagogically phased cycle of *awareness*, *knowledge*, *critique*, and *action* (originally developed by Auerbach and Wallerstein 1987). It has since been suggested that this cycle can be used for nursing education (Sally Candlin 1995) and, more recently, for demonstrating to overseas trained medical graduates how 'clinically effective empathy' can be interactionally accomplished in primary health care settings (O'Grady 2011). There is little doubt that this procedure could be used more broadly, as in the education and development of accounting professionals.

From this brief overview of research into professional development, and the ways in which it may be facilitated, it is readily seen that applied linguistic understandings, enriched by accumulating insights into specialised fields, registers and knowledges, and the systematic study of professional discourse in mediated as well as face-to-face interaction, make it possible to develop a systematic and comprehensive model accounting for professional practice, development and expertise. In this model, language plays a pivotal role. We know that, of all the human semiotic systems, language is the most complex. It is a prerequisite for other semiotic systems but remains the most powerful of these (Halliday 2003: 3). Language mediates all of our more important social activities and functions, including professional practice, and ideally at least adds subtlety and art to the various types of interactions that largely constitute that practice. This insight represents something of a challenge for accounting professionals and their institutions, as the interactional and language-dependent aspects of professional accounting work are only just now being recognised as central to and, to some extent, constitutive of professional accounting practice. Yet the accounting profession has always been distinguished by a strong concern to understand its own nature as a discipline and its role in society, as evidenced by a long tradition of practice-focused research and critical reflection in a range of dedicated journals. Accountancy has also been traditionally marked by its consistent aim of educating its practitioners to the highest possible standards. Hence one can confidently predict that these crucial communicative dimensions of professional accounting work will soon be more widely acknowledged and embraced.

Related topics

theoretical frameworks; analysing discourse variation; knowledge making; business communication

Key readings

Amernic, Joel, and Craig, Russell (2004). 'Reform of accounting education in the post-Enron era: Moving accounting "out of the shadows"', *ABACUS*, 40(3), 342–78. (The authors discuss 'the need for accounting educators to have students appreciate the idiosyncratic, political, rhetorical, ideological and non-objective nature of accounting' and suggest ways in which this might be done (p. 343).)

Bargiela-Chiappini, Francesca (ed.) (2009). *The Handbook of Business Discourse*, Edinburgh: Edinburgh University Press. (This collection provides authoritative scholarly introductions to a wide range of historical, disciplinary, methodological, and cultural perspectives on Business Discourse as a new field of research and analysis – and one that, of course, includes accounting as an important sub-field.)

Cutler, Sally F. (2010). *A Few Good Words: How Internal Auditors Can Write Better, More Insightful Reports*. Publisher: iUniverse. (This book is a particularly good example of a new type of profession-specific communication manual. This particular book is designed to help internal auditors acquire important strategies and skills for the effective writing of internal audit reports and for managing report writers. Realistic examples make the author's suggestions immediately relevant and provide models for their adoption.)

Doupnik, Timothy S. (2008). 'Influence of Culture on Earnings Management: A Note', *ABACUS*, 44(3), 317–40. (This article builds usefully on Geert Hofstede's work on ways in which culture influences organisations, professional values and professional practices, showing that common accounting practices are culture-sensitive. (See e.g. Geert Hofstede, Gert Jan Hofstede, and Michael Minkov (1991). *Cultures and Organizations: Software of the Mind*, Maidenhead, UK: McGraw-Hill.))

Poovey, Mary (1998). *A History of the Modern Fact. Problems of Knowledge in the Sciences of Wealth and Society*, Chicago: University Of Chicago Press. (Poovey describes how, in Britain, between the sixteenth and nineteenth centuries, numerical representations became the preferred form of evidence for government decision-making, as well as how a reliance on double-entry book-keeping, record-keeping and more recently statistics constantly leads back to the intractable problem of induction: How can any amount of observed and codified 'facts' justify a particular theory, belief or decision? This is a philosophical question that regularly recurs in one guise or another in the various literatures of accounting.)

Notes

1. *Professional accounting work* here refers specifically to work conducted by accountants with formal accounting qualifications and professional credentials in any of the various sub-fields of accounting (i.e. not simply 'bookkeepers').
2. Reflecting Patricia Benner's (1982, 1984) five levels of experience and expertise in nursing. Sally Candlin (2002) has recently drawn on Benner's schema in her discourse-analytic exploration of risk as an essential facet of professional communication.
3. Prepared by the Public Sector Accounting Standards Board of the Australian Accounting Research Foundation and by the Australian Accounting Standards Board.
4. The Australian Society of Certified Practising Accountants (ASCPA) is now known as CPA Australia.
5. His research was in fact sponsored by the two professional bodies in question.
6. Birkett thought Bloom's distinction between affective and cognitive skills was unsustainable; he also collapsed Bloom's six categories of cognitive skills to just three (leaving aside entirely the most basic one involving knowledge and its simple recall) (Birkett 1993). The final set contrasts cognitive skills with behavioural skills, and communication appears both in the form of specific separate skills or, more implicitly, as types of behaviour entailed by behavioural skills (Whitefield and Kloot 2006).
7. The passage in question can be found for example on the website of the University of Edinburgh: www.employability.ed.ac.uk/GraduateAttributes.htm (accessed 3 October 2013).
8. Readers are invited to compare this model and the one presented further below as Figure 21.2 with the models of professional expertise and extensive discussion of this concept provided in Bhatia (2004: 142–52).
9. This concerns the fact that successful professionals can consistently 'read' a situation and identify what is causing a practice problem, and then 'match' the problem with a uniquely appropriate solution. Schön (1983) noted that no practice situation is identical to the ones that preceded it, hence successful problem-solving in professional practice is always 'contingent'.
10. Effective practitioners possess well-developed 'diagnostic maps' – generated through reflection on practice – that assist them to figure out what is going on in any new problem situation and to identify appropriate solutions.
11. We have to distinguish between professions that are founded on research into given natural phenomena (e.g. medicine) and professions founded on conceptual schemas and taxonomies of a more prescriptive kind. In the former discourse is an adjunct to practice, but in the latter (e.g. the law and accounting) it is constitutive.
12. J. P. Gee postulated the existence of Discourses (written with a capital 'D') that are peculiar to specific groups of people and that encompass the totality of their tacitly accepted and expected ways of behaving, valuing and thinking, as well as their characteristic modes of speaking and writing (Gee 1996: viii).
13. The project is based at Victoria University of Wellington, in New Zealand.
14. Holmes and Riddiford (2010) compared the different strategies used by a professional accountant from Hong Kong and a senior public relations adviser from Russia to manage identity construction in the context of workplace interactions. The intercultural dimension of their enterprise amplified the level of interpersonal risk.
15. This qualification goes to the theoretical heart of the model. There are two types of realisation. Halliday and Martin (1993) explain the theoretical implications of one type of realisation in terms of 'metaredundancies' – i.e. mutual expectancies at each level are absorbed into higher levels of mutual expectancy at the next highest level. They note, significantly for my own use of the model, that '[m]etaredundancy theory has the advantage of being directional as far as degrees of abstraction are concerned but non-directional as far as cause and effect are concerned' (1993: 42). Realisation of a different kind builds on a concept known as instantiation; and I am not claiming here that the

successive levels in Figure 21.2 represent successive realisations qua instantiations or objectivations of the one preceding it.
16 Although these authors distinguish between professional practices that are more and less dependent on communicative expertise (2005: 4), they note (2010: 4):

> The contingencies surrounding professional practice defy a logical, patterned, indiscriminate application of what is learnt as part of professional education and training. It goes beyond the dogma of 'communication skills' as currently ingrained in many professional curricula, especially in healthcare, which runs the risk of creating an over-proceduralized order through which 'we drive out wisdom, artistry and the feel for the phenomena' all of which depend on 'judgement' and 'discretionary freedom' (Schön 1987).

17 Anderberg *et al.* (2008: 15) build on Svensson's (1978) key insight into what we might call the inherent opacity of intended meaning: 'Svensson (1978) illustrated how a particular conception could be expressed in very different words, while widely differing conceptions were expressed in rather similar language'.
18 I am using genre here somewhat narrowly to mean institutionalised communicative forms or patterned 'activities' defined in terms of purpose and structure. The types of lexicogrammatical resources that accompany and realise genres, so defined, as well as rhetorical skills, belong to my third 'linguistic' layer.

Appendix

Core Curriculum in Generic Skills Areas

[These are the skills and/or attributes that the Institute of Chartered Accountants in Australia and CPA Australia (2009) deemed necessary for accreditation of tertiary level courses in accounting. These two bodies recommended that the acquisition of generic skills be taken into account in curriculum design.]

I Cognitive Skills

1. Routine Skills
– report writing
– computer literacy
2. Analytic/Design Skills

Particularly the ability to:

– identify, find, evaluate, organise and manage information and evidence
– initiate and conduct research
– analyse, reason logically, conceptualise issues
– solve problems and construct arguments
– interpret data and reports
– engage in ethical reasoning.
3. Appreciative Skills

Particularly the ability to:

– receive, evaluate and react to new ideas
– adapt and respond positively to challenges

- make judgements derived from one's own value framework
- think and act critically
- know what questions to ask
- engage in lifelong learning
- recognise own strength and limitations
- appreciate ethical dimensions of situations
- apply disciplinary and multi-disciplinary perspectives
- appreciate processes of professional adaptation and behaviour.

II Behavioural Skills

4. Personal Skills

Particularly:

- a commitment to think and behave ethically
- flexibility in new/different situations
- to act strategically
- to think and act independently
- to be focused on outcomes;
- to tolerate ambiguity
- to think creatively.

5. Interpersonal Skills

Particularly the ability to:

- listen effectively
- present, discuss and defend views
- transfer and receive knowledge
- negotiate with people from different backgrounds and with different value systems
- understand group dynamics
- collaborate with colleagues.

Bibliography

Abrandt Dahlgren, M., Hult, H., Dahlgren, L. O., Hård af Segerstad, H. and Johansson, K. (2006). 'From senior student to novice worker: Learning trajectories in political science, psychology and mechanical engineering', *Studies in Higher Education*, *31*, 569–86.

Abrandt Dahlgren, M., Reid, A., Dahlgren, L. and Petocz, P. (2008). 'Learning for the professions: Lessons from linking international research projects', *Higher Education: An International Journal of Higher Education and Educational Planning*, *56*, 129–48.

Ahrens, T. (1997). 'Talking accounting: An ethnography of management knowledge in British and German brewers', *Accounting, Organizations and Society*, *22*(7), 617–37.

Ahrens, T. and Chapman, C. S. (2007a). 'Management accounting as practice', *Accounting, Organizations and Society*, *32*(1–2), 1–27.

——(2007b). 'Theorizing practice in management accounting research', in C. S. Chapman, A. G. Hopwood and M. D. Shields (eds), *Handbook of Management Accounting Research. Volume 1* (pp. 99–112), Elsevier Science.

Alvegård, C., Anderberg, E., Svensson, L. and Johansson, T. (2010). 'The interplay between content, expressions and their meaning when expressing understanding', *Science & Education*, *19*(3), 283–303.

American Institute of Certified Public Accountants (1999). *AICPA Core Competency Framework for Entry into the Accounting Profession*. Available at www.aicpa.org (accessed 3 March 2006).
Anderberg, E. (2000). 'Word meaning and conceptions: An empirical study of relationships between students' thinking and use of language when reasoning about a problem', *Instructional Science*, 28(2), 89–1.
Anderberg, E., Svensson, L., Alvegård, C. and Johansson, T. (2008). 'The epistemological role of language use in learning: A phenomenographic intentional-expressive approach', *Educational Research Review*, 3(1), 14–29.
Auerbach, E. R. and Wallerstein, N. (1987). *ESL for Action: Problem Posing at Work*, Reading, MA: Addison-Wesley.
Australian Society of CPAs and Institute of Chartered Accountants in Australia (1996). *Guidelines for Joint Administration of Accreditation of Tertiary Courses by the Professional Accounting Bodies*, Melbourne VIC: Australian Society of CPAs.
Australian Society of CPAs and the Institute of Chartered Accountants in Australia (1997). *Revised Guidelines for Joint Administration of Accreditation of Tertiary Courses by Professional Accounting Bodies*, Melbourne VIC: Australian Society of CPAs and the Institute of Chartered Accountants in Australia.
Baartman, L. K. J. and de Bruijn, E. (2011). 'Integrating knowledge, skills and attitudes: Conceptualising learning processes towards vocational competence', *Educational Research Review*, 6(2), 125–34.
Bame-Aldred, C. W. and Kida, T. (2007). 'A comparison of the auditor and client initial negotiation positions and tactics', *Accounting, Organizations and Society*, 32(6), 497–511.
Barnett, R. (1994). *The Limit of Competence: Knowledge, Higher Education and Society*, Bristol: Open University.
Barrie, S. (2004). 'A research-based approach to generic graduate attributes policy', *Higher Education Research and Development*, 23, 261–75.
Benner, P. (1982). 'From novice to expert', *American Journal of Nursing*, 82(3), 402–7.
——(1984). *From Novice to Expert: Excellence and Power in Clinical Nursing Practice*, Menlo Park, CA: Addison-Wesley.
Benner, P. and Tanner, C. A. (1987). 'Clinical judgment: How expert nurses use intuition', *American Journal of Nursing*, 87(1), 23–31.
Berkenkotter, C. and Huckin, T. (1995). *Genre Knowledge in Disciplinary Communication: Cognition/Culture/Power*, Hillsdale, NJ: Erlbaum Associates.
Bhatia, V. K. (1993). *Analysing Genre – Language Use in Professional Settings*, Applied Linguistics and Language Study Series, London: Longman.
——(1999). 'Disciplinary variation in business English', in M. Hewings and C. Nickerson (eds.), *Business English: Research into Practice* (pp. 129–43), Harlow: Prentice Hall.
——(2004). *Worlds of Written Discourse: A Genre-Based View*, London and New York: Continuum.
——(2006). 'Discursive practices in disciplinary and professional contexts', *Linguistic and Human Sciences*, 2(1), 5–28.
——(2008a). 'Creativity and accessibility in written professional discourse', *World Englishes*, 27(3–4), 319–26.
——(2008b). 'Genre analysis, ESP and professional practice', *English for Specific Purposes*, 27, 161–74.
——(2010). 'Interdiscursivity in professional communication', *Discourse & Communication*, 21(1), 32–50.
Birkett, W. P. (1993). *Competency Based Standards for Professional Accountants in Australia and New Zealand*, Discussion paper, Melbourne: Australian Society of Certified Practising Accountants, Institute of Chartered Accountants in Australia and the New Zealand Society of Accountants.
——(2002). *Competency Profiles for Management Accounting Practice and Practitioners, Study 12*, New York: International Federation of Accountants (IFAC).
——(2003). *Competency Based Standards for Professional Accountants in Australia and New Zealand*, Sydney: Link Publishing.
Bloom, B. S. (1956). *Taxonomy of Educational Objectives, Handbook I: The Cognitive Domain*, New York: David McKay Co Inc.
Bordage, G. (1994). 'Elaborated knowledge: A key to successful diagnostic thinking', *Academic Medicine*, 69(11), 883–85.
Boud, D., Keogh, R. and Walker, D. (1985). 'Promoting reflection in learning: A model', in D. Boud and R. Keogh and D. Walker (eds), *Reflection: Turning Experience into Learning* (pp. 18–40), London: Kogan Page.
Bourdieu, P. (1977). *Outline of a Theory of Practice*, Cambridge: Cambridge University Press.
Bowden, J., Hart, G., King, B., Trigwell, K. and Watts, O. (2000). *Generic Capabilities of ATN University Graduates*, Canberra: Australian Government Department of Education, Training and Youth Affairs.
Bowker, G. C. and Star, S. L. (1999). *Sorting Things Out: Classification and Its Consequences*, Cambridge, MA: MIT Press.

Bui, B. and Porter, B. (2010). 'The expectation-performance gap in accounting education: An exploratory study', *Accounting Education: An International Journal*, *19*(1–2), 23–50.
Byram, M. (1997). *Teaching and Assessing Intercultural Communicative Competence*, Clevedon: Multilingual Matters.
Canadian Institute of Chartered Accountants (2012). *The UFE Candidates' Competency Map: Understanding the Professional Competencies Evaluated on the UFE* (See specifically pp. 21–30). (accessed 31 August 2013).
Candlin, C. N. (1999). 'How can discourse be a measure of expertise?' Unpublished address, International Association for Dialogue Analysis, Symposium: *Expert Talk*. University of Birmingham, 8–10 April 1999.
——(2006). 'Accounting for interdiscursivity: Challenges to professional expertise' in M. Gotti and D. Giannone (eds), *New Trends in Specialized Discourse Analysis* (pp. 21–46), Bern: Peter Lang Verlag.
Candlin, C. N. and Lucas, J. (1986). 'Interpretations and explanations in discourse: Modes of 'advising' in family planning', in T. Ensink, A. van Essen and T. van der Geest (eds), *Discourse Analysis and Public Life* (pp. 13–38), Dordrecht: Foris.
Candlin, C. N., Maley, Y., Crichton, J. and Koster, P. (1995). 'Orientations in lawyer-client interviews', *Forensic Linguistics* 2, 1 International Association for Forensic Phonetics and Acoustics.
Candlin, S. (1995). *Towards Excellence in Nursing: An Analysis of the Discourse of Nurse and Patients in the Context of Health Assessments*, Lancaster: University of Lancaster.
——(2002). 'Taking risks: An indicator of expertise', in C. N. Candlin and S. Candlin (eds), *Expert Talk and Risk in Health Care*, A Special Issue of *Research and Social Interaction*, *35*(2), 173–94.
Child, J. (1972). 'Organizational structure, environment and performance: The role of strategic choice', *Sociology*, *6*(1), 1–22.
Clanchy, J. and Ballard, B. (1995). 'Generic skills in the context of higher education', *Higher Education Research and Development*, *14*(2), 155–66.
Daff, L. (2012). 'Lessons from successes in medical communication training and their applications to accounting education', *Accounting Education: An International Journal*, *21*(4), 385–405.
Dall'Alba, G. and Barnacle, R. (2007). 'An ontological turn for higher education', *Studies in Higher Education*, *32*(6), 679–91.
Dean, M. (1999). *Governmentality: Power and Rule in Modern Society*, London: Sage.
Dent, J. F. (1986). 'Organisational research in accounting: Perspectives, issues and a commentary', in M. Bromwich and A. G. Hopwood (eds), *Research and Current Issues in Management Accounting*, London: Pitman.
Devitt, A. J. (1991). 'Intertextuality in tax accounting: Generic, referential, and functional', in C. Bazerman and J. Paradis (eds), *Textual Dynamics Of The Professions: Historical And Contemporary Studies Of Writing In Professional Communities* (pp. 336–57), Madison, USA: University Of Wisconsin.
diSessa, A. A. and Sherin, B. L. (1998). 'What changes in conceptual change?' *International Journal of Science Education*, *20*(10), 1155–91.
Dreyfus, H. L. and Dreyfus, S. E. (1986). *Mind over Machine: The Power of Human Intuition and Expertise in the Age of the Computer*, Oxford: Basil Blackwell.
Early, M., Potts, D. and Mohan, B. (2005). 'Teachers' professional knowledge in scaffolding academic literacies for English language learners', *Prospect*, *20*(3), 63–76.
Entwistle, N. J. and Ramsden, P. (1983). *Understanding Student Learning*, London: Croom Helm.
Fouch, S. R. (2004). 'Developing functional and personal competencies through an interactive tax research case study', *Journal of Accounting Education*, *22*(4), 275–87.
Gee, J. P. (1996 [1990]). *Social Linguistics and Literacies: Ideology in Discourses*. (*Critical Perspectives on Literacy and Education*.), 2nd edition, London: Falmer Press.
Giddens, A. (1984). *The Constitution of Society*, Cambridge: Polity Press.
Goleman, D. (1995). *Emotional Intelligence: Why it Can Matter More Than IQ for Character, Health and Lifelong Achievement*, New York: Bantam Books.
Goodwin, C. (1994). 'Professional vision', *American Anthropologist* (New Series), *96*(4), 606–33.
Goodwin, J. (2002). 'Auditors' conflict management styles: An exploratory study', *ABACUS*, *38*(3), 378–405.
Gray, E. and Murray, N. (2011). '"A distinguishing factor": Oral communication skills in new accountancy graduates', *Accounting Education: An International Journal*, *20*(3), 275–94.
Halliday, M. A. K. (1978). *Language as Social Semiotic: The Social Interpretation of Language and Meaning*, London: Arnold.
——(2003). 'On the "architecture" of human language', in Jonathan Webster (ed.), *On Language and Linguistics. Vol. 3 in the Collected Works of M. A. K. Halliday* (pp. 1–29), London: Continuum.
Halliday, M. A. K. and Martin, J. R. (1993). *Writing Science: Literacy and Discursive Power*, London: Falmer Press.

Hancock, P., Freeman, M. and Associates (2010). *Learning and Teaching Academic Standards Project: Business, Management and Economics: Learning and Teaching Academic Standards Statement for ACCOUNTING*, Sydney, NSW: Australian Learning & Teaching Council. Available online: www.abdc.edu.au/download.php?id=325154,282,1 (accessed 5 May 2013).

Hocking, D. and Fieldhouse, W. (2011). 'Implementing academic literacies in practice', *New Zealand Journal of Education Studies*, 46(1), 35–47.

Hollindale, J., Kent, P. and McNamara, R. (2008). *Auditor Orientation, Strategies, and Tactics in Audit Negotiations*, Bond University: Business Papers. Available at http://epublications.bond.edu.au/cgi/viewcontent.cgi?article=1123&context=business_pubs (accessed 10 April 2012).

——(2011). 'Auditor tactics in negotiations: A research note', *International Journal of Auditing*, 15(3), 288–300.

Holmes, J. (2000). 'Doing collegiality and keeping control at work: Small talk in government departments', in J. Coupland (ed.), *Small Talk* (pp. 32–61), London: Longman.

——(2005). 'Story-telling at work: A complex discursive resource for integrating personal, professional and social identities', *Discourse Studies*, 7(6), 671–700.

——(2006). 'Workplace narratives, professional identity and relational practice', in Anna De Fina, Deborah Schiffrin and Michael Bamberg (eds), *Discourse and Identity* (Studies in Interactional Sociolinguistics No. 23) (pp. 166–87), New York: Cambridge University Press.

Holmes, J. and Marra, M. (2006). 'Humor and leadership style', *Humor*, 19(2), 119–38.

——(2011). 'Harnessing storytelling as a sociopragmatic skill: Applying narrative research to workplace English courses', *TESOL Quarterly*, 45(3), 510–34.

Holmes, J. and Riddiford, N. M. (2010). 'Professional and personal identity at work: Achieving a synthesis through intercultural workplace talk', *Journal of Intercultural Communication*, 22, January. Available online: www.immi.se/jicc/

——(2011). 'From classroom to workplace: Tracking socio-pragmatic development', *ELT Journal*, 65(4), 376–86.

Holmes, J., Stubbe, M. and Vine, B. (1999). 'Constructing professional identity: "Doing power" in policy units', in S. Sarangi and C. Roberts (eds), *Talk, Work and Institutional Order: Discourse in Medical, Mediation and Management Settings* (Language, Power & Social Process), Berlin, New York: Mouton de Gruyter.

Hopwood, A. G. (1989). 'Organizational contingencies and accounting configurations', in B. Fridman and L. Østman (eds), *Accounting Development: Some Perspectives – A Book in Honor of Sven-Erik Johansson* (pp. 23–44), Stockholm: Economic Research Institute.

Hopwood, A. G. and Miller, P. (eds) (1994). *Accounting as Social and Institutional Practice*, Cambridge: Cambridge University Press.

Howieson, B. (2003). 'Accounting practice in the new millennium: Is accounting education ready to meet the challenge?' *The British Accounting Review*, 35(2), 69–103.

Hyland, T. and Johnson, S. (1998). 'Of cabbages and key skills: Exploding the mythology of core transferable skills in post-school education', *Journal of Further and Higher Education*, 22(2), 163–72.

Iedema, R. (2001). 'Resemiotization', *Semiotica*, 137(1/4), 23–39.

——(2003). *Discourses of Post-bureaucratic Organisations*, Document Design Companion Series, Amsterdam: Benjamins.

Institute of Chartered Accountants in Australia and CPA Australia (2009). *Professional Accreditation Guidelines for Higher Education Programs*, Melbourne VIC: Australian Society of CPAs and the Institute of Chartered Accountants in Australia. Available online: www.cpaaustralia.com.au/cps/rde/xbcr/cpasite/Professional_accreditation_guidelines_ for_higher_education_programs.pdf (accessed 6 May 2013).

Järvinen, H.-M. (2009). *Handbook – Language in Content Instruction* (LICI), Turku: University of Turku.

Jones, A. (Anna) (2010). 'Generic attributes in accounting: The significance of the disciplinary context', *Accounting Education: An International Journal*, 19(1–2), 5–21.

Jones, A. and McCracken, S. (2007). 'Teaching the discourse of legal risk to finance professionals: Foundations for a linguistically scaffolded curriculum', in R. Wilkinson and V. Zegers (eds), *Researching Content and Language Integration in Higher Education* (pp. 122–36), Maastricht: Maastricht University.

——(2011). 'Crossing the boundary between finance and law: The collaborative problematisation of professional learning in a postgraduate classroom', in C. N. Candlin and S. Sarangi (eds), *Handbook of Communication in Organisations and Professions* (pp. 499–518), Berlin: Mouton De Gruyter.

Jones, A. and Sin, S. (2003). *Generic Skills in Accounting: Competencies for Students and Graduates*, Sydney: Pearson Prentice Hall.

——(2004). 'Integrating language with content in first year accounting: Student profiles, perceptions and performance', in R. Wilkinson (ed.), *Integrating Content and Language: Meeting the Challenge of a Multilingual Higher Education* (pp. 478–92), Maastricht: Maastricht University Press.
——(2005). 'Perceptions and priorities of two diverse groups of first year accounting students', *Australian Journal of Accounting Education*, 1(1), 21–50.
——(2013). 'Achieving professional trustworthiness: Communicative expertise and identity work in professional accounting practice', in C. Candlin and J. Crichton (eds), *Discourses of Trust* (pp. 151–66), Houndmills, Basingstoke: Palgrave Macmillan.
Kamberelis, G. (1995). 'Genre as institutionally-informed social practice', *Journal of Contemporary Legal Issues*, 6, 115–71.
Kavanagh, M. H. and Drennan, L. (2008). 'What skills and attributes does an accounting graduate need? Evidence from student perceptions and employer expectations', *Accounting and Finance*, 48(2), 279–300.
Kemmis, S. (1985). 'Action research and the politics of reflection', in D. Boud, R. Keogh and D. Walker (eds), *Reflection: Turning Experience into Learning* (pp. 139–63), London: Kogan Page.
——(2005). 'Knowing practice: Searching for saliences', *Pedagogy, Culture and Society*, 13(3), 391–426.
Levinson, S. (1979). 'Activity types and language', *Linguistics*, 17(5–6), 365–99. (Reprinted in P. Drew and J. Heritage (eds), *Talk at Work: Interaction in Institutional Settings* (pp. 66–100), Cambridge: Cambridge University Press.)
Lingard, L., Garwood, K., Schryer, C. F. and Spafford, M. M. (2003). 'A certain art of uncertainty: Case presentation and the development of professional identity', *Social Science & Medicine*, 56(3), 603–16.
Llewellyn, S. and Milne, M. J. (2007). 'Accounting as codified discourse', *Accounting, Auditing & Accountability Journal*, 20(6), 805–24.
Lucas, U. and Tan, P. (2007). *Developing a Reflective Capacity within Undergraduate Education: The Role of Work-based Placement Learning*, York: Higher Education Academy. Available at www.heacademy.ac.uk/assets/York/documents/resources/publications/LucasLengTan.pdf (accessed 30 June 2012).
Maljers, A., Marsh, D., Wolff, D., Genesee, F., Frigols-Martín, M. and Mehisto, P. (2010). *Diverse Contexts – Converging Goals: CLIL in Europe*, Frankfurt: Peter Lang.
Marra, M. (2008). 'Meeting talk: Aligning the classroom with the workplace', *Communication Journal of New Zealand*, 9(1), 63–82.
McLaughlin, M. E., Carnevale, P. and Lim, R. G. (1991). 'Professional mediators' judgments of mediation tactics: Multidimensional scaling and cluster analyses', *Journal of Applied Psychology*, 76, 465–72.
Mercer, N. and Howe, C. (2012). 'Explaining the dialogic processes of teaching and learning: The value and potential of sociocultural theory', *Learning, Culture and Social Interaction*, 1(1), 12–21.
Mertz, E. (2007). *The Language of Law School: Learning to 'Think Like a Lawyer'*, Oxford: Oxford University Press.
Mezirow, J. (1991). *Transformative Dimensions of Adult Learning*, San Francisco: Jossey-Bass.
——(2003). 'Transformative learning as discourse', *Journal of Transformative Education*, 1(1), 58–63.
Miller, C. (1984). 'Genre as social action', *Quarterly Journal of Speech*, 70, 151–67.
Miller, P. (1994). 'Accounting as social and institutional practice: An introduction', in Hopwood, A. G. and Miller, P. (eds), *Accounting as Social and Institutional Practice* (pp. 1–39), Cambridge: Cambridge University Press.
Misztal, B. A. (2000). *Informality: Social Theory and Contemporary Practice*, London: Routledge.
——(2001). 'Normality and trust in Goffman's theory of interaction order', *Sociological Theory*, 19(3), 312–24.
Mohan, B. (1986). *Language and Content*, Reading, MA: Addison-Wesley.
O'Grady, Catherine (2011). 'Teaching the communication of empathy in patient-centred medicine', in B. Hoekje and S. Tipton (eds), *English Language and the Medical Profession: Instructing and Assessing the Communication Skills of International Physicians* (Innovation And Leadership In English Language Teaching) (pp. 43–72), Bradford, UK: Emerald Group Publishing Limited.
Park, J. S. Y. and Bucholtz, M. (2009). 'Introduction. Public transcripts: Entextualization and linguistic representation in institutional contexts', *Text & Talk: An Interdisciplinary Journal of Language, Discourse & Communication*, 29(5), 485–502.
Peursem, K. A. van (2005). 'Conversations with internal auditors: The power of ambiguity', *Managerial Auditing Journal*, 20(5), 489–512.
Potter, B. N. (2005) 'Accounting as a social and institutional practice: Perspectives to enrich our understanding of accounting change', *ABACUS*, 41(3), 265–89.
Power, M. (1999). *The Audit Society: Rituals of Verification*, New York, NY: Oxford University Press.
Reid, A. and Petocz, P. (2004). 'The professional entity: Researching the relationship between students' conceptions of learning and their future profession', in Chris Rust (ed.), *Improving Student Learning:*

Theory, Research and Scholarship (pp. 145–57), Oxford: The Oxford Centre for Staff Learning & Development.
Reid, A., Abrandt-Dahlgren, M., Petocz, P. and Dahlgren, L. O. (2011). *From Expert Student to Novice Professional*, Dordrecht: Springer.
Sarangi, S. (2000). 'Activity types, discourse types and interactional hybridity: The case of genetic counselling', in S. Sarangi and M. Coulthard (eds) *Discourse and Social Life* (pp. 1–27), London: Pearson.
——(2002). 'Discourse practitioners as a community of interprofessional practice: Some insights from health communication research', in C. N. C. Candlin (ed.), *Research and Practice in Professional Discourse* (pp. 95–135), Hong Kong: City University of Hong Kong Press.
——(2005). 'The conditions and consequences of professional discourse studies', *Journal of Applied Linguistics*, 2(3), 371–94.
Sarangi, S. and Candlin, C. N. (2010). 'Editorial: Applied linguistics and professional practice: Mapping a future agenda', *Journal of Applied Linguistics and Professional Practice*, 7(1), 1–9.
——(2011). 'Professional and organisational practice: A discourse/communication perspective', in C. N. Candlin and S. Sarangi (eds), *Handbook of Communication in Professions and Organisations* (pp. 3–58), Berlin: Mouton de Gruyter.
Schön, D. (1983). *The Reflective Practitioner*, New York: Basic Books.
——(1987). *Educating the Reflective Practitioner: Toward a New Design for Teaching and Learning in the Professions*, San Francisco: Jossey Bass.
Scollon, R. and Scollon, S. W. (2001). *Intercultural Communication: A Discourse Approach* (2nd edn; 1st edn 1995), Malden, MA: Blackwell Publishers.
Scott, G. (2003). *Learning Principles. Leadership Capability and Learning Research in the New South Wales Department of Education and Training*, Sydney, NSW: New South Wales Department of Education and Training, Professional Support and Curriculum Directorate. Available at www.det.nsw.edu.au/proflearn/docs/pdf/sld_lpw.pdf (accessed 5 May 2013).
Scott, G. and Yates, W. (2002). 'Using successful graduates to improve the quality of undergraduate engineering programmes', *European Journal of Engineering Education*, 27(4), 363–78.
Scott, G. and Wilson, D. (2002). *Tracking and Profiling Successful IT Graduates*, ACIS Proceedings 2002. Available at www.uws.edu.au/-data/assets/pdf_file/0009/146745/Scott–and–Wilson_Successful_IT_Graduates.pdf (accessed 30 June 2012).
Scott, G., Yates, W. and Wilson, D. (2001). *Tracking and Profiling Successful Graduates*, UTS Sydney.
Senatra, P. T. (1980). 'Role conflict, role ambiguity, and organizational climate in a public accounting firm', *The Accounting Review*, 55(4), 594–603.
Sin, S. (2011). *An Investigation of Practitioners' and Students' Conceptions of Accounting Work*, Linkoping: Linkoping University Press.
Sin, S., Jones, A. and Petocz, P. (2007). 'Evaluating a method of integrating generic skills with accounting content based on a functional theory of meaning', *Accounting & Finance*, 47(1), 143–63.
Sin, S., Reid, A. and Jones, A (2012). 'An exploration of students' conceptions of accounting work', *Accounting Education: An International Journal*, 21(4), 323–40.
Sin, S., Reid, A. and Dahlgren, L. O. (2011). 'The conceptions of work in the accounting profession in the 21st century from the experiences of practitioners', *Studies in Continuing Education*, 33(2), 139–56.
Sinclair, S. (1997). *Making Doctors: An Institutional Apprenticeship* (Explorations in Anthropology), London: Berg Publishers.
Slembrouck, S. and Hall, C. (2011). 'Family support and home visiting: Understanding communication, "good practice" and interactional skills', in C. Candlin and S. Sarangi, *Handbook of Communication in Organisations and Professions* (pp. 481–98), Berlin: Mouton de Gruyter.
Suzuki, T. (2003). 'The accounting figuration of business statistics as a foundation for the spread of economic ideas', *Accounting, Organizations and Society*, 28(1), 65–95.
Svensson, L. (1978). *Some Notes on a Methodological Problem in the Study of the Relationship between Thought and Language: Describing the Thought Content in Terms of Different Conceptions of the Same Phenomenon* (Reports from the Institute of Education, Gothenburg University, no 69.), Gothenburg: Gothenburg University, Department of Education and Educational Research.
Van Rossum, E. J. and Schenk, S. M. (1984). 'The relationship between learning conception, study strategy and learning outcome', *British Journal of Educational Psychology*, 54, 73–83.
Vine, B. (2004). *Getting Things Done at Work: The Discourse of Power in Workplace Interaction*, Amsterdam and Philadelphia: John Benjamins.

Vosniadou, S. (1994). 'Capturing and modeling the process of conceptual change', *Learning & Instruction*, 4, 45–69.
Wacquant, L. (2005). 'Habitus', in J. Beckert and M. Zafirovski (eds), *International Encyclopedia of Economic Sociology* (pp. 315–19), London: Routledge.
Wells, G. (1999). *Dialogic Inquiry: Towards a Sociocultural Practice and Theory of Education*, Cambridge: Cambridge University Press.
Wells, P., Gerbic, P., Kranenburg, I. and Bygrave, J. (2009). 'Professional skills and capabilities of accounting graduates: The New Zealand expectation gap?' *Accounting Education: An International Journal*, 18(4), 403–20.
Whitefield, D. and Kloot, L. (2006). 'Personal and interpersonal skills: The process of prescribing definitions in an Accounting degree', *Asian Review of Accounting*, 14(1 & 2), 101–21.
Whitehead, D. (2005). 'Empirical or tacit knowledge as a basis for theory development', *Journal of Clinical Nursing*, 14(2), 299–305.
Willing, K. (1992). *Talking it Through: Clarification and Problem-Solving in Professional Work*, Sydney, Australia: National Centre for English Language Teaching.

22
Professional communication in the legal domain

Christoph A. Hafner

The language of the law, which lawyers use to communicate in the legal domain, has a notorious reputation as a highly complex, overly technical register, accessible only to the initiated. This perception can be traced back over many centuries. For example, in the 1726 novel *Gulliver's Travels*, the writer Jonathon Swift refers to the community of legal practitioners and comments that 'this Society hath a peculiar Cant and Jargon of their own, that no other Mortal can understand' (Swift 1967: 297). Yet, in spite of such observations, it is through the language of the law that the everyday social lives of ordinary people are routinely regulated. The language of the law plays a central role in the legal process, from the construction of legal rules, to their enforcement by police and their interpretation in a court of law. It should be obvious, therefore, that professional communication in the legal domain goes far beyond professional encounters between specialist lawyers and includes a much wider range of interactions. For the purposes of this chapter, professional legal communication refers broadly to discourse practices in legal contexts: it includes the language of the law and the way this language is used by both specialists and non-specialists as they negotiate the legal process. Scholars interested in professional legal communication in this broad sense belong to a range of different scholarly traditions, including genre analysis, conversation analysis, forensic linguistics, semiotics, linguistic anthropology, jurisprudence, legal writing and drafting, law and society. They have focused on everything from the construction of written legal texts to spoken interactions in police interviews, lawyer-client interviews, legal proceedings, as well as intercultural interactions in multilingual and multicultural contexts which are often complicated by language barriers and call for the involvement of translators and interpreters.

This chapter aims to provide an overview of the existing research into professional communication in the legal domain. It is argued that, in order to reach a satisfactory understanding of specialised legal genres and interactions, it is necessary to go beyond a focus on texts and take into account the full socio-cultural context. In particular, the discourse practices of the legal professional community are shaped by the social goals of those practices, as well as the jointly held, tacit system of values and beliefs of community members. Here again, the notion of 'legal professional community' is broadly construed to go beyond judges and lawyers to include other kinds of legal professionals: legal draftspersons, arbitrators, mediators, conciliators, law enforcement officers and, to a lesser extent perhaps, legal translators and paralegals. The chapter therefore begins by explaining the cultural assumptions that legal professionals may bring to the construction and interpretation of legal texts, often referred to among lawyers as 'legal reasoning' or 'thinking like a lawyer.' Next, the chapter reviews three main areas of scholarly activity in professional legal communication research: 1) descriptive studies of written professional genres, 2) interpretive studies of talk and interaction, and 3) studies of multilingual and multicultural legal contexts. The chapter concludes with a summary of critical issues that arise in these different areas of research and makes suggestions about how the study of professional legal communication might usefully develop in the future.

The socio-cultural context

As indicated above, professional legal communication can occur across a range of contexts of situation, involving diverse participants. In addition, the texts and interactions that are produced in those settings are shaped by the shared goals of the legal community of practice, as well as the shared values and beliefs of the members of that community. Frequently, such values and beliefs, rather than being explicitly stated, are tacitly held and assumed by members of the community when they communicate with one another. Those who do not share their assumptions are likely to encounter barriers to successful communication and so it is instructive to consider the nature of such shared values and beliefs. However, a caveat is in order. While it may be convenient to talk of the 'legal community' as a single, unified entity, such a 'legal community' is in fact an abstraction. This abstraction is useful for the purposes of discourse analysis, allowing for the generation of insights into discourse practices, but it is an abstraction nonetheless. In reality, a multitude of different kinds of legal communities can be identified, and practices vary between them. The most obvious example of this is the systematic variation in discourse practices found between civil and common law legal contexts, such that legal rules (for example) are formulated in quite different ways (Gotti 2008b). Similarly, variations in discourse practices are also found within communities, as Mather *et al.* (2001) note in their description of the practices of divorce lawyers in Maine and New Hampshire, USA. As they point out, this community presents 'a highly differentiated world of legal practice' (p. 8) where diverse rather than uniform professional legal communication practices are observed.

In spite of these limitations, considerable insight can be gained into professional legal communication by understanding the common assumptions that legal professionals make when they engage in the legal process. Studies of legal discourse in a range of contexts (e.g. law school, courtrooms) show how successful communication depends on the adoption of a particular legal ideology or worldview. For example, in their study of lay litigants interacting with judges in informal courts (small claims tribunals) in the US, Conley and O'Barr (1990) identify two main kinds of lay litigant, described as 'relational' and 'rule-oriented'. These two kinds of litigants differ mainly in the ideological assumptions that they make when they are presenting their case to the court. Relational litigants tend to analyse their legal problems in terms of status and social relationships and they assume that the court is able to make awards on the basis of 'broad notions of social need and entitlement' (p. 58). Consequently, such litigants find it necessary to describe the details of their social lives to the judge when they provide their accounts. By contrast, rule-oriented litigants are those who tend to see the law as a system of rules to promote individual rights and responsibilities, irrespective of notions of status and social relationships. According to Conley and O'Barr, such litigants 'structure their accounts as a deductive search for blame' (p. 59), invoking legal rules and categories in order to justify their claims. This second orientation, that of the rule-oriented litigant, is the one which corresponds most closely to the ideology of the court and consequently enjoys the most success. The accounts given by relational litigants, on the other hand, are typically perceived by the court as 'imprecise, rambling, and straying from the central issues' (p. 58). As Merry (1990) notes, lay participants in interactions in lower courts and mediation sessions often find that their accounts are 'reframed' in terms of the dominant legal discourse by courtroom personnel and mediators.

Mertz's (2007) study of the socialisation of law students, based on the spoken discourse of law school classrooms in the US, also highlights the way in which law students come to adopt a rule-oriented perspective to legal problems, as described above. Her study shows how the discourse of the law school classroom, in which law professors emphasise certain elements of legal cases and de-emphasise others, encourages law students to read legal cases from such a rule-oriented perspective. In the process, law students learn to think, read and talk like lawyers, adopting a specialised form of 'legal reasoning'. In the common law context, legal reasoning involves analysing a specific factual situation in order to identify legal issues, identify relevant legal rules, select legally 'material' facts and apply the rules to those facts in order to arrive at a legal outcome (see Holland and Webb 2003; Vandevelde 1996 for detailed accounts). Thus, in this process there is an interaction between the 'ideal world' of legal rules on the one hand and the 'real world' of facts on the other (Bhatia 2004). Only those facts that are relevant to the abstract categories of the legal rules in question can play a role in the analysis, and, as a result, legal reasoning involves a reduction of complex social situations. The resulting 'legal story' that is constructed follows the dominant discourse of the law and is often very different from the accounts presented by lay participants in the legal process. This leads to what Mertz (p. 132) refers to as 'cultural invisibility', as elements of the social context (e.g. race, social class) are ideologically backgrounded at the same time as dominant cultural values (e.g. freedom of contract) become highly visible.

Thus, these studies reveal the preference of legal professionals for general, abstract categories over 'details' of the social context, in the application of legal rules to particular disputes. Many of the features of professional legal communication, as well as many of the challenges that it creates, can be explained in terms of the underlying 'rule-oriented' ideology and associated 'legal reasoning' that is adopted. The particular ways in which this ideology is linguistically realised forms the subject of many studies of legal language and communication. The following section considers studies of legal genres, which describe the rhetorical, grammatical and lexical features identified in legal texts related to the construction and interpretation of the law.

Legal professional written genres

Early studies of legal language and professional communication attempt to describe and explain the formal features of the legal register, especially, but not exclusively, those found in written legal texts. Useful summaries of such formal features can be found in Bhatia (1993), Crystal and Davy (1969), Danet (1985, 1990), Maley (1994), Mellinkoff (1963) and Tiersma (1999). Among the formal features that are usually mentioned as characteristic of legal text are the use of long, complex sentences with minimal punctuation, nominalisation and post-modification, the passive voice, archaic language, Latin phrases, technical legal terminology, and a lack of anaphoric references, to name just a few. For the purposes of this review, descriptions of written legal genres in this tradition can be organised into three main categories according to the context:

Christoph A. Hafner

1 genres used to construct the law (e.g. legislation)
2 genres used to interpret the law (e.g. judgments)
3 genres in the legal workplace.

Constructing the law

A key function of written professional legal genres is to define the rights, obligations and powers of members of society. This function is observed in both the public sphere (legislation) and in the private sphere (written agreements/contracts and deeds). Thus, legislation and agreements are genres that serve to 'construct' the law through the creation of legal rules: they are 'normative texts'. In cases of disagreement, the meaning of such texts can be disputed in a court of law, where they will be subjected to intense scrutiny. Drafting legislation and agreements therefore poses a unique challenge: as Bhatia (1993) notes, the draftsperson must attempt to be clear, precise and unambiguous, while at the same time drafting a document that is all-inclusive in that the general principles that it establishes anticipate an unlimited number of real world scenarios to which the rules might apply. Accordingly, in his work on legislative provisions, Bhatia (1993) identifies the following 'syntactic properties': the use of long sentences, nominalisation and passive voice, complex prepositional phrases (e.g. *in accordance with*), binomial and multinomial expressions (e.g. *act or omission, advice and consent*), initial case descriptions that describe circumstances when the rule applies, qualifications that limit the application of the rule, and syntactic discontinuities.

The language of normative texts is often portrayed as overly reliant on formal and archaic expressions, so that it is often difficult to read, especially for the non-specialist. In legislation and agreements, the over-riding concern of the legal draftsperson is, of course, to create a text that successfully establishes the desired legal rights, obligations and powers. As such, the primary audience for these texts is often not the general public or the parties to an agreement, but other legal specialists (chiefly lawyers and judges), who will jointly decide what exactly the document means. In some cases, particular 'formalities' must be complied with to achieve the desired ends. As Tiersma (1999: 102) notes, 'formal and ritualistic language in wills and similar documents can signal to the parties that this is a legal act with significant consequences'. In addition, for reasons of safety and convenience, legal professionals tend to be very conservative in their own document drafting practices. The usual practice is to adapt existing forms or precedents that have been 'tried and tested' over time, whose meanings have been argued over by lawyers and interpreted in court by judges. Such documents are seen as more certain and reliable, and, as a result, innovation in legal drafting is rare. All of these factors contribute to the highly formal, ritualistic and archaic nature of much professional legal communication.

A common justification for the communicative shortcomings of legal writing is that the features described above make it clear and precise. This notion has been strongly criticised, for example by Mellinkoff (1963: 290) who notes that

> lawyers have been telling each other for so many years that the language of the law is *precise* that they have come to believe it, even though long preoccupation with litigation caused by their language should have by this time made them at least sceptical.

Others have pointed out that language is inherently vague and indeterminate, and that the language of the law is no exception to this principle (Bhatia *et al.* 2005). Furthermore, such vagueness can be used as a strategic resource by the legal draftsperson, who may deliberately make use of unspecified terms, leaving it to the courts to decide their precise meanings when a case of dispute arises. Finally, some critical scholars point out that the purpose of legal language is not so much to provide clarity but rather to obscure the mechanisms of power that legal texts create in order to serve dominant interests in society (Wagner and Cacciaguidi-Fahy 2008).

Interpreting the law

A second important function of legal writing is to interpret the law as it applies to a particular situation by providing what one could broadly refer to as a 'legal opinion'. This happens when judges render judgments (see below), when lawyers provide legal advice (Hafner 2010, 2013; Tessuto 2006), and even when law students demonstrate to their professors their understanding of legal principles by providing answers to simulated 'legal problem questions' (Howe 1990). Out of this group of genres, the most prominent is the judgment. An early study of a single judgment by Maley (1985: 160) identifies a number of generic elements, described as follows: 'Facts, F, an account of events and/or the relevant history of the case; Issues, I, either of fact or of law; Reasoning, R; Conclusion, C, the principle or rule declared applicable for the instant case, and Order or Finding, O.' Reasoning typically, though not always, follows the rule-based (see above) pattern of stating the relevant legal rule, then applying the rule to the particular facts of the case in order to arrive at a legal outcome. A range of other studies have described this genre, also referred to as legal cases (Bhatia 1993) and law case reports (Harris 1997), as well as how such texts are typically read (Lundeberg 1987). In addition, the very closely related genre of newspaper law report (Badger 2003) has also received attention in the literature.

As with normative texts, one of the challenges in writing the kinds of legal opinions described here relates to the multiple potential audiences encountered: a judge writing a judgment is not just rendering a decision for the parties involved (and their legal counsel) but also constructing a text, which will be scrutinised by the wider community, including judges, lawyers, scholars, law students and even the wider public in some important cases. In delivering their judgments, judges usually pay particular attention to contentious issues in case the judgment is appealed, in which case it will be read and analysed by the appellate court. Furthermore, in common law jurisdictions, according to the principle of binding precedent (also referred to as *stare decisis,* literally 'to stand by what has been decided'), judges can make law by deciding 'precedent cases', which must be followed by lower court judges in future. Other kinds of opinions, notably the barrister's opinion, must also cater to a range of audiences: barristers write their opinions for an instructing solicitor and that solicitor's lay client, and the opinion could be further shared with a range of other audiences (including the court) which are difficult for the barrister to anticipate (see Hafner 2010).

The kinds of legal opinions described here are highly intertextual. Writers draw on existing sources of law, such as legislation, agreements and cases, in order to establish principles of law. In addition, to establish the facts of a particular case (especially those in dispute), they may refer to correspondence between parties or other such documentation. In a study of three legal textbooks, Swales (1982) identifies three different ways of referring to cases: 1) 'parenthetical' (the most common form, the case name is inserted in parentheses after the proposition of law it supports); 2) 'locative' (the next most common form, the case name and a description of the facts of that case follows the locative preposition *in*); 3) 'marked' (the least common form, in which the writer marks the significance of the case as in 'The leading case is *Astbury Railway Co. Ltd.*'). Another very important discursive feature of legal opinions is the frequent use of modality and conditional structures. These forms are necessary in order to carefully weigh the possibilities of different arguments, argue hypothetically, and provide conclusions that are appropriately hedged. Accounts of the difficulties that law students face with respect to this use of modality can be found in Hafner (2008) and Langton (2002).

Practising the law

Beyond the genres described above, there has been relatively little research conducted into written genres specific to the legal workplace (e.g. communication within a law firm). In addition to the provision of advice, lawyers perform an important function of negotiating agreements for their clients, a function that is in part performed through written communication. Candlin and Bhatia (1998) have done a survey of the communication needs of lawyers in Hong Kong law firms. The study, which adopted a survey and questionnaire methodology, identified a range of text types written in practice, including: in-house correspondence, letters to clients, letters to solicitors, files/attendance notes, agreements and contracts, promotional materials, briefs and reports, plain English documents.

Legal professional spoken interaction

In addition to the studies of written genres described above, considerable effort has been put into the analysis of spoken interaction in the professional legal context. Three main communicative contexts of use have been investigated: the trial, the police interview and the lawyer-client interview. In all three of these contexts, legal professionals are engaged in communication with non-specialists, and balancing the expectations of these non-specialists with specialist participants who may be present requires considerable skill and expertise. The three contexts are detailed below; for a more thorough, book-length treatment of the research in this area see Eades (2010).

Courtroom interaction

Sociolinguistic studies of courtroom interaction cover hearings in a range of settings, including small claims tribunals, tribunals of inquiry, criminal court, and mediation and arbitration settings. These studies characterise legal proceedings as formal, ritualised events, similar to a drama with a number of clearly defined participants. For example, in a common law criminal trial one will typically find judges, lawyers (for the prosecution and defence), court officials, defendants, witnesses, members of the jury, members of the press, members of the public. These various participants will be recognisable by their dress, their actions and the role they play, and even their physical position in the courtroom (with the judge(s) always occupying a physically dominant position). The trial itself will have a number of pre-determined stages in which various participants play pre-determined roles. Cotterill (2003) shows how the jury trial procedure can be likened to the development of a narrative that proceeds through the stages of opening statements, witness examination, closing arguments, verdict, sentencing or release. Furthermore, each of these stages has its own rules and conventions about who may contribute and what kind of contribution is allowable. These rules and conventions tend to create an imbalance of power, with judges and lawyers having greater conversational privileges than other participants in the trial (in particular, they are allowed to ask questions). In this way, courtroom interaction is heavily constrained by the ritual conventions of the trial as well as rules of evidence (e.g. the rule against 'hearsay evidence' or against 'leading questions' in examination in chief) that have been developed in order to ensure a fair trial.

Much of the literature on courtroom interaction has focused on witness examination in the common law context. In this phase of the trial, the lawyer attempts to elicit or challenge the witness's story by asking a series of questions, which the witness is obliged to answer. Early studies of witness examination considered the way that lawyers use their questions to control or manipulate the testimony of the witness, especially in combative cross-examinations (Danet et al. 1980; Harris 1984; Philips 1987; Walker 1987; Woodbury 1984). For example, Woodbury (1984) identifies a range of formal question types that are used in witness examination, from least controlling to most controlling forms: broad wh-questions, narrow wh-questions, alternative questions, grammatical yes/no questions, negative grammatical yes/no questions, prosodic questions and tag questions. Other studies go beyond this focus on grammatical form to analyse the lexical choices and conversational strategies used by lawyers (Atkinson and Drew 1979; Cotterill 2004; Drew 1990, 1992; Hobbs 2003; Matoesian 2001, 2005). Atkinson and Drew's (1979) conversation analysis of witness examination shows, among other things, how lawyers design sequences of questions in order to manage their accusations incrementally, seeking the witness's agreement to damaging inferences in earlier questions before revealing the accusation (at which point it is too late for the witness to repair the earlier inference).

Some studies also focus on the way that witnesses (especially powerful ones) are able to resist lawyers' courtroom strategies. In an interesting study of this kind, Ehrlich and Sidnell (2006) describe a witness (the then Premier of Ontario, Canada, Michael Harris testifying in a provincial inquiry) who skilfully deconstructed the inferences hidden in counsel's questions, at one point saying 'Well, you assumed that I didn't intervene in the business process and I think that's – that's not an assumption you ought to make' (p. 666). Other studies of witness resistance in cross-examination in a different context (rape trials) include Drew (1992), Matoesian (2005) and Ehrlich (2001).

On the whole, the studies of witness examination described here demonstrate the considerable skill employed by lawyers in this specialised form of professional communication. Other phases of the trial have also been analysed in terms of their specialised discourse, in particular the ritual opening of the trial (Atkinson and Drew 1979), defendants' guilty pleas (Philips 1998), lawyers' opening statements and closing arguments (Cotterill 2003; Matoesian 2001), and judges' summing up and instructions to the jury (Charrow and Charrow 1979; Heffer 2005).

Police interviews

Research into professional legal communication in law enforcement has also focused heavily on interactions between specialists (police officers) and non-specialists (witnesses and suspects in police investigations). As with courtroom interaction, police interviews also involve an inherent power imbalance, with certain participants institutionally empowered to ask questions while others answer. In addition, the interaction is complicated by the presence of multiple roles and audiences, as well as legal requirements, for example that police officers inform interviewees of their rights (Rock 2007). Heydon (2005) divides the police interview into a three-part structure: Opening, Information Gathering and Closing. The purpose of the Opening/Closing is to adhere to legislative requirements, while the purpose of the Information Gathering is, ideally, to produce a voluntary confession (see Heydon 2005: 73). The goals of the interaction can thus be defined in institutional terms: as police carry out their interviews, they are attending not only to the immediate interaction, but how this interaction will be perceived and legally evaluated if admitted in evidence at a future prosecution. Leo (2008) is highly critical of what he refers to as 'police interrogation', suggesting that police tactics go beyond the normal 'investigative' function and take on a 'prosecutorial' quality, becoming highly adversarial. Other critical research has focused on the forms of 'police cautions', also known in the United States as 'Miranda warnings', in which police officers inform interviewees of their rights (e.g. to remain silent, to request a lawyer). The language of such warnings, which are written to be read, has been criticised for being overly formal and complex (Brière 1978; Gibbons 1990, 2003; Shuy 1997). In addition, police may use forms of coercion and deception in order to encourage interviewees to waive their rights (Berk-Seligson 2009; Pavlenko 2008).

Lawyer–client interaction

Because of its confidential nature, it is quite rare for researchers of professional legal communication to gain access to interactions between lawyers and their clients. Nevertheless a few studies have been carried out, with a range of settings covered: law offices (Maley *et al.* 1995; Sarat and Felstiner 1995), legal aid offices (Bogoch 1994), a police station (Halldorsdottir 2006) and a courthouse cell (Scheffer 2006). The studies show how the differing orientations (i.e. 'rule-based' and 'relational', see above) of specialist lawyers and non-specialist clients play an important role in this kind of professional communication. A legal and rational approach to the problem is called for, rather than a social and emotional perspective. The lawyer's role is to shuttle between the different discursive worlds of lawyer and client, both by listening to the client's 'story' and creating a coherent 'legal narrative' out of it and by explaining legal options in a language that the client can relate to. Maley *et al.* (1995) show how, in lawyer-client interviews, lawyers appropriate the discursive resources of the everyday for persuasive effect. Sarat and Felstiner (1995) examine such interviews in the context of divorce law, an area that is particularly fraught because it is so emotionally charged. In this context, when clients speak about the failure of their marriage they frequently resort to the 'language of guilt, fault and responsibility' (p. 50), and when confronted with such talk (usually seen as irrelevant) lawyers respond with silence or, alternatively, with tactical advice considering only legal issues. Although they attempt to avoid the emotional worlds of their clients, paradoxically, in attempting to resolve their clients' legal problems, lawyers discuss human aspects (personalities, emotions) of important players in the system (e.g. a particular judge), where such consideration is necessary from a legal tactical perspective (Sarat and Felstiner 1995: 95).

Multilingual and multicultural contexts

As noted at the outset, one important focus of research into professional legal communication investigates intercultural communication that occurs in multilingual and multicultural contexts. Such studies can be broken down into two main kinds: 1) studies of intercultural contact *within the system*, for example when individuals from indigenous or immigrant ethnic groups interact with individuals from the dominant culture; 2) studies of intercultural contact *between systems*, for example in globalised legal practices such as international commercial arbitration.

Intercultural contact within the legal system

Intercultural contact can occur within a given legal system when individuals from indigenous or immigrant groups become involved in the legal process and need to communicate with representatives of the legal institution. Such representatives typically act according to the communicative norms of the dominant culture in society, which underpin communication in the legal system. However, individuals from minority ethnic groups may make different cultural assumptions about norms of communication in the legal process, resulting in challenges to successful communication. A number of insights can be gleaned from research carried out in the Australian context. First, the practice, so common to courtroom interaction, of asking and answering questions, may be perceived as inappropriate by some indigenous Australians, who may expect access to certain kinds of knowledge to be limited and gained in more indirect ways (Eades 1994; Walsh 1994). This may lead such witnesses to appear to evade questions as they attempt to signal that they consider the questions inappropriate. Eades (2007) further observes that some indigenous Australians may begin their answers to questions with silence, which can be misinterpreted by dominant culture individuals and contribute to a poor impression of the witness, who may be seen as lacking credibility. Similarly, indigenous Australians may avoid direct eye contact, which is considered by them to be inappropriately threatening and rude. A particularly damaging practice that has been observed in some indigenous Australians is that of 'gratuitous concurrence' (see Liberman 1981). These findings are not intended to suggest that all members of a particular minority ethnic group will encounter communication challenges in the legal process. They do, however, suggest the need for legal professionals to understand the communication challenges that can arise with individuals from particular minority ethnic groups.

The challenges of intercultural contact within the legal system can also be linguistic in nature, with some individuals not fully proficient in the dominant language of the legal system. Again in the Australian context, Cooke (1995, 2002) has shown how L1 interference can cause breakdowns in communication, pointing out that certain kinds of yes/no questions are answered differently in different languages. This raises the issue of when to use an interpreter, a practice that is not very popular with legal professionals and is usually left up to the presiding judicial officer (Eades 2010: 66). While the general perception is that an interpreter is there to remove the language barrier (Hale 2004), they are sometimes observed to act as a kind of 'cultural broker' and clarify some of the cultural presuppositions that hinder effective communication at times (Hale 2007). In addition, the practice of courtroom interpreting is not as simple as it is thought to be and limitations on interpretation can have far-reaching effects. Lee (2009, 2010) shows how the lack of equivalent grammatical categories in English and Korean prevented an interpreter from providing an appropriately specific response to a lawyer's question in a rape trial, a fact that was seized upon by the lawyer as evidence of a lack of credibility on the part of the witness. Interpreters can also encounter significant pragmatic challenges in their interpretations, sometimes failing to interpret pragmatic markers such as 'well', which often convey important information about attitude, which could be quite crucial in a hostile cross-examination (Berk-Seligson 1999; Hale 2004).

Intercultural contact between legal systems

Another kind of intercultural contact can occur when different legal systems come into contact, especially as a result of global political and economic trends. In terms of professional legal communication, there are two principal contexts that have been studied, both of which have led to the establishment of multilingual and multicultural contexts with innovative legal communication practices. The political union of Europe leading to the creation of the EU constitutes one such context while the practice of international commercial arbitration (ICA) as the preferred method of dispute resolution for multinational corporations acting as global trading partners is another. In both of these contexts, the legal professional communication practices observed transcend national boundaries and therefore involve legal professionals from a range of different legal and national backgrounds in communication with each other. Both the EU and ICA involve the creation of a supra-national legal regulatory framework, which must be incorporated into domestic legislation, in a process that involves the creation of normative texts across systems and cultures (Bhatia *et al.* 2003, 2008).

Studies of the formal features of such normative texts show that systematic variation can be observed in texts constructed in different settings and that such variation is the result of varying drafting conventions, linguistic constraints and socio-cultural constraints (Gotti 2008a). For example, EU directives incorporated into English legal texts drafted in the common law tradition show a preference for detail and specificity when compared with Italian texts drafted in the civil law tradition (Catenaccio 2008). Similar variation can also be found in other kinds of texts, such as awards in ICA, which may differ in terms of the rhetorical patterns of professional reasoning adopted, depending on whether the dispute is one that is based on common law or civil law (Hafner 2011). In these contexts, the translation of supra-national legal documents can be particularly problematic, as certain legal concepts may be missing from the legal lexicon of the target legal language. As a result, some translation scholars suggest a functional approach to legal translation, advocating that source and target texts should not only be formally equivalent but also functionally equivalent, in that they achieve the same legal ends (Chromá 2004; Gémar 2001; Šarčević 1997). As legal professionals from different jurisdictions increasingly come into contact with one another, one should expect to see more innovative language practices, including various kinds of borrowing and code-switching (Powell and Hashim 2011). While there is clearly some potential for the practices of legal professionals in multilingual and multicultural contexts to 'harmonize' and accommodate one another, evidence from discourse analysis suggests that this is likely to be a slow process, as the cultural assumptions embedded in discourse practices are tacitly held and below the level of consciousness (Gotti 2008a, 2008b).

Critical issues and future directions

This chapter has summarised existing research into professional communication in the legal domain by describing the socio-cultural context, written legal genres, spoken interaction and communication in multilingual and multicultural contexts. One key issue that appears repeatedly in the literature is the role of legal language in allowing or restricting individuals' access to the legal process. The specialised language of the law that is used to formulate legal texts can often interfere with clear communication, whether this be in the context of written legal documents or spoken interactions in the courtroom, lawyer's office or police station. As a consequence, a number of scholars and practitioners have argued for language reform, in particular promoting the use of 'plain language' (Asprey 2003) in order to make written legal texts more accessible to non-specialist readers. There is a balance to be struck here, as many of the features of legal language that make it difficult to access are also those features that are required in order to create a legally effective document. Critical applied linguistic research into the language of the law clearly has an ongoing role to play in highlighting the linguistic complexities of institutional texts and suggesting practical change, as for example in the work of Gibbons (2001), which informed the re-drafting of standard police cautions in Australia. Such work promoting access to the legal process could usefully be extended to evaluate the effectiveness of other kinds of texts for non-specialists, for example legal popularisations, which attempt to convey an understanding of a given area of law to a non-specialist audience.

A second issue for professional legal communication relates to the changing nature of participants in the legal process. With the trend towards increasing globalisation of the workforce and the resulting diversification of domestic populations, participants in the legal process will in future come from a wider range of cultural backgrounds, bringing with them different assumptions about communication in legal settings. In addition, legal practices are themselves becoming more globalised in nature because of increasing opportunities for international trade. As a result, legal professionals will increasingly need to develop good intercultural communicative competence and there is therefore likely to be some need for training in this area as well. While existing work provides a useful sketch of the terrain in terms of some of the intercultural communication challenges in the legal context, this research will need to be expanded in future in order to cater to newly emerging immigrant groups in particular local contexts. Furthermore, there is little in the way of research that examines legal professionals' awareness of cultural issues in communication in legal contexts, nor how they might seek to accommodate to or exploit cultural differences in communication. Future research could address the question of how to facilitate communication across different cultural groups and should lead to the development of resources that can benefit legal professionals working in culturally diverse settings (as an example of such resources see the practitioners' manual developed by Eades (1992)).

Finally, there is evidence that professional legal communication practices are evolving in response to developments in information and communication technologies. For example, Robbins-Tiscione (2008) documents lawyers' increasing reliance on email to fulfil functions traditionally performed by the legal memorandum. Such a switch to computer-mediated communication could of course have an effect on professional legal communication practices with the potential for innovation there. However, this issue has so far received little attention in the literature and there is therefore a need for research that evaluates the effect of mediated communication on legal writing and drafting practices and potentially also on courtroom discourse (as, for example, when certain vulnerable witnesses appear in court via a CCTV link, in accordance with rape shield laws and other similar legislation). New technologies and the internet also have the potential to increase participation in the legal process, as was recently observed when a 'crowd-sourced' constitution, which had been developed with reference to comments received through social media like Twitter and Facebook, was approved by the people of Iceland (Morris 2012). Such innovations point to reversals in traditional power structures, with non-specialists deeply involved in practices that are traditionally reserved for specialists. Above all, innovations in professional legal communication practices highlight the fact that professional legal communication is dynamic and evolving in the face of changing contexts, so that a complete understanding of the field requires a sustained research effort.

Related topics

Analysing discourse variation in professional contexts; the role of translation in professional communication; the formation of a professional communicator: a socio-rhetorical approach

Key readings

Asprey, M. M. (2003). *Plain Language for Lawyers*, 3rd edition, Sydney: Federation Press. (Aimed at a legal professional audience, this book provides a history of the plain language movement and describes some of the principles of plain language drafting.)

Bhatia, V. K. (1993). *Analysing Genre: Language Use in Professional Settings*, London: Longman. (Introduces principles of genre analysis and applies them to written legal discourse, especially legislation and legal cases.)

Conley, J. M. and O'Barr, W. M. (1990). *Rules Versus Relationships: The Ethnography of Legal Discourse*, Chicago: University of Chicago Press. (Describes a study of lay litigants in small claims tribunals in the US and shows how challenges to communication are influenced by the orientation ('rule-based' or 'relational') adopted by these litigants.)

Cotterill, J. (2003). *Language and Power in Court: A Linguistic Analysis of the O. J. Simpson Trial*, Basingstoke, Hampshire: Palgrave Macmillan. (A recent analysis of court-room discourse based on the transcripts of the high profile O. J. Simpson trial.)

Eades, D. (2010). *Sociolinguistics and the Legal Process*, Bristol: Multilingual Matters. (Provides a thorough overview of forensic linguistic research in a range of situational contexts.)

References

Asprey, M. M. (2003). *Plain Language for Lawyers*, 3rd edition, Sydney: Federation Press.
Atkinson, J. M. and Drew, P. (1979). *Order in Court: The Organization of Verbal Interaction in Judicial Settings*, Atlantic Highlands, NJ: Humanities Press.
Badger, R. (2003). 'Legal and general: Towards a genre analysis of newspaper law reports', *English for Specific Purposes*, 22(3), 249–63.
Berk-Seligson, S. (1999). 'The impact of court interpreting on the coerciveness of leading questions', *Forensic Linguistics*, 6(1), 30–56.
——(2009). *Coerced Confessions: The Discourse of Bilingual Police Interrogations*, Berlin: Mouton de Gruyter.
Bhatia, V. K. (1993). *Analysing Genre: Language Use in Professional Settings*, London: Longman.
——(2004). *Worlds of Written Discourse: A Genre-based View*, London: Continuum.
Bhatia, V. K., Candlin, C. N. and Engberg, J. (eds) (2008). *Legal Discourse Across Cultures and Systems*, Hong Kong: Hong Kong University Press.
Bhatia, V. K., Candlin, C. N., Engberg, J. and Trosborg, A. (eds) (2003). *Multilingual and Multicultural Contexts of Legislation: An International Perspective*, Bern: Peter Lang.
Bhatia, V. K., Engberg, J., Gotti, M. and Heller, D. (eds) (2005). *Vagueness in Normative Texts*, Bern: Peter Lang.
Bogoch, B. (1994). 'Power, distance and solidarity: Models of professional-client interaction in an Israeli legal aid setting', *Discourse & Society*, 5(1), 65–88.
Brière, E. J. (1978) 'Limited English speakers and the Miranda rights', *TESOL Quarterly*, 12(3), 235–45.
Candlin, C. N. and Bhatia, V. K. (1998). *Strategies and Competencies in Legal Communication: A Study to Investigate the Communicative Needs of Legal Professionals*, Hong Kong: The Law Society of Hong Kong.
Catenaccio, P. (2008). 'Implementing Council Directive 1993/13/EEU on unfair terms in consumer contracts in Great Britain: A case for intra-linguistic translation?', in V. K. Bhatia, C. N. Candlin and P. Evangelisti Allori (eds), *Language, Culture and the Law: The Formulation of Legal Concepts across Systems and Cultures* (pp. 259–80), Bern: Peter Lang.
Charrow, R. P. and Charrow, V. R. (1979). 'Making legal language understandable: A psycholinguistic study of jury instructions', *Columbia Law Review*, 79(7), 1306–74.
Chromá, M. (2004), 'Cross-cultural traps in legal translation', in C. Candlin and M. Gotti (eds), *Intercultural Aspects of Specialized Communication* (pp. 197–222), Bern: Peter Lang.
Conley, J. M. and O'Barr, W. M. (1990). *Rules Versus Relationships: The Ethnography of Legal Discourse*, Chicago: University of Chicago Press.
Cooke, M. (1995). 'Aboriginal evidence in the cross-cultural courtroom', in D. Eades (ed.), *Language in Evidence: Issues Confronting Aboriginal and Multicultural Australia* (pp. 55–96), Sydney: University of New South Wales Press.
——(2002). *Indigenous Interpreting Issues for Courts*, Carlton, VA: Australian Institute of Judicial Administration.
Cotterill, J. (2003). *Language and Power in Court: A Linguistic Analysis of the O.J. Simpson Trial*, Basingstoke, Hampshire: Palgrave Macmillan.
——(2004). 'Collocation, connotation, and courtroom semantics: Lawyers' control of witness testimony through lexical negotiation', *Applied Linguistics*, 25(4), 513–37.
Crystal, D. and Davy, D. (1969). 'The language of legal documents', in D. Crystal and D. Davy (eds), *Investigating English Style* (pp. 193–217), Harlow: Longman.
Danet, B. (1985). 'Legal discourse', in T. A. Van Dijk (ed.), *Handbook of Discourse Analysis: Volume 1: Disciplines of Discourse* (pp. 273–91), London: Academic Press.
——(1990). 'Language and law: An overview of 15 years of research', in H. Giles and W. P. Robinson (eds), *Handbook of Language and Social Psychology* (pp. 537–59), Chichester: Wiley.
Danet, B., Hoffman, K. B., Kermish, N. C., Rahn, H. J. and Stayman, D. G. (1980). 'An ethnography of questioning in the courtroom', in R. W. Shuy and A. Shnukal (eds), *Language Use and the Uses of Language* (pp. 222–34), Washington, DC: Georgetown University Press.
Drew, P. (1990). 'Strategies in the contest between lawyer and witness in cross-examination', in J. N. Levi and A. G. Walker (eds), *Language in the Judicial Process* (pp. 39–64), New York: Plenum Press.

——(1992). 'Contested evidence in courtroom cross-examination: The case of a trial for rape', in P. Drew and J. Heritage (eds), *Talk at Work: Interaction in Institutional Settings* (pp.470–520), Cambridge: Cambridge University Press.
Eades, D. (1992). *Aboriginal English and the Law: Communicating with Aboriginal English Speaking Clients: A Handbook for Legal Practitioners*, Brisbane: Queensland Law Society.
——(1994). 'A case of communicative clash: Aboriginal English and the legal system', in J. Gibbons (ed.), *Language and the Law* (pp. 234–64), London: Longman.
——(2007). 'Aboriginal English in the criminal justice system', in G. Leitner and I. Malcolm (eds), *The Habitat of Australia's Aboriginal Languages: Past, Present and Future* (pp. 299–326), Berlin: Mouton de Gruyter.
——(2010). *Sociolinguistics and the Legal Process*, Bristol: Multilingual Matters.
Ehrlich, S. (2001). *Representing Rape: Language and Sexual Consent*, London: Routledge.
Ehrlich, S. and Sidnell, J. (2006). '"I think that's not an assumption you ought to make": Challenging presuppositions in inquiry testimony', *Language in Society*, 35(5), 655–76.
Gémar, J.-C. (2001). 'Seven pillars for the legal translator: Knowledge, know-how and art', in S. Šarčević (ed.), *Legal Translation: Preparation for Accession to the European Union* (pp. 111–38), Rijeka: University of Rijeka.
Gibbons, J. (1990). 'Applied linguistics in court', *Applied Linguistics*, 11(3), 229–37.
——(2001). 'Revising the language of New South Wales police procedures: Applied linguistics in action', *Applied Linguistics*, 22, 439–69.
——(2003). *Forensic Linguistics: An Introduction to Language in the Justice System*, Malden, MA: Blackwell.
Gotti, M. (2008a). 'Cultural constraints on arbitration discourse', in V. K. Bhatia, C. N. Candlin and J. Engberg (eds), *Legal Discourse across Cultures and Systems* (pp. 221–52), Hong Kong: Hong Kong University Press.
——(2008b). 'The formulation of legal concepts in arbitration normative texts in a multilingual, multicultural context', in V. K. Bhatia, C. N. Candlin and P. Evangelisti Allori (eds), *Language, Culture and the Law: The Formulation of Legal Concepts across Systems and Cultures* (pp. 23–45), Bern: Peter Lang.
Hafner, C. A. (2008). 'Designing, implementing and evaluating an online resource for professional legal communication skills', Unpublished doctoral thesis, Macquarie University, Sydney.
——(2010). 'A multi-perspective genre analysis of the barrister's opinion: Writing context, generic structure, and textualization', *Written Communication*, 27(4), 410–41.
——(2011). 'Professional reasoning, legal cultures, and arbitral awards', *World Englishes*, 30(1), 117–28.
——(2013). 'The discursive construction of expertise: Appeals to authority in barrister's opinions', *English for Specific Purposes*, 32(3), 131–43.
Hale, S. (2004). *The Discourse of Court Interpreting: Discourse Practices of the Law, the Witness, and the Interpreter*, Amsterdam: John Benjamins.
——(2007). *Community Interpreting*, Basingstoke: Palgrave Macmillan.
Halldorsdottir, I. (2006). 'Orientations to law, guidelines, and codes in lawyer–client interaction', *Research on Language & Social Interaction*, 39(3), 263–301.
Harris, S. (1984). 'Questions as a mode of control in magistrates' courts', *International Journal of the Sociology of Language*, 49, 5–28.
——(1997). 'Procedural vocabulary in law case reports', *English for Specific Purposes*, 16(4), 289–308.
Heffer, C. (2005). *The Language of Jury Trial: A Corpus-aided Analysis of Legal-lay Discourse*, Basingstoke: Palgrave Macmillan.
Heydon, G. (2005). *The Language of Police Interviewing: A Critical Analysis*, Basingstoke: Palgrave Macmillan.
Hobbs, P. (2003). '"You must say it for him": Reformulating a witness' testimony on cross-examination at trial', *Text*, 23(4), 477–511.
Holland, J. A. and Webb, J. (2003). *Learning Legal Rules*, New York: Oxford University Press.
Howe, P. M. (1990). 'The problem of the problem question in English for academic legal purposes', *English for Specific Purposes*, 9(3), 215–36.
Langton, N. (2002). 'Hedging argument in legal writing', *Perspectives: Working Papers in English and Communication*, 14(1), 16–51.
Lee, J. (2009). 'Interpreting inexplicit language during courtroom examination', *Applied Linguistics*, 30(1), 93–114.
——(2010). 'Interpreting reported speech in witnesses' evidence', *Interpreting*, 12(1), 60–82.
Leo, R. A. (2008). *Police Interrogation and American Justice*, Cambridge, MA: Harvard University Press.
Liberman, K. (1981). 'Understanding Aborigines in Australian courts of law', *Human Organization*, 40, 247–55.

Lundeberg, M. A. (1987). 'Metacognitive aspects of reading comprehension: Studying understanding in legal case analysis', *Reading Research Quarterly*, 22(4), 407–32.

Maley, Y. (1985). 'Judicial discourse: The case of the legal judgment', *Beitrage zur Phonetik und Linguistik*, 48, 159–73.

——(1994). 'The language of the law', in J. Gibson (ed.), *Language and the Law* (pp. 11–50), Harlow: Longman.

Maley, Y., Candlin, C. N., Crichton, J. and Koster, P. (1995). 'Orientations in lawyer-client interviews', *Forensic Linguistics*, 2(1), 42–55.

Mather, L., McEwen, C. A. and Maiman, R. J. (2001). *Divorce Lawyers at Work*, New York: Oxford University Press.

Matoesian, G. M. (2001). *Law and the Language of Identity: Discourse in the William Kennedy Smith Rape Trial*, Oxford: Oxford University Press.

——(2005). 'Nailing down an answer: Participations of power in trial talk', *Discourse Studies*, 7(6), 733–59.

Mellinkoff, D. (1963). *The Language of the Law*, Boston: Little, Brown.

Merry, S. E. (1990). *Getting Justice and Getting Even: Legal Consciousness Among Working-class Americans*, Chicago: University of Chicago Press.

Mertz, E. (2007). *The Language of Law School: Learning to Think like a Lawyer*, New York: Oxford University Press.

Morris, H. (2012). 'Crowdsourcing Iceland's constitution', *International Herald Tribune*. Available at: http://rendezvous.blogs.nytimes.com/2012/10/24/crowdsourcing-icelands-constitution/ (accessed 22 December 2012).

Pavlenko, A. (2008). '"I'm very not about the law part": Nonnative speakers of English and the Miranda warnings', *TESOL Quarterly*, 42, 1–30.

Philips, S. U. (1987). 'The social organization of questions and answers in courtroom discourse', in L. Kedar (ed.) *Power through Discourse* (pp. 83–113), Norwood NJ: Ablex.

——(1998). *Ideology in the Language of Judges: How Judges Practice Law, Politics, and Courtroom Control*, New York: Oxford University Press.

Powell, R. and Hashim, A. (2011). 'Language disadvantage in multilingual contexts: Policy and practice in Malaysian litigation and alternative dispute resolution', *World Englishes*, 30(1), 92–105.

Robbins-Tiscione, K. K. (2008). 'From snail mail to e-mail: The traditional legal memorandum in the twenty-first century', *Journal of Legal Education*, 58, 32–60.

Rock, F. (2007). *Communicating Rights: The Language of Arrest and Detention*, Basingstoke: Palgrave Macmillan.

Sarat, A. and Felstiner, W. L. F. (1995). *Divorce Lawyers and their Clients: Power and Meaning in the Legal Process*, New York: Oxford University Press.

Šarčević, S. (1997). *New Approaches to Legal Translation*, The Hague: Kluwer Law International.

Scheffer, T. (2006). 'The microformation of criminal defense: On the lawyer's notes, speech production, and a field of presence', *Research on Language and Social Interaction*, 39(3), 303–42.

Shuy, R. W. (1997). 'Ten unanswered language questions about Miranda', *Forensic Linguistics*, 4(2), 175–96.

Swales, J. M. (1982). 'The case of cases in English for academic legal purposes', *IRAL*, 20, 139–48.

Swift, J. (1967). *Gulliver's Travels*, Harmondsworth, Middlesex: Penguin.

Tessuto, G. (2006). 'Opinions of counsel: An exploratory survey of generic features', in V. K. Bhatia and M. Gotti (eds), *Explorations in Specialized Genres* (pp. 291–308), Bern: Peter Lang.

Tiersma, P. (1999). *Legal Language*, Chicago: The University of Chicago Press.

Vandevelde, K. J. (1996). *Thinking like a Lawyer*, Boulder, CO: Westview Press.

Wagner, A. and Cacciaguidi-Fahy, S. (eds) (2008). *Obscurity and Clarity in the Law: Prospects and Challenges*, Aldershot: Ashgate.

Walker, A. G. (1987). 'Linguistic manipulation, power, and the legal setting', in L. Kedar (ed.), *Power Through Discourse* (pp. 57–83), Norwood, NJ: Ablex.

Walsh, M. (1994). 'Interactional styles in the courtroom: An example from northern Australia', in J. Gibbons (ed.), *Language and the Law* (pp. 217–33), London: Longman.

Woodbury, H. (1984). 'The strategic use of questions in court', *Semiotica*, 48(3–4), 197–228.

23
Communication in the construction industry

Michael Handford

Introduction

The construction industry is one of the largest sectors in the world, accounting for 10 per cent of global GDP (PricewaterhouseCoopers 2010), employing between 10 and 20 per cent of many national workforces, and involving professionals and organisations from the public, private and NPO/NGO sectors. Despite its economic power and social impact, surprisingly little research has been conducted on written or spoken naturally occurring discourse in the construction industry (exceptions include Medway 1996; Cheng and Mok 2008; Gluch and Raisanen 2009; Baxter and Wallace 2009; Handford and Matous 2011; Handford forthcoming).

If we broaden the search to look at 'construction communication' (hereafter CC), then a somewhat scattered history of research into communication in the construction industry (hereafter CI) becomes apparent (see Emmitt and Gorse 2003 Chapter 2 for an overview). Much of this research has been conducted in the UK, although the last two decades have seen an increase in the number of other national and international studies (Dainty *et al.* 2006). In the early 1960s the British government commissioned the first of many reports into problems in CI (Emmerson 1962): it pinpointed ineffective communication as the biggest issue facing the industry. A few years later, a highly influential study by a psychologist and a statistician (Higgin and Jessop 1965) was conducted that focused wholly on communication. It assumed that CC was indeed problematic, and then argued that the complex and adversarial nature of the relationships in CI was the primary cause of the problems. Forty years later, a book length study of CC by a professional architect/professor in Innovation in Building and a construction manager/professor in Civil Engineering argues that there has been 'little improvement' in communication in CI, with an increase in complexity having occurred: there are more specialists and more specialised registers, more court-cases, and there is greater fragmentation, more complex technology, and more information to process (Emmitt and Gorse 2003: 16). A similar conclusion is reached by other book-length studies by academic civil engineers with professional experience (Dainty *et al.* 2006; Tijhuis and Fellows 2012), and is the tone of much of the research into CC (see section 2).

This chapter will outline some of the studies that have been conducted into CC, and will discuss an ongoing discourse-based project that I am involved in. More specifically, the chapter is divided into five sections. In sections 1–3, the following areas will be addressed: how the construction process is structured, with particular reference to the different parties involved; how communication within the industry is portrayed in academic and professional studies, and the types of research that have been conducted; thirdly, how Candlin's (2002) exhortation for studies into professional discourse to have practical relevance might be operationalised in this context. The final two sections will then outline a methodology, developed in Handford (2010), which attempts to take up Candlin's recommendations, and demonstrate how it has been applied to audio, video and ethnographic data collected on a Hong Kong construction project. Section 5 will conclude the chapter by making some brief recommendations for future discourse-analysis informed research.

1 The construction process

Traditionally, construction projects can be broken into two phases: the design phase and the construction phase, both of which can last years on large projects (Dainty *et al.* 2006). In the design phase, the design of the product (building, bridge, tunnel, etc.) is proposed and agreed upon. Bids are then invited by construction companies, and the company/companies who win the contract will embark on stage two of the process.

The above description of the process is highly simplistic, not least because it neglects to mention the different parties who are involved. Emmitt and Gorse group them into the following five categories (2003: 16):

1 The client: 'The client' is the person(s), organisation or organisations who pay for the project, and may be private individuals or companies, governments, development banks and so on.
2 Professional consultants: There may be many types of consultants in projects. In one construction meeting I recorded[1] in South Asia (Handford forthcoming), there were design consultants (whose role it was to design a bridge), an environmental consultant, several construction consultants (academic engineers who were employed to evaluate the design), a resettlement expert and an independent checking engineer.
3 Main contractor and sub-contractors: These are the organisations and groups who are typically employed at the outset of the second phase of the process.
4 Legislative bodies: Depending on the project and the parties involved, sanctioned parties will outline how international, domestic and local building codes and other related legislation will have to be complied with.
5 Interested parties: These can include special interest groups, future users of the structure, and members of the community.

The key communicative relationships in CI can be roughly categorised as follows (Dainty *et al.* 2006):

1 between clients and consultants
2 between consultants
3 between the designers and the contractor
4 on-site between contractors, and between contractors and sub-contractors.

Generally speaking, the first two categories occur during the first (design) phase of the project, and the third and fourth constitute the second (construction) phase. Nevertheless, other communication can also take place, such as between the client and the contractor, depending on the issue at hand and the role played by the client in the overall process.

2 Communication in the construction industry

Given the wide range of stakeholders involved in CI, the potential for problematic communication is clear. As Tijhuis and Fellows (2012: i) state:

> Despite the wide range of technologies involved, the construction industry still relies heavily on people. Clients, managers, designers, investors and a whole host of other stakeholders are all involved in a crucial series of relationships that may be more important for project success than technical know-how. As construction projects become increasingly international, as well as interdisciplinary, the risks and costs of disharmonious working become ever larger. The growth of IT and the increased occurrences of mergers and joint ventures have created new problems, which require new solutions.

This quotation touches on recent changes in CI that have also occurred in many other industries, such as the growth of mergers and joint ventures and the prevalence of IT. The quotation also highlights the importance of relationships in ensuring the successful completion of the project, in other words the importance of the interpersonal in achieving transactional goals (Holmes and Stubbe 2003; Koester 2006; Handford 2010).

One issue with relationships in CI is that the parties, as shown above, are from different professions. Emmitt and Gorse state (2003: 30), 'The building industry is notorious for its adversarial behaviour and distrust between different professional groups', an evaluative stance that seems to be widely accepted in various studies of CC (see below). However, the presence of differing groups does not necessarily entail conflict, which begs the question, why is CI so prone to it? One explanation is that, although construction projects involve different groups working on the same project, this does not mean they work as teams. Each group or organisation is not concerned with collaborating with other groups, but with looking after the interests of its members. Emmitt and Gorse argue 'The "project team" appears to be a myth, instead there are a series of poorly connected teams or groups that carry out specific functions for a particular project' (Emmitt and Gorse 2003: 4). They go on to explain that, unless the project is well-managed, conflict can easily spiral upwards with the only beneficiaries being the legal profession.

The centrality of goals in professional communication is well understood (Charles 1996; Sarangi and Roberts 1999; Holmes and Stubbe 2003; Bhatia 2004; Koester 2006; Handford 2010), and can be used to explain the potentially conflictual nature of much CC. According to Dainty *et al.* (2006: 23):

> the industry is made up of many disparate organisations which come together in pursuit of shared project objectives, but also individual organisational goals. These are not necessarily compatible or mutually supportive and they may not align with people's personal objectives.

For instance, the goals of the professional consultants and the goals of the designers or contractors can all be very different (e.g. Handford forthcoming).

Furthermore, the practice in CI of sub-contracting out jobs, the lack of continuity in participants working together within and across jobs, the time pressure on all parties once a contract is awarded, the uniqueness of each project, the jargon used by different groups, the noise on-site, the male-dominated culture, an increasingly diverse workforce, variable language proficiency, and the need to deal with members of the public mean that CI faces a plethora of communication challenges (Emmitt and Gorse 2003; Dainty *et al.* 2006). Several of these issues have been the focus of research, largely by academics and professionals in Civil Engineering departments: the challenges facing women in CI (Dainty *et al.* 2006; Loosemore and Waters 2004; USDL 1999); the problems that a strong male genderlect can cause (Loosemore and Galea 2008; Baxter and Wallace 2009); diversity in terms of organisational and national culture (Loosemore and Al Muslmani 1999; Gajendran *et al.* 2012; Tijhuis and Fellows 2012; Handford and Matous 2012); issues of language proficiency (Trajkovski and Loosemore 2006; Handford and Matous 2011); differences in terminology used by architects and engineers (Dadji 1988, referenced in Dainty *et al.* 2006); understanding community-based protests against construction projects (Teo and Loosemore 2010) as well as managing public perceptions of risk (Loosemore 2007). In two key book studies of CC (Emmitt and Gorse 2003; Dainty *et al.* 2006), which are targeted primarily towards academic and professional engineering audiences, several more general themes are taken up. These include communicating abstract ideas, interpersonal communication, group communication, organisational communication, corporate communication, building an effective communication culture, managing meetings, conflict management, selecting appropriate communication media and using ICT in CI.[2] Notably, very few of these studies analyse naturally occurring language between people at work.

While many of the above studies paint a conflictual picture of communication and relationships in CI, it should be added that the majority of these studies involve English-speaking contexts, and that other regions may have different communicative practices because of differing expectations and relationships. For instance, Tijhuis and Fellows (2012: 66) report that in the Chinese and Japanese contexts, a form of 'deterrent based trust' may operate, which mitigates against conflict. This is not because of any sense of altruism, but because of there being many long-term relationships between companies and other stakeholders. A further factor mitigating against conflict in Japan is the nature of the relationships between the companies: there are a handful of very powerful construction companies, who then appoint smaller contractors, and it would very much be against the long-term interests of these smaller contractors to disagree with the larger companies. Indeed, several smaller companies are in fact subsidiary companies of the larger firm (see Woodall 1996).[3]

3 Towards a practically relevant corpus-informed discourse analysis of construction communication

As we can see, CI is a potentially rich arena for discourse analysis, given both the apparent range of issues the industry faces, and the scarcity of work into real interactions between the various parties and their organisations. Furthermore, communicating findings to the industry and other interested groups is possible, as the study below demonstrates.

Candlin (2002) proposes the need for discourse analysis in professional contexts to move beyond both the *description* of lexicogrammar at the textual level and the *interpretation* of the discourse and its practices, to an *evaluation* of the data and its context. In other words, if we are to achieve what Cicourel (1992) terms 'ecological validity', the researcher needs to see a key motivation for the research as feeding back into the research site in some way and thus achieving 'practical relevance' (Candlin 2006: 42). Candlin (ibid.) acknowledges that this is a contentious stance, potentially fraught with ideological, ethical and practical difficulties, a view shared by Scollon *et al.* They recognise the need for mutual trust between the researcher and the 'gatekeepers' in the organisations, but state:

> It is not unusual, however, in such situations for either researchers or members of the organisation to come to the conclusion during the course of the research that there is a

mismatch in goals or values. The researcher might, for instance, witness practices that he or she might consider in some way unethical, or members of the organisation may expect the researcher to provide services to the organisation to promote the organisation in publications in ways the researcher is unwilling to do.

(2012: 204)

This is indeed a genuine issue facing researchers of professional discourse, and one that may reflect substantial differences in professional culture and values (Scollon *et al.* ibid.). Researching CC may present the researcher with a range of dilemmas, given that the environmental, social and economic costs of the products of the industry itself can be contentious.

One perspective on the differing evaluative, interventionist roles open to researchers is suggested by work into organisational culture in construction projects by Gajendran *et al.* (2012). They draw from Alvesson's (2002) organisational framework of interventionist research orientations (technical – the removal of irrationality, practical – the removal of misunderstanding, and emancipatory – the removal of unnecessary suffering) and on Martin's (2002, 2004) 'philosophical' perspectives to culture, to suggest a hybrid approach to researching culture in CI – see Box 23.1.

Box 23.1: **Approaches to culture in CC**

1   Integration-Technical
    Focus: to identify and manipulate cultural variables to generate the intended culture

2   Differentiation-Practical
    Focus: to assist cultural understanding and remove misunderstanding

3   Fragmentation-Emancipatory
    Focus: to expose domination and exploitation aspects of a culture

---

Gajendran *et al.* (2012) argue that the Integration-Technical stance supports managers who believe they can *control* the output of subordinates through the manipulation of culture. As such it is positivistic, and censors deviation from the cultural norm. The Differentiation-Practical and the Fragmentation-Emancipatory positions, concerned with the clarification of misunderstandings and the alleviation of unnecessary suffering respectively, may be more attractive for researchers than the first position.[4] Indeed, there seems to be clear overlap between the Differentiation-Practical position and much work in discourse analysis and applied linguistics (e.g. Gumperz 1982; Yamada 1997), and the Fragmentation-Emancipatory position and critical discourse analysis (e.g. Van Dijk 1991; Gee *et al.* 1996; Roberts and Campbell 2005). The tension to which Candlin (2006) and Scollon *et al.* (2012) allude may be caused by many company executives expecting support from research along the lines of the Integration-Technical approach, whereas researchers are intending to either help participants overcome problems in miscommunication, improve their working conditions or ability to negotiate better conditions, or both. While Gajendran *et al.* (2012) recommend a hybrid approach, taking account of all three stances, an alternative approach is to persuade the decision-makers in the organisation that improving communication and giving a voice to the voiceless within the organisation may lead to higher levels of job satisfaction and employee empowerment. In turn, this could mean the mission statement's goals are more likely to be met. However, such an argument is unlikely to carry weight with all decision-makers.

4 Example of discourse-based construction communication research

In 2007 I was approached by the Construction Management Laboratory in the Department of Civil Engineering at the University of Tokyo, and invited to discuss how joint research into communication in the construction industry might be conducted. The rationale was an interdisciplinary approach to CC, with the academics in the laboratory (Professor K. Ozawa and Dr Petr Matous) bringing expertise and contacts in the industry, and my bringing the tools and insights of discourse analysis. This section will discuss the results of one aspect of this collaboration, which is still ongoing.

4.1 Background to the study

The Japanese construction industry is one of the largest in the world, although much of its business comes from domestic projects (Woodall 1996; Ministry of Land Infrastructure, Transport and Tourism 2010). Given that the domestic market is at a mature stage, there is pressure both internally and from the Japanese government for the industry to obtain more business from overseas (Ministry of Land Infrastructure, Transport and Tourism 2010).[5] The University of Tokyo has traditionally had a close relationship with both Japanese state bureaucracy and businesses, and we were given considerable support in setting up this project. Company decision-makers told us that young Japanese engineers can have difficulties working abroad because of English proficiency and various cultural issues, as well as a steeper learning curve in terms of the higher professional expectations and responsibilities that tend to occur on overseas projects. Furthermore, companies can save money by having junior staff manage projects that traditionally more experienced engineers would have overseen.

After consulting managers and other employees of Japanese construction companies, we decided that the analysis of on-site communication on a large international construction project would enable us to research the communicative requirements of young Japanese engineers. Dr Petr Matous visited four potential sites in Hong Kong in early 2008, and we eventually chose one large joint venture tunnelling project because of assumed levels of support, and the presence of two young Japanese engineers (in their early 30s) working on the project. Figure 23.1 shows the key relationships that we focused on during our recordings, with Kita and Arai the two Japanese engineers, and Marvin and TT the two HK foremen. Figure 23.2 shows the overall organisational framework of the whole project, with the relationships of Figure 23.1 fitting in the box titled 'Sites 1 & 2' in Figure 23.2. 'Ishihara' is the synonym for the Japanese construction company.

In December 2008 Petr Matous and I went out to Hong Kong for a week of recordings and interviews with the employees. We were also accompanied by a long-term employee of the HR department of the Japanese construction company, who was at the time a researcher in the Construction Management Laboratory, and who was able to offer insights into the project and give us his opinions of 'the mindset of the Japanese' and of 'foreign workers'.[6]

The project thus benefited from our being able to collect a wide range of data sources. These include audio and video recordings of the interactions between the on-site employees and other engineers, various interviews with the engineers and other staff and follow up interviews with expert informants, and access to various documents. Flowerdew (2012: 253), in a review of a preliminary article by Handford and Matous (2011), states 'The study is notable for its use of multiple data sources and ethnographic dimension to understand how the discursive practices of NNS (non-native speaker) engineers in their daily working life on-site are construed through the lexicogrammar'.

4.2 Methodology

The ongoing research project itself can be broken down into three parts, which roughly overlap with Candlin's (2002) three aims of professional discourse analysis (description, interpretation,

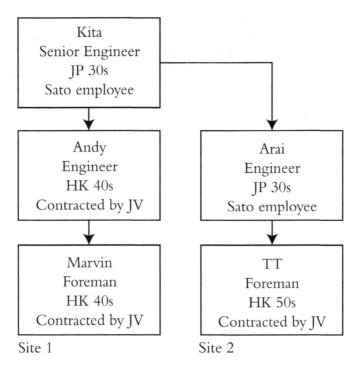

Figure 23.1 Relationships among speakers

evaluation/explanation). In terms of description, we conducted a corpus-informed analysis of frequent lexicogrammatical items, which led on to an analysis of nonverbal communication (Handford and Matous 2011). In terms of interpretation, we have analysed the discursive patterns of problem-solving encounters from discursive and cultural perspectives (ibid.; Handford and Matous in preparation). Evaluation, or in other words, achieving practical relevance, is being achieved through feeding the findings back to our postgraduate civil engineering students, many of whom have worked or will work in CI, and we are developing training materials for young in-company engineers who are required to work abroad, usually for the first time. These postgraduate and in-house materials partly take the form of analysis of cultural and professional 'critical incidents'. Furthermore, an article for the Japanese professional engineering audience was published in *The Japan Society of Civil Engineers* journal about the content and aims of our training (Handford 2012).

The methodology used in this project, developed in Handford (2010), can be outlined as follows:

1. collect and transcribe relevant textual and ethnographic data
2. pinpoint potentially important lexicogrammatical items and linguistic/paralinguistic features
3. understand how the situated meaning of the chosen item or feature is invoked in its specific context
4. infer the practices, goals, socially situated identities and social structures that orient the participants through the discourse (or genres) in which the item occurs
5. develop teaching and training material based on the above for the researched community, and disseminate findings among wider professional community.

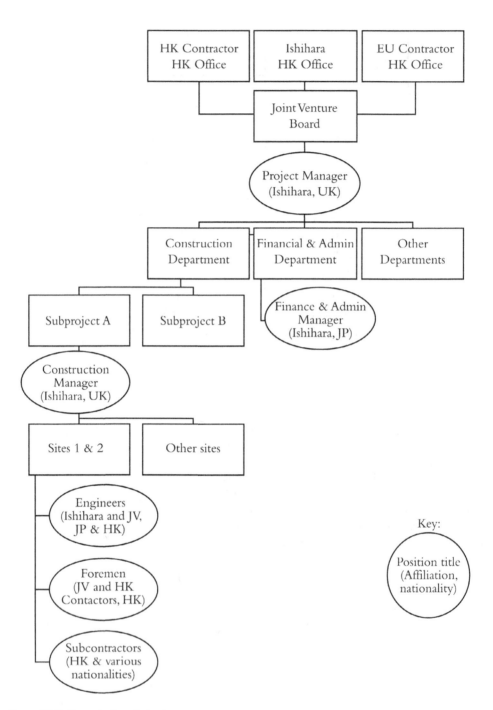

Figure 23.2 Organisational chart

Communication in the construction industry

It should be noted that the analysis is cyclical rather than purely linear, in that in order to explore the relationship between the text and the context, it is often necessary and indeed fruitful to move between the two. This is most typical with steps 3 and 4, which draw heavily on the work of Gee (1992, 2005) and Bhatia (2004). For instance the notion of 'situated meanings' (Gee 2005), which ties in closely with indexicality (Ochs 1996), indicates how we need to explore items in context to understand them, and that it is through shared communicative practices that items achieve their meaning. Gee's (2005) concept of Discourse (ways of performing and recognising socially situated identities through the use of symbols, tools, technologies and communicative practices to achieve certain shared goals) is also operationalised in this methodology. Indeed, the research is in large part an attempt to understand and map the Discourses of Japanese young engineers on international projects, and consider how changes might be made to the Discourse to improve their situation, and that of those with whom they interact.

Bhatia's (2004, 2008) categorisation of social, professional and discursive practices is combined with Gee's (1992, 2005) approach to social practices and Discourses, to account for the relationship between the text (in terms of situated meanings of important items and features) and the context it reflexively indexes. For instance, an engineer asking the foreman on-site 'No oil – oil is empty?' can be categorised as follows (Figure 23.3; the arrow represents the widening level of context):

Discourse:	Being an engineer
Social practice:	Managing projects
Professional practice(s):	Ensuring resources are used appropriately/problem-solving
Discursive practice:	Checking
Text:	No oil – oil is empty?

Figure 23.3 Language and practice relationship

The research is also cyclical in that the insights gained from interacting with the professional community (step 5) can lead to new understandings in step 3, and can also inform future data collection (step 1).

The next section will describe how Candlin's three areas of professional discourse analysis (description, interpretation, evaluation) have been addressed in this research project.

4.3 Description: Lexicogrammar and discursive practices

This section offers a summary of the preliminary findings from this research (taken from Handford and Matous 2011), which explored the lexicogrammar and the discursive practices used on-site, mainly between the young Japanese engineers and the HK foremen (see Figure 23.1). Initially, corpus comparisons between the 12,000 words of on-site encounters with two larger reference corpora were conducted, one of everyday spoken English (CANCODE), and one of spoken business English (CANBEC). This was to answer the first research question: How do the interactions recorded in a Japanese company in Hong Kong compare at the lexicogrammatical level to everyday English and business English?

From previous conversations with expert informants, such as the HR employee who was conducting research at the Management Construction Laboratory, and much of the literature on construction communication (see above) we were led to expect a high level of directness in on-site interactions, which would contrast with the communicative norms in many other professional settings. For instance, Holmes and Stubbe's assertion that 'most workplace interactions provide evidence of mutual respect and concern for the feelings or face needs of others' (2003: 7) seemed unlikely to be replicated. It was therefore surprising that, not only was much of the most frequent language in the (ELF) HK interactions interpersonal, but that it also featured many of the same items that occurred most typically in (largely L1) business meetings. Box 23.2 shows several of the statistically significant interpersonal and textual keywords (Scott 1999), with the underlined items also being statistically significant in the CANBEC corpus (compared to CANCODE: Handford 2010).

Box 23.2: **Key interpersonal items**

Back channels: *hmm, yes, okay, hai*
Modal verbs: *cannot, need, will*
Pronouns: *we*
Conjunctions: *so, because*
Hedges, fillers: *umm, uh*
Markers: *okay, alright*
(Evaluative nouns: *problem*)
Place deictics: *this, here*

Place deictics was the only category that was unique to the HK data, and will be discussed further below.

The analysis of the most frequent two-, three- and four-word clusters (phraseological items that index recurrent discursive practices) further unearthed a high number of interpersonal items, many of which are partly comprised of the keywords. Box 23.3 shows a collection of some of these, categorised according to type, once again with the underlined items also being found among the most frequent clusters in the CANBEC corpus.

Box 23.3: **Frequent clusters**

Hedging: *I think, I don't know*
Deontic modals: (*we/I*) *need to, no need to, we can, have to*
'If': *if we, (even if we fix), if we can*
Problem-decision: *I agree with you, to make a decision*
Combinations (face): *I think this is, er you need to*
Deictics: *this is (the), this one (is), put it here*

In terms of the discursive practices that such items invoke, there was again considerable overlap with other professional contexts. For instance, hedges (such as *I think*) serve to negotiate power over knowledge, or in other words soften the speaker's claim to expertise. Deontic modality negotiates power over obligation, and the particular deontic (semi) modal verb often combines with the pronoun *we*. Extract 1, a typical exchange, shows the foreman combining the hedges *I think* and *er* with the modal cluster *we don't have to*, with the deictic *here*. The use of the back channel *hmm* by the Japanese engineer is also of note, as it is statistically significant here and in CANBEC, and is widely used in senior-subordinate meetings in other settings (Handford 2010: 161).

Extract 1

TT: I think + er we don't have to consider about the safety + in here
ARAI: Hmm

Interestingly, the deontic forms *need to* and *have to* are the preferred verbs of choice, as opposed to the semantically synonymous but pragmatically different *must*. This is interesting for two reasons: the same pattern occurs in business meetings (Handford 2010); secondly, one expert informant predicted before the recordings that engineers on-site would use *you must* rather than the less face-threatening *we need to/have to*. We found that, in interactions between the HK foremen, the Japanese engineers and other engineers on the joint venture, this was not the case, suggesting that the on-site interactions we recorded may display a preference for face-saving communication at the lexicogrammatical level that is found in other professional contexts. While more data in other equivalent settings is needed to make any generalisations, the findings do contrast with the construction communication literature's comments on conflict. One interpretation is that the interactions are between participants who align themselves as working for the same side, hence the chance for conflict is less, and they are keen to downplay any potential disagreements. This is supported by the frequent usage of inclusive (as opposed to exclusive) *we* to signal their social identities and relationships. Analysis of construction interactions involving parties from differing organisations and professions shows a far greater usage of exclusive *we*, as well as less attention to face (Handford forthcoming).

However, it should also be stated that many of the responses of the Japanese engineers were notably brief, and there was little 'small talk' or evidence of relationship-building beyond the above recurrent lexicogrammatical preferences.

Deictic items indexing place are not statistically significant in business meetings (CANBEC vs CANCODE, see Handford 2010), which suggests that place deictics do not feature strongly in such interactions. However, as mentioned above, they are frequent in the HK interactions, for instance the keywords *here* and *this*, and the clusters *this is*, *this one*, and *put it here*. Through a close analysis of their occurrence on the video recordings, we were able to see that they combined with gestures and actions to invoke certain discursive practices. For instance, in extract 2, the Japanese engineer uses several deictics while drawing to clarify the explanation. The *they* in Arai's first turn refers to the sub-contractors: it is TT's responsibility to communicate directly with the sub-contractors on behalf of the joint venture management, for instance the instructions outlined by Arai.

Extract 2

ARAI: And then and (I go to this here) they can connect + here ...
TT: Hmm
ARAI: ... with (an opposite) side ...
TT: Hmm
ARAI: ... and then and then we measure there
TT: Hmm
ARAI: and there

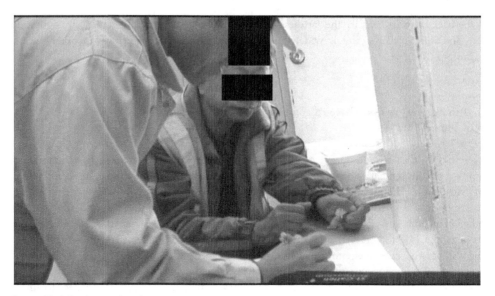

Figure 23.4 Engineer drawing

Given the noise on construction sites, the widespread use of deictics in combination with gestures is easy to explain. Furthermore, they form part of a wider network of physical semiotics we saw being used on-site. These include photos, diagrams, equations, maps and drawings.

4.4 Interpretation: Discourse patterns (e.g. problem-solving)

The next stage of the analysis looks at the interactions in terms of underlying discourse patterns. The most frequent pattern we found is that of problem-solving, which according to Sarangi and Roberts (1999) is one of the defining functions of the workplace. From the interactions, our observations and the interviews, several questions relating to the problems and differing ways of dealing with them were pinpointed:

1   What type of problem is it?
2   How big a problem is it?
3   Is it a recurrent, but unavoidable problem?
4   Is/Was the problem predicted to happen, or has it happened unexpectedly?
5   Can it be dealt with immediately, or is it more nebulous?
6   Is the problem a contractual issue?
7   Is there any chance of the problem requiring litigation?
8   Who will carry out the action of solving the problem, if anyone?
9   Who needs consulting for the problem to be dealt with?
10 Who is responsible for the problem if anyone (i.e. to blame)?
11 Who has the responsibility for dealing with the problem?

Questions 1–7 largely refer to the nature of the problem itself; questions 8–11 concern the potential parties involved, in terms of the responsibility for the problem, the management communication channels, the decision-makers and the agents who will act. Question 6 is a crucial question, as the contract plays a pivotal role in the progress of the project, with the potential for conflict (Tijhuis and Fellows 2012). Negotiating the abstruse areas of the contract requires knowledge, expertise and interpersonal skills. Furthermore, the avoidance of litigation (question 7) is a core concern of the various parties (ibid.), given the costs in terms of money, time and goodwill. The size of the contract itself can differ according to culture, with our interviewees commenting that Japanese domestic contracts tend to be much shorter than their equivalent international contracts, because of the multiple shared social practices of the domestic environment.

Nevertheless, from our observations and discussions, on-site problems tend to be far more mundane, and requiring a quick and direct response. A large part of an on-site supervising engineer or foreman's day-to-day life involves watching what is happening on the site itself, in order to react to incidents and direct when necessary. Such problems include the movement of equipment, reacting to the physical environment (e.g. the land, the weather, the position of trees, etc.), or reacting to immediate but unavoidable delays and thus ensuring the sub-contracted labourers are given work to carry on with (as they are paid per hour).

The role culture plays in workplace problem-solving has been the focus of much research, and a widely held assumption is that 'Westerners' solve problems in a linear fashion, whereas 'Asians' solve problems in a more circular way (Hofstede 1991; Lewis 2005). Handford and Matous (in preparation) examined the problem-solving interactions to see whether there was a preference for circular problem-solving among these HK and Japanese engineers. What we found was, straightforward problems tend to be solved in a linear fashion, whereas more nebulous problems are approached and returned to later, to be put aside and taken up at different times and among different participants, i.e. addressed in a more circular or cyclical fashion. This ties in with findings on English L1 workplace interactions by Boden (1994), Holmes and Stubbe (2003) and Handford (2010), in that it is the local level of the issue itself, rather than the nationality, etc. of the speakers, that most strongly influences the way the problem is addressed.

4.5 Evaluation: Achieving intervention

There are at least three main audiences for this research project. The first audience, and the easiest for us to communicate with, are the civil engineering postgraduates in our institution. The second is professional engineers in companies we have contacts with (including the company we recorded), specifically younger engineers who are required to work internationally, and the third is the wider profession. As stated above, we have been exploring the findings with our postgraduates, have written for the wider professional audience, and are developing training materials for the in-house audience. Our stance has been primarily Differentiation-Practical (Gajendran *et al.* 2012), in other words looking for examples of miscommunication, ineffective communication or other communication-related issues. However, enabling people to communicate more effectively, to develop better relationships and to query their own stereotypes, may also address a more emancipatory need.

The lectures and workshops we have conducted with our postgraduates have involved analysis of the language and discourse patterns outlined above, followed by discussion of several critical incidents. These critical incidents have been drawn from our observations, interviews with the participants and our knowledge of the field; some of the incidents are primarily relational whereas others are more transactional/professional. While the latter explore issues of, for example, interpreting the contract, the former are more 'soft'. For instance, we noticed that the Japanese engineers, who are managing the project, never eat lunch or dinner with the other members of the joint venture. Given that good relationships are of such value in CI (and yet seemingly rather difficult to achieve, according to the literature), we felt that this was perhaps a missed opportunity. We interviewed the Japanese engineers and the Hong Kong engineers and foremen about this, and the latter stated that they felt the Japanese managers could do more to develop stronger ties with their non-Japanese colleagues. The question we gave to students is:

> The Japanese engineers always eat separately from the other staff, because it means they can relax and talk Japanese to each other. Is this a problem? Why/Why not?

A sizeable majority of the (Japanese and non-Japanese) postgraduate students agreed that this was a problem, and below are a couple of typical answers.

> This is a problem because the Japanese and the other staff can't understand the way of thinking to their jobs each other.
>
> In my opinion, this is a problem. They have to interact with other staff while eating to make the working environment friendly.

Also, many Japanese employees of differing companies who have commented on this say that, while it is not good, it is rather commonplace. However, a minority of (Japanese) students did say that they felt such behaviour was acceptable and 'natural':

> It is not a problem. When we Japanese want to relax, it is natural for us to eat separately from the other staff.

While the above critical incident questions are rather brief, it is also possible to develop longer case studies. For instance, Dainty *et al.* (2006) feature several case studies that aim to develop problem-solving skills for project managers, and Tijhuis and Fellows (2012) explore culture in CI through case studies.

In order to reach the wider professional audience, an article for the *Japan Society of Civil Engineers*, a professional journal for practising engineers and decision-makers was published (Handford 2012). The article touched on some of the research we have conducted, and argued that companies need to move beyond equating communication training with TEFL-type classes, and to focus on issues like cultural awareness-raising, effective intercultural communication and relationship-building, as well as the ability to negotiate typical workplace genres. In this article, ongoing research into 'communication training' in Japanese construction companies is outlined by Dr Akiko Otsu, who has found that such training can follow a rigid TEFL approach focusing on strict error correction, with little or no reference to the communicative needs of the employees.

A next step is to present our findings to some of the CI company heads, and to carry out workshops in companies.[7] In terms of what can be covered in in-house training, Box 23.4 is a list of topics:

Box 23.4: Topics for in-house training

Language
- Key words in the profession
- Jargon of each profession
  (architects vs civil engineers)

- Gestures

Genres
- Emails
- Short reports
- (Interpreting) Contracts
- Meetings
- Negotiations
- On-site checks.

Problem-solving
- Case studies, exploring different aspects of the process (see questions 1–11 above)
- Linear vs circular approaches, when and by whom

Culture
- Cultural awareness – not trusting to stereotypes
- Exploring what cultural differences exist
- Seeing through another's eyes
- Dealing with cultural differences
- Leveraging culture

Relationships
- Different goals
- Building relationships
- Managing relationships

Conflict
- Understanding conflict's causes
- Recognising conflict
- Predicting conflict
- Dealing with conflict

Working in teams
- Team building stages
- Developing trust
- The benefits of difference

5 Conclusion

This chapter has provided a brief summary of the types of research that are being conducted into CC, as well as the relatively nascent studies into CC from a discourse perspective. It is argued here that CI presents both possibilities and challenges for the discourse analyst: possibilities because so little research has been carried out into actual communication in the context of one of the largest industries in the world and one that could arguably benefit from expert insights; challenges because the industry itself is inherently contentious, at times adversarial, and may be involved in practices that may lead to the ethical dilemmas alluded to by Scollon et al. (2012). However, because of the communicative (and indeed social) issues in the industry, it provides a rich context for researchers seeking to answer Candlin's call to achieve socially responsible intervention, thus answering the 'So what?' question of why we do research and how it can be truly 'applied research'.

The potential for assisting in cultural understanding and removing misunderstanding (what Gajendran et al. (2012) refer to as the Differentiation-Practical approach) in such a complex and at times conflictual sector as the CI is considerable. One of the crucial factors, as indeed is the case in any type of professional discourse analysis, is obtaining the trust of the participants, but once this has been gained then interviews, discussions and recordings of interactions should provide rich material. The list of topics for in-house training (Table 23.4) could also serve as a rough agenda for research into the field. For instance, areas like understanding the importance and issues around specialised language and how it is used across different professions, raising awareness of our tendency to negatively stereotype and developing techniques to combat this, and recognising the importance of solid relationships which can help employees overcome conflict are all key areas.

For researchers wishing to explore CC from a more emancipatory stance, there are several disturbing social issues that feature a discursive element. For instance, homelessness of unskilled labourers is very high in some countries: around 60 per cent of homeless men in Japan were previously labourers (Hasegawa 2005), and there are many reports of such individuals being unable to access benefits and negotiate rights to which they are legally entitled (ibid.). Gender issues in CI are mentioned above, and the difficulties of women in the industry seem transnational. In the US for instance, verbal and physical sexual harassment, power harassment and other forms of discrimination are seemingly endemic, with the US CI reporting the second highest levels of sexual harassment among all industries (USDL 1999).

According to Emmitt and Gorse, 'construction communication research is in its infancy' (2003: 18). If we tighten the definition to cover discourse-based research, that is, research of actual interactions in workplaces, we might even term it embryonic. As such, it is provides a vista of opportunities for discourse analysts, especially those wanting to conduct interdisciplinary research.

Related topics

communication in the construction industry; achieving practical relevance; culture in construction; mixed methods approach; professional discourse analysis

Key readings

Dainty, A., Moore, D. and Murray, M. (2006). *Communication in Construction: Theory and Practice*, London: Taylor and Francis. (This gives an overview of the key areas and concerns in construction communication, with an emphasis on professionals in the field.)

Emmitt, S. and Gorse, C. (2003). *Construction Communication*, Oxford: Blackwell. (This also gives an overview of the field, and is less focused on project managers.)

Handford, M. and Matous, P. (2011). 'Lexicogrammar in the international construction industry: A corpus-based case study of Japanese-Hong-Kongese on-site interactions in English', *English for Specific Purposes, 30*(2), 87–100. (The methodology discussed here is applied in this prize-winning article.)

Handford, M. (forthcoming). 'Context in spoken professional discourse: Language and practice in an international bridge design meeting', in J. Flowerdew, (ed.), *Discourse in Context*. London: Continuum. (This chapter explores the role of context in construction communication.)

Tijhuis, W. and Fellows, R. (2012) *Culture in International Construction*, London: Spon Press. (As with readings 1 and 2, this is not written for discourse analysts, but it provides interesting analyses of the role of culture in the industry.)

Notes

1 The recording was conducted as a part of the Corpus of International Professional Discourse (CIPED) project (JSPS, Project no.: 22520390, April 2010–April 2012 Director: Michael Handford, University of Tokyo).[date?listed?]
2 Emmitt and Gorse (2003) also have a chapter on social network theory, an approach that Matous and I combine with discourse analysis to gain a more systematic understanding of the key relationships on-site.
3 Another key factor is the intimate relationship between politicians, bureaucrats and private companies involved in the Japanese CI (UITBB 2012), which again reduces the likelihood of inter-group conflict.
4 This is because I am assuming many researchers of communication share Scollon et al.'s view that part of our job is to 'attempt to make people's lives better in any way we can' (2012: 204), and that helping executives to control employees may be politically incompatible with such a stance.
5 In fact, Japanese construction companies obtain much of their overseas work through overseas development aid projects, which are funded by the Japanese government (Lancaster 2010).
6 Ironically, his views reinforced our opinion that training on the dangers of stereotyping others was needed, and that the causes of communication problems are often deeper than the linguistic level. This was further reinforced by some of the views expressed during interviews we conducted with the Japanese and HK Chinese staff in Hong Kong.
7 In 2012 I was awarded a grant from the Kajima Foundation to develop such a training booklet for its international engineers.

Transcription conventions

[laughs]	Paralinguistic features in square brackets
…	Pause of up to one second
(3)	Pause of specified number of seconds
(hello)	Transcriber's best guess at an unclear utterance
-	Incomplete or cut-off utterance

References

Alvesson, M. (2002). *Understanding Organisational Culture*, London: Sage.
Baxter, J. and Wallace, K. (2009). 'Outside in-group and out-group identities? Constructing male solidarity and female exclusion in UK builders' talk', *Discourse in Society*, 20, 411–31.
Bhatia, V. K. (2004). *Worlds of Written Discourse*, London: Continuum.
——(2008). 'Towards critical genre analysis', in V. K. Bhatia, J. Flowerdew and R. Jones (eds), *Advances in Discourse Studies* (pp. 166–77), Abingdon: Routledge.
Boden, D. (1994). *The Business of Talk: Organizations in Action*, Cambridge: Polity Press.
Candlin, C. (2002). 'Introduction', in C. Candlin (ed.), *Research and Practice in Professional Discourse* (pp. 1–22), Hong Kong: City University of Hong Kong Press.
——(2006). 'Accounting for interdiscursivity: Challenges to professional expertise', in M. Gotti and D. Giannone (eds), *New Trends in Specialized Discourse Analysis* (pp. 21–45), Bern: Peter Lang Verlag.
Charles, M. (1996). 'Business negotiations: Interdependence between discourse and the business relationship', *English for Specific Purposes*, 15, 19–36.
Cheng, W. and Mok, E. (2008). 'Discourse processes and products: Land surveyors in Hong Kong', *English for Specific Purposes*, 27, 57–73.
Dadji, M. (1988). 'Are you talking to M&E?' *RIBA Journal* (Switch Supplement), October, 102–3.
Dainty, A., Moore, D. and Murray, M. (2006). *Communication in Construction: Theory and Practice*, London: Taylor and Francis.
Emmerson, H. (1962). *Survey of Problems before the Construction Industry: A Report Prepared for the Ministry of Works*, HMSO: London
Emmitt, S. and Gorse, C. (2003). *Construction Communication*, Oxford: Blackwell.
Flowerdew, L. (2012). *Corpora and Language Education*, London: Palgrave Macmillan.
Gajendran, T., Brewer, G., Dainty, A. and Runeson, G. (2012). 'A conceptual approach to studying the organisational culture of construction projects', *Australasian Journal of Construction Economics and Building*, 12(2), 1–26.

Gee, J. P. (1992). *The Social Mind: Language, Ideology and Practice*, New York: Bergin & Garvey.
——(2005). *An Introduction to Discourse Analysis: Theory and Method*, Abingdon: Routledge.
Gee, J. P., Hull, G. and Lankshear, C. (1996). *The New Work Order: Behind the Language of New Capitalism*, Boulder: Westview.
Gluch, P. and Raisanen, C. (2009). 'Interactional perspective on environmental communication in construction projects', *Building Research and Information*, 37(2), 164–75.
Gumperz, J. (1982). *Discourse Strategies*, Cambridge: Cambridge University Press.
Handford, M. (2010). *The Language of Business Meetings*, Cambridge: Cambridge University Press.
——(2012). 'Construction communication training: Aims and issues', *Journal of Japan Society of Civil Engineers* 67(11), 73–6.
——(forthcoming). 'Context in spoken professional discourse: Language and practice in an international bridge design meeting', in J. Flowerdew (ed.), *Discourse(s) in Context(s)*, London: Continuum.
Handford, M. and Matous, P. (2011). 'Lexicogrammar in the international construction industry: A corpus-based case study of Japanese-Hong-Kongese on-site interactions in English', *English for Specific Purposes*, 30(2), 87–100.
——(in preparation). 'Problem-solving discourse on an international construction site: Patterns and practices'.
Hasegawa, M. (2005). 'Economic globalization and homelessness in Japan', *American Behavioral Scientist*, 48, 989–1012.
Higgin, G. and Jessop, N. (1965). *Communications in the Building Industry: The Report of a Pilot Study*, Tavistock: London.
Hofstede, G. (1991). *Cultures and Organizations: Software of the Mind*, London: McGraw-Hill.
Holmes, J. and Stubbe, M. (2003). *Power and Politeness in the Workplace. A Sociolinguistic Analysis of Talk at Work*, Edinburgh: Pearson.
Koester, A. (2006). *Investigating Workplace Discourse*, London: Routledge.
Lancaster, C. (2010). 'Japan's ODA: naiatsu and gaiatsu, domestic sources and transnational influences', in D. Leheny and K. Warren (eds), *Japanese Aid and the Construction of Global Development: Inescapable Solutions* (pp. 29–53), London: Routledge.
Lewis, R. (2005). *When Cultures Collide: Leading Across Cultures*, Yarmouth, ME: Nicholas Brealey Publishing.
Loosemore, M. (2007). 'Managing public perceptions of risk on construction projects – how to involve stakeholders in business directions', in *Proceedings of CRIOCM 2007 International Research Symposium on Advancement of Construction Management and Real Estate*, UNSW, Sydney, pp. 15–24.
Loosemore, M. and Al Muslmani, H. S. (1999). 'Construction project management in the Persian Gulf: Inter-cultural communication', *International Journal of Project Management*, 17, 95–100.
Loosemore, M. and Galea, N. (2008). 'Genderlect and conflict in the Australian construction industry', *Construction Management and Economics*, 26, 125–35.
Loosemore, M. and Waters, T. (2004). 'Gender differences in occupational stress among professionals in the construction industry', *Journal of Management in Engineering*, 20(3), 126–31.
Martin, J. (2002). *Organisational Culture: Mapping the Terrain*, Sage: Newbury Park.
——(2004). 'Organisational culture', *Research Paper Series, Stanford*, Research Paper No. 1847.
Medway, P. (1996). 'Virtual and material buildings: Construction and constructivism in architecture and writing', *Written Communication*, 13, 473–514.
Ministry of Land Infrastructure, Transport and Tourism (2010). *Kokusai tenkai kanmin renkei bun'ya* (Report of the division for international expansion and public private linkages). Available at www.mlit.go.jp/common/000115371.pdf. (accessed 11 November 2012).
Ochs, E. (1996). 'Linguistic resources for socializing humanity', in J. Gumperz, (ed.), *Rethinking Linguistic Relativity* (pp. 407–37), Cambridge: Cambridge University Press.
PricewaterhouseCoopers (2010). *Engineering and Construction Report*. Available at www.pwc.com/gx/en/engineering-construction (accessed October 2011).
Roberts, C. and Campbell, S. (2005). 'Fitting stories into boxes: Rhetorical and contextual constraints on candidates' performances in British job interviews', *Journal of Applied Linguistics*, 2(1), 45–73.
Sarangi, S. and Roberts, C. (1999). 'The dynamics of interactional and institutional orders in work-related settings', in S. Sarangi and C. Roberts (eds), *Talk, Work and Institutional Order* (pp. 2–57), Berlin: Mouton de Gruyter.
Scollon, R., Scollon Wong, S. and Jones, R. (2012). *Intercultural Communication: A Discourse Approach*, Oxford: Wiley Blackwell.
Scott, M. (1999). *Wordsmith Tools Version 3*, Oxford: Oxford University Press.

Teo, M. and Loosemore, M. (2010). 'Community-based protest against construction projects: The social determinants of protest movement continuity', *International Journal of Project Management in Business*, 3(2), 216–36.

Tijhuis, W. and Fellows, R. (2012). *Culture in International Construction*, London: Spon Press.

Trajkovski, S. and Loosemore, M. (2006). 'Safety implications of low-English proficiency among migrant construction site operatives', *International Journal of Project Management*, 24(5), 446–52.

UITBB (2012). 'Current state of Japanese construction industry', *Trades Union International of Workers in the Building, Building Materials and Allied Industries*. Available at www.uitbb.org/index.php?option=com_content&task=view&id=85&Itemid=30 (accessed 7 November 2012).

USDL (1999). 'Women in the construction workplace: Providing equitable safety and health protection', *United States Department of Labour*. Available at www.osha.gov/doc/accsh/haswicformal.html (accessed 9 November 2012).

Van Dijk, T. (1991). *Racism and the Press*, London: Routledge.

Woodall, B. (1996). *Japan Under Construction: Corruption, Politics and Public Works*, Berkeley: University of California Press.

Yamada, H. (1997). *Different Games Different Rules: Why Americans and Japanese Misunderstand Each Other*, Oxford University Press: Oxford.

24
Offshore outsourcing
The need for appliable linguistics

Gail Forey

Introduction

The market for the global Information Technology – Business Process Outsourcing (BPO) industry is predicted to triple in size from USD 500 billion to USD 1.5–1.6 trillion by 2020 (NASSCOM 2009a). Such explosive growth has huge economic benefits for Asia, and in particular for India and the Philippines. Both India and the Philippines are leading global Offshore Outsourcing (O&O) destinations for the BPO industry. Within the industry both countries' success and economic development is directly related to English and the potential of employment in English-based back office work, call centres and other professional services. In order to maintain and expand further, improvement in English language proficiency is crucial for this industry. Trade groups and chambers of commerce in both destinations explicitly support, promote and encourage English language development through educational, economic and social initiatives. The BPO trade organisation in the Philippines, the Business Processing Association of the Philippines (BPAP), is motivated to develop the industry. A recent report by the Oxford Business Group (OBG 2012: 120) states that the 'Philippine BPO employed some 640,000 workers and generated some $10.9bn in 2011, displaying over 22% growth over 2010'. Both India and the Philippines are actively encouraging, through multiple routes, the promotion and cultivation of the earning potential of the industry. This encouragement is manifested in a number of ways, for example in India, NASSCOM (the BPO trade group) are currently undertaking a drive to increase the number of women in the BPO workforce by a staggering 50 per cent (NASSCOM 2009b; Forey forthcoming). The implications of such a huge push will have tremendous social impact, and yet this and other initiatives are rarely the focus of research. In general the explosive growth of the industry and the associated educational, economic and social initiatives underpinning change are moving at a pace far faster than academic research.

In the Philippines, the BPO industry is expanding and evolving; this expansion involves moving from voice back office work (call centres) to knowledge processing outsourcing (KPO), and investing heavily in infrastructure and education (OBG 2012). However, on the road to expansion, there are multiple initiatives and institutional challenges which the industry faces, including political, economic and educational ones. It could also be argued that there is a need to challenge what is meant by 'language' in the world of work and in educational circles. The OGB

(2012: 122) report states that both India and the Philippines need to confront the challenges of 'corruption, an inefficient labour market, and low quality primary education'. In response to the need for improved education there has been a major policy shift in the Philippines, resulting in the introduction of a K-12 education policy, which will have an enormous impact on the country. School attendance has been extended by two years and the deadline for implementation is 2016 (OBG 2012). A major factor influencing this change has been the need for greater English proficiency in order to support further development of the economy. A deep-rooted belief is that educational development will lead to economic and employment advancements for a country (UNPD 2010). An area which is of principal concern and directly related to the future of the BPO in the Philippines is English, and a focus on fostering English proficiency is seen as paramount. Tayag, Country Manager for Accenture (a leading BPO), has been quoted as saying 'proficiency in English is one of the country's major competitive advantages, [and] it is vital that the government develops a comprehensive education system that develops English language skills from an early age' (OBG 2012: 124).

There are a number of mismatches between the industry and academe's perception of what is meant when talking about 'language'. This perennial problem has led to a consistent disjunct between education concerns and industry needs. As Selingo (2012) points out, 'right now, employers see themselves as detached consumers of what colleges produce, and academics are sometimes hostile to the notion that they are simply training students for jobs'. The distinction seems to be that as pointed out by Bremner (2010), Eraut (2009), Forey (2004) and Lockwood (2012a, b), namely that there is a knowledge gap between the academic knowledge gained within academia and the tacit knowledge needed within the workplace. In addition to the type of knowledge needed, there are also difficulties in the concept of language. During our involvement in the BPO industry, carrying out research for over eight years and after visiting, interviewing and conducting research in 15–20 different BPO sites, we have found inconsistencies in the conception of how language is perceived within the BPO industry compared to academe (see Forey forthcoming; Hood and Forey 2008; Forey and Lockwood 2007, 2010; Lockwood 2012a, b). Within the industry, and even within research from the field of business, language is seen as 'grammar' and 'accent', i.e. discrete grammar items as identified in written or 'correct' grammar, and the need to have a neutral accent when speaking. However, the language we are referring to in call centres is spoken, dialogic language where the lexis and grammar function to make meaning very differently from written language. As researchers collaborating in the workplace, we need to find a model of language that enables a meta-discourse (a language to talk about language) relating to how language functions in particular texts such as service encounters. In this chapter we focus on the BPO industry, and through the framework of Systemic Functional Linguistics (SFL), outline differences between written and spoken discourse, with the aim of building a bridge between what we know within applied linguistics and how language is understood in the workplace. The view that written and spoken language uses the same grammar needs to be addressed within the industry. For example, if the industry wants to hire and train a Customer Service Representative (CSR) to deal effectively with customer service enquiries, it may be futile to test and train them through models of written language.

The differences between spoken and written language demonstrate what we know as applied linguists through evidence-based research and through how language is perceived within the industry. There are a number of other 'gaps' or disparities between how language is perceived in the industry and academe. Initial studies focusing on language and call centres were undertaken in onshore destinations: for example Cameron (2001a, b) and Adolphs et al. (2004) present studies based on data from the UK. Research in O&O destinations, where the language needs of the industry are very different, and where English is not the first language of those working in the BPO, have only recently been undertaken. These studies tend to focus on features of language such as accent (Cowie 2007; Cowie and Murty 2010; Friginal 2007), assessment (Davies 2010; Hamp-Lyons and Lockwood 2009; Lockwood *et al.* 2009; Lockwood 2012a,b) or discourse analysis (Forey and Lam forthcoming; Forey and Lockwood 2007, 2010; Hood and Forey 2008; Lockwood *et al.* 2009; Xu *et al.* 2011). Studies on specific language choices and with particular reference to grammar in the service encounters tend to be extremely limited. Forey and Lam (forthcoming) focus on the distinction between declarative, imperative and interrogative choices in calls assessed as being effective along industry standards. Hood and Forey (2008) discuss the discourse semantic flow of emotional language in customer service encounters where complaints and conflict are realised. The findings from these studies are revealing and demonstrate a disparity between authentic language in the BPO industry and the linguistic demands, the training and the curriculum found in authentic call centre interaction. However, these studies have viewed language as the site of research and although they infer the difference of the industry's perceptions of language, they do not address the need for a model of language that is functional and that allows the researcher to talk about language in a coherent and informed manner that is convincing to the industry.

At the other end of the scale, reflecting current research in the field of business, the BPO industry generally views language as different from 'communication'. Within the industry, language tends to be viewed as either grammar rules or accent, whereas communication is often framed in an abstract manner such as soft skills. Communication is classified as a 'high end soft skill' (Bain *et al.* 2002; Bolton and Houlihan 2005; Gilmore 2001; Porter and Tanner 2004; Taylor and Bain 2005), or sometimes it is referred to as 'emotional labour' (Deery *et al.* 2002); within such studies, communication is seen in vague and mainly commonsense, nebulous terms. There needs to be a middle ground where applied linguists make meaning and demonstrate, based on evidence, the value of understanding how language functions in particular contexts.

In this chapter I wish to consider ways in which an applied linguist can take a role in intervening in this problematic area and based on evidence, demonstrate the value of applied linguistics in modelling and supporting the language (and communication) needs of service encounters. I begin with a discussion for the need of 'appliable linguistics', that is, a view of language as a meaning-making system of choice that varies in relation to shifts in the context. As pointed out by Halliday and Hasan (1985: 7) 'the value of a theory lies in the use that can be made of it'. With this in mind, I outline some of the ways we are working with the BPO industry to investigate language and feed back our findings to the industry, in order to advance knowledge, support training and recruitment, and practice about language. Through an analysis of the transcriptions of authentic telephone service encounters, I take the seemingly small issue of 'discourse marker' and 'feedback tokens' and review the meanings made. The aim of the study described here is to demonstrate the potential of appliable linguistics and how it can inform practice, and hopefully persuade the industry to revisit its notion of language and communication.

Language and register in the workplace

As noted, for many in the workplace and education, language refers to what many believe to be 'rules' that govern the composition of sentences, phrases and words in a given natural language. Traditional approaches to language subsume all aspects of sentence patterning, including phonology, syntax and semantics. In approaches to language such as traditional or generative grammar, the focus is on the structure and the form of the sentence as the unit of analysis, and the sentence is taken as the unit for understanding how language works (Chomsky 1975; Leitner 1991; Williams 2005).

In contrast, language can also be viewed very differently as a system of 'choices' and not 'rules' (Halliday and Matthiessen 2004). This is the approach taken within Systemic Functional Linguistics (SFL), a theoretical framework, developed by Michael Halliday in the 1960s. The term 'systemic' refers to the view of language as 'a network of systems, or interrelated sets of options for making meaning' (Halliday 1994:15) and the term 'functional' indicates that the approach is concerned with the contextualised, practical uses to which language is put. SFL is concerned primarily with the choices the language makes available to speakers and writers.

In the present chapter I outline the language choices made that reflect workplace discourse. I establish that language within workplace settings reflects the goal or purpose of the utterance or written word and depending on what the topic is (Field), or who is involved (Tenor), and the channel of communication whether written, spoken, face to face, one-to-one or one to multiparty (Mode), the choices we make within the clause will vary. The framework of Field, Tenor and Mode helps the analyst to identify why different choices are made in different texts. Following Martin and Rose (2008) among others, these are explained in more detail below:

Field: the 'what', what is being talked about? What is the aim of the text?
Tenor: the 'who', who is doing the talking or writing? The relationship between the speaker or writer and the listener or reader.
Mode: the 'how', how is the text represented? The kind of text that has been made – spoken, written?

Field, Tenor and Mode are the variables of register (or the context of situation) as they reflect the main functions of language (Halliday et al. 1964; Halliday 1994; Martin 1997; Martin and Rose 2008). The relationship between register and language is seen to be 'connotative' in that they are both semiotic systems that make use of each other, but which are not the same, and which function within their own plane. Register is 'designed to interface the analysis of social context naturally with the metafunctionally diversified organization of language resources' (Martin 1997: 6). The register variables, Field, Tenor and Mode, influence the grammar. The functional diversification of language choice within clause level grammar is modelled through three metafunctions: ideational, interpersonal and textual. Ideational resources encode our experiences of the world, interpersonal resources encode interaction, and textual resources are concerned with how language is used to organise our experiential and interactional meaning into a coherent whole (Halliday 1994: 35). Through adopting an SFL approach to understanding language, I outline the choices and the influence that particular institutional settings have on the output, i.e. the discourse found within a workplace.

In the call centre interaction we have a speaker and a listener co-constructing a text where the customer requests services or information and a customer service representative (CSR) provides service or information. If we take language as reflecting the institution, we can also say that the workplace, or the text being constructed within the workplace, influences the choices in the language. We are able to, as Martin (2009) points out, shunt back and forth between what may seem to be extremely small choices in the language such as choices of the phoneme, the word, the grammatical form, rise or falling tone, or within the clause, the realisations of meaningful units such as the nominal, verbal group and discourse markers; and how such features of spoken language relate to the text. By relating these choices to the text we can better understand the prosodic features of the text, for example the generic structure (Martin and Rose 2008) and the discourse semantic choices such as evaluative/persuasive choices (Hood and Forey 2008; Martin and White 2005). In this chapter the findings demonstrate how the language varies if we move from written to spoken (Mode), or if the Tenor changes e.g.

empathising with a friend compared to a customer, or if the Field changes e.g. presenting real estate compared to a customer service call related to insurance. In all cases when the register variables change, the language choices change.

Methodology

In this section, I outline the data and approach that is used to reflect specific choices found in the telephone service encounters. The data comes from large multinational organisations where the customer is based in the US and the CSR is in the Philippines (Forey and Lockwood 2007, 2010). The data is drawn from the transcription of over 120 authentic calls from different industries such as banking, insurance, travel and tourism, product support and other commercial ventures. The transcriptions have been anonymised and any sensitive data such as names, numbers, dates, etc., have been changed.

The data represents inbound telephone service encounters (where the customer calls the service centre), in which the relationship between the CSR and customer is different from outbound calls (where the CSR calls the customer as a follow up, or to collect outstanding bills or for sales purposes). Variation in Field, Tenor and Mode within an institutional or other setting will affect language choices. For example, if the Field is concerned with an inbound customer service encounter related to a personal banking issue over the telephone, the language choices would be very different from an outbound collection call within a bank. Both texts would have some similarities in that they are both a spoken telephone call centre interaction, involving spoken grammar, and that the customer service representative (CSR) and customer take turns in co-constructing the text. However, when we change from an inbound to an outbound, or from one industry to another, discourse and lexico-grammatical differences may be found, such as who uses interrogatives, the type of mood structure, the role of modality in the call, the choices of discourse markers, the dispreferred responses, etc.

In general, customer service encounters are pragmatically focused, i.e. they have a clear goal in mind, void of any body language or gesture, and often the relationship is between a CSR who provides their name (often a pseudonym) and the customer who identifies themselves by name, an identification reference and perhaps other security checks. The speakers' relationship is institutionalised as a CSR and a customer. Institutional registerial variation is bound to be present when members of different institutions come from different social and racial backgrounds and write/speak in different contexts. Thus we do not expect speakers from a multinational banking company to have the same institutional choices as speakers working in IT, tourism, electronic goods, health care, income tax, etc. For example, within the BPO industry a customer service representative working for a large multinational banking organisation will make very different language choices within a text when compared to an IT professional working for Microsoft offering support to IT specialists around the world. Thus we take it that language and social context realise and influence meaning within each other's domain. Social context construes the meanings made in language, and choices made in the language we use influence how we interpret and understand social patterns.

Spoken language: Discourse markers in authentic data, recruitment and training

As established by Heritage (1984) (see also Biber and Conrad 2009; Carter and McCarthy 2006; Coffin *et al.* 2009; Conrad and Biber 2009; Halliday 2001), the difference between spoken and written language is phenomenal. According to Halliday (2001), spoken language tends to be more varied in mood structure, more focused around the verbal group, and incorporative of a great deal of ellipsis (missing words), short forms such as *don't* or *I'll,* grammatically intricate clauses where the clause relationship is far looser than written language (Carter and McCarthy 2006), adjustment markers such as *just, already, once* (Hood and Forey 2008), and discourse markers such as *ok, alright, uhuh,* etc. (Muller 2005). In this chapter I show how discourse markers are common features in the spoken data, and yet tend to be overlooked or nonexistent in some recruitment and training material.

Spoken interaction gives rise to particular meanings and particular choices in the language, and has a wide variety of 'grammatical options' to choose from to signal intimacy, distance, organise and sequence the message, and to signal evaluation and attitude (Carter and McCarthy 2006). One common feature found in the call centre data, and a feature that is key to the development of the telephonic exchange, is what is termed in the industry as 'verbal nods' or more commonly known in applied linguistics as 'discourse markers' (Muller 2005). Carter and McCarthy (2006: 209) suggest that discourse markers are lexical rather than grammatical, whereas others view discourse markers as grammatical or a combination of lexical and grammatical (Ingels 2005; Frank-Job 2006). Frank-Job (2006: 396) points out that discourse markers are polysemic in two ways: 'a polysemy resulting from a diachronic process in which additional metacommunicative meanings appear. Second, we are dealing with a polysemy that consists of several pragmatic meanings working simultaneously on different levels of discourse processing.' Discourse markers are polysemic and multifunctional; whether they change in meaning over time or within a particular context, they are a key resource chosen to 'structure and organize speech in interpersonal, referential, structural, and cognitive categories' (Fung and Carter 2007: 435). They help to develop a relationship between speakers, to reference other meanings, to link ideas and express emotion. They are common and extremely important features of telephone service encounters interaction which lubricate the unfolding of the discourse and are often found in the language choices of both the CSR and customer. Unfortunately, one of the disparities I outlined in the introduction is that such language resources are ignored in textbooks or training manuals and material (Fung and Carter 2007; Forey and Lockwood 2010; Lam 2009). In what follows, I show how discourse markers are frequently occurring features in the authentic transcripts but overlooked in the recruitment and training process of the BPO industry, and further afield, which are neglected in the education system that aims to prepare students for English language use beyond educational contexts.

Discourse markers may come in the form of single words, two-word phrases, fixed phrases or semi-fixed phrases (Lam 2010). For example, in the call centre data we find single words such as *OK, right, oh, so, well, uhuh*; two-word phrases e.g. *you know*; fixed phrases such as *let's see, I think, that is to say*; and semi-fixed phrases e.g. *bear with me* (see Fung and Carter 2007; Lam 2010; Muller 2005). As pointed out by Leech and Svartvik (2002), their presence is fundamental to conversational cooperation, and in telephone conversations such acknowledgements and discourse features are key to reassuring both parties that the other person is listening and still there.

In spoken interaction the speaker tends to use discourse markers such as *uhuh, yea, right, OK, oh* to signal a variety of responses, for example as continuers e.g. *um hm, ah, uhuh,* often representing an active listener, where the listener is signalling *I'm still here,* and providing minimal feedback while not interrupting the flow of the current speaker's utterance (Bolden 2006; Castro 2009, Fischer 2006; Lam 2009); or as newsmarkers, e.g. *really* could propose that the listener has undergone some kind of change in his or her locally current state of knowledge, information, orientation or awareness (Heritage 1984). There are also markers of dispreferred responses, e.g. *well,* which reflect a lack of interest, indifference and impatience (Lam 2009);

Table 24.1 Summary of discourse marker functions

Textual functions	Opening frame marker	So; ok; now
	Closing frame marker	Ok; right; well
	Turn takers/(Turn givers)	Ok; yeah; and; err; well
	Fillers/Turn keeper	Um; err; and
	Topic switchers	Ok; well; now
	New/old information indicators	And; because; so
	Sequence/relevance markers	So; and; and then; because
	Repair marker	Well; I mean; you know; like
Interpersonal functions	Back channel signals	Mhm; uh huh; yea
	Cooperation, agreement marker	Ok; yes; yeah; mhm
	Disagreement marker	But; no
	Response/reaction markers	Yeah; oh; ah; but; oh yeah; well; eh; oh really?
	Checking and understanding markers	Right? OK?
	Confirmation markers	Ah; I know; yeah; mhm; yes

Source: (Castro 2009: 61)

or perhaps *well* might be chosen to show a lack of understanding (Brunner 1973; Stenstrom 1994). Castro (2009) provides a useful summary of discourse markers, drawing a similar distinction to Frank-Job (2006): that of grammatical (textual function) and lexical (interpersonal function).

Within the call centre data it is possible to find a wide variety of discourse markers, and each discourse marker may have multiple meanings. In order to understand the meaning, the co-text and the context need to be taken into consideration, as meanings are not fixed but function in relation to co-text and are influenced by the Field, Tenor and Mode. As pointed out by Fung and Carter (2007), discourse markers are not a single grammatical class, but have varied meaning potential and draw from various grammatical groups.

(1)

```
101   CSR34:   You'll get that soon. … err did you receive your annual statement?
102   C34:     Not yet.
103   CSR34:   Uhuh Just give me a few more days. You should be getting that, maam.
104   C34:     OK, alright … thank you. You've been very helpful.
105   CSR34:                                              =OK, you're welcome, maam.
                                                         You have a good day.
```

In Example 1, this extract comes at the end of a very long call, where the CSR has performed his job in a positive manner and developed a good rapport with his customer. The discourse markers have a positive tone and add to the development of the solidarity between the interlocutors. Most discourse markers are in an initial position, as seen here with *uhuh* and *ok*, and function to signal backchannel signals and confirmation markers. The CSR in Turn 101 responds to the customer and then after a short pause retains the floor through the choice of *err*, a discourse marker used to keep the turn. Attending to the voice quality and the rise and fall of the discourse markers and other semiotic resources such as voice quality or breathiness are also important considerations, as shown in Example 2.

(2)

23	C:	And how long will this be?
24	CSR:	OK our call back normally takes a week.
25	C:	A week?
26	CSR:	*uh huh*
27	C:	*Well*, why does the underwriter tell me … this was the big dilemma? They told me it would probably take 24 hours and this was back on November 18th.

In Example 2, the discourse markers of *OK, uhuh* and *well* are all in initial position, indicating various meanings. Here *OK* signals confirmation of the amount of time it will take for the call back. On the other hand *uhuh* signals agreement, whereas *well,* Turn 27, is marking an evaluative response of negative attitude from the caller, who is highly dissatisfied with the amount of time it has taken to get a call back from the call centre. The discourse marker *Well* here probably would have involved a wider range of resources, perhaps breathiness, a falling tone and lengthening of the word, all such voice quality features combining to express interpersonal meaning in this one discourse marker (see Wan 2010 for a discussion of voice quality in call centre communication).

In Example 3 below, the discourse markers are generally in an initial position as seen with *so, right, OK, err* and *yeah*. The position and semantic potential of these discourse markers have been discussed and the function is generally to indicate that the speaker will carry on speaking, or for the listener to affirm and respond that they understand the information given (Gardner 1999). Other discourse markers in an initial position such as *so* and *well* function as units as a form of consequence linking previous ideas to those that follow e.g. as cause and effect or evidence and conclusion (Martin and Rose 2008: 119). In Example 3, Turn 26, the customer again chooses *well* to indicate his disagreement with the process of notification of loans and follows the *well* with *err* as a turn keeper to ensure the customer has the opportunity to question the billing procedures. Again in the following two turns, Turn 27 and 28, both the CSR and the customer use *well* to initiate and take the turn. In all instances in these three turns, *well* is followed by turn keepers, *err, yea*. It could be suggested that simply modelling the use of discourse markers such as *well* and *so*, reaction markers and other discourse markers would really support trainee CSRs and would help the fluency during the interaction.

(3)

24	C39:	*So* they will never notify me if there is another loan against it until they start charging interest on it.
25	CSR39:	*Right*, the interest is just being billed once a year during your anniversary date, they just send it out once a year for that matter.
26	C39:	*OK well* … it doesn't really make sense either … because they're saying from May–September it was $6.00 worth of interest charged against it and then from September to September another $6.00 worth against it, so it doesn't make any difference … *I mean* how do they figure the interest on it? It's like you get $6.36 for 4 months then $6.79 for a whole year.
27	CSR39:	*Err … Well … yeah …* that's the amount of … interest … erm that's incurred during … during the year for that year … but how may I help you regards to this, Sir?

28	C39:	*Well, err.* It's just that is I just think it's confusing myself … I think there should just be a bit more accounting if they're going to do that. But exactly how much do I owe on that policy now?
	CSR39:	*Err* right now I'm seeing $63.94 that's the pay off amount $63.94
	C39:	OK and that's good for how long?
29	CSR39:	*Err* up to date – it's $63.94, so you can send in that payment if you want to pay out that loan.
30	C39:	OK, and there'll be no other interest or anything charged against it, right?
31	CSR39:	Yeah, right.
32	C39:=	*Ok, alright* that's what I'll do-I'll get it out, but I *erm, you know*, think the billing policy screwed up a bit, if they're going to charge, if they're going to make an automatic loan they should at least notify you that it was done =
33	CSR39:	= *mm, hm* =
34	C39:	= but I guess that … =
35	CSR39:	= Automatic, yes, Sir. =
36	C39:	It's not your fault, but it sure pisses me off {laughs}

Also, depending on voice quality, these discourse markers may also function to express sarcasm. In this instance in Turn 31 above, the representative states *yeah right* as a confirmation marker. In other authentic material transcribed we have heard from the customer *yeah* with a falling tone and then followed by *right* with a rising tone to express disbelief. This caveat acts as a reminder that discourse markers and other lexicogrammatical features construct meaning in context, and that items or phrases may be multifunctional/polysemic with the potential to construe different meanings in different contexts (Frank-Job 2006).

The discourse markers identified in the call centre interactions analysed are, at the same time, construing solidarity between the interactants. Martin and White (2005) outline a system for creating solidarity, which is referred to as 'engagement'. This notion of solidarity, an element within 'engagement', is key to the call centre industry. Within the industry time and energy is invested in developing 'empathy' between the customer and the CSR. Empathy, a key soft skill (see www.callcentrehelper.com or other resources on soft skills, culture and training), is a crucial skill the industry looks for when hiring, and it is also an area that is emphasised during training. However, concepts of empathy within the training resources and also in the minds of trainers and human resource managers are an enigma that is often referred to through the idiom *putting yourself in the customer's shoes*. Such abstraction of empathising with others is perhaps not that useful to Filipino or Indian CSRs who do not have insurance, or a bank account, or computers in their homes, and where putting themselves in 'someone else's shoes' is an existential exercise with very limited reality. The two days or two weeks of intercultural training they may receive may not be enough for a CSR to understand how to deal with sensitive issues of death or finances, which are common occurrences in insurance or a banking BPO. However, an analysis of calls can provide real evidence about how empathy can be construed in a telephone service encounter. Empathy can be construed through a range of different choices; one choice that clearly construes empathy or discord is the use of discourse markers.

This is illustrated in Example 4 below: the CSR here is clearly reducing the social distance between himself and his customer through a range of different resources such as laughter overlaps and discourse markers. In Turn 31, the CSR reassures the customer that an email address is not essential through the repetition of *OK, OK* and then by a positive encouragement through the discourse phrase *that's fine*. This positive solidarity building theme continues throughout this short extract showing how the Filipino speaking in English, his second language (or perhaps third language as there are over 120 different Filipino dialects, and all speakers also speak Tagalog, see Bautista and Bolton (2008)) is extremely effective in concurring and supporting the dialogic development of this interaction. In Turn 33, the CSR again reassures the customer by adding *ah, that's alright*. The CSR never apologises; he is simply agreeing with the customer in order to show he understands, and moves on to the final generic stage of ending the call. They share laughter together in Turn 34, with the CSR demonstrating that he has completely understood the situation experienced by the customer, and that he can empathise with having a very old computer. The CSR even adds his own interpretation of events by including a rhetorical question *we can do without it, right?*

(4)

29	CSR 95:	thank you maam, and lastly, just to assure you of the best customer services, what'll be your email address, please, maam?
30	C95:	I don't have one. {laughs}
31	CSR95:	*OK, OK, that's fine*
32	C95:	I have the oldest computer in the office, so I don't have an email address.=
33	CSR95:	=*Ah, that's alright, and err.*
34	C95:	=sorry *err*, I'm sorry too ... {both laugh}
35	CSR95:	*That's alright maam*. We can do it without it right? *Hm,*
36	C95:	cos I have the oldest, I have
37	CSR95:	=*mhm* =
38	C95:	=I have
39	CSR95:	=*really*=
40	C95:	=as a matter of fact I had someone come in here the other day and he couldn't believe it
42	CSR95:	=*mhm*=
43	C95:	=I have the oldest Dell around

This rhetorical question has a discourse marker of completion *hm* at the end. The customer here is, to a certain extent, moving from the role of a distant customer calling an offshore call centre to more of an acquaintance sharing an experience, and sharing in a manner more reflective of casual conversation than pragmatic talk. Eggins and Slade (2006) and many others illustrate a clear distinction between casual conversation (interactional talk) and pragmatic conversation (transactional talk). In casual conversations the speakers take on a role that is more equal and represents close social distance. In Example 4, it is evident that the CSR is able to develop a relationship where overlaps, laughter and discourse markers are building a more informal relationship. The evidence of the empathy, or what is referred to as 'solidarity' within Appraisal Analysis (see Martin and White 2005), is mediated through the choice of such resources. If it is possible to identify such resources and how they are used effectively in a text, then it is possible to model these choices and train others using evidential resources how to construe 'empathy'. Such models are far more explicit than asking someone to 'put themselves in another person's shoes', which is opaque and abstract. A full discussion of solidarity and resources for solidarity in call centre interactions can be found in Martin and White (2005).

Discourse markers as a resource can be used to construe negative as well as positive attitude. For instance in Example 5, the customer is using discourse markers to indicate dissatisfaction with the length of time it takes an organisation to address an issue.

(5)

29 C9:   Oh ... well yeah, your policy is to hold it as long as possible uh?
30 CSR9: We can fax it out like what we've said, that would be faster if you can have someone you know or a friend or someone that we can fax it.

In Turn 29, the customer starts with the discourse marker *oh ... well, yeah* and if the CSR were an expert user of English, from the falling tone, the breathiness and the elongated stretching of the words, the CSR would be able to identify the dissatisfaction and negative attitude of the customer, even before the sarcastic comment about the time the company takes *holding on to* policies. Again, whether such elements of spoken interaction are made explicit to the CSRs during their training has not been evident during the research visits to multiple sites, where the research team have collected data on recruitment, training, assessment and texts, i.e. audio recordings of call centre interactions.

Grammar in recruitment proficiency assessment

In the BPO industry we found that the recruitment and training material often tended to be based on written discourse, written grammar and discrete grammar items. Example 6 is an extract from an assessment tool used for proficiency measures in the BPO industry, which has items such as:

(6)

Read Aloud
Read the passage aloud smoothly and naturally in a clear voice. You will be stopped after 30 seconds. This is not a speed reading test. You may not be able to finish reading the entire passage, but that is okay. When your time is up, you will automatically move on to the next item.
   1 We have several offices for rent in a large office building. The building is surrounded by trees. All offices have private balconies and hardwood floors. There are many features including an outdoor eating area and a shower. The location is within a few steps of many shops and cafes.

D Sentence Builds
Please rearrange the word groups into a sentence.
Example: You hear: 'finished by April' ... 'must be' ... 'our projects'
          You say: 'Our projects must be finished by April'

(Versant 2012)

This is an example of a common test used for initial screening of potential employees in the BPO industry. The test, Versant, is a spoken English test developed by Pearson to assess an individual's spoken proficiency in a 15-minute test taken online or over the phone where the scores are available within minutes. Versant argues that the results are similar to face-to-face assessments and that the test assesses 'phonological fluency, sentence construction and comprehension, passive and active vocabulary use, listening skill, and pronunciation of rhythmic and segmental units' (Pearson Education 2011: 3). If we focus more specifically on the 'Read aloud' component, it is possible to read the extract 'we have several offices for rent ... ' within the 30-second time limit. However, in this example we find complete clauses, sentences, punctuation, and a lack of discourse markers. The topic in this example reflects more of a real estate agent's pitch than a customer service encounter. Such features bear little resemblance to the lexicogrammatical and discourse features found in the authentic data shown in Examples 1–5.

Furthermore, Section D (Sentence Builds) again resembles the grammar of written English and requires the candidate to build sentences following an SVO structure. In certain contexts it would be completely acceptable for a speaker to respond to a question such as Q: *When must the projects be finished? A: By April, our projects must be finished.* However, this response although grammatically accurate would rarely be heard in spoken interaction where ellipsis is common, and a response such as *A: By April* would suffice and in fact be more of an unmarked choice. However, for the purpose of the assessment given by Versant only one answer is acceptable – *our projects must be finished by April* – and any other variation would be deemed incorrect. Reading aloud echoes some of the frequent bad habits and negative criticism often faced by the BPO, where customers comment negatively that the CSR sounds 'unnatural' and 'scripted'.

Another commonly used spoken proficiency test is MeriTrac (www.merittrac.com). In MeriTrac speakers are rated on a remedial basis and scored based on the number of pronunciation errors made. They even adopt a 'Fatal Error' analysis where pronunciation errors are graded, and when a speaker makes five pronunciation errors that are detrimental to the communication they are rejected for further recruitment procedures. Such tests do not reflect the demands of the work or the authentic interaction that is found in customer service encounters. During one field trip when observing an interview I witnessed a fluent competent speaker who possessed the interpersonal skills you would admire in a customer service representative. The Human Resource (HR) recruitment officer rejected this candidate. When interviewed after the recruitment process the HR officer stated that the candidate used too many 'fillers', or what we are referring to in this chapter as discourse markers. However, as shown in the authentic data in the present chapter and as argued in other studies, these discourse markers are fundamental to the co-construction of a successful dialogic interaction.

Training material and language

During our numerous studies in the BPO we have observed many training sessions and reviewed and reported back on training material used. However, due to copyright and privacy we cannot publish any of the authentic examples that we have encountered. On the internet though there are a range of examples of training material for call centres. One example available is representative of the material we have encountered over the eight years. This material, which focuses on 'empathy training', is available from callcentrehelper.com and states that empathy is 'the ability of one individual to understand another by placing themselves hypothetically in their position'. The website goes on to recommend role playing 'empathy' (www.callcentrehelper.com) as seen in Example 7:

(7)

Role plays

Role playing games in a learning environment can be a very flexible and effective tool, helping to build teams, develop employee motivation and improve communication skills. Plan your role plays and be mindful of the following objectives and guidelines:

- Be clear and concise when communicating your objective – what do you want people to learn from this experience?
- All sides of the role play should be unambiguous and aligned to the objectives set out
- The brief should contain enough information for the delegate to engage in a believable conversation
- Paint the picture – explain the background of the characters; why is this role player angry, what has made him angry?
- Give the role players adequate preparation time
- Allow the observers time to provide feedback after the exercise
- Make sure time is set aside to discuss what worked, what didn't work and what could have been done better within the exercise.

(www.callcentrehelper.com)

On the Call Centre Helper website, they suggest listening to calls and focusing on the role of empathy. However, a clear understanding of how empathy is construed in the language is not available, and in all of our involvement with the industry, empathy has been seen to be a vague and nebulous term, meaning different things for different people. The 'right tone' is often referred to as important, and 'asking the right questions' is another key feature. However, clear evidence-based examples are rarely ever provided. A more common approach is to conduct role plays in the trainee classroom and to allow the CSR to experiment with ways of expressing empathy in a second language. The role play presented in Example 7 is frequently used in training classrooms in the BPO industry. Often the empathy or the roles are designed and developed by the trainees and may involve elements from their own social, family or workplace experience, which may or may not be related to the American customer's experience. This material is perhaps useful in helping the trainees to develop group dynamics and allows for the development of a relaxed and friendly atmosphere, but it may bear little resemblance to what happens in authentic call centre interactions. Often such role plays have no language or grammar focus and limited consideration of other language points.

On another website focusing on teaching material for call centres in India, some specific material is available outlining the language used in call centres. The material presented on this website is well designed and looks impressive. However, the video 'English Grammar – Sentence' starts by defining a sentence: 'When we speak we use a sentence. A sentence is a group of words used to communicate a complete thought'; the narrator continues to explain that 'we must have a Subject in every sentence'. Slides are included in the podcast to help prospective CSRs to identify the Subject and verb, as shown in Examples 8 and 9 (the use of lower and upper case letters, and the use of 'round' instead of 'around' are as shown on the slides):

(8)

Watch the following sentences to identify subject and the predicate
The Sun Sets

Ram is Playing
The cat Chases the Rat

(9)

Lets [sic] find out the subject and the predicate in the following sentence.
The ship went out to sea
The Earth moves round the sun
Don't make a noise
Forgive Me Father
A Hermit lives in a jungle
Mumbai is a big city.

If we consider this training material, the language focuses on written and not spoken language. The examples used to illustrate the point are completely unrelated to call centre interaction and bear little resemblance to any of the authentic data found in Examples 1–5. For example, it would be difficult to imagine the clause *a hermit lives in a jungle* ever being used by an Indian or Filipino CSR or American or any other English-speaking customer. Furthermore the premise on which this whole unit of work is based i.e. the focus on 'the sentence', is unrelated to spoken language. As pointed out by McCarthy and Carter (2006) and many others researching spoken English, we do not speak in sentences but in grammatically intricate clauses, and these clauses may be complete clauses with a subject and verb, but they may also be simply made up of a minor clause or a discourse marker and an incomplete clause.

The material presented in Examples 7–9 is truly representative of BPO training material and illustrates two extremes, with Example 7 having a focus on 'soft skills', following more of a post-modernist paradigm, and overlooking language per se, and Examples 8–9 adopting a traditional, structuralist view of language that is only concerned with written language and does not reflect the current research nor authentic grammatical choices found in spoken English. The model of language we adopt is essential for the tacit appreciation of language and communication within the workplace. In the examples outlined above the model of language found in the authentic data reflects current research into spoken language. However, the view of language adopted in the assessment and training procedures introduced in the present chapter appears to be anchored in constructs of 'sentences' and 'rules'. Yet we do not speak in sentences and we are not bound by rules; we make choices, whether consciously or subconsciously, in order to make meaning when we speak and write. We can undertake studies to investigate and model the patterns and genres found within the workplace. If we can model the patterns, then we can teach these patterns for others to follow and develop their own understanding and use of such patterns. Before we do this, again we need to have an established and shared appreciation of what we mean by language.

Conclusion

When we, as researchers, are demanding time and resources from an organisation, the question we often face is 'what's in it for us?'. If an organisation is prepared to make time for a research team to conduct interviews and ethnographic studies, to select and share texts, and to open up their workplace as a site for research, then there should be some benefits for the organisation. We have found that having a strong theoretical framework that can provide a blueprint for understanding how lexico-grammatical or phonological choices at the micro level are directly influenced by and directly influence the choices made at a macro level is an extremely powerful and reliable tool. The work of applied linguists within the field of English for Specific Purposes is to ensure that their work is 'appliable', relevant and useable for those who we are researching. However, as argued above, the concept of language used in any study is dependent upon the models that are relevant for the 'intended users of one's work' (Berry 1996: 4).

The rationale for selecting SFL as a model of language is that it incorporates the notion that language is a social phenomenon, and in dealing with language SFL relates language choices, whether spoken or written, to meaning. What we understand by the term 'language' needs to be shared with the industry and the evolution of metalanguage where we are all starting from the same page needs to be addressed. Through an analysis of spoken language, we are able to identify certain features and patterns common to spoken telephonic customer service interactions, which may not have previously been as explicitly identified and modelled in traditional approaches to language. In order to be able to share findings with the workplace a certain degree of metalanguage is needed, and an agreement of terms such as language and grammar needs to be developed. As it stands, and in reviewing the recruitment and training material, it appears that 'language' is a term that is largely equated with 'written language'. More recent research about the distinction between written and spoken language has yet to penetrate the world of work.

In the brief discussion of discourse markers in the present chapter we have demonstrated the role of one specific polysemic language feature, which is key to efficacy in telephonic spoken interaction. Discourse markers have been shown to perform various roles in spoken interaction, and this is true of service encounters. In addition, discourse markers are also suggested to be a key resource used to develop solidarity within the workplace. Authentic texts can be used to identify the different roles of discourse markers and to model for trainees one way in which solidarity (or empathy as it is vaguely described as within the industry) is construed.

In a comparison of the spoken language of the authentic data with the focus on language in the recruitment process it seems that there is a disparity between the 'fit-for-good purpose' of the recruitment instruments and the authentic interactions within the BPO industry. The commercial organisations profess to provide assessment instruments that are specific to the call centre industry, which were developed for the purpose of recruitment (see Lockwood 2012b). Such tools may provide a cost-effective initial screening process. However, for developmental and training processes there is a need to move towards a language that better reflects the choices within the target text i.e. the telephone service encounter. In order to understand the language resources found within the target texts we need to conduct further micro-based research into the lexico-grammatical resources found within the clause; the discourse semantic choices found within the text; and at the same time investigate the macro-influence of culture, customer service expectations, industry-specific needs, and information technology-enabled support. An initial prerequisite is that we have a clear identifiable framework that allows us as researchers to explicitly discuss language choices and their function in an appliable manner within the workplace.

Related topics

call centres and globalisation; systemic functional linguistics; the grammar of spoken and written language; authentic language use in training and teaching material

Key readings

Carter, R. and McCarthy, M. (2006). *Cambridge Grammar of English*, Cambridge: Cambridge University Press. (This book provides an extremely useful overview of grammar and in particular provides valuable insights into the difference between spoken and written grammar.)

Forey, G. and Lockwood, J. (eds) (2010). *Globalisation, Communication and the Workplace*, London: Continuum. (This edited volume contains a range of papers all related to the BPO industry. The chapters involve studies that focus on curriculum, corpus analysis, phonology, assessment and sociolinguistic features found in the BPO industry in both the Philippines and India.)

Hood, S. and Forey, G. (2008). 'The interpersonal dynamics of call-centre interactions: Co-constructing the rise and fall of emotion', *Discourse and Communication*, 2(4), 389–409. (In this paper Hood and Forey provide an introduction to Appraisal Analysis and demonstrate some of the key features related to linguistic realisations construing emotion and empathy (or not) in customer service interactions.)

Martin, J. R. and White, P. (2005). *The Language of Evaluation: Appraisal in English*, London: Palgrave Macmillan. (Martin and White in this book introduce a systematic framework that provides the discourse analyst with an extremely useful tool that can be adopted to understand how a writer or speaker persuades and aligns the listener or reader to agree with his or her position.)

References

Adolphs, S., Brown, B., Carter, R., Crawford, P. and Sahota, O. (2004). 'Applying corpus linguistics in a health care context', *Journal of Applied Linguistics*, 1, 9-28.

Agar, M., (1985). 'Institutional discourse', *Text*, 5, 147–68.

Bain, P., Watson, A., Mulvey, G., Taylor, P. and Gall, G (2002). 'Taylorism, targets and the pursuit of quantity and quality by call centre management', *New Technology, Work and Employment.* 17(3): 170–85.

Bautista, Ma Lourdes (2004a). 'The verb in Philippine English: A preliminary analysis of modal would', *World Englishes,* 23(1), 113–28.

——(2004b). 'Researching English in the Philippines: Bibliographical resources', *World Englishes,* 23(1).

Bautista, M. L. S. and Bolton, K. (eds) (2008). *Philippine English: Linguistic and Literary Perspectives*, Hong Kong: Hong Kong University Press.

Berry, M. (1996). 'What is Theme? A(nother) personal view', in M. Berry, R. Fawcett and G. Huang (eds), *Meaning and Form: Systemic Functional Interpretations* (pp. 1–64), Norwood: Ablex Publishing Company.

Bhatia, V. (2004). *Worlds of Written Discourse: A Genre-Based View*, London: Continuum.

Biber, D. and Conrad, S. (2009). *Register, Genre and Style*, Cambridge: Cambridge University Press.

Bjorge, A. K. (2010). 'Conflict or cooperation: The use of back channelling in ELF negotiations', *English for Specific Purposes,* 29, 191–203

Bolden, G. B. (2006). 'Little words that matter: Discourse markers "so" and "oh" and the doing of other-attentiveness in social interaction', *Journal of Communication,* 56, 661–88.

Bolton, S. and Houlihan, M. (2005). 'The (mis)representation of customer service', *Work, Employment and Society,* 19(4), 685–703.

Bremner, S. (2010). 'Collaborative writing: Bridging the gap between the textbook and the workplace', *English for Specific Purposes,* 29, 121–32.

Call Centre Helper (2013). *How to Improve Empathy in the Call Centre.* Available at www.callcentrehelper.com (accessed 9 March 2013).

Cameron, D. (2000a). 'Styling the worker: Gender and the commodification of language in the globalized service economy', *Journal of Sociolinguistics,* 4(3), 323–47.

——(2000b). *Good to Talk? Living and Working in a Communication Culture.* London: Sage.

Carter, R. and McCarthy, M. (2006). *Cambridge Grammar of English*, Cambridge: Cambridge University Press.

Castro, C. M. C. (2009). 'The use and functions of discourse markers in EFL classroom interaction', *Profile,* 11, 55–77.

Chomsky, N. (1957). 'Three models for the description of language', *Transactions on Information Theory,* 2(3), 113–24.

——(1975). *Reflections on Language,* New York: Pantheon.

Coffin, C. (2001). 'Theoretical approaches to written language – a TESOL perspective', in A. Burns and C. Coffin (eds), *Analysing English in a Global Context* (pp. 93–122), London: Routledge.

Coffin, C., Donohue, J. and North, S. (2009). *Exploring English Grammar: From Formal to Functional*, London: Routledge.

Conrad, S. and Biber, D. (2009). *Register, Genre, and Style*, Cambridge: Cambridge University Press, 2009.

Corporate Training Material (2011). Available at www.corporatetrainingmaterials.com (accessed 13 March 2013).

Cowie, C. (2007) 'The accents of outsourcing: The meanings of "neutral" in the Indian call centre industry', *World Englishes*, 26(3), 316–30.

Cowie, C. and Murty, L. (2010) 'Researching and understanding accent shifts in Indian call centre agents', in G. Forey and J. Lockwood (eds), *Globalisation, Communication and the Workplace* (pp. 125–146), London: Continuum.

Davies, A. (2010). 'Language assessment in call centres: The case of the customer service representatives', in G. Forey and J. Lockwood (eds), *Globalisation, Communication and the Workplace* (pp. 242–250), London: Continuum.

Deery, S., Iverson, R. and Walsh, J. (2002). Work relationships in telephone call centres: Understanding emotional exhaustion and employee withdrawal. *Journal of Management Studies*, 39(4), 471–96.

Eggins, S. and Slade, D. (2006). *Analysing Casual Conversation*. London: Equinox.

Eraut, M. (2009). 'Transfer of knowledge between education and workplace settings', in H. Daniels, H. Lauder and J. Porter (eds), *Knowledge, Values and Educational Policy: A Critical Perspective* (pp. 65–84), New York: London.

Fischer, K. (2006). *Approaches to Discourse Particles*, Amsterdam: Elsevier.

Forey, G. (2004). 'Workplace texts: Do they mean the same for teachers and business people?' *English for Specific Purposes*, 23(4), 447–69.

——(forthcoming). 'Globalisation, English language and call centre communication in India: Its impact on women', *World Englishes*.

Forey, G. and Lam, M. (forthcoming 2013) 'Applying systemic functional linguistics: Understanding the choices of quality in the workplace. The impact of SFL on professional discourse', Special Focus Issue of *Journal of Applied Linguistics and Professional Practice*.

Forey, G. and Lockwood, J. (2007). '"I'd love to put someone in jail for this": An initial investigation of English in the business processing outsourcing' (BPO) Industry, *English for Specific Purposes*, 26(3), 308–26.

——(eds) (2010). *Globalisation, Communication and the Workplace*, London: Continuum.

Forey, G., and Thompson, G. (eds) (2009). *Text Type and Texture*, London: Equinox.

Frank-Job, B. (2006). 'A dynamic-interactional approach to discourse markers', in K. Fischer (ed.), *Approaches to Discourse Particles (SiP 1), Volume 1 (Studies in Pragmatics)* (pp. 359–74), Oxford: Elsevier Ltd.

Friginal, Eric (2007). 'Outsourced call centres and English in the Philippines', *World Englishes*, 26(3), 331–45.

——(2010). 'Call centre training and language in the Philippines', in Gail Forey and Jane Lockwood (eds), *Globalisation, Communication & the Workplace* (pp. 190–203), London: Continuum.

Fung, L. and Carter, R. (2007). 'Discourse markers and spoken English: Native and learner use in pedagogic settings', *Applied Linguistics*, 28(3), 410–39.

Gardner, R. (1999). *When Listeners Talk: Response Tokens and Listener Stance*, Amsterdam: John Benjamins Publishing.

Gilmore, A. (2001). 'Call centre management: Is service quality a priority?', *Managing Service Quality*, 11(3), 153–159.

Halliday, M. A. K. (1994). *An Introduction to Functional Grammar*, 2nd edn, London: Edward Arnold.

——(2001). 'Literacy and linguistics: Relationships between spoken and written language', in C. Coffin and A. Burns (eds), *Analysing English in a Global Context: A Reader* (pp. 181–93), London: Routledge.

Halliday, M. A. K. and Hasan, R. (1985). *Language, Context and Text: Aspects of Language in a Social-semiotic Perspective*, Victoria: Deakin University Press. Republished by Oxford University Press, 1989.

Halliday, M. A. K. and Matthiessen, Christian M. I. M. (2004). *An Introduction to Functional Grammar 3rd edition*, London: Edward Arnold.

Halliday, M. A. K., McIntosh, A. and Strevens, P. (1964). *The Linguistic Sciences and Language Teaching*, Longman: London.

Hamp-Lyons, L. and Lockwood, J. (2009). 'The workplace, the society and the wider world: The offshoring and outsourcing industry', *Annual Review of Applied Linguistics (ARAL)*, 29, 145–167.

Heritage, J. (1984). *Garfinkel and Ethnomethodology*, Cambridge: Polity Press.
Hood, S. and Forey, G. (2008). 'The interpersonal dynamics of call-centre interactions: Co-constructing the rise and fall of emotion', *Discourse and Communication*, 2(4), 389–409.
Ingels, M. (2005). *Legal English Communication Skills: Introduction to Writing Skills and Vocabulary Acquisition for the Legal Profession*, Leuven: Academische Cooperative Venootschap cvba.
Lam, P. W. Y. (2009). 'Discourse particles in corpus data and textbooks: The case of well', *Applied Linguistics*, 31(2), 260–81
——(2010). 'Toward a functional framework for discourse particles: A comparison of well and so', *Text and Talk*, 30(6), 657–77.
Leech, G. and Svartvik, J. (2002). *A Communicative Grammar of English*, Harlow: Longman.
Leitner, G. (1991). *English Traditional Grammars: An International Perspective*, Amsterdam: John Benjamins.
Let's talk (2013). Available at www.letstalkpodcast.com (accessed 1 March 2013).
Lockwood, Jane (2008). 'What does the Business Processing Outsourcing (BPO) industry want from English language assessment?' *Prospect*, 23(2) (Special Issue), 67–78.
——(2012a). 'Language assessment practices in Asian business processing outsourcing (BPO) worksites', *Journal of Business Communication*.
——(2012b). 'Are we getting the right people for the job? A study of English language recruitment assessment practices in the Business Processing Outsourcing sector: India and the Philippines', *Journal of Business Communication*, 49(2), 107–27.
Lockwood, J., Forey, G. and Elias, N. (2009). 'Call centre communication: Measurement processes in non-English speaking contexts', in D. Belcher (ed.) *English for Specific Purposes in Theory and Practice* (pp. 143–164), Ann Arbor, Michigan: Michigan University Press.
McCarthy, M. and Carter, R. (2006). *Cambridge Grammar of English: A Comprehensive Guide: Spoken and Written English Grammar Usage*, Cambridge: Cambridge University Press.
Martin, J. R. (1997). 'Analysing genre: Functional parameters', in F. Christie and J. R. Martin (eds), *Genre and Institutions: Social Processes in the Workplace and School* (pp. 3–39), London: Cassell.
——(2009). 'Boomer dreaming: The texture of re-colonisation in a lifestyle magazine', in G. Forey and G. Thompson (eds), *Text Type and Texture* (pp. 252–84), London: Equinox.
Martin, J. R. and Rose, D. (2008). *Genre Relations: Mapping Culture*, London: Equinox.
Martin, J. R. and White, P. (2005). *The Language of Evaluation: Appraisal in English*, London: Palgrave Macmillan.
MeriTrac. www.merittrac.com (accessed 1 March 2013).
Muller, S. (2005). *Discourse Markers in Native and Non-native English Discourse*, John Benjamins.
NASSCOM (2009a). *Gender Inclusivity in India: Building an Empowered Organisation*. Available at www.nasscom.in (accessed December 2012).
——(2009b). *Impact of IT-BPO Industry in India: A Decade in Review*. Available at www.nasscom.in/impact-itbpo-industry-india-decade-review (accessed 4 February 2013).
——(2012). *The IT-BPO Sector in India: Strategic Review 2012*. Available at www.nasscom.org (accessed 8 December 2012).
OBG (Oxford Business Group) (2012) *The Report: The Philippines 2012*. Manila, Philippines: Oxford Business Group.
Pearson Education (2011). *Versant English Test: Test Description and Validation Summary*. Available at www.versanttest.com (accessed 1 March 2013).
Porter, L.J. and Tanner, S. J. (2004). *Assessing Business Excellence*. Amsterdam: Elsevier
Selingo, J. (2012). 'Skills gap? Employers and colleges point fingers at each other', *The Chronicle of Higher Education*, Available at www.chronicle.com (accessed 5 October 2012).
Stenstrom, A. (1994). *An Introduction to Spoken Interaction*, London: Longman.
Taylor, P. and Bain, P. (2005). '"India calling to the far away towns": The call centre labour process and globalization', *Work Employment and Society*, 19, 261–82.
UNPD (2010). *Power Voice and Rights: A Turning Point for Gender Equality in Asia and the Pacific*. Available at www2.unpd.org (accessed 10 September 2013).
Versant (2012). Available at http://versanttest.com/ (accessed 26 September 2012).
Wan, Y. N. (2010). 'Call centre discourse: Graduation in relation to voice quality and attitudinal profile', in G. Forey and J. Lockwood (eds), *Globalisation, Communication and the Workplace*, London: Continuum.
Williams, J. D. (2005). *The Teacher's Grammar Book*, New York: Taylor & Francis.
Xu, Xun-feng., Wang, Yan, Forey, Gail and Li, Lan (2010). 'Analyzing the genre structure of Chinese call-center communication', *Journal of Business and Technical Communication*, 24(4), 445–75.

25
Media communication
Current trends and future challenges

Isabel Corona

Introduction

Media communication involves a complex and dynamic range of texts, genres, processes, practices, users, institutions and organisations. It is constructed within a network of social, economic and political constraints while at the same time it is currently going through an unprecedented expansion with the new era of computer-mediated communication.

The first necessary step for this overview of media communication is to delimit the scope of the term 'media', a term that is 'notoriously polyvalent' (Spitulnik 2001: 143), as it tries to describe an 'elusive concept' (Finnegan 2002: 40), as we may consider that anything can be a 'medium' for social interaction, and consequently it has in the last decade become 'overloaded in meaning' (Wales 2007).

In the strict sense the term is the plural of the Latin term 'medium' and refers to channels of communication. With the development of newspapers, television and radio, the term was used to refer to these institutions and their professionals, as the 'mass media', characterised by their one-to-many centralised address (Hartley 2002: 142). The advent of the IT revolution has brought in a profound change, from the centralised address of one institution-to-many to new, unprecedented possibilities for communication of one individual to many, and many to many taking place simultaneously, as well as new channels, new products, new audiences, new institutions, and even new realities of the physical workplace. A different premodifier to the term 'media' has been needed, and the 'new media' has taken the stage.

Thus, the term 'media' can be seen to show the convergence of three senses currently coexisting: first, the 'technical' media, as 'the very tangible devices needed to materialise instances of media types' (Elleström 2010: 12), whose radical changes have revolutionised the media landscape in terms of literacy, social relations and professional practices; secondly, the 'institutional' media, as the main means of mass communication, through media types or genres produced in newspapers, television, radio, advertising agencies, publishing companies, PR firms or film industries; finally, the most specific use of the term 'the media', which refers to the organisations and professionals engaged in the practice of news reporting. Professional communication in the media has to take into consideration all these senses. As we shall see, the three of them are necessarily intertwined in all the areas dealt with in the present and brief overview of professional communication in the media.

This chapter works towards clarifying the current state of media communication by taking a threefold perspective and considering media as a discipline, as professional practice and as object of research for discourse analysts. Media as a discipline is concerned with media studies in the curriculum and in tertiary education as part of communication studies with a traditional interdisciplinary theoretical nature but with new technologically based curricular demands. Media as professional practice involve encompassing a multiplicity of professions and practices, with an increasing demand for both specialised knowledge and adaptability to respond to evolving new media texts and genres and globalising contexts for production and dissemination processes. Finally, media as an object of research respond to an increasing demand for interdisciplinarity as shown by the main current trends and methodological approaches in the study of media discourse.

In sum, this chapter tries to find some common ground for an integrated view of the problems and challenges posed by technological, social and globalisation factors that have a strong impact on the current developments in media studies, practice and research. The last section offers some reflections on future lines of research with an eye to the realities of professional media.

1 Studying the media

One necessary clarification that is the source of not little misunderstanding is the distinction among several terms that are frequently confused in the educational arena and have to do with the different meanings of the term 'media': media education, media literacy and educational media.

Media education is the process of teaching and learning about the media. It is implemented in a variety of ways: at its best, as a specialised discipline in the curriculum (usually referred to as 'media studies'), but more commonly as an aspect of mother tongue teaching, that is, as material integrated into the teaching of a variety of subjects (also called 'media across the curriculum'), and even just as technology lessons (IT).

The outcome of this teaching and learning process is what is now widely known as 'media literacy'. Being media literate has become one of the main educational challenges in our new information technology society and is being currently developed in primary and secondary education programmes in many English-speaking countries: the UK, the US, Australia, New Zealand, Canada and also in South Africa, Israel and in many European nations.[1] The European Commission has issued specific guidelines for this 'skill', considered, as stated in the factsheet of its Media Programme webpage[2] 'a fundamental part of our basic entitlement to full citizenship and democratic participation'. The European Commission's Media Programme defines 'media literacy' as 'the ability to access the media, to understand and to critically evaluate different aspects of the media and media content and to create communications in a variety of contexts'.[3] So it involves two aspects, content and channel – more appropriately understood as technology – and the ability to deal with both. A media literate citizen is both able to have a critical understanding of the media and able to actively participate in media channels.

On the other hand, 'educational media' refers to the use of media as teaching aids, as new means of delivering information, that is, teaching *through* and *with* the media' (Buckingham 2003: 4). Thus, a media educator is not one who uses technology or teaches how to 'use the machine' (that would be an IT teacher), but one whose aim is 'to ensure that new media technologies are used effectively and critically' (QCA 2005: 66).

It can also be understood from this little clarification of terms that access to media studies as a specialised discipline is the most desirable scenario for becoming media literate. The methodology applied for the measurement of media literacy competences has used a set of 'key concepts' that somehow seek a unifying criterion for the diverse disciplinary backgrounds of practitioners and scholars in the field, which include communication, sociology, psychology, cultural studies and media studies, to name but a few (Hobbs 2005). More significantly, these concepts have mirrored the co-existing social assumptions regarding the nature and function of the media and have followed the dominating trends in media research during the last century. Masterman's (1997) historical review of media education reveals a tendency that moved from 'ignoring' the mass media, as a first reaction to its existence, to 'distrust' of its effects and thus reacting against the mass media by developing a pedagogy of discrimination, according to ethical and aesthetic 'values' of good and bad media texts. This 'protectionist' attitude moved towards a more 'dialogical' approach, more interested in understanding, rather than condemning (Cappello 2008). The developments in semiotics, theories of ideology and sociology expanded the study of the media to see them as representations of reality, as sites of struggle and as being not only 'texts' but also as part of the social contexts of production and reception. Masterman (1997: 41) elaborated a list of analytical tools intended 'to make the textual investigation of any medium more systematic and rigorous'. They included:

> [D]enotation and connotation, genre, selection, nonverbal communication, media language, naturalism and realism, audience, institution, construction, mediation, representation, code/encoding/decoding, audience, segmentation, narrative structure, sources, ideology, anchorage, rhetoric, discourse, and subjectivity.

In his seminal book, *Media Education*, Buckingham (2003) regrouped them into four main interconnected concepts that still define the field of study: language (texts and genres), representation (as portrayals of ideas, values and ideologies), production (how organisations operate) and audience (how users select and interpret products).

To sum up, the basic tenet for media education at school is, in Hobbs's (2005: 27) words, 'a pedagogy of enquiry', defined as 'the act of asking questions about media texts', accompanied by the ability to produce media texts critically and creatively, going through 'a self-determined process of deconstruction/reconstruction of knowledge' (Cappello 2008: 16).

There has also been observed some concern for career paths and a call for more involvement of media practitioners in media education. Thus, the British QCA report (2005) calls for taking a more explicitly vocational purpose and a more sustainable model for continuing professional development in media studies, sensitive to the needs of media industries. There also seems to be a lack of an effective cooperative attitude between professionals and educators (Cappello 2008).

As for tertiary education, from its beginnings in the Anglo-American world (the first university course in journalism was given at the University of Missouri in the period 1879–84, and the first journalism school was founded in 1908 at Columbia University in New York), media studies in higher education has expanded in the last 50 years all over the world as an academic field (sometimes still considered a 'Mickey Mouse' subject by the more traditionally recognised academic disciplines) in various forms: as a major or minor subject, as a full degree, and with a diversity of content, drawing from cultural studies, film studies, journalism, communication studies, visual design, semiotics, linguistics and even IT. The field has become strongly diversified, with branches that respond to a main focus on the channel of communication (television, radio, newspapers, or cinema), on the content and professional practices of communication (journalism, advertising, PR, culture, arts), or on purely technical approaches, encouraged by the developments in new media. Again, we see the consequences of the blurriness or multiplicity of meanings of the terms 'media' and 'communication'.

Both media and journalism studies are now frequently linked to Professional Communication as a single degree or academic programme in many universities all over the world with a rapidly growing demand. The courses may cover corporate relations (from organisational communication, health communication and public relations, to newspapers and nonfiction),[4] writing for the media (including writing in the legal professions, grant and proposal writing, sport writing or public relations writing) to digital media (referring to film as well as television, digital imaging or graphic design). Studies in the professional communication arena are as varied as they can be and the lines between the traditional notion of journalism and other professional communication practices are increasingly blurring. This is, according to Sévigny and Flynn (2011: 9) 'a consequence of the mashing together of communication channels and the democratization of publishing through electronic media'. To take just an example, the BS Degree in Professional Communication and Emerging Media offered by the University of Wisconsin has a 'concentration' in 'Applied Journalism'. The promotional information webpage[5] asserts that 'Journalism is not dead', but 'general interest journalism may be fading'. The answer for that is 'applied journalism' which, they argue, is meant to 'bring content to a particular business sector' by 'exploring multimedia, interactivity and content repurposing'. The different careers listed under 'applied journalism' studies include editor, web content manager, PR writer, blogger, trade journal writer, freelance writer, researcher, copy editor, publisher *and* journalist. The profession of journalist is commonly subsumed as part of an umbrella profession that could be described roughly as 'communication practitioner'.[6]

Before moving on to the realities of work to be discussed in the next section, it is necessary to point out two aspects of media studies and media education that cannot be underestimated and which at first may be seem contradictory but are becoming more and more complementary from an international and linguistic perspective: the call for the internationalisation of studies and the need for developing more educational opportunities for the study of English as a foreign language *for* the media.

Twenty years after Silverstone (1999) gave his much-quoted book the title *Why Study the Media?* the question has been slightly modified to 'Why internationalize media studies?' (Thussu 2009b). Silverstone's question shows that 20 years ago it was necessary to explain the importance of media studies because it had not been taken too seriously by academia; the answer then, still valid today, was that the media are central to our lives and we need to understand them to make sense of our world. The second question encapsulates the complexity of globalisation and its consequences in the twenty-first-century mediascape, with the rise and growth of the media in the non-Western world, an example of which can be observed in the internationalisation of news networks, such as Aljazeera in English, Telesur (the Latin-American broadcaster), Russia Today, China's CCTV or India's NDTV, which are all offering distinctive perspectives on regional, national and international issues on a global scale.

Taking the more general meaning of internationalisation of media studies as the exchanging of knowledge and understandings across borders (Livingstone 2007), it follows that two opposing perspectives can be taken: either viewing the world with Western eyes and extrapolating that view to the media world in general, particularly the Anglo-centred scope of media studies, or viewing it, as many voices who criticise the dependency on Western paradigms do, as a truly diverse interconnected scenario that needs a de-Westernised approach (Curran and Park 2000) that looks at global and local media and audiences with a comparative and transnational focus (Thussu 2009a).

Another academic and educational necessity – demanded by the growing internationalisation and mobility of students worldwide, by the access to job opportunities and by the globalisation of information through the internet – is concerned with competence in the language of communication.[7] Ever since English has been consolidated as the hegemonic language of international communication in professional practices, we have witnessed a rapid spread of English for Specific Purposes (ESP) publications: English as a second language for law, business, accounting, nursing, aviation, marketing, the military, engineering, human resources ... and also English for more general professional communicative practices, such as English for telephoning and conferencing, for successful presentations in English, meetings in English, and even job hunting in English. Surprisingly enough, publications and pedagogic materials dealing with English for journalists are meant to provide native speakers of English with the necessary writing skills for their professional practice. Publications that specifically offer ESP courses of English *for* the media, that is, targeted at non-Anglo prospective media practitioners, are certainly very rare. However, international courses on English and media organised by international schools and universities in mainly English-speaking countries are far more common. To take just a random example, the course 'Media and English' of the London School of English and Finance promotes the course in its webpage as 'tailored for the specific needs of non-native English speakers with a desire to embark on a career in the media, [...] perfect for anyone who wants to hit the ground running in this exciting industry'.

It seems that the time has come to take, using Graddol's words (2006: 87), 'the most radical and controversial approach to thinking about English under globalisation'. In this globalised environment, it is necessary for the younger population to learn English and to develop not only language competence but also intercultural competence. English as a lingua franca (ELF) is becoming established as a standard tool for international and intercultural communication.

2 Working in the media

From the beginning of the last century, journalism as a profession developed with the increasing organisation of working journalists and their growing sense of social responsibility. Sociological studies of the problems and techniques of mass communication, together with awareness of the determining influence of media messages, made clear the need for some specialised education. Journalism rapidly moved from being considered a craft learned by working as apprentices at the newsrooms to a socially valued profession.

The succinct definition of journalism provided by the *New Encyclopaedia Britannica* in 1986 (Volume 6: 627) as 'the collection, preparation and distribution of news and related materials' remains basically the same as the one given today more generally to media professionals, as 'the people who select or create the material that a media company produces, distributes, or exhibits' (Turow 2011: 36). However, the 'people' come from more diversified professional media fields; the 'material' refers not only to news reports and other specific journalistic genres, but also to those produced in advertising, public relations, or advocacy; the new technological affordances have made the whole process of collection, preparation and distribution a much more complex endeavour in the digital world.

For nearly a hundred years, news organisations worked with a media form that had not changed for the most part. Now they have to rethink every step and be imbued with a sense of constant innovation. The internet phenomenon has changed many areas of the media industry. Digital convergences, understood as 'the coming together of computer technologies as the basis for production, distribution, and even exhibition in any media industries' (Turow 2011: 177) have changed the media ecosystem. The increase in ways to distribute and exhibit materials has produced media fragmentation and audience segmentation, targeting different types of people according to their characteristics. The policies of the media are increasingly governed by marketing experts, who make news decisions to reflect focus-group results, rather than by editors

(McPhail 2010: 15). In order to cover costs and achieve a good share, the same content is used in different media, from the print paper to the online version, to the cable news network, the tablet or the smart phone, and distributed to countries around the globe by companies holding different media industries under a single corporate umbrella. The primary goal, Turow (2011: 175) explains, is 'synergy', 'the ability of mass media organizations to channel content into a wide variety of mass media on a global scale through control over production, distribution, and exhibition in as many of those media as possible'. This is changing the way in which media firms do business. In fact, most people in the news business have begun to see the digital revolution as the enemy. As happened to other industries at other times, for example in the case of the railway revolution, or the printing revolution, disruption has not come from the rulers of those industries, but from outside. Frank Bennack, Vice Chair and CEO of Hearst Corporation, declared in April 2012: 'what I have learnt is that, despite 50 years in the business, I am running a huge start-up company. That's what it feels like.' In fact, every industry, not only the media, has been hit and forced to reorganise and to rethink what they are doing. Traditional old models are no longer working. The industry has been devastated by declining revenue as news and information are 'shoveled' (Estok 2011: 23) onto the internet for free. Printed newspapers are going out of business and broadcasters are finding it harder and harder to keep themselves above water. The basic 5-Whs rule for writing news reports has been reworded for media organisations: Who cares about the information? What are they willing to pay? Where can we reach these people? When is it profitable to provide this information? And why is this profitable? (Finberg 2010). The paywall system, an attempt to ensure content generates some revenue, has been tested in some leading newspapers and magazines, with economic results still to be fully estimated. The feeling is that paywalls will only work for a very few selected publications around the world. The future appears to be bleak (Estok 2011: 25):

> Unless newspapers can find a sustainable way to charge for online content, or discover methods to produce revenue from digitized content, they will have no other choice but to continue cutting staff, newspaper size, and other expenses to reduce costs. These cuts will ultimately have an impact on quality.

John Paton (2012), CEO of Digital First Media, sees it as 'a period of transition which is going to last five to ten years, when it is going to be extremely difficult', while Richard Gingrass (2012), Google's Head of News Products, believes that 'three years ago we were talking about social as the key component of the information ecosystem. What does it tell us? In three years from now we are going to be talking about something very different again.'

What does it all mean for journalists working in institutions struggling to be financially sustainable? Journalists are in the process of redefining themselves with new tools and skills. If organisations are thinking of ways to strategically provide value for their online content, and finding new ways to distribute it, journalists' first challenge is to deal with the huge quantities of information pouring onto the internet. Content is not scarce. It is making sense of the current information overload that is daunting. The US-based and 40-year-old Media Communications Association-International (MCA-I) asserts in its webpage[8] that 'a media professional is first and foremost a content provider or content producer', and continues: 'Without creative content, technology is just wires and chips and screens.' More importantly still, new technologies have also changed the way to tell stories, that is, to 'produce' that content. Being a good writer is no longer enough. As Richard Gingrass (2012) explains, 'the investigative report of tomorrow is not 15,000 words of narrative about the story, but a report produced in query strings and fusion tables'.

In a survey carried out in 2009 by Middleberg Communications and the Society for New Communications Research (SNCR) in the US, as reported by Jeremy Porter (2009a) in his blog, 70 per cent of journalists said they use social networks to assist in reporting. The survey also found that 69 per cent of journalists go to company websites, while 66 per cent use blogs, and 47 per cent use Twitter and other microblogging services.

A well known example of the useful application of social media in real time news reporting and open source journalism is the coverage of Libya's uprising by Andy Carvin, a social media strategist for US public service radio broadcaster NPR. He tweeted nearly 1,200 times in 48 hours (Kiss 2011) on the ground and verified facts and sources through other Twitter users, proving to news organisations the value of social media as a tool for real time newsgathering and the feasibility of aggregating and of verifying information in that platform.[9] News corporations are now well aware of the power of these networking sites – Twitter, Facebook, MySpace and others – and are finding new ways to use them, as breaking news in the news desks, as hyperlinks to people's sites (instead of quoting them), but also to profile their businesses. Reporters themselves are building their trust through blogs and Facebook as personal branding, helping them construe a bona fide web presence as well as a way to connect with their readers.

In the current media environment, the Decalogue of challenges cited by journalists, as reported by Porter (2009b), is the following:

1. Having to write content across multiple formats (print, Web, blog, etc.) – being asked to produce more content than ever before.
2. Dealing with constant changes to coverage areas and beats.
3. Working in an uncertain economic environment – layoffs are happening all over the place.
4. Being forced to do more with less – staff cuts means there's more work for those left behind.
5. Competing against other outlets for the best stories – working around challenges of a 24/7, global news climate.
6. Adapting to new media – social networking and Twitter, for example.
7. Processing and filtering incoming information efficiently – including the high-volume of pitches and press releases.
8. Managing relationships and sources for ongoing story development.
9. Dealing with uninformed PR reps and off-topic pitches.
10. Finding necessary information from PR reps and online press rooms.

Apart from those aspects dealing with the consequences of job cuts, financial uncertainty, and competition, three 'challenges' are of interest here. First, the pressing need for learning to repurpose genres in multimodal texts and multimedia channels, an area that has started to concern discourse analysts. Secondly, the close relationship of journalists with the work of PR reps, mainly through their press releases. In the US, there are almost four public relations specialists for every working journalist (Porter 2009c). According to Hickey (2008), 'the press release is the least loved document in the media universe' (some journalists referring to them as 'spam'), but its influence and benefits are expanding. The traditional press release genre has given way to a new breed with a variety of formats to serve different audiences and purposes. Thus the SEO (Search Engine Optimised) releases, targeted at customers, are used by wire services and integrate key words, phrases and embedded links to provide assistance to customers seeking solutions through search; the more recent SMR (Social Media Release), for press, bloggers and customers alike, uses one single resource that provides everything that the user may need. As Hickey (2008) explains, 'it's not just about multimedia content; it's about connecting information across social networks, the people looking for it, as well as the conversations that bind them together'. The latest generation of press releases has repurposed itself to help the user to discover, share and retell a story. The third challenge for journalists, as the two previous aspects have made clear, is the professional awareness that journalism is not a product, but a process that needs collaborative work. As Robinson (2011: 137) argues, news is 'a shared, distributed *action* with multiple authors, shifting institution-audience relationships and altered labour dynamics for everyone involved'. If one of the most welcomed innovations in online newspapers genres was the interactional factor provided by the 'comments' section, where readers can have their say on the piece of news or information right after its publication online and share it with other readers, now journalists can ask their readers before or during the elaboration process, asking the online audience about the ongoing events so that there is a new, unprecedented participation, in which, more than ever, 'the job of a journalist', as Jarvis (2010) reminds us, 'is to help the community to organise its knowledge'.

To sum up, journalists now need to write, edit video, edit pictures and, more generally, be technically savvy, managing and understanding critically the social media, and building a strong professional network. According to Peter Horrocks (2010), Director of BBC World Service, 'the future of journalism is about networking, between journalists within organizations, between organizations and, crucially, networking with the audience, having a two-way dialogue with them'. Furthermore, they need to develop their journalism in all the new forms and different genres, repurposing them, translating them from one platform to the next. In the years to come, the profile of the new journalist is going to be that of an individual entrepreneur, independent and capable of doing everything by themselves, working for a variety of media outlets in a variety of different contexts in a world or real time media. The old days are long gone, some experts say, when journalists were advised to stay away from business, because it was considered 'corrupting' (Jarvis 2010). Now the new generation of journalists have to function as freelancers, struggling for financial sustainability as well.

The challenges for journalists, and for so many professionals working in and for the media-as-institutions or as freelancers, seem at variance with academics' interests. The speed of technological innovations is challenging traditional media studies, which are felt to have become obsolete. A common rebuke received by young journalists from their more experienced workmates on their first day's work is 'what have you learnt at university?' Or better, 'what have they taught you?' In the working arena the dominant feeling is that academia is divorced from reality. For online publisher and journalism blogger Paul Bradshaw (2010), 'journalism schools are like zombies, brainlessly repeating the habits of their former lives'. The problem, he contends, is that 'online journalism is so young that it can't be taught. We need space for experimentation.'

A new debate among professional communication practitioners and educators is one of integration (in terms of education, training and accreditation) of journalism, promotionalism, and public relations. According to Sévigny and Flynn (2011), these fields – to which they add communication metrics – seem to be converging in the skills that are needed, the sharing of interests, and the facing of similar ethical questions.

In non-English speaking countries there are other demands to add. To take just an example, *Periodistas* (Journalists), published by the Spanish Federation of Associations of Journalists (FAPE) devoted its summer 2012 issue (*Periodismo: una carrera de obstáculos*, Journalism: an obstacle course) to the current situation regarding the relationship between journalism studies and employment in a country, Spain, where there are 3,000 new graduates in journalism each year, of whom only one sixth would be able to enter the professional world. The needs analyses explored in the different contributions to the issue reveal two interconnected demands – technologisation and internationalisation as consequences of globalisation – which could easily be extended to other countries: the call for more IT courses in schools of journalism (that is, an emphasis on the technologisation of media practices), and the demand for more courses on English, as it is considered the way to increase their opportunities for personal development and also their chances of professional and social integration in their own country and in an international environment.

3 Researching the media

Media research, that is, the use of specific analytical methods to study the media, started more than one hundred years ago. From its early stages, conceptual as well as empirical media research was interested in the power of the mass media to guide people's understanding of the world. Some of their main concerns and observations then can still be seen as having an important role in current research. One of them is their power 'to connect'. Turow (2011) observes that early studies of mass media, carried out by sociologists from the University of Chicago at the beginning of the last century, suggested that the new emerging mass media – newspapers and magazines – 'allowed for the creation of a new type of community' in the US (Turow 2011: 124), connecting diverse and separate individuals that were then forming the new cities, made up of immigrants, people pouring to the cities from the farms, and new working classes. A century later, the director of the BBC, interviewed by Arlidge (2002) from *The Observer*, decided to add a new buzzword to the famous three-word mantra of the BBC for more than eighty years: to 'inform, entertain, educate' he added 'and connect'.

Another 'finding' of serious concern in that early research was the issue of the social function of the press, as servant and guardian of institutions. Lippmann, a journalist and Pulitzer Prize winner, wrote in his famous work *Public Opinion* (1922) that journalism was not a firsthand report of the raw material, but a report of that material after it had been 'stylized', that is, transformed by a twofold process that had nothing to do with the sacrosanct notion of objectivity. First, a journalist's version of the truth was in his view only his [sic] version, subjective and limited to how he or she constructs reality. A second but equally important factor against the assumption of objectivity was the need for economy of time and effort and the professional conventions or practices in the production processes. As Lippmann (1922) saw it 90 years ago, specific practices of the professional community and individual factors, that is, personal opinions, codes, stereotypes and interests, inevitably produced restricted – or biased – views of the world:

> Every newspaper when it reaches the reader is the result of a whole series of selections as to what items shall be printed, in what position they shall be printed, how much space each shall occupy, what emphasis each shall have. There are no objective standards here.
>
> *(1922: 128)*

This early understanding of the realities of professional practices and their social function and effects has developed into a vast amount of research. Describing and explaining what people can do with media and what the media do to people have led research for more than a hundred years.

The phenomenal growth of communication and media studies and its internal division as a multidisciplinary field makes it impossible to draw a clear-cut panorama of research in this vast area. Nordenstreng (2009: 261) describes the field as 'loosely constructed', because it 'refers broadly to all approaches to media and communication within the humanities, social sciences and arts, apart from purely technical approaches, and it covers both research and education' (Nordenstreng 2009: 256). Communication research presents a mosaic of disciplines that includes historians, sociologists, political scientists, philosophers, economists, psychologists, linguists and more precisely communication researchers proper, those identified by Heinderyckx (2007: 357) as 'communication-natives', that is, those initially trained in communication departments and holding communication degrees.

Linguists, or, more generally, discourse analysts, comprise a large and in itself heterogeneous group of scholars described by Heinderyckx (2007: 357) as 'communication-migrants'. Compared with the research in sociology, anthropology or cultural studies, the study of the media by linguists is relatively young. Research in this communication studies 'subfield' of media discourse within Linguistics also comes from different disciplinary backgrounds, drawing on different theoretical frameworks and methodological approaches. Matheson (2005) reports on a common complaint from students that there isn't a straightforward and 'definitive' textbook on media discourse that tells them what to do. From the much-quoted book on leading approaches to media discourse edited by Bell and Garrett (1998), to more recent overviews, most work approaches language from a critical perspective to show how different media make meanings through language (Conboy 2007; Richardson 2007; Johnson and Ensslin 2007; Durant 2010). A fine introduction can be found in Durant and Lambrou's (2009) resource book for students of media discourse.

A useful point of departure is the four key concepts used in the study of media in schools referred to earlier in the first section: language, representation, institutions and audience. Media language has always been a main interest among linguists asking the same key questions: how media language works and what it tells us about the media. Their contribution to the macro-field of media communication has been paramount in many schools of journalism, since the pioneering work of Fowler *et al.* (1979) and Kress and Hodge (1979), with outstanding work addressed to media students but also to researchers. The media have been approached from two main perspectives: as linguistic institutions, looking at how language is used in different media, and as social institutions, as representations of political, social and cultural realities.

An overview of the reviews of media discourse research carried out by different authors in the last two decades may throw some light on the development of media discourse research in linguistics and discourse analysis. Reviews are usually approached from the perspective of the different analytical frameworks applied and the leading scholars that have developed them. Thus Boyd-Barrett's 1994 review explored three approaches to the study of media, those of Van Dijk's (1985, 1988) structure of news, Fowler's (1991) ideology in news language and Bell's (1991) news production processes, because, he explained, 'they have highlighted many features of journalistic production that media scholars, even those whose interest is in the dynamics of professional practice, tend to take for granted' (Boyd-Barrett 1994: 38).

Bell's 1995 review of language and the media focused on the same leading theorists as Boyd-Barrett, adding Fairclough's (1989, 1992, 1995) important contribution with his application of Bakhtin's intertextuality for the analysis of texts and discourses and of Foucault's social theory for social practice analysis in the written media. More widely known as Critical Discourse Analysis (CDA), this theoretical approach is the one that has been most profusely applied in the analysis of media texts by discourse analysts, emphasising issues of ideology and power in specific journalistic genres, namely news and editorials.

By the second half of the 1990s some scholars in Linguistics had started to call for a change of analytical frameworks as a consequence of the major shift in the notion of 'text'. Linguistic work, some claimed, focused on written forms – whether as discourse analysis or as genre analysis, or as text analysis. Kress and Van Leeuwen's (1996) groundbreaking work on multimodality, *The Grammar of Visual Design*, shattered the foundations of traditional studies in the field. The journal *Text* devoted an issue in 2004 (No. 24, vol. 3) to media discourse. In the Introduction to the issue, Östman and Simon-Vandenbergen (2004) identified the then main concerns of media research in the field. First, the hybrid nature of many types of discourse if one starts from traditional genre distinctions and defining criteria; the theoretical question was to what extent the traditional genre categories needed to be rethought. Secondly, the need for interdisciplinary research to answer fundamental questions of functioning and effect of media texts. Thirdly, that ideology, be it in political, economic, social or moral matters, was the explanatory factor of the linguistic choices made in the texts, and the only way to get at the driving forces behind these choices was through the study of the functioning of the texts in society. Finally, the authors expressed a serious concern with extending and improving current methodological frameworks; collaboration with sociology was explicitly advocated. Its editor, Srikant Sarangi (2004: 299), called for a 'bracketing in of different analytic insights', and the use of an 'eclectic' framework, because 'the analyst has to approach the text from multiple perspectives in order to recover as much of the context as possible to aid the *interpretation potential*'. Kress (2004) pointed out the limitations of current linguistic analysis and urged the consideration of certain items to figure in a new 'pressing' agenda of work in media studies: the different analytical approaches needed for the different modes, 'brought together in a semiotic theory', the question of medium and the ways it shapes texts, and the new social frames encouraged by what Kress (2004: 445) called the 'cohabitation of text types', deeply related to what is now commonly known as convergence. 'The new constellation', Kress (2004: 446) concluded, 'is that of the *mode* of the image and the *medium* of the screen. This will lead to quite new representational forms, new possibilities for communicational action, and new understandings of human social meaning making' (italics my own). Multimodal analysis has been consistently developed in the last decade by scholars drawing mainly on Systemic Functional Linguistics, while being almost ignored by researchers following other theoretical standings. Van Leeuwen (2011: 679–80) lists three main desirables: the need to combine different methods and draw on different disciplines; the need for attending to cultural diversity, and the need for engaging with technology:

> A multimodal approach to studying technologically mediated communication, combining close attention to their built-in resources and structuring devices, as well as to the ways these are used in different settings, would have much to contribute to our understanding of contemporary mediated communication.

Cotter's (2001) insightful review of approaches and methods in media discourse analysis also asserts that 'the interdisciplinarity of media research is more firmly established, the issues under consideration tend to focus less on the methodological or theoretical limitations than on what the different approaches – taken together – can usefully reveal' (Cotter 2001: 421). Although she does not consider the emerging multimodal endeavours, she offers a somewhat novel perspective for continued research. Taking two dimensions of media analysis as a point of departure, namely texts and processes of text production, she points out that, of the two, 'the processes of newsgathering, reporting, and editing have not been addressed in any degree of depth' (Cotter 2001: 428). Cotter proposed a change in focus from text to process and more ethnographic, community-situated research.

More recent work has explored this path, to include the study of news production processes: the norms, constraints and routines that shape the texts and discourses of news practitioners.

Bell's (1991) groundbreaking analyses, and more recently Cotter's (2010), both former journalists turned into linguists, have brought in the practitioner's perspective on production processes. Their work has bridged the gap that has characterised media discourse research, in that it has overlooked professional practices, that is, workplace contextualisation. It is true that the inclusion of the wider context, the relationships between specific language use and the wider social structures, such as the institutions, and the implications of the notion of news as business, has been widely researched in other fields, but linguists have largely avoided entering the newsroom and observing the actions and dynamics of practitioners, that is, the way that journalists construct news texts as outcomes of a series of discourse processes and professional practices.

In the same vein, the journal *Pragmatics* devoted an issue in 2008 to the discourse of news management, bringing together insights from news sociology, anthropology and discourse analysis in the exploration of the practices and forces acting, from PR to journalism, in news making practices. In its Introduction, Jacobs *et al.* (2008: 2) explain the concept of 'news management' as 'the triumvirate of news access (source-media interaction), news selection (editorial decision-making) and news production (entextualization)'. This movement towards a more ethnographically oriented linguistics of news production comes mainly from the projects carried out at the NewsTalkandText (NT&T) Research Centre at the University of Ghent in Belgium and at the Zurich University of Applied Sciences' Institute of Applied Media Studies in Switzerland. A special issue of the *Journal of Pragmatics* (2011) continued along similar lines, exploring different discursive perspectives on news production. In the introductory paper the NT&T Group establishes that their aim is 'to fill a blind spot in news scholarship' (Catenaccio *et al.* 2011: 1843), namely the linguistically situated production stage. 'We believe', the authors (Catenaccio *et al.* 2011: 1845–46) argue,

> that this is where ethnographic, field based, interaction-oriented news production research is needed: with the researcher sitting in on the story meeting, looking over the journalist's shoulder at the computer screen, out on assignment, and listening to watercooler or coffee break chat.

In sum, they advocate for research on media from a threefold perspective: as text, as professional practice and as interaction, and claim to revitalise 'the ethnographic methodologies of sociologists who entered newsrooms in the 1970s and 1980s' (Catenaccio *et al.* 2011: 1847) together with 'linguistically sensitive micro-analysis'. The NT&T Group resumes its analytical paradigm endorsing what Rampton *et al.* (2004, quoted by Catenaccio *et al.* 2011: 1847) identify as a 'tension' of 'tying ethnography down' and 'opening linguistics up'. Their final focus is limited to the exploration of the writing processes and outcomes.

O'Keefe's 2011 review adds to the well-developed frameworks Conversational Analysis (CA) and Critical Discourse Analysis (CDA) the potential of Corpus Linguistics (CL) to complement both. O'Keefe (2011: 76) takes into account the changes brought about by the new media, which she sees as 'a new order of things' that 'renders many old metaphors and frameworks anachronistic', as 'the new democratized nature of things in the media begs for a new paradigm to encapsulate the changed dynamics, power structures, participation frameworks and discourses that are ever-emerging' (O'Keefe 2011: 77).

Certainly the new media has become a fast-growing area of academic enquiry, particularly in Sociolinguistics. Thurlow and Mroczek's (2011) perspective on new media sociolinguistics identifies four main organising principles for research: discourse, technology, multimodality, and ideology. According to Hoffmann (2010: 12), research 'is only scratching the surface of the internet's sociolinguistic dimension'. Hoffman divides it in two phases: a first wave in Computer Mediated Communication research aimed at general features and strategies of new media discourse, and a second wave 'currently underway', which is 'laying open the sociopragmatic and discursive characteristics of communication in new media', where 'there is a pressing need to elicit which compositional and functional properties define internet genres and which ones describe its "digital" context', for which, Hoffman points out, there are few existing corpus-based studies to help uncover certain forms of realisations. There is thus a call for new computational linguistic models to study online content, in verbal, visual and audio forms.

To conclude, research on media discourse analysis has broadened in its interdisciplinarity and in its scope. The key concepts language, production, representation and audience still remain fully accountable, but have evolved. Texts are multimodal, genres are 'translated', channels converge in different platforms, media products are the result of complex processes on a global scale and audiences have become users and distributors of media products. For the media scholar, new technologies have opened whole new fields of research and have enabled new ways of enquiry, of recording, collecting, storing and organising data. However, they also demand rethinking investigative and analytic methods. Furthermore, compared to the vast research carried out on texts as final products, research on the new multimodal and multimedial production processes and the new ways of interaction in the workplace, from freelancers to local and global media organisations, has still a long way to go.

Final remarks

At this stage, we can reasonably say that media communication is a truly complex, multifaceted and multidisciplinary area of study, professional practice and research. Nordenstreng (2009: 255) critiques that 'the multiplication of branches, approaches, methodologies and foci runs the risk of deserting its scholarly roots', and warns against 'diversity turning into surfing', and thus 'becoming more and more dependent on empirical and practical aspects of reality'. Similarly, Heinderyckx (2007: 362) observes the increasing pressure from academic institutions for scholars to 'behave more and more as *experts* and less and less as scholars'. However, this is more or less what is expected of applied linguistics research.

Linguistic research needs to refocus and reinforce its applied goal. Research in the media has to build a practical eye; it has to contribute to the development of the training ground to produce experts in techniques of repurposing content, 'translating' genres and building relationships in the interconnected social media. Some of the questions to answer in the near future for a better understanding and assisting professional communication in the media scenario are summarised by Sévigny and Flynn (2011: 7):

> [H]ow people relate to one another, how governments communicate, how persuasion, influence and rhetoric operate, how communicative effects and impacts can be measured, and how relationships between journalists and other communicators are being renegotiated in this emerging new professional context.

In this new area, Ekecrantz (2009: 75) asks one key question: 'How is media research to be conducted in a globalized world?' He argues that media studies shares with sociology and political science difficulties in coming to grips with the realities of a transnationalised and transforming world and calls for an agenda of 'de-' catch words: 'de-Westernizing' (meaning to make room for perspectives from the East and South), 'de-colonizing', and 'de-disciplining' (that is, 'reinserting media in the social and the cultural' (Ekecrantz 2009: 82)). In other words, he calls for 'new alliances in media studies, both between and beyond disciplines and their national habitats' (2009: 85). We need to show the complex relationships between the new work order of globalised media practices, the new technological affordances and the increasing mobility of professionals across the world.

We have seen how professional practices have changed as they go online. We need to reconsider, as Roberts (2011) advocates, Goffman's (1959) distinction between frontstage and backstage performances in the work of media communicators, even more so when the line between producers and audiences is more and more blurred: the latter, previously identified as viewers, readers or audiences in general, have become 'media users' who exert an influence on the content of the mediated communication. As Matheson (2005: 169) explains, 'from a discourse analytical perspective, a key issue is the way a discursive context is negotiated between participants online and the way participants perform particular selves in their interactions through the forms of language deployed'. We would need a media system approach to understand how professional communication works in multimodal, multimedial, global and transcultural terms.

Although some authors warn us against the fetishisation of technology (Thurlow and Mroczek 2011), it certainly provides new communicative affordances, and plays a new role in the journalist's construction of stories, enabling the audiences, now users of the same technologies, to be both co-participants and distributors of those stories (an example of which is the so-called citizen journalism). Although it should also be remembered that the technological present appears to be just a transitional moment and the affirmation of change has become the ontological condition of existence (Cappello 2008). Technology has changed the ways in which people work, but, consequently, and most importantly, economic realities are playing a crucial role in shaping work in the media. In many nations inequalities of access to technology and thus to information and development opportunities are far from diminishing, creating a new form of exclusion, a reality known as the *digital divide*. Some interesting work is being done in development journalism, a concept that tries 'to deal with the needs, strengths, and aspirations of journalistic endeavours in the emerging developing nation-states' (McPhail 2010: 41), an area of study that has not been addressed by applied linguistics or discourse analysts so far.

Furthermore, there is a persistent problem in new media scholarship as most of the research being carried out is in and on English. Bell's 1995 review of studies in language and the media already observed that research was embedded in Western media environments. The apparent dominance of English as the medium of publication and as subject of analysis is also considered 'a persistent problem in new media scholarship' (Thurlow and Mroczek 2011: xxiii). There are many voices (Thussu 2009a) urging media researchers to move away from the Anglo-centred scope of media research, with the rise of the media worldwide, particularly in the Asian countries of China and India (the Chindia mediascape).

Furthermore, the globalisation of news, information, entertainment, businesses and society in general is also calling for applied work in International English, that is, English as a lingua franca (ELF), aimed at enabling Anglo and non-Anglo prospective professionals alike to use the language they need in the new media professional world, with its old and new repertoires of written and spoken genres, and their increasing demand for knowledge dissemination and communicative exchange. An assessment of the actual use of ELF (Seidlhofer 2011) may be a next step for applied linguists working in professional communication in the media.

Finally, another aspect worth mentioning is the question of our specific academic jargon. Maybe it is time to rethink metalanguage if we want our research to be of application in the professional world. Bell's (1995: 33) review of applied linguistics studies on media noted the existence of 'a caveat' regarding the accessibility and applicability of the frameworks: 'the frameworks themselves can be difficult to understand', 'the terminologies used and the explanations of categories and methods are not always clearly presented', and 'the analyses are time-consuming' if done properly. Turow's (2011) mass communication textbook *Media Today*, addressed to media students in US universities, also agrees that the linguistic models are not straightforward or easy to understand:

> They tend to use the complex phraseology of linguistics … to make their points. That is unfortunate, because some of the scholars involved in this area often proclaim that their goal is to encourage viewers and readers to 'resist' the dominant models of society that are suggested in the text.
>
> *(Turow 2011: 145)*

Any text, any communicative artifact, any technologically mediated product has a history, and its 'final' shape is affected by very complex processes of mediatisation. There is a lot of work to be done if we discourse analysts want to understand better what is going on in the media workplace, be it online or offline, face-to-face or digitally mediated, on paper, through the waves or on the screen. The applied linguist researcher should engage with the emerging and shifting sands of professional communication in the social media and first, be in contact with media practitioners in their sites of engagements and second, be open to research endeavours and publications that may apparently be situated far from the circle of applied linguistics research. More than ever, we need to go beyond the text and analyse the professional practices and practitioners' needs, the professional cultures, local and global, national and international, that shape genres and texts (Bhatia 2004, 2008, 2010), to understand the realities of professional communication and thus be able to contribute and participate in the current challenges and problems of educating, training and working in the twenty-first-century media, so that our research efforts can be profitably applied in the real world. The future is inter and cross-disciplinary, inter and cross-professional. It is already here. And it is truly demanding.

Acknowledgements

I would like to acknowledge projects FFI2009–09792, funded by the Spanish Ministerio de Ciencia e Innovación and FFI2012–37346, funded by the Spanish Ministerio de Economía y Competitividad.

Related topics

media studies; media literacy; new media genres; globalisation of information; the future of journalism

Key readings

Buckingham, David (2003). *Media Education: Literacy, Learning and Contemporary Culture*, Cambridge: Polity Press. (It offers a historical evolution of approaches to media education in the UK to outline the main challenges lying ahead for media educators today, providing a valuable set of principles for a media curriculum.)

Cotter, Colleen (2010). *News Talk: Investigating the Language of Journalism*, Cambridge: Cambridge University Press. (It takes an ethnographic approach to the study of the language of journalism. By showing the professional practices of journalists in the US and the UK, it explores the behind-the-scenes processes of news production to explain how news texts are shaped.)

McPhail, Thomas L. (2010). *Global Communication: Theories, Stakeholders, and Trends*, London: Wiley-Blackwell. (It assesses the current trends that influence global communication and media conglomerates and gives insights into the role of international media in the shaping of information and entertainment in our global community in the near future.)

Turow, Joseph (1999) (2011). *Media Today: An Introduction to Mass Communication*, New York and London: Routledge. (A textbook on mass communication aimed at media students in US universities, organised around the notion of mass media as an interconnected system of industries, and covering the latest economic, technical and cultural trends affecting the media sector, taking digital convergence as a central aspect.)

Notes

1 In fact the situation in Europe is as varied as it can be, and media education ranges from being nonexistent to being fully integrated in the curriculum. For an analysis of the common elements and differences in the implementation of media education in European nations see E. Bernhard and D. Süss (2008) 'Media education in Europe. Common trends and differences', in *European Research on Media Education 2008*, European Commission Project Number 142299–LLP–1–2008–1–IT–COMENIUS–CMP, Available at www.onair.medmediaeducation.it/userfiles/European_research_on_Media_Education.pdf.
2 Available at http://ec.europa.eu/culture/media/media-content/medialiteracy/factsheet_media_literacy.pdf.
3 Available at http://ec.europa.eu/culture/media/media-literacy/index_en.htm.
4 All these courses fall under the 'specialisation track' of 'Corporate/Community Relations' in the Major 'Media and Professional Communications' at the University of Pittsburgh (US). Available at www.oafa.pitt.edu.
5 Available at www.uwstout.edu/programs/bspcem/upload/bspcem_aj_info.pdf.
6 Certainly this tendency co-exists with specific schools of journalism, with very fine examples, such as the Columbia University Graduate School of Journalism or the undergraduate and graduate courses in journalism at the City University London.
7 The dominance of English on the internet has started to be questioned. While some say that English-language users 'are being overtaken by Chinese, Japanese, Korean, Spanish, Russian and other language communities', particularly in the 'domestication of various internet technologies' (Goggin and McLelland 2009: 295), others assert that 'for every page on the internet which is non-English, there are at least 100 pages of English text' (McPhail 2010: 143).
8 Available at www.mca-i.org/en/cms/?179.
9 In June 2011 Twitter made available a tool for journalists. *Twitter for Newsrooms #Tfn* is a guide for journalists to use Twitter with the purpose of, according to the platform, 'finding sources, verifying facts, publishing stories, promoting your work and yourself – and doing all of it faster and faster all the time' (https://dev.twitter.com/media/newsrooms).

Bibliography

Arlidge, John (2002). 'Dyke's new mantra for the future BBC: Only connect', *The Observer*, 6 January 2002. Available at www.guardian.co.uk/media/2002/jan/06/bbc.broadcasting1 (accessed 14 January 2011).
Bell, Allan (1991). *The Language of News Media*, Oxford: Blackwell.
——(1995). 'Language and the media', *Annual Review of Applied Linguistics*, 15, 23–41.
Bell, Allan and Garrett, Peter (eds) (1998). *Approaches to Media Discourse*, London: Blackwell.
Bennack, Frank (2012). 'News at the speed of life: A global conversation on the reinvention of journalism', International Media Council (IC2012), Available at www.elpais.com/encuentros/international-council/videos/ (accessed 3 May 2012).
Bhatia, Vijay K. (2004). *Worlds of Written Discourse: A Genre-Based View*, London: Continuum.
——(2008). 'Towards critical genre analysis', in V. K. Bhatia, J. Flowerdew and R. H. Jones (eds), *Advances in Discourse Studies* (pp. 166–77), London: Routledge.
——(2010). 'Interdiscursivity in professional communication', *Discourse & Communication*, 4(1), 32–50.

Boyd-Barrett, Oliver (1994). 'Language and media: A question of convergence', in David Graddol and Oliver Boyd-Barrett (eds), *Media Texts: Authors and Readers* (pp. 22–39), Clevendon: The Open University.

Bradshaw, Paul (2010). 'A journalism curriculum for the 21st century', European Journalism Centre (EJC). Available at http://futureofjournalism.net/index.php/EJC_at_PICNIC2010 (accessed 10 May 2012).

Buckingham, David (2003). *Media Education: Literacy, Learning and Contemporary Culture*, Cambridge: Polity Press.

Cappello, Gianna (2008). 'Educating in a media-saturated society: The contribution of Media Education', in *Transnational Research on Media Education*. European Media Education Project (142299-LLP-1-2008-1 -IT-COMENIUS-CPM), 9–18.

Catenaccio, Paola, Colleen Cotter, Mark De Smedt, Giuliana Garzone, Geert Jacobs, Felicitas Macgilchrist, Lugard Lams, Daniel Perrin and John E. Richardson, Tom van Hout and Ellen Van Praet (2011). 'Towards a linguistics of news production', *Journal of Pragmatics*, 43,1843–52.

Conboy, Martin (2007).*The Language of the News*, London: Routledge.

Cotter, Colleen (2001). 'Discourse and Media', in Deborah Chiffrin, D. Tannen and H.E. Hamilton (eds), *The Handbook of Discourse Analysis* (pp. 416–36), Cornwall: Blackwell.

——(2010). *News Talk: Investigating the Language of Journalism*, Cambridge: Cambridge University Press.

Curran, James and Park, Myung-Jin-J. (2000). 'Beyond globalization theory', in J. Curran and M.-J. Park (eds), *De-Westernizing Media Studies* (pp. 3–18), London: Routledge.

Dijk, T. A. van (1985). 'Structures of news in the press', in T. A. van Dijk (ed.), *Discourse and Communication: New Approaches to the Analysis of Mass Media Discourse and Communication* (pp. 69–93), Berlin: de Gruyter.

——(1988). *News as Discourse*, Illsdale, N.J.: Erlbaum.

Downing, John D. H. (2009). 'International media studies in the US Academy', in Daya Kihan Thussu (ed.), *Internationalizing Media Studies* (pp. 267–76), London: Routledge.

Durant, Alan (2010). *Meaning in the Media: Discourse, Controversy and Debate*, Cambridge: Cambridge University Press.

Durant, Alan and Lambrou, Marina (2009). *Language and Media: A Resource Book for Students*, London: Routledge.

Ekecrantz, Jan (2009). 'Media Studies going global', in Daya Kihan Thussu (ed.), *Internationalizing Media Studies* (pp. 75–89), London: Routledge.

Elleström, Lars (2010). 'The modalities of media: A model for understanding intermedial relations', in L. Elleström (ed.), *Media Borders, Multimodaldity and Intermediality* (pp. 11–48), London: Palgrave.

Estok, David M. (2011). 'Paywalls', *Journal of Professional Communication*, 1(1), 23–26.

Fairclough, Norman (1989). *Language and Power*, London: Longman.

——(1992). 'Discourse and text: Linguistic and intertextual analysis within discourse analysis', *Discourse & Society*, 3(2), 193–217.

——(1995). *Media Discourse*, London: Arnold.

FAPE Periodistas (2012). *Federación de Asociaciones de Periodistas Españoles*, Vol. 29. Available at www.fape.es/periodistas-29_fape_revista-periodistas-818345291421752.htm (accessed 21 July 2012).

Finberg, Howard I. (2010). 'The future of journalism and journalists: What we know, what questions we need to ask', European Journalism Centre, PICNIC2010, Amsterdam. Available at http://vimeo.com/15355988 (accessed 10 May 2012).

Finnegan, Ruth (2002). *Communicating: The Multiple Modes of Human Interconnection*, London: Routledge.

Fowler, Roger (1991). *Language in the News: Discourse and Ideology in the Press*, London: Routledge.

Fowler, Roger, Hodge, Robert, Kress, Gunther and Trew, Tony (1979). *Language and Control*, London: Routledge.

Gingrass, Richard (2012). 'News at the speed of life: A global conversation on the reinvention of journalism', International Media Council (IC2012). Available at www.elpais.com/encuentros/international-council/videos/ (accessed 3 May 2012).

Goffman, Erving (1959). *The Presentation of Self in Everyday Life*, London: Penguin.

Goggin, Gerard and McLelland, Mark (2009). 'The internationalization of the internet', in Daya Kihan Thussu (ed.), *Internationalizing Media Studies* (pp. 294–307), London: Routledge.

Graddol, David (2006). *English Next*, London: The British Council. Available at www.britishcouncil.org/learning-research-english-next (accessed 20 October 2010).

Hartley, John (2002). *Communication, Cultural and Media Studies: The Key Concepts*, London: Routledge.

Heinderyckx, François (2007). 'The academic identity crisis of the European communication researcher', in N. Carpentier, P. Pruulmann-Vergerfeldt, K. Nordenstreng, M. Hartmann, P. Vihalemm, B. Cammaerts and H. Nieminen (eds), *Media Technologies and Democracy in an Enlarged Europe* (pp. 357–62), Tartu: Tartu University Press.

Hickey, Matt (2008). 'The evolution of the press release'. Available at http://techcrunch.com/2008/05/11/the-evolution-of-the-press-release (accessed 7 April 2009).

Hobbs, Renée (2005). 'The state of media literacy education', *Journal of Communication*, 55(4), 865–71.

Hoffmann, Christian R. (2010). 'Narrative revisited: Telling a story in the age of new media', in C. Hoffmann (ed.) *Narrative Revisited* (pp. 1–18), Amsterdam: Benjamins.

Horrocks, Peter (2010). 'The future of journalism'. Available at www.youtube.com/watch?v=rrpqbE5-dO0 (accessed 21 December 2010).

Jacobs, Geert, Maat, Henk Pander and Van Hout, Tom (2008). 'Introduction: The discourse of news management', *Pragmatics*, 18(1), 1–8.

Jarvis, Jeff (2010). 'Journalists as entrepeneurs', in PICNIC2010, European Journalism Centre, Amsterdam. Available at http://futureofjournalism.net/index.php/EJC_at_PICNIC2010 (accessed 10 May 2012).

Johnson, Sally and Ensslin, Astrid (2007). *Language in the Media*, London: Continuum.

Kiss, Jemina (2011). 'Andy Carvin: The man who tweets revolutions', *The Guardian*, 4 September 2011. Available at www.guardian.co.uk/media/2011/sep/04/andy-carvin-tweets-revolutions (accessed 4 September 2011).

Kress, Gunther (2004). 'Commentary: Media discourse – extensions, mixes, and hybrids: Some comments on pressing issues', in *Text*, 24(3), 443–46.

Kress, Gunther and Hodge, Robert (1979). *Language as Ideology*, London: Routledge.

Kress, Gunther and Leeuwen, Theo van (1996). *Reading Images: The Grammar of Visual Design*, London: Routledge.

Leeuwen, Theo van (2011). 'Multimodality', in James Simpson (ed.), *The Routledge Handbook of Applied Linguistics* (pp. 668–82), London: Routledge.

Lippmann, Walter (1922). *Public Opinion*. Available at www.gutenberg.org/cache/epub/6456/pg6456.html (accessed 17 January 2010).

Livingstone, Sonia (2007). 'Internationalizing media and communication studies: Reflections on the International Communication Association', *Global Media and Communication*, 3(3), 273–88. Available at http://eprints.lse.ac.uk/4253/ (accessed 21 March 2010).

Machin, David and Leeuwen, Theo van (2007). *Global Media Discourse*, London: Routledge.

McPhail, Thomas L. (2010). *Global Communication: Theories, Stakeholders, and Trends*, London: Wiley-Blackwell.

Masterman, Len (1997). 'A rationale for media education', in Robert W. Kubey (ed.), *Media Literacy in the Information Age: Current Perspectives* (pp. 15–68), New Jersey (US): Transactions Publishing.

Matheson, Donald M. (2005). *Media Discourses: Analysing Media Texts*, Milton Keynes: Open University Press.

The New Encylopaedia Britannica (1768) (1986). 'Journalism', Vol. 6, Chicago: The University of Chicago, 637–38.

Nordenstreng, Kaarle (2009). 'Media studies as an academic discipline', in Daya Kishan Thussu (ed.), *Internationalizing Media Studies* (pp. 254–66), London: Routledge.

O'Keeffe, Anne (2011). 'The media', in James, Simpson (ed.), *The Routledge Handbook of Applied Linguistics* (pp. 67–80), London: Routledge.

Östman, Jan-Ola and Simon-Vandenbergen, Anne-Marie (2004). 'Introduction', *Text*, 24(3), 303–6. (Special Issue on Media Discourse).

Paton, John (2012). 'News at the speed of life: A global conversation on the reinvention of journalism', International Media Council (IC2012). Available at www.elpais.com/encuentros/international-council/videos/ (accessed 3 May 2012).

Porter, Jeremy (2009a). '70 percent of journalists use social networks to assist in reporting'. Available at http://blog.journalistics.com/2009/70-percent-of-journalists-use-social-networks-to-assist-in-reporting/ (accessed 16 October 2011).

——(2009b). 'Big challenges for journalists in the current media environment'. Available at http://blog.journalistics.com/2009/big-challenges-for-journalists/ (accessed 16 October 2011).

——(2009c). 'Are journalists outnumbered in the PR game?' Available at http://blog.journalistics.com/2009/are-journalists-outnumbered-in-the-pr-game/ (accessed 16 October 2011).

QCA (Qualifications and Curriculum Authority) (2005). *Media Matters: A Review of Media Studies in Schools and Colleges*. Available at www.qcda.gov.uk/resources/publication.aspx?id=202c33a0-e5e3-49cf-b3c6-0cd1a817862f (accessed 16 October 2011).

Richardson, John E. (2007). *Analysing Newspapers: An Approach from Critical Discourse Analysis*, London: Palgrave.

Roberts, Celia (2011). 'Institutional discourse', in R. Carter, G. Cook, D. Larsen-Freeman and A. Tsui (eds), *The Routledge Handbook of Applied Linguistics* (pp. 81–95), London: Routledge.

Robinson, Sue (2011). 'Journalism as process: The organizational implications of participatory online news', *Journalism & Communication Monographs*, *13*(3), 137–210.

Sarangi, Srikant (2004). 'Editorial: Mediated interpretation of hybrid textual environments', *Text*, *24*(3), 297–301.

Seidlhofer, Barbara (2011). *Understanding English as a Lingua Franca*, Oxford: Oxford University Press.

Sévigny, Alex and Flynn, Terry (2011). 'A reflection on the evolution of the field of professional communication', *Journal of Professional Communication*, *1*(1), 3–14.

Silverstone, R. (1999). *Why Study the Media*, London: Sage.

Spitulnik, Debra (2001). 'Media', in A. Duranti (ed.), *Key Terms in Language and Culture* (pp. 143–45), Oxford: Blackwell.

Thurlow, Crispin and Mroczek, Kristine (2011). 'Introduction: Fresh perspectives on new media sociolinguistics', in Crispin Thurlow and Kristine Mroczek (eds), *Digital Discourse: Language in the New Media* (pp. xix–xliv), Oxford: Oxford University Press.

Thussu, Daya Kishan (2009a). 'Introduction', in Daya Kishan Thussu (ed.), *Internationalizing Media Studies* (pp. 1–10), London: Routledge.

——(2009b). 'Why internationalize media studies and how?' in Daya Kishan Thussu (ed.), *Internationalizing Media Studies* (pp. 13–31), London: Routledge.

Turow, Joseph (1999) (2011). *Media Today: An Introduction to Mass Communication*, New York and London: Routledge.

Wales, Katie (2007). 'Keywords revisited: Media', *Critical Quarterly*, *49*(1), 6–17.

26
The public relations industry and its place in professional communication theory and practice

Past, present and future perspectives

Anne Peirson-Smith

Public relations practitioners rely on the linguistic capital of words to shape organisational reputations, (re-)position products and services in the marketplace, promote issues and public policy, negotiate and establish community, employee, media and customer relations. In essence, they do this by shaping how people see and interact with the organisation whose position they are representing whilst competing to be seen and heard. In this way, public relations professionals utilise the symbols of appeal by crafting key messages, to influence their audiences and form their opinions in the competing marketplace of words and ideas across cultures.

Public relations (PR) is also a complex professional communication based profession whose rationale is founded on theories and practices from a range of academic and applied fields such as business, management, psychology, sociology, media studies, marketing and communication. This complexity, added to the wide scope of professional activities that public relations activities increasingly encompass, both technical such as news releases and annual report writing, and strategic as in planning and executing corporate image, health care or public affairs campaigns for example, demonstrates that public relations is a ubiquitous part of everyday organisational communications management.

This chapter aims to focus on the main theories and debates surrounding the current role of public relations as professional practice and as a subject for academic study. The key areas to be addressed are definitions of public relations, the history and origins of the public relations profession, its role within the integrated marketing communications framework, why it is needed – that is, the rationale behind public relations, stakeholder relationships, the development of public relations and the application of professional communication theories to analyse and direct public relations activities. Finally, some pointers will be addressed about where the academy and the profession believe that public relations education and practice are heading in future given the rapidly changing nature of the communication system with the application and dominance of new technology in getting the PR message across to its key stakeholders.

Anne Peirson-Smith

Background to public relations activity

The exact starting date of public relations practices is unclear, although we may take flags and coins as early examples of corporate identity/positioning in most early civilisations and the use of slogan and symbols by American Revolutionaries in the eighteenth century War of Independence (Cutlip 1995; Seitel 2010). The emergence of modern public relations in the United States and Western Europe was rooted in the growth of private industry in the 1930s (Nessman 2000) and local politics in the UK (L'Etang 2004). Whereas in Hong Kong and other former Asian colonies, for example, public relations was founded by expatriate companies during the 1960s, in Taiwan it resided in the role of government spokespersons in the 1950s (Huang 2000). In other geographic areas, such as Africa and Vietnam, the Middle East, Mexico and Indonesia, public relations is still a relatively new and emerging profession (Sriramesh and Verčič 2009a). Today according to the Holmes Report, which provides annual global rankings of the world's top 250 PR firms such as Edelman, Weber Shandwick, Burson Marstellar, Fleishman Hillard and the MSL group, which form the top five, there are 66,000 people employed by PR agencies worldwide. Whilst this does not account for PR executives working inside corporate communications divisions of organisations or independent PR companies, the report concluded that globally the public relations agency business is today at least a $10 billion business, and the report concludes 'It is clear from this research that PR is a significant global business, and that it is growing faster than the world economy as a whole' (Holmes 2012).

Public relations definitions

For an industry whose mainstay is the management of communication and corporate image there are numerous common misperceptions about the term and practice of public relations. Many negative associations are made with the profession including the term 'spin-doctoring' often used in news media articles to describe 'subterfuge and deception' (Ewen 1996), or 'whitewash' (L'Etang 1998) on behalf of political and entertainment personnel, or by management teams in organisations failing to successfully communicate messages to their stakeholders. The negative framing of public relations as a propaganda tool or as paid lying (Stauber and Rampton 1995) may have its origins in the wartime usage by the UK and US governments (Jowett and O'Donnell 1992). Although early PR theorists used the term in a positive light, the 'father of PR' Edward Bernays, in his seminal work on the subject, equated public relations with propaganda as an important aspect of a democratic society in either wartime or peacetime. According to Bernays, the manufacture of social responses to fulfil organisational objectives required 'the conscious and intelligent manipulation of the organised habits and opinions of the masses' (1928: 38). Clearly, persuasion is critical to the public relations effort as we shall see below in the business of attempting to change the cognitive, affective and behavioural states of the audience on the receiving end of public relations messages. But the debates surrounding the profession are symptomatic of its relative modernity, its persuasive purpose and its wide-ranging communication practices.

Academic debates persist as to whether public relations is a management-based or communication-oriented discipline, a technical, social or cultural practice (White and Manzur 1995) or an accredited profession in its own right (Cheney and Christensen 2001) as opposed to being an adjunct of marketing and advertising (Kotler and Mindak 1978). When the author interviewed a senior public relations manager recently, in the answer to the question, 'How do you explain your job to those outside of the public relations field, including prospective clients?' the MD of an international public relations firm based in Hong Kong replied:

Public relations professionals dread that question because it's a bit like defining an elephant ... and generally we are all too busy doing it anyway to explain what it is. The main thing is that it should be effective in getting the right message across about the client to the right people.

Public relations companies are also finding explanations of their raison d'être to be a communications challenge as evidenced by the wide range of terms referring to public relations found in job advertisements and company brochures from communications planning to perception and ideas management. This trend is evidenced in a company advertisement for the world's oldest and leading public relations firm, Burson Marsteller, which re-branded itself as a perception management consultancy as their advertisement explained:

> Our activities help organisations build 'Intellectual Capital'. We help differentiate brands, improve customer loyalty, and motivate employees. We help win the support of key stakeholders by developing informed opinion about products, issues and corporate activities. And to safeguard those assets no one's better at helping you prepare for, and resolve a crisis.
> *(Asian PR News 2000: 6)*

This challenge in explaining what public relations is may in part stem from the fact that if it is to be successful then the practice of public relations should be invisible and natural. In other words, from a professional perspective, the act of promoting organisations, countries, products, services, people and issues should appear to be a transparent process of disseminating information to those who need it and should not be regarded as cynical acts of persuading the community to think, believe and act as the persuader or agent wishes them to do. Essentially, it is a professional communications practice based on putting words into CEOs' mouths by writing their speeches, for example, or writing the content of a corporate website or social media campaign in the name of an organisation. As public relations professionals operate as ghost writers on behalf of their clients with no by-lines attached to their work, then their professional role is very much below the line and is perhaps not as relatable to observers as are above the line communication activities such as advertising.

Secondly, the multi-disciplinary complexity of public relations activities, added to the wide scope of professional activities that public relations encompasses, both technical, such as news release writing, and strategic, as in planning and executing health care campaigns, and viral marketing campaigns on YouTube, for example, demonstrates that public relations assumes a broad based communications management role. As such, this may also make PR practice hard to comprehend by those outside of the field of operation.

PR as a definable management function

Some scholars represent public relations as a 'management function that establishes and maintains mutually beneficial relationships between an organization and its publics on whom its success or failure depends' (Cutlip, Center and Broom 2006: 5). Here the outcomes or relationships take precedence in understanding the PR rationale. Other PR definitions focus on processes and outputs (communication) regarding PR as 'the management of communication between an organization and its publics' (Grunig and Hunt 1984: 4). In the absence of a universally applicable definition to satisfy both academic perspectives and practitioner needs, and in an attempt to demystify the emerging profession, the definition offered by the Institute of Professional Public Relations (IPR), the professional association for the UK, provides a useful starting point. This view of public relations blends the notions of ethical international strategic communication operating at all levels of organisation and society over a sustained time-line, based on mutually beneficial relationships between an organisation and its stakeholders to sustain positive opinion in the public interest:

> Public relations is about reputation – the result of what you do, what you say and what others say about you. Public relations practice is the discipline, which looks after reputation – with the aim of earning understanding and support, and influencing opinion and behaviour. It is the planned and sustained effort to establish and maintain goodwill and mutual understanding between an organization and its publics.
>
> *(CIPR 2013)*

This accessible definition perhaps comes closest to representing both the current academic and practitioner based views of this creative communication industry and its professional discursive, transactional, dialogic practices. Yet, it still omits to mention the importance of global practices, linguistic differences and cultural contexts. In grounded terms, the aim of public relations is to establish a co-creational communication flow between an organisation and its publics across a range of global and cultural contexts to gain:

> acknowledgment of achievement ... not just an acknowledgment of corporate action – but rather of an action that has made a difference in a given community such as a fuel company sponsoring a beach clean-up day ... Companies use public relations to get the message across to their relevant communities of interest that they are doing good things in the best interest of all concerned and are consequently gaining favorable recognition for that.
>
> *(Devereux and Peirson-Smith 2009: 12)*

What PR is not

Over the past decade, PR has been seen as one of the most increasingly significant components of the promotional marketing mix, distinguishing itself as low cost, below the line communication, in contrast to expensive, above the line advertising with the rise of the former being predicted above the death of latter (Ries and Ries 2002). Other critics have suggested that the failure of the profession to clearly define itself or professionalise through a globally recognised set of accredited professional training programmes has compromised its future and it is seen as an erosion of its operations to management consultants or branding departments (Morris and Goldsworthy 2008).

Academic and industry research surveys demonstrate (Childers Hon and Grunig 1999; CIPR 2011; Toth 2002) that a significant amount of time is still devoted to tactical communications production work involved in generating media publicity and writing tasks (Napoli, Taylor and Powers 1999). Increasingly, however, public relations managers operate at more strategic levels, directing research into stakeholder perceptions and counselling management about the implementation of communication campaigns (Grunig and Repper 1992). This clearly represents a move away from old perceptions of a publicity-oriented, news media driven profession, and only represents part of the job overall.

Public relations in practice is seen as an increasingly significant part of the organisational strategic communications effort. Hence, PR professionals often work closely together with other marketing executives on advertising and sales promotions to launch a new consumer product or banking services, for example. Typical public relations activities range from launching and sustaining the market position of a brand, such as Starbucks, to raising awareness amongst key stakeholders about the human papilloma virus (HPV) in a student health care campaign, for example. In essence, public relations is an integrated and increasingly important part of the promotional mix in marketing, being recognised as such by practitioners and academics alike. The emphasis of public relations on relationship building and developing sustainable consumer relationships as its core ethos may also have contributed to this increasing recognition of its added value role in marketing communications. The multi-levelled and adaptive public relations approach, from using print media to social media in crafting and delivering targeted promotional messages across multiple communications platforms, has validated its existence within the corporate sphere as a communication management based profession.

PR and communication management roles

From a functional systems perspective, Dozier and Broom (1995) identified two dominant public relations roles, focusing on the communication technician and the communication manager. According to this model, the former highly skilled individual carries out programmes and activities such as news releases, editing newsletters, developing websites and social media campaigns, for example, and is generally not involved in organisational strategic decision-making. The second role of the public relations professional – the communication manager – positions the public relations executive as an integral part of the dominant coalition who plans, manages, and facilitates the communications programme, provides counsel for senior management and makes policy decisions. It would appear that within the profession these two roles occupy a hierarchical position with the managerial role being equated with a perception of enhanced worth and standing (Grunig et al. 2002) and a proportionately higher salary.

Other studies found a gender bias correlating technical, lower managerial jobs with women's work (Aldoory and Toth 2002). Despite findings suggesting that the public relations profession worldwide has more women employees than men (Grunig et al. 2001; Frolich and Peters 2007) the latter still hold the majority of senior managerial positions, which some feminist scholars consider to be an inequitable trend within the industry on a worldwide basis (Edwards 2012).

Yet, although junior level staff often appear to assume most of the technical level jobs, in practice there is a functional overlap: 'most public relations professionals play both manager and technician roles as part of their job' (Devereux and Peirson-Smith 2009: 10). The degree to which they are communication manager or technician will depend on the cultural context, the size of the public relations organisation, length of tenure and the client's needs. The roles that PR or communications managers within organisations are engaged in throughout their working week include monitoring and evaluating the progress of public relations activities; advising on strategic policy for senior management, troubleshooting and crisis management on key issues for an organisation or client, tracking and analysing trends and data of relevance to the client, and technical communication tasks linked to the public relations effort such as writing press releases, web content and annual reports.

In reality, this cross-hatching of strategic and technical duties undertaken by the public relations executive is a consequence of the collaborative nature of the public relations effort (Peirson-Smith et al. 2011). Whether the practitioner works in a public relations agency or in-house in a corporate communications department, the work effort is team based and as such each member of the team will take some role in the cyclical process of research, planning, writing and editing of a text such as a news release, for example as 'generalized specialists' (Seitel 2010: 492).

The practice of public relations across small, medium and large scale enterprises, whether in-house or PR agency-based, is very broad in scope and includes planning, managing and implementing awareness campaigns, managing corporate affairs, identifying issues of relevance to the public interest, crisis communication, public affairs, organisational communication, stakeholder management and technical writing. It has also become increasingly issues based resulting in specialist public relations expertise on health care, consumer, fashion and lifestyle, environment, investor relations and technology communications, for example, being offered inside the corporate communications department of an organisation, within an agency or in the form of small-scale public relations companies. Crisis communications in particular has been a growth field within PR practice over the past 20 years given the realities of product crises – milk powder shortages, product tampering and periodic oil spills to cite a few – and practitioners have been able to offer this under the banner of preparedness planning to clients as a form of insurance. Crises are an inevitable fact of corporate life and can be classified from natural to technological or management misconduct (Lerbinger 2012) or as snakes (Seymour and Moore 2000) and as such can be planned for but not necessarily prevented, despite views to the contrary (Coombs 2010). There are many analyses and dissections of the stages that a typical crisis goes through (Fearn Banks 2007; Coombs 2010), and prescriptive guidelines as to how to manage this situation (Cohn 2000; Anthonissen 2008). At the end of the day, as complexity theory suggests, we inhabit a complex and uncertain world and ideally public relations can assist organisations to prepare for, respond to and manage these unpredictable scenarios using competencies such as monitoring, risk assessment, improvisation, creativity and reflection in order to become proactive, enabling entities (Weick 1979).

Theoretical underpinnings to the practice of PR – how it's analysed

Every profession strives to have a theoretical base with conceptual models that are continuously and empirically tested on the job as a means of establishing and maintaining professional best practice and communications excellence (Grunig 1984; Grunig *et al.* 2002) echoing the normative search for managerial excellence (Peters and Waterman 1982). A good grasp of theory is considered to be a necessary precursor for strategic thinking and planning (Pavlik 1987) as theory enhances practice and provides a way of testing out new ways of doing things.

Public relations is a relative newcomer on the academic scene and on the university syllabus and currently is without a unifying theoretical framework. Hence, it has borrowed concepts from diverse disciplines such as sociology, business, management, marketing, psychology, media and communications, for example, in building an emerging body of public relations theory that provides a variety of perspectives on the profession in terms of how and why it operates as it does.

Despite the consensus-building nature of public relations as an occupation, there is a significant amount of contestation surrounding the theoretical debates that attempt to explain public relations as a phenomenon. Broadly, the academic analysis of public relations resides in dual camps, reflecting two different, but largely Western-framed paradigms based on distinct qualitative and quantitative research approaches and methodologies.

On the one hand, the more prescriptive, functional or systems oriented analytical approach to public relations examines how it operates in practice and how effective it is in the process of establishing social consensus. On the other hand, some approaches to the subject have taken a more critical and less prescriptive analytical angle by focusing on the cultural and societal impact and implications of public relations as a profession and a communications process. Although these are all abstracted representations of public relations reality, and are not mutually exclusive in their application, they are useful models for demonstrating the range of possible public relations approaches in theory and practice and the varying relationships between practitioner and publics across a variety of contexts in the persuasive communications process.

Management theory and public relations

In addition to being accepted as part of the promotional aspects of the marketing function or marketing mix alongside advertising and sponsorship (Kotler 1984), public relations has also been situated within the organisational management system by some scholars (Grunig and Hunt 1984). According to this model, public relations professionals, as communication intermediaries or boundary spanners, enable clients or companies to communicate across organisational lines, both within and outside of the organisation. In this way, public relations professionals become systems managers, where public relations itself is regarded as a key component of the managerial subsystem, having a clear organisational function. Public relations professionals are characterised in this approach as helping other internal corporate subsystems, enabling effective communication within the organisation itself and also by facilitating communication with external audiences or stakeholders. In this way, public relations practice can provide an 'early warning system' or an intelligence gathering system and assumes a counselling role for the organisation by advising on what, and how, to communicate the organisation's philosophy, policy and programmes to identified stakeholders.

As with most communications industries, including advertising and branding, public relations practice has ascribed to the management by objectives model (Drucker 2006; Watson and Noble 2011) utilising the discourse of war (Marchand 1998) to underscore the communications mission, planning strategies and tactics to win the campaign and target the audience. Public relations' strategic role is premised on the basis that its function is to manage communication for the organisations' internal and external stakeholders to ensure that each understands the other. The strategic public relations process aims to facilitate dialogue between the organisation and its multiple audiences in order to communicate a positive message about its activities and achievements. The capacity to formulate strategy is the intellectual talent setting PR apart from the routine aspects of the marketing communications process and the ability to put this into tactical operation is seen by some as the value added characteristic of the PR professional. Implementing the strategic vision for PR practice is framed in terms of the military precision that is prescribed in the form of a blueprint (Gregory 2010) outlining the planning stages and invariably including objectives, situation analysis, strategy, communication messages, implementation and tactics and evaluation. In the interests of effectiveness and good management, evaluating is increasingly seen as an ongoing and critical part of the PR process, rather than simply taking place at the final stages of the programme, and ranges from informal to formal metrics (Macnamara 2011). Yet, in practice there is no unified evaluative benchmark and the debate still rages between the most effective metrics, especially given the increasing adoption of digital media channels and the qualitative versus quantitative nature of the professional evaluation.

The decade long 'Excellence Study' (Grunig 1992; Grunig *et al.* 2002), largely funded by the International Association of Business Communicators (IABC), attempted to identify the ways in which PR could be fully understood and improved by identifying generic benchmarks for effective practice. Ideally, to be effective in delivering the PR effort according to this study, the internal and external communications effort must operate across programme, departmental, organisational and economic levels. At the same time, organisational effectiveness through the public relations effort should align organisational goals with stakeholder interests resulting in monetary profit and long-term strategic alliances. The involvement of senior management is an essential component of this model, as Grunig observes:

> Public relations according to the findings of the study is most likely to contribute to effectiveness when the senor public relations manager is a member of the dominant

collation where he or she is able to shape the organization's goals and to help determine which external public are most strategic.

(1992: 6)

According to this model, in real life public relations scenarios, asymmetric and symmetric communication reside on a continuum at the centre point of which lies a symmetric 'mixed motive' or 'win-win' zone of communication, accommodating the interests and viewpoints of both parties. In addition, the outer ranges of the model represent the public position at one end and the dominant coalition at the other, reflecting the range of dialogue driven by self-interest that prevails across various public relations moments, both asymmetric and symmetric, whose outcomes are tempered by strategies of argument, conciliation and cooperation.

James Grunig and Todd Hunt (1984) also developed an earlier typological model charting the evolution of public relations, albeit from a Western centric viewpoint. This theoretical/practical construct consists of four sections: the propaganda-oriented press agentry/publicity model based on one-way communication often used by emerging governments and product promoters in developing countries in delivering a one sided, angled message; the public information model of truthful one-way communication typified by non-profit organisations, local government departments and some small businesses; the two-way asymmetric model comprising an interactive, yet imbalanced communication flow in favour of the agent or sender as practised by most competitive businesses and political campaigning outfits; and the two-way symmetric model or public relations 'ideal' (abstracted) scenario based on two-way balanced communication resulting in mutual understanding and equal dialogue as used by regulated organisations. The latter was considered to be the benchmark of excellent public relations, yet more recently functional scholars (Dozier, Grunig and Grunig 1995: 2001) concede that the reality of public relations practice tends to reside somewhere between two-way asymmetric and symmetric communication and have reworked their original model, again borrowing notions from game theory premised on the need to balance the interests of the public with the organisations that they interact with (Murphy 1989).

Communications theory and public relations

Public relations is a communications-based profession, in the sense that its rationale is to facilitate mutual symbolic message exchange between an organisation and its stakeholders. In this sense, communication models such as Harold Lasswell's 'who says, what, to whom and with what effect?' (Lasswell 1950) are a valid starting point, yet only present a linear view of PR reminiscent of Grunig's press agentry model (Grunig and Hunt 1984) and other simple one-way or basic two-way sender/receiver communication models such as those of Shannon and Weaver or Wesley and McLean (McQuail and Windhal 1993). The actual effect of mediated messages on receivers is still a matter of debate, and practitioners may ascribe to this view of the all-powerful media machine particularly when pitching to clients as it is more useful to believe that your communications campaign will have the desired persuasive impact than none at all.

Other communications theorists view the actions of the sender to be irrelevant, and focus instead on the role of the receiver in making sense of the communicated message. This audience reception focus is becoming increasingly important with the increased use of social media channels (Cambie and Ooi 2009; Breakenridge 2012). Understanding how audiences decode messages both verbally, visually and aurally depending on their ideological viewpoint and cultural expectations (Fiske 1990) is useful for public relations practitioners as this knowledge can avoid miscommunication or misunderstanding. The uses and gratifications (McQuail 1994; Windhal, Signitzer and Olson 1993), such as entertainment values, and information-seeking behaviours that motivate media audiences, also provide useful insights for the public relations practitioner when choosing effective communication channels to ensure their messages reach their publics and that the message output causes the desired outcome whether cognitive, affective or behavioural. The public relations practitioner can also use Maslow's hierarchy of needs (1954) to identify the perceived wants and self-interests of stakeholders such as basic, safety, social, ego or self-fulfilment needs and then articulate those in public relations messages.

PR preparedness planning and audience response models

Communications can break down resulting in a distortion of the PR message due to a variety of factors, including physical channel noise, psychological noise exercised by the selective receiver, semantic noise due to linguistic misunderstandings, information overload or time constraints, for example. This is always a useful reminder that not all public relations efforts in the public domain succeed or fulfil their objectives. Game theory is one of the ways of reducing the impact of communications failure by enabling the public relations practitioner to determine the best strategy for the intended communication outcome (Murphy 1991) as part of preparedness planning strategy implemented for clients. Equally useful for public relations analysis are models such as the diffusion of innovation theory (Lionberger 1960) outlining how people process data and adopt new ideas by following a staged path of awareness, interest, trial, evaluation and adoption. Equally, Kotler's cognitive, affective, behavioural response hierarchy (Kotler 1984) for eliciting the required consumer response provides insights into the mind of the prospect by showing how public relations messages can be crafted to have the desired effect in an awareness raising campaign for a new product launch, or when launching a public health initiative, for example.

The concepts of information diffusion, opinion formation and the psychological needs of audiences have significant practical applications for public relations practitioners by providing evaluative tools for useful insights into the complexities of how individuals respond to persuasive messages. According to the diffusion of innovation model (Rogers 1971), for example, the audience's cognitive state must be changed first by raising the awareness and developing their interests through mass mediated messages before they accept the product or idea by following peer group reinforcement and word of mouth marketing. Armed with this knowledge, the public relations practitioner may tailor his or her message dissemination to the awareness and interest stages of this process.

The importance of persuasive communication for PR practice is also relevant here (Miller 1989; Pfau and Wan 2006). But beyond the historic link between public relations and propaganda, recent discussions have tended to focus more on negotiation as being key to the communication process. This may be down to the tendency for functional analysis of PR to focus on the process as opposed to the aims and the outcomes, which some suggest are geared at constructing a positive corporate image. A critical extension of this view is taken up by rhetorical theorists who are largely concerned with the language and discourse exchanged between PR professionals and their audiences (Heath and Vasquez 2001), and the actual reception or decoding of promotional messages by audiences, which is addressed in more detail below. Here, the concern lies not so much on what promotional messages can do to the cognitive, affective and behavioural states of receivers in terms of their impact, but with how audiences decipher them and how and why they are used post-reception.

Anne Peirson-Smith

Identifying and sustaining relationships with publics/stakeholders

As public relations is a communications-based profession, most of its daily activity includes interacting with a range of audiences to convey carefully crafted key messages on behalf of clients and organisations. Public relations practitioners do not communicate with the general public, as this is too simplistic and all-encompassing a way of representing what are essentially complex segments of people, or publics, in the plural form, who compose/constitute the audience for public relations messages. These stakeholders (a term originally borrowed from political communication theory) (Freeman 1984; Johnson and Scholes 2008) are linked together by the fact that they often share common demographic (age, gender, income, education, location) and psychographic (lifestyle and aspirational) features and are affected by the organisation whilst also being able to impact on its operations. As such, this can include employees, customers, suppliers, government departments, investors, interest groups and media organisations.

Often the terms 'publics' and stakeholders are used synonymously in the literature, referring to audiences in the public domain that public relations professionals enter into dialogue with. Yet, a distinction has been made between publics and stakeholders in terms of their levels of involvement and engagement with an organisation. According to this approach, publics are seen as active subsets of stakeholders who identify with a specific need because of a perceived issue or problem and decide to do something about it by vocalising their concerns (Grunig and Hunt 1984, 1994). Hence, when people are concerned about healthy lifestyles they may evolve from being generic stakeholders of fast food and soft drinks companies to becoming key publics concerned about the damaging effect of the high levels of sugar and salt contained in their food-based products. Similarly, in practice, public relations professionals would identify the range of stakeholders who are within the remit of an organisation, such as employees, consumers and government officials, and then further classify this universe into primary and secondary publics depending on the key messages that the organisation wants to issue and the audiences that it needs to communicate with on a given issue.

In a further application of the diffusion of innovation model Grunig (1984) and Grunig and Repper (1992) put forward a tripartite typology of audiences termed active, passive and latent. The premise of this model is that passive or inactive audiences with a low knowledge of, and involvement in, the company, product, service or issue being promoted need encouragement to accept the persuasive message. Dynamic strategies, therefore, are devised for engaging passive audiences at the basic level of awareness creation based on attention grabbing communication tactics involving dramatic visuals, arresting sounds, and short, memorable slogans. By comparison, active audiences, having reached the interest stage of the diffusion model, are aware of the product, service or issue and require more complex information through the use of brochures, lengthy news and feature style articles, videos, speeches, and display boards. In reality, passive, active and latent audiences exist in each communications campaign across a sliding scale requiring knowledge and involvement with an issue or an organization and its outputs before engagement takes place (Bao 2009; Hallahan 2000). This is why multiple messages are prepared for a variety of mediated channels to reach target publics, as the multiple links provided on a corporate website or the use of Facebook or Instagram driven promotions, for example, demonstrate.

The linear, one-way asymmetric, centralised communication message flow from one organisation to many has shifted to a more distributed two-way or multi-way communications model affording more control in the hands of the user. Both practitioners and academics from various perspectives recognise that stakeholder relationships for most organisations operating in developed economies are becoming more transactional because of the widespread access to, and use of, digital media platforms by their customers, from emails to blogs. Within this digitised domain the audience or stakeholder is more in control of the message and their ability to comment and feed back on the activities of organisations is enhanced and accelerated. This offers both challenges and opportunities for the profession. On the one hand, it increases the range of communication tools at the disposal of the practitioner to connect in a segmented and targeted way with their intended stakeholders from consumer to pressure group with the opportunity to engage with them more closely and develop a deeper understanding of their attitudes and behaviours. On the other hand, it increases the importance of monitoring the external environment via the enabling technology to determine issues of relevance to the organisation and public perceptions in the interests of accounting for and managing corporate reputation (Forbrun and Van Riel 2004).

Critical responses to the functional systemic models

These abstracted representations of public relations practice and the notion of prescriptive excellence in public relations have been seen by other scholars as idealistic, mythical and misrepresentative of the real communication process, which is more likely to represent the views of vested interests rather than an equitable and pluralistic dialogue (L'Etang 2006; Pieczka 2006). These critiques are centred on the notion that this view of public relations practice is supremely managerial, linking organisational success to efficient management. In addition, it is premised on the notion that PR must be sanctioned and driven by senior management and as such represents elite, top down, rather than horizontal two-way communication (Sriramesh 2007a) requiring 'someone at senior level who can function as a peer professional among other members of the organisation's dominant coalition' (Grunig and Grunig 2009: 638). In addition, the systems based 'excellence' approach to public relations has been criticised for its Western neo-liberal bias and market orientation (Miller and Dinan 2000) equating PR effectiveness with economic success and an assured positive impact on the organisational bottom line (Dutta and Pal 2011).

Other perspectives on public relations as a communications profession have emerged less from the perspective of, and perhaps in opposition to, the prescriptive idea of how public relations should best be done, and are more concerned with whether it should be done at all. Other critics concede that if public relations is to become an accepted part of corporate and professional life then it should be subjected to a critical interpretation of its socio-cultural and economic impact across time, space and place. On the whole, critical approaches to public relations have focused on a critique of public relations as a tool of capitalist oppression used in the interests of propagating the ideologies of powerful entities in political, economic, cultural, organisational, textual and discursive contexts. They also tend to operate at the theoretical level.

Taking a producer focus, critical scholars claim that public relations tends to be part of the capitalist agenda employed in the vested interest of the dominating forces in society such as government and industry. According to this view, the public relations industry, as an active part of the culture industries (Adorno and Horkheimer 1994), is used to protect elite economic interests by representing these dominant viewpoints to the exclusion of other less powerful voices in a given society. This belief is premised on the notion that structurally the economic and political producers control and run the media industry and the news stories in which public relations messages are managed, compounded by the increasing pressure on journalists to generate large amounts of copy across multiple platforms, resulting in a dependence on the PR industry to generate the content for these stories. In addition, other postmodern perspectives on PR (Edwards 2011) suggest that the language embodied in PR messages by practitioners and the metanarrative content of those stories signals which social groups are privileged and covered and which are marginalised and ignored. As Holtzhausen posits, language is used to entrench existing power relations to the detriment of those who are less powerful; or marginalized in society, particularly because their discourses are drowned out by the discourse of those in power. The powerful can do this because they use people such as public relations practitioners to present their ideas as rational and truthful.

(2011: 144)

According to this view, the dominant and powerful social groups gain a voice, whilst the stories and voices of those considered less worthwhile or troublesome remain untold and voiceless. Notably this is the case in emerging economies where there is still an information divide with the powerful elite having more access to, and controlling the communication channels from traditional to digital.

PR in the public sphere

Whilst functional scholars have examined public relations primarily at the transitional level, critical European-based scholars have preferred to research the profession in the societal domain (Jensen 2001) after Habermas' notion (1989) of the public sphere. Here, the debate occurs between political and private entities and the principles of communicative action, which aims ideally for a symmetrical outcome between contesting parties using the language of symmetrical communication, as we might see in discussions between trade unions and companies during industrial action over wage claims. This approach is interested in how all parties – PR professionals, organisations, politicians and stakeholders all contribute on different levels through different and changing discourses (Raupp 2004) to creating social rules and standards through discursive practices in the public domain or the 'persuasive sphere' (Moloney 2006) where all citizens are assumed to have the responsibility to actively decode promotional messages. A good example of this would be the public debates surrounding corporate and social responsibility in general and specifically environmentally responsible practices in the textile industry, where most recently the collapse of a clothing factory in Bangladesh resulted in over 1,000 employee deaths (Associated Press 2013). This catastrophe has sparked a global debate about the lack of regulation in the industry in developing countries and the need for tighter production controls and ethical standards of production and consumption. Ethical concerns with the practice and content of PR have spurred some critical approaches to develop more prescriptive models of how public relations should be practised in the public sphere, from exhorting citizens to be more aware of decoding the persuasive messages they consume, to encouraging PR practitioners to make their communication more truthful and sincere in anticipation of impending public criticism and accountability.

In practical terms, this approach merges both organisational interests with the social impact of their operations in devising consensus-oriented theories or prescriptive models facilitating open and public dialogue with impacted stakeholders. However, rhetorical theorists suggest that, as with the functional symmetrical model, this is too simplistic to be meaningful and it places idealistic emphasis on the ability of all stakeholders to assume equal and ethical responsibility when in fact unequal power relations tend to prevail.

Rhetorical approach to public relations

The rhetorical interpretive approach to analysing public relations that developed alongside, and partly in opposition to, the positivist functional 'excellence' PR school of thought is also concerned with ethics and power relations and how public relations practitioners and their publics might use 'persuasive strategies and argumentative discourse' (L'Etang 2006: 359) to facilitate a consensual dialogue between the parties involved in the debate or the pluralistic wrangle of voices (Heath 2009). This perspective is based on the notion that 'individuals, groups and organisations make meaning, through argument and counter-argument, to create issues, resolve uncertainty, compete to achieve a preferable position or to build coalitions – to solve problems' (Toth 2009: 50). This approach suggests that rhetorical theory can be used to understand the public relations process and its impact on society in its use of narrative, performance, activism and oratory, for example, and in issues management (Heath 2006).

Through the lens of discourse theory and new rhetorical theory public relations is represented as creating and propagating symbolic cultural meaning for organisations and products through a range of modalities whether from the individual practitioners or Foulcauldian 'discourse technologists' (Motion and Leitch 2002, 2007) or the organisational rhetor. In this regard, multinational corporations such as Nike and McDonald's, for example, are seen to peddle the mythic discourse of the American Dream, equating consumption with self-actualisation (Curtin and Gaither 2007) as 'the news and information they disseminate reflect the political and commercial ideologies that define their home nation and ... the developed world' (Edwards 2011: 40). Taking this line, the global health campaigns launched by Coca-Cola could be seen to be a way of deflecting criticism of the harmful cumulative effects of consuming sugar-based drinks. Here, public relations is also seen to construct mediated representations of reality by intensifying discourses such as consumerism that are used selectively by journalists to frame stories and angle events according to the dominant news agenda influenced by the media owner, from Murdoch's Sky News to the Xin Hua news agency.

Cultural, global and international takes on PR

More recently, there has been a focus on public relations within the context of the circuit of culture and communication. This has partly emerged from a concern on the part of some that whilst the public relations industry has a global reach, being increasingly practised across the world (Sriramesh and Verčič 2009b), traversing various cultures, languages and multiple-scapes (Appadurai 1996), it has largely been part of a 'West to Rest' (Hall 1996) trend both in practice and in its theoretical interpretation thereby ignoring local realities and identities. Two schools of thought have emerged with regard to the growing practice of public relations. On the one hand, emerging from a functionalist perspective is the view that PR is a global practice benchmarked against notions of excellence (Verčič, Grunig and Grunig 1996; Sriramesh and White 1992) where, for example, in a multinational corporation all communication for its global subsidiaries is controlled from head office, as the global operations of the Walt Disney Corporation or Nike exemplify. An opposing view suggests that PR is an international practice that should take into consideration, and be led by, considerations of local cultures and social structures at all levels of its transnational operations. According to this approach, Western-style public relations practised by multinational organisations has been imported around the world with US-centred models of public relations excellence being used to benchmark the rest of the world's PR efforts, driven by global firms, who are often owned by multinational conglomerates (Wilcox and Cameron 2010). Local employees are merely cast in the role of cultural interpreters of local culture and language for multinational companies. Equally, they contest, PR pedagogy is dominated by US textbooks and prescribed knowledge leaving continents such as Africa and Asia off the PR map (McKie and Munshi 2007). A more equitable solution perhaps resides in local offices in international enterprises driving the creation and management of products and services and their promotional campaigns to create a symbiotic communication exchange and a closer cultural connection. In support of this point, a recent grounded ethnographic study examining language use and collaborative work practices in Hong Kong public relations firms

(Peirson-Smith et al. 2011) found that in practice people operated in hierarchical dyads consisting of a more experienced writer and a less experienced writer, with the latter researching and gathering materials and the former writing, for example, or the less experienced one doing the first draft and the more experienced one editing it. Naturally, people with different language abilities and backgrounds also took up particular roles in the life cycle of texts such as translation (done by bilingual Chinese staff) and final proofreading (normally done by native English speakers).

Some scholars regard such inequality in power relations as potentially jeopardising the process of successful collaboration, restricting multivocality and stifling the creative tensions that emerge from shifting and multiple authorship roles (Ede and Lunsford 1990).

However, seemingly hierarchical relationships in this study usually appeared to enhance creative collaboration, providing scaffolding for less experienced members to enhance their linguistic and creative skills (Jones et al. 2012) across a range of spoken and written genres of public relations texts.

The relationship between public relations and culture has also been explored from an intercultural communication perspective adopting Hofstede's cultural dimensions (1997) to explain the impact of PR activities on culture and relationships in organisational contexts (Sriramesh and White 1992) based on fixed and stereotypical cultural categories (Kent and Taylor 2002). A few PR scholars and practitioners have examined the relationship between culture and public relations in a relatively static managerial or organisational framework, bounded by territory or by the nation state in separate geographic locations, from Mexico to China, in a particularist case study format that appears to be quite limited in scope (Sriramesh and Verčič 2009, 2012; Chen and Culbertson 2009). Yet, in reality, public relations operates in a broader, glocalised world characterised by a compression of time, space and place where ideas and goods flow across global scapes aided by an increasing reliance on digital technology to disseminate the promotional message. As such, this local-global discourse 'has fundamentally unseated the notion that public relations practices of nations can be captured, compared and evaluated in large scale studies that seek to articulate master narratives of public relations practice' (Pal and Dutta 2008: 164).

A complementary theoretical approach to understanding public relations, its cultural dimensions and its intersections with power, identity and difference has also been offered by Curtin and Gaither's culture-economic model (2007) representing public relations as a cultural practice – being part of the culture in which it operates and being in turn shaped by it. Drawing on the circuit of culture model (Du Gay 1997) the practice of public relations is founded on socio-cultural discursive representations on behalf of clients, producing meaning through texts such as news releases, websites, stories, blogs etc., and constructing various client and stakeholder identities in the process of promoting consumption habits in the promotional culture (Wernick 1991).

In response, some writers, blending theory and praxis, have proposed to focus on a reworked value system and stakeholder engagement process by revising Maslow's hierarchy of needs (1943) into a circular model based on 'authentic, localised cultural motivators', explaining why stakeholders in different cultures operate according to different value systems. In the Asia-Pacific context, for example, appeals to community responsibility may be used as an effective promotional message in a public health campaign. This can be usefully exemplified by grounded operational specifics: 'if you were launching a government funded program in the region to make people more environmentally responsible by recycling all of their household waste, the key message would focus on everyone's responsibility as part of a community effort to develop community ownership of the idea' with the caveat that 'as countries and societies develop, their needs and priorities may change' (Devereux and Peirson-Smith 2009: 9).

On a related topic, the professional culture of public relations as a community or field of practice, or as an occupational group, is a relatively under-researched area. Some studies have focused on the professional culture of public relations in terms of the PR professional's role as cultural intermediary as a channel for the cultural norms and values that are negotiated between organisations and stakeholders. The professional culture of this occupational group comprises their lifeworlds, habitus (Bourdieu 1992) or perceptions about their job, reinforced via socialisation with other professionals and the impact of their actions on a given culture and society in which they work. Other postmodern critics have advocated a new role for the public relations professional in the form of 'the practitioner as organizational activist' operating from within as the 'conscience in the organization resisting dominant power structures', privileging 'employees' and external publics' discourse over that of management' (Holtzhausen and Voto 2002: 64). Such a role is most likely in practice to be assumed by staff associations and trade union representatives or the employee turned blogger, who increasingly use public relations strategies and tactics in framing their viewpoints and representing them to management and the media in cases of employee disputes or corporate malpractice.

Critique of public relations theories

As seen above, the functionalist approach to public relations has been criticised for its prescriptive orientation and positivist perspective, lacking a depth of investigation, or championing metanarratives of economic progress embedded in the discourse of corporate public relations messages (Miller and Dinan 2000). Equally the critical and postmodern theoretical studies have equally been challenged for lacking any substantive contribution to PR practice (Grunig 2001; Tyma 2008) or for supporting a one-sided argument offering disruptive activism as the only viable rationale for public relations practice (Edwards 2011). Equally, others have charged the critical take on public relations practice as being too theoretical and neglecting to accommodate 'a discursive space for engaging with the voices of stakeholders who are typically marginalized though the dominant practice of public relations' (Pal and Dutta 2008: 173) as audience reception research in media studies have done. Furthermore, public relations strategies and tactics are not the sole preserve of corporatised PR and are increasingly being used successfully by NGOs such as Oxfam, Save the Children and Orbis in the interests of promoting causes and aiding the underprivileged. Also, critical theorists and writers are actively involved in some cases in monitoring and publicising the malpractices of the public relations industry, aiming to bring about change, as is the case with the US based PR Watch 'a nonprofit, public interest organization dedicated to investigative reporting on the public relations industry' (PR Watch 2013) that publishes the work of critical public relations scholars, and the UK organisation Spinwatch, which campaigns for greater transparency in UK and EU governance (Spinwatch 2013). Yet, critical theorists may risk the danger of academic elitism pontificating from the safety of their ivory towers, far removed from the workplace realities of public relations. The postmodern analysis of public relations as the representation of multiple viewpoints and identities in a transglobal world also usually has its critics who suggest that it represents another form of colonialism, replacing old sets of metanarratives with new ones of fragmentation and fluidity, still privileging the interests of more powerful educated groups over weaker ones, particularly in developing or newly industrialised countries.

Future directions – where public relations is going

The future challenges for the public relations profession are of concern to both practitioners working in, and academics researching the field. Public relations appears to be consolidating its supremacy in the communications and marketing industries as a key part of the strategic promotional effort based on establishing closer dialogue between an organisation and its publics in the interest of maintaining corporate reputation and acknowledgement of achievement.

Practitioners and functional academics alike believe that the profession's ability to fulfil its promise as a top strategic management function will be achieved through greater professionalism, a more unified industry, adherence to ethical codes of practice, enhanced creativity, integrated communication, and closer ties being forged between public relations education and the workplace to boost core skills and validated qualifications, and to equalise ethnic, subaltern and gender relations. The increased demands for fast-paced globalised message delivery and integrated communications efforts will require the careful management of human resources within the profession in terms of providing guidance on attaining a work-life balance across cultures.

The challenges and opportunities presented by enhanced digital technology channels will have to be met both through strategic corporate reputation management and tactical message delivery via corporate websites by servicing stakeholder/media relations through evolving digital communication channels. Digital communication channels clearly provide more opportunity for dialogic exchange between practitioner and publics that re-addresses power relations in terms of who is and should be in control of the message and who has access to the debate. These digital democracies offered to stakeholders have implications for normative practices and critical considerations of public relations practice serving as a reminder of the dynamic environments in which human, intercultural and corporate communication exchanges operate.

The twenty-first-century public relations industry operates increasingly at an international level traversing cultural, linguistic, political and economic differences across some of the largest and smallest populations, active and inactive markets, richest and poorest nations and most educated and under-educated countries throughout the globe. This presents considerable challenges for PR practice in public and private sector transnational and local organisations and NGOs. Public relations could play an important role in giving voice to diversity, new market activity and social responsibility given the decline of Western market supremacy and the emergence of a new world political order with a focus on non-Western social, cultural and economic issues. This necessitates a good working knowledge of local market needs and stakeholder inclusion by public relations practitioners in their work at all levels. It also requires the development of global capabilities accommodating local cultural sensitivities – enabling the dialogue to flow from outside-in and inside-out aligned with dynamic transglobal trade exchanges. At the same time, the future role of PR and those who work in the industry will be concerned with ensuring that all voices are accommodated in public relations discourses around key issues across a range of communication platforms to ensure that equitable and ethical decisions and choices are implemented across local, national and international contexts.

Related topics

public relations; corporate communications, promotional discourse; strategic communications, communications management; persuasive communication

Key readings

Devereux, M. M. and Peirson-Smith, A. (2009). *Public Relations in Asia Pacific: Communicating Effectively across Cultures*, Singapore: John Wiley & Sons. (A unique professional insight into the strategic and tactical approaches to international public relations practice across the Asia-Pacific region with grounded case examples to illustrate best practice.)

L'Etang, J. and Pieczka, M. (eds) (2006). *Public Relations: Critical Debates and Contemporary Practice*, Mahwah, NJ: Lawrence Erlbaum Associates. (An interdisciplinary reader covering key critical theoretical debates from a range of authors on public relations issues.)

Grunig, L. A., Grunig, J. E. and Dozier, D. M. (2002). *Excellent Public Relations and Effective Organizations: A Study of Communication Management in Three Countries*, Mahwah, NJ: Lawrence Erlbaum. (The final output of the IABC funded 'Excellence' project provides a functional, quantitative and comparative analysis of public relations practice across selected global locations that has been widely followed in practice and much debated by PR theorists.)

Heath, R. L., Toth, E. L. and Waymer, D. (2009). *Rhetorical and Critical Approaches to Public Relations II*, New York: Routledge. (A rhetorical/critical approach to public relations practice from a range of writers covering the theory and practice of public relations from various rhetorical angles including ethics, advocacy and activism.)

Sriramesh, K. and Verčič, D. (2009). *The Global Public Relations Handbook: Theory, Research, and Practice*, Mahwah, NJ: Lawrence Erlbaum. (A comprehensive nation by nation case reader focussing on public relations theory and practice from a global and cultural public relations perspective.)

Bibliography

Adorno, T. and Horkheimer, M. (1944). 'The culture industry: Enlightenment as mass deception', in T. Adorno and M. Horkheimer (eds) (1972), *Dialectics of Enlightenment* (translated by John Cumming), New York: Herder and Herder.

Aldoory, L. and Toth, E. (2002). 'Gender discrepancies in a gendered profession. A developing theory for public relations', *Journal of Public Relations Research*, 14(2), 103–26.

Anthonissen, P. F. (2008). *Crisis Communication: Practical PR Strategies for Reputation Management and Company Survival*, London: Kogan Page.

Appadurai, A. (1996). *Modernity at Large: Cultural Dimensions of Globalization*, Minneapolis, MN: University of Minnesota Press.

Asian PR News (2000). 'The billion dollar asset that's hard to see, and even harder to manage. Full-page advertisement for Burson Marsteller', *Asian PR News*, February 28, 5.

Associated Press (2013). 'Tragedy shows dark heart of garment trade', *South China Morning Post*, 30 April, A12.

Bao, X. (2009). *Inactive Publics in Organizational Crisis a Test of Crisis Communication Strategies' Effects on Information-seeking Behavior and Attitudes*, Gainesville, FL: University of Florida.

Bernays, E. L. (1928). *Propaganda*, New York: H. Liveright.

Bourdieu, P. (1992). *The Field of Cultural Production: Essays in Art and Literature*, Cambridge, UK: Polity Press.

Breakenridge, D. (2012). *Social Media and Public Relations: Eight New Practices for the PR Professional*, Upper Saddle River, NJ: FT Press.

Cambie, S. and Ooi, Y. (2009). *International Communications Strategy Developments in Cross-cultural Communications, PR and Social Media*, London: Kogan Page.

Chen, N. (1996). 'Public relations in China: The introduction and development of an occupational field', in Ni Chen and Hugh Culbertson (eds), *International Public Relations: A Comparative Analysis* (pp. 121–54), Mahwah, NJ: Lawrence Erlbaum Associates.

Chen, N. and Culbertson, H. M. (2009). 'Public relations in Mainland China. An adolescent with growing pains', in K. Sriramesh and D. Verčič, *The Global Public Relations Handbook: Theory, Research, and Practice* (pp. 22–45), Mahwah, NJ: Lawrence Erlbaum.

Cheney, G. and Christensen, L. T. (2001). 'Public relations as a contested terrain: A critical response', in R. L. Heath and G. Vasquez, *Handbook of Public Relations* (pp. 167–203), Thousand Oaks, CA: Sage Publications.

Childers Hon, L. and Grunig, J. E. (1999). *Guidelines for Measuring Relationships in Public Relation*, Institute of Public Relations Report (IPR), November 1999. Available at www.instituteforpr.org (accessed 15 January 2013).

CIPR (2011). *CIPR: State of the PR Profession Benchmark Survey*, December 2011, London: CIPR, Communication Research Ltd.

Cohn, R. (2000). *The PR Crisis Bible: How to Take Charge of the Media When All Hell Breaks Loose*, New York: St Martin's Press.

Coombs, W. T. (2010). 'Parameters for crisis communications', in W. T. Coombs and S. J. Holiday (eds), *The Handbook of Crisis Communications* (pp. 17–53), Chichester, UK: Blackwell Publishing.

Council of Public Relations (CIPR) (2010). *State of the Public Relations Profession: Benchmarking Survey*, London: CIPR/ComRes, Available at www.cipr.co.uk/sites/default/files/CIPR%20State%20of%20the%20profession%20benchmarking%20survey%202010%20Sept.pdf. (accessed 9 September 2010).

——(2013). *What is PR?* Available at www.cipr.co.uk/content/careers-cpd/careers-pr/what-pr (accessed 6 February, 2013).

Curtin, P. A. and Gaither, T. K. (2007). *International Public Relations: Negotiating Culture, Identity, and Power*, Thousand Oaks, CA: Sage Publications.

——(2012). *Globalization and Public Relations in Postcolonial Nations*, Amherst, NY: Cambria Press.

Cutlip, S. M. (1995). *Public Relations History: From the 17th to the 20th Century: The Antecedents*, Hillsdale, NJ: Erlbaum.

Cutlip, S. M, Center, A. and Broom, G. (2006). *Effective Public Relations* (9th edn), Upper Saddle River, NJ: Pearson Prentice Hall.

Devereux, M. M. and Peirson-Smith, A. (2009). *Public Relations in Asia Pacific: Communicating Effectively Across Cultures*, Singapore: John Wiley & Sons.

Dozier, D. M. and Broom, G. M. (1995). 'Evolution of the manager role in public relations practices', *Journal of Public Relations Research*, 7(1), 3–26.

——(2006). 'The centrality of practitioner roles to public relations theory', in C. H. Botan and V. Hazleton (eds), *Public Relations Theory II* (pp. 137–70), Mahwah, NJ: Lawrence Erlbaum Associates.

Dozier, D. M., Grunig, L. A. and Grunig, J. E. (1995). *Manager's Guide to Excellence in Public Relations and Communication Management*, Mahwah, NJ: Lawrence Erlbaum & Associates.

Drucker, P. F. (2006). *The Practice of Management*, New York, NY: Collins.

Du Gay, P. (1997). *Doing Cultural Studies: The Story of the Sony Walkman*, London: Sage, in association with The Open University.

Dutta, M.J. and Pal, M. (2011). 'Public relations and marginalization in a global context: A postcolonial critique', in N. Bardhan and C. K. Weaver (pp. 195–225), *Public Relations in Global Cultural Contexts: Multi-Paradigmatic Perspectives*, New York: Routledge.

Ede, L. and Lunsford, S. (1990). *Singular Texts/Plural Authors: Perspectives on Collaborative Writing*, Carbondale: Southern Illinois University.

Edwards, L. (2011). 'Critical perspectives in global public relations: Theorizing power', in N. Bardhan and C. K. Weaver, *Public Relations in Global Cultural Contexts: Multi-Paradigmatic Perspectives* (pp. 29–49), New York: Routledge.

——(2012). 'Public relations occupational culture: Habitus, exclusion and resistance in the UK context', in K. Sriramesh and D. Verčič, *Culture and Public Relations: Links and Implications* (pp. 142–62), New York, NY: Routledge.

Ewen, S. (1996). *A Social History of Spin*, New York: Basic Books.

Fearn Banks, K. (2007). *Crisis Communications: A Casebook Approach* (3rd edn), Mahwah, NJ: Lawrence Erlbaum Associates.

Fiske, J. (1990). *Introduction to Communication Studies*, London: Routledge.

Forbrun, C. J. and van Riel, C. B. M. (2004). *How Successful Companies Build Winning Reputations*, New York: Prentice Hall, Financial Times.

Forrest, A. (2002). 'PR now the force behind the product', *Sunday Money, Sunday Morning Post*, 13 October, 5.

Freeman, R. E. (1984). *Strategic Management: A Stakeholder Approach*, Boston: Pitman.

Frolich, H. and Peters, S. (2007). 'PR bunnies caught in the agency ghetto? Gender stereotypes, organizational factors and women's careers in PR agencies', *Journal of Public Relations Research*, 19(3), 229–54.

Gregory, A. (2010). *Planning and Managing Public Relations Campaigns: A Strategic Approach* (3rd edn), London: Kogan Page.

Grunig, J. E. (1984). 'Organisations, environments and models of public relations', *Public Relations Research and Education*, 1(4), 6–29.

——(1992). *Excellence in Public Relations and Communication Management* (9th edn), Hillsdale, NJ: L. Erlbaum Associates.

——(2001). 'Two-way symmetrical public relations: Past, present and future', in R. L. Heath (ed.), *Handbook of Public Relations* (pp. 11–30), Thousand Oaks, CA: Sage.

Grunig, J. E. and Grunig, L. (2009). 'Public relations in the United States: A generation of maturation', in K. Sriramesh, and D. Verčič, *The Global Public Relations Handbook: Theory, Research, and Practice* (pp. 621–53), Mahwah, NJ: Lawrence Erlbaum.

Grunig, L. A., Grunig, J. E. and Dozier, D. M. (2002). *Excellent Public Relations and Effective Organizations: A Study of Communication Management in Three Countries*, Mahwah, NJ: Lawrence Erlbaum.
Grunig, J. E. and Hunt, T. (1984). *Managing Public Relations*, New York: Holt, Rinehart & Winston.
Grunig, J. and Repper, F. (1992). 'Strategic management, publics and issues', in J. Grunig (ed.), *Excellence in Public Relations and Communications Management* (pp. 117–57), Mahwah, NJ: Lawrence Erlbaum.
Grunig, L. A., Toth, E. L. and Hon, L. C. (2001). *Women in Public Relations: How Gender Influences Practice*, New York: Guilford Press.
Habermas, J. (1989). *The Structural Transformation of the Public Sphere: An Inquiry into a Category of Bourgeois Society*, Cambridge: Polity Press.
Hagley, T. (2002). 'Public relations: A necessary component of an MBA', *The Public Relations Strategist*, Summer, 32–33.
Hall, S. (1996), 'The west and the rest: Discourse and power', in S. Hall, D. Held, D. Hubert and K. Thompson (eds), *Modernity: An Introduction to Modern Societies* (pp. 185–227), Malden, MA: Blackwell.
Hallahan, K. (1999). 'Seven models of framing implications for public relations', *Public Relations Review*, 11(3), 205–42.
——(2000). 'Inactive publics: The forgotten publics in public relations', *Public Relations Review*, 26(4). 499–515.
Heath, R. L. (1991). 'Public relations research and education: Agendas for the 1990s', *Public Relations Review*, 17(2), Summer, 185–94.
——(2006). 'A rhetorical approach to issues management', in C. Botan and V. Hazelton (eds), *Public Relations Theory II* (pp. 499–522), NJ: Lawrence Erlbaum Associates.
——(2009). 'The rhetorical tradition: Wrangle in the marketplace', in R. L. Heath, E. L. Toth and D. Waymer, *Rhetorical and Critical Approaches to Public Relations II* (pp. 17–47), New York: Routledge.
——(2010). *The SAGE Handbook of Public Relations* (2nd edn), London: Sage.
Heath, R. L. and Vasquez, G. (2001). *Handbook of Public Relations*, Thousand Oaks, CA: Sage.
Hofstede, G. (1997). *Cultures and Organizations, Software of the Mind: Intercultural Cooperation and its Importance for Survival*, New York: McGraw Hill.
Holmes, P. (2012). 'Global PR industry up 10 per cent to 10 billion'. Available at www.holmesreport.com; http://globalpragencies.com/top-250 (accessed 8 May 2013).
Holtzhausen, D. (2011). 'The need for a postmodern turn in public relations', in N. Bardhan, *Public Relations in Global Cultural Contexts: Multi-paradigmatic Perspectives* (pp. 140–66), New York: Routledge.
Holtzhausen, D. and Voto, R. (2002). 'Resistance from the margins: The postmodern political relations practitioner as organizational activity', *Journal of Public Relations Research*, 14(1) 57–84.
Horkheimer, M. and Adorno, T. W. (1972). *Dialectic of Enlightenment*. New York: Herder and Herder.
Huang, Y. H. (2000). 'The personal influence model and Gao Guanxi in Taiwan Chinese public relations', *Public Relations Review*, Summer, 26(2), 219–36.
Hunt, T. and Grunig, J. E. (1994). *Public Relations Techniques*, Boston: Harcourt Brace Publishers.
Jensen, I. (2001). 'Public relations and emerging functions of the public sphere: An analytical framework', *Journal of Communication Management*, 6(2), 133–47.
Johnson, G. and Scholes, K. (2008). *Exploring Corporate Strategy* (8th edn), Harlow: Financial Times Prentice Hall.
Jones, R., Bhatia, V. K., Bremner, S. and Peirson-Smith, A. (2012) 'Creative collaboration in the public relations industry', in R. Jones (ed.), *Discourse and Creativity* (pp. 93–107), Harlow, UK: Pearson Education.
Jowett, G. S. and O'Donnell, V. (1992). *Propaganda and Persuasion*, 2nd Edition, Belmont, CA: Wadsworth.
Kent, M. L. and Taylor, M. (2002). 'Toward a dialogic theory of public relations', *Public Relations Review*, 28(1), 21–37.
Kotler, P. (1984). *Marketing Management*, Englewood Cliffs, NJ: Prentice Hall.
Kotler, P. and Mindak, W. (1978). 'Marketing and public relations: Should they be partners or rivals?' *Journal of Marketing*, 42(10), 13–20.
L'Etang, J. (1998). *The Development of British Public Relations in the Twentieth Century*, Paper delivered to IAMCR Conference, Glasgow, 23–26 July 1998.
——(2004). *Public Relations in Britain: A History of Professional Practice in the Twentieth Century*, Mahwah, NJ: Lawrence Erlbaum Associates.
——(2006) 'Public relations and propaganda: Conceptual issues, methodological problems and public relations discourse', in J. Etang and M. Pieczka (eds), *Public Relations: Critical Debates and Contemporary Practice* (pp. 23–40), Mahwah, NJ: Lawrence Erlbaum Associates.

——(2008). *Public Relations: Concepts, Practice, Critique*, London: Sage.
Lasswell, H. D. (1950). *A Study of Power*, Glencoe, IL: Free Press.
Lerbinger, O. (2012). *The Crisis Manager: Facing Disasters, Conflicts, and Failures* (2nd edn), New York: Routledge.
Lionberger, H. (1960). *Adoption of New Ideas and Practices*, Ames: Iowa State University Press.
Macnamara, J. R. (2011). *Public Relations: Theories, Practices, Critiques*, Frenchs Forest, NSW: Pearson Australia.
Marchand, R. (1998). *Creating the Corporate Soul: The Rise of Public Relations and Corporate Imagery in American Big Business*, Berkeley and Los Angeles, CA: University of California Press.
McKie, D. and Munshi, D. (2007). *Reconfiguring Public Relations: Ecology, Equity, and Enterprise*, London: Routledge.
McQuail, D. (1994). *Mass Communication Theory*, London: Sage.
McQuail, D. and Windahl, S. (1993). *Communication Models for the Study of Mass Communications*, 2nd edn, London: Longman.
Maslow, A. H. (1943). 'A theory of human motivation', *Psychological Review*, 50(4), 370–96.
Maslow, A. (1954). *Motivation and Personality*, New York: Harper and Row.
Miller, G. A. (1989). 'Persuasion and public relations: Two 'Ps' in a pod?' in C. H. Botan and V. Hazleton (eds), *Public Relations Theory* (pp. 45–66), Hillsdale, NJ: L. Erlbaum Associates.
Miller, D. and Dinan, W. (2000). 'The rise of the PR industry in Britain, 1979–88', *European Journal of Communication*, 15(1), 5–35.
Moloney, K. (2006). *Rethinking Public Relations: PR Propaganda and Democracy* (2nd edn), London: Routledge.
Morris, T. and Goldsworthy, S. (2008). *PR – a Persuasive Industry? Spin, Public Relations, and the Shaping of the Modern Media*, Basingstoke, England: Palgrave Macmillan.
Motion, J. and Leitch, S. (2002). 'The technologies of corporate identity', *International Studies of Management & Organization*, 32(3), 45–64.
Murphy, P. (1989). 'Game theory as a paradigm for the public relations process', in C. Botan and V. Hazelton (eds), *Public Relations Theory* (pp. 173–92), NJ: Lawrence Erlbaum Associates.
——(1991). 'The limits of symmetry: A game theory approach to symmetric and asymmetric public relations', *Public Relations Research Annual*, 3(1–4), 115–31.
Napoli, P. M., Taylor, M. and Powers, G. (1999) 'Writing activities of public relations practice: The relationship between experience and writing tasks', *Public Relations Review*, 25(3), Autumn 1999, 369–80.
Nessman, K. (2000). 'The origins and development of public relations in Germany and Austria', in D. Moss, D. Verčič and G. Warnaby, *Perspectives on Public Relations Research* (pp. 211–225), London: Routledge.
Pal, M. and Dutta, M. J. (2008). 'Public relations in global contexts: The relevance of critical modernism as a theoretical lens', *Journal of Public Relations Research*, 20(2) 159–79.
Pavlik, J. V. (1987). *Public Relations: What the Research Tells Us*, Beverly Hills, CA: Sage Publications.
Peirson-Smith, A., Bhatia, V. K., Bremner, S. and Jones, R. (2011). 'Creative English and public relations in Hong Kong', *World Englishes*, 29(4), 523–35.
Peters, T. J. and Waterman, R. H. (1982). *In Search of Excellence: Lessons from America's Best-run Companies*, New York: Harper & Row.
Pfau, M. and Wan, Hua-Hsin (2006). 'Persuasion: An intrinsic function of public relations', in C. Botan and V. Hazleton (eds), *Public Relations Theory II* (pp. 101–36), Mahwah, NJ: Lawrence Erlbaum Associates.
Pieczka, M. (2006). 'Paradigms, systems theory and public relations', in J. L'Etang, and M. Pieczka, *Public Relations: Critical Debates and Contemporary Practice* (pp. 331–58), Mahwah: Lawrence Erlbaum Associates Inc.
PR Watch (2013). Available at www.prwatch.org (accessed 7 February 2013).
Raupp, J. (2004). 'Public sphere as a central concept of public relations', in B. van Ruler and D. Verčič (eds), *Public Relations and Communications Management in Europe* (pp. 309–16), Berlin: Mouton de Gruyter.
Riel, C. B. and Fombrun, C. J. (2007). *Essentials of Corporate Communication: Implementing Practices for Effective Reputation Management*, London: Routledge.
Ries, A. and Ries, L. (2002). *The Fall of Advertising and the Rise of PR*, New York: Harper Business.
Rogers, E. M. (1971). *Communication of Innovations: A Cross-cultural Approach*, (2nd edn), New York: Free Press.
Seitel, Fraser P. (2010). *The Practice of Public Relations*, 11th edn, Englewood Cliffs, NJ: Prentice Hall.

Seymour, M. and Moore, S. (2000). *Effective Crisis Management: Worldwide Principles and Practice*, London: Cassell.

Spinwatch (2013). Available at www.spinwatch.org (accessed 10 February 2013).

Sriramesh, K. (2007a) 'The relation between culture and public relations', in E. L. Toth (ed.), *The Future of Excellence in Public Relations and Communications Management: Challenges for the Next Generation* (pp. 507–26), Mahwah, NJ: Lawrence Erlbaum Associates.

Sriramesh, K. (2007b). *Impact of Globalization on Public Relations: A Special Section from the BledCom 2007 Conference*, Amsterdam: Elsevier.

Sriramesh, K. and Verčič, D. (2009a). *The Global Public Relations Handbook: Theory, Research, and Practice*, Mahwah, NJ: Lawrence Erlbaum.

——(2009b). 'A theoretical framework for global public relations research and practice', in K. Sriramesh and D. Verčič (eds), *The Global Public Relations Handbook: Theory, Research, and Practice* (pp. 1–19), Mahwah, NJ.: Lawrence Erlbaum.

——(2012). *Culture and Public Relations: Links and Implications*, New York, NY: Routledge.

Sriramesh, K. and White, J. (1992). 'Societal culture and public relations', in *Excellence in Public Relations and Communication Management* (9th edn) (pp. 597–614), Hillsdale, NJ: L. Erlbaum Associates.

Stauber, J. C. and Rampton, S. (1995). *Toxic Sludge is Good For You: Lies, Damn Lies, and the Public Relations Industry*, Monroe, ME: Common Courage Press.

Taylor, M. (2001). 'Internationalizing the public relations curriculum', *Public Relations Review*, 27(1), Spring, 73–88.

Toth, E. (2009). 'The case for pluralistic studies of public relations', in R. L. Heath, E. Toth and D. Waymer (eds), *Rhetorical and Critical Approaches to Public Relations*. Volume 2 (pp. 48–60), New York: Routledge.

Toth, O. (2002). 'Are you well rewarded?' *PR Week*, 11 October, 8–12.

Tyma, A. (2008). 'Public relations through a new lens: Critical praxis via the "Excellence Theory"', *International Journal of Communications*, 2, 193–205.

Verčič, D., Grunig, J. E. and Grunig, L. A. (1996). 'Global and specific principles of public relations: Evidence from Slovenia', in H. M. Culbertoson and N. Chen, *International Public Relations: A Comparative Analysis* (pp. 31–65), Mahwah, NJ: Erlbaum.

Watson, T. and Noble, P. (2007). *Evaluating Public Relations: A Best Practice Guide to Public Relations Planning, Research and Evaluation* (2nd edn), London: Kogan Page.

Weick, K. E. (1979). *The Social Psychology of Organizing*, Reading, MA: Addison-Wesley.

Wenger, E., McDermott, R. A. and Snyder, W. (2002). *Cultivating Communities of Practice: A Guide to Managing Knowledge*, Boston, MA: Harvard Business School Press.

Wernick, A. (1991). *Promotional Culture: Advertising, Ideology, and Symbolic Expression*, London: Sage Publications.

White, J. and Manzur, L. (1995) *Strategic Communications Management: Making Public Relations Work*, Wokingham, UK: Addison-Wesley.

Wilcox, D. L. and Cameron, G. T. (2009). *Public Relations: Strategies and Tactics* (9th edn), Boston, MA: Pearson, Allen & Bacon.

——(2010). *Public Relations: Strategies and Tactics*, 9th edition, Upper Saddle River, NJ: Pearson Education.

Windhal, J., Signitzer, B. and Olson, J. (1993). *Using Communication Theory*, London: Sage.

Section 3
Acquisition of professional competence

27
Communities in studies of discursive practices and discursive practices in communities

Becky S. C. Kwan

Introduction

For more than two decades now, the field of Applied Linguistics has witnessed much research interest in discursive practices in a wide range of academic and professional settings as also reflected in some of the chapters in this volume. The wealth of studies conducted has mostly been motivated to serve practical ends such as those in ESP instruction and corporate communication training. Despite the diversity in their focuses and methodological approaches, many such studies share some of the same terminology when referring to their contexts of investigation, and among the most common is the notion of *community*, a term that has been linguistically modified in a variety of ways. We have, for example, *discourse community, community of practice and scientific community*, which have now become widely invoked in the literature. In this chapter, I will provide a brief overview of the epistemic origins of the three notions of community, how they have been characterised, how they have been taken up in early and current studies of professional communication, and what the plethora of language studies have revealed about discursive practices in specific communities. I will end the chapter by proposing some of the directions that future studies of discursive practices in specific communities may consider.

Origins of the three notions of community

Though originating from different epistemic domains, the three notions of *discourse community, scientific community* and *community of practice* have interesting parallels with a notable one being that the introduction of all three has been marked by a social constructionist turn in their own domains to the study of production of knowledge and discourse. The notion of *scientific community*, though dating back to the 1942 speech delivered by Michael Polyani to the Manchester Literary and Philosophical Society (Guerrero 1980 cited in Gaillard 1994), was actually popularised by sociologists and philosophers of science two decades later in their critiques of the essentialist as well as realist views of scientific knowledge and knowledge production that dominated the time (e.g. Hagstrom 1965; Kuhn 1962, 1977; Merton 1973; Rorty 1979). Warren Hagstrom (1965), for example, provided a detailed account that shows that science is the activity of a human group and that it is shaped by various mechanisms of social control and in particular reward systems established within the group. Taking a more critical stance, Richard Rorty (1979), in his seminal work *Philosophy and the Mirror of Nature*, disputes the entrenched belief that the mind can faithfully mirror an external reality, and argues that knowledge is only what a particular society produces based on its accepted norms and rules, as such knowledge itself involves a social justification of belief. Likewise, Thomas Kuhn in his *Structure of Scientific Revolution* (1962) sees that scientific discoveries and inventions such as those of physical optics, electricity and heat are made possible by the paradigms (i.e. the theories and tools) that have been developed through past achievements within a scientific tradition (community) and that are shared and upheld by its followers. By relying on the paradigms, scientists in a community generate knowledge that can be accumulated to explain a phenomenon in a puzzle-solving manner, which Kuhn describes as normal science.

Discussions of 'discourse community' started to emerge in the 80s in some of the literature of composition studies and technical communication. Among the earliest pieces in which the notion was used is *The Invisible College* by Bartholomae (1985), which expounds the struggles facing university students in the US as they write for their professors, as captured in the following famous excerpt:

> Every time a student sits down to write for us, he has to invent the university for the occasion – invent the university, that is, or a branch of it, like history or anthropology or economics or English. The student has to learn to speak our language, to speak as we do, to try on the peculiar ways of knowing, selecting, evaluating, reporting, concluding, and arguing that define the discourse of our community.
>
> *(Bartholomae 1985: 134)*

The university in Bartholomae's quote was considered, probably for the first time, to be a discourse community that has its own shared language, its own shared ways of knowing and reasoning, and its own shared ways of speaking. His work came at a time when composition scholars started to realise the failure of the expressivist and cognitivist (process) writing pedagogies in helping students to master the conventions and norms of the academic discourse needed in their own disciplines. Bartholomae's work was among the more vocal calls for revamping the writing curriculum in US to help in initiating students into the discourse community of the university.

Another piece of early work, from which the notion of discourse community was thought to have come, is *Is There a Text in This Class?* by Fish (1980) who introduced the notion of interpretive community to represent the institution of literary study. The community, as Fish argues, carries its own assumptions and norms that govern how literary texts should be interpreted. The term has later been cited as discourse community by scholars of composition studies, scientific and technical communication studies to mean various disciplinary communities (see e.g. Zappen 1989). Both Bartholomae's and Fish's descriptions of discourse community suggest that it is the social norms within a community that shape the ways language is used therein.

While the exact origin of the notion remains unknown, Swales (1990) has traced its formative influences to some of the seminal works of Anthropology, Literary Studies, New Rhetoric, and Sociology of Science written by 'the leading "relativist" or "social constructionist" thinkers" of our time' (Swales 1990: 21). Citing from Bruffee (1986), Herzberg (1986) and Porter (1988), Swales listed *The New Rhetoric* by Chaïm Perelman and Lucie Olbrechts-Tyteca (1969), *Structure of Scientific Revolutions* by Thomas Kuhn (1970), *Is There a Text in This Class?* by

Stanley Fish (1980), *The Archaeology of Knowledge* by Michel Foucault (1972), *Philosophy and the Mirror of Nature* by Richard Rorty (1979), *Local Knowledge* by Clifford Geertz (1983) and *Philosophical Investigations* by (Wittgenstein 1958).

The notion of 'community of practice' first appeared in Lave and Wenger's (1991) widely cited volume *Situated Learning: Legitimate Peripheral Participation*, which is considered by many to mark a major paradigm shift in conceptualising learning. The volume came at a time when education scholars and especially anthropologists of education became concerned about the failures in education in preparing students for participating in the daily activities of their professional life. The authors illustrated how learning takes place in the real world and how different it is from that in formal educational settings by drawing on studies that examined apprenticeships in five different domains (namely Yucatec midwives, Vai and Gola Tailors, US naval quartermasters, butcher's apprentices in supermarkets, and Alcoholics Anonymous), each of which was referred to as a community of practice. One central argument in the volume is that newcomers to a community develop their knowledge and skills (i.e. norms, values, world views and practices) *in situ*, often through participating in its activities and through interactions with old-timers and other artifacts of the community; hence learning is very much a social process.

Attempts to define the notions

When they first appeared in the literature, all three notions of community were used in a rather loose manner. Their meanings were only clarified in subsequent works, often though after contested uses in the literature and criticisms from other scholars. For example, responding to critiques of his *Structure of Scientific Revolutions*, Kuhn in his *The Essential Tension* (*Tension* henceforth) (1977) openly admitted that:

> Throughout *Structure of Scientific Revolutions* I identify and differentiate scientific communities by subject matter, implying, for example, that such terms as 'physical optics,' 'electricity', and 'heat' can serve to designate individual scientific communities just because they also designate subject matters for research. Once pointed out, the anachronism is obvious. I would now insist that scientific communities must be discovered by examining patterns of education and communication before asking which particular research problems engage each group.
>
> *(Kuhn 1977: xvi)*

In *Tension*, Kuhn (1977) characterised a scientific community as one that 'consists of ... practitioners of a scientific speciality', who are 'bound together by common elements in their education and apprenticeship'. Members of a scientific community 'see themselves and are seen by others as the men responsible for the pursuit of a set of shared goals, and also share in values, symbolic generalizations, models, ontology, metaphysical commitment and scientific techniques' (1977: 296). Kuhn goes on to explain that a scientific community can be identified through its professional societies, the journals read by its members, the conferences and seminars they attend, and the informal and formal networks of communication, as well as the connections among citations. To Kuhn, such scientific communities can exist at different levels. Natural scientists take up one level of scientific community, which subsumes the different communities of physicists, chemists, astronomers and zoologists, each of which in turn subsumes different specialist groups, which too can be regarded as scientific communities. A scientific community, as seen by Kuhn and assumed by many sociologists of science of the time, is not only a social but also an autonomous entity that has its own internal mechanisms regulating and shaping scientific pursuits. This assumption is increasingly challenged by contemporary scholars of higher education, and I will return to this issue in a later section.

Likewise, *discourse community* was also used rather intuitively in earlier discussions and probably for this reason its meaning has also been disputed by some of the scholars of the time (see e.g. Kent 1991; Harris 1989; Bizzell 1992). Swales (1987; cited in Bizzell 1992, 1990) is probably the only person who has attempted to define the notion. To Swales, a discourse community is a group of people who pursue a broadly agreed set of common public goals which may be tacit or formally documented. Members of the group communicate with each other through specific mechanisms such as meetings, telecommunications, correspondence, newsletters and conversations. Its members are involved in information exchanges. The group over time develops and possesses one or more genres that are used 'in the communicative furtherance of its aims' (Swales 1990: 26). It also develops and possesses its own specific lexis, abbreviations and acronyms that take on specific meanings known to members of the group. Finally, a community has a threshold level of members with a suitable degree of relevant content and discoursal expertise. Members of the community enter as apprentices, implying that their content and discoursal knowledge is developed *in situ* through participating in the community. Swales illustrates the six criteria by using the Hong Kong Stamps Association of which he is a distant (rather inactive) member. Swales also adds that at any one time, a person may belong to more than one discourse community, and thus may need to develop the discoursal skills required in the different communities. Much like previous interpretations of the notion, Swales underscores shared discursive conventions and norms as the major criteria used to define a discourse community.

The meaning of a community of practice was clarified in a later volume by Wenger (1998). According to Wenger, the notion is both a theoretical construct and a unit of analysis. To Wenger, what makes a group of people a community of practice is the practice in which the group is engaged, and practice is a construct that consists of three dimensions that confer coherence to the community. One is the enterprise that its members jointly pursue. Wenger exemplifies this dimension by referring to the claims-processing centre in an insurance company that he observed. The joint enterprise the centre pursues is processing insurance claims. The second dimension is mutual engagement, meaning the members interact with each other, share information, and make themselves accountable to each other in their joint pursuit of the enterprise. In the claim-processing unit that Wenger refers to, the mutual engagement includes that of information exchanges about work among the members of the unit as well as personal conversations such as sharing of jokes and gossip. The third dimension of practice is the repertoire shared by members of the community, which includes among others, knowledge, history, language, communication tools and other artifacts all related to the community.

While community of practice is a theoretical concept, it is also shorthand for the social theory of learning that Lave and Wenger (1991) attempted to develop in their seminal volume. The theory provides an elaborate account of learning that takes place *in situ*. To learn in a community means to participate in its tasks and more importantly to develop one's mastery of skills and knowledge required in the tasks. Learning in this regard does not take place in an explicit, organised manner as it does in formal education settings. Rather, it is an outcome or a by-product of participation in a community. That is, one develops his/her knowledge of practices and acquires the repertoire of a community through engaging in its tasks. Newcomers entering a community often start by participating on the periphery, working on light, less complex or attenuated tasks. Lave and Wenger (1991) refer to this form of engagement in the community as legitimate peripheral participation, which is usually scaffolded in that newcomers often receive support of various sorts from experienced colleagues, which makes Lave and Wenger's theory a social one. Through participation in tasks on the periphery, and with help from other members, newcomers develop the knowledge and skills associated with the tasks. Gradually, they move on to take up more central tasks which confer on them full membership of the community.

As can be seen from this overview of definitions, the three notions of community share some core characterising attributes despite the fact that they have been developed by scholars from different intellectual traditions. For a group of people to be qualified as a community, there needs to be coherence within the group, which is manifested in different ways. One is the joint goal(s) the community pursues, which shapes the activities in which the group engage. The set of norms and values shared and upheld by its members also contributes to its coherence, which in turn shapes the ways its members behave. As a community develops, so does its repertoire, which encompasses its knowledge, techniques, tools, semiotic resources and communicative mechanisms, which are all essential to the sustenance of the community.

Despite these commonalities, the emphasis on and elaboration of each distinguishing feature not surprisingly vary across the three notions as a result of their epistemic origins and orientations. In Kuhn's description of scientific community, developed mainly to describe work of scientists whose main tasks are to produce knowledge, ontology, symbols, language, research techniques, professional societies, conferences and journals are at the forefront of the characterisation of a community's repertoire. In defining a discourse community – an invention of language and literary scholars – Swales provides a much more elaborate description of the linguistic resources and communicative channels that make up the repertoire possessed by a discourse community, which include, among others, its lexis, genres, genre chains, communication mechanisms and communicative practices, which are not specified in the characterisations of the other two notions. Still, despite the different emphases, the shared attributes of the three notions at the general level as described above may explain why the three notions of community have been invoked in studies of discursive practices, a phenomenon that will be discussed in the following section.

Notions of community in studies of discursive practices

The notion of scientific community has been employed in a number of early studies of science discourse conducted by sociologists of science. Though the term has been used in general to refer to a discipline or a specialism, focuses in the studies have often been on specific networks of scientists investigating a specific phenomenon or a problem. In their seminal ethnographic account *Opening Pandora's Box*, for example, Gilbert and Mulkay (1984) detailed a large-scale study in which they followed and interviewed a network of scientists working on bioenergetics in different parts of the world to examine the discourse the scientists used in describing their work. Gilbert and Mulkay discovered the two distinct empirical and contingency repertoires that the scientists selectively used in accounting for their research and writing experiences. The empiricist repertoire refers to the way of talk and the line of reasoning that create an objective representation of scientific actions and facts. It is the repertoire that one sees in public domains such as publications. Gilbert and Mulkay noted that the repertoire was also occasionally used by the scientists during the interviews to justify their own research actions. The contingency repertoire is the kind of discourse that is seldom made accessible to the public, which, as Gilbert and Mulkay observed, was used by their informants to recount the contingent events and actions that arose in the course of their research (e.g. human errors and mistaken beliefs), and the private motivations (e.g. the social connections, collegiality and social indebtedness) behind the citations they provided in some of their publications. Latour's (1987) ethnographic accounts also unveil similar social and contingent dimensions in the supposedly objective and empirical discourse of discovery.

In the early days of its development, the notion of discourse community was mostly used to refer to various types of academic contexts. In the literature of composition studies, it became almost a buzzword used to recast writing classrooms as sites of discourse communities. In later studies, it was used to refer to a variety of academic domains, including specific disciplines (e.g. Duff 2010; Hyland 1997), scientists in particular national contexts (see e.g. Ahmad 1997; Duszak 1997; Myers 1990). The term has also been appropriated to signify various professional groupings at various levels, ranging from a specific profession (see e.g. Killingsworth and Gilbertson 1992; Pogner 2003) to a particular institution, a unit or a team of people therein (see e.g. Beaufort 1997, 1999; Flowerdew and Wan 2006; Smart 1998; Yates and Orlikowski 2002). The body of work has mostly drawn on social theories of discourse production developed in New Rhetoric, and Composition Studies and English for Specific Purposes (ESP) studies[1] with attention directed at lexico-grammatical features as well as patterned discursive practices in specific communities.

The term 'community of practice' started to appear in the mid-1990s in a few ESP and professional discourse studies that provided anecdotal accounts of how newcomers mastered the discursive practices in academic and professional communities of practice. The studies specifically drew on the theoretical perspectives associated with the notion of community of practice as discussed in Lave and Wenger's earlier volume (Lave and Wenger 1991). Belcher (1994) and Blakeslee (1997) were among the first few that examined how novice research students are initiated into their communities of practice in specific disciplines and how their past discursive and research practices, as well as their alignments or dis-alignments with their disciplinary goals and mentors, facilitated and hindered their mastery of the discursive practices in the disciplines. Freeman and Adam (1996) compared the discursive practices in two communities of practice, namely the university and the workplace, and examined how a group of intern students interpreted the practices in both communities, and how their interpretations facilitated and hindered their learning in the workplace. Later studies have adopted the term to refer to communities of practice of science at both international and national levels. For example, Li (2006), in her study of a doctoral student of chemistry, framed the discipline as an international community of practice and the department in which the student was based as a local community of practice. Her work examined how the doctoral student negotiated the discursive practices in the two communities and highlighted the socio-political issues that the newcomer needed to deal with when developing discourse in the two communities of practice.

In recent years, the three notions have been increasingly used together. For example, in their discussion of how a group of doctoral students selected their research topics, Harasti and Street (2009) invoke all three notions of community to describe the contexts in which the students were located. It is also not uncommon to see that the notions are used synonymously. Discourse community is very often used interchangeably with scientific community and also some other notions such as academic communities, disciplinary communities, research communities (see e.g. Ayers 2008; Flowerdew 2000; Koutsantoni 2004; Kuo 1999; Tardy 2010), professional as well as specialist communities (see e.g. Bhatia 2008, 2011; Bhatia and Bremner 2012). It is also interesting to note that in many studies, the three notions are used without any specific reference made to any of the work from which the notions originate. It may be the case that the meanings of the notions are now established and require no explanation. But, it is clear that in some cases the notions have been only used as shorthand for a discipline or a profession rather than a group of people who pursue a joint goal(s) and who interact with each other to pursue a joint enterprise. Notwithstanding, there are still some studies that use the notions to mean what they have been originally intended to mean and have also been informed by their associated theories (see e.g. Berkenkotter and Huckin 1995; Bhatia 2008, 2011; Harasti and Street 2009; Ivanič 1997; Myers 1990; Palmeri 2004).

Discursive practices in communities

The plethora of discourse studies conducted in specific communities, regardless of which notion of community they use and their theoretical allegiances, have provided illuminating accounts of the discoursal features of texts produced in specific academic and non-academic contexts, which include, among many others, the socio-pragmatic functions (e.g. Hyland 1997; Salager-Meyer 2001) and evaluative language in research texts (e.g. Gil-Salom and Soler-Monreal 2010), and stylistics of politeness in tax computation letters (Flowerdew and Wan 2006), as well as the rhetorical structures in a host of genres (e.g. Basturkmen 2009; Golebiowski 2009; Jorgensen 2005; Martinez-Escudero 2011; Phong 2008).

The predominant focus on discoursal attributes of specific genres in specific communities seems to have overshadowed work that deals with other less pursued and yet important aspects of the writing practices in some communities. One such theme deals with the sets of genres that members of a specific community read or write as part of their normal professional duties. Despite the few studies conducted in this area, there are interesting insights generated about how genre sets differ across communities as a result of their goals and the types of activities that go on in the communities. Swales (2004) exemplifies the set of genres in which US graduate students engage. The set includes course assignments, seminar research papers, texts of conference presentations, research articles and the dissertation. Hyon and Chen (2004) in their study of the genres that faculty need to write identified three distinct sets of texts they need to produce. The first set includes mainly teaching-related genres such as course materials, lecture notes, quizzes and exams and comments on students' work. The second set consists of research genres, which include conference abstracts, research grant applications, and manuscripts for publication. The last set is mostly service-related, and among examples that Hyon and Chen provide are class visitation reports, memos or letters to colleagues, letters of recommendation, faculty activity reports (FAR), annual activities reports (AAR), evaluation reports such as those of policy and curriculum documents and reports of retention, promotion, tenure (PRT) and faculty merit increase (FMI).

The set of graduate genres exemplified by Swales (2004), as well as the faculty genres identified by Hyon and Chen (2004) in the US academic community are very different from those identified in studies of other non-academic communities. For example, in their study of the discourse processes in which land surveyors are engaged and the texts they produce, Cheng and Mok (2008) observed two distinct sets of genres that experts in the profession produce (see Tables 27.1 and 27.2).

In another study of the discursive practices in a US Job Resource Center (JRC) whose survival relies heavily on external sources of funding, Beaufort (1997, 1999) found that her informants did not just communicate with staff of the centre but also members of four external fund-granting communities (the federal government, the local government, business communities, and private foundations) through different sets of genres (Figure 27.1). Beaufort also noted that the genres were accorded different statuses in JRC in terms of the relative importance of the constituencies they addressed as well as the time and the resources that needed to be expended on the genres. High status genres are those that involve texts produced to request government funding or donations from the local business community or philanthropic organisations. Genres of lower statuses are mostly produced for internal communication.

Some of the studies that examined genre sets possessed by specific communities also looked at how genres in the sets are related to or inter-locked with each other. There has been a variety of terms coined to describe the connections among members of a genre set, which include genre systems or genre networks (Orlikowski and Yates 1994; Yates and Orlikowski 2002), and

Becky S. C. Kwan

Table 27.1 Discourse processes and products among parties in external communication

Parties involved in external communication	External discourse products between different parties and Contractor and Sub-contractors
Client (Highways Department, Hong Kong Government SAR)	Contracts
The consultancy firm	Letters
Resident land surveyor in LS Department of Consultancy Firm	Meetings, emails, project works (text, maps, graphs, diagrams)
Senior surveying officer in LS Department of Consultancy Firm	Meetings, emails, phase division of project works
Surveying officer in LS Department of Consultancy Firm	'Request for Inspection' pro-forma, 'Request for Information' pro-forma, phase division of project works, meetings, emails

Source: Cheng and Mok 2008: 65

Table 27.2 Discourse processes and products among parties in internal communication

Parties involved in internal communication	Upward communication	Downward communication
The consultancy firm	Meetings (including telephone meetings), emails, project works (text, maps, graphs, diagrams)	Meetings (including telephone meetings), emails, project works (text, maps, graphs, diagrams)
Resident land surveyor	Emails, phase division of project works (text, maps, graphs, diagrams)	Project works (text, maps, graphs, diagrams), phase division of project works (text, maps, graphs, diagrams)
Senior surveying officer	Emails, meetings, phase division of project works (texts, maps, graphs, diagrams)	Meetings, emails, phase division of project works (text, maps, graphs, diagrams)
Surveying officer		'Request for Inspection Form', 'Request for Information Form', emails

Source: Cheng and Mok 2008: 65

genre chains (Räisänen 1999; cited in Swales 2004). Illustrating their notions of genre systems, Yates and Orlikowski (2002) draw examples from the series of genres of oral presentations, dialogue and voting in meetings, and the interrelated texts involved in major project contracts, which include a request for a proposal initiated by an organisation, a proposal submitted as a response to the request to the initiating organisation, an evaluation document about the proposal, and the contract signed by the two organisations.

Work on genre chains provides interesting insights about how genres in specific professional communities are sequenced. In their study of the discourse processes in which land surveyors engaged and the texts they produced, Cheng and Mok (2008 cited earlier) observed the two chains shown in Figure 27.1.

Taking one step further, some researchers have also examined how genres in a chain may draw on each other in what Kristeva (1980) refers to as intertextual ways. Devitt (1999), for example, in her analysis of the texts produced in six accounting firms, distinguished three types

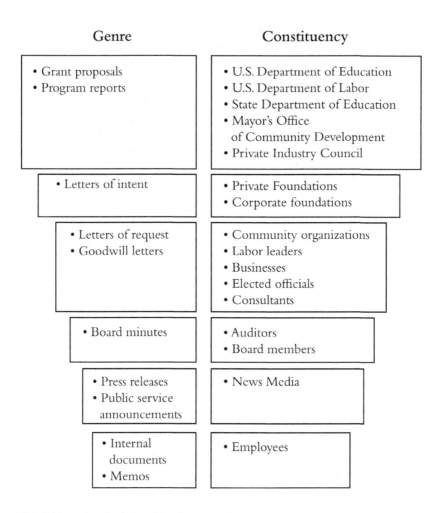

Figure 27.1 A hierarchical relationship of texts at JRC (Beaufort 1997: 496)

of intertextuality, namely generic, referential, and functional. Generic intertextuality refers to how discoursal features of prior texts produced as responses to similar writing exigencies are drawn on as models or samples to complete a writing task. Referential intertextuality means references made to prior texts for information in order to complete a current text. Functional intertextuality refers to the interactions of texts produced by accountants at different levels of an accounting firm as part of quality control. The set of interacting texts (a macro-text) usually bears consequences and is usually what a senior accountant makes use of to form a picture of an entire firm's work.

Drawing on Devitt's taxonomy, Flowerdew and Wan (2006), in their ethnographic study examining the discursive practices of a group of tax accountants in an accounting firm in Hong Kong, also identified similar types of intertextuality among the texts produced by their informants, as summarised below:

> One of the most interesting findings from this study is that intertextuality both defines and serves the needs of the accounting community, as exemplified in Devitt's (1991) study.

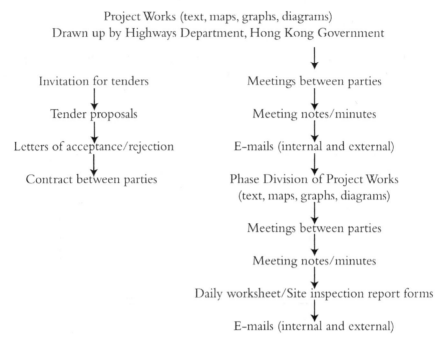

Figure 27.2 Discourse flow of land surveying project management (Cheng and Mok 2008: 66)

The accountants repeatedly draw on previous texts to produce a letter in response to similar situations by the use of the template (Devitt's generic intertextuality). In addition, whenever an accountant writes a tax computation letter, they are making a connection to the enclosed computation and to the audit report (Devitt's referential intertextuality). Further, while the tax computation letter is based on an audit report, the latter itself results from an audit visit. At the same time the tax computation letter also anticipates acknowledgment and signature of approval from the representative of the company concerned, before another letter is written to the Inland Revenue Department (Devitt's functional intertextuality).

(Flowerdew and Wan 2006: 150)

Intertextual writing practices have also been noted in other professional settings. Smart (1998), in his analysis of how texts were produced by economists at different levels in the Bank of Canada, noted how texts were recycled in producing knowledge to inform formulations of monetary policies. In the two chains of genres they identified (see Figure 27.2), Cheng and Mok (2008 cited earlier) also found that the genres are related in various intertextual ways.

Collaborative writing has also been a focus of some of the studies conducted in specific communities, which have revealed a variety of interesting aspects of this form of writing at the workplace. Examples include Beaufort's (1997, 1999 cited earlier) study of the discursive practices in JRC in which the author showed how old-timers and newcomers collaborated in writing projects through which the newcomers were enculturated into the discursive practices of the centre. The collaboration in which newcomers were involved took on different forms such as ghost writing, editing, formatting documents and writing up small sections of important documents when they worked with more experienced members of the job centre. The types of collaborative writing differ markedly from the more complex types practised in team projects that involved experts of different professional backgrounds. Pogner's (2003) investigation for example examined how an energy concept proposal in a Danish consulting firm was co-produced by a group of engineers (electrical, mechanical and other experts) and a project manager for a municipal government in Germany. While the task was a collaborative undertaking, different members of the team were assigned to different parts of the document, and the parts produced were circulated for comments and revision by different members, it was the project manager who having a better sense of the audiences the document was addressing made the final decision regarding the parts to keep and the parts to leave out. Meanwhile, Palmeri (2004) provides an account of how collaborative writing of four major legal documents (demand letter, complaint, punitive packet and medical review) took place in a medically oriented law firm. As Palmeri describes, the writing process normally involved an attorney, a nurse consultant and a professional writer. The contents of a document were first generated by the attorney and the nurse consultant, and these were collected either orally or in writing by the professional writer, who synthesised the contents into a draft document. The draft document was then reviewed by the attorneys and nurse consultants. The documents were then edited by the professional writer for language accuracy and clarity for non-specialist audiences.

Another less pursued strand of research has to do with the fluid nature of communities and how this may implicate the discourse and the discursive practices in some communities. Illustrating this aspect of discourse communities, Bhatia (2004) draws on Sarangi and Robert's notions of medical professional discourse and institutional discourse of health professionals:

> A medical setting would include the clinician's narratives which work up patients as cases, the diagnosis of the medical problem in doctor-patient interaction, or the display of medical authority as evidence. The institutional discourses would include the gate-keeping functions of selection, training and assessment, the discourses around the management of hospitals, General Practitioners' surgery and so on, and the voices used by the institution to represent itself to the outside world.
> *(Sarangi and Roberts 1999: 16; cited from Bhatia 2004: 149–50)*

Likewise, Beaufort's study of JRC also noted the overlapping nature of the communities in her study: while communicating with the internal units of the centre, her informants also needed to communicate with four other communities when applying for funding (Beaufort 1997, 1999 cited earlier). Addressing the porosity and overlapping nature of discourse communities, Beaufort postulated a community-specific discursive competence model to describe the domains of knowledge that writers at JRC needed to develop in order to function effectively in the organisation. The five domains are knowledge of the discourse communities (internal and external), knowledge of subject matter to communicate about, knowledge of the genres one uses to communicate with members of the various discourse communities, rhetorical knowledge and writing process knowledge.

Adopting critical approaches to the notion of community, some scholars have also noted various types of processes (e.g. hybridisation, colonisation and contestations) shaping the discoursal features and discursive practices in some communities, which are results of the multi-memberships of their participants (e.g. Bhatia 2008, 2010, 2011; Ivanič 1997; Johns 1997; Palmeri 2004; Li 2006; Starfield 2001). Drawing on texts from different professional communities, and in particular those of business and international arbitration, Bhatia (2010), for example, provides evidence of appropriation of semiotic resources across different domains, which give rise to hybridised discourse in a community as a result of the co-participation of members from different professional communities in joint production of discourse. One piece of evidence is from the corporate annual reports collected from the business community of listed companies in Hong Kong. Bhatia identified the four types of discourse laminated into the genre, which, as he contends, are appropriated from four professional communities, namely accounting, economics, public relations and law. He explains them thus:

- *Accounting discourse*, which forms a major part of the Annual Reports, duly endorsed, certified by public accountants;
- *Discourse of economics*, in the form of what is conventionally known as the financial review section of the report [normally written by people of the company specializing in financial management].
- *Public relations discourse*, in the form of the chairman's letter to shareholders, for which public accounting firms do not take any responsibility.
- *Legal discourse,* which forms a major part of disclaimers, often necessary to comprehend the full implications of the information disclosed in the report.

(Bhatia 2010: 39)

In the same article, as well as in his other work (Bhatia 2011), Bhatia illustrates the possibility of colonisation of discourse in newly developed professional communities by drawing on his observations made in a large-scale study of international arbitration practices, which have been introduced in some countries as an alternative to settling disputes outside of the courts. In many cases, as Bhatia notes, disputing parties tend to go to legal experts rather than non-legal experts as arbitrators. This tendency has now made arbitration more like litigation both in terms of its discoursal features and procedures, an observation that has also been borne out by different studies carried out in various contexts (see e.g. Anesa 2012; Bhatia, Candlin and Hafner 2012; Gotti 2012; Gotti and Anesa 2011; Kathpalia 2012). For example, arbitration awards have been found to display a strong presence of impersonal style of language, complex co-ordination and subordination structures, and frequent references made to other legal documents, which are all characteristics of a lawyer's style of writing. Likewise, legal discoursal features have also been observed in arbitration proceedings. While such proceedings normally take place in offices and are presumably less formal, it has been found that arbitrators acted in ways similar to those acted by judges in court trials, which include interrupting interlocutors, allocating turns, calling out a particular party to speak, to repeat or to reformulate what they said, granting or refusing objections or questions (see e.g. Anesa 2012; Bhatia, Candlin and Hafner 2012; Gotti 2012; Gotti and Anesa 2011).

Contestations of discourse in specific communities have also been highlighted in work that has taken a more critical approach in exposing the power struggles in such communities (e.g. Harris 1989; Bizzell 1992; Ivanič 1997; Johns 1997; Palmeri 2004; Starfield 2001). Palmeri's (2004 cited earlier) study of how documents were produced in a law firm documented the epistemological and discursive conflicts between nursing consultants and attorneys that often occurred in their collaborative writing and which might result in 'muddled' documents. Ivanič (1997) in her examination of how a group of mature students negotiated the academic discourse in a university in the UK, noted the dissonances the students experienced when they were required to conform to the discourse conventions of academia. Likewise, Starfield (2001), who triangulated data from a markers' meeting about the assessment of students' essays in a South African university and interviews with faculty as well as students, provided evidence that challenges the 'static, rule-governed and fixed' view of the academic community. Both Ivanič's and Starfield's studies suggest how underprivileged members may lose in the battles to win control of their own discourses in academic communities.

Conclusion

In this chapter, I have traced the origins of three frequently used notions of community: scientific community, discourse community and community of practice. Discourse community, originating from rhetoric and written communication studies, places an emphasis on the predominant discursive attributes and practices in specific communities. Community of practice, on the other hand, coming from studies of anthropological education, focuses more on the various mechanisms and in particular social relationships through which newcomers to a specific community develop key types of competence they need to participate in the daily life and activities of a specific community. Scientific community, coming from sociology of science, stresses how paradigms, rewards, affiliations and networking may impact on knowledge production, research and the discourse of science. The three notions, as well as other similar notions of community, have been increasingly used interchangeably in the current literature of discursive practices in specific contexts. Nonetheless, the body of work that has drawn on the three notions and their associated theoretical assumptions has illuminated, on the one hand, our understanding about the patterned discourse as well as norms of communicative practices of various communities, and on the other hand has revealed the possible heterogeneity and contestations of discourses therein, suggesting the fluidity, porosity, and overlapping nature of communities. Drawing on some of these insights, I will end this chapter by proposing several areas of work that practitioners and researchers may further pursue.

On the practical front, designers and instructors of ESP courses as well as corporate professional training programmes may consider familiarising students or trainees with the high-status genres in which they are likely to engage. Attention can be directed not only to the discoursal features of the genres (e.g. rhetorical purposes content, organisation, and lexico-grammatical attributes), but how the genres may be linked to form a genre chain. Attention can also be accorded to the receptive and productive skills and strategies that need to be exercised when reading and writing the genres in the chain.

Students or trainees can also be familiarised with the kinds of collaborative writing typical of the setting in which they participate. They may be shown how joint text production proceeds in the context, the distribution of work and the roles that participants play in the process. They also need to be sensitised to the negotiations and contestations that characterise such joint writing practices. More importantly, they need to be shown various ways and strategies to work with others to resolve conflicts when they arise.

These above two areas of training are particularly lacking in both educational and corporate training settings, and they are also under-addressed in many existing professional communication textbooks, which tend to provide rather general advice on these aspects of professional writing practices (see the two textbook surveys in Bremner 2008, 2010). It is thus much desired that when designing simulated communication tasks, practitioners consider creating rhetorical exigencies that require students to read and produce texts that form a meaningful genre chain that models on one of those in the community which they are prepared to enter. It is also important that students be guided to assign different types of roles in joint writing tasks, which may include the facilitator or the convenor overseeing a writing project, or an editor(s) looking after the language accuracy and clarity of the written product. Students may also be required to produce a post-writing reflection evaluating how well they have managed themselves in the text production process, how conflicts have been resolved and the lessons they have learned through the co-authoring experience.

Meanwhile, following calls from critical analysts, action research can also be conducted to identify ways to empower the underprivileged members of a community (e.g. ESL students,

EAL scholars and new migrants in the workplace) and to help them to resist the dominant discourses and assert their own voices in the community.

On the research front, while future studies of discursive practices may continue to examine patterned features of texts produced in specific communities, there is a bigger need to investigate the less pursued areas such as the genre sets of specific communities and how genres in the sets are intertextually linked. For example, it would be interesting to investigate the intertextuality of the texts involved in multi-tiered review exercises such as those of promotion, tenure and grant applications. Focuses can be put on how reviewers in each level read the details provided in the document trail prepared by or provided for a reviewee, how the details of the reviewee are appropriated and represented orally in the discussions in a review meeting, how the discussions are drawn on to form the basis of evaluation and in particular the joint production of an evaluation report, and how the evaluation report is read and appropriated at a higher level of review.

Following a critical approach, researchers can also study hybridisation, colonisation and contestations of discourses and discursive practices in communities whose members at the same time belong to other communities. For example, investigations can be directed at such processes in newly formed interdisciplinary departments, interdisciplinary research project teams, board meetings of business and non-business organisations as well as meetings of legislative councils with members whose academic, professional, ethnic and political affiliations are becoming increasingly diverse. Where conflicts arise, attention can be directed at how the contestations may be resolved.

Studies can also be conducted on discourses of people with transient memberships in communities and how they negotiate their own membership, and how their perceived memberships as well as alignment with a primary (home) community may shape their discourses in the contact zone in the secondary (host) community (e.g. host organisations where student interns are placed).

The areas of study proposed above can draw on the latest work on community of practice and sociology of science published in other disciplines such as business management, higher education and vocational training. For example, there has been work published in the disciplines of management and education concerning how experienced newcomers can contribute to a community of practice (Fuller *et al.* 2005), which earlier work on the theory has seldom explored. Work in this regard will be useful to inform studies of how newcomers with expertise of specific types may shape the discursive practices or may breed new types of practices in a host community.

Likewise, there have been a wealth of studies published in journals and books of higher education that document the macro social and business processes (e.g. globalisation, internationalisation and marketisation), various top-down educational initiatives (e.g. problem-solving, outcome-based learning, interdisciplinary programmes and student exchange programmes), and research initiatives (e.g. interdisciplinary research programmes, overseas research collaboration) that are taking place in universities around the world and that have impacted on what have previously been assumed to be autonomous faculty practices and monolithic disciplinary pursuits. It would be interesting to see how these developing phenomena in academia may have shaped the world views of academics and how they may have changed the ways they frame and conduct their research and teaching, and how all these have in turn impacted on the discursive practices in communities of specific disciplines and individual institutions (e.g. the genre repertoire, intertextuality, lexis and rhetorical structures of the genres). A diachronic approach to such studies would be a fruitful one as has been followed in some prior work (see e.g. Bazerman 1988).

In short, although various notions of community have been around for some time and a great number of studies have been conducted on the communication practices in numerous settings, the proliferation of new communities at the professional and the institutional levels implicated by various social and business processes means that discursive practices situated in specific communities will continue to be an exciting topic of research. Work in this regard is still very much needed to inform teaching practices in ESP and corporate training.

Related topics

community of practice; discourse community; scientific community

Key readings

Readers may consult the following references to learn more about some of the issues discussed in this chapter.
Becher, T. and Trowler, P. R. (2001). *Academic Tribes and Territories (2nd edition)*, Buckingham: The Society for Research and Higher Education & Open University Press.
Benesch, S. (2001). *Critical English for Academic Purposes: Theory, Politics and Practice*, Mahwah, NJ: Erlbaum.
Boud, D., Cressey, P. and Docherty, P. (eds) (2006). *Productive Reflection at Work*, New York: Routledge.
Hughes, J., Jewson, N. and Unwin, L. (eds) (2007). *Communities of Practice: Critical Perspectives*, New York: Routledge.

Note

1 Some of these theories have also drawn on theories developed by sociologists of science as noted by Swales (1990, cited earlier).

Bibliography

Ahmad, U. K. (1997). 'Research article introductions in Malay: Rhetoric in an emerging research community', in A. Duszak (ed.), *Culture and Styles of Academic Discourse* (pp. 273–303), Berlin: Mouton de Gruyter.
Anesa, P. (2012). 'Language and power in arbitration proceedings: Insights into theory and practice', in B. K. Bhatia, C. N. Candlin and M. Gotti (eds), *Discourse and Practice in International Commercial Arbitration* (pp. 93–111), Burlington, US: Ashgate.
Ayers, G. (2008). 'The evolutionary nature of genre: An investigation of the short texts accompanying research articles in the scientific journal *Nature*', *English for Specific Purposes*, 27, 22–41.
Bartholomae, D. (1985). 'Inventing the university', in M. Rose (ed.), *When a Writer can't Write: Studies in Writer's Block and other Composing-process Problems* (pp. 134–65), New York: Guilford.
Basturkmen, H. (2009). 'Commenting on results in published research articles and masters dissertations in language teaching', *Journal of English for Academic Purposes*, 8, 241–51.
Bazerman, C. (1988). *Shaping Written Knowledge: The Genre and Activity of the Experimental Article in Science*, Madison, Wisconsin: University of Wisconsin Press.
Beaufort, A. (1997). 'Operationalizing the concept of discourse community: A case study of one institutional site of composing', *Research in the Teaching of English*, 31(4), 486–529.
——(1999). *Writing in the Real World: Making the Transition from School to Work*, New York: Teachers College Press.
Belcher, D. (1994). 'The apprenticeship approach to advanced academic literacy: Graduate students and their mentors', *English for Specific Purposes*, 13(1), 23–34.
Berkenkotter, C. and Huckin, T. N. (1995). *Genre Knowledge in Disciplinary Communication: Cognition, Culture, Power*, Hillsdale, NJ: Lawrence Erlbaum Associates.
Bhatia, V. K. (2004). *Discourse Worlds of Written Discourse: A Genre-based View*, New York: Continuum.
——(2008). 'Genre analysis, ESP and professional practice', *English for Specific Purposes*, 27, 161–74.

——(2010). 'Interdiscursivity in professional communication', *Discourse and Communication*, *21*(1), 32–50.
——(2011). 'Interdiscursive colonisation of arbitration practice', *World Englishes*, *30*(1), 76–80.
Bhatia, V. K. and Bremner, S. (2012). 'English for business communication', *Language Teaching*, *45*(4), 410–45.
Bhatia, V. K., Candlin, C. N. and Hafner, C. A. (2012). 'Arbitration awards as accounts', in V. K. Bhatia, C. N. Candlin and C. A. Hafner (eds), *Discourse and Practice in International Commercial Arbitration: Issues, Challenges and Prospects* (pp. 147–61), Burlington, US: Ashgate.
Bizzell, P. (1992). *Academic Discourse and Critical Consciousness*, Pittsburgh: University of Pittsburgh Press.
Blakeslee, A. M. (1997). 'Activity, context, interaction and authority: Learning to write scientific papers in situ', *Journal of Business and Technical Communication*, *11*(2), 125–69.
Bremner, S. (2008). 'Intertextuality and business communication textbooks: Why students need more textual support', *English for Specific Purposes*, *27*, 308–21.
——(2010). 'Collaborative writing: Bridging the gap between the textbook and the workplace', *English for Specific Purposes*, *29*, 121–32.
Bruffee, K. A. (1986). 'Social construction, language and the authority of knowledge: A bibliographical essay', *College English*, *48*, 773–90.
Cheng, W. and Mok, E. (2008). 'Discourse processes and products: Land surveyors in Hong Kong', *English for Specific Purpose*, *27*, 57–73.
Devitt, A. (1999). 'Intertextuality in tax accounting: Generic, referential and functional', in C. Bazerman and J. Paradis (eds), *Textual Dynamics in the Professions: Historical and Contemporary Studies of Writing in Professional Communities* (pp. 336–57), Madison, Wisconsin: University of Wisconsin Press.
Duff, P. (2010). 'Socialization into academic discourse communities', *Language Annual Review of Applied Linguistics*, *30*, 169–92.
Duszak, A. (1997). 'Cross-cultural academic communication: A discourse-community view', in A. Duszak (ed.), *Culture and Styles of Academic Discourse* (pp. 11–40), Berlin: Mouton de Gruyter.
Fish, S. (1980). *Is There a Text in this Class? The Authority of Interpretive Communities*, Cambridge, Massachusetts: Harvard University Press.
Flowerdew, J. (2000). 'Discourse community, legitimate peripheral participation, and the non-native-English-Speaking scholar', *TESOL Quarterly*, *34*(1), 127–50.
Flowerdew, J. and Wan, A. (2006). 'Genre analysis of tax computation letters: How and why tax accountants write the way they do', *English for Specific Purposes*, *25*, 133–53.
Freeman, A. and Adam, C. (1996). 'Learning to write professionally: "Situated learning" and the transition from university to professional discourse', *Journal of Business and Technical Communication*, *10*(4), 395–427.
Fuller, A., Hodkinson, H., Hodkinson, P. and Unwin, L. (2005). 'Learning as peripheral participation in communities of practice: A reassessment of key concepts in workplace learning', *British Educational Research Journal*, *31*(1), 49–68.
Foucault, M. (1972). *The Archaeology of Knowledge*, New York: Harper & Row.
Gaillard, J. (1994). 'The behaviour of scientists and scientific communities', in J.-J. Salomon, F. R. Sagasti and C. Sachs-Jeantet (eds), *The Uncertain Quest: Service, Technology and Development* (pp. 201–36), New York, US: United Nations University Press.
Geertz, C. (1973). *Local Knowledge*, New York: Basic Books.
Gilbert, G. N. and Mulkay, M. (1984). *Opening Pandora's Box: A Sociological Analysis of Scientists' Discourse*, Cambridge: Cambridge University Press.
Gil-Salom, L. and Soler-Monreal, C. (2010). 'Appraisal resources in scientific research article discussions', in M. L. Gea-Valor, I. Garcia-Izquierdo and M.-J. Esteve (eds), *Linguistic and Translation Studies in Scientific Communication* (pp. 69–90), Berlin: Peter Lang.
Golebiowski, Z. (2009). 'Prominent messages in Education and Applied Linguistic abstracts: How do authors appeal to their prospective readers?' *Journal of Pragmatics*, *41*, 753–69.
Gotti, M. (2012). 'The judicialization of arbitration discourse in the Italian context', in B. K. Bhatia, C. N. Candlikn and M. Gotti (eds), *Discourse and Practice in International Commercial Arbitration* (pp. 129–46). Burlington, US: Ashgate.
Gotti, M. and Anesa, P. (2011). 'Professional identities in Italian arbitral awards: The spread of lawyers' language', in V. K. Bhatia and P. E. Allori (eds), *Discourse and Identity in the Professions* (pp. 189–212), Berlin: Peter Lang.
Guerrero, R.C. (1980). 'La idea de comunidad científica: su significado teórico y su contenido ideológico', *Revista Mexicana de Sociología*, *42*(2), 1217–30.
Hagstrom, W. (1965). *The Scientific Community*, New York: Basic Books.

Harasti, M. and Street, B. (2009). 'PhD topic arrangement in 'D'iscourse communities of engineers and social sciences/humanities', *Journal of English for Academic Purposes*, 8, 14–25.
Harris, J. (1989). 'The idea of community in the study of writing', *College Composition and Communication*, 40(1), 11–22.
Herzberg, B. (1986). 'The politics of discourse communities', Paper presented at the CCC Convention, New Orleans, La, March, 1986.
Hyland, K. (1997). 'Scientific claims and community values: Articulating an academic culture', *Language & Communication*, 17(1), 19–31.
Hyon, S. and Chen, R. (2004). 'Beyond the research article: University faculty genres and EAP graduate preparation', *English for Specific Purposes*, 23, 233–63.
Ivanič, R. (1997). *Writing and Identity: The Discoursal Construction of Identity in Academic Writing*, Philadelphia: John Benjamins Publishing Co.
Johns, A. (1997). *Text, Role, and Context: Developing Academic Literacies*, Cambridge: Cambridge University Press.
Jorgensen, P. E. F. (2005). 'The dynamics of business letters: Defining creative variation in established genres', in P. Gillaerts and P. Gotti (eds), *Genre Variations in Business Letters* (pp. 147–78), Berlin: Peter Lang.
Kathpalia, S. (2012). 'Is arbitration being colonized by litigation – Practitioners' views in the Singapore context', in B. K. Bhatia, C. N. Candlikn and M. Gotti (eds), *Discourse and Practice in International Commercial Arbitration* (pp. 263–81), Burlington, US: Ashgate.
Kent, T. (1991). 'On the very idea of a discourse community', *College Composition and Communication*, 42(4), 425–45.
Killingsworth, M. J. and Gilbertson, M. K. (1992). *Signs, Genres, and Communities in Technical Communication*, Amityville, US: Baywood Publishing Co.
Koutsantoni, D. (2004). 'Relations of power and solidarity in scientific communities: A cross-cultural comparison of politeness strategies in the writing of native English speaking and Greek engineers', *Multilingua*, 23, 111–43.
Kristeva, J. (1980). *Desire in Language: A Semiotic Approach to Literature and Art*, Oxford: Blackwell.
Kuhn, T. S. (1962). *The Structure of Scientific Revolutions*, Chicago, US: University of Chicago Press.
——(1970). *The Structure of Scientific Revolutions* (2nd edition), Chicago: University of Chicago Press.
——(1977). *The Essential Tension*. Chicago, US: University of Chicago Press.
Kuo, C. H. (1999). 'The use of personal pronouns: Role relationships in scientific journal articles', *English for Specific Purposes*, 18(2), 121–38.
Latour, B. (1987). *Science in Action*. Cambridge, MA: Harvard University Press.
Lave, J. and Wenger, E. (1991). *Situated Learning: Legitimate Peripheral Participation*, New York: Cambridge University Press.
Li, Y. Y. (2006). 'A doctoral student of physics writing for publication: A sociopolitically-oriented case study', *English for Specific Purposes*, 25, 456–78.
Martinez-Escudero, L. (2011). 'A corpus-based insight into genre: The case of WIPO domain name arbitration decisions', *Discourse & Communication*, 5(4), 375–92.
Merton, R. K. (1973). *The Sociology of Science*, Chicago: University of Chicago Press.
Myers, G. (1990). *Writing Biology: Texts in the Social Construction of Scientific Knowledge*, Madison: University of Wisconsin Press.
Orlikowski, W. J. and Yates, J. (1994). 'Genre repertoire: Examining the structuring of communicative practices in organizations', *Administrative Science Quarterly*, 39, 541–74.
Palmeri, J. (2004). 'When discourses collide: A case study of interprofessional collaborative writing in a medically oriented law firm', *Journal of Business Communication*, 41(1), 37–65.
Perelman, C. and Olbrechts-Tyteca, L. (1969). *The New Rhetoric: A Treatise on Argumentation*. Trans. J. Wilkinson and Purcell Weaver, Notre Dame, Ind.: University of Notre Dame Press.
Phong, P. D. (2008). 'Research article abstracts in applied linguistics and educational technology: A study of linguistic realizations of rhetorical structure and authorial stance', *Discourse Studies*, 10(2), 231–50.
Pogner, K. H. (2003). 'Writing and interacting in the discourse community of engineering', *Journal of Pragmatics*, 35, 855–67.
Porter, J. E. (1988). 'The problem of defining discourse communities', Paper presented at the CCC Convention, St Louis, March, 1986.
Räisänen, C. (1999). *The Conference Forum as a System of Genres*, Gothenberg, Sweden: Acta Universitatis Gothoburgensis.

Rorty, R. (1979). *Philosophy and the Mirror of Nature*, Princeton, NJ: Princeton University Press.
Salager-Meyer, F. (2001). 'From self-highlightedness to self-effacement: A genre-based study of the socio-pragmatic function of criticism in medical discourse', *LSP & Professional Communication*, 1(2), 63–84.
Sarangi, S. and Roberts, C. (1999). 'The dynamics of interactional and institutional orders in work-related settings', in S. Sarangi and C. Roberts (eds), *Talk, Work, and the Institutional Order: Discourse in Medical, Mediation and Management Settings* (pp. 1–57), Berlin: Mouton De Gruyter.
Smart, G. (1998). 'Mapping conceptual worlds: Using interpretive ethnography to explore knowledge-making in a professional community', *Journal of Business Communication*, 35, 111–27.
Starfield, S. (2001). '"I'll go with the group": Rethinking "discourse community" in EAP', in J. Flowerdew and M. Peacock (eds), *Research Perspectives on English for Academic Purpose* (pp. 132–47), Cambridge, UK: Cambridge University Press.
Swales, J. M. (1990). *Genre Analysis: English in Academic and Research Settings*, New York: Cambridge University Press.
——(2004). *Academic Genres: Explorations and Applications*, New York: Cambridge University Press.
Tardy, C. M. (2010). *Building Genre Knowledge*, West Lafayette, West Indiana: Parlor Press.
Wenger, E. (1998). *Communities of Practice: Learning, Meaning and Identity*, New York, US: Cambridge University Press.
Wittgenstein, L. (1958). *Philosophical Investigations*, Oxford: Basil Blackwell.
Yates, J. and Orlikowski, W. J. (2002). 'Genre systems: Structuring interaction through communicative norms', *Journal of Business Communication*, 39, 13–35.
Zappen, J. P. (1989). 'The discourse community in scientific and technical communication: Institutional and social views', *Journal of Technical Writing and Communication*, 19(1), 1–11.

28
The formation of a professional communicator
A socio-rhetorical approach[1]

Natasha Artemeva and Janna Fox

Over the past 35 years, scholars who study professional communication have explored various ways in which novices develop as competent communicators within their professions (e.g. Anson and Forsberg 1990; Dias and Paré 2000; Winsor 1996). This research has been motivated by the desire to better understand whether and how professionals can be taught and trained 'to communicate appropriately in specific contexts to achieve their disciplinary and/or professional objectives' (Bhatia and Bremner, this volume: xvii). Many studies that addressed these issues revealed that 'novices typically go through a fairly slow process of organizational acculturation before they acquire and can successfully use' genres of workplace communication (Artemeva 2006: 9). Some researchers have questioned the very possibility of portability (e.g., Dias *et al.* 1999; Freedman 1995) of communication skills and strategies from one context to another.

In this chapter, we would like to reconsider the notion of portability as it pertains to the transition from academia to the workplace. Traditionally, conceptions of successful transition from one context to another were narrowly viewed as the effect of the mastery of prior tasks on subsequent task performance at the same level of complexity (Säljö 2003; Tuomi-Gröhn and Engeström 2003a, 2003b). However, as Brent (2011: 397) observes, recently, there has been considerable scepticism among researchers about 'whether students can transfer their … knowledge and skill to neighboring academic disciplines'. Further, and of direct relevance to the discussion in this chapter, Brent questions whether students can transfer what they learn in academia to the professional workplace (see also, Dias *et al.* 1999; Ford 2004; Freedman and Adam 1996; Freedman, Adam and Smart 1994).

Currently, researchers see successful transition as continual learning that occurs across changing situations of increasing complexity (Säljö 2003; Tuomi-Gröhn and Engeström 2003b). From this perspective, one's ability to successfully move from academia to the workplace is enabled by the ability to apply learning and knowledge acquired in the classroom setting to the workplace setting, as one becomes an ever more productive professional communicator. Thus, the possibility of *transfer of learning* is a key question for both novices who are preparing for the workplace in the global economy, and for the educators who are attempting to prepare future professional communicators for the world of work.

Historically, the development of research into the academia-to-workplace transition in technical and professional communication accompanied the 1970s–1980s increase in research in the teaching of English language. Language teaching researchers were investigating professional and technical communication in order to elaborate pedagogical approaches, typically for speakers of English as an additional language (EAL), who were studying or working in specific professional contexts of use (e.g. engineering, business, medicine). This research developed into the English for Specific Purposes (ESP) tradition with its focus on texts in contexts of use (e.g. Hutchinson and Waters 1987; Swales 1971, 1985; see also Belcher, Johns and Paltridge 2011). As Swales (1988: 17) pointed out, ESP grew out of the recognition that 'the descriptive techniques of Modern Linguistics ... could be successfully applied to the language of science and technology'.

The perspective that informs this chapter is shaped by the North American research tradition in Writing Studies, or Composition and Rhetoric. During the 1980s, scholars working within this rich research tradition began to turn their attention from general university writing courses to discipline-specific ones (e.g. Petraglia 1995) and to 'writing outside academic settings' (Beaufort 2006: 217). A large number of these studies were conducted focusing on university students' writing in engineering, finance, law, and other disciplines, and on the writing of professionals in various fields (e.g. Anderson, Brockmann and Miller 1983; Anson and Forsberg 1990; Bazerman 1988; Doheny-Farina 1986, 1989, 1992; Faigley 1985; Odell and Goswami 1985; Witte and Faigley 1983).

Whereas the ESP tradition has continued to focus to a large extent on the *textual* realisations of oral and written professional communication by speakers of EAL, the Writing Studies tradition in North America has investigated academic and workplace writing as situated within socio-cultural, historical, or *rhetorical*, contexts of predominantly English speaking students and professionals.

Within Writing Studies, one of the attractions of studying written communication in workplace settings was that investigations of settings other than academic ones 'shed light back on classrooms as social sites for composing' (Beaufort 2006: 225). This interest in non-academic writing led to the development and growing disciplinary maturity of the new field of Technical and Professional Communication and thus, to new research opportunities. Drawing on a variety of theoretical and methodological research approaches, professional communication scholars investigated rhetorical strategies used in various professions and explored the learning of these strategies by novices (e.g. Dias and Paré 2000; Smart 2006; Starke-Meyerring *et al.* 2011; Wickman 2010; Witte and Haas 2001; Winsor 1996).

As the research evolved, in-depth longitudinal studies were conducted, investigating ways in which students and novices developed (or failed to develop) as competent communicators within their professions (e.g. Couture 1986; Brown and Herndl 1986; Medway 1993). These studies, in turn, led to the development of a specific area of professional communication research that focuses on what has come to be called 'school-to-work transition' (e.g. Beaufort 1999; Katz 1998; Dias *et al.* 1999). This research investigates the processes that novices go through when moving from academic institutions, such as colleges and universities, to the workplace (e.g. Artemeva and Freedman 2001; Dias and Paré 2000; Medway 2000; Winsor 1996, 2003). Analysing these processes is a complicated endeavour not only because of the complexities of cognitive, social, and other processes involved, but also because the transition itself may occur in a variety of ways. For example, many students work while still in school. Others, unable to find professional employment upon graduation, are either forced into or select jobs other than those they were trained for, and so on.

In order to situate our discussion of the current literature on transitions between academic and workplace contexts, which takes into account these complexities, we begin with a review of the theoretical approaches, which have informed much of the scholarship in this area, namely, Rhetorical Genre Studies (RGS), activity theory (AT), theories of situated learning (SL), and distributed cognition. 'The relationship between theory and empirical data is interactive,' as Freedman (2006: 102) has pointed out. 'The data flesh out and specify the theory, modifying, elaborating, and necessarily reshaping it in the context of what is observed'; further, 'sometimes the data force researchers to reconsider the theory'. Therefore, this chapter discusses some of the empirical research, which was informed by these theories and, ultimately, contributed to their further development. By the end of the 1990s, once a large body of empirical research of the school-to-work transition in professional communications had become part of the discussion in the field, researchers were prompted to reconsider and modify the theoretical frameworks informing their studies. The chapter continues by discussing more recent theoretical reconceptualisations and the studies they have informed (cf. Artemeva 2008; Bazerman 2013; Bazerman and Russell 2002; Dias *et al.* 1999). We conclude by discussing issues in the area of the school-to-work transition research that require further investigation, including pedagogical implications of this research, and suggest future trends.

Theoretical approaches informing research in the school-to-work transition

The theoretical approaches discussed below have been productively used in the study of professional communication and, in particular, of the school-to-work transition in different disciplines and professions.

Rhetorical Genre Studies

By the 1980s, due to the changing perception of the social aspects of writing, writing began to be considered as located in the social world and, thus, to be fundamentally structured by the social milieu (e.g. Cooper 1986; Cooper and Holzman 1989; Miller 1984). A renewed interest in rhetoric and the development of the New Rhetoric in the twentieth century (Perelman and Olbrechts-Tyteca 1969) have led to the integration of rhetorical approaches into the study and teaching of technical and professional communication in the USA and Canada. In his 1980 article 'Functional Communication: A Situational Perspective', Bitzer proposed to consider 'rhetoric as a functional, or pragmatic, communication and thus a critical mode of functional interaction in which the chief interacting grounds are persons on the one hand and the environment on the other' (1980: 21). In a more narrow sense, functional communication is sometimes defined as communication within the tasks of one's profession such as law, accounting and administration (e.g. Beaudet 1998; Clerc and Beaudet 2002; Faber 2002). In other words, it is the type of communication, in which novices entering professional settings are expected to demonstrate proficiency. This type of communication has come to be called *technical* or *professional communication*.

The development of the field of professional communication coincided with Miller's (1984) reconceptualisation of genre as social action and the publication of the work of Russian literary critic Michail Bakhtin (1981, 1986) in English.[2] Genre, according to Miller (1984), is seen as developing in response to social need and in co-construction with a recognisable construal of a rhetorical situation (Bawarshi 2000; Paré and Smart 1994), perceived as a combination of purpose, audience, and occasion (Artemeva and Freedman 2001; Bitzer 1968; Coe and Freedman 1998). This understanding of genres of professional communication provided a foundation for the development of Rhetorical Genre Studies (RGS) (also known as North American, or New Rhetoric, genre theory) (e.g. Freedman and Medway 1994a, 1994b; Miller 1984; Schryer 1993) and a new theoretical approach to the study of *non-literary* genres. RGS treats textual regularities in genres as traces of the social, political, and rhetorical actions implicit in texts (e.g. Artemeva and Freedman 2006; Coe, Lingard and Teslenko 2002). It recognises that genres are 'flexible, plastic and free' (Bakhtin 1986: 79) – not static, but rather changing, decaying, and disappearing with time, to paraphrase Miller (1984), or 'stabilized-for-now' (Schryer 1993: 204). Far from being rigid templates, genres can be modified according to rhetorical circumstances (e.g. Berkenkotter and Huckin 1995). And, because genres involve both form and content (Giltrow 2002), which are inseparable, the forms of discourse in a discipline or profession change along with the changing intellectual content.

RGS considers genre learning as a situated process that occurs while communicators are immersed in the situational context (Miller 1992), which allows users to use genres 'expertly ... even though they may be unaware of generic parameters' (Hanks 1987: 681). This rhetorical approach to genres of professional communication has allowed researchers to illuminate the historical evolution of genres (see for example, Bazerman 1988; Bazerman and Paradis 1991), the development of genres in response to evolving socio-cultural, ideological, and political circumstances, and the process of genre acquisition and use during the school-to-work transition (e.g. Bazerman, Bonini and Figueiredo 2009; Coe *et al.* 2002; Russell 1997).

In the 1980s and 1990s, the rhetorical approach to genre analysis primarily focused on uncovering and documenting genres used in academic and workplace contexts, such as the experimental article (Bazerman 1988), reports by tax accountants (Devitt 1991), student writing in content areas (e.g. Berkenkotter and Huckin 1993, 1995; Giltrow and Valiquette 1994), engineering documents (e.g. Paradis, Dobrin and Miller, 1995), business memoranda (Yates 1989), financial documents and social workers' records (Paré and Smart 1994), health communication (e.g. Berkenkotter 2001; Schryer 1993; Segal 2005), and so on (for further discussion, see Bazerman, Bonini and Figueiredo 2009; Coe *et al.* 2002; Dias and Paré 2000; Freedman and Medway 1994a). This research provided much needed information about the norms and practices of rhetorical communities (Miller 1994). Once a relatively large body of knowledge about genres was accumulated, it became clear that in order to unpack complex communicative phenomena it was necessary to study 'the relationships among genres within a community' (Yates and Orlikowski 2002: 103), or what Spinuzzi (2004) called *genre assemblages*. Several concepts that described interactions among genres were proposed: for example, in her study of tax accountants' work, Devitt (1991) introduced the notion of a *genre set*. A genre set represents all types of texts produced by a person in a particular occupation in the process of his/her work. Orlikowski and Yates (1994) and Spinuzzi (2004) suggested that sets of genres overlap, and introduced the notion of genre *repertoire* to describe overlapping sets routinely used by members of a particular community. Bazerman's (1994: 97) concept of *genre systems* – the full set of 'interrelated genres that interact with each other in specific settings' – extends these notions. These perspectives on genres as interacting with each other proved useful to the investigation of the development of workplace literacies and the school-to-work transition (e.g. Coe *et al.* 2002).

More recently, in addition to the concepts reviewed above, the concept of *agency* (agent, social actor) has become central to RGS research. Schryer (2002), for example, insists that when analysing genres, researchers should bear in mind that the recurrence of the construal of a rhetorical situation (Miller 1984) might be identified *only* by 'the social actors involved in that social setting' (2002: 77) (also see Bitzer 1968; Dias *et al.* 1999: 234).

Although RGS provides a powerful social theoretical framework for the study of learning and use of genres by professionals and by novices transitioning from the academy to the workplace, lately, it has been used in conjunction with other rhetorical, psychological, and social theories in order to better flesh out relationships between the *individual* and the *social* (cf. Berger and Luckmann 1967), and between *agency* and *structure* (cf. Giddens 1984; Schryer 2000, 2002). At present, it is difficult to find a study that would rely on RGS as a sole theoretical framework. Many studies have successfully demonstrated that a combination of complementary social theories provides further insight into the questions that RGS attempts to answer (e.g. Artemeva 2008, 2009, 2011; Artemeva and Freedman 2001; Dias *et al.* 1999; Le Maistre and Paré 2004; Russell 1997; Winsor 1996, 2001, 2003). This combination of complementary yet distinct theoretical perspectives, such as, for example, activity theory and theories of situated learning, has allowed researchers to explore the interplay of the individual and the social in the study of genre learning in the process of novices' transition from school to the workplace (e.g. Artemeva and Freedman 2001; Freedman and Adam 2000; Freedman and Smart 1997; Dannels 2000, 2003, 2009; Dannels and Norris Martin 2008; Dias *et al.* 1999; Le Maistre and Paré 2004; Schryer 2000, 2002, 2005; Winsor 2001).

Both theories of activity and situated learning consider the social context in which human activity takes place as an *integral* part of activity rather than just its surrounding environment. Activity and situated learning theorists agree that 'every cognitive act must be viewed as a specific response to a specific set of circumstances. Only by understanding the circumstances and the participants' construal of the situation can a valid interpretation of the cognitive activity be made' (Resnick 1991: 4). This view of human activity is highly compatible with the RGS perspective on the reciprocal relationship between genre and its social context (cf. Bawarshi 2000; Paré and Smart 1994).

In the following sub-sections, we review theories of human activity and situated learning as they relate to the study of the school-to-work transition and genre learning.

Activity theory

Activity theory is based on Vygotsky's (1934, 1986) view of the relationships between an individual and objects of the environment as mediated by cultural means, tools and signs. An earlier version of AT was developed by Leont'ev (e.g. 1981, 1989) drawing on Marx's concept of labour, or production of use values. Leont'ev saw work as mediated by tools and performed in conditions of *collective* activity. In his depiction, mediated human activity is represented by a triad (often depicted as a triangle) – consisting of the subject, the object, and the mediating artifact, a culturally constructed material or symbolic tool. The three-level model of activity proposed by Leont'ev provides distinction between collective *activity*, individual *action*, and *operation*. The uppermost level of collective activity is driven by an object-related motive; the middle level of individual (or group) action is driven by a conscious goal, and the bottom level of automatic operations is driven by the conditions and available tools (e.g. Artemeva 2011; Engeström 1987; Engeström and Miettinen 1999; Leont'ev 1981; Wertsch 1981, 1985).

For example, Artemeva (2011) applied this model in her study of an engineering student learning to communicate as a novice engineer in the workplace. Leont'ev's three-level model allowed Artemeva to unpack the levels of the student's activity when the student was involved in communication tasks at university and in the workplace. Artemeva found that some transfer of learning from the university engineering communication classroom did occur as the student gradually engaged in workplace activity, and as some actions that she had performed consciously in the classroom, dropped to the level of more or less automatic operations in the workplace.

Leont'ev's theoretical representation of human activity was later critiqued by a number of scholars (e.g. Engeström 1999; Davydov and Zinchenko 1989; Davydov and Radzikhovski 1980, 1981, 1985; Witte 1992, 1999) for a major contradiction that lies at its heart: the use of object-oriented activity *both* as an explanatory principle of the theory *and* the object of the study. These ambiguities of the three-level model have been overcome to some extent in further development in AT with the introduction of the concept of an *activity system*, which includes, at a minimum, 'the object, subject, mediating artifacts (signs and tools), rules, community, and division of labor' (Engeström and Miettinen 1999: 9). Engeström (1987) proposed to use the activity system as a unit of analysis in order to account for the socially distributed and interactive nature of human activity. Activity systems are characterised by inner contradictions (e.g. Engeström 1987, 1996); these internal tensions and contradictions 'are the motive force of change and development' (Engeström and Miettinen 1999: 9) in human activity.

Russell (1997) and Dias (2000) were among the first to demonstrate the compatibility and complementarity of RGS and AT in their applications of these theories to the study of academic and professional communication. Their research paved the way to a large number of more recent studies that rely on a combination of these theoretical approaches (e.g. Bazerman and Russell 2002).

All in all, when compared to RGS, AT provides 'a higher level of theorization to account for change as well as resistance and conflict' (Artemeva and Freedman 2001: 170) and a complementary perspective on 'social motive, and on the action aspect of genre' (Dias *et al.* 1999: 23), thus serving as a powerful theoretical tool that can be legitimately combined with RGS to be used in professional communication research.

Theories of situated learning

Theories of situated learning (e.g. Freedman and Adam 2000; Lave and Wenger 1991; Rogoff 1990) are based on the view of learning and knowing as social, rooted in the experiences of daily life. Sharing its origins with AT, the view of learning as situated in the social is also based on the Vygotskian understanding of higher mental functions (1986) in the individual as being derived from social life (Wertsch 1991) and on his recognition of the social as primary. Such theorists as, for example, Brown, Collins and Duguid (1989) and Lave and Wenger (1991) see all knowledge as situated. Central to the literature on situated learning, therefore, are the notions that learning and knowing are context-specific, that learning is active and accomplished through co-participation, and that cognition is socially shared (e.g. Freedman and Adam 1996, 2000; Hanks 1991; Hutchins 1993). The emphasis that Vygotsky and his followers placed on activity, on person-in-activity, and on mediation through socio-cultural tools such as language, is central for the concept of situated learning, as is Vygotsky's understanding of higher mental functions as internalised social relationships (1986). As Rogoff (1990) observed, Vygotsky had developed his theories 'on the premise that individual intellectual development of higher mental processes cannot be understood without reference to the social milieu in which the individual is embedded' and without consideration of 'the social roots of both the tools for thinking that … [novices] are learning to use and the social interactions that guide' their use of these tools (1990: 35). Situated activity perspectives, developed on the basis of Vygotsky's theories, perceive learning occurring as part of the changing participation and practices of people engaged in an ongoing activity (Lave 1996a; Lave and Wenger 1991), or, in other words, as Lave and Wenger observed, 'there is no activity that is not situated' (p. 33). Central to the theories of situated learning is Vygotsky's (1934, 1986) concept of the *zone of proximal development* (ZPD).

ZONE OF PROXIMAL DEVELOPMENT

Another of Vygotsky's contributions to this view of human activity and learning was his revolutionary concept of the ZPD, defined as 'the distance between the mental age, or the level of actual development, determined by means of independently solved problems and the level, which a child achieves when solving problems not individually but in collaboration' (Vygotsky 1934: 218, translated by Artemeva). Vygotsky claimed that individual cognitive change is effected by the social and, thus, we conclude that this view is compatible with RGS. Sometimes, in the Western literature the ZPD is mistakenly defined as the distance between the levels of *task difficulty*; however, this definition switches the focus from human development to the complexity of the tasks (cf. Chaiklin 2003) and takes researchers away from the issues of the development of higher mental functions in a social interactive environment. Vygotsky (1934, 1986) observed that the actual developmental level characterises the child's development as of yesterday while the zone of proximal development characterises her development as of tomorrow. Therefore, the recognition of the important role of the ZPD becomes essential to our understanding of the development of higher mental functions and hence, to learning.

For example, Artemeva (2008, 2009, 2011) and Artemeva and Fox (2010) showed in their studies of students going back and forth between university courses in engineering communications and work placements that some students who had had an opportunity to work within their ZPDs with workplace mentors and participate in workplace interactions in collaboration with experienced employees were able to expand their genre repertoires. When these students returned to the classroom, they had an expanded professional genre repertoire to draw on in performing classroom tasks.

Freedman and Adam (1996) pointed to two distinct analytical perspectives on learning which had emerged from the literature on situated learning: Rogoff's *guided participation* (GP) (1990) and Lave and Wenger's *legitimate peripheral participation* (LPP), which places in the centre the concept of *communities of practice* (CoPs) (1991). As their common origins suggest, these two perspectives share fundamental conceptions of learning; however, there are important differences, which in turn reveal the differences between learning in conventional university settings and learning in the workplace.

Guided participation

Rogoff (1990) developed the notion of guided participation from Vygotsky's observation that what children can do in collaboration, with assistance today, they will be able to do alone tomorrow; in other words, that learning takes place through processes of co-participation in the ZPD. For Rogoff, both guidance and participation are essential to a maturing child's *apprenticeship in thinking*. This view of learning accounts powerfully for the interactions between child and caretaker. The main focus in GP is on the learners and their learning. As Freedman and Adam (1996) argue, it describes most learning that occurs in school situations, including higher education. By contrast, in the workplace, newcomers and old-timers are involved in activities that have a purpose above and beyond the initiation of newcomers and their learning. As Freedman and Adam observe, when students move from the university context to the workplace, they typically not only have to learn new genres but, more significantly, they need to learn new ways to learn. However, the learning that takes place in workplace settings cannot be fully accounted for by the GP perspective (e.g. Freedman and Adam 1996, 2000). Lave and Wenger's (1991) LPP, with its central concept of *communities of practice* (CoPs) (Lave 1988, 1991,

1996a, 1996b; Lave and Wenger 1991; Wenger 1998a, 1998b, 2005), was specifically developed to reflect workplace learning scenarios.

Lave and Wenger's version of situated learning

Lave and Wenger's version of situated learning (1991) reflects a workplace scenario in which novices start by working on necessary but less involved tasks under the guidance of more experienced practitioners and gradually become practitioners themselves. The unit of analysis they use in their study of learning that occurs in workplace settings is *community of practice*, mentioned above.

Communities of practice

Wenger (2005) defines community of practice as a group of people who 'share a concern or a passion for something they do and who interact regularly to learn how to do it better' (n. p.). For such a group of people to be considered a CoP, it needs to consist of 'peers in the execution of real work'; these peers share 'a common sense of purpose and a real need to know what each other knows' (Brown and Gray 1995: paragraph 27). CoPs cannot be equated with formal teams because they are defined by what their members *do* (Dias et al. 1999: 29). For CoPs, 'learning ... is not a separate activity. It is not something we do when we do nothing else or stop doing when we do something else' (Wenger 1998b: 8). Each CoP is constituted by distinct intellectual and social conventions. Members of the community are practitioners who share a repertoire of stories and resources such as materials, tools, documents, routines, vocabulary, symbols, artifacts, etc., that embody the accumulated knowledge of the community. This *shared repertoire* serves as a foundation for future learning (Wenger 2005). As situated learning theorists (e.g. Lave 1996a, 1996b; Lave and Wenger 1991; Wenger 1998b) observe, a primary, and most effective, form of one's increasing engagement in this shared repertoire, that is, in situated learning, is *apprenticeship*, where the notion of apprenticeship includes so-called *cognitive apprenticeship* (Brown, Collins and Duguid 1989: 32). In situated learning theories, apprenticeship is understood as a process in which newcomers to a CoP, including interns and students, learn the local expert practices by being actively engaged in them with limited responsibility for the outcome and under the guidance of more experienced 'oldtimers' (Smart and Brown 2002: 119). This process represents learning that occurs within the ZPD. In fact, Wenger (2005) describes the process of learning in CoPs as a 'living curriculum' (n. p.) for apprentices.

The notion of CoP, though widely used in various fields for many years, has met some criticism. For example, Eraut (2002: 13) criticised it for its narrowness and argued that 'a profession is [a] much larger and more diverse community than any community of practice'. He described a range of archetypal workplace scenarios that extended from a fully democratic learning community with a high status for novices, high commitment to learning, and participation as the dominant form of learning, to a scenario in which the organisational commitment to learning is never meant to be transformed into action. He further asserted that only one of these scenarios corresponded to Lave and Wenger's definition of CoP – that in which novices 'have lower status, but are seen as starting on trajectories that raise their status over time. A ... characteristic of such communities is their acceptance of clear progression models developed as part of their tradition of practice' (2002: 10; for further discussion of alternative views on situated learning, see Jackson 2011).

In his discussion of CoPs, Wenger (1998b) pays particular attention to the theoretical constructs of *participation* and *reification*. Participation, Wenger argues, 'is a constituent of [our] identities, and as such, participation is not something we turn on or off' (1998b: 57). Reification, Wenger explains, refers to 'the process of giving form to our experience by producing objects that congeal this experience into "thingness"' and to the ability of humans 'to project [themselves] onto the world and ... attribute to [their] meanings an independent existence' (1998b: 58). In other words, reification refers to *projection*. Wenger proposed to use the concepts of participation and reification in conjunction in order to describe the engagement of humans with the world in a process of meaning production. Participation and reification are two intrinsic and inseparable constituents of negotiation of meaning, which, in turn, is one of the major constituents of CoP.

Legitimate peripheral participation

Lave and Wenger's (1991) version of situated learning in which they use CoP as the unit of analysis, is called *legitimate peripheral participation*. They define LPP as an *analytical perspective* on or a *descriptor* of situated learning. LPP focuses on the action itself and on its social outcome, and describes a range of apprenticeships. It views learning as taking place in the process of creation or action and as accomplished through co-participation, where co-participation refers to active engagement in a CoP and construction of 'identities in relation to these communities' (Wenger 1998b: 4).

Lave and Wenger (1991) unpack the term *legitimate peripheral participation* by noting that the term should be considered as a whole and not as an opposition to some 'illegitimated' peripheral participation. They continue by saying that 'with regard to "peripherality" there may well be no such thing as "central participation" in a community of practice' (1991: 35–36). That is, peripheral participation of newcomers, in this view, gradually leads to full participation and full membership in a CoP. In their discussion of movement from peripheral to full participation in a CoP, Lave and Wenger (1991) see learning as one of the primary characteristics of social practice. Through their engagement in practice, legitimate peripheral participants (i.e. newcomers) can develop a view of what the whole enterprise is about, and what there is to be learned. LPP focuses on novices developing 'knowledgeably skilled identities in practice' (Lave and Wenger 1991: 55) and gaining comprehensive understanding of how 'agent, activity, and the world mutually constitute each other' (1991: 33).

In other words, in contrast to Rogoff's 1990 caregiver and child perspective on situated learning as *guided* participation in *educational* tasks, Lave and Wenger argue that in the workplace, apprentices are initiated into CoPs by participating in *authentic* tasks that are *not* invented as educational opportunities (Freedman and Adam 2000; Hanks 1991). In LPP, learning is, therefore, seen as *improvised practice*. In order for this kind of learning to be effective, newcomers to the CoP need to have broad access to different parts of the activity and gradually proceed to full participation in core tasks; be engaged in abundant interaction with other participants, 'mediated ... by stories of problematic situations and their solutions' (Engeström 1991: 252), or 'war stories' (Lave and Wenger 1991: 109); and have direct access to the CoP's technologies and structures, so that the 'inner workings [of these technologies and structures] can become available' to them (Engeström 1991: 252).

Wenger (1998b) observed that the process of the development of knowledgeably skilled or master identities and movement from peripheral to full participation create generational discontinuities in CoPs as relative newcomers are gradually turning into oldtimers. In other words, while members of a CoP are dependent on each other (i.e. newcomers are not able to learn without oldtimers, while oldtimers are not able to carry on the practice through time without newcomers), 'the success of both new and old members depends on the eventual replacement of oldtimers by newcomers-become-oldtimers themselves. The tensions this introduces into processes of learning are fundamental' (1998b: 74), and the unpacking of these tensions becomes crucial for the complete understanding of the mechanisms of situated learning.

In the past 20 years or so, the notion of CoP has attracted significant attention from professional communication scholars and researchers (e.g. Amin and Roberts 2008; Artemeva 2008; Barton and Tusting 2005; Beaufort 2000; Fisher and Bennion 2005) because through the process of situated learning in CoPs novices learn the genres of professional communication (cf. Artemeva 2008; Dannels and Norris Martin 2008; Freedman, Adam and Smart 1994). In other words, the learning of job-specific speaking and writing is seen in the situated learning framework as a profoundly social process directed toward the shared goals of the CoP. The concept of CoP has been productively used in the study and teaching of professional communication (e.g. Dias *et al.* 1999; Dias and Paré 2000; Freedman and Adam 1996; Starke-Meyerring *et al.* 2011). In the current climate of globalisation, it has been applied across international contexts (e.g. Johnson 2007).

As noted above, learning that occurs in the process of social participation in CoPs and learning that takes place in a classroom setting and is expected to occur as a result of teaching are often contrasted (e.g. Freedman and Adam 2000; Rogoff 1990) because 'learning through legitimate peripheral participation takes place' regardless of the setting and regardless of 'whether there is any intentional education at all' (Lave and Wenger 1991: 40). However, recently, some productive innovations that draw on LPP have been introduced into educational settings (e.g. Artemeva 2005, 2008, 2011; Artemeva, Logie and St-Martin 1999; Rogoff, Turkanis and Bartlett 2001; see McLaughlin 2003 for a discussion of the role of CoPs in education).

Another theoretical approach to learning and activity, which has been applied in the study of professional communication and the school-to-work transition (e.g. Freedman and Smart 1997; Paré 2000; Winsor 2001) is *distributed cognition* (Hutchins 1993, 1995a, 1995b, 2000, 2006).

Distributed cognition

Hutchins developed the theory by observing a ship crew manoeuvring a ship into the harbour (1993, 1995a) and investigating the work of pilots in an aircraft cockpit (1995b). These observations made him realise that none of the people involved in these activities was able to complete the task without other people participating and contributing their knowledge, memory and understanding of the situation. Knowledge was distributed among the participants so that in addition to some shared (or redundant) knowledge or memory, each participant possessed knowledge that was different from all other participants'. In other words, Hutchins saw knowledge, memory and intelligence as 'distributed across' people, 'social practices ... and the various tools' (Gee 2000: 181) rather than it being 'encompassed by the skin or skull of an individual' (Hutchins 2000: 1). By mediational tools he understood both material and symbolic tools, such as language. The distributed cognition perspective is rooted in the Vygotskian view of human cognition and closely related to the theories of situated learning and activity discussed above.

In her study of engineering students entering the workplace and learning to do 'knowledge work', Winsor (2001) relied on the theory of distributed cognition to capture the processes in which the students participated in the engineering company. She observed that in the workplace, knowledge was distributed among participants in an activity and the mediational tools they used. To be engaged in the workplace activity, students needed to participate in the system of distributed cognition formed in the workplace. In addition to materials tools, they needed to become skilful users of 'disciplinary or organizational language conventions' (i.e., workplace genres) to be able to communicate with members of the system. These conventional genres allowed both students and employees to access 'previously stabilized knowledge that has been distributed into them' (2001: 26), and develop the knowledge further. As Winsor noted, knowledge in the engineering company was constantly in flux, thus making it more difficult for the students to join the workplace system of distributed cognition.

Some scholars (e.g. Artemeva 2008, 2009; Dias *et al.* 1999; Bazerman and Russell 2002) have suggested that the integration of rhetorical theory with theories of activity, situated learning, and distributed cognition provides a more complex and rich theoretical framework that allows researchers to see beyond 'the textual dynamics of the professions' (Bazerman and Paradis 1991) into larger organisational contexts and ideologies.

Further theorising coupled with extensive empirical work has provided professional communication researchers with a rich body of largely qualitative work that has investigated the discursive practices of students, novices, and professionals in both academic and workplace settings (e.g. Artemeva and Freedman 2006; Bazerman *et al.* 2009). This research has prompted professional communication scholars to reconceptualise theoretical frameworks to account for new findings. In the section below, we summarise some of this empirical research.

Novice-to-expert transition in professional communication: Past to present

Empirical research in the mid-1980s and early 1990s contributed to the development of an increased understanding of writing within academic disciplines (e.g. Berkenkotter and Huckin 1995; Herrington 1985; Carter 1990) and non-academic settings (e.g. Bazerman and Paradis 1991; Couture and Rymer 1993; Faigley 1985; Odell and Goswami 1985; Spilka 1993). Theoretically, this research was predominantly informed by the developing field of RGS. These early studies accounted for discursive *form* within different settings, 'in which treatment of function/use/effect tended toward anthropological description, in part because many studies were oriented by the practical task of helping apprentice writers gain access to existing communities of discourse' (Coe, Lingard and Teslenko 2002: 5). This rich period of research resulted in new recognitions of differences in 'school' and workplace communication (e.g. Anson and Forsberg 1990; Dias and Paré 2000; Winsor 1994). Questions were raised about the relations between writing in university and writing in the workplace, the *transition from school to work*, and novices' ability to competently engage in professional communication (e.g. Dias and Paré 2000; Dias *et al.* 1999; Winsor 1996, 2003).

In response to these questions, a number of longitudinal programmes of research were undertaken. In general, they investigated transitions of novices to different professional settings, for example: in architecture (e.g. Dias *et al.* 1999; Medway 2000); in finance, law and government (e.g. Freedman and Adam 1996, 2000; Freedman, Adam and Smart 1994; MacKinnon 1993; Smart 2000); in engineering (e.g. Artemeva and Freedman 2001; Dannels 2000, 2003; Winsor 1994, 1996); in medicine and veterinary (e.g. Berkenkotter 2001; Schryer 1993; Segal 2005); in social work and education (e.g. Paré 2000; Le Maistre and Paré 2004), in management, political science and communication studies (e.g. Schneider and Andre 2005), and in other fields.

In our view, these programmes of research reflected the main trends in the school-to-work transitions scholarship and directly contributed to the reconceptualisations of school and workplace as learning environments. Not only were these programmes of research longitudinal, but they also tended to employ similar holistic methodological approaches, 'variously labelled as phenomenological, ethnographic, hermeneutic, and qualitative' (Beaufort 1999: 199). As Beaufort points out, the use of such holistic approaches was 'logical', given the recognition that 'literacy is culturally embedded and that written texts or acts of composing cannot be understood apart from the social systems of both producer and product' (1999: 199). In other words, in contrast to early professional communication studies, these programmes of research focused less on questions related to texts and discursive forms (cf. Coe, Lingard and Teslenko 2002), and more 'on questions of social knowledge' (Herndl, Fennell and Miller 1991: 304).

For example, the seminal seven-year study by Dias *et al.* (1999) focused on novices' transitions between matched academic and workplace sites. The authors directly addressed the question, 'What are the relations between writing in university and writing in the workplace?' (1999: 222). In commenting on the results of their study, they remarked, 'for a book about writing, surprisingly little writing, in the usual sense of texts, gets quoted and discussed', and continued by noting that 'we had to completely refocus our operating notions of what writing is'. They explained that in the course of their study, their views of writing changed 'toward a vision of a complex network of activities in which composition represents only one strand'. They came to understand that texts 'derive their meaning as much from the activity systems in which they are embedded as from their denotational content'. In other words, texts carry the meanings of the *places* or *spaces* that they inhabit, construe and are construed by: 'Writing, it turns out and in a manner of speaking, will be known by the company it keeps' (1999: 222). Dias *et al.* (1999) reflect a shift in school-to-work transition research, evident in other longitudinal studies of the time, as researchers moved from a predominant focus on 'archeological unearthing' (Freedman and Adam 2000: 58) of texts to a focus on social context and knowledge construction. In addition, by drawing on RGS and theories of situated learning and activity, researchers reconceptualised the construct of *context* (Bazerman 2013; Bracewell and Witte 2003; Schryer 2011; Witte 1992). New theoretical perspectives were developed on the basis of the integration of the theories reviewed in this chapter, such as activity-based genre theory (e.g. Berkenkotter and Huckin 1993; Smart 2003); writing, activity and genre research (WAGR) (e.g. Spinuzzi 2010); a unified theoretical perspective on genre learning and use (e.g. Artemeva 2008, 2009, 2011), and others. These theoretical approaches have further enriched the study of school-to-work transitions in professional communications.

For example, having demonstrated the compatibility and complementarity of RGS, AT and LPP, in her longitudinal study of engineering students' trajectories on their way to becoming professionals, Artemeva (2008) illustrated how the theoretical framework that integrated these theoretical perspectives facilitated an in-depth exploration of genre learning in a professional activity system as a component of the novice's movement from peripheral to full participation, accomplished under the mentorship of oldtimers.

At the same time, notions of situatedness continued to be further problematised (Beaufort 2000; Gee 2000). New reconceptualisations allowed 'researchers to avoid the subject/object or center/periphery' (Zachry 2007: x) dichotomies that had resulted from a predominant focus on context alone (Spinuzzi 2011). Zachry (2007: v) further observes that 'theories of communication have become increasingly complex', beginning to emphasise 'such considerations as power, contingency, and unpredictability and their relationship' to communication practices. Expanded by recognitions of the need for more 'critical examination' (Freedman and Medway 1994a: 15), recent research has increasingly drawn attention to issues of relationality, agency and identity (e.g. Artemeva and Freedman 2006; Dannels 2000, 2009; Schryer *et al.* 2002; Spinuzzi 2003; Zachry and Thralls 2007). Researchers interested in the school-to-work transition have begun to focus more on professional identity formation, as novices acquire

> not only the *regulated* resources of their profession but also (and more importantly) *regularized* ways of knowing. Both forms of knowing embody professional values and are essential to the process of professional identity formation.
>
> *(Schryer, Lingard and Spafford 2007: 23)*

Issues related to identity formation have led to increased interest in ideology, values, and the distribution of power (Coe *et al.* 2002; Starke-Meyerring *et al.* 2011). Some researchers have focused on these issues in academic contexts (e.g. Devitt 2004, 2009; Herrington and Moran 2005; Lee and Maguire 2011; Paré 2000; Paré, Starke-Meyerring and McAlpine 2011), others have looked at power relations in the workplace (e.g. Schneider 2002, 2007; Spinuzzi 2010), but of greatest interest to us are the studies that investigate transitions from school to workplace (e.g. Artemeva and Freedman 2006; Schryer *et al.* 2002; Schryer *et al.* 2006; Spafford *et al.* 2004). Amongst these are studies in which academic institutions themselves are considered workplaces (e.g. Artemeva and Fox 2011; Fox and Artemeva 2011; Tardy 2003).

Not only have theoretical notions of context been problematised and expanded, notions of professional communication itself have also been subject to revision, modification and elaboration. The technological revolution in professional communications has, inevitably, had a dramatic impact on how we construct, learn and enact meanings in school and the workplace and school-to-work transition. At the same time, recognition of the embodied (e.g. Haas and Witte 2001), or *multimodal*, nature of professional writing/communications has required new methodological approaches, for which technological advances have provided the investigative means (e.g. O'Halloran *et al.* 2011).

Multimodal perspectives on professional communication

Within the tradition of Systemic Functional Linguistics (SFL) (cf. Halliday 1973, 1978), Hodge and Kress (1988), O'Toole (1994), and Kress and van Leeuwen (1996) pioneered the treatment of text and image as multimodal. However, as Bhatia, Flowerdew and Jones (2008: 129) observe, such text- and image-centred approaches were initially too 'static' in their rendering of multimodality. Informed by this tradition of research, more recent work (e.g. O'Halloran 2004; Jewitt 2009) extended these initial approaches, which evolved into a new stream of multimodal discourse analysis (e.g. Jewitt and Kress 2003; Kress 2010). As Norris (2012) points out, theories of mediated discourse analysis are theories of *action,* which take the view 'that meanings are created in texts and interactions in a complex interplay of semiosis across multiple modes, which include but are not limited to written and spoken language' (Bhatia *et al.* 2008: 129). Norris (2004, 2011, 2012), drawing on the insights of previous research, has introduced what she refers to as multimodal interaction analysis. For example, she applies this analysis in her ethnographic study of identity construction through the workplace interactions and communications (e.g. 2008) of two co-owners of a web design business.

In Writing Studies, although Haas (1995), Sauer (1998), and Haas and Witte (2001) were amongst the first researchers to highlight the embodied nature of professional communication, they did not refer to it as multimodal. Rather, their view of communication as an embodied practice recognised 'its intimate linking with technologies and with knowledge [which] are always enacted in part through bodily and sensory means' (Haas and Witte 2001: 416). Such notions are consistent with currently developing perspectives on communication as a multimodal phenomenon, and a growing recognition that focusing only on written texts reduces and even distorts the nature of communication (e.g. Artemeva and Fox 2011; Levine and Scollon 2004):

> multimodality has always and everywhere been present as representations are propagated across multiple media and as any situated event is indexically fed by all the modes present. ... In this sense, all genres are irremediably multimodal.
>
> *(Prior 2009: 27)*

These more dynamic approaches consider discourse as 'integrated in the flow of concrete social actions that go to make up ordinary and professional human practices' (Bhatia *et al.* 2008: 130). Indeed, theories of human activity and situated learning, as well as RGS, and the integrated theoretical perspective, are consistent with this view of professional communication as multimodal, social action.

Our own research (e.g. Artemeva and Fox 2011; Fox and Artemeva 2011) has been informed by this perspective as we examine professional communication practices of mathematics instructors teaching within the university-as-workplace. The purpose of this research is to understand the process of school-to-work transition that graduate students and novice instructors go through as they become experienced university mathematics teachers. Our research indicates that the locus of the professional practices of this disciplinary community is a multi-modal pedagogical genre characterised by layered modes (Jewitt as cited in Norris 2012: 5) of speaking, writing, and movement (Fox and Artemeva 2011). Current technologies allow for the creation of multimodal records of professional communication practices,

> in which talk is kept in context and all modes are recorded ... [enabling] researchers to rigorously and systematically examine resources and practices through which participants ... build their social activities and how their talk, facial expression, gaze, gesture, and body elaborate one another.
>
> *(Jewitt 2012: 6)*

Such multimodal records create new opportunities for researchers to investigate and simultaneously relate micro-level with macro-level realisations of professional communication. Analysis of these records, informed by the theoretical perspectives reviewed in this chapter, promises to contribute not only to further theorising of school-to-work transition, but also to an increased understanding of how to provide support to novices. For example, in their consideration of classroom discourses, Jewitt and Jones (2008: 149) point out, 'multimodal micro-descriptions of how discourses are realized in the classroom can contribute both to discourse theory and to educational practices'. This is also the case for professional communication in the workplace.

Pedagogical implications

On the basis of their empirical research into school-to-work transition, in the 1990s some scholars (e.g. Dias *et al.* 1999; Freedman 1993, 1995; Freedman and Adam 1996, 2000a, b; Freedman, Adam and Smart 1994) expressed doubts that workplace communications could be taught and learned in the academic classroom. More recently, researchers (e.g. Artemeva 2005, 2008; Artemeva and Fox 2010; Bawarshi and Reiff 2010; Beaufort 1999; Brent 2011, 2012; Devitt 2004; Ford 2004; Tuomi-Gröhn and Engeström 2003a) have observed that some *transfer of learning* across school and workplace contexts does occur under specific circumstances. It appears that students in school can learn how to engage in, navigate, and act on new rhetorical contexts. Rather than expecting *skills* to transfer from school to workplace, what can be expected to 'transfer' is a sense of how *to learn* to communicate in new workplace environments. In other words, new research (e.g. Artemeva 2005, 2008, 2009, 2011; Starke-Meyerring *et al.* 2011) provides confirmatory evidence that although writing and speaking in school and in the workplace are fundamentally different (cf. Dias *et al.* 1999), what can be taught are rhetorical strategies that students may draw on, adapt and apply to new contexts or circumstances (cf. Devitt 2004).

This brings us back to the discussion of the notion of portability as it pertains to the transition from academia to the workplace, which framed this chapter. As recent publications discussed in this chapter indicate, *transfer of learning* can occur if the classroom is set up for it (cf. Artemeva 2005, 2008; Dias *et al.* 1999). It appears that professional communication pedagogy can, in fact, support novices going through the work-to-school transition – but only if this pedagogy is informed by richly theorised and carefully constructed studies of multimodal rhetorical practices realised in professional settings. Such studies would contribute to needs analyses, which could inform curricular models. As argued in the foundational school-to-work research (Dias *et al.* 1999), the purely *academic* classroom setting has only a limited chance of providing support for novices transitioning into workplaces.

In the past decade or so, alongside more traditional classroom instruction and online courses (e.g. St Amant 2007), technical communication programmes have incorporated internships and co-operative education, where students join professional organisations for a limited time and work there as employees (e.g. Anson and Forsberg 1990; Artemeva 2005, 2009; Billett 2004; Smart and Brown 2002). A more recent approach to teaching that has gained popularity in the US and Canada is *service learning* (e.g. Arney and Jones 2006). This approach involves students in communication activities while engaging them in the work of their community, not-for-profit organisations, and non-governmental organisations. This civic engagement both educates students as future professional communicators and provides them with an 'education in citizenship' (Bazerman 2002; McMillan 2011; Sapp and Crabtree 2002). Pedagogical approaches such as these may enhance the potential for transfer of learning.

One of the major challenges that technical and professional communication educators face at the moment is the need to remain critical in their expectations of what can and cannot be transferred from the classroom to workplace contexts. Further research may help account for the strategies that can be reapplied to workplace situations (cf. Brent 2011). Freedman's call, articulated as early as 1987, 'for far more research, directed towards understanding how,' among other things, novices learn to communicate effectively 'in the context of the social exigencies entailed in entering a new discourse community' (p. 112) has been echoed in Brent's recent publications (2011, 2012).

Future directions for research

Technological advances are transforming our capacity to generate multimodal records of professional communication in academic and workplace settings. For example, O'Halloran *et al.* (2011) have developed software that allows for sophisticated, layered multimodal representations of data. More recent versions of computer-based tools for qualitative analysis (e.g. NVivo, Atlas, etc.) permit the coding of video data. Electronic tools that are currently applied to the analysis of written and spoken corpora data (e.g. WordSmith, Antconc, etc.), will, undoubtedly, in the future be further developed to accommodate visual modes. The capacity for multimodal investigation of professional communication will allow researchers to integrate the analysis of written and oral rhetorical strategies with studies of non-verbal communication strategies, which have often remained overlooked in traditional professional communication research. Such research can further contribute to greater understanding of how to support novices in their transition from school to workplace.

Already, internet capabilities (e.g. Skype, social media, etc.) allow for multimodal data collection in the public domain and increase the potential for large-scale studies. These capabilities will increase and influence professional communication research in the coming years. New questions about the nature and learning of professional communication will emerge. These questions will, in turn, require the application of new methods. For example, the potential for large-scale studies will increasingly encourage researchers to complement qualitative approaches with quantitative ones. A combination of qualitative and quantitative approaches – mixed methods – will add to the study of school-to-work transition and respond to questions that otherwise could not have been addressed. For example, in our multimodal study of pedagogical genres in university mathematics classrooms, we have collected data that provide a multimodal record of genre enactment across a large and representative sample of mathematics instructors (Artemeva and Fox 2011; Fox and Artemeva 2011). As a result, we have begun to address questions about what repeats and what differs in the genre performance in the community of practice of university mathematics teachers across contexts and levels of experience.

As McMillan and Schumacher (2010) suggest, the recent increase in the number of mixed methods studies can in part be explained by researchers' needs to apply 'both quantitative and qualitative methods in the same study ... when using solely a quantitative or qualitative method would be insufficient to provide complete answers that meet the goal or purpose of the study' (2010: 395). In our view, future research into school-to-work transition will be further enhanced by new technological advances, thus leading to the development of new theoretical, methodological and analytical approaches.

Related topics

knowledge-making in professional discourses; genre analysis; needs analysis; communities in studies of discursive practices

Key readings

Artemeva, N. and Freedman, A. (eds) (2006). *Rhetorical Genre Studies and Beyond*, Winnipeg, Manitoba, Canada: Inkshed Publications. (A collection of chapters that discuss the need for complementing rhetorical genre studies (RGS) with additional compatible theoretical perspectives necessary to further develop RGS as a theoretical framework for the study of the school-to-work transition; the collection includes empirical studies based on these theoretical approaches.)

Dias, P., Freedman, A., Medway, P. and Paré, A. (1999). *Worlds Apart: Acting and Writing in Academic and Workplace Contexts*, Mahwah, NJ: Lawrence Erlbaum Associates. (A unique longitudinal multi-site study of the nature of professional communication and its acquisition by novices during their school-to-work transition in different matching academic disciplines and fields; the study uses as its theoretical framework activity-based genre theory complemented by the theories of situated learning.)

Dias, P. and Paré, A. (eds) (2000). *Transitions: Writing in Academic and Workplace Settings*, Cresskill, NJ: Hampton. (A collection of chapters that focus on different aspects of the school-to-work transition in the fields of engineering, finance, social work, etc.)

Freedman, A. and Medway, P. (eds) (1994a). *Genre and the New Rhetoric*, London: Taylor & Francis. (A foundational collection that assembles some of the most important international publications in Rhetorical Genre Studies as of the early 1990s.)

Tuomi-Gröhn, T. and Engeström, Y. (eds) (2003a). *Between School and Work: New Perspectives on Transfer and Boundary Crossing*, Kidlington, UK: Elsevier Science. (A comprehensive collection that includes theoretical discussions and empirical studies of the phenomenon of transfer, predominantly in vocational training settings.)

Notes

1 Authors' Note: Portions of this chapter originally appeared in Artemeva, N. and Freedman, A. (eds) (2006). *Rhetorical Genre Studies and Beyond*. (pp. 9–99). Inkshed Publications: Winnipeg, Canada © Copyright 2006 the authors of each chapter.

2 Recently, some Western scholars have claimed that Bakhtin's work cannot be considered original (see, for example, Bronckart and Bota 2011). The authors of this chapter do not share this view and choose to rely on Bakhtin's published work, verified against original Russian publications.

Bibliography

Amin, A. and Roberts, J. (2008). 'Knowing in action: Beyond communities of practice', *Research Policy*, 37, 353–69.
Anderson, P. V., Brockmann, R. J. and Miller, C. R. (eds) (1983). *New Essays in Technical and Scientific Communication: Research, Theory, Practice*, Farmingdale, NY: Baywood.
Anson, C. M. and Forsberg, L. L. (1990). 'Moving beyond the academic community: Transitional stages in professional writing', *Written Communication*, 7(2), 200–31. DOI: 10.1177/0741088390007002002.
Arney, J. B. and Jones, I. (2006). 'Uniting community and university through service learning,' *Business Communication Quarterly*, 69(2), 195–98. DOI:10.1177/108056990606900211.
Artemeva, N. (2005). 'A time to speak, a time to act: A rhetorical genre analysis of the calculated risk-taking by a novice engineer', *Journal of Business and Technical Communication*, 19(4), 389–421.
——(2006). 'Approaches to learning genres: A bibliographical essay', in N. Artemeva and A. Freedman (eds), *Rhetorical Genre Studies and Beyond* (pp. 9–99), Winnipeg, MA, Canada: Inkshed. Available at http://http-server.carleton.ca/~nartemev/Artemeva%20&%20Freedman%20Rhetorical%20Genre%20Studies%20and%20beyond.pdf (accessed 3 September 2013) (Original work published in print by Inkshed, Winnipeg, MA, Canada).
——(2008). 'Toward a unified theory of genre learning', *Journal of Business and Technical Communication*, 22(2), 160–85. DOI 10.1177/1050651907311925.
——(2009). 'Stories of becoming: A study of novice engineers learning genres of their profession', in C. Bazerman, A. Bonini and D. Figueiredo (eds), *Genre in a Changing World* (pp. 158–78), Perspectives on Writing, Fort Collins, Colorado: The WAC Clearinghouse and Parlor Press. Available at http://wac.colostate.edu/books/genre/chapter8.pdf (accessed 3 September 2013).
——(2011). '"An engrained part of my career": The formation of a knowledge worker in the dual space of engineering knowledge and rhetorical process', in D. Starke-Meyerring, A. Paré, N. Artemeva, M. Horne and L. Yousoubova (eds), *Writing in Knowledge Societies* (pp. 321–50), Perspectives on Writing, Fort Collins, CO: The WAC Clearinghouse and Parlor Press. Available at http://wac.colostate.edu/books/winks/chapter16.pdf (accessed 3 September 2013).
Artemeva, N. and Freedman, A. (2001). '"Just the boys playing on computers": An activity theory analysis of differences in the cultures of two engineering firms', *Journal of Business and Technical Communication*, 15(2), 164–94.
Artemeva, N. and Fox, J. (2010). 'Awareness vs. production: Probing students' antecedent genre knowledge', *Journal of Business and Technical Communication*, 24, 476–515. DOI:10.1177/1050651910371302.
——(2011). 'The writing's on the board: The global and the local in teaching undergraduate mathematics through chalk talk', *Written Communication*, 28, 345–79. DOI:10.1177/0741088311419630.
Artemeva, N. and Freedman, A. (eds) (2006). *Rhetorical Genre Studies and Beyond*, Winnipeg, Manitoba, Canada: Inkshed Publications.
Artemeva, N., Logie, S. and St-Martin, J. (1999). 'From page to stage: How theories of genre and situated learning help introduce engineering students to discipline-specific communication', *Technical Communication Quarterly*, 8(3), 301–16.
Bakhtin, M. M. (1981). *The Dialogic Imagination*, M. Holquist (ed.), C. Emerson and M. Holquist (trans.), Austin: University of Texas Press.
——(1986). 'The problem of speech genres', in C. Emerson and M. Holquist (eds), V. W. McGee (trans.), *Speech Genres and Other Late Essays* (pp. 60–102), Austin, TX: University of Texas Press.
Barton, D. and Tusting, K. (2005). *Beyond Communities of Practice: Language, Power and Social Context*, Cambridge: Cambridge University Press.
Bawarshi, A. (2000). 'The genre function', *College English*, 62(3), 335–60.
Bawarshi, A. and Reiff, M. J. (2010). *Genre: An Introduction to History, Theory, Research, and Pedagogy*, West Lafayette, in Parlor Press and the WAC Clearinghouse. Available at http://wac.colostate.edu/books/bawarshi_reiff/ (accessed 3 September 2013).
Bazerman, C. (1988). *Shaping Written Knowledge: The Genre and Activity of the Experimental Article in Science*, Madison, WI: University of Wisconsin Press.

——(1994). 'Systems of genres and the enactment of social intentions', in A. Freedman and P. Medway (eds), *Genre and the New Rhetoric* (pp. 79–101), London: Taylor & Francis.

——(2002). 'Genre and identity: Citizenship in the age of the internet and the age of global capitalism', in R. Coe, L. Lingard and T. Teslenko (eds), *The Rhetoric and Ideology of Genre* (pp. 13–37), Cresskill, NJ: Hampton Press.

Bazerman, C. (2013). *A Rhetoric of Literate Action: Literate Action*. Vol. 1. Perspectives on Writing. Fort Collins, Colorado: The WAC Clearinghouse and Parlor Press. Available at http://wac.colostate.edu/books/literateaction/v1/ (accessed 3 September 2013).

Bazerman, C., Bonini, A. and Figueiredo, D. (eds) (2009). *Genre in a Changing World*, Perspectives on Writing, Fort Collins, Colorado: The WAC Clearinghouse and Parlor Press. Available at http://wac.colostate.edu/books/genre/ (accessed 3 September 2013).

Bazerman, C. and Paradis, J. (eds) (1991). *Textual Dynamics of the Professions: Historical and Contemporary Studies of Writing in Professional Communities*, Madison, WI: University of Wisconsin Press.

Bazerman, C. and Russell, D. (eds) (2002). *Writing Selves/Writing Societies: Research from Activity Perspectives*, Perspectives on Writing. Fort Collins, Colorado: The WAC Clearinghouse and Mind, Culture, and Activity. Available at http://wac.colostate.edu/books/selves_societies/ (accessed 3 September 2013).

Beaudet, C. (1998). 'Littératie et rédaction: vers la définition d'une pratique professionnelle' ['Literacy and writing: Toward the definition of professional practice'], in G. A. Legault (ed.), *L'intervention: usages et méthodes* [*An Intervention: Applications and Methods*] (pp. 69–88), Sherbrooke, Canada: GGC Publishing.

Beaufort, A. (1999). *Writing in the Real World: Making the Transition from School to Work*, New York: Teachers College Press.

——(2000). 'Learning the trade: A social apprenticeship model for gaining writing expertise', *Written Communication*, 17(2), 185–223.

——(2006). 'Writing in the professions', in P. Smagorinsky (ed.), *Perspectives on Composition: Multiple Perspectives on Two Decades of Change* (pp. 217–42), New York: Teachers College Press.

Belcher, D., Johns, A. and Paltridge, B. (eds) (2011). *New Directions in English for Specific Purposes Research*, Ann Arbor: University of Michigan Press.

Berger, P. L. and Luckmann, T. (1967). *The Social Construction of Reality: A Treatise in the Sociology of Knowledge*, Garden City, NY: Anchor Books.

Berkenkotter, C. (2001). 'Genre systems at work: DSM-IV and rhetorical recontextualization in psychotherapy paperwork', *Written Communication*, 18, 326–49.

Berkenkotter, C. and Huckin, T. N. (1993). 'Rethinking genre from a sociocognitive perspective', *Written Communication*, 10(4), 475–509.

——(1995). *Genre Knowledge in Disciplinary Communication: Cognition/Culture/Power*, Hillsdale, NJ: Lawrence Erlbaum Associates.

Billett, S. (2004). 'Workplace participatory practices: Conceptualising workplaces as learning environments', *Journal of Workplace Learning*, 16(6), 312–24. DOI: 10.1108/13665620410550295.

Bitzer, L. F. (1968). 'The rhetorical situation', *Philosophy and Rhetoric*, 1, 1–14.

——(1980). 'Functional communication: A situational perspective', in E. E. White (ed.), *Rhetoric in Transition: Studies in the Nature and Uses of Rhetoric* (pp. 21–38), University Park: Pennsylvania State University Press.

Bhatia, V. K., Flowerdew, J. and Jones, R. H. (2008). *Advances in Discourse Studies*, London, UK: Routledge.

Bracewell, R. and Witte, S. (2003). 'Tasks, ensembles, and activity: Linkages between text production and situation of use in the workplace', *Written Communication*, 20, 511–59.

Brent, D. (2011). 'Transfer, transformation, and rhetorical knowledge: Insights from transfer theory', *Journal of Business and Technical Communication*, 25(4), 396–420. DOI: 10.1177/1050651911410951.

——(2012). 'Crossing boundaries: Co-op students relearning to write', *College Composition and Communication*, 63(4), 558–92.

Bronckart, J.-P. and Bota, C. (2011). *Bakhtin démasqué: Histoire d'un menteur, d'une excroqueries et d'un délire collectif*, Geneva: Librarie Droz.

Brown, J. S., Collins, A. and Duguid, P. (1989). 'Situated cognition and the culture of learning', *Educational Researcher*, 18(1), 32–42.

Brown, J. S. and Gray, E. S. (1995). 'The people are the company: How to build your company around your people', *FastCompany Magazine*, 1, 78. Available at www.fastcompany.com/26238/people-are-company (accessed 3 September 2013).

Brown, R. L. and Herndl, C. G. (1986). 'An ethnographic study of corporate writing: Job status as reflected in written text', in B. Couture (ed.), *Functional Approaches to Writing: Research Perspectives* (pp. 11–28), London: Frances Pinter.

Carter, M. (1990). 'The idea of expertise: An exploration of cognitive and social dimensions of writing', *College Composition and Communication*, *41*(3), 265–86.
Chaiklin, S. (2003). 'The Zone of Proximal Development in Vygotsky's analysis of learning and instruction', in A. Kozulin, B. Gindis, V. Ageyev and S. Miller (eds), *Vygotsky's Educational Theory and Practice in Cultural Context* (pp. 39–64), Cambridge: Cambridge University Press.
Clerc, I. and Beaudet, C. (2002). 'Pour un enseignement de la rédaction professionnelle ou de la rédaction technique?' ['For the teaching of professional or technical writing?'] *Technostyle*, *18*(1), 27–44.
Coe, R. M. and Freedman, A. (1998). 'Genre theory: Australian and North American approaches', in M. L. Kennedy (ed.), *Theorizing Composition: A Critical Sourcebook of Theory and Scholarship in Contemporary Composition Studies* (pp. 136–47), Westport, CT: Greenwood Press.
Coe, R., Lingard, L. and Teslenko, T. (eds) (2002). *The Rhetoric and Ideology of Genre*, Cresskill, NJ: Hampton Press.
Cole, M. and Engeström, Y. (1993). 'A cultural-historical approach to distributed cognition', in G. Salomon (ed.), *Distributed Cognitions: Psychological and Educational Considerations* (pp. 1–45), Cambridge: Cambridge University Press.
Cooper, M. (1986). 'The ecology of writing', *College English*, *48*(4), 364–75.
Cooper, M. M. and Holzman, M. (eds) (1989). *Writing as Social Action*, Portsmouth, NH: Boynton/Cook Heinemann.
Couture, B. (ed.) (1986). *Functional Approaches to Writing: Research Perspectives*, London: Frances Pinter.
Couture, B. and Rymer, J. (1993). 'Situational exigence: Composing processes on the job by writer's role and task value', in R. Spilka (ed.), *Writing in the Workplace: New Research Perspectives* (pp. 4–20), Carbondale: South Illinois University Press.
Dannels, D. P. (2000). 'Learning to be professional: Technical classroom discourse, practice, and professional identity construction', *Journal of Business and Technical Communication*, *14*, 5–37. DOI:10.1177/105065190001400101.
——(2003). 'Teaching and learning design presentations in engineering: Contradictions between academic and workplace activity systems', *Journal of Business and Technical Communication*, *17*(2), 139–69. DOI: 10.1177/1050651902250946.
——(2009). 'Features of success in engineering design presentations: A call for relational genre knowledge', *Journal of Business & Technical Communication*, *23*(4), 399–427. DOI: 10.1177/1050651909338790.
Dannels, D. and Norris Martin, K. (2008). 'Critiquing critiques: A genre analysis of feedback across novice to expert design studios', *Journal of Business and Technical Communication*, *22*(2), 135–59. DOI: 10.1177/1050651907311923.
Davydov, V. D. and Radzikhovski, L. A. (1980). 'Teoria L. S. Vygotskogo i deiatel'nostnii podhod v psihologii' ['L. S. Vygotsky's theory and the activity-oriented approach in psychology']. Part 1, *Voprosy psikhologii*, *6*, 48–59.
——(1981). 'Teoria L. S. Vygotskogo i deiatel'nostnii podhod v psihologii' ['L. S. Vygotsky's theory and the activity approach in psychology']. Part 2. *Voprosy psikhologii*, *1*, 67–80.
——(1985). 'Vygotsky's theory and the activity-oriented approach in psychology', in J. V. Wertsch (ed.), *Culture, Communication and Cognition: Vygotskyan Perspectives* (pp. 35–65), Cambridge: Cambridge University Press.
Davydov, V. D. and Zinchenko, V. P. (1989). 'Vygotsky's contribution to the development of psychology', *Soviet Psychology*, *27*(2), 22–36.
Devitt, A. J. (1991). 'Intertextuality in tax accounting: Generic, referential, and functional', in C. Bazerman and J. Paradis (eds), *Textual Dynamics of the Professions: Historical and Contemporary Studies of Writing in Professional Communities* (pp. 336–57), Madison: University of Wisconsin Press.
——(2004). *Writing Genres*, Carbondale: Southern Illinois University Press.
——(2009). 'Teaching critical genre awareness', in C. Bazerman, A. Bonini and D. Figueiredo (eds), *Genre in a Changing World: Perspectives on Writing*, Fort Collins, CO: The WAC Clearinghouse and Parlor Pres. Available at http://was.colostate.edu/books/genre/chapter17.pdf (accessed 3 September 2013).
Dias, P. (2000). 'Writing classrooms as activity systems', in P. Dias and A. Paré (eds), *Transitions: Writing in Academic and Workplace Settings* (pp. 11–29), Mahwah, NJ: Hampton Press.
Dias, P., Freedman, A., Medway, P. and Paré, A. (1999). *Worlds Apart: Acting and Writing in Academic and Workplace Contexts*, Mahwah, NJ: Lawrence Erlbaum Associates.
Dias, P. and Paré, A. (eds) (2000). *Transitions: Writing in Academic and Workplace Settings*, Cresskill, NJ: Hampton.
Doheny-Farina, S. (1986). 'Writing in an emerging organization', *Written Communication*, *3*, 158–85.

——(1989). 'A case study of one adult writing in academic and nonacademic discourse communities', in C. B. Matalene (ed.), *Worlds of Writing: Teaching and Learning in Discourse Communities of Work* (pp. 17–42), New York: Random House.
——(1992). 'The individual, the organization and kairos: Making transitions from college to careers', in, S. P. Witte, N. Nakadate and R. D. Cherry (ed.), *A Rhetoric of Doing: Essays on Written Discourse in Honor of James L. Kinneavy* (pp. 293–309), Carbondale: Southern Illinois University Press.
Engeström, Y. (1987). *Learning by Expanding: An Activity-theoretical Approach to Developmental Research*, Helsinki, Finland: Orienta-Konsultit Oy.
——(1991). '*Non scolae sed vitae discimos:* Toward overcoming the encapsulation of school learning', *Learning and Instruction*, 1, 243–59.
——(1992). *Interactive Expertise: Studies in Distributed Working Intelligence. Research Bulletin 83*, Helsinki: University of Helsinki, Department of Education.
——(1996). 'Developmental studies of work as a testbench of activity theory: The case of primary care medical practice', in S. Chaiklin and J. Lave (eds), *Understanding Practice: Perspectives on Activity and Context* (pp. 64–103), Cambridge: Cambridge University Press.
——(1999). 'Activity theory and individual and social transformation', in Y. Engeström, R. Miettinen and R. L. Punamäki (eds), *Perspectives on Activity Theory* (pp. 19–38), Cambridge: Cambridge University Press.
Engeström, Y. and Miettinen, R. (1999). 'Introduction', in Y. Engeström, R. Miettinen and R. L. Punamäki (eds), *Perspectives on Activity Theory* (pp. 1–16), Cambridge: Cambridge University Press.
Eraut, M. (2002, April). *Conceptual Analysis and Research Questions: Do the Concepts of 'Learning Community' and 'Community of Practice' Provide Added Value?* Paper presented at the annual meeting of the American Education Research Association, New Orleans (ERIC Document Reproduction Service No. ED 466 030).
Faber, B. (2002). 'Professional identities: What is professional about professional communication?' *Journal of Business and Technical Communication*, 16(3), 306–37.
Faigley, L. (1985). 'Nonacademic writing: The social perspective', in L. Odell and D. Goswami (eds), *Writing in Nonacademic Settings* (pp. 231–48), New York: Guilford Press.
Fisher, L. and Bennion, L. (2005). 'Organizational implications of the future development of technical communication: Fostering communities of practice in the workplace', *Technical Communication*, 52(3), 277–88.
Ford, J. D. (2004). 'Knowledge transfer across disciplines: Tracking rhetorical strategies from a technical communication classroom to an engineering classroom', *IEEE Transactions on Professional Communication*, 17, 301–15. DOI: 10.1109/TPC.2004.840486.
Fox, J. and Artemeva, N. (2011). 'The cinematic art of teaching university mathematics: Chalk talk as embodied practice', *Multimodal Communication*, 1(1), 83–103.
Freedman, A. (1987). 'Learning to write again', *Carleton Papers in Applied Language Studies*, 4, 95–116.
——(1993). 'Show and tell? The role of explicit teaching in the learning of new genres', *Research in the Teaching of English*, 27, 222–51.
——(1995). 'The what, where, when, why, and how of classroom genres', in J. Petraglia (ed.), *Reconceiving Writing, Rethinking Writing Instruction* (pp. 121–44), Mahwah, NJ: Lawrence Erlbaum.
——(2006). 'Interaction between theory and research: RGS and a study of students and professionals working "in computers"', in N. Artemeva and A. Freedman (eds), *Rhetorical Genre Studies and Beyond* (pp. 102–20), Winnipeg, MA, Canada: Inkshed.
Freedman, A. and Adam, C. (1996). 'Learning to write professionally: "Situated learning" and the transition from university to professional discourse', *Journal of Business and Technical Communication*, 10(4), 395–427.
——(2000a). 'Bridging the gap: University-based writing that is more than simulation', in P. Dias and A. Paré (eds), *Transitions: Writing in Academic and Workplace Settings* (pp. 129–44). Cresskills, NJ: Hampton.
——(2000b). 'Write where you are: Situating learning to write in university and workplace settings', in P. Dias and A. Paré (eds), *Transitions: Writing in Academic and Workplace Settings* (pp. 31–60), Cresskills, NJ: Hampton.
Freedman, A., Adam, C. and Smart, G. (1994). 'Wearing suits to class: Simulating genres and simulations as genre', *Written Communication*, 11(2), 193–226. DOI:10.1177/0741088394011002002.
Freedman, A. and Medway, P. (eds) (1994a). *Genre and the New Rhetoric*. London: Taylor & Francis.
——(1994b). *Learning and Teaching Genre*, Portsmouth, NH: Boynton/Cook.
Freedman, A. and Smart, G. (1997). 'Navigating the current of economic policy: Written genres and the distribution of cognitive work at a financial institution', *Mind, Culture, and Activity*, 4(4), 238–55.
Gee, J. P. (2000). 'The new literacy studies: From "socially situated" to the work of the social', in D. Barton, M. Hamilton and R. Ivanič (eds), *Situated Literacies: Reading and Writing in Context* (pp. 180–96), London, UK: Routledge.

Giddens, A. (1984). *The Constitution of Society: Outline of the Theory of Structuration*, Berkeley, CA: University of California Press.
Giltrow, J. (2002). *Academic Writing: Writing and Reading in the Disciplines*, Peterborough, Canada: Broadview Press.
Giltrow, J. and Valiquette, M. (1994). 'Genre and knowledge: Students writing in the disciplines', in A. Freedman and P. Medway (eds), *Learning and Teaching Genre* (pp. 47–62), Portsmouth, NH: Boynton/Cook.
Haas, C. (1995). *Writing Technology: Studies on the Materiality of Literacy*, Hillsdale, NJ: Lawrence Erlbaum Associates.
Haas, C. and Witte, S. (2001). 'Writing as an embodied practice: The case of engineering standards', *Journal of Business and Technical Communication*, 15(4), 413–57.
Halliday, M. A. K. (1973). 'Explorations in the functions of language', London, UK: Edward Arnold.
——(1978). 'Language as a social semiotic', London, UK: Edward Arnold.
Hanks, W. F. (1987). 'Discourse genres in a theory of practice', *American Ethnologist*, 14(4), 668–92.
——(1991). 'Foreword', in J. Lave and E. Wenger (eds), *Situated Learning: Legitimate Peripheral Participation* (pp. 11–21), Cambridge: Cambridge University Press.
Herndl, C. C., Fennell, B. A. and Miller, C. R. (1991). 'Understanding failures in organizational discourse: The accident at Three Mile Island and the Shuttle Challenger disaster', in C. Bazerman and J. Paradis (eds), *Textual Dynamics of the Professions: Historical and Contemporary Studies of Writing in Professional Communities* (pp. 279–395), Madison: University of Wisconsin Press.
Herrington, A. J. (1985). 'Classrooms as forums for reasoning and writing', *College Composition and Communication*, 36(4), 404–13.
Herrington, A. and Moran, C. (eds) (2005). *Genre Across the Curriculum*, Logan, UT: Utah State University Press.
Hodge, R. and Kress, G. (1988). *Social Semiotics*, Ithaca, NY: Cornell UP.
Hutchins, E. (1993). 'Learning to navigate', in S. Chaiklin and J. Lave (eds), *Understanding Practice: Perspectives on Activity and Context* (pp. 35–63), Cambridge, UK: Cambridge University Press.
——(1995a). *Cognition in the Wild*, Cambridge, MA: MIT Press.
——(1995b). 'How a cockpit remembers its speed', *Cognitive Science*, 19, 265–88.
——(2000). 'Distributed cognition', *International Encyclopaedia of the Social and Behavioral Sciences*. Available at www.artmap-research.com/wp-content/uploads/2009/11/Hutchins_DistributedCognition.pdf (accessed 3 September 2013).
——(2006). 'The distributed cognition perspective on human interaction', in N. J. Enfield and S. C. Levinson (eds), *Roots of Human Sociality: Culture, Cognition and Interaction* (pp. 375–98), New York, NY: Berg Publishers.
Hutchinson, T. and Waters, A. (1987). *English for Specific Purposes – A Learning-centred Approach*, Cambridge: Cambridge University Press.
Jackson, N. (ed.) (2011). *Learning to be Professional Through a Higher Education*, Surrey Centre for Excellence in Professional Training and Education (SCEPTrE). Available at http://learningtobeprofessional.pbworks.com/w/page/15914981/Learning to be Professional through a Higher Education e-Book (accessed 3 September 2013).
Jewitt, C. (ed.) (2009) *The Routledge Handbook of Multimodal Analysis*, London: Routledge.
——(2012). 'An introduction to using video for research', National Centre for Research Methods (NCRM) unpublished working paper. Institute of Education, University of London. Available at http://mode.ioe.ac.uk/2012/03/17/an-introduction-to-using-video-for-research/ (accessed 3 September 2013).
Jewitt, C. and Jones, K. (2008). 'Multimodal discourse analysis: The case of "ability" in UK secondary school English', in V. K. Bhatia, J. Flowerdew and R. H. Jones (eds), *Advances in Discourse Studies* (pp. 149–60), London, UK: Routledge.
Jewitt, C. and Kress, G. R. (2003). *Multimodal Literacy*, New York, NY: P. Lang.
Johnson, H. (2007). 'Communities of practice and international development', *Progress in Development Studies*, 7(4), 277–90.
Kaptelinin, V. (1996). 'Activity Theory: Implications for human-computer interaction', in B. Nardi (ed.), *Context and Consciousness: Activity Theory and Human–Computer Interaction*, Cambridge, MA: MIT Press. Available at www.quasar.ualberta.ca/edpy597/readings/m15_kaptelin.htm (accessed 19 May 2003).
Kaptelinin, V. and Nardi, B. A. (1997). 'Activity Theory: Basic concepts and applications', *CHI97 Electronic Publications: Tutorials*. Available at www.acm.org/sigchi/chi97/proceedings/tutorial/bn.htm (accessed 19 May 2003).

Katz, S. M. (1998). *The Dynamics of Writing Review: Opportunities for Growth and Change in the Workplace*, Stamford, CT: Ablex.
Kress, G. (2010). *Multimodality: A Social Semiotic Approach to Contemporary Communication*, London and New York: Routledge.
Kress, G. and Van Leeuwen, T. (1996). *Reading Images: The Grammar of Visual Design*, London: Routledge.
Kress, G. and Van Leeuwen, T. (2001). *Multimodal Discourses: The Modes and Media of Contemporary Communication*, London, UK: Arnold.
Lave, J. (1988). *Cognition in Practice*, Cambridge: Cambridge University Press.
——(1991). 'Situating learning in communities of practice', in L. B. Resnick, J. M. Levine and S. D. Teasley (eds), *Perspectives on Socially Shared Cognition* (pp. 63–82), Washington, DC: APA.
——(1996a). 'Teaching, as learning, in practice', *Mind, Culture, and Activity*, 3(3), 149–64.
——(1996b). 'The practice of learning', in S. Chaiklin and J. Lave (eds), *Understanding Practice: Perspectives on Activity and Context* (pp. 3–32), Cambridge: Cambridge University Press.
Lave, J. and Wenger, E. (1991). *Situated Learning: Legitimate Peripheral Participation*, Cambridge: Cambridge University Press.
Le Maistre, C. and Paré, A. (2004). 'Learning in two communities: The challenges for universities and workplaces', *Journal of Workplace Learning*, 16(1/2), 44–52.
Lee, H. and Maguire, M. H. (2011). 'International students and identity: Resisting dominant ways of writing and knowing in academe', in D. Starke-Meyerring, A. Paré, N. Artemeva, M. Horne and L. Yousoubova (eds), *Writing in Knowledge Societies* (pp. 351–70), Perspectives on writing. Fort Collins, CO: The WAC Clearinghouse and Parlor Press. Available at http://wac.colostate.edu/books/winks/chapter17.pdf (accessed 3 September 2013).
Leont'ev, A. N. (1981). 'The problem of activity in psychology', in J. V. Wertsch (ed.), *The Concept of Activity in Soviet Psychology* (pp. 37–71), Armonk, NY: Sharpe.
——(1989). 'The problem of activity in the history of Soviet Psychology', *Soviet Psychology*, 27(1), 22–39.
Levine, P. and Scollon, R. (eds) (2004). *Discourse and Technology: Multimodal Discourse Analysis*, Washington, DC: Georgetown University Press.
MacKinnon, J. (1993). 'Becoming a rhetor: Developing writing ability in a mature, writing-intensive organization', in R. Spilka (ed.), *Writing in the Workplace: New Research Perspectives.* (pp. 41–55), Carbondale, IL.: Southern Illinois University Press.
McLaughlin, T. (2003). 'Teaching as practice and a community of practice: The limits of commonality and the demands of diversity', *Journals of Philosophy of Education*, 37(2), 339–52.
McMillan, J. (2011). 'What happens when the university meets the community? Service learning, boundary work and boundary workers', *Teaching in Higher Education*, 16(5), 553–64, DOI: 10.1080/13562517.2011.580839.
McMillan, J. H. and Schumacher, S. (2010). *Research in Education: Evidence-based Inquiry*. 7th edition, Upper Saddle River, NJ: Pearson.
Medway, P. (1993). *Shifting Relations: Science, Technology, and Technoscience*, Geelong, Australia: Deakin University.
——(2000). 'Writing and design in architectural education', in P. Dias and A. Paré (eds), *Transitions: Writing in Academic and Workplace Settings* (pp. 89–128), Mahwah, NJ: Hampton Press.
Miller, C. (1984). 'Genre as social action', *Quarterly Journal of Speech*, 70, 151–67.
——(1992). 'Kairos in the rhetoric of science', in S. P. Witte, N. Nakadate and R. D. Cherry (eds), *A Rhetoric of Doing: Essays on Written Discourse in Honor of James L. Kinneavy* (pp. 310–27), Carbondale: Southern Illinois University Press.
——(1994). 'Rhetorical community: The cultural basis of genre', in A. Freedman and P. Medway (eds), *Genre and the New Rhetoric* (pp. 67–78), London: Taylor & Francis.
Norris, S. (2004). *Analyzing Multimodal Interaction: A Methodological Framework*, New York: Routledge.
——(2008). 'Some thoughts on personal identity construction: A multimodal perspective', in V. K. Bhatia, J. Flowerdew and R.H. Jones (eds), *Advances in Discourse Studies* (pp. 132–48), London, UK: Routledge.
——(2011). *Identity in (Inter)action: Introducing Multimodal (Inter)action Analysis*, Göttingen: De Gruyter Mouton.
——(ed.) (2012). *Multimodality in Practice: Investigating Theory-in-practice-through-methodology*, New York: Routledge.
O'Halloran, K. (2004). *Mathematical Discourse: Language, Symbolism and Visual Images*, London, UK: Continuum.
O'Halloran, K. L., Tan, S., Smith, B. A. and Podlasov, A. (2011). 'Multimodal discourse: Critical analysis within an Interactive Software Environment', *Critical Discourse Studies*, 8(2), 109–25.

O'Toole, M. (1994). *The Language of Displayed Art*, Cranbury, NJ: Associated University Presses.
Odell, L. and Goswami, D. (eds) (1985). *Writing in Nonacademic Settings*, New York: Guilford Press.
Orlikowski, W. and Yates, J. A. (1994). 'Genre repertoire: The structuring of communicative practices in organizations', *Administrative Science Quarterly, 39*, 541–74.
Paradis, J., Dobrin, D. and Miller, R. (1995). 'Writing at Exxon ITD: Notes on the writing environment of an R&D organization', in L. Odell and D. Goswami (eds), *Writing in Non-Academic Settings* (pp. 281–307), New York: Guilford Press.
Paré, A. (2000). 'Writing as a way into social work: Genre sets, genre systems, and distributed cognition', in P. Dias and A. Paré (eds), *Transitions: Writing in Academic and Workplace Settings* (pp. 145–66), Cresskill, NJ: Hampton Press.
Paré, A. and Smart, G. (1994). 'Observing genres in action: Towards a research methodology', in A. Freedman and P. Medway (eds), *Genre and the New Rhetoric* (pp. 146–55), London: Taylor & Francis.
Paré, A., Starke-Meyerring, D. and McAlpine, L. (2011). 'Knowledge and identity work in the supervison of doctoral student writing: Shaping rhetorical subjects', in D. Starke-Meyerring, A. Paré, N. Artemeva, M. Horne and L. Yousoubova, (eds), *Writing in Knowledge Societies* (pp. 215–36), Perspectives on Writing. Fort Collins, Colorado: The WAC Clearinghouse and Parlor Press. Available at http://wac.colostate.edu/books/winks/chapter11.pdf (accessed 3 September 2013).
Perelman, C. and Olbrechts-Tyteca, L. (1969). *The New Rhetoric: A Treatise on Argumentation*, Notre Dame, IN: Notre Dame Press.
Prior, P. (2009). 'From speech genres to mediated multimodal genre systems: Bakhtin, Voloshinov, and the question of writing', in C. Bazerman, A. Bonini and D. Figueiredo (eds), *Genre in a Changing World* (pp. 17–34), Perspectives on Writing. Fort Collins, Colorado: The WAC Clearinghouse and Parlor Press. Available at http://wac.colostate.edu/books/genre/ (accessed 3 September 2013).
Resnick, L. B. (1991). 'Shared cognition: Thinking as social practice', in L. B. Resnick, J. M. Levine and S. D. Teasley (eds), *Perspectives on Socially Shared Cognition* (pp. 1–20), Washington, DC: APA.
Rogoff, B. (1990). *Apprenticeship in Thinking: Cognitive Development in Social Context*, New York: Oxford University Press.
Rogoff, B., Turkanis, C. G. and Bartlett, L. (eds) (2001). *Learning Together: Children and Adults in a School Community*, New York, NY: Oxford University Press.
Russell, D. R. (1997). 'Rethinking genre in school and society: An activity theory analysis', *Written Communication, 14*(4), 504–54.
Säljö, R. (2003). 'Epilogue: From transfer to boundary-crossing', in T. Tuomi-Gröhn and Y. Engeström (eds), *Between School and Work: New Perspectives on Transfer and Boundary Crossing* (pp. 311–22), Kidlington, UK: Elsevier Science.
Sapp, D. A. and Crabtree, R. D. (2002). 'A laboratory in citizenship: Service learning in the technical communication classroom', *Technical Communication Quarterly, 11*(4), 411–32. DOI: 10.1207/s15427625tcq1104_3.
Sauer, B. (1998). 'Embodied knowledge: The textual representation of embodied sensory information in dynamic and uncertain material environment', *Written Communication, 15*(2), 131–69.
Schneider, B. (2002). 'Theorizing structure and agency in workplace writing: An ethnomethodological approach', *Journal of Business and Technical Communication, 16*, 170–95.
——(2007). 'Power and regulation of workplace communication', in M. Zachry and C. Thralls (eds), *Communicative Practices in Workplaces and Professions: Cultural Perspectives on the Regulations of Discourse and Organizations* (pp. 181–99), Amityville, NY: Baywood Publishing.
Schneider, B. and Andre, J.-A. (2005). 'University preparation for workplace writing: An exploratory study of the perceptions of students in three disciplines', *Journal of Business Communication, 42*(3), 195–218.
Schryer, C. (1993). 'Records as genre', *Written Communication, 10*(2), 200–34.
——(2000). 'Walking a fine line: Writing negative letters in an insurance company', *Journal of Business and Technical Communication, 14*(4), 445–97.
——(2002). 'Genre and power: A chronotopic analysis', in R. Coe, L. Lingard and T. Teslenko (eds), *The Rhetoric and Ideology of Genre* (pp. 73–102), Cresskill, NJ: Hampton Press.
——(2011). 'Investigating texts in their social contexts: The promise and peril of rhetorical genre studies', in D. Starke-Meyerring, A. Paré, N. Artemeva, M. Horne and L. Yousoubova (eds), *Writing in Knowledge Societies* (pp. 31–52), Perspectives on Writing. Fort Collins, Colorado: The WAC Clearinghouse and Parlor Press. Available at http://wac.colostate.edu/books/winks/chapter2.pdf (accessed 3 September 2013).

Schryer, C. F., Campbell, S. L., Spafford, M. M. and Lingard, L. (2006), 'You are how you cite: Citing patient information in health care settings', in N. Artemeva, and A. Freedman (eds), *Rhetorical Genre Studies and Beyond* (pp. 143–87), Winnipeg, Manitoba, Canada: Inkshed.

Schryer, C. F., Lingard, L., Spafford, M. and Garwood, K. (2002). 'Structure and agency in medical case presentations', in C. Bazerman and D. Russell (ed.), *Writing Selves/Writing Societies: Research from Activity Perspectives*, Perspectives on Writing. Fort Collins, CO: The WAC Clearinghouse and Mind, Culture and Activity. Available at http://wac.colostate.edu/books/selves_societies/schryer/schryer.pdf (accessed 3 September 2013).

Schryer, C. F., Lingard, L. and Spafford, M. (2007). 'Regulated and regularized: Genres, improvisations, and identity formation in healthcare professions', in M. Zachry and C. Thralls (eds), *Communicative Practice in Workplaces and the Professions: Cultural Perspectives on the Regulations of Discourse and Organizations* (pp. 21–44), Amityville, NY: Baywood Publishing.

Segal, J. Z. (2005). *Health and the Rhetoric of Medicine*, Carbondale: Southern Illinois UP.

Smart, G. (2000). 'Reinventing expertise: Experienced writers in the workplace encounter a new genre', in P. Dias and A. Paré (eds), *Transitions: Writing in Academic and Workplace Settings* (pp. 223–52), Cresskill, NJ: Hampton Press.

——(2003). 'Commentary: Using activity-based genre theory as a framework for analysing fund-raising discourse', *The CASE International Journal of Educational Advancement*, 4(2), 191–93.

——(2006). *Writing the Economy: Activity, Genre and Technology in the World of Banking*, London: Equinox.

Smart, G., and Brown, N. (2002). 'Learning transfer or transforming learning? Student interns reinventing expert writing practices in the workplace', *Technostyle*, 18(1), 117–41.

Spafford, M. M., Lingard, L., Schryer, C. F. and Hrynchak, P. K. (2004). 'Tensions in the field: Teaching standards of practice in optometry case presentations', *Optometry & Vision Science*, 81, 800–6.

Spilka, R. (ed.) (1993). *Writing in the Workplace: New Research Perspectives*, Carbondale: Southern Illinois University Press.

Spinuzzi, C. (2003). *Tracing Genres through Organizations: A Sociocultural Approach to Information design*, Cambridge, MA: The MIT Press.

——(2004). 'Describing assemblages: Genre sets, systems, repertoires, and ecologies', *Computer Writing and Research Lab. White Paper Series: #040505–2*. Available at www.dwrl.utexas.edu/sites/www.dwrl.utexas.edu/files/assemblages.pdf (accessed 3 September 2013).

——(2010). 'Secret sauce and snake oil: Writing monthly reports in a highly contingent environment', *Written Communication*, 27(4) 363–409. DOI: 10.1177/0741088310380518.

——(2011). 'Losing by expanding: Coralling the runaway object', *Journal of Business and Technical Communication*, 25(4), 449–86.

St Amant, K. (2007). 'Online education in an age of globalization: Foundational perspectives and practices for technical communication instructors and trainers', *Technical Communication Quarterly*, 16(1), 13–30. DOI: 10.1080/10572250709336575.

Starke-Meyerring, D., Paré, A., Artemeva, N., Horne, M. and Yousoubova, L. (eds) (2011). *Writing in Knowledge Societies*, Perspectives on Writing. Fort Collins, Colorado: The WAC Clearinghouse and Parlor Press. Available at http://wac.colostate.edu/books/winks/ (accessed 3 September 2013).

Swales, J. (1971). *Writing Scientific English*, Walton-on-Thames: Nelson.

——(1985). *Episodes in ESP*, Oxford: Pergamon Institute of English.

——(1988). *Episodes in ESP: A Source and Reference Book on the Development of English for Science and Technology*, New York: Prentice-Hall.

Tardy, C. M. (2003). 'A genre system view of the funding of academic research', *Written Communication*, 20(1), 7–36.

Tuomi-Gröhn, T. and Engeström, Y. (eds) (2003a). *Between School and Work: New Perspectives on Transfer and Boundary Crossing*, Kidlington, UK: Elsevier Science.

——(2003b). 'Conceptualizing transfer: From standard notions to developmental perspectives', in T. Tuomi-Gröhn and Y. Engeström (eds), *Between School and Work: New Perspectives on Transfer and Boundary Crossing* (pp. 19–38), Kidlington, UK: Elsevier Science.

Vygotsky, L. S. (1934). *Mishlenie i rech* [*Thinking and Speech*], Moscow: Glavlit. Available at http://psychlib.ru/mgppu/VMr-1934/VMR-001.HTM (accessed 3 September 2013).

——(1986). *Thought and Language* (A. Kosulin, trans.), Cambridge, MA: MIT Press.

Wenger, E. (1998a). 'Communities of practice: Learning as a social system', *Systems Thinker*. Available at www.co-i-l.com/coil/knowledge-garden/cop/lss.shtml (accessed 3 September 2013).

——(1998b). *Communities of Practice: Learning, Meaning, and Identity*, Cambridge: Cambridge University Press.
——(2005). *Communities of Practice: A Brief Introduction*. Available at www.ewenger.com/theory/index.htm (accessed 3 September 2013).
Wertsch, J. V. (ed.) (1981). *The Concept of Activity in Soviet Psychology*, Armonk, NY: M. E. Sharpe.
——(1985). *Vygotsky and the Social Formation of Mind*, Cambridge, MA: Harvard University Press.
——(1991). *Voices of the Mind: A Sociocultural Approach to Mediated Action*, Cambridge, MA: Harvard University Press.
Wickman, C. (2010). 'Writing material in chemical physics research: The laboratory notebook as locus of technical and textual integration', *Written Communication*, 27, 259–92.
Winsor, D. A. (1994). 'Invention and writing in technical work: Representing the object', *Written Communication*, 11, 227–50.
——(1996). *Writing like an Engineer: A Rhetorical Education*, Mahwah, NJ: Erlbaum.
——(2001). 'Learning to do knowledge work in systems of distributed cognition', *Journal of Business and Technical Communication*, 15(1), 5–28.
——(2003). *Writing Power: Communication in an Engineering Center*, Albany, NY: SUNY Press.
Witte, S. P. (1992). 'Context, text, intertext: Toward a constructivist semiotics of writing', *Written Communication*, 9(2), 237–308.
——(1999, May). *Tools, Technologies, Artifacts of Speedbumps*, Paper presented at the Carleton University Seminar in Applied Language Studies, Ottawa, ON, Canada.
Witte, S. P. and Faigley, L. (1983). *Evaluating College Writing Programs*, Carbondale, IL: Southern Illinois Press.
Witte, S. P. and Haas, C. (2001). 'Writing as an embodied practice: The case of engineering standards', *Journal of Business and Technical Communication*, 15(4), 413–57.
Yates, J. (1989). *Control Through Communication*, Baltimore, MD: Johns Hopkins University Press.
Yates, J. and Orlikowski, W. (2002). 'Genre systems: Chronos and kairos in communicative interaction', in R. Coe, L. Lingard and T. Teslenko (eds), *The Rhetoric and Ideology of Genre*. (pp. 103–21), Cresskill, NJ: Lawrence Erlbaum Publishing.
Zachry, M. (2007). 'Regulation and communicative practices', in M. Zachry and C. Thralls (eds), *Communicative Practice in Workplaces and the Professions: Cultural Perspectives on the Regulations of Discourse and Organizations* (pp. v–xv), Amityville, NY: Baywood Publishing.
Zachry, M. and Thralls, C. (eds) (2007). *Communicative Practice in Workplaces and the Professions: Cultural Perspectives on the Regulations of Discourse and Organizations*, Amityville, NY: Baywood Publishing.

29
Collaborative writing
Challenges for research and teaching

Stephen Bremner

Collaborative writing is integral to almost any organisation; indeed, Burnett (2001) suggests that as much as 75 per cent to 85 per cent of writing is collaborative in nature, and numerous studies emphasise the collaborative nature of writing in professional settings (e.g. Colen and Petelin 2004; Jones 2007). Considerable attention has been paid to this feature of workplace activity over the last 20 or 30 years: since the pioneering research in this area conducted by Faigley and Miller (1982), and Paradis, Dobrin and Miller (1985), there has been a range of studies aimed at describing and categorising different aspects of collaborative writing (e.g. Couture and Rymer 1989; Witte 1992; Lowry, Curtis and Lowry 2004); there is also a growing body of ethnographic research investigating collaborative writing in organisational settings (e.g. Cross 1994, 2001; Wegner 2004). We are perennially reminded of the continuing importance of collaborative writing as a topic for research (Forman 1991, 2004; Thompson 2001; Jones 2005, 2007), with the last of these contending that it is 'worthy of additional research since it is crucial to the jobs of many writers' (2007: 283).

Collaborative writing can be viewed in the broader context of teams and teamwork in professional settings. The importance of teamwork in general has been stressed 'as organizations move to cross-functional teams to improve effectiveness' (Thacker and Yost 2002: 89), and Keyton and Beck claim that 'teams have become the fundamental unit of organizational structure' (2008: 488); meanwhile Chen, Donahue and Klimoski suggest that 'teamwork KSAs (knowledge, skills and abilities) have become an integral component of workforce readiness' (2004: 35). While acknowledging this trend as significant, and recognising that there is a considerable bank of research and literature that looks at issues relating to team building, team management and so on, this chapter is primarily focused on the ways in which groups interact and collaborate in the workplace in order to produce written texts.

In this chapter I look at the role of collaborative writing in professional communication, discussing the definitions and taxonomies that have emerged from research. A central issue is the extent to which collaborative writing activity is entwined in the contexts in which it takes place; I consider the implications this has for research aimed at defining and delineating collaborative writing, and the challenges that this constitutive relationship between writing and context poses for teaching. I conclude the chapter with a look at research areas related to collaborative writing that might be worthy of further investigation.

Definitions and taxonomies of collaborative writing

Gollin (1999) talks of the 'complexity and interactivity' of collaborative writing, and says that there is no generally agreed notion of exactly what it is. Meanwhile Thompson (2001) and Lowry et al. (2004) note the profusion of terminology used to describe different aspects of collaborative writing, which is further indication of the complexity of the processes associated with it. Reither captures the involved nature of writing in general with his contention that 'writing is "social", "collaborative", "intertextual" in that authors challenge, modify, use, build on, and add to the utterances of others to join in "co-operative competition" with them in the process of text and knowledge making' (1993: 198), a point also made by Prior (2004). Thus a central challenge for researchers in this area is the fact that collaboration is so imbricated in workplace activity that it is difficult to decide where the boundaries of collaborative writing lie for the purposes of analysis.

Nevertheless many researchers have risen to this challenge, and various definitions of collaborative writing have emerged. Ede and Lunsford (1990: 15–16), for example, provide a broad definition, describing it as 'any writing done in collaboration with one or more persons'. Most perspectives on collaborative writing, however, extend the notion well beyond the basic idea of groups of people coming together to produce texts. Couture and Rymer (1989: 79) see collaborative writing as the interaction before or after drafting, rather than simply producing a document within a group. They talk about 'discourse interactions' or the 'oral and written communication pertaining to a document during the process of planning, drafting and revising it'; 'it may be fair to conclude that significant writing is enveloped in talk', they say, a point echoed by Debs (1991), and Louhiala-Salminen (2002). Jones (2005) considers factors beyond the participants, and defines collaborative writing as 'interaction by an author or authors with people, documents and organizational rules in the process of creating documents' (2005: 450). Meanwhile Lowry et al. have developed a very detailed definition of collaborative writing (CW):

> an iterative and social process that involves a team focused on a common objective that negotiates, coordinates, and communicates during the creation of a common document. The potential scope of CW goes beyond the more basic act of joint composition to include the likelihood of pre- and posttask activities, team formation, and planning. Furthermore, based on the desired writing task, CW includes the possibility of many different writing strategies, activities, document control approaches, team roles, and work modes.
>
> *(2004: 72–74)*

As can be seen, this definition, based on the authors' examination of a substantial number of studies of the field, appears intended to provide a comprehensive explanation of collaborative writing. However, as with any definition, it may not always be possible to produce one that can be applied to all situations, given the wide variety of workplaces in which collaborative writing takes place. Indeed, the definition Lowry et al. (2004) propose implies a sense of collective purpose and order that is not necessarily seen in certain group writing endeavours that some researchers would nevertheless label collaborative, a point that will be revisited later. Finally, a caveat in regard to definitions is offered by Jones (2007: 290), based on the finding from his survey of technical writers, which 'suggests that practitioners, teachers, and researchers all should view collaboration as consisting of a rich, varied group of activities and not simply rely on a single narrow definition'.

Thus it can be seen that there is a range of definitions of collaborative writing – those mentioned above are just a few examples – from the general (Ede and Lunsford 1990) to more detailed explanations (Lowry *et al.* 2004). There is concern over the lack of agreement on definitions, and also over the lack of commonly agreed terminology to discuss collaborative practices. The fact that the phenomenon is visited from so many directions and different disciplines is a central factor in this lack of agreement on common terminology. A quick look at the references section of this chapter, and the journals that have included articles relating to collaboration, gives an indication of the diversity of perspectives from which collaborative writing might be viewed and analysed. Forman explains the challenges this presents:

> most issues (e.g., group conflict, writers' roles, groupware choice and use) cut across disciplinary boundaries, bringing into play the mix of theoretical perspectives, assumptions, and lexicons that can lead to confusion when researchers from one discipline import from other disciplines.
>
> *(2004: 28)*

Not only this, the focus of these various disciplines will be different. She cites her own experience of working on an interdisciplinary research project to illustrate this point, explaining that information systems specialists, business communication specialists and group process specialists will concern themselves with different aspects of the same process (Forman 2004, 2005).

There have been a number of attempts at categorising or creating taxonomies of collaborative writing activity. One of the earlier examples can be seen in the work of Witte (1992), who outlines four broad types of collaboration: the 'traditional' mode involves two or more writers working together, with each having an equal share of the responsibility for the final product; in the 'committee' mode the degree of responsibility assumed by the writers may vary; 'incidental' collaboration consists of 'brief, often highly focused interactions … through any medium', while 'covert' collaboration consists of interactions among writers, conscious or otherwise, through 'both linguistic and non-linguistic texts' (1992: 296). Two fairly recent studies (Lowry *et al.* 2004; Jones 2005) represent efforts to provide more detailed taxonomies. These are discussed below; what is significant about these is the fact that they pull together, draw on and build upon much of the relevant literature, and they serve as useful frameworks within which to discuss other research relating to collaborative writing.

Lowry *et al.* (2004), like Forman (2004) cited above, are concerned about the 'disjointed' nature of interdisciplinary collaborative writing research, saying that it 'lacks a common taxonomy and nomenclature for interdisciplinary discussion' (2004: 67); they go on to point out that this lack 'undermines the ability of researchers and practitioners to solve the core issues' (2004: 68). Drawing on previous work in the area, they identify a huge range of such issues, from group dynamics to creativity to conflict (for a fuller list of issues see Lowry *et al.* 2004: 69), that they believe a common taxonomy and nomenclature would assist in addressing.

The taxonomy they propose, which they acknowledge is to some extent built on the work of Horton *et al.* (1991), is explained in terms of writing strategies, activities, document control modes and roles. They define strategies as 'a team's overall approach for coordinating the writing of a collaborative document' (2004: 74).

They go on to explain that collaborative writing involves a range of activities, from prewriting to postwriting. An important feature of these activities is that they are dynamic and iterative in nature, an element seen in Paradis *et al.*'s (1985) notion of 'document cycling', and also emphasised by Freedman and Adam (1996). Lowry *et al.* also point out that other activities can take place at 'unpredictable times' (2004: 79), which contribute to the writing task and which can be seen as part of the iterative process of collaboration; these include, for example, socialisation, research, communication and negotiation. This aspect of collaborative activity is an indication of both the richness and complexity of what takes place when people work together in professional settings; it also bears out the observation made earlier that collaboration is very much entangled with other workplace phenomena, and thus adds to the challenges faced by researchers trying to demarcate collaborative writing from the activity surrounding it. As for the third component of their taxonomy, this concerns what they call document control modes: 'the chosen approaches used to manage control of a collaborative document' (2004: 83), while the fourth component is the different roles that participants play in the collaborative writing process.

The final aspect of the collaborative writing process that they talk about is what they term 'work modes', which relate to the degree of proximity and synchronicity that is seen in a collaborative writing group. The representation of these modes, adapted from the work of Ellis, Gibbs and Rein (1991), shows face-to-face activity, for example, as displaying a high degree of both proximity and synchronicity, while if groups are working both in different locations and at different times, this is described as 'asynchronous-distributed'; differences in proximity and synchronicity have an impact on the level of group awareness among group members. This is an important consideration, given the multiple ways in which writers can collaborate, particularly with the immense possibilities for asynchronous and distributed work afforded by the internet, an issue considered later in this chapter.

Jones (2005, 2007), meanwhile, has developed a taxonomy of collaborative practices along what he calls the Comprehensive Collaborative Continuum; this comprises three categories of collaborative interaction, namely contextual collaboration, so called because it 'involves the context of the organization itself' (2005: 451); hierarchical collaboration, a term he takes from Ede and Lunsford along with its definition: 'carefully, and often rigidly, structured, driven by highly specific goals, and carried out by people playing clearly defined and delimited goals' (1990: 133); and group collaboration, which 'involves a collection of people who largely plan, draft, and revise together' (2005: 454). These three categories are positioned along Jones's Continuum according to the degree of overtness of the collaboration, with contextual at the least overt end, and group at the most overt.

Contextual collaboration serves as a very useful label in that it attempts to account for elements of collaboration beyond people simply interacting together. It has some similarities with Witte's (1992) concept of 'covert' collaboration, mentioned above. Contextual collaboration is related to the fact that texts produced within an organisation are to some degree shaped by other texts and practices that are found there i.e. to the notion of intertextuality. This is broadly captured by Winsor's explanation of collaborative writing as meaning that 'any individual's writing is called forth and shaped by the needs and aims of the organization, and that to be understood it must draw on vocabulary, knowledge, and beliefs other organization members share' (1989: 271). Thus writers will often call upon previous examples of particular text types to compose new ones, or will use templates or boilerplates. A key article in this regard is that of Devitt (1991), who discusses relevant notions of intertextuality in some detail in the context of accounting documents. The practice of actively drawing on preexisting templates and other organisational texts, a central feature of contextual collaboration, is referred to by Jones (2005) as 'document borrowing', echoing the findings of Freedman, Adam and Smart, who say that 'workplace writing is resonant with the discourse of colleagues and the ongoing conversation of the institution ... the fact of such intertextual borrowing is a reality and a perceived good' (1994: 210). The issue is also discussed in the context of teaching business communication by Bremner (2008, 2010). What is clear is that this is an important type of collaborative writing activity that is commonly reported as workplace practice (e.g. Beaufort 1999; Flowerdew and Wan 2006).

Hierarchical collaboration relates to the ways in which groups or teams are configured, and the roles that different participants play. Discussion of hierarchical collaboration when writing can be seen, as noted above, in the work of Ede and Lunsford (1990) and also Killingsworth and Jones (1989). An important element in hierarchical collaboration and the attendant interactions is what Bhatia (2004) calls 'participatory mechanisms', the idea of who can contribute what to a particular process, and when they can contribute; in this way he echoes the concerns of Yates and Orlikowski, who consider the question of 'who is not empowered to initiate or receive certain genres' (2002: 17). Connected with this are notions of power and power relationships, and the ways in which the hierarchy – or lack of it – within an organisation can impact on the collaborative writing process (Gollin 1999; Holmes and Stubbe 2003). Hierarchical distribution of power in collaborative writing processes is an issue mentioned by Cross (1994) and is discussed as a source of conflict by Hansen (1995), while Angouri and Harwood (2008) consider how the relative seniority of an employee can be a factor in collaborative writing activity. It should be remembered that while the term 'collaboration' can evoke cosy visions of people working together, the workplace is a context where not everyone is equal, and that this plays out in the way that writing is divided up within an organisation; issues of power are an important consideration in understanding the nature of collaborative activity in professional settings.

Group collaboration, as mentioned above, sits at the most overt end of the Jones's Continuum. The key elements of this process are a 'sense of group identity', the fact that the group have a shared goal, and that they 'largely view the product as a collective, or jointly authored, effort' (2005: 454). This to a considerable extent invokes elements from Lowry *et al.*'s (2004) definition of collaborative writing, cited earlier, in that these explanations imply collective purpose.

The work of Lowry *et al.* (2004) and Jones (2005) represents very substantial efforts to bring together the wealth of research that has been carried out relating to collaborative writing, and it is for this reason that their studies have been discussed at length. Indeed, the very fact that Jones makes considerable reference to Lowry *et al.*'s work indicates the value of their efforts in helping provide the means to describe collaborative activity in different settings. But taxonomies are potentially restrictive (Forman 2004), and definitions of collaborative writing can appear somewhat idealised, in the sense of the order that is implied by phrases (taken from Lowry *et al.*'s (2004) definition) like 'focused on a common objective' or 'team formation', but which does not necessarily prevail in every workplace. The complex and dynamic nature of collaborative processes, something acknowledged by Lowry *et al.* themselves, makes their attempts to bring order to this area that much more challenging – and laudable.

Nevertheless we cannot escape from the fact that the collaborative construction of texts is not always the predictable, linear process that is sometimes implied by definitions from research or prescriptions from business communication textbooks. The disordered nature of text creation is well attested: Dourish and Bellotti (1992), for example, see collaborative writing as 'a relatively unstructured task' (cited in Lowry *et al.* 2004: 88); Winsor (2000: 172) describes a study in which work orders 'served as an orderly surface representation of a whole array of improvised activity'; Swales (2000: 63) meanwhile, stresses the 'need to see that contemporary specialized texts are distanced reconstructions of mangled experience'. Researchers who operate within the confines of taxonomies and definitions, while these are welcome, run the risk of overlooking the more organic and unscripted aspects of collaborative activity, and this may lead to incomplete accounts of what actually happens in workplace contexts.

Collaborative writing and context

The potential for collaborative activity to resist easy categorisation is very much tied up with the role of context, which is a key factor in collaborative writing, and one that is likely to complicate the picture. Much of the research into collaborative processes is premised on the idea that writing and the processes surrounding it are intrinsically linked to the contexts in which they occur i.e. that they are socially situated and socially constructed (Berkenkotter and Huckin 1995; Bargiela-Chiappini and Nickerson 1999; Angouri and Harwood 2008). Taking the social constructionist position that there is a strong constitutive relationship between text and context leads to a view of collaborative activities as being socially embedded in and dynamically linked with their particular contexts. As Cross points out, 'Culture, text, and process ... are not discrete facets of collaborative writing' (1993: 143). There is an increasing number of longitudinal studies of workplace writing in specific settings: some deal with collaboration as part of the wider cycle of activity in the contexts under study (e.g. Beaufort 1997, 1999, 2000; Haas and Witte 2001; Pogner 2003; Winsor 2003; Smart 2006), while others look more specifically at the collaborative aspect (Paradis *et al.* 1985; Gollin 1999; Yates and Orlikowski 2002; Wegner 2004). In the latter category, it is worth singling out the work of Geoffrey Cross, who has conducted a number of in-depth ethnographic studies of collaborative processes, looking at the role of conflict (1994), at large-scale collaboration (2001) and most recently at the role of collaboration in verbal-visual communication (2011).

The evidence from these and other studies suggests that collaboration does not always run smoothly. A central factor that can affect the functioning of a collaborative endeavour is the potential for conflict that arises when groups from different workplace cultures or disciplines come into contact, an issue discussed by Spilka (1993) and Burnett (1993, 1996). Conflict in the workplace has been examined in particular by Cross (1994, 2001), as noted above, and Palmeri (2004), the latter making the point that 'conflict in interprofessional collaboration is not inherently positive or negative' (2004: 60); indeed, researchers such as Burnett (1993), and Dautermann (1993) have demonstrated the potential benefits of substantive conflict in collaboration.

In relation to the issue of conflict, interdisciplinary differences are a growing source of research interest, and have been studied among others by Schryer (1994), who discusses the tensions between researchers and clinicians, Palmeri (2004), looking at the collaborative practices at a law firm, and Gooch (2005), who examined the interactions surrounding group proposal writing. The importance of understanding this aspect of collaboration is iterated by Palmeri, who says 'we need more research (both broad surveys and local case studies) of interprofessional collaboration and conflict in the workplace so that we can develop a variety of strategies for effectively managing interprofessional conflict' (2004: 60).

An important consideration in this regard is what can be learnt from studying the breakdown of collaborative processes. Cross (2001), for example, conducted an intensive ethnography of a financial conglomerate, and in highlighting moments when collaboration in the organisation broke down and also the subsequent salvage and resurrection of the process, or the formation of a 'collective mind', which he explains is 'found in the heedful interrelation of group members' (2000: 79), provides invaluable insights into how collaboration can operate.

Teaching and learning collaborative writing

The work of Lowry *et al.* (2004) and Jones (2005), and many others can be seen as attempts to bring order to an area of professional communication that, as noted, is somewhat messy, and to some extent resists being tied down and categorised. But this tension has ramifications for teaching: if collaborative writing is resistant to being broken down into types of behaviour, this poses a challenge to the teacher of workplace writing who is concerned with making students aware of the collaborative nature of writing and providing them with appropriate tasks and assignments. This question has been the subject of considerable interest, and it is fair to say that given the centrality of collaborative writing to workplace communication, there is general recognition of the need to provide students with appropriate experience, a need summed up by Nelson (2003: 274): 'it is important to expose students to ... collaborative writing practices in the classroom if we want them to seek out these practices as professionals'. Other researchers who suggest the need to teach students how to write collaboratively include Gollin (1999), Colen and Petelin (2004) and Dovey (2006). The value of collaboration in the classroom, largely with an eye to its application in the workplace, is attested by many researchers: building interactivity and teamwork and developing negotiation skills (Spilka 1993); improved decision-making (Hansen 2006); the benefits that accrue from 'working out disagreements' (Rentz et al. 2009: 108–9); achieving 'understanding about diversity in the workplace, and experience coping with group dynamics' (Ding and Ding 2008: 458). Meanwhile Nelson (2003) suggests that the group is of itself a 'learning mechanism'.

There is a variety of views regarding how the teaching of collaborative writing should be approached, which relate mainly to the differences between the academy and the workplace, the portability of relevant skills from one context to another, and the degree to which collaborative writing should be actively taught.

This first issue, namely the difference between the academy and the workplace, is particularly problematic, with some researchers suggesting that the gap between the two contexts is considerable; Mabrito is one of them: 'we will never be able to exactly duplicate in our classrooms many of the constraints and pressures that writers experience in the workplace' (1999: 105), he says, mentioning in this regard the different types of relationships found in the these different settings, a point also made by Debs (1991). Certainly there are many features of collaborative writing that differ in the two contexts. Central among these is the reason why people write in the academy when compared to the workplace, and the reason why they collaborate, as well as the audiences they are writing for. There are also often significant differences in terms of the constitution of the groups that collaborate: these relate to issues such as power, levels of knowledge and ability, diversity of roles and so on. Student groups tend to be more homogenous in their make-up, and the ways in which they interact will thus often be quite different from the interactions seen in workplace settings. Another difference might be seen in the type and range of texts that writers can draw on i.e. the levels of intertextuality and thus the levels of contextual collaboration (Jones 2005), described earlier. For further discussion of the differences found in the workplace and the academy in relation to collaborative writing, see Freedman, Adam and Smart (1994), Freedman and Adam (1996) and Bremner (2010).

The second concern when approaching the teaching of collaborative writing is the issue of portability of collaborative skills from the classroom to the workplace; this is to a large extent linked to the notion that context and activity are essentially inseparable, and that, as explained above, the academy and the workplace are distinct discourse communities. As Freedman, Adam and Smart (1994: 221) point out, 'the nature of the institutional context necessarily and inevitably shapes the writing in ways that cannot be altered'. Much of the research and discussion about this issue of portability is concerned with how written genres taught in professional writing classes can be transferred to the workplace, and while some researchers question whether this is possible (Anson and Forsberg 1990; Dias and Paré 2000; Freedman and Adam 2000), recent work by Artemeva (2005, 2009) suggests that it may be possible to teach domain-specific communication separately from the local context. A more detailed discussion of the question of portability can be found in Artemeva and Fox (this volume).

The issue of portability in relation to collaborative writing often involves the identification of the particular skills and competencies that can lead to successful collaboration. Of those that have been identified, some relate to teamwork more generally, and others to collaborative writing more specifically. Newstrom and Scannell (1998: xi), for example, looking at the ingredients of a high-performance team, say that such teams 'usually exhibit an overall team purpose, mutual accountability, collective work products, shared leadership roles, high cohesiveness, collaboration in deciding task assignments and procedures, and collective assessment of their own success'. Other desirable behaviours for members of successful writing groups are mentioned by Rentz et al. (2009): these include listening to each other and trying not to dominate. Rehling (1994: 42) looks at the question of document ownership attributions, and suggests that newcomers to professional workplaces could be helped in their transitions 'by foregrounding ownership attitudes'. It is helpful to identify practices and characteristics such as these, but from a teaching perspective they might translate into little more than general recommendations or exhortations. There have, however, been attempts to translate team characteristics into individual competencies. Chen et al. (2004), for example, have extracted five KSA (knowledge, skills and abilities) dimensions from the work of Stevens and Campion (1994): conflict resolution, collaborative problem solving, communication, goal setting and performance management, and planning and task coordination. A slightly different perspective is taken by Onrubia and Engel (2009: 1260), who identify and evaluate five main strategies 'for collaborative elaboration of written products', which relate to the ways in which group members in a collaborative process divide up and tackle elements of the task.

The third issue relating to the teaching of collaborative writing is the extent to which it should be actively taught. As observed earlier, the need to give students opportunities to collaborate is recognised by many (Nelson 2003; Colen and Petelin 2004; Dovey 2006). Yet a number of researchers suggest that this aspect of learning is given insufficient attention (e.g. Chen et al. 2004; Rentz et al. 2009). Indeed, Hansen (2006: 15) contends that 'it appears that the majority of faculty who place students into teams do nothing more than that', a claim made by Snyder (2009) too. Research by Bremner (2010) also indicates that business communication textbooks rarely provide focused advice or activities with regard to collaboration.

There have been numerous studies addressing the challenge of preparing students for the types of collaborative writing that they might encounter in the workplace. It was noted earlier that much of the research into collaborative writing takes a social constructionist position, and some suggestions relate to the need to provide some kind of social context and community in the classroom (Doheny-Farina 1986; Gollin 1999). Beaufort builds on this, saying that we should 'capitalize on social motives for writing' (2000: 218) and proposes the adoption of collaborative models for writing rather than competitive ones. As well as general calls for the provision of opportunities to collaborate and interact (Couture and Rymer 1989; Schneider and Andre 2005), there is some focus on the need for students to play multiple roles (Dias et al. 1999); Paré and Smart look at the larger picture, and suggest that students need to engage with 'a set of texts, the composing processes involved in creating those texts ... and the social roles played by writers and readers' (1994: 147). Wallace (1994) also makes the important point relating to social context that by engaging in collaborative activity, students can gain an increased understanding of both context and audience. Finally Palmeri, whose research is concerned with collaboration among different professional groups, calls for pedagogical models 'for merging discourses in interprofessional communication' (2004: 61).

Thus what we see is a range of approaches to the conundrum of how to approach the teaching of collaborative writing. At one end of the spectrum are activities that essentially consist of putting students in groups – the observation made by Hansen (2006); further along the spectrum are activities designed to give students opportunities to collaborate in conditions that replicate the workplace to a greater or lesser extent; finally there is the school of thought that recommends more active and focused teaching: 'Collaborative writing is a complex activity and needs to be actively taught', says Gollin (1999: 289), and Fredrick (2008) is also of this opinion, saying that rather than simply providing students with opportunities to collaborate, teachers need to act as facilitators, to interact with student teams, and also to develop 'evaluations that value the process of teamwork' (2008: 439).

A number of studies have examined the pedagogical effects of instigating collaborative processes in academic settings. Baker (1991), for example, devised an entire course focused on shared document writing and observed ways in which different groups managed the process, concluding that 'organized flexibility' was a major factor influencing the outcome of the collaboration. Hemby *et al.* (2004) looked at students' reactions to a group simulation focusing on planning meetings culminating in a presentation and report, while Bekins and Merriam (2004) instituted an experiential learning project that required students to carry out research on a local organisation and help it with its documentation needs, the final product coming in the form of a submitted grant proposal.

One other area that needs to be considered in relation to collaborative writing and teaching and learning is the issue of collaborative participation in professional communities of practice (i.e. in the workplace) leading to the acquisition of particular skills. This is linked to the notion of cognitive apprenticeships that Lave and Wenger (1991) talk about in their highly influential work on situated learning and legitimate peripheral participation (LPP), whereby newcomers to a community, by participating in the activities of that community, and through interacting (i.e. collaborating) with oldtimers, develop relevant knowledge and skills. (For further discussion of this phenomenon, see Kwan, this volume). Also relevant is Rogoff's (1991) notion of 'guided participation', which along with LPP is linked philosophically to Vygotsky's (1978) 'zone of proximal development', a zone in which the learner operates – and learns – alongside an experienced practitioner. Freedman and Adam (1996) propose the concepts of 'facilitated performance' and 'attentuated authentic participation', which are respectively based on Rogoff's guided participation and Lave and Wenger's notion of LPP. Attenuated authentic participation is a workplace-based scenario whereby learners are given tasks within their ability which 'engage(d) them in processes that ultimately enable(d) fuller participation' (1996: 412), and is important as a way of accounting for collaborative activity between guide and learner in a workplace setting.

An important example of research that has considered collaborative interactions between newcomers and managers as part of the process of learning to write is that of Beaufort (1999). Also in this connection, the work of Dias *et al.* (1999), and Paré (2000) has taken a sociocognitive perspective on writing; their work draws on theories of situated learning and situated cognition. Paré (2000: 152) explains that from this perspective, like writing, 'cognition is best conceived of as a social phenomenon embedded in activity', and that it is 'always social ... the individual is cognitively enabled, constrained, inspired, and influenced by situation and history, by increasingly wider circles of collectivity: family, friends, school, religion, race, society, culture'. This perspective casts light on the sociocognitive aspect of collaborative writing processes, and as Beaufort concludes: 'Collaborative writing is not just a division of labor; rather it entails interactive cognitive processes among writers, editors, and managers' (2008: 230).

Current and future research

An area of growing interest is the effect of technology on writing. Beaufort (2008: 224) suggests that two main areas of investigation have emerged in relation to the impact of technology on writing in the professions generally: '(a) how technologies affect writers' processes (or don't), and (b) how technologies spawn new genres or new communicative patterns (or don't)'. These also relate to collaborative writing, with Jones (2005), for example, considering the effects of advances in technology on how technical writers collaborate.

Interest in the relationship between technology and collaboration has led to the notion of e-collaboration, defined by Kock *et al.* (2001: 1) as 'collaboration among individuals engaged in a common task using electronic technologies'. The area of e-collaboration is discussed in some detail by Kock and Nosek (2005) in a special issue of *IEEE Transactions on Professional Communication*, in which, among other questions, they consider research interest in group decision support systems (GDSSs) and computer supported cooperative work (CSCW). Not all e-collaboration relates specifically to writing, but the resources available for collaborating are having an impact on organisational structure and patterns of communication generally, and with that an effect, direct or indirect, on how people collaborate to produce texts.

A huge variety of software exists for professionals to collaborate in virtual, distributed work settings, allowing for document authoring and sharing, from wikis to content management systems. It is beyond the scope of this chapter to enumerate these, but a special issue of the *Journal of Business and Technical Communication* looking at social software in professional communication (July 2009) considers many of the relevant issues. Hewett and Robidoux (2010) take a detailed look at virtual collaborative writing in workplace settings; their collection considers the many computer-mediated communication (CMC) technologies that are used in workplaces to facilitate collaboration. An interesting feature of this particular work is that it was collaboratively written through the use of wikis and Google Docs.

As CMC technologies will no doubt continue to proliferate, there is ample scope for future research into the ways in which they might afford different collaborative opportunities and processes in professional settings, a point made by Jones, who issues a call for further studies 'to enable us to expand our notions of collaboration and the writing process in general' (2007: 292). Similarly there is a need for further research on the ways in which technology might be harnessed to helping students adjust to the possibility of working in environments where virtual collaboration is common. Work has been done on this area by, for example, Eastman and Swift (2002), Rehling (2005), and Buechler (2010), but developments in technology are ongoing and rapid; as Paretti, McNair and Holloway-Attaway suggest, noting transformations in the workplace in relating to distributed work, 'such transformations ... require concomitant transformations in our educational practices' (2007: 328).

Finally, it should be pointed out, and it is perhaps fairly evident from the studies enumerated and discussed in this chapter, that most of the research into collaborative writing has been conducted in North American settings. Gollin's (1999) work in Australia is an exception, and the work of researchers in Europe such as Louhiala-Salminen (2002) and Gunnarsson (1997), for example, while not focusing on collaboration, nevertheless takes account of the collaborative nature of text production in workplace settings. As for English for Specific Purposes, this has traditionally focused on text analysis and making genres of different types accessible to non-native speakers of English. While frameworks for investigating the broader contexts in which texts are constructed, such as that of Bhatia (2004), suggest a need to look beyond the text to the production processes in social and professional contexts, the collaborative element of these contexts has not as yet been the focus of research in this field. In Asia, again there is little in the way of research related to collaborative writing, aside from a recent examination of collaborative practices in the PR industry in Hong Kong (Peirson-Smith *et al.* 2010).

It would seem, then, that there are many opportunities for further research into collaborative writing in settings beyond North America that can build on the valuable foundations established by the work conducted there. Roughly ten years ago Forman contended that there is 'an acute gap in our knowledge of collaborative writing within specific local conditions' (2004: 28); there is certainly scope for investigating collaborative writing in other regions around the world, but also for looking further at the kinds of collaborative practices that take place in the increasingly globalised workplace, particularly as different cultural groups and their expectations come together to produce texts.

Related topics

business communication; communities and discursive practices; discourse variation in professional contexts; formation of a professional communicator; management communication

Key readings

Cross, G. (2001). *Forming the Collective Mind: A Contextual Exploration of Large-scale Collaborative Writing in Industry*, Cresskill, NJ: Hampton. (An excellent ethnography of large-scale collaborative writing that covers a wide range of issues relating to this topic.)

Ede, L. and Lunsford, A. (1990). *Singular Texts/Plural Authors: Perspectives on Collaborative Learning*, Carbondale: Southern Illinois University Press. (An early classic that deals with many of the issues relating to collaborative writing.)

Lowry, P., Curtis, A. and Lowry, M. (2004). 'Building a taxonomy and nomenclature of collaborative writing to improve interdisciplinary research and practice', *Journal of Business Communication*, 41(1), 66–99. (An attempt at providing a comprehensive taxonomy of collaborative writing.)

Palmeri, J. (2004). 'When discourses collide: A case study of interprofessional collaborative writing in a medically oriented law firm', *Journal of Business Communication*, 41(1), 37–65. (An interesting case study of interprofessional conflict and collaboration.)

Bibliography

Angouri, J. and Harwood, N. (2008). 'This is too formal for us ... A case study of variation in the written products of a multinational consortium', *Journal of Business and Technical Communication*, 22(1), 38–64.

Anson, C. and Forsberg, L. (1990). 'Moving beyond the academic community: Transitional stages in professional writing', *Written Communication*, 7(2), 200–31.

Artemeva, N. (2005). 'A time to speak, a time to act: A rhetorical genre analysis of a novice engineer's calculated risk taking', *Journal of Business and Technical Communication*, 19(4), 389–421.

——(2009). 'Stories of becoming: A study of novice engineers learning genres of their profession', in C. Bazerman, A. Bonini and D. Figuieredo (eds), *Genre in a Changing World: Perspectives on Writing* (pp. 158–78), Fort Collins, Colorado: The WAC Clearinghouse and Parlor Press.

Baker, T. (1991). 'Collaborating the course: Organized flexibility in professional writing', *Journal of Business and Technical Communication*, 5(3), 275–84.

Bargiela-Chiappini, F. and Nickerson, C. (1999). 'Business writing as social action', in F. Bargiela-Chiappini and C. Nickerson (eds), *Writing Business: Genres, Media and Discourses* (pp. 1–32), London: Longman.

Beaufort, A. (1997). 'Operationalizing the concept of discourse community: A case study of one institutional site of composing', *Research in the Teaching of English*, 31(4): 486–529.

——(1999). *Writing in the Real World: Making the Transition from School to Work*, New York, NY: Teachers College Press.

——(2000). 'Learning the trade: A social apprenticeship model for gaining writing expertise', *Written Communication*, 17, 185–224.

——(2008). 'Writing in the professions', in C. Bazerman (ed.), *Handbook of Research on Writing: History, Society, School, Individual, Text* (pp. 221–35), New York: Lawrence Erlbaum Associates.

Bekins, L. and Merriam, S. (2004). 'Consulting and collaborative writing connections', *Academic Exchange Quarterly*, 8(3), 233–37.

Berkenkotter, C. and Huckin, T. (1995). *Genre Knowledge in Disciplinary Communication: Cognition/Culture/Power*, New Jersey: Lawrence Erlbaum Associates.

Bhatia, V. (2004). *Worlds of Written Discourse: A Genre-based View*, London: Continuum.
Bremner, S. (2008). 'Intertextuality and business communication textbooks: Why students need more textual support', *English for Specific Purposes*, 27, 306–21.
——(2010). 'Collaborative writing: Bridging the gap between the textbook and the workplace', *English for Specific Purposes*, 29(2), 121–32.
Buechler, S. (2010). 'Using Web 2.0 to collaborate', *Business Communication Quarterly*, 73(4), 439–43.
Burnett, R. (1993). 'Conflict in collaborative decision-making', in N. Blyler and C. Thralls (eds), *Professional Communication: The Social Perspective* (pp. 145–63), Newbury Park, CA: Sage.
——(1996). '"Some people weren't able to contribute anything but their technical knowledge": The anatomy of a dysfunctional team', in A. Duin and C. Hansen (eds), *Nonacademic Writing: Social Theory and Technology* (pp. 123–56), Mahwah, NJ: Lawrence Erlbaum.
——(2001). *Technical Communication*, Fort Worth, TX: Harcourt Brace.
Chen, G., Donahue, L. and Klimoski, R. (2004). 'Training undergraduates to work in organizational teams', *Academy of Management Learning and Education*, 3(1), 27–40.
Colen, K. and Petelin, R. (2004). 'Challenges in collaborative writing in the contemporary corporation', *Corporate Communications*, 9(2), 136–45.
Couture, B. and Rymer, J. (1989). 'Interactive writing on the job: Definitions and implications of "collaboration"', in M. Kogan (ed.), *Writing in the Business Professions* (pp. 73–93), Urbana, IL: National Council of Teachers of English and Association for Business Communication.
Cross, G. (1993). 'The interrelation of genre, context, and process in the collaborative writing of two corporate documents', in R. Spilka (ed.), *Writing in the Workplace: New Research Perspectives* (pp. 141–52), Carbondale: Southern Illinois Press.
——(1994). *Collaboration and Conflict: A Contextual Exploration of Group Writing and Positive Emphasis*, Cresskill, NJ: Hampton.
——(2000). 'Collective form: An exploration of large-group writing', 1998 Outstanding Researcher Lecture, *Journal of Business Communication*, 37(1), 77–100.
——(2001). *Forming the Collective Mind: A Contextual Exploration of Large-scale Collaborative Writing in Industry*, Cresskill, NJ: Hampton.
——(2011). *Envisioning Collaboration: Group Verbal-visual Composing in a System of Creativity*, Amityville, NY: Baywood Publishing Company, Inc.
Dautermann, J. (1993). 'Negotiating meaning in a hospital discourse community', in R. Spilka (ed.), *Writing in the Workplace: New Research Perspectives* (pp. 98–111), Carbondale: Southern Illinois University Press.
Debs, M. (1991). 'Recent research on collaborative writing in industry', *Technical Communication*, Fourth quarter, 476–84.
Devitt, A. (1991). 'Intertextuality in tax accounting: Generic, referential, and functional', in C. Bazerman and J. Paradis (eds), *Textual Dynamics of the Professions: Historical and Contemporary Studies of Writing in Professional Communities* (pp. 336–57), Madison: University of Wisconsin Press.
Dias, P. and Paré, A. (eds) (2000). *Transitions: Writing in Academic and Workplace Settings*, Cresskill, NJ: Hampton Press, Inc.
Dias, P., Freedman, A., Medway. P. and Paré, A. (1999). *Worlds Apart: Acting and Writing in Academic and Workplace Contexts*, Mahwah, NJ: Erlbaum.
Ding, H. and Ding, X. (2008) 'Project management, critical praxis, and process-oriented approach to teamwork', *Business Communication Quarterly*, 71, 456–71.
Doheny-Farina, S. (1986). 'Writing in an emerging organization: An ethnographic study", *Written Communication*, 3(2), 158–85.
Dourish, P. and Bellotti, V. (1992). 'Awareness and coordination in shared workspaces', Paper presented at the International Conference on Computer Supported Cooperative Work.
Dovey, T. (2006). 'What purposes, specifically? Re-thinking purposes and specificity in the context of the "new vocationalism"', *English for Specific Purposes*, 25, 387–402.
Eastman, J. and Swift, C. (2002) 'Enhancing collaborative learning: Discussion boards and chat rooms as project communication tools', *Business Communication Quarterly*, 65(3), 29–41.
Ede, L. and Lunsford, A. (1990). *Singular Texts/Plural Authors: Perspectives on Collaborative Learning*, Carbondale: Southern Illinois University Press.
Ellis, C., Gibbs, S. and Rein, G. (1991) 'Groupware: Some issues and experiences', *Communications of the ACM*, 34(1), 39–58.
Faigley, L. and Miller, T. (1982). 'What we learn from writing on the job', *College English*, 44(6), 557–69.

Flowerdew, J. and Wan, A. (2006). 'Genre analysis of tax computation letters: How and why tax accountants write the way they do', *English for Specific Purposes*, 25(2), 133–53.

Forman, J. (1991). 'Collaborative business writing: A Burkean perspective for future research', *Journal of Business Communication*, 28(3), 233–57.

——(2004). 'Opening the aperture: Research and theory on collaborative writing', *Journal of Business Communication*, 41(1), 27–36.

——(2005). 'Research on collaboration, business communication, and technology', *Journal of Business Communication*, 42(1), 78–102.

Fredrick, T. (2008). 'Facilitating better teamwork: Analyzing the challenges and strategies of classroom-based collaboration', *Business Communication Quarterly*, 71, 439–55.

Freedman, A. and Adam, C. (1996). 'Learning to write professionally: "Situated learning" and the transition from university to professional discourse', *Journal of Business and Technical Communication*, 10, 395–427.

——(2000). 'Bridging the gap: University-based writing that is more than simulation', in P. Dias and A. Paré (eds), *Transitions: Writing in Academic and Workplace Settings* (pp. 129–44), Cresskill, NJ: Hampton Press.

Freedman, A., Adam, C. and Smart, G. (1994). 'Wearing suits to class: Simulating genres and simulations as genres', *Written Communication*, 11(2), 193–226.

Gollin, S. (1999). '"Why? I thought we'd talked about it before": Collaborative writing in a professional workplace setting', in C. Candlin and K. Hyland (eds), *Writing: Texts, Processes and Practices* (pp. 267–90), London: Longman.

Gooch, J. (2005). 'The dynamics and challenges of interdisciplinary collaboration: A case study of "cortical depth of bench" in group proposal writing', *IEEE Transactions on Professional Communication*, 48(2), 177–90.

Gunnarsson, B.-L. (1997). 'The writing process from a sociolinguistic viewpoint', *Written Communication*, 14(2), 139–88.

Haas, C. and Witte, S. (2001). 'Writing as an embodied practice: The case of engineering standards', *Journal of Business and Technical Communication*, 15(4), 413–57.

Hansen, C. (1995) 'Writing the project team: Authority and intertextuality in a corporate setting', *Journal of Business Communication*, 32(2), 103–22.

Hansen, R. (2006). 'Benefits and problems with student teams: Suggestions for improving team projects', *Journal of Education for Business*, 82(1), 11–19.

Hemby, V., McPherson, B., Moore, W., Szul, L., Woodland, D. and Wilkinson, K. (2004). 'A meeting planning project: A major component in developing teamwork and collaborative writing skills', *Journal of Organizational Culture, Communications and Conflict*, 8(2), 27–45.

Hewett, B. and Robidoux, C. (2010). *Virtual Collaborative Writing in the Workplace: Computer-mediated Communication Technologies and Processes*, Hershey, PA: IGI Global.

Holmes, J. and Stubbe, M. (2003). *Power and Politeness in the Workplace*, London: Pearson Education.

Horton, M., Rogers, P., Austin, L. and McCormick, M. (1991). 'Exploring the impact of face-to-face collaborative technology on group writing', *Journal of Management Information Systems*, 8(3), 27–48.

Jones, S. (2005). 'From writers to information coodinators', *Journal of Business and Technical Communication*, 19(4), 449–67.

——(2007). 'How we collaborate: Reported frequency of technical communicators' collaborative writing activities', *Technical Communication*, 54(3), 283–94.

Keyton, J. and Beck, S. (2008). 'Team attributes, processes, and values: A pedagogical framework', *Business Communication Quarterly*, 71, 488–504.

Killingsworth, M. and Jones, B. (1989). 'Division of labor or integrated teams: A crux in the management of technical communication?' *Technical Communication*, 36(3), 210–21.

Kock, N. and Nosek, J. (2005). 'Expanding the boundaries of e-collaboration', *IEEE Transactions on Professional Communication*, 48(1), 1–9.

Kock, N., Davison, R., Ocker, R. and Wazlawick, R. (2001). 'E-collaboration: A look at past and future challenges', *Journal of Systems and Information Technology*, 5(1), 1–9.

Lave, J. and Wenger, E. (1991). *Situated Learning: Legitimate Peripheral Participation*, Cambridge: Cambridge University Press.

Louhiala-Salminen, L. (2002). 'The fly's perspective: Discourse in the daily routine of a business manager', *English for Specific Purposes*, 21, 211–31.

Lowry, P., Curtis, A. and Lowry, M. (2004). 'Building a taxonomy and nomenclature of collaborative writing to improve interdisciplinary research and practice', *Journal of Business Communication*, 41(1), 66–99.

Mabrito, M. (1999). 'From workplace to classroom: Teaching professional writing', *Business Communication Quarterly*, 62(3), 101–4.
Nelson, S. (2003). 'Engineering and technology student perceptions of collaborative writing practices', *IEEE Transactions on Professional Communication*, 46(4), 265–76.
Newstrom, J. and Scannell, E. (1998). *The Big Book of Team Building Games: Trust-building Activities, Team Spirit Exercises, and Other Fun Things*, New York: McGraw-Hill.
Onrubia, J. and Engel, A. (2009). 'Strategies for collaborative writing and phases of knowledge construction in CSCL environments', *Computers and Education*, 53, 1256–65.
Palmeri, J. (2004). 'When discourses collide: A case study of interprofessional collaborative writing in a medically oriented law firm', *Journal of Business Communication*, 41(1), 37–65.
Paradis, J., Dobrin, D. and Miller, R. (1985). 'Writing at Exxon: Notes on the writing environment of an R & D organization', in L. Odell and D. Goswami (eds), *Writing in Non-Academic Settings* (pp. 281–308), New York: Guilford.
Paré, A. (2000). 'Writing as a way into social work: Genre sets, genre systems, and distributed cognition', in P. Dias and A. Paré (eds), *Transitions: Writing in Academic and Workplace Settings* (pp. 145–66), Cresskill, NJ: Hampton Press, Inc.
Paré, A. and Smart, G. (1994). 'Observing genres in action: Towards a research methodology', in A. Freedman and P. Medway (eds), *Genre and the New Rhetoric* (pp. 146–54), London: Taylor & Francis.
Paretti, M., McNair, L. and Holloway-Attaway, L. (2007). 'Teaching technical communication in an era of distributed work: A case study of collaboration between US and Swedish students', *Technical Communication Quarterly*, 16(3), 327–52.
Peirson-Smith, A., Bhatia, V., Bremner, S. and Jones, R. (2010). 'Creative English and public relations in Hong Kong', *World Englishes*, 29(4), 523–35.
Pogner, K. H. (2003). 'Writing and interacting in the discourse community of engineering', *Journal of Pragmatics*, 35, 855–67.
Posner, I. and Baecker, R. (1992). 'How people write together', Paper presented at the Twenty-Fifth Hawaii International Conference on System Sciences, Kauai.
Prior, P. (2004). 'Tracing process: How texts come into being', in C. Bazerman and P. Prior (eds), *What Writing Does and How it Does it: An Introduction to Analyzing Texts and Textual Practices* (pp. 167–200), Mahwah, NJ: Lawrence Erlbaum.
Rehling, L. (1994). '"Is it theirs, mine, or ours?" Ownership, collaboration, and cultures', *IEEE Transactions on Professional Communication*, 37(1), 42–49.
——(2005). 'Teaching in a high-tech conference room: Academic adaptations and workplace simulations', *Journal of Business and Technical Communication*, 19(1), 98–113.
Reither, J. (1993). 'Scenic motives for collaborative writing in workplace and school', in R. Spilka (ed.), *Writing in the Workplace: New Research Perspectives* (pp. 195–206), Carbondale, IL: Southern Illinois University Press.
Rentz, K., Arduser, L., Meloncon, L. and Debs, M. (2009). 'Designing a successful group-report experience', *Business Communication Quarterly*, 72(1), 79–84.
Rogoff, B. (1991). 'Social interaction as apprenticeship in thinking: Guided participation in spatial planning', in L. Resnick, J. Levine and S. Teasley (eds), *Perspectives on Socially Shared Cognition* (pp. 349–64), Washington, DC: American Psychological Association.
Schneider, B. and Andre, J. (2005). 'University preparation for workplace writing: An exploratory study of the perceptions of students in three disciplines', *Journal of Business Communication*, 42(2), 195–218.
Schryer, C. (1994). 'The lab vs. the clinic: Sites of competing genres', in A. Freedman and P. Medway (eds), *Genre and the New Rhetoric* (pp. 105–24), Bristol: Taylor & Francis.
Smart, G. (1993). 'Genre as a community invention: A central bank's response to its executives' expectations as readers', in R. Spilka (ed.), *Writing in the Workplace: New Research Perspectives* (pp. 124–40), Carbondale, Illinois: Southern Illinois University Press.
——(2006). *Writing the Economy: Activity, Genre and Technology in the World of Banking*, London: Equinox.
Snyder, L. (2009). 'Teaching teams about teamwork: Preparation, practice, and performance review', *Business Communication Quarterly*, 72(1), 74–79.
Spilka, R. (1993). 'Collaboration across multiple organizational cultures', *Technical Communication Quarterly*, 2(2), 125–45.
Stevens, M. and Campion, M. (1994). 'The knowledge, skill, and ability requirements for teamwork: Implications for human resource management', *Journal of Management*, 20, 505–30.
Swales, J. (2000). 'Languages for specific purposes', *Annual Review of Applied Linguistics*, 20, 59–76.

Thacker, R. and Yost, C. (2002). 'Training students to become effective workplace team leaders', *Team Performance Management, 8*(3/4), 89–94.
Thompson, I. (2001). 'Collaboration in technical communication: A quantitative content analysis of journal articles, 1990–99', *IEEE Transactions on Professional Communication, 44*(3), 161–73.
Vygotsky, L. (1978). *Mind in Society*, Cambridge, MA: Harvard University Press.
Wallace, D. L. (1994). 'Collaborative planning and transforming knowledge', *Journal of Business Communication, 3*(1), 41–60.
Wegner, D. (2004). 'The collaborative construction of a management report in a municipal community of practice: Text and context, genre and learning', *Journal of Business and Technical Communication, 18*(4), 411–51.
Winsor, D. (1989). 'An engineer's writing and the corporate construction of knowledge', *Written Communication, 6*, 270–85.
——(2000). 'Ordering work: Blue-collar literacy and the political nature of genre', *Written Communication, 17*(2), 155–84.
——(2003). *Writing Power: Communication in an Engineering Center*, Albany, NY: State University of New York Press.
Witte, S. (1992). 'Context, text, intertext: Toward a constructivist semiotic of writing', *Written Communication, 9*(2), 237–308.
Yates, J. and Orlikowski, W. (2002). 'Genre systems: structuring interaction through communicative norms', *Journal of Business Communication, 39*(1), 13–35.

30
Training the call centre communications trainers in the Asian BPO industry

Jane Lockwood

Introduction

The context of this chapter is the call centre worksite in off-shored and outsourced destinations such as the Philippines and India where young graduates, employed as call centre customer services representatives (CSRs), talk to Western English speaking customers, mostly American, throughout the night. These CSRs have good levels of English but the transactional and interactional nature of what they are doing on the phones is carried out in an unfamiliar cultural milieu and is extremely challenging, especially as they are second, not first language speakers of English.

This chapter will first briefly explore the communication needs of the CSRs as a way of then describing what is required of English language communications trainers in the call centre workplace context in Asia. I will address the following two key questions: what is the knowledge and skills set required of these English language communications trainers and what is the nature of CSR communication breakdown that they are expected to prevent and remediate?

First, I will outline the context of the call centre worksite and the nature of the communication breakdown drawing on research completed to date. I will then move on to describe how CSRs are currently being supported through English language communications training and coaching at the workplace. I will situate this discussion within the research in the applied linguistic English for Specific Purposes (ESP) discipline, in teacher education and in the discourse analysis of communication breakdown in call centres. However, I will also take an interdisciplinary approach by considering the business requirements for communications training drawing on relevant business management research as it relates to training in the workplace. Finally, I will suggest what might go into an English for Specific Purposes (ESP) call centre communication 'train the trainer program' and briefly discuss how this could be implemented. Throughout this chapter, I will include the voice of the call centre trainer based on both CSR and worksite trainer interview data collected over the period 2004–7 whilst consulting and researching in call centres in Manila, Bangalore and Hyderabad.

The Business Processing Outsourcing context and the work of the call centres

Businesses in the USA, UK and Australia are increasingly moving their 'back office' functions, such as customer services, to cheaper destinations in Asia, Eastern Europe and South America. This industry is known as Business Processing Outsourcing (BPO) and has a current estimated worth of over USD 100 billion (BPAP 2009, NASSCOM 2012). In the early years of 2000, routine back office functions and call centres were first migrated and building on the early success of these, more complex work has been sent to these cheaper destinations in developing countries such as India and the Philippines. This is sometimes referred to as Knowledge Processing Outsourcing (KPO) and includes work such as medical and legal research, publishing, animation and financial advising. In the call centres in the Philippines there is a developing success story as reported in *The Report – The Philippines 2012* compiled by the Oxford Business Group (2012: 122):

> As companies capitalized on the abundant, qualified, English speaking labour pool, the Philippine BPO industry employed some 640,000 workers and generated some US 10.9 billion in 2011, displaying over 22 per cent growth over 2010, the year in which the country over-took India as the world leader in the standalone voice business (call centres) ... the country's BPO industry is a centerpiece of the Philippine Development Plan 2011–16.

However, as the report goes onto warn:

> Direct hires by companies makes up less than 8 per cent of applicants due to insufficient language or critical analysis skills, although this can be boosted by additional training.
>
> *(p.163)*

Companies that decide to send work to these destinations do so in two ways. First, a large multinational may simply set up its own dedicated site overseas and employ local staff; this is known as a 'captive' or an 'off-shored' site. Banks such as HSBC fall into this category. Alternatively, businesses may contract a '3rd party' to provide such services. These are known as 'outsourced' providers, the largest being Sykes, People Support and Convergys, which operate globally.

Understanding the English language demands of the call centre CSR in off-shored or outsourced (O&O) companies in Manila or Bangalore requires an understanding not only of the needs of second language speakers of English, but also of the demands of the business itself. Over the last decade, call centres have proliferated in Asian destinations for primarily economic reasons. Arguments have also been mounted by outsourced and off-shored (O&O) multinational companies (MNCs), that this migration of jobs also leads to quality improvements in customer care, due to the natural affinity of many Asian cultures (e.g. Filipinas) for good care and service; as well, CSRs in these new destinations tend to be degree holders, not school leavers as is the case on-shore (Hamp-Lyons and Lockwood 2009). However, given that there are significant financial and quality gains to be made, the question needs to posed as to whether these MNCs really understood the linguistic and cultural challenges of customer service on the phones with a CSR population who speak English as a second rather than a first language?

Most of the Asian call centres are inbound businesses (BPAP 2006; NASSCOM 2009) where the customers ring in only when they have a particular problem or an enquiry; the complexity of such calls can range from plotting the best route by coach from the west to the east side of the USA to providing customer advice on a range of complex financial or insurance products. Whilst the content demands of such calls can vary, so can the callers. Callers from the USA for example, represent different socio-economic groupings, different ethnic groupings (e.g. USA Hispanic and Chinese speakers represent a high percentage of the adult population, particularly in the Western and Southern states), different genders, age groups and personalities. This huge variety of inbound callers from the USA puts pressure on the Asian CSRs who may have intercultural and linguistic challenges in assisting them. One new CSR, working for an off-shored American insurance company in Manila described the challenges of her new CSR job in the following way:

> At the moment I get anxious about just picking up the phone as I only started 7 weeks ago. You never know who you are going to get next on the phone; it might be a west coast financial advisor wanting advice himself on our range of insurance products or, on the other hand it might be mid-states retiree wanting to cash in a policy ... you need to know your product line; you need to profile your customer right away; is he joking?; is she being sarcastic or is he really mad at me or is she grieving? ... and you need to make sure you comply with all the company regulations and give the customer a good experience. My bonus each year depends on me getting all this right first time round ... most of my friends at this call centre leave within 6 months because they can't hit their quality targets and they burn out.
> *(Manila – female CSR in off-shored USA insurance call centre 2005)*

Within the call centres themselves, the different accounts pose vastly different challenges as mentioned above. In the outsourced 3rd party provider surveyed, there were different 'vertical' accounts – companies whose businesses were finance, insurance, travel and hospitality, retail, IT and telecommunications were all represented. Within each 'vertical', denoting for example 'insurance', there may be three different companies domiciled on-shore with outsourced call centres in Asia. It is common therefore for an outsourced 3rd party provider, for example, to be doing work for three different insurance companies, each with its own culture of doing things, each company with its own products and each with its own customer bases maybe representing different demographic backgrounds and cultural backgrounds. How can all these specialist needs be identified and trained for in the different accounts in the call centre?

The business demands are relentless and expectations high, in terms of good communication skills ensuring customer satisfaction on the calls. Understandably English language communication is viewed as a 'core commodity' for customer service success in these businesses; but how are these CSRs sourced, supported and measured for quality in the call centres? How are the communications trainers trained? And critically, what is the impact on the business if communication goes wrong and customers complain?

Many call centres have quite unrealistic expectations about how quickly and easily CSRs will become comfortable in their transactions and interactions with customers on the phones and how quickly they will perform to the very high standard expected in their regular quality checks on the floor. Research shows the high complexity in call centre work, especially where the CSRs are L2 speakers (Forey and Lockwood 2007; Hood 2010), but unfortunately this is not reflected in how the CSRs are currently being supported in the call centre worksites. This is causing CSR burn-out as evidenced in the very high attrition rates that often exceed a 100 per cent turnover of CSRs (BPAP 2006).

Research into the specific communication needs of L2 CSRs on the phones to L1 customers is still in its infancy as it has only been in the last few years that research has been conducted into communication breakdown on the phones (see, for example, Forey and Lockwood 2007; Clark *et al.* 2008) in off-shored/outsourced call centres. Whilst much of this research is illuminating, the outcomes are slow to be applied to mainstream training in this industry, as this requires call centre training expertise in linking appropriate applied linguistic theory to the call centre practices.

It is not easy to get a job in a call centre and the industry in Asia bemoans low employment rates from frequent recruitment drives where the average conversion rate is between 5 and 10 per cent (BPAP 2006). It has been argued elsewhere that the quality of the assessment tools and processes of the communication measure used in the Asian call centres lack validity, reliability, practicality and therefore internal credibility and value (Lockwood 2008, 2012a). An example of this is where recruitment and training specialists administer an elaborate range of communication assessment tasks, sometimes requiring two days, only to be told by the account manager that the prospective hire is not suitable. As one Indian trainer said:

> Sometimes it can be very frustrating in recruitment as we give the prospective 'hires' grammar tests, pronunciation tests, oral interviews, reading and listening tests and then when we endorse them over to an account often the account manager will say he doesn't think their language is good enough ... maybe because they have some kind of mother tongue interference in their pronunciation or maybe they made a grammar mistake ... no matter how hard we try to convince them they're OK in language they get the final veto ... They clearly don't trust our judgment.
>
> *(Indian female communications trainer – mid-30s)*

The account manager on the floor is ultimately responsible for the quality of English language communication for their account and there is little room for negotiation. In a language audit I carried out in an outsourced 3rd party provider in Manila in July 2004, one of the business objectives was 'to evaluate the existing English language training, induction and support infrastructure set up to support English language communication in Operations' (Lockwood 2004, Audit Report). There were a number of key findings and recommendations. First, the quality and skills of the communications trainers were highly problematic with a small number with low English proficiency skills and a majority of them with no TESOL training nor TESOL classroom experience.

> The quality and skills of the English trainers are insufficient. Problematic pronunciation and language problems were observed and poor language training skills were evident where CSR participants waste time doing speaking activities that have unclear goals and no formative feedback processes for language improvement. CSR communications course participants were rarely corrected and many trainers were very 'teacher-centred' using a lecture type approach to language learning in a language communication classroom where the participants should be the main contributors.
>
> *(Lockwood 2004, Company X Audit Report)*

This is discussed later in this chapter as there appears to be a serious disconnect between the professional expertise required of the English language trainer, their work, and how their role is ultimately viewed and valued within the business. From a business standpoint there appears to be a tension in taking the advice from their internally hired communications trainers who are merely expected to deliver courses with unrealistic outcomes.

What do business stakeholders view to be the problems in English language communication?

There is a pervasive view within the Asian call centre industry that mother tongue interference (MTI) has a deleterious effect on the ability of the CSR to speak good English on the phones. This view is exacerbated by the early politics of O&O where businesses would unrealistically require American accents and names of their newly recruited local CSRs to mask the new O&O service locations. Despite recent research to the contrary, businesses persist in their beliefs that MTI, particularly in the mistakes of pronunciation and grammar production, are the main causes of communication breakdown. As a result, communications training programs often comprise only 'remedial' type English language training often done by giving CSRs grammar accuracy tasks to complete, and by conducting 'accent neutralisation lessons', which are a mixture of accent training and 'drilling out' MTI 'mistakes'. The communications training and coaching on-the-floor courses reflect similar business perceptions of communication need as described above, and unfortunately these are also evident in the recruitment and quality assurance processes. One training manager in a large bank with globalised call centres in India and the Philippines, talked about 'the best of bad practice' syndrome in call centre communications training where the industry all copy each other's programs and are all driven by these narrow beliefs. It is regrettable that this somewhat outmoded paradigm of language understood by the business stakeholders has negatively affected the English language communications agenda to date.

The call centre communication problems, as described in the current research outlined below, show a much broader array of causes, based on sociolinguistic and constructivist views of language.

Who are the communications trainers in the call centres and how are they supported?

In a survey of 45 trainers carried out in 2005 in a large outsourced 3rd party provider in Manila and in an off-shored provider (Manila and Hyderabad), it was found that most (over 80 per cent) of the trainers had been recruited from within the call centres themselves and were either experienced CSRs or quality assurance specialists; some working in concurrent roles. Good CSRs are constantly looking for any kind of career advancement within the centre after working on the phones through the night, and the trainer department is a popular choice. A smaller number of trainers (about 20 per cent) were recruited from outside; these were generally sourced because of their experience in teaching English as a speakers of other languages (TESOL). Of this latter group, the usual TESOL qualification was at a Certificate level (e.g. Certificate of English Language Teaching to Adults – CELTA offered by Cambridge ESOL), and it was rare to find a trainer with a master's level in TESOL. Given the complexity of the TESOL work in curriculum and assessment development in the call centres, this lack of expertise is highly problematic. As one training coordinator said:

> We don't even know what we don't know! ... but we can't say that to the business managers. The accounts managers expect us to fix their problems overnight with a 6-hour course on say 'Showing empathy'; or to eradicate MTI in spoken communication within a few days ... None of this is realistic, we know it can't be done, but we feel both powerless and underprepared for our roles here, we need good ESP training ... we need to know why we can't do these things and how to articulate this to our business managers, and we need to know what is realistic and how to do it!
>
> *(Manila training team coordinator – TESOL trained, outsourced 3rd party call centre)*

Within this outsourced 3rd party call centre there was constant antagonism between the business accounts and the training team; both parties feeling that the other did not understand, nor had the knowledge, nor the skills, to fix the problems on the phones. Such communication problems were jeopardising Service Level Agreements (SLAs). The issue appeared to me to be circular where there seemed to be very little trainer understanding of TESOL principles and applied linguistic theory as they related to the call centre business; and because services provided by these trainers demonstrated little impact, the business managers became sceptical about the advice and support they were getting with their L2 CSR workforce. As well, little research had been completed at this time by applied linguists on the nature of the communication breakdown in the newly O&O call centres as this has only opened up as an applied linguistic research area in the last ten years.

Several disenchanted account managers had resorted to outsourcing their English language communications training to outside commercial and university-based English language specialists with disappointing results. One account manager complained:

> Last year our on-shore (meaning USA) bosses decided not to use the internal training team because they couldn't see any results and things were getting worse; so we decided to contract English language trainers from one of the best universities here in Manila. This ended up being equally problematic, and a lot more expensive. This group of English trainers did not understand our business expectations and just spent the lessons teaching pronunciation and using an 'English for Business' book that bore no relation to the work of call centre agents here ... it was a very expensive mistake. We know we need someone who knows or could find out about the communication needs of our business and tailor a program ... but these people are difficult to find.
>
> *(Manila account manager – male, outsourced 3rd party call centre)*

In-house trainers constantly complained that their roles were difficult. They typically adapted, bought, or imported from the on-shore parent company, developed sets of communications materials. The syllabus for communications training was often fragmented into what was called 'language training' – meaning accent neutralisation and grammar classes; soft skills training – meaning customer care courses usually transported from USA; and USA culture training – meaning fact and figure downloads from the internet. This fragmented organisation reflected a poor level of business understanding of how language, soft skills and intercultural training are necessarily intertwined in communication. The on-shore source of such training materials was also problematic for the following reasons:

> Because of the limited training materials specifically designed for Filipinos, many language and culture training programs in the Philippine call centers use materials from the US. These references and activity manuals on call handling practices and mock transactions are primarily written for native speakers of English with high-level language proficiency. Training topics in telephone support that address service competence include appropriate speech techniques; establishing rapport and personalization of support; and clarity, effectiveness and accuracy of information. The foci of these topics already assume fluency in the English language ... the need is for more grounding of these skills in cross-cultural competence, and consequently language usage ... In sum, Filipino agents need well-designed language and culture training as well as sufficient experience serving American callers to slowly gain cultural awareness that is vital in successful outsourced call center interactions.
>
> *(Friginal 2009: 63)*

The better qualified and experienced communications trainers often bemoan the narrow view taken by the business when they talk about language, but they themselves also seem daunted by the complexity of the problem and many have not been TESOL (Teaching English to Speakers of other Languages) trained:

> In our call centre language, communication, culture and product training are all treated as separate things; we do the language training, meaning grammar accuracy and accent training; quality specialists do communications soft skills training; subject matter experts do the product training and in our call centre an outside vendor comes in and does the culture training as we feel it should be conducted by a native speaker of American English. The result is a mess and I am sure there is a lot of overlap and that we as trainers should have more of a role in communications training ... I mean we do role plays of calls on the phones, so in a sense we are doing all these things ... it's just hard to see how they can all be connected. I mean where does language stop and communications start? The business talks about them as different things but there is definitely an overlap.
>
> *(Manila trainer – male, off-shored call centre)*

Others said:

> I find this job difficult as we are delivering training about 30 hours a week and we have little time to develop materials and revise the syllabus. Even if we could revise the syllabus the business would not allow it as we have to carry out pre and post course language assessments that determine whether the agent will finally get a job. It's not really a training course, it's just another hurdle the CSRs need to jump.
>
> *(Manila female trainer – outsourced 3rd party provider)*

> The business has high expectations of what the trainers can do in such a short period of time ... we often fail our CSRs before they can get started and then if they don't make the first quality score, they are either out or given coaching. Coaching is also problematic because these sessions are usually run by quality specialists who have no training in diagnosing communication issues and giving feedback. I saw one CSR last week who had got a low score because the customer lost his temper and she froze on the call. The caller berated her because she was an Indian and said he couldn't understand her but it wasn't that at all ... but the coach just drilled her on MTI pronunciation mistakes ... the CSR just didn't know how to handle this type of really aggrieved and racist customer. Whose problem is this?
>
> *(Indian female trainer – off-shored call centre)*

Clearly the CSRs struggle through the first few months of doing the job and whilst the trainers can see they have a problem, they have difficulty analysing it and finding the cause; they are therefore challenged when advising the business on how communication can be improved. To exacerbate these problems, the businesses are directed by on-shore managers who use metrics, based on native speaker norms to gauge communication success. Unfortunately, they themselves have little understanding of the needs of non-native speakers of English nor how they should be trained and supported.

In summary, English language communication is a core business commodity for the Asian call centres; yet how to source this at recruitment, how to develop and support it at training and coaching and how to evaluate it for quality assurance safeguards is not well understood. This is why CSR communications programs, based on current research and well-trained trainers and coaches, are key to this success. The content of such training is discussed later in this chapter.

Jane Lockwood

What does the research tell us about the nature of spoken communication and the needs of ESP trainers in the workplace?

(i) The nature of spoken communication in the call centres

Most of the current research into the nature of the discourse of call centre interaction is seen through the sociolinguistic frameworks using conversation analysis (CA) (Clark *et al.* 2008; Friginal 2007, 2008), discourse analysis, corpus studies (Friginal 2007, 2008), and systemic functional linguistics (SFL) (Forey and Lockwood 2007; Wan 2010; Hood and Forey 2008; Hood 2010). This integrated way of looking and analysing language and context has been revealing for the business:

> This all makes sense as our business practices and what you call functional language are part of the same picture ... when I tell the L2 CSR to show more empathy, it's not a 'know what soft skills is' question we train for, it's a 'know how to express it in English' question we train for ... one is content and one is communication skills development
>
> *(European account manager, mid-50s – off-shored call centre)*

An early study carried out by Forey and Lockwood (2007) on 500 USA insurance calls made into the Philippines revealed a set of obligatory and optional moves in the telephone exchange, each of which being realised through a range of lexico-grammatical choices. This research highlighted where the call communication appeared to be most problematic and the 'purpose' and 'servicing' moves, where resolution of the problem typically takes place, were found to be where communication breakdown frequently occurred. They report:

> The caller interactions which appear to cause difficulties for the agents are the complaint itself; frustration, reiteration, vagueness, silence, no feedback, no apology, overuse of technical language and formulaic responses and personalization.
>
> *(Forey and Lockwood 2007: 318)*

Problems with discourse or extensive turn-taking were also revealed in a later study (Lockwood *et al.* 2008) causing breakdown of communication in the Philippine-based calls:

> We suggest that there may be something in the discourse structure of Philippine English that is, at times, incompatible with conventional discourse patterns of Standard American English (SAE). This manifests itself in claims by customers and clients that the (Philippine) CSR sounds as if they are 'beating around the bush' or 'long-winded' in their explanations.
>
> *(p. 235)*

An analysis of rapport development and the use of interpersonal language was undertaken by Hood and Forey (2008) using Appraisal Theory (Martin and White 2005). Appraisal Theory attempts to highlight in the language system where interpersonal meaning is made and the short extract below is illustrative of this. Here the caller is having difficulty in paying an account that is being billed in her husband's, rather than in her company's name. Whilst the customer does not openly lose her temper, there is implicit anger in her responses, for example, frustration is nuanced in her word stress (as indicated below) and intonation patterns; by uncontracting negative auxiliaries and in repeating herself.

CALLER: **No one** seems to be able to work out the right account on my payment ... it **should** be under the company name Litmus Construction Ltd ... I've made this request **so many times** and **nothing** happens.

AGENT: Uh, because we can actually change the account ... this account name ...

CALLER: But they **haven't**. I've done it already. ... a **number** of times. If they were changing it, they would have **done** it by **now**, and they wouldn't have sent me a new invoice, **which has not happened**

Hood (2010) has also used Appraisal Theory to investigate the issue of using names to build rapport; this is an area for which many call centres provide specific training in the form of prescribing CSRs to use the customer's first name at least three times on the call. Business intuition and prescription, however, is not borne out in the research. This issue of naming appears to rely very much on the caller personality and call concern where the naming may change from formal to casual depending on what is being said as well as the context. In other words, CSRs need to make good judgments about how to address their callers. Using a systemic functional linguistic framework, Wan (2010) also uses an SFL framework to demonstrate how pronunciation and voice quality can make meaning on the phones: 'The purpose of voice quality analysis is to allow us to understand how voice quality features construe interpersonal meaning within a particular context' (p. 115).

Elias (2010) provides an analysis of current intercultural training in call centre training. The first point he makes is that, given a sociolinguistic framework in training (e.g. genre-based approaches and SFL theory), intercultural issues will be grounded in the interaction on the phones and will be evidenced in the language. In a sociolinguistic framework, language, behaviour and culture are continuously negotiated in a dialogic process. He says:

> In the BPO context and in call centres in particular, the ideational meaning (the field or content of what is being transacted and discussed); the tenor, i.e. the interpersonal meaning (the complex relationship between the CSR and the customer) and the mode (the textual unfolding of the call on the phone) interact with each other to produce very specific intercultural registers.
>
> *(p. 160)*

He is critical of much of the current culture training in the BPO industry as he claims it relies solely on information and facts downloaded from websites. He proposes a multidimensional intercultural training framework that encapsulates language, motivation, behaviours, skills and selected knowledge for syllabus development (Byram 2000; Earley and Ang 2003).

These studies all promote a sociolinguistic paradigm as a way of understanding the dynamic interrelatedness of context, culture, soft skills, language choices, and pronunciation in something called 'English language communication' on the phones. Such an understanding enriches not only curriculum and assessment development (Lockwood 2010, 2012b), but, just as importantly, it informs and enriches the professional development agenda for the call centre trainers.

(ii) English for Specific Purposes research

English for Specific Purposes (ESP) is a branch of applied linguistics that has developed to delineate boundaries between generic English language teaching (ELT) programmes and the ever-increasing number of tailored programmes for business, for study and for occupational purposes. However, over the last decade this construct has become more refined with a strong interdisciplinary approach, largely in response to the demands for improved English language skills in the globalised business and professional sectors. In recent times, ESP research and practice has been emphasising the role of cultural, institutional and discipline specific practices as their starting points; St John (1996) says:

> An interdisciplinary approach (to ESP for business) is called for to take account of language, interpersonal communication skills, business know-how and cultural issues.
>
> (St John 1996: 3)

However, it is not well researched;

> Business English is an area of ESP that is relatively poorly researched. Rigorous linguistic analysis is fragmented and is more frequently based on written forms of language such as correspondence, annual reports and articles in business journals. Some kinds of analyses have been carried out with respect to the language of meetings and discussions, but there is still little to support course developers beyond their first-hand experience gained in the field.
>
> (Ellis and Johnson 1994: 8)

Bargiela-Chiappini and Nickerson (1999) also call for ESP and business English in particular, to become theoretically grounded drawing on discourse analysis, rhetorical analysis, organisational communication and social reconstructivism. In call centres the business perspective and the context of the sites themselves have also been important in understanding the communication needs of the CSRs. The bridging of what Bhatia has called the 'integration of discursive and professional practices' (2008: 161) into critical genre analysis is also becoming a preoccupation in ESP and is relevant to the subject of this chapter.

(iii) The nature of teacher expertise and its development

There is a broad literature exploring the developmental stages in teacher expertise and changes in teacher perceptions about their professional performance over time (Adams 1992; Bereiter and Scadamalia 1993; Berliner 1995; Huberman 1993; Tsui 2003) as well as a literature investigating the nature of the development, in a more general sense, of professional expertise (Dreyfus and Dreyfus 1996; Eraut 1994). Whilst the education literature is mostly based in the school and college system, the findings, combined with those in a non-education sector, are relevant to this chapter. There appears, however, to be little research completed in workplace settings regarding the formal professional training support of workplace trainers, and the developmental stages of English language communications trainers in the call centre workplace.

A starting point may be to look at the developmental models that have proved useful in other occupations. Dreyfus (1997) and Dreyfus and Dreyfus (1996) argued that 'knowing how' not 'knowing that' is at the very core of human experience. They proposed a five-stage model of skills acquisition from novice to expert summarised as follows:

> Thus according to our description of skill acquisition, the novice and advanced beginner exercise no judgment, the competent performer judges by means of conscious deliberation,

and those who are proficient or expert make judgments based upon their prior concrete experiences in a manner that defies explanation.

(Dreyfus and Dreyfus 1996: 36)

This chapter does not attempt to unpack the detailed implications of a developmental model for training the call centre industry but this literature provides a useful framework for conceptualising how the 'what' could be organised in a systematic and long-term professional development programme for call centre trainers and coaches. This is an interesting and important area of research for the industry going forward.

Given what we know about the call centre worksite and how the research may assist, let us now unpack the knowledge and skills set required by call centre communications trainers.

What is the knowledge and skills set required by call centre communications trainers?

The role of the worksite English language communications trainers is a highly demanding one (Nunan 1988; Dudley-Evans and St John 1998; Boswood and Marriott 1994; Belcher 2009).

> ESP business practitioners need to reconceptualise their task as language teachers and gain access to the discourse communities of business people, training professionals and other ESP business practitioners ... This understanding must include: the values of the community e.g. returns on investment and value for money; operational details, such as the influence of budgetary planning on training courses; and relationships within the community ... In dealing with training managers, ESP practitioners must appreciate the training paradigm, specifically the concepts of accountability, corporate orientation and human resources management, budgetary realities, training objectives, professionalism in training, as well as expectations of training managers and business stakeholders in terms of course design.
>
> *(Boswood and Marriott 1994: 16)*

As discussed in the previous section, there is a strong interdisciplinary requirement for working within this industry. Trainers who have been excellent CSRs are ideal candidates for training prospective CSRs in communications skills. But what knowledge and skills do they need from the disciplines of applied linguistics and education to do this well?

I would suggest that the call centre worksite communications trainer needs to consider her/himself as having multiple and concurrent roles within the worksite as follows, acquiring each in a systematic and staged way. These different roles are described below.

1 The trainer as ESP curriculum and syllabus developer

As part of my doctoral studies, which focused on curriculum and evaluation processes in Hong Kong workplaces, I needed to conceptualise a way of looking at the very complex tasks of ESP syllabus design in Hong Kong workplaces. Clearly, the demands on the ESP practitioner delivering generic English for business courses for career development (e.g. Business English Certificate – Cambridge ESOL) to bank employees for career development purposes, is very different from developing a course for bank tellers that addresses problematic communication service problems and which needs to show performance improvement. 30.1 provides a way into thinking about the ESP syllabus design process:

	Language performance training with business focus		
GENERIC	Short training packages with performance gain outcomes e.g. presentation skills; meeting skills	Short tailor-made packages for individual workplace settings with performance gain outcomes e.g. telephoning skills for Hong Kong gas company; sales assistants courses for a UK retail outlet	SPECIFIC
	Teaching programmes with proficiency gain outcomes e.g. Business English certificate programmes (100 hours) offered at different CEFR levels	Teaching programmes specialised to an industry/professional association standards with proficiency outcomes e.g. Writing courses (100 hours) for accountants (Hong Kong Society of Accountants)	
	Language proficiency teaching with education focus		

Figure 30.1 Workplace ESP syllabus development

This figure illustrates English for Specific Purposes (ESP) workplace programs plotted on a matrix with two axes. The first axis is drawn horizontally from generic to specific; this axis represents the continuum of specialisation of the course design required by the workplace. The second and vertical axis denotes whether the needs and expectations for the training are education (meaning more language proficiency development based) or business oriented (meaning more language performance based). I have suggested earlier that in high stakes business-oriented language training that requires performance improvement or change (e.g. specific accounts problems in call centres), there is more demand on the knowledge and skills of an ESP trainer than courses that are language proficiency based (e.g. near hire training in call centres) and outcomes centre on language skills improvement. This is because the trainer cannot simply draw on pre-packaged materials and is required to analyse the authentic data as a way into establishing the needs of the target group and what should be taught.

This detailed representation of the ESP syllabus framework for the call centre industry is contained in Figure 30.2 below:

The more specific and performance-based the syllabus, the more likely the trainer needs to be a subject matter expert or a subject matter expert needs to be collaborating with the applied linguistic expert. This model can also be used to conceptualise the professional development needs of call centre trainers and where to place them initially as they develop enhanced ESP knowledge and skills.

There are two fundamental issues to be considered before the syllabus can be designed, delivered and evaluated. First, the curriculum developer needs to be intimately aware and experienced in:

	Language performance training with call centre focus		
GENERIC	**Short training packages with performance gain outcomes** e.g. Dealing with irate customers; showing empathy; active listening	**Short tailor-made packages for individual call centre accounts with performance gain outcomes** e.g. Upselling in the Sincere Insurance product X; collections targets for Bank Z. **Pre-hire** training package in call centres	**SPECIFIC**
	Teaching programmes with proficiency gain outcomes e.g. Near-hire training to reach a designated benchmark level	**Teaching programmes specialised to call centres industry/professional association standards with proficiency outcomes** e.g. TESDA call centre qualifying communications programme	
	Language proficiency teaching with education focus		

Figure 30.2 Call centre ESP syllabus development

(i) The **curriculum context** of the business requirements and subject matter related to the work of the call centre agent for whom the course is targeted.
(ii) The **curriculum construct**, which relates to the relevant and appropriate theoretical constructs (in this case taken from business management, applied linguistics and adult education).

Unlike school and college settings where there is a centralised curriculum planning process where experts design the syllabus and develop the materials and teachers implement the programmes in the classroom, workplace language trainers perform all these functions.

2 The trainer as applied linguistic expert and researcher

Given the small amount of applied linguistic research into the nature of the call centre interaction and transaction, trainers working in this sector need the appropriate tools of discourse analyses when working with the authentic calls from the various accounts in their workplaces. Many have what has been called 'first-hand experience gained in the field' (Ellis and Johnson 1994: 8) but there is a paucity of workplace trainers in the call centre industry with relevant research and applied linguistic skills such as discourse analysis. Developing such skills and turning targeted research into usable English language materials, tools and processes for workplace trainers is in high demand.

Jane Lockwood

> With our language communications team we are now looking for something that is more sophisticated than base-line TESOL training of how to deliver generic pre-hire English language communications sessions. We know our workplace situation is unique; we have over 45 different accounts all clamouring for high level English language communications services ... but it requires going into those different accounts, listening to the business needs from the account manager's and CSRs' points of view; gathering and analyzing the authentic data and turning the findings into training and coaching materials ... we need help in getting our language team to the point where they can produce highly specific syllabus documents for each account in their caseload ... typically they have 4–5 accounts. We brought in ESP specialists from a well-known university, but it didn't help ... our trainers spent all the time teaching them about the context ...
>
> *(Training manager – 3rd party provider – Manila 2012)*

How much subject/content knowledge an ESP trainer needs of the specialist area they are training for remains hotly debated (Dudley-Evans and St John 1998; Weigle and Nelson 2001; Belcher 2009). Training in the call centre industry, which is the subject of this chapter, relies on trainers and coaches clearly understanding that English language communication is a core commodity for its business. The success of each call, as measured regularly by customer satisfaction surveys, can make or break the business as quality targets for communication are written into the service level agreements (SLAs), so excellent performance is key. The higher the business expectation, the more in-depth knowledge and skills seem to be required of call centre trainers. However, some existing ESP courses across different call centre accounts that I have seen appear to be little more than lists of technical vocabulary and terms used in the account. As one senior trainer in a call centre said:

> We have lists of insurance terms and jargon for our insurance accounts; we have lists of retails terms and jargon for our retail accounts ... but it doesn't work ... this isn't the real specialist language of what is going on and technical vocab knowledge doesn't seem to be connected to communication difficulty on the calls ... most CSRs say they learn this technical stuff and jargon in their product training.
>
> *(Filipina senior trainer – 3rd party call centre)*

Using a knowledge of sociolinguistic construct(s) to understand the spoken text in call centre accounts is key to the ESP trainer. As research to date has demonstrated, sociolinguistic lines of enquiry have all contributed to a deeper understanding of why communication is happening.

3 The language communications trainer as internal consultant

From observations made during the last decade in the call centre industry in both the Philippines and India, language communications trainers have regrettably lacked business credibility. Call centre businesses currently have difficulty in relying on their own internal training team for advice because of a lack of applied linguistic professional development and resort to paying dearly for outside advice, which also is mostly not research based (Lockwood 2012b). Ultimately, investing in and developing internal trainers to a stage where they are able to convincingly persuade businesses that the knowledge and skills reside in them when it comes to effective English communications improvement would ensure that their credibility as internal consultants is established. One trainer said:

> We need a course in assertiveness training ... we get treated as second class citizens here and no one values our opinions.
>
> *(Female Filipina trainer, mid-30s, off-shore bank)*

4 The trainer as trainer and coach

Call centre trainers have the dual role of trainer and coach. These roles can demand different kinds of knowledge and skills as follows. As can be seen in Figure 30.2, training programmes for new hires in the call centres fall into three main categories. First what has become known as 'near-hire' training. This category relates to those courses that aim to ensure language proficiency gains in listening and speaking in English (see Figure 30.2). These courses have been mounted by the call centres because they are having difficulty getting the required numbers at recruitment who are ready for work on the phones. They have therefore made a business decision to invest in English language proficiency development. The second kind of course is 'pre-hire' training (see Figure 30.2). This relates to language 'performance' training that is directly related to the work CSRs will be expected to do on the phones. Typically this performance training will take place at the same time as the account product training and this includes language, soft skills and intercultural training as outlined previously. The third kind of training course relates to highly specific training that is 'account specific' (see Figure 30.2). This is possibly the most challenging training as an analysis of where communication is breaking down in the account and/or where new training needs to be developed because a new business requirement is needed. Here, both an intimate knowledge of the business as well as a good grasp of applied linguistic theory and practice is needed.

Trainers also provide a quality assurance function in mounting coaching courses for individual CSRs who are not meeting their targets. Some call centres require all their CSRs to undertake regular coaching sessions, while others provide it on a needs basis. However, the coach is expected to listen to problematic recorded calls, diagnose the problems, provide feedback and devise relevant follow up improvement tasks for the CSR. These are high order skills requiring a good knowledge of applied linguistics as well as the research to date on communication breakdown on the phones. It also requires an understanding of how language communication may develop and which problems to deal with first; as one senior coach said:

> The account manager wants a 'quick fix' of language problems on the floor because these are affecting the team's performance targets and the business ... but if a CSR has just joined and is new there is no way that these problems will be fixed overnight ... from my experience it takes 3–6 months for new CSRs to get comfortable and confident on the phones
>
> *(Senior Indian coach – mid-40s)*

The adult learning literature (Eraut 1994; Dreyfus and Dreyfus 1996) would corroborate this view in that novice professionals develop a feeling of competence in their work only after few weeks/months of working on the job. Why should CSRs be any different?

5 The trainer as assessor and program evaluator

Trainers also take on the role of language assessor in the call centre workplace. The 'core commodity' of the call centres is good English language communication skills, which means sourcing it at recruitment; training for it at near- and pre-hire programs; coaching it on the floor and measuring it for quality assurance puts great demands on English language assessment tools and processes (Lockwood 2008, 2010, 2012a). It also puts great demand on the trainers who need to understand, use and support others in developing good language assessment skills for the purpose(s) they are required. For example, one trainer in a large call centre in Manila complained:

> Our QA team are not trained to understand and use the new assessment tool and they keep feeding back on MTI mistakes which bear no relation to why the communication is breaking down ... if they understood the assessment criteria well, they would be doing something very different in their coaching sessions ... I said this to Stan (account manager) yesterday and he asked me to train them up using XYZ.
> *(Filipina Trainer – 30s, 3rd party provider)*

It is often said that when business budgets get tight, training departments are often the first to suffer cuts. In the call centre industry it is crucial that English language trainers promote themselves as protectors of the quality of the business' core commodity of language communication. In order to do this, demonstrating how the language services and skills offer direct benefits to the business is key (Kirkpatrick 1994). For example, in one account in Manila, the trainers were able to demonstrate improved quality as measured on the internal scorecard and CSATs as a result of a new coaching programme that introduced improved measures to diagnose interactional, discourse and intercultural issues.

> For the first time the account manager saw some hard data that convinced him that we are adding value to the business and he is sharing much more information with us now and asking our advice ... actually we are getting busier and busier
> *(Canadian trainer, USA bank call centre – based in Manila)*

Discussion and conclusions

Business worksites such as the call centres in India and the Philippines remain under-researched and there is much yet to be learned. However, given that English language communication is such a central requirement to this new business now employing second language speakers, the pressure to recruit, train for and evaluate CSR English communication ability is key; and much of this work requires the expertise of the English language trainers. Therefore training these English language communications trainers is of critical importance to the call centre industry. It would seem that the following ten key theoretical and practical areas would be relevant in training and supporting teams of trainers in the call centre industry and this content may set a clear agenda for professional development in the call centre industry:

i **Current knowledge of the nature of language theory and how it works in different settings.** In carrying out analyses of authentic data of call centre exchanges (including email exchanges), discourse analysis skills are required as underpinned by a sociolinguistic language construct e.g. conversational analysis, systemic functional linguistics.
ii **Skills development with specific focus on listening and speaking.** Whilst there are demands in some accounts for reading and writing (e.g. email exchange and chat online); most of the customer service work to date is carried out on the phones. Profiling the customer in the first few seconds of the call and providing efficient customer care, sometimes called 'soft skills', is key.
iii **Language learning theory.** For trainers who are providing near-hire training and pre-training, a knowledge of how language is acquired and how language choices may be made depending on the proficiency level is key.

iv **Adult learning principles.** Not only is an understanding of learner styles and strategies important in acquiring new skills in adult learners, but also an appreciation of how professional knowledge and skills are developed will ensure that trainer support programmes correlate with the existing stage of development of the trainers. Clearly asking novice trainers to develop highly specific ESP programmes is beyond their capabilities.
v **Issues in syllabus design for ESP.** Some syllabus planning e.g. the adaptation of syllabus documents for generic near- and pre-hire proficiency development as illustrated in Figure 30.2 is an easier task to carry out than highly specific and tailored ESP course development that relies on the outcomes of needs analysis (business and linguistic) of particular call centre accounts. This process also requires the ability to transfer research findings into teaching and learning materials.
vi **Intercultural understanding and its relationship to language.** Using frameworks for intercultural training that look beyond the 'facts' approach prevalent in many industry courses requires an understanding of how culture is manifested in language and interaction.
vii **Interdisciplinary approaches**; i.e. the interface of business requirements and communication need. Understanding the business needs of the call centres is critical to the advice given by communications trainers to the business stakeholders. Trainer credibility revolves around being able to persuade the account managers, for example, to train for quality improvements in communications or to modify a particular business requirement that may be compromising smooth communication.
viii **Language communications assessment.** Understanding how formative and summative assessment can inform recruitment, placement and quality assurance is a basic requirement in the call centres. Using, modifying and developing communications assessment are key skills for trainers in this industry.
ix **Language programme evaluation.** In workplace training, linking the outcomes of training to individual trainee success is only part of the process of workplace communications evaluation. Linking the outcomes of training to improved workplace performance is a key requirement. This ensures the business sees value for money in its training investments, thus ensuring training is not a marginalised activity.
x **Research methodology.** Needs analysis research for each new ESP call centre account is required in an ongoing way by the trainers. As discussed, the research carried out to date in the emerging Asian call centre industry is in its infancy; practitioners in the field are ideally situated to carry this research agenda forward.

How such training and development content can be systematic is another big question. Perhaps we should apply the same principles of adult learning and a staged development theory of professional expertise acquisition (Eraut 1994; Dreyfus and Dreyfus 1996; Dreyfus 1997). One large bank with off-shored call centres in India, Manila, Southern China and Malaysia has employed over 100 English language communications trainers in the region and has been working on this issue of how specialist work and training is allocated:

> We initially put all our trainers through the British Council's CELTA programme. Although this was expensive and although many of our trainers did not require the kind of classroom management skills needed for TESOL, it was a beginning and it seemed to be the only thing around. But then we needed almost immediately something more in depth and more geared towards the specific English language training issues in call centres. Some of our trainers just deliver programmes that have been prepared for them, but they still need to know about the principles behind the programmes ... if they don't understand these, they don't use the materials properly. And then other trainers go into accounts and

shadow their work and come up with highly specialised training packages to meet very particular needs ... this is much harder and requires specific support ... and can be a very creative process. Finally we want a sustainable model – so we may need online professional development support for our trainers and links with universities that know our field.

(Indian training manager – doctorate in applied linguistics)

The hierarchy of training needs for this group of industry trainers appears to fall into three main categories. First, the fundamental need of all trainers to understand the theoretical principles and to use appropriate classroom strategies to deliver prepared programmes in near- and pre-hire training programmes. These same trainers may also be asked to administer prepared assessments as part of recruitment and/or end of course summative assessment, in which case it is important for them to also understand the theoretical construct upon which the assessments are based; these courses may be termed TESOL support programmes. It is interesting to note that in CELTA training, there is much emphasis on the practical classroom skills of TESOL with little attention to the theoretical principles of language syllabus and assessment development. Interestingly, a large proportion of the BPO trainers have come up through the ranks of product training, quality assurance support and coaching and demonstrate confidence in managing small group and classroom dynamics.

A second tier of training needs lies in the development and adaptation of syllabus documents, materials and assessments. This will involve all of the above, but may pay special attention to the adaptation of existing materials and the skills of language syllabus and assessment development for specific accounts with specific problems within the call centre; or what we would call English for Specific Purposes course developers. This group would also perhaps be part of the quality assurance team providing on-the-spot diagnostic feedback to individual CSRs experiencing communication difficulties; these may be termed ESP support programmes.

A possible third tier may comprise those trainers with TESOL breadth and depth in the call centre context who are researching and creating new communications products and services to meet industry need. It is perhaps not appropriate to think of this group requiring formal support unless undertaking supervised research awards or carrying out funded research and development projects; but perhaps providing access to research articles and research opportunities and possible postgraduate research opportunities within the academy.

As long as applied linguistic research based in businesses remains scant, the issue of supporting TESOL professionals at the workplace, from outside (e.g. the academy) will be problematic. To overcome this, businesses may need to allow applied linguists from universities easier access to the communication issues and consider partnering programmes that meet the needs of workplace trainers. As one business manager said:

I can see that the industry needs expert applied linguistic professionals to advise on recruitment, training and quality assurance ... the problem is we've got mostly novice and competent deliverers. My question is, do we grow them or do we outsource all this to specialists in the field ... I don't know. We need to get universities more involved to help us.

Related topics

discourse variation in professional communities; a situated genre approach for business communication education; business communication; off-shore outsourcing

Key readings

Belcher, D. (ed.) (2009). *English for Specific Purposes in Theory and Practice*. University of Michigan Press. (This is an excellent edited collection of ESP articles exploring new paradigms for ESP in the university and workplace sectors. Very good overview introduction provided by the editor and Afterword by Brian Paltridge.)

Forey, G. and Lockwood, J. (2007). '"I'd love to put someone in jail for this": An initial investigation of English needs in the Business Processing Outsourcing (BPO) industry', *English for Specific Purposes*, 26, 308–26. (This is one of the first studies carried out on call centre authentic data in the Philippines revealing the generic moves and linguistic features of successful calls where the customer services representatives (CSRs) are second language speakers.)

Hood, S. and Forey, G. (2008). 'The interpersonal dynamics of call centre interactions: Co-constructing the rise and fall of emotion', *Discourse and Communication*, 2(4), 389–409. (Through the application of Systemic Functional Linguistics (SFL) theory, the authors demonstrate how interpersonal attitude is realised in call centre exchanges. This is then followed by comments on how this research may be applied to training CSRs.)

Lockwood, J. (2012b). 'Developing an English for Specific Purpose curriculum for Asian call centres: How the theory can inform practice', *English for Specific Purposes*, 31, 14–24. (This article explores the theoretical constructs, with particular reference to sociolingiuistic theory, that have informed the practical process of developing an English for Specific Purposes curriculum for the call centre industry.)

Tsui, A. (2003). *Understanding Expertise in Teaching: Case Studies of ESL Studies of ESL Teachers*, Cambridge University Press. (Presents a comprehensive framework to explore the developing expertise of teacher expertise. This can be applied to settings outside the school education context and is particularly useful in understanding how trainers need to operate and their work on professional workplace settings.)

Bibliography

Adams, R. (1992) 'Teacher development: A look at changes in teachers' perceptions across time', *Journal of Teacher Education*, 23(4), 40–43.

Bargiela-Chiappini, F. and Nickerson, C. (eds) (1999) *Writing Business: Genres, Media and Discourses*, London: Longman.

Bereiter, C. and Scadamalia, M. (1993). *Surpassing Ourselves: An Inquiry into the Nature and Implications of Expertise*, Illinois: Open Court.

Belcher, D. (ed.) (2009) *English for Specific Purposes in Theory and Practice*, Ann Arbor: University of Michigan.

Berliner, D. C. (1995). 'The development of pedagogical expertise', in P. K. Siu and P. T. K. Tam (eds), *Quality in Education: Insights from Different Perspectives* (pp. 1–14), Hong Kong: Hong Kong Educational Research Association.

Bhatia, V. (2008). 'Genre analysis: ESP and professional practice', *ESP Journal*, 27, 161–74.

Boswood, T. and Marriott, A. (1994) 'Ethnography for special purposes: Teaching and training in parallel', *ESP Journal*, 13(1), 3–21.

Business Processing Association of the Philippines (BPAP) (2006a). *Annual Report*. Available at www.bpab.org.ph (retrieved 7 February 2009).

BPAP (2006b). 'English is not the problem! Communication skills in the BPO industry', *BPAP Annual Report*. Available at www.bpab.org/bpap/bpaprese.arch.asp (retrieved 28 August 2006).

Byram, M. (2000). 'Assessing intercultural competence in language teaching', in *Sprogforum*, 6, 8–13.

Clark, C., Rogers, P., Murfett, U. and Ang, S. (2008). *Is Courtesy Not Enough? 'Solidarity' in Call Center Interactions*, University of Michigan, Ross School of Business Working Paper.

Dreyfus, H. (1997). 'Models of expert performance', in C. E. Zsambok and G. Klien (eds), *Naturalistic Decision Making* (pp. 17–28), New Jersey: Lawrence Erlbaum.

Dreyfus, H. L. and Dreyfus, S. E. (1996). 'The relationship of theory and practice in the acquisition of skill', in P. Benner, C. A. Tanner and C. A. Chesla (eds), *Expertise in Nursing Practice* (pp. 29–48), New York: Springer Publishing Company.

Dudley-Evans, T. and St John, M. J. (1998). *Development in English for Specific Purposes: A Multi-disciplinary Approach*, New York: Cambridge University Press.

Earley, P. and Ang, S. (2003). *Cultural Intelligence: Individual Interactions Across Borders*, Stanford: Stanford University Press.

Elias, N. (2010) 'Reconceptualizing culture for workplace communication', in G. Forey and J. Lockwood (eds), *Globalization, Communication and the Workplace: Talking Across the World*, UK: Continuum.

Ellis, M. and Johnson, C. (1994) *Teaching Business English*, Oxford: Oxford University Press.

Eraut, M. (1994). *Developing Professional Knowledge and Competence*, UK: The Falmer Press.
Forey, G. and Lockwood, J. (2007). '"I'd love to put someone in jail for this": An initial investigation of English needs in the Business Processing Outsourcing (BPO) Industry', *English for Specific Purposes, 26*, 308–26.
Friginal, E. (2007). 'Outsourced call centres and English in the Philippines', *World Englishes, 26*(3), 331–45.
——(2008). 'Linguistic variation in the discourse of outsourced call centers', *Discourse Studies, 10*, 715–36.
——(2009). 'Threats to the sustainability of the outsourced call centre industry in the Philippines: Implications for language policy', *Language Policy, 8*, 51–68.
Hamp-Lyons, L. and Lockwood, J. (2009). 'The workplace, the society and the wider world: The offshoring and outsourcing industry', *Annual Review of Applied Linguistics (ARAL), 29*, 145–167.
Hood, S. (2010). 'Naming and negotiating relationships in call centre talk', in G. Forey and J. Lockwood (eds), *Globalization, Communication and the Workplace: Talking Across the World* (pp. 88–105), London, Continuum.
Hood, S. and Forey, G. (2008). 'The interpersonal dynamics of call centre interactions: Co-constructing the rise and fall of emotion', *Discourse and Communication, 2*(4), 389–409.
Huberman, M. (1993) 'Steps towards a developmental model of the teaching career', in L. Kremer-Hayon, H. Vonk and R. Fessler (eds), *Teacher Professional Development: A Multiple Perspective Approach* (pp. 93–118), Amsterdam: Swets and Zeitlinger.
Hyon, S. (1996). 'Genre in three traditions: Implications for ESL', *TESOL Quarterly*, 693–722.
Jenkins, J. (2005) *World Englishes*, London: Routledge.
Kirkpatrick, D. (1994). *Evaluating Training Programs: The Four Levels*, USA: Berrett-Koehler Publishers.
Lockwood, J. (2004). 'Sykes audit report', Unpublished.
——(2008). 'What does the Business Processing Outsourcing (BPO) Industry want from English language assessment?' *Prospect, 23*(2) (Special Issue), 67–78.
——(2010). 'Consulting assessment for the BPO industry in the Philippines', in G. Forey and J. Lockwood (eds), *Globalization, Communication and the Workplace* (pp. 221–41), UK: Continuum International Publishing Group Ltd.
——(2012a). 'Are we getting the right people for the job? A study of English Language recruitment assessment practices in the Business Processing Outsourcing (BPO) sector: India and the Philippines', *Journal of Business Communication, 49*(2), 107–27.
——(2012b). 'Developing an English for specific purpose curriculum for Asian call centres: How the theory can inform practice', *English for Specific Purposes, 31*, 14–24.
——(2013). 'Assessment of business and professional Language for Specific Purposes', in C. A. Chapelle (ed.), *The Encyclopedia of Applied Linguistics*, Oxford, UK: Wiley-Blackwell.
Lockwood, J., Forey, G. and Price, H. (2008). 'Englishes in the Philippine Business Processing Outsourcing industry: Issues, opportunities and research', in M. L. S. Bautista and K. Bolton (eds), *Philippine English: Linguistic and Literary Perspectives* (pp.157–72), Hong Kong: Hong Kong University Press.
Lockwood, J., Forey, G. and Elias, N (2009). 'Call centre measurement processes in non-English speaking contexts', in D. Belcher (ed.), *English for Specific Purposes in Theory and Practice* (pp. 143–65), USA: University of Michigan Press.
Martin, J. (1992). *English Text: System and Structure*, Amsterdam: John Benjamins.
Martin, J. and White, P. (2005). *The Language of Evaluation: Appraisal in English*, London: Palgrave Macmillan.
NASSCOM (2009). 'Perspectives 2020: Transform Business: Transform India (Executive Summary)', Available at www.nasscom.in (retrieved April 2012).
NASSCOM (2012). Available at www.nasscom.in/indian-itbpo-industry.
Nunan, D. (1988). *Syllabus Design*, Oxford: OUP.
Oxford Business Group (2012). *The Report – The Philippines*. Available at www.oxfordbusinessgroup.com.
Pal, M. and Buzzanell, P. (2008). 'The Indian call center experience: A case study in changing discourses of identity, identification, and career in a global context', *Journal of Business Communication, 45*, 31–58.
Paltridge, B. (2009). 'Afterword: Where have we come from and where are we now?' in D. Belcher (ed.), *English for Specific Purposes in Theory and Practice* (pp. 289–96), Ann Arbor: University of Michigan Press.
St John, M. J. (1996). 'Business is booming: Business English in the 1990s', *ESP Journal,15*(1), 3–18.
Tsui, A. (2003). *Understanding Expertise in Teaching: Case Studies of ESL Studies of ESL Teachers*, UK: Cambridge University Press.
Wan, J. (2010) 'Call centre discourse: Graduation in relation to voice quality and attitudinal profile', in G. Forey and J. Lockwood (eds), *Globalization, Communication and the Workplace: Talking Across the World* (pp. 106–124), London: Continuum.
Weigle, S. C. and Nelson, G. (2001). 'Academic writing for university examinations', in I. Leki (ed.), *Academic Writing Programs* (pp. 121–36), Alexandria, VA: TESOL.

31
Credentialing of communication professionals

Saul Carliner

Introduction

Credentialing of practising professionals is one of the most significant developments in the practice of professional communication since the 1980s. Since then, most of the major professional associations in the field have launched programs to provide communication professionals with some external means of validating their professional skill. (One launched its program in the 1960s.) Almost every major association serving communication professionals offers a credential, including the International Association of Business Communicators (IABC) (which serves employee communications specialists and communications generalists), Public Relations Society of America (PRSA), Council of Science Editors (formerly the Council of Biology Editors), American Medical Writers Association (AMWA), Board of Editors in Life Sciences (BELS), tekom (the German organisation for technical communicators) and, most recently, the Society for Technical Communication (STC).

These organisations have the same general motivations for offering credentials: to formally acknowledge the skills of professionals, many of whom work in the field without formal degrees in communication; provide professionals with a means of distinguishing themselves in the job market; and providing employers with a means of distinguishing qualified candidates for open positions.

In this chapter, I explore these credentialing programs. In it, I first provide a foundation for a discussion of credentialing, defining the various types of credentials available then identifying the certifications available to professional communicators. Next, I critically explore the concept of credentialing for professional communicators. After describing the arguments for and against credentialing, I explore several ramifications of credentials for professional communicators, some of immediate practical concern, others with longer-term implications. When exploring certification, I do so from the perspective of someone who recently chaired the committee certifying policies and procedures for certification of training and development professionals in Canada, and served as a member of the founding board of the Society for Technical Communication Certification Commission.

521

Background

This section provides the basis for a discussion of credentialing and its impact on professional communication. In it, I first define the concept of credentialing and describe the different types of credentials for practising professionals, then identify the specific credentials available to people working in the field.

The concept of credentialing

For the purpose of this discussion, credentialing refers to programs that formally recognise professional accomplishments of communication professionals. All credentialing efforts try to demonstrate that these professionals bring unique expertise. (In other discussions, credentialing has a more narrow definition, referring to the process of licensing or certifying professionals.) Several types of credentials exist, most of which are available to professional communicators. These include certification, licensure, certificates, degrees and accreditation.

Certification

Certification is the validation of demonstrated competence in a particular field by a third party assessor (Hale 2000). Certification candidates demonstrate competence through one or more of these means:

- Passing examinations. These examinations typically assess familiarity with a *body of knowledge*, a 'complete set of concepts, terms, and activities that make up a professional domain' (Coppola 2010: 12).
- Demonstrating skills. In some certifications of communication skills, applicants are provided with a work-related situation and asked to prepare a sample communication product or some similar deliverable. In other certifications, applicants submit an existing work sample. In both types of certifications, applicants also provide an explanation of the choices made while producing their work product. Assessors evaluate the resulting work product and explanation to ensure that they conform to the stated criteria. A skill demonstration like this often comprises part of an overall assessment that also involves an examination.
- Submitting a portfolio for evaluation by external assessors and that validates the originality of the work. The portfolio assessment operates similarly to a skill demonstration, except that applicants have produced the work products for their jobs rather exclusively for the certification. As in a skill demonstration, applicants explain their choices in addition to providing work samples. Assessors use established criteria to assess the work samples and explanations, just as they use when assessing a skill demonstration.

Candidates who successfully complete a certification process are required to adhere to the code of ethics for their profession. These codes of ethics encourage honest and forthright practice of the profession in accordance with the law and typically address issues such as the responsibilities to the client, users, and employers, as well as to other communicators and the profession (AMWA 2008; IABC 2012a; PRSA 2012a). Most codes of ethics for professions with certification also include provisions to sanction certified professionals who violate the code.

Most certification programs also require that professionals maintain their certifications by participating in ongoing professional development activities. Some organisations only recognise completion of formal continuing education programs while others accept a wide range of activities, including continuing education courses, independent study, service to professional organisations, and the production of new knowledge (that is, publishing articles and books) to fulfil this requirement (CSTD 2011).

Certification is voluntary (Jong 2010), both on the part of the candidate who can choose whether or not to seek it and on the part of employers, who can choose whether or not to recognise the certification when hiring and promoting individuals. Emphasising the voluntary nature of certification, STC promotes its Certified Professional Technical Communicatior by suggesting 'Take your career to the next level by obtaining the CPTC™ credential' (STC Certification Commission 2012a).

Licensure

While certification is voluntary licensure is not. Only those with valid licences can practise in licensed professions. Like certification, licensure involves demonstrating competence in a given field. In addition to a requirement to work in certain occupations, only those who have graduated from accredited programs that teach a required curriculum for licensure may take the certification examination. The law that requires licensing for a profession also identifies which professional organisation manages the licensing process. Most licenses also require that professionals maintain their licenses by participating in ongoing professional development activities.

Certificates

Certification also differs from a *certificate*. Certification attests to competence in a given profession; a *certificate* attests to successful completion of requirements for a particular program of study (Carliner 2012a). It does not attest to competence. For example, receiving a certificate from a program on technical writing only means that the person who received the certificate completed the requirements for the program. It does not validate that the person can effectively communicate in workplace settings.

Degrees

Although many professional communicators seek certification and certificates to recognise their knowledge and skills in communication, others receive formal education through academic institutions. The resulting degrees offer a credential and often help in the job search, especially the search for a first job. A degree represents completion of an approved curriculum of study at an accredited institution.

Colleges and universities offer degrees in various branches of communication. Some institutions offer generalist degrees in communication studies (usually offered through a Communications department) and professional communication (usually offered through an English department), and offer elective courses that let students explore different types of communication. Other institutions offer programs in specific branches of communication, such as business communication, organisational communication, public relations, and technical communication. In most countries, institutions offer these degrees at the bachelor's and master's levels, with some offering doctoral degrees. In some countries, like Canada and Germany, institutions also offer associate's degrees (community college degree) in communication.

In addition, the continuing education arms of many academic institutions offer certificate programs in communication (often in competition with degree programs). These programs are like the ones described earlier.

Accreditation

When many institutions offer degrees in communication, accreditation provides a means of ensuring that these programs are 'meeting the essential requirements' and providing 'academic excellence' (Dictionary.com 2012). Most universities undergo a general accreditation process for all of their programs and programs like accountancy, engineering, and medicine that prepare students for licensing exams require specialised accreditation. Accreditation processes usually assess the appropriateness of the curriculum and the extent to which it matches recommendations (if available), and the extent and suitability of resources to support the teaching of the curriculum, such as the holdings in the library and the coverage of faculty.

Some professions also accredit organisations that provide continuing education and non-credit courses, especially if professionals require education but do not need to complete a particular degree program to enter the field, such as real estate.

No program of accreditation exists for academic programs in professional communication, much less for private providers of continuing education.

Also note that the term accreditation is sometimes used as a synonym for certification of individual professionals (Dictionary.com 2012). As a practical measure, using accreditation for such a purpose creates avoidable confusion with its more widely acknowledged use in relation to academic programs and with *certification*, the more commonly used term for recognition of individual competence.

Credentials available to professional communicators

Nearly all of the major professional organisations serving professional communicators offer opportunities to earn credentials. The types of credentials, their cost, and participation rates vary widely among organisations. The following sections list the certificates and certifications available to practising professionals. Note that no organisation offers licences to practise nor do any formal accreditations exist for academic and training programs.

Certificates

Several organisations serving professional communicators offer certificate programs: that is, programs of study that lead to a formal certificate – or acknowledgement – of completion of study. In most instances, the certificate attests to achievement of the learning objectives of the program, usually through an examination or capstone (concluding) project. In some instances, however, the certificate merely attests to attendance in the course. Although people who successfully complete a certificate program receive confirmation of completion, these programs generally do not lead to a credential that one can include in their signature (as a Project Management Professional (PMP) might use). Communicators can choose among certificates offered by professional associations, universities and colleges, and for-profit training organisations. Table 31.1 lists a sample selection of certificate programs available from professional associations.

Certifications

More commonly than they offer certificate programs, organisations serving professional communicators offer certification: that is, validation of demonstrated competence in a particular field by a third party assessor. As noted earlier, some organisations refer to this as certification, others refer to it as accreditation. Professionals who successfully complete a certification process receive

Table 31.1 Certificates available from professional associations

Organisation	Certificates available
American Medical Writers Association	Offers separate certificates in each of the following topics (AMWA 2012): Essential skills Business Composition and publication Concepts in science and medicine Regulatory and research Each certificate involves attendance at a selection of workshops (usually more than three) and completion of pre-course assignments.
Council of Science Editors	Offers a Publishing Certificate Program that focuses on scholarly publishing. Requirements for the certificate (sometimes referred to as *certification* on the website of the organisation) include participation in conferences, webinars, and short courses, and knowledge is verified through preparation of a research paper and conference poster (Council of Science Editors 2012).
Society for Technical Communication	Offers a variety of certificate programs. The topics change each year, but staples include basic technical writing, Darwin Information Typing Architecture (DITA), and technical communication management. Each certificate program includes either a face-to-face workshop of several days or several online sessions. Each instructor also assesses learning through assignments (Society for Technical Communication 2012).
tekom (the German association for technical communicators)	The tekom program involves completion of a program of study and a capstone project (Herzke and Fritz 2003). Originally offered only in German, the organisation is launching an English language version in 2012 or 2013. Note that tekom refers to its program as accreditation or certification, but using terminology as defined in this chapter, certificate is a more apt description.

a designation, a credential that one can include in their signature (such as a Certified Professional Technical Communicator). Table 31.2 provides a comprehensive list of certifications available to professional communicators as of early 2013. Most of the credentials emerge from North America, especially the United States. One reason for this is that most of the international organisations are based in the United States; these organisations also have sufficiently large membership bases to fund the development of certification programs. Communicators in other countries determine whether these credentialing programs meet their needs. For example, technical communicators in Australia and New Zealand are working together to determine whether the tekom certificate or the STC-offered CPTC better suits their needs (Sunter 2012).

In addition to certifications in their areas of communication, certifications in related fields are often popular with professionals in this field. Among the most popular is the Project Management Professional (PMP) designation offered by the Project Management Institute (PMI). The credential, earned by successfully completing an examination, validates competence in planning and overseeing projects of any type, not just communication projects.

Other professionals seek certification in related fields, such as training and development. Several certifications exist for training and development professionals, such as the Certified Professional in Learning and Performance offered by the American Society for Training and Development, Certified Training and Development Professional and Certified Training Practitioner (instructor only) offered by the Canadian Society for Training and Development, the

Table 31.2 Certifications available to professional communicators

Organisation	Certification(s) Available
Board of Editors in the Life Sciences (BELS)	Offers the Editor in the Life Sciences, Diplomate (sic) in the Life Sciences, Honored Editor in the Life Sciences. Professionals earn these certifications by completing the related examinations.
International Association of Business Communicators	Offers the Accredited Business Communicator (ABC) designation. Professionals earn this certification by submitting a portfolio and completing an examination (International Association of Business Communicators 2012b).
Public Relations Society of America	Has offered the credential, Accredited in Public Relations (APR) since 1964, making it the oldest credential for professional communicators. The organisation offers a specialised version of the credential for professionals serving the military (APR+M). Professionals earn this credential by successfully completing an examination (PRSA 2012b).
Society for Technical Communication	Launched the Certified Professional Technical Communicator™, (CPTC™) program in 2012 and the Certified Professional Technical Writer™, (CPTW™) in 2013, making these the newest credentials for professional communicators. Professionals earn these credentials by submitting an annotated portfolio, which is assessed against a set of criteria by a trained evaluation team (STC Certification Commission 2012b).

Certified Technical Trainer (instructor) offered by CompTIA, and the Certified Performance Technologist offered by the International Society for Performance Improvement.

Others, especially those working in technical communication, might seek certification in usability (also known as ergonomics and human factors). The Board of Certification in Professional Ergonomics offers several certifications, including the Certified Human Factors Professional, Associate Human Factors Professional, Certified User Experience Professional, and Associate User Experience Professional (BCPE 2011).

Still other professionals seek certification in the industry that they serve, such as the telecommunications or banking industries.

Last, some professional communicators seek certification in a particular technique, such as certification as a FutureSearch facilitator or to teach the Information Mapping method.

Critically exploring the concept of credentialing for professional communicators

From this foundation of the general nature of credentials and the credentials available to professional communicators, I critically explore the concept of credentialing for professional communicators. After describing the arguments for and against credentialing, I explore several implications of credentials for professional communicators, some of immediate practical concern, others with longer-term implications.

The pros and cons of credentialing for professional communicators

The websites for each certification program extol the benefits of credentialing. For example, IABC notes that its 'professional credential program recognize[es] communicators who have reached a globally accepted standard of knowledge and proficiency in their chosen field' (IABC 2012c). Similarly, BELS notes that (2006):

Potential employers and clients of manuscript editors usually have no objective way to assess the proficiency of editors. For their part, editors are frustrated by the difficulty of demonstrating their ability. That is why both employers and editors so often resort to personal references or ad hoc tests, not always with satisfactory results. The need for an objective test of editorial skill has long been recognized.

(BELS 2006)

On a more personal level, Erin Page, Director of Communications and Marketing at the Oklahoma Heritage Association and the Gaylord-Pickens Museum, commented that:

Having my [Accreditation in Public Relations] APR has given me added credibility and has helped my boss, board, and co-workers view me more as a strategic adviser than just a tactician.

(PRSA 2012b)

These promotional comments sum up most of the key arguments in favour of credentialing professional communicators. Coppola (2010) suggests an additional benefit, received through the preparation process. It familiarises professionals with the body of knowledge of their communication discipline as well as the characteristics of effective practice.

Although one might wonder, who could argue with these benefits? Credentialing stirs strong emotions all the same. Different concerns arise with each type of credential. Among the key concerns with certificate programs is that they certify nothing other than attendance. Some certificate programs lack required assignments although most include them. Of those programs that do, concerns arise that learners receive credit merely for submitting assignments that instructors never actually review. Besides, most certificate programs, especially those offered by professional associations, only offer pass-fail grades and no transcripts are available. Indeed, the record keeping for certificate programs that involve several sessions, much less several classes, is often a nuisance to the organisations offering the programs. Even those programs that take assessment seriously only assess whether learners can perform under classroom conditions, not on the job, which is the type of assessment employers seek.

Although certification assesses work under workplace conditions, it arouses even stronger passions than certificates. For example, some professionals see certification as a route to strengthening the profession while others see it as a useless exercise (Carliner 2012b). One of the key objections is that communication – even specialised forms like technical communication – primarily involves specialised, industry-specific work so no common competency framework adequately addresses the work of any individual in the field. A typical response to this is that everyone working in the field has a common job title; certification focuses on what's similar among these professionals, rather than on the differences.

Another key concern is that, even if the field can be defined, doing so narrows its scope and excludes opportunity to professionals in the field. For example, by defining technical communication primarily as the preparation of user assistance, it might preclude a technical communicator from marketing him or herself as a usability specialist. Proponents of certification typically respond that the competency models that guide certification programs must be drafted broadly to reflect the diversity of work of people who use the same job title.

A third key concern is that employers will not recognise the credential. Proponents acknowledge that, but believe that will change as the percentage of certified professionals increases.

Accreditation also raises strong passions, especially within the academic community. Primary concerns are that outside parties, such as a professional organisations, and people who are practising professionals will dictate what academic programs should and should not cover (Barker 2012). At the least, the concern exists that these parties lack the qualifications to design academic programs. At the most, the concern exists that the accreditation process compromises academic freedom. Some faculty object, too, to giving 'corporate' interests a say in academic curricula (Blakeslee and Spilka 2004).

Underlying all of these credentialing efforts is a sincere effort to ensure effective practice and protect clients from malpractice. But because participation in all of these credentialing programs is voluntary, they do not limit entry into the field. Furthermore, even when people have acquired credentials, they only validate knowledge, skill, or competence in particular situations and at a particular point in time. Even with credentials, professionals might still fail to perform to the satisfaction of a client or manager.

Broader implications of credentialing

Credentialing is a long-term investment in the profession. Although some of its benefits accrue in the short-run, many of the benefits do not accrue until later. (Short-run varies substantially among situations and organisations. Because committed professionals might work in a given field for as many as 50 years, 'short-run' in a professional context substantially differs from short-run in other contexts, such as the high technology industry, where technology still changes every year or two). In this section, I explore some of the potential issues that credentialing poses for professional communication – both benefits and limitations.

Implication 1: Consistent knowledge and expectations of performance

Because of the complexity of compiling a body of knowledge, most organisations only engage in the effort if they intend to certify or license professionals and need to develop either an examination, evaluation criteria for work products, or both. But bodies of knowledge offer benefits far beyond the immediate ones to certification and licensure. By defining a common body of knowledge and standards of performance, certification has the potential to ensure some level of consistency in knowledge among practising professionals who otherwise come from diverse educational backgrounds, work in diverse industries, and have diverse work experiences. Similarly, by defining a competent performance for a given branch of communication, this effort also has the potential to more clearly and effectively differentiate among the branches of communication and help clients determine when they might want, say, a technical communicator rather than a public relations specialist.

Employers can use these standards of performance to create job descriptions and performance plans for communication professionals, as well as guide the performance evaluation process. Similarly, educational institutions can use these bodies of knowledge as the foundations for their curricula and individual courses. The content in a body of knowledge helps academics develop their programs, by defining the knowledge students need and describing the levels of performance expected of graduates when they enter the workplace.

Implication 2: Uniquely branding the different branches of professional communication

As part of the process of defining its body of knowledge, different branches of professional communication also differentiate themselves from one another. For example, the process of defining the body of knowledge for medical writing differentiates it from more general technical writing.

This, in turn, offers branches of professional communication the opportunity to uniquely brand themselves in the eyes of potential clients and professionals. This can be vital in efforts to market a profession. For example, a study of the sponsors of technical communication services first asked sponsors whether technical communicators added value to their organisations. Sponsors said yes. When asked how technical communicators added value, however, sponsors could not offer specific ways (Cash 1995). Similarly, public relations professionals are concerned about the ways that customers perceive them; but studies of the perceptions of public relations professionals do not typically explore the issue of competent performance.

The emic distinctions of branches of communication developed by people in the field might also pose problems, however. If a branch defines itself too broadly (for example, if employee communication includes the technical manuals and training offered by Information Technology groups), it might either be unrecognisable to its core constituencies or professionals might fail to perform properly when given these assignments. Only by validating definitions of specific branches of communication with client groups and comparing bodies of knowledge for one group with those of other branches of communication can one branch of communication assure that it has clearly and appropriately defined itself. Similarly, in some instances, job descriptions used by one branch match those used by professionals in another branch, even though the job title might differ, as happens with the description of an information designer and content strategist (Carliner 2012b). Such overlaps confuse hiring managers and bother professional communicators.

Implication 3: Confusion over competing credentials

Although one of the proposed benefits of credentialing is that it helps employers and clients make informed decisions when hiring and evaluating the work of professional communicators, the availability of so many credentials, many of which overlap and compete with one another, and similar overlap of terminology, might backfire and create confusion.

One area of potential confusion is terminology. Although precise definitions exist for the terms certificate, certification, and accreditation, professional organisations use the terms interchangeably and, in some cases, outside of standard use. This is especially surprising because managing terminology is a major concern of communication professionals. As a result, both the credentialed professional and employers might be confused about the meaning of the credential. For example, someone who receives a certificate – even one with a rigorous capstone project – is not technically certified, even if the professional organisation suggests otherwise.

Another area of potential confusion is competing credentials. For example, although the credentials offered by tekom and the Society for Technical Communication are technically different (the former is a certificate, the latter is a certification), both are marketed in similar ways and aimed at the same markets of employers and professionals. Although the competition might strengthen both programs, it also has the potential to backfire and discredit both programs among their key constituencies.

Implication 4: The possibilities of building or dividing the professional community

Absent or playing limited roles in the development of many of these programs is the academic community. In some instances when members of the academic community did participate, the decision to offer certification was already made and academics merely helped to shape the implementation of the program.

This, in turn, has several implications. The most significant is that the academic community might not support certification and, in some cases, could actively resist it. One particular area of possible concern to the academic community is the focus on competencies in certification programs. To some academics, competencies only pertain to job-related skills. As a result, programs that focus on job skills primarily offer training; the purpose of academic programs is education and to develop critical thinking skills. But that perceived dichotomy might change with time as emerging approaches to higher education increasingly emphasise outcomes and competencies over credit hours. For example, in the US, Western Governor's University, and the state university systems of Arizona and Wisconsin (Kolowich 2012; Young 2012) – the latter two of which are homes to some ranking programs in professional communication – emphasise competencies. Although primarily used within the context of the workplace, the concept of competency is not limited to it, nor is it limited to job-related skills. A competency is 'the quality of being adequately or well qualified physically and intellectually' (Dictionary.com 2013), a definition that encompasses critical thinking. Furthermore, most professional decisions, especially in the earliest phases of design – when professional communicators must devise an approach that communicates an intended message to a designated audience using the resources available – require critical thinking.

Another concern is that certification should align with academic curricula that prepare students to enter particular branches of communication. Without academic buy-in, supporters of certification lose one potential incentive to align university curricula.

Some professional organisations might like to accredit programs that prepare students for certification but, without academic buy-in, this could prove difficult. Some associations might try a softer approach, such as that used by the Canadian Society for Training and Development, with its recognised programs (CSTD 2011). Recognition involves a brief review of a curriculum to make sure that it covers the competencies addressed by certification; it is not as thorough a process as accreditation.

Academic programs could also find themselves competing against professional associations that offer their certification preparation programs. In some instances, professional organisations might recognise other organisations that offer these curricula in their name, such as private providers and continuing education groups within universities.

Implication 5: Credentials without credibility

But perhaps the most significant concern with credentialing is that it won't achieve its intended goals. That might happen because none of the credentialing programs reach a 'critical mass', meaning that a large minority of the profession (about 30 to 40 per cent of the membership of a professional organisation) chooses to certify. After a certain period of time, perhaps 15 to 20 years, such a credential essentially becomes worthless. Or even if credentialing programs do reach a critical mass, employers might not recognise them or might only recognise them marginally. As a result, the profession does not realise the anticipated benefits of clearly branding the branch of communication or of limiting entry by those who lack appropriate qualifications and training.

Concluding thoughts

It's too early to tell, however, what the impact of credentialing will ultimately be. Certification programs build slowly. For example, the certification program for the Society for Human Resource Management was launched in the 1980s, but has only reached critical mass in the past ten years. The situation is the same with the certification in project management. Most certifications of professional communicators are much newer. In other words, patience might be the most important factor in determining the success of a certification program.

Trademarks

Certified Professional Technical Communicator, Certified Professional Technical Writer, CPTC and CPTW are trademarks of the Society for Technical Communication Certification Commission.

Related topics

accreditation; certification; credentialing; certification of professional communication

Key readings

Hale, J. (2012). *Performance-Based Certification: How to Design a Valid, Defensible, Cost Effective Program* (2nd edn), San Francisco, CA: Jossey-Bass/Pfeiffer. (A useful reference to learn how to establish a certification program.)

Livingston, S. and Zieke, M. (2006). 'Passing scores: A manual for setting standards of performance on educational and occupational tests', excerpted in M. Zieke and M. Perie, *A Primer on Setting Cut Scores on Tests of Educational Achievement*, Princeton, NJ: Educational Testing Service. Available at www.ets.org/Media/Research/pdf/Cut_Scores_Primer.pdf (accessed 21 April 2013). (Explains how to establish standards for evaluating certifications.)

Learn about the individual certification programs themselves:
- American Medical Writers Association (2012). AMWA Education Programs and Certificates. Available at www.amwa.org/default.asp?id=250 (accessed 25 June 2012).
- Board of Certification in Professional Ergonomics (2011). BCPE certifications at a glance. Available at www.bcpe.org/page/BCPE-Certifications-at-a-Glance (accessed 25 June 2012).
- Board of Editors in the Life Sciences (2006). Welcome to BELS. Available at www.bels.org/index.cfm (accessed 25 June 2012).
- Council of Science Editors (2012). CSE Publication Certificate Program. Available at www.councilscienceeditors.org/i4a/pages/index.cfm?pageid=3617 (accessed 25 June 2012).
- International Association of Business Communicators (2012). IABC Accreditation. Available at www.iabc.com/abc/ (accessed 25 June 2012).
- Public Relations Society of America (2012). Accreditation. Available at www.prsa.org/Learning/Accreditation/ (accessed 25 June 2012).
- Society for Technical Communication (2012). Certification. Available at www.stc.org/education/certification/certification-main (accessed 23 May 2013).

Bibliography

American Medical Writers Association (AMWA) (2008.) 'AMWA Code of Ethics'. Available at www.amwa.org/default.asp?Mode=DirectoryDisplay&DirectoryUseAbsoluteOnSearch=True&id=114 (accessed 25 June 2012).

——(2012). 'AMWA Education Programs and Certificates'. Available at www.amwa.org/default.asp?id=250 (accessed 25 June 2012).

Barker, T. (2012.) 'CPTC certification: What's in it for academics? (Part 1)', *Intercom*, *59*(3). Available at http://intercom.stc.org/2012/03/the-academic-conversationcptc-certification-what%E2%80%99s-in-it-for-academicspart-1/ (accessed 25 June 2012).

Blakeslee, A. M. and Spilka, R. (2004). 'The state of research in Technical Communication', *Technical Communication Quarterly*, *13*(1), 73–92.

Board of Certification in Professional Ergonomics (BCPE) (2011). 'BCPE certifications at a glance'. Available at www.bcpe.org/page/BCPE-Certifications-at-a-Glance (accessed 25 June 2012).

Board of Editors in the Life Sciences (BELS) (2006). 'Welcome to BELS'. Available at www.bels.org/index.cfm (accessed 25 June 2012).
Canadian Society for Training and Development (CSTD) (2011). *Certification Maintenance Handbook*, Toronto, Canada: Canadian Society for Training and Development.
Carliner, S. (2012a). 'Certification and the branding of HRD', *HRD Quarterly*, 23(3), 411–19.
——(2012b). 'Three approaches to professionalization in Technical Communication', *Technical Communication*, 59(1), 49–65.
Cash, M. (1995). 'Manual labor: Professional input helps Canadian firms satisfy customers', *Intercom*, 42(4), 9.
Coppola, N. (2010). 'The technical communication body of knowledge initiative: An academic–practitioner partnership', *Technical Communication*, 57(1), 11–25.
Council of Science Editors (CSE) (2012). *CSE Publication Certificate Program*. Available at www.councilscienceeditors.org/i4a/pages/index.cfm?pageid=3617 (accessed 25 June 2012).
Dictionary.com (2012). 'Definition of accredited'. Available at http://dictionary.reference.com/browse/accredited (accessed 25 June 2012).
——(2013). *Definition of Competence from Wordnet 3.0*. Available at www.thefreedictionary.com/competency (accessed 22 February 2013).
Hale, J. (2000). *Performance-Based Certification: How to Design a Valid, Defensible, and Cost Effective Program*, San Francisco, CA: Jossey-Bass/Pfeiffer.
Herzke, H. and Fritz, M. (2003). 'Certificate through modules', *technische kommunikation*, 25(3), 37. Available at www.tekom.de/index_neu.jsp?url=/servlet/ControllerGUI?action=voll&id=202 (accessed 25 June 2012).
International Association of Business Communicators (IABC) (2012a). 'IABC code of ethics for professional communicators'. Available at www.iabc.com/about/code.htm (accessed 25 June 2012).
——(2012b). 'Accreditation for prospective candidates'. Available at www.iabc.com/abc/prospective/ (accessed 25 June 2012).
——(2012c). 'IABC accreditation'. Available at www.iabc.com/abc/ (accessed 25 June 2012).
Jong, S. (2010). 'Technical communication certification', Presented at the Technical Communication Summit, the 57th Annual Conference of the Society for Technical Communication. Dallas, TX, 2 May 2010.
Kolowich, S. (11 July 2012). 'Competency loves company', *InsideHigherEd*, 11 July 2012. Available at www.insidehighered.com/news/2012/07/11/northern-arizona-u-partners-pearson-competency-based-degree-programs (accessed 14 December 2012).
Public Relations Society of America (PRSA) (2012a). 'Public Relations Society of America (PRSA) member code of ethics'. Available at www.prsa.org/AboutPRSA/Ethics/CodeEnglish/ (accessed 25 June 2012).
——(2012b). 'Accreditation'. Available at www.prsa.org/Learning/Accreditation/ (accessed 25 June 2012).
Society for Technical Communication (2012). 'Online certificate courses'. Available at www.stc.org/education/online-education/certificate-courses (accessed 25 June 2012).
STC Certification Commission (2012a). 'Home page of the STC Certification website'. Available at www.stccert.org (accessed 25 June 2012).
——(2012b). 'Application process'. Available at www.stccert.org/?q=node/138 (accessed 25 June 2012).
Sunter, B. (25 October 2012). 'Presentation at the Technical Communicators Association of New Zealand (TCANZ) conference', Auckland, NZ, 25 October 2012.
Young, E. (9 July 2012). 'Another state to assess skills', *InsideHigherEd.com*, 9 July 2012. Available at www.insidehighered.com/news/2012/07/09/wisconsin-seeks-competency-based-degree-program-without-help-western-governors (accessed 19 December 2012).

Section 4
View from the professions

32
Banking

Interviewee: Banker (B), who would like to remain anonymous, has been a banking professional for about 25 years, and has held very senior management positions in American, British and European as well as Asian banking institutions. He has been in the Asian region for the last several years.

(R – Researcher – Vijay Bhatia; B – Banker)

R I would like to begin by asking you how do you describe a good, ideal, and successful banker? How do you identify a good banker when you need to look for one?

B There are a couple of things that a banker has to have. Firstly, banking is a very broad board ... I mean there are a whole lot of things which have changed the industry in the last 20–30 years. Historically, banking used to be understood as a place where you borrow and lend money ... and when you borrow money, you borrow cheap, and you lend, you lend at a higher rate, so that's where the bank used to make profit. And that was the basic game. There were depositors who would send money to the bank and the creditors would borrow money from the bank. But in the last 20–25 years banking has changed a lot. Basically there are a few things which are important for a banker. Firstly, ethical standards personally have to be at a very high level. It's very difficult to identify those standards on day one, but it is something that one has to look for and gaze in the past experience and in the research report that we do on the individual. And obviously, the ability to understand clients' needs is very important as well. I mean, every client is different ... you have clients today from 25 years to 75 years of age. Obviously, their requirements and demands are different, so one needs to understand the requirements and needs well, and the ability to suggest and explain the kinds of products or schemes that your clients may find attractive. So these two things are absolutely necessary. A good banker is not necessarily driven by only individual profits ... unless a client makes money, the bank can never make money ... so it's very important for the banker to understand that. And many times, that doesn't really happen. So, it can be a struggle.

R I understand, things have become difficult especially in the last 15 years or so ...

B Absolutely, so that's where people have lost that value system to some extent, and most of the things are driven by short-term profits and short-term gains. It's also an important factor

535

because the corporate world looks at the shareholder's values and the trends ... I mean, from the time the quarterly reporting in the US has been enforced ... so every shareholder, chairman, and every board are driven by quarterly profits. When you have the requirement of quarterly performance, then it trickles down to the lowest level. So we as bankers, when dealing with the clients, also need to look at this kind of quarterly game ... from the client's perspective, he may often look at a three-year/five-year span down the line, and then what happens is that you are selling a three-year product or five-year product ... not knowing, how it will perform or really take its own shape and turn in two or three years if the market goes the other way.

R So it's a high pressure activity ... because the targets are set on a quarterly basis.

B Absolutely, so over the years, it has become a very much profit driven culture, which is not likely to happen in the industry, but that's how the industry works. And in the last three to four years, after the crisis in 2008 and 2009, things have dramatically changed ... stringent regulations are being put in place to a great extent.

R And in all these activities that you have actually told us about, what's the role of language?

B Language plays a dramatic role in it because if there are ten preconditions for a certain product, then you need to articulate these to the client, and if you only tell the client eight conditions and the most important two conditions which will probably affect him or for the next one to two years are hidden from him, then he would not ever understand the entire risk parameters that he's going to go through in a particular deal. The use of language is crucial, how the bankers use it, or how the compliance people word it, or how the legal people approve it when they write it on the term sheet. So, in earlier days, the risk disclosure was in the smallest fonts and it was not really possible for people to understand or read thoroughly. But over the last four years, things have changed, so there is one page of term sheet, which contains the details of the product, there will still be four pages of disclaimers which are in the same size font. So things have changed and language has a crucial role.

R And what kind of language do you expect your employees or bankers to use? Is it the general ability to use language or a highly specialised language, for example, language of banking, the written language or technical documents, or the general ability to use language?

B The bankers should be in a position to understand broad aspects of language, I mean they need to understand the technical language, which is used in the banking documents, and they should have the ability to transform that banking information into simple language for a layman, for an individual investor who is not hugely qualified to understand the jargon. That's very important, and that's what we always look for in a good banker ... for example, if I use knock in and knock out ... the client would not understand it ... so we should be able to explain it. Similarly, if you strike at a particular level, that means at this level you will buy, and at this level you will sell.

R How do you really identify such characteristics in a person you are recruiting for your unit? Suppose there are three candidates to choose from, what is it that you look for in all three of them? Are there any typical characteristics you look for?

B Different roles require different abilities and sets of competencies and characteristics. I have been leading the teams which deal with clients directly, so we are absolutely the front line ... we are the face of the bank. So what we look for ... I can give you a really good example of our team. I look for bankers to deal with clients directly, or I may look for advisors, who will have a desk role and they would be doing a lot of research, so their requirements are slightly different. When we look for someone for the front line, we look for an ability to articulate. The past background is extremely important, that's where credibility comes in, so if he or she has lost a lot of money for the client in the previous job, then obviously he or she is not

really a good candidate for a front-line job, because the business world is very small and people know about these bankers …
R But would you still use him, put him behind the scene?
B If he or she comes from a different kind of background, if his ability matches with what you are looking for, probably yes. I cannot say for sure that it would be a completely no, there would still be a chance … as long as articulating standards are okay. At the same time, ability to convince the other side of truthfulness and the genuineness is important. Bankers have to be very fair to the clients. If so, you can be a successful banker in a short time. If the clients don't make money, you cannot continue to bid for big business. …
R You have to build the confidence of the clients.
B That's right. Banking is all about one word, trust. So the moment trust is lost, there's nothing left. So trust is what you are working on, and the entire life for a banker goes in building trust with the clients, so when the client trusts you, then he or she can be a partner with you in good times and bad times as well. So, that's very very important.
R There is also another aspect of trust. To what extent do you actually look for trust between the employer and the employee, or the loyalty between the employer and the employee … I mean, between the boss and the subordinate?
B Sure. It is driven from the culture of every organisation … it's driven from the top to a great extent. In the good old days before 2007 and 2008 … before the crisis, every market was booming, everywhere there was high growth, and everything was absolutely fine. So at that point of time, trust between employer and employee was also very high … trust between the employee and the client was also very high … everybody was making money. Having said that, when the times are not so good … then the ability of the institution's culture comes into play … it depends on whether they want to take a short-term or a long-term view of building it up slowly … and continuing with the organic growth … that's where the chairman comes in and says … I have only so much and I want to double the revenue. Then obviously a similar pressure comes onto the front line, and the front line ends up doing some silly stuff, which is not really necessary. Firstly the difficult market conditions … and then the clients have lost their money … and then there is a mismatch between expectations of the organisation and the ability to make it work on the front line. Obviously, if the front line has to move on, they have to change their ways. In most of the cases, the organisations don't change their ways, the front line has to move on, or do something different … and look for organisations where they find the same mentality to grow the business.
R If you look at a typical banker, a good successful banker, where do you think he or she really acquires his expertise, in the university or in the workplace?
B I would really not think … that at this stage universities do a great job. To be honest, I am sorry to say there are not many banking courses. It's only in the last few years that we have found certain courses in places like Singapore; I think, one or two places in Hong Kong … there are certain schools which are giving specific courses on banking and they have started to train bankers for one and a half year courses. Prior to that, bankers came from very diverse backgrounds, I mean there were accountants, people who have been in accountancy have come to banking, people who have done … law have come into banking, people who have done science have come into banking, people who have done statistics have gone into banking, and have taken on different roles. Guys with a background in statistics will go into modelling, or statistical evaluation.
R You do need all kinds of expertise.
B All kinds of expertise in different units. But typically, universities don't have many courses … it's very common for people to choose banking as a career after graduation …

R That's not enough as specialism.
B That's not enough.
R Generally people go for MBA and they think MBA ...
B MBA can manage anything in that sense, they may not be able to prepare a balance sheet, but they can analyse a balance sheet very well ...
R So what we are trying to hint at is that most of the times, they become expert bankers only when they start working for the bank.
B Primarily, training is given on the job and there are a lot of training courses, which every bank runs. Whether it is consumer banking or retail banking or corporate banking or investment banking or finance and strategy function or it's a staff function.
R So every bank has such facilities?
B Every bank has various internal programmes for training, which are given at different points and times ... to different levels of people. There are leadership trainings for higher managerial level ... there are product trainings at the base level ...
R So everybody is given a chance to retrain oneself?
B Yes, there are mandatory courses, and there are optional courses. Mandatory, you have to do it, because it signifies your role, whereas optional, if you have extra time or you are interested, then you can do all those optional courses. But again, it's not enough, because what happens is everybody works under high pressure ... and it's not that 99 per cent of the people really do optional courses. I would imagine only 1 per cent of the entire workforce will do and try one of those courses. Banks try to differentiate themselves by saying that we do a lot of training for staff. That's one of the ways where they can attract talents.
R And how do you, at the end of the day ... I mean after working with somebody for two, three, four, five years, appraise his or her work? How do you evaluate a person? Are there any fixed ways of doing it? Or do you go by hunch, or you go by his performance?
B Right, apart from obviously performing on the key performance indicators, what we call KPI, those things are typically based on what your role entails. So whether you are in the front line and your role is revenue generation ... you've got to look at how much revenue target you should be able to manage and how much you are able to generate ... if your target is five million dollars, and you reached three million dollars, then obviously you do not perform well. But if you are able to generate six million, you have achieved your target. Consistency and KPI measurements, they are assessed in the management ... you have to make sure your total losses for the year in your line is no more than 10 per cent of your total revenue generation. Those are various ways of measuring the key performances. Apart from that, ability to grow his or her credentials has to be looked at. It's not enough that every year on year, a person is only able to manage his numbers. There are a lot of people who can manage their numbers very well, who can be very smart and just manage their numbers very well. But then, they probably work for the salary and the ethics of bonuses, which is called a performance bonus at a given time of the year based on certain formulae in individual banks. Apart from that, if you want to develop your managerial skills, and if you want to grow into different careers, from a private banker you want to become a corporate banker, you have to be able to identify certain deals which other banks have been able to make. So those are the key factors that come into play. And that's what we look for in promoting a person to a next level, which shows that you can take on more pressure and more number of people under you. We can bring some juniors under you if you have become a seasoned banker.
R So people do specialise over a period of time?

B That's right, some people have managerial ambitions ... but obviously not everybody is capable of doing so and may not be able to do so. That requires a lot of people management. Apart from client management, we also do a lot on people management. It's not easy ...

R In your unit, or the units that you have handled, obviously there are people who are given different kinds of jobs depending upon their specialism and they all have their ways of performing. How often do they work individually? Or do they work together? People coming from different sub-disciplines ... how do they work together? How important is it for them to work together in groups?

B Most of the times, organisations would want them to work in teams, but individuals being individuals, they are all driven by their selfish motives. It's a manager's job to bring all of them together and make them work together, because it is most effective for the clients. Whether it is a corporate client or individual client, it always makes sense if you see three or four different facets of the bank, and that's all coming from different angles. If I am dealing with a high net-worth family, and they have the requirement of say a structure specialist, because they have to structure their 20 different companies and 15 different family members ... equally shared, looking for a succession plan and all that. Now for that, it has to be a 'do with me or be on the call with me and the client' during various meetings with the client. And then there are investment specialists ... say a fixed income specialist, or ethic specialist, who comes in and talks about how the markets are expected to behave and how they are looking into the past and what has happened globally and things like that. And there could be a credit specialist, who is looking into whether you can extract value from this company, you can take as much of leverage from her, or you cannot take ... you should reduce your exposure to these things here. As long as there is an effective approach to put in front of your client, it is always more effective to work in teams. If I were to go to a client and talk about all these things, he will only see one face. His level of confidence only increases when he sees the team ... though I am still the centrepiece, and he talks to me if there is a problem, the issue, there is a cost issue, things like that.

R So, team work and collaboration is absolutely crucial?

B It's very very crucial to be with larger business, to be with big clients.

R One of the problems ... I don't know whether you face it or not, could be when people come with different backgrounds, with different specialisms, they also have their own point of view, which may probably be contested in a particular situation.

B Let me tell you, and it happens many times. And in my experience, when we are in front of our clients, we should not ever go prepared that this is what we have to say. If you are at that point of time, if there is a discussion going on, let's say, dollar to euro, if you view as a specialist, is it one euro to 1.20 and if my view is 1.25, then we both have arguments to support that view. And we could have that argument ... it happens many times with me personally, maybe he is confused at the time of the day because two people are talking ... the issue for the client is who to trust or what view to take. But he also has a view ... the point that if he doesn't have a view, he is looking through his specialist view, but he sees both the reasons. If I say that the European Union will not stay for long and it will go, and he has a view that 'No ... no ... no ... it's too far' he can reason to prove his view at that point in time. I have a view when I said it may not happen in one year but may happen in two or three years.

R So it's good to have a diversity of views.

B It is good to have a diversity of views, but at the same time, it shouldn't be too much conflicting ...

R It can't be too diversified.

B Exactly, at that point in time, the house view comes into play and every institution has their own house views and we, as bankers, many times are supposed to say, it is not my view but this is the house view, or vice versa ... we also sometimes have to override the house view.

R We have been talking a lot about spoken interaction with the clients, the negotiation with the clients, but there are also documents that people normally write, and I am sure you write quite a lot. So when you write, is there any collaboration across people, members of the unit ... do they write individually or do they write together? Or maybe, one person writes it and the other people look at it. How do you go about it?

B To be very honest, it is really a good question. In an ideal situation, one would appreciate the involvement of all the concerned parties and the document based on everyone's feedback. Having said that, in practice one finds that it probably happens 10 per cent of the time. 90 per cent of the time, it is driven by different business units who have a function to prepare documents or people sitting in compliance, legal departments, are preparing those documents, trying to include every aspect of their back-sight, or the bank's back-sight, but you know some of them may not make enough sense to take them in front of the client.

R But the documents are circulated to other units in order to get their feedback ...

B Many times, it is not circulated ... many times, it is just prepared, and people are told that it is to be used. They have prepared the documents based on an actuator's requirement, if an actuator sends a letter to you that, 'we want you to check whether the time fraction of these types are only done with professional investors'. They don't say too much in that letter, but if they try to interplay ... one can say, 'okay, I will do this check, I will do this'. Instead of five checks, you can end up with 50 checks, because it is a very loose sentence that an actuator has said. To that extent, does one go and analyse it? Different banks will do different things ... unless the actuator says what exactly needs to be done.

R If a document is produced by a specific department, I assume that there must be several people working there; how do they produce it? Do they work individually, or collaboratively?

B No, normally there is a head in the department, and the team on the lead will work, and obviously the head will have to sign it.

R The head will have to sign. Obviously most people are consulted, they have their input, and so it's not one individual writing it ...

B Yes, the parties who are going to be using it could be slightly different from parties who may have created it. That party may also have a group of people.

R Let's move to recruitment and training procedures. I think you have already answered a few questions. To what extent do you actually pay importance to the qualifications that the universities normally provide? So if you have a person with a specific qualification, do you pay much attention to that?

B It definitely counts, it's not completely ignored, but if you are looking for an experienced person who has crossed ten plus years of office experience, then it typically ends up taking a little backseat ... then what happens is you look for the practical experience and whether it is relevant experience of past five years that is brought into your job profile. But qualification does give you an initial basic parameter a person has to have. There is an intelligence level of X amount ... you have taken up these subjects today leading to basic understanding ... I am not hiring a science graduate and then trying to tell him what are debtors and creditors. So if he is a commerce graduate, he will understand what are debtors and creditors.

R So the basic understanding of discipline is necessary?

B Yes, it is important.

R What if you have, say for example, two people ... one has a degree in economics, and the other person doesn't have a degree in economics, but he has a degree in, say social sciences, government and management or some administrative field. But if you compare the two people, they have different degrees, different specialisms, but the one actually who is a social science graduate is much brighter, and has a higher level of achievement than the one who has done a degree in economics. Who would you tend to prefer?

B In such situations, there is obviously a requirement of the roles that you are looking for in a particular person. And if that role has a relevant experience behind it, if that social science graduate has done similar things in his previous job, and he has practical knowledge about it, and if the economics graduate has not done much in that particular area, then the one who has the experience will be followed up. Experience always takes precedence over degree in such situations. If it is a research function, and it is an economics graduate, who does have a research background, he will probably be preferred; but if it is a sales function or it's a marketing function, when there is an economics graduate and a social science graduate, and the social science graduate has done some marketing roles, he would be preferred to an economics graduate.

R What are the other kinds of training that are considered necessary to enter the banking profession?

B There is something called CFA, which are Chartered Financial Analyst. This is something that takes care of the last 10 to 12 years of development into a lot of derivative areas, the various models have come out for derivatives. Businesses typically like banks that have given market loans. Now you package all these market loans and sell it to someone else, who buys it from you ... that is called securitisation. That guy has finally got these hundreds of mortgages, wherein that manager does not have to really work on each case but he buys a complete portfolio, so it's much simpler for someone to buy it from you and have similar returns, whereas the person who has done these hundreds of mortgages, must have worked for years. So various things under the CFA program give you a boost, but there are again corporate bankers who would be typically dealing with the corporate requirement, that's really to understand how to read the balance sheet and where to find the flaws in the balance sheet, and how much credit can be given, where the cash flows are positive, or not positive, and things like that. So they should have a very clear understanding of their accountancy side of the balance sheet, whereas an investment banker should have a very detailed understanding of various derivatives, models and market scenarios, the market would move from say ... something like 2001, 9/11 happens, and the market crashes in a day. Then what would happen and how contingency would operate, or things like that. So we have people who work on statistics and models and do all these assessments and evaluations. Then on the front line, it's more about learning of these products, and using them to explain such scenarios to clients. These tasks require different skills. There is no individual course that can cover all these aspects ... they need specialised courses ...

R Yea, so people normally do such short-term specialised courses ...

B Six months or a year if you are working, if you want to be a private banker. Singapore has started recently some courses for private bankers. So that would encompass every asset class, so you need to have a basic understanding of every asset class ... whereas a research analyst sitting and doing telecom research doesn't need to understand how the industry works. He only needs to understand complete details ... complete depth of telecom world. How the ARPU (Average Revenue Per User) works, if there are a hundred thousand forms being sold in Hong Kong in one month, then how much average revenue these forms are generating for that company. So here one has to go to a lot more details of spectrum for the layman ...

R Are these specialised courses some kind of substitutes for bankers? I understand they also recruit trainees.

B Yes, exactly. Banks still have graduate trainees, the trainees come on board for six months, one year or two years in different functions, where they pick up a few things, then they are

View from the professions

given a chance where they would like to go and work and when there are vacancies, they will move there. Typically these are bright kids who are picked up from universities, maybe just after graduation. They will be typically handling six different areas in a three-year period ... six months in each area. And then they are asked whether they would want to go into this area or that area, and then based on their interests and openings they will be matched to their area of interest and expertise.

R In your unit, and of course, in banking generally in Hong Kong, how important are English and Chinese, particularly for front line staff?

B Internally the entire email system of the bank works in English. Everybody understands English, everybody speaks and everybody communicates in English. However, documents can also be bilingual ... Chinese clients have started to grow in numbers through the years in this part of the world. So there is a demand for front line documents and presentations to be bilingual. I mean when we make presentations to clients, they are bilingual many a time.

R But there are no government operative conditions that you have to have bilingual documents?

B No, English language still prevails in a legal sense, but at the same time, there are translators who are qualified translators employed by the banks right now. Their role is just to translate the documents and then send for printing ... and things like that.

R And what are the general modes of communication? How often do they use email?

B I would say email is kind of misused these days. The number of emails keeps flowing from one unit to another and the number of people or the groups being copied or copying those emails ... because what happens is every unit is working with say five, seven, or ten people ... so if there is a middle office, back office, a front office or it's a legal department ... it's a compliance department, or HR function ... all of them may have six or seven people, for instance, frontline has ten teams and every team has seven to eight people ... If one message has to go to credit, credit has created their own group, credit guys would say to you, 'okay don't send it to me, because I am not responsible. Please mark it to the group.' Now if in a group, one person is going to act on it, seven people will get the message ... so six of them would just ignore it ... because they know that person number one has to deal with it. But it gets to all of them because if he is not on the desk or he is already sick or he is not available, then at least somebody else can take care of it.

R So that's how it multiplies tasks.

B It just multiplies. And because of that, there are systems and ways by which bankers started doing the internal chat system. So we have an inter-enterprise chat system whereby ... if I need just to deal with you ... I would work on the chat rather than sending an email. That is also a genuine mode of communication ... that's also stored, and recorded. But it is one on one. You know, and informally I can ask you something. I don't need to send you an email that is copied to seven other people. On the other hand, there is also a tendency in the culture of Hong Kong ... that is, if you call up somebody, then he may not either pick up the phone or sometimes may respond a little late. He would not feel so much responsible to respond. You know, if they have sent an answer to say 'No, it's not possible', then there is no way to argue on the phone and then to get a 'yes' on them ... whereas if there is an email exchange, everybody takes it extremely seriously, because that can be copied and sent across to whoever he wants. So everybody is very particular to respond to emails ... and they feel obliged to reply to email even if it does not make much sense. So sometimes ... a 'thank you' message also comes back, which is completely nonsense ... it wastes all our resources and time.

R There are no guidelines?

B There are basic behavioural things such as that one is not supposed to send 'Thank you, Mrs.' ... but every person is different, and their behaviour is also different ... they just do not follow guidelines all the time.
R Don't you think there is a need or perhaps it is necessary to have some kind of an office system which will actually put all these messages into relevant and not so relevant categories ... so people are not bothered by that immediately.
B You can do this at your level ... at an individual computer level ... but it cannot be set at the enterprise or organisation or a team level for that matter ... because you cannot ask the system to identify which is relevant and which is not ... it cannot do that.
R But the way the computer can actually identify spam and most of the other messages, you can filter them out.
B Yes.
R But in the same way, an institution can internally develop a programme that does something similar.
B It is a good thought, but I don't think ... every technology unit within the banks ... the organisations are so stretched to deliver various requirements of various parts of the banks that these things are not given that much of importance.
R Now, let's look at the perspective of the employees as against the management. In any profession people often work under constraints. In banking, what kind of work constraints do you think employees face?
B Main constraints could be related to the ability to deliver the product sets ... inability to meet client's expectations or requirement. Clients are very different ... every client is different ... and they may have different needs. One may be based in Hong Kong ... and have a residence in India ... similarly somebody based in Singapore may have a residence in Hong Kong ... or somebody based here has a residence in Australia ... and they may want mortgage facility on their properties. One bank ... one institution may not be in a position to give mortgages in Australia, Singapore and India at the same at competitive levels. Different institutions are good for different things. So with a global bank, typically the set of products become a big constraint, 'okay, we can do these things', there are a lot of things which are doable, lot of things which are not doable. It's like going to an Indian restaurant and asking for Chinese food or vice versa. You know you can go to a specialised restaurant to get that food, that cuisine. So ... there are lots of times policy issues ... the policies are imposed or monitored and sometimes they are not very flexible, and they impose constraints ... sometimes they are very different from what the market is offering ... So a front line person will typically benchmark the policy of an institution where he or she is working to an outsider policy. Whereas the back office people would look at the policy from where we were three months ago and where we are now. They will not consider anything that five other institutions outside are dealing with. For everybody the benchmarks are slightly different. So to bring everyone on the same platform ... to have the same benchmark is the job of a CEO. I have to balance both the things ... if the market demands this and internally we were very backward and we move forward to some extent, but we have not moved forward enough to compare with the market. So probably you have to move forward. So, he has to balance both the things.
R But these are the constraints coming from the profession. But they could also be constraints ... at a slightly different level, for example, if a person has come from a different bank and moved across banks ... for instance, if you come with a background say from Bank 'A', and then you come to Bank 'B', when you come here, then if you are working under somebody else who has been in Bank B for a long time, then of course you'll bring different

kinds of ideas, different kinds of attitudes, different kinds of values. Then is that something that is important or seen as a constraint or may be a source of conflict?

B I would say it is a strength, when one organisation tries to get people from different places … it creates a new culture … it brings in value addition within the existing set up, but sometimes people on the other side do feel constrained. Like if Bank A is technically far advanced, and Bank B is not very advanced, they use five different systems on the technology front, … then obviously Bank B has to learn, but I also understand that at the same time, this cannot be changed immediately, so one has also to manage expectations … what can be changed and what cannot be changed, and what will take a medium term, short term and long-term perspective … there could be … I would not say, conflicts among people. It is an opportunity to share ideas, and everybody being positive to pick up good things. And sometimes, yes you also have to look at their points of view, their bank culture … and where they come from and to understand their culture and try to fit yourself into that culture.

R Yeah, that's part of your personality … so it's not easy to change it overnight … that you will change an organisation or change yourself completely.

B And at the same time, you can't expect the organisation to change simply because you have changed the organisation. So it happens over a period of time. It's a constant endeavour … constant work that the people have to do with the senior management, the senior management has to appreciate and understand and take it in the right spirit … if they go wrong about it, then I don't think the relationship would last very long.

R The good thing in your industry is that the movement is so quick and fast, so if you don't like it you can always go to the next organisation …

B It is not always very simple to find the right fit … it's not very easy, and employers today always crib about not getting the right set of people to hire … At the same time, if you look at the industry and unemployment rate, it is only increasing. So there are people who have been left without a job and are not able to find the right job … either the organisations are not finding them fit to be hired or the employees are not wanting to go because of the preconceived notions.

R From that, let us move on to broader questions about professional culture. We have talked about people coming from different kinds of organisations … now the thing is if a banker comes from an organisation which has a very different kind of organisational culture, organisational identity, and at the same time, he has an identity as a professional banker, which has a banker's identity which identifies him as a banker, but at the same time … he is also seen as a banker who works with Bank A or Bank B, and also of course, as a human being, he has his own identity … all these identities can be projected at the same time. Which identity is more important for you? As a professional banker or a banker in a particular organisation, when you are looking for somebody for your bank … Is it more valuable than organisational identity because organisation identities can change?

B That also depends on how much time you have worked. If you have worked for 25 years, then one can say you are a true (Bank A) banker if you have worked for a long period of time. If you have worked for four years or five years, then it is a professional identity which carries you into different places, and gives you the ability to develop from there rather than organisational identities imposed on you.

R So people do regard professional identity perhaps at the top, but at the same time, when you look at these identities, professionals who have the ability to have an identity … who have a reputation of their own, and they move from one institution to the other, the third and the fourth … is there any kind of mechanism in the banking industry to monitor the movement of people, monitor the value system. The professional organisation like banking organisations, there must be something …

B   Oh yeah, in developed markets, say four–five cities, if I can name, New York, London, Tokyo, Hong Kong, Singapore, Dubai, all these cities as major financial centres in the world, typically there are a lot of headhunting firms who have been tracking the career movement of very many senior bankers ... and they know exactly how they have performed or what their perception has been, either by talking to an internal resource through HR or to clients, because all these ... they are part of various social gatherings and functions, where they meet their clients as well as they meet their bankers, on the other side. They have been there for many years, so they know the people within the industry, they are real gatekeepers. So there are lots of headhunting firms which have had presence for two or three decades. They would check ... for a very senior banker. So they would know typically ... and if somebody is trying to identify a person, he would go to a headhunting firm and tell them that here is the guy he's targeting. They would give him within 24 hours what the situation is right now, what he is doing, what he has done in past and things like that.

R   What does it mean to be a member of a profession, banking profession ... that is individuals, who are trusted, highly reputed members of an established profession? What does it mean, does it carry any value for the individuals?

B   Seeing at different points in time, different processes will come ... but for most of the time, if you have spent x amount of time in a particular profession, obviously you like that profession, you love that profession, that's why you are there. But obviously, it's not always a straight line up, there are pitfalls, and there are times when there are depressions, and you don't feel like being in that organisation or in that role or in that industry altogether. Of late, in the last five years, there have been more lows than highs, but in the last 24 years, if I were to say, for myself, I would say, there have been far more highs than lows.

R   To what extent is it the function of the market ... the economy going up and down ...

B   In fact, this industry is very much skewed to ... how the market performs ... there is very high correlation. One could say to a great extent, it's a very highly correlated industry from the market perspective. So when the economy is doing well, generally people have jobs, then people are spending money and they are getting good salaries, unemployment rate is low, things are going smooth, and banking does very well. When things go wrong ... for instance, if there is a housing crisis, or there is some kind of 9/11 event, then in those kind of situations, the market takes a tumble, and banking immediately takes a tumble, and then certain parts of the banking industry ... if you look at the investment bank typically, they always work on very quick hire and fire kind of a mode. It can be very unstable in that sense, when there are a lot of mergers and acquisitions happening, there are a lot of companies being bought and sold, and things like that. There will be a lot of requirement of demand for these M&A specialist people ... they will go hire from different institutions by paying very high salaries. But immediately when the market goes down, and there are not many transactions, they really add high cost for the bank. They also get cut the fastest ... because in two years, you make decent revenues ... you have a lot of deals. All of a sudden when the deals have dried up, there's nothing more that they can do, so they are being asked to go. So there are times when bankers go to those places where they don't have jobs, and either they move in different industries, head for different industries such as hedge fund management, or you just start your own private equity firm, and things like that.

R   But that also somehow disturbs the relationship between society and the profession ... how society views a particular profession.

B   Frankly in the last four or five years, to call yourself a banker has not been a great thing. To be honest, there were times in 2008 and 2009, people who are bankers would not call themselves bankers, because they expected that kind of rebuttal from the society. You guys are the guys who have created this mess for the entire world. It will take at least a couple of years to come over this. We also had a lot of people with high blood pressure and stress as a result of this.

R That's perhaps because the industry has been functioning basically on the basis of how much profit an institution can generate. The profit is the only motive and the social concern takes a back seat.

B That's right, at the time of the day ... banking worldwide some 30 years ago was seen as more of a public utility ... In the last 25–30 years of openness, of capitalism, the world has become a smaller place and banks have also become a big shareholder value driven thing. So they are profit-making organisations, not a charity organisation, they also have to make a profit. There are various ways of making profits, so whether you are happy at five billion, ten billion or twenty billion ... there is no limit.

R One, final question ... if you look at a normal banker, who has worked for five years, seven years, in a particular organisation. Is it possible to see that a person who is professionally competent as a banker will also find a personal satisfaction in his job? It means the relationship between the personal satisfaction and the professional competency ... is it a direct one? So for instance, if you are a good professional banker, then you are likely to get more satisfaction from your job, or are there other factors that disturb this balance? You may be an excellent banker, but still, in your profession, because of other things, because of the market demand, you don't find personal satisfaction in your job. Does it happen?

B Yes, it is possible. I would say it is very much driven by individual personality ... it would mean different things to different people. I can give you certain examples ... I can't name the persons here, but there are people who have been in the same role, same function for the last ten years. If their personality is such that they have seen this is what they want to achieve and they are happy with it, and are not very ambitious to take five steps ahead, they are happy with this set-up and will continue ... they will continue to sell to their clients in the same fashion as long as the institution doesn't throw them out or the demand of the institution doesn't really drastically change, but it could work the other way round too ... if the institution demands that they have to grow 15 per cent organically every year, then what you are talking about is in five years' time, you have to double the revenue, and double every five years, so in ten years, you basically quadruple what you started off with in your career. There may not be a person capable of working individually, and that's where the conflict arises. So, one needs to find the right fit with the right organisation ... sometimes there can be a difficult situation but it happens probably in a small number of cases. Most of the time, and as long as the organisation is growing, you grow with the organisation, and things go okay. It has to be commensurate, it cannot be that the organisation goes very fast high up and you continue to stagnate ... you will see some people who were your peers have overtaken you. This situation is possible, which will not be a very happy situation ... On the other hand, if you want to go very fast and the organisation is taking a very slow movement, then you will find another place to go very fast. The mentality has to match with individual personality and expectations.

33
Law

Interviewee: George Anthony David Dass was a partner at Shahrizat, Rashid and Lee for over 25 years. He continues as a consultant and a board member of Perbadanan Insurans Deposit Malaysia, and also of United Bintang Berhad in Malaysia.
(R – Researcher – Vijay Bhatia; L – Lawyer)

L When I went to school, the language of instruction was English. And so it was for our generation at the University of Singapore between 1967 and 1971 – we used English. Most Malaysians either went to Singapore or to the UK to train as lawyers as there was no law school in Malaysia until 1972. At that time the attitude of many senior practitioners in Malaya was that you could only be a good lawyer if you were trained in one of the Inns of Court. They were quite sceptical about standards at the University of Singapore. But training was vigorous in Singapore. They had, what they called the broad spectrum intake approach. Candidates were interviewed to gauge aptitude and motivation. The interviewers didn't really care what kind of grades the candidates had for their A-levels. A large number of students were admitted into the first year but half to two-thirds were eliminated after the first year. In my year, the policy had begun to change. You had to get at least four A-levels to get in. This approach was more humane as fewer would fail. At least that was the theory. In actual fact, about 120 students came into the first year in 1966/67 and only about 60 graduated four years later. Some took a bit longer to complete the course. But it was given that English language was the language of law and the language for the training of lawyers. In the context of Singapore and Malaysia, English was the language of the professions, of the middle-class, and it certainly was the language of the law. Both the teaching of law and the practice of law required you to look up cases, and the cases you looked at, including judgements reported in Malaysia or Singapore, were all in English and many of the judges at that time were also English judges. There were locals, but they were locals trained in England. Law was considered a noble profession. It was a demanding profession and the number of lawyers was very small. So when I graduated, one of the things that was insisted on by employers as well as the bar committees was the importance of knowing other practitioners and knowing all the stakeholders and participants in the legal process – high court clerks, low court clerks, registrars, interpreters, magistrates, judges, etc., so your relationship with the

View from the professions

people who administered the system, including bar council members and bar committee members, mattered and was important so you very quickly got yourself connected with the profession and to the seniors in the profession.

R Did you also practise in Singapore?

L No, I didn't. Although I did a lot of cross-border work which required me to interact with Singapore lawyers. In those days, it would have been a simple matter for me to be called to the Singapore bar. A lot of my friends got called and appeared in the Singapore courts. I really wasn't interested, although I was offered a job with the Singapore legal service. I began to practise in a corporate law firm in Kuala Lumpur, which also did civil and a little criminal litigation. I did a few criminal cases in the beginning but decided very quickly that I was not going to be a criminal lawyer and so did civil work. I then left, took a couple of years off and went to the UK, did a master's, came back and joined another corporate law firm in Kuala Lumpur. I began with civil litigation and general civil work, but I, very quickly, gave up litigation to focus on banking and corporate law. And that was to be my practice for the rest of my career.

R So when you look back to all your experience, your accumulated experience ... how would you actually categorise the legal behaviour ... how would you identify a good lawyer or a bad lawyer, or not so good a lawyer?

L That's easy enough to do – in recruiting lawyers we first look at their academic results – the schools they attended, the grades obtained, the law school, class, second degree, etc. But changes in the legal environment over the years have made the problem more complex ... For a start, the number of lawyers has increased from less than 1,000 when I graduated, to 15 to 16,000 today so it's a much larger number. The relationship between lawyers is not the same as it was then, and this has resulted in a big change in the way lawyers practise law. In the early days many problems resulting in litigation were resolved simply by lawyers settling matters amicably. But now cases that should be settled are often litigated at the expense of the client. Each lawyer takes the position that his client has got a good case. And you drag it out. A good attribute for a lawyer therefore, is the ability to skilfully interact with other lawyers. Many conflicts can be resolved through discussions and through conciliation and mediation. You now have mediation and conciliation as part of the structure of the legal process. So the character of a lawyer is important – is he able to relate effectively with others? Most lawyers today are trained locally, and relatively very few lawyers are trained in England. A number of them are trained in Australia, and very few are trained in Singapore. Many who are trained locally are trained for external degrees through tutorial colleges. English language proficiency is also important both for training and for practice. We have lost the English language proficiency, which came from training in the UK. And the local universities clearly have not engaged in a sensible and a practical way with the use of English in the training of lawyers. Malay is the language of instruction in schools and a mix of Malay and English is used for the law courses in Public Universities. Law Faculties have not been able to remedy the lack of English language proficiency for the purpose of law studies and the result is evident in the language skills of many lawyers.

R Is it that they don't actually recognise the need or that they do not have the expertise to do it?

L I think, if you speak to the senior members of Law Faculties, they recognise the importance of English, but they think it's beyond them to try to repair or remedy the language deficiency in the time students have at the university. And I think it goes across all the professions, but looking at law in particular, your textbooks are in English, your law reports are in English. Kids come in with varying degrees of, varying levels of proficiency, there are some who come from families where English is virtually their first language, so they are good. Some embrace bilingualism, so they are okay. But a lot of them don't have English language the way we had. Most kids don't read as much as they used to. This appears to be a universal problem.

R That's right.

L But more so here because, over 90 per cent of the Chinese kids go to Chinese primary schools and over 50 per cent of the Indian kids go to Tamil schools. Most Malay kids are monolingual to a large extent. In the old days, they recognised the relevance of English in their lives – we used to have a higher level of spoken English because that's how we communicated across the races. And in Singapore, because the population was mainly Chinese, they spoke in Chinese dialects, so we used to think that we spoke better English than Singaporeans. And then Singapore experimented with Mandarin – things went downhill and they had to have remedial courses at the universities ... But in Malaysia nobody, neither the government nor the law teachers has decisively recognised this problem. Some law teachers recognise it, but think it's beyond them ... But even the law teachers do not fully recognise the importance of English in the training of the lawyer, in the training of the legal mind. In Singapore they used cases to teach the law. They used the Harvard case method of instruction. It was a stressful but effective way of teaching us law through the cases. Textbooks were in English, universities used English textbooks and cases were published/reported in the English language and we were required to plough through the original case reports, reading judgements, summarising them, trying to understand the dissenting judgements – it took me a long while to understand the nuances to understand the concept of the reasoned judgement. Today my own experience with young lawyers is that many just don't have the language to think analytically. There is also some confusion as to what the Rule of Law means when one has a written constitution. That there is embedded in law notions of justice, human rights, individual freedom, etc. That all law must be measured against the standards established by the Constitution, which is the Supreme Law of the country.

R But obviously, that is not actually really because they don't have the language ...

L But it is related to language ... how do you train lawyers. I often use this example, how do you train the security guard? How do you train a policeman? How do you make an honest security guard – one whom you are asking to watch over somebody else's property? How do you know that at the end of the training, he will be an honest security guard? How do you know at the end of the training, he will be an honest, good policeman? So when you train a lawyer, how do you ensure that he is a lawyer imbued with the right ethics, the right principles? Motivated to ensure that at the end justice is served? This is where language plays a part – a good lawyer needs to be able to fully understand and appreciate the concepts and nuances and to be able to read widely to understand the philosophy and jurisprudence underpinning the legal system. And the fact remains that we have chosen the English Common law as our system of law.

R That's one of the main questions I have.

L So, it becomes an important part of the training ... the legal mind is not just somebody technically competent, it's somebody who is also ethical and somebody who is passionate about justice. I think in the old days, when we graduated, the vast majority of us had ideals, at least at that point in time ... we were concerned with the ideals of law. After a few years some may have got lost in the corporate world and begun to think of making money above all else. Individuals take different pathways but at least as far as possible, law faculties should try to instil in lawyers noble ideals. Throughout the world, lawyers talk about certain judges – Lord Denning, for instance, is a name that would be known anywhere in the world when people look at common law cases and why is there this excitement about a man like Lord Denning and others like Lord Wright and Lord Atkins? Why? Because of the decisions they made, the values they spoke of and the way they pushed for justice. And their judgements were rich and compelling, speaking loudly for justice.

R Is this something to do with the local culture? Or the local legal system?

L It's always the tension between old ways and new institutions and processes, and I always make this point to a lot of my friends and in talks I give. The Chinese don't come from a history of democratic traditions. Traditional Chinese society was largely feudal, and all rights of the people reposed with the emperor and subsequent dictators. India was the same, 600 maharajas had absolute power over others. The Malays had their traditional rulers. So none of us, none of the indigenous people, had a tradition and history of democratic rights and traditions. The British brought these things in and it's very recent but it was amazing how quickly it became part of the local scene and how quickly the elite group of people subscribed to these forms and institutions and it became part of our lives. And many of us think it is a good thing. But there has always been resistance to the idea that law could be a greater force than the power of politicians. There was a recent prime minister who challenged the notion that courts should be independent of the executive.

R In one sense, the legal profession is slightly different from other professions. Other professions have some kind of training in place – as they enter the profession they are given training, and they are occasionally sent back for training in law. You have actually identified a number of key competencies that a good lawyer should have, but is it possible to incorporate these in the university programmes?

L I think it is possible. First, let's look at the way to train someone as a doctor. It's clear what skills he must have. And there's no politics about it, the key competencies you need to have in a doctor or accountant, not a problem, like most of the other professions. When it comes to law, it's a bit difficult. I am talking about the constitution, about the objectives and aims of a legal system, which is justice, and achieving the right kind of tension and dynamic between the rights of the state and the individual. At the best of times it's a difficult balancing act, and if the power is weighed in favour of the government, that leads to us being autocratic or authoritarian. So can you train lawyers to be competent in specific areas of the law? I think if you are looking at the corporate and the commercial side of things, it's not difficult. You can train a lawyer to be a good conveyance or banking lawyer, which is not difficult. You just need to identify the areas and the skills you need to have training specifically in, and language is an important part of that. For instance, in drafting agreements and pleadings and doing research and writing opinions and submissions. A lawyer can also be trained in courtroom skills – to be a skilful cross-examiner. Moots aim to do that but the question must be asked as to their adequacy. And I think quite possibly these are better treated as postgraduate kinds of courses. I think law courses could be more rigorous. But for them to be more rigorous, you have to deal with the issue of language, and if it's Malaysia, it's got to be bilingualism – English and Malay lawyers have to be trained to use both the languages to the highest levels possible. English is used extensively in the High Courts and Malay is used extensively in the lower courts. Many magistrates are not very proficient in the use of English and all lawyers are comfortable today in using Malay in the lower courts but submissions are made with the use of cases that are reported in English.

R One of the issues that comes up quite regularly in the universities, both here and elsewhere – in Hong Kong, in Singapore, and even in Britain, that is that when they start devoting time to different courses, most of the law professors complain that they don't have enough time to devote to English language.

L That's right. It is the same thing here. But a lecturer must be concerned about the ability of his students to understand him. He must also be concerned about the ability of the students to express their ideas in the relevant languages. It is not possible to teach or learn law under our common law system without English language proficiency. It also depends on which university you are in. Some universities conduct their courses entirely in English. But the point is – the issue of English language proficiency must be addressed. One solution may be to require those who are not proficient in English to spend an additional year for language proficiency and then to go into the law course proper. But the point is that if you don't address that problem, you will not be able to teach effectively.

R How different is the legal profession compared to, for example, business, accounting or medicine in terms of appraisal of people's professional work? If a lawyer joins a particular organisation or a law firm, how is he actually appraised every year or every two years? Is there a mechanism for appraisal?

L The banking and corporate law services provided by the legal profession form part of the financial system and in that respect they are no different from the other professions in the financial system. We have a financial system which is quite sophisticated, we have people who are quite brilliant with first world thinking, and they are everywhere, they are in government, central bank, ministry of finance, ministry of trade, they are very clever people, who are outstanding. We have outstanding judges and outstanding lawyers. These people would function at the same level as the top lawyers anywhere around the world. Law firms would provide expertise in certain areas. It is usual for work to be handled by teams comprising lawyers with varying levels of experience. Most project and transactional work would have to be handled within agreed time frames. Lawyers would work to deadlines. The team must work cohesively. Good lawyers will learn on the hop as it were. Lawyers would be appraised annually and would be rewarded by bonuses. Some may not make the grade. So when you are looking for lawyers, you want lawyers to support you, to do your work. And we are all aware that there are different levels of experience and expertise required. One should generally expect little from a first year lawyer. As a general rule it takes approximately three intense years in a good firm for one to become a useful lawyer, in five years, you become senior and able to do some work on your own and after seven years, you are ready for a partnership, so at that level, you make decisions about a lawyer's technical skills, his people skills, his leadership skills. Appraisal is a continuing process and usually with time and experience it would become clear who makes the cut. The specific forms that appraisal takes would vary from firm to firm.

R Unless they come from a good university.

L It doesn't matter which university you come from. You are clever, but you cannot be immediately useful. And it will take you some time to pick up the practical skills – you don't learn practical skills at a university.

R So, is that a kind of apprenticeship or understudy?

L The first two years of your training contract are meant to be that. But I know from my own son's experience in the UK that they may, perhaps, on the first day, put you in the deep end. Some kids are bright enough to be able to pick things up. Anyway, the point I am making is, they are paying you a lot of money, even in the first year, especially in the UK, so expectations are very high and the pressure on young lawyers is very high and some make it and some don't. Some lawyers need a reasonable period to pick up experience and confidence and some collapse under the pressure and give up law practice.

R And obviously, in early days, when you enter the profession, you are working with other people maybe in small groups. But as you become senior, as you grow in the profession, do you still have to work together with other people in teams? Or do people normally practise individually if they are working in a firm?

L It varies. I don't think it's possible to do corporate transactions without teams. I know a few practitioners who love doing everything by themselves. But I think they are old school generally, because in a transaction, there is work which is very complex, it requires the senior guy. There is also work which is very simple and basic, and can be handled by juniors. So the team should comprise people of different types, different levels of experience and expertise …

R Even when you write documents, produce documents, briefs, memos …

L Very often, some of the documents can be produced by less senior lawyers and looked at by the senior lawyers. So, it's again a different level of collaboration and today, for most transactions, you work off precedents, you work off documents you have, so it's adaptation …

R So adaptation of most of the documents …

L Unless it's a new type of transaction which requires drafting from scratch.

R How do you actually identify people when they join the profession?

L The first thing to do is to look at the CV, which school they come from, look at the school, look at the university, look at the subjects they have done, look at their grades and class. And increasingly firms are looking for people with a second degree. Again, maybe it's a result of falling standards, but we are looking for people who can write, who can research and write well. And generally, we assume that if you have a master's degree, you have learnt to do research more effectively.

R Is there any requirement that people should have some kind of experience either outside the profession or within the profession? So you don't look like other professions.

L There is generally no such requirement. But it could be advantageous for those wanting to practise in certain areas to have either specialised knowledge or experience. For instance engineers or architects who subsequently become lawyers and do construction law.

R Now you have in Malaysia and in a number of other countries, the local language and the language of the courts but in addition to that in a number of these countries, expertise in English. Is this equally relevant, or more relevant, or perhaps less so when you look at the people with both the languages, or three languages?

L As I explained earlier on proficiency in English is still a requirement and the commercial sector functions almost entirely in English, so yes it is relevant.

R In spite of the fact that the language of court is mostly in Malay?

L English is used quite extensively in the higher courts although the requirement is that you file your pleadings and submissions in Malay with English translations. Of course, the knowledge of other languages is good. You assume that most lawyers will be reasonably proficient in Malay because they have gone through the school system, which is Malay. So you assume that they have the ability to look at documentation, look at forms, correspondence with government, departments and they will be able to do translation for documents, for the courts. So, basically in many instances all drafting is still done in English but for translation, firms employ professional translators or lawyers themselves translate, they translate English into Malay. So knowledge of both languages is essential. Knowledge of other languages which have commercial value – Mandarin or other Chinese dialects – would be useful for lawyers.

R Do you actually ever have, when you are working in a team, and when you are not performing on the stage, that is a courtroom setting, but discussing a case in a committee room with team members, conflicts, misunderstandings, discussions within the lawyers themselves in the team?

L You mean fights or arguments?

R Not fights, but arguments, different points of view, contested views?

L Within the same site, the same firm, a good firm would encourage this kind of thing. The young lawyers will come into my firm and that's my expectation. And they will develop the confidence and have the confidence to disagree with me. Good firms understand the need for people who can think independently.

R Because onstage performance is generally finished agreement, indicating the view of the company, the view of the lawyer, and the team of lawyers, but inside they actually argue and disagree when discussing the case.

L But I'm not sure whether there is a standard, because this kind of internal discussion/argument is more likely to occur in the larger firms and the majority of law firms in this country are very small firms, one-man, two-men, three-men firms. There are some firms, there are maybe, six, seven firms which have more than 50 lawyers and there are a couple of firms with more than 100 lawyers.

R Is there a very substantial difference between the local legal culture and the legal culture in neighbouring countries, Singapore, Hong Kong, India?

L I think the theoretical constructs are not different. Maybe there is a huge gap between the theoretical construct and the actual implementation and the actual behaviour or conduct of the people. The commercial law of England became the commercial law of the colonies. The Contract law of England was codified and became the Contracts Act of India, which Malaysia followed. The Companies Act of the UK became that of Australia, which in turn was followed by Malaysia and Singapore. So to a large extent, corporate law or commercial law of the developed world is a codification of English common law principles, so it will not be dissimilar … there is almost homogenisation of commercial law principles. Except for Sharia type financing transactions the concepts underlying commercial transactions are becoming universal, so it doesn't matter whether it's an English lawyer who writes it or an Indian lawyer who writes it, or the Malaysian lawyer who writes it. You choose a system of law you are competent to practise. Today, for huge commercial law transactions, you choose the law of New York, you choose the law of England, you choose the law of Singapore, you choose the law of Malaysia, or you can choose arbitration to be the main way of resolving disputes. We can choose then the principles depending on where you want to arbitrate. The culture, to me, matters only where the legal systems are dissimilar. What is the law in Saudi Arabia? What is the law in Russia? What is the law in China? The legal systems are so different.

R So it all depends on the legal system.

L You have to make the assumption that to some extent, the legal system of the country will reflect the way people behave. It doesn't necessarily follow, because you can write brilliant contracts for a particular country but the people may ignore the written word and do exactly what they like and the courts may not be helpful. So a good lawyer will be very aware of the behaviour of people and the integrity of the judicial system so he tells his client that you write your contract here, but don't rely on enforcement of your contract in some countries. A lot of people get into problems, they write the contracts and even provide for arbitration in some other country but the contract is not enforced/enforceable.

R How is this legal profession in Malaysia viewed by the stakeholders or members of the public?

L This is really a big question. But generally people are positive about the system. There are misgivings about political cases and sometimes cases with a religious element. But Malaysians generally respect the law. And as far as Malaysia is concerned, it really depends on enforcement and it depends on the courts. If the courts are vigilant and quick to enforce, the legal principles and processes are clear. So Malaysians participating in commercial life in this country don't have a choice. They will have to abide by agreements they make because they should not expect the court to help them subvert/breach the terms of the agreement. So this is the expectation we have here. But generally, we write contracts with the expectation that people will honour commitments made and that courts will enforce such contracts. I think that people – the stakeholders – generally think that the system works – not perfectly – but to a reasonable standard.

R One final general question … In most countries the impression of the law in the last 10–15 years has been that like medicine or accountancy and to some extent other professions, law has also been extremely commercialised, with the result that it is losing its prestige that it once enjoyed. The lawyers have some kind of social responsibility, but in most countries, it is being commercialised.

L The nature of law hasn't changed. Law as a profession is like any other profession – lawyers are becoming more money-minded. I think there have always been money-minded lawyers in any time. There are also lawyers who are more concerned about justice, more concerned about the work they are doing to help the dispossessed, disenfranchised. And there are lawyers who are only concerned about making money and servicing the big client. This will always be there.

R Is that proportion increasing?

L The multinational law firms dominate, and they are generally only concerned with the commercial law. They have no interest in the ideals of justice, which are generally the concern of the criminal law and constitutional law. So to that extent, this is true. The major law firms in the world, the multinational law firms in the world are generally only concerned about commercial corporate law, they have little interest in criminal law in the country, so it's for each country to sort that out, for each country to make sure that you have lots of lawyers who are concerned about justice. In that sense, I am very proud of the Malaysian legal profession … I think we are one of the more dynamic bars; the Malaysian bar has consistently fought for the oppressed. There are a lot of brilliant Malaysian lawyers, who operate as single practitioners or in small firms, earning not very much money but doing a lot of good work. Unfortunately, big money is in commercial law, a lot of very clever lawyers don't even think twice, they go to the law school, come out and all they want to do is commercial law, corporate law. But when I first began, we had to do litigation work, you had to have been a litigation lawyer for few years before you could make a choice of becoming an office lawyer, but we abandoned that some years ago. So there are lawyers who will never go to court, have never been to courts, it is a tragedy because you really develop strength and resilience by going to court for a few years.

34
Accounting

Accountant (A), who would like to remain anonymous, works for an accountancy firm in Hong Kong.
(R – Researcher – Alina Wan; A – Accountant)

R Alright, so ... Thank you very much for participating in this interview. The first question I'd like to ask is, how would you characterise or describe an expert accountant?
A It depends on how you define expert, the term expert. A qualified accountant may specialise in a particular area, such as auditing, taxation, accounting and so on. Under, say, in the auditing field, he may also further specialise in some specialist areas. Very specialised or just in a particular field, such as auditing or accounting.
R Let's talk about auditing. Because you have more experience in auditing – is that right?
A Yes, most of the time I've been working in auditing.
R Okay, so how would you describe an expert qualified, you know, an accountant who is an auditor working in an accounting firm?
A First of all, having past experience, passing all the examinations, that's basic. The experience can vary a lot; auditing people mainly learn from experience, I should say.
R Okay, so what about the expert behaviour of an auditor?
A Nothing too special. Maybe able to carry out an audit assignment properly within a required time. Maybe giving the outsiders an impression that we are professionals.
R So you are professional by, perhaps, going through your responsibilities as an auditor going through audits, going to other organisations and conducting audits and talking to clients?
A Yes.
R Does discursive competence, your ability to write professional documents or to participate in spoken communication in professional contexts play a role in professional practice?
A I think it plays an important role. However, there is not a way to assess whether a student possesses such competence before he can be called qualified, because students have to pass examinations, have to go through all the training. But there's not a particular subject on discursive competence and the way they communicate. Perhaps, maybe, let's say in Hong Kong, the Institute requires students under the qualifying programmes to attend workshops. Let me explain a bit: under the qualifying programme – the QP, we call it – there are four

modules, four main subjects. Before the students can sit for examinations for each module, they have to attend workshops for each. Each workshop lasts for two days, each of eight hours. During the workshop, students have to participate in group discussions, case studies, in order to be assessed. But the pass rate is over 99 per cent – as long as they've prepared for the workshop, as long as they participate in the discussions and the teamwork, they can pass. We consider communication skills, but it is not the main point. It's so easy to pass. It's not a good way to assess their communication skills.

R So you're saying that it does play a very important role in the professional practice of accountants, of auditors, but it's not sufficiently really taught at school. Then, how does it play a role in the professional practice, so in terms of writing documents and going to meetings, how does that play a role – discursive competence?

A We have to write a lot apart from dealing with figures. We have to write a lot, such as planning documents, and reports and so on. Generally, we communicate with each other in English, by email and phone calls. Also we have to deal with clients – clients from everywhere, maybe local clients, maybe PRC, maybe other parts of the world.

R Oh I see, OK, alright, so the next question would be: Is it possible to specify expertise in terms of key competencies? What are they, what do you think, for an auditor?

A Yes, maybe. First of all, may I define key competencies? Do you have anything in mind?

R A key competency would be something measurable e.g. knowledge or skills, abilities or even personal attributes. So for example, communication would be a key competency. Leadership, team focus, accountability. So these are some examples of key competencies. So do you think that you can ... is it possible to specify expertise in terms of these key competencies as an auditor? What do you think?

A Yes, at least to an extent. May I divide them into ... maybe technical competencies. Technical competencies can be assessed mainly through examinations, built up through practice and through working experience. At work, the performance of a student or maybe an employee is assessed through some internal assessment in order to determine whether they're entitled to promotion or standard increase. Also apart from technical competencies, I can say the other one is, say generic competencies. They include cognitive thinking, communication skills that we mentioned just now, language ability, teamwork, ethical behaviour and so on. There's no clearly defined way to assess these. Especially when, during an examination, we cannot ... It's difficult to assess – there's no sort of interview that students have to sit for before they're qualified. But in the workplace, these competencies can also be assessed through internal assessments. The performance at work can be reviewed.

R So as an expert auditor, some key competencies of an auditor, you include communication, language skills, the ability to use technology, some technical skills as well, perhaps even working with others in teams, that would be another competency. Are there any other key competencies of an auditor?

A I think these are the two main areas, technical and generic. I can't think of them at the moment ... But maybe there are others under these two big headings.

R And then you mentioned that these competencies ... do you think are these teachable or learnable?

A Yes, teachable, I think ... I believe ... especially the technical ones, through examinations, through learning and also through training at work.

R So maybe through the academy, through school and also in the workplace. So both, right?

A Yes, both.

R How would you appraise or measure these competencies or expertise in your workplace? Some of these technical competencies that you mentioned or the generic competencies, how would you measure these in your workplace?

A In the workplace, first of all, their qualifications. As a basic requirement, they have to be professionally qualified. On top of that, their relevant experience, recognised and approved experience.
R This would be in other accounting firms in Hong Kong, or even overseas?
A I think everywhere.
R So I'd like to ask, who are the specialists in your field?
A Do you mean the experts or the specialists?
R Yes, so you know, you're working in an accounting firm, for example, and then you've got auditors, perhaps, tax accountants, you might also have reporting accountants, forensic accountants, so who are the specialists in your field?
A In the auditing field? I think different auditors may specialise in different areas – maybe some are specialised in IPOs, maybe some are specialised in takeovers, some are more specialised in corporate governance. I consider these have special knowledge in specific areas.
R Are there any significant disciplinary differences in terms of academic study? Like how do you become specialised in IPOs or how do you become specialised in ... or is it through training again?
A Training and experience.
R Are there any special courses one might have to take?
A Yes, there are some special courses in special fields.
R And how many specialists actually work with you or do you normally work with?
A I'm not too specialised in my workplace and there aren't too many specialists around. Some may be better in some areas but I cannot say whether they're specialists or not.
R Do you normally work individually or do you work in groups?
A Both.
R Do you write your documents individually or collaboratively? So the reports that you write ...
A I usually write individually.
R You write these individually but what kinds of documents do you normally have to write, then?
A Audit type documents, audit completion memorandums, audit reports, draft audit reports, and also management letters, and so on, and also some ad hoc documents.
R When you mentioned the audit report that you have to draft ... Now, that – you do individually but what about the audit work itself though, is that collaborative?
A Well, actually I draft or write these individually, and they are being reviewed by more senior staff such as audit partners.
R Right, so it does go through an editing or maybe an approval process?
A Yes.
R Who do you normally interact with as part of your daily work?
A I'm just in the middle, I interact with the audit partners, and also with staff underneath, interact with clients, also interact with other colleagues of a similar grade because different people may specialise in different areas. I may consult with tax departments, tax managers for their opinion or their advice, also consult technical departments for technical matters. So I interact with all people.
R When you say technical matters, what do you mean by technical matters?
A There's a technical department, they specialise in going through the standards, guidelines, regulations and ordinance – all things. Usually we consult them in some difficult matters or some grey areas, how we can deal with them.
R In terms of ordinance or regulation?

A Hmm.
R So they're more like ... do you mean they're more versed with the accounting standards and guidelines, is that what you mean?
A Yes, I can say they specialise in that.
R So there's actually a separate department, called the technical department. These are also qualified accountants?
A Yes.
R Personal question, what sort of education do you have?
A Qualified accountant. Do you mean academic or professional qualification? Academic, I've got a BA in Accounting Studies, I got a BA and an MSc in Accounting and Finance.
R And did you get your degree in Hong Kong or overseas?
A Overseas.
R How did you get trained to become a qualified accountant?
A After my graduation, I joined a small firm in London as a trainee. I got a trainee contract, and for the next four years, I worked there.
R And then after that you came back to Hong Kong?
A Yes.
R Did you go through the QP programme again or is it the ACCA?
A No, it was in the 90s, before the QP programme in Hong Kong. It came into effect a few years ago. At that time there was a sort of transfer, so I got ... Apart from the UK qualification, I can also get the Hong Kong qualification.
R So you are professionally qualified in the UK as well as in Hong Kong.
A Yes.
R So normally how are accountants, or more particularly auditors, how are they recruited in Hong Kong?
A They are usually recruited to a professional firm, an accountancy firm ...
R Are there exams, or is there a procedure involved, even in your experience in the UK and in Hong Kong?
A Usually there are two ways. One is they can apply just like a normal job ... apply for a job in a particular firm. The other way is some audit firms, accountancy firms go to universities to recruit students, the final year students.
R So they have their own procedures for those students in universities in Hong Kong. And then you mentioned you've got to be professionally qualified, so in terms of qualifications now you also mentioned a QP route and then I think before that there's an ACCA route, is that right? So what qualifications are required in Hong Kong?
A I can't quite get your question, can you repeat that?
R Yea, sure, if you want to be a qualified accountant in Hong Kong, what is the qualification that you need ... that is required?
A First of all, you need to have a university degree, then you go through the QP (Qualifying Programme) and then the final examinations.
R This takes how many years ... to go through QP?
A I'm not too sure, I think at least two ... because according to the number of modules and the number of examinations and workshops, it may take about 3 years or maybe as long as 10 years. It depends if you can pass the examinations.
R So it depends on the individual, right?
A Yes.
R And you also mentioned that you were a trainee. How many years do you have to work as a trainee then? In general or in your case ... please you can talk about your case.

A   As far as I can remember it was a three-year trainee contract, at least, three years. In Hong Kong, the general requirement is also three years.
R   So training for three years and then you need to go through the QP programme, and then after you've achieved these two, then you're a qualified accountant, is that right?
A   Yes, the experience and the programme and all the examinations and experience can go together. You can acquire them at the same time.
R   Acquire them at the same time. So while you're training, you're also studying for the QP, is that right?
A   Yes.
R   So really it depends on how determined or how ambitious a particular person is?
A   Yes.
R   Are there any procedures available for work appraisals? So how does that work in terms of appraising someone's work, is it yearly, is there a reward system, is there a rank system, how does that work?
A   Usually half a year.
R   Who appraises whom, how does that work?
A   A senior member of the firm appraises a junior member. It's usually a supervisor or a manager appraising a staff and the appraisal is then reviewed by the partner.
R   And there are set forms available to fill out, is that right?
A   Yes.
R   And this is viewed by both the appraiser and the appraisee?
A   Yes.
R   Do they discuss this? Is there a meeting between the appraiser and the appraisee?
A   Yes, there's always a discussion.
R   What languages do you often use? I think you've mentioned English, but do you use both English and Cantonese? You know – from your experience in different firms in Hong Kong, both, right?
A   Both.
R   What about Putonghua? What's the role of that?
A   Only when you deal with PRC or Taiwan clients.
R   And another question will be, what mode of interaction do you prefer, or do you normally use? Is it email, telephone, face-to-face interaction, group meetings? Your preference … and what's the normal practice?
A   I prefer email and face-to-face, both. Normal practice, we use all types of these.
R   So all types, group meetings, face to face … Now another question I wanted to ask you would be about any constraints that you work under. So what kinds of … or are there any institutional constraints that you work under?
A   We have to work, we have to follow the ethical guidelines. For example, if we audit a company or group, we or our immediate family cannot hold shares in that company, that's the basic requirement. And also there are a few others … quite a lot of these ethical requirements.
R   So more ethical requirements for accountants and auditors? And what kinds of conflicts do you often have to face at work?
A   What do you mean by conflicts? Do you mean …
R   Perhaps, conflicting goals, maybe with a particular client, or any conflicts of interest?
A   We have to avoid that as far as possible according to the ethical requirements, avoid conflicts of interest. So we don't face … As long as the conflicts can be avoided, we don't face a lot of these.
R   Any particular conflicts with perhaps partners of the firm, maybe disagreement?

View from the professions

A Oh, you mean disagreement? Yes, but not a lot.
R And then more generally, if you're to hire someone, what do you look for in a potential employee?
A First of all, technical ability, that means 'can do'. And also, I put a lot of emphasis on the ability to communicate properly, both oral and written communication. And also maybe the candidate's willingness to work, to advance.
R Another question would be, what kind of identity do you display in your daily tasks, as an auditor? Is it more professional, is it more of a corporate identity, is it individual? For you in particular.
A For me, myself … just individual.
R It will be more individual?
A Yeah, I should say, I can say that. But it depends on how you define 'individual'.
R What kind of identity are you required to display as an auditor?
A To be professional.
R More professional than individual?
A Yes.
R What kind of gate-keeping mechanism does your profession have? You mentioned something about, you need a university degree first, so if you don't have a university degree, then you're out – probably you wouldn't be able to qualify as an accountant nowadays. And then besides having a university degree you need to go through a programme, the QP programme. You also have to have a training contract, is that right?
A Yes. In Hong Kong, it's not a training contract because a candidate can always change employment, as long as the change is not excessive.
R So how do you define 'excessive'? Like more than three times?
A I think within the … two to three times. There's a requirement, you cannot change more than … Within the qualifying period, the training period, you cannot change more than two or three times, otherwise that bit of experience will not be counted.
R So that bit of experience will not be counted, but let's say you change twice, then you can accumulate the experience from the first training period you worked and then the second, then you can accumulate that. That would have to be two to three years of experience, right?
A Yes, sort of.
R Can I ask you about the professional associations that you're part of?
A I'm part of, in the UK, the Institute of Chartered Accountants in England and Wales; in Hong Kong, it's the Hong Kong Institute of CPA (Certified Public Accountants).
R Can I ask you just about the professional culture? What sort of professional culture do you find in your profession?
A It's not obvious.
R Oh, it's not obvious, so what is it? What sort of professional culture is it? Could it be a very supportive culture? What do you think? Is it a culture of teamwork? Or is it very individualistic?
A It's more teamwork and perhaps I can say we're all prepared to overwork.
R Oh, I see. So it is definitely a hardcore working culture, isn't it?
A Yes.
R And then I just have two more questions. What kind of recognition do you get from your employers, your previous employers, what kind of recognition do you get at work?
A What do you mean by recognition in this case?
R If you've done a good job, you've clocked in a number of years of experience, is there a promotion or is there a rank that after a certain number of years of good work, you're promoted to another rank and then you're also rewarded with more money?

A I think pay increase and promotion are common.
R Within the accounting profession. And is there like a set pay scale?
A No, not a pay scale. Maybe for the new trainees or for the fresh graduates, they have a pay scale. First year, maybe first and second year, they have a promotion scale, also a pay scale for the first maybe two or three years. And after that, it really depends on performance or recognition inside the firm.
R So they have that for more junior ranking employees of the firm. Okay, and then just one last question, how other members of society, especially from outside your profession, how do you think these other members of society view accountants or view auditors?
A I think accountants are perceived as very good at dealing with figures but this may not actually be the case.
R So this might not necessarily be the case. Why do you say that?
A We don't have to be very good at calculation, dealing with figures. In the examinations, many questions are not number-crunching questions. You don't have to be particularly strong in dealing with figures.
R That's very interesting, because most people perceive accountants as number crunchers, you know, they work really well with numbers. But you're saying that that's not really a key competency to number crunch.
A Not necessarily.
R Oh I see. So you view other competencies like communication, other technical skills, these are more important than actually dealing with numbers.
A Yes.
R Okay. I think that's about it.

35
PR

Interviewee: PR practitioner (P), who would like to remain anonymous, is the Managing Director of a PR company in Hong Kong.
(R – Researcher – Stephen Bremner; P – PR practitioner)

R Basically what we are trying to find out is what constitutes expert knowledge in your field and what makes a PR practitioner a PR practitioner rather than, say, a lawyer, what is particular about the way that people become PR people and work as PR people. The first thing we are interested in is the whole nature of the specialist community of PR practitioners. To start with, how do you work? Do you work individually? Do you work in groups? What kind of groups?

P Never individually, always collaboratively. We are a small consultancy of ~10 staff. Always in a group, we have a director which is me … We have a member who has a project management responsibility. And then, in terms of formulating … The first part that we become involved in would be the big process. Generally, myself and my appointed proposal manager would then brainstorm the issues. To be honest, we generally would involve three or four of us to think of the issues, to think of the types of challenges, the type of work to do to impress …

R So, right from the beginning.

P Literally, with almost all … I don't think that that we'd ever do it even with just two, I think the collective wisdom is always better, and we have got different parts that we have: we do public relations where it's building a brand and then a subset of that would be where the communication is between a brand and its consumers. And we have a subset which is public affairs, where the communication is basically between government relations and public affairs, so it's corporate to government. So those are different types of PR people, and then we do quite a lot on communication where it's more infrastructure and development, so it's stakeholder communication with public engagement, public consultation, and they are all slightly differing characteristics that we have.

R Could you put all of these together and say the overall aim of these activities as one common … ?

P Yeah, it's just basically communicating with your target, from a branding point of view – brand building, you are wanting simply to effectively target a response in your consumers or your publics or whatever it might be. So I think it's that. Definitely a good way of looking – both in terms of the public relations and the public affairs – is to think about it in terms of perception – changing perception. Quite often, on the public affairs side, for example, government may bring a new law or policy in that could materially affect negatively and materially affect a business, perhaps even destroy the business. But we will often then get brought in, A – to understand the corporate's position, B – then to discuss the government's position, what are they trying to do under the new legislation.

R Discuss with the government?

P With the government, directly – 'Tell me a little bit more, government, tell me a little bit about what you're trying to do'. And then putting the two together and trying to see how you can broker a compromise. So here, the corporate wants this, the government wants this. Where is the overlap in the Venn diagram that can allow both parties to achieve their aims?

R But in this case, your client would not be the government.

P Yes, we always ... it's actually a very one-way street, so it's always corporate to government, influencing government, brokering a workable, liveable compromise. That's the public affairs. So definitely, there is a lot of changing perception, and in terms of the brand building and the PR, you're basically wanting to change the perception of your audience, your consumer, whether it's physical, whether it's product, whether it's service – affect them to basically either buy your products, or hire your service.

R But it's a collaborative enterprise throughout ...

P Oh, right, yes, the proposal process is very collaborative, brainstorming ... and you invest a lot of effort in thinking about it. What is actually quite interesting is that because we have to cost, we have to ... generally ... 'Give me a quote to do this work', generally on a retainer basis, so you have an amount of hours, or an amount of money basically to support your client, to influence, change perceptions of their consumers. But there is a lot of thought that goes into the actual process of 'Right, what do they need, what is the minimum amount of support that we can give, in terms of manpower, in terms of supporting and making a difference.' So there's that cost side of it. But what's interesting is that as a company, we generally don't want to share all of our brilliant ideas with the client until we are hired, because it's IP, it's like Microsoft ... We have a lot of ideas, but it's actually ... as a communication exercise or bidding process, it's really fascinating, because you're not wanting to give away all of your secrets, because, you know, if you give too much to the clients, and appear to be more expensive, then they don't need to hire you ... You've given them all the goodies. So they can go, okay, XX was asking for 380,000 dollars and someone else said 240,000 dollars a month. We'll just engage them and tell them to do all the clever ideas. In a writing sense and also in a verbal communication, you have to put this down in writing enough to allow the client to think you really understand their needs without giving away all your secrets. And then you generally are invited into a process where you have to make a presentation, where, generally I will give more ideas out than on paper, and I'll do it quite quickly.

R So you are still withholding ... ?

P But then, hopefully you get onto the job, so that's just winning the work – definitely highly collaborative. And then, it really is, I think, the collective intellect of a group. The reason I preface that with ... there are different types of demand. We have recently been invited to do public relations, brand building work for ZZZ, which is an alternative investment company, and they are wanting to expand into Hong Kong, and their basic intention, is actually to have this as a new asset class, so instead of buying wine or fine art, or gold or property, this is another alternative investment. So in that one, when we put in our proposal, and there was some pitching for it and then they awarded it, then we'll sit down with the ideas we didn't initially share with client. But we might then convene the group again, and say, right, okay what are the priorities. And once working on the account we'll bring different people in … We have people who are more on the stakeholder side of it, so they'll kind of think more about who are the targets, who are we wanting to influence.

R You mean people from … ?

P Within our company, so to collaboratively come up with ideas, smart ideas. And then we've got the more PR side of it, but always really brainstorming ideas …

R So within even a small company, you have people who you feel have strengths in particular areas that …

P Definitely. I genuinely … I think actually more so with … I think there is one thing that's not really your question, but there's one thing that I think is quite interesting. Within all companies in my experience, whether they're small or large, in terms of communication, I will often sit down and do some brainstorming … I will have thought about it, I'll have done a little mind-map – I use that quite a lot … to kind of flesh out issues. I'll generally sit down and what I need to do is then get my group … It's to get them to not be afraid of saying something … So I generally will say 'Look, come on, I've got some ideas, I'm going to start the ball rolling with one' … But if I've got ten ideas, I always think that five of them are pretty good, five of them are probably weak. Then the team need to help me identify the ones that are ok and add new ideas from their different perspectives. It's that sort of collective wisdom. So in a small company, it's making the whole team unafraid of saying something stupid. Actually I might say 'I'm going to come up with some really daft ideas, you've got to help me identify the silly ideas.' I think in bigger companies, you have the sycophants, where you have the CEO … One thing that's quite interesting with CEOs: quite often we're hired to do a public relations task, for a stakeholder engagement or it might be copywriting or some other services. Six to seven months into a job we've developed such a relationship of trust, that sometimes they'll call up, they'll just say … I had one recently … a financial firm where the head called me up and said, 'Oh T, are you free for lunch in a week's time?' 'Yes, what's it about? Is there anything particular?' And he goes, 'No, I just want to tell you some ideas.' He basically sat down and explained, that they were wanting to buy another firm. Basically he discussed it … discussed his ideas with all of his team, and of course they all said that it's brilliant, it's really good … As he's the boss, he's paying their salary and bonus. I knew the company really well, I knew what he was trying to achieve, and he just went through and said 'What do you think?' and I said, 'Well you know, Company A, you've always said you would never … so why is that on the list?' And he says, 'Yes I agree – it's off the list'. Anyway, with team brainstorming, I think, you've got to be at pains to take out the embarrassment factor in collaborative thinking.

R Would you say that was characteristic of this company because it's small or of PR in general?

P Well, I've worked for bigger agencies, and that was much less collaborative, but I think they kind of run on a very lean mix of fuel, and I think that quite often – I can explain why – most PR companies spend some of their time bidding for work, and some of the time doing the work, whereas, we spend all of our clients' time and money on their work, and only our time bidding for work. But the model for some PR firms, the way they win work is … It's like waiting at your in-tray or inbox for a letter to come in, saying … from 'Soft drink firm A' saying 'We want to hire a PR firm for two years, so are you interested?' And then basically the PR firm then bid, because they're constantly bidding for more work. The law of averages will mean that occasionally they win, and largely they don't win, because there would probably be 15 firms invited to put in an expression of interest, and they'll shortlist three or four. So they are always in bid mode.

R So they spend huge amounts of time bidding?
P I call it the beauty contest, because it is ... Whereas our company ... Generally, to be frank, if we know it's a competitive bid, we'll politely tell them that we're really a small company, and we don't really have the resources. But actually, the reason for that is that if we're bidding competitively, we're always going to be more expensive. So generally most of our work comes through the referral process, through our happy clients. Company A says: 'You know I keep seeing your company's name on the branding. How do you do that? We have a company that we'd like you to support.' So we then get someone who has almost prequalified us, done their due diligence through the client of ours. So they know we're honest, we achieve results. We've got a smart team. They'll generally come to us, and just say 'Right', like ZZZ, through a lead, 'We've got a very good recommendation, this is what we want to do, how much will it be?' So you spend a very short period of time collaboratively working out how much support they need to achieve their objectives and the cost. But we're not always in bidding mode. I think many of the bigger PR firms ... are spending virtually all the time in bid mode. So I don't think ... From my experience, they generally do it very uncollaboratively. It's like 'Right, you ... here', and that person literally just works away and gives it to the person who assigns the work. They will go, 'Oh no, too much money or too little money' or whatever, probably not change a lot, because it's a little bit of a production line, because if you're bidding all the time, you just use a template type PR proposal, but it's more the money side that they focus on. So, when we're bidding ... all of the work, all of our writing are very collaboratively done. Even down to thinking about structure when we're writing, or structure of servicing is very collaborative.
R What we're also interested in – I think you've already answered very comprehensively the idea of how people work together – is ... What does it take to be a successful PR person? Is there a formal side to training and learning how to be a PR person?
P We have used CCC University quite a lot, in terms of our hiring and we want someone who's got a good solid degree – and there's a lot of those – in communications ... professional training. So, a CCCU course that – is really good – it teaches people how to really understand, the theory, but it also ... one of the things that interests us a lot is the fact that people are exposed to business through the internship process. And if I'm honest with you, there's a lot of people with good degrees, fewer with very good degrees, but there is a large pool. We'll put in a job advert for an entry-level PR person, and we'll probably get 50 CVs, then we'll weed those down. The other thing I'm actually really interested in, because of point 1, ... what I want to know is, 'Yes, you've studied, what else did you do apart from study? Did you get involved in a charity? Did you do an internship? Several internships?' And then grilling people: 'What did you actually do in that internship? What were you physically responsible for? Was there any output? What did you learn?' The reason why it's really important is that, with what I would call a fresh graduate, is that if they don't have that internship process, then they can be fairly unproductive for a fairly long time. Like, even ... How do I use the photocopier? How do I ... ? Whereas when we hire people, when we intern people, we give them stuff that they can really talk about, that they've actually worked on, but we give them some experience in terms of the office environment, the collaborative nature of working. Actually what I really like is someone who's got at least one or two internships under their belt and that really can talk to me and explain what they did. When I interview, one of my stock interview questions is 'You've got a communications degree, have you looked at our website?' – everyone has – 'You tell me what you learnt in your course that is relevant to me and building my business.' So, qualifications, working

experience and then all the other social skills – did they get involved in university union life or did they get involved in a charity or sport or not?

R So basically experiences which help them make these connections between the theories and courses and the realities …

P Yes, I mean someone with just theoretical knowledge really is not an enormous amount of use in business. One thing I would say that I do like – my son is doing IB, International Baccalaureate, which has a wider curriculum than A levels – I do like the General Education or Liberal Arts education. As an employer, and I think particularly for PR employers, I really like that, because of having to have a knowledge of the world around them in terms of culture, tradition, religion, geography and art, all of those things. I am a huge fan – as an employer – of those, because they deliver me much more useful people. When I then introduce them to a client, who they've to develop a working relationship with, working, they can actually have an informed discussion about the world around them. It's more than just the work. That type of knowledge … Or they understand if we have an American client with cultural differences or an Indian client for example. I need to hire PR graduates who have knowledge about more than just a subject, which Liberal Arts or General Education provides, because … Obviously they need to be really good communicators, and that can be through the written word, say a press release or a briefing or a position paper or whatever, but in terms of engagement with the client, and engagement with media, there has to be really high levels of social skills. Why I often mention press releases, there's the 'Send to world' press release approach of many PR firms. What we do with all of our clients, is that … we would not necessarily 'send to the world', but collaboratively, identify, where does this need to go – I use the word 'pop up' – where does this need to pop up, where are the targets, and what do they read, and what do they listen to. So rather than sending out to the world, we identify where we want it to be, where we want it to end up if it is a press release. If we want it to be the *Sunday Morning Post* for example … We'll actually think of the article, what it's going to look like mentally, and then draft text to catch the interest and conform with the style needed.

R So it's much more focused.

P Also, it's much more communication, which is expensive. So we send out a press release, with one of our team members very often, someone literally pitching, selling those stories to journalists. They've got to be quite compelling in terms of marketing that to this person because this person gets pitched, you know, has hundreds of emails every day, pitched at by people, so having someone who's persuasive, friendly, respectful, understands what a journalist's life is, which is not getting up, putting on the suit, sitting on the train at 8:30 … It's probably grabbing a coffee on the way to the office at 11, so it's different. That respectfulness, understanding the deadlines, so having someone who can call, and so what we do – we're always maintaining and nurturing relationships with media. So we'll do all the time … what I'm doing would be aligned with the type of clients we have. I'll quite often be sending … I'll read something in the paper and I'll quite often send a quick email: 'Really good piece'. Just that. 'Really good piece – I enjoyed that', 'I liked that idea – it was really clever', so you can keep the relationship up, I think that's for a PR professional, highly sociable. The other thing is that it's a hard thing for Hong Kong to be creative, you just can't educate people into being creative, but I think when it comes to brainstorming, being creative, coming out, thinking – awful term – 'outside the box', that's really important. When I'm trying to hire people … I don't think I would hire anyone anymore who didn't have an internship or two. Our model of employing someone is we take on an intern in their final year particularly through CCC University – and we have interns from the UK and from the US. We hire them for maybe a couple of months. Two months is a good period of time, because it's enough to get quite a lot under their belt, for them to go through a bit of learning, and then start to be more productive. So we'll do that for a couple of months. We generally then might have three or four people as interns, and then after that, if they are really a good intern, then we'll say, 'Okay, if you have a bit of time – never interrupting your studies – but if you have an afternoon, you could come in … ' So we'll then have … they'll basically be an employee, a part-time employee. Then when we come round to them graduating, I know whether I think they are good, efficient and a good hire. More importantly, equally, they know this is a company that they like the shape of – we're not normal, we're a little abnormal in that sense. So then, rather than just recruit, which we do when we really urgently need people, we're sort of going in eyes wide shut, whereas your eyes are wide open if you are able to nurture an intern into an employee and for both with that model: it is easy for me to make them an offer, easy – hopefully – for them to at least know this is a company they would want to work for … That worldliness I think is what PR people need … they're having a lot of interface, General Education qualification, Communication qualification to understand the theory, and then the internship to actually rub … A graduate – if they haven't had an internship is a fairly angular object … Whereas the pebble, turning that into … smoothing off the corners … The other thing that we do with all of our staff – which I'm a great fan of – and interns also, is bringing them along to these events and saying, 'Maybe you can take a few notes, and just sit here, see how business is conducted.'

R So kind of socialising them into the business culture.

P Socialising them, so basically there's a point at which that they become able to manage. They go on the road with stabilisers, type of thing.

R You've pretty much answered all the questions I was going to ask. That's really good. I was just going to say, are there formal qualifications in PR that are a central part of the industry or are they peripheral?

P Well … You don't have a chartership. If you are an engineer, you're chartered. And that doesn't mean that you have always very good engineers, I hasten to say … There isn't that type of thing. We have – it's a very good question – we have in the past taken people who don't have the theoretical training behind them. And I would say I wouldn't do that again because … I've got hundreds of CVs on my desk. In the past I thought: 'That was really good, it's a very well written letter'. And they are not quite … they haven't got that training behind them. But we do … as you can probably tell, we invest a lot in training – on the job training and nurturing. But the amount of effort to recreate the technological knowledge that goes into a three or four-year degree, I can't bear that. By 'bear' I mean in terms of bearing the cost. So I actually will … of all of the criteria above the first one is to have that theoretical knowledge, so a good course when you do some PR training, when you learn how to structure a press release, academically and theoretically.

R And other texts besides press releases?

P Yes … there's writing style and that's what I was talking to ———'s students about. It's always asking the question – audience. Who is the audience? Our first question is to understand our audience. In our writing that we do, probably press releases are what we do least of. We do a lot of writing of corporate websites, not the IT side, but the writing. There's an interesting research project definitely that CCCU should do, because we find that websites don't last very long. We're now ten years old and our website is constantly changing and being refined. But a lot of companies … We work with FFF Engineering; about seven years ago we wrote all their website, and then about five years later, we objectively reviewed it and said we think it looks really old, it has far too many words, and now people are much more interested in brevity. So we do a lot of that, we do a lot of brochure writing, we do quite a lot of PR work which I call selling the invisible services – PR, marketing services. There's a lot of kind of collateral writing there. Because they don't have a product, so you've got to basically craft the product – generally the website or the collateral ... We do a lot on the more government relations side, we do a lot of position papers, green papers, white papers – that type of thing.

R So, a huge range.

P Let me do the public engagement side again. I was trying to explain to our students the public engagement side: the audience is Joe Chan, on a public housing estate, so you've got to de-jargonise everything – plain 'lay language' is king. It's all got to be – not quite words of one syllable – but it's all got to be easy for all people to understand. That's something that we as a company are really good at – working on big ... For example the major infrastructure project we're working with. We do a lot of that, and it's distilling very complex, often very technical, development, infrastructural planning, whatever. And actually you're seeing, understanding that our audience are not engineers or planners or developers – they're ordinary people, thinking about what their interest is. We took on a big engagement – the expansion of TTT new town for government. And so I was saying you need to think about: this is expanding the new town, so there's going to be some reclamation, and lots of building, whatever, but I said a better way to think of it is making TTT a better place to live, work, rest and play. So suddenly if you start thinking about it in that sense, then the way you write everything ... You're not saying we're going to build XXX hundred hectares of this, you're going to say you're going to identify and provide better quality living space, you're going to provide more community services that people need, you're going to be trying to introduce employment opportunities, you're wanting to protect the environment, so that people can recreate and relax and recharge ... making a better place to work, rest and play.

R One last question that we are interested in, is this whole idea of culture and identity, and there are a couple of questions that intrigue me. What do you see as the role of PR profession in society?

P The role is connection, connecting a product or service with its consumers or procurers ... I mean that's really what it is – it's trying to do that in an honest and genuine way in terms of how you present that, the ethical side of it, never overselling. We often encourage modesty in our clients ... Our mantra is more of a sort of 'underpromise and overdeliver' type thing, particularly on the products and services. We try and understate things a little bit, because I think that's more sensible and plausible.

R How do you think you are perceived by society as a group?

P That's a really good question. I don't think the industry is that well perceived. The thing is that there's the communication, the spin-doctoring, the spinning ... I think that society might have reasons – there are good and bad – have good reasons to be quite sceptical. I think in that sense as a PR provider, you've got to be subtle and creative, using third parties, ideally to try and support it, developing ripples and word of mouth, rather than something that's an obvious placement of a piece that a journalist received at 12 o'clock, and just tops and tails and that fills a blank space – 'Done'. I think there is a good reason for society to be critical. On the PR side of it, there are those overblown claims or 'green wash' that I think are bad. You've then got the PR-ing of tragedy and crisis. Then you've got the very current situation of Oscar Pistorius, who's hired the ex-head of a major UK tabloid newspaper to be his 'PR'. I think that PR can be trying to put lipstick on a pig sometimes ... And I think on the government relations side of things, there are a million ways that you can communicate with government, but I think most people – it's more extreme – understand the Washington model of lobbying, it's sort of grubby. I think on government relations, the American model is incredibly overt and overbearing. Whereas our style of government relations communication is very subtle, just getting a message across in a very subtle manner. I think it's good, but I think often, what hits headlines is the more aggressive and brash PR or communication. I think most PR practitioners would think of themselves as promoting their brands, raising the awareness of a client's brand or service. Again, practitioners have to get it and buy into it, whether it's a dream, or whatever. They've got to be enthusiastic – most people are very ... they become very good advocates of the work. Again, there are a lot of issues, like big oil, why PR might be perceived as the bad guy in an overbearing way, disguising or covering up or adding doubt into the debate. I think most PR people would see it as a service to the community: people don't know about this product or service, we're just putting it out there, we're not saying you have to buy it, we're just putting it out there so that you're aware of it.

Appendix

View from the professions – questions

The questions were for our guidance and not necessarily systematically used in a particular order. The idea was not to look for brief and precise answers to the question we had in mind, but to seek their extended 'narratives of experience'. At the end of the interviews, the recorded interviews were transcribed and then edited closely for focus on relevant topics, and also to make them more readable. The edited transcripts were then sent back to the specialists for their approval.

General question: How do we specify, acquire, teach and measure professional expertise?

1. What constitutes expert behaviour in a specific professional field? In other words, how do we characterise an expert banker, accountant, lawyer or any other professional?
2. What role does discursive competence (ability to write professional documents, or participate in spoken communication in professional contexts) play in professional practice?
3. Is it possible to specify professional expertise in terms of key competencies?
4. How does one acquire and use these professional competencies?
5. Are these competencies teachable/learnable? If so, what is the role of the setting i.e. the academy or the workplace? Do they perceive any significant gap in this respect between the academy and the workplace?
6. How does one appraise/measure expertise in a specialist workplace/professional context?

More specific questions to be used selectively

7. Who do they work with? Do they work individually, or in groups?
8. Do they write their documents individually or collaboratively?
9. How does this collaboration work? Can they give details and examples?
10. How do they join the profession?
11. What qualifications and experience are required?
12. More generally, what do they look for in potential employees?
13. What do they see as the role of their profession in society?
14. How do other members of society, especially from outside the profession, view them?

Index

Note: Italics indicate figures; boldface type indicates tables

academic-professional relationships 46, 523–24, 529–30

academic programmes: academic settings 41, 46–47; accreditation 524, 527–28, 530; for banking 537–38, 541; for business communication 50–52; continuing education 522–23, 524, 530; for law 547–51; for management communication 166–68; for the MBA 166–68; for professional communication 523–24; for technical communication 107

accountants: auditors 329–30, 334, 335; competencies acquisition among 322–23, 332–33, 336–39; employer expectations of 325–29; high dependence of on face-to-face communication 325–26, 329, 335; high dependence of on interpersonal skills 321, 325–26, 329–30, 332–33, 335, 340n14; need of for rhetorical talents 329, 334–35; need of for verbal explanatory talents 330, 331

accounting: codified discourse in 330–31; communications research in 331, 334, 336–39; contextualised nature of 323–24, 327; decision-making and outcomes as focal points of 329, 331; as discourse 329, 330–36; goals of curricula for 324–27, 336–39, 341–42; Professional Capability Framework 327–28; types and functions of 321, 322, 323–24

annual report: as a strategic management tool 238, 239–47; evolution of the 239–40; influence of on analyst reporting 246; link of to corporate image, identity, and reputation 240–45, 249; multimodal messaging in the 238, 240, 243–45; presentational conventions of the 240–42; relationship of to other corporate communication tools 239, 240–41

applied linguistics: as a tool for solving BPO language dilemma 384, 513, 515, 518; influence of on BC 57, 58, 59–60; influence of on technical communication 105; use of in ESP 3; use of to analyse textual patterns 73

Aristotelian philosophy 29, 87, 89

audiences: collaborative writing for 453–54, 492, 493, 562–63, 566; as conceived in communication as constitutive of organising CCO studies 213; corporate communications with global 136–43, 238–48, 247–48; dichotomy of original and foreign for translators 149, 150, 157; empowerment of by web technologies 403, 407, 412, 413, 428–29; fragmentation of by new media technologies 404; influence of on presentation of arguments 87–89; in legal discourse 352, 353, 354; management of using genre systems 176–77; perception of translated text by recipients 150; PR communication flows with 422–23, 426–29, 428–29, 562–63; PR concept of as an information-processing spectrum 427–28; PR concept of as cultural entities 426–28, 430–32; PR concept of passive, active, and latent 428; relationships of to reporting professionals 406–7; significance of responses 170–73, 427–28; workplace intermingling of different types of 170; writing for targeted 536, 562–63, 566, 567

auditors: communicative challenges of 329–30, 334, 335; essential competencies for 556–57

571

Index

Bargiela-Chiappini, Francesca 56–57, 73
Bhatia, Vijay: on the annual report 242, 243; contributions of to the genre studies approach 72; on discourse communities 453–54; influence of in BC 60, 61; legal discourse project 80, 352; on professional communication 208; on the use of CGA with needs analysis 261–62, 267–69
blogs: addressed to corporate stakeholders 141–43; I'd Rather Be Writing (technical communication) 107; micro-blogging 142–43; use of by journalists 403, 406; webzine (technical communication) 107; *see also* websites
branding: organisational 227–28, 232, 238, 243, 530; personal 406; and PR 425, 562, 565; protection of corporate brands using social media 131–32, 138–39; risk management of corporate brands on the internet 138, 238; use of Really Simple Syndication (RSS) feeds for corporate 137
business communication (BC): academic programmes for 50–52; advantages of face-to-face 278–81; basic situational types 68; Chinese expo sales study 31–36; corporate websites 130, 133, 139–40, 275–77, 406; effect of on business operations 50, 71; forms of communication studied in 58, 59–61, 72; future directions for 61, 78–80; geographic influences on 54, 58, 59, 61; globalisation of 68–69; influence of communication theory on 3; internal corporate networks 70; jungle versus orchard dichotomy 72, 76–77, 81; LESCANT model 78; media preferences spectrum for 277–84; multimodal communication types 54, 61; overlap of with related disciplines 50, 57, 58, 59, 69, 71; pedagogy in 51–53, 55, 61, 71, 80–81, 282–85; primary concerns of 50–51, 59; research in 51–54, 54, 59–60, 61, 78–80; Singapore case study 275–82; social influence theory 278; socio-cultural symbolism of media used 278; with strangers 280, 281, 283; theoretical approaches to 54, 72, 78–79; time as a criterion for media selection 277–82; traditional versus technological modes 54, 277, 277–82; video- and teleconferencing tools for 276–81; Zones model 77
business discourse versus workplace communication 112–13
Business English as a Lingua Franca (BELF): as a concern of BC 53, 54, 56, 58, 59, 61; compared to English language perspective 174, 175; integration of with Zones model 78, 79; in MC 173, 174–75; in special vocabulary environments 73; *see also* English
Business Process Outsourcing (BPO) industry: business models of 502; case study of Philippine call centre 386–92; concepts of language versus communication in 384–85, 504; emphasis of on English language use 382–83, 502, 505, 514; gaps in language preparation for 383–84, 503; problem of cultural differences between callers and CSRs 390, 394, 503, 505–6; recruitment and training materials in use 392–95, 504–5; research on 383–84, 386, 509–11, 516–18; researchers' obligations to organisations studied 395–96; training of CSRs for 383, 387, 389–96, 503–4, 507, 509–10; typical speech patterns in 394–95; *see also* outsourcing and offshoring

call centres: concept of conversational cooperation 387, 389, 390–91, 394, 396, 508–9; CSR-customer interactions 385–92, 507, 508–9; function of empathy in interactions 390–91, 393–94, 396, 508, 513; incoming versus outgoing calls 386, 502, 503; plight of CSR trainers in 504–7, 510–16; reliance of on spoken English 383, 502, 505, 514; research on language use in 384, 386–93; research on training challenges for O&O 509–11, 516–18; role play training for 393–94, 507; use of ESP to train trainers in 501, 509–14, 517–18; variation of among industries 386, 503; *see also* outsourcing and offshoring
Candlin, Christopher N., on discourse analysis 366–67, 369
case studies: research projects on the creation of scientific knowledge 90–91; versus ethnography 86–87
co-occurrence 13, 14, 20, 23
cognition: cognitive reasoning 325, 328, 338; cognitive skills 337, 340n6, 341–42, 549, 550, 566; distributed 463, 470–71; role of in interlingual translation 149, 154; role of in learning 465, 468, 474; in the school-to-work transition 462, 467, 474, 537–38, 540–41; situated 28–29, 35–36, 466, 494
collaboration: in accounting 557–58, 559–60; in banking 539; facilitation of through wikis 130, 136; inspiration as a product of 45; in law 551–53; in PR 562–64; role of diversity in creative 214; in writing projects 486–91, 540
collaborative writing 552; as a subject of research 491, 492, 494–96; attempts to define 487–90; impact of technology on 494–96; impacts of power and hierarchy on 488–93; intertextual features of 489, 492; pedagogical concerns in teaching 491–94; spectrum of team relationships in 489–91
collocation analysis 14–15, 17–18, 20, 21, 22
communication: body language as 265, 357; casual conversation 391; challenges for auditors 329–30, 334, 335; change management 212; clause-based versus sentence-based 394–95; communicative competencies 293, 535–36; communicative purposes 5, 27, 30–31, 33,

572

261–62, 266; as compared to transmission 77; competencies for accountants 322–23, 325–29, 331–36, 338; Competing Values Framework (CVF) tool to assess 178–80; complementarity of verbal and non-verbal 46–47, 77–78, 151, 193; complicating factors in 472–73; conceptualisation of ideas as an influence on structure of 4–5; constitutive approach to 207; corporate visual identity (CVI) 243; face-to-face in accounting 325, 329–30, 335, 338; functional 463; impact as a key goal in 4; importance of listening proficiency in ESP 257, 260, 264–65, 309–12; integrated marketing communication (IMC) 227–29; interaction of speech with non-verbal modes 41, 43; internal versus external **450**; interrelationships of genres 449–52, 453; key elements of 207; language acquisition 292–93; media discourse 409–10; message overload in the workplace 173, 221–22; meta-communicative purposes 44, 47–48; multimodal nature of 473–75; multimodal studies of 410; multimodal techniques for 40–48; nature of in BPO industry 384; news reporting 400, 405–7, 410–11; non-verbal 41, 122, 475; Nonverbal Immediacy Scale 177; nuance 13, 40, 214, 279, 508–9, 549; pauses and silence as 20, 283–84; research into verbal 243–44, 246, 248; research into visual 243–44, 249; SocioCommunicative Style Scale 177; the specialist-layman interface in 536, 568; targeted 562–63, 566, 567; uncontrollable nature of 170–71; verbal 43–44, 114, 147, 152; visual representation as 45–46, 90, 105, 224–25, 244

communities: as the basic unit of knowledge production 443–47; colonisation phenomenon between 454; communal networks 445, 447; community of practice 445, 446, 448, 455, 467–70, 494; concepts of participation and reification 468–69; conflict within professional 454, 455, 469–70; defining characteristics of 444–47, 454; discourse 443, 444, 446–48, 455; empowerment of weak members in 455–56; impact of educational initiatives on knowledge 456–57; interdependence of novices and veterans in 456, 469–70; legal 350, 547–51; overlap among knowledge 453–54; scientific 443, 445, 447, 448, 455; three notions of knowledge-based 443–47, 448, 455; as transmitters of norms and assumptions 444–45, 452–53

competence: as a target of study by BC scholars 59–60; academic degrees and 548; acquisition of by novices 448, 461, 466, 510, 515; body of knowledge concept 331–32, 522, 527–28; certification of for business communication 526; certification of for public relations 526; certification of for technical communicators 103, 106, 107–8, 521, 525–26; certification versus certificate 523, 527; and collaborative writing 492–93; communicative 60, 71, 80, 535–36, 567; credentialing 522–24, 527–30; cultural 79, 404, 566, 567; demonstration of 522–26, 528, 530; demonstration of in accounting 322–29, 331–36, 341–42, 555–60; demonstration of in banking 535, 538, 541; demonstration of in law 548–51; EST approaches to establishing language 310–17; experience versus academics 540–41, 565, 566; and job satisfaction 546; licensure 523; linguistic matching 77, 78, 79; model to establish generic 27, 30–36; research on acquisition of by novices 462–75; third party assessments of 524, 527; in web technologies 282–85, 401–2

concgrams, defined 20

concordances: Camiciotolli study in finance 16–17; Chinese language study using people.com.cn 18; defined 13; Nelson study in business 15; online legal concordancer for students 17; study of American television 18; study of British National Party (BNP) language changes 22; study using European Union speeches 21–22; 'thank you study' in the Hong Kong Corpus of Spoken English (HKCSE) *14*

conferences and symposia: for business communications 51, 53; for corporate communication 233; for management communication 166; for technical communication 107

conflict *see* collaboration

Confucian social philosophy 26, 29

construction communication (CC): adversarial versus business meeting models of 363, 371, 372–73; basic communicative relationships 364; case study of Japanese engineers in Hong Kong 368–75; the contract as a point of conflict 373–74; corpus comparisons of 371, 372, 373; deictics and gestures as necessary to 373; discourse analysis of 366–67, 369, 371, 373–74, 376; elements of complexity in 363, 365; emancipatory potential of research in 367, 374, 378; ethical tensions between managers and researchers studying 366, 367; face-saving and problem-solving discourse 372, 373–74; influence of culture on 373, 375–76, 378, 379n6; influence of on working conditions 367, 374, 378; at internationally-run sites 368–75; lexicogrammatical analyses of 369, 371, 372–73; pedagogical materials for international 375–77; research in 363, 366–67, 369, 378

Content and Language Integrated Learning (CLIL) 337

context: crucial role of in BPO industry training 384; discourse markers as elements of 388–90;

Index

importance of in translation 149, 151, 154, 157–58; influence of institutional protocols on 386; influence of on collaborative writing 486, 490–92; influence of on grammar 385; influence of on meaning-making 75, 384, 385–86; re-contextualisation for target audiences 87–88; recovery and management of by the media 410–11; register as 385, 386; role of in genre analysis 6–7; significance of in workplace communication 112–14, 120, 121–22, 123

conventions: as a defining product of community 9, 27, 444, 446, 454; as basic elements of acculturation 470–71; role of in communications among specialists 5, 27–28, 34; Western versus Chinese business **33**, 34–35

coordination: common starting points (CSP) model 228; levels of corporate 227–28; Stakeholder Management Capability (SMC) 229; strategic continuum 227–28; sustainable corporate story (SCS) 228

corpora: American National Corpus (ANCS) 18; Bank of English (BoE) 17; British National Commercial Corpus (BNC) 15, 16, 17; business 15–20; Business English Corpus (BEC) 15; business periodical and journal articles (BPJA) 18; Cambridge and Nottingham Business Corpus (CANBEC) 19, 20, 370–71, 372, 373; Cambridge and Nottingham Corpus of Discourse in English (CANCODE) 19, 370–71, 373; concordance analysis of 13–15, 17; Corpus of American Soap Operas (SOAP) 14; Corpus of Contemporary American English (COCA) 14–15; Corpus of EU English (CEUE) 17; Enron 16; financial 16, 17; G-Corpus 17; GeM for multimodal page-based annotations 42; general language 14; Hong Kong Corpus of Spoken English (HKCSE) 13; legal 17; media 20–21; multimodal 23; Narrative Corpus (NC) 20; NHS Direct 19; political 20–21, 22; small specialised 14–15; Socialising and Intimate subcorpora (SOCINT) 19, 20; UK Operating and Financial Review (OFR) 17; Wolverhampton Corpus of Business English (WBE Corpus) 16

corporate brands *see* branding

corporate communication: as a strategic management function 220, 222, 223, 227–30, 240, 242; common starting points (CSP) model 228; as compared to public relations 221, 223; as compared to related disciplines 50, 220, 232, 238; concepts of image versus reputation 225–26; corporate versus organisational identity 225; definition of 220, 222–24, 237; equivocal character of 238–39; ethical responsibilities in 237, 239; financial reporting 238, 239, 240, 241, 246; Global RepTrak Pulse (Reputation Quotient) model 226; image-defining activities of 238, 239; image versus reputation 226; integration 226–29, 231–32; investor relations 238–45; local versus globalised messaging 247–48; management ideal of 231–32, 237, 238; management of consumer resistance 229; research in 224–33, 237–39, 241–49; role of annual report in 238–45; role of in change and crisis management 221, 226, 237; role of in Competing Values Framework (CVF) 223, 228; role of in generating a consistent corporate story 237, 239, 244; role of in organisational positioning 222; roles of corporate social responsibility (CSR) in 238, 240, 242, 244, 246, 248; significance of to corporate identity 224–25; stakeholder relations studies 229–31; sustainable corporate story model (SCS) 228; use of gender ideologies in 242–43; use of web technologies 237, 241, 245–46, 248; versus corporate branding 232, 243; visual rhetoric in 239–41, 243–45

corporate communicators: designated employee systems 138, 142; relationships of to various stakeholders 130–31, 138–43; strategies regarding web technologies used by 132, 133–34; and third parties 141–42, 144; use of automatic alert systems among 138–39; use of blogs and micro-blogs by 143–44; use of Really Simple Syndication (RSS) feeds by 137; use of eXtensible Business Reporting Language (XBRL) by 139–41

corpus analysis: *ConcGram* software 20–21; corpus downsizing methodologies 22; methods 15; study of lexical compounds for 'climate change' 21; study of the lemma RISK 15; use of to expose linguistic subtleties 17–18; *wMatrix* software 16, 20

corpus linguistics (CL): chronological analysis in 21–22; defined 13–14; future research for 22–23; genres studied 15; integration of with critical discourse analysis 20, 21–22; methodologies of various studies 18, 22; pronoun studies 19; studies performed in China 18, 20–21; study of Enron email 16; use of for sound and intonation analysis 13; use of semantic prosody 14; use of word frequency analysis 16

Critical Discourse Analysis (CDA): for analysis of unequal social relationships 8–9; compared to interactional sociolinguistic analysis 121, 125n1; EU narrative study 21; integration of with corpus linguistics 20; study of BNP language changes 22; study of 'human rights' as a lexical item 20; use of in analysing workplace dynamics 115, 121–23

Critical Genre Analysis (CGA): as a complement to needs analysis 257, 261–62, 266–67, 269–70; defined 8; demystifying role of 8–9, 262, 268; goals of 8–9 cross-cultural communication: coherence of translated text in 148, 150, 157; genre approach to 26, 27, 32; individualism versus collectivism in 26; knowledge and learning 28, 29, 30, 35–36; overlap of with BC 50; persuasion in 29–30; role of etiquette in 30, 32–33, 74

culture: as a consideration in language learning 311–12, 509–10; behaviour as an element of professional 74–75; as context for translation 151, 154–57, 160–61; Cultural Intelligence (CQ) quotient 74; establishing fluency in a foreign 34; influence of on international corporate communications 247–48; influence of on legal systems 351, 356–58, 549–50, 553; as an influence on communication 74; legal documents as specific products of 154, 155–59, 161; and miscommunication 74, 79; organisational 74, 543–44, 567; professional 74–75, 547, 553–54, 560; stereotyping and generalizations 26; translation as a means of exposing differences in 148; translation in context of organisational 157–60; unilingual versus multilingual 156–57

customer service representatives (CSR): in BPO industry 386–92, 503–10; contributions of to annual reports 240, 242, 244, 246; role of in protecting corporate images and reputations 226, 228, 238, 245, 248

data meta-tagging using XBRL 140–41
disagreement *see* collaboration
discipline-specific knowledge *see* knowledge
disclosure: corporate 134, 136–40, 240, 243, 246, 248; financial genres 15, 16, 536; financial risk 536; Regulation Fair Disclosure (Reg. FD) 140, 141

discourse: call centre 501, 508, 516; colonisation phenomenon between communities 454; discourse and genre analysis 3–4, *4*; discourse community 4–5, 6, 27–28, 31, 36, 72; discourse interactions of managers 180–82; discursive strategies to establish relationships 45–47, 566; establishing cross-cultural competency in 26; institutional 113; legal 349–51, 354–59; organisational discourse studies (ODS) 193; research on communal 449–56; role of in knowledge-making 85, 87, 91–94; role of in organisational politics 195–96; studies of use of among scientists 87–89, 91, 92–93; theme-rheme dichotomy 150; variation 3, 9; within knowledge-producing communities 447; workplace 385

discourse analysis: business meetings 19–20, 73; of call centre communication 501, 513, 516; Candlin on 366–67, 369–70; in CC 366, 376; defined 73; of face-to-face communication 333–34; influence of on EST 308; lexico-grammatical approach to 4, 17, 209, 386, 396,

455; media discourse analysis 401, 409–12; multimodal 124, 473; problem-solving patterns in 373–74; use of in BC 50; of written communication 261

discourse markers: analysis of 386–92; function of 387–92, 396; ignored in language texts 387; polysemic nature of 387, 390, 396

editing: in collaborative writing 452, 557; in media analysis 410; in PR 423, 432; in technical communication 102–5, 106, 108

emotionality: in language 18–19; *pathos* and *qing* 29–30, 32, 33

empirical research: in BC 52–53, 56, 58–61, 75, 77; of BELF in communication networks 73; case studies versus ethnographies 86; in CL 13; in cultural studies 74; Language in the Workplace Project (LWP) (New Zealand) 60; qualitative 85–86, 92–93, 94–95; in technical communication 99, 100, 102

English: as a global lingua franca 19, 57, 158, 404, 413, 542, 559; as a globalising tool 403–4, 408, 413, 415n7; Certificate of English Language Teaching to Adults (CELTA) 505, 517–18; compared to BELF **174**; English as a Foreign Language (EFL) 288, 289, 291, 299; English for Academic Purposes (EAP) 288, 289–90; English for Professional Communication Purposes (EPCP) 257, 270; English for Specific Business Purposes (ESBP) 58–59; ESP versus General English (GE) 304; and globalisation of English common law 358, 549, 551, 553; Mother Tongue Interference (MTI) problem 504–5, 507, 516; in native-to-nonnative interactions 70, 386–92, 507–9; in nonnative-to-nonnative interactions 70, 547–53; spoken versus written in BPO industry 382–83; Teaching English to Speakers of Other Languages (TESOL) 504–7, 514, 517–18; typology of courses *305*; use of as a linking language 70, 158; use of as a working language 70, 542, 547–50; *see also* Business English as a Lingua Franca (BELF)

English for Science and Technology (EST): case study of Argentine brewers 312–13; case study of Hong Kong engineering students 310–11; case study of Hong Kong science students 315–17; case study of immigrant nurses in Australia 311–12; context as a major pedagogical determinant in 305–6, 309–10, 314; course materials selection in 310–16; development of 307–10; genre-based approach to 314; Introduction, Methods, Results, Discussion (IMRD) protocol 315; influence of student needs on 311–312, 313, 315; listening activities for 309–11, 315; relation of to ESP 304–5, 317; teaching contexts of 306; textbook development in 308–10; training non-scientists

who teach 310, 311, 312; use of multiple media and modes by 309–10, 316–17
English for Specific Purposes (ESP): development of 304–5, 307; influence of applied linguistics on 3; influence of on BC 53, 57, 59; integration of into other areas of professional communication 10; and learners' cognitive processes 289, 297, 299; needs analysis for 306–7; overlap of with EFL pedagogy 289, 299–300; pedagogical principles for 287–300; primary journals for 288; research in call centres 509–10; syllabus development for call centre CSRs 509, 511–13, 516–18; textbook development in 307–10; use of in training call centre personnel 509–14, 517–18
ethics: as a concern among lawyers 549–50, 553–54; as a concern in corporate communication 237, 241, 246; as a concern in professional communication 75, 133, 210, 522, 538, 549; as a concern in public relations 430; in financial reporting 55, 325, 332, 559
ethnography: as a tool for creating EST curricula 315; research projects on the creation of scientific knowledge 91–94; versus case study 86–87
etiquette: case study of British-Chinese sociality 115; Chinese concepts of 30, 32–33; in hierarchical work environments 172; hotelier 265–66; importance of in cross-cultural communications 74; on the internet 130–31, 275; politeness theory 114
expertise *see* competence

Face Threatening Acts (FTAs) 173–74
Facebook: influence of on globalisation 72; use of as a social networking tool 130; use of by activists 130, 132, 135; use of by corporations 130, 131–32, 139, 143–44; use of for investor relations 141; use of Really Simple Syndication (RSS) feeds by 137
facts: audience influence on presentation of 89; as creations 87, 92–94, 303
Fahnestock, Jeanne 88–89
film versus 3D study 40–48
financial reporting 55, 139, 176, 239, 246; balance sheet 140, 240; of cash flow 323, 330, 541; financial analysis 139–41; for global audiences 248

gaming, CL studies of 16
genre: chains 450–52, 455; concepts of 27, 28; intertextuality of 450–52, 456; RGS approach 463–65; text and audience examples *451*
genre analysis: Critical Genre Analysis (CGA) 8–9, 262, 267–69; frameworks for the study of 72–73; goals of 4–7, 9; multi-perspective approach in 261; situated genre approach 27–30, 36; use of in BC 50, 53, 61; use of in EST pedagogy 309, 314; use of in Zones model 77

globalisation: impact of on communications 26, 69–71, 232, 244, 358, 408; and the media 401, 403, 413; symbiosis of English with 61, 123, 257, 404, 469; symbiosis of technology with 274–75

IBM social computing guidelines 133–34
identity: as a focus of corporate communication 224; as a personal construct in the workplace 116–17, 120, 212, 544, 545, 559; as a product of organisational discourse 193, 194, 201; as a product of relationships to others 214; as a research topic in organisational communication 210–11; corporate 224–25; employees' many with organisations 221; formation of professional 472–73, 537–38, 545; gender 116; group in collaborative writing 489–91; identity studies 224; personal *habitus* concept 337–38; stigmatised work and 212, 214
image: corporate 225–26, 238–41; role of investor relations in shaping corporate 238–41, 243–48; Similarity-Attraction paradigm of 247; symbolic versus behavioural 231; use of annual report to shape corporate 241–45; versus reputation 225–26, 238–39
individualism versus collectivism dichotomy 26, 74
informality 18–19; as an advantage of instant messaging 279; in language 18–19; role of in establishing professional identities 46–47; in written communication 34–35
information: flow of in PR-audience communications 426–28; flow of on the internet 130, 137, 143–44; globalisation of 403, 413; managing overload of in the workplace 173, 221–22; manipulation of through the media 405–8, 410, 413; presentation of through annual reports 238–46; the press release as spam 406–7; problems of collecting 176–77; processing of as a PR concern 421–23, 427–28, 431; profitability of for the media 405; repurposing of among journalists 405, 406; Search Engine Optimised (SEO) releases 406–7; Social Media Release (SMR) 406–7; use of BELF for presenting 175
Information and Communication Technologies (ICTs) *see* web technologies
Insight Out series (2006–8) 43–44, 46, 47
intention: as a concern for translators 153; and cognition 328, 330, 335, 336; corporate 17, 247; private 5, 7, 9, 262
interdiscursivity: annual reports as products of 242, 249; of communication 6–7, *8*, 9, 267, 268, 326; in legal discourse 17
internet: as a medium for corporate outsourcing 135–36; advantages and disadvantages of for corporations 129, 135, 144; alert systems 137–38, 138–39; amplification properties of the

134–35, 137–38; as an application of intertextuality 34; blogs and micro-blogs 129, 133, 141–43, 406; chronological speed of the 130, *131*, 144; NIRI standards for corporations using the 140, 141–42; pranks 135; RSS feeds and Google alerts 130, 137; Securities and Exchange Commission (SEC) *Interpretive Guidance for Websites* 140; usage statistics 130; use of by activists 135; use of mobile devices to access the 143–44; wikis 130, 136; YouTube 135, 143–44, 316–17; *see also* web technologies

interpretation: in accounting 322, 323, 324, 331; as an act of exclusion 196, 200, 228; concept of the terministic screen 88; divergence of between presenter and recipient 90, 154, 156, 161, 247–48; ethnographic context of 114; versus translation 152–53

intertextuality: annual reports as products of 242, 249; of collaborative writing 489, 492; to facilitate learning 30, 36; features of 6, 28, 75; in genre chains 450–52, 456; internet websites as sources of 34; in legal discourse 17; types of 451–52; versus interdiscursivity 7

interviews: as a source of data for further exploration 117; for Chinese–New Zealander case study 34–35, 37n2; in multimodality case study 42–47; use of in case studies 86, 90, 92; use of in ethnographic research 93, 120; use of in workplace communication research 117; used in the *Journal of Business Communication* 54; in workplace communication 114, 124

investor relations: communication genres of 238–45; functions of 239; and stakeholder perceptions 238–39

journalism: as a process 407, 410–11; as a subject of research 408–14; as an academic discipline 402–4, 409; financial threats to 405; importance of English competency in 403; internationalisation of institutions 403, 408; as the presentation of opinions 408–9

journalists: evolution of practices among 404, 405–8, 412; management of information overload by 405, 406; relationships of to audiences 406–7, 413; as research subjects 406, 411, 414; social responsibilities of 404, 408

journals: primary for business communication 51–56; primary for corporate communication 221, 226, 233; primary for EST 307; primary for management communication 166, 168, 185–87; primary for technical communication 107

jungle versus orchard dichotomy *see* business communication (BC)

keyword analysis 19, 21, 138, 143, 371
Knorr-Cetina, Karin 93–94

knowledge: as a product of communal interactions 44, 443–45, 447; assumptions of distributed cognition concerning 470; assumptions of LPP concerning 469–70; body of 331–32, 522, 527–28; collective wisdom concept 562, 564; commodification of in PR 563; communicating specialised in accounting 329–30, 332–33; concept of stabilised 471; cultural attitudes toward acquisition of 357; demystification of specialised as a goal 8–9, 10, 262, 268; disciplinary and genre 28; importance of achieving local 26, 27; Knowledge Processing Outsourcing (KPO) industry 382, 502; Language in Content Instruction (LICI) 337; portability of between academia and the workplace 461; transmission of within disciplines 5, 8, 9–10, 44; updating of as a professional requirement 522; use of online concordancers to facilitate 17; use of subject to facilitate language learning 514–15

knowledge-making: role of collaboration in 88, 92–93; role of discourse in 85, 89, 91, 92–94; role of qualitative research in 85, 86, 88–89, 90; role of quantitative research in 85; role of rhetoric in 87, 92–94

language: as a product of communal norms 444, 446, 447, 453, 454, 455; as a social phenomenon 385, 396; appropriations of 5–7; importance of discourse markers in spoken 386–92; influence of proficiency on business communication 70, 78; influences of metafunctions on 385; language approach to BC 72–74; Language in Content Instruction (LICI) 337; Language in the Workplace Project (LWP) 60, 114, 118–19; media language 408, 409, 411–12; positive, as a goal 16, 33; proficiency in multilingual settings 157–60, 547–50, 552; SFL concept of as a system of choices 385, 396

Language for Specific Purposes (LSP) 257, 270, 288, 290

Language in the Workplace Project (LWP) 333

language learning: analytic versus experiential approaches to 295; bilingualism as a necessity 542, 548–49, 550; for BPO industry 382–86; the communicative approach to 292–93, 305; communicative competencies 293, 294, 297, 299; communicative continuum **298**; and the concept of methodology 291–92; connection of form and meaning in 293, 298; context as a major pedagogical determinant 305–6, 309–10, 314; curriculum development for 258–62, 269, *270*; documentary-creation as a tool in 316–17; environment for 261; EST 307–17; experiential approach to 294; extracurricular elements of 311–12; gaps among learners' needs, wants and goals 258–61, 264–65, 269; genre-based approach to 314; impact of web technologies on 314–15; the importance of context in 292–93; integration of with knowledge content 337–38, 549–51; lexico-grammatical approach to 307, 308, 309; listening as a basic goal of 260, 309–12, 315; milestones in the pedagogical literature 289–90; Mother Tongue Interference (MTI) problem 504–5, 507, 516; the nature of language acquisition 292–93; oral-written recontextualisation in 316–17; pedagogical principles for 296–99; Presentation-Practice-Production (PPP) approach to 291, 294; research in BPO industry 509–11, 516–18; for science and technology 304–10; segmentation approach to 293–94; significance of discourse markers in 387; situation-specific 257, 306; students' roles in 313, 314; subject knowledge as a complement to 310, 311, 312, 514–15; target needs versus learning needs in 288; task-based approach to 289–90, 309–10, 313–14, 316, 327; traditional methodologies for 291, 293–94, 308–9

learning: as a by-product of participation 444–48, 453, 465, 469–70; Activity Theory of 465–66; apprenticeship as a vehicle for 446, 467–69, 474, 475; classroom versus workplace 470; collaborative writing 491–94; context as a determinant of 462, 465, 466, 467; continuing education 522–23, 524, 530, 538; guided participation approach 467–68, 469; Legitimate Peripheral Participation (LPP) approach 469–70; situated genre approach to 27, 31–32, 35–36; Situated Learning (SL) approach 466–67, 468–70; through workplace training 394, 396, 455, 516, 541, 551–53; zone of proximal development concept 466–67

legal discourse 17; arbitration practices study 80; arguments over the cognitive accessibility of 358–59; assumptions underlying 350, 357–58; audiences for 352, 353, 354; clashes of cultural values in 356–58; courtroom interactions 354–55; distinguishing features of 351–52, 358; influence of local community of practice on 349, 350; influence of web technologies on 359; intermediary role of lawyers in 356; international 357–59; interpretation and judgments in 352, 353–54, 358; interpreters as a complicating factor in 357; intertextual qualities of 353; by lay litigants 350–51; legal reasoning 350, 351; legislation 352, 353, 357, 359; logic of using precedents in 352, 353; multilingual interactions inside a system 356–57; normative texts 352–53, 357–58; police interviews 355–56; purpose of formal language in 352, 358; questioning protocols in 354–57; rational versus relational approaches to 350–51; research in 349–59; ritualised elements of 352, 354–55; rule-oriented perspective in 350–51; socialization of law students 351, 353; sociocultural contexts of 349, 350, 356–58; sociolinguistics of 354, 357–58; special concerns for translators of legal texts 149, 150, 151, 154, 155–59, 161; between specialists and non-specialists 349, 350, 355–56, 358–59; spoken genres of 354–56; typology of 349, 354; written genres of 351–54, 357–58

Legitimate Peripheral Participation (LPP) see peripheral participation

LESCANT model 78, 79

lexicology: in CL 13–14, 17–18, 20, 21; discourse markers 387, 388; lexical choices 120, 155, 293–94, 309, 336; lexico-grammar 3–6

linking language (link-pin channels) 70

listening: as a basic goal of language learning 260, 264–65, 309–12; inclusion of as a needs analysis goal 260, 263–64, 269; as part of language learning curriculum 309–11, 312

localisation of terminology in technical communication 104

Louhiala-Salminen, Leena, research of in BC 50, 52, 57, 61, 117

management communication (MC): compared to other communication fields 168–69, 183–84; Competing Values Framework (CVF) tool 178–80, **181**; genre sets and systems 176–77; goals of 165, 168–69; interdisciplinary nature of 168; measurement tools for hiring and placement 177–78; memorandum versus letter 176; multiparty interactions 176; narrative as a useful tool in 173–74; organisational genres in 175–76, 177; overlap of with BC 50; predictive analysis of audience responses 171–73; research areas in 165–66, 170, 173, 174, 176, 181–83; significance of BELF protocols in 173, 174–75; significance of clarity in 183; significance of media type 171; significance of message relevance, timing, and type 171; significance of rhetorical options in 173; significance of sentence-level constructions in 174, 175; theories 183

managers: as a teaching resource 34–35; assessing the effectiveness of 178–81; change management studies 212, 221; core communication activities of 170; diversity management 213–14; handling of face-threatening acts (FTAs) by 173–74; influence of on information flow 165, 169, 182, 183; interaction of with novices 182–83; need of for cooperative relationships 172; performance appraisal and measurements 178; persuasion as a tool of 183; responsibilities of 165, 169–70, 183; use of discourse interaction by 180–83; use of indirect versus direct language by 173–74; use of online risk alert systems by 138–39

marketing: attention, interest, desire and action (AIDA) model 32, 34; meta-communications in 44, 47; multi-resource kits study 40–48

meaning-making: in BPO communications 384; contribution of semiotic modes to 41–42; importance of underlying meaning to 75; influence of context on 384–86, 396; in the news media 410–11; polysemic words and phrases 387, 390, 396; in PR 431, 568; role of discourse markers in 387, 390; through participation and reification 468–69

media: as a tool for creating a sense of community 408; analytical tools for investigating a medium 402; definitions of 400, 401; disconnect between educators and professionals in the 402, 407, 412, 414; discourse analysis of the 409–12; educational 401; English as the lingua franca for the 403–4, 408, 413; globalisation of the 403, 408, 412–14; historical responses to the 402; as an inherently subjective entity 408–9; institutional elements of the 400, 405, 409; journalism 402–14; mass messaging power of the 400, 404, 405, 408; media literacy 401; media studies 401, 402, 403, 415n1; press releases 406–7; problems of information management 405–7; research on the 401, 406, 408–12; sociolinguistics studies of the 411–12

medium, defined 41

meta-communications 44, 47

metaphors and metaphorical expressions: appearance of in knowledge-building discourses 89–90; in CDA of workplace communications 115; in ethnic humour 120–21; Gareth Morgan on 232; as the objects of CL studies 18; in translation 159

miscommunication: as a planning consideration in PR 427; intercultural 74, 79; in the workplace 113–14, 115

mode defined 41–42

multi-resource kits for professional communication 40–48

multimodal analysis 41–42; loss of generic integrity among modes 43–44; use of transcription in 42

National Investor Relations Institute (NIRI) 137, 140, 141–42

needs analysis: approaches to 260, 261; blended (BNA) 263–64, 267–69; employment of for EST curricula 310, 315; for language curricula 257–62, 307; Macao hospitality study 262–67, 269; methodological concerns of 258–59, 270; methods used for conduct of 259–60; use of CGA for language pedagogy 257; use of experienced informants in 259, 265

netiquette 130, 131, 275, 284

networks: actor network theory (ANT) 230–31; communication 68, 70, 73

new media: definition of 400; research on the 401, 402, 411–12, 413

news aggregation and automation 137–38

nuance: advantages of telephone use in capturing 279; detection of as an insight into cultures 26; enhancement of using semiotic modes 40

organisational communication: actor network theory (ANT) 213; communication as constitutive of organising (CCO) studies 213–14; as compared to professional communication 207–8; concept-based studies in 211–12; cybervetting studies in 211; definition of 207; discursive approach to difference studies in 213, 214; the employee work–life balance phenomenon 211–12; interdisciplinary character of 209; management of change studies 212; meaning and meaningfulness of work 211; non-human elements as an organisational influence 213; the organisation as communication 207, 212–15; research in 207–8, 209–15

organisational discourse: as a tool of organisations 196–204; climate change example 194, 195, 197, 198–203; conflict of facts and alternate realities 195, 196, 198–200, 203; definition of 193; focus of on the role of power 194, 200; framing of problems by their solutions in 197, 198–202, 203; function of everyday talk 195–96; interplay of actors in 195–96, 199–202; interplay of concepts, objects, and subjects in 194, 195–96, 198, 203–4; marketing strategies as 201; operation of at different levels 194; social reality as a construct of 193, 195, 196, 200, 201, 203; space of action 196, 197; tame versus wicked versus crisis problems 197–203; there-is-no-alternative (TINA) principle 197; use of as a crisis avoidance tool 198–202

outsourcing and offshoring: facilitated by the internet 135–36; use of in technical communications 103–4; see also Business Process Outsourcing (BPO) industry; call centres

participant-observers as researchers 86, 91–95, 118–23

patterns: collocational 15, 18, 20; communication as an object of study in genre analysis 72–73; detection of in multimodal transcription 42; importance of in empirical research 75; lexico-grammatical 17; prepatterned conventions 27; textual as an object of study in applied linguistics 73; use of CL to detect 13; within genre conventions 28

Index

pedagogy: in ESP, 291–92, 299; genre-based, 287; of journalistic enquiry, 402; in MC, 166; textbooks in BC 58, 61, 71, 76, 77, 283; use of technology-driven, 317
peer review in journals 86, 91, 102
peripheral participation as a means of enhancing generic competence 27, 28–29, 30, 33–34, 35–36
perspective: influence of on discursive interactions 90–91; of managers versus novices when collaborating 182–83
persuasion: in a cross-cultural context 27, 29–30, 32; alternatives as noise 93; basic principles of 183; Boyle's use of mental images for 90; in the context of accounting 329, 331, 333–35; organisational discourse example 198–99; purpose of in knowledge-building 87, 89–90, 92–94; role of emotionality in 29–30; use of in technical communication 102; *see also* rhetoric
plain language approach 74, 101
political discourse: example of BNP manipulation of language 22; use of social media tools in 130–31
pragmatics: influence of on translation 148, 150, 152, 161; use of with CL analysis 13, 15, 23
productivity enhancement through the use of wikis 130, 136
professional-academic relationships 46, 523–24, 529–30
Professional Capability Framework 327–28
professional communication: Activity Theory (AT) approach to 463, 465–66; among accountants and auditors 556; among insiders sharing knowledge 44; among lawyers 547–53; among scientists 90–95; applied linguistics approach to 322, 334, 336, 338, 339; case study of engineering students 465, 467, 470–71, 472; case study of mathematicians 474, 476; certifications available for **525**, **526**; CL research studies 15–22; collaborative writing 486–91; combination of theoretical approaches to study 464–65, 466–68, 471–72; employment of multimodality in 41–48; genre-based approach to 26; guided participation learning 467–68; between insiders and outsiders 44; as an integrative product of ESP and BC 3, 10; interdisciplinary studies in 403; by journalists 400, 407, 412–13, 414; Legitimate Peripheral Participation (LPP) approach 469–70; multimodal nature of 473–75; multimodal research approaches to 473–76; overlap of with BC 59; overlapping of genres in multimodal presentations 43; from participants to user-observers 47; portability of knowledge for novices in 461; Rhetorical Genre Studies (RGS) approach 463–65; Situated Learning (SL) approach 465, 466–67, 468–70; studies of the school-to-work transition 462–65, 470–76; use of genre theory to analyse 6
professional identities: case study of the film industry 40–48; dynamic character of 41, 44–47, 537–38, 544–46; multimodal capture of the dynamic nature of 40, 44–47; shifting of using non-verbal modes 44–47; and use of discursive strategies 45–47
professional organisations: assessment and credentialing by 522, 524–29; for business communication 51, 52, 53; continuing education through 541; for corporate communication 221; for management communication 165, 166; responsibility of for ethical practices 522; for technical communication 99, 100, 106–7, 521, 525–26; use of continuing education 522–23, 524, 530
pronoun: studies of usage in CL 19–20; use of to establish communal relationships 45
public relations (PR): as a function of organisational management 421–22, 425; as a subject of research 422, 425, 430, 431–33; advocacy functions of 420, 425–31; commodification of knowledge in 563; consensus-building functions of 420, 423, 424–26, 430–31; cultural values as a source of conflict for 430–33; definitions of 420–22; establishing competence in 565–67; focus of on achieving planned outcomes 425, 426, 427, 430, 562–63; globalisation of 420, 428, 431–33; influence of technology on 426–29, 432, 434; information management functions of 421–23, 427–28, 431, 568; interdisciplinary nature of 419–22, 424, 562; intermediating functions of 421, 422, 425, 427–29, 433; negative portrayals of 420, 421, 429–31, 433; one-way and two-way communications in 426; and the problem of dominant versus minority viewpoints 429–30; reconciliation of global with local needs in 431–32; relationships of with stakeholders 562–63, 564, 566; role of defending organisational reputation 422–24, 429; role of in crisis management 421, 423, 424, 427; small versus large firms 563, 564–65; social and ethical concerns of 423, 430–31, 433, 568–69; spectrum of functions 419–24, 430, 562; strategic planning function of 421, 422–23, 425–27, 433–34, 564; theoretical bases for practice of 420, 424–26, 430, 432, 433; versus advertising 420, 421, 422; versus marketing 420, 422, 423, 425; writing functions in 421–24, 431–32, 567, 568

qualitative analysis: of conversations 19; forms of 13; for researching school-to-work transition 475–76; use of concordance format for 13 quantitative analysis: as an element of corpus linguistics (CL) 13; for researching school-to-work transition 476

questionnaires for workplace communication analysis 117

Rapport Theory (workplace communication) 114–15

reader: divergence in understanding between author and 90–91; as the focal point in translation 148–49; placement of in SL context 149

real world: as a teaching tool 27, 29, 31, 35, 469, 471; consulting projects in the for MBA candidates 167–68; post-internship reflections on the 338; student transitions into the 461, 474

Really Simple Syndication (RSS) 130, 137

recontextualisation of discourse and genre 6, 7, 40

register: definition of 385; register analysis 3–4, 9

relationships, Confucian concept of 29–30

reputation: and financial performance 238; public perception of accountants 561; public perceptions of banking 545–46; public perceptions of PR 568–69; The Reputation Institute (New York City) 226; versus image 226, 238–39

research documentation preparation by technical communicators 101–2

research methodologies: match between questions and framework 123; used in business communication 54

rhetoric: as a PR function 420, 425–31; CEO styles of 240, 242; Classical concepts of 87, 89; importance of to a manager's effectiveness 173, 183; influence of on BC 51, 54, 56, 57–58; influence of on technical communication 105; in language learning 314; modern definition of 87; New Rhetoric theory 461, 463, 474; studies of use of among scientists 87–88, 91–94; visual 243, 244; *see also* persuasion

scientific research: case studies of 90–92; ethnographic studies of 92–94

semantics: CL studies of positive and negative 15; Pollyanna effect 16–17; in translation 149

semiotic modes: as a complement to language 40–43, 48; contribution of to meaning-making 41–42; influence of on translation 148, 149, 151, 152, 161; resemiotisation 42; as tools to communicate knowledge 44

situated learning as a complement to peripheral participation 27, 33, 35

skills *see* knowledge; language learning

social constructionist theory of scientific knowledge 90, 91, 93–94

social media: as a powerful political tool 129, 130–31; as a threat to corporate brands 131–32; corporate policies regarding 132–33, 136–37; NIRI guidelines 136–37; types of 129–30; use of by activists 135; use of by small firms 143; use of to discredit corporations 130, 133

social relationships, as defined by language 8–9

socio-pragmatic influences on communications 5–8

sociolinguistics: as a complement to ethnographic research 120; interactional for workplace discourse analysis 113–14, 120, 121, 125n1; language use among specialists 3–4; significance of shared values to 9; studies in new media 411–12, 414; studies of workplace communication 112

software: coding 119; *ConcGram* 20–21; Speech Interpretation and Recognition Interface (SIRI) 144; use of for text analysis 13; *wMatrix* 16, 20; XBRL 130, 139–41

source language (SL): borrowing from for translation 148; translating concepts from the 149, 152, 154, 155, 156; translation methods focusing on the 149

source text (ST): importance of context to 149–50, 154–56; as social discourse 151; specialised 153, 160–61; theory of translation 148, 151; as translation at the author's level 149, 150, 153, 156

speaking: discourse markers 386–92; intonation 389–90; telephone interactions in BPO industry 384, 385, 507, 508–9; verbal signage 387, 508–9; versus writing 386–87

stakeholders: as a basis for strategic management 229–30; actor network theory (ANT) 230–31; concept of social integration 228; corporate relations with capital providers 238–41, 246–48; corporate relations with foreign 247–48; corporate returns to 245; definition of 229; as a focus of corporate communication studies 220, 229–31; interdependence of with corporation 228; intermediating function of PR with 419, 421–22, 424, 425–29, 432–33, 562–63; interrelationships among various 223, 230–31; Legitimacy Theory 246; perceptions of an organisation among 225–26, 238, 239, 243–47; power of to damage corporate images 238, 245; research on 229–31; Similarity-Attraction paradigm 247; Stakeholder Management Capability (SMC) 229; theory 229–30; versus PR concept of publics 428

stereotyping in the workplace 116

strategic management: the annual report as a tool of 239; corporate communication as a function of 220, 222, 223; investor relations as a function of 239; Stakeholder Management Capability (SMC) 229; and voluntarism 229

Index

students: as a teaching resource 35–36; internship experiences of 30–32, 35; the learning and unlearning processes of 35–36
survey research: European Communication Monitor (ECM) 221; use of in workplace communication analysis 117
sustainability: and corporate environmental strategies 194, 195, 198–201, 202; CSR reports of 54, 56, 249; discourses concerning corporate 61
symposia *see* conferences and symposia
Systematic Functional Linguistics (SFL): Field-Tenor-Mode framework 385; perception of language as a system of choices 385, 396; use of to analyse spoken versus written English 383

taboos *see* etiquette
target language (TL): interpretation into a 152, 156; as part of the receiving environment 154, 155, 158, 159, 161; the role of adaptation in translating to a 148, 151; translation methods focusing on the 149
target text (TT): function of the 149, 150, 152, 154–55; in the functional approach to translation 149, 152, 160–61; theory of translation 148
task genres in Zones model 77
teaching: instructors as facilitators 36; mismatch of with reality found in workplace communication studies 123–24; peripheral participation as a tool for 28–29; and research in business communication 60–61, 69; and research in technical communication 107–8; and training in business communication 71, 80–81
teamwork *see* collaboration
technical communication: competence certifications in 521, 525–26; definition of 99, 463; evaluation of technical content 106; influence of internet on 104; instructional role of 99–100; localisation of documentation in 104, 105; for non-specialists 101, 102; outsourcing and offshoring of 103–4; preparation of research documentation 101–2, 105, 106; procedural element of presenting information 101, 106; production options 105–6; proposals, grants, and feasibility studies 102; roles of in content development 103; by scientists and technicians 104; service documentation 101; for specialists 101, 102; theoretical orientations of 105; translation of documentation 103–4, 105; typology of materials 100; use of audio-visual media in 105; use of plain language for 101; use of references to present facts 101; use of serial questioning to solve problems 101; user assistance 100–1, 107

technology: channels of communication based on 72; influence of on business communication 76; influence of on technical communications 104, 105; *see also* web technologies
television as a subject of CL studies 18
text: as a research focus for MC 168–69; authentic as a teaching tool 31, 34, 36; text-based analysis 88–90, 95n1; text-external factors 3, 7; text-internal factors 3, 7
text typologies in translation 149
theme-rheme dichotomy 150
theory: in analysing workplace discourse 113–16, 124; building 85, 86, 91–94; defined 86; function of as a framework for argumentation 88, 90; function of as an analytical lens 88; influence of audience on presentation of 87–89; linking of to practice through real-world experiences 33–34; purpose and uses of 85, 86; versus concept 86
translation: adaptation procedure 148; benefits of pragmatic approach for recipients 149, 152, 157; borrowing procedure 148; calque word borrowing 148; charts depicting process *152, 153*; communicative strategy 149; computer-aided 104; defined 147–48; description and explanation in 156; dichotomy of options for 149, 152; direct strategy 148; effect of assumptions on 151, 155; equivalence procedure 148–49, 150, 154–56, 157; free 148, 149; functional approach to 149–52, 155–56; gloss 149; instrumental 150; interpretive theory of 149, 151; interrelationships of source text (ST), source language (SL), target text (TT) and target language (TL) 154–55, 161; intralingual 151; of legal texts 149, 150, 151, 154, 155–59, 161; at lexis level 155; literal (or direct) strategy 148; as mediated communication 151–52; misunderstanding, mistranslation, and incompleteness in 151, 159, 161, 162; modulation procedure 148; oblique strategy 148; pragmatic approach to 148, 150, 152–54, 156, 157, 160; preservation of concepts in 155; processing phase of 152; recipients versus original audience 148–52, 155, 157, 161; semiotic approach to 148, 149, 151, 152, 161; *skopos* theory of 150, 155; as social discourse 152; of specialised text 153, 160–61; syntactic versus communicative functions in 150; temporality of interpretation 152–53; theories of 148–50, 152, 155, 162; transposition procedure 148; typologies 151; in unilingual versus multilingual environments 156–57; verbal 147, 151, 152; word-for-word procedure 148
translator: as a bilingual mediator 152; agency of in selecting translation procedure 148, 157; cognitive background of the 149, 151, 154;

electronic 160, 162; factors affecting a 153–57, 159; the non-professional 159–61, 162
transparency: enhancement of by web technologies 129, 133, 139; impact of Enron frauds on 15, 16, 221, 239; informational facilitated by web technologies 129, 132, 133, 139; need for corporate 132, 237, 239, 241, 246, 433; Reg. FD guidelines 140–43
Twitter: enhancement of news reporting through 406, 415n9; influence of on globalisation 72; original uses of 129, 142; powerful real-time reporting capabilities of 143; use of as a political tool 134, 142; use of as an emergency tool 142; use of by activists 135; use of by corporations and small local businesses 143; use of for investor relations 141, 142; use statistics for 142

user assistance concept 101, 102, 107

values: as the basis for distinguishing image from reputation 226; common starting points (CSP) 228; Competing Values Framework (CVF) 178–81, 223, 228; Competing Values Framework for Corporate Communication (CVFCC) 228; influence of on corporate communication 246–48; organisational 225
Vygotsky, L. S., theories of learning 465, 466–67, 470

web technologies: in a banking environment 542–43; access to 412, 413; advantages of email 278–83; challenges of to content-makers 405, 406; Channel Expansion Theory 279–80; criteria for uses of 277–83; cybervetting 211; democratising effects of on publishing options 403, 407, 412; electronic media types 129–30, 278–82; empowerment of audiences by 428–29, 432; enhancement of press release media through 406–7, 415n9; expanded further by mobile devices 143–44; exploitation of to promote negative agendas 134–35; high versus low bandwidth types 274, 278–79; influence of on collaborative writing 494–96; influence of on shaping of texts 406, 410; influence of on the news media 400, 404, 406; influence of on workplace communications 274–75; instant messaging as a tool for BC 279, 281, 284; intranets 136, 276–78, 280; and language learning 314–15, 316–17; networking capabilities of 129; penetration of in Singapore 275; role of in corporate communications 237, 239, 243–46, 248; SEC regulations affecting 140–41; social media 72, 129–37; speed of 130, 137, 144; teleconferencing as a tool for BC 276, 277–78, 280–81; use and abuse of by employees 131–32, 136–39; use of as part of BC pedagogy 282–85; videoconferencing as a tool for BC 277–78, 279–81; the website as a confrontational space 130, 135; the website as a corporate tool 239–42, 284, 421, 428, 434, 567; *see also* internet; technology
websites: aacsb.edu 187; KeyContent.org (technical communication) 107; www1.english.cityu.edu.hk/acadlit/index.php?q=node/21 316; www.victoria.ac.nz/lals/lwp/ (Language in the Workplace) 60; *see also* blogs
wikis 130, 136, 495
work, definitions of 212, 214
workplace, informal and formal networks 170; politics of the 172, 209–10, 504–5
workplace communication: in banking 536, 539–41; collaborative writing 486–91; community of practice concept 114, 445–46; data collection methodologies 117–19; defined 112–13; distributed cognition theory of 470; ethnographic analysis of 118; gender identities in 115–16; importance of assumptions in 114, 118, 122; influence of on personal identity 113, 116, 117; interviews 114, 124; LPP approach to 469–70; managerial tactics to achieve desired goals 114–16, 120–23; micro and macro aspects of 267, 268; overt versus covert 121–23; power and politeness in 113–14, 116, 122–23; Rapport Theory for analysis of 114–15; Singapore case study 275–82; social constructionist framework for analysing 116–17; theoretical frameworks for analysing 113–17; use of CDA to analyse dynamics of 115; use of digressions and evasiveness to exert control in the 122; use of ethnic communications in 116, 120; use of foreign languages in 118; use of humour in 116, 120–21, 122; use of non-verbal behaviour in 122, 124; use of post-structural theory to analyse dynamics of 115–16; versus business discourse 112–13; workplace meetings 116, 118–23
workplace environment: as a research topic in organisational communication 210; stereotyping in the 116
writing: as a basic function of PR 421–24, 431–32; annual report narratives 240–41, 244; business writing 26, 30, 33, 36; collaborative 452–53, 455, 486–96, 552; communal practices of 447, 449, 454–55; Competing Values Framework (CVF) tool to assess 178–80; fluency in a cross-cultural context 27, 31, 34; genre chains 450–52; genres 451; GMAT tools to assess 178; informality in 34–35; interaction

of with non-verbal modes 41; intertextuality in 451, 452, 552; Lunsford and Ede (1990) survey 182–83; memorandum versus letter 176; overemphasis on by BPO industry 384, 392–93; pedagogies 444, 455; portability of from academia to workplace 462, 492; in technical communication 103–5; versus speaking 386–87, 392–93; writing studies research 88–89; Writing Studies theory 462–63, 470–72

YouTube 143–44, 316–17

Zones model 77